BIOLOGY

BIOLOGY
Chemistry, Cells, and Genetics
Units 1, 2, and 3

Selected Materials from

BIOLOGY

Second Edition

Robert J. Brooker
University of Minnesota – Minneapolis

Eric P. Widmaier
Boston University

Linda Graham
University of Wisconsin – Madison

Peter Stiling
University of South Florida

Boston   Burr Ridge, IL   Dubuque, IA   New York   San Francisco   St. Louis
Bangkok   Bogotá   Caracas   Lisbon   London   Madrid
Mexico City   Milan   New Delhi   Seoul   Singapore   Sydney   Taipei   Toronto

The McGraw·Hill Companies

BIOLOGY
Chemistry, Cells, and Genetics
Units 1, 2, and 3
Selected Material from
Biology, Second Edition

3 4 5 6 7 8 9 0 DOW DOW 12 11

ISBN-13: 978-0-07-740565-6
ISBN-10: 0-07-740565-X

Learning Solutions Specialist: Shirley Grall
Production Editor: Tina Hermsen
Printer/Binder: RR Donnelley

Brief Contents

About the Authors

Robert J. Brooker

Rob Brooker (Ph.D., Yale University) received his B.A. in biology at Wittenberg University in 1978. At Harvard, he studied the lactose permease, the product of the *lacY* gene of the *lac* operon. He continues working on transporters at the University of Minnesota, where he is a Professor in the Department of Genetics, Cell Biology, and Development and has an active research laboratory. At the University of Minnesota, Dr. Brooker teaches undergraduate courses in biology, genetics, and cell biology. In addition to many other publications, he has written three editions of the undergraduate genetics text *Genetics: Analysis & Principles*, McGraw-Hill, copyright 2009.

Eric P. Widmaier

Eric Widmaier received his Ph.D. in 1984 in endocrinology from the University of California at San Francisco. His research is focused on the control of body mass and metabolism in mammals, the hormonal correlates of obesity, and the effects of high-fat diets on intestinal cell function. Dr. Widmaier is currently Professor of Biology at Boston University, where he recently received the university's highest honor for excellence in teaching. Among other publications, he is a coauthor of *Vander's Human Physiology: The Mechanisms of Body Function*, 11th edition, published by McGraw-Hill, copyright 2008.

Linda E. Graham

Linda Graham received her Ph.D. in botany from the University of Michigan, Ann Arbor. Her research explores the evolutionary origin of land-adapted plants, focusing on their cell and molecular biology as well as ecological interactions. Dr. Graham is now Professor of Botany at the University of Wisconsin–Madison. She teaches undergraduate courses in biology and plant biology. She is the coauthor of, among other publications, *Algae*, copyright 2000, a major's textbook on algal biology, and *Plant Biology*, copyright 2006, both published by Prentice Hall/Pearson.

Left to right: Eric Widmaier, Linda Graham, Peter Stiling, and Rob Brooker

Peter D. Stiling

Peter Stiling obtained his Ph.D. from University College, Cardiff, Wales, in 1979. Subsequently, he became a postdoc at Florida State University and later spent 2 years as a lecturer at the University of the West Indies, Trinidad. During this time, he began photographing and writing about butterflies and other insects, which led to publication of several books on local insects. Dr. Stiling is currently a Professor of Biology at the University of South Florida at Tampa. He teaches graduate and undergraduate courses in ecology and environmental science as well as introductory biology. He has published many scientific papers and is the author of *Ecology: Global Insights and Investigations*, soon to be published by McGraw-Hill. Dr. Stiling's research interests include plant-insect relationships, parasite-host relationships, biological control, restoration ecology, and the effects of elevated carbon dioxide levels on plant herbivore interactions.

The authors are grateful for the help, support,
and patience of their families, friends, and students,
Deb, Dan, Nate, and Sarah Brooker,
Maria, Rick, and Carrie Widmaier,
Jim, Michael, and Melissa Graham, and
Jacqui, Zoe, Leah, and Jenna Stiling.

Improving Biology Education: We Listened to You

A Step Ahead

A Step Ahead describes what we set out to accomplish with this second-edition textbook. As authors and educators, we know your goal is to ensure your students are prepared for the future—their future course work, lab experiences, and careers in the sciences. Building a strong foundation in biology will put your students a step ahead on this path.

The illustrations are outstanding and better than in most textbooks. They are clear, eye-catching, and compactly illustrate the important features without the cluttering that so often accompanies diagrams. The essential features can be seen and understood at a glance.

Harold Heatwole, North Carolina State University

Through our classroom experiences and research work, we became inspired by the prospect that the first edition of *Biology* could move biology education forward. We are confident that this new edition of *Biology* is a step ahead because we listened to you. Based on our own experience and our discussions with educators and students, we continue to concentrate our efforts on these crucial areas:

- Experimentation and the process of science
- Modern content
- Evolutionary perspective
- Emphasis on visuals
- Accuracy and consistency
- Critical thinking
- Media—active teaching and learning with technology

Continued feedback from instructors using this textbook has been extremely valuable in refining the presentation of the material. Likewise, we have used the textbook in our own classrooms. This hands-on experience has provided much insight regarding areas for improvement. Our textbook continues to be comprehensive and cutting-edge, featuring an evolutionary focus and an emphasis on scientific inquiry.

The first edition of *Biology* was truly innovative in its visual program, and with the second edition it remains a step ahead. In watching students study as well as in extensive interviews, it is clear that students rely heavily on the artwork as their primary study tool. As you will see when you scan through our book, the illustrations have been crafted with the student's perspective in mind. They are very easy to follow, particularly those that have multiple steps, and have very complete explanations of key concepts. We have taken the approach that students should be able to look at the figures and understand the key concepts, without having to glance back and forth between the text and art. Many figures contain text boxes that explain what the illustration is showing. In those figures with multiple steps, the boxes are numbered and thereby guide the students through biological processes.

A Step Ahead in Serving Teachers and Learners

To accurately and thoroughly cover a course as wide ranging as biology, we felt it was essential that our team reflect the diversity of the field. We saw an opportunity to reach students at an early stage in their education and provide their biology training with a solid and up-to-date foundation. We have worked to balance coverage of classic research with recent discoveries that extend biological concepts in surprising new directions or that forge new concepts. Some new discoveries were selected because they highlight scientific controversies, showing students that we don't have all the answers yet. There is still a lot of work for new generations of biologists. With this in mind, we've also spotlighted discoveries made by diverse people doing research in different countries to illustrate the global nature of modern biological science.

As active teachers and writers, one of the great joys of this process for us is that we have been able to meet many more educators and students during the creation of this textbook. It is humbling to see the level of dedication our peers bring to their teaching. Likewise, it is encouraging to see the energy and enthusiasm so many students bring to their studies. We hope this book and its media package will serve to aid both faculty and students in meeting the challenges of this dynamic and exciting course. For us, this remains a work in progress, and we encourage you to let us know what you think of our efforts and what we can do to serve you better.

This is an excellent textbook for biology majors, and the students should keep the book as a future reference. The thoughts flow very well from one topic to the next.

Gary Walker, Youngstown State University

Rob Brooker, Eric Widmaier, Linda Graham, Peter Stiling

CHANGES TO THIS EDITION

The author team is dedicated to producing the most engaging and current textbook that is available for undergraduate students who are majoring in biology. We want our students to be inspired by the field of biology and to become critical thinkers. To this end, we have made the following changes throughout the entire book.

- Each chapter in the second edition begins with an interesting story or a set of observations that will capture the students' interests as they begin to read a chapter.

- To help students test their knowledge and critical-thinking skills, we have increased the number of Concept check questions that are associated with the figure legends and revised many of the questions at the end of each chapter so they are at a higher level in Bloom's taxonomy. An answer key for the questions is now provided in an appendix at the end of the book.

- To further help students appreciate the scientific process, the Feature Investigation in each chapter now includes three new elements: a Conclusion, the original journal citation for the experiment, and questions that are directly related to the experiment.

- Many photographs and micrographs have been enlarged or replaced with better images.

- The presentation of the material has been refined by dividing some of the chapters into smaller sections and by the editing of complex sentences.

With regard to the scientific content in the textbook, the author team has worked with hundreds of faculty reviewers to refine the first edition and to update the content so that our students are exposed to the most cutting-edge material. Some of the key changes that have occurred are summarized below.

Chemistry Unit

- **Chapter 2. The Chemical Basis of Life I: Atoms, Molecules, and Water:** This stage-setting chapter now introduces the concepts of matter and energy, chemical equilibrium, condensation/hydrolysis reactions, and expands upon the properties of water (for example, introducing such concepts as specific heat). The nature and importance of radioisotopes in biology and medicine has also been expanded and clarified, along with a new photo of a whole-body PET scan of a person with cancer.

- **Chapter 3. The Chemical Basis of Life II: Organic Molecules:** Enzymes are now defined in this early chapter. A new figure has been added that reinforces and elaborates upon the mechanism and importance of dehydration and hydrolysis reactions, which were first introduced in Chapter 2. This figure includes the principles of polymer formation and breakdown. Carbohydrates, lipids, proteins, and nucleic acids have been reorganized into distinct major headings for sharper focus.

Cell Unit

- **Chapter 4. General Features of Cells:** You will find improved illustrations of the cytoskeleton and new content regarding the origin of peroxisomes. The chapter has a new section on Protein Sorting to Organelles and ends with a new

section called System Biology of Cells: A Summary, which summarizes the content of Chapter 4 from a systems biology perspective.

- **Chapter 5. Membrane Structure, Synthesis, and Transport:** This chapter has a new section on the Synthesis of Membrane Components in Eukaryotic Cells. In this section, you will find a description of how cells make phospholipids, a critical topic that is often neglected.

- **Chapter 6. An Introduction to Energy, Enzymes, and Metabolism:** Based on reviewer comments, this newly created chapter splits the material that was originally in Chapter 7 of the first edition. Chapter 6 provides an introduction to energy, enzymes, and metabolism. It includes added material on ribozymes and a novel section at the end of the chapter that describes the important topic of how cells recycle the building blocks of their organic macromolecules.

- **Chapter 7. Cellular Respiration, Fermentation, and Secondary Metabolism:** In the second edition, Chapter 7 is now divided into three sections: Cellular Respiration in the Presence of Oxygen, Anaerobic Respiration and Fermentation, and Secondary Metabolism.

- **Chapter 8. Photosynthesis:** The discussion of the light-dependent reactions is now divided into two sections: Reactions that Harness Light Energy and Molecular Features of Photosystems.

- **Chapter 9. Cell Communication:** Two sections that were in the first edition on Cellular Receptors and Signal Transduction and the Cellular Response have been streamlined and simplified. A new section called Apoptosis: Programmed Cell Death has been added, which includes a pioneering Feature Investigation that describes how apoptosis was originally discovered.

- **Chapter 10. Multicellularity:** The figures in this chapter have been greatly improved with a greater emphasis on orientation diagrams that help students visualize where an event is occurring in the cell or in a multicellular organism.

Genetics Unit

- **Chapter 11. Nucleic Acid Structure, DNA Replication, and Chromosome Structure:** The section on Chromosome Structure has been moved from Chapter 15 in the first edition to this chapter so that the main molecular features of the genetic material are contained within a single chapter. To help students grasp the major concepts, the topic of DNA replication has been split into two sections: Overview of DNA Replication and Molecular Mechanism of DNA Replication.

- **Chapter 12. Gene Expression at the Molecular Level:** Several topics in this chapter have been streamlined to make it easier for students to grasp the big picture of gene expression.

- **Chapter 13. Gene Regulation:** Topics in gene regulation, such as micro RNAs, have been updated.

- **Chapter 14. Mutation, DNA Repair, and Cancer:** Information regarding the effects of oncogenes has been modified so that students can appreciate how mutations in particular oncogenes and tumor suppressor genes promote cancer.

- **Chapter 15. The Eukaryotic Cell Cycle, Mitosis, and Meiosis:** This chapter now begins with a section on the eukaryotic cell cycle, which was in Chapter 9 of the first edition. This new organization allows students to connect how the cell cycle is related to mitosis and meiosis. Also, a new Genomes and Proteomes Connection on cytokinesis has been added, which explains new information on how cells divide.
- **Chapter 16. Simple Patterns of Inheritance:** To make the topics stand out better for students, this chapter has been subdivided into six sections: Mendel's Laws of Inheritance, The Chromosome Theory of Inheritance, Pedigree Analysis of Human Traits, Sex Chromosomes and X-Linked Inheritance Patterns, Variations in Inheritance Patterns and Their Molecular Basis, and Genetics and Probability.
- **Chapter 17. Complex Patterns of Inheritance:** The coverage of X inactivation, genomic imprinting, and maternal effect genes has been streamlined to focus on their impacts on phenotypes.
- **Chapter 18. Genetics of Viruses and Bacteria:** In response to reviewers of the first edition, this chapter now begins with viruses. The topics of viroids and prions are set apart in their own section. Also, the information regarding bacterial genetics comes at the end of the chapter and is divided into two sections on Genetic Properties of Bacteria and on Gene Transfer Between Bacteria.
- **Chapter 19. Developmental Genetics:** Invertebrate development has been streamlined to focus on the major themes of development. The topic of stem cells has been updated with new information regarding their importance in development and their potential uses in medicine.
- **Chapter 20. Genetic Technology:** New changes to this chapter include an improved figure on polymerase chain reaction (PCR) and new information regarding the engineering of Bt crops in agriculture.
- **Chapter 21. Genomes, Proteomes, and Bioinformatics:** This chapter has been updated with the newest information regarding genome sequences. Students are introduced to the NCBI website, and a collaborative problem at the end of the chapter asks the students to identify a mystery gene sequence using the BLAST program.

Evolution Unit

- **Chapter 22. The Origin and History of Life:** The topic of fossils has been separated into its own section. The second edition has some new information regarding ideas about how polymers can be formed abiotically in an aqueous setting. The role of oxygen has been expanded.
- **Chapter 23. An Introduction to Evolution:** To help the students make connections between genes and traits, newly discovered examples, such as the role of allelic differences in the *Igf2* gene among dog breeds, have been added.

- **Chapter 24. Population Genetics:** To bring the topics into sharper focus, this chapter is now subdivided into five sections: Genes in Populations, Natural Selection, Sexual Selection, Genetic Drift, and Migration and Nonrandom Mating. The important topic of single nucleotide polymorphisms is highlighted near the beginning of the chapter along with its connection to personalized medicine.
- **Chapter 25. Origin of Species and Macroevolution:** The topic of species concepts has been updated with an emphasis on the general lineage concept. Sympatric speciation has been divided into three subtopics: Polyploidy, Adaptation to Local Environments, and Sexual Selection.
- **Chapter 26. Taxonomy and Systematics:** The chapter begins with a modern description of taxonomy that divides eukaryotes into eight supergroups. To make each topic easier to follow, the chapter is now subdivided into five sections: Taxonomy, Phylogenetic Trees, Cladistics, Molecular Clocks, and Horizontal Gene Transfer.

Diversity Unit

- **Chapter 27. Bacteria and Archaea:** In this chapter featuring bacterial and archeal diversity, several illustrations have been improved. New information has been added to the Feature Investigation highlighting radiation resistance in Deinococcus.
- **Chapter 28. Protists:** In this exploration of protist diversity, recent research findings have been incorporated into chapter organization and phylogenetic trees. The evolutionary and ecological importance of cryptomonads and haptophytes are emphasized more completely. Life-cycle diagrams have been improved for clarity. A new Genomes and Proteomes Connection features genomic studies of the human pathogens trichomonas and giardia.
- **Chapter 29. Plants and the Conquest of Land:** This chapter on seedless plant diversity incorporates new molecular phylogenetic information on relationships. A new Genomes and Proteomes Connection features the model fern genus *Ceratopteris*. Life cycles have been improved for greater clarity.
- **Chapter 30. The Evolution and Diversity of Modern Gymnosperms and Angiosperms:** This chapter, highlighting seed plant diversity, features a new Genomes and Proteomes Connection on the role of whole genome duplication via autopolyploidy and allopolyploidy in the evolution of seed plants.
- **Chapter 31. Fungi:** The fungal diversity chapter's position has been changed to emphasize the close relationship of fungi to animals. There is an increased emphasis upon the role of fungi as pathogens and in other biotic associations. For example, a new Genomes and Proteomes Connection explores the genetic basis of beneficial plant associations with ectomycorrhizal fungi, and a new Feature Investigation features experiments that reveal a partnership between a virus and endophytic fungi that increases heat tolerance in plants. Life cycles of higher fungi have been modified to highlight heterokaryotic phases.

- **Chapter 32: An Introduction to Animal Diversity:** A brief evolutionary history of animal life has been added. A new figure shows the similarity of a sponge to its likely ancestor, a colonial choanoflagellate. The summary characteristics of the major animal phyla have been simplified.

- **Chapter 33: The Invertebrates:** With the huge number of invertebrate species and the medical importance of many, a new Genomes and Proteomes Connection discusses DNA barcoding, which may allow for rapid classification of species. The taxonomy of the annelids, arthropods, and chordates has been updated.

- **Chapter 34: The Vertebrates:** The organization of the section headings now follows the vertebrate cladogram introduced at the start of the chapter. A more modern approach to the taxonomy of vertebrates has been adopted, particularly in the discussion of primates. In addition, there is an extended treatment of human evolution and a new Genomes and Proteomes Connection comparing the human and chimpanzee genetic codes.

Plant Unit

- **Chapter 35. An Introduction to Flowering Plant Form and Function:** This overview of flowering plant structure and function has been revised to better serve as an introduction to Chapters 36–39. A new Genomes and Proteomes Connection features the genetic control of stomatal development and emphasizes the role of asymmetric division in the formation of specialized plant cells. A new Feature Investigation reveals how recent experiments have demonstrated the adaptive value of palmate venation in leaves.

- **Chapter 36. Flowering Plants: Behavior:** In this chapter on plant behavior, the general function of plant hormones in reducing gene repression, thereby allowing gene expression, provides a new unifying theme. As an example, new findings on the stepwise evolution of the interaction between gibberellin and DELLA proteins are highlighted. The Feature Investigation, highlighting classic discoveries concerning auxin's role in phototropism, has been condensed to achieve greater impact.

- **Chapter 37. Flowering Plants: Nutrition:** In this chapter on plant nutrition, a new Genomes and Proteomes Connection features the development of legume-rhizobium symbioses.

- **Chapter 38. Flowering Plants: Transport:** In this chapter on plant transport, the recent use of synthetic tree models has been added to further highlight experimental approaches toward understanding plant structure-function relationships.

- **Chapter 39. Flowering Plants: Reproduction:** In this chapter on flowering plant reproduction, greater attention is paid to the trade-offs of sexual versus asexual reproduction, explaining why both commonly occur and are important in nature and agricultural applications. A new Genomes and Proteomes Connection describes a study of the evolution of plants that reproduce via only asexual means from sexually reproducing ancestral species.

Animal Unit

Key changes to the animal unit include reorganization of the chapters such that animal nervous systems are presented first, an expanded emphasis on comparative features of invertebrate and vertebrate animal biology, and updates to each of the Impact on Public Health sections.

- **Chapter 40. Animal Bodies and Homeostasis:** This opening chapter has numerous new and improved photos and illustrations, such as those associated with an expanded discussion of different types of connective and epithelial tissue. The utility of the Fick diffusion equation has now been explained, and the very important relationship between surface area and volume in animals has been more thoroughly developed.

- **Chapter 41. Neuroscience I: Cells of the Nervous System:** Discussion of animal nervous systems has been moved to the beginning chapters of the animal unit, rather than appearing midway through the unit. This was done to better set the stage for all subsequent chapters. In this way, students will gain an appreciation for how the nervous system regulates the functions of all other organ systems. This concept will be continually reinforced as the students progress through the unit. Specific changes to Chapter 41 include an expanded treatment of equilibrium potential, a new discussion and figure on spatial and temporal summation in neurons, and a false-color SEM image of a synapse.

- **Chapter 42. Neuroscience II: Evolution and Function of the Brain and Nervous Systems:** In this second chapter devoted to nervous systems, the many functions of individual regions of animals' brains have been more extensively described and also summarized for easy reference in a new table. The epithalamus is now included in this discussion, and the structure and function of the autonomic nervous system has received expanded coverage.

- **Chapter 43. Neuroscience III: Sensory Systems:** An expanded, detailed, and step-by-step treatment of visual and auditory signaling mechanisms has been added to this third and concluding chapter on animal nervous systems. A fascinating comparison of the visual fields of predator and prey animals has been added, along with a figure illustrating the differences. A new figure illustrating how people see the world through eyes that are diseased due to glaucoma, macular degeneration, or cataracts is now included.

- **Chapter 44. Muscular-Skeletal System and Locomotion:** The events occurring during cross-bridge cycling in muscle have been newly illustrated and detailed. A new figure showing the histologic appearance of healthy versus osteoporotic bones, and the skeleton of a child with rickets has been added.

- **Chapter 45. Nutrition, Digestion, and Absorption:** An overview figure illustrating the four basic features of energy assimiliation in animals has been added to the beginning of the chapter to set the stage for the later discussions of ingestion, digestion, absorption, and elimination. A more developed comparative emphasis on ingestive and digestive processes in animals has been added, with expanded treatment of adaptations that occur in animals that live in freshwater or marine environments. This is accompanied by newly added photographs of different animals' teeth being used to chew, tear, grasp, and nip food in their native environments.

- **Chapter 46. Control of Energy Balance, Metabolic Rate, and Body Temperature:** The text and artwork in this chapter have been considerably streamlined to emphasize major principles of fat digestion and absorption in animals.
- **Chapter 47. Circulatory Systems:** The local and systemic relationships between pressure, blood flow, and resistance are now distinguished more clearly from each other and described in separate sections to emphasize the differences between them. The organization of major topics has been adjusted to better reflect general principles of circulatory systems that apply across taxa, as well as comparative features of vertebrate circulatory systems.
- **Chapter 48. Respiratory Systems:** This chapter has benefited from a general upgrade in artwork, but particularly that of the human respiratory system, including the addition of a cross section through alveoli to illustrate their cellular structures and associations with capillaries.
- **Chapter 49. Excretory Systems and Salt and Water Balance:** A new photo of proximal tubule cells that reveals their extensive microvilli has been added to reinforce the general principle of surface-area adaptations described in earlier chapters. A major reorganization of the manner in which the anatomy and function of nephrons has been introduced; each part of the nephron has now been separated into multiple figures for easier understanding.
- **Chapter 50. Endocrine Systems:** The layout of many figures has been adjusted to improve readability and flow; this has also been facilitated with new orientation illustrations that reveal where within the body a given endocrine organ is located. Along with the new layouts, several figures have been simplified to better illustrate major concepts of hormone synthesis, action, and function. As part of a unit-wide attempt to increase quantitative descriptions of animal biology, additional data have been added in the form of a bar graph to this chapter's Feature Investigation.
- **Chapter 51. Animal Reproduction:** The major concepts of asexual and sexual reproduction have been pulled together from various sections of the text into a newly organized single section immediately at the start of the chapter. This reorganization and consolidation of material has eliminated some redundancy, but more importantly allows for a direct, integrated comparison of the two major reproductive processes found in animals. In keeping with a unit-wide effort to improve the flow of major illustrations, certain complex, multipart figures have been broken into multiple figures linked with the text.
- **Chapter 52. Animal Development:** To better allow this chapter to be understood on its own, a new introductory section has been added that reinforces basic concepts of cellular

and molecular control of animal development that were first introduced in Chapter 19 (Developmental Genetics). The complex processes occurring during gastrulation have been rendered in a newly simplified and clarified series of illustrations. The treatment of Frzb and Wnt proteins in the Genomes and Proteomes Connection has been removed and replaced with a discussion of Spemann's organizer to better reflect the genetic basis of development across taxa in animals. An amazing series of photographs depicting cleft lip/palate and its surgical reconstruction has also been added to the Impact on Public Health section.

- **Chapter 53. Immune Systems:** A key change in this chapter is the effective use of additional or reformatted text boxes in illustrations of multistep processes. The layout of nearly every figure has been modified for clarity and ease of understanding. The topic of specific immunity has been reorganized such that the cellular and humoral aspects of immunity are clearly defined and distinguished. A new figure illustrating clonal selection has been added.

Ecology Unit

- **Chapter 54: An Introduction to Ecology and Biomes:** A new table summarizes the various abiotic factors and their effects on organisms. New information on greenhouse gases is provided, including their contributions to global warming.
- **Chapter 55: Behavioral Ecology:** Portions of the section on mating systems have been rewritten in this updated chapter on behavior.
- **Chapter 56: Population Ecology:** Additional information on population growth models has been provided by discussing the finite rate of increase, λ, and by discussing growth of black-footed ferret populations in Wyoming, which are recovering after being pushed to the brink of extinction.
- **Chapter 57: Species Interactions:** This new treatment of species interactions has been streamlined, but at the same time, new information is provided on how shark fishing along the eastern seaboard of the United States has disrupted marine food webs.
- **Chapter 58: Community Ecology:** The content of this chapter has been updated and rewritten, and historical information regarding community recovery following volcanic eruption on the island of Krakatau, Indonesia, has been added. The section of species richness has also been reorganized.
- **Chapter 59: Ecosystems Ecology:** New art and text on the pyramid of numbers has been provided in the first section. The carbon cycle has been rewritten, and information on net primary production in different biomes has been updated.
- **Chapter 60: Biodiversity and Conservation Biology:** The link between biodiversity and ecosystem function has been underscored by better explaining Tilman's field experiments. The chapter also provides a new section on climate change as a cause of species extinction and loss of biodiversity. A new discussion of bioremediation has been provided in the restoration ecology section.

A STEP AHEAD IN PREPARING STUDENTS FOR THE FUTURE

> *I really like the Feature Investigation so students can begin to grasp how scientists come to the conclusions that are simply presented as facts in these introductory texts.*
>
> Richard Murray, Hendrix College

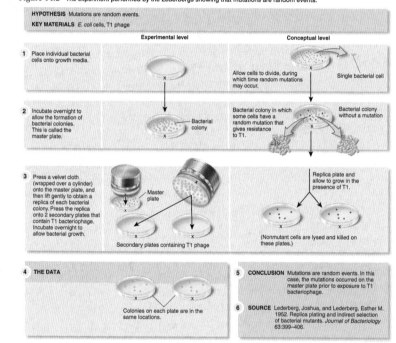

FEATURE INVESTIGATION

The Lederbergs Used Replica Plating to Show That Mutations Are Random Events

Mutations can affect the expression of genes in a variety of ways. Let's now consider the following question: Do mutations that affect the traits of an individual occur as a result of pre-existing circumstances, or are they random events that may happen in any gene of any individual? In the 19th century, French naturalist Jean Baptiste Lamarck proposed that physiological events (such as use or disuse) determine whether traits are passed along to offspring. For example, his hypothesis suggested that an individual who practiced and became adept at a physical activity, such as the long jump, would pass that quality on to his or her offspring. Alternatively, geneticists in the early 1900s suggested that genetic variation occurs as a matter of chance. According to this view, those individuals whose genes happen to contain beneficial mutations are more likely to survive and pass those genes to their offspring.

These opposing views were tested in bacterial studies in the 1940s and 1950s. One such study, by Joshua and Esther Lederberg, focused on the occurrence of mutations in bacteria (Figure 14.2). First, they placed a large number of *E. coli* bac-

Figure 14.2   The experiment performed by the Lederbergs showing that mutations are random events.

EXPERIMENTAL APPROACH

Feature Investigations provide a complete description of experiments, including data analysis, so students can understand how experimentation leads to an understanding of biological concepts. There are two types of *Feature Investigations*. Most describe experiments according to the scientific method. They begin with observations and then progress through the hypothesis, experiment, data, and the interpretation of the data (conclusion). Some *Feature Investigations* involve discovery-based science, which does not rely on a preconceived hypothesis. The illustrations of the *Feature Investigations* are particularly innovative by having parallel drawings at the experimental and conceptual levels. By comparing the two levels, students will be able to understand how the researchers were able to interpret the data and arrive at their conclusions.

This is one of the best features of these chapters. It is absolutely important to emphasize evolution themes at the molecular level in undergraduate biology courses.

Jorge Busciglio, University of California – Irvine

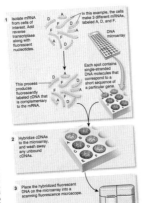

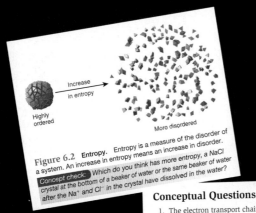

Figure 6.2 Entropy. Entropy is a measure of the disorder of a system. An increase in entropy means an increase in disorder.

Concept check: Which do you think has more entropy, a NaCl crystal at the bottom of a beaker of water or the same beaker of water after the Na⁺ and Cl⁻ in the crystal have dissolved in the water?

Conceptual Questions

1. The electron transport chain is so named because electrons are transported from one component to another. Describe the purpose of the electron transport chain.

2. What causes the rotation of the γ subunit of the ATP synthase? How does this rotation promote ATP synthesis?

3. During fermentation, explain why it is important to oxidize NADH to NAD⁺.

EVOLUTIONARY PERSPECTIVE

Modern techniques have enabled researchers to study many genes simultaneously, allowing them to explore genomes (all the genes an organism has) and proteomes (all the proteins encoded by those genes). This allows us to understand biology in a more broad way. Beginning in Chapter 3, each chapter has a topic called the *Genomes & Proteomes Connection* that provides an understanding of how genomes and proteomes underlie the inner workings of cells and explains how evolution works at the molecular level. The topics that are covered in the *Genomes & Proteomes Connection* are very useful in preparing students for future careers in biology. The study of genomes and proteomes has revolutionized many careers in biology, including those in medicine, research, biotechnology, and many others.

CRITICAL THINKING

Students can test their knowledge and critical thinking skills with the *Concept check* questions that are associated with the figure legends. These questions go beyond simple recall of information and ask students to apply or interpret information presented in the illustrations.

Conceptual Questions can be found at the end of each chapter. Again, these questions take students a step ahead in their thought process by asking them to explain, describe, differentiate, distinguish, and so on, key concepts of the chapter.

A VISUAL OUTLINE

Working with a large team of editors, scientific illustrators, photographers, educators, and students, the authors have created an accurate, up-to-date, and visually appealing illustration program that is easy to follow, realistic, and instructive. The artwork and photos serve as a "visual outline" and guide students through complex processes.

I'm very impressed with the accuracy and quality of the figures. I especially like the explanatory captions within certain figures.

Ernest DuBrul, University of Toledo

The illustrations were very effective in detailing the processes. The drawings were more detailed than our current book, which allowed for a better idea of what the proteins' (or whatever the object) structure was.

Amy Weber, student, Ohio University

COMPANION WEBSITE

Students can enhance their understanding of the concepts with the rich study materials available at www.brookerbiology.com. This open access website provides self-study options with chapter quizzes to assess current understanding, animations that highlight topics students typically struggle with and textbook images that can be used for notetaking and study.

Overall, this is a great chapter where the text, photos, and diagrams come together to make for easy reading and easy understanding of concepts and terminology. Depth of coverage is right on, and bringing in current research results is a winner.

Donald Baud, University of Memphis

General Features of Cells

4

E mily had a persistent cough ever since she started smoking cigarettes in college. However, at age 35, it seemed to be getting worse, and she was alarmed by the occasional pain in her chest. When she began to lose weight and noticed that she became easily fatigued, Emily decided to see a doctor. The diagnosis was lung cancer. Despite aggressive treatment of the disease with chemotherapy and radiation therapy, she succumbed to lung cancer 14 months after the initial diagnosis. Emily was 36.

Topics such as cancer are within the field of **cell biology**—the study of individual cells and their interactions with each other. Researchers in this field want to understand the basic features of cells and apply their knowledge in the treatment of diseases such as cystic fibrosis, sickle-cell disease, and lung cancer.

The idea that organisms are composed of cells originated in the mid-1800s. German botanist Matthias Schleiden studied plant material under the microscope and was struck by the presence of many similar-looking compartments, each of which contained a dark area. Today we call those compartments cells, and the dark area is the nucleus. In 1838, Schleiden speculated that cells are living entities

A cell from the pituitary gland. The cell in this micro[graph] viewed by a technique called transmission electron m[icroscopy] which is described in this chapter. The micrograph wa[s] colored using a computer to enhance the visualizatio[n of] cell structures.

experiments provided the first evidence that secreted proteins are synthesized into the rough ER and move through a series of cellular compartments before they are secreted. These findings also caused researchers to wonder how proteins are targeted to particular organelles and how they move from one compartment to another. These topics are described later in Section 4.6.

Experimental Questions

1. Explain the procedure of a pulse-chase experiment. W[hat] is the pulse, and what is the chase? What was the pur[pose] of the approach?

2. Why were pancreatic cells used for this investigation?

3. What were the key results of the experiment of Figure 4.19? What did the researchers conclude?

Concept check: What is the advantage of having a highly invaginated inner membrane?

Summary of Key Concepts

4.1   Microscopy

• Three important parameters in microscopy are magnification, resolution, and contrast. A light microscope utilizes light for

Assess and Discuss

Test Yourself

1. The cell doctrine states
   a. all living things are composed of cells.
   b. cells are the smallest units of living organisms.
   c. new cells come from pre-existing cells by cell division.

Conceptual Questions

1. Describe two specific ways that protein-protein interactions are involved with cell structure or cell function.

2. Explain how motor proteins and cytoskeletal filaments can interact to promote three different types of movements: movement of a cargo, movement of a filament, and bending of a filament.

3. Describe the functions of the Golgi apparatus.

Collaborative Questions

1. Discuss the roles of the genome and proteome in determining cell structure and function.

2. Discuss and draw the structural relationship between the nucleus, the rough endoplasmic reticulum, and the Golgi apparatus.

Online Resource

www.brookerbiology.com

Mc Graw Hill connect
|BIOLOGY

Stay a step ahead in your studies with animations that bring concepts to life and practice tests to assess your understanding. Your instructor may also recommend the interactive ebook, individualized learning tools, and more.

THE LEARNING SYSTEM

Each chapter starts with a simple outline and engaging story that highlights why the information in the chapter is important and intriguing. Concept checks and the questions with the Feature Investigations throughout the chapter continually ask the student to check their understanding and push a bit further. We end each chapter with a thorough review section that returns to our outline and emphasizes higher-level learning through multiple-question types.

A STEP AHEAD IN PREPARING YOUR COURSE

McGRAW-HILL CONNECT PLUS™ BIOLOGY

Connect™ Biology is a web-based assignment and assessment platform that gives students the means to better connect with their course work, with their instructors, and with the important concepts that they will need to know for success now and in the future.

With Connect Biology, you can deliver assignments, quizzes, and tests online. A robust set of questions and activities are presented and tied to the textbook's learning objectives. As an instructor, you can edit existing questions and author entirely new problems. Track individual student performance—by question, assignment, or in relation to the class overall—with detailed grade reports. Integrate grade reports easily with Learning Management Systems (LMS) such as WebCT and Blackboard. And much more.

ConnectPlus™ Biology provides students with all the advantages of Connect Biology, plus 24/7 access to an eBook—a media-rich version of the book that includes animations, videos,

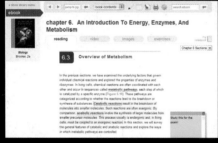

and inline assessments placed appropriately throughout the chapter. ConnectPlus Biology allows students to practice important skills at their own pace and on their own schedule. By purchasing eBooks from McGraw-Hill students can save as much as 50% on selected titles delivered on the most advanced eBook platforms available. Contact your McGraw-Hill sales representative to discuss eBook packaging options.

Powerful Presentation Tools

Everything you need for outstanding presentation in one place!

- FlexArt Image PowerPoints—including every piece of art that has been sized and cropped specifically for superior presentations as well as labels that you can edit, flexible art that can be picked up and moved, tables, and photographs.
- Animation PowerPoints—numerous full-color animations illustrating important processes. Harness the visual impact of concepts in motion by importing these slides into classroom presentations or online course materials.
- Lecture PowerPoints with animations fully embedded.
- Labeled and unlabeled JPEG images—full-color digital files of all illustrations that can be readily incorporated into presentations, exams, or custom-made classroom materials.

Presentation Center

In addition to the images from your book, this online digital library contains photos, artwork, animations, and other media from an array of McGraw-Hill textbooks that can be used to create customized lectures, visually enhanced tests and quizzes, compelling course websites, or attractive printed support materials.

Quality Test Bank

All questions have been written to fully align with the learning objectives and content of the textbook. Provided within a computerized test bank powered by McGraw-Hill's flexible electronic testing program EZ Test Online, instructors can create paper and online tests or quizzes in this easy-to-use program! A new tagging scheme allows you to sort questions by difficulty level, topic, and section. Now, with EZ Test Online, instructors can select questions from multiple McGraw-Hill test banks or author their own, and then either print the test for paper distribution or give it online.

Active Learning Exercises

Supporting biology faculty in their efforts to make introductory courses more active and student-centered is critical to improving undergraduate biological education. Active learning can broadly be described as strategies and techniques in which students are engaged in their own learning, and is typically characterized by the utilization of higher order critical thinking skills. The use of these techniques is critical to biological education because of their powerful impact on students' learning and development of scientific professional skills.

Active learning strategies are highly valued and have been shown to:

- Help make content relevant
- Be particularly adept at addressing common misconceptions
- Help students to think about their own learning (metacognition)

- Promote meaningful learning of content by emphasizing application
- Foster student interest in science

Guided Activities have been provided for instructors to use in their course for both in-class and out-of-class activities. The Guided Activities make it easy for you to incorporate active learning into your course and are flexible to fit your specific needs.

FLEXIBLE DELIVERY OPTIONS

Brooker et al. *Biology* is available in many formats in addition to the traditional textbook to give instructors and students more choices when deciding on the format of their biology text.

Also available, customized versions for all of your course needs. You're in charge of your course, so why not be in control of the content of your textbook? At McGraw-Hill Custom Publishing, we can help you create the ideal text—the one you've always imagined. Quickly. Easily. With more than 20 years of experience in custom publishing, we're experts. But at McGraw-Hill, we're also innovators, leading the way with new methods and means for creating simplified, value-added custom textbooks.

The options are never-ending when you work with McGraw-Hill. You already know what will work best for you and your students. And here, you can choose it.

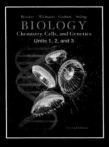

Foundations of Life—Chemistry, Cells, and Genetics
ISBN: 007740565X
Units 1, 2, and 3

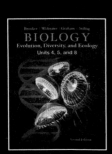

Evolution, Diversity, and Ecology
ISBN: 0077405889
Units 4, 5, and 8

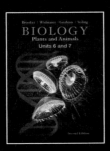

Plants and Animals
ISBN: 0077405897
Units 6 and 7

LABORATORY MANUALS

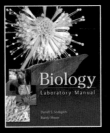

Biology Lab Manual, Ninth Edition, Vodopich/Moore
ISBN 0073383066

This laboratory manual is designed for an introductory majors biology course with a broad survey of basic laboratory techniques. The experiments and procedures are simple, safe, easy to perform, and especially appropriate for large classes. Few experiments require a second class-meeting to complete the procedure. Each exercise includes many photographs, traditional topics, and experiments that help students learn about life. Procedures within each exercise are numerous and discrete so that an exercise can be tailored to the needs of the students, the style of the instructor, and the facilities available.

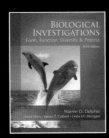

Biological Investigations, **Ninth Edition,** Dolphin et al.
ISBN 0073383058

This independent laboratory manual can be used for a one- or two-semester majors-level general biology lab and can be used with any majors-level general biology textbook. The labs are investigative and ask students to use more critical thinking and hands-on learning. The author emphasizes investigative, quantitative, and comparative approaches to studying the life sciences.

FOCUS ON EVOLUTION

Understanding Evolution, **Seventh Edition,** by Rosenbaum and Volpe
ISBN 0073383236

As an introduction to the principles of evolution, this paperback textbook is ideally suited as a main textbook for general evolution or as a supplement for general biology, genetics, zoology, botany, anthropology, or any life science course that utilizes evolution as the underlying theme of all life.

A STEP AHEAD IN QUALITY

360° DEVELOPMENT PROCESS

McGraw-Hill's 360° Development Process is an ongoing, never-ending, education-oriented approach to building accurate and innovative print and digital products. It is dedicated to continual large-scale and incremental improvement, driven by multiple user feedback loops and checkpoints. This is initiated during the early planning stages of our new products, intensifies during the development and production stages, then begins again upon publication in anticipation of the next edition.

This process is designed to provide a broad, comprehensive spectrum of feedback for refinement and innovation of our learning tools, for both student and instructor. The 360° Development Process includes market research, content reviews, course- and product-specific symposia, accuracy checks, and art reviews. We appreciate the expertise of the many individuals involved in this process.

Contributing Authors

Photo Consultant - Alvin Telser, *Northwestern University*
Instructors Manual - Mark Hens, *University of North Carolina–Greensboro*
Integrated eBook Study Quizzes - Anita Baines, *University of Wisconsin–LaCrosse;* **Matthew Neatrour,** *North Kentucky University*
Test Bank - Bruce Stallsmith, *University of Alabama–Huntsville*
Regina Wiggins-Speights, *Houston Community College–Northeast*
Punnee Soonthornpoct, *Blinn College*
Sheila Wicks, *Malcom X Junior College*
James Mickle, *North Carolina State University*
Website - Lisa Burgess, *Broward Community College;* **Marceau Ratard,** *Delgado Community College;* **Amanda Rosenzweig,** *Delgado Community College*
Instructor Media - Sharon Thoma, *University of Wisconsin–Madison;* **Brenda Leady,** *University of Toledo*
Active Learning - Frank Bailey, *Middle Tennessee State University,* **Steve Howard,** *Middle Tennessee State University;* **Michael Rutledge,** *Middle Tennessee State University*

Connect Content Contributors

Russell Borski, *North Carolina State University*
Scott Cooper, *University of Wisconsin—LaCrosse*
Phil Gibson, *Oklahoma University*
Susan Hengeveld, *Indiana University*
Lelsie Jones, *Valdosta State*
Morris Maduro, *University of California– Riverside*
Matt Neatrour, *Northern Kentucky University*
Lynn Preston, *Tarrant County College*
Brian Shmaefsky, *Lone Star College*

Digital Board of Advisors

We are indebted to the valuable advice and direction of an outstanding group of advisors, led by Melissa Michael, University of Illinois at Urbana-Champaign. Other board members include

Russel Borski, *North Carolina State University*
Karen Gerhart, *University of California—Davis*
Jean Heitz, *University of Wisconsin—Madison*
Mark Lyford, *University of Wyoming*
John Merrill, *Michigan State*
Randy Phillis, *University of Massachusetts*
Deb Pires, *University of California—Los Angeles*
Lynn Preston, *Tarrant County College*
Michael Rutledge, *Middle Tennessee State*

David Scicchitano, *New York University*
Bill Wischusen, *Louisiana State University*

General Biology Symposia

Every year McGraw-Hill conducts several General Biology Symposia, which are attended by instructors from across the country. These events are an opportunity for editors from McGraw-Hill to gather information about the needs and challenges of instructors teaching the major's biology course. It also offers a forum for the attendees to exchange ideas and experiences with colleagues they might not have otherwise met. The feedback we have received has been invaluable, and has contributed to the development of Biology and its supplements. A special thank you to recent attendees:

Sylvester Allred, *Northern Arizona University*
Michael Bell, *Richland College*
Arlene Billock, *University of Louisiana–Lafayette*
Stephane Boissinot, *Queens College, the City University of New York*
David Bos, *Purdue University*
Scott Bowling, *Auburn University*
Jacqueline Bowman, *Arkansas Technical University*
Arthur Buikema, *Virginia Polytechnic Institute*
Anne Bullerjahn, *Owens Community College*
Helaine Burstein, *Ohio University*
Raymond Burton, *Germanna Community College*
Peter Busher, *Boston University*
Richard Cardullo, *University of California–Riverside*
Jennifer Ciaccio, *Dixie State College*
Anne Barrett Clark, *Binghamton University*
Allison Cleveland, *University of South Florida–Tampa*
Jennifer Coleman, *University of Massachusetts–Amherst*
Sehoya Cotner, *University of Minnesota*
Mitch Cruzan, *Portland State University*
Laura DiCaprio, *Ohio University*
Kathyrn Dickson, *California State College–Fullerton*
Cathy Donald-Whitney, *Collin County Community College*
Stanley Faeth, *Arizona State University*
Donald French, *Oklahoma State University*
Douglas Gaffin, *University of Oklahoma*
Karen Gerhart, *University of California–Davis*
Cynthia Giffen, *University of Wisconsin–Madison*

William Glider, *University of Nebraska–Lincoln*
Christopher Gregg, *Louisiana State University*
Stan Guffey, *The University of Tennessee*
Bernard Hauser, *University of Florida–Gainesville*
Jean Heitz, *Unversity of Wisconsin–Madison*
Mark Hens, *University of North Carolina–Greensboro*
Albert Herrera, *University of Southern California*
Ralph James Hickey, *Miami University of Ohio–Oxford*
Brad Hyman, *University of California–Riverside*
Kyoungtae Kim, *Missouri State University*
Sherry Krayesky, *University of Louisiana–Lafayette*
Jerry Kudenov, *University of Alaska–Anchorage*
Josephine Kurdziel, *University of Michigan*
Ellen Lamb, *University of North Carolina–Greensboro*
Brenda Leady, *University of Toledo*
Graeme Lindbeck, *Valencia Community College*
Susan Meiers, *Western Illinois University*
Michael Meighan, *University of California–Berkeley*
John Mersfelder, *Sinclair Community College*
Melissa Michael, *University of Illinois–Urbana-Champaign*
Leonore Neary, *Joliet Junior College*
Shawn Nordell, *Saint Louis University*
John Osterman, *University of Nebraska–Lincoln*
Stephanie Pandolfi, *Michigan State University*
C.O. Patterson, *Texas A&M University*
Nancy Pencoe, *University of West Georgia*
Roger Persell, *Hunter College*
Marius Pfeiffer, *Tarrant County College NE*
Steve Phelps, *University of Florida*
Debra Pires, *University of California–Los Angeles*
Lynn Preston, *Tarrant County College*
Rajinder Ranu, *Colorado State University*
Marceau Ratard, *Delgado Community College–City Park*
Melanie Rathburn, *Boston University*
Robin Richardson, *Winona State University*
Amanda Rosenzweig, *Delgado Community College–City Park*
Connie Russell, *Angelo State University*
Laurie Russell, *St. Louis University*
David Scicchitano, *New York University*
Timothy Shannon, *Francis Marion University*
Brian Shmaefsky, *Lone Star College–Kingwood*
Richard Showman, *University of South Carolina*
Robert Simons, *University of California–Los Angeles*
Steve Skarda, *Linn Benton Community College*
Steven D. Skopik, *University of Delaware*

Phillip Sokolove, *University of Maryland—Baltimore County*
Brad Swanson, *Cental Michigan University*
David Thompson, *Northern Kentucky University*
Maureen Tubbiola, *St. Cloud State University*
Ashok Upadhyaya, *University of South Florida–Tampa*
Anthony Uzwiak, *Rutgers University*
Rani Vajravelu, *University of Central Florida*
Gary Walker, *Appalachian State University*
Pat Walsh, *University of Delaware*
Elizabeth Weiss-Kuziel, *University of Texas–Austin*
David Williams, *Valencia Community College, East Campus*
Holly Williams, *Seminole Community College*
Michael Windelspecht, *Appalachian State University*
Mary Wisgirda, *San Jacinto College, South Campus*
Jay Zimmerman, *St. John's University*

Second Edition Reviewers

Eyualem Abebe, *Elizabeth City State University*
Nihal Ahmad, *University of Wisconsin–Madison*
John Alcock, *Arizona State University*
Myriam Alhadefl-Feldman, *Lake Washington Technical College*
Dennis Arvidson, *Michigan State University*
David K. Asch, *Youngstown State University*
Tami Asplin, *North Dakota State University*
Amir Assad-Rad, *Delta College*
Karl Aufderheide, *Texas A&M University*
Idelisa Ayala, *Broward Community College*
Anita Davelos Baines, *University of Texas–Pan American*
Adebiyi Banjoko, *Chandler-Gilbert Community College*
Gerry Barclay, *Highline Community College*
Susan Barrett, *Massasoit Community College*
Donald Reon Baud, *University of Memphis*
Vernon Bauer, *Francis Marion University*
Chris Bazinet, *St. John's University*
Michael C. Bell, *Richland College Giacomo Bernardi University of California–Santa Cruz*
Giacomo Bernardi, *University of California–Santa Cruz*
Deborah Bielser, *University of Illinois–Urbana–Champaign*
Arlene G. Billock, *University of Louisiana–Lafayette*
Eric Blackwell, *Delta State University*
Andrew R. Blaustein, *Oregon State University*
Harriette Howard-Lee Block, *Prairie View A&M University*
Steve Blumenshine, *California State University–Fresno*
Jason Bond, *East Carolina University*
Russel Borski, *North Carolina State University*
James Bottesch, *Brevard Community College/Cocoa Campus*
Scott Bowling, *Auburn University*
Robert S. Boyd, *Auburn University*
Robert Brewer, *Cleveland State Community College*
Randy Brewton, *University of Tennessee*
George Briggs, *State Univerity College–Geneseo*
Mirjana M. Brockett, *Georgia Institute of Technology*
W. Randy Brooks, *Florida Atlantic University*
Jack Brown, *Paris Junior College*
Rodolfo Buiser, *University of Wisconsin–Eau Claire*
Anne Bullerjahn, *Owens Community College*
Carolyn J.W. Bunde, *Idaho State University*
Scott Burt, *Truman State University*
Stephen R. Burton, *Grand Valley State University*
Jorge Busciglio, *University of California*
Thomas Bushart, *University of Texas–Austin*
Malcolm Butler, *North Dakota State University*
David Byres, *Florida Community College South Campus*
Jennifer Campbell, *North Carolina State University*

Jeff Carmichael, *University of North Dakota*
Timothy H. Carter, *St. John's University*
Domenic Castignetti, *Loyola University of Chicago*
Deborah A. Cato, *Wheaton College*
Tien-Hsien Chang, *Ohio State University*
Estella Chen, *Kennesaw State University*
Sixue Chen, *University of Florida*
Brenda Chinnery-Allgeier, *University of Texas–Austin*
Young Cho, *Eastern New Mexico University*
Genevieve Chung, *Broward Community College–Central*
Philip Clampitt, *Oakland University*
T. Denise Clark, *Mesa Community College*
Allison Cleveland Roberts, *University of South Florida–Tampa*
Randy W. Cohen, *California State University–Northridge*
Patricia Colberg, *University of Wyoming*
Joanne Conover, *University of Connecticut*
John Cooley, *Yale University*
Craig Coleman, *Brigham Young University–Provo*
Ronald H. Cooper, *University of California–Los Angeles*
Vicki Corbin, *University of Kansas–Lawrence*
Anthony Cornett, *Valencia Community College*
Will Crampton, *University of Central Florida*
Charles Creutz, *University of Toledo*
Karen Curto, *University of Pittsburgh*
Kenneth A. Cutler, *North Carolina Central University*
Cara Davies, *Ohio Northern University*
Donald H. Dean, *The Ohio State University*
James Dearworth, *Lafayette College*
John Dennehy, *Queens College*
William Dentler, *University of Kansas*
Smruti A. Desai, *Lonestar College–Cy Fair*
Donald Deters, *Bowling Green State University*
Laura DiCaprio, *Ohio University*
David S. Domozych, *Skidmore College*
Kristiann M. Dougherty, *Valencia Community College*
Kari M.H. Doyle, *San Jacinto College*
John Drummond, *Lafayette College*
Ernest Dubrul, *University of Toledo*
James N. Dumond, *Texas Southern University*
Tod Duncan, *University of Colorado–Denver*
Richard Duhrkopf, *Baylor University*
Susan Dunford, *University of Cincinnati*
Roland Dute, *Auburn University*
Ralph P. Eckerlin, *Northern Virginia Community College*
Jose L. Egremy, *Northwest Vista College*
David W. Eldridge, *Baylor University*
Lisa K. Elfring, *University of Arizona*
Kurt J. Elliot, *Northwest Vista College*
Seema Endley, *Blinn College*
Bill Ensign, *Kennesaw State University*
David S. Epstein, *J. Sergeant Reynolds Community College*
Gary N. Ervin, *Mississippi State University*
Frederick Essig, *University of Southern Florida*
Brent E. Ewers, *University of Wyoming*
Susan Fahrbach, *Wake Forest University*
Peter Fajer, *Florida State University*
Zen Faulkes, *University of Texas–Pan American*
Miriam Ferzli, *North Carolina State University*
Fleur Ferro, *Community College of Denver*
Jose Fierro, *Florida State College–Jacksonville*
Melanie Fierro, *Florida State College–Jacksonville*
Teresa G. Fischer, *Indian River College*
David Fitch, *New York University*
Sandra Fraley, *Dutchess Community College*
Steven N. Francoeur, *Eastern Michigan University*
Barbara Frase, *Bradley University*
Robert Friedman, *University of South Carolina*
Bernard L. Frye, *University of Texas–Arlington*
Caitlin Gabor, *Texas State University–San Marcos*
Mike Ganger, *Gannon University*
Deborah Garrity, *Colorado State University*
Shannon Gerry, *Wellesley College*
Cindee Giffen, *University of Wisconsin–Madison*

Chris Gissendanner, *University of Louisiana at Monroe*
Florence K. Gleason, *University of Minnesota*
Elmer Godeny, *Baton Rough Community College*
Elizabeth Godrick, *Boston University*
Robert Gorham, *Northern Virginia Community College*
Brian Grafton, *Kent State University*
John Graham, *Bowling Green State University*
Christopher Gregg, *Louisiana State University*
John Griffis, *Joliet Junior College*
LeeAnn Griggs, *Massasoit Community College*
Tim Grogan, *Valencia Community College–Osceola*
Richard S. Groover, *J. Sergeant Reynolds Community College*
Gretel Guest, *Durham Technical Community College*
Cameron Gundersen, *University of California*
Patricia Halpin, *UCLA*
George Hale, *University of West Georgia*
William Hanna, *Massasoit Community College*
David T. Hanson, *University of New Mexico*
Christopher J. Harendza, *Montgomery County Community College*
Sally E. Harmych, *University of Toledo*
Betsy Harris, *Appalachian State University*
M.C. Hart, *Minnesota State University–Mankato*
Barbara Harvey, *Kirkwood Community College*
Mary Beth Hawkins, *North Carolina State University*
Harold Heatwole, *North Carolina State University*
Cheryl Heinz, *Benedictine University*
Jutta B. Heller, *Loyola University–Chicago*
Susan Hengeveld, *Indiana University–Bloomington*
Mark Hens, *University of North Carolina–Greensboro*
Steven K. Herbert, *University of Wyoming–Laramie*
Edgar Javier Hernandez, *University of Missouri–St. Louis*
Albert A. Herrera, *University of Southern California*
David S. Hibbert, *Clark University*
R. James Hickey, *Miami University of Ohio–Oxford*
Terri Hildebrand, *Southern Utah University*
Juliana Hinton, *McNeese State University*
Anne Hitt, *Oakland University*
Robert D. Hollister, *Grand Valley State University*
Richard G Holloway, *Northern Arizona University*
Dianella Howarth, *St. John's University*
Carrie Hughes, *San Jacinto College*
Kelly Howe, *University of New Mexico*
Barbara Hunnicutt, *Seminole Community College*
Bradley Hyman, *University of California–Riverside*
Vicki J. Isola, *Hope College*
Joseph J. Jacquot, *Grand Valley State University*
Desirée Jackson, *Texas Southern University*
John Jaenike, *University of Rochester*
Ashok Jain, *Albany State University*
Eric Jellen, *Brigham Young University*
Elizabeth A. Jordan, *Moorpark College*
Robyn Jordan, *University of Louisiana at Monroe*
Susan Jorstad, *University of Arizona*
Nick Kaplinsky, *Swarthmore College*
Vesna Karaman, *University of Texas at El Paso*
Istvan Karsai, *East Tennessee State University*
Nancy Kaufmann, *University of Pittsburgh*
Stephen R. Kelso, *University of Illinois–Chicago*
Denice D. King, *Cleveland State Community College*
Bridgette Kirkpatrick, *Collin County Community College*
Ted Klenk, *Valencia Community College–West*
Anna Koshy, *Houston Community College–NW*
David Krauss, *Borough of Manhattan Community College*
William Kroll, *Loyola University–Chicago*
Pramod Kumar, *University of Texas–San Antonio*
Allen Kurta, *Eastern Michigan University*
William Lamberts, *College of St. Benedict/Saint John's University*
David Lampe, *Duquesne University*
John C. Law, *Community College of Allegheny County*
Jonathan N. Lawson, *Collin County Community College*
Brenda Leady, *University of Toledo*

David Leaf, *Western Washington University*
John Lepri, *University of North Carolina–Greensboro*
Hugh Lefcort, *Gonzaga University*
Army Lester, *Kennesaw State University*
Q Quinn Li, *Miami University, Ohio*
Nardos Lijam, *Columbus State Community College*
Yusheng Liu, *East Tennessee State University*
Robert Locy, *Auburn University*
Albert R. Loeblich III, *University of Houston*
Thomas A. Lonergan, *University of New Orleans*
Craig Longtine, *North Hennepin Community College*
Donald Lovett, *The College of New Jersey*
Paul T. Magee, *University of Minnesota–Minneapolis*
Jay Mager, *Ohio Northern University*
Charles H. Mallery, *University of Miami*
Nilo Marin, *Broward College*
Joe Matanoski, *Stevenson University*
Patricia Matthews, *Grand Valley State University*
Barbara May, *College of St. Benedict/St. John's University*
Kamau Mbuthia, *Bowling Green State University*
Norah McCabe, *Washington State University*
Chuck McClaugherty, *Mount Union College*
Regina S. McClinton, *Grand Valley State University*
Mark A. McGinley, *Texas Tech University*
Kerry McKenna, *Lord Fairfax College*
Carrie McMahon Hughes, *San Jacinto College–Central Campus*
Joseph McPhee, *LaGuardia Community College*
Judith Megaw, *Indian River Community College*
Mona C. Mehdy, *University of Texas–Austin*
Brad Mehrtens, *University of Illinois–Urbana-Champaign*
Susan Meiers, *Western Illinois University*
Michael Meighan, *University of California–Berkeley*
Catherine Merovich, *West Virginia University*
Richard Merritt, *Houston Community College*
Jennifer Metzler, *Ball State University*
James Mickle, *North Carolina State University*
Brian T. Miller, *Middle Tennessee State University*
Manuel Miranda-Arango, *University of Texas at El Paso*
Michael Misamore, *Texas Christian University*
Jasleen Mishra, *Houston Community College–Southwest*
Alan Molumby, *University of Illinois, Chicago*
W. Linn Montgomery, *Northern Arizona University*
Daniel Moon, *University of North Florida*
Jennifer Moon, *University of Texas–Austin*
Richard C. Moore, *Miami University*
David Morgan, *University of West Georgia*
Roderick M. Morgan, *Grand Valley State University*
Ann C. Morris, *Florida State University*
Christa P.H. Mulder, *University of Alaska–Fairbanks*
Mike Muller, *University of Illinois–Chicago*
Darrel C. Murray, *University of Illinois–Chicago*
Richard J. Murray, *Hendrix College*
Jennifer Nauen, *University of Delaware*
Raymond Neubauer, *University of Texas–Austin*
Jacalyn Newman, *University of Pittsburgh*
Robert Newman, *University of North Dakota*
Laila Nimri, *Seminole Community College*
Shawn E. Nordell, *St. Louis University*
Olumide Ogunmosin, *Texas Southern University*
Wan Ooi, *Houston Community College–Central*
John C. Osterman, *University of Nebraska–Lincoln*
Ravishankar Palanivelu, *University of Arizona*
Peter Pappas, *Community College of Morris*
Lisa Parks, *North Carolina State University*
David Pennock, *Miami University*
Beverly Perry, *Houston Community College*
John S. Peters, *College of Charleston*
David K. Peyton, *Morehead State University*
Marius Pfeiffer, *Tarrant County College NE*

Jerry Phillips, *University of Colorado–Colorado Springs*
Susan Phillips, *Brevard Community College*
Paul Pilliterri, *Southern Utah University*
Debra B. Pires, *University of California–Los Angeles*
Terry Platt, *University of Rochester*
Peggy E. Pollack, *Northern Arizona University*
Uwe Pott, *University of Wisconsin-Green Bay*
Linda F. Potts, *University of North Carolina–Wilmington*
Jessica Poulin, *University at Buffalo, SUNY*
Kumkum Prabhakar, *Nassau Community College*
Joelle Presson, *University of Maryland*
Gregory Pryor, *Francis Marion University*
Penny L. Ragland, *Auburn University*
Rajinder S. Ranu, *Colorado State University*
Marceau Ratard, *Delgado Community College*
Melanie K. Rathburn, *Boston University*
Flona Redway, *Barry University*
Melissa Murray Reedy, *University of Illinois Urbana-Champaign*
Stuart Reichler, *University of Texas–Austin*
Jill D. Reid, *Virginia Commonwealth University*
Anne E. Reilly, *Florida Atlantic University*
Kim Risley, *Mount Union College*
Elisa Rivera-Boyles, *Valencia Community College*
Laurel B. Roberts, *University of Pittsburgh*
James V. Robinson, *The University of Texas–Arlington*
Kenneth R. Robinson, *Purdue University*
Luis A. Rodriguez, *San Antonio College*
Chris Romero, *Front Range Community College–Larimer Campus*
Doug Rouse, *University of Wisconsin–Madison*
Ann E. Rushing, *Baylor University*
Laurie K. Russell, *St. Louis University*
Sheridan Samano, *Community College of Aurora*
Hildegarde Sanders, *Stevenson University*
David K. Saunders, *Augusta State University*
H. Jochen Schenk, *California State University–Fullerton*
Deemah Schirf, *University of Texas–San Antonio*
Chris Schneider, *Boston University*
Susan Schreier, *Towson University*
David Schwartz, *Houston Community College–Southwest*
David A. Scicchitano, *New York University*
Erik Scully, *Towson University*
Robin Searles-Adenegan, *University of Maryland*
Pat Selelyo, *College of Southern Idaho*
Pramila Sen, *Houston Community College–Central*
Tim Shannon, *Francis Marion University*
Jonathan Shaver, *North Hennepin Community College*
Brandon Sheafor, *Mount Union College*
Ellen Shepherd Lamb, *The University of North Carolina-Greensboro*
Mark Sheridan, *North Dakota State University*
Dennis Shevlin, *The College of New Jersey*
Patty Shields, *University of Maryland*
Cara Shillington, *Eastern Michigan University*
Richard M. Showman, *University of South Carolina*
Scott Siechen, *University of Illinois–Urbana-Champaign*
Anne Simon, *University of Maryland*
Sue Simon Westendorf, *Ohio University–Athens*
John B. Skillman, *California State University–San Bernadino*
Lee Smee, *Texas A&M University*
Dianne Snyder, *Augusta State University*
Nancy Solomon, *Miami University*
Sally Sommers Smith, *Boston University*
Punnee Soonthornpoct, *Blinn College*
Vladimir Spiegelman, *University of Wisconsin–Madison*
Bryan Spohn, *Florida State College at Jacksonville*
Bruce Stallsmith, *University of Alabama–Huntsville*
Richard Stalter, *St. John's University*
Susan J. Stamler, *College of Dupage*
William Stein, *Binghampton University*
Mark E. Stephansky, *Massasoit Community College*

Dean Stetler, *University of Kansas–Lawrence*
Brian Stout, *Northwest Vista College*
Mark Sturtevant, *Oakland University*
C.B. Subrahmanvam, *Florida A&M University*
Mark Sutherland, *Hendrix College*
Brook Swanson, *Gonzaga University*
Debbie Swarthout, *Hope College*
Judy Taylor, *Motlow State Community College*
Randall G. Terry, *Lamar University*
Sharon Thoma, *University of Wisconsin*
Carol Thornber, *University of Rhode Island*
Patrick A. Thorpe, *Grand Valley State University*
Scott Tiegs, *Oakland University*
Kristina Timmerman, *St. John's University*
Paul Trombley, *Florida State University*
John R. True, *Stony Brook University*
Encarni Trueba, *Community College of Baltimore County Essex*
Cathy Tugmon, *Augusta State University*
Marshall Turell, *Houston Community College*
Ashok Upadhyaya, *University of South Florida–Tampa*
Anthony J. Uzwiak, *Rutgers University*
William Velhagen, *New York University*
Wendy Vermillion, *Columbus State Community College*
Sara Via, *University of Maryland*
Thomas V. Vogel, *Western Illinois University*
R. Steven Wagner, *Central Washington University–Ellensburg*
John Waldman, *Queens College-CUNY*
Randall Walikonis, *University of Connecticut*
Gary R. Walker, *Youngstown State University*
Sean E. Walker, *California State University–Fullerton*
Delon E. Washo-Krupps, *Arizona State University*
Fred Wasserman, *Boston University*
R. Douglas Watson, *University of Alabama–Birmingham*
Doug Wendell, *Oakland University*
Jennifer Wiatrowski, *Pasco-Hernando Community College*
Sheila Wicks, *Malcolm X College*
Donna Wiersema, *Houston Community College*
Regina Wiggins-Speights, *Houston Community College–Northeast*
David H. Williams, *Valencia Community College*
Lawrence R. Williams, *University of Houston*
Ned Williams, *Minnesota State University–Mankato*
E. Gay Williamson, *Mississippi State University*
Mark S. Wilson, *Humboldt State University*
Bob Winning, *Eastern Michigan University*
David Wood, *California State University–Chico*
Bruce Wunder, *Colorado State University*
Mark Wygoda, *McNeese State University*
Joanna Wysocka-Diller, *Auburn University*
Marlena Yost, *Mississippi State University*
Robert Yost, *Indiana University—Purdue*
Kelly Young, *California State University–Long Beach*
Linda Young, *Ohio Northern University*
Ted Zerucha, *Appalachian State University*

First Edition Reviewers and Contributors

James K. Adams, *Dalton State College*
Sylvester Allred, *Northern Arizona University*
Jonathan W. Armbruster, *Auburn University*
Joseph E. Armstrong, *Illinois State University*
David K. Asch, *Youngstown State University*
Amir M. Assadi-Rad, *Delta College*
Karl J. Aufderheide, *Texas A&M University*
Anita Davelos Baines, *University of Texas–Pan American*
Lisa M. Baird, *University of San Diego*
Diane Bassham, *Iowa State University*
Donald Baud, *University of Memphis*
Vernon W. Bauer, *Francis Marion University*
Ruth E. Beattie, *University of Kentucky*
Michael C. Bell, *Richland College*

Steve Berg, *Winona State University*
Arlene G. Billock, *University of Louisiana–Lafayette*
Kristopher A. Blee, *California State University–Chico*
Heidi B. Borgeas, *University of Tampa*
Russell Borski, *North Carolina State University*
Scott A. Bowling, *Auburn University*
Robert Boyd, *Auburn University*
Eldon J. Braun, *University of Arizona*
Michael Breed, *University of Colorado–Boulder*
Randy Brewton, *University of Tennessee–Knoxville*
Peggy Brickman, *University of Georgia*
Cheryl Briggs, *University of California–Berkeley*
Peter S. Brown, *Mesa Community College*
Mark Browning, *Purdue University*
Cedric O. Buckley, *Jackson State University*
Don Buckley, *Quinnipiac University*
Arthur L. Buikema, Jr., *Virginia Tech University*
Anne Bullerjahn, *Owens Community College*
Ray D. Burkett, *Southeast Tennessee Community College*
Stephen P. Bush, *Coastal Carolina University*
Peter E. Busher, *Boston University*
Jeff Carmichael, *University of North Dakota*
Clint E. Carter, *Vanderbilt University*
Patrick A. Carter, *Washington State University*
Merri Lynn Casem, *California State University–Fullerton*
Domenic Castignetti, *Loyola University–Chicago*
Maria V. Cattell
David T. Champlin, *University of Southern Maine*
Jung H. Choi, *Georgia Institute of Technology*
Curtis Clark, *Cal Poly–Pomona*
Allison Cleveland, *University of South Florida*
Janice J. Clymer, *San Diego Mesa College*
Linda T. Collins, *University of Tennessee–Chattanooga*
William Collins, *Stony Brook University*
Jay L. Comeaux, *Louisiana State University*
Bob Connor II, *Owens Community College*
Daniel Costa, *University of California–Santa Cruz*
Sehoya Cotner, *University of Minnesota*
Mack E. Crayton III, *Xavier University of Louisiana*
Louis Crescitelli, *Bergen Community College*
Charles Creutz, *University of Toledo*
Karen A. Curto, *University of Pittsburgh*
Mark A. Davis, *Macalester College*
Mark D. Decker, *University of Minnesota*
Jeffery P. Demuth, *Indiana University*
Phil Denette, *Delgado Community College*
Donald W. Deters, *Bowling Green State University*
Hudson R. DeYoe, *University of Texas–Pan American*
Laura DiCaprio, *Ohio University*
Randy DiDomenico, *University of Colorado–Boulder*
Robert S. Dill, *Bergen Community College*
Kevin Dixon, *University of Illinois–Urbana–Champaign*
John S. Doctor, *Duquesne University*
Warren D. Dolphin, *Iowa State University*
Cathy A. Donald-Whitney, *Collin County Community College*
Robert P. Donaldson, *George Washington University*
Kristiann Dougherty, *Valencia Community College*
Marjorie Doyle, *University of Wisconsin–Madison*
Ernest F. Dubrul, *University of Toledo*
Jeffry L. Dudycha, *William Patterson University of New Jersey*
Charles Duggins, Jr., *University of South Carolina*
Roland R. Dute, *Auburn University*
William D. Eldred, *Boston University*
Johnny El-Rady, *University of South Florida*
Dave Eldridge, *Baylor University*
Inge Eley, *Hudson Valley Community College*
Frederick B. Essig, *University of South Florida*
Sharon Eversman, *Montana State University*
Stan Faeth, *Arizona State University*
Peter Fajer, *Florida State University*
Paul Farnsworth, *University of Texas–San Antonio*

Paul D. Ferguson, *University of Illinois–Urbana–Champaign*
Margaret F. Field, *Saint Mary's College of California*
Jorge A. Flores, *West Virginia University*
Irwin Forseth, *University of Maryland*
David Foster, *North Idaho College*
Paul Fox, *Danville Community College*
Pete Franco, *University of Minnesota*
Wayne D. Frasch, *Arizona State University*
Barbara Frase, *Bradley University*
Adam J. Fry, *University of Connecticut*
Caitlin R. Gabor, *Texas State University–San Marcos*
Anne M. Galbraith, *University of Wisconsin–La Crosse*
John R. Geiser, *Western Michigan University*
Nicholas R. Geist, *Sonoma State University*
Patricia A. Geppert, *University of Texas–San Antonio*
Frank S. Gilliam, *Marshall University*
Chris R. Gissendanner, *University of Louisiana–Monroe*
Jon Glase, *Cornell University*
Florence K. Gleason, *University of Minnesota*
Elizabeth Godrick, *Boston University*
James M. Grady, *University of New Orleans*
John S. Graham, *Bowling Green State University*
Barbara E. Graham-Evans, *Jackson State University*
Christine E. Gray, *Blinn College*
Stan Guffey, *University of Tennessee*
Rodney D. Hagley, *University of North Carolina–Wilmington*
Gary L. Hannan, *Eastern Michigan University*
Kyle E. Harms, *Louisiana State University*
M. C. Hart, *Minnesota State University–Mankato*
Carla Ann Hass, *The Pennsylvania State University*
Brian T. Hazlett, *Briar Cliff University*
Harold Heatwole, *North Carolina State University*
Mark D. Hens, *University of North Carolina*
Stephen K. Herbert, *University of Wyoming*
Albert A. Herrera, *University of Southern California*
David L. Herrin, *University of Texas–Austin*
Helen Hess, *College of the Atlantic*
R. James Hickey, *Miami University*
Tracey E. Hickox, *University of Illinois–Urbana–Champaign*
Mark A. Holbrook, *University of Iowa*
Ella Ingram, *Rose-Hulman Institute of Technology*
Jeffrey Jack, *University of Louisville*
Judy Jernstedt, *University of California–Davis*
Lee Johnson, *Ohio State University*
Robyn Jordan, *University of Louisiana–Monroe*
Walter S. Judd, *University of Florida*
David Julian, *University of Florida*
Stephen R. Kelso, *University of Illinois–Chicago*
Heather R. Ketchum, *Blinn College*
Eunsoo Kim, *University of Wisconsin–Madison*
Stephen J. King, *University of Missouri–Kansas City*
John Z. Kiss, *Miami University*
Ted Klenk, *Valencia Community College*
David M. Kohl, *University of California–Santa Barbara*
Anna Koshy, *Houston Community College System*
Sherry Krayesky, *University of Louisiana–Lafayette*
John Krenetsky, *Metropolitan State College–Denver*
Karin E. Krieger, *University of Wisconsin–Green Bay*
Paul Kugrens, *Colorado State University*
Josephine Kurdziel, *University of Michigan*
David T. Kurjiaka, *Ohio University*
Allen Kurta, *Eastern Michigan University*
Paul K. Lago, *University of Mississippi*
Ellen Shepherd Lamb, *University of North Carolina–Greensboro*
Pamela Lanford, *University of Maryland*
Marianne M. Laporte, *Eastern Michigan University*

Arlen T. Larson, *University of Colorado–Denver*
John Latto, *University of California–Berkeley*
Brenda Leady, *University of Toledo*
Shannon Erickson Lee, *California State University–Northridge*
Tali D. Lee, *University of Wisconsin–Eau Claire*
Michael Lentz, *University of North Florida*
Jennifer J. Lewis, *San Juan College*
Pauline A. Lizotte, *Valencia Community College*
Jason L. Locklin, *Temple College*
Robert Locy, *Auburn University*
James A. Long, *Boise State University*
David Lonzarich, *University of Wisconsin–Eau Claire*
James B. Ludden, *College of DuPage*
Albert MacKrell, *Bradley University*
P. T. Magee, *University of Minnesota*
Christi Magrath, *Troy University*
Richard Malkin, *University of California–Berkeley*
Charles H. Mallery, *University of Miami*
Kathleen A. Marrs, *IUPUI–Indianapolis*
Diane L. Marshall, *University of New Mexico*
Peter J. Martinat, *Xavier University of Louisiana*
Joel Maruniak, *University of Missouri*
Kamau Mbuthia, *Bowling Green State University*
Greg McCormac, *American River College*
Andrew McCubbin, *Washington State University*
David L. McCulloch, *Collin County Community College*
Tanya K. McKinney, *Xavier University of Louisiana*
Brad Mehrtens, *University of Illinois–Urbana–Champaign*
Michael Meighan, *University of California–Berkeley*
Douglas Meikle, *Miami University*
Allen F. Mensinger, *University of Minnesota–Duluth*
John Merrill, *Michigan State University*
Richard Merritt, *Houston Community College*
Melissa Michael, *University of Illinois–Urbana–Champaign*
Brian T. Miller, *Middle Tennessee State University*
Hugh A. Miller III, *East Tennessee State University*
Thomas E. Miller, *Florida State University*
Sarah L. Milton, *Florida Atlantic University*
Dennis J. Minchella, *Purdue University*
Subhash C. Minocha, *University of New Hampshire*
Patricia Mire, *University of Louisiana-Lafayette*
Daniela S. Monk, *Washington State University*
Daniel C. Moon, *University of North Florida*
Janice Moore, *Colorado State University*
Mathew D. Moran, *Hendrix College*
Jorge A. Moreno, *University of Colorado–Boulder*
Roderick M. Morgan, *Grand Valley State University*
James V. Moroney, *Louisiana State University*
Molly R. Morris, *Ohio University*
Michael Muller, *University of Illinois–Chicago*
Michelle Mynlieff, *Marquette University*
Allan D. Nelson, *Tarleton State University*
Raymond L. Neubauer, *University of Texas–Austin*
Jacalyn S. Newman, *University of Pittsburgh*
Colleen J. Nolan, *St. Mary's University*
Shawn E. Nordell, *St. Louis University*
Margaret Nsofor, *Southern Illinois University–Carbondale*
Dennis W. Nyberg, *University of Illinois–Chicago*
Nicole S. Obert, *University of Illinois–Urbana–Champaign*
David G. Oppenheimer, *University of Florida*
John C. Osterman, *University of Nebraska– Lincoln*
Brian Palestis, *Wagner College*
Julie M. Palmer, *University of Texas–Austin*
C. O. Patterson, *Texas A&M University*
Ronald J. Patterson, *Michigan State University*
Linda M. Peck, *University of Findlay*
David Pennock, *Miami University*
Shelley W. Penrod, *North Harris College*
Beverly J. Perry, *Houston Community College System*
Chris Petersen, *College of the Atlantic*
Jay Phelan, *UCLA*

Randall Phillis, *University of Massachusetts–Amherst*
Eric R. Pianka, *The University of Texas–Austin*
Thomas Pitzer, *Florida International University*
Peggy E. Pollak, *Northern Arizona University*
Mitch Price, *Pennsylvania State University*
Richard B. Primack, *Boston University*
Lynda Randa, *College of Dupage*
Marceau Ratard, *Delgado Community College*
Robert S. Rawding, *Gannon University*
Jennifer Regan, *University of Southern Mississippi*
Stuart Reichler, *University of Texas–Austin*
Jill D. Reid, *Virginia Commonwealth University*
Anne E. Reilly, *Florida Atlantic University*
Linda R. Richardson, *Blinn College*
Laurel Roberts, *University of Pittsburgh*
Kenneth R. Robinson, *Purdue University*
Chris Ross, *Kansas State University*
Anthony M. Rossi, *University of North Florida*
Kenneth H. Roux, *Florida State University*
Ann E. Rushing, *Baylor University*
Scott Russell, *University of Oklahoma*
Christina T. Russin, *Northwestern University*
Charles L. Rutherford, *Virginia Tech University*
Margaret Saha, *College of William and Mary*
Kanagasabapathi Sathasivan, *University of Texas–Austin*
Stephen G. Saupe, *College of St. Benedict*
Jon B. Scales, *Midwestern State University*
Daniel C. Scheirer, *Northeastern University*
H. Jochen Schenk, *California State University–Fullerton*
John Schiefelbein, *University of Michigan*
Deemah N. Schirf, *University of Texas–San Antonio*
Mark Schlueter, *College of Saint Mary*
Scott Schuette, *Southern Illinois University–Carbondale*
Dean D. Schwartz, *Auburn University*
Timothy E. Shannon, *Francis Marion University*
Richard M. Showman, *University of South Carolina*
Michele Shuster, *New Mexico State University*
Martin Silberberg, *McGraw-Hill chemistry author*
Robert Simons, *UCLA*
J. Henry Slone, *Francis Marion University*
Phillip Snider, Jr., *Gadsden State Community College*
Nancy G. Solomon, *Miami University*
Lekha Sreedhar, *University of Missouri–Kansas City*
Bruce Stallsmith, *University of Alabama–Huntsville*

Susan J. Stamler, *College of Dupage*
Mark P. Staves, *Grand Valley State University*
William Stein, *Binghamton University*
Philip J. Stephens, *Villanova University*
Kevin Strang, *University of Wisconsin-Madison*
Antony Stretton, *University of Wisconsin–Madison*
Gregory W. Stunz, *Texas A&M University–Corpus Christi*
Julie Sutherland, *College of Dupage*
David Tam, *University of North Texas*
Roy A. Tassava, *Ohio State University*
Sharon Thoma, *University of Wisconsin–Madison*
Shawn A. Thomas, *College of St. Benedict/St. John's University*
Daniel B. Tinker, *University of Wyoming*
Marty Tracey, *Florida International University*
Marsha Turell, *Houston Community College*
J. M. Turbeville, *Virginia Commonwealth University*
Rani Vajravelu, *University of Central Florida*
Neal J. Voelz, *St. Cloud State University*
Samuel E. Wages, *South Plains College*
Jyoti R. Wagle, *Houston Community College System–Central*
Charles Walcott, *Cornell University*
Randall Walikonis, *University of Connecticut*
Jeffrey A. Walker, *University of Southern Maine*
Delon E. Washo-Krupps, *Arizona State University*
Frederick Wasserman, *Boston University*
Steven A. Wasserman, *University of California–San Diego*
R. Douglas Watson, *University of Alabama–Birmingham*
Cindy Martinez Wedig, *University of Texas–Pan American*
Arthur E. Weis, *University of California–Irvine*
Sue Simon Westendorf, *Ohio University*
Howard Whiteman, *Murray State University*
Susan Whittemore, *Keene State College*
David L. Wilson, *University of Miami*
Robert Winning, *Eastern Michigan University*
Jane E. Wissinger, *University of Minnesota*
Michelle D. Withers, *Louisiana State University*
Clarence C. Wolfe, *Northern Virginia Community College*
Gene K. Wong, *Quinnipiac University*
Richard P. Wunderlin, *University of South Florida*
Joanna Wysocka-Diller, *Auburn University*
H. Randall Yoder, *Lamar University*
Marilyn Yoder, *University of Missouri–Kansas City*
Scott D. Zimmerman, *Southwest Missouri State University*

International Reviewers

Dr. Alyaa Ragaei, *Future University, Cairo*
Heather Addy, *University of Calgary*
Mari L. Acevedo, *University of Puerto Rico at Arecibo*
Heather E. Allison, *University of Liverpool, UK*
David Backhouse, *University of New England*
Andrew Bendall, *University of Guelph*
Marinda Bloom, *Stellenbosch University, South Africa*
Tony Bradshaw, *Oxford-Brookes University, UK*
Alison Campbell, *University of Waikato*
Bruce Campbell, *Okanagan College*
Clara E. Carrasco, Ph.D., *University of Puerto Rico–Ponce Campus*
Keith Charnley, *University of Bath, UK*
Ian Cock, *Griffith University*
Margaret Cooley, *University of NSW*
R. S. Currah, *University of Alberta*
Logan Donaldson, *York University*
Theo Elzenga, *Rijks Universiteit Groningen, Netherlands*
Neil C. Haave, *University of Alberta*
Tom Haffie, *University of Western Ontario*
Louise M. Hafner, *Queensland University of Technology*
Annika F. M. Haywood, *Memorial University of Newfoundland*
William Huddleston, *University of Calgary*
Shin-Sung Kang, *KyungBuk University*
Wendy J. Keenleyside, *University of Guelph*
Christopher J. Kennedy, *Simon Fraser University*
Bob Lauder, *Lancaster University*
Richard C. Leegood, *Sheffield University, UK*
Thomas H. MacRae, *Dalhousie University*
R. Ian Menz, *Flinders University*
Kirsten Poling, *University of Windsor*
Jim Provan, *Queens University, Belfast, UK*
Richard Roy, *McGill University*
Han A.B. Wösten, *Utrecht University, Netherlands*

A NOTE FROM THE AUTHORS

The lives of most science-textbook authors do not revolve around an analysis of writing techniques. Instead, we are people who understand science and are inspired by it, and we want to communicate that information to our students. Simply put, we need a lot of help to get it right.

Editors are a key component that help the authors modify the content of their book so it is logical, easy to read, and inspiring. The editorial team for this *Biology* textbook has been a catalyst that kept this project rolling. The members played various roles in the editorial process. Lisa Bruflodt, Senior Developmental Editor, has been the master organizer. Coordinating the efforts of dozens of people and keeping them on schedule is not always fun. Lisa's success at keeping us on schedule has been truly amazing.

Our Freelance Developmental Editors worked directly with the authors to greatly improve the presentation of the textbook's content. Suzanne Olivier and Joni Frasier did an outstanding job in editing chapters and advising the authors on improvements for the second edition. Deborah Brooker painstakingly analyzed all of the illustrations in the textbook to make sure they are accurate, consistent, and student-friendly. She also took the lead role in the editing of the glossary. We would also like to acknowledge our copy editor, Jane DeShaw, for keeping our grammar on track.

Another important aspect of the editorial process is the actual design, presentation, and layout of materials. It's confusing if the text and art aren't on the same page or if a figure is too large or too small. We are indebted to the tireless efforts of Peggy Selle, Lead Project Manager, and David Hash, Senior Designer of McGraw-Hill. Their artistic talents, ability to size and arrange figures, and attention to the consistency of the figures have been remarkable.

We would like to acknowledge the ongoing efforts of the superb marketing staff at McGraw-Hill. Kent Peterson, Vice President, Director of Marketing, oversees a talented staff of people who work tirelessly to promote our book. Special thanks to Michelle Watnick, Marketing Director, and Chris Loewenberg, Marketing Manager, for their ideas and enthusiasm for this book.

Finally, other staff members at McGraw-Hill Higher Education have ensured that the authors and editors were provided with adequate resources to achieve the goal of producing a superior textbook. These include Kurt Strand, President, Science, Engineering, and Math; Marty Lange, Vice President, Editor-in-Chief; and Janice Roerig-Blong, Publisher.

Contents

UNIT I   Chemistry

UNIT II   Cell

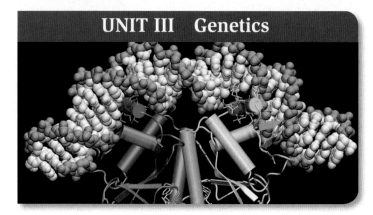

UNIT III   Genetics

CONTENTS

BIOLOGY

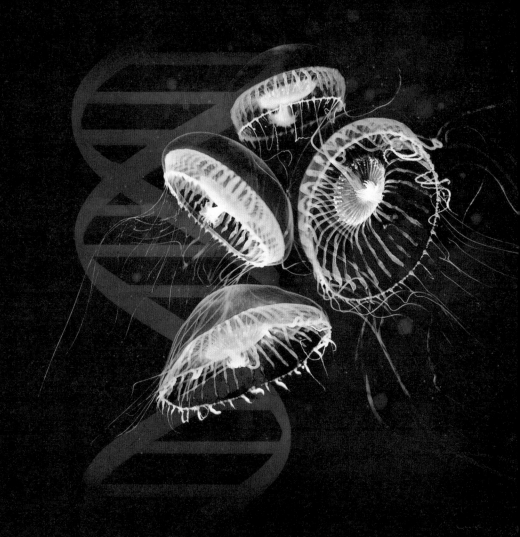

An Introduction to Biology

1

Biology is the study of life. The diverse forms of life found on Earth provide biologists with an amazing array of organisms to study. In many cases, the investigation of living things leads to unforeseen discoveries that no one would have imagined. For example, researchers determined that the venom from certain poisonous snakes contains a chemical that lowers blood pressure in humans. By analyzing that chemical, drugs were later developed to treat high blood pressure (Figure 1.1). Certain ancient civilizations, such as the Greeks, Romans, and Egyptians, discovered that the bark of the white willow tree can be used to fight fever. Modern chemists determined that willow bark contains a substance called salicylic acid, which led to the development of the related compound acetylsalicylic acid, more commonly known as aspirin (Figure 1.2). In the last century, biologists studied soil bacteria that naturally produce "chemical weapons" to kill competing bacteria in their native environment. These chemicals have been characterized and used to develop antibiotics such as streptomycin to treat bacterial infections (Figure 1.3). Finally, for many decades, biologists have known that the Pacific yew tree produces a toxin in its bark and needles that kills insects.

The crystal jelly (*Aequorea victoria*), which produces a green fluorescent protein (GFP). The gene that encodes GFP has been widely used by researchers to study gene expression and to determine the locations of proteins in cells.

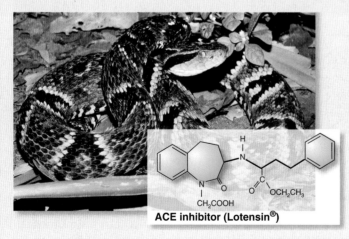

ACE inhibitor (Lotensin®)

Figure 1.1 **The Brazilian arrowhead viper and inhibitors of high blood pressure.** Derivatives of a chemical found in the venom of the Brazilian arrowhead viper, called angiotensin-converting enzyme (ACE) inhibitors, are commonly used to treat high blood pressure.

Aspirin

Figure 1.2 **The white willow and aspirin.** Modern aspirin, acetylsalicylic acid, was developed after analyzing a chemical found in the bark of the white willow tree.

Since the 1990s, this toxin, known by the drug name Taxol, has been used to treat patients with ovarian and breast cancer (**Figure 1.4**). These are but a few of the many discoveries that make biology an intriguing discipline. The study of life not only reveals the fascinating characteristics of living species but also leads to the development of drugs and research tools that benefit the lives of people.

To make new discoveries, biologists view life from many different perspectives. What is the composition of living things? How is life organized? How do organisms reproduce? Sometimes the questions posed by biologists are fundamental and even philosophical in nature. How did living organisms originate? Can we live forever? What is the physical basis for memory? Can we save endangered species? Can we understand intriguing changes in body function, such as the green light given off by certain jellyfish?

Future biologists will continue to make important advances. Biologists are scientific explorers looking for answers to some of the world's most enduring mysteries. Unraveling these mysteries presents an exciting challenge to the best and brightest minds. The rewards of a career in biology include the excitement of forging into uncharted territory, the thrill of making discoveries that can improve the health and lives of people, and the impact of biology on the preservation of the environment and endangered species. For these and many other compelling reasons, students seeking challenging and rewarding careers may wish to choose biology as a lifelong pursuit.

In this chapter, we will begin our survey of biology by examining the basic features that are common to all living organisms. We will consider how evolution has led to the development of modern genomes—the entire genetic compositions of living organisms—which can explain the unity and diversity that we observe among modern species. Finally, we will explore the general approaches that scientists follow when making new discoveries.

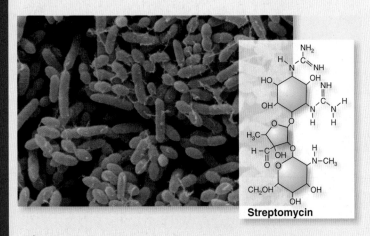

Figure 1.3 **The soil bacterium *Streptomyces griseus*, which naturally produces streptomycin that kills competing bacteria in the soil.** Doctors administer streptomycin to people to treat bacterial infections.

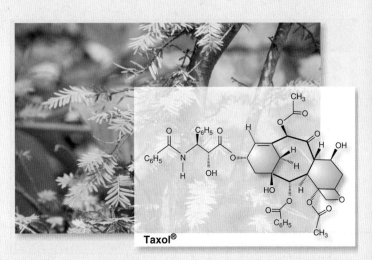

Figure 1.4 **The Pacific yew and Taxol.** A toxin called Taxol, found in the Pacific yew tree, is effective in the treatment of certain cancers.

Concept check: How does biology—the study of life—benefit humans?

1.1 The Properties of Life

A good way to begin a biology textbook is to distinguish living organisms from nonliving objects. At first, the distinction might seem intuitively obvious. A person is alive, but a rock is not. However, the distinction between living and nonliving may seem less obvious when we consider microscopic entities. Is a bacterium alive? What about a virus or a chromosome? In this section, we will examine the characteristics that are common to all forms of life and consider the levels of organization that biologists study.

A Set of Characteristics Is Common to All Forms of Modern Life

Living organisms have consistent features that set them apart from nonliving things. Biologists have determined that all living organisms display seven common characteristics, as described next.

Cells and Organization The concept of organization is so fundamental to biology that the term **organism** can be applied to all living species. Organisms maintain an internal order that is separated from the environment (**Figure 1.5a**). The simplest unit of such organization is the **cell**, which we will examine in Unit II. The **cell theory** states that (1) all organisms are made of cells, (2) cells are the smallest units of life, and (3) cells come from pre-existing cells via cell division. Unicellular organisms are composed of one cell, whereas multicellular organisms such as plants and animals contain many cells. In plants and animals, each cell has internal order, and the cells within the body have specific arrangements and functions.

Energy Use and Metabolism The maintenance of organization requires energy. Therefore, all living organisms acquire

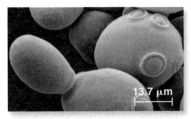

(a) Cells and organization:
Organisms maintain an internal order. The simplest unit of organization is the cell. Yeast cells are shown here.

13.7 μm

(b) Energy use and metabolism:
Organisms need energy to maintain internal order. These algae harness light energy via photosynthesis. Energy is used in chemical reactions collectively known as metabolism.

(c) Response to environmental changes:
Organisms react to environmental changes that promote their survival.

(d) Regulation and homeostasis:
Organisms regulate their cells and bodies, maintaining relatively stable internal conditions, a process called homeostasis.

(e) Growth and development:
Growth produces more or larger cells, whereas development produces organisms with a defined set of characteristics.

(f) Reproduction:
To sustain life over many generations, organisms must reproduce. Due to the transmission of genetic material, offspring tend to have traits like their parents.

(g) Biological evolution:
Populations of organisms change over the course of many generations. Evolution results in traits that promote survival and reproductive success.

Figure 1.5 Seven characteristics common to life.

energy from the environment and use that energy to maintain their internal order. Cells carry out a variety of chemical reactions that are responsible for the breakdown of nutrients. Such reactions often release energy in a process called **respiration**. The energy may be used to synthesize the components that make up individual cells and living organisms. Chemical reactions involved with the breakdown and synthesis of cellular molecules are collectively known as **metabolism**. Plants, algae, and certain bacteria can directly harness light energy to produce their own nutrients in the process of **photosynthesis** (Figure 1.5b). They are primary producers of food on Earth. In contrast, some organisms, such as animals and fungi, are consumers—they must use other organisms as food to obtain energy.

Response to Environmental Changes   To survive, living organisms must be able to respond to environmental changes. For example, bacterial cells have mechanisms to detect that certain nutrients in the environment are in short supply while others are readily available. In the winter, many species of mammals develop a thicker coat of fur that protects them from the cold temperatures. Also, plants can respond to changes in the angle of the sun. If you place a plant in a window, it will grow toward the light (Figure 1.5c). The response shown in Figure 1.5c is a short-term response. As discussed later, biological evolution over the course of many generations can lead to more permanent adaptations of a species to its environment.

Regulation and Homeostasis   As we have just seen, one way that organisms can respond to environmental variation is to change themselves. The growth of thick fur in the wintertime is an example. Although life is a dynamic process, living cells and organisms regulate their cells and bodies to maintain relatively stable internal conditions, a process called **homeostasis** (from the Greek, meaning to stay the same). The degree to which homeostasis is achieved varies among different organisms. For example, most mammals and birds maintain a relatively stable body temperature in spite of changing environmental temperatures (Figure 1.5d), whereas reptiles and amphibians tolerate a wider fluctuation in body temperature. By comparison, all organisms continually regulate their cellular metabolism so that nutrient molecules are used at an appropriate rate and new cellular components are synthesized when they are needed.

Growth and Development   All living things grow and develop. **Growth** produces more or larger cells, whereas **development** is a series of changes in the state of a cell, tissue, organ, or organism. The process of development produces organisms with a defined set of characteristics. Among unicellular organisms such as bacteria, new cells are relatively small, and they increase in volume by the synthesis of additional cellular components. Multicellular organisms, such as plants and animals, begin life at a single-cell stage (for example, a fertilized egg) and then undergo multiple cell divisions to develop into a complete organism with many cells (Figure 1.5e).

Reproduction All living organisms have a finite life span. To sustain life over many generations, organisms must **reproduce** (**Figure 1.5f**). A key feature of reproduction is that offspring tend to have characteristics that greatly resemble those of their parent(s). How is this possible? All living organisms contain genetic material composed of **DNA** (**deoxyribonucleic acid**), which provides a blueprint for the organization, development, and function of living things. During reproduction, a copy of this blueprint is transmitted from parent to offspring. As discussed in Unit III, **genes**, which are segments of DNA, govern the characteristics, or traits, of organisms. Most genes are transcribed into a type of **RNA** (**ribonucleic acid**) molecule called messenger RNA (mRNA) that is then translated into a **polypeptide** with a specific amino acid sequence. A **protein** is composed of one or more polypeptides. The structures and functions of proteins are largely responsible for the traits of living organisms.

Biological Evolution The first six characteristics of life, which we have just considered, apply to individual organisms over the short run. Over the long run, another universal characteristic of life is **biological evolution**, which refers to the phenomenon that populations of organisms change from generation to generation. As a result of evolution, organisms may become more successful at survival and reproduction. Populations become better adapted to the environment in which they live. For example, the long snout of an anteater is an adaptation that enhances its ability to obtain food, namely ants, from hard-to-reach places (**Figure 1.5g**). Over the course of many generations, the long snout occurred via biological evolution in which modern anteaters evolved from populations of organisms that did not have such long snouts. Unit IV is devoted to the topic of evolution, and Unit V surveys the evolutionary diversity among different forms of life.

Living Organisms Can Be Viewed at Different Levels of Organization

As we have just learned, life exhibits a set of characteristics, beginning with the concept of organization. The organization of living organisms can be analyzed at different levels of complexity, starting with the tiniest level of organization and progressing to levels that are physically much larger and more complex. **Figure 1.6** depicts a scientist's view of biological organization at different levels.

1. **Atoms:** An **atom** is the smallest unit of an element that has the chemical properties of the element. All matter is composed of atoms.
2. **Molecules and macromolecules:** As discussed in Unit I, atoms bond with each other to form **molecules**. Many molecules bonded together to form a polymer such as a polypeptide is called a **macromolecule**. Carbohydrates, proteins, and nucleic acids (for example, DNA and RNA) are important macromolecules found in living organisms.

3. **Cells:** Molecules and macromolecules associate with each other to form larger structures such as membranes. A **cell** is formed from the association of these larger structures.
4. **Tissues:** In the case of multicellular organisms such as plants and animals, many cells of the same type associate with each other to form **tissues**. An example is muscle tissue (Figure 1.6).
5. **Organs:** In complex multicellular organisms, an **organ** is composed of two or more types of tissue. For example, the heart is composed of several types of tissues, including muscle, nervous, and connective tissue.
6. **Organism:** All living things can be called **organisms**. A single organism possesses the set of characteristics that define life. Biologists classify organisms as belonging to a particular **species**, which is a related group of organisms that share a distinctive form and set of attributes in nature. The members of the same species are closely related genetically. In Units VI and VII, we will examine plants and animals at the level of cells, tissues, organs, and complete organisms.
7. **Population:** A group of organisms of the same species that occupy the same environment is called a **population**.
8. **Community:** A biological **community** is an assemblage of populations of different species. The types of species found in a community are determined by the environment and by the interactions of species with each other.
9. **Ecosystem:** Researchers may extend their work beyond living organisms and also study the environment. Ecologists analyze **ecosystems**, which are formed by interactions of a community of organisms with their physical environment. Unit VIII considers biology from populations to ecosystems.
10. **Biosphere:** The **biosphere** includes all of the places on the Earth where living organisms exist. Life is found in the air, in bodies of water, on the land, and in the soil.

1.2 The Unity and Diversity of Life

Unity and diversity are two words that often are used to describe the living world. As we have seen, all modern forms of life display a common set of characteristics that distinguish them from nonliving objects. In this section, we will explore how this unity of common traits is rooted in the phenomenon of biological evolution. As you will learn, life on Earth is united by an evolutionary past in which modern organisms have evolved from pre-existing organisms.

Evolutionary unity does not mean that organisms are exactly alike. The Earth has many different types of environments, ranging from tropical rain forests to salty oceans, hot and dry deserts, and cold mountaintops. Diverse forms of life have evolved in ways that help them prosper in the diverse environments the Earth has to offer. In this section, we will begin to examine the diversity that exists within the biological world.

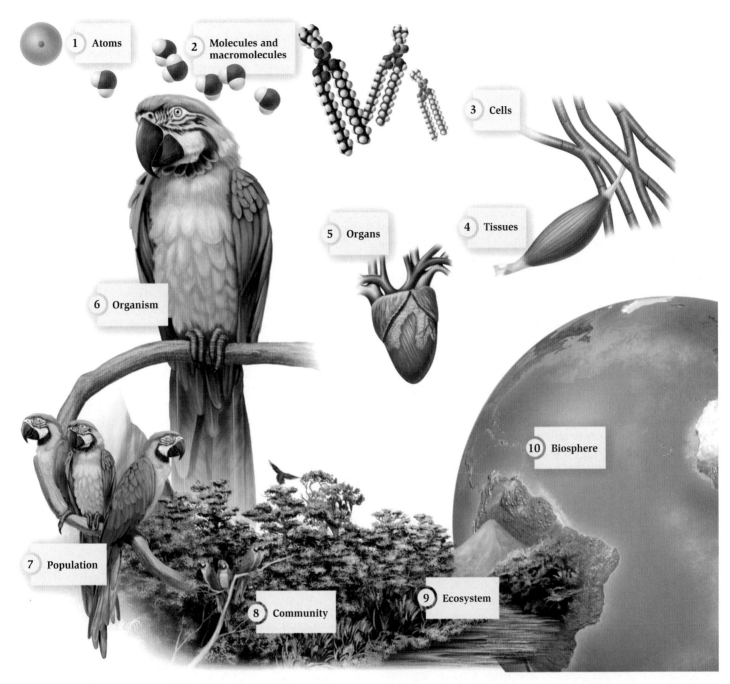

Figure 1.6 The levels of biological organization.

Concept check: *At which level of biological organization would you place a herd of buffalo?*

Modern Forms of Life Are Connected by an Evolutionary History

Life began on Earth as primitive cells about 3.5 to 4 billion years ago. Since that time, those primitive cells underwent evolutionary changes that ultimately gave rise to the species we see today. Understanding the evolutionary history of species often provides key insights into the structure and function of an organism's body. As a way to help you appreciate this idea, **Figure 1.7** shows a photograph of a bird using a milk carton

in which to build a nest. If we did not already know that the milk carton had served an earlier purpose—namely, to contain milk—we might wonder why the bird had made a nesting site with this shape. Obviously, we do not need to wonder about this because we immediately grasp that the milk carton had a previous history and that it has been modified by a person to serve a new purpose—a nesting site for a bird. Understanding history allows us to make sense out of this nest.

Likewise, evolutionary change involves modifications of characteristics in pre-existing populations. Over long periods of time, populations may change such that structures with a particular function may become modified to serve a new function. For example, the wing of a bat is used for flying, and the flipper of a dolphin is used for swimming. Both structures were modified from a limb that was used for walking in a pre-existing ancestor (Figure 1.8).

Evolutionary change occurs by two mechanisms: vertical descent with mutation and horizontal gene transfer. Let's take a brief look at each of these mechanisms.

Vertical Descent with Mutation   The traditional way to view evolution is in a vertical manner, which involves a progression of changes in a series of ancestors. Such a series is called a **lineage**. Figure 1.9 shows a portion of the lineage that gave rise to modern horses. This type of evolution is called **vertical evolution** because it occurs in a lineage. Biologists have traditionally depicted such evolutionary change in a diagram like the one shown in Figure 1.9. In this mechanism of evolution, new species evolve from pre-existing species by the accumulation of **mutations**, which are random changes in the genetic material of organisms. But why would some mutations accumulate in a population and eventually change the characteristics of an entire species? One reason is that a mutation may alter the traits of organisms in a way that increases their chances of survival and reproduction. When a mutation causes such a beneficial change, the frequency of the mutation may increase in a population from one generation to the next, a process called **natural selection**. This process is discussed in Units IV and V. Evolution also involves the accumulation of neutral changes that do not either benefit or harm a species, and sometimes even involves rare changes that may be harmful.

With regard to the horses shown in Figure 1.9, the fossil record has revealed adaptive changes in various traits such as size and tooth morphology. The first horses were the size of dogs, whereas modern horses typically weigh more than a half ton. The teeth of *Hyracotherium* were relatively small compared to those of modern horses. Over the course of millions of years, horse teeth have increased in size, and a complex pattern of ridges has developed on the molars. How do evolutionary biologists explain these changes in horse characteristics? They can be attributed to natural selection producing adaptations to changing global climates. Over North America, where much of horse evolution occurred, large areas changed from dense forests to grasslands. The horses' increase in size allowed them to escape predators and travel great distances in search of food. The changes seen in horses' teeth are consistent with a dietary shift from eating more tender leaves to eating grasses and other vegetation that are more abrasive and require more chewing.

Horizontal Gene Transfer   The most common way for genes to be transferred is in a vertical manner. This can involve the transfer of genetic material from a mother cell to daughter cells, or it can occur via gametes—sperm and egg—that unite to form a new organism. However, as discussed in later chapters, genes are sometimes transferred between organisms by other mechanisms. These other mechanisms are collectively known as **horizontal gene transfer**. In some cases, horizontal gene transfer can occur between members of different species. For example, you may have heard in the news media that resistance to antibiotics among bacteria is a growing medical problem. As discussed in Chapter 18, genes that confer antibiotic resistance are sometimes transferred between different bacterial species (Figure 1.10).

Figure 1.7 **An example of modification of a structure for a new function.**   The bird shown here has used a modified milk carton in which to build its nest. By analogy, evolution also involves the modification of pre-existing structures for a new function.

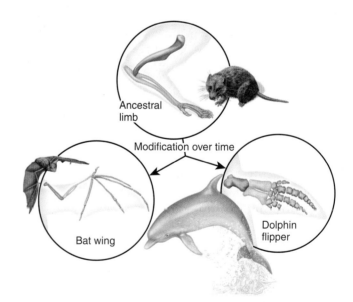

Figure 1.8 **An example showing a modification that has occurred as a result of biological evolution.**   The wing of a bat and the flipper of a dolphin were modified from a limb that was used for walking in a pre-existing ancestor.

Concept check: *Among mammals, give two examples of how the tail has been modified for different purposes.*

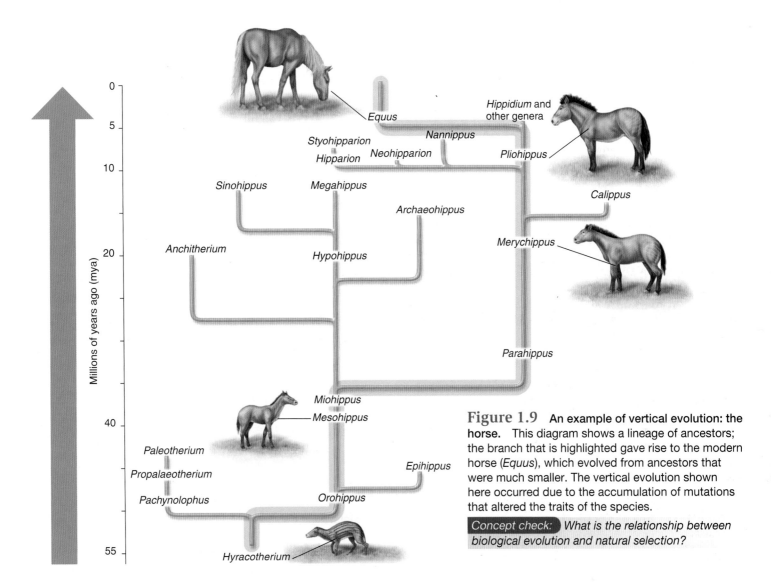

Figure 1.9   **An example of vertical evolution: the horse.**   This diagram shows a lineage of ancestors; the branch that is highlighted gave rise to the modern horse (*Equus*), which evolved from ancestors that were much smaller. The vertical evolution shown here occurred due to the accumulation of mutations that altered the traits of the species.

Concept check: *What is the relationship between biological evolution and natural selection?*

In a lineage in which the time scale is depicted on a vertical axis, horizontal gene transfer between different species is shown as a horizontal line (**Figure 1.11**). Genes transferred horizontally may be subjected to natural selection and promote changes in an entire species. This has been an important mechanism of evolutionary change, particularly among bacterial species. In addition, during the early stages of evolution, which occurred a few billion years ago, horizontal gene transfer was an important part of the process that gave rise to all modern species.

Traditionally, biologists have described evolution using diagrams that depict the vertical evolution of species on a long time scale. This is the type of evolutionary tree that was shown in Figure 1.9. For many decades, the simplistic view held that all living organisms evolved from a common ancestor, resulting in a "tree of life" that could describe the vertical evolution that gave rise to all modern species. Now that we understand the great importance of horizontal gene transfer in the evolution of life on Earth, biologists have needed to re-evaluate the concept of evolution as it occurs over time. Rather than a tree of life, a more appropriate way to view the unity of living organisms is

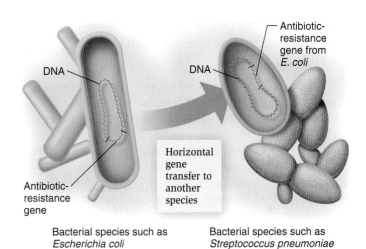

Figure 1.10   **An example of horizontal gene transfer: antibiotic resistance.**   One bacterial species may transfer a gene to a different bacterial species, such as a gene that confers resistance to an antibiotic.

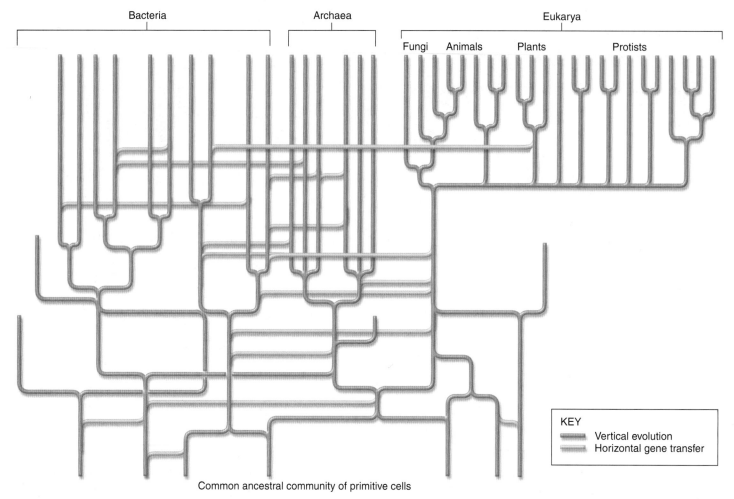

Common ancestral community of primitive cells

Figure 1.11   The web of life, showing both vertical evolution and horizontal gene transfer.   This diagram of evolution includes both of these important mechanisms in the evolution of life on Earth. Note: Archaea are unicellular species.

Concept check: *How does the concept of a tree of life differ from that of a web of life?*

to describe it as a "web of life," which accounts for both vertical evolution and horizontal gene transfer (Figure 1.11).

The Classification of Living Organisms Allows Biologists to Appreciate the Unity and Diversity of Life

As biologists discover new species, they try to place them in groups based on their evolutionary history. This is a difficult task because researchers estimate the Earth has between 10 and 100 million different species! The rationale for categorization is usually based on vertical descent. Species with a recent common ancestor are grouped together, whereas species whose common ancestor is in the very distant past are placed into different groups. The grouping of species is termed **taxonomy**.

Let's first consider taxonomy on a broad scale. You may have noticed that Figure 1.11 showed three main groups of organisms. All forms of life can be placed into three large categories, or domains, called **Bacteria**, **Archaea**, and **Eukarya** (**Figure 1.12**). Bacteria and Archaea are microorganisms that are also termed **prokaryotic** because their cell structure is

relatively simple. At the molecular level, bacterial and archaeal cells show significant differences in their compositions. By comparison, organisms in domain Eukarya are **eukaryotic** and have larger cells with internal compartments that serve various functions. A defining distinction between prokaryotic and eukaryotic cells is that eukaryotic cells have a **cell nucleus** in which the genetic material is surrounded by a membrane. The organisms in domain Eukarya had once been subdivided into four major categories, or kingdoms, called Protista (protists), Plantae (plants), Fungi, and Animalia (animals). However, as discussed in Chapter 26 and Unit V, this traditional view has become invalid as biologists have gathered new information regarding the evolutionary relationships of these organisms. We now know that the protists do not form a single kingdom but instead can be divided into seven broad groups.

Taxonomy involves multiple levels in which particular species are placed into progressively smaller and smaller groups of organisms that are more closely related to each other evolutionarily. Such an approach emphasizes the unity and diversity of different species. As an example, let's consider the clownfish, which is a common saltwater aquarium fish (**Figure 1.13**).

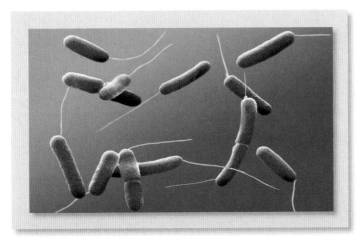

(a) Domain Bacteria: Mostly unicellular prokaryotes that inhabit many diverse environments on Earth.

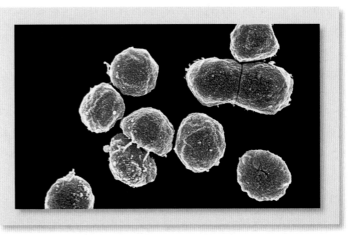

(b) Domain Archaea: Unicellular prokaryotes that often live in extreme environments, such as hot springs.

Protists: Unicellular and small multicellular organisms that are now subdivided into seven broad groups based on their evolutionary relationships.

Plants: Multicellular organisms that can carry out photosynthesis.

Fungi: Unicellular and multicellular organisms that have a cell wall but cannot carry out photosynthesis. Fungi usually survive on decaying organic material.

Animals: Multicellular organisms that usually have a nervous system and are capable of locomotion. They must eat other organisms or the products of other organisms to live.

(c) Domain Eukarya: Unicellular and multicellular organisms having cells with internal compartments that serve various functions.

Figure 1.12   **The three domains of life.**   Two of these domains, **(a)** Bacteria and **(b)** Archaea, are prokaryotes. The third domain, **(c)** Eukarya, comprises species that are eukaryotes.

Taxonomic group	Clown anemonefish is found in	Approximate time when the common ancestor for this group arose	Approximate number of modern species in this group	Examples
Domain	Eukarya	2,000 mya	> 5,000,000	
Kingdom	Animalia	600 mya	> 1,000,000	
Phylum	Chordata	525 mya	50,000	
Class	Actinopterygii	420 mya	30,000	
Order	Perciformes	80 mya	7,000	
Family	Pomacentridae	~ 40 mya	360	
Genus	*Amphiprion*	~ 9 mya	28	
Species	*ocellaris*	< 3 mya	1	

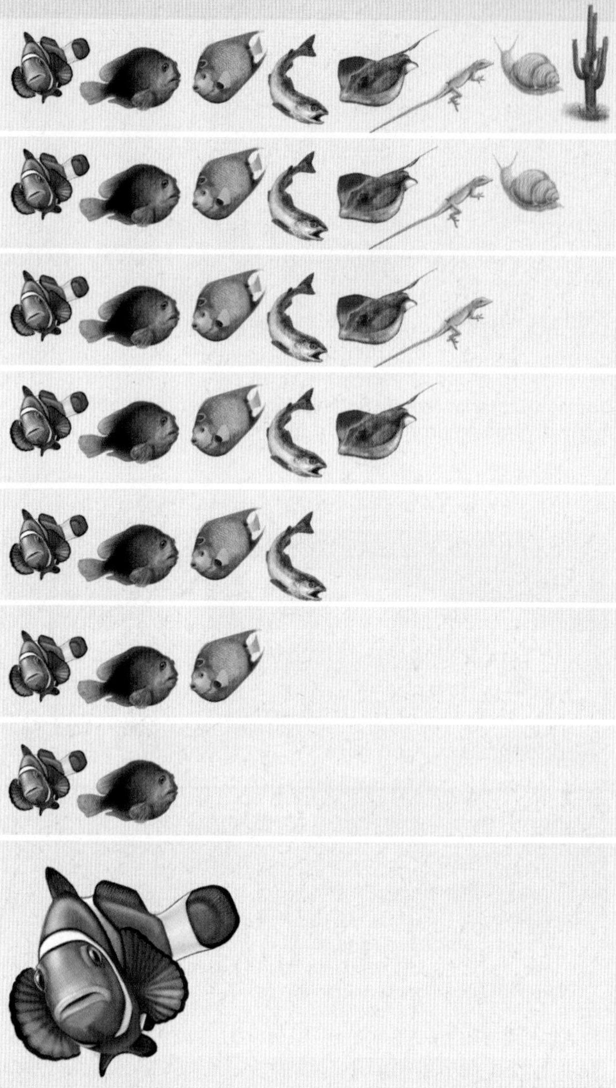

Figure 1.13 Taxonomic and evolutionary groupings leading to the clownfish.

Concept check: *Why is it useful to place organisms into taxonomic groupings?*

Several species of clownfish, also called clown anemonefish, have been identified. One species of clownfish, which is orange with white stripes, has several common names, including Ocellaris clownfish, false clownfish, and false-clown anemonefish. The broadest grouping for this clownfish is the domain, namely, Eukarya, followed by progressively smaller divisions, from kingdom (Animalia) to species. In the animal kingdom, clownfish are part of a phylum, Chordata, the chordates, which is subdivided into classes. Clownfish are in a class called Actinopterygii, which includes all ray-finned fishes. The common ancestor that gave rise to ray-finned fishes arose about 420 million years ago (mya). Actinopterygii is subdivided into several smaller orders. The clownfish are in the order Perciformes (bony fish). The order is, in turn, divided into families; the clownfish belong to the family of marine fish called Pomacentridae, which are often brightly colored. Families are divided into

genera (singular, genus). The genus *Amphiprion* is composed of 28 different species; these are various types of clownfish. Therefore, the genus contains species that are very similar to each other in form and have evolved from a common (extinct) ancestor that lived relatively recently on an evolutionary time scale.

Biologists use a two-part description, called **binomial nomenclature**, to provide each species with a unique scientific name. The scientific name of the Ocellaris clownfish is *Amphiprion ocellaris.* The first part is the genus, and the second part is the specific epithet or species descriptor. By convention, the genus name is capitalized, whereas the specific epithet is not. Both names are italicized. Scientific names are usually Latinized, which means they are made similar in appearance to Latin words. The origins of scientific names are typically Latin or Greek, but they can come from a variety of sources, such as a person's name.

Genomes & Proteomes Connection

The Study of Genomes and Proteomes Provides an Evolutionary Foundation for Our Understanding of Biology

The unifying concept in biology is evolution. We can understand the unity of modern organisms by realizing that all living species evolved from an interrelated group of ancestors. However, from an experimental perspective, this realization presents a dilemma—we cannot take a time machine back over the course of 4 billion years to carefully study the characteristics of extinct organisms and fully appreciate the series of changes that have led to modern species. Fortunately though, evolution has given biologists some wonderful puzzles to study, including the fossil record and, more recently, the genomes of modern species. As mentioned, the term **genome** refers to the complete genetic composition of an organism (**Figure 1.14a**). The genome is critical to life because it performs these functions:

- *Stores information in a stable form:* The genome of every organism stores information that provides a blueprint to create its characteristics.

- *Provides continuity from generation to generation:* The genome is copied and transmitted from generation to generation.

- *Acts as an instrument of evolutionary change:* Every now and then, the genome undergoes a mutation that may alter the characteristics of an organism. In addition, a genome may acquire new genes by horizontal gene transfer. The accumulation of such changes from generation to generation produces the evolutionary changes that alter species and produce new species.

The evolutionary history and relatedness of all living organisms can be illuminated by genome analysis. The genome of every organism carries the results and the evidence of millions of years of evolution. The genomes of prokaryotes usually contain a few thousand genes, whereas those of eukaryotes may contain tens of thousands. An exciting advance in biology over the past couple of decades has been the ability to analyze the DNA sequence of genomes, a technology called **genomics**. For instance, we can compare the genomes of a frog, a giraffe, and a petunia and discover intriguing similarities and differences. These comparisons help us to understand how new traits evolved. For example, all three types of organisms have the same kinds of genes needed for the breakdown of nutrients such as sugars. In contrast, only the petunia has genes that allow it to carry out photosynthesis.

An extension of genome analysis is the study of **proteomes**, which refers to all of the proteins that a cell or organism can make. The function of most genes is to encode polypeptides that become units in proteins. As shown in **Figure 1.14b**, these include proteins that form a cytoskeleton, proteins that function in cell organization and as enzymes, transport proteins, cell signaling proteins, and extracellular proteins. The genome of each species carries the information to make its proteome, the hundreds or thousands of proteins that each cell of that species makes. Proteins are largely responsible for the structures and functions of cells and organisms. The technical approach called **proteomics** involves the analysis of the proteome of a single species and the comparison of the proteomes of different species. Proteomics helps us understand how the various levels of biology are related to one another, from the molecular level—at the level of protein molecules—to the higher levels, such as how the functioning of proteins produces the characteristics of cells and organisms and affects the ability of populations of organisms to survive in their natural environments.

As a concrete way to understand the unifying concept of evolution in biology, a recurring theme in the chapters that follow is a brief topic called "Genomes & Proteomes Connection" that will allow you to appreciate how evolution produced the characteristics of modern species. These topics explore how the genomes of different species are similar to each other and how they are different. You will learn how genome changes affect the proteome and thereby control the traits of modern species. Ultimately, these concepts provide you with a way to relate information at the molecular level to the traits of organisms and their survival within ecosystems.

The Textbook Cover Provides an Example of How Genomes and Proteomes Are Fundamental to an Organism's Characteristics

As shown on the cover of your textbook, the crystal jelly (*Aequorea victoria*) is a bioluminescent jellyfish found off the west coast of North America. What is **bioluminescence**? The term refers to the ability of some living organisms, such as jellyfish, to produce and emit light due to reactions in which chemical energy is converted to light energy. Biologists currently do not know the function of bioluminescence in this species. Possible roles could be defense against predators or attracting prey.

In the case of the crystal jelly, most of the organism is transparent and not bioluminescent. The bioluminescence is largely restricted to a ring of discrete spots around the bell margin (**Figure 1.15a**). The spots occasionally give off flashes of green light, which is due to a protein the jellyfish makes, called green fluorescent protein (GFP). From the perspective of genomes and proteomes, biologists would say that the GFP gene is found in the genome of this jellyfish, but the green fluorescent protein is expressed only in the proteome of the cells that form these spots around the bell margin.

Researchers interested in bioluminescence have studied how it occurs at the molecular level. The crystal jelly produces light in a two-step process. First, the release of Ca^{2+} in a cell interacts with a protein called aequorin, which produces a blue light. Why don't the jellyfish glow blue? The answer is that, in a second step, the blue light is absorbed by GFP, which then emits a green light.

Because GFP is easily activated by UV or blue light and then specifically gives off green light, researchers have also adapted and used GFP as a visualization tool in medicine, research,

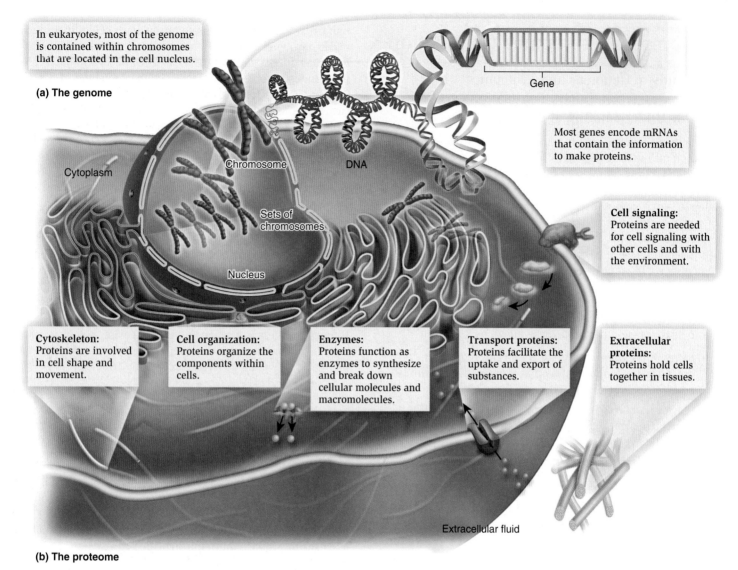

In eukaryotes, most of the genome is contained within chromosomes that are located in the cell nucleus.

(a) The genome

Gene

Most genes encode mRNAs that contain the information to make proteins.

Cytoplasm

Chromosome   DNA

Sets of chromosomes

Nucleus

Cell signaling: Proteins are needed for cell signaling with other cells and with the environment.

Cytoskeleton: Proteins are involved in cell shape and movement.

Cell organization: Proteins organize the components within cells.

Enzymes: Proteins function as enzymes to synthesize and break down cellular molecules and macromolecules.

Transport proteins: Proteins facilitate the uptake and export of substances.

Extracellular proteins: Proteins hold cells together in tissues.

Extracellular fluid

(b) The proteome

Figure 1.14   **Genomes and proteomes.**   **(a)** The genome, which is composed of DNA, is the entire genetic composition of an organism. Most of the genetic material in eukaryotic cells is found in the cell nucleus. Its primary function is to encode the proteome. **(b)** The proteome is the entire protein complement of a cell or organism. Six general categories of proteins are illustrated. Proteins are largely responsible for the structure and function of cells and complete organisms.

Concept check: *Biologists sometimes say the genome is a storage unit, whereas the proteome is largely the functional unit of life. Explain this statement.*

and biotechnology. With the aid of GFP, researchers can "see" where genes are expressed in a multicellular organism and where in a cell a particular protein is located. How is this possible? As mentioned, the gene for GFP is found in the genome of the crystal jelly. Using molecular techniques, copies of the GFP gene have been made from this species and placed into the cells of other species. Researchers can create hybrid genes in which a gene from a species of interest is fused with the GFP gene. For example, **Figure 1.15b** shows the results of an experiment where researchers created a hybrid gene by fusing a gene that encodes a protein called tubulin to the GFP gene. Tubulin is a component of microtubules that form a spindle in dividing cells. This hybrid gene encodes a protein in which tubulin is linked to GFP. When this hybrid protein is made in dividing cells and the

cells are exposed to UV light, the spindle glows green, enabling researchers to visualize its location. These results confirm that tubulin is a component of the spindle.

The discovery of GFP and its development as a molecular tool has involved the efforts of several scientists. In the 1960s, Osamu Shimomura was the first researcher to identify and purify GFP from *Aequorea victoria*. Over 20 years later, Martin Chalfie and colleagues obtained the GFP gene from Douglas Prasher, who was also interested in GFP as a molecular tool. Chalfie's work demonstrated that GFP could be used as a colored tag in both bacteria and animals. In addition, Roger Tsien studied the molecular properties of GFP, enabling biologists to understand how GFP gives off light and leading to the development of altered forms of GFP that glow in different colors

(a) Bioluminescence in *Aequorea victoria*

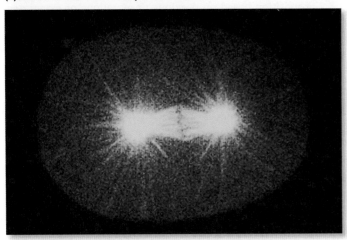

(b) Using GFP to label a spindle in a dividing cell

Figure 1.15 Expression of green fluorescent protein (GFP) in the crystal jelly and its use as a molecular tool. **(a)** This jellyfish is mostly transparent. GFP is naturally expressed in spots along the bell margin. **(b)** When GFP is linked to tubulin, the spindle (described in Chapter 15) glows green.

such as cyan, yellow, and red. In 2008, Shimomura, Chalfie, and Tsien received the Nobel Prize for the discovery and the development of GFP, which has become a widely used tool in biology.

1.3 Biology as a Scientific Discipline

What is science? Surprisingly, the definition of science is not easy to state. Most people have an idea of what science is, but actually articulating that idea proves difficult. In biology, we might define **science** as the observation, identification, experimental investigation, and theoretical explanation of natural phenomena.

Science is conducted in different ways and at different levels. Some biologists study the molecules that compose life, while others try to understand how organisms survive in their natural environments. In some cases, experiments are designed to test the validity of ideas suggested by researchers. In this section, we will examine how biologists follow a standard approach, called the **scientific method**, to test their ideas. We will learn that scientific insight is not based solely on intuition. Instead, scientific knowledge makes predictions that can be experimentally tested.

Even so, not all discoveries are the result of researchers following the scientific method. Some discoveries are simply made by gathering new information. As described earlier in Figures 1.1 to 1.4, the characterization of many plants and animals has led to the development of many important medicines and research tools. In this section, we will also consider how researchers often set out on "fact-finding missions" that are aimed at uncovering new information that may eventually lead to modern discoveries in biology.

Biologists Investigate Life at Different Levels of Organization

Earlier, in Figure 1.6, we examined the various levels of biological organization. The study of these different levels depends not only on the scientific interests of biologists but also on the tools available to them. The study of organisms in their natural environments is a branch of biology called **ecology** (Figure 1.16a). In addition, researchers examine the structures and functions of plants and animals, which are disciplines called **anatomy** and **physiology** (Figure 1.16b). With the advent of microscopy, **cell biology**, which is the study of cells, became an important branch of biology in the early 1900s and remains so today (Figure 1.16c). In the 1970s, genetic tools became available to study single genes and the proteins they encode. This genetic technology enabled researchers to study individual molecules, such as proteins, in living cells and thereby spawned the field of **molecular biology**. Together with chemists and biochemists, molecular biologists focus their efforts on the structure and function of the molecules of life (Figure 1.16d). Such researchers want to understand how biology works at the molecular and even atomic levels. Overall, the 20th century saw a progressive increase in the number of biologists who used a reductionist approach to understanding biology. **Reductionism** involves reducing complex systems to simpler components as a way to understand how the system works. In biology, reductionists study the parts of a cell or organism as individual units.

In the 1980s, the pendulum began to swing in the other direction. Scientists have invented new tools that allow us to study groups of genes (genomic techniques) and groups of proteins (proteomic techniques). Biologists now use the term **systems biology** to describe research aimed at understanding how the properties of life arise by complex interactions. This term is often applied to the study of cells. In this context, systems biology may involve the investigation of groups of proteins with a common purpose (Figure 1.16e). For example, a systems biologist may conduct experiments that try to characterize an entire cellular process, which is driven by dozens of different proteins.

Ecologists study species in their native environments.

(a) Ecology—population/ community/ecosystem levels

Anatomists and physiologists study how the structures of organisms are related to their functions.

(b) Anatomy and physiology— tissue/organ/organism levels

Cell biologists often use microscopes to learn how cells function.

(c) Cell biology—cellular levels

Molecular biologists and biochemists study the molecules and macromolecules that make up cells.

(d) Molecular biology— atomic/molecular levels

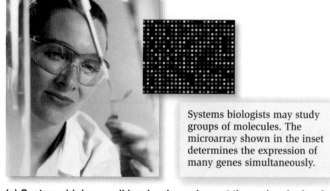

Systems biologists may study groups of molecules. The microarray shown in the inset determines the expression of many genes simultaneously.

(e) Systems biology—all levels, shown here at the molecular level

Figure 1.16 Biological investigation at different levels.

However, systems biology is not new. Animal and plant physiologists have been studying the functions of complex organ systems for centuries. Likewise, ecologists have been characterizing ecosystems for a very long time. The novelty and excitement of systems biology in recent years have been the result of new experimental tools that allow us to study complex interactions at the molecular level. As described throughout this textbook, the investigation of genomes and proteomes has provided important insights regarding many interesting topics in systems biology.

A Hypothesis Is a Proposed Idea, Whereas a Theory Is a Broad Explanation Backed by Extensive Evidence

Let's now consider the process of science. In biology, a **hypothesis** is a proposed explanation for a natural phenomenon. It is a proposition based on previous observations or experimental studies. For example, with knowledge of seasonal changes, you might hypothesize that maple trees drop their leaves in the autumn because of the shortened amount of daylight. An alternative hypothesis might be that the trees drop their leaves because of colder temperatures. In biology, a hypothesis requires more work by researchers to evaluate its validity.

A useful hypothesis must make **predictions**—expected outcomes that can be shown to be correct or incorrect. In other words, a useful hypothesis is testable. If a hypothesis is incorrect, it should be **falsifiable**, which means that it can be shown to be incorrect by additional observations or experimentation. Alternatively, a hypothesis may be correct, so further work will not disprove it. In such cases, we would say that the researcher(s) has failed to reject the hypothesis. Even so, a hypothesis is never really proven but rather always remains provisional. Researchers accept the possibility that perhaps they have not yet conceived of the correct hypothesis. After many experiments, biologists may conclude that their hypothesis is consistent with known data, but they should never say the hypothesis is proven.

By comparison, the term **theory**, as it is used in biology, is a broad explanation of some aspect of the natural world that is substantiated by a large body of evidence. Biological theories incorporate observations, hypothesis testing, and the laws of other disciplines such as chemistry and physics. The power of theories is they allow us to make many predictions regarding the properties of living organisms. As an example, let's consider the theory that DNA is the genetic material and that it is organized into units called genes. An overwhelming body of evidence has substantiated this theory. Thousands of living species have been analyzed at the molecular level. All of them have been found to use DNA as their genetic material and to express genes that produce the proteins that lead to their characteristics. This theory makes many valid predictions. For example, certain types of mutations in genes are expected to affect the traits of organisms. This prediction has been confirmed experimentally. Similarly, this theory predicts that genetic material is copied and transmitted from parents to offspring. By comparing the DNA of parents and offspring, this prediction has also been confirmed. Furthermore, the theory explains the observation that offspring resemble their parents. Overall, two key attributes of a scientific theory are (1) consistency with a vast amount of known data and (2) the ability to make many correct predictions. Two other important biological theories we have touched on in this chapter are the cell theory and the theory of evolution by natural selection.

The meaning of the term theory is sometimes muddled because it is used in different situations. In everyday language, a "theory" is often viewed as little more than a guess or a hypothesis. For example, a person might say, "My theory is that Professor Simpson did not come to class today because he went to the beach." However, in biology, a theory is much more than a guess. A theory is an established set of ideas that explains a vast amount of data and offers valid predictions that can be tested. Like a hypothesis, a theory can never be proven to be true. Scientists acknowledge that they do not know everything. Even so, biologists would say that theories are extremely likely to be true, based on all known information. In this regard, theories are viewed as **knowledge**, which is the awareness and understanding of information.

Discovery-Based Science and Hypothesis Testing Are Scientific Approaches That Help Us Understand Biology

The path that leads to an important discovery is rarely a straight line. Rather, scientists ask questions, make observations, ask modified questions, and may eventually conduct experiments to test their hypotheses. The first attempts at experimentation may fail, and new experimental approaches may be needed. To suggest that scientists follow a rigid scientific method is an oversimplification of the process of science. Scientific advances often occur as scientists dig deeper and deeper into a topic that interests them. Curiosity is the key phenomenon that sparks scientific inquiry. How is biology actually conducted? As discussed next, researchers typically follow two general types of approaches—discovery-based science and hypothesis testing.

Discovery-Based Science The collection and analysis of data without the need for a preconceived hypothesis is called **discovery-based science**, or simply **discovery science**. Why is discovery-based science carried out? The information gained from discovery-based science may lead to the formation of new hypotheses, and, in the long run, may have practical applications that benefit people. Drug companies, for example, may test hundreds or even thousands of compounds to determine if any of them are useful in the treatment of disease (**Figure 1.17a**). Once a drug has been discovered that is effective in disease treatment, researchers may dig deeper and try to understand how the drug exerts its effects. In this way, discovery-based science may help us learn about basic concepts in medicine and biology. Another example involves the study of

genomes (**Figure 1.17b**). Over the past few decades, researchers have identified and begun to investigate newly discovered genes within the human genome without already knowing the function of the gene they are studying. The goal is to gather additional clues that may eventually allow them to propose a hypothesis that explains the gene's function. Discovery-based science often leads to hypothesis testing.

Drug companies may screen hundreds or thousands of different compounds, trying to discover ones that may prove effective in the treatment of a particular disease.

(a) Drug discovery

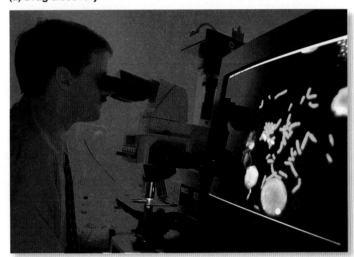

Genetic researchers search through the genomes of humans and other species, trying to discover new genes. Such discoveries may help us understand molecular biology and provide insight into the causes of inherited diseases in people.

(b) Discovery of genes

Figure 1.17 Discovery-based science.

Concept check: *How is discovery-based science different from hypothesis testing?*

Hypothesis Testing   In biological science, the scientific method, also known as **hypothesis testing**, is usually followed to test the validity of a hypothesis. This strategy may be described as a five-stage process:

1. Observations are made regarding natural phenomena.
2. These observations lead to a hypothesis that tries to explain the phenomena. A useful hypothesis is one that is testable because it makes specific predictions.
3. Experimentation is conducted to determine if the predictions are correct.
4. The data from the experiment are analyzed.
5. The hypothesis is considered to be consistent with the data, or it is rejected.

The scientific method is intended to be an objective way to gather knowledge. As an example, let's return to our scenario of maple trees dropping their leaves in autumn. By observing the length of daylight throughout the year and comparing that data with the time of the year when leaves fall, one hypothesis might be that shorter daylight causes the leaves to fall (**Figure 1.18**). This hypothesis makes a prediction—exposure of maple trees to shorter daylight will cause their leaves to fall. To test this prediction, researchers would design and conduct an experiment.

How is hypothesis testing conducted? Although hypothesis testing may follow many paths, certain experimental features are common to this approach. First, data are often collected in two parallel manners. One set of experiments is done on the **control group**, while another set is conducted on the **experimental group**. In an ideal experiment, the control and experimental groups differ by only one factor. For example, an experiment could be conducted in which two groups of trees would be observed and the only difference between their environments would be the length of light each day. To conduct such an experiment, researchers would grow small trees in a greenhouse where they could keep factors such as temperature and water the same between the control and experimental groups, while providing them with different amounts of daylight. In the control group, the number of hours of light provided by lightbulbs would be kept constant each day, while in the experimental group, the amount of light each day would become progressively shorter to mimic seasonal light changes. The researchers would then record the number of leaves dropped by the two groups of trees over a certain period of time.

Another key feature of hypothesis testing is data analysis. The result of experimentation is a set of data from which a biologist tries to draw conclusions. Biology is a quantitative science. When experimentation involves control and experimental groups, a common form of analysis is to determine if

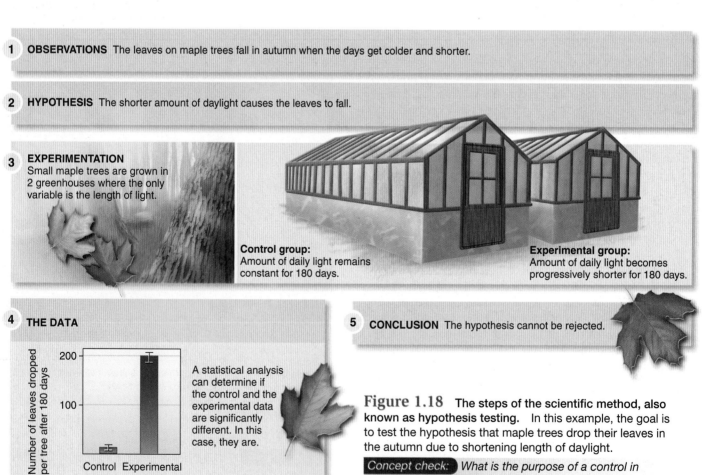

1 OBSERVATIONS The leaves on maple trees fall in autumn when the days get colder and shorter.

2 HYPOTHESIS The shorter amount of daylight causes the leaves to fall.

3 EXPERIMENTATION Small maple trees are grown in 2 greenhouses where the only variable is the length of light.

Control group: Amount of daily light remains constant for 180 days.

Experimental group: Amount of daily light becomes progressively shorter for 180 days.

4 THE DATA

A statistical analysis can determine if the control and the experimental data are significantly different. In this case, they are.

Number of leaves dropped per tree after 180 days

200 —

100 —

Control group   Experimental group

5 CONCLUSION The hypothesis cannot be rejected.

Figure 1.18   **The steps of the scientific method, also known as hypothesis testing.**   In this example, the goal is to test the hypothesis that maple trees drop their leaves in the autumn due to shortening length of daylight.

Concept check: *What is the purpose of a control in hypothesis testing?*

the data collected from the two groups are truly different from each other. Biologists apply statistical analyses to their data to determine if the control and experimental groups are likely to be different from each other because of the single variable that is different between the two groups. When they are statistically significant, this means that the differences between the control and experimental data are not likely to have occurred as a matter of random chance. In our tree example shown in Figure 1.18, the trees in the control group dropped far fewer leaves than did those in the experimental group. A statistical analysis could determine if the data collected from the two greenhouses are significantly different from each other. If the two sets of data are found not to be significantly different, the hypothesis would be rejected. Alternatively, if the differences between the two sets of data are significant, as shown in Figure 1.18, biologists would conclude that the hypothesis is consistent with the data, though it is not proven. These results may cause researchers to ask further questions. For example, they may want to understand how decreases in the length of daylight promote cellular changes that cause the leaves to fall.

As described next, discovery-based science and hypothesis testing are often used together to learn more about a particular scientific topic. As an example, let's look at how both approaches have led to successes in the study of the disease called cystic fibrosis.

The Study of Cystic Fibrosis Provides Examples of Both Discovery-Based Science and Hypothesis Testing

Let's consider how biologists made discoveries related to the disease cystic fibrosis (CF), which affects about 1 in every 3,500 Americans. Persons with CF produce abnormally thick and sticky mucus that obstructs the lungs and leads to life-threatening lung infections. The thick mucus also blocks the pancreas, which prevents the digestive enzymes this organ produces from reaching the intestine. For this reason, CF patients tend to have excessive appetites but poor weight gain. Persons with this disease may also experience liver damage because the thick mucus can obstruct the liver. The average life span for people with CF is currently in their mid- to late 30s. Fortunately, as more advances have been made in treatment, this number has steadily increased.

Because of its medical significance, many scientists are interested in cystic fibrosis and have conducted studies aimed at gaining greater information regarding its underlying cause. The hope is that a better understanding of the disease may lead to improved treatment options, and perhaps even a cure. As described next, discovery-based science and hypothesis testing have been critical to gaining a better understanding of this disease.

The CF Gene and Discovery-Based Science   In 1945, Dorothy Anderson determined that cystic fibrosis is a genetic disorder. Persons with CF have inherited two faulty *CF* genes, one from each parent. Over 40 years later, researchers used discovery-based science to identify this gene. Their search

for the *CF* gene did not require any preconceived hypothesis regarding the function of the gene. Rather, they used genetic strategies similar to those described in Chapter 20. In 1989, research groups headed by Lap-Chi Tsui, Francis Collins, and John Riordan identified the *CF* gene.

The discovery of the gene made it possible to devise diagnostic testing methods to determine if a person carries a faulty *CF* gene. In addition, the characterization of the *CF* gene provided important clues regarding its function. Researchers observed striking similarities between the *CF* gene and other genes that were already known to encode proteins called transporters, which function in the transport of substances across membranes. Based on this observation, as well as other kinds of data, the researchers hypothesized that the function of the normal *CF* gene is to encode a transporter. In this way, the identification of the *CF* gene led researchers to conduct experiments aimed at testing a hypothesis of its function.

The CF Gene and Hypothesis Testing   Researchers considered the characterization of the *CF* gene along with other studies showing that patients with the disorder have an abnormal regulation of salt balance across their plasma membranes. They hypothesized that the normal *CF* gene encodes a transporter that functions in the transport of chloride ions (Cl^-), a component of common table salt (NaCl), across the membranes of cells (**Figure 1.19**). This hypothesis led to experimentation in which researchers tested normal cells and cells from CF patients

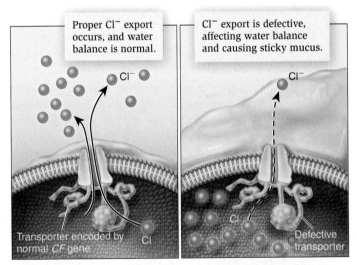

| Lung cell with normal *CF* gene | Lung cell with faulty *CF* gene |

Figure 1.19 A hypothesis that suggests an explanation for the function of the gene that is defective in patients with cystic fibrosis. The normal *CF* gene, which does not carry a mutation, encodes a transporter that transports chloride ions (Cl^-) across the plasma membrane to the outside of the cell. In persons with CF, this transporter is defective due to a mutation in the *CF* gene.

Concept check: *Explain how discovery-based science helped researchers to hypothesize that the CF gene encodes a transporter.*

for their ability to transport Cl^-. The CF cells were found to be defective in chloride transport. In 1990, scientists successfully transferred the normal *CF* gene into CF cells in the laboratory. The introduction of the normal gene corrected the cells' defect in chloride transport. Overall, the results showed that the *CF* gene encodes a transporter that transports Cl^- across the plasma membrane. A mutation in this gene causes it to encode a defective transporter, leading to a salt imbalance that affects water levels outside the cell, which explains the thick and sticky mucus in CF patients. In this example, hypothesis testing has provided a way to evaluate a hypothesis regarding how a disease is caused by a genetic change.

FEATURE INVESTIGATION

Observation and Experimentation Form the Core of Biology

Because biology is the study of life, a biology textbook that focuses only on a description of living organisms would miss the main point. Biology is largely about the process of discovery. Therefore, a recurring theme of this textbook is discovery-based science and hypothesis testing. While each chapter contains many examples of data collection and experiments, a consistent element is a "Feature Investigation"—an actual study by current or past researchers. Some of these involve discovery-based science in which biologists collect and analyze data in an attempt to make discoveries that are not hypothesis driven. Alternatively, most Feature Investigations involve hypothesis testing in which a hypothesis is stated and the experiment and resulting data are presented. See Figure 1.18 to see the form of these Feature Investigations.

The Feature Investigations allow you to appreciate the connection between science and scientific theories. We hope you will find this a more interesting and rewarding way to learn about biology. As you read a Feature Investigation, you may find yourself thinking about different approaches and alternative hypotheses. Different people can view the same data and arrive at very different conclusions. As you progress through the experiments in this textbook, you will enjoy biology far more if you try to develop your own skills at formulating hypotheses, designing experiments, and interpreting data.

Experimental Questions

1. Discuss the difference between discovery-based science and hypothesis testing.

2. What are the steps in the scientific method, also called hypothesis testing?

3. When conducting an experiment, explain how a control group and an experimental group differ from each other.

Science as a Social Discipline

Finally, it is worthwhile to point out that science is a social discipline. After performing observations and experiments, biologists communicate their results in different ways. Most importantly, papers are submitted to scientific journals. Following submission, most papers undergo a **peer-review process** in which other scientists, who are experts in the area, evaluate the paper and make suggestions regarding its quality. Following peer review, a paper is either accepted for publication, rejected, or the authors of the paper may be given suggestions for how to revise the work or conduct additional experiments before it will be acceptable for publication.

Another social aspect of research is that biologists often attend meetings where they report their most recent work to the scientific community (**Figure 1.20**). They comment on each other's ideas and work, eventually shaping together the information that builds into scientific theories over many years. As you develop your skills at scrutinizing experiments, it is satisfying to discuss your ideas with other people, including fellow students and faculty members. Importantly, you do not need to "know all the answers" before you enter into a scientific discussion. Instead, a more rewarding way to view science is as an ongoing and never-ending series of questions.

Figure 1.20 The social aspects of science. At scientific meetings, researchers gather to discuss new data and discoveries. Research conducted by professors, students, lab technicians, and industrial participants is sometimes hotly debated.

Summary of Key Concepts

- Biology is the study of life. Discoveries in biology help us understand how life exists, and they also have many practical applications, such as the development of drugs to treat human diseases. (Figures 1.1, 1.2, 1.3, 1.4)

1.1 The Properties of Life

- Seven characteristics are common to all forms of life. All living things (1) are composed of cells; (2) use energy; (3) respond to environmental changes; (4) regulate their internal conditions (homeostasis); (5) grow and develop; (6) reproduce; and (7) evolve over the course of many generations. (Figure 1.5)

- Living organisms can be viewed at different levels of complexity: atoms, molecules and macromolecules, cells, tissues, organs, organisms, populations, communities, ecosystems, and the biosphere. (Figure 1.6)

1.2 The Unity and Diversity of Life

- Changes in species often occur as a result of modification of pre-existing structures. (Figures 1.7, 1.8)

- Vertical evolution involves mutations in a lineage that alter the characteristics of species over many generations. During this process, natural selection results in the survival of individuals with greater reproductive success. Over the long run, this process alters species and may produce new species. In addition, evolution involves the accumulation of neutral changes. (Figure 1.9)

- Horizontal gene transfer may involve the transfer of genes between different species. Along with vertical evolution, it is an important force in biological evolution, producing a web of life. (Figures 1.10, 1.11)

- Taxonomy involves the grouping of species according to their evolutionary relatedness to other species. Going from broad to narrow, each species is placed into a domain, kingdom, phylum, class, order, family, and genus. (Figures 1.12, 1.13)

- The genome is the genetic composition of a species. It provides a blueprint for the traits of an organism, is transmitted from parents to offspring, and acts as an instrument for evolutionary change. The proteome is the collection of proteins that a cell or organism can make. Beginning with Chapter 3, each chapter in this textbook has a brief discussion called "Genomes & Proteomes Connection." (Figure 1.14)

- An analysis of genomes and proteomes helps us to understand the characteristics of individuals and how they survive in their native environments. (Figure 1.15)

1.3 Biology as a Scientific Discipline

- Biological science involves the observation, identification, experimental investigation, and theoretical explanation of natural phenomena.

- Biologists study life at different levels, ranging from ecosystems to molecular components in cells. (Figure 1.16)

- A hypothesis is a proposal to explain a natural phenomenon. A useful hypothesis makes a testable prediction. A biological theory is a broad explanation based on vast amounts of data and makes many valid predictions.

- Discovery-based science is an approach in which researchers conduct experiments without a preconceived hypothesis. It is a fact-finding mission. (Figure 1.17)

- The scientific method, also called hypothesis testing, is a series of steps to test the validity of a hypothesis. The experimentation often involves a comparison between control and experimental groups. (Figure 1.18)

- The study of cystic fibrosis is an interesting example in which both discovery-based science and hypothesis testing have provided key insights regarding the nature of the disease. (Figure 1.19)

- Each chapter in this textbook has a "Feature Investigation" to help you appreciate how science has led to key discoveries in biology.

- To be published, scientific papers are usually subjected to peer review. Advances in science often occur when scientists gather and discuss their data. (Figure 1.20)

Assess and Discuss

Test Yourself

1. The process where living organisms maintain a relatively stable internal condition is
   a. adaptation.   d. homeostasis.
   b. evolution.   e. development.
   c. metabolism.

2. Populations of organisms change over the course of many generations. Many of these changes result in increased survival and reproduction. This phenomenon is
   a. evolution.   d. genetics.
   b. homeostasis.   e. metabolism.
   c. development.

3. All of the places on Earth where living organisms are found is
   a. the ecosystem.   d. a viable land mass.
   b. a community.   e. a population.
   c. the biosphere.

4. Which of the following would be an example of horizontal gene transfer?
   a. the transmission of an eye color gene from father to daughter
   b. the transmission of a mutant gene causing cystic fibrosis from father to daughter
   c. the transmission of a gene conferring pathogenicity (the ability to cause disease) from one bacterial species to another
   d. the transmission of a gene conferring antibiotic resistance from a mother cell to its two daughter cells
   e. all of the above

5. The scientific name for humans is *Homo sapiens*. The name *Homo* is the _____ to which humans are classified.
   a. kingdom   d. genus
   b. phylum   e. species
   c. order

6. The complete genetic makeup of an organism is called
   a. the genus.
   b. the genome.
   c. the proteome.
   d. the genotype.
   e. the phenotype.

7. A proposed explanation for a natural phenomenon is
   a. a theory.
   b. a law.
   c. a prediction.
   d. a hypothesis.
   e. an assay.

8. In science, a theory should
   a. be equated with knowledge.
   b. be supported by a substantial body of evidence.
   c. provide the ability to make many correct predictions.
   d. all of the above.
   e. b and c only.

9. Conducting research without a preconceived hypothesis is called
   a. discovery-based science.
   b. the scientific method.
   c. hypothesis testing.
   d. a control experiment.
   e. none of the above.

10. What is the purpose of using a control in scientific experiments?
    a. A control allows the researcher to practice the experiment first before actually conducting it.
    b. A researcher can compare the results in the experimental group and control group to determine if a single variable is causing a particular outcome in the experimental group.
    c. A control provides the framework for the entire experiment so the researcher can recall the procedures that should be conducted.
    d. A control allows the researcher to conduct other experimental changes without disturbing the original experiment.
    e. All of the above are correct.

Conceptual Questions

1. What are the seven characteristics of life? Explain a little about each.

2. Explain how it is possible for evolution to result in unity among different species yet also create amazing diversity.

3. Which two taxonomic groups are very diverse? Which two are the least diverse (see Figure 1.13)?

Collaborative Questions

1. Discuss whether or not you think that theories in biology are true. Outside of biology, how do you decide if something is true?

2. In certain animals, such as alligators, sex is determined by temperature. When alligator eggs are exposed to low temperatures, most alligator embryos develop into females. Discuss how this phenomenon is related to genomes and proteomes.

Online Resource

www.brookerbiology.com

Stay a step ahead in your studies with animations that bring concepts to life and practice tests to assess your understanding. Your instructor may also recommend the interactive ebook, individualized learning tools, and more.

The Chemical Basis of Life I:
Atoms, Molecules, and Water

2

Biology—the study of life—is founded on the principles of chemistry and physics. All living organisms are a collection of atoms and molecules bound together and interacting with each other through the forces of nature. Throughout this textbook, we will see how chemistry can be applied to living organisms as we discuss the components of cells, the functions of proteins, the flow of nutrients in plants and animals, and the evolution of new genes. This chapter lays the groundwork for understanding these and other concepts. We begin with an overview of **inorganic chemistry**—that is, the nature of atoms and molecules, with the exception of those that contain rings or chains of carbon. Such carbon-containing molecules form the basis of **organic chemistry** and are covered in Chapter 3.

Crystals of sodium chloride (NaCl), a molecule composed of two elements.

2.1 Atoms

All life-forms are composed of **matter**, which is defined as anything that contains mass and occupies space. In living organisms, matter may exist in any of three states: solid, liquid, or gas. All matter is composed of **atoms**, which are the smallest functional units of matter that form all chemical substances and ultimately all organisms; they cannot be further broken down into other substances by ordinary chemical or physical means. Atoms, in turn, are composed of smaller, subatomic components collectively referred to as particles. Chemists are interested in the properties of atoms and **molecules**, which are two or more atoms bonded together. A major role of the physicist, by contrast, is to uncover the properties of subatomic particles. Chemistry and physics merge when one attempts to understand the mechanisms by which atoms and molecules interact. When atoms and molecules are studied in the context of a living organism, the science of biochemistry emerges. No living creature is immortal, but atoms never "die." Instead, they exist *ad infinitum* as solitary atoms or as components of a single molecule, or they shuttle between countless molecules over vast eons of time. (An exception to this are unstable atoms called radioisotopes, described later.) In this section, we explore the physical properties of atoms so we can understand how atoms combine to form molecules of biological importance.

Atoms Are Comprised of Subatomic Particles

There are many types of atoms in living organisms. The simplest atom, hydrogen, is approximately 0.1 nanometers (1×10^{-10} meters) in diameter, roughly one-millionth the diameter of a human hair. Each specific type of atom—nitrogen, hydrogen, oxygen, and so on—is called an **element** (or chemical element), which is defined as a pure substance of only one kind of atom.

Three subatomic particles—**protons**, **neutrons**, and **electrons**—are found within atoms. The protons and neutrons are confined to a very small volume at the center of an atom, the **atomic nucleus**, whereas the electrons are found in regions at various distances from the nucleus. With the exception of ions—atoms that have gained or lost one or more electrons (described later in this chapter)—the numbers of protons and electrons in a given type of atom are identical, but the number of neutrons may vary. Each of the subatomic particles has a different electric charge. Protons have one unit of positive charge, electrons have one unit of negative charge, and neutrons are electrically neutral. Like charges always repel each other, and opposite charges always attract each other. It is the opposite charges of the protons and electrons that create an atom—the positive charges in the nucleus attract the negatively charged electrons.

Because the protons are located in the atomic nucleus, the nucleus has a net positive charge equal to the number of protons it contains. The entire atom has no net electric charge, however, because the number of negatively charged electrons around the nucleus is equal to the number of positively charged protons in the nucleus.

The basic structure of the atom was discovered by Ernest Rutherford in a landmark experiment conducted during the years 1909–1911, as described next.

FEATURE INVESTIGATION

Rutherford Determined the Modern Model of the Atom

Nobel laureate Ernest Rutherford was born in 1871 in New Zealand, but he did his greatest work at McGill University in Montreal, Canada, and later at the University of Manchester in England. At that time, scientists knew that atoms contained charged particles but had no idea how those particles were arranged. Neutrons had not yet been discovered, and many scientists, including Rutherford, hypothesized that the positive charge and the mass of an atom were evenly dispersed throughout the atom.

In a now-classic experiment, Rutherford aimed a fine beam of positively charged α (alpha) particles at an extremely thin sheet of gold foil only 400 atoms thick (**Figure 2.1**). Alpha particles are the two protons and two neutrons that comprise the nuclei of helium atoms; you can think of them as helium atoms without their electrons. Surrounding the gold foil were zinc sulfide screens that registered any α particles passing through or bouncing off the foil, much like film in a camera detects light. Rutherford hypothesized that if the positive charges of the gold atoms were uniformly distributed, many of the positively charged α particles would be slightly deflected, because one of the most important features of electric charge is that like charges repel each other. Due to their much smaller mass, he did not expect electrons in the gold atoms to have any impact on the ability of an α particle to move through the metal foil.

Surprisingly, Rutherford discovered that more than 98% of the α particles passed right through as if the foil was not there and only a small percent were slightly deflected; a few even bounced back at a sharp angle! To explain the 98% that passed right through, Rutherford concluded that most of the volume of an atom is empty space. To explain the few α particles that bounced back at a sharp angle, he postulated that most of the

Figure 2.1 Rutherford's gold foil experiment, demonstrating that most of the volume of an atom is empty space.

HYPOTHESIS Atoms in gold foil are composed of diffuse, evenly distributed positive charges that should usually cause α particles to be slightly deflected as they pass through.

KEY MATERIALS Thin sheet of gold foil, α particle emitter, zinc sulfide detection screen.

Experimental level   Conceptual level

1 Emit beam of α particles.

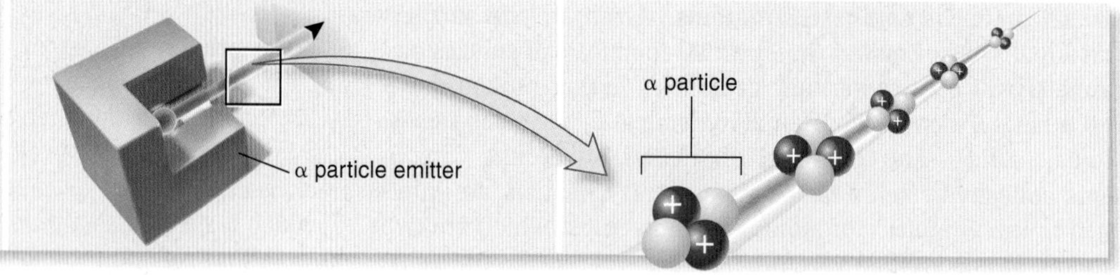

α particle emitter

α particle

2 Pass beam through gold foil.

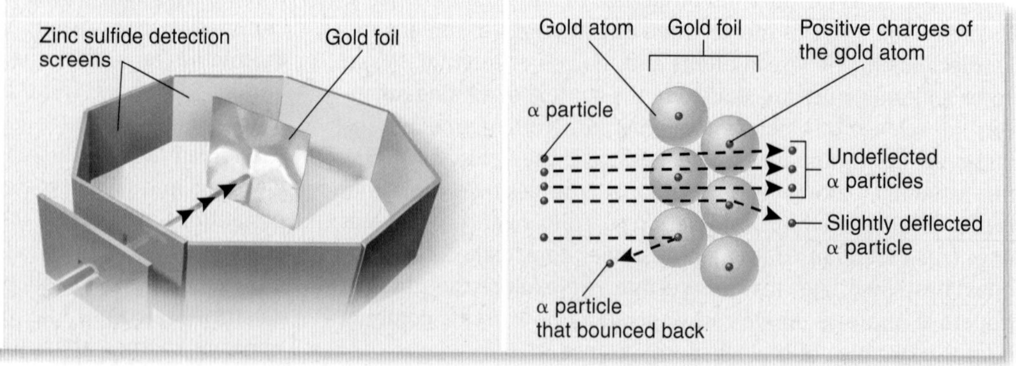

Zinc sulfide detection screens   Gold foil

Gold atom   Gold foil   Positive charges of the gold atom

α particle

Undeflected α particles

Slightly deflected α particle

α particle that bounced back

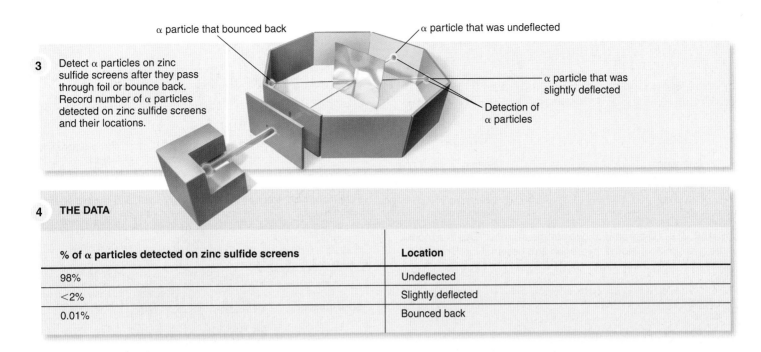

3   Detect α particles on zinc sulfide screens after they pass through foil or bounce back. Record number of α particles detected on zinc sulfide screens and their locations.

α particle that bounced back

α particle that was undeflected

α particle that was slightly deflected

Detection of α particles

4   THE DATA

% of α particles detected on zinc sulfide screens	Location
98%	Undeflected
<2%	Slightly deflected
0.01%	Bounced back

5   CONCLUSION Most of the volume of an atom is empty space, with the positive charges concentrated in a small volume.

6   SOURCE Rutherford, E. 1911. The scattering of α and β particles by matter and the structure of the atom. *Philosophical Magazine* 21:669–688.

atom's positive charge was localized in a highly compact area at the center of the atom. The existence of this small, dense region of highly concentrated positive charge—which today we call the atomic nucleus—explains how some α particles could be so strongly deflected by the gold foil. The α particles would bounce back on the rare occasion when they directly collided with an atomic nucleus. Therefore, based on these results, Rutherford rejected his original hypothesis that atoms are composed of diffuse, evenly distributed positive charges.

From this experiment, Rutherford proposed a transitional model of an atom, with its small, positively charged nucleus surrounded at relatively great distances by negatively charged electrons. Today we know that more than 99.99% of an atom's volume is outside the nucleus. Indeed, the nucleus accounts for only about 1/10,000 of an atom's diameter—most of an atom is empty space!

Experimental Questions

1. Before the experiment conducted by Ernest Rutherford, how did many scientists envision the structure of an atom?

2. What was the hypothesis tested by Rutherford?

3. What were the results of the experiment? How did Rutherford interpret the results?

Electrons Occupy Orbitals Around an Atom's Nucleus

At one time, scientists visualized an atom as a mini–solar system, with the nucleus being the sun and the electrons traveling in clearly defined orbits around it. **Figure 2.2** shows a diagram of the two simplest atoms, hydrogen and helium, which have the smallest numbers of protons. This model of the atom is now known to be an oversimplification, because as described shortly, electrons do not actually orbit the nucleus in a defined path like planets around the sun. However, this depiction of an atom remains a convenient way to diagram atoms in two dimensions.

Electrons move at terrific speeds. Some estimates suggest that the electron in a typical hydrogen atom could circle the Earth in less than 20 seconds! Partly for this reason, it is difficult to precisely predict the exact location of a given electron. In fact, we can only describe the region of space surrounding the nucleus in which there is a high probability of finding that electron. These regions are called **orbitals**. A better model of an atom, therefore, is a central nucleus surrounded by cloud-like orbitals. The cloud represents the region in which a given electron is most likely to be found. Some orbitals are spherical, called *s* orbitals, whereas others assume a shape that is often described as similar to a propeller or dumbbell and are called *p* orbitals (**Figure 2.3**). An orbital can contain a maximum of two

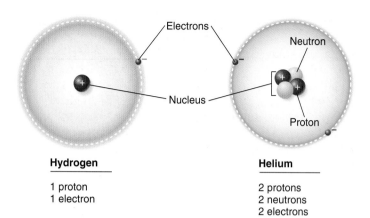

Hydrogen

1 proton
1 electron

Helium

2 protons
2 neutrons
2 electrons

Figure 2.2 **Diagrams of two simple atoms.** This is a model of the two simplest atoms, hydrogen and helium. Note: In all figures of atoms, the sizes and distances are not to scale.

Orbital name	1s	2s	2p
	Nucleus		
Number of electrons per energy shell	2	2 per orbital; 8 total	
Orbital shape	Spherical	First orbital: spherical	Second to fourth orbital: dumbbell-shaped

Figure 2.3 **Diagrams of individual electron orbitals.** Electrons are found outside the nucleus in orbitals that may resemble spherical or dumbbell-shaped clouds. The orbital cloud represents a region in which the probability is high of locating a particular electron. For this illustration, only two shells are shown; the heaviest elements contain a total of seven shells.

electrons. Consequently, any atom with more than two electrons must contain additional orbitals.

Orbitals occupy so-called **energy shells**, or energy levels. **Energy** can be defined as the capacity to do work or effect a change. In biology, we often refer to various types of energy, such as light energy, mechanical energy, and chemical energy. Electrons orbiting a nucleus have kinetic energy, that is, the energy of moving matter. Atoms with progressively more electrons have orbitals within energy shells that are at greater and greater distances from the nucleus. These shells are numbered, with shell number 1 closest to the nucleus. Different energy shells may contain one or more orbitals, each orbital with up to two electrons. The innermost energy shell of all atoms has room for only two electrons, which spin in opposite directions within a spherical *s* orbital (1*s*). The second energy shell is composed of one spherical *s* orbital (2*s*) and three dumbbell-shaped *p*

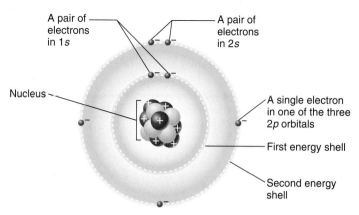

(a) Simplified depiction of a nitrogen atom (7 electrons; 2 electrons in first energy shell, 5 in second energy shell)

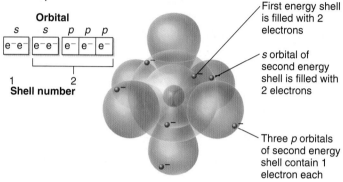

(b) Nitrogen atom showing electrons in orbitals

Figure 2.4 **Diagrams showing the multiple energy shells and orbitals of a nitrogen atom.** The nitrogen atom is shown **(a)** simplified and **(b)** with all of its orbitals and shells. An atom's shells fill up one by one. In shells containing more than one orbital, the orbital with lowest energy fills first. Subsequent orbitals gain one electron at a time, shown schematically in boxes, where *e* represents an electron. Heavier elements contain additional shells and orbitals.

Concept check: *Explain the difference between an energy shell and an orbital.*

orbitals (2*p*). Therefore, the second shell can hold up to four pairs of electrons, or eight electrons altogether (Figure 2.3).

Electrons vary in the amount of energy they have. The shell closest to the nucleus fills up with the lowest energy electrons first, and then each subsequent shell fills with higher and higher energy electrons, one shell at a time. Within a given shell, the energy of electrons can also vary among different orbitals. In the second shell, for example, the *s* orbital has lower energy, while the three *p* orbitals have slightly higher and roughly equal energies. In that case, therefore, two electrons fill the *s* orbital first. Any additional electrons fill the *p* orbitals one electron at a time.

Although electrons are actually found in orbitals of varying shapes, as shown in Figure 2.3, chemists often use more simplified diagrams when depicting the energy shells of electrons. Figure 2.4a illustrates an example involving the element nitrogen. An atom of this element has seven protons and seven electrons. Two electrons fill the first shell, and five electrons are found in the outer shell. Two of these fill the 2*s* orbital and are shown as a pair of electrons in the second shell. The other three electrons in the second shell are found singly in each of the three *p* orbitals. The diagram in Figure 2.4a makes it easy to see whether electrons are paired within the same orbital and whether the outer shell is full. **Figure 2.4b** shows a more scientifically accurate depiction of a nitrogen atom, showing how the electrons occupy orbitals with different shapes.

Most atoms have outer shells that are not completely filled with electrons. Nitrogen, as we just saw, has a first shell filled with two electrons and a second shell with five electrons (Figure 2.4a). Because the second shell can actually hold eight electrons, the outer shell of a nitrogen atom is not full. As discussed later in this chapter, atoms that have unfilled energy shells tend to share, release, or obtain electrons to fill their outer shell. Those electrons in the outermost shell are called the **valence electrons**. As you will learn shortly, in certain cases such electrons allow atoms to form chemical bonds with each other, in which two or more atoms become joined together to create a new substance.

Each Element Has a Unique Number of Protons

Each chemical element has a specific and unique number of protons that distinguishes it from another element. The number of protons in an atom is its **atomic number**. For example, hydrogen, the simplest atom, has an atomic number of 1,

corresponding to its single proton. Magnesium has an atomic number of 12, corresponding to its 12 protons. Recall that except for ions, the number of protons and electrons in a given atom are identical. Therefore, the atomic number is also equal to the number of electrons in the atom, resulting in a net charge of zero.

Figure 2.5 shows the first three rows of the periodic table of the elements, which arranges the known elements according to their atomic number and electron shells (see Appendix for the complete periodic table). A one- or two-letter symbol is used as an abbreviation for each element. The rows (known as "periods") indicate the number of energy shells. For example, hydrogen (H) has one shell, lithium (Li) has two shells, and sodium (Na) has three shells. The columns (called "groups"), from left to right, indicate the numbers of electrons in the outer shell. The outer shell of lithium (Li) has one electron, beryllium (Be) has two, boron (B) has three, and so forth. This organization of the periodic table tends to arrange elements based on similar chemical properties. For example, magnesium (Mg) and calcium (Ca) each have two electrons in their outer shell, so these two elements tend to combine with many of the same other elements. The similarities of elements within a group occur because they have the same number of electrons in their outer shells, and therefore, they have similar chemical

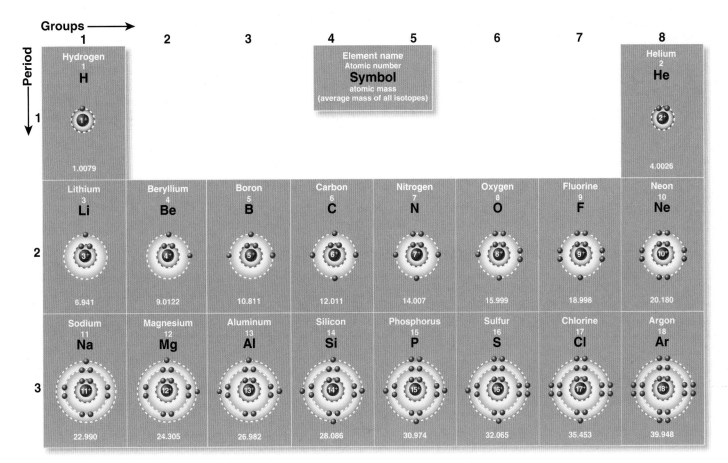

Figure 2.5 **The first three rows of the periodic table of the elements.** The elements are shown in models that depict the energy shells in different colors and the total number of electrons in each shell. The occupancy of orbitals is that of the elements in their pure state. The red sphere represents the nucleus of the atom, and the numerical value with the $^+$ designation represents the number of protons and, therefore, the positive charge of the nucleus. Elements are arranged in groups (columns) and periods (rows). For the complete periodic table, see Appendix.

bonding properties. These properties will be discussed later in this chapter.

Atoms Have a Small but Measurable Mass

Atoms are extremely small and therefore have very little mass. A single hydrogen atom, for example, has a mass of about 1.67×10^{-24} g (grams). Protons and neutrons are nearly equal in mass, and each are more than 1,800 times the mass of an electron (**Table 2.1**). Because of their tiny size relative to protons and neutrons, the mass of the electrons in an atom is ignored in calculations of atomic mass.

The **atomic mass** scale indicates an atom's mass relative to the mass of other atoms. By convention, the most common type of carbon atom, which has six protons and six neutrons, is assigned an atomic mass of exactly 12. On this scale, a hydrogen atom has an atomic mass of 1, indicating that it has 1/12 the mass of a carbon atom. A magnesium atom, with an atomic mass of 24, has twice the mass of a carbon atom.

The term mass is sometimes confused with weight, but these two terms refer to different features of matter. Weight is derived from the gravitational pull on a given mass. For example, a man who weighs 154 pounds on Earth would weigh only 25 pounds if he were standing on the moon, and he would weigh 21 trillion pounds if he could stand on a neutron star. However, his mass is the same in all locations because he has the same amount of matter. Because we are discussing mass on Earth, we can assume that the gravitational tug on all matter is roughly equivalent, and thus the terms become essentially interchangeable for our purpose.

Atomic mass is measured in units called daltons, after the English chemist John Dalton, who, in postulating that matter is composed of tiny indivisible units he called atoms, laid the groundwork for atomic theory. One **Dalton** (**Da**), also known as an atomic mass unit (amu), equals 1/12 the mass of a carbon atom, or about the mass of a proton or a hydrogen atom. Therefore, the most common type of carbon atom has an atomic mass of 12 daltons.

Because atoms such as hydrogen have a small mass, while atoms such as carbon have a larger mass, 1 g of hydrogen would have more atoms than 1 g of carbon. A **mole** of any substance contains the same number of particles as there are atoms in exactly 12 g of carbon. Twelve grams of carbon equals 1 mole of carbon, while 1 g of hydrogen equals 1 mole of hydrogen. As first described by Italian physicist Amedeo Avogadro, 1 mole of any element contains the same number of atoms—6.022×10^{23}. For example, 12 g of carbon contain 6.022×10^{23} atoms, and 1 g of hydrogen, whose atoms have 1/12 the mass of a carbon atom, also contains 6.022×10^{23} atoms. This number, which is known today as **Avogadro's number**, is large enough to be somewhat mind-boggling, and thus gives us an idea of just how small atoms really are. To visualize the enormity of this number, imagine that people could move through a turnstile at a rate of 1 million people per second. Even at that incredible rate, it would require almost 20 billion years for 6.022×10^{23} people to move through that turnstile!

Isotopes Vary in Their Number of Neutrons

Although the number of neutrons in most biologically relevant atoms is often equal to the number of protons, many elements can exist in multiple forms, called **isotopes**, that differ in the number of neutrons they contain. For example, the most abundant form of the carbon atom, ^{12}C, contains six protons and six neutrons, and thus has an atomic number of 6 and an atomic mass of 12 daltons, as described earlier. The superscript placed to the left of ^{12}C is the sum of the protons and neutrons. The rare carbon isotope ^{14}C, however, contains six protons and eight neutrons. While ^{14}C has an atomic number of 6, it has an atomic mass of 14 Da. Nearly 99% of the carbon in living organisms is ^{12}C. Consequently, the average atomic mass of carbon is very close to, but actually slightly greater than, 12 Da because of the existence of a small amount of heavier isotopes. This explains why the atomic masses given in the periodic table do not add up exactly to the predicted masses based on the atomic number and the number of neutrons of a given atom (see Figure 2.5).

Isotopes of an atom often have similar chemical properties but may have very different physical properties. For example, many isotopes found in nature are inherently unstable; the length of time they persist is measured in half-lives—the time it takes for 50% of the isotope to decay. Some persist for very long times; for example, ^{14}C has a half-life of more than 5,000 years. Such unstable isotopes are called **radioisotopes**, and they lose energy by emitting subatomic particles and/or radiation. At the very low amounts found in nature, radioisotopes usually pose no serious threat to life, but exposure of living organisms to high amounts of radioactivity can result in the disruption of cellular function, cancer, and even death.

Modern medical treatment and diagnosis make use of the special properties of radioactive compounds in many ways. For example, beams of high-energy radiation can be directed onto cancerous parts of the body to kill cancer cells. In another example, one or more atoms in a metabolically important molecule, such as the sugar glucose, can be chemically replaced with a radioactive isotope of fluorine. ^{18}F has a half-life of about 110 minutes. When a solution containing such a modified radioactive glucose is injected into a person's bloodstream, the organs of the body will take it up from the blood just as they would ordinary glucose. Special imaging techniques, such as the PET scan shown in **Figure 2.6**, can detect the amount of the radioactive glucose in the body's organs. In this way, it is

Table 2.1	Characteristics of Major Subatomic Particles			
Particle		**Location**	**Charge**	**Mass relative to electron**
Proton	+	Nucleus	+1	1,836
Neutron		Nucleus	0	1,839
Electron	•–	Around the nucleus	–1	1

although hydrogen makes up a small percentage of the mass of the human body, it accounts for about 63% of all the atoms in the body. That is because the atomic mass of hydrogen is so much smaller than that of heavier elements such as oxygen.

Other essential elements in living organisms include the mineral elements. Calcium and phosphorus, for example, are important constituents of the skeletons and shells of animals. Minerals such as potassium and sodium are key regulators of water movement and electrical currents that occur across the surfaces of many cells.

In addition, all living organisms require **trace elements**. These elements are present in extremely small quantities but still are essential for normal growth and function. For example, iron

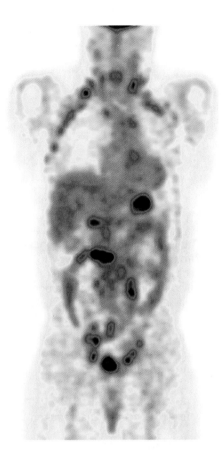

Figure 2.6 Diagnostic image of the human body using radioisotopes. A procedure called positron-emission tomography (PET) scanning highlights regions of the body that are actively using glucose, the body's major energy source. Radioactivity in this image shows up as a color. The dark patches are regions of extremely intense activity, which were later determined to be cancer in this patient.

possible to visualize whether or not organs such as the heart or brain are functioning normally, or at an increased or decreased rate. For example, a PET scan of the heart that showed reduced uptake of glucose from the blood might indicate the blood vessels of the heart were damaged and thereby depriving the heart of nutrients. PET scans can also reveal the presence of cancer— a disease characterized by uncontrolled cell growth. The scan of the individual shown in Figure 2.6, for example, identified numerous regions of high activity, suggestive of cancer.

The Mass of All Living Organisms Is Largely Composed of Four Elements

Just four elements—oxygen, carbon, hydrogen, and nitrogen— account for the vast majority of atoms in living organisms (**Table 2.2**). These elements typically make up about 95% of the mass of living organisms. Much of the oxygen and hydrogen occur in the form of water, which accounts for approximately 60% of the mass of most animals and up to 95% or more in some plants. Carbon is a major building block of all living matter, and nitrogen is a vital element in all proteins. Note in Table 2.2 that

Table 2.2	Chemical Elements Essential for Life in Most Organisms*		
Element	**Symbol**	**% Human body mass**	**% All atoms in human body**
Most abundant in living organisms (approximately 95% of total mass)			
Oxygen	O	65	25.5
Carbon	C	18	9.5
Hydrogen	H	9	63.0
Nitrogen	N	3	1.4
Mineral elements (less than 1% of total mass)			
Calcium	Ca		
Chlorine	Cl		
Magnesium	Mg		
Phosphorus	P		
Potassium	K		
Sodium	Na		
Sulfur	S		
Trace elements (less than 0.01% of total mass)			
Chromium	Cr		
Cobalt	Co		
Copper	Cu		
Fluorine	F		
Iodine	I		
Iron	Fe		
Manganese	Mn		
Molybdenum	Mo		
Selenium	Se		
Silicon	Si		
Tin	Sn		
Vanadium	V		
Zinc	Zn		

* While these are the most common elements in living organisms, many other trace and mineral elements have reported functions. For example, aluminum is believed to be a cofactor for certain chemical reactions in animals, but it is generally toxic to plants.

plays an important role in how vertebrates store oxygen in their blood, and copper serves a similar role in some invertebrates.

2.2 Chemical Bonds and Molecules

The linkage of atoms with other atoms serves as the basis for life and also gives life its great diversity. Two or more atoms bonded together make up a molecule. Atoms can combine with each other in several ways. For example, two oxygen atoms can combine to form one oxygen molecule, represented as O_2. This representation is called a **molecular formula**. It consists of the chemical symbols for all of the atoms that are present (here, O for oxygen) and a subscript that tells you how many of those atoms are present in the molecule (in this case, two). The term **compound** refers to a molecule composed of two or more different elements. Examples include water (H_2O), with two hydrogen atoms and one oxygen atom, and the sugar glucose ($C_6H_{12}O_6$), which has 6 carbon atoms, 12 hydrogen atoms, and 6 oxygen atoms.

One of the most important features of compounds is their emergent physical properties. This means that the properties of a compound differ greatly from those of its elements. Let's consider sodium as an example. Pure sodium (Na), also called elemental sodium, is a soft, silvery white metal that you can cut with a knife. When sodium forms a compound with chlorine (Cl), table salt (NaCl) is made. NaCl is a white, relatively hard crystal (as seen in the chapter-opening photo) that dissolves in water. Thus, the properties of sodium in a compound can be dramatically different from its properties as a pure element.

The atoms in molecules are held together by chemical bonds. In this section, we will examine the different types of chemical bonds, how these bonds form, and how they determine the structures of molecules.

Covalent Bonds Join Atoms Through the Sharing of Electrons

Covalent bonds, in which atoms share a pair of electrons, can occur between atoms whose outer shells are not full. A fundamental principle of chemistry is that *atoms tend to be most stable when their outer shells are filled with electrons.* Figure 2.7 shows this principle as it applies to the formation of hydrogen fluoride, a molecule with many important industrial and medical applications such as petroleum refining and fluorocarbon formation. The outer shell of a hydrogen atom is full when it contains two electrons, though a hydrogen atom has only one electron. The outer shell of a fluorine atom is full when it contains eight electrons, though a fluorine atom has only seven electrons in its outer shell. When hydrogen fluoride (HF) is made, the two atoms share a pair of electrons, which spend time orbiting both nuclei. This allows both of the outer shells of those atoms to be full. Covalent bonds are strong chemical bonds, because the shared electrons behave as if they belong to each atom.

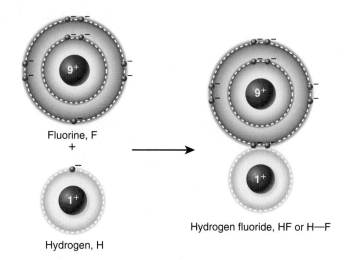

Fluorine, F
+
Hydrogen, H

Hydrogen fluoride, HF or H—F

Figure 2.7 **The formation of covalent bonds.** In covalent bonds, electrons from the outer shell of two atoms are shared with each other in order to complete the outer shells of both atoms. This simplified illustration shows hydrogen forming a covalent bond with fluorine.

When the structure of a molecule is diagrammed, each covalent bond is represented by a line indicating a pair of shared electrons. For example, hydrogen fluoride is diagrammed as

H—F

A molecule of water (H_2O) can be diagrammed as

H—O—H

The structural formula of water indicates that the oxygen atom is covalently bound to two hydrogen atoms.

Each atom forms a characteristic number of covalent bonds, which depends on the number of electrons required to fill the outer shell. The atoms of some elements important for life, notably carbon, form more than one covalent bond and become linked simultaneously to two or more other atoms. Figure 2.8 shows the number of covalent bonds formed by several atoms commonly found in the molecules of living cells.

For many types of atoms, their outermost shell is full when they contain eight electrons, an octet. The **octet rule** states that atoms are stable when they have eight electrons in their outermost shell. This rule applies to most atoms found in living organisms, including oxygen, nitrogen, carbon, phosphorus, and sulfur. These atoms form a characteristic number of covalent bonds to make an octet in their outermost shell (Figure 2.8). However, the octet rule does not always apply. For example, hydrogen has an outermost shell that can contain only two electrons, not eight.

In some molecules, a **double bond** occurs when atoms share two pairs of electrons (four electrons) rather than one pair. As shown in Figure 2.9, this is the case for an oxygen molecule (O_2), which can be diagrammed as

O=O

Another common example occurs when two carbon atoms form bonds in compounds. They may share one pair of electrons (single bond) or two pairs (double bond), depending on how many other covalent bonds each carbon forms with other

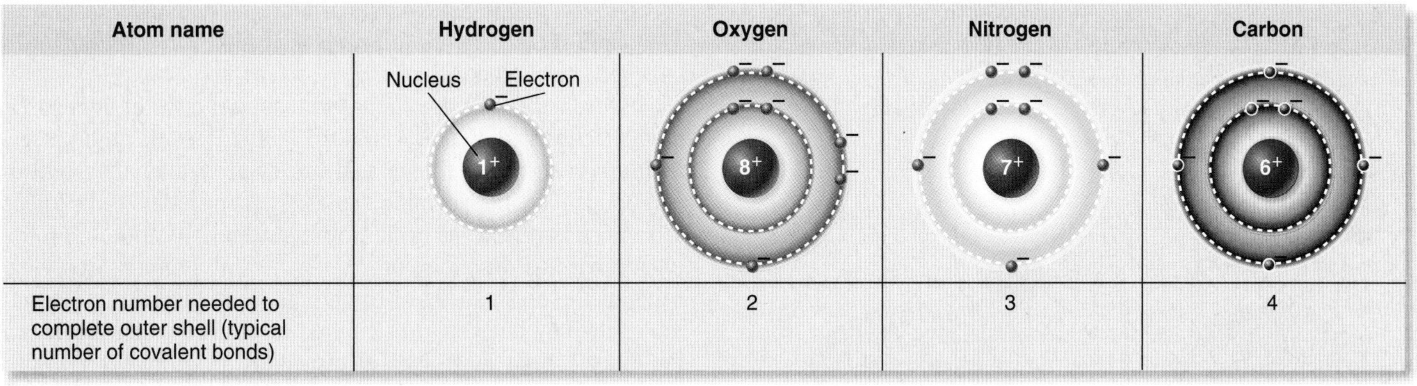

Atom name	Hydrogen	Oxygen	Nitrogen	Carbon
	Nucleus Electron 1+	8+	7+	6+
Electron number needed to complete outer shell (typical number of covalent bonds)	1	2	3	4

Figure 2.8 **The number of covalent bonds formed by common essential elements found in living organisms.** These elements form different numbers of covalent bonds due to the electron configurations in their outer shells.

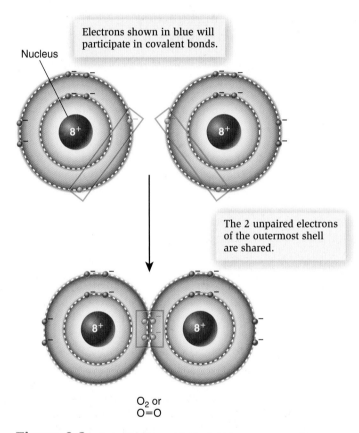

Electrons shown in blue will participate in covalent bonds.

Nucleus

The 2 unpaired electrons of the outermost shell are shared.

O₂ or
O=O

Figure 2.9 A double bond between two oxygen atoms.

Concept check: *Explain how an oxygen molecule obeys the octet rule.*

atoms. In rare cases, carbon can even form triple bonds, where three pairs of electrons are shared between two atoms.

Electrons Are Not Always Evenly Shared Between Atoms

Some atoms attract shared electrons more readily than do other atoms. The **electronegativity** of an atom is a measure of its ability to attract electrons in a bond with another atom. When two atoms with different electronegativities form a covalent bond, the shared electrons are more likely to be closer to the nucleus of the atom of higher electronegativity rather than the atom of lower electronegativity. Such bonds are called **polar covalent bonds**, because the distribution of electrons around the nuclei creates a polarity, or difference in electric charge, across the molecule. Water is the classic example of a molecule containing polar covalent bonds. The shared electrons at any moment tend to be closer to the oxygen nucleus rather than to either of the hydrogens. This unequal sharing of electrons gives the molecule a region of partial negative charge and two regions of partial positive charge (**Figure 2.10**).

Atoms with high electronegativity, such as oxygen and nitrogen, have a relatively strong attraction for electrons. These atoms form polar covalent bonds with hydrogen atoms, which have low electronegativity. Examples of polar covalent bonds include O—H and N—H. In contrast, bonds between atoms with similar electronegativities, for example between two carbon atoms (C—C) or between carbon and hydrogen atoms (C—H), are called **nonpolar covalent bonds**. Molecules containing significant numbers of polar bonds are known as **polar molecules**, whereas molecules composed predominantly of nonpolar bonds are called **nonpolar molecules**. A single molecule may have different regions with nonpolar bonds and polar bonds. As we will explore later, the physical characteristics of polar and nonpolar molecules, especially their solubility in water, are quite different.

Hydrogen Bonds Allow Interactions Between and Within Molecules

An important result of certain polar covalent bonds is the ability of one molecule to loosely associate with another molecule through a weak interaction called a **hydrogen bond**. A hydrogen bond forms when a hydrogen atom from one polar molecule becomes electrically attracted to an electronegative atom, such as an oxygen or nitrogen atom, in another polar molecule. Hydrogen bonds, like those between water molecules, are represented in diagrams by dashed or dotted lines to distinguish them from covalent bonds (**Figure 2.11a**). A single hydrogen

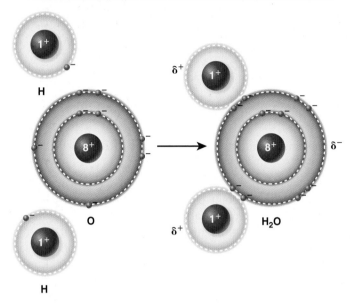

In water, the shared electrons spend more time near the oxygen atom. This gives oxygen a partial negative charge (δ^-) and each hydrogen a partial positive charge (δ^+).

Figure 2.10 **Polar covalent bonds in water molecules.** In a water molecule, two hydrogen atoms share electrons with an oxygen atom. Because oxygen has a higher electronegativity, the shared electrons spend more time closer to oxygen. This gives oxygen a partial negative charge, designated δ^-, and each hydrogen a partial positive charge, designated δ^+.

bond is very weak. The strength of a hydrogen bond is only a few percent of the strength of the polar covalent bonds linking the hydrogen and oxygen within a water molecule.

Hydrogen bonds can also occur within a single large molecule. Many large molecules may have dozens, hundreds, or more of hydrogen bonds within their structure. Collectively, many hydrogen bonds add up to a strong force that helps maintain the three-dimensional structure of a molecule. This is particularly true in deoxyribonucleic acid (DNA)—the molecule that makes up the genetic material of living organisms. DNA exists as two long, twisting strands of many thousands of atoms. The two strands are held together along their length by hydrogen bonds between different portions of the molecule (Figure 2.11b). Due to the large number of hydrogen bonds, it takes considerable energy to separate the strands of DNA.

In contrast to the cumulative strength of many hydrogen bonds, the weakness of individual bonds is also important. When an interaction between two molecules involves relatively few hydrogen bonds, such interactions tend to be weak and may be readily broken. The reversible nature of hydrogen bonds allows molecules to interact and then to become separated again. For example, as discussed in Chapter 7, small molecules may bind to proteins called enzymes via hydrogen bonds. **Enzymes** are molecules found in all cells that facilitate

or catalyze many biologically important chemical reactions. The small molecules are later released after the enzymes have changed their structure.

Hydrogen bonds are similar to a special class of bonds that are collectively known as **van der Waals forces**. In some cases, temporary attractive forces that are even weaker than hydrogen bonds form between molecules. These van der Waals forces arise because electrons orbit atomic nuclei in a random, probabilistic way, as described previously. At any moment, the electrons in the outer shells of the atoms in an electrically neutral molecule may be evenly distributed or unevenly distributed. In the latter case, a short-lived electrical attraction may arise with other nearby molecules. Like hydrogen bonds, the collective strength of temporary attractive forces between molecules can be quite strong.

Ionic Bonds Involve an Attraction Between Positive and Negative Ions

Atoms are electrically neutral because they contain equal numbers of negative electrons and positive protons. If an atom or molecule gains or loses one or more electrons, it acquires a net electric charge and becomes an **ion** (Figure 2.12a). For example, when a sodium atom (Na), which has 11 electrons, loses one electron, it becomes a sodium ion (Na^+) with a net positive charge. Ions that have a net positive charge are called **cations**. A sodium ion still has 11 protons, but only 10 electrons. Ions such as Na^+ are depicted with a superscript that indicates the net charge of the ion. A chlorine atom (Cl), which has 17 electrons, can gain an electron and become a chloride ion (Cl^-) with a net negative charge—it has 18 electrons but only 17 protons. Ions with a net negative charge are **anions**.

Table 2.3 lists the ionic forms of several elements. Hydrogen atoms and most mineral and trace elements readily form ions. The ions listed in this table are relatively stable because the outer electron shells of the ions are full. For example, a sodium atom has one electron in its third (outermost) shell. If it loses this electron to become Na^+, it no longer has a third shell, and the second shell, which is full, becomes its outermost shell.

Alternatively, a Cl atom has seven electrons in its outermost shell. If it gains an electron to become a chloride ion (Cl^-), its outer shell becomes full with eight electrons. Some atoms can gain or lose more than one electron. For instance, a calcium atom, which has 20 electrons, loses 2 electrons to become a calcium ion, depicted as Ca^{2+}.

An **ionic bond** occurs when a cation binds to an anion. Figure 2.12a shows an ionic bond between Na^+ and Cl^- to form NaCl. Salt is the general name given to compounds formed from an attraction between a positively charged ion (a cation) and negatively charged ion (an anion). Examples of salts include NaCl, KCl, and $CaCl_2$. Salts may form crystals in which the cations and anions form a regular array. **Figure 2.12b** shows a NaCl crystal, in which the sodium and chloride ions are held together by ionic bonds. Ionic bonds are easily broken in water—the environment of the cell.

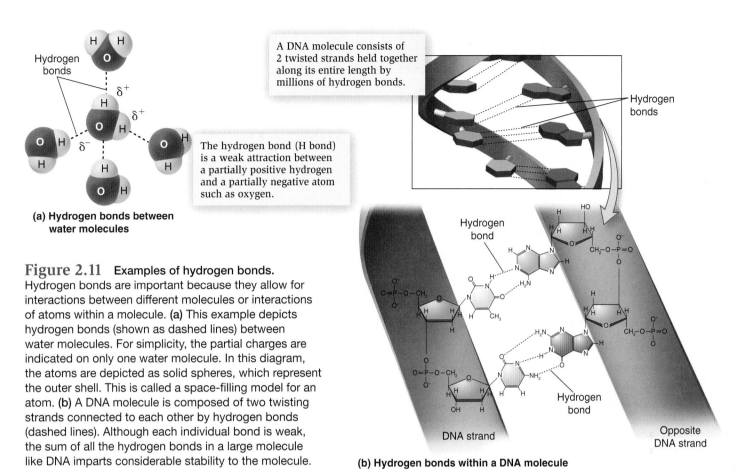

Figure 2.11   Examples of hydrogen bonds. Hydrogen bonds are important because they allow for interactions between different molecules or interactions of atoms within a molecule. **(a)** This example depicts hydrogen bonds (shown as dashed lines) between water molecules. For simplicity, the partial charges are indicated on only one water molecule. In this diagram, the atoms are depicted as solid spheres, which represent the outer shell. This is called a space-filling model for an atom. **(b)** A DNA molecule is composed of two twisting strands connected to each other by hydrogen bonds (dashed lines). Although each individual bond is weak, the sum of all the hydrogen bonds in a large molecule like DNA imparts considerable stability to the molecule.

Concept check: In Chapter 11, you will learn that the two DNA strands must first separate into two single strands for DNA to be replicated. Do you think the process of strand separation requires energy, or do you think the strands can separate spontaneously?

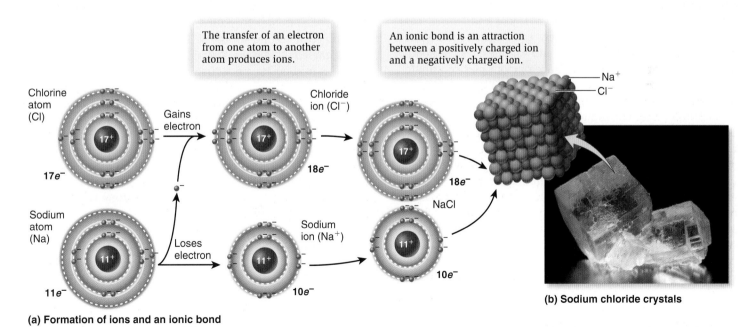

(a) Formation of ions and an ionic bond

Figure 2.12   Ionic bonding in table salt (NaCl). **(a)** When an electron is transferred from a sodium atom to a chlorine atom, the resulting ions are attracted to each other via an ionic bond. **(b)** In a salt crystal, a lattice is formed in which the positively charged sodium ions (Na$^+$) are attracted to negatively charged chloride ions (Cl$^-$).

Table 2.3	Ionic Forms of Some Common Elements			
Atom	Chemical symbol	Ion	Ion symbol	Electrons gained or lost
Calcium	Ca	Calcium ion	Ca^{2+}	2 lost
Chlorine	Cl	Chloride ion	Cl^-	1 gained
Hydrogen	H	Hydrogen ion	H^+	1 lost
Magnesium	Mg	Magnesium ion	Mg^{2+}	2 lost
Potassium	K	Potassium ion	K^+	1 lost
Sodium	Na	Sodium ion	Na^+	1 lost

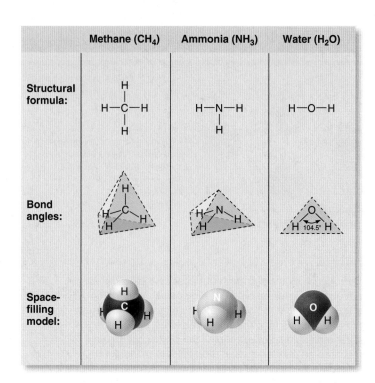

Figure 2.13 **Shapes of molecules.** Molecules may assume different shapes depending on the types of bonds between their atoms. The angles between groups of atoms are well defined. For example, in liquid water at room temperature, the angle formed by the bonds between the two hydrogen atoms and the oxygen atom is approximately 104.5°. This bond angle can vary slightly depending on the temperature and degree of hydrogen bonding between adjacent water molecules.

Molecules May Change Their Shapes

When atoms combine, they can form molecules with various three-dimensional shapes, depending on the arrangements and numbers of bonds between their atoms. As an example, let's consider the arrangements of covalent bonds in a few simple molecules, including water (Figure 2.13). These molecules form new orbitals that cause the atoms to have defined angles relative to each other. This gives groups of atoms very specific shapes, as shown in the three examples of Figure 2.13.

Molecules containing covalent bonds are not rigid, inflexible structures. Think of a single covalent bond, for example, as an axle around which the joined atoms can rotate. Within certain limits, the shape of a molecule can change without breaking its covalent bonds. As illustrated in Figure 2.14a, a molecule of six carbon atoms bonded together can assume a number of shapes as a result of rotations around various covalent bonds. The three-dimensional, flexible shape of molecules contributes to their biological properties. As shown in Figure 2.14b, the binding of one molecule to another may affect the shape of one of the molecules. An animal can taste food, for instance, because food molecules interact with special proteins called receptors on its tongue. When a food molecule encounters a receptor, the two molecules recognize each other by their unique shapes, somewhat like a key fitting into a lock. As molecules in the food interact with the receptor, the shape of the receptor changes. When we look at how an animal's brain receives information from other parts of the body, we will see that the altered shape of the receptor initiates a signal that communicates information about the taste of the food to the animal's brain (see Chapter 43).

Free Radicals Are a Special Class of Highly Reactive Molecules

Recall that an atom or an ion is most stable when each of its orbitals is occupied by its full complement of electrons. A molecule containing an atom with a single, unpaired electron in its outer shell is known as a **free radical**. Free radicals can react with other molecules to "steal" an electron from one of their atoms, thereby filling the orbital in the free radical. In the process, this may create a new free radical in the donor molecule, setting off a chain reaction.

Free radicals can be formed in several ways, including exposure of cells to radiation and toxins. Free radicals can do considerable harm to living cells—for example, by causing a cell to rupture or by damaging the genetic material. Surprisingly, the lethal effect of free radicals is sometimes put to good use. Some cells in animals' bodies create free radicals and use them to kill invading cells such as bacteria. Likewise, people use hydrogen peroxide to kill bacteria, as in a dirty skin wound. Hydrogen peroxide can break down to create free radicals, which can then attack bacteria in the wound.

Despite the exceptional case of fighting off bacteria, though, most free radicals that arise in an organism need to be inactivated so they do not kill healthy cells. Protection from free radicals is afforded by molecules that can donate electrons to the free radicals without becoming highly reactive themselves. Examples of such protective compounds are certain vitamins known as antioxidants (for example, vitamins C and E), found in fruits and vegetables, and the numerous plant compounds

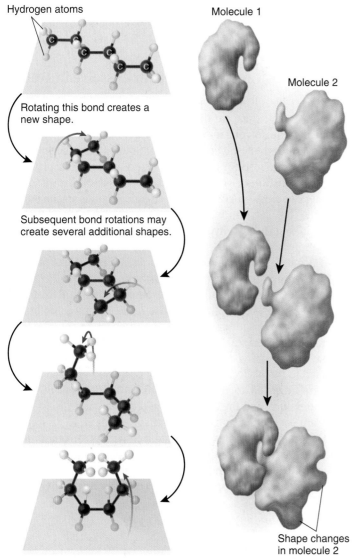

Hydrogen atoms

Rotating this bond creates a new shape.

Subsequent bond rotations may create several additional shapes.

Molecule 1

Molecule 2

Shape changes in molecule 2

(a) Bond rotation in a small molecule

(b) Noncovalent interactions that may alter the shape of molecules

Figure 2.14 **Shape changes in molecules.** A single molecule may assume different three-dimensional shapes without breaking any of the covalent bonds between its atoms, as shown in **(a)** for a six-carbon molecule. Hydrogen atoms above the blue plane are shown in white; those below the blue plane are blue. **(b)** Two molecules are shown schematically as having complementary shapes that permit them to interact. Upon interacting, the flexible nature of the molecules causes molecule 2 to twist sufficiently to assume a new shape. This change in shape is often an important mechanism by which one molecule influences the activity of another.

known as flavonoids. This is one reason why a diet rich in fruits and vegetables is beneficial to our health.

Free radicals are diagrammed with a dot next to the atomic symbol. Examples of biologically important free radicals are superoxide anion, $O_2 \cdot^-$; hydroxyl radical, $\cdot OH$; and nitric oxide, $NO \cdot$. Note that free radicals can be either charged or neutral.

Chemical Reactions Change Elements or Compounds into Different Compounds

A **chemical reaction** occurs when one or more substances are changed into other substances. This can happen when two or more elements or compounds combine with each other to form a new compound, when one compound breaks down into two or more molecules, or when electrons are added to or removed from an atom.

Chemical reactions share many similar properties. First, they all require a source of energy for molecules to encounter each other. The energy required for atoms and molecules to interact is provided partly by heat, or thermal, energy. In the complete absence of any heat (a temperature called absolute zero), atoms and molecules would be totally stationary and unable to interact. Heat energy causes atoms and molecules to vibrate and move, a phenomenon known as Brownian motion. Second, chemical reactions that occur in living organisms often require more than just Brownian motion to proceed at a reasonable rate. Such reactions need to be catalyzed. As discussed in Chapter 6, a catalyst is a substance that speeds up a chemical reaction. As noted earlier, all cells contain many kinds of catalysts called enzymes. Third, chemical reactions tend to proceed in a particular direction but will eventually reach a state of equilibrium unless something happens to prevent equilibrium.

To understand what we mean by "direction" and "equilibrium" in this context, let's consider a chemical reaction between methane (a component found in natural gas) and oxygen. When a single molecule of methane reacts with two molecules of oxygen, one molecule of carbon dioxide and two molecules of water are produced:

$$CH_4 + 2 O_2 \rightleftharpoons CO_2 + 2 H_2O$$

(methane) (oxygen)   (carbon dioxide) (water)

As it is written here, methane and oxygen are the **reactants**, and carbon dioxide and water are the **products**. The bidirectional arrows indicate that this reaction can proceed in both directions. Whether a chemical reaction is likely to proceed in a forward ("left to right") or reverse ("right to left") direction depends on changes in free energy, which you will learn about in Chapter 6. If we began with only methane and oxygen, the forward reaction would be very favorable. The reaction would produce a large amount of carbon dioxide and water, as well as heat. This is why natural gas is used as a fuel to heat homes. However, all chemical reactions will eventually reach **chemical equilibrium**, in which the rate of the forward reaction is balanced by the rate of the reverse reaction; in other words, there would no longer be a change in the concentrations of products and reactants. In the case of the reaction involving methane and oxygen, this equilibrium would occur when nearly all of the reactants had been converted to products. In biological systems, however, many reactions do not have a chance to reach chemical equilibrium. For example, the products of a reaction may immediately be converted within a cell to a different product through a second reaction, or used by a cell to carry out some function. When a product is removed from a reaction as fast as it is formed, the reactants continue to form new product until all the reactants are used up.

A final feature common to chemical reactions in living organisms is that many reactions occur in watery environments. Such chemical reactions involve reactants and products that are dissolved in water. Next, we will examine the properties of this amazing liquid.

2.3 Properties of Water

It would be difficult to imagine life without water. People can survive for a month or more without food but usually die in less than a week without water. The bodies of all organisms are composed largely of water; most of the cells in an organism's body not only are filled with water, but are surrounded by water. Up to 95% of the weight of certain plants comes from water. In humans, typically 60–70% of body weight is from water. The brain is roughly 70% water, blood is about 80% water, and the lungs are nearly 90% water. Even our bones are about 20% water! In addition, water is an important liquid in the surrounding environments of living organisms. For example, vast numbers of species are aquatic organisms that live in watery environments.

Thus far in this chapter, we have considered the features of atoms and molecules and the nature of bonds and chemical reactions between atoms and molecules. In this section, we will turn our attention to issues related to the liquid properties of living organisms and the environment in which they live. Most of the chemical reactions that occur in nature involve molecules that are dissolved in water, including those reactions that happen inside cells and in the spaces that surround cells of living organisms (**Figure 2.15**).

However, not all molecules dissolve in water. In this section, we will examine the properties of chemicals that influence whether they dissolve in water, and we will consider how biologists measure the amounts of dissolved substances. In addition,

we will examine some of the other special properties of water that make it a vital component of living organisms and their environments.

Ions and Polar Molecules Readily Dissolve in Water

Substances dissolved in a liquid are known as **solutes**, and the liquid in which they are dissolved is the **solvent**. In all living organisms, the solvent for chemical reactions is water, which is the most abundant solvent in nature. Solutes dissolve in a solvent to form a **solution**. Solutions made with water are called **aqueous solutions**. To understand why a substance dissolves in water, we need to consider the chemical bonds in the solute molecule and those in water. As discussed earlier, the covalent bonds linking the two hydrogen atoms to the oxygen atom in a water molecule are polar. Therefore, the oxygen in water has a slight negative charge, and each hydrogen has a slight positive charge. To dissolve in water, a substance must be electrically attracted to water molecules. For example, table salt (NaCl) is a solid crystalline substance because of the strong ionic bonds between positive sodium ions (Na^+) and negative chloride ions (Cl^-). When a crystal of sodium chloride is placed in water, the partially negatively charged oxygens of water molecules are attracted to the Na^+, and the partially positively charged hydrogens are attracted to the Cl^- (**Figure 2.16**). Clusters of water molecules surround the ions, allowing the Na^+ and Cl^- to separate from each other and enter the water—that is, to dissolve.

Generally, molecules that contain ionic and/or polar covalent bonds will dissolve in water. Such molecules are said to be **hydrophilic**, which literally means "water-loving." In contrast, molecules composed predominantly of carbon and hydrogen

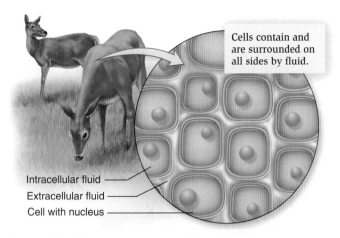

Figure 2.15 Fluids inside and outside of cells. Aqueous solutions exist in the intracellular fluid and in the extracellular fluid. Chemical reactions are always ongoing in both fluids.

Figure 2.16 NaCl crystals dissolving in water. The ability of water to dissolve sodium chloride crystals depends on the electrical attraction between the polar water molecules and the charged sodium and chloride ions. Water molecules surround each ion as it becomes dissolved. For simplicity, the partial charges are indicated for only one water molecule.

are relatively insoluble in water, because carbon-carbon and carbon-hydrogen bonds are nonpolar. These molecules do not have partial positive and negative charges and, therefore, are not attracted to water molecules. Such molecules are **hydrophobic**, or "water-fearing." Oils are a familiar example of hydrophobic molecules. Try mixing vegetable oil with water and observe the result. The two liquids separate into an oil phase and water phase. Very little oil dissolves in the water.

Although hydrophobic molecules dissolve poorly in water, they normally dissolve readily in nonpolar solvents. For example, cholesterol is a compound found in the blood and cells of animals. It is a hydrophobic molecule that is barely soluble in water but easily dissolves in nonpolar solvents used in chemical laboratories, such as ether. Biological membranes like those that encase cells are made up in large part of nonpolar compounds. Because of this, cholesterol also inserts into biological membranes, where it helps to maintain the membrane structure.

Molecules that have both polar or ionized regions at one or more sites and nonpolar regions at other sites are called **amphipathic** (or amphiphilic, from the Greek for "both loves"). When mixed with water, long amphipathic molecules may aggregate into spheres called **micelles**, with their polar (hydrophilic) regions at the surface of the micelle, where they are attracted to the surrounding water molecules. The nonpolar (hydrophobic) ends are oriented toward the interior of the micelle (**Figure 2.17**). Such an arrangement minimizes the interaction between water molecules and the nonpolar ends of the amphipathic molecules. Nonpolar molecules can dissolve in the central nonpolar regions of these clusters and thus exist in an aqueous environment in far higher amounts than would otherwise be possible based on their low solubility in water. One familiar example of amphipathic molecules are those in detergents, which can form micelles that help to dissolve oils and nonpolar molecules found in dirt. The detergent molecules found in soap have polar and nonpolar ends. Oils on your skin dissolve in the nonpolar regions of the detergent, and the polar ends help the detergent rinse off in water, taking the oil with it.

In addition to micelles, amphipathic molecules may form structures called bilayers. As you will learn in Chapter 5, lipid bilayers play a key role in cellular membrane structure.

The Amount of a Dissolved Solute per Unit Volume of Liquid Is Its Concentration

Solute **concentration** is defined as the amount of a solute dissolved in a unit volume of solution. For example, if 1 gram (g) of NaCl were dissolved in enough water to make 1 liter of solution, we would say that its solute concentration is 1 g/L.

A comparison of the concentrations of two different substances on the basis of the number of grams per liter of solution does not directly indicate how many molecules of each substance are present. For example, let's compare 10 g each of glucose ($C_6H_{12}O_6$) and sodium chloride (NaCl). Because the individual molecules of glucose have more mass than those of NaCl, 10 g of glucose will contain fewer molecules than 10 g

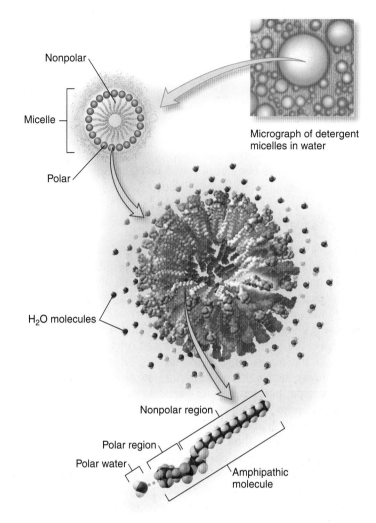

Micrograph of detergent micelles in water

Figure 2.17   The formation of micelles by amphipathic molecules.   In water, amphipathic molecules tend to arrange themselves so their nonpolar regions are directed away from water molecules and the polar regions are directed toward the water and can form hydrogen bonds with it.

Concept check: *When oil dissolves in soap, where is the oil found?*

of NaCl. Therefore, another way to describe solute concentration is according to the moles of dissolved solute per volume of solution. To make this calculation, we must know three things: the amount of dissolved solute, the molecular mass of the dissolved solute, and the volume of the solution.

The **molecular mass** of a molecule is equal to the sum of the atomic masses of all the atoms in the molecule. For example, glucose ($C_6H_{12}O_6$) has a molecular mass of 180 ([6 × 12] + [12 × 1] + [6 × 16] = 180). As mentioned earlier, 1 mole (abbreviated mol) of a substance is the amount of the substance in grams equal to its atomic or molecular mass. The **molarity** of a solution is defined as the number of moles of a solute dissolved in 1 L of solution. A solution containing 180 g of glucose (1 mol) dissolved in enough water to make 1 L is a 1 **molar** solution of glucose (1 mol/L). By convention, a

1 mol/L solution is usually written as 1 M, where the capital M stands for molar and is defined as mol/L. If 90 g of glucose (half its molecular mass) were dissolved in enough water to make 1 L, the solution would have a concentration of 0.5 mol/L, or 0.5 M.

The concentrations of solutes dissolved in the fluids of living organisms are usually much less than 1 M. Many have concentrations in the range of millimoles per liter (1 mM = 0.001 M = 10^{-3} M), and others are present in even smaller concentrations—micromoles per liter (1 μM = 0.000001 M = 10^{-6} M) or nanomoles per liter (1 nM = 0.000000001 M = 10^{-9} M).

Water Exists in Three States

Let's now consider some general features of water and how dissolved solutes affect its properties. Water is an abundant compound on Earth that exists in all three states of matter—solid (ice), liquid (water), and gas (water vapor). At the temperatures found over most regions of the planet, water is found primarily as a liquid in which the weak hydrogen bonds between molecules are continuously being formed, broken, and formed again. If the temperature rises, the rate at which hydrogen bonds break increases, and molecules of water escape into the gaseous state, becoming water vapor. If the temperature falls, hydrogen bonds are broken less frequently, so larger and larger clusters of water molecules are formed, until at 0°C water freezes into a crystalline matrix—ice. The water molecules in ice tend to lie in a more orderly and "open" arrangement, that is, with greater intermolecular distances, which makes ice less dense than water. This is why ice floats on water (**Figure 2.18**). Compared to water, ice is also less likely to participate in most types of chemical reactions.

Changes in state, such as changes between the solid, liquid, and gaseous states of water, involve an input or a release of energy. For example, when energy is supplied to make water boil, it changes from the liquid to the gaseous state. This is called vaporization. The heat required to vaporize 1 mole of any substance at its boiling point is called the substance's **heat of vaporization**. For water, this value is very high, because of the high number of hydrogen bonds between the molecules. It takes more than five times as much heat to vaporize water than it does to raise the temperature of water from 0°C to 100°C. In contrast, energy is released when water freezes to form ice. Water also has a high **heat of fusion**, which is the amount of heat energy that must be withdrawn or released from a substance to cause it to change from the liquid to the solid state. These two features, the high heats of vaporization and fusion, mean that water is extremely stable as a liquid. Not surprisingly, therefore, living organisms have evolved to function best within a range of temperatures consistent with the liquid phase of water.

The temperature at which a solution freezes or vaporizes is influenced by the amounts of dissolved solutes. These are examples of **colligative properties**, defined as those properties that depend strictly on the total number of dissolved solutes, not on the specific type of solute. Pure water freezes at 0°C

Figure 2.18 **Structure of liquid water and ice.** In its liquid form, the hydrogen bonds between water molecules continually form, break, and re-form, resulting in a changing arrangement of molecules from instant to instant. At temperatures at or below its freezing point, water forms a crystalline matrix called ice. In this solid form, hydrogen bonds are more stable. Ice has a hexagonally shaped crystal structure. The greater space between H_2O molecules in this crystal structure causes ice to have a lower density compared to water. For this reason, ice floats on water.

and vaporizes at 100°C. Addition of solutes to water lowers its freezing point below 0°C and raises its boiling point above 100°C. Adding a small amount of the compound ethylene glycol—antifreeze—to the water in a car's radiator, for instance, lowers the freezing point of the water and consequently prevents it from freezing in cold weather. Similarly, the presence of large amounts of solutes partly explains why the oceans do not freeze when the temperature falls below 0°C. Likewise, the colligative properties of water also account for the remarkable ability of certain ectothermic animals, which are unable to maintain warm body temperatures in cold environments, to nonetheless escape becoming frozen solid. Such animals produce antifreeze molecules that dissolve in their body fluids in very large numbers, thereby lowering the freezing point of the fluids and preventing their blood and cells from freezing in the extreme cold. The emerald rockcod (*Trematomus bernacchii*), found in the waters of Antarctica, for example, manages to live in ocean waters that are at or below 0°C (**Figure 2.19a**). Similarly, many insects, such as the larvae of the parasitic wasp (*Bracon cephi*), also make use of natural antifreeze to stay alive in extreme conditions (**Figure 2.19b**).

Figure 2.19 Antifreeze in living organisms.   Many animals, such as **(a)** the emerald rockcod (*Trematomus bernacchii*) and **(b)** the larvae of the parasitic wasp (*Bracon cephi*), can withstand extremely cold temperatures thanks to natural antifreeze molecules in their body fluids.

(a) Emerald rockcod in the waters of Antarctica

(b) Wasp larvae, which can withstand freezing temperatures

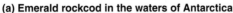

Concept check: *The liquid portion of blood of animals, including humans, is a watery solution containing many dissolved solutes, such as Na⁺ and Cl⁻. Would you predict that the freezing point of blood is above, below, or the same as that of water?*

Water Performs Many Other Important Tasks in Living Organisms

As discussed earlier, water is the primary solvent in the fluids of all living organisms, from unicellular bacteria to the largest sequoia tree. Water permits atoms and molecules to interact in ways that would be impossible in their nondissolved states. In Unit II, we will consider many ions and molecules that are solutes in living cells. Even so, it is important to recognize that in addition to acting as a solvent, water serves many other remarkable functions that are critical for the survival of living organisms. For example, water molecules themselves take part in many chemical reactions of this general type:

$$R1{-}R2 + H{-}O{-}H \quad \rightarrow \quad R1{-}OH + H{-}R2$$

R is a general symbol used in this case to represent a group of atoms. In this equation, R1 and R2 are distinct groups of atoms. On the left side, R1—R2 is a compound in which the groups of atoms are connected by a covalent bond. To be converted to products, a covalent bond is broken in each reactant, R1—R2 and H—O—H, and OH and H (from water) form covalent bonds with R1 and R2, respectively. Reactions of this type are known as **hydrolysis** reactions (from the Greek *hydro*, meaning water, and *lysis*, meaning to break apart), because water is used to break apart another molecule (**Figure 2.20a**). As discussed in Chapter 3 and later chapters, many large molecules are broken down into smaller, biologically important units by hydrolysis.

Alternatively, other chemical reactions in living organisms involve the removal of a water molecule so that a covalent bond can be formed between two separate molecules. For example, let's consider a chemical reaction that is the reverse of our previous hydrolysis reaction:

$$R1{-}OH + H{-}R2 \quad \rightarrow \quad R1{-}R2 + H{-}O{-}H$$

Such a reaction involves the formation of a covalent bond between two molecules. Two or more molecules combining to form one larger molecule with the loss of a small molecule is called a **condensation reaction**. In the example shown here, a molecule of water is lost during the reaction; this is a specific type of condensation reaction called a **dehydration reaction**. As discussed in later chapters, this is a common reaction used to build larger molecules in living organisms.

Another feature of water is that it is incompressible—its volume does not significantly decrease when subjected to high pressure. This has biological importance for many organisms that use water to provide force or support (**Figure 2.20b**). For example, water supports the bodies of worms and some other invertebrates, and it provides turgidity (stiffness) and support for plants.

Water is also the means by which unneeded and potentially toxic waste compounds are eliminated from an animal's body (**Figure 2.20c**). In mammals, for example, the kidneys filter out soluble waste products derived from the breakdown of proteins and other compounds. The filtered products remain in solution in a watery fluid, which eventually becomes urine and is excreted.

Recall from our discussion of water's properties that it takes considerable energy in the form of heat to convert water from a liquid to a gas. This feature has great biological significance. Although everyone is familiar with the fact that boiling water is converted to water vapor, water can vaporize into the gaseous state even at ordinary temperatures. This process is known as **evaporation**. The simplest way to understand this is to imagine that in any volume of water at any temperature, some vibrating water molecules will have higher energy than others. Those with the highest energy break their hydrogen bonds and escape into the gaseous state. The important point, however, is that even at ordinary temperatures, it still requires the same energy to change water from liquid to gas. Therefore,

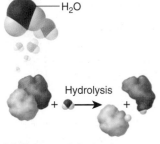

Hydrolysis

(a) Water participates in chemical reactions.

(b) Water provides support. The plant on the right is wilting due to lack of water.

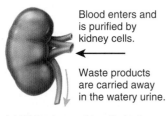

Blood enters and is purified by kidney cells.

Waste products are carried away in the watery urine.

(c) Water is used to eliminate soluble wastes.

(d) Evaporation helps some animals dissipate body heat.

(e) The cohesive force of water molecules aids in the movement of fluid through vessels in plants.

(f) Water in saliva serves as a lubricant during—or as shown here, in anticipation of—feeding.

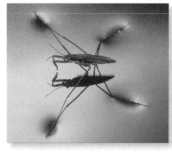

(g) The surface tension of water explains why this water strider doesn't sink.

Figure 2.20 Some of the amazing roles of water in biology. In addition to acting as a solvent, water serves many crucial functions in nature.

the evaporation of sweat from an animal's skin requires considerable energy in the form of body heat, which is then lost to the environment. Evaporation is an important mechanism by which many animals cool themselves on hot days (**Figure 2.20d**).

Another important feature for living organisms is that water has a very high **specific heat**, defined as the amount of heat energy required to raise the temperature of 1 gram of a substance by 1°C (or conversely, the amount of heat energy that must be lost to lower the temperature by 1°C). This means that it takes considerable heat to raise the temperature of water. A related concept is heat capacity; this refers to the amount of heat energy required to raise the temperature of an entire object or substance. A lake has a greater heat capacity than does a bathtub filled with water, but both have the same specific heat because both are the same substance (ignoring for the moment that a lake is not pure water). These properties of water contribute to the relatively stable temperatures of large bodies of water compared to inland temperatures. Large bodies of water tend to have a moderating effect on the temperature of nearby land masses.

The hydrogen-bonding properties of water affect its ability to form droplets and to adhere to surfaces. The phenomenon of water molecules attracting each other is called **cohesion**. Water exhibits strong cohesion due to hydrogen bonding. Cohesion aids in the movement of water through the vessels of plants (**Figure 2.20e**). A property similar to cohesion is **adhesion**, which refers to the ability of water to be attracted to, and thus adhere to, a surface that is not electrically neutral. Water tends to cling to surfaces to which it can hydrogen bond, such as a paper towel. In organisms, the adhesive properties of water allow it, for example, to coat the surfaces of the digestive tract of animals and act as a lubricant for the passage of food (**Figure 2.20f**).

Surface tension is a measure of the attraction between molecules at the surface of a liquid. In the case of water, the attractive force between hydrogen-bonded water molecules at the interface between water and air is what causes water to form droplets. The surface water molecules attract each other into a configuration (roughly that of a sphere) that reduces the number of water molecules in contact with air. You can see this by slightly overfilling a glass with water; the water will form an oval shape above the rim. Likewise, surface tension allows certain insects, such as water striders, to walk on the surface of a pond without sinking (**Figure 2.20g**) and plays a significant role in the filling of lungs with air in humans and many other animals.

Hydrogen Ion Concentrations Are Changed by Acids and Bases

Pure water has the ability to ionize to a very small extent into hydrogen ions that exist as single protons (H^+) and **hydroxide ions** (OH^-). (In nature or in laboratory conditions, hydrogen atoms may exist as any of several rare types of positively or negatively charged ions; in this text, we will use the term hydrogen ion to refer to the common H^+ form). In pure water, the concentrations of H^+ and OH^- are both 10^{-7} mol/L, or 10^{-7} M. An inherent property of water is that the product of the concentrations of H^+ and OH^- is always 10^{-14} M at 25°C. Therefore, in pure water, $[H^+][OH^-] = [10^{-7}\ M][10^{-7}\ M] = 10^{-14}$ M. (The brackets around the symbols for the hydrogen and hydroxide ions indicate concentration.)

When certain substances are dissolved in water, they may release or absorb H^+ or OH^-, thereby altering the relative concentrations of these ions. Substances that release hydrogen ions in solution are called **acids**. Two examples are hydrochloric acid and carbonic acid:

$$HCl \rightarrow H^+ + Cl^-$$

(hydrochloric acid)   (chloride ion)

$$H_2CO_3 \rightleftharpoons H^+ + HCO_3^-$$

(carbonic acid)   (bicarbonate ion)

Hydrochloric acid is called a **strong acid** because it almost completely dissociates into H^+ and Cl^- when added to water. By comparison, carbonic acid is a **weak acid** because some of it will remain in the H_2CO_3 state when dissolved in water.

Compared to an acid, a **base** has the opposite effect when dissolved in water—it absorbs hydrogen ions in solution. This can occur in different ways. Some bases, such as sodium hydroxide (NaOH), release OH^- when dissolved in water:

$$NaOH \rightarrow Na^+ + OH^-$$

(sodium hydroxide)   (sodium ion)

Recall that the product of $[H^+]$ and $[OH^-]$ is always 10^{-14} M. When a base such as NaOH raises the OH^- concentration, some of the hydrogen ions bind to these hydroxide ions to form water. Therefore, increasing the OH^- concentration lowers the H^+ concentration. Alternatively, other bases, such as ammonia, react with water to produce ammonium ion:

$$NH_3 + H_2O \rightleftharpoons NH_4^+ + OH^-$$

(ammonia)   (ammonium ion)

Both NaOH and ammonia have the same effect—they lower the concentration of H^+. NaOH achieves this by directly increasing the OH^- concentration, whereas NH_3 reacts with water to produce OH^-.

The H^+ Concentration of a Solution Determines the Solution's pH

The addition of acids and bases to water can greatly change the H^+ and OH^- concentrations over a very broad range. Therefore, chemists and biologists use a log scale to describe the concentrations of these ions. The H^+ concentration is expressed as the solution's **pH**, which is defined as the negative logarithm to the base 10 of the H^+ concentration.

$$pH = -\log_{10}[H^+]$$

To understand what this equation means, let's consider a few examples. A solution with a H^+ concentration of 10^{-7} M has a pH of 7. A concentration of 10^{-7} M is the same as 0.1 μM. A solution in which $[H^+] = 10^{-6}$ M has a pH of 6. 10^{-6} M is the same as 1.0 μM. A solution at pH 6 is said to be more **acidic**, because the H^+ concentration is 10-fold higher than a solution at pH 7. Note that as the acidity increases, the pH decreases. A solution where the pH is 7 is said to be neutral because $[H^+]$ and $[OH^-]$ are equal. An acidic solution has a pH below 7, and an **alkaline** solution has a pH above 7. **Figure 2.21** considers the pH values of some familiar fluids.

Why is pH of importance to biologists? The answer lies in the observation that H^+ and OH^- can readily bind to many

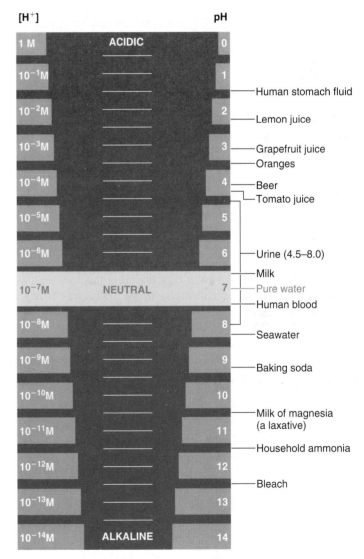

Figure 2.21 The pH scale and the relative acidities of common substances.

Concept check: What is the OH^- concentration at pH 8?

kinds of ions and molecules. For this reason, the pH of a solution can affect

- the shapes and functions of molecules;
- the rates of many chemical reactions;
- the ability of two molecules to bind to each other;
- the ability of ions or molecules to dissolve in water.

Due to the various effects of pH, many biological processes function best within very narrow ranges of pH, and even small shifts can have a negative effect. In living cells, the pH ranges from about 6.5 to 7.8 and is carefully regulated to avoid major shifts in pH. The blood of the human body has a normal range of about pH 7.35 to 7.45 and is therefore slightly alkaline. Certain diseases, such as kidney disease, or acute illnesses, such as prolonged vomiting (in which stomach acid is vomited) can decrease or increase blood pH by a few tenths of a unit. When this happens, the enzymes in the body that are required for normal metabolism can no longer function optimally, leading to additional illness. As described next, living organisms have molecules called buffers to help prevent such changes in pH.

Buffers Minimize Fluctuations in the pH of Fluids

What factors might alter the pH of an organism's fluids? External factors such as acid rain and other forms of pollution can reduce the pH of water entering the roots of plants. In animals, exercise generates lactic acid, and certain diseases can raise or lower the pH of blood.

Organisms have several ways to cope with changes in pH. Vertebrate animals such as mammals, for example, use structures like the kidney to secrete acidic or alkaline compounds into the bloodstream when the blood pH becomes imbalanced. Similarly, the kidneys can transfer hydrogen ions from the fluids of the body into the urine and adjust the pH of the body's fluids in that way. Another mechanism by which pH balance is regulated in diverse organisms involves the actions of acid-base buffers. A **buffer** is composed of a weak acid and its related base. One such buffer is the bicarbonate pathway, which works to keep the pH of an animal's body fluids within a narrow range.

$$CO_2 + H_2O \rightleftharpoons H_2CO_3 \rightleftharpoons H^+ + HCO_3^-$$
$$\text{(carbonic acid)} \qquad \text{(bicarbonate)}$$

This buffer system can work in both directions. For example, if the pH of an animal's blood were to increase (that is, the H^+ concentration decreased), the bicarbonate pathway would proceed from left to right. Carbon dioxide would combine with water to make carbonic acid, and then the carbonic acid would dissociate into H^+ and HCO_3^-. This would raise the H^+ concentration and thereby lower the pH. Alternatively, when the pH of an animal's blood decreases, this pathway runs in reverse. Bicarbonate combines with H^+ to make H_2CO_3, which then dissociates to CO_2 and H_2O. This process removes H^+ from the blood, restoring it to its normal pH, and the CO_2 is exhaled

from the lungs. Many buffers exist in nature. Buffers found in living organisms are adapted to function most efficiently at the normal range of pH values seen in that organism.

 Summary of Key Concepts

2.1 Atoms

- Atoms are the smallest functional units of matter that form all chemical elements and cannot be further broken down into other substances by ordinary chemical or physical means. Atoms are composed of protons (positive charge), electrons (negative charge), and (except for hydrogen) neutrons (electrically neutral). Electrons are found in orbitals around the nucleus. (Table 2.1, Figures 2.1, 2.2, 2.3, 2.4)
- Each element contains a unique number of protons—its atomic number. The periodic table organizes all known elements by atomic number and energy shells. (Figure 2.5)
- Each atom has a small but measurable mass, measured in daltons. The atomic mass scale indicates an atom's mass relative to the mass of other atoms.
- Many atoms exist as isotopes, which differ in the number of neutrons they contain. Some isotopes are unstable radioisotopes and emit radiation. (Figure 2.6)
- Four elements—oxygen, carbon, hydrogen, and nitrogen—account for the vast majority of atoms in living organisms. In addition, living organisms require mineral and trace elements that are essential for growth and function. (Table 2.2)

2.2 Chemical Bonds and Molecules

- A molecule consists of two or more atoms bonded together. The properties of a molecule are different from the properties of the atoms that combined to form it. A compound is composed of two or more different elements.
- Atoms tend to form bonds that fill their outer shell with electrons.
- Covalent bonds, in which atoms share electrons, are strong chemical bonds. Atoms form two covalent bonds—a double bond—when they share two pairs of electrons. (Figures 2.7, 2.8, 2.9)
- The electronegativity of an atom is a measure of its ability to attract bonded electrons. When two atoms with different electronegativities combine, the atoms form a polar covalent bond because the distribution of electrons around the atoms creates polarity, or difference in electric charge, across the molecule. Polar molecules, such as water, are largely composed of polar bonds, and nonpolar molecules are composed predominantly of nonpolar bonds. (Figure 2.10)
- An important result of polar covalent bonds is the ability of one molecule to loosely associate with another molecule through weak interactions called hydrogen bonds. The van der Waals

forces are weak electrical attractions that arise between molecules due to the probabilistic orbiting of electrons in atoms. (Figure 2.11)

- If an atom or molecule gains or loses one or more electrons, it acquires a net electric charge and becomes an ion. The strong attraction between two oppositely charged ions forms an ionic bond. (Table 2.3, Figure 2.12)

- The three-dimensional, flexible shape of molecules allows them to interact and contributes to their biological properties. (Figures 2.13, 2.14)

- A free radical is an unstable molecule that interacts with other molecules by taking away electrons from their atoms.

- A chemical reaction occurs when one or more substances are changed into different substances. All chemical reactions will eventually reach an equilibrium, unless the products of the reaction are continually removed.

2.3 Properties of Water

- Water is the solvent for most chemical reactions in all living organisms, both inside and outside of cells. Atoms and molecules dissolved in water interact in ways that would be impossible in their nondissolved states. All chemical reactions require energy. (Figure 2.15)

- Solutes dissolve in a solvent to form a solution. Solute concentration refers to the amount of a solute dissolved in a unit volume of solution. The molarity of a solution is defined as the number of moles of a solute dissolved in 1 L of solution. (Figure 2.16)

- Polar molecules are hydrophilic, whereas nonpolar molecules, composed predominantly of carbon and hydrogen, are hydrophobic. Amphipathic molecules, such as detergents, have polar and nonpolar regions. (Figure 2.17)

- H_2O exists as ice, liquid water, and water vapor (gas). (Figure 2.18)

- The colligative properties of water depend on the number of dissolved solutes and allow it to function as an antifreeze in certain organisms. (Figure 2.19)

- Water's high heat of vaporization and high heat of fusion make it very stable in liquid form.

- Water molecules participate in many chemical reactions in living organisms. Hydrolysis breaks down large molecules into smaller units, and dehydration reactions combine two smaller molecules into one larger one. In living organisms, water provides support, is used to eliminate wastes, dissipates body heat, aids in the movement of liquid through vessels, and serves as a lubricant. Surface tension allows certain insects to walk on water. (Figure 2.20)

- The pH of a solution refers to its hydrogen ion concentration. The pH of pure water is 7 (a neutral solution). Alkaline solutions have a pH higher than 7, and acidic solutions have a pH lower than 7. (Figure 2.21)

- Buffers are compounds that act to minimize pH fluctuations in the fluids of living organisms. Buffer systems can raise or lower pH as required.

 # Assess and Discuss

Test Yourself

1. _____ make(s) up the nucleus of an atom.
   a. Protons and electrons
   b. Protons and neutrons
   c. DNA and RNA
   d. Neutrons and electrons
   e. DNA only

2. Living organisms are composed mainly of which atoms?
   a. calcium, hydrogen, nitrogen, and oxygen
   b. carbon, hydrogen, nitrogen, and oxygen
   c. hydrogen, nitrogen, oxygen, and helium
   d. carbon, helium, nitrogen, and oxygen
   e. carbon, calcium, hydrogen, and oxygen

3. The ability of an atom to attract electrons in a bond with another atom is termed its
   a. hydrophobicity.
   b. electronegativity.
   c. solubility.
   d. valence.
   e. both a and b

4. Hydrogen bonds differ from covalent bonds in that
   a. covalent bonds can form between any type of atom and hydrogen bonds form only between H and O.
   b. covalent bonds involve sharing of electrons and hydrogen bonds involve the complete transfer of electrons.
   c. covalent bonds result from equal sharing of electrons but hydrogen bonds involve unequal sharing of electrons.
   d. covalent bonds involve sharing of electrons between atoms but hydrogen bonds are the result of weak attractions between a hydrogen atom of a polar molecule and an electronegative atom of another polar molecule.
   e. covalent bonds are weak bonds that break easily but hydrogen bonds are strong links between atoms that are not easily broken.

5. A free radical
   a. is a positively charged ion.
   b. is an atom with one unpaired electron in its outer shell.
   c. is a stable atom that is not bonded to another atom.
   d. can cause considerable cellular damage.
   e. both b and d

6. Chemical reactions in living organisms
   a. require energy to begin.
   b. usually require a catalyst to speed up the process.
   c. are usually reversible.
   d. occur in liquid environments, such as water.
   e. all of the above

7. Solutes that easily dissolve in water are said to be
   a. hydrophobic.
   b. hydrophilic.
   c. polar molecules.
   d. all of the above.
   e. b and c only.

8. The sum of the atomic masses of all the atoms of a molecule is its
   a. atomic weight.
   b. molarity.
   c. molecular mass.
   d. concentration.
   e. polarity.

9. Reactions that involve water in the breaking apart of other molecules are known as _____ reactions.
   a. hydrophilic
   b. hydrophobic
   c. dehydration
   d. anabolic
   e. hydrolytic

10. A difference between a strong acid and a weak acid is
    a. strong acids have a higher molecular mass than weak acids.
    b. strong acids completely (or almost completely) ionize in solution, but weak acids do not completely ionize in solution.
    c. strong acids give off two hydrogen ions per molecule, but weak acids give off only one hydrogen ion per molecule.
    d. strong acids are water-soluble, but weak acids are not.
    e. strong acids give off hydrogen ions, and weak acids give off hydroxyl groups.

Conceptual Questions

1. Distinguish between the types of bonds commonly found in biological molecules.

2. Distinguish between the terms hydrophobic and hydrophilic.

3. What is the significance of molecular shape, and what may change the shape of molecules?

Collaborative Questions

1. Discuss the properties of the three subatomic particles of atoms.

2. Discuss several properties of water that make it possible for life to exist.

Online Resource

www.brookerbiology.com

Stay a step ahead in your studies with animations that bring concepts to life and practice tests to assess your understanding. Your instructor may also recommend the interactive ebook, individualized learning tools, and more.

The Chemical Basis of Life II:
Organic Molecules

3

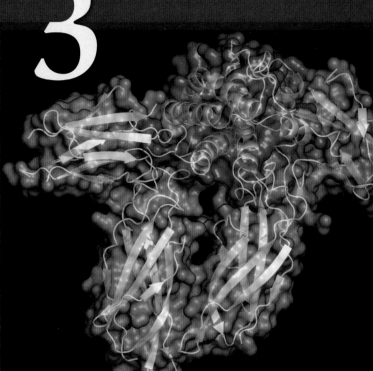

A model showing the structure of a protein—a type of organic macromolecule.

I n Chapter 2, we learned that all life is composed of sub-atomic particles that form atoms, which, in turn, combine to form molecules. Molecules may be simple in atomic composition, as in water (H_2O) or hydrogen gas (H_2), or may bind with other molecules to form larger molecules. Of the countless possible molecules that can be produced from the known elements in nature, certain types contain carbon and are found in all forms of life. These carbon-containing molecules are collectively referred to as **organic molecules**, so named because they were first discovered in living organisms. Among these are lipids and large, complex compounds called **macromolecules**, which include carbohydrates, proteins, and nucleic acids. In this chapter, we will survey the structures of these molecules and examine their chief functions. We begin with the element whose chemical properties are fundamental to the formation of biologically important molecules: carbon. This element provides the atomic scaffold upon which life is built.

3.1 The Carbon Atom and the Study of Organic Molecules

The science of carbon-containing molecules is known as **organic chemistry**. In this section, we will examine the bonding properties of carbon that create groups of atoms with distinct functions and shapes.

Interestingly, the study of organic molecules was long considered a fruitless endeavor because of a concept called vitalism that persisted into the 19th century. Vitalism held that organic molecules were created by, and therefore imparted with, a vital life force that was contained within a plant or an animal's body. Supporters of vitalism argued there was no point in trying to synthesize an organic compound, because such molecules could arise only through the intervention of mysterious qualities associated with life. As described next, this would all change due to the pioneering experiments of Friedrich Wöhler in 1828.

Wöhler's Synthesis of an Organic Compound Transformed Misconceptions About the Molecules of Life

Friedrich Wöhler was a German physician and chemist interested in the properties of inorganic and organic compounds. He spent some time studying urea ($(NH_2)_2CO$), a natural organic product formed from the breakdown of proteins in an animal's body. In mammals, urea accumulates in the urine, which is formed by the kidneys, and then is excreted from the body. During the course of his studies, Wöhler purified urea from the urine of mammals. He noted the color, size, shape, and other characteristics of the crystals that formed when urea was isolated. This experience would serve him well in later years when he quite accidentally helped to put the concept of vitalism to rest.

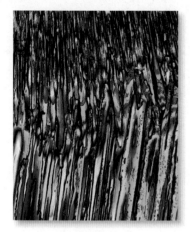

Figure 3.1 Crystals of urea as viewed with a polarizing microscope (approximately 80x magnification).

Concept check: *How did prior knowledge of urea allow Wöhler to realize he had synthesized urea outside of the body?*

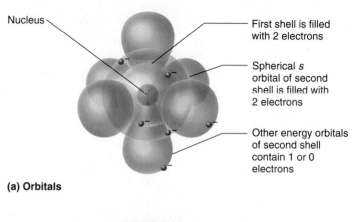

(a) Orbitals

Nucleus

First shell is filled with 2 electrons

Spherical *s* orbital of second shell is filled with 2 electrons

Other energy orbitals of second shell contain 1 or 0 electrons

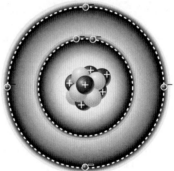

(b) Simplified depiction of energy shells

Figure 3.2   Models for the electron orbitals and energy shells of carbon.   Carbon atoms have only four electrons in their outer (second) energy shell, which allows carbon to form four covalent bonds. When carbon forms four covalent bonds, the result is four hybrid orbitals of equal energy.

In 1828, while exploring the reactive properties of ammonia and cyanic acid, Wöhler attempted to synthesize an inorganic molecule, ammonium cyanate (NH_4OCN). Instead, to his surprise, Wöhler discovered that ammonia and cyanic acid reacted to produce a third compound, which, when heated, formed familiar-looking crystals (**Figure 3.1**). After careful analysis, he concluded that these crystals were in fact urea. He announced to the scientific community that he had synthesized urea, an organic compound, "without the use of kidneys, either man or dog." In other words, no mysterious life force was required to create this organic molecule. Other scientists, such as Hermann Kolbe, would soon demonstrate that organic compounds such as acetic acid (CH_3COOH) could be synthesized directly from simpler molecules. These studies were a major breakthrough in the way in which scientists viewed life, and so began the field of science now called organic chemistry. From that time to the present, the fields of chemistry and biology have been understood to be intricately related.

Central to Wöhler's and Kolbe's reactions is the carbon atom. Urea and acetic acid, like all organic compounds, contain carbon atoms bound to other atoms. Let's now consider the chemical features that make carbon such an important element in living organisms.

Carbon Forms Four Covalent Bonds with Other Atoms

One of the properties of the carbon atom that makes life possible is its ability to form four covalent bonds with other atoms, including other carbon atoms. This occurs because carbon has four electrons in its outer shell, and it requires four additional electrons for its outer shell to be full (**Figure 3.2**). In living organisms, carbon atoms most commonly form covalent bonds with other carbon atoms and with hydrogen, oxygen, nitrogen, and sulfur atoms. Bonds between two carbon atoms, between carbon and oxygen, or between carbon and nitrogen can be single or double, or in the case of certain C≡C and C≡N bonds, triple. The variation in bonding of carbon with other carbon atoms and with different elements allows a vast number of organic compounds to be formed from only a few chemical elements. This is made all the more impressive because carbon bonds may occur in configurations that are linear, ringlike, or highly branched. Such molecular shapes can produce molecules with a variety of functions.

Carbon and hydrogen have similar electronegativities (see Chapter 2); therefore, carbon-carbon and carbon-hydrogen bonds are nonpolar. As a consequence, molecules with predominantly or entirely hydrogen-carbon bonds, called **hydrocarbons**, tend to be poorly soluble in water. In contrast, when carbon forms polar covalent bonds with more electronegative atoms, such as oxygen or nitrogen, the molecule is much more soluble in water due to the electrical attraction of polar water molecules. The ability of carbon to form both polar and nonpolar bonds (**Figure 3.3**) contributes to its ability to serve as the backbone for an astonishing variety of biologically important molecules.

One last feature of carbon that is important to biology is that carbon bonds are stable in the large range of temperatures associated with life. This property arises in part because the carbon atom is very small compared to most other atoms; therefore, the distance between carbon atoms forming a carbon-carbon bond is quite short. Shorter bonds tend to be stronger and more stable than longer bonds between two large atoms. Thus, carbon bonds are compatible with what we observe about life-forms today; namely, living organisms can inhabit

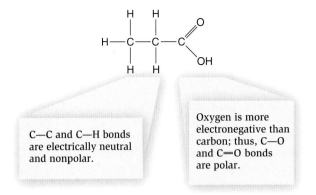

Figure 3.3 Nonpolar and polar bonds in an organic molecule. Carbon can form both nonpolar and polar bonds, and single and double bonds, as shown here for the molecule propionic acid, a common food preservative.

Table 3.1	Some Biologically Important Functional Groups That Bond to Carbon	
Functional group* (with shorthand notation)	**Formula**	**Examples of where they are found**
Amino $-NH_2$	R—N with H and H	Amino acids (proteins)
Carbonyl** $-CO$ Ketone	$R-\overset{O}{\overset{\|}{C}}-R'$	Steroids, waxes, and proteins
Aldehyde	$R-\overset{O}{\overset{\|}{C}}-H$	
Carboxyl $-COOH$	$R-C\overset{O}{\underset{OH}{}}$	Amino acids, fatty acids
Hydroxyl $-OH$	$R-OH$	Steroids, alcohol, carbohydrates, some amino acids
Methyl $-CH_3$	$R-\overset{H}{\underset{H}{\overset{\|}{C}}}-H$	May be attached to DNA, proteins, and carbohydrates
Phosphate $-PO_4^{2-}$	$R-O-\overset{O}{\overset{\|}{P}}-O^-$ with O^-	Nucleic acids, ATP, attached to amino acids
Sulfate $-SO_4^-$	$R-O-\overset{O}{\underset{O}{\overset{\|}{\underset{\|}{S}}}}-O^-$	May be attached to carbohydrates, proteins, and lipids
Sulfhydryl $-SH$	$R-SH$	Proteins that contain the amino acid cysteine

* This list contains many of the functional groups that are important in biology. However, many more functional groups have been identified by biochemists. R and R' represent the remainder of the molecule.

** A carbonyl group is C═O. In a ketone, the carbon forms covalent bonds with two other carbon atoms. In an aldehyde, the carbon is linked to a hydrogen atom.

environments ranging from the Earth's frigid icy poles to the superheated water of deep-sea vents.

Carbon Atoms Can Bond to Several Biologically Important Functional Groups

Aside from the simplest hydrocarbons, most organic molecules and macromolecules contain **functional groups**—groups of atoms with characteristic chemical features and properties. Each type of functional group exhibits similar chemical properties in all molecules in which it occurs. For example, the amino group (NH_2) acts like a base. At the pH found in living organisms, amino groups readily bind H^+ to become NH_3^+, thereby removing H^+ from an aqueous solution and raising the pH. As discussed later in this chapter, amino groups are widely found in proteins and also in other types of organic molecules. **Table 3.1** describes examples of functional groups found in many different types of organic molecules. We will discuss each of these groups at numerous points throughout this textbook.

Carbon-Containing Molecules May Exist in Multiple Forms Called Isomers

When Wöhler did his now-famous experiment, he was surprised to discover that urea and ammonium cyanate apparently contained the exact same ratio of carbon, nitrogen, hydrogen, and oxygen atoms, yet they were different molecules with distinct chemical and biological properties. Two structures with an identical molecular formula but different structures and characteristics are called **isomers**.

Figure 3.4 depicts three ways in which isomers may occur. **Structural isomers** contain the same atoms but in different bonding relationships. Urea and ammonium cyanate fall into this category; a simpler example of a structural isomer is illustrated in Figure 3.4a.

Stereoisomers have identical bonding relationships, but the spatial positioning of the atoms differs in the two isomers. Two types of stereoisomers are *cis-trans* isomers and enantiomers. In **cis-trans** isomers, like those shown in Figure 3.4b, the

two hydrogen atoms linked to the two carbons of a C═C double bond may be on the same side of the carbons, in which case the C═C bond is called a *cis* double bond. If the hydrogens are on opposite sides, it is a *trans* double bond. *Cis-trans* isomers may have very different chemical properties from each other, most notably their stability and sensitivity to heat and light. For instance, the light-sensitive region of your eye contains a molecule called retinal, which may exist in either a *cis* or *trans* form because of a pair of double-bonded carbons in its string of carbon atoms. In darkness, the *cis*-retinal form predominates.

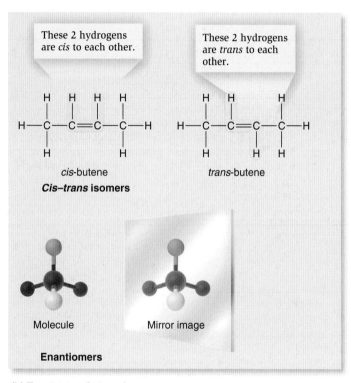

Because this –OH group is attached to a different carbon, these 2 molecules are structural isomers.

Isopropyl alcohol   Propyl alcohol

(a) Structural isomers

These 2 hydrogens are *cis* to each other.

These 2 hydrogens are *trans* to each other.

cis-butene   *trans*-butene

***Cis–trans* isomers**

Molecule   Mirror image

Enantiomers

(b) Two types of stereoisomers

Figure 3.4 Types of isomers. Isomers are compounds with the same molecular formula but different structures. The differences in structure, though small, are sufficient to result in very different biological properties. Isomers can be grouped into **(a)** structural isomers and **(b)** stereoisomers.

The energy of sunlight, however, causes retinal to isomerize to the *trans* form. The *trans*-retinal activates the light-capturing cells in the eye.

A second type of stereoisomer, called an **enantiomer**, exists as a pair of molecules that are mirror images. Four different atoms can bind to a single carbon atom in two possible ways, designated a left-handed and a right-handed structure. The resulting structures are not identical, but instead are mirror images of each other (Figure 3.4b). A convenient way to visualize the mirror-image properties of enantiomers is to look at a pair of gloves. No matter which way you turn or hold a left-hand glove, for example, it cannot fit properly on your right hand. Any given pair of enantiomers shares identical chemical properties, such as solubility and melting point. However, due to the different orientation of atoms in space, their ability to noncovalently bind to other molecules can be strikingly different. For example, as you learned in Chapter 2, **enzymes** are molecules that catalyze, or speed up, the rates of many biologically important chemical reactions. Typically, a given enzyme is very specific in its action, and an enzyme that recognizes one enantiomer of a pair often does not recognize the other. That is because the actions of enzymes depend upon the spatial arrangements of the particular atoms in a molecule.

3.2 Formation of Organic Molecules and Macromolecules

As we have seen, organic molecules have various shapes due to the bonding properties of carbon. During the past two centuries, biochemists have studied many organic molecules found in living organisms and determined their structures at the molecular level. Many of these compounds are relatively small molecules, containing a few or a few dozen atoms. However, some organic molecules are extremely large macromolecules composed of thousands or even millions of atoms. Such large molecules are formed by linking together many smaller molecules called **monomers** (meaning one part) and are thus also known as **polymers** (meaning many parts). The structure of macromolecules depends on the structure of their monomers, the number of monomers linked together, and the three-dimensional way in which the monomers are linked.

As introduced in Chapter 2, the process by which two or more molecules combine into a larger one is called a **condensation reaction**. Such reactions are accompanied by the loss of a small molecule formed as a result of the condensation. When an organic macromolecule is formed, two smaller molecules combine by condensation, producing a larger molecule along with the loss of a molecule of water. This specific type of condensation reaction is called a **dehydration reaction**, because a molecule of water is removed when the monomers combine.

An idealized dehydration reaction is illustrated in **Figure 3.5a**. Notice that the length of a polymer may be extended again and again with additional dehydration reactions. Some polymers can reach great lengths by this mechanism. For example, as you will learn in Chapter 46, nutrients in an animal's food are transported out of the digestive tract into the body fluids as monomers. If more energy-yielding nutrients are consumed than are required for an animal's activities, the excess nutrients may be processed by certain organs into extremely long polymers consisting of tens of thousands of monomers. The polymers are then stored in this convenient form to provide a source of energy when food is not available. An example would be during sleep, when an animal is not eating but nevertheless still requires energy to carry out all the various activities required to maintain cellular function.

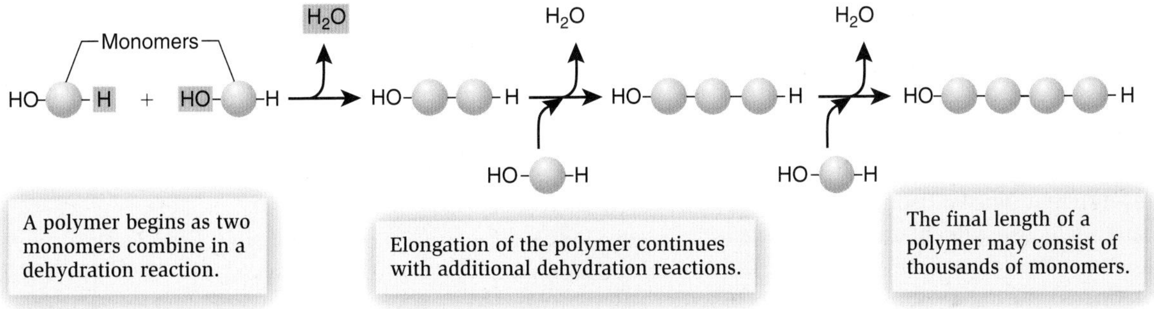

(a) Polymer formation by dehydration reactions

A polymer begins as two monomers combine in a dehydration reaction.

Elongation of the polymer continues with additional dehydration reactions.

The final length of a polymer may consist of thousands of monomers.

Polymers are broken down one monomer at a time by hydrolysis reactions.

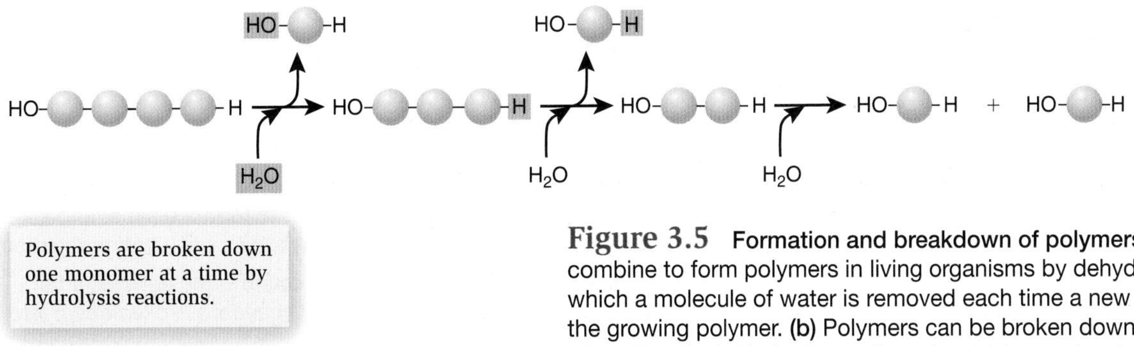

(b) Breakdown of a polymer by hydrolysis reactions

Figure 3.5 **Formation and breakdown of polymers.** **(a)** Monomers combine to form polymers in living organisms by dehydration reactions, in which a molecule of water is removed each time a new monomer is added to the growing polymer. **(b)** Polymers can be broken down into their constituent monomers by hydrolysis reactions, in which a molecule of water is added each time a monomer is released.

Polymers, however, are not recognized by the cellular machinery that functions to release the chemical energy stored in the bonds of molecules. Consequently, polymers must first be broken down into their constituent monomers, which then, under the right conditions, can release some of the energy stored in their bonds. The process by which a polymer is broken down into monomers is called a **hydrolysis reaction** (Figure 3.5b) (from the Greek *hydro*, meaning water, and *lysis*, meaning to separate), because a molecule of water is added back each time a monomer is released. Therefore, the formation of polymers in organisms is generally reversible; once formed, a polymer can later be broken down. These processes may repeat themselves over and over again as dictated by changes in the various cellular activities of an organism. Both condensation/dehydration reactions and hydrolysis reactions are catalyzed by enzymes.

By analyzing the cells of many different species, researchers have determined that all forms of life have organic molecules and macromolecules that fall into four broad categories, based on their chemical and biological properties: carbohydrates, lipids, proteins, and nucleic acids. In the next sections, we will survey the structures of these organic compounds and begin to examine their biological functions.

3.3 Carbohydrates

Carbohydrates are composed of carbon, hydrogen, and oxygen atoms in or close to the proportions represented by the general formula $C_n(H_2O)_n$, where n is a whole number. This formula gives carbohydrates their name—carbon-containing compounds

that are hydrated (that is, contain water). Most of the carbon atoms in a carbohydrate are linked to a hydrogen atom and a hydroxyl functional group. However, other functional groups, such as amino and carboxyl groups, are also found in certain carbohydrates. As discussed next, sugars are relatively small carbohydrates, whereas polysaccharides are large macromolecules.

Sugars Are Carbohydrate Monomers That May Taste Sweet

Sugars are small carbohydrates that in some, but not all, cases taste sweet. The simplest sugars are the monomers known as **monosaccharides** (from the Greek, meaning single sugars). The most common types are molecules with five carbons, called pentoses, and with six carbons, called hexoses. Important pentoses are ribose ($C_5H_{10}O_5$) and the closely related deoxyribose ($C_5H_{10}O_4$), which are part of RNA and DNA molecules, respectively, which are described later in this chapter. The most common hexose is glucose ($C_6H_{12}O_6$). Like other monosaccharides, glucose is very water-soluble and thus circulates in the blood or fluids of animals, where it can be transported across plasma membranes. Once inside a cell, enzymes can break down glucose into smaller molecules, releasing energy that was stored in the chemical bonds of glucose. This energy is then stored in the bonds of another molecule, called adenosine triphosphate, or ATP (see Chapter 7), which, in turn, powers a variety of cellular processes. In this way, sugar is often used as a source of energy by living organisms.

Figure 3.6a depicts the bonds between atoms in a monosaccharide in both linear and ring forms. The ring structure is a better approximation of the true shape of the molecule as it mostly exists in solution, with the carbon atoms numbered by convention as shown. The ring is made from the linear structure by an oxygen atom, which forms a bond that bridges two carbons. The hydrogen atoms and the hydroxyl groups may lie above or below the plane of the ring structure.

Figure 3.6b compares different types of isomers of glucose. Glucose can exist as D- and L-glucose, which are mirror images of each other, or enantiomers. (The letters D and L are derived from dextrorotatory—rotating to the right—and levorotatory—rotating to the left—which describe the ways in which a beam of polarized light is altered by some molecules.) Other types of isomers are formed by changing the relative positions of the hydrogens and hydroxyl groups along the sugar ring. For example, glucose exists in two interconvertible forms, with the hydroxyl group attached to the number 1 carbon atom lying either above (the β form of glucose, Figure 3.6b) or below (the α form, Figure 3.6a) the plane of the ring. As discussed later, these different isomers of glucose have different biological properties. In another example, if the hydroxyl group on carbon atom number 4 of glucose is switched from below to above the plane of the ring, the sugar called galactose is created (Figure 3.6b).

Monosaccharides can join together by dehydration to form larger carbohydrates. **Disaccharides** (meaning two sugars) are carbohydrates composed of two monosaccharides. A familiar

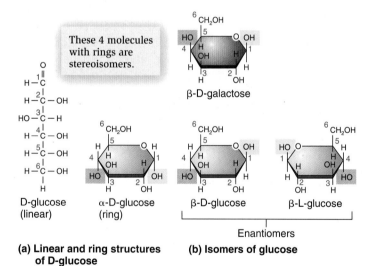

(a) Linear and ring structures of D-glucose

(b) Isomers of glucose

Figure 3.6   Monosaccharide structure.   (a) A comparison of the linear and ring structures of glucose. In solution, such as the fluids of organisms, nearly all glucose is in the ring form. (b) Isomers of glucose. The locations of the C-1 and C-4 hydroxyl groups are emphasized with green and orange boxes, respectively. Glucose exists as stereoisomers designated α- and β-glucose, which differ in the position of the —OH group attached to carbon atom number 1. Glucose and galactose differ in the position of the —OH group attached to carbon atom number 4. Enantiomers of glucose, called D-glucose and L-glucose, are mirror images of each other. D-glucose is the form used by living cells.

Concept check: *With regard to their binding to enzymes, why do enantiomers such as D- and L-glucose have different biological properties?*

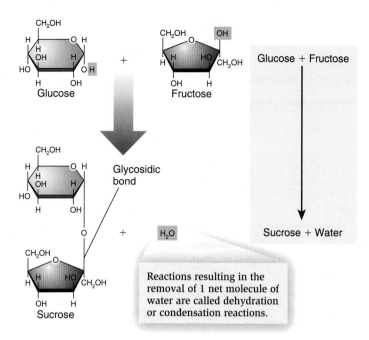

Figure 3.7   Formation of a disaccharide.   Two monosaccharides can bond to each other to form a disaccharide, such as sucrose, maltose, or lactose, by a dehydration reaction.

Concept check: *What type of reaction is the reverse of the ones shown here, in which a disaccharide is broken down into two monosaccharides?*

disaccharide is sucrose, or table sugar, which is composed of the monomers glucose and fructose (**Figure 3.7**). Sucrose is the major transport form of sugar in plants. The linking together of most monosaccharides involves the removal of a hydroxyl group from one monosaccharide and a hydrogen atom from the other, giving rise to a molecule of water and bonding the two sugars together through an oxygen atom. The bond formed between two sugar molecules is called a **glycosidic bond**. Conversely, hydrolysis of a glycosidic bond in a disaccharide breaks the bond by adding back the water, thereby uncoupling the two monosaccharides. Other disaccharides frequently found in nature are maltose, formed in animals during the digestion of large carbohydrates in the intestinal tract, and lactose, present in the milk of mammals. Maltose is α-D-glucose linked to α-D-glucose, and lactose is β-D-galactose linked to β-D-glucose.

Polysaccharides Are Carbohydrate Polymers That Include Starch and Glycogen

When many monosaccharides are linked together to form long polymers, **polysaccharides** (meaning many sugars) are made. **Starch**, found in plant cells, and **glycogen**, present in animal cells and sometimes called animal starch, are examples of polysaccharides (**Figure 3.8**). Both of these polysaccharides are composed of thousands of α-D-glucose molecules linked together in long, branched chains, differing only in the extent of branching along the chain. The bonds that form in polysaccharides are not random but instead form between specific carbon atoms of each molecule. The carbon atoms are numbered according to convention, as shown in Figure 3.8. The higher degree of branching in glycogen contributes to its solubility in animal tissues, such as muscle. This is because the extensive branching creates a more open structure, in which many hydrophilic hydroxyl (—OH) side groups have access to water and can hydrogen-bond with it. Starch, because it is less branched, is less soluble and contributes to the properties of plant structures (think of a potato or a kernel of corn).

Some polysaccharides, such as starch and glycogen, are used to store energy in cells. Like disaccharides, polysaccharides can be hydrolyzed in the presence of water to yield monosaccharides, which are broken down to provide the energy to make ATP. Starch and glycogen, the polymers of α-glucose, provide efficient means of storing energy for those times when a plant or animal cannot obtain sufficient energy from its environment or diet for its metabolic requirements.

Other polysaccharides provide a structural role, rather than storing energy. The plant polysaccharide **cellulose** is a polymer of β-D-glucose, with a linear arrangement of carbon-carbon bonds and no branching (see Figure 3.8). Each glucose monomer in cellulose is in an opposite orientation from its adjacent monomers ("flipped over"), forming long chains of several thousand glucose monomers. The bond orientations in β-D-glucose prevent cellulose from being hydrolyzed for ATP production in most types of organisms. This is because many enzymes are highly specific for one type of molecule, as noted earlier. The enzymes that break the bonds between monomers of α-D-glucose in starch do not recognize the shape of the polymer made by the bonds between β-D-glucose monomers in cellulose. Therefore, plant cells can break down starch without breaking down cellulose. In this way, cellulose can be used for other functions, notably in the formation of the rigid cell-wall structure characteristic of plants. The linear arrangement of bonds in cellulose provides opportunities for vast numbers of hydrogen bonds between cellulose

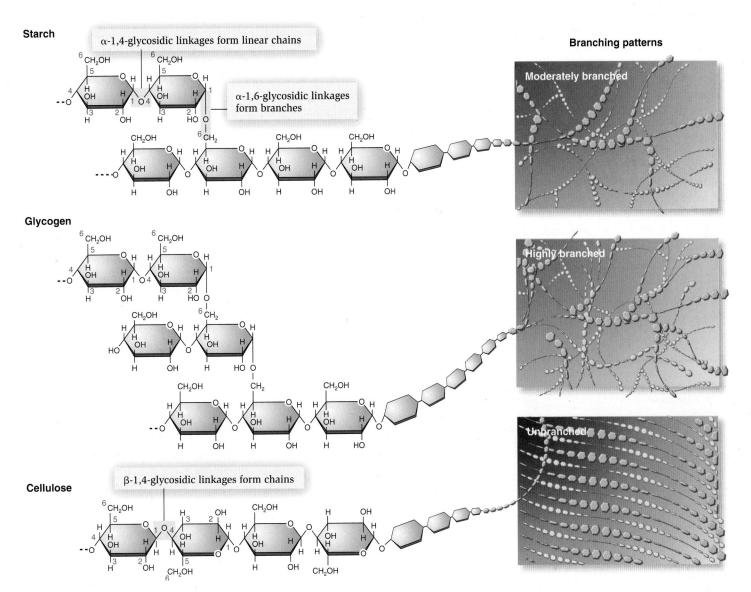

Figure 3.8 **Polysaccharides that are polymers of glucose.** These polysaccharides differ in their arrangement, extent of branching, and type of glucose isomer. Note: In cellulose, the bonding arrangements cause every other glucose to be upside down with respect to its neighbors.

molecules, which stack together in sheets and provide great strength to structures like plant cell walls. Cellulose accounts for up to half of all the carbon contained within a typical plant, making it the most common organic compound on Earth.

Unlike most animals and plants, some organisms do have an enzyme capable of breaking down cellulose. For example, certain bacteria present in the gastrointestinal tracts of grass and wood eaters, such as cows and termites, respectively, can digest cellulose into usable monosaccharides because they contain an enzyme that can hydrolyze the bonds between β-D-glucose monomers. Humans lack this enzyme; therefore, we eliminate in the feces most of the cellulose ingested in our diet. Undigestible plant matter we consume is commonly referred to as fiber.

Other polysaccharides also play structural roles. **Chitin**, a tough, structural polysaccharide, forms the external skeleton of insects and the cell walls of fungi. The sugar monomers within chitin have nitrogen-containing groups attached to them. **Glycosaminoglycans** are large polysaccharides that play a structural role in animals. For example, they are abundantly found in cartilage, the tough, fibrous material found in bone and certain other animal structures. Glycosaminoglycans are also abundant in the extracellular matrix that provides a structural framework surrounding many of the cells in an animal's body (this will be covered in Chapter 10).

3.4 Lipids

Lipids are hydrophobic molecules composed mainly of hydrogen and carbon atoms. The defining feature of lipids is that they are nonpolar and therefore insoluble in water. Lipids account for about 40% of the organic matter in the average human body and include fats, phospholipids, steroids, and waxes.

Fats Are Made from Glycerol and Fatty Acids

Fats, also known as **triglycerides** or **triacylglycerols**, are formed by bonding glycerol to three fatty acids (**Figure 3.9**).

Glycerol is a three-carbon molecule with one hydroxyl group (—OH) bonded to each carbon. A fatty acid is a chain of carbon and hydrogen atoms with a carboxyl group (—COOH) at one end. Each of the hydroxyl groups in glycerol is linked to the carboxyl group of a fatty acid by the removal of a molecule of water by a dehydration reaction. The resulting bond is an example of a type of chemical bond called an ester bond.

The fatty acids found in fats and other lipids may differ with regard to their lengths and the presence of double bonds (**Figure 3.10**). Fatty acids are synthesized by the linking of two-carbon fragments. Therefore, most fatty acids in nature have an even number of carbon atoms, with 16- and 18-carbon fatty acids being the most common in the cells of plants and animals. Fatty acids also differ with regard to the presence of double bonds. When all the carbons in a fatty acid are linked by single covalent bonds, the fatty acid is said to be a **saturated fatty acid**, because all the carbons are saturated with covalently bound hydrogen. Alternatively, some fatty acids contain one or more C=C double bonds and are known as **unsaturated fatty acids**. A fatty acid with one C=C bond is a monounsaturated fatty acid, whereas a fatty acid with two or more C=C bonds constitutes a polyunsaturated fatty acid. In organisms such as mammals, some fatty acids are necessary for good health but cannot be synthesized by the body. Such fatty acids are called essential fatty acids, because they must be obtained in the diet; an example is linoleic acid (Figure 3.10).

Fats (triglycerides) that contain high amounts of saturated fatty acids can pack together tightly, resulting in numerous intermolecular interactions that stabilize the fat. Saturated fats have high melting points and tend to be solid at room temperature. Animal fats generally contain a high proportion of saturated fatty acids. For example, beef fat contains high amounts of stearic acid, a saturated fatty acid with a melting point of 70°C (Figure 3.10). When you heat a hamburger on the stove, the saturated animal fats melt, and liquid grease appears in the

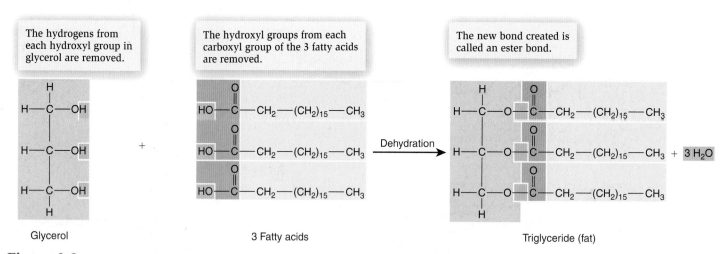

Figure 3.9 **The formation of a fat.** The formation of a triglyceride requires three dehydration reactions in which fatty acids are bonded to glycerol. Note in this figure and in Figure 3.10, a common shorthand notation is used for depicting fatty acid chains, in which a portion of the CH_2 groups are illustrated as $(CH_2)_n$, where n may be 2 or greater.

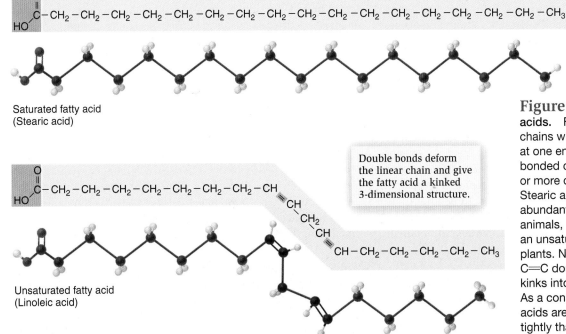

Saturated fatty acid
(Stearic acid)

Unsaturated fatty acid
(Linoleic acid)

Double bonds deform the linear chain and give the fatty acid a kinked 3-dimensional structure.

Figure 3.10 **Examples of fatty acids.** Fatty acids are hydrocarbon chains with a carboxyl functional group at one end and either no double-bonded carbons (saturated) or one or more double bonds (unsaturated). Stearic acid, for example, is an abundant saturated fatty acid in animals, whereas linoleic acid is an unsaturated fatty acid found in plants. Note that the presence of two C=C double bonds introduces two kinks into the shape of linoleic acid. As a consequence, saturated fatty acids are able to pack together more tightly than unsaturated fatty acids.

frying pan (**Figure 3.11**). When allowed to cool, however, the liquid grease in the pan returns to its solid form.

As illustrated in Figure 3.10, the presence of an unsaturated bond in a fatty acid introduces a kink into the linear shape of a fatty acid. Because of kinks in their chains, unsaturated fatty acids cannot stack together as tightly as saturated fatty acids. Fats high in unsaturated fatty acids usually have low melting points and are liquids at room temperature. Such fats are called oils. Fats derived from plants generally contain unsaturated fatty acids. Olive oil contains high amounts of oleic acid, a monounsaturated fatty acid with a melting point of 16°C. Fatty acids with additional double bonds have even lower melting points; linoleic acid (see Figure 3.10), found in soybeans and other plants, has two double bonds and melts at −5°C.

Most unsaturated fatty acids, including linoleic acid, exist in nature in the *cis* form (see Figures 3.4 and 3.10). Of particular importance to human health, however, are *trans* fatty acids, which are formed by a synthetic process in which the natural *cis* form is altered to a *trans* configuration. This gives the fats that contain such fatty acids a more linear structure and, therefore, a higher melting point. Although this process has been used for many years to produce fats with a longer shelf-life and with better characteristics for baking, it is now understood that *trans* fats are linked with human disease. Notable among these is coronary artery disease, caused by a narrowing of the blood vessels that supply the muscle cells of the heart with blood.

Like starch and glycogen, fats are important for storing energy. The hydrolysis of triglycerides releases the fatty acids

High temperature converts solid, saturated fats to liquid.

After cooling, saturated fats return to their solid form.

Unsaturated fats are oils at room temperature and below.

(a) Animal fats at high and low temperatures

(b) Vegetable fats at low temperature

Figure 3.11 **Fats at different temperatures.** Saturated fats found in animals tend to have high melting points compared to unsaturated fats found in plants.

Concept check: Certain types of fats used in baking are called shortenings. They are solid at room temperature. Shortenings are often made from vegetable oils by a process called hydrogenation. What do you think happens to the structure of an oil when it is hydrogenated?

from glycerol, and these products can then be metabolized to provide energy to make ATP (see Chapter 7). Certain organisms, most notably mammals, have the ability to store large amounts of energy by accumulating fats. As you will learn in Chapter 7, the number of C—H bonds in a molecule of fat or carbohydrate determines in part how much energy the molecule can yield. Fats are primarily long chains of C—H bonds, whereas glucose and other carbohydrates have numerous C—OH bonds. Consequently, 1 gram of fat stores more energy than does 1 gram of starch or glycogen. Fat is therefore an efficient means of energy storage for mobile organisms in which excess body mass may be a disadvantage. In animals, fats can also play a structural role by forming cushions that support organs. In addition, fats provide insulation under the skin that helps protect many terrestrial animals during cold weather and marine mammals in cold water.

Phospholipids Are Amphipathic Lipids

Another class of lipids, **phospholipids**, are similar in structure to triglycerides but with one important difference. The third hydroxyl group of glycerol is linked to a phosphate group instead of a fatty acid. In most phospholipids, a small polar or charged nitrogen-containing molecule is attached to this phosphate (**Figure 3.12a**). The glycerol backbone, phosphate group, and charged molecule constitute a polar hydrophilic region at one end of the phospholipid, whereas the fatty acid chains provide a nonpolar hydrophobic region at the opposite end. Recall from Chapter 2 that molecules with polar and nonpolar regions are called amphipathic molecules.

In water, phospholipids become organized into bilayers, because their hydrophilic polar ends are attracted to the water molecules and their hydrophobic nonpolar ends exclude water. As you will learn in Chapter 5, this bilayer arrangement of phospholipids is critical for determining the structure of cellular membranes, as shown in **Figure 3.12b**.

Steroids Contain Ring Structures

Steroids have a distinctly different chemical structure from that of the other types of lipid molecules discussed thus far. Four fused rings of carbon atoms form the skeleton of all steroids.

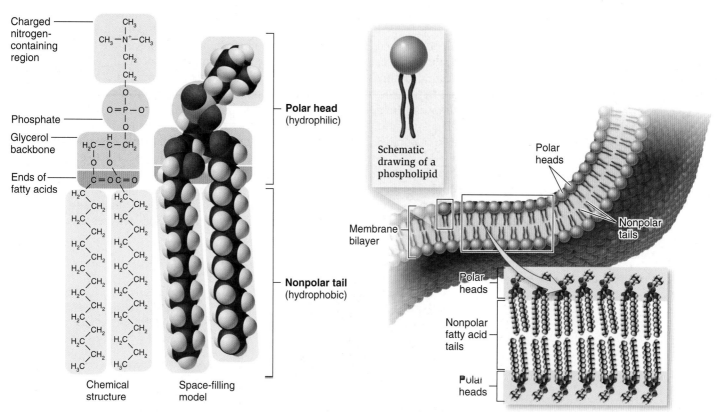

(a) Structure and model of a phospholipid

(b) Arrangement of phospholipids in a bilayer

Figure 3.12   Structure of phospholipids.   (a) Chemical structure and space-filling model of phosphatidylcholine, a common phospholipid found in living organisms. Phospholipids contain both polar and nonpolar regions, making them amphipathic. The fatty-acid tails are the nonpolar region. The rest of the molecule is polar. **(b)** Arrangement of phospholipids in a biological membrane, such as the plasma membrane that encloses cells. The hydrophilic regions of the phospholipid face the watery environments on either side of the membrane, while the hydrophobic regions associate with each other in the interior of the membrane, forming a bilayer.

Concept check: When water and oil are added to a test tube, the two liquids form two separate layers (think of oil and vinegar in a bottle of salad dressing). If a solution of phospholipids were added to a mixture of water and oil, where would the phospholipids dissolve?

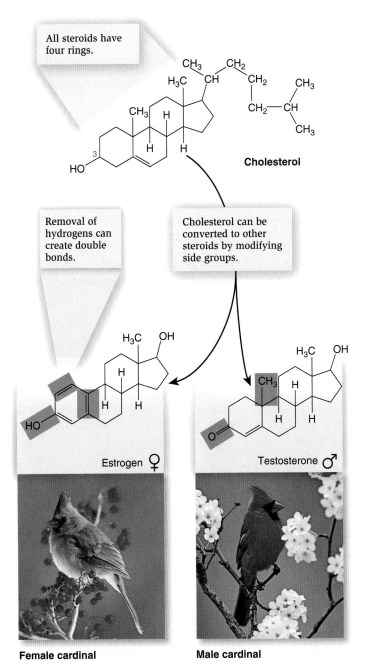

Figure 3.13 Structure of cholesterol and steroid hormones derived from cholesterol.   The structure of a steroid has four rings. Steroids include cholesterol and molecules derived from cholesterol, such as steroid hormones. These include the reproductive hormones estrogen and testosterone.

One or more polar hydroxyl groups are attached to this ring structure, but they are not numerous enough to make a steroid highly water-soluble. For example, steroids with a hydroxyl group are known as sterols—one of the most well known being cholesterol (Figure 3.13, top). Cholesterol is found in the blood and plasma membranes of animals. Due to its low solubility in water, at high concentrations cholesterol can contribute to the formation of blockages in major blood vessels.

In steroids, tiny differences in chemical structure can lead to profoundly different biological properties. For example, estrogen is a steroid found in high amounts in female vertebrates. Estrogen differs from testosterone, a steroid found largely in

males, by having one less methyl group, a hydroxyl group instead of a ketone group, and additional double bonds in one of its rings (Figure 3.13, bottom). However, these seemingly small differences are sufficient to make these two molecules largely responsible for whether an animal exhibits male or female characteristics, including feather color.

Waxes Are Complex Lipids That Help Prevent Water Loss from Organisms

Many plants and animals produce lipids called waxes that are typically secreted onto their surface, such as the leaves of plants and the cuticles of insects. Although any wax may contain hundreds of different compounds, all waxes contain one or more hydrocarbons and long structures that resemble a fatty acid attached by its carboxyl group to another long hydrocarbon chain. Most waxes are very nonpolar and therefore exclude water, providing a barrier to water loss. They may also be used as structural elements in colonies like those of bees, where beeswax forms the honeycomb of the hive.

3.5   Proteins

Proteins are polymers found in all cells and play critical roles in nearly all life processes (**Table 3.2**). The word protein comes from the Greek *proteios* (meaning of the first rank), which aptly describes their importance. Proteins account for about 50% of the organic material in a typical animal's body.

Proteins Are Made Up of Amino Acid Monomers

Proteins are composed of carbon, hydrogen, oxygen, nitrogen, and small amounts of other elements, notably sulfur. The building blocks of proteins are **amino acids**, compounds with a structure in which a carbon atom, called the α-carbon, is linked to an amino group (NH_2) and a carboxyl group (COOH). The α-carbon also is linked to a hydrogen atom and a side chain, which is given a general designation R. Proteins are polymers of amino acids.

When dissolved in water at neutral pH, the amino group accepts a hydrogen ion and is positively charged, whereas the carboxyl group loses a hydrogen ion and is negatively charged. The term amino acid is the name given to such molecules because they have an amino group and also a carboxyl group that behaves like an acid.

Table 3.2   Major Categories and Functions of Proteins

Category	Functions	Examples
Proteins involved in gene expression and regulation	Make mRNA from a DNA template; synthesize polypeptides from mRNA; regulate genes	RNA polymerase assists in synthesizing RNA from DNA. Transcription factor proteins are involved in gene regulation.
Motor proteins	Initiate movement	Myosin provides the contractile force of muscles. Kinesin is a key protein that helps cells to sort their chromosomes.
Defense proteins	Protect organisms against disease	Antibodies ward off infection due to bacteria or viruses.
Metabolic enzymes	Increase rates of chemical reactions	Hexokinase is an enzyme involved in sugar metabolism.
Cell signaling proteins	Enable cells to communicate with each other and with the environment	Taste receptors in the tongue allow animals to taste molecules in food.
Structural proteins	Support and strengthen structures	Actin provides shape to the cytoplasm of cells, such as plant and animal cells. Collagen gives strength to tendons.
Transporters	Promote movement of solutes across plasma membranes	Glucose transporters move glucose from outside cells to inside cells, where it can be used for energy.

All amino acids except glycine may exist in more than one isomeric form, called the D and L forms, which are enantiomers. Note that glycine cannot exist in D and L forms because there are two hydrogens bound to its α-carbon. Only L-amino acids and glycine are found in proteins. D-isomers are found in the cell walls of certain bacteria, where they may play a protective role against molecules secreted by the host organism in which the bacteria live.

The 20 amino acids found in proteins are distinguished by their side chains (**Figure 3.14**). The amino acids are categorized as those in which the side chains are nonpolar, or polar and uncharged, or polar and charged. The varying structures of the side chains are critical features of protein structure and function. The arrangement and chemical features of the side chains cause proteins to fold and adopt their three-dimensional shapes. In addition, certain amino acids may be critical in protein function. For example, amino acid side chains found within the active sites of enzymes are important in catalyzing chemical reactions.

Amino acids are joined together by a dehydration reaction that links the carboxyl group of one amino acid to the amino group of another (**Figure 3.15a**). The covalent bond formed between a carboxyl and amino group is called a **peptide bond**. When many amino acids are joined by peptide bonds, the resulting molecule is called a **polypeptide** (**Figure 3.15b**). The backbone of the polypeptide in Figure 3.15 is highlighted in yellow. The amino acid side chains project from the backbone. When two or more amino acids are linked together, one end of the resulting molecule has a free amino group. This is the amino end, or N-terminus. The other end of the polypeptide, called the carboxyl end, or C-terminus, has a free carboxyl group. As shown in **Figure 3.15c**, amino acids within a polypeptide are numbered from the amino end to the carboxyl end.

The term polypeptide refers to a structural unit composed of a single chain of amino acids. In contrast, a protein is a functional unit composed of one or more polypeptides that have been folded and twisted into a precise three-dimensional shape that carries out a particular function. Many proteins also have carbohydrates (glycoproteins) or lipids (lipoproteins) attached at various points along their amino acid chain; these modifications impart unique functions to such proteins.

Proteins Have a Hierarchy of Structure

Scientists view protein structure at four progressive levels: primary, secondary, tertiary, and quaternary, shown schematically in **Figure 3.16**. Each higher level of structure depends on the preceding levels. For example, changing the primary structure may affect the secondary, tertiary, and quaternary structures. Let's now consider each level separately.

Primary Structure   The **primary structure** (see Figure 3.16) of a polypeptide is its amino acid sequence, from beginning to end. The primary structures of polypeptides are determined by genes. As we will explore in Chapter 12, genes carry the information for the production of polypeptides with a specific amino acid sequence.

Figure 3.17 shows the primary structure of ribonuclease, which functions as an enzyme to degrade ribonucleic acid (RNA) molecules after they are no longer required by a cell. As described later and in Unit III of this textbook, RNA is a key part of the mechanism by which proteins are synthesized. Ribonuclease is composed of a relatively short polypeptide with 124 amino acids. An average polypeptide is about 300–500 amino acids in length, and some genes encode polypeptides that are a few thousand amino acids long.

Secondary Structure   The amino acid sequence of a polypeptide, together with the fundamental constraints of chemistry and physics, cause a polypeptide to fold into a more compact structure. Amino acids can rotate around bonds within a polypeptide. Consequently, polypeptides and proteins are flexible and can fold into a number of shapes, just as a string of beads can be twisted into many configurations. Folding can be irregular or certain regions can have a repeating folding pattern. Such repeating patterns are called **secondary structure**. The two basic types of secondary structure are the α helix and the β pleated sheet.

In an **α helix**, the polypeptide backbone forms a repeating helical structure that is stabilized by hydrogen bonds along the length of the backbone. As shown in Figure 3.16, the hydrogen linked to a nitrogen atom forms a hydrogen bond with an oxygen atom that is double-bonded to a carbon atom. These

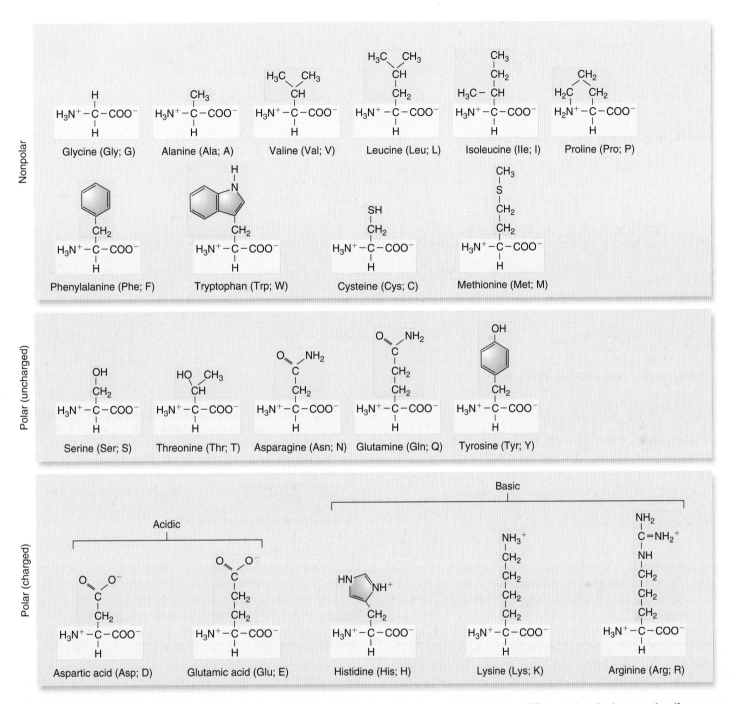

Figure 3.14 **The 20 amino acids found in living organisms.** The various amino acids have different chemical properties (for example, nonpolar versus polar) due to the nature of their different side chains. These properties contribute to the differences in the three-dimensional shapes and chemical properties of proteins, which, in turn, influence their biological functions. Tyrosine has both polar and nonpolar characteristics and is listed in just one category for simplicity. The common three-letter and one-letter abbreviations for each amino acid are shown in parentheses.

hydrogen bonds occur at regular intervals within the polypeptide backbone and cause the backbone to twist into a helix.

In a **β pleated sheet**, regions of the polypeptide backbone come to lie parallel to each other. Hydrogen bonds between a hydrogen linked to a nitrogen atom and a double-bonded oxygen form between these adjacent, parallel regions. When this occurs, the polypeptide backbone adopts a repeating zigzag—or pleated—shape.

The α helices and β pleated sheets are key determinants of a protein's characteristics. For example, α helices in certain proteins are composed primarily of nonpolar amino acids. Proteins containing many such regions with an α helix structure tend to anchor themselves into a lipid-rich environment, such as a cell's plasma membrane. In this way, a protein whose function is required in a specific location such as a plasma membrane can be retained there. Secondary structure also contributes to

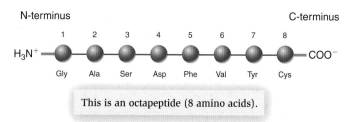

(a) Formation of a peptide bond between 2 amino acids

The amino end of a polypeptide is called the N-terminus.

The backbone of the polypeptide is highlighted in yellow.

The carboxyl end of a polypeptide is called the C-terminus.

(b) Polypeptide—a linear chain of amino acids

N-terminus   C-terminus

1 2 3 4 5 6 7 8

H_3N^+ — Gly Ala Ser Asp Phe Val Tyr Cys — COO^-

This is an octapeptide (8 amino acids).

(c) Numbering system of amino acids in a polypeptide

Figure 3.15   **The chemistry of polypeptide formation.** Polypeptides are polymers of amino acids. They are formed by linking amino acids via dehydration reactions to make peptide bonds. Every polypeptide has an amino end, or N-terminus, and a carboxyl end, or C-terminus.

Concept check: How many water molecules would be produced in making a polypeptide that is 72 amino acids long by dehydration reactions?

the great strength of certain proteins, including the keratins found in hair and hooves; the proteins that make up the silk webs of spiders; and collagen, the chief component of cartilage in vertebrate animals.

Some regions along a polypeptide chain do not assume an α helix or β pleated sheet conformation and consequently do not have a secondary structure. These regions are sometimes called random coiled regions. However, this term is somewhat misleading because the shapes of random coiled regions are usually very specific and important for the protein's function.

Tertiary Structure   As the secondary structure of a polypeptide chain becomes established due to the particular primary structure, the polypeptide folds and refolds upon itself to assume a complex three-dimensional shape—its **tertiary structure** (see Figure 3.16). The tertiary structure is the three-dimensional shape of a single polypeptide. Tertiary structure includes all secondary structures plus any interactions involving amino acid side chains. For some proteins, such as ribonuclease, the tertiary structure is the final structure of a functional protein. However, as described next, other proteins are composed of two or more polypeptides and adopt a quaternary structure.

Quaternary Structure   Most functional proteins are composed of two or more polypeptides that each adopt a tertiary structure and then assemble with each other (see Figure 3.16). The individual polypeptides are called **protein subunits**. Subunits may be identical polypeptides or they may be different. When proteins consist of more than one polypeptide chain, they are said to have **quaternary structure** and are also known as **multimeric proteins** (meaning multiple parts). Multimeric proteins are widespread in organisms. A common example is the oxygen-binding protein called hemoglobin, found in the red blood cells of vertebrate animals. As you will learn in Chapter 48, four protein subunits combine to form one molecule of hemoglobin. Each subunit can bind a single molecule of oxygen; therefore, each hemoglobin molecule can carry four molecules of oxygen in the blood.

Protein Structure Is Influenced by Several Factors

The amino acid sequences of polypeptides are the defining features that distinguish the structure of one protein from another. As polypeptides are synthesized in a cell, they fold into secondary and tertiary structures, which assemble into quaternary

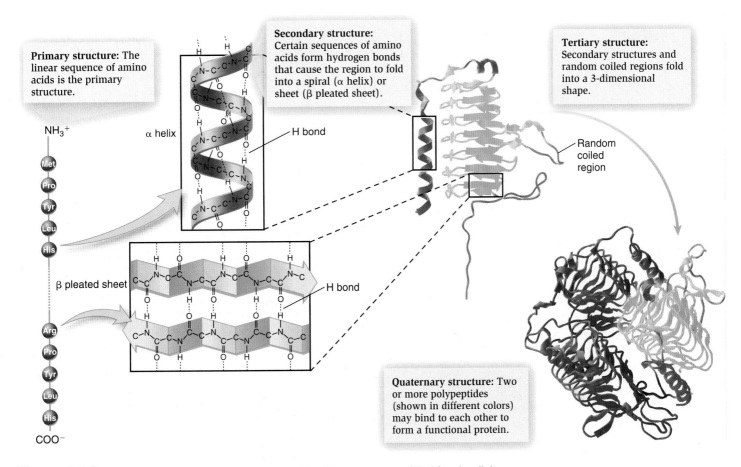

Figure 3.16   The hierarchy of protein structure.   The R groups are omitted for simplicity.

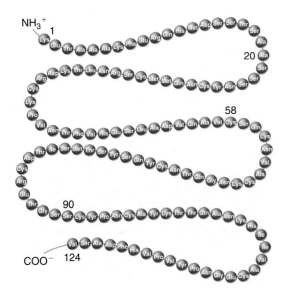

Figure 3.17   The primary structure of ribonuclease.
The example shown here is ribonuclease from cows.

structures for many proteins. Several factors determine the way that polypeptides adopt their secondary, tertiary, and quaternary structures. As mentioned, the laws of chemistry and physics, together with the amino acid sequence, govern this process.

As shown in **Figure 3.18**, five factors are critical for protein folding and stability:

1. *Hydrogen bonds*—The large number of weak hydrogen bonds within a polypeptide and between polypeptides adds up to a collectively strong force that promotes protein folding and stability. As we have already learned, hydrogen bonding is a critical determinant of protein secondary structure and also is important in tertiary and quaternary structure.

2. *Ionic bonds and other polar interactions*—Some amino acid side chains are positively or negatively charged. Positively charged side chains may bind to negatively charged side chains via ionic bonds. Similarly, uncharged polar side chains in a protein may bind to ionic amino acids. Ionic bonds and polar interactions are particularly important in tertiary and quaternary structure.

3. *Hydrophobic effect*—Some amino acid side chains are nonpolar. These amino acids tend to exclude water. As a protein folds, the hydrophobic amino acids are likely to be found in the center of the protein, minimizing contact with water. As mentioned, some proteins have stretches of nonpolar amino acids that anchor them in the hydrophobic portion of membranes. The hydrophobic effect plays a major role in tertiary and quaternary structures.

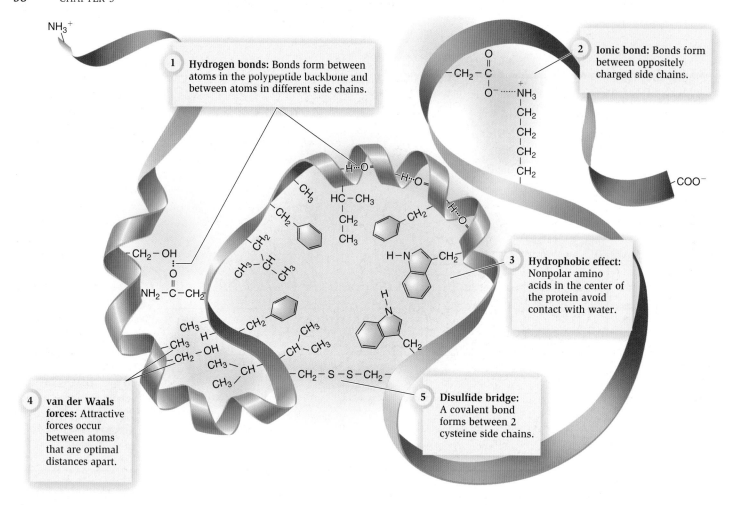

Figure 3.18   Factors that influence protein folding and stability.

4. *van der Waals forces*—Atoms within molecules have weak attractions for each other if they are an optimal distance apart. This optimal distance is called the van der Waals radius, and the weak attraction is the van der Waals force (see Chapter 2). If two atoms are very close together, their electron clouds will repel each other. If they are far apart, the van der Waals force will diminish. The van der Waals forces are particularly important for tertiary structure.

5. *Disulfide bridges*—The side chain of the amino acid cysteine contains a sulfhydryl group (—SH), which can react with a sulfhydryl group in another cysteine side chain. The result is a disulfide bridge or bond, which links the two amino acid side chains together (—S—S—). Disulfide bonds are covalent bonds that can occur within a polypeptide or between different polypeptides. Though other forces are usually more important in protein folding, the covalent nature of disulfide bonds can help to stabilize the tertiary structure of a protein.

The first four factors just described are also important in the ability of different proteins to interact with each other. As discussed throughout Unit II and other parts of this textbook, many cellular processes involve steps in which two or more different proteins interact with each other. For this to occur, the surface of one protein must bind to the surface of the other. Such binding is usually very specific. The surface of one protein

precisely fits into the surface of another (**Figure 3.19**). Such **protein-protein interactions** are critically important so that cellular processes can occur in a series of defined steps. In addition, protein-protein interactions are important in building cellular structures that provide shape and organization to cells.

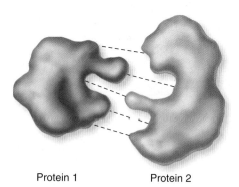

Protein 1   Protein 2

Figure 3.19   **Protein-protein interaction.**   Two different proteins may interact with each other due to hydrogen bonding, ionic bonding, the hydrophobic effect, and van der Waals forces.

Concept check: If the primary structure of Protein 1 in this figure were experimentally altered by the substitution of several incorrect amino acids for the correct ones, would Protein 1 still be able to interact with Protein 2?

FEATURE INVESTIGATION

Anfinsen Showed That the Primary Structure of Ribonuclease Determines Its Three-Dimensional Structure

Prior to the 1960s, the mechanisms by which proteins assume their three-dimensional structures were not understood. Scientists believed either that correct folding required unknown cellular factors or that ribosomes, the site where polypeptides are synthesized, somehow shaped proteins as they were being made. American researcher Christian Anfinsen, however, postulated that proteins contain all the information necessary to fold into their proper conformation without the need for cellular factors or organelles. He hypothesized that proteins spontaneously assume their most stable conformation based on the laws of chemistry and physics (**Figure 3.20**).

To test this hypothesis, Anfinsen studied ribonuclease, an enzyme that degrades RNA molecules (see Figure 3.17). Biochemists had already determined that ribonuclease has four disulfide bonds between eight cysteine amino acids. Anfinsen began with purified ribonuclease. The key point is that other cellular components were not present, only the purified protein. He exposed ribonuclease to a chemical called β-mercaptoethanol, which broke the S—S bonds, and to urea, which disrupted the hydrogen and ionic bonds. Following this treatment, he measured the ability of the treated enzyme to degrade RNA. The enzyme had lost nearly all of its ability to degrade RNA. Therefore, Anfinsen concluded that when ribonuclease was unfolded or denatured, it was no longer functional.

The key step in this experiment came when Anfinsen removed the urea and β-mercaptoethanol from the solution. Because these molecules are much smaller than ribonuclease, removing them from the solution was accomplished with a technique called size-exclusion chromatography. In size-exclusion chromatography, solutions are layered atop a glass column of beadlike particles and allowed to filter down through the column to an open collection port at the bottom. The particles in the column have microscopic pores that trap small molecules like urea and mercaptoethanol but that permit large molecules such as ribonuclease to pass down the length of the column and out the collection port.

Using size-exclusion chromatography, Anfinsen was able to purify the ribonuclease out of the original solution. He then allowed the purified enzyme to sit in water for up to 20 hours, after which he retested the ribonuclease for its ability to degrade RNA. The result revolutionized our understanding of proteins. The activity of the ribonuclease was almost completely restored! This meant that even in the complete absence of any cellular factors or organelles, an unfolded protein can refold into its correct, functional structure. This was later confirmed by chemical analyses that demonstrated the disulfide bonds had re-formed at the proper locations.

Since Anfinsen's time, we have learned that ribonuclease's ability to refold into its functional structure is not seen in all proteins. Some proteins do require enzymes and other proteins (known as chaperone proteins; see Chapter 4) to assist in their proper folding. Nonetheless, Anfinsen's experiments provided

Figure 3.20   Anfinsen's experiments with ribonuclease, demonstrating that the primary structure of a polypeptide plays a key role in protein folding.

HYPOTHESIS Within their amino acid sequence, proteins contain all the information needed to fold into their correct, 3-dimensional shapes.

KEY MATERIALS Purified ribonuclease, RNA, denaturing chemicals, size-exclusion columns.

Experimental level   Conceptual level

1   Incubate purified ribonuclease in test tube with RNA, and measure its ability to degrade RNA.

Purified ribonuclease

Numerous H bonds (not shown) and 4 S—S bonds. Protein is properly folded.

2   Denature ribonuclease by adding β-mercaptoethanol (breaks S—S bonds) and urea (breaks H bonds and ionic bonds). Measure its ability to degrade RNA.

β-mercaptoethanol + Urea

Denatured ribonuclease

No more H bonds, ionic bonds, or S—S bonds. Protein is unfolded.

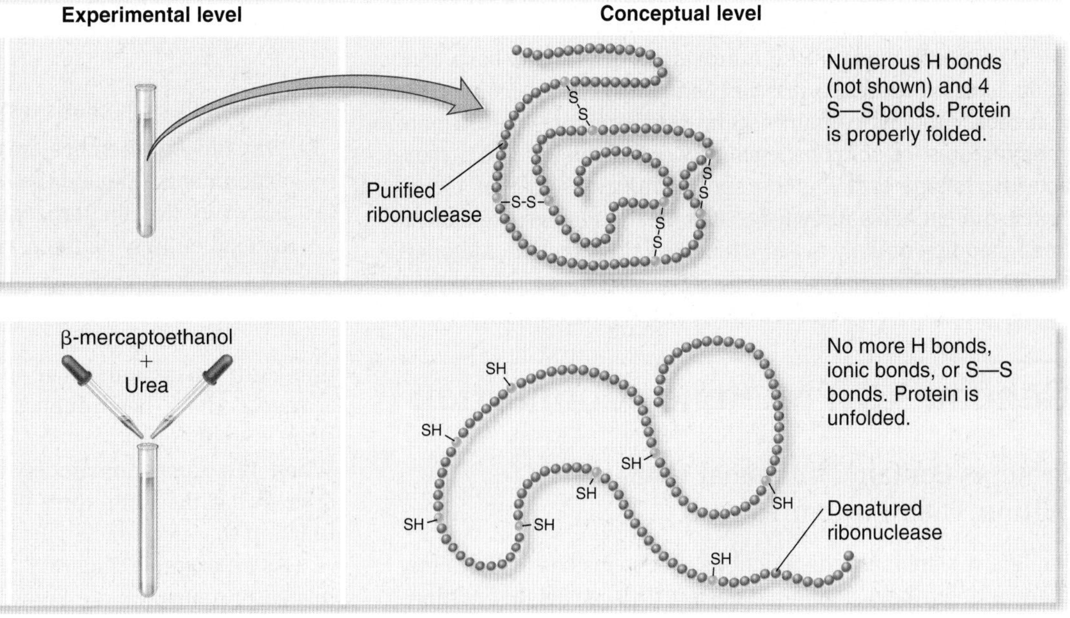

3 Layer mixture from step 2 atop a chromatography column. Beads in the column allow ribonuclease to escape, while β-mercaptoethanol and urea are retained. Collect ribonuclease in a test tube and measure its ability to degrade RNA.

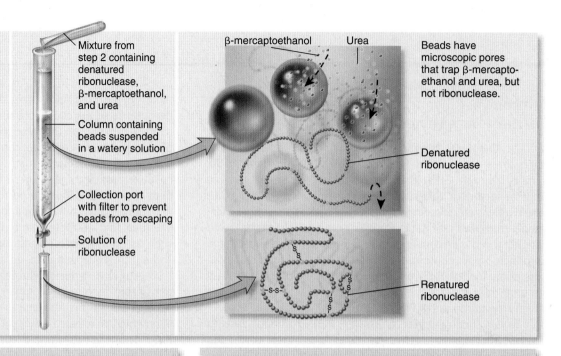

Mixture from step 2 containing denatured ribonuclease, β-mercaptoethanol, and urea

Column containing beads suspended in a watery solution

Collection port with filter to prevent beads from escaping

Solution of ribonuclease

β-mercaptoethanol　　Urea

Beads have microscopic pores that trap β-mercapto-ethanol and urea, but not ribonuclease.

Denatured ribonuclease

Renatured ribonuclease

4 **THE DATA**

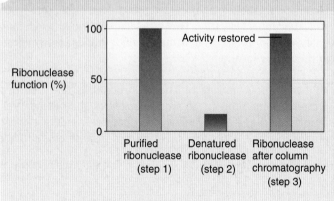

Ribonuclease function (%)

Activity restored

Purified ribonuclease (step 1)　Denatured ribonuclease (step 2)　Ribonuclease after column chromatography (step 3)

5 **CONCLUSION** Certain proteins, like ribonuclease, can spontaneously fold into their final, functional shapes without assistance from other cellular structures or factors. (However, as described in your text, this is not true of many other proteins.)

6 **SOURCE** Haber, E., and Anfinsen, C.B. 1961. Regeneration of enzyme activity by air oxidation of reduced subtilisin-modified ribonuclease. *Journal of Biological Chemistry* 236:422–424.

compelling evidence that the primary structure of a polypeptide is the key determinant of a protein's tertiary structure, an observation that earned him a Nobel Prize in 1972.

As investigations into the properties of proteins have continued since Anfinsen's classic experiments, it has become clear that most proteins contain within their structure one or more substructures, or domains, each of which is folded into a characteristic shape that imparts special functions to that region of the protein. This knowledge has greatly changed scientists' understanding of the ways in which proteins function and interact, as described next.

Experimental Questions

1. Before the experiments conducted by Anfinsen, what were the common beliefs among scientists about protein folding?

2. Explain the hypothesis tested by Anfinsen.

3. Why did Anfinsen use urea and β-mercaptoethanol in his experiments? Explain the result that was crucial to the discovery that the tertiary structure of ribonuclease may depend entirely on the primary structure.

Genomes & Proteomes Connection

Proteins Contain Functional Domains Within Their Structures

Modern research into the functions of proteins has revealed that many proteins have a modular design. This means that portions within proteins, called modules, motifs, or **domains**, have distinct structures and functions. These units of amino acid sequences have been duplicated during evolution so that the same kind of domain may be found in several different proteins. When the same domain is found in different proteins, the domain has the same three-dimensional shape and performs a function that is characteristic of that domain.

As an example, **Figure 3.21** shows a member of a family of related proteins that are known to play critical roles in regulating how certain genes are turned on and off in living cells. This

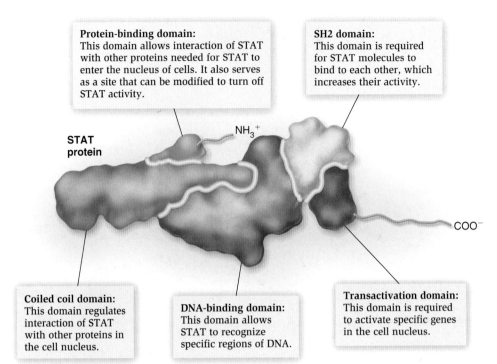

Protein-binding domain:
This domain allows interaction of STAT with other proteins needed for STAT to enter the nucleus of cells. It also serves as a site that can be modified to turn off STAT activity.

SH2 domain:
This domain is required for STAT molecules to bind to each other, which increases their activity.

STAT protein

$NH_3{}^+$

COO^-

Coiled coil domain:
This domain regulates interaction of STAT with other proteins in the cell nucleus.

DNA-binding domain:
This domain allows STAT to recognize specific regions of DNA.

Transactivation domain:
This domain is required to activate specific genes in the cell nucleus.

Figure 3.21 The domain structure of a STAT protein.

protein bears the cumbersome name of s̲ignal t̲ransducer and a̲ctivator of t̲ranscription (STAT) protein.

Each domain of this protein is involved in a distinct biological function, a common occurrence in proteins with multiple domains. For example, one of the domains is labeled the SH2 domain (Figure 3.21). Many different proteins contain this domain. It allows such proteins to recognize other proteins in a very specific way. The function of SH2 domains is to bind to tyrosine amino acids to which phosphate groups have been added by cellular enzymes. When an amino acid receives a phosphate group in this way, it is said to be phosphorylated (as is the protein in which the tyrosine exists). As might be predicted, proteins that contain SH2 domains all bind to phosphorylated tyrosines in the proteins they recognize.

As a second example, a STAT protein has another domain called a DNA-binding domain. This portion of the protein has a structure that specifically binds to DNA. Overall, the domain structure of proteins enables them to have multiple, discrete regions, each with its own structure and purpose in the functioning of the protein.

3.6 Nucleic Acids

Nucleic acids account for only about 2% of the weight of animals like ourselves, yet these molecules are extremely important because they are responsible for the storage, expression, and transmission of genetic information. The expression of genetic information in the form of specific proteins determines whether one is a human, a frog, an onion, or a bacterium. Likewise, genetic information determines whether a cell is part of a muscle or a bone, a leaf or a root.

Nucleic Acids Are Polymers Made of Nucleotides

The two classes of nucleic acids are **deoxyribonucleic acid** (**DNA**) and **ribonucleic acid** (**RNA**). DNA molecules store genetic information coded in the sequence of their monomer building blocks. RNA molecules are involved in decoding this information into instructions for linking a specific sequence of amino acids to form a polypeptide chain. The monomers in DNA must be arranged in a precise way so that the correct code can be read. As an analogy, think of the difference in the meanings of the words "marital" and "martial," in which the sequence of two letters is altered.

Like other macromolecules, both types of nucleic acids are polymers and consist of linear sequences of repeating monomers. Each monomer, known as a **nucleotide**, has three components: a phosphate group, a pentose (five-carbon) sugar (either ribose or deoxyribose), and a single or a double ring of carbon and nitrogen atoms known as a **base** (Figure 3.22). Nucleotides in a DNA strand are covalently held together by phosphodiester linkages between adjacent phosphate and sugar molecules, with the bases protruding from the side of the phosphate-sugar backbone (Figure 3.23).

DNA Is Composed of Purines and Pyrimidines

The nucleotides in DNA contain the five-carbon sugar **deoxyribose**. Four different nucleotides are present in DNA, corresponding to the four different bases that can be linked to deoxyribose. The **purine** bases, **adenine** (**A**) and **guanine** (**G**), have double rings of carbon and nitrogen atoms, and the **pyrimidine** bases, **cytosine** (**C**) and **thymine** (**T**), have a single ring (Figure 3.23).

A DNA molecule consists of two strands of nucleotides coiled around each other to form a double helix (Figure 3.24).

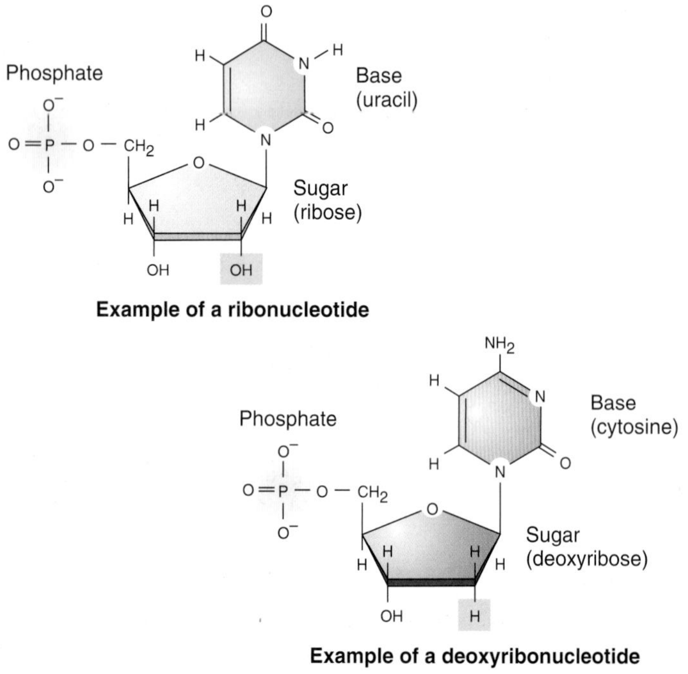

Phosphate

Base
(uracil)

Sugar
(ribose)

Example of a ribonucleotide

Phosphate

Base
(cytosine)

Sugar
(deoxyribose)

Example of a deoxyribonucleotide

Figure 3.22 **Examples of two nucleotides.** A nucleotide has a phosphate group, a five-carbon sugar, and a nitrogenous base.

Purines and pyrimidines occur in both strands. The two strands are held together by hydrogen bonds between a purine base in one strand and a pyrimidine base in the opposite strand. The ring structure of each base lies in a flat plane perpendicular to the sugar-phosphate backbone, somewhat like steps on a spiral staircase. This base pairing maintains a constant distance between the sugar-phosphate backbones of the two strands as they coil around each other.

As we will see in Chapter 11, only certain bases can pair with others, due to the location of the hydrogen-bonding groups in the four bases (Figure 3.24). Two hydrogen bonds can be formed between adenine and thymine (A-T pairing), while three hydrogen bonds are formed between guanine and cytosine (G-C pairing). In a DNA molecule, A on one strand is always paired with T on another strand, and G with C. If we know the amount of one type of base in a DNA molecule, we can predict the relative amounts of each of the other three bases. For example, if a DNA molecule were composed of 20% A bases, then there must also be 20% T bases. That leaves 60% of the bases that must be G and C combined. Because the amounts of G and C must be equal, this particular DNA molecule must be composed of 30% each of G and C. This specificity provides the mechanism for duplicating and transferring genetic information (see Chapter 11).

RNA Is Usually Single Stranded and Comes in Several Forms

RNA molecules differ in only a few respects from DNA. Except in some viruses, RNA consists of a single rather than double strand of nucleotides. In RNA, the sugar in each nucleotide is **ribose** rather than deoxyribose. Also, the pyrimidine base

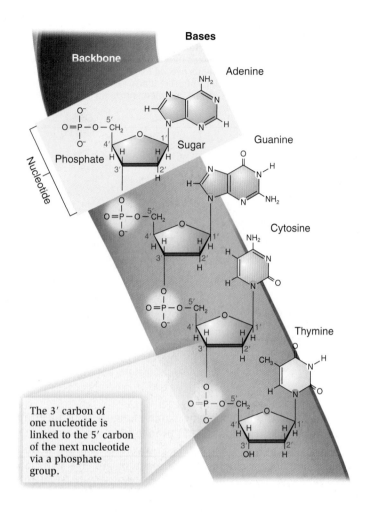

The 3′ carbon of one nucleotide is linked to the 5′ carbon of the next nucleotide via a phosphate group.

Figure 3.23 **Structure of a DNA strand.** Nucleotides are linked to each other to form a strand of DNA. The four bases found in DNA are shown. A strand of RNA would be similar except the sugar would be ribose, and uracil would be substituted for thymine.

thymine in DNA is replaced in RNA with the pyrimidine base **uracil** (**U**) (see Figure 3.22). The other three bases—adenine, guanine, and cytosine—are found in both DNA and RNA. Certain forms of RNA called messenger RNA (mRNA), ribosomal RNA (rRNA), and transfer RNA (tRNA) are responsible for converting the information contained in DNA into the formation of a new polypeptide. This topic will be discussed in Chapter 12.

▶ Summary of Key Concepts

3.1 The Carbon Atom and the Study of Organic Molecules

- Organic chemistry is the science of studying carbon-containing molecules, which are found in living organisms. (Figure 3.1)

- One property of the carbon atom that makes life possible is its ability to form four covalent bonds (polar or nonpolar) with other atoms. The combination of different elements and different types of bonds allows a vast number of organic

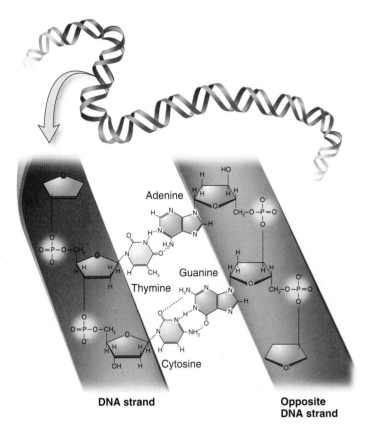

Figure 3.24 **The double-stranded structure of DNA.** DNA consists of two strands coiled together into a double helix. The bases form hydrogen bonds in which A pairs with T, and G pairs with C.

Concept check: *If the sequence of bases in one strand of a DNA double helix is known, can the base sequence of the opposite strand be predicted?*

compounds to be formed from only a few chemical elements. (Figures 3.2, 3.3)

- Organic molecules may occur in various shapes. The structures of molecules determine their functions.

- Carbon bonds are stable at the different temperatures associated with life.

- Organic compounds may contain functional groups. (Table 3.1)

- Carbon-containing molecules can exist as isomers, which have identical molecular composition but different structures and characteristics. Structural isomers contain the same atoms but in different bonding relationships. Stereoisomers have identical bonding relationships but different spatial positioning of their atoms. Two types of stereoisomers are *cis-trans* isomers and enantiomers. (Figure 3.4)

3.2 Formation of Organic Molecules and Macromolecules

- The four major classes of organic molecules are carbohydrates, lipids, proteins, and nucleic acids. Organic molecules exist as monomers or polymers. Polymers are large macromolecules

built up by dehydration reactions in which individual monomers combine with each other. Polymers are broken down into monomers by hydrolysis reactions. (Figure 3.5)

3.3 Carbohydrates

- Carbohydrates are composed of carbon, hydrogen, and oxygen atoms. Cells can break down carbohydrates, releasing energy and forming bonds in ATP.

- Carbohydrates include monosaccharides (the simplest sugars), disaccharides, and polysaccharides. The polysaccharides starch (in plant cells) and glycogen (in animal cells) are energy stores. The plant polysaccharide cellulose serves a support or structural function. (Figures 3.6, 3.7, 3.8)

3.4 Lipids

- Lipids, composed predominantly of hydrogen and carbon atoms, are nonpolar and very insoluble in water. Major classes of lipids include fats, phospholipids, steroids, and waxes.

- Fats, also called triglycerides and triacylglycerols, are formed by bonding glycerol with three fatty acids. In a saturated fatty acid, all the carbons are linked by single covalent bonds. Unsaturated fatty acids contain one or more C=C double bonds. Animal fats generally contain a high proportion of saturated fatty acids, and vegetable fats contain more unsaturated fatty acids. (Figures 3.9, 3.10, 3.11)

- Phospholipids are similar in structure to triglycerides, except they are amphipathic because one fatty acid is replaced with a charged polar group that includes a phosphate group. (Figure 3.12)

- Steroids are constructed of four fused rings of carbon atoms. Small differences in steroid structure can lead to profoundly different biological properties, such as the differences between estrogen and testosterone. (Figure 3.13)

- Waxes, another class of lipids, are nonpolar and repel water, and they are often found as protective coatings on the leaves of plants and the outer surfaces of animals' bodies.

3.5 Proteins

- Proteins are composed of carbon, hydrogen, oxygen, nitrogen, and small amounts of other elements, such as sulfur. Proteins are macromolecules that play critical roles in almost all life processes. The proteins of all living organisms are composed of the same set of 20 amino acids, corresponding to 20 different side chains. (Figure 3.14, Table 3.2)

- Amino acids are joined by linking the carboxyl group of one amino acid to the amino group of another, forming a peptide bond. A polypeptide is a structural unit composed of amino acids. A protein is a functional unit composed of one or more polypeptides that have been folded and twisted into precise three-dimensional shapes. (Figure 3.15)

- The four levels of protein structure are primary (its amino acid sequence), secondary (α helices or β pleated sheets), tertiary (folding to assume a three-dimensional shape), and quaternary (multimeric proteins that consist of more than one polypeptide chain). The three-dimensional structure of a protein determines its function—for example, by creating binding sites for other molecules. (Figures 3.16, 3.17, 3.18, 3.19, 3.20, 3.21)

3.6 Nucleic Acids

- Nucleic acids are responsible for the storage, expression, and transmission of genetic information. The two types of nucleic acids are deoxyribonucleic acid (DNA) and ribonucleic acid (RNA). (Figures 3.22, 3.23)

- DNA molecules store genetic information coded in the sequence of their monomers. A DNA molecule consists of two strands of nucleotides coiled around each other to form a double helix, held together by hydrogen bonds between a purine base on one strand and a pyrimidine base on the opposite strand. (Figure 3.24)

- RNA molecules are involved in decoding this information into instructions for linking amino acids in a specific sequence to form a polypeptide chain. RNA consists of a single strand of nucleotides. The sugar in each nucleotide is ribose rather than deoxyribose, and the base uracil replaces thymine.

Assess and Discuss

Test Yourself

1. Molecules that contain the element _____ are considered organic molecules.
   a. hydrogen   d. nitrogen
   b. carbon   e. calcium
   c. oxygen

2. _____ was the first scientist to synthesize an organic molecule. The organic molecule synthesized was _____.
   a. Kolbe, urea   d. Kolbe, acetic acid
   b. Wöhler, urea   e. Wöhler, glucose
   c. Wöhler, acetic acid

3. The versatility of carbon to serve as the backbone for a variety of different molecules is due to
   a. the ability of carbon atoms to form four covalent bonds.
   b. the fact that carbon usually forms ionic bonds with many different atoms.
   c. the abundance of carbon in the environment.
   d. the ability of carbon to form covalent bonds with many different types of atoms.
   e. both a and d.

4. _____ are molecules that have the same molecular composition but differ in structure and/or bonding association.
   a. Isotopes   d. Analogues
   b. Isomers   e. Ions
   c. Free radicals

5. _____ is a storage polysaccharide commonly found in the cells of animals.
   a. Glucose   d. Starch
   b. Sucrose   e. Cellulose
   c. Glycogen

6. In contrast to other fatty acids, essential fatty acids
   a. are always saturated fats.
   b. cannot be synthesized by the organism and are necessary for survival.
   c. can act as building blocks for large, more complex macromolecules.
   d. are the simplest form of lipids found in plant cells.
   e. are structural components of plasma membranes.

7. Phospholipids are amphipathic, which means they
   a. are partially hydrolyzed during cellular metabolism.
   b. are composed of a hydrophilic portion and a hydrophobic portion.
   c. may be poisonous to organisms if in combination with certain other molecules.
   d. are molecules composed of lipids and proteins.
   e. are all of the above.

8. The monomers of proteins are _____, and these are linked by polar covalent bonds commonly referred to as _____ bonds.
   a. nucleotides, peptide   d. amino acids, peptide
   b. amino acids, ester   e. monosaccharides, glycosidic
   c. hydroxyl groups, ester

9. The _____ of a nucleotide determines whether it is a component of DNA or a component of RNA.
   a. phosphate group   d. fatty acid
   b. five-carbon sugar   e. Both b and d are correct.
   c. side chain

10. A _____ is a portion of protein with a particular structure and function.
    a. peptide bond   d. wax
    b. domain   e. monosaccharide
    c. phospholipid

Conceptual Questions

1. Define isomers.
2. List the four classes of organic molecules; give a function of each.
3. Explain the difference between saturated and unsaturated fatty acids.

Collaborative Questions

1. Discuss the differences between different types of carbohydrates.
2. Discuss some of the roles that proteins play in organisms.

Online Resource

www.brookerbiology.com

Stay a step ahead in your studies with animations that bring concepts to life and practice tests to assess your understanding. Your instructor may also recommend the interactive ebook, individualized learning tools, and more.

General Features of Cells

4

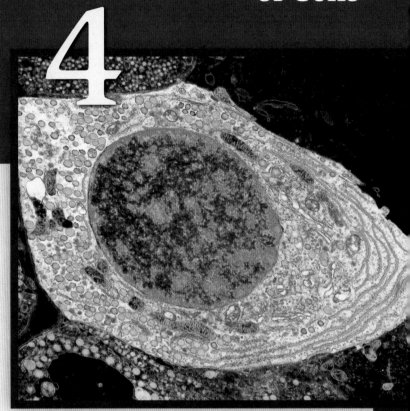

A cell from the pituitary gland. The cell in this micrograph was viewed by a technique called transmission electron microscopy, which is described in this chapter. The micrograph was artificially colored using a computer to enhance the visualization of certain cell structures.

E mily had a persistent cough ever since she started smoking cigarettes in college. However, at age 35, it seemed to be getting worse, and she was alarmed by the occasional pain in her chest. When she began to lose weight and noticed that she became easily fatigued, Emily decided to see a doctor. The diagnosis was lung cancer. Despite aggressive treatment of the disease with chemotherapy and radiation therapy, she succumbed to lung cancer 14 months after the initial diagnosis. Emily was 36.

Topics such as cancer are within the field of **cell biology**— the study of individual cells and their interactions with each other. Researchers in this field want to understand the basic features of cells and apply their knowledge in the treatment of diseases such as cystic fibrosis, sickle-cell disease, and lung cancer.

The idea that organisms are composed of cells originated in the mid-1800s. German botanist Matthias Schleiden studied plant material under the microscope and was struck by the presence of many similar-looking compartments, each of which contained a dark area. Today we call those compartments cells, and the dark area is the nucleus. In 1838, Schleiden speculated that cells are living entities and plants are aggregates of cells arranged according to definite laws.

Schleiden was a good friend of the German physiologist Theodor Schwann. Over dinner one evening, their conversation turned to the nuclei of plant cells, and Schwann remembered having seen similar structures in animal tissue. Schwann conducted additional studies that showed large numbers of nuclei in animal tissue at regular intervals and also located in cell-like compartments. In 1839, Schwann extended Schleiden's hypothesis to animals. About two decades later, German biologist Rudolf Virchow proposed that *omnis cellula e cellula*, or "every cell originates from another cell." This idea arose from his research, which showed that diseased cells divide to produce more diseased cells.

The **cell theory**, or **cell doctrine**, which is credited to both Schleiden and Schwann with contributions from Virchow, has three parts.

1. *All living organisms are composed of one or more cells.*
2. *Cells are the smallest units of life.*
3. *New cells come only from pre-existing cells by cell division.*

Most cells are so small they cannot be seen with the naked eye. However, as cell biologists have begun to unravel cell structure and function at the molecular level, the cell has emerged as a unit of wonderful complexity and adaptability. In this chapter, we will begin our examination of cells with an overview of their structures and functions. Later chapters in this unit will explore certain aspects of cell biology in greater detail. But first, let's look at the tools and techniques that allow us to observe cells.

4.1 Microscopy

The **microscope** is a magnification tool that enables researchers to study the structure and function of cells. A **micrograph** is an image taken with the aid of a microscope. The first compound microscope—a microscope with more than one lens—was invented in 1595 by Zacharias Jansen of Holland. In 1665, an English biologist, Robert Hooke, studied cork under a primitive compound microscope he had made. He actually observed cell

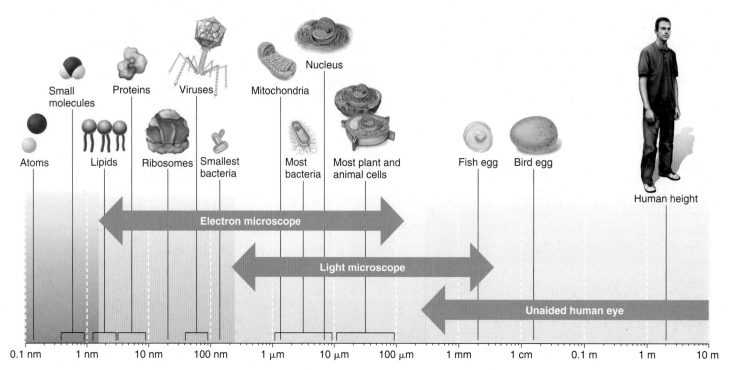

Figure 4.1 A comparison of the sizes of chemical and biological structures, and the resolving power of the naked eye, light microscope, and electron microscope. The scale at the bottom is logarithmic to accommodate the wide range of sizes in this drawing.

Concept check: Which type of microscope would you use to observe a virus?

walls because cork cells are dead and have lost their internal components. Hooke coined the word cell, derived from the Latin word *cellula*, meaning small compartment, to describe the structures he observed. Ten years later, the Dutch merchant Anton van Leeuwenhoek refined techniques of making lenses and was able to observe single-celled microorganisms such as bacteria.

Three important parameters in microscopy are resolution, contrast, and magnification. **Resolution**, a measure of the clarity of an image, is the ability to observe two adjacent objects as distinct from one another. For example, a microscope with good resolution enables a researcher to distinguish two adjacent chromosomes as separate objects, which would appear as a single object under a microscope with poor resolution. The second important parameter in microscopy is **contrast**. The ability to visualize a particular cell structure may depend on how different it looks from an adjacent structure. If the cellular structure of interest can be specifically stained with a colored dye, this makes viewing much easier. The application of stains, which selectively label individual components of the cell, greatly improves contrast. As described later, fluorescent molecules are often used to selectively stain cellular components. However, staining should not be confused with colorization. Many of the micrographs shown in this textbook are colorized to emphasize certain cellular structures (see the chapter opener, for example). In colorization, particular colors are added to micrographs with the aid of a computer. This is done for educational purposes. For example, colorization can help to emphasize different parts of a cell. Finally, **magnification** is the ratio between the size of an image produced by a

microscope and its actual size. For example, if the image size is 100 times larger than its actual size, the magnification is designated 100X. Depending on the quality of the lens and illumination source, every microscope has an optimal range of magnification before objects appear too blurry to be readily observed.

Microscopes are categorized into two groups based on the source of illumination. A **light microscope** utilizes light for illumination, whereas an **electron microscope** uses electrons for illumination. Very good light microscopes can resolve structures that are as close as 0.2 μm (micron, or micrometer) from each other. The resolving power of a microscope depends on several factors, including the wavelength of the source of illumination. Resolution is improved when the illumination source has a shorter wavelength. A major advance in microscopy occurred in 1931 when Max Knoll and Ernst Ruska invented the first electron microscope. Because the wavelength of an electron beam is much shorter than visible light, the resolution of the electron microscope is far better than any light microscope. For biological samples, the resolution limit is typically around 2 nm (nanometers), which is about 100 times better than the light microscope. **Figure 4.1** shows the range of resolving powers of the electron microscope, light microscope, and unaided eye and compares them to various cells and cell structures.

Over the past several decades, enormous technological advances have made light microscopy a powerful research tool. Improvements in lens technology, microscope organization, sample preparation, sample illumination, and computerized image processing have enabled researchers to create different

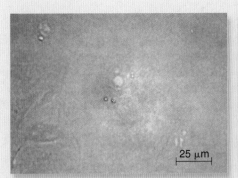

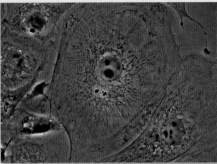

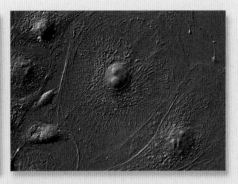

Standard light microscope (bright field, unstained sample). Light is passed directly through a sample, and the light is focused using glass lenses. Simple, inexpensive, and easy to use but offers little contrast with unstained samples.

Phase contrast microscope. As an alternative to staining, this microscope controls the path of light and amplifies differences in the phase of light transmitted or reflected by a sample. The dense structures appear darker than the background, thereby improving the contrast in different parts of the specimen. Can be used to view living, unstained cells.

Differential-interference-contrast (Nomarski) microscope. Similar to a phase contrast microscope in that it uses optical modifications to improve contrast in unstained specimens. Can be used to visualize the internal structures of cells, and is commonly used to view whole cells or larger cell structures such as nuclei.

(a) Light microscopy on unstained samples

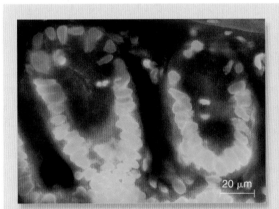

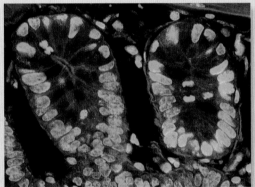

Standard (wide-field) fluorescence microscope. Fluorescent molecules specifically label a particular type of cellular protein or organelle. A fluorescent molecule absorbs light at a particular wavelength and emits light at a longer wavelength. This microscope has filters that illuminate the sample with the wavelength of light that a fluorescent molecule absorbs, and then only the light that is emitted by the fluorescent molecules is allowed to reach the observer. To detect their cellular location, researchers often label specific cellular proteins using fluorescent antibodies that bind specifically to a particular protein.

Confocal fluorescence microscope. Uses lasers that illuminate various points in the sample. These points are processed by a computer to give a very sharp focal plane. In this example, this microscope technique is used in conjunction with fluorescence microscopy to view fluorescent molecules within a cell.

(b) Fluorescence microscopy

Figure 4.2   Examples of light microscopy.   (a) These micrographs compare three microscopic techniques on the same unstained sample of cells. These cells are endothelial cells that line the interior surface of arteries in the lungs. **(b)** These two micrographs compare standard (wide-field) fluorescence microscopy with confocal fluorescence microscopy. The sample is a section through a mouse intestine, showing two villi, which are described in Chapter 45. In this sample, the nuclei are stained green, and the actin filaments (discussed later in this chapter) are stained red.

types of light microscopes, each with its own advantages and disadvantages (**Figure 4.2**).

Similarly, improvements in electron microscopy occurred during the 1930s and 1940s, and by the 1950s, the electron microscope was playing a major role in advancing our understanding of cell structure. Two general types of electron microscopy have been developed: transmission electron microscopy and scanning electron microscopy. In **transmission electron**

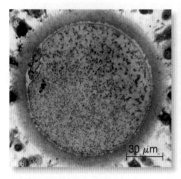

(a) Transmission electron micrograph

(b) Scanning electron micrograph

Figure 4.3   A comparison of transmission and scanning electron microscopy.   **(a)** Section through a developing human egg cell, observed by TEM, shortly before it was released from an ovary. **(b)** An egg cell, with an attached sperm, was coated with heavy metal and observed via SEM. This SEM is colorized.

Concept check: *What is the primary advantage of SEM?*

microscopy (**TEM**), a beam of electrons is transmitted through a biological sample. In preparation for TEM, a sample is treated with a chemical that binds to cellular molecules and fixes them in place. The sample is placed in a liquid resin, and the resin polymerizes to form a hardened block. To view cells, the sample embedded within the block is sliced into very thin sections, typically less than 0.2 μm in thickness. To provide contrast, the sample is stained with a heavy metal. During staining, the metal binds to certain cellular structures such as membranes. The thin sections of the sample that have been stained with heavy metal are then adhered to a copper grid and placed in a transmission electron microscope. When the beam of electrons strikes the sample, some of them hit the heavy metal and are scattered, while those that pass through without being scattered are focused to form an image on a photographic plate or screen (**Figure 4.3a**). Because the scattered electrons are lost from the beam, the metal-stained regions of the sample that scatter electrons appear as darker areas, due to reduced electron penetration. TEM provides a cross-sectional view of a cell and its organelles and gives the greatest resolution compared with other forms of microscopy. However, such microscopes are expensive and are not used to view living cells.

Scanning electron microscopy (**SEM**) is used to view the surface of a sample. A biological sample is coated with a thin layer of heavy metal, such as gold or palladium, and then is exposed to an electron beam that scans its surface. Secondary electrons are emitted from the sample, which are detected and create an image of the three-dimensional surface of the sample (**Figure 4.3b**).

4.2   Overview of Cell Structure

Cell structure is primarily determined by four factors: (1) matter, (2) energy, (3) organization, and (4) information. In Chapters 2 and 3, we considered the first factor. The matter found in living

organisms is composed of atoms, molecules, and macromolecules. Each type of cell synthesizes a unique set of molecules and macromolecules that contribute to cell structure.

We will discuss the second factor, energy, throughout this unit, particularly in Chapters 6 through 8. Energy is needed to produce molecules and macromolecules and to carry out many cellular functions.

The third phenomenon that underlies cell structure is organization. A cell is not a haphazard bag of components. The molecules and macromolecules that constitute cells have specific sites where they are found. For instance, if we compare the structure of a nerve cell in two different humans, or two nerve cells within the same individual, we would see striking similarities in their overall structures. All living cells have the ability to build and maintain their internal organization. **Protein-protein interactions** are critical to cell structure and function. Proteins often bind to each other in much the same way that building blocks snap together. These types of interactions can build complicated cell structures and also facilitate processes in which proteins interact in a consistent series of steps.

Finally, a fourth critical factor is information. Cell structure requires instructions. These instructions are found in the blueprint of life, namely the genetic material, which is discussed in Unit III. Every species has a distinctive **genome**, which is defined as the entire complement of its genetic material. Likewise, each living cell has a copy of the genome; the **genes** within each species' genome contain the information to create cells with particular structures and functions. This information is passed from cell to cell and from parent to offspring to yield new generations of cells and new generations of life. In this section, we will explore the general structure of cells and examine how the genome contributes to cell structure and function.

Prokaryotic Cells Have a Simple Structure

Based on cell structure, all forms of life can be placed into two categories called prokaryotes and eukaryotes. We will first consider the **prokaryotes**, which have a relatively simple structure. The term comes from the Greek *pro* and *karyon*, which means before a kernel—a reference to the kernel-like appearance of what would later be named the cell nucleus. Prokaryotic cells lack a membrane-enclosed nucleus.

From an evolutionary perspective, the two categories of prokaryotes are **bacteria** and **archaea**. Both types are microorganisms that are relatively small. Bacteria are abundant throughout the world, being found in soil, water, and even our digestive tracts. Most bacterial species are not harmful to humans, and they play vital roles in ecology. However, a few species are pathogenic—they cause disease. Examples of pathogenic bacteria include *Vibrio cholerae*, the source of cholera, and *Bacillus anthracis*, which causes anthrax. Archaea are also widely found throughout the world, though they are less common than bacteria and often occupy extreme environments such as hot springs and deep-sea vents.

Figure 4.4 shows a typical prokaryotic cell. The **plasma membrane**, which is a double layer of phospholipids and

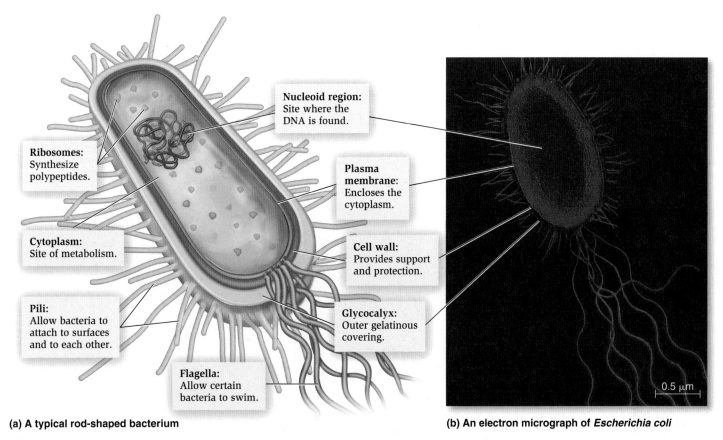

Ribosomes:
Synthesize polypeptides.

Nucleoid region:
Site where the DNA is found.

Plasma membrane:
Encloses the cytoplasm.

Cytoplasm:
Site of metabolism.

Cell wall:
Provides support and protection.

Pili:
Allow bacteria to attach to surfaces and to each other.

Glycocalyx:
Outer gelatinous covering.

Flagella:
Allow certain bacteria to swim.

0.5 μm

(a) A typical rod-shaped bacterium

(b) An electron micrograph of *Escherichia coli*

Figure 4.4   Structure of a typical prokaryotic cell.   Prokaryotic cells, which include bacteria and archaea, lack internal compartmentalization.

embedded proteins, forms an important barrier between the cell and its external environment. The **cytoplasm** is the region of the cell contained within the plasma membrane. Certain structures in the bacterial cytoplasm are visible via microscopy. These include the **nucleoid region**, which is where its genetic material (DNA) is located, and **ribosomes**, which are involved in polypeptide synthesis.

Some bacterial structures are located outside the plasma membrane. Nearly all species of prokaryotes have a relatively rigid **cell wall** that supports and protects the plasma membrane and cytoplasm. The cell wall composition varies widely among prokaryotes but commonly contains peptides and carbohydrate. The cell wall, which is relatively porous, allows most nutrients in the environment to reach the plasma membrane. Many bacteria also secrete a **glycocalyx**, an outer viscous covering surrounding the bacterium. The glycocalyx traps water and helps protect bacteria from drying out. Certain strains of bacteria that invade animals' bodies produce a very thick, gelatinous glycocalyx called a **capsule** that may help them avoid being destroyed by the animal's immune (defense) system or may aid in the attachment to cell surfaces. Finally, many prokaryotes have appendages such as **pili** and **flagella**. Pili allow prokaryotes to attach to surfaces and to each other. Flagella provide prokaryotes with a way to move, also called motility.

Eukaryotic Cells Are Compartmentalized by Internal Membranes to Create Organelles

Aside from prokaryotes, all other species are **eukaryotes** (from the Greek, meaning true nucleus), which include protists, fungi, plants, and animals. Paramecia and algae are types of protists; yeasts and molds are types of fungi. **Figure 4.5** describes the morphology of a typical animal cell. Eukaryotic cells possess a true nucleus where most of the DNA is housed. A nucleus is a type of **organelle**—a membrane-bound compartment with its own unique structure and function. In contrast to prokaryotes, eukaryotic cells exhibit **compartmentalization**, which means they have many membrane-bound organelles that separate the cell into different regions. Cellular compartmentalization allows a cell to carry out specialized chemical reactions in different places. For example, protein synthesis and protein breakdown occur in different compartments in the cell.

Some general features of cell organization, such as a nucleus, are found in nearly all eukaryotic cells. Even so, be aware that the shape, size, and organization of cells vary considerably among different species and even among different cell types of the same species. For example, micrographs of a human skin cell and a human nerve cell show that, although these cells contain the same types of organelles, their overall morphologies are quite different (**Figure 4.6**).

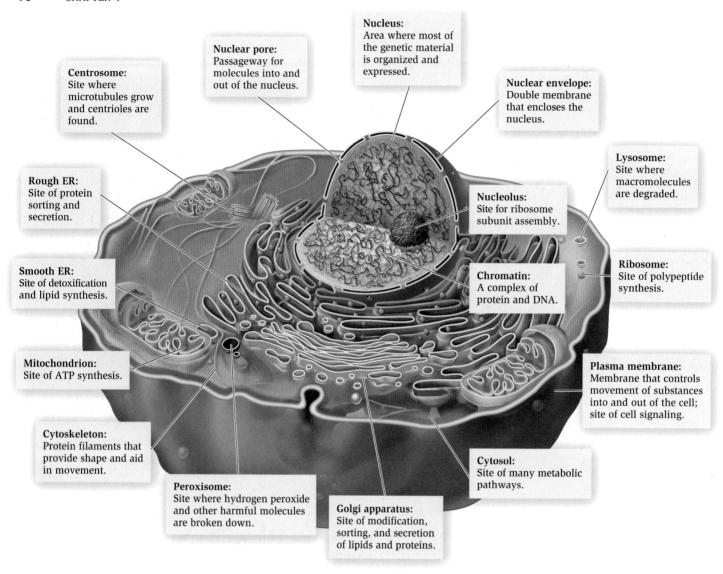

Centrosome: Site where microtubules grow and centrioles are found.

Nuclear pore: Passageway for molecules into and out of the nucleus.

Nucleus: Area where most of the genetic material is organized and expressed.

Nuclear envelope: Double membrane that encloses the nucleus.

Rough ER: Site of protein sorting and secretion.

Lysosome: Site where macromolecules are degraded.

Nucleolus: Site for ribosome subunit assembly.

Smooth ER: Site of detoxification and lipid synthesis.

Chromatin: A complex of protein and DNA.

Ribosome: Site of polypeptide synthesis.

Mitochondrion: Site of ATP synthesis.

Plasma membrane: Membrane that controls movement of substances into and out of the cell; site of cell signaling.

Cytoskeleton: Protein filaments that provide shape and aid in movement.

Cytosol: Site of many metabolic pathways.

Peroxisome: Site where hydrogen peroxide and other harmful molecules are broken down.

Golgi apparatus: Site of modification, sorting, and secretion of lipids and proteins.

Figure 4.5   General structure of an animal cell.

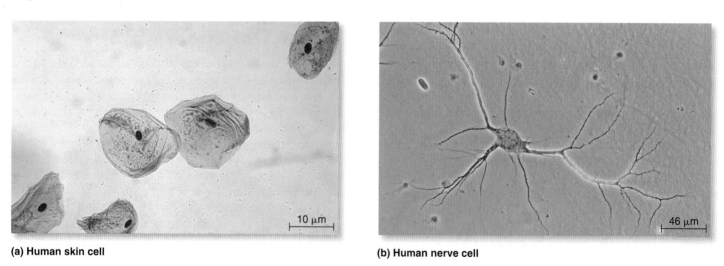

(a) Human skin cell

10 µm

(b) Human nerve cell

46 µm

Figure 4.6   **Variation in morphology of eukaryotic cells.**   Light micrographs of **(a)** a human skin cell and **(b)** a human nerve cell. Although these cells have the same genome and the same types of organelles, note that their general morphologies are quite different.

Concept check: *What is the underlying reason why skin and nerve cells have such different morphologies?*

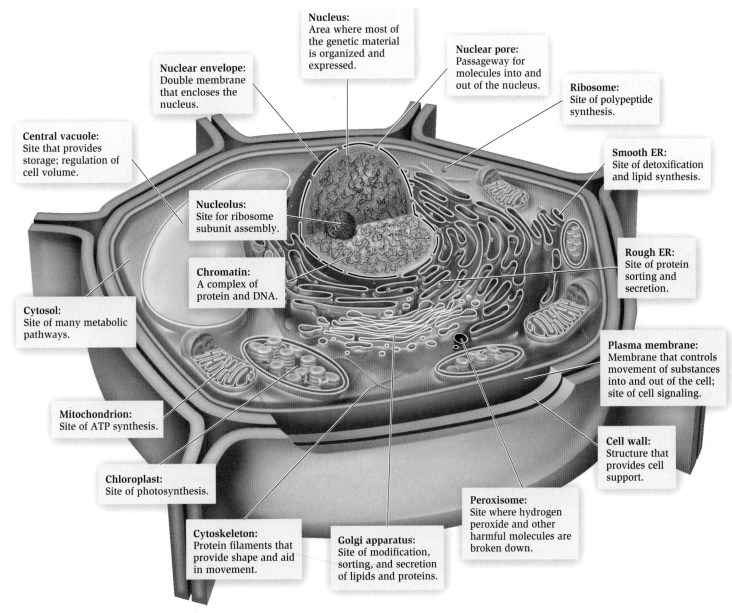

Nucleus:
Area where most of the genetic material is organized and expressed.

Nuclear pore:
Passageway for molecules into and out of the nucleus.

Ribosome:
Site of polypeptide synthesis.

Nuclear envelope:
Double membrane that encloses the nucleus.

Smooth ER:
Site of detoxification and lipid synthesis.

Central vacuole:
Site that provides storage; regulation of cell volume.

Nucleolus:
Site for ribosome subunit assembly.

Rough ER:
Site of protein sorting and secretion.

Chromatin:
A complex of protein and DNA.

Cytosol:
Site of many metabolic pathways.

Plasma membrane:
Membrane that controls movement of substances into and out of the cell; site of cell signaling.

Mitochondrion:
Site of ATP synthesis.

Cell wall:
Structure that provides cell support.

Chloroplast:
Site of photosynthesis.

Peroxisome:
Site where hydrogen peroxide and other harmful molecules are broken down.

Cytoskeleton:
Protein filaments that provide shape and aid in movement.

Golgi apparatus:
Site of modification, sorting, and secretion of lipids and proteins.

Figure 4.7   **General structure of a plant cell.**   Plant cells lack lysosomes and centrioles. Unlike animal cells, plant cells have an outer cell wall; a large central vacuole that functions in storage, digestion, and cell volume; and chloroplasts, which carry out photosynthesis.

Concept check: *What are the functions of the cell structures and organelles that are not found in both animal and plant cells?*

Plant cells possess a collection of organelles similar to animal cells (**Figure 4.7**). Additional structures found in plant cells but not animal cells include chloroplasts, a central vacuole, and a cell wall.

Genomes & Proteomes Connection

The Proteome Determines the Characteristics of a Cell

Many organisms, such as animals and plants, are multicellular, meaning that a single organism is composed of many cells. However, the cells of a multicellular organism are not all iden-

tical. For example, your body contains skin cells, nerve cells, muscle cells, and many other types. An intriguing question, therefore, is how does a single organism produce different types of cells?

To answer this question, we need to consider the distinction between genomes and proteomes. Recall that the genome constitutes all types of genetic material, namely DNA, that an organism has. Most genes encode the production of polypeptides, which assemble into functional proteins. An emerging theme discussed in this unit is that the structures and functions of proteins are primarily responsible for the structures and functions of cells. The **proteome** is defined as all of the types and relative amounts of proteins that are made in a particular cell at a particular time and under specific conditions. As an example, let's consider skin cells and nerve cells—two cell types that have dramatically different organization and structure (see Figure 4.6). In any particular individual, the genes in a human skin cell are identical to those in a human nerve cell. However, their proteomes are different. The proteome of a cell largely determines its structure and function. Several phenomena underlie the differences observed in the proteomes of different cell types.

1. *Certain proteins found in one cell type may not be produced in another cell type.* This phenomenon is due to differential gene regulation, discussed in Chapter 13.
2. *Two cell types may produce the same protein but in different amounts.* This is also due to gene regulation and to the rates at which a protein is synthesized and degraded.
3. *The amino acid sequences of particular proteins can vary in different cell types.* As discussed in Chapter 13, the mRNA from a single gene can produce two or more polypeptides with slightly different amino acid sequences via a process called alternative splicing.
4. *Two cell types may alter their proteins in different ways.* After a protein is made, its structure may be changed in a variety of ways. These include the covalent attachment of molecules such as phosphate and carbohydrate, and the cleavage of a protein to a smaller size.

These four phenomena enable skin and nerve cells to produce different proteomes and therefore different structures and functions. Likewise, the proteomes of skin and nerve cells differ from those of other cell types such as muscle and liver cells. Ultimately, the proteomes of cells are largely responsible for producing the traits of organisms, such as the color of a person's eyes.

During the last few decades, researchers have also discovered an association between proteome changes and disease. For example, the proteomes of healthy lung cells are different from the proteomes of lung cancer cells. Furthermore, the proteomes of cancer cells change as the disease progresses. One reason for studying cancer-cell proteomes is to improve the early detection of cancer by identifying proteins that are made in the early stages, when the disease is most treatable. In addition, information about the ways that the proteomes of cancer cells change may help researchers uncover new treatment options. A key challenge for biologists is to understand the synthesis and function of proteomes in different cell types and how proteome changes may lead to disease conditions.

4.3 The Cytosol

Thus far, we have focused on the general features of prokaryotic and eukaryotic cells. In the rest of this chapter, we will survey the various compartments of eukaryotic cells with a greater emphasis on structure and function. **Figure 4.8** highlights an animal and plant cell according to four different regions. We will start with the **cytosol** (shown in yellow), the region of a

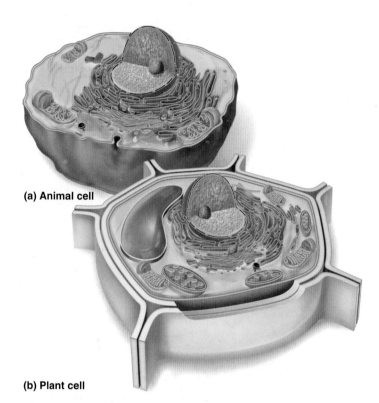

(a) Animal cell

(b) Plant cell

Figure 4.8 Compartments within (a) animal and (b) plant cells.   The cytosol, which is outside the organelles but inside the plasma membrane, is shown in yellow. The membranes of the endomembrane system are shown in purple, and the fluid-filled interiors are pink. The peroxisome is dark purple. The interior of the nucleus is blue. Semiautonomous organelles are shown in orange (mitochondria) and green (chloroplasts).

eukaryotic cell that is outside the membrane-bound organelles but inside the plasma membrane. The other regions of the cell, which we will examine later in this chapter, include the interior of the nucleus (blue), the endomembrane system (purple and pink), and the semiautonomous organelles (orange and green). As in prokaryotes, the term cytoplasm refers to the region enclosed by the plasma membrane. This includes the cytosol and the organelles.

Though the amount varies among different types of cells, the cytosol is an aqueous environment that typically occupies about 20 to 50% of the total cell volume. In this section, we will consider the primary functions of the cytosol. First, it is the site of many chemical reactions that produce the materials that are necessary for life. Second, we will examine the structure and function of large protein filaments that provide organization to cells and allow cells to move.

Synthesis and Breakdown of Molecules Occur in the Cytosol

Metabolism is defined as the sum of the chemical reactions by which cells produce the materials and utilize the energy that are necessary to sustain life. Although specific steps of metabolism also occur in cell organelles, the cytosol is a central coordinating region for many metabolic activities of eukaryotic cells.

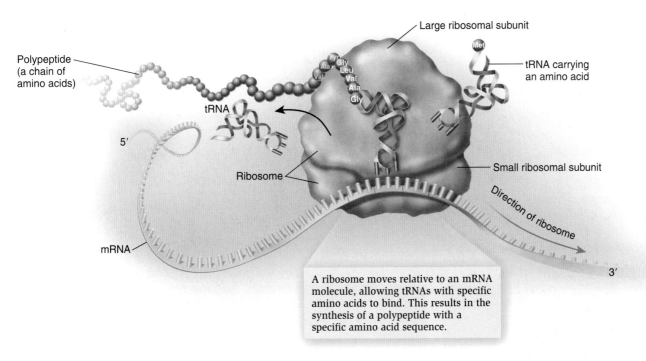

Polypeptide (a chain of amino acids)

Large ribosomal subunit

tRNA carrying an amino acid

tRNA

5′

Ribosome

Small ribosomal subunit

Direction of ribosome

mRNA

3′

A ribosome moves relative to an mRNA molecule, allowing tRNAs with specific amino acids to bind. This results in the synthesis of a polypeptide with a specific amino acid sequence.

Figure 4.9   **Translation: the process of polypeptide synthesis.**   A ribosome is the site of polypeptide synthesis. It is composed of a small and large subunit. Messenger RNA (mRNA) provides the information for the amino acid sequence of a polypeptide.

Metabolism often involves a series of steps called a metabolic pathway. Each step in a metabolic pathway is catalyzed by a specific **enzyme**—a protein that accelerates the rate of a chemical reaction. In Chapters 6 and 7, we will examine the functional properties of enzymes and consider a few metabolic pathways that occur in the cytosol and cell organelles.

Some pathways involve the breakdown of a molecule into smaller components, a process termed **catabolism**. Such pathways are needed by the cell to utilize energy and also to generate molecules that provide the building blocks to construct cellular macromolecules. Conversely, other pathways are involved in **anabolism**, the synthesis of cellular molecules and macromolecules. For example, polysaccharides are made by linking sugar molecules. To create proteins, amino acids are covalently connected to form a polypeptide. An overview of this process, called translation, is shown in Figure 4.9. It is described in greater detail in Chapter 12. Translation occurs on ribosomes, which are found in various locations in the cell. Some ribosomes may float free in the cytosol, others are attached to the endoplasmic reticulum membrane, and still others are found within the mitochondria or chloroplasts.

The Cytoskeleton Provides Cell Shape, Organization, and Movement

The **cytoskeleton** is a network of three different types of protein filaments: **microtubules, intermediate filaments**, and **actin filaments** (Table 4.1). Each type is constructed from many protein monomers. The cytoskeleton is a striking example of protein-protein interactions. The cytoskeleton is found primarily in the cytosol and also in the nucleus along the inner nuclear membrane. Let's first consider the structure of cytoskeletal filaments and their roles in the construction and organization of cells. Later, we will examine how they are involved in cell movement.

Microtubules   Microtubules are long, hollow, cylindrical structures about 25 nm in diameter composed of subunits called α and β protein tubulin. The assembly of tubulin to form a microtubule results in a polar structure with a plus end and a minus end (Table 4.1). Microtubules grow at the plus end, although they can shorten at either the plus or minus end. A single microtubule can oscillate between growing and shortening phases, a phenomenon termed **dynamic instability**. Dynamic instability is important in many cellular activities, including the sorting of chromosomes during cell division.

The sites where microtubules form within a cell can vary among different types of organisms. Nondividing animal cells contain a single structure near their nucleus called the **centrosome**, or **microtubule-organizing center** (Table 4.1). Within the centrosome are the **centrioles**, a conspicuous pair of structures arranged perpendicular to each other. In animal cells, microtubule growth typically starts at the centrosome in such a way that the minus end is anchored there. In contrast, most plant cells and many protists lack centrosomes and centrioles. Microtubules are created at many sites that are scattered throughout a plant cell. In plants, the nuclear membrane appears to function as a microtubule-organizing center.

Table 4.1   Types of Cytoskeletal Filaments Found in Eukaryotic Cells

Characteristic	Microtubules	Intermediate filaments	Actin filaments
Diameter	25 nm	10 nm	7 nm
Structure	Hollow tubule	Twisted filament	Spiral filament

Protein composition	Hollow tubule composed of the protein tubulin	Can be composed of different proteins including desmin, keratin, lamin, and others that form twisted filaments	Two intertwined strands composed of the protein actin

Common functions	Cell shape; organization of cell organelles; chromosome sorting in cell division; intracellular movement of cargo; cell motility (cilia and flagella)	Cell shape; provide cells with mechanical strength; anchorage of cell and nuclear membranes	Cell shape; cell strength; muscle contraction; intracellular movement of cargo; cell movement (amoeboid movement); cytokinesis in animal cells

Microtubules are important for cell shape and organization. Organelles such as the Golgi apparatus often are attached to microtubules. In addition, microtubules are involved in the organization and movement of chromosomes during mitosis and in the orientation of cells during cell division. We will examine these events in Chapter 15.

Intermediate Filaments   Intermediate filaments are another class of cytoskeletal filament found in the cells of many but not all animal species. Their name is derived from the observation that they are intermediate in diameter between actin filaments and myosin filaments. (Myosin filaments are described in Chapter 44.) Intermediate filament proteins bind to each other in a staggered array to form a twisted, ropelike structure with a diameter of approximately 10 nm (Table 4.1). They function as tension-bearing fibers that help maintain cell shape and rigidity. Intermediate filaments tend to be relatively stable. By comparison, microtubules and actin filaments readily grow by the addition of more protein monomers and shorten by the loss of monomers.

Several types of proteins can assemble into intermediate filaments. Desmins form intermediate filaments in muscle cells and provide mechanical strength. Keratins form intermediate filaments in skin, intestinal, and kidney cells, where they are important for cell shape and mechanical strength. They are also a major constituent of hair and nails. In addition, intermediate filaments are found inside the cell nucleus. As discussed later in this chapter, nuclear lamins form a network of intermediate filaments that line the inner nuclear membrane and provide anchorage points for the nuclear pores.

Actin Filaments   Actin filaments—also known as **microfilaments** because they are the thinnest cytoskeletal filaments—are long, thin fibers approximately 7 nm in diameter (Table 4.1). Like microtubules, actin filaments have plus and minus ends, and they are very dynamic structures in which each strand grows at the plus end by the addition of actin monomers. This assembly process produces a fiber composed of two strands of actin monomers that spiral around each other.

Despite their thinness, actin filaments play a key role in cell shape and strength. Although actin filaments are dispersed throughout the cytosol, they tend to be highly concentrated near the plasma membrane. In many types of cells, actin filaments support the plasma membrane and provide shape and strength to the cell. The sides of actin filaments are often anchored to other proteins near the plasma membrane, which explains why actin filaments are typically found there. The plus ends grow toward the plasma membrane and can play a key role in cell shape and movement.

Motor Proteins Interact with Microtubules or Actin Filaments to Promote Movements

Motor proteins are a category of proteins that use ATP as a source of energy to promote various types of movements. As shown in **Figure 4.10a**, a motor protein consists of three domains called the head, hinge, and tail. The head is the site where ATP binds and is hydrolyzed to ADP and P_i. ATP binding and hydrolysis cause a bend in the hinge, which results in movement. The tail region is attached to other proteins or to other kinds of cellular molecules.

To promote movement, the head region of a motor protein interacts with a cytoskeletal filament (**Figure 4.10b**). When ATP binds and is hydrolyzed, the motor protein attempts to "walk" along the filament. The head of the motor protein is initially attached to a filament. To move forward, the head detaches from the filament, cocks forward, binds to the filament, and cocks backward. To picture how this works, consider the act of walking and imagine that the ground is a cytoskeletal filament, your leg is the head of the motor protein, and your hip is the hinge. To walk, you lift your leg up, you move it forward, you place it on the ground, and then you cock it backward (which propels you forward). This series of events is analogous to how a motor protein moves along a cytoskeletal filament.

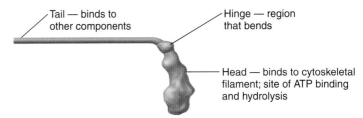

(a) Three-domain structure of a motor protein

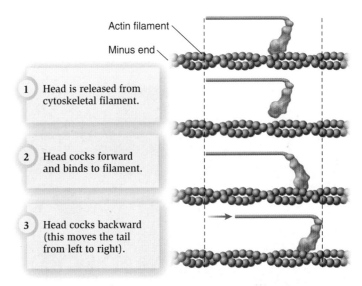

(b) Movement of a motor protein along a cytoskeletal filament

Figure 4.10   Motor proteins and their interactions with cytoskeletal filaments.   The example shown here is the motor protein myosin (discussed in Chapter 44), which interacts with actin filaments. (a) Three-domain structure of a motor protein. Note: The protein subunits of motor proteins often associate with each other along their tails, such that the motor has two tails, two hinges, and two heads. (b) Conformational changes in a motor protein that allow it to "walk" along a cytoskeletal filament.

Interestingly, cells have utilized the actions of motor proteins to promote three different kinds of movements: movement of cargo via the motor protein, movement of the filament, or bending of the filament. In the example shown in **Figure 4.11a**, the tail region of a motor protein called kinesin is attached to a cargo, so the motor protein moves the cargo from one location to another. Alternatively, a motor protein can remain in place and cause the filament to move (**Figure 4.11b**). As discussed in Chapter 44, this occurs during muscle contraction (see Figure 44.7). A third possibility is that both the motor protein and filament are restricted in their movement. In this case, when the motor proteins called dynein attempt to walk toward the minus end, they exert a force that causes microtubules to bend (**Figure 4.11c**). As described next, this occurs during the bending of flagella and cilia.

In certain kinds of cells, microtubules and motor proteins facilitate movement involving cell appendages called **flagella** and **cilia** (singular, flagellum and cilium). Flagella are usually longer than cilia and are found singly or in pairs. Both flagella and cilia cause movement by a bending motion. In flagella, movement occurs by a whiplike motion that is due to the propagation of a bend from the base to the tip. A single flagellum may

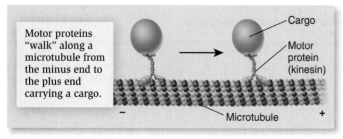

(a) Motor protein moves

Motor proteins "walk" along a microtubule from the minus end to the plus end carrying a cargo.

Cargo

Motor protein (kinesin)

Microtubule

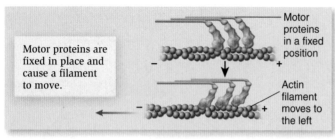

(b) Filament moves

Motor proteins are fixed in place and cause a filament to move.

Motor proteins in a fixed position

Actin filament moves to the left

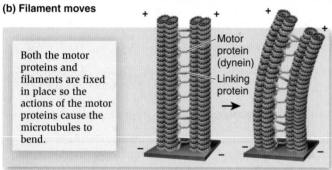

(c) Filaments bend

Both the motor proteins and filaments are fixed in place so the actions of the motor proteins cause the microtubules to bend.

Motor protein (dynein)

Linking protein

Figure 4.11   Three ways that motor proteins and cytoskeletal filaments cause movement.

propel a cell such as a sperm cell with a whiplike motion (Figure 4.12a). Alternatively, a pair of flagella may move in a synchronized manner to pull a microorganism through the water (think of a human swimmer doing the breaststroke). Certain unicellular algae swim in this manner (Figure 4.12b). By comparison, cilia are often shorter than flagella and tend to cover all or part of the surface of a cell. Protists such as paramecia may have hundreds of adjacent cilia that beat in a coordinated fashion to propel the organism through the water (Figure 4.12c).

Despite their differences in length, flagella and cilia share the same internal structure called the **axoneme**. The axoneme contains microtubules, the motor protein dynein, and linking proteins (Figure 4.13). In the cilia and flagella of most eukaryotic organisms, the microtubules form an arrangement called a 9 + 2 array. The outer nine are doublet microtubules, which are composed of a partial microtubule attached to a complete microtubule. Each of the two central microtubules consists of a single microtubule. Radial spokes connect the outer doublet microtubules to the central pair. The microtubules in flagella and cilia emanate from **basal bodies**, which are anchored to the cytoplasmic side of the plasma membrane. At the basal body, the microtubules form a triplet structure. Much like the centrosome of animal cells, the basal bodies provide a site for microtubules to grow.

The movement of both flagella and cilia involves the propagation of a bend, which begins at the base of the structure and proceeds toward the tip (see Figure 4.12a). The bending occurs because dynein is activated to walk toward the minus end of the microtubules. ATP hydrolysis is required for this process. However, the microtubules and dynein are not free to move relative to each other because of linking proteins. Therefore, instead of dyneins freely walking along the microtubules, they exert a force that bends the microtubules (see Figure 4.11c). The dyneins at the base of the structure are activated first, followed by dyneins that are progressively closer to the tip of the appendage. The resulting movement propels the organism.

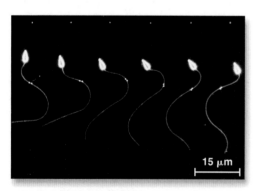

(a) Time-lapse photography of a human sperm moving its flagellum

15 μm

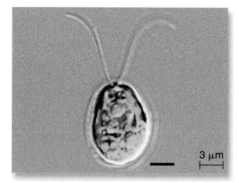

(b) *Chlamydomonas* with 2 flagella

3 μm

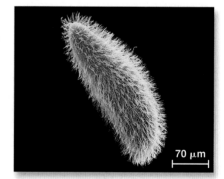

(c) *Paramecium* with many cilia

70 μm

Figure 4.12   Cellular movements due to the actions of flagella and cilia.   (a) Sperm swim by means of a single, long flagellum that moves in a whiplike motion, as shown by this human sperm. (b) The swimming of *Chlamydomonas reinhardtii* also involves a whiplike motion at the base, but the motion is precisely coordinated between two flagella. This results in swimming behavior that resembles a breaststroke. (c) Ciliated protozoa such as this *Paramecium* swim via many shorter cilia.

Concept check: *During the movement of a cilium or flagellum, describe the type of movements that are occurring between the motor proteins and microtubules.*

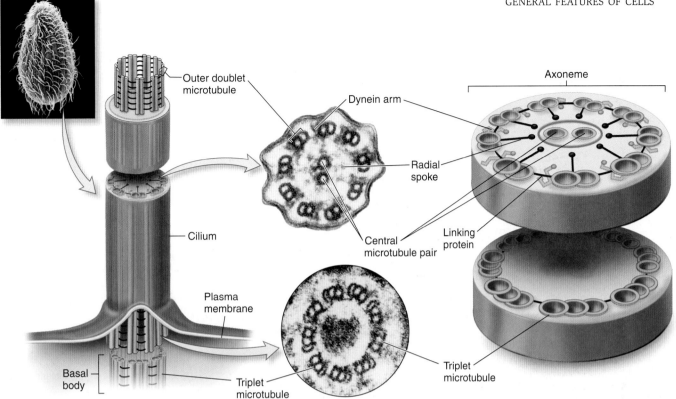

Figure 4.13 **Structure of a eukaryotic cilium.** **(inset)** SEM of a protist, *Tetrahymena themophila*. The core structure consists of a 9 + 2 arrangement of nine outer doublet microtubules and two central microtubules. This structure is anchored to the basal body, which has nine triplet microtubules, in which three microtubules are fused together. Note: The structure of the basal body is very similar to centrioles in animal cells.

4.4 The Nucleus and Endomembrane System

In Chapter 2, we learned that the nucleus of an atom contains protons and neutrons. In cell biology, the term **nucleus** has a different meaning. It is an organelle found in eukaryotic cells that contains most of the cell's genetic material. A small amount of genetic material is also found in mitochondria and chloroplasts.

The membranes that enclose the nucleus are part of a larger network of membranes called the **endomembrane system**. This system includes not only the nuclear envelope, which encloses the nucleus, but also the endoplasmic reticulum, Golgi apparatus, lysosomes, vacuoles, and peroxisomes. The prefix *endo* (from the Greek, meaning inside) originally referred only to these organelles and internal membranes. However, we now know that the plasma membrane is also part of this integrated membrane system (**Figure 4.14**). Some of these membranes, such as the nuclear envelope and the membrane of the

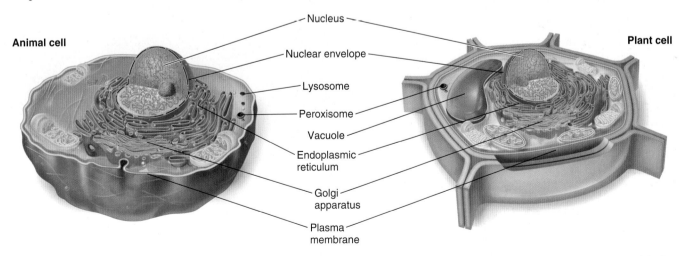

Figure 4.14 **The nucleus and endomembrane system.** This figure highlights the internal compartment of the nucleus (blue), the membranes of the endomembrane system (purple), and the fluid-filled interiors of the endomembrane system (pink). The nuclear envelope is considered part of the endomembrane system, but the interior of the nucleus is not.

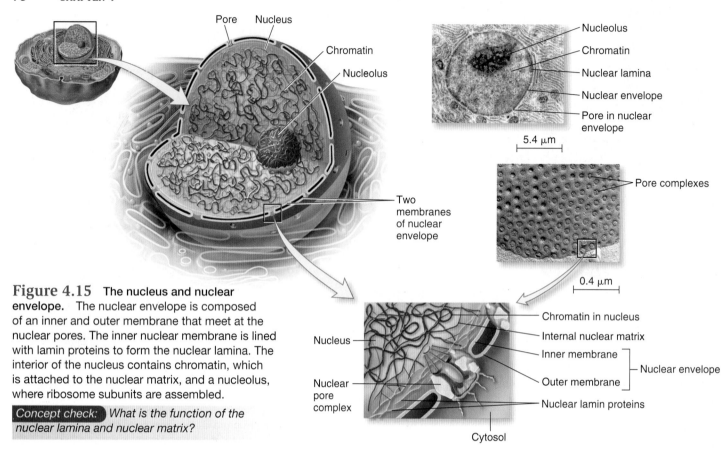

Figure 4.15 **The nucleus and nuclear envelope.** The nuclear envelope is composed of an inner and outer membrane that meet at the nuclear pores. The inner nuclear membrane is lined with lamin proteins to form the nuclear lamina. The interior of the nucleus contains chromatin, which is attached to the nuclear matrix, and a nucleolus, where ribosome subunits are assembled.

Concept check: What is the function of the nuclear lamina and nuclear matrix?

endoplasmic reticulum, have direct connections to one another. Other organelles of the endomembrane system pass materials to each other via **vesicles**—small membrane-enclosed spheres (look ahead to Figure 4.18). In this section, we will examine the nucleus and survey the structures and functions of the organelles and membranes of the endomembrane system.

The Eukaryotic Nucleus Contains Chromosomes

The nucleus is the internal compartment that is enclosed by a double-membrane structure termed the **nuclear envelope** (Figure 4.15). In most cells, the nucleus is a relatively large organelle that typically occupies 10–20% of the total cell volume. The outer membrane of the nuclear envelope is continuous with the endoplasmic reticulum membrane. **Nuclear pores** are formed where the inner and outer nuclear membranes make contact with each other. The pores provide a passageway for the movement of molecules and macromolecules into and out of the nucleus. Although cell biologists view the nuclear envelope as part of the endomembrane system, the materials within the nucleus are not (Figure 4.15).

Inside the nucleus are the chromosomes and a filamentous network of proteins called the nuclear matrix. Each **chromosome** is composed of genetic material, namely DNA, and many types of proteins that help to compact the chromosome to fit inside the nucleus. The complex formed by DNA and such proteins is termed **chromatin**. The **nuclear matrix** consists of two parts: the nuclear lamina, which is composed of intermediate filaments that line the inner nuclear membrane, and an internal nuclear matrix, which is connected to the lamina and fills

the interior of the nucleus. The nuclear matrix serves to organize the chromosomes within the nucleus. Each chromosome is located in a distinct, nonoverlapping **chromosome territory**, which is visible when cells are exposed to dyes that label specific types of chromosomes (**Figure 4.16**).

The primary function of the nucleus involves the protection, organization, replication, and expression of the genetic material. These topics are discussed in Unit III. Another important

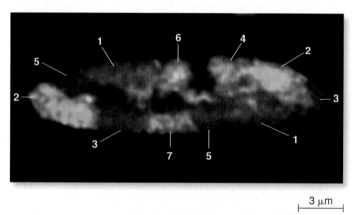

Figure 4.16 **Chromosome territories in the cell nucleus.** Chromosomes from a chicken were labeled with chromosome-specific probes. Seven types of chicken chromosomes are colored with a different dye. Each chromosome occupies its own distinct, nonoverlapping territory within the cell nucleus. Reprinted by permission from Macmillan Publishers Ltd. Cremer, T., and Cremer, C. Chromosome territories, nuclear architecture and gene regulation in mammalian cells. *Nature Reviews/ Genetics*, Vol. 2(4), Figure 2, 292–301, 2001.

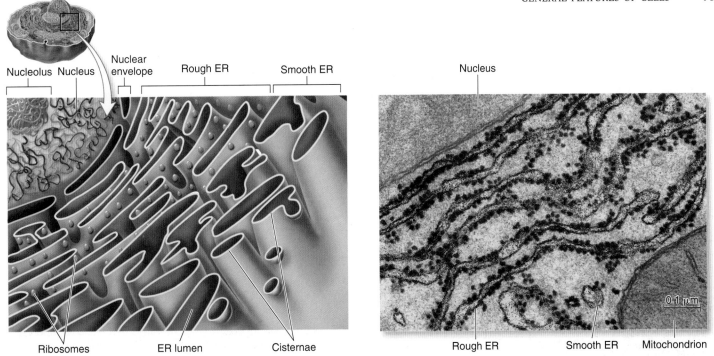

Figure 4.17 Structure of the endoplasmic reticulum.   (Left side) The ER is composed of a network of flattened tubules called cisternae that enclose a continuous ER lumen. The rough ER is studded with ribosomes, whereas the smooth ER lacks ribosomes. The rough ER is continuous with the outer nuclear membrane. (Right side) A colorized TEM. The lumen of the ER is colored yellow and the ribosomes are red.

function is the assembly of ribosome subunits—cellular structures involved in producing polypeptides during the process of translation. The assembly of ribosome subunits occurs in the **nucleolus** (plural, nucleoli), a prominent region in the nucleus of nondividing cells. A ribosome is composed of two subunits, one small and one large (see Figure 4.9). Each subunit contains one or more RNA molecules and several types of proteins. Most of the RNA molecules that are components of ribosomes are made in the vicinity of the nucleolus. This occurs because the chromosomes that carry the genes that encode most types of ribosomal RNA molecules are located there. By comparison, the ribosomal proteins are produced in the cytosol and then imported into the nucleus through the nuclear pores. The ribosomal proteins and RNA molecules then assemble in the nucleolus to form the ribosomal subunits. Finally, the subunits exit through the nuclear pores into the cytosol, where they are needed for protein synthesis.

The Endoplasmic Reticulum Initiates Protein Sorting and Carries Out Certain Metabolic Functions

The **endoplasmic reticulum** (**ER**) is a network of membranes that form flattened, fluid-filled tubules, or **cisternae** (Figure 4.17). The terms endoplasmic (Greek, for in the cytoplasm) and reticulum (Latin, for little net) refer to the location and shape of this organelle when viewed under a microscope. The term **lumen** describes the internal space of an organelle. The ER membrane encloses a single compartment called the **ER lumen**. In some cells, the ER membrane makes up more than half of the total membrane in the cell. The rough ER has its outer surface studded with ribosomes, giving it a bumpy appearance. Once bound

to the ER membrane, the ribosomes actively synthesize proteins through the ER membrane. The smooth ER lacks ribosomes.

Rough ER The **rough endoplasmic reticulum** (**rough ER**) plays a key role in the sorting of proteins that are destined for the ER, Golgi apparatus, lysosomes, vacuoles, plasma membrane, or outside of the cell. This topic is described later in Section 4.6. In conjunction with protein sorting, a second function of the rough ER is the insertion of certain newly made proteins into the ER membrane. A third important function of the rough ER is the attachment of carbohydrate to proteins and lipids. This process is called **glycosylation**. The topics of membrane protein insertion and protein glycosylation will be discussed in Chapter 5, because they are important features of cell membranes.

Smooth ER The **smooth endoplasmic reticulum** (**smooth ER**), which is continuous with the rough ER, functions in diverse metabolic processes. The extensive network of smooth ER membranes provides an increased surface area for key enzymes that play important metabolic roles. In liver cells, enzymes in the smooth ER detoxify many potentially harmful organic molecules, including barbiturate drugs and ethanol. These enzymes convert hydrophobic toxic molecules into more hydrophilic molecules, which are easily excreted from the body. Chronic alcohol consumption, as in alcoholics, leads to a greater amount of smooth ER in liver cells, which increases the rate of alcohol breakdown. This explains why people who consume alcohol regularly must ingest more alcohol to experience its effects. It also explains why alcoholics often have enlarged livers.

The smooth ER of liver cells also plays a role in carbohydrate metabolism. The liver cells of animals store energy in

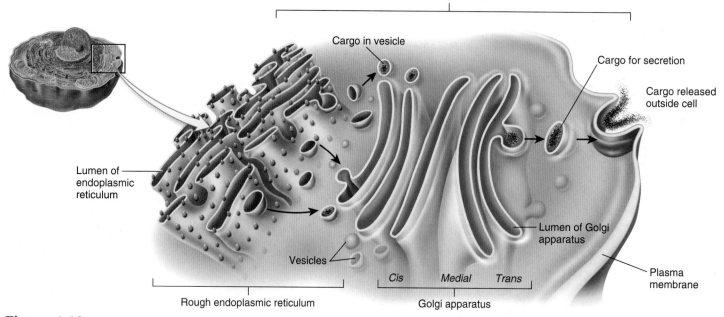

Figure 4.18 **The Golgi apparatus and secretory pathway.** The Golgi is composed of stacks of membranes that enclose separate compartments. Transport to and from the Golgi compartments occurs via membrane vesicles. Vesicles can bud from the ER and go to the Golgi, and vesicles from the Golgi can fuse with the plasma membrane to release cargo to the outside. The pathway from the ER to the Golgi to the plasma membrane is termed the secretory pathway.

Concept check: *If we consider the Golgi apparatus as three compartments (cis, medial, and trans), describe the compartments that a protein will travel through to be secreted.*

the form of glycogen, which is a polymer of glucose. Glycogen granules, which are in the cytosol, sit very close to the smooth ER membrane. When chemical energy is needed, enzymes are activated that break down the glycogen to glucose-6-phosphate. Then, an enzyme in the smooth ER called glucose-6-phosphatase removes the phosphate group, and glucose is released into the bloodstream.

Another important function of the smooth ER in all eukaryotes is the accumulation of calcium ions. The smooth ER contains calcium pumps that transport Ca^{2+} into the ER lumen. The regulated release of Ca^{2+} into the cytosol is involved in many vital cellular processes, including muscle contraction in animals.

Finally, enzymes in the smooth ER are critical in the synthesis and modification of lipids. For example, steroid hormones such as estrogen and testosterone are derived from the lipid cholesterol. Enzymes in the smooth ER are necessary for certain modifications that are needed to produce these hormones. In addition, the smooth ER is the primary site for the synthesis of phospholipids, which are the main lipid component of eukaryotic cell membranes. This topic is described in Chapter 5.

The Golgi Apparatus Directs the Processing, Sorting, and Secretion of Cellular Molecules

The **Golgi apparatus** (also called the Golgi body, Golgi complex, or simply Golgi) was discovered by the Italian microscopist Camillo Golgi in 1898. It consists of a stack of flattened membranes; each flattened membrane encloses a single compartment. The Golgi stacks are named according to their orientation in the cell. The *cis* Golgi is close to the ER membrane, the *trans* Golgi is near the plasma membrane, and the *medial*

Golgi is found in the middle. Materials are transported between the Golgi stacks via membrane vesicles that bud from one compartment in the Golgi (for example, the *cis* Golgi) and fuse with another compartment (for example, the *medial* Golgi).

The Golgi apparatus performs three overlapping functions: (1) processing, (2) protein sorting, and (3) secretion. We will discuss protein sorting in Section 4.6. Enzymes in the Golgi apparatus modify, or process, certain proteins and lipids. As mentioned earlier, carbohydrates can be attached to proteins and lipids in the endoplasmic reticulum. Glycosylation continues in the Golgi. For this to occur, a protein or lipid is transported via vesicles from the ER to the *cis* Golgi. Most of the glycosylation occurs in the *medial* Golgi.

A second type of processing event is **proteolysis**, whereby enzymes called **proteases** cut proteins into smaller polypeptides. For example, the hormone insulin is first made as a large precursor protein termed proinsulin. In the Golgi apparatus, proinsulin is packaged with proteases into vesicles. The proteases cut out a portion of the proinsulin to create a smaller insulin molecule that is a functional hormone. This happens just prior to secretion, which is described next.

The Golgi apparatus packages different types of materials into **secretory vesicles** that later fuse with the plasma membrane, thereby releasing their contents outside the plasma membrane. Proteins destined for secretion are synthesized into the ER, travel to the Golgi, and then are transported by vesicles to the plasma membrane for secretion. The entire route is called the **secretory pathway** (Figure 4.18). The later stage in this process in which vesicles fuse with the plasma membrane is called **exocytosis**. This process can also run in reverse to take substances into the cell; this is called **endocytosis**. This topic is discussed further in Chapter 5.

FEATURE INVESTIGATION

Palade Demonstrated That Secreted Proteins Move Sequentially Through Organelles of the Endomembrane System

As we have seen, one of the key functions of the endomembrane system is protein secretion. The identification of the secretory pathway came from studies of George Palade and his colleagues in the 1960s. He hypothesized that proteins follow a particular intracellular pathway in order to be secreted. Palade's team conducted **pulse-chase experiments**, in which the researchers administered a pulse of radioactive amino acids to cells so they made radioactive proteins. A few minutes later, the cells were given a large amount of nonradioactive amino acids. This is called a "chase" because it chases away the ability of the cells to make any more radioactive proteins. In this way, radioactive proteins were produced only briefly. Because they were labeled with radioactivity, the fate of these proteins could be monitored over time. The goal of a pulse-chase experiment is to determine where the radioactive proteins are produced and the pathway they take as they travel through a cell.

Palade chose to study the cells of the pancreas. This organ secretes enzymes and protein hormones that play a role in digestion and metabolism. Therefore, these cells were chosen because their primary activity is protein secretion. To study the pathway for protein secretion, Palade and colleagues injected a radioactive version of the amino acid leucine into the bloodstream of male guinea pigs. The radiolabeled leucine would travel in the bloodstream and be quickly taken up by cells of the body, including those in the pancreas. Three minutes later, they injected nonradioactive leucine (**Figure 4.19**). At various times after the second injection, samples of pancreatic cells were removed from the animals. The cells were then prepared for transmission electron microscopy. The sample was stained with osmium tetroxide, a heavy metal that became bound to membranes and showed the locations of the cell organelles. In addition, the sample was coated with a radiation-sensitive emulsion containing silver. When radiation was emitted from radioactive proteins, it interacted with the emulsion in a way that caused the precipitation of silver, which became tightly bound to the sample. In this way, the precipitated silver marked the location of the radiolabeled proteins. Unprecipitated silver in the emulsion was later washed away. Because silver atoms are electron dense, they produce dark spots in a transmission electron micrograph. Therefore, dark spots revealed the locations of radioactive proteins.

The micrograph in the data of Figure 4.19 illustrates the results that were observed 5 minutes after the completion of the pulse-chase injections. Very dark objects, namely radioactive proteins, were observed in the rough ER. As shown schematically to the right of the actual data, later time points indicated that the radioactive proteins moved from the ER to the Golgi, and then to secretory vesicles near the plasma membrane. In this way, Palade followed the intracellular pathway of protein movement. His

Figure 4.19 Palade's use of the pulse-chase method to study protein secretion.

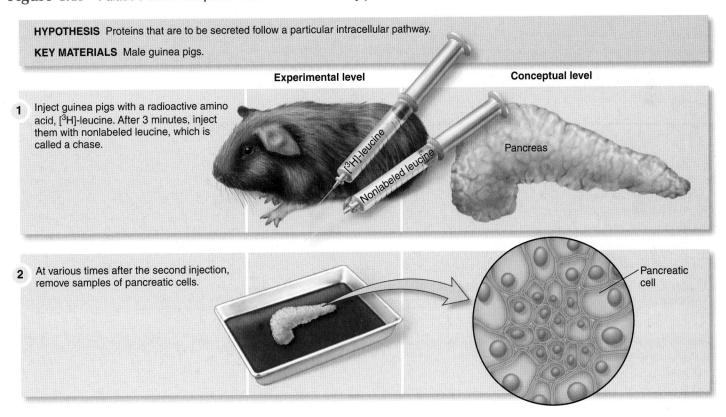

HYPOTHESIS Proteins that are to be secreted follow a particular intracellular pathway.

KEY MATERIALS Male guinea pigs.

Experimental level   Conceptual level

1. Inject guinea pigs with a radioactive amino acid, [³H]-leucine. After 3 minutes, inject them with nonlabeled leucine, which is called a chase.

[³H]-leucine

Nonlabeled leucine

Pancreas

2. At various times after the second injection, remove samples of pancreatic cells.

Pancreatic cell

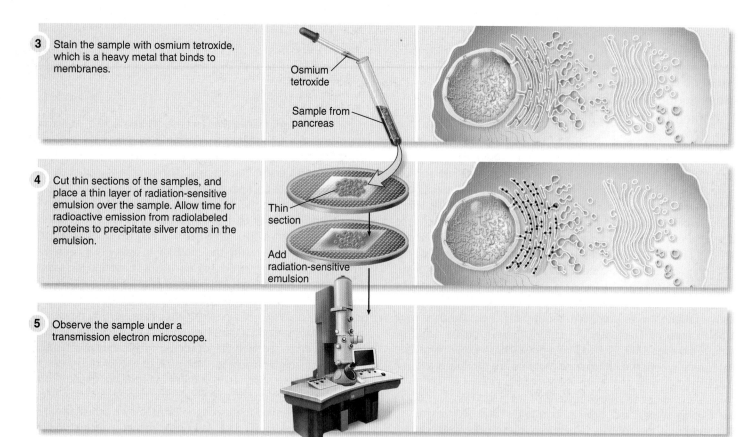

3 Stain the sample with osmium tetroxide, which is a heavy metal that binds to membranes.

Osmium tetroxide

Sample from pancreas

4 Cut thin sections of the samples, and place a thin layer of radiation-sensitive emulsion over the sample. Allow time for radioactive emission from radiolabeled proteins to precipitate silver atoms in the emulsion.

Thin section

Add radiation-sensitive emulsion

5 Observe the sample under a transmission electron microscope.

6 THE DATA

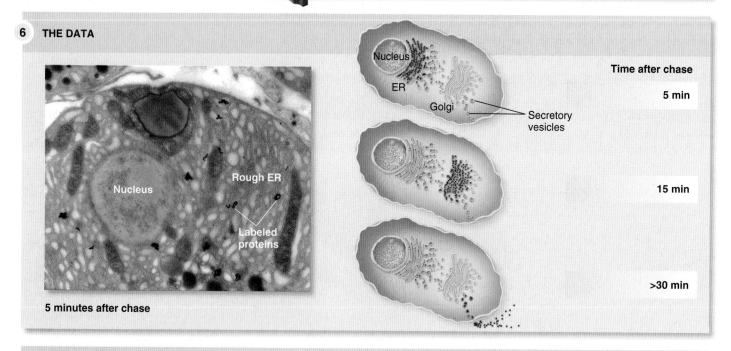

Nucleus

Rough ER

Labeled proteins

5 minutes after chase

Nucleus

ER

Golgi

Secretory vesicles

Time after chase

5 min

15 min

>30 min

7 **CONCLUSION** To be secreted, proteins move from the ER to the Golgi to secretory vesicles and then to the plasma membrane, where they are released to the outside of the cell.

8 **SOURCE** Caro, L.G., and Palade, G.E. 1964. Protein synthesis, storage, and discharge in the pancreatic exocrine cell. An autoradiographic study. *Journal of Cell Biology* 20:473–495.

experiments provided the first evidence that secreted proteins are synthesized into the rough ER and move through a series of cellular compartments before they are secreted. These findings also caused researchers to wonder how proteins are targeted to particular organelles and how they move from one compartment to another. These topics are described later in Section 4.6.

Experimental Questions

1. Explain the procedure of a pulse-chase experiment. What is the pulse, and what is the chase? What was the purpose of the approach?

2. Why were pancreatic cells used for this investigation?

3. What were the key results of the experiment of Figure 4.19? What did the researchers conclude?

Lysosomes Are Involved in the Intracellular Digestion of Macromolecules

We now turn to another organelle of the endomembrane system, **lysosomes**, which are small organelles found in animal cells that are able to lyse macromolecules. Lysosomes contain many **acid hydrolases**, which are hydrolytic enzymes that use a molecule of water to break a covalent bond. This type of chemical reaction is called hydrolysis:

$$R_1 - R_2 + H_2O \xrightarrow{\text{Acid hydrolase}} R_1 - OH + R_2 - H$$

The hydrolases found in a lysosome function optimally at an acidic pH. The fluid-filled interior of a lysosome has a pH of approximately 4.8. If a lysosomal membrane breaks, releasing acid hydrolases into the cytosol, the enzymes are not very active because the cytosolic pH is neutral (approximately pH 7.0) and buffered. This prevents significant damage to the cell from accidental leakage.

Lysosomes contain many different types of acid hydrolases that can break down carbohydrates, proteins, lipids, and nucleic acids. This enzymatic function enables lysosomes to break down complex materials. One function of lysosomes involves the digestion of substances that are taken up from outside the cell via endocytosis. In addition, lysosomes help to break down cellular molecules and macromolecules to recycle their building blocks to make new molecules and macromolecules in a process called autophagy (see Chapter 6).

Vacuoles Are Specialized Compartments That Function in Storage, the Regulation of Cell Volume, and Degradation

The term **vacuole** (Latin, for empty space) came from early microscopic observations of these compartments. We now know that vacuoles are not empty but instead contain fluid and sometimes even solid substances. Most vacuoles are made from the fusion of many smaller membrane vesicles. Vacuoles are prominent organelles in plant cells, fungal cells, and certain protists. In animal cells, vacuoles tend to be smaller and are more commonly used to temporarily store materials or transport substances. In animals, such vacuoles are sometimes called storage vesicles.

The functions of vacuoles are extremely varied, and they differ among cell types and even environmental conditions. The best way to appreciate vacuole function is to consider a few examples. Mature plant cells often have a large **central vacuole** that occupies 80% or more of the cell volume (**Figure 4.20a**). The membrane of this vacuole is called the **tonoplast**. The central vacuole serves two important purposes. First, it stores a large amount of water, enzymes, and inorganic ions such as calcium; it also stores other materials including proteins and pigments. Second, it performs a space-filling function. The large size of the vacuole exerts a pressure on the cell wall, called turgor pressure. If a plant becomes dehydrated and this pressure is lost, a plant will wilt. Turgor pressure is important in maintaining the structure of plant cells and the plant itself, and it helps to drive the expansion of the cell wall, which is necessary for growth.

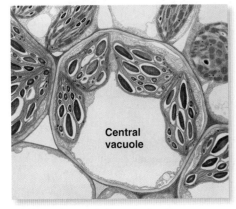

(a) Central vacuole in a plant cell

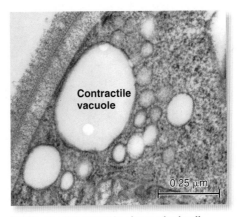

(b) Contractile vacuoles in an algal cell

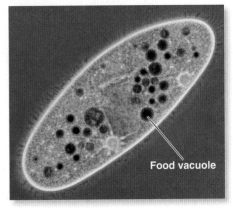

(c) Food vacuoles in a paramecium

Figure 4.20 **Examples of vacuoles.** These are transmission electron micrographs. Part (c) is colorized.

Certain species of protists also use vacuoles to maintain cell volume. Freshwater organisms such as the alga *Chlamydomonas reinhardtii* have small, water-filled **contractile vacuoles** that expand as water enters the cell (**Figure 4.20b**). Once they reach a certain size, the vacuoles suddenly contract, expelling their contents to the exterior of the cell. This mechanism is necessary to remove the excess water that continually enters the cell by diffusion across the plasma membrane.

Another function of vacuoles is degradation. Some protists engulf their food into large **phagocytic vacuoles**, or **food vacuoles** (**Figure 4.20c**). As in the lysosomes of animal cells, food vacuoles contain digestive enzymes to break down the macromolecules within the food. Macrophages, a type of cell found in animals' immune systems, engulf bacterial cells into phagocytic vacuoles, where the bacteria are destroyed.

Peroxisomes Catalyze Detoxifying Reactions

Peroxisomes, discovered by Christian de Duve in 1965, are relatively small organelles found in all eukaryotic cells. Peroxisomes consist of a single membrane that encloses a fluid-filled lumen. A typical eukaryotic cell contains several hundred of them.

The general function of peroxisomes is to catalyze certain chemical reactions, typically those that break down molecules by removing hydrogen or adding oxygen. In mammals, for example, large numbers of peroxisomes can be found in the cells of the liver, where toxic molecules accumulate and are broken down. A by-product of this type of chemical reaction is hydrogen peroxide, H_2O_2:

$$RH_2 + O_2 \rightarrow R + H_2O_2$$

Hydrogen peroxide has the potential to be highly toxic. In the presence of metals such as iron (Fe^{2+}) that are found naturally in living cells, hydrogen peroxide can be broken down to form a hydroxide ion (OH^-) and a molecule called a hydroxide free-radical ($\cdot OH$):

$$Fe^{2+} + H_2O_2 \rightarrow Fe^{3+} + OH^- + \cdot OH \text{ (hydroxide free-radical)}$$

The hydroxide free-radical is highly reactive and can damage proteins, lipids, and DNA. Therefore, it is beneficial for cells to break down hydrogen peroxide in an alternative manner that does not form a hydroxide free-radical. Peroxisomes contain an enzyme called **catalase** that breaks down hydrogen peroxide to make water and oxygen gas (hence the name peroxisome):

$$2\ H_2O_2 \xrightarrow{\text{Catalase}} 2\ H_2O + O_2$$

Aside from detoxification, peroxisomes usually contain enzymes involved in the metabolism of fats and amino acids. For example, plant seeds contain specialized organelles called **glyoxysomes**, which are similar to peroxisomes. Seeds often store fats instead of carbohydrates. Because fats have higher energy per unit mass, a plant can make seeds that are smaller and less heavy. Glyoxysomes contain enzymes that are needed to convert fats to sugars. These enzymes become active when a seed germinates and the seedling begins to grow.

Peroxisomes were once viewed as semiautonomous because peroxisomal proteins are imported into the peroxisome in a manner that is very similar to the targeting of proteins to the mitochondria and chloroplasts, as described later in this chapter. Another similarity is that new peroxisomes can be produced by the division of pre-existing peroxisomes. However, recent research indicates that peroxisomes are derived from the endomembrane system. A general model for peroxisome formation is shown in **Figure 4.21**, though the details may differ among animal, plant, and fungal cells. To initiate peroxisome

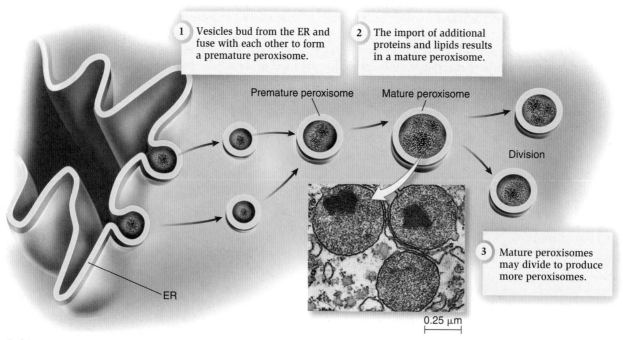

1. Vesicles bud from the ER and fuse with each other to form a premature peroxisome.

2. The import of additional proteins and lipids results in a mature peroxisome.

Premature peroxisome   Mature peroxisome

Division

3. Mature peroxisomes may divide to produce more peroxisomes.

ER

0.25 μm

Figure 4.21 Formation of peroxisomes. The inset is a TEM of mature peroxisomes.

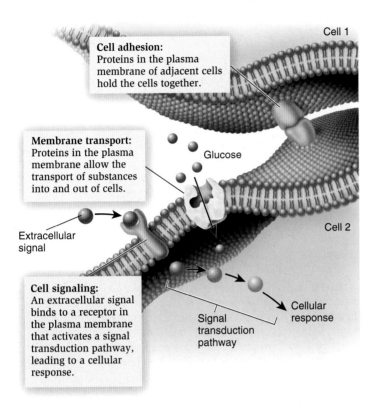

Cell adhesion:
Proteins in the plasma membrane of adjacent cells hold the cells together.

Cell 1

Membrane transport:
Proteins in the plasma membrane allow the transport of substances into and out of cells.

Glucose

Extracellular signal

Cell 2

Cell signaling:
An extracellular signal binds to a receptor in the plasma membrane that activates a signal transduction pathway, leading to a cellular response.

Signal transduction pathway

Cellular response

Figure 4.22 Major functions of the plasma membrane. These include membrane transport, cell signaling, and cell adhesion.

Concept check: Which of these three functions do you think is the most important for cell metabolism?

formation, vesicles bud from the ER membrane and form a premature peroxisome. Following the import of additional proteins, the premature peroxisome becomes a mature peroxisome. Once the mature peroxisome has formed, it may then divide to further increase the number of peroxisomes in the cell.

The Plasma Membrane Is the Interface Between a Cell and Its Environment

The cytoplasm of eukaryotic cells is surrounded by a plasma membrane, which is part of the endomembrane system and provides a boundary between a cell and the extracellular environment. Proteins in the plasma membrane perform many important functions that affect the activities inside the cell. First, many plasma membrane proteins are involved in **membrane transport** (Figure 4.22). Some of these proteins function to transport essential nutrients or ions into the cell, and others are involved in the export of substances. Due to the functioning of these transporters, the plasma membrane is selectively permeable; it allows only certain substances in and out. We will examine the structures and functions of a variety of transporters in Chapter 5.

A second vital function of the plasma membrane is **cell signaling**. To survive and adapt to changing conditions, cells must be able to sense changes in their environment. In addition, the cells of a multicellular organism need to communicate with each

other to coordinate their activities. The plasma membrane of all cells contains receptors that recognize signaling molecules—either environmental agents or molecules secreted by other cells. Once signaling molecules bind to a receptor, this elicits a signal transduction pathway—a series of steps that cause the cell to respond to the signal (Figure 4.22). For example, when you eat a meal, the hormone insulin is secreted into your bloodstream. This hormone binds to receptors in the plasma membrane of your cells, which results in a cellular response that allows your cells to increase their uptake of certain molecules found in food, such as glucose. We will explore the details of cell signaling in Chapter 9.

A third important role of the plasma membrane in animal cells is **cell adhesion**. Protein-protein interactions among proteins in the plasma membranes of adjacent cells promote cell-to-cell adhesion (Figure 4.22). This phenomenon is critical for animal cells to properly interact to form a multicellular organism and allows cells to recognize each other. The structures and functions of proteins involved in cell adhesion will be examined in Chapter 10.

4.5 Semiautonomous Organelles

We now turn to those organelles in eukaryotic cells that are considered semiautonomous: mitochondria and chloroplasts. These organelles can grow and divide to reproduce themselves, but they are not completely autonomous because they depend on other parts of the cell for their internal components (**Figure 4.23**). For example, most of the proteins found in mitochondria are imported from the cytosol. In this section, we will survey the structures and functions of the semiautonomous organelles

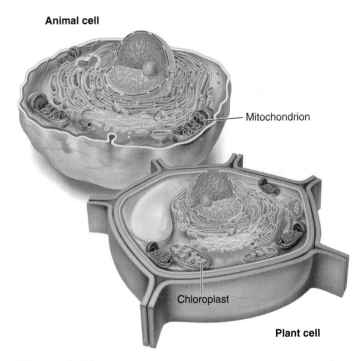

Animal cell

Mitochondrion

Chloroplast

Plant cell

Figure 4.23 Semiautonomous organelles. These are the mitochondria and chloroplasts.

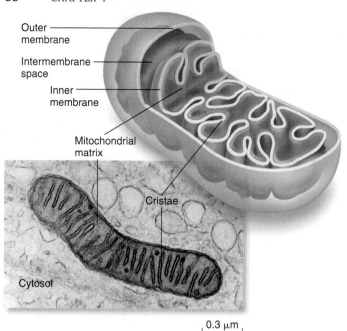

Figure 4.24 **Structure of a mitochondrion.** This organelle is enclosed in two membranes. The invaginations of the inner membrane are called cristae. The mitochondrial matrix lies inside the inner membrane. The micrograph is a colorized TEM.

Concept check: *What is the advantage of having a highly invaginated inner membrane?*

in eukaryotic cells and consider their evolutionary origins. In Chapters 7 and 8, we will explore the functions of mitochondria and chloroplasts in greater depth.

Mitochondria Supply Cells with Most of Their ATP

Mitochondrion (plural, mitochondria) literally means thread granule, which is what mitochondria look like under a light microscope. They are similar in size to bacteria. Depending on a cell's function, it may contain a few hundred to a few thousand mitochondria. Cells with particularly heavy energy demands, such as muscle cells, have more mitochondria than other cells. Research has shown that regular exercise increases the number and size of mitochondria in human muscle cells to meet the expanded demand for energy.

A mitochondrion has an outer membrane and an inner membrane separated by a region called the intermembrane space (**Figure 4.24**). The inner membrane is highly invaginated (folded) to form projections called **cristae**. These invaginations greatly increase the surface area of the inner membrane, which is the site where ATP is made. The compartment enclosed by the inner membrane is the **mitochondrial matrix**.

The primary role of mitochondria is to make ATP. Even though mitochondria produce most of a cell's ATP, mitochondria do not create energy. Rather, their primary function is to convert chemical energy that is stored within the covalent bonds of organic molecules into a form that can be readily used by cells. Covalent bonds in sugars, fats, and amino acids store a large amount of energy. The breakdown of these molecules into

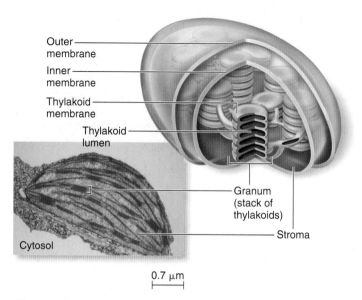

Figure 4.25 **Structure of a chloroplast.** Like a mitochondrion, a chloroplast is enclosed in a double membrane. In addition, it has an internal thylakoid membrane system that forms flattened compartments. These compartments stack on each other to form grana. The stroma is located inside the inner membrane but outside the thylakoid membrane. This micrograph is a colorized TEM.

simpler molecules releases energy that is used to make ATP. Many proteins in living cells utilize ATP to carry out their functions, such as muscle contraction, uptake of nutrients, cell division, and many other cellular processes.

Mitochondria perform other functions as well. They are involved in the synthesis, modification, and breakdown of several types of cellular molecules. For example, the synthesis of certain hormones requires enzymes that are found in mitochondria. Another interesting role of mitochondria is to generate heat in specialized fat cells known as brown fat cells. Groups of brown fat cells serve as "heating pads" that help to revive hibernating animals and protect sensitive areas of young animals from the cold.

Chloroplasts Carry Out Photosynthesis

Chloroplasts are organelles that can capture light energy and use some of that energy to synthesize organic molecules such as glucose. This process, called **photosynthesis**, is described in Chapter 8. Chloroplasts are found in nearly all species of plants and algae. **Figure 4.25** shows the structure of a typical chloroplast. Like the mitochondrion, a chloroplast contains an outer and inner membrane. An intermembrane space lies between these two membranes. A third system of membranes, the **thylakoid membrane**, forms many flattened, fluid-filled tubules that enclose a single, convoluted compartment. These tubules tend to stack on top of each other to form a structure called a **granum** (plural, grana). The **stroma** is the compartment of the chloroplast that is enclosed by the inner membrane but outside the thylakoid membrane. The **thylakoid lumen** is enclosed by the thylakoid membrane.

Chloroplasts are a specialized version of plant organelles that are more generally known as **plastids**. All plastids are derived from unspecialized **proplastids**. The various types of plastids are distinguished by their synthetic abilities and the types of pigments they contain. Chloroplasts, which carry out photosynthesis, contain the green pigment chlorophyll. The abundant number of chloroplasts in the leaves of plants gives them their green color. Chromoplasts, a second type of plastid, function in synthesizing and storing the yellow, orange, and red pigments known as carotenoids. Chromoplasts give many fruits and flowers their colors. In autumn, the chromoplasts also give many leaves their yellow, orange, and red colors. A third type of plastid, leucoplasts, typically lacks pigment molecules. An amyloplast is a leucoplast that synthesizes and stores starch. Amyloplasts are common in underground structures such as roots and tubers.

Mitochondria and Chloroplasts Contain Their Own Genetic Material and Divide by Binary Fission

To fully appreciate the structure and organization of mitochondria and chloroplasts, we also need to briefly examine their genetic properties. In 1951, Y. Chiba exposed plant cells to Feulgen, a DNA-specific dye, and discovered that the chloroplasts became stained. Based on this observation, he was the first to suggest that chloroplasts contain their own DNA. Researchers in the 1970s and 1980s isolated DNA from both chloroplasts and mitochondria. These studies revealed that the DNA of these organelles resembled smaller versions of bacterial chromosomes.

The chromosomes found in mitochondria and chloroplasts are referred to as the **mitochondrial genome** and **chloroplast genome**, respectively, and the chromosomes found in the nucleus of the cell constitute the **nuclear genome**. Like bacteria, the genomes of most mitochondria and chloroplasts are composed of a single circular chromosome. Compared to the nuclear genome, they are very small. For example, the amount of DNA in the human nuclear genome (about 3 billion base pairs) is about 200,000 times greater than the mitochondrial genome. In terms of genes, the human genome has approximately 20,000 to 25,000 different genes, whereas the human mitochondrial genome has only a few dozen. Chloroplast genomes tend to be larger than mitochondrial genomes, and they have a correspondingly greater number of genes. Depending on the particular species of plant or algae, a chloroplast genome is about 10 times larger than the mitochondrial genome of human cells.

Just as the genomes of mitochondria and chloroplasts resemble bacterial genomes, the production of new mitochondria and chloroplasts bears a striking resemblance to the division of bacterial cells. Like their bacterial counterparts, mitochondria and chloroplasts increase in number via **binary fission**, or splitting in two. **Figure 4.26** illustrates the process for a mitochondrion. The mitochondrial genome, which is found in a region called the nucleoid, is duplicated, and the organelle divides into two separate organelles. Mitochondrial and chloroplast division are needed to maintain a full complement of these organelles when cell growth occurs following cell

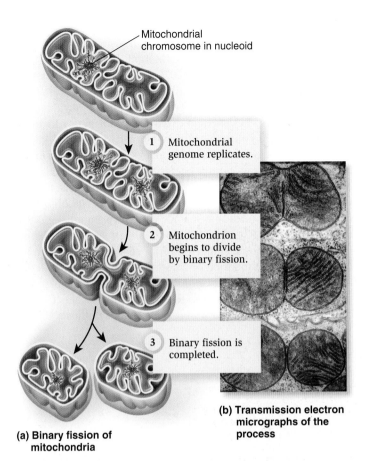

(a) Binary fission of mitochondria

(b) Transmission electron micrographs of the process

Figure 4.26 Division of mitochondria by binary fission.

division. In addition, environmental conditions may influence the sizes and numbers of these organelles. For example, when plants are exposed to more sunlight, the number of chloroplasts in leaf cells increases.

Mitochondria and Chloroplasts Are Derived from Ancient Symbiotic Relationships

The observation that mitochondria and chloroplasts contain their own genetic material may seem puzzling. Perhaps you might think that it would be simpler for a eukaryotic cell to have all of its genetic material in the nucleus. The distinct genomes of mitochondria and chloroplasts can be traced to their evolutionary origin, which involved an ancient symbiotic association.

A symbiotic relationship occurs when two different species live in direct contact with each other. **Endosymbiosis** describes a symbiotic relationship in which the smaller species—the symbiont—actually lives inside the larger species. In 1883, Andreas Schimper proposed that chloroplasts were descended from an endosymbiotic relationship between cyanobacteria (a bacterium capable of photosynthesis) and eukaryotic cells. In 1922, Ivan Wallin also hypothesized an endosymbiotic origin for mitochondria.

In spite of these interesting ideas, the question of endosymbiosis was largely ignored until the discovery that mitochondria and chloroplasts contain their own genetic material. In 1970, the issue of endosymbiosis as the origin of mitochondria and chloroplasts was revived by Lynn Margulis in her book *Origin of Eukaryotic Cells*. During the 1970s and 1980s, the advent of molecular genetic techniques allowed researchers to analyze genes from mitochondria, chloroplasts, bacteria, and eukaryotic nuclear genomes. Researchers discovered that genes in mitochondria and chloroplasts are very similar to bacterial genes. Likewise, mitochondria and chloroplasts are strikingly similar in size and shape to certain bacterial species. These observations provided strong support for the **endosymbiosis theory**, which proposes that mitochondria and chloroplasts originated from bacteria that took up residence within a primordial eukaryotic cell (**Figure 4.27**). Over the next 2 billion years, the characteristics of these intracellular bacterial cells gradually changed to those of a mitochondrion or chloroplast. A more in-depth discussion of the origin of eukaryotic cells is found in Chapter 22.

Symbiosis occurs because the relationship is beneficial to one or both species. According to the endosymbiosis theory,

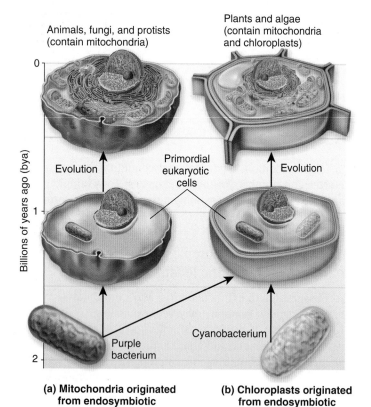

(a) Mitochondria originated from endosymbiotic purple bacteria.

(b) Chloroplasts originated from endosymbiotic cyanobacteria.

Figure 4.27   A simplified view of the endosymbiosis theory. (a) According to this concept, modern mitochondria were derived from purple bacteria, also called α-proteobacteria. Over the course of evolution, their characteristics changed into those found in mitochondria today. **(b)** A similar phenomenon occurred for chloroplasts, which were derived from cyanobacteria, a bacterium that is capable of photosynthesis.

Concept check: Discuss the similarities and differences between modern bacteria and mitochondria.

this relationship provided eukaryotic cells with useful cellular characteristics. Chloroplasts, which were derived from cyanobacteria, have the ability to carry out photosynthesis. This benefits plant cells by giving them the ability to use the energy from sunlight. By comparison, mitochondria are thought to have been derived from a different type of bacteria known as purple bacteria or α-proteobacteria. In this case, the endosymbiotic relationship enabled eukaryotic cells to synthesize greater amounts of ATP. How the relationship would have been beneficial to a cyanobacterium or purple bacterium is less clear, though the cytosol of a eukaryotic cell may have provided a stable environment with an adequate supply of nutrients.

During the evolution of eukaryotic species, many genes that were originally found in the genome of the primordial purple bacteria and cyanobacteria have been transferred from the organelles to the nucleus. This has occurred many times throughout evolution, so modern mitochondria and chloroplasts have lost most of the genes that still exist in present-day purple bacteria and cyanobacteria. Some researchers speculate that the movement of genes into the nucleus makes it easier for the cell to control the structure, function, and division of mitochondria and chloroplasts. In modern cells, hundreds of different proteins that make up these organelles are encoded by genes that have been transferred to the nucleus. These proteins are made in the cytosol and then taken up into mitochondria or chloroplasts. We will discuss this topic next.

4.6   Protein Sorting to Organelles

Thus far, we have considered how eukaryotic cells contain a variety of membrane-bound organelles. Each protein that a cell makes usually functions within one cellular compartment or is secreted from the cell. How does each protein reach its appropriate destination? For example, how does a mitochondrial protein get sent to the mitochondrion rather than to a different organelle such as a lysosome? In eukaryotes, most proteins contain short stretches of amino acid sequences that direct them to their correct cellular location. These sequences are called **sorting signals**, or **traffic signals**. Each sorting signal is recognized by specific cellular components that facilitate the proper routing of that protein to its correct location.

Most eukaryotic proteins begin their synthesis on ribosomes in the cytosol, using messenger RNA (mRNA) that contains the information for polypeptide synthesis (**Figure 4.28**). The cytosol provides amino acids, which are used as building blocks to make these proteins during translation. Cytosolic proteins lack any sorting signal, so they stay there. By comparison, the synthesis of some eukaryotic proteins begins in the cytosol and then halts temporarily until the ribosome has become bound to the ER membrane. After this occurs, translation resumes and the polypeptide is synthesized into the ER lumen or ER membrane. Proteins that are destined for the ER, Golgi, lysosome, vacuole, plasma membrane, or secretion are first directed to the ER. This is called **cotranslational sorting** because the first step in the sorting process begins while translation is occurring.

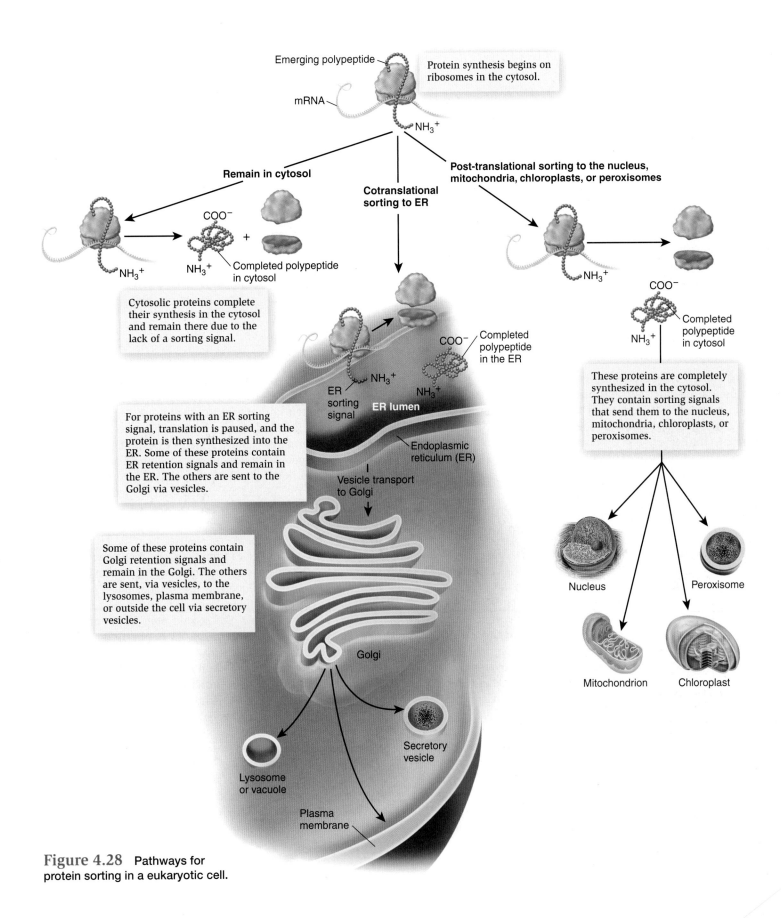

Emerging polypeptide

Protein synthesis begins on ribosomes in the cytosol.

mRNA

NH$_3^+$

Remain in cytosol

Cotranslational sorting to ER

Post-translational sorting to the nucleus, mitochondria, chloroplasts, or peroxisomes

COO$^-$

NH$_3^+$

NH$_3^+$ +

Completed polypeptide in cytosol

NH$_3^+$

COO$^-$

Completed polypeptide in cytosol

NH$_3^+$

Cytosolic proteins complete their synthesis in the cytosol and remain there due to the lack of a sorting signal.

ER sorting signal

Completed polypeptide in the ER

COO$^-$

NH$_3^+$

NH$_3^+$

ER lumen

For proteins with an ER sorting signal, translation is paused, and the protein is then synthesized into the ER. Some of these proteins contain ER retention signals and remain in the ER. The others are sent to the Golgi via vesicles.

Endoplasmic reticulum (ER)

Vesicle transport to Golgi

These proteins are completely synthesized in the cytosol. They contain sorting signals that send them to the nucleus, mitochondria, chloroplasts, or peroxisomes.

Some of these proteins contain Golgi retention signals and remain in the Golgi. The others are sent, via vesicles, to the lysosomes, plasma membrane, or outside the cell via secretory vesicles.

Golgi

Nucleus

Peroxisome

Mitochondrion

Chloroplast

Secretory vesicle

Lysosome or vacuole

Plasma membrane

Figure 4.28 Pathways for protein sorting in a eukaryotic cell.

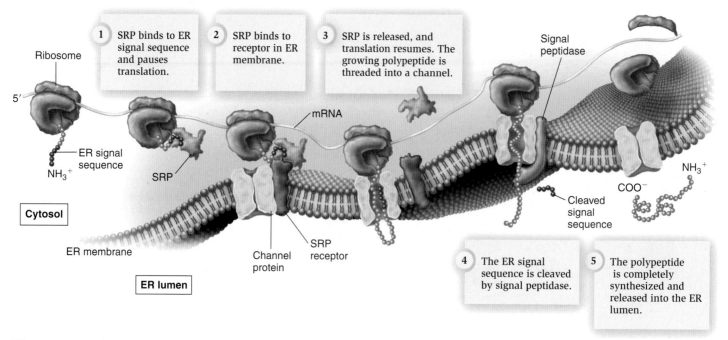

Figure 4.29   First step in cotranslational protein localization: cotranslational sorting.

Concept check: What prevents an ER protein from being completely synthesized in the cytosol?

Finally, the uptake of most proteins into the nucleus, mitochondria, chloroplasts, and peroxisomes occurs after the protein is completely made (that is, completely translated). This is called **post-translational sorting** because sorting does not happen until translation is finished. In this section, we will consider how cells carry out cotranslational and post-translational sorting.

The Cotranslational Sorting of Some Proteins Occurs at the Endoplasmic Reticulum Membrane

The concept of sorting signals in proteins was first proposed by Günter Blobel in the 1970s. Blobel and colleagues discovered a sorting signal in proteins that sends them to the ER membrane, which is the first step in cotranslational sorting (**Figure 4.29**). To be directed to the rough ER membrane, a polypeptide must contain a sorting signal called an **ER signal sequence**, which is a sequence of about 6 to 12 amino acids that are predominantly hydrophobic and usually located near the amino terminus. As the ribosome is making the polypeptide in the cytosol, the ER signal sequence emerges from the ribosome and is recognized by a protein/RNA complex called **signal recognition particle (SRP)**. SRP has two functions. First, it recognizes the ER signal sequence and pauses translation. Second, SRP binds to a receptor in the ER membrane, which docks the ribosome over a channel protein. At this stage, SRP is released and translation resumes. The growing polypeptide is threaded through the channel to cross the ER membrane. In most cases, the ER signal sequence is removed by signal peptidase. If the protein is not a membrane protein, it will be released into the lumen of the ER. In 1999, Blobel won the Nobel Prize for his discovery of sorting signals in proteins. The process shown in Figure 4.29 illustrates another important role of

protein-protein interactions—a series of interactions causes the steps of a process to occur in a specific order.

Some proteins are meant to function in the ER. Such proteins contain ER retention signals in addition to the ER signal sequence. Alternatively, other proteins that are destined for the Golgi, lysosomes, vacuoles, plasma membrane, or secretion must be sorted to these other locations (see Figure 4.28). Such proteins leave the ER and are transported to their correct location. This transport process occurs via vesicles that are formed from one compartment and then move through the cytosol and fuse with another compartment. Vesicles from the ER may go to the Golgi, and then vesicles from the Golgi may go to the lysosomes, vacuoles, or plasma membrane. Sorting signals within proteins' amino acid sequences are responsible for directing them to the correct location.

Figure 4.30 describes the second step in cotranslational sorting, vesicle transport from the ER to the Golgi. A cargo, such as protein molecules, is loaded into a developing vesicle by binding to cargo receptors in the ER membrane. Vesicle formation is facilitated by **coat proteins**, which help a vesicle to bud from a given membrane. As a vesicle forms, other proteins called **v-snares** are incorporated into the vesicle membrane (hence the name v-snare). Many types of v-snares are known to exist; the particular v-snare that is found in a vesicle membrane depends on the type of cargo it carries. After a vesicle is released from one compartment such as the ER, the coat is shed. The vesicle then travels through the cytosol. But how does the vesicle know where to go? The answer is that the v-snares in the vesicle membrane are recognized by **t-snares** in a target membrane. After v-snares recognize t-snares, the vesicle fuses with the membrane containing the t-snares. The recognition between v-snares and t-snares ensures that a vesicle carrying a

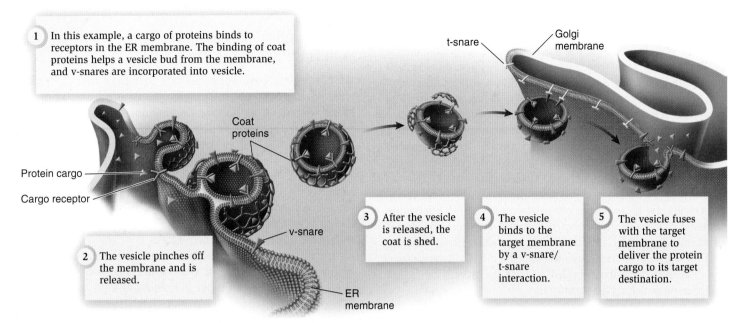

1 In this example, a cargo of proteins binds to receptors in the ER membrane. The binding of coat proteins helps a vesicle bud from the membrane, and v-snares are incorporated into vesicle.

Golgi membrane

t-snare

Coat proteins

Protein cargo

Cargo receptor

v-snare

2 The vesicle pinches off the membrane and is released.

ER membrane

3 After the vesicle is released, the coat is shed.

4 The vesicle binds to the target membrane by a v-snare/ t-snare interaction.

5 The vesicle fuses with the target membrane to deliver the protein cargo to its target destination.

Figure 4.30   Second step in cotranslational protein localization: vesicle transport from the endoplasmic reticulum.

specific cargo moves to the correct target membrane in the cell. Like the sorting of proteins to the ER membrane, the formation and sorting of vesicles also involves a series of protein-protein interactions that cause the steps to occur in a defined manner.

Proteins Are Sorted Post-Translationally to the Nucleus, Peroxisomes, Mitochondria, and Chloroplasts

The organization and function of the nucleus, peroxisomes, and semiautonomous organelles are dependent on the uptake of proteins from the cytosol. Most of their proteins are synthesized

in the cytosol and then taken up into their respective organelles. For example, most proteins involved in ATP synthesis are made in the cytosol and taken up into mitochondria after they have been completely synthesized. For this to occur, a protein must have the appropriate sorting signal as part of its amino acid sequence.

As one example of post-translational sorting, let's consider how a protein is directed to the mitochondrial matrix. Such a protein would have a matrix-targeting sequence as part of its structure, which is a short sequence at the amino terminus with several positively charged amino acids that folds into an α helix. As shown in **Figure 4.31**, the process of protein import into

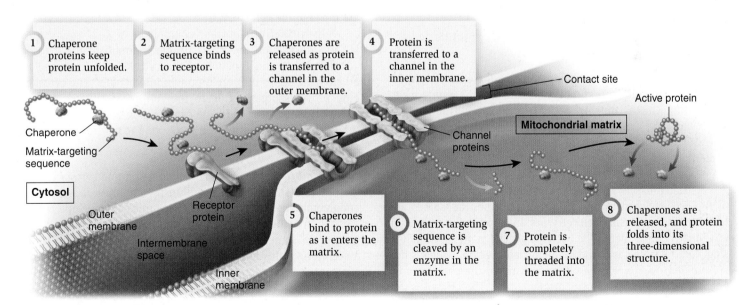

1 Chaperone proteins keep protein unfolded.

2 Matrix-targeting sequence binds to receptor.

3 Chaperones are released as protein is transferred to a channel in the outer membrane.

4 Protein is transferred to a channel in the inner membrane.

Contact site

Active protein

Chaperone

Matrix-targeting sequence

Mitochondrial matrix

Channel proteins

Cytosol

Outer membrane

Receptor protein

Intermembrane space

Inner membrane

5 Chaperones bind to protein as it enters the matrix.

6 Matrix-targeting sequence is cleaved by an enzyme in the matrix.

7 Protein is completely threaded into the matrix.

8 Chaperones are released, and protein folds into its three-dimensional structure.

Figure 4.31   Post-translational sorting of a protein to the mitochondrial matrix.

Concept check: *What do you think would happen if chaperone proteins did not bind to a mitochondrial matrix protein before it was imported into the mitochondrion?*

the matrix involves a series of intricate protein-protein interactions. A protein destined for the mitochondrial matrix is first made in the cytosol, where proteins called **chaperones** keep it in an unfolded state. A receptor protein in the outer mitochondrial membrane recognizes the matrix-targeting sequence. The protein is released from the chaperone as it is transferred to a channel in the outer mitochondrial membrane. Because it is in an unfolded state, the mitochondrial protein can be threaded through this channel, and then through another channel in the inner mitochondrial membrane. These channels lie close to each other at contact sites between the outer and inner membranes. As the protein emerges in the matrix, other chaperone proteins that were already in the matrix continue to keep it unfolded. Eventually, the matrix-targeting sequence is cleaved, and the entire protein is threaded into the matrix. At this stage, the chaperone proteins are released, and the protein can adopt its three-dimensional active structure.

4.7 Systems Biology of Cells: A Summary

We will conclude this chapter by reviewing cell structure and function from a perspective called systems biology. In **systems biology**, researchers view living organisms in terms of their underlying network structure—groups of structural and functional connections—rather than their individual molecular components. A "system" can be anything from a metabolic pathway to a cell, an organ, or even an entire organism. In this section, we focus on the cell as a system. First, we will compare prokaryotic and eukaryotic cells as systems, and then examine the four interconnected parts that make up the system that is the eukaryotic cell.

Bacterial Cells Are Relatively Simple Systems Compared to Eukaryotic Cells

Bacterial cells are relatively small and lack the extensive internal compartmentalization characteristic of eukaryotic cells (**Table 4.2**). On the outside, bacterial cells are surrounded by a cell wall, and many species have flagella. Animal cells lack a cell wall, and only certain cell types have flagella or cilia. Like bacteria, plant cells also have cell walls but only rarely have flagella.

As stated earlier in this chapter, the cytoplasm is the region of the cell enclosed by the plasma membrane. Ribosomes are found in the cytoplasm of all cell types. In bacteria, the cytoplasm is a single compartment. The bacterial genetic material, usually a single chromosome, is found in the nucleoid region, which is not surrounded by a membrane. By comparison, the cytoplasm of eukaryotic cells is highly compartmentalized. The cytosol is the area that surrounds many different types of membrane-bound organelles. For example, eukaryotic chromosomes are found in the nucleus that is surrounded by a double membrane. In addition, all eukaryotic cells have an endomembrane system and mitochondria, and plant cells also have chloroplasts.

A Eukaryotic Cell Is a System with Four Interacting Parts

We can view a eukaryotic cell as a system of four interacting parts: the interior of the nucleus, the cytosol, the endomembrane system, and the semiautonomous organelles (**Figure 4.32**). These four regions play a role in their own structure and organization, as well as the structure and organization of the entire cell.

Nucleus The nucleus houses the genome. Earlier in this chapter, we learned how the genome plays a key role in producing the proteome through the process of gene expression. The collection of proteins that a cell makes is primarily responsible for the structure and function of the entire cell. Gene regulation, which largely occurs in the cell nucleus, is very important in creating specific cell types and enabling cells to respond to environmental changes. The nucleus itself is organized by a collection of filamentous proteins called the nuclear matrix.

Cytosol The cytosol is the region that is enclosed by the plasma membrane but outside of the organelles. It is an important coordination center for cell function and organization. Along with the plasma membrane, the cytosol coordinates responses to the environment. Factors in the environment may stimulate signaling pathways in the cytosol that affect the functions of cellular proteins and the regulation of genes in the cell nucleus.

The cytosol also has a large impact on cell structure because it is the compartment where many small molecules are metabolized in the cell. This region receives molecules that are taken up from the environment. In addition, many pathways for the synthesis and breakdown of cellular molecules are found in the cytosol, and pathways in organelles are often regulated by events there. Most of the proteins that constitute the proteome are made in the cytosol.

A particularly important component of cell organization is the cytoskeleton, which is primarily found in the cytosol. The formation and function of the cytoskeleton is caused by an amazing series of protein-protein interactions. The cytoskeleton provides organization to the cell and facilitates cellular movements. In most cells, the cytoskeleton is a dynamic structure, enabling its composition to respond to environmental and developmental changes.

Endomembrane System The endomembrane system can be viewed as a smaller system within the confines of a cell. The endomembrane system includes the nuclear envelope, endoplasmic reticulum (ER), Golgi apparatus, lysosomes, vacuoles, peroxisomes, and plasma membrane. This system forms a secretory pathway that is crucial in the movement of larger substances, such as carbohydrates and proteins, out of the cell. The export of carbohydrates and proteins plays a key role in the organization of materials that surround cells.

The endomembrane system also contributes to the overall structure and organization of eukaryotic cells in other ways. The ER and Golgi are involved in protein sorting and in the attachment of carbohydrates to lipids and proteins. In addition,

Table 4.2   A Comparison of Cell Complexity Among Bacterial, Animal, and Plant Cells

Structures	Bacteria	Animal cells	Plant cells
Extracellular structures			
Cell wall*	Present	Absent	Present
Flagella/cilia	Flagella sometimes present	Cilia or flagella present on certain cell types	Rarely present**
Plasma membrane	Present	Present	Present
Interior structures			
Cytoplasm	Usually a single compartment inside the plasma membrane	Composed of membrane-bound organelles that are surrounded by the cytosol	Composed of membrane-bound organelles that are surrounded by the cytosol
Ribosomes	Present	Present	Present
Chromosomes and their location	Typically one circular chromosome per nucleoid region; nucleoid region is not a separate compartment	Multiple linear chromosomes in the nucleus; nucleus is surrounded by a double membrane. Mitochondria also have chromosomes.	Multiple linear chromosomes in the nucleus; nucleus is surrounded by a double membrane. Mitochondria and chloroplasts also have chromosomes.
Endomembrane system	Absent	Present	Present
Mitochondria	Absent	Present	Present
Chloroplasts	Absent	Absent	Present

*The biochemical composition of bacterial cell walls is very different from plant cell walls.
**Some plant species produce sperm cells with flagella, but flowering plants produce sperm within pollen grains that lack flagella.

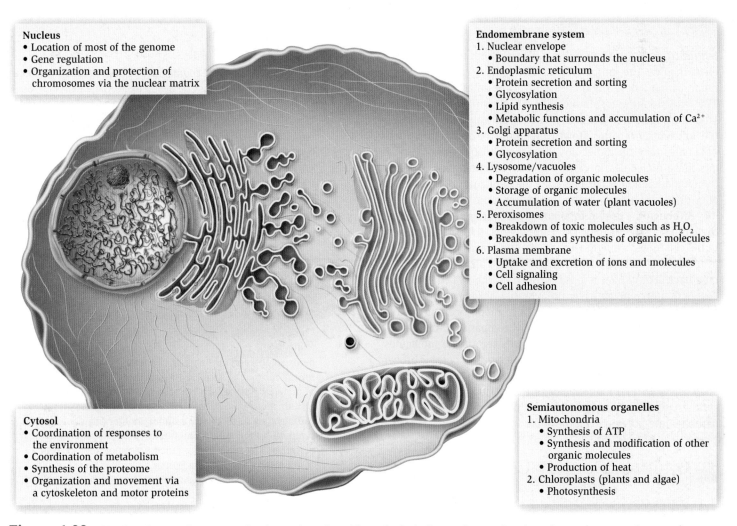

Nucleus
- Location of most of the genome
- Gene regulation
- Organization and protection of chromosomes via the nuclear matrix

Endomembrane system
1. Nuclear envelope
   - Boundary that surrounds the nucleus
2. Endoplasmic reticulum
   - Protein secretion and sorting
   - Glycosylation
   - Lipid synthesis
   - Metabolic functions and accumulation of Ca^{2+}
3. Golgi apparatus
   - Protein secretion and sorting
   - Glycosylation
4. Lysosome/vacuoles
   - Degradation of organic molecules
   - Storage of organic molecules
   - Accumulation of water (plant vacuoles)
5. Peroxisomes
   - Breakdown of toxic molecules such as H_2O_2
   - Breakdown and synthesis of organic molecules
6. Plasma membrane
   - Uptake and excretion of ions and molecules
   - Cell signaling
   - Cell adhesion

Cytosol
- Coordination of responses to the environment
- Coordination of metabolism
- Synthesis of the proteome
- Organization and movement via a cytoskeleton and motor proteins

Semiautonomous organelles
1. Mitochondria
   - Synthesis of ATP
   - Synthesis and modification of other organic molecules
   - Production of heat
2. Chloroplasts (plants and algae)
   - Photosynthesis

Figure 4.32   The four interacting parts of eukaryotic cells.   These include the nucleus, cytosol, endomembrane system, and semiautonomous organelles.

most of a cell's lipids are made in the smooth ER membrane and distributed to other parts of the cell. The smooth ER also plays a role in certain metabolic functions, such as the elimination of alcohol, and is important in the accumulation of Ca^{2+}.

Another important function of the endomembrane system that serves the needs of the entire cell is the breakdown and storage of organic molecules. Lysosomes in animal cells and vacuoles in the cells of other organisms assist in breaking down various types of macromolecules. The building blocks are then recycled back to the cytosol and used to construct new macromolecules. Vacuoles often play a role in the storage of organic molecules such as carbohydrates, proteins, and fats. In plants, vacuoles may store large amounts of water. Finally, peroxisomes are involved in the breakdown and synthesis of organic molecules and can degrade toxic molecules such as hydrogen peroxide.

The plasma membrane is also considered a part of the endomembrane system. It plays an important role as a selective barrier that allows the uptake of nutrients and the excretion of waste products. The plasma membrane also contains different types of receptors that provide a way for a cell to sense changes in its environment and communicate with other cells. Finally, in animals, proteins in the plasma membrane promote the adhesion of adjacent cells.

Semiautonomous Organelles The semiautonomous organelles include the mitochondria and chloroplasts. Regarding organization, these organelles tend to be rather independent. They exist in the cytosol much like a bacterium would grow in a laboratory medium. Whereas a bacterium would take up essential nutrients from the growth medium, the semiautonomous organelles take up molecules from the cytosol. The organelles use these molecules to carry out their functions and maintain their organization. Like bacteria, the semiautonomous organelles divide by binary fission to produce more of themselves.

Although the semiautonomous organelles rely on the rest of the cell for many of their key components, they also give back to the cell in ways that are vital to maintaining cell organization. Mitochondria take up organic molecules from the cytosol and give back ATP, which is used throughout the cell to drive processes that are energetically unfavorable. This energy is crucial for cell organization. Mitochondria also modify certain organic molecules and may produce heat. By comparison, the chloroplasts capture light energy and synthesize organic molecules. These organic molecules also store energy and can be broken down when energy is needed. In addition, organic molecules, such as sugars and amino acids, are used as building blocks to synthesize many different types of cellular molecules, such as carbohydrate polymers and proteins.

▌ Summary of Key Concepts

4.1 Microscopy

- Three important parameters in microscopy are magnification, resolution, and contrast. A light microscope utilizes light for

illumination, whereas an electron microscope uses an electron beam. Transmission electron microscopy (TEM) provides the best resolution of any form of microscopy, and scanning electron microscopy (SEM) produces an image of a three-dimensional surface. (Figures 4.1, 4.2, 4.3)

4.2 Overview of Cell Structure

- Cell structure relies on four factors: matter, energy, organization, and information. Every living organism has a genome. The genes within the genome contain the information to create cells with particular structures and functions.

- We can classify all forms of life into two categories based on cell structure: prokaryotes and eukaryotes.

- The prokaryotes have a relatively simple structure and lack a membrane-enclosed nucleus. The two categories of prokaryotes are bacteria and archaea. Structures in prokaryotic cells include the plasma membrane, cytoplasm, nucleoid region, and ribosomes. Prokaryotes also have a cell wall and many have a glycocalyx. (Figure 4.4)

- Eukaryotic cells are compartmentalized into organelles and contain a nucleus that houses most of their DNA. (Figures 4.5, 4.6, 4.7)

- The proteome of a cell determines its structure and function.

4.3 The Cytosol

- The cytosol is a central coordinating region for many metabolic activities of eukaryotic cells, including polypeptide synthesis. (Figures 4.8, 4.9)

- The cytoskeleton is a network of three different types of protein filaments: microtubules, intermediate filaments, and actin filaments. Microtubules are important for cell shape, organization, and movement. Intermediate filaments help maintain cell shape and rigidity. Actin filaments support the plasma membrane and play a key role in cell strength, shape, and movement. (Table 4.1, Figures 4.10, 4.11, 4.12, 4.13)

4.4 The Nucleus and Endomembrane System

- The primary function of the nucleus involves the organization and expression of the cell's genetic material. A second important function is the assembly of ribosomes in the nucleolus. (Figures 4.14, 4.15, 4.16)

- The endomembrane system includes the nuclear envelope, endoplasmic reticulum, Golgi apparatus, lysosomes, vacuoles, peroxisomes, and plasma membrane. The rough endoplasmic reticulum (rough ER) plays a key role in the initial sorting of proteins. The smooth endoplasmic reticulum (smooth ER) functions in metabolic processes such as detoxification, carbohydrate metabolism, accumulation of calcium ions, and synthesis and modification of lipids. The Golgi apparatus performs three overlapping functions: processing, protein sorting, and secretion. Lysosomes degrade macromolecules and help digest substances taken up from outside the cell (endocytosis) and inside the cell. (Figures 4.17, 4.18)

- Palade's pulse-chase experiments demonstrated that secreted proteins move sequentially through the ER and Golgi apparatus. (Figure 4.19)

- Types and functions of vacuoles include central vacuoles; contractile vacuoles; and phagocytic, or food, vacuoles. (Figure 4.20)

- Peroxisomes catalyze certain chemical reactions, typically those that break down molecules by removing hydrogen or adding oxygen. Peroxisomes usually contain enzymes involved in the metabolism of fats and amino acids. Peroxisomes are made via budding from the ER, followed by maturation and division. (Figure 4.21)

- Proteins in the plasma membrane perform many important roles that affect activities inside the cell, including membrane transport, cell signaling, and cell adhesion. (Figure 4.22)

4.5 Semiautonomous Organelles

- Mitochondria and chloroplasts are considered semiautonomous because they can grow and divide, but they still depend on other parts of the cell for their internal components. (Figure 4.23)

- Mitochondria produce most of a cell's ATP, which is utilized by many proteins to carry out their functions. Other mitochondrial functions include the synthesis, modification, and breakdown of cellular molecules and the generation of heat in specialized fat cells. (Figure 4.24)

- Chloroplasts, which are found in nearly all species of plants and algae, carry out photosynthesis. (Figure 4.25)

- Plastids, such as chloroplasts, chromoplasts, and amyloplasts, differ in their function and the pigments they store.

- Mitochondria and chloroplasts contain their own genetic material and divide by binary fission. (Figure 4.26)

- According to the endosymbiosis theory, mitochondria and chloroplasts have evolved from bacteria that took up residence in early eukaryotic cells. (Figure 4.27)

4.6 Protein Sorting to Organelles

- Eukaryotic proteins are sorted to their correct cellular destination. (Figure 4.28)

- The cotranslational sorting of ER, Golgi, lysosomal, vacuolar, plasma membrane, and secreted proteins involves sorting signals and vesicle transport. (Figures 4.29, 4.30)

- Most proteins are sorted to the nucleus, mitochondria, chloroplasts, and peroxisomes post-translationally. (Figure 4.31)

4.7 Systems Biology of Cells: A Summary

- In systems biology, researchers study living organisms in terms of their structural and functional connections, rather than their individual molecular components.

- Prokaryotic and eukaryotic cells differ in their levels of organization. (Table 4.2)

- In eukaryotic cells, four regions—the nucleus, cytosol, endomembrane system, and semiautonomous organelles— work together to produce dynamic organization. (Figure 4.32)

Assess and Discuss

Test Yourself

1. The cell doctrine states
   a. all living things are composed of cells.
   b. cells are the smallest units of living organisms.
   c. new cells come from pre-existing cells by cell division.
   d. all of the above.
   e. a and b only.

2. When using microscopes, the resolution refers to
   a. the ratio between the size of the image produced by the microscope and the actual size of the object.
   b. the degree to which a particular structure looks different from other structures around it.
   c. how well a structure takes up certain dyes.
   d. the ability to observe two adjacent objects as being distinct from each other.
   e. the degree to which the image is magnified.

3. If a motor protein were held in place and a cytoskeletal filament were free to move, what type of motion would occur when the motor protein was active?
   a. The motor protein would "walk" along the filament.
   b. The filament would move.
   c. The filament would bend.
   d. All of the above would happen.
   e. Only b and c would happen.

4. The process of polypeptide synthesis is called
   a. metabolism.   d. hydrolysis.
   b. transcription.   e. both c and d.
   c. translation.

5. Each of the following is part of the endomembrane system except
   a. the nuclear envelope.   d. lysosomes.
   b. the endoplasmic reticulum. e. mitochondria.
   c. the Golgi apparatus.

6. Vesicle transport occurs between the ER and the Golgi in both directions. Let's suppose a researcher added a drug to cells that inhibited vesicle transport from the Golgi to the ER but did not affect vesicle transport from the ER to the Golgi. If you observed cells microscopically after the drug was added, what would you expect to see happen over the course of 1 hour?
   a. The ER would get smaller, and the Golgi would get larger.
   b. The ER would get larger, and the Golgi would get smaller.
   c. The ER and Golgi would stay the same size.
   d. Both the ER and Golgi would get larger.
   e. Both the ER and Golgi would get smaller.

7. Functions of the smooth endoplasmic reticulum include
   a. detoxification of harmful organic molecules.
   b. metabolism of carbohydrates.
   c. protein sorting.
   d. all of the above.
   e. a and b only.

8. The central vacuole in many plant cells is important for
   a. storage.
   b. photosynthesis.
   c. structural support.
   d. all of the above.
   e. a and c only.

9. Let's suppose an abnormal protein contains three targeting sequences: an ER signal sequence, an ER retention sequence, and a mitochondrial-matrix targeting sequence. The ER retention sequence is supposed to keep proteins within the ER. Where would you expect this abnormal protein to go? Note: Think carefully about the timing of events in protein sorting and which events occur cotranslationally and which occur post-translationally.
   a. It would go to the ER.
   b. It would go the mitochondria.
   c. It would go to both the ER and mitochondria equally.
   d. It would remain in the cytosol.
   e. It would be secreted.

10. Which of the following observations would <u>not</u> be considered evidence for the endosymbiosis theory?
   a. Mitochondria and chloroplasts have genomes that resemble smaller versions of bacterial genomes.
   b. Mitochondria, chloroplasts, and bacteria all divide by binary fission.
   c. Mitochondria, chloroplasts, and bacteria all have ribosomes.
   d. Mitochondria, chloroplasts, and bacteria all have similar sizes and shapes.
   e. all of the above

Conceptual Questions

1. Describe two specific ways that protein-protein interactions are involved with cell structure or cell function.

2. Explain how motor proteins and cytoskeletal filaments can interact to promote three different types of movements: movement of a cargo, movement of a filament, and bending of a filament.

3. Describe the functions of the Golgi apparatus.

Collaborative Questions

1. Discuss the roles of the genome and proteome in determining cell structure and function.

2. Discuss and draw the structural relationship between the nucleus, the rough endoplasmic reticulum, and the Golgi apparatus.

Online Resource

www.brookerbiology.com

Stay a step ahead in your studies with animations that bring concepts to life and practice tests to assess your understanding. Your instructor may also recommend the interactive ebook, individualized learning tools, and more.

Membrane Structure, Synthesis, and Transport

5

When he was 28, Andrew began to develop a combination of symptoms that included fatigue, joint pain, abdominal pain, and a loss of sex drive. His doctor conducted some tests and discovered that Andrew had abnormally high levels of iron in his body. Iron is a mineral found in many foods. Andrew was diagnosed with a genetic disease called hemochromatosis, which caused him to absorb more iron than he needed. This was due to an overactive protein involved in the transport of iron through the membranes of intestinal cells and into the body. Unfortunately, when the human body takes up too much iron, it is stored in body tissues, especially the liver, heart, pancreas, and joints. The extra iron can damage a person's organs. In Andrew's case, the disease was caught relatively early, and treatment—which includes a modification in diet along with medication that inhibits the absorption of iron—prevented more severe symptoms. Without treatment, however, hemochromatosis can cause a person's organs to fail. Later signs and symptoms include arthritis, liver disease, heart failure, and skin discoloration.

The disease hemochromatosis illustrates the importance of membranes in regulating the traffic of ions and molecules into and out of cells. Cellular membranes, also known as biological membranes or biomembranes, are an essential characteristic of all living cells. The **plasma membrane** separates the internal contents of a cell from its external environment. With such a role, you might imagine that the plasma membrane would be thick and rigid. Remarkably, the opposite is true. All cellular membranes, including the plasma membrane, are thin (typically 5–10 nm) and somewhat fluid. It would take 5,000 to 10,000 membranes stacked on top of each other to equal the thickness of the page you are reading! Despite their thinness, membranes are impressively dynamic structures that effectively maintain the separation between a cell and its surroundings. Membranes provide an interface to carry out many vital cellular activities (**Table 5.1**).

In this chapter, we will begin by considering the components that provide the structure of membranes and then explore how they are made. Finally, we will examine one of a membrane's primary functions, membrane transport. Biomembranes regulate the traffic of substances into and out of the cell and its organelles.

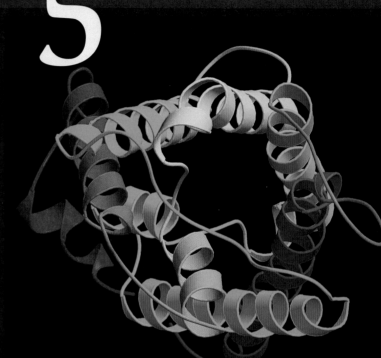

A model for the structure of aquaporin. This protein, found in the plasma membrane of many cell types, such as red blood cells and plant cells, allows the rapid movement of water molecules across the membrane.

Table 5.1	Important Functions of Cellular Membranes
Function	
Selective uptake and export of ions and molecules	
Cell compartmentalization	
Protein sorting	
Anchoring of the cytoskeleton	
Production of energy intermediates such as ATP and NADPH	
Cell signaling	
Cell and nuclear division	
Adhesion of cells to each other and to the extracellular matrix	

5.1 Membrane Structure

As we progress through this textbook, a theme that will emerge is that structure determines function. This paradigm is particularly interesting when we consider how the structure of cellular membranes enables them to compartmentalize the cell while selectively importing and exporting vital substances. The two primary components of membranes are phospholipids, which form the basic matrix of a membrane, and proteins, which are embedded in the membrane or loosely attached to its surface. A third component is carbohydrate, which may be attached to membrane lipids and proteins. In this section, we will be mainly concerned with the organization of these components to form a biological membrane and how they are important in the overall function of membranes. We will also consider some interesting experiments that provided insight into the dynamic properties of membranes.

Biological Membranes Are a Mosaic of Lipids, Proteins, and Carbohydrates

Figure 5.1 shows the biochemical organization of cellular membranes, which are similar in composition among all living organisms. The framework of the membrane is the **phospholipid bilayer**, which consists of two layers of phospholipids. The most abundant lipids found in membranes are the phospholipids. Recall from Chapter 3 that phospholipids are **amphipathic** molecules. They have a hydrophobic (water-fearing) or nonpolar region, and also a hydrophilic (water-loving) or polar region. The hydrophobic tails of the lipids, referred to as fatty acyl tails, form the interior of the membrane, and the hydrophilic head groups are on the surface.

Cellular membranes also contain proteins, and most membranes have carbohydrates attached to lipids and proteins. The relative amounts of lipids, proteins, and carbohydrates vary among different membranes. Some membranes, such as the inner mitochondrial membrane, have relatively little

carbohydrate, whereas the plasma membrane of eukaryotic cells can have a large amount. A typical membrane found in cell organelles contains 50% protein by mass; the remainder is mostly lipids. However, the smaller lipid molecules outnumber the proteins by about 50 to 1 because the mass of one lipid molecule is much less than the mass of a protein.

Overall, the membrane is considered a mosaic of lipid, protein, and carbohydrate molecules. The membrane structure illustrated in Figure 5.1 is referred to as the **fluid-mosaic model**, originally proposed by S. Jonathan Singer and Garth Nicolson in 1972. As discussed later, the membrane exhibits properties that resemble a fluid because lipids and proteins can move relative to each other within the membrane. **Table 5.2** summarizes some of the historical experiments that led to the formulation of the fluid-mosaic model.

Half of a phospholipid bilayer is termed a **leaflet**. Each leaflet faces a different region. For example, the plasma membrane contains a cytosolic leaflet and an extracellular leaflet (see Figure 5.1). With regard to lipid composition, the two leaflets of cellular membranes are highly asymmetrical. Certain types of lipids may be more abundant in one leaflet compared to the other. A striking asymmetry occurs with glycolipids—lipids with carbohydrate attached. These are found primarily in the extracellular leaflet such that the carbohydrate portion of a glycolipid protrudes into the extracellular medium.

Membrane Proteins Associate with Membranes in Different Ways

Although the phospholipid bilayer forms the basic foundation of cellular membranes, the protein component carries out many

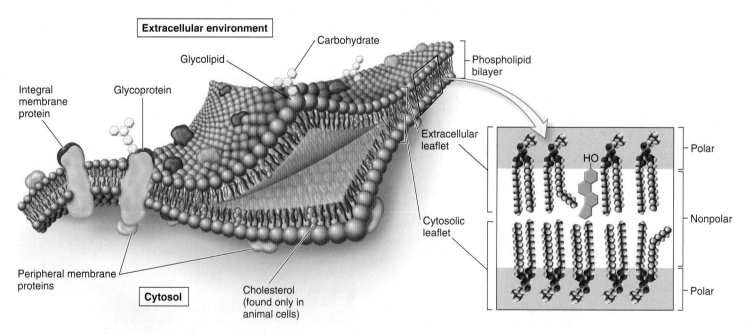

Figure 5.1 **Fluid-mosaic model of membrane structure.**   The basic framework of a plasma membrane is a phospholipid bilayer. Proteins may span the membrane and may be bound on the surface to other proteins or to lipids. Proteins and lipids, which have covalently bound carbohydrate, are called glycoproteins and glycolipids, respectively.

Table 5.2	Historical Developments That Led to the Formulation of the Fluid-Mosaic Model

Date	Description
1917	Irving Langmuir made artificial membranes experimentally by creating a monolayer of lipids on the surface of water. The polar heads interacted with water, and nonpolar tails projected into the air.
1925	Evert Gorter and F. Grendel proposed that lipids form bilayers around cells. This was based on measurements of lipid content enclosing red blood cells that showed there was just enough lipid to surround the cell with two layers.
1935	Because proteins were also found in membranes, Hugh Davson and James Danielli proposed incorrectly that a phospholipid bilayer was sandwiched between two layers of protein.
1950s	Electron microscopy studies carried out by J.D. Robertson and others revealed that membranes look like a train track—two dark lines separated by a light space. Initially, these results were misinterpreted. Researchers thought the two dark lines were layers of proteins and the light area was the phospholipid bilayer. Later, it was correctly determined that the dark lines in these experiments are the phospholipid heads, which were heavily stained, and the light region is their phospholipid tails.
1966	Using freeze fracture electron microscopy (described later in this chapter), Daniel Branton concluded that membranes are bilayers because the freeze fracture procedure splits membranes in half, thus revealing proteins in the two membrane leaflets.
1972	S. Jonathan Singer and Garth Nicolson proposed the fluid-mosaic model described in Figure 5.1. Their model was consistent with the observation that membrane proteins are globular, and some are known to span the phospholipid bilayer and project from both sides.

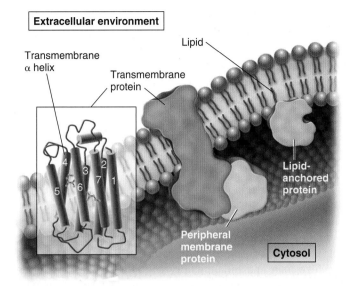

Figure 5.2 **Types of membrane proteins.** Integral membrane proteins are of two types: transmembrane proteins and lipid-anchored proteins. Peripheral membrane proteins are noncovalently bound to the hydrophilic regions of integral membrane proteins or to the polar head groups of lipids. Inset: The protein shown in the inset contains seven transmembrane segments in an α helix structure. The transmembrane α helices are depicted as cylinders. This particular protein, bacteriorhodopsin, functions as an ion pump in halophilic (salt-loving) archaea.

other functions. Some of these functions were considered in Chapter 4. For example, we examined how membrane proteins in the smooth ER membrane function as enzymes that break down glycogen. Later in this chapter, we will explore how membrane proteins are involved in transporting ions and molecules across membranes. Other key functions of membrane proteins are examined in later chapters, including ATP synthesis (Chapter 7), photosynthesis (Chapter 8), cell signaling (Chapter 9), and cell-to-cell adhesion (Chapter 10).

Membrane proteins have different ways of associating with a membrane (**Figure 5.2**). An **integral membrane protein**, also called an intrinsic membrane protein, cannot be released from the membrane unless the membrane is dissolved with an organic solvent or detergent—in other words, you would have to disrupt the integrity of the membrane to remove it. The most common type of integral membrane protein is a **transmembrane protein**, which has one or more regions that are physically inserted into the hydrophobic region of the phospholipid bilayer. These regions, the **transmembrane segments**, are stretches of nonpolar amino acids that span or traverse the membrane from one leaflet to the

other. In most transmembrane proteins, each transmembrane segment is folded into an α helix structure. Such a segment is stable in a membrane because the nonpolar amino acids can interact favorably with the hydrophobic fatty acyl tails of the lipid molecules.

A second type of integral membrane protein, known as a **lipid-anchored protein**, has a lipid molecule that is covalently attached to an amino acid side chain within the protein. The fatty acyl tails are inserted into the hydrophobic portion of the membrane and thereby keep the protein firmly attached to the membrane.

Peripheral membrane proteins, also called extrinsic proteins, are another category of membrane protein. They do not interact with the hydrophobic interior of the phospholipid bilayer. Instead, they are noncovalently bound to regions of integral membrane proteins that project out from the membrane, or they are bound to the polar head groups of phospholipids. Peripheral membrane proteins are typically bound to the membrane by hydrogen and/or ionic bonds. For this reason, they usually can be removed from the membrane experimentally by varying the pH or salt concentration.

Genomes & Proteomes Connection

Approximately 25% of All Genes Encode Transmembrane Proteins

Membrane proteins participate in some of the most important and interesting cellular processes. These include transport, energy transduction, cell signaling, secretion, cell recognition, metabolism, and cell-to-cell contact. Research studies have revealed that cells devote a sizeable fraction of their energy and metabolic machinery to the synthesis of membrane proteins. These proteins are particularly important in human medicine—approximately 70% of all medications exert their effects by binding to membrane proteins. Examples include the drugs aspirin, ibuprofen, and acetaminophen, which are widely used to relieve pain and inflammatory conditions such as arthritis. These drugs bind to cyclooxygenase, a protein in the ER membrane that is necessary for the synthesis of chemicals that play a role in inflammation and pain sensation.

Because membrane proteins are so important biologically and medically, researchers have analyzed the genomes of many species and asked the question, What percentage of genes encodes transmembrane proteins? To answer this question, they have developed tools to predict the likelihood that a gene encodes a transmembrane protein. For example, the occurrence of transmembrane α helices can be predicted from the amino acid sequence of a protein. All 20 amino acids can be ranked according to their tendency to enter a hydrophobic or hydrophilic environment. With these values, the amino acid sequence of a protein can be analyzed using computer software to determine the average hydrophobicity of short amino acid sequences within the protein. A stretch of 18 to 20 amino acids in an α helix is long enough to span the membrane. If such a stretch contains a high percentage of hydrophobic amino acids, it is predicted to be a transmembrane α helix. However, such computer predictions must eventually be verified by experimentation.

Using a computer approach, many research groups have attempted to calculate the percentage of genes that encode transmembrane proteins in various species. **Table 5.3** shows the results of one such study. The estimated percentage of transmembrane proteins is substantial: 20–30% of all genes may encode transmembrane proteins. This trend is found throughout all domains of life, including archaea, bacteria, and eukaryotes. For example, about 30% of human genes encode transmembrane proteins. With a genome size of 20,000 to 25,000 different genes, the total number of genes that encode different transmembrane proteins is estimated at 6,000 to 7,500. The functions of many of them have yet to be determined. Identifying their functions will help researchers gain a better understanding of human biology. Likewise, medical researchers and pharmaceutical companies are interested in the identification of new transmembrane proteins that could be targets for effective new medications.

Table 5.3 Estimated Percentage of Genes That Encode Transmembrane Proteins*

Organism	Percentage of genes that encode transmembrane proteins
Archaea	
Archaeoglobus fulgidus	24.2
Methanococcus jannaschii	20.4
Pyrococcus horikoshii	29.9
Bacteria	
Escherichia coli	29.9
Bacillus subtilis	29.2
Haemophilus influenzae	25.3
Eukaryotes	
Homo sapiens	29.7
Drosophila melanogaster	24.9
Arabidopsis thaliana	30.5
Saccharomyces cerevisiae	28.2

*Data from Stevens and Arkin (2000) *Proteins: Structure, Function, and Genetics* 39: 417–420. While the numbers may vary due to different computer programs and estimation techniques, the same general trends have been observed in other similar studies.

Membranes Are Semifluid

Let's now turn our attention to the dynamic properties of membranes. Although a membrane provides a critical interface between a cell and its environment, it is not a solid, rigid structure. Rather, biomembranes exhibit properties of **fluidity**, which means that individual molecules remain in close association yet have the ability to readily move within the membrane. Though membranes are often described as fluid, it is more appropriate to say they are **semifluid**. In a fluid substance, molecules can move in three dimensions. By comparison, most phospholipids can rotate freely around their long axes and move laterally within the membrane leaflet (**Figure 5.3a**). This type of motion is considered two-dimensional, which means it occurs within the plane of the membrane. Because rotational and lateral movements keep the fatty acyl tails within the hydrophobic interior, such movements are energetically favorable. At 37°C, a typical lipid molecule exchanges places with its neighbors about 10^7 times per second, and it can move several micrometers per second. At this rate, a lipid could traverse the length of a bacterial cell (approximately 1 μm) in only 1 second and the length of a typical animal cell in 10–20 seconds.

In contrast to rotational and lateral movements, the "flip-flop" of lipids from one leaflet to the opposite leaflet does not occur spontaneously. Energetically, such movements are unfavorable because the polar head of a phospholipid would have to be transported through the hydrophobic interior of the membrane. How are lipids moved from one leaflet to the other? The transport of lipids between leaflets requires the action of the enzyme flippase, which provides energy from the hydrolysis of ATP (**Figure 5.3b**).

Although most lipids tend to diffuse rotationally and laterally within the plane of the lipid bilayer, researchers have discovered that certain types of lipids in animal cells tend to strongly

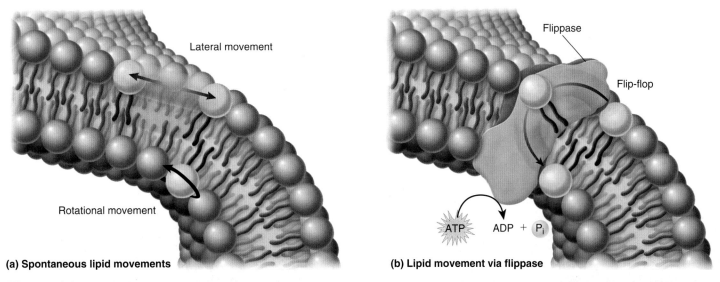

Figure 5.3 **Semifluidity of the lipid bilayer.** **(a)** Spontaneous movements in the bilayer. Lipids can rotate (that is, move 360°) and move laterally (for example, from left to right in the plane of the bilayer). **(b)** Flip-flop does not happen spontaneously, because the polar head group would have to pass through the hydrophobic region of the bilayer. Instead, the enzyme flippase uses ATP to flip phospholipids from one leaflet to the other.

Concept check: *In an animal cell, how can changes in lipid composition affect membrane fluidity?*

associate with each other to form structures called lipid rafts. As the term raft suggests, a **lipid raft** is a group of lipids that float together as a unit within a larger sea of lipids. Lipid rafts have a lipid composition that differs from the surrounding membrane. For example, they usually have a high amount of cholesterol. In addition, lipid rafts may contain unique sets of lipid-anchored proteins and transmembrane proteins. The functional importance of lipid rafts is the subject of a large amount of current research. Lipid rafts may play an important role in endocytosis (discussed later in this chapter) and cell signaling (Chapter 9).

Lipid Composition Affects Membrane Fluidity

The biochemical properties of phospholipids have a profound effect on the fluidity of the phospholipid bilayer. One key factor is the length of fatty acyl tails, which range from 14 to 24 carbon atoms, with 18 to 20 carbons being the most common. Shorter acyl tails are less likely to interact with each other, which makes the membrane more fluid. A second important factor is the presence of double bonds in the acyl tails. When a double bond is present, the lipid is said to be **unsaturated** with respect to the number of hydrogens that can be bound to the carbon atoms (refer back to Figure 3.10). A double bond creates a kink in the fatty acyl tail (see inset to Figure 5.1), making it more difficult for neighboring tails to interact and making the bilayer more fluid. As described in Chapter 3, unsaturated lipids tend to be more liquid compared to saturated lipids that often form solids at room temperature (refer back to Figure 3.11).

A third factor affecting fluidity is the presence of cholesterol, which is a short and rigid planar molecule produced by animal cells (see inset to Figure 5.1). Plant cell membranes contain phytosterols that resemble cholesterol in their chemical structure.

Cholesterol tends to stabilize membranes; its effects depend on temperature. At higher temperatures, such as those observed in mammals that maintain a constant body temperature, cholesterol makes the membrane less fluid. At lower temperatures, such as icy water, cholesterol has the opposite effect. It makes the membrane more fluid and prevents it from freezing.

An optimal level of bilayer fluidity is essential for normal cell function, growth, and division. If a membrane is too fluid, which may occur at higher temperatures, it can become leaky. However, if a membrane becomes too solid, which may occur at lower temperatures, the functioning of membrane proteins will be inhibited. How can organisms cope with changes in temperature? The cells of many species adapt to changes in temperature by altering the lipid composition of their membranes. For example, when the water temperature drops, the cells of certain fish will incorporate more cholesterol in their membranes. If a plant cell is exposed to high temperatures for many hours or days, it will alter its lipid composition to have longer fatty acyl tails and fewer double bonds.

Membrane Proteins May Diffuse in the Plane of the Membrane or Be Restricted in Their Movement

Like lipids, many transmembrane proteins may rotate and laterally move throughout the plane of a membrane. Because transmembrane proteins are larger than lipids, they move within the membrane at a much slower rate. Flip-flop of transmembrane proteins does not occur because the proteins also contain hydrophilic regions that project out from the phospholipid bilayer. It would be energetically unfavorable for the hydrophilic regions of membrane proteins to pass through the hydrophobic portion of the phospholipid bilayer.

Researchers can examine the lateral movements of lipids and transmembrane proteins by a variety of methods. In 1970, Larry Frye and Michael Edidin conducted an experiment that verified the lateral movement of transmembrane proteins (Figure 5.4). Mouse and human cells were mixed together and exposed to agents that caused them to fuse with each other. Some cells were cooled to 0°C, while others were incubated at 37°C before being cooled. Both sets of cells were then exposed to fluorescently labeled antibodies that became specifically bound to a mouse transmembrane protein called H-2. The fluorescent label was observed with a fluorescence microscope. If the cells were maintained at 0°C, a temperature that greatly inhibits lateral movement, the fluorescence was seen on only one side of the fused cell. However, if the cells were incubated for several hours at 37°C and then cooled to 0°C, the fluorescence was distributed throughout the plasma membrane of the fused cell. This occurred because the higher temperature allowed the lateral movement of the H-2 protein throughout the fused cell.

Unlike the example shown in Figure 5.4, not all transmembrane proteins are capable of rotational and lateral movement. Depending on the cell type, 10–70% of membrane proteins may be restricted in their movement. Transmembrane proteins may be bound to components of the cytoskeleton, which restricts the proteins from moving (Figure 5.5). Also, membrane proteins may be attached to molecules that are outside the cell, such as the interconnected network of proteins that forms the extracellular matrix of animal cells.

Glycosylation of Lipids and Proteins Serves a Variety of Cellular Functions

As mentioned earlier, the third constituent of cellular membranes is carbohydrate. **Glycosylation** refers to the process of covalently attaching a carbohydrate to a lipid or protein. When a carbohydrate is attached to a lipid, this creates a **glycolipid**, whereas attachment to a protein produces a **glycoprotein**.

What is the function of glycosylation? Though the roles of carbohydrate in cell structure and function are not entirely understood, some functional consequences of glycosylation have emerged. The carbohydrates attached to proteins and lipids have well-defined structures that, in some cases, serve as recognition signals for other cellular proteins. For example, proteins destined for the lysosome are glycosylated and have a sugar (mannose-6-phosphate) that is recognized by other proteins in the cell that target the glycosylated protein from the Golgi to the lysosome. Similarly, glycolipids and glycoproteins often play a role in cell surface recognition. When glycolipid and glycoproteins are found in the plasma membrane, the carbohydrate portion is located in the extracellular region. During embryonic development in animals, significant cell movement occurs. Layers of cells slide over each other to create body structures such as the spinal cord and internal organs. The proper migration of individual cells and cell layers relies on the recognition of cell types via the carbohydrates on their cell surfaces.

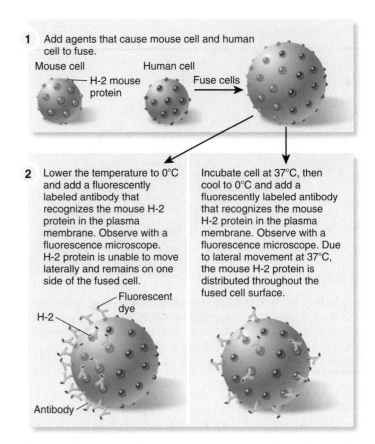

1 Add agents that cause mouse cell and human cell to fuse.

Mouse cell   Human cell

H-2 mouse protein   Fuse cells

2 Lower the temperature to 0°C and add a fluorescently labeled antibody that recognizes the mouse H-2 protein in the plasma membrane. Observe with a fluorescence microscope. H-2 protein is unable to move laterally and remains on one side of the fused cell.

Incubate cell at 37°C, then cool to 0°C and add a fluorescently labeled antibody that recognizes the mouse H-2 protein in the plasma membrane. Observe with a fluorescence microscope. Due to lateral movement at 37°C, the mouse H-2 protein is distributed throughout the fused cell surface.

Fluorescent dye

H-2

Antibody

Figure 5.4 A method to measure the lateral movement of membrane proteins.

Concept check: *Explain why the H-2 proteins are found on only one side of the cell when the cells were incubated at 0°C.*

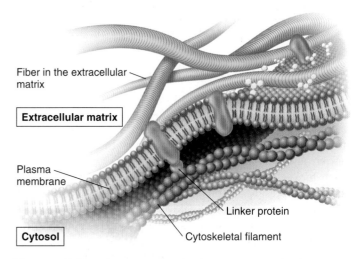

Fiber in the extracellular matrix

Extracellular matrix

Plasma membrane

Linker protein

Cytosol

Cytoskeletal filament

Figure 5.5 Attachment of transmembrane proteins to the cytoskeleton and extracellular matrix of an animal cell. Some transmembrane proteins have regions that project into the cytosol and are anchored to large cytoskeletal filaments via linker proteins. Being bound to these filaments restricts the movement of these proteins. Similarly, transmembrane proteins may bind to large, immobile components in the extracellular matrix that also restrict the movement of the proteins.

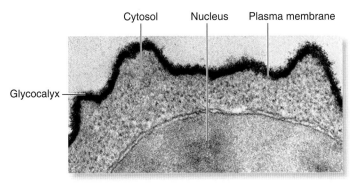

Cytosol   Nucleus   Plasma membrane

Glycocalyx

200 nm

Figure 5.6   A micrograph of the cell coat, or glycocalyx, of an animal cell.   This figure shows a lymphocyte—a type of white blood cell—stained with ethidium red, which emphasizes the thick carbohydrate layer that surrounds the cell. Note: The term glycocalyx (from the Greek, meaning sugar coat) is also used to describe other carbohydrate surfaces, such as a carbohydrate layer that surrounds certain strains of bacteria (refer back to Figure 4.4).

Concept check: *What is an important function of the glycocalyx?*

Carbohydrates also play a role in determining blood type, which is described in Chapter 16 (look ahead to Table 16.3).

Carbohydrates can also have a protective effect. The term **cell coat**, or **glycocalyx**, is used to describe the carbohydrate-rich zone on the surface of certain animal cells that shields the cell from mechanical and physical damage (**Figure 5.6**). The carbohydrate portion of glycosylated proteins protects them from the harsh conditions of the extracellular environment and degradation by extracellular proteases, which are enzymes that digest proteins.

Membrane Structure Can Be Viewed with an Electron Microscope

Electron microscopy, discussed in Chapter 4, is a valuable tool to probe membrane structure and function. In transmission electron microscopy (TEM), a biological sample is thin sectioned and stained with heavy-metal dyes such as osmium tetroxide. This compound binds tightly to the polar head groups of phospholipids, but it does not bind well to the fatty acyl tails. As shown in **Figure 5.7a**, membranes stained with osmium tetroxide resemble a railroad track. Two thin dark lines, which are the stained polar head groups, are separated by a uniform light space about 2 nm thick. This railroad track morphology is seen when cell membranes are subjected to electron microscopy.

Due to the incredibly small size of biological membranes, scientists have not been able to invent instruments small enough to dissect them. However, a specialized form of TEM, freeze fracture electron microscopy (FFEM), can be used to

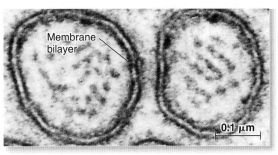

Membrane bilayer

0.1 μm

(a) Transmission electron microscopy (TEM)

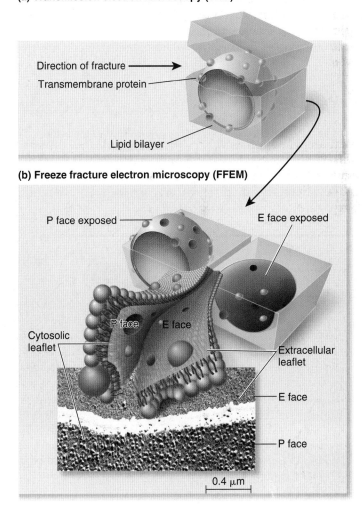

Direction of fracture

Transmembrane protein

Lipid bilayer

(b) Freeze fracture electron microscopy (FFEM)

P face exposed

E face exposed

Cytosolic leaflet

P face   E face

Extracellular leaflet

E face

P face

0.4 μm

Figure 5.7   Electron micrographs of a cellular membrane. **(a)** In the standard form of TEM, a membrane appears as two dark parallel lines. These lines are the lipid head groups, which stain darkly with osmium tetroxide. The fatty acyl tails do not stain well and appear as a light region sandwiched between the dark lines. **(b)** In the technique of freeze fracture electron microscopy, a sample is frozen in liquid nitrogen and fractured. The sample is then coated with metal and viewed under the electron microscope.

Concept check: *If a heavy metal labeled the hydrophobic tails rather than the polar head groups (as osmium tetroxide does), do you think you would see a bilayer (that is, a railroad track) under TEM?*

analyze the interiors of phospholipid bilayers. Russell Steere invented this method in 1957. In FFEM, a sample is frozen in liquid nitrogen and split with a knife (**Figure 5.7b**). The knife does not actually cut through the bilayer, but it fractures the frozen sample. Due to the weakness of the central membrane region, the leaflets separate into a P face (the protoplasmic face that was next to the cytosol) and the E face (the extracellular face). Most transmembrane proteins do not break in half. They remain embedded within one of the leaflets, usually in the P face. The samples, which are under a vacuum, are then sprayed with a heavy metal such as platinum, which coats the sample and reveals architectural features within each leaflet. When viewed with an electron microscope, membrane proteins are visible as bumps that provide significant three-dimensional detail about their form and shape.

5.2 Synthesis of Membrane Components in Eukaryotic Cells

As we have seen, cellular membranes are composed of lipids, proteins, and carbohydrates. Most of the membrane components of eukaryotic cells are made at the endoplasmic reticulum (ER). In this section, we will begin by considering how phospholipids are synthesized at the ER membrane. We will then examine the process by which transmembrane proteins

are inserted into the ER membrane and explore how some proteins are glycosylated.

Lipid Synthesis Occurs at the ER Membrane

In eukaryotic cells, the cytosol and endomembrane system work together to synthesize most lipids. This process occurs at the cytosolic leaflet of the smooth ER membrane. **Figure 5.8** shows a simplified pathway for the synthesis of phospholipids. The building blocks for a phospholipid are two fatty acids, each with an acyl tail, one glycerol molecule, one phosphate, and a polar head group. These building blocks are made via enzymes in the cytosol, or they are taken into cells from food. To begin the process of phospholipid synthesis, the fatty acids are activated by attachment to an organic molecule called coenzyme A (CoA). This activation promotes the bonding of the two fatty acids to a glycerol-phosphate molecule, and the resulting molecule is inserted into the cytosolic leaflet of the ER membrane. The phosphate is removed from glycerol, and then a polar molecule already linked to phosphate is attached to glycerol. In the example shown in Figure 5.8, the polar head group contains choline, but many other types are possible. Phospholipids are initially inserted into the cytosolic leaflet. Flippases in the ER membrane transfer some of the newly made lipids to the other leaflet so that similar amounts of lipids are in both leaflets.

The lipids made in the ER membrane can be transferred to other membranes in the cell by a variety of mechan-

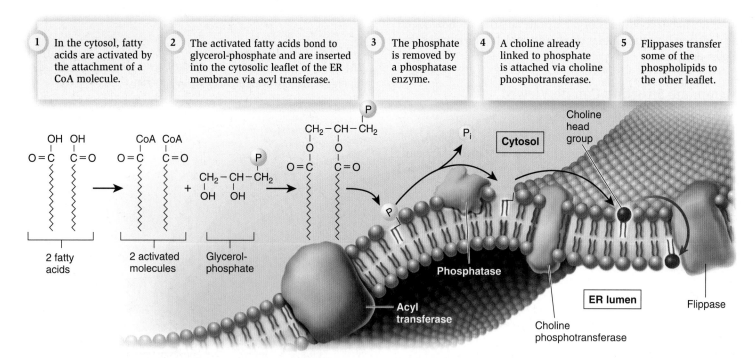

Figure 5.8 A simplified pathway for the synthesis of membrane phospholipids at the ER membrane. Note: Phosphate is abbreviated P when it is attached to an organic molecule and P_i when it is unattached. The subscript i refers to the inorganic form of phosphate.

Concept check: How are lipids transferred to the other leaflet of the ER membrane?

isms. Phospholipids in the ER can diffuse laterally to the nuclear envelope. In addition, lipids can be transported via vesicles to the Golgi, lysosomes, vacuoles, or plasma membrane. A third mode of lipid transfer involves **lipid exchange proteins**, which extract a lipid from one membrane, diffuse through the cell, and insert the lipid into another membrane. Such transfer can occur between any two membranes, even between the endomembrane system and semiautonomous organelles. For example, lipid exchange proteins can transfer lipids between the ER and mitochondria. In addition, chloroplasts and mitochondria can synthesize certain types of lipids that can be transferred from these organelles to other cellular membranes via lipid exchange proteins.

Most Transmembrane Proteins Are First Inserted into the ER Membrane

In Chapter 4 (Section 4.6), we learned that eukaryotic proteins contain sorting signals that direct them to their proper destination. With the exception of proteins destined for semiautonomous organelles, most transmembrane proteins contain an ER signal sequence that directs them to the ER membrane. If a polypeptide also contains a stretch of 20 amino acids that are mostly hydrophobic and form an α helix, this region will become a transmembrane segment. In the example shown in **Figure 5.9**, the polypeptide contains one such sequence. After the ER signal sequence is removed by signal peptidase (refer back to Figure

4.29), a membrane protein with a single transmembrane segment is the result. Other polypeptides may contain more than one transmembrane segment. Each time a polypeptide sequence contains a stretch of 20 hydrophobic amino acids that forms an α helix, an additional transmembrane segment is synthesized into the membrane. From the ER, membrane proteins can be transferred via vesicles to other regions of the cell, such as the Golgi, lysosomes, vacuoles, or plasma membrane.

Glycosylation of Proteins Occurs in the ER and Golgi Apparatus

As mentioned, glycosylation is the attachment of carbohydrate to a lipid or protein, producing a glycolipid or glycoprotein. Two forms of protein glycosylation occur in eukaryotes: N-linked and O-linked. N-linked glycosylation, which also occurs in archaea, involves the attachment of a carbohydrate to the amino acid asparagine in a polypeptide chain. It is called N-linked because the carbohydrate attaches to a nitrogen atom of the asparagine side chain. For this to occur, a group of 14 sugar molecules are built onto a lipid called dolichol, which is found in the ER membrane. This carbohydrate tree is then transferred to an asparagine as a polypeptide is synthesized into the ER lumen through a channel protein (**Figure 5.10**). The carbohydrate

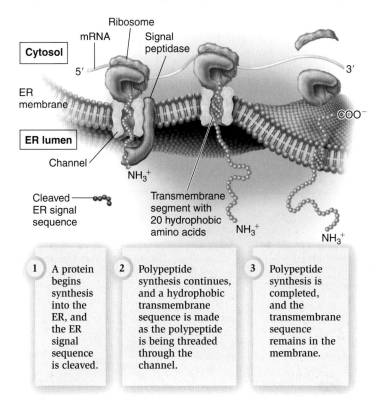

1. A protein begins synthesis into the ER, and the ER signal sequence is cleaved.

2. Polypeptide synthesis continues, and a hydrophobic transmembrane sequence is made as the polypeptide is being threaded through the channel.

3. Polypeptide synthesis is completed, and the transmembrane sequence remains in the membrane.

Figure 5.9 Insertion of membrane proteins into the ER membrane.

Concept check: *What structural feature of a protein causes a region to form a transmembrane segment?*

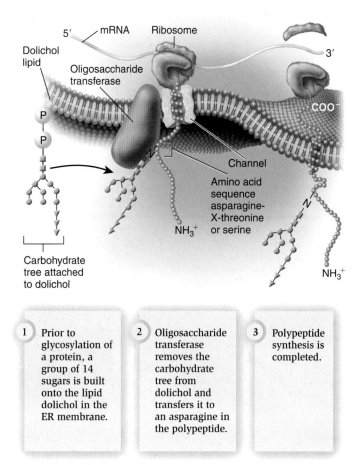

1. Prior to glycosylation of a protein, a group of 14 sugars is built onto the lipid dolichol in the ER membrane.

2. Oligosaccharide transferase removes the carbohydrate tree from dolichol and transfers it to an asparagine in the polypeptide.

3. Polypeptide synthesis is completed.

Figure 5.10 N-linked glycosylation in the endoplasmic reticulum.

tree is attached only to asparagines occurring in the sequence asparagine—X—threonine or asparagine—X—serine, where X could be any amino acid except proline. An enzyme in the ER, oligosaccharide transferase, recognizes this sequence and transfers the carbohydrate tree from dolichol to the asparagine. Following this initial glycosylation step, the carbohydrate tree is further modified as other enzymes in the ER attach additional sugars or remove sugars. After a glycosylated protein is transferred to the Golgi by vesicle transport, enzymes in the Golgi usually modify the carbohydrate tree as well. N-linked glycosylation commonly occurs on membrane proteins that are transported to the cell surface.

The second form of glycosylation, O-linked glycosylation, occurs only in the Golgi apparatus. This form involves the addition of a string of sugars to the oxygen atom of serine or threonine side chains in polypeptides. In animals, O-linked glycosylation is important for the production of proteoglycans, which are highly glycosylated proteins that are secreted from cells and help to organize the extracellular matrix that surrounds cells. Proteoglycans are also a component of mucus, a slimy material that coats many cell surfaces and is secreted into fluids such as saliva. High concentrations of carbohydrates give mucus its slimy texture.

5.3 Membrane Transport

We now turn to one of the key functions of membranes, **membrane transport**—the movement of ions and molecules across biological membranes. All cells contain a plasma membrane that is a **selectively permeable** barrier between a cell and its external environment. As a protective envelope, its structure ensures that essential molecules such as glucose and amino acids enter the cell, metabolic intermediates remain in the cell, and waste products exit. The selective permeability of the plasma membrane allows the cell to maintain a favorable internal environment.

Substances can move across a membrane in three general ways (Figure 5.11). **Diffusion** occurs when a substance moves from a region of high concentration to a region of lower concentration. Some substances can move directly through a phospholipid bilayer via diffusion. A second way that substances can move across membranes is via **facilitated diffusion**. In this case, a transport protein provides a passageway for the substance to cross the membrane. Both diffusion and facilitated diffusion are examples of **passive transport**—the transport of a substance across a membrane from a region of high concentration to a region of lower concentration. Passive transport does not require an input of energy. In contrast, a third mode of transport, called **active transport**, moves a substance from an area of low concentration to high concentration or against a concentration gradient with the aid of a transport protein. This type of transport requires an input of energy, such as ATP hydrolysis.

In this section, we begin with a discussion of how the phospholipid bilayer presents a barrier to the movement of ions and molecules across membranes, and then consider the concept of gradients across membranes. We will then focus on transport proteins, which carry out facilitated diffusion and active transport. Such proteins play a key role in the selective permeability of biological membranes. Finally, we will examine two mechanisms found in eukaryotic cells for the transport of substances via membrane vesicles.

The Phospholipid Bilayer Is a Barrier to the Diffusion of Hydrophilic Solutes

Because of their hydrophobic interiors, phospholipid bilayers present a formidable barrier to the movement of ions and hydrophilic molecules. Such ions and molecules are called solutes; they are dissolved in water, which is a solvent. The rate of diffusion across a phospholipid bilayer depends on the chemistry of the solute and its concentration. Figure 5.12 compares the relative permeabilities of various solutes through an artificial phospholipid bilayer that does not contain any proteins or carbohydrates. Gases and a few small, uncharged molecules can passively diffuse across the bilayer. However, the rate of diffusion of ions and larger polar molecules, such as sugars,

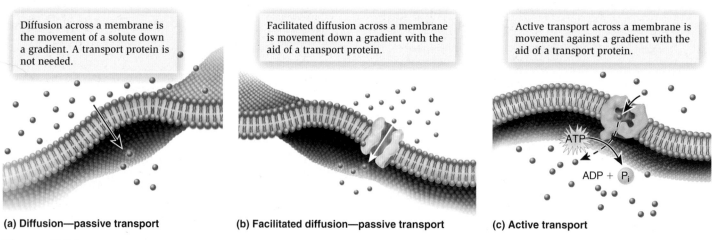

(a) Diffusion—passive transport (b) Facilitated diffusion—passive transport (c) Active transport

Figure 5.11 Three general types of membrane transport.

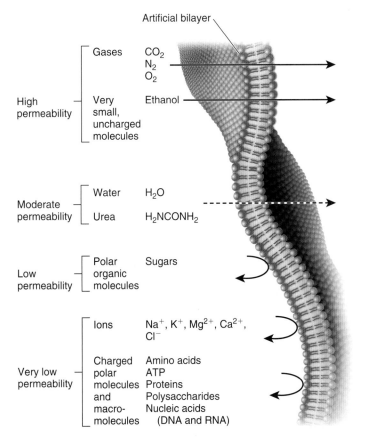

Figure 5.12 Relative permeability of an artificial phospholipid bilayer to a variety of solutes. Solutes that easily penetrate are shown with a straight arrow that passes through the bilayer. The dotted line indicates solutes that have moderate permeability. The remaining solutes shown at the bottom are relatively impermeable.

Concept check: Which amino acid (described in Chapter 3; see Figure 3.14) would you expect to cross an artificial membrane more quickly, leucine or lysine?

$$NH_2-\overset{\overset{\displaystyle O}{\|}}{C}-NH_2 \qquad CH_3-CH_2-NH-\overset{\overset{\displaystyle O}{\|}}{C}-NH-CH_2-CH_3$$

Urea   Diethylurea

Figure 5.13 Structures of urea and diethylurea.

Concept check: Which molecule would you expect to pass through a phospholipid bilayer more quickly, methanol (CH_3OH) or methane (CH_4)?

is relatively slow. Similarly, macromolecules, such as proteins and polysaccharides, do not readily cross a lipid bilayer.

When we consider the steps of diffusion among different solutes, the greatest variation occurs in the ability of solutes to enter the hydrophobic interior of the bilayer. As an example, let's compare urea and diethylurea. Compared to urea, diethylurea is much more hydrophobic because it contains two nonpolar ethyl groups ($-CH_2CH_3$) (**Figure 5.13**). For this reason, it can more readily pass through the hydrophobic region of the bilayer. The rate of diffusion of diethylurea through a phospholipid bilayer is about 50 times faster than urea.

Cells Maintain Gradients Across Their Membranes

A hallmark of living cells is their ability to maintain a relatively constant internal environment that is distinctively different from their external environment. This involves establishing gradients of solutes across the plasma membrane and organellar membranes. When we speak of a **transmembrane gradient**, we mean the concentration of a solute is higher on one side of a membrane than the other. For example, immediately after you eat a meal containing carbohydrates, a higher concentration of glucose is found outside your cells compared to inside (**Figure 5.14a**). This is an example of a chemical gradient.

Gradients involving ions have two components—electrical and chemical. An **electrochemical gradient** is a dual gradient that has both electrical and chemical components (**Figure 5.14b**). It occurs with solutes that have a net positive or negative charge. For example, let's consider a gradient involving Na^+. An electrical gradient could exist in which the amount of net positive charge outside a cell is greater than inside. In

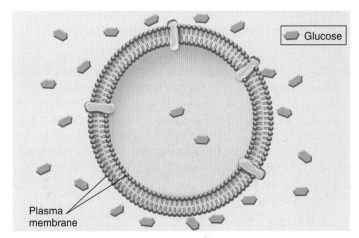

(a) Chemical gradient for glucose—a higher glucose concentration outside the cell

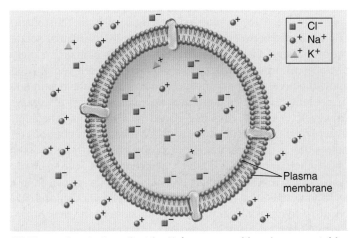

(b) Electrochemical gradient for Na^+—more positive charges outside the cell and a higher Na^+ concentration outside the cell

Figure 5.14 Gradients across cell membranes.

Figure 5.14b, an electrical gradient is due to differences in the amounts of different types of ions across the membrane, including Na^+, K^+, and Cl^-. At the same time, a chemical gradient—a difference in Na^+ concentration across the membrane—could exist in which the concentration of Na^+ outside is greater than inside. The Na^+ electrochemical gradient is composed of both an electrical gradient due to charge differences across the membrane along with a chemical gradient for Na^+. Transmembrane gradients of ions and other solutes are a universal feature of all living cells.

One way to view the transport of solutes across membranes is to consider how the transport process affects the pre-existing gradients across membranes. Passive transport tends to dissipate a pre-existing gradient. It is a process that is energetically favorable and does not require an input of energy. As mentioned, passive transport can occur in two ways, via diffusion or facilitated diffusion (see Figure 5.11a,b). By comparison, active transport produces a chemical gradient or electrochemical gradient. The formation of a gradient requires an input of energy.

Osmosis Is the Movement of Water Across Membranes to Balance Solute Concentrations

Let's now turn our attention to how gradients affect the movement of water across membranes. When the solute concentrations on both sides of the plasma membrane are equal, the two solutions are said to be **isotonic** (Figure 5.15a). However, we have also seen that transmembrane gradients commonly exist across membranes. When the solute concentration outside the cell is higher, it is said to be **hypertonic** relative to the inside of the cell (Figure 5.15b). Alternatively, the outside of the cell could be **hypotonic**—have a lower solute concentration relative to the inside (Figure 5.15c).

If solutes cannot readily move across the membrane, water will move and tend to balance the solute concentrations. In this process, called **osmosis**, water diffuses across a membrane from the hypotonic compartment into the hypertonic compartment. Cells generally have a high internal concentration of a variety of solutes, including ions, sugars, amino acids, and so on. Animal cells, which are not surrounded by a rigid cell wall, must maintain a balance between the extracellular and intracellular solute concentrations; they are isotonic. Animal cells contain a variety of transport proteins that can sense changes in cell volume and allow the necessary movements of solutes across the membrane to prevent osmotic changes and maintain normal cell shape. However, if animal cells are placed in a hypotonic medium, water will diffuse into them to equalize solute concentrations on both sides of the membrane. In extreme cases, a cell may take up so much water that it ruptures, a phenomenon called **osmotic lysis** (Figure 5.16a). Alternatively, if animal cells are placed in a hypertonic medium, water will exit the cells via osmosis and equalize solute concentrations on both sides of the membrane, causing them to shrink in a process called **crenation**.

How does osmosis affect cells with a rigid cell wall, such as bacteria, fungi, algae, and plant cells? If the extracellular fluid is hypotonic, a plant cell will take up a small amount of water, but the cell wall prevents major changes in cell size (Figure

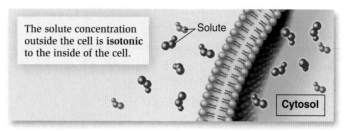

(a) Outside isotonic

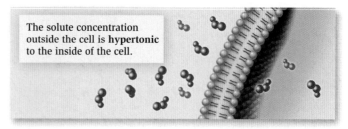

(b) Outside hypertonic

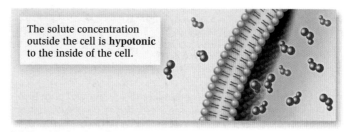

(c) Outside hypotonic

Figure 5.15   Relative solute concentrations outside and inside cells.

5.16b). Alternatively, if the extracellular fluid surrounding a plant cell is hypertonic, water will exit the cell and the plasma membrane will pull away from the cell wall, a process called **plasmolysis**.

The tendency of water to move into a cell creates an **osmotic pressure**, which is defined as the hydrostatic pressure required to stop the net flow of water across a membrane due to osmosis. In plant cells, osmotic pressure is also called **turgor pressure** or, simply, cell turgor. The turgor pressure pushes the plasma membrane against the rigid cell wall. An appropriate level of turgor is needed for plant cells to maintain their proper structure (Figure 5.17). If a plant has insufficient water, the extracellular fluid surrounding plant cells becomes hypertonic. This causes the plasma membrane to pull away from the cell wall, and the turgor pressure drops. Such a loss of turgor pressure is associated with wilting.

Some freshwater microorganisms, such as amoebae and paramecia, can exist in extremely hypotonic environments where the external solute concentration is always much lower than the concentration of solutes in their cytosol. Because of the great tendency for water to move into the cell by osmosis, such organisms contain one or more contractile vacuoles to prevent osmotic lysis. A contractile vacuole takes up water from the cytosol and periodically discharges it by fusing the vacuole with the plasma membrane (Figure 5.18).

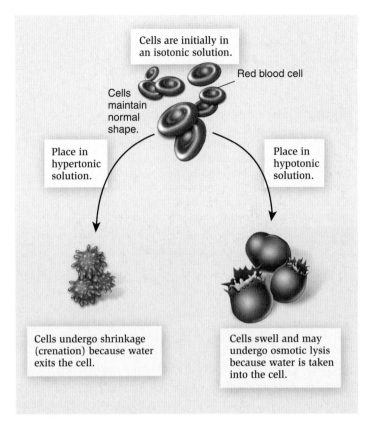

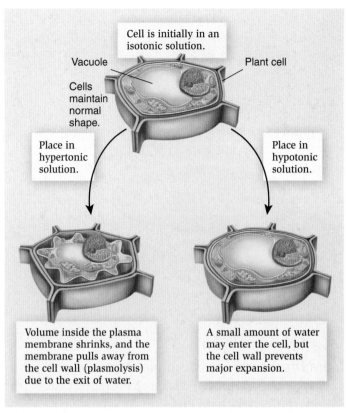

Cells are initially in an isotonic solution.

Red blood cell

Cells maintain normal shape.

Place in hypertonic solution.

Place in hypotonic solution.

Cells undergo shrinkage (crenation) because water exits the cell.

Cells swell and may undergo osmotic lysis because water is taken into the cell.

(a) Osmosis in animal cells

Cell is initially in an isotonic solution.

Vacuole

Plant cell

Cells maintain normal shape.

Place in hypertonic solution.

Place in hypotonic solution.

Volume inside the plasma membrane shrinks, and the membrane pulls away from the cell wall (plasmolysis) due to the exit of water.

A small amount of water may enter the cell, but the cell wall prevents major expansion.

(b) Osmosis in plant cells

Figure 5.16 **The phenomenon of osmosis.** (a) In cells that lack a cell wall, such as animal cells, osmosis may promote cell swelling or shrinkage (crenation). (b) In cells that have a rigid cell wall, such as plant cells, a hypotonic medium causes only a minor amount of expansion, whereas a hypertonic medium causes the plasma membrane to pull away from the cell wall.

Concept check: *Let's suppose the inside of a cell has a solute concentration of 0.3 M, while the outside is 0.2 M. If the membrane is impermeable to the solutes, which direction will water move?*

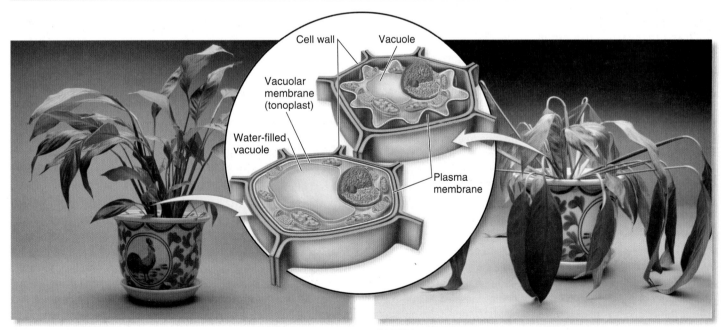

Cell wall

Vacuole

Vacuolar membrane (tonoplast)

Water-filled vacuole

Plasma membrane

(a) Sufficient water

(b) Wilting

Figure 5.17 **Wilting in plants.** (a) When a plant has plenty of water, the slightly hypotonic surroundings cause the vacuole to store water. The increased size of the vacuole influences the volume of the cytosol, thereby exerting a turgor pressure against the cell wall. (b) Under dry conditions, water is released from the cytosol into the hypertonic extracellular medium. The vacuole also shrinks, because it loses water to the cytosol. Turgor pressure is lost, which causes the plant to wilt.

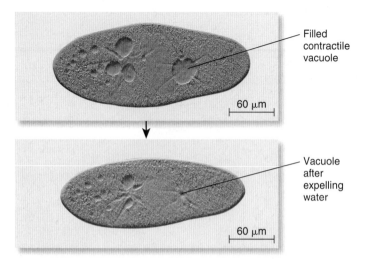

Filled contractile vacuole

60 μm

Vacuole after expelling water

60 μm

Figure 5.18   The contractile vacuole in *Paramecium caudatum.*   In the upper photo, a contractile vacuole is filled with water from radiating canals that collect fluid from the cytosol. The lower photo shows the cell after the contractile vacuole has fused with the plasma membrane (which would be above the plane of this page) and released the water from the cell.

Concept check: Why do freshwater protists, such as P. caudatum, need contractile vacuoles?

FEATURE INVESTIGATION

Agre Discovered That Osmosis Occurs More Quickly in Cells with Transport Proteins That Allow the Facilitated Diffusion of Water

In living cells, the flow of water may occur by diffusion through the phospholipid bilayer. However, in the 1980s, researchers also discovered that certain cell types allow water to move across the plasma membrane at a much faster rate than would be predicted by diffusion. For example, water moves very quickly across the membrane of red blood cells, which causes them to shrink and swell in response to changes in extracellular solute concentrations. Likewise, bladder and kidney cells, which play a key role in regulating water balance in the bodies of vertebrates, allow the rapid movement of water across their membranes. Based on these observations, researchers speculated that certain cell types might have proteins in their plasma membranes that permit the rapid movement of water.

One approach to characterize a new protein is to first identify a protein based on its relative abundance in a particular cell type and then attempt to determine the protein's function. This rationale was applied to the discovery of proteins that allow the rapid movement of water across membranes. Peter Agre and his colleagues first identified a protein that was abundant in red blood cells and kidney cells but not found in many other cell types. Though they initially did not know the function of the protein, its physical structure was similar to other proteins that were already known to function as transport proteins. They named this protein CHIP28, which stands for <u>c</u>hannel-forming <u>i</u>ntegral membrane <u>p</u>rotein with a molecular mass of <u>28</u>,000 Da. During the course of their studies, they also identified and isolated the gene that encodes CHIP28.

In 1992, Agre and his colleagues conducted experiments to determine if CHIP28 functions in the transport of water across membranes (**Figure 5.19**). Because they already had iso-

lated the gene that encodes CHIP28, they could make many copies of this gene in a test tube (in vitro) using gene cloning techniques (see Chapter 20). Starting with many copies of the gene in vitro, they added an enzyme to transcribe the gene into mRNA that encodes the CHIP28 protein. This mRNA was then injected into frog oocytes, chosen because frog oocytes are large, easy to inject, and lack pre-existing proteins in their plasma membranes that allow the rapid movement of water. Following injection, the mRNA was expected to be translated into CHIP28 proteins that should be inserted into the plasma membrane of the oocytes. After allowing sufficient time for this to occur, the oocytes were placed in a hypotonic medium. As a control, oocytes that had not been injected with CHIP28 mRNA were also exposed to a hypotonic medium.

As you can see in the data, a striking difference was observed between oocytes that expressed CHIP28 versus the control. Within minutes, oocytes that contained the CHIP28 protein were seen to swell due to the rapid uptake of water. Three to 5 minutes after being placed in a hypotonic medium, they actually burst! By comparison, the control oocytes did not swell as rapidly, and they did not rupture even after 1 hour. Taken together, these results are consistent with the hypothesis that CHIP28 functions as a transport protein that allows the facilitated diffusion of water across the membrane. Many subsequent studies confirmed this observation. Later, CHIP28 was renamed **aquaporin** to indicate its newly identified function of allowing water to diffuse through a pore in the membrane (**Figure 5.20**). More recently, the three-dimensional structure of aquaporin was determined (see chapter-opening photo). Agre was awarded the Nobel Prize in 2003 for this work.

Aquaporin is an example of a transport protein called a channel. Next, we will discuss the characteristics of channels and other types of transport proteins.

Figure 5.19   The discovery of water channels by Agre.

HYPOTHESIS CHIP28 may function as a water channel.

KEY MATERIALS Prior to this work, a protein called CHIP28 was identified that is abundant in red blood cells and kidney cells. The gene that encodes this protein was cloned, which means that many copies of the gene were made in a test tube.

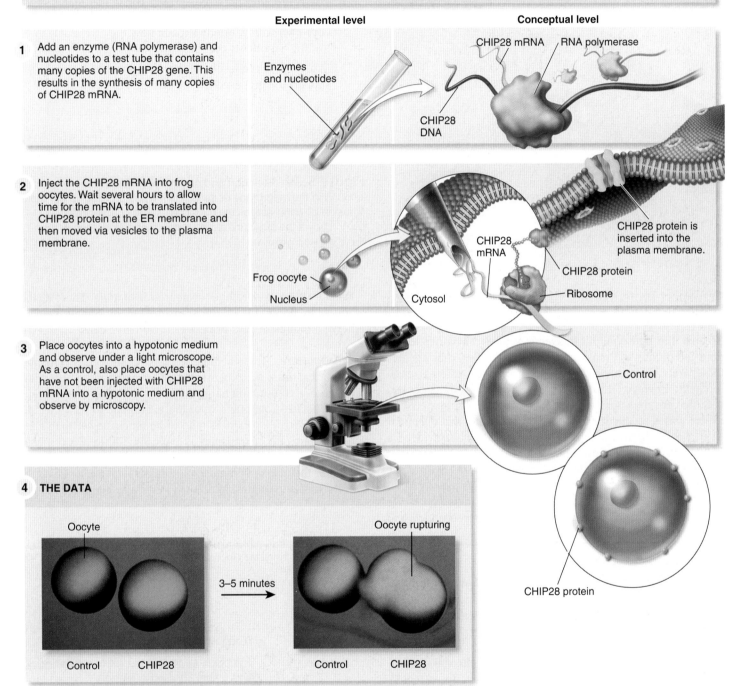

Experimental level

Conceptual level

1 Add an enzyme (RNA polymerase) and nucleotides to a test tube that contains many copies of the CHIP28 gene. This results in the synthesis of many copies of CHIP28 mRNA.

Enzymes and nucleotides

CHIP28 DNA

CHIP28 mRNA   RNA polymerase

2 Inject the CHIP28 mRNA into frog oocytes. Wait several hours to allow time for the mRNA to be translated into CHIP28 protein at the ER membrane and then moved via vesicles to the plasma membrane.

Frog oocyte

Nucleus

CHIP28 mRNA

Cytosol

CHIP28 protein is inserted into the plasma membrane.

CHIP28 protein

Ribosome

3 Place oocytes into a hypotonic medium and observe under a light microscope. As a control, also place oocytes that have not been injected with CHIP28 mRNA into a hypotonic medium and observe by microscopy.

Control

4 **THE DATA**

Oocyte

Oocyte rupturing

3–5 minutes

Control   CHIP28

Control   CHIP28

CHIP28 protein

5 **CONCLUSION** The CHIP28 protein, now called aquaporin, allows the rapid movement of water across the membrane.

6 **SOURCE** Preston, G.M., Carroll, T.P., Guggino, W.B., and Agre, P. 1992. Appearance of water channels in *Xenopus* oocytes expressing red cell CHIP28 protein. *Science* 256:385–387.

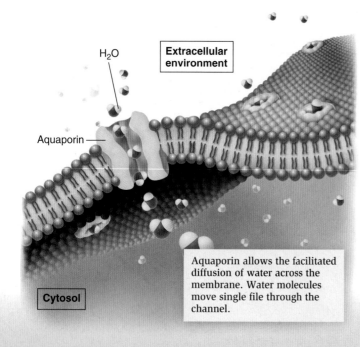

Aquaporin allows the facilitated diffusion of water across the membrane. Water molecules move single file through the channel.

1. What observations about particular cell types in the human body led to the experimental strategy of Figure 5.19?

2. What were the characteristics of CHIP28 that made Agre and associates speculate that it may transport water? In your own words, briefly explain how they were able to test the hypothesis that CHIP28 may have this function.

3. Explain how the results of the experiment of Figure 5.19 support the proposed hypothesis.

Figure 5.20   Function and structure of aquaporin.   Aquaporin is found in the membrane of certain cell types and allows the rapid diffusion of water across the membrane. The chapter-opening photo shows the structure of aquaporin that was determined by X-ray crystallography.

Transport Proteins Alter the Selective Permeability of Biological Membranes

Because the phospholipid bilayer is a physical barrier to the diffusion of ions and most hydrophilic molecules, cells are able to separate their internal contents from their external environment. However, this barrier also poses a severe problem because cells must take up nutrients from the environment and export waste products. How do cells overcome this dilemma? Over the course of millions of years, species have evolved a multitude of **transport proteins**—transmembrane proteins that provide a passageway for the movement of ions and hydrophilic molecules across membranes. Transport proteins play a central role in the selective permeability of biological membranes. We can categorize transport proteins into two classes, channels and transporters, based on the manner in which they move solutes across the membrane.

Channels   Transmembrane proteins called **channels** form an open passageway for the facilitated diffusion of ions or molecules across the membrane (Figure 5.21). Solutes move directly through a channel to get to the other side. Aquaporin, discussed in the Feature Investigation, is a channel that allows the movement of water across the membrane. When a channel is open, the transmembrane movement of solutes can be extremely rapid, up to 100 million ions or molecules per second!

Most channels are **gated**, which means they can open to allow the diffusion of solutes and close to prohibit diffusion. The phenomenon of gating allows cells to regulate the movement of solutes. For example, gating sometimes involves the direct binding of a molecule to the channel protein itself. One category of channels are ligand-gated channels, which are controlled by the noncovalent binding of small molecules—called

ligands—such as hormones or neurotransmitters. These ligands are often important in the transmission of signals between nerve and muscle cells or between two nerve cells.

Transporters   Transmembrane proteins known as **transporters**, or **carriers**, bind their solutes in a hydrophilic pocket and undergo a conformational change that switches the exposure of the pocket from one side of the membrane to the other side (Figure 5.22). Transporters tend to be much slower than channels. Their rate of transport is typically 100 to 1,000 ions or molecules per second. Transporters provide the principal pathway for the uptake of organic molecules, such as sugars, amino acids, and nucleotides. In animals, they also allow cells to take

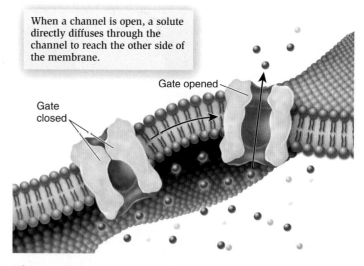

When a channel is open, a solute directly diffuses through the channel to reach the other side of the membrane.

Gate opened

Gate closed

Figure 5.21   Mechanism of transport by a channel protein.

Concept check: *What is the purpose of gating?*

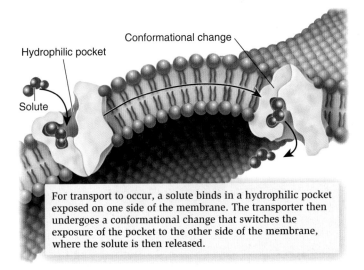

Figure 5.22 Mechanism of transport by a transporter, also called a carrier.

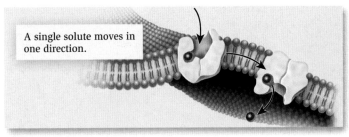

(a) Uniporter

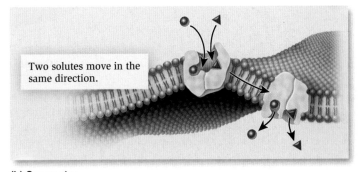

(b) Symporter

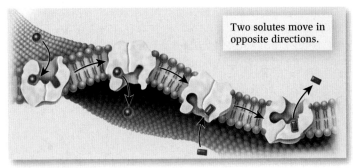

(c) Antiporter

Figure 5.23 Types of transporters based on the direction of transport.

up certain hormones and neurotransmitters. In addition, many transporters play a key role in export. Waste products of cellular metabolism must be released from cells before they reach toxic levels. For example, a transporter removes lactic acid, a by-product of muscle cells during exercise. Other transporters, which are involved with ion transport, play an important role in regulating internal pH and controlling cell volume.

Transporters are named according to the number of solutes they bind and the direction in which they transport those solutes (Figure 5.23). **Uniporters** bind a single ion or molecule and transport it across the membrane. **Symporters**, or **cotransporters**, bind two or more ions or molecules and transport them in the same direction. **Antiporters** bind two or more ions or molecules and transport them in opposite directions.

Active Transport Is the Movement of Solutes Against a Gradient

As mentioned, active transport is the movement of a solute across a membrane against its gradient—that is, from a region of low concentration to higher concentration. Active transport is energetically unfavorable and requires the input of energy. **Primary active transport** involves the functioning of a **pump**—a type of transporter that directly uses energy to transport a solute against a gradient. Figure 5.24a shows a pump that uses ATP to transport H^+ against a gradient. Such a pump can establish a large H^+ electrochemical gradient across a membrane.

Secondary active transport involves the use of a pre-existing gradient to drive the active transport of another solute. For example, a H^+/sucrose symporter can use a H^+ electrochemical gradient, established by an ion pump, to move sucrose against its concentration gradient (Figure 5.24b). In this regard, only sucrose is actively transported. Hydrogen ions move down their electrochemical gradient. H^+/solute symporters are more common in bacteria, fungi, algae, and plant cells, because H^+ pumps are found in their plasma membranes. In animal cells, a pump that exports Na^+ maintains a Na^+ gradient across the plasma membrane. Na^+/solute symporters are prevalent in animal cells.

Symporters enable cells to actively import nutrients against a gradient. These proteins use the energy stored in the electrochemical gradient of H^+ or Na^+ to power the uphill movement of organic solutes such as sugars, amino acids, and other needed solutes. Therefore, with symporters in their plasma membrane, cells can scavenge nutrients from the extracellular environment and accumulate them to high levels within the cytoplasm.

Different ATP-Driven Ion Pumps Generate Ion Electrochemical Gradients

The phenomenon of active transport was discovered in the 1940s based on the study of ion movements using radioisotopes of Na^+ and K^+. After analyzing the movement of these ions across the plasma membrane of muscle cells, nerve cells, and red blood cells, researchers determined that the export of sodium ions (Na^+) is coupled to the import of potassium ions (K^+). In the late 1950s, Danish biochemist Jens Skou proposed

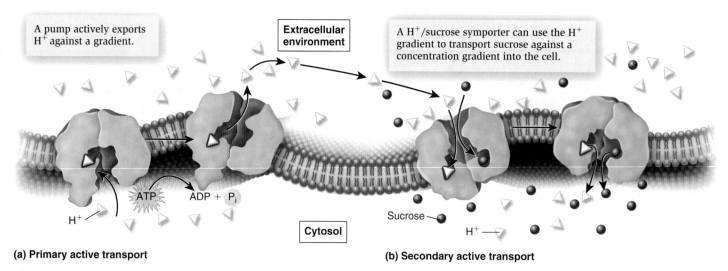

Figure 5.24 Types of active transport. **(a)** During primary active transport, a pump directly uses energy, in this case from ATP, to transport a solute against a gradient. The pump shown here uses ATP to establish a H$^+$ electrochemical gradient. **(b)** Secondary active transport via symport involves the use of this gradient to drive the active transport of a solute, such as sucrose.

that a single transporter is responsible for this phenomenon. He was the first person to describe an ATP-driven ion pump, which was later named the Na$^+$/K$^+$-ATPase. This pump can actively transport Na$^+$ and K$^+$ against their gradients by using the energy from ATP hydrolysis (**Figure 5.25a**). The plasma membrane of a typical animal cell contains thousands of Na$^+$/K$^+$-ATPase pumps. These pumps establish large gradients in which the concentration of Na$^+$ is higher outside the cell and the concentration of K$^+$ is higher inside the cell.

Interestingly, Skou initially had trouble characterizing this pump. He focused his work on the large nerve cells found in the shore crab (*Carcinus maenas*). After isolating membranes from these cells, he was able to identify a transporter that could hydrolyze ATP, but the rate of hydrolysis was too low compared to the level of ATP hydrolysis that was observed in living cells that pump Na$^+$ and K$^+$. When he added Na$^+$ to his membranes, the ATP hydrolysis rate was not greatly affected. Then he tried adding K$^+$, but the ATP hydrolysis rate still did not

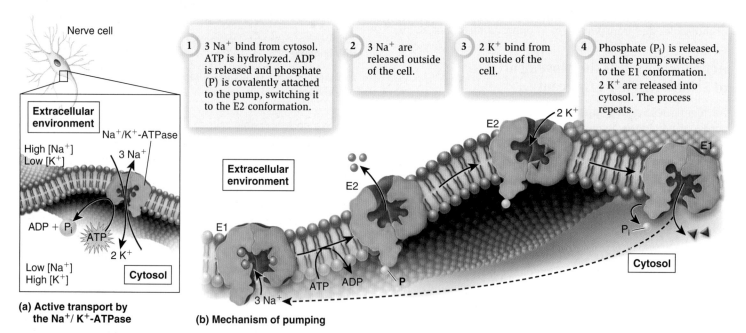

Figure 5.25 Structure and function of the Na$^+$/K$^+$-ATPase. **(a)** Active transport by the Na$^+$/K$^+$-ATPase. Each time this protein hydrolyzes one ATP molecule, it pumps out three Na$^+$ and pumps in two K$^+$. **(b)** Pumping mechanism. The figure illustrates the protein conformational changes between E1 and E2. As this occurs, ATP is hydrolyzed to ADP and phosphate. During the process, phosphate is covalently attached to the protein but is released after two K$^+$ bind.

Concept check: If a cell had ATP and Na$^+$, but K$^+$ were missing from the extracellular medium, how far through these steps could the Na$^+$/K$^+$-ATPase proceed?

increase. Eventually, he did the critical experiment in which he added both Na^+ and K^+ to his membranes. With both ions present, ATP hydrolysis soared dramatically. This observation led to the identification and purification of the Na^+/K^+-ATPase. Jens Skou was awarded the Nobel Prize in 1997, over 40 years after his original work.

Let's take a closer look at the Na^+/K^+-ATPase that Skou discovered. Every time one ATP is hydrolyzed, the Na^+/K^+-ATPase functions as an antiporter that pumps three Na^+ into the extracellular environment and two K^+ into the cytosol. Because one cycle of pumping results in the net export of one positive charge, the Na^+/K^+-ATPase also produces an electrical gradient across the membrane. For this reason, it is considered an **electrogenic pump**—it generates an electrical gradient.

By studying the interactions of Na^+, K^+, and ATP with the Na^+/K^+-ATPase, researchers have pieced together a molecular road map of the steps that direct the pumping of ions across the membrane (**Figure 5.25b**). The Na^+/K^+-ATPase can alternate between two conformations, designated E1 and E2. In E1, the ion-binding sites are accessible from the cytosol—Na^+ binds tightly to this conformation, whereas K^+ has a low affinity. In E2, the ion-binding sites are accessible from the extracellular environment—Na^+ has a low affinity, and K^+ binds tightly.

To examine the pumping mechanism of the Na^+/K^+-ATPase, let's begin with the E1 conformation. Three Na^+ bind to the Na^+/K^+-ATPase from the cytosol (Figure 5.25b). When this occurs, ATP is hydrolyzed to ADP and phosphate. Temporarily, the phosphate is covalently bound to the pump, an event called phosphorylation. The pump then switches to the E2 conformation. The three Na^+ are released into the extracellular environment because they have a lower affinity for the E2 conformation, and then two K^+ bind from the outside. The binding of two K^+ causes the release of phosphate, which, in turn, causes a switch to E1. Because the E1 conformation has a low affinity for K^+, the two K^+ are released into the cytosol. The Na^+/K^+-ATPase is now ready for another round of pumping.

The Na^+/K^+-ATPase is a critical ion pump in animal cells because it maintains Na^+ and K^+ gradients across the plasma membrane. Many other types of ion pumps are also found in the plasma membrane and in organellar membranes. Ion pumps play the primary role in the formation and maintenance of ion gradients that drive many important cellular processes (**Table 5.4**). ATP is commonly the source of energy to drive ion pumps, and cells typically use a substantial portion of their ATP to keep them working. For example, nerve cells use up to 70% of their ATP just to operate ion pumps!

Macromolecules and Large Particles Are Transported via Exocytosis and Endocytosis

We have seen that most small substances are transported via membrane proteins such as channels and transporters, which provide a passageway for the movement of ions and molecules across the membrane. Eukaryotic cells have two other mechanisms, exocytosis and endocytosis, to transport larger molecules such as proteins and polysaccharides, and even very large particles. Both mechanisms involve the packaging of the transported substance, sometimes called the cargo, into a membrane vesicle or vacuole. Table 5.5 describes some examples.

Exocytosis   During **exocytosis**, material inside the cell is packaged into vesicles and then excreted into the extracellular environment (**Figure 5.26**). These vesicles are usually derived from

Table 5.4	Important Functions of Ion Electrochemical Gradients
Function	**Description**
Transport of ions and molecules	Symporters and antiporters use H^+ and Na^+ gradients to take up nutrients and export waste products.
Production of energy intermediates	In the mitochondrion and chloroplast, H^+ gradients are used to synthesize ATP.
Osmotic regulation	Animal cells control their internal volume by regulating ion gradients between the cytosol and extracellular fluid.
Nerve signaling	Na^+ and K^+ gradients are involved in conducting action potentials, the signals transmitted by nerve cells.
Muscle contraction	Ca^{2+} gradients regulate the ability of muscle fibers to contract.
Bacterial swimming	H^+ gradients drive the rotation of bacterial flagella.

Table 5.5	Examples of Exocytosis and Endocytosis		
Exocytosis	**Description**	**Endocytosis**	**Description**
Hormones	Certain hormones, such as insulin, are composed of polypeptides. To exert its effect, insulin is secreted via exocytosis into the bloodstream from B cells of the pancreas.	Uptake of vital nutrients	Many important nutrients are insoluble in the bloodstream. Therefore, they are bound to proteins in the blood and then taken into cells via endocytosis. Examples include the uptake of lipids (bound to low-density lipoprotein) and iron (bound to transferrin protein).
Digestive enzymes	Digestive enzymes that function in the lumen of the small intestine are secreted via exocytosis from cells of the pancreas.	Root nodules	Nitrogen-fixing root nodules found in certain species of plants, such as legumes, are formed by the endocytosis of bacteria. After endocytosis, the bacterial cells are contained within a membrane-enclosed compartment in the nitrogen-fixing tissue of root nodules.
Extracellular matrix	Most of the components of the extracellular matrix that surrounds animal cells are secreted via exocytosis.	Immune system	Cells of the immune system, known as macrophages, engulf and destroy bacteria via phagocytosis.

the Golgi apparatus. As the vesicles form, a specific cargo is loaded into their interior. The budding process involves the formation of a protein coat around the emerging vesicle. The assembly of coat proteins on the surface of the Golgi membrane causes the bud to form. Eventually, the bud separates from the membrane to form a vesicle. After the vesicle is released, the coat is shed. Finally, the vesicle fuses with the plasma membrane and releases the cargo into the extracellular environment.

Endocytosis   During **endocytosis**, the plasma membrane invaginates, or folds inward, to form a vesicle that brings substances into the cell. A common form of endocytosis is **receptor-mediated endocytosis**, in which a receptor in the plasma membrane is specific for a given cargo (**Figure 5.27**). Cargo molecules binding to their specific receptors stimulate many receptors to aggregate, and then coat proteins bind to the membrane. The protein coat causes the membrane to invaginate and form a vesicle.

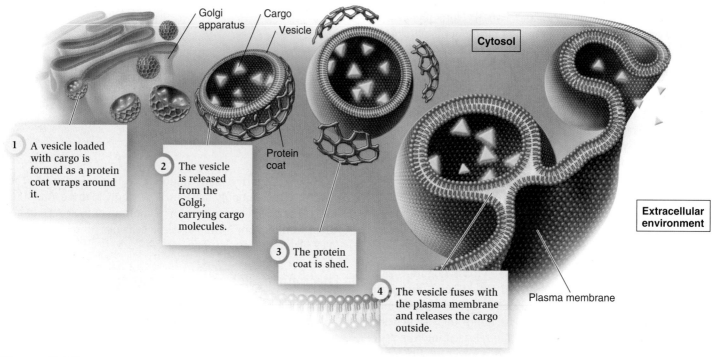

Golgi apparatus

Cargo

Vesicle

Cytosol

1. A vesicle loaded with cargo is formed as a protein coat wraps around it.

2. The vesicle is released from the Golgi, carrying cargo molecules.

Protein coat

3. The protein coat is shed.

4. The vesicle fuses with the plasma membrane and releases the cargo outside.

Plasma membrane

Extracellular environment

Figure 5.26   Exocytosis.

Concept check: *What is the function of the protein coat?*

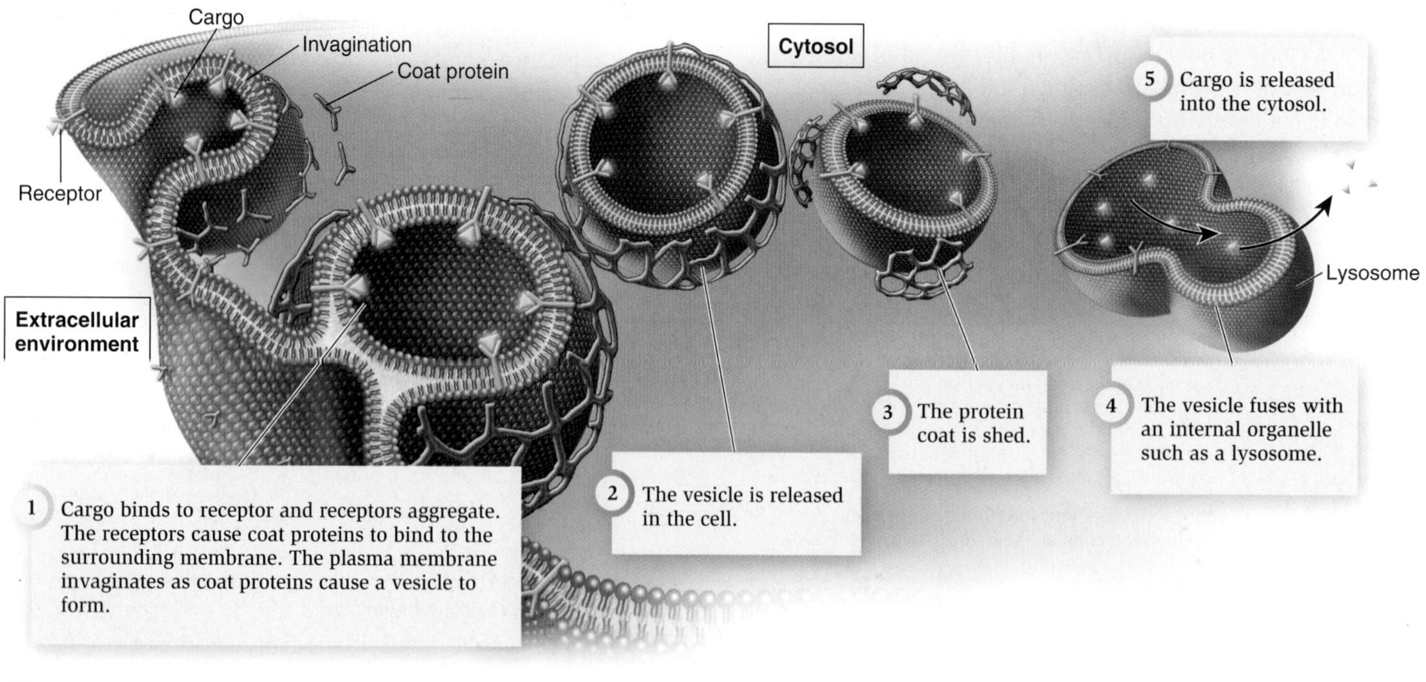

Cargo

Invagination

Coat protein

Cytosol

5. Cargo is released into the cytosol.

Receptor

Extracellular environment

3. The protein coat is shed.

4. The vesicle fuses with an internal organelle such as a lysosome.

Lysosome

1. Cargo binds to receptor and receptors aggregate. The receptors cause coat proteins to bind to the surrounding membrane. The plasma membrane invaginates as coat proteins cause a vesicle to form.

2. The vesicle is released in the cell.

Figure 5.27   Receptor-mediated endocytosis.

Once it is released into the cell, the vesicle sheds its coat. In most cases, the vesicle fuses with an internal membrane organelle, such as a lysosome, and the receptor releases its cargo. Depending on the cargo, the lysosome may release it directly into the cytosol or digest it into simpler building blocks before releasing it.

Other specialized forms of endocytosis occur in certain types of cells. **Pinocytosis** (from the Greek, meaning cell drinking) involves the formation of membrane vesicles from the plasma membrane as a way for cells to internalize the extracellular fluid. This allows cells to sample the extracellular solutes. Pinocytosis is particularly important in cells that are actively involved in nutrient absorption, such as cells that line the intestine in animals.

Phagocytosis (from the Greek, meaning cell eating) is an extreme form of endocytosis. It involves the formation of an enormous membrane vesicle called a phagosome, or phagocytic vacuole, that engulfs a large particle such as a bacterium. Only certain kinds of cells can carry out phagocytosis. For example, macrophages, which are cells of the immune system in mammals, kill bacteria via phagocytosis. Once inside the cell, the phagosome fuses with lysosomes, and the digestive enzymes within the lysosomes destroy the bacterium.

Summary of Key Concepts

5.1 Membrane Structure

- Plasma membranes separate a cell from its surroundings, and organellar membranes provide interfaces to carry out vital cellular activities. (Table 5.1)

- The accepted model of membranes is the fluid-mosaic model, and its basic framework is the phospholipid bilayer. Cellular membranes also contain proteins, and most membranes have attached carbohydrates. (Figure 5.1, Table 5.2)

- The three main types of membrane proteins are transmembrane proteins, lipid-anchored proteins, and peripheral membrane proteins. Transmembrane proteins and lipid-anchored proteins are classified as integral membrane proteins. Researchers are working to identify new membrane proteins and their functions because these proteins are important biologically and medically. (Figure 5.2, Table 5.3)

- Bilayer semifluidity is essential for normal cell function, growth, and division. Lipids can move rotationally and laterally, but flip-flop does not occur spontaneously. The chemical properties of phospholipids—such as tail length and the presence of double bonds—and the amount of cholesterol have a profound effect on the fluidity of membranes. (Figures 5.3, 5.4, 5.5)

- Glycosylation, which produces glycolipids or glycoproteins, has a variety of cellular functions. Carbohydrate can serve as a recognition marker or a protective cell coat. (Figure 5.6)

- Electron microscopy is a valuable tool for studying membrane structure and function. Freeze fracture electron microscopy (FFEM) can be used to analyze the interiors of phospholipid bilayers. (Figure 5.7)

5.2 Synthesis of Membrane Components in Eukaryotic Cells

- In eukaryotic cells, most membrane phospholipids are synthesized at the cytosolic leaflet of the smooth ER membrane. Flippases move some phospholipids to the other leaflet. (Figure 5.8)

- Most transmembrane proteins are first inserted into the ER membrane. (Figure 5.9)

- Glycosylation of proteins occurs in the ER and Golgi apparatus. (Figure 5.10)

5.3 Membrane Transport

- Biological membranes are selectively permeable. Diffusion occurs when a solute moves from a region of high concentration to a region of lower concentration. Passive transport of a solute across a membrane can occur via diffusion or facilitated diffusion. Active transport is the movement of a substance against a gradient. (Figure 5.11)

- The lipid bilayers of membranes are relatively impermeable to many substances. (Figures 5.12, 5.13)

- Living cells maintain an internal environment that is separated from their external environment. This involves establishing transmembrane gradients across the plasma membrane and organellar membranes. (Figure 5.14, Table 5.4)

- In the process of osmosis, water diffuses through a membrane from a solution that is hypotonic (lower solute concentration) into a solution that is hypertonic (higher solute concentration). Solutions with identical solute concentrations are isotonic. The tendency of water to move into a cell creates an osmotic (turgor) pressure. (Figures 5.15, 5.16, 5.17, 5.18)

- The two classes of transport proteins are channels and transporters. Channels form an open passageway for the direct diffusion of solutes across the membrane; one example is aquaporin, which allows the movement of water. Most channels are gated, which allows cells to regulate the movement of solutes. (Figures 5.19, 5.20, 5.21)

- Transporters, which tend to be slower than channels, bind their solutes in a hydrophilic pocket and undergo a conformational change that switches the exposure of the pocket to the other side of the membrane. They can be uniporters, symporters, or antiporters. (Figures 5.22, 5.23)

- Primary active transport involves pumps that directly use energy to generate a solute gradient. Secondary active transport uses a pre-existing gradient. (Figure 5.24)

- The Na^+/K^+-ATPase is an electrogenic ATP-driven pump. This protein follows a series of steps that direct the pumping of ions across the membrane. (Figure 5.25, Table 5.4)

- In eukaryotes, exocytosis and endocytosis are used to transport large molecules and particles. Exocytosis is a process in which material inside the cell is packaged into vesicles and excreted into the extracellular environment. During endocytosis, the plasma membrane folds inward to form a vesicle that brings substances into the cell. Forms of endocytosis include receptor-mediated endocytosis, pinocytosis, and phagocytosis. (Figures 5.26, 5.27, Table 5.5)

Assess and Discuss

Test Yourself

1. Which of the following statements best describes the chemical composition of biomembranes?
   a. Biomembranes are bilayers of proteins with associated lipids and carbohydrates.
   b. Biomembranes are composed of two layers—one layer of phospholipids and one layer of proteins.
   c. Biomembranes are bilayers of phospholipids with associated proteins and carbohydrates.
   d. Biomembranes are composed of equal numbers of phospholipids, proteins, and carbohydrates.
   e. Biomembranes are composed of lipids with proteins attached to the outer surface.

2. Which of the following events in a biological membrane would not be energetically favorable and therefore not occur spontaneously?
   a. the rotation of phospholipids
   b. the lateral movement of phospholipids
   c. the flip-flop of phospholipids to the opposite leaflet
   d. the rotation of membrane proteins
   e. the lateral movement of membrane proteins

3. Let's suppose an insect, which doesn't maintain a constant body temperature, was exposed to a shift in temperature from 60°F to 80°F. Which of the following types of cellular changes would be the most beneficial to help this animal cope with the temperature shift?
   a. increase the number of double bonds in the fatty acyl tails of phospholipids
   b. increase the length of the fatty acyl tails of phospholipids
   c. decrease the amount of cholesterol in the membrane
   d. decrease the amount of carbohydrate attached to membrane proteins
   e. decrease the amount of carbohydrate attached to phospholipids

4. Carbohydrates of the plasma membrane
   a. are associated with a protein or lipid.
   b. are located on the outer surface of the plasma membrane.
   c. can function as cell markers for recognition by other cells.
   d. all of the above
   e. a and c only

5. A transmembrane protein in the plasma membrane is glycosylated at two sites in the polypeptide sequence. One site is Asn—Val—Ser and the other site is Asn—Gly—Thr. Where in this protein would you expect these two sites to be found?
   a. in transmembrane segments
   b. in hydrophilic regions that project into the extracellular environment
   c. in hydrophilic regions that project into the cytosol
   d. could be anywhere
   e. b and c only

6. The tendency for Na^+ to move into the cell could be due to
   a. the higher numbers of Na^+ outside the cell, resulting in a chemical concentration gradient.
   b. the net negative charge inside the cell attracting the positively charged Na^+.
   c. the attractive force of K^+ inside the cell pulling Na^+ into the cell.
   d. all of the above.
   e. a and b only.

7. Let's suppose the solute concentration inside the cells of a plant is 0.3 M and outside is 0.2 M. If we assume that the solutes do not readily cross the membrane, which of the following statements best describes what will happen?
   a. The plant cells will lose water, and the plant will wilt.
   b. The plant cells will lose water, which will result in a higher turgor pressure.
   c. The plant cells will take up a lot of water and undergo osmotic lysis.
   d. The plant cells will take up a little water and have a higher turgor pressure.
   e. Both a and b are correct.

8. What structural features of a membrane are major contributors to its selective permeability?
   a. phospholipid bilayer
   b. transport proteins
   c. glycolipids on the outer surface of the membrane
   d. peripheral membrane proteins on the inside of the membrane
   e. both a and b

9. What is the name given to the process in which solutes are moved across a membrane against their concentration gradient?
   a. diffusion   d. passive diffusion
   b. facilitated diffusion   e. active transport
   c. osmosis

10. Large particles or large volumes of fluid can be brought into the cell by
   a. facilitated diffusion.   d. exocytosis.
   b. active transport.   e. all of the above.
   c. endocytosis.

Conceptual Questions

1. With your textbook closed, draw and describe the fluid-mosaic model of membrane structure.

2. Describe two different ways that integral membrane proteins are anchored to a membrane. How do peripheral membrane proteins associate with a membrane?

3. Solutes can move across membranes via diffusion, facilitated diffusion, active transport, exocytosis, and endocytosis. During which of these five processes would you expect the solute to physically touch the tails of phospholipids in the membrane? For the other processes, describe how the solute avoids an interaction with the phospholipid tails in the membrane.

Collaborative Questions

1. Proteins in the plasma membrane are often the target of medicines. Discuss why you think this is the case. How would you determine experimentally that a specific membrane protein was the target of a drug?

2. With regard to bringing solutes into the cell across the plasma membrane, discuss the advantages and disadvantages of diffusion, facilitated diffusion, active transport, and endocytosis.

Online Resource

www.brookerbiology.com

Stay a step ahead in your studies with animations that bring concepts to life and practice tests to assess your understanding. Your instructor may also recommend the interactive ebook, individualized learning tools, and more.

An Introduction to Energy, Enzymes, and Metabolism

6

Common drugs that are enzyme inhibitors.   Drugs such as aspirin and ibuprofen exert their effects by inhibiting an enzyme that speeds up a chemical reaction in the cell.

Have you ever taken aspirin or ibuprofen to relieve a headache or reduce a fever? Do you know how it works? If you answered "no" to the second question, you're not alone. Over 2,000 years ago, humans began treating pain with powder from the bark and leaves of the willow tree, which contains a compound called salicylic acid. Modern aspirin is composed of a derivative of salicylic acid called acetylsalicylic acid, which is gentler to the stomach. Only recently, however, have we learned how such drugs work. Aspirin and ibuprofen are examples of drugs that inhibit specific enzymes found in cells. In this case, these drugs inhibit an enzyme called cyclooxygenase. This enzyme is needed to synthesize molecules called prostaglandins, which play a role in inflammation and pain. Aspirin and ibuprofen exert their effects by inhibiting cyclooxygenase, thereby decreasing the levels of prostaglandins.

Enzymes are proteins that act as critical catalysts to speed up thousands of different reactions in cells. As discussed in Chapter 2, a **chemical reaction** is a process in which one or more substances are changed into other substances. Such reactions may involve molecules attaching to each other to form larger molecules, molecules breaking apart to form two or more smaller molecules, rearrangements of atoms within molecules, or the transfer of electrons from one atom to another. Every living cell continuously performs thousands of such chemical reactions to sustain life. The term **metabolism** is used to describe the sum total of all chemical reactions that occur within an organism. The term also refers to a specific set of chemical reactions occurring at the cellular level. For example, biologists may speak of sugar metabolism or fat metabolism. Most types of metabolism involve the breakdown or synthesis of organic molecules. Cells maintain their structure by using organic molecules. Such molecules provide the building blocks to construct cells, and the chemical bonds within organic molecules store energy that can be used to drive cellular processes.

In this chapter, we begin with a general discussion of chemical reactions. We will examine what factors control the direction of a chemical reaction and what determines its rate, paying particular attention to the role of enzymes. We then consider metabolism at the cellular level. First, we will examine some of the general features of chemical reactions that are vital for the energy needs of living cells. We will also explore the variety of ways in which metabolic processes are regulated and how macromolecules are recycled.

6.1   Energy and Chemical Reactions

Two general factors govern the fate of a given chemical reaction in a living cell—its direction and rate. To illustrate this point, let's consider a generalized chemical reaction such as

$$a\text{A} + b\text{B} \rightleftharpoons c\text{C} + d\text{D}$$

where A and B are the reactants, C and D are the products, and a, b, c, and d are the number of moles of reactants and products. This reaction is reversible, which means that A + B could be converted to C + D, or C + D could be converted to A + B. The direction of the reaction, whether C + D are made (the forward direction) or A + B are made (the reverse direction), depends on energy and on the concentrations of A, B, C, and D. In this section, we will begin by examining the interplay of energy and the concentration of reactants as they govern the direction of a chemical reaction. You will learn that cells use energy intermediate molecules, such as ATP, to drive chemical reactions in a desired direction.

Energy Exists in Many Forms

To understand why a chemical reaction occurs, we first need to consider **energy**, which we will define as the ability to promote change or do work. Physicists often consider energy in two forms: kinetic energy and potential energy (**Figure 6.1**). **Kinetic energy** is energy associated with movement, such as the movement of a baseball bat from one location to another. By comparison, **potential energy** is the energy that a substance possesses due to its structure or location. The energy contained within covalent bonds in molecules is also a type of potential energy called **chemical energy**. The breakage of those bonds is one way that living cells can harness this energy to perform cellular functions. **Table 6.1** summarizes chemical and other forms of energy important in biological systems.

An important issue in biology is the ability of energy to be converted from one form to another. The study of energy interconversions is called **thermodynamics**. Physicists have determined that two laws govern energy interconversions:

1. **The first law of thermodynamics**—The first law states that energy cannot be created or destroyed; it is also called the law of conservation of energy. However, energy can be transferred from one place to another and can be transformed from one type to another (as when, for example, chemical energy is transformed into heat).

2. **The second law of thermodynamics**—The second law states that the transfer of energy or the transformation of energy from one form to another increases the **entropy**, or degree of disorder of a system (**Figure 6.2**). Entropy is a measure of the randomness of molecules in a system. When a physical system becomes more disordered, the entropy increases. As the energy becomes more evenly distributed, that energy is less able to promote change or do work. When energy is converted from one form to another, some energy may become unusable by living organisms. For example, unusable heat may be released during a chemical reaction.

(a) Kinetic energy   **(b) Potential energy**

Figure 6.1   **Examples of energy.**   (a) Kinetic energy, such as swinging a bat, is energy associated with motion. (b) Potential energy is stored energy, as in a bow that is ready to fire an arrow.

Next, we will see how the two laws of thermodynamics place limits on the ways that living cells can use energy for their own needs.

The Change in Free Energy Determines the Direction of a Chemical Reaction or Any Other Cellular Process

Energy is necessary for living organisms to exist. Energy is required for many cellular processes, including chemical reactions, cellular movements such as those occurring in muscle contraction, and the maintenance of cell organization. To understand how living organisms use energy, we need to distinguish between the energy that can be used to promote change or do work (usable energy) and the energy that cannot (unusable energy).

Total energy = Usable energy + Unusable energy

Why is some energy unusable? The main culprit is entropy. As stated by the second law of thermodynamics, energy transformations involve an increase in entropy, a measure of the disorder that cannot be harnessed in a useful way. The total energy is termed **enthalpy** (**H**), and the usable energy—the

Table 6.1	Types of Energy That Are Important in Biology	
Energy type	**Description**	**Biological example**
Light	Light is a form of electromagnetic radiation. The energy of light is packaged in photons.	During photosynthesis, light energy is captured by pigments (see Chapter 8). Ultimately, this energy is used to reduce carbon and produce organic molecules.
Heat	Heat is the transfer of kinetic energy from one object to another or from an energy source to an object. In biology, heat is often viewed as energy that can be transferred due to a difference in temperature between two objects or locations.	Many organisms, such as humans, maintain their bodies at a constant temperature. This is achieved, in part, by chemical reactions that generate heat.
Mechanical	Mechanical energy is the energy possessed by an object due to its motion or its position relative to other objects.	In animals, mechanical energy is associated with movements due to muscle contraction, such as walking.
Chemical	Chemical energy is stored in the chemical bonds of molecules. When the bonds are broken and rearranged, large amounts of energy can be released.	The covalent bonds in organic molecules, such as glucose and ATP, store large amounts of energy. When bonds are broken in larger molecules to form smaller molecules, the chemical energy that is released can be used to drive cellular processes.
Electrical/ion gradient	The movement of charge or the separation of charge can provide energy. Also, a difference in ion concentration across a membrane constitutes an electrochemical gradient, which is a source of potential energy.	During oxidative phosphorylation (described in Chapter 7), a H^+ gradient provides the energy to drive ATP synthesis.

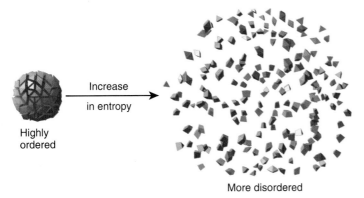

Figure 6.2 Entropy. Entropy is a measure of the disorder of a system. An increase in entropy means an increase in disorder.

Concept check: *Which do you think has more entropy, a NaCl crystal at the bottom of a beaker of water or the same beaker of water after the Na⁺ and Cl⁻ in the crystal have dissolved in the water?*

amount of available energy that can be used to promote change or do work—is called the **free energy** (**G**). The letter G is in recognition of J. Willard Gibbs, who proposed the concept of free energy in 1878. The unusable energy is the system's entropy (S). Gibbs proposed that these three factors are related to each other in the following way:

$$H = G + TS$$

where T is the absolute temperature in Kelvin (K). Because our focus is on free energy, we can rearrange this equation as

$$G = H - TS$$

A critical issue in biology is whether a process will or will not occur spontaneously. For example, will glucose be broken down into carbon dioxide and water? Another way of framing this question is to ask: Is the breakdown of glucose a spontaneous reaction? A spontaneous reaction or process is one that will occur without being driven by an input of energy. However, a spontaneous reaction does not necessarily proceed quickly. In some cases, the rate of a spontaneous reaction can be quite slow. For example, the breakdown of sugar is a spontaneous reaction, but the rate at which sugar in a sugar bowl would break down into CO_2 and H_2O would be very slow.

The key way to evaluate if a chemical reaction is spontaneous is to determine the free-energy change that occurs as a result of the reaction:

$$\Delta G = \Delta H - T\Delta S$$

where the Δ sign (the Greek letter delta) indicates a change, such as before and after a chemical reaction. If a chemical reaction has a negative free-energy change ($\Delta G < 0$), this means that the products have less free energy than the reactants, and, therefore, free energy is released during product formation. Such a reaction is said to be **exergonic**. Exergonic reactions are spontaneous. Alternatively, if a reaction has a positive free-energy change ($\Delta G > 0$), requiring the addition of free energy from the environment, it is termed **endergonic**. An endergonic reaction is not a spontaneous reaction.

If ΔG for a chemical reaction is negative, the reaction favors the formation of products, whereas a reaction with a positive ΔG favors the formation of reactants. Chemists have determined

Adenine (A)

Phosphate groups

Adenosine triphosphate (ATP)

Hydrolysis of ATP

Adenosine diphosphate (ADP)   **Phosphate (P$_i$)**

$$\Delta G = -7.3 \text{ kcal/mol}$$

Figure 6.3 **The hydrolysis of ATP to ADP and P$_i$.** As shown in this figure, ATP has a net charge of −4, and ADP and P$_i$ are shown with net charges of −2 each. When these compounds are shown in chemical reactions with other molecules, the net charges will also be indicated. Otherwise, these compounds will simply be designated ATP, ADP, and P$_i$. At neutral pH, ADP^{2-} will dissociate to ADP^{3-} and H$^+$.

Concept check: *Because ΔG is negative, what does that tell us about the direction of this chemical reaction? What does it tell us about the rate?*

free-energy changes for a variety of chemical reactions, which allows them to predict their direction. As an example, let's consider **adenosine triphosphate** (**ATP**), which is a molecule that is a common energy source for all cells. ATP is broken down to adenosine diphosphate (ADP) and inorganic phosphate (P$_i$). Because water is used to remove a phosphate group, chemists refer to this as the hydrolysis of ATP (**Figure 6.3**). In the reaction of converting 1 mole of ATP to 1 mole of ADP and P$_i$, ΔG equals −7.3 kcal/mole. Because this is a negative value, the reaction strongly favors the formation of products. As discussed later in this chapter, the energy liberated by the hydrolysis of ATP is used to drive a variety of cellular processes.

Chemical Reactions Will Eventually Reach a State of Equilibrium

Even when a chemical reaction is associated with a negative free-energy change, not all of the reactants are converted to products. The reaction reaches a state of **chemical equilibrium** in which the rate of formation of products equals the rate of formation of reactants. Let's consider the generalized reaction

$$a\text{A} + b\text{B} \rightleftharpoons c\text{C} + d\text{D}$$

where again A and B are the reactants, C and D are the products, and a, b, c, and d are the number of moles of reactants and products. An equilibrium occurs, such that:

$$K_{eq} = \frac{[\text{C}]^c[\text{D}]^d}{[\text{A}]^a[\text{B}]^b}$$

where K_{eq} is the equilibrium constant. Each type of chemical reaction will have a specific value for K_{eq}.

Biologists make two simplifying assumptions when determining values for equilibrium constants. First, the concentration of water does not change during the reaction, and the pH remains constant at pH 7. The equilibrium constant under these conditions is designated K_{eq}' (' is the prime symbol). If water is one of the reactants, as in a hydrolysis reaction, it is not included in the chemical equilibrium equation. As an example, let's consider the chemical equilibrium for the hydrolysis of ATP.

$$\text{ATP}^{4-} + \text{H}_2\text{O} \rightleftharpoons \text{ADP}^{2-} + \text{P}_i^{2-}$$

$$K_{eq}' = \frac{[\text{ADP}][\text{P}_i]}{[\text{ATP}]}$$

Experimentally, the value for K_{eq}' for this reaction has been determined and found to be approximately 1,650,000 M. Such a large value indicates that the equilibrium greatly favors the formation of products—ADP and P_i.

Cells Use ATP to Drive Endergonic Reactions

In living organisms, many vital processes require the addition of free energy; that is, they are endergonic and will not occur spontaneously. Fortunately, organisms have a way to overcome this problem. Rather than catalyzing exothermic reactions that release energy in the form of unusable heat, cells often couple exergonic reactions with endergonic reactions. If an exergonic reaction is coupled to an endergonic reaction, the endergonic reaction will proceed spontaneously if the net free-energy change for both processes combined is negative. For example, consider the following reactions:

Glucose + phosphate^{2-} → Glucose-6-phosphate^{2-} + H$_2$O

$$\Delta G = +3.3 \text{ kcal/mole}$$

ATP^{4-} + H$_2$O → ADP^{2-} + P$_i^{2-}$ $\Delta G = -7.3$ kcal/mole

Coupled reaction:

Glucose + ATP^{4-} → Glucose-6-phosphate^{2-} + ADP^{2-}

$$\Delta G = -4.0 \text{ kcal/mole}$$

The first reaction, in which phosphate is covalently attached to glucose, is endergonic, whereas the second, the hydrolysis

of ATP, is exergonic. By itself, the first reaction would not be spontaneous. If the two reactions are coupled, however, the net free-energy change for both reactions combined is exergonic. In the coupled reaction, a phosphate is directly transferred from ATP to glucose in a process called **phosphorylation**. This coupled reaction proceeds spontaneously because the net free-energy change is negative. Exergonic reactions, such as the breakdown of ATP, are commonly coupled to cellular processes that would otherwise be endergonic or require energy.

6.2 Enzymes and Ribozymes

For most chemical reactions in cells to proceed at a rapid pace, such as the breakdown of sugar, a catalyst is needed. A **catalyst** is an agent that speeds up the rate of a chemical reaction without being permanently changed or consumed. In living cells, the most common catalysts are enzymes. The term was coined in 1876 by a German physiologist, Wilhelm Kühne, who discovered trypsin, an enzyme in pancreatic juice that is needed for digestion of food proteins. In this section, we will explore how enzymes are able to increase the rate of chemical reactions. Interestingly, some biological catalysts are RNA molecules called ribozymes. We will also examine a few examples in which RNA molecules carry out catalytic functions.

Enzymes Increase the Rates of Chemical Reactions

Thus far, we have examined aspects of energy and considered how the laws of thermodynamics are related to the direction of chemical reactions. If a chemical reaction has a negative free-energy change, the reaction will be spontaneous; it will tend to proceed in the direction of reactants to products. Although thermodynamics governs the direction of an energy transformation, it does not control the rate of a chemical reaction. For example, the breakdown of the molecules in gasoline to smaller molecules is a highly exergonic reaction. Even so, we could place gasoline and oxygen in a container and nothing much would happen (provided it wasn't near a flame). If we came back several days later, we would expect to see the gasoline still sitting there. Perhaps if we came back in a few million years, the gasoline would have been broken down. On a timescale of months or a few years, however, the chemical reaction would proceed very slowly.

In living cells, the rates of enzyme-catalyzed reactions typically occur millions of times faster than the corresponding uncatalyzed reactions. An extreme example is the enzyme catalase, which is found in peroxisomes (see Chapter 4). This enzyme catalyzes the breakdown of hydrogen peroxide (H_2O_2) into water and oxygen. Catalase speeds up this reaction 10^{15}-fold faster than the uncatalyzed reaction!

Why are catalysts necessary to speed up a chemical reaction? When a covalent bond is broken or formed, this process initially involves the straining or stretching of one or more bonds in the starting molecule(s), and/or it may involve the positioning of two molecules so they interact with each other properly. Let's consider the reaction in which ATP is used to phosphorylate glucose.

$$\text{Glucose} + \text{ATP}^{4-} \rightarrow \text{Glucose-phosphate}^{2-} + \text{ADP}^{2-}$$

For a reaction to occur between glucose and ATP, the molecules must collide in the correct orientation and possess enough energy so that chemical bonds can be changed. As glucose and ATP approach each other, their electron clouds cause repulsion. To overcome this repulsion, an initial input of energy, called the **activation energy**, is required (**Figure 6.4**). Activation energy allows the molecules to get close enough to cause a rearrangement of bonds. With the input of activation energy, glucose and ATP can achieve a **transition state** in which the original bonds have stretched to their limit. Once the reactants have reached the transition state, the chemical reaction can readily proceed to the formation of products, which in this case is glucose-phosphate and ADP.

The activation energy required to achieve the transition state is a barrier to the formation of products. This barrier is the reason why the rate of many chemical reactions is very slow. There are two common ways to overcome this barrier and thereby accelerate a chemical reaction. First, the reactants could be exposed to a large amount of heat. For example, as we noted previously, if gasoline is sitting at room temperature, nothing much happens. However, if the gasoline is exposed to a flame or spark, it breaks down rapidly, perhaps at an explosive rate! Alternatively, a second strategy is to lower the activation energy barrier. Enzymes lower the activation energy to a point where a small amount of available heat can push the reactants to a transition state (Figure 6.4).

How do enzymes lower the activation energy barrier of chemical reactions? Enzymes are generally large proteins that bind relatively small reactants (Figure 6.4). When bound to an enzyme, the bonds in the reactants can be strained, thereby making it easier for them to achieve the transition state. This is one way that enzymes lower the activation energy. In addition, when a chemical reaction involves two or more reactants, the enzyme provides a site in which the reactants are positioned very close to each other in an orientation that facilitates the formation of new covalent bonds. This also lowers the necessary activation energy for a chemical reaction.

Straining the reactants and bringing them close together are two common ways that enzymes lower the activation energy barrier. In addition, enzymes may facilitate a chemical reaction by changing the local environment of the reactants. For example, amino acids in an enzyme may have charges that affect the chemistry of the reactants. In some cases, enzymes lower the activation energy by directly participating in the chemical reaction. For example, certain enzymes that hydrolyze ATP form a covalent bond between phosphate and an amino acid in the enzyme. However, this is a temporary condition. The covalent bond between phosphate and the amino acid is quickly broken, releasing the phosphate and returning the amino acid back to its original condition. An example of such an enzyme is Na$^+$/K$^+$-ATPase, described in Chapter 5 (refer back to Figure 5.25).

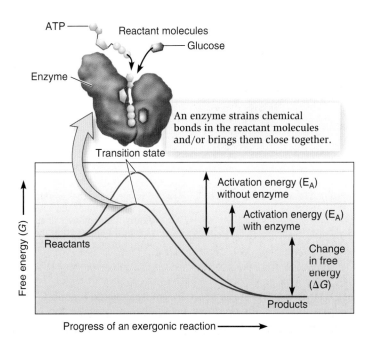

Figure 6.4 **Activation energy of a chemical reaction.** This figure depicts an exergonic reaction. The activation energy is needed for molecules to achieve a transition state. One way that enzymes lower the activation energy is by straining the reactants so that less energy is required to attain the transition state. A second way is by binding two reactants so they are close to each other and in a favorable orientation.

Concept check: *How does lowering the activation energy affect the rate of a chemical reaction? How does it affect the direction?*

Enzymes Recognize Their Substrates with High Specificity and Undergo Conformational Changes

Thus far, we have considered how enzymes lower the activation energy of a chemical reaction and thereby increase its rate. Let's consider some other features of enzymes that enable them to serve as effective catalysts in chemical reactions. The **active site** is the location in an enzyme where the chemical reaction takes place. The **substrates** for an enzyme are the reactant molecules that bind to an enzyme at the active site and participate in the chemical reaction. For example, hexokinase is an enzyme whose substrates are glucose and ATP (**Figure 6.5**). The binding between an enzyme and substrate produces an **enzyme-substrate complex**.

A key feature of nearly all enzymes is they bind their substrates with a high degree of **specificity**. For example, hexokinase recognizes glucose but does not recognize other similar sugars very well, such as fructose and galactose. In 1894, the German scientist Emil Fischer proposed that the recognition of a substrate by an enzyme resembles the interaction between a lock and key: only the right-sized key (the substrate) will fit into the keyhole (active site) of the lock (the enzyme). Further research revealed that the interaction between an enzyme and its substrates also involves movements or conformational changes in the enzyme itself. As shown in Figure 6.5, these

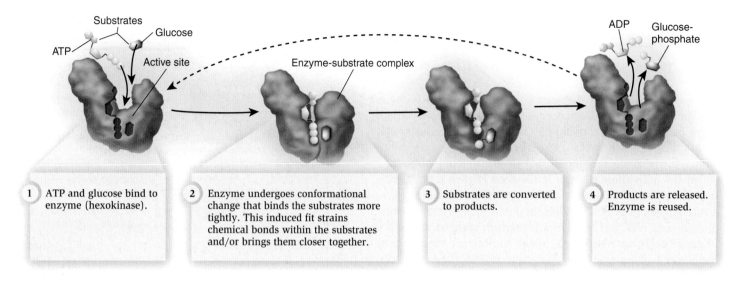

| 1 | ATP and glucose bind to enzyme (hexokinase). | 2 | Enzyme undergoes conformational change that binds the substrates more tightly. This induced fit strains chemical bonds within the substrates and/or brings them closer together. | 3 | Substrates are converted to products. | 4 | Products are released. Enzyme is reused. |

Figure 6.5   **The steps of an enzyme-catalyzed reaction.**   The example shown here involves the enzyme hexokinase, which binds glucose and ATP. The products are glucose-phosphate and ADP, which are released from the enzyme.

Concept check: *During which step is the activation energy lowered?*

conformational changes cause the substrates to bind more tightly to the enzyme, a phenomenon called **induced fit**, which was proposed by American biochemist Daniel Koshland in 1958. Only after this conformational change takes place does the enzyme catalyze the conversion of reactants to products.

Competitive and Noncompetitive Inhibitors Affect Enzyme Function

Molecules or ions may bind to enzymes and inhibit their function. To understand how such inhibitors work, researchers compare the function of enzymes in the absence or presence of inhibitors. Let's first consider enzyme function in the absence of an inhibitor. In the experiment of **Figure 6.6a**, tubes labeled A, B, C, and D each contained one microgram of enzyme. This enzyme recognizes a single type of substrate and converts it to a product. For each data point, the substrate concentration added to each tube was varied from a low to a high level. The samples were incubated for 60 seconds, and then the amount of product in each tube was measured. In this example, the velocity of the chemical reaction is expressed as the amount of product produced per second. As we see in Figure 6.6a, the velocity increases as the substrate concentration increases, but eventually reaches a plateau. Why does the plateau occur? At high substrate concentrations, nearly all of the active sites of the enzyme are occupied with substrate, so increasing the substrate concentration further has a negligible effect. At this point, the enzyme is saturated with substrate, and the velocity of the chemical reaction is near its maximal rate, called its V_{max}.

Figure 6.6a also helps us understand the relationship between substrate concentration and velocity. The K_M is the substrate concentration at which the velocity is half its maximal value. The K_M is also called the Michaelis constant in honor

of the German biochemist Leonor Michaelis, who carried out pioneering work with the Canadian biochemist Maud Menten on the study of enzymes. The K_M is a measure of the substrate concentration required for catalysis to occur. An enzyme with a high K_M requires a higher substrate concentration to achieve a particular reaction velocity compared to an enzyme with a lower K_M.

For an enzyme-catalyzed reaction, we can view the formation of product as occurring in two steps: (1) binding or release of substrate and (2) formation of product.

$$E + S \rightleftharpoons ES \rightarrow E + P$$

where

E is the enzyme

S is the substrate

ES is the enzyme-substrate complex

P is the product

If the second step—the rate of product formation—is much slower than the rate of substrate release, the K_M is inversely related to the **affinity** degree of attraction—between the enzyme and substrate. For example, let's consider an enzyme that breaks down ATP into ADP and P_i. If the rate of formation of ADP and P_i is much slower than the rate of ATP release, the K_M for such an enzyme is a measure of its affinity for ATP. In such cases, the K_M and affinity show an inverse relationship. Enzymes with a high K_M have a low affinity for their substrates—they bind them more weakly. By comparison, enzymes with a low K_M have a high affinity for their substrates—they bind them more tightly.

Now that we understand the relationship between substrate concentration and the velocity of an enzyme-catalyzed

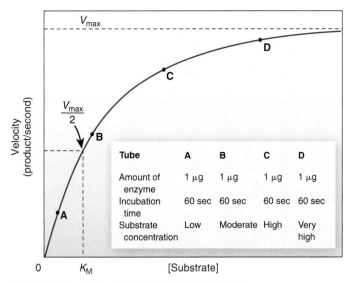

(a) Reaction velocity in the absence of inhibitors

Tube	A	B	C	D
Amount of enzyme	1 μg	1 μg	1 μg	1 μg
Incubation time	60 sec	60 sec	60 sec	60 sec
Substrate concentration	Low	Moderate	High	Very high

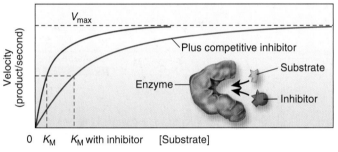

(b) Competitive inhibition

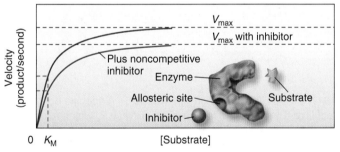

(c) Noncompetitive inhibition

Figure 6.6 **The relationship between velocity and substrate concentration in an enzyme-catalyzed reaction, and the effects of inhibitors.** **(a)** In the absence of an inhibitor, the maximal velocity (V_{max}) is achieved when the substrate concentration is high enough to be saturating. The K_M value is the substrate concentration where the velocity is half the maximal velocity. **(b)** A competitive inhibitor binds to the active site of an enzyme and raises the K_M for the substrate. **(c)** A noncompetitive inhibitor binds outside the active site to an allosteric site and lowers the V_{max} for the reaction.

Concept check: *Enzyme A has a K_M of 0.1 mM, whereas enzyme B has a K_M of 1.0 mM. They both have the same V_{max}. If the substrate concentration was 0.5 mM, which reaction—the one catalyzed by enzyme A or B—would have the higher velocity?*

reaction, we can explore how inhibitors may affect enzyme function. **Competitive inhibitors** are molecules that bind to the active site of an enzyme and inhibit the ability of the substrate to bind. Such inhibitors compete with the substrate for the ability to bind to the enzyme. Competitive inhibitors usually have a structure or a portion of their structure that mimics the structure of the enzyme's substrate. As seen in **Figure 6.6b**, when competitive inhibitors are present, the apparent K_M for the substrate increases—a higher concentration of substrate is needed to achieve the same velocity of the chemical reaction. In this case, the effects of the competitive inhibitor can be overcome by increasing the concentration of the substrate.

By comparison, **Figure 6.6c** illustrates the effects of a **noncompetitive inhibitor**. As seen here, this type of inhibitor lowers the V_{max} for the reaction without affecting the K_M. A noncompetitive inhibitor binds noncovalently to an enzyme at a location outside the active site, called an **allosteric site**, and inhibits the enzyme's function. In this example, a molecule binding to the allosteric site inhibits the enzyme's function, but for other enzymes, such binding can enhance their function.

Additional Factors Influence Enzyme Function

Enzymes, which are composed of protein, sometimes require additional nonprotein molecules or ions to carry out their functions. **Prosthetic groups** are small molecules that are permanently attached to the surface of an enzyme and aid in catalysis. **Cofactors** are usually inorganic ions, such as Fe^{3+} or Zn^{2+}, that temporarily bind to the surface of an enzyme and promote a chemical reaction. Finally, some enzymes use **coenzymes**, organic molecules that temporarily bind to an enzyme and participate in the chemical reaction but are left unchanged after the reaction is completed. Some of these coenzymes can be synthesized by cells, but many of them are taken in as dietary vitamins by animal cells.

The ability of enzymes to increase the rate of a chemical reaction is also affected by the surrounding conditions. In particular, the temperature, pH, and ionic conditions play an important role in the proper functioning of enzymes. Most enzymes function maximally in a narrow range of temperature and pH. For example, many human enzymes work best at 37°C (98.6°F), which is the body's normal temperature. If the temperature was several degrees above or below this value due to infection or environmental causes, the function of many enzymes would be greatly inhibited (**Figure 6.7**). Increasing the temperature may have more severe effects on enzyme function if the protein structure of an enzyme is greatly altered. Very high temperatures may denature a protein—cause it to become unfolded. Denaturing an enzyme is expected to inhibit its function.

Enzyme function is also sensitive to pH. Certain enzymes in the stomach function best at the acidic pH found in this organ. For example, pepsin is a protease—an enzyme that digests proteins—that is released into the stomach. Its function is to degrade food proteins into shorter peptides. The optimal pH for pepsin function is around pH 2.0, which is extremely

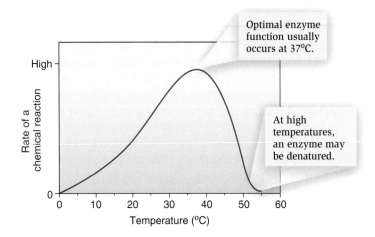

Optimal enzyme function usually occurs at 37°C.

At high temperatures, an enzyme may be denatured.

Figure 6.7 **Effects of temperature on a typical human enzyme.** Most enzymes function optimally within a narrow range of temperature. Many human enzymes function best at 37°C, which is body temperature.

acidic. By comparison, many cytosolic enzymes function optimally at a more neutral pH, such as pH 7.2, which is the pH normally found in the cytosol of human cells. If the pH was significantly above or below this value, enzyme function would be decreased for cytosolic enzymes.

FEATURE INVESTIGATION

The Discovery of Ribozymes by Sidney Altman Revealed That RNA Molecules May Also Function as Catalysts

Until the 1980s, scientists thought that all biological catalysts are proteins. One avenue of study that dramatically changed this view came from the analysis of ribonuclease P (RNase P), a catalyst initially found in the bacterium *Escherichia coli* and later identified in all species examined. RNase P is involved in the processing of tRNA molecules—a type of molecule required for protein synthesis. Such tRNA molecules are synthesized as longer precursor molecules called ptRNAs, which have 5′ and 3′ ends. (The 5′ and 3′ directionality of RNA molecules is described in Chapter 11.) RNase P breaks a covalent bond at a specific site in precursor tRNAs, which releases a fragment at the 5′ end and makes them shorter (**Figure 6.8**).

Sidney Altman and his colleagues became interested in the processing of tRNA molecules and turned their attention to RNase P in *E. coli*. During the course of their studies, they purified this enzyme and, to their surprise, discovered it has two subunits—one is an RNA molecule that contains 377 nucleotides, and the other is a small protein with a mass of 14 kDa. A complex between RNA and a protein is called a **ribonucleoprotein**. In 1990, the finding that a catalyst has an RNA subunit was very unexpected. Even so, a second property of RNase P would prove even more exciting.

Altman and colleagues were able to purify RNase P and study its properties in vitro. As mentioned earlier in this chapter, the functioning of enzymes is affected by the surrounding conditions. Cecilia Guerrier-Takada in Altman's laboratory determined that Mg^{2+} had a stimulatory effect on RNase P function. In the experiment described in **Figure 6.9**, the effects of Mg^{2+} were studied in greater detail. The researchers analyzed the effects of low (10 mM $MgCl_2$) and high (100 mM $MgCl_2$) magnesium concentrations on the processing of a ptRNA. At low or high magnesium concentrations, the ptRNA was incubated without RNase P (as a control); with the RNA subunit alone; or with intact RNase P (RNA subunit and protein sub-

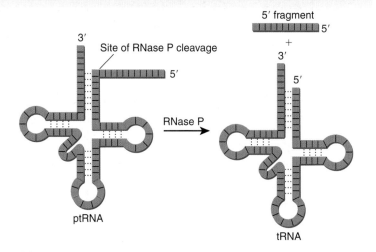

Figure 6.8 **The function of RNase P.** A specific bond in a precursor tRNA (ptRNA) is cleaved by RNase P, which releases a small fragment at the 5′ end. This results in the formation of a mature tRNA.

unit). Following incubation, they performed gel electrophoresis on the samples to determine if the ptRNAs had been cleaved into two pieces—the tRNA and a 5′ fragment.

Let's now look at the data. As a control, ptRNAs were incubated with low (lane 1) or high (lane 4) $MgCl_2$ in the absence of RNase P. As expected, no processing to a lower molecular mass tRNA was observed. When the RNA subunit alone was incubated with ptRNA molecules in the presence of low $MgCl_2$ (lane 2), no processing occurred, but it did occur if the protein subunit was also included (lane 3).

The surprising result is shown in lane 5. In this case, the RNA subunit alone was incubated with ptRNAs in the presence of high $MgCl_2$. The RNA subunit by itself was able to cleave the ptRNA to a smaller tRNA and a 5′ fragment! These results indicate that RNA molecules alone can act as catalysts that facilitate the breakage of a covalent bond. In this case, the RNA subunit

Figure 6.9   The discovery that the RNA subunit of RNase P is a catalyst.

HYPOTHESIS   The catalytic function of RNase P could be carried out by its RNA subunit or by its protein subunit.

KEY MATERIALS   Purified precursor tRNA (ptRNA) and purified RNA and protein subunits of RNase P from *E. coli*.

Experimental level   Conceptual level

1   Into each of five tubes, add ptRNA.

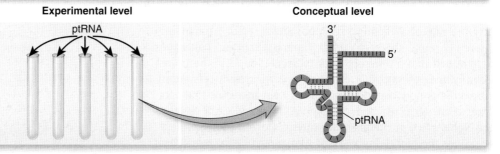

2   In tubes 1–3, add a low
concentration of MgCl$_2$;
in tubes 4 and 5, add a
high MgCl$_2$ concentration.

Low MgCl$_2$ High MgCl$_2$
(10 mM)   (100 mM)

3   Into tubes 2 and 5, add the RNA
subunit of RNase P alone; into tube
3, add both the RNA subunit and the
protein subunit of RNAase P.
Incubate to allow digestion to occur.
Note: Tubes 1 and 4 are controls that
have no added subunits of RNase P.

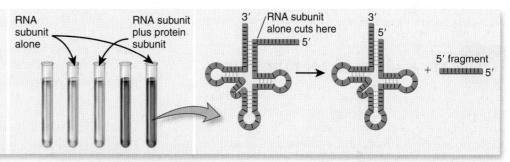

4   Carry out gel electrophoresis on
each sample. In this technique,
samples are loaded into a well on a
gel and exposed to an electric field
as described in Chapter 20. The
molecules move toward the bottom
of the gel and are separated
according to their masses: Molecules
with higher masses are closer to the
top of the gel. The gel is exposed to
ethidium bromide, which stains RNA.

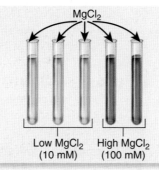

Catalytic function will
result in the digestion
of ptRNA into tRNA and
a smaller 5′ fragment.

5   **THE DATA**

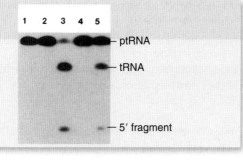

6   **CONCLUSION**   The RNA subunit alone can catalyze the breakage
of a covalent bond in ptRNA at high Mg
concentrations. It is a ribozyme.

7   **SOURCE**   Altman, S. 1990. Enzymatic cleavage of RNA by RNA.
Bioscience Reports 10:317–337.

is necessary and sufficient for ptRNA cleavage. Presumably, the high MgCl$_2$ concentration helps to keep the RNA subunit in a conformation that is catalytically active. Alternatively, the protein subunit plays a similar role in a living cell.

Subsequent work confirmed these observations and showed that the RNA subunit of RNase P is a true catalyst—it accelerates the rate of a chemical reaction, and it is not permanently altered. Around the same time, Thomas Cech and colleagues determined that a different RNA molecule found in the protist *Tetrahymena thermophila* also had catalytic activity. The term **ribozyme** is now used to describe an RNA molecule that catalyzes a chemical reaction. In 1989, Altman and Cech received the Nobel Prize in chemistry for their discovery of ribozymes.

Since the pioneering work of Altman and Cech, researchers have discovered that ribozymes play key catalytic roles in cells (**Table 6.2**). They are primarily involved in the processing of RNA molecules from precursor to mature forms. In addition, a ribozyme in the ribosome catalyzes the formation of covalent bonds between adjacent amino acids during polypeptide synthesis.

Experimental Questions

1. Briefly explain why it was necessary to purify the individual subunits of RNase P to show that it is a ribozyme.

2. In the Altman experiment involving RNase P, explain how the researchers experimentally determined if RNase P or

Table 6.2	Types of Ribozyme
General function	**Biological examples**
Processing of RNA molecules	1. RNase P: As described in this chapter, RNase P cleaves precursor tRNA molecules (ptRNAs) to a mature form.
	2. Spliceosomal RNA: As described in Chapter 12, eukaryotic pre-mRNAs often have regions called introns that are later removed. These introns are removed by a spliceosome composed of RNA and protein subunits. The RNA within the spliceosome is believed to function as a ribozyme that removes the introns from pre-mRNA.
	3. Certain introns found in mitochondrial, chloroplast, and prokaryotic RNAs are removed by a self-splicing mechanism.
Synthesis of polypeptides	The ribosome has an RNA component that catalyzes the formation of covalent bonds between adjacent amino acids during polypeptide synthesis.

subunits of RNase P were catalytically active or not. Why were two controls—one without protein and one without RNA—needed in this experiment?

3. Describe the critical results that showed RNase P is a ribozyme. How does the concentration of Mg^{2+} affect the function of the RNA in RNase P?

6.3 Overview of Metabolism

In the previous sections, we have examined the underlying factors that govern individual chemical reactions and explored the properties of enzymes and ribozymes. In living cells, chemical reactions are often coordinated with each other and occur in sequences called **metabolic pathways**, each step of which is catalyzed by a specific enzyme (**Figure 6.10**). These pathways are categorized according to whether the reactions lead to the breakdown or synthesis of substances. **Catabolic reactions** result in the breakdown of molecules into smaller molecules. Such reactions are often exergonic. By comparison, **anabolic reactions** involve the synthesis of larger molecules from smaller precursor molecules. This process usually is endergonic and, in living cells, must be coupled to an exergonic reaction. In this section, we will survey the general features of catabolic and anabolic reactions and explore the ways in which metabolic pathways are controlled.

Catabolic Reactions Recycle Organic Building Blocks and Produce Energy Intermediates Such as ATP and NADH

Catabolic reactions result in the breakdown of larger molecules into smaller ones. One reason for the breakdown of macromolecules is to recycle their building blocks to construct new macromolecules. For example, RNA molecules are composed of building blocks called nucleotides. The breakdown of RNA by enzymes called nucleases produces nucleotides that can be used in the synthesis of new RNA molecules.

$$\text{RNA} \xrightarrow{\text{Nucleases}} \text{Many individual nucleotides}$$

Polypeptides, which comprise proteins, are composed of a linear sequence of amino acids. When a protein is improperly folded or is no longer needed by a cell, the peptide bonds between amino acids in the protein are broken by enzymes called proteases. This generates amino acids that can be used in the construction of new proteins.

$$\text{Protein} \xrightarrow{\text{Proteases}} \text{Many individual amino acids}$$

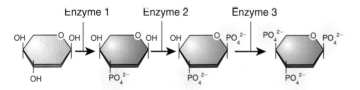

Figure 6.10   A metabolic pathway.   In this metabolic pathway, a series of different enzymes catalyze the attachment of phosphate groups to various sugars, beginning with a starting substrate and ending with a final product.

The breakdown of macromolecules, such as RNA molecules and proteins that are no longer needed, allows a cell to recycle the building blocks and use them to make new macromolecules. We will consider the mechanisms of recycling later in this chapter.

A second reason for the breakdown of macromolecules and smaller organic molecules is to obtain energy that can be used to drive endergonic processes in the cell. Covalent bonds store a large amount of energy. However, when cells break covalent bonds in organic molecules such as carbohydrates and proteins, they do not directly use the energy released in this process. Instead, the released energy is stored in **energy intermediates**, molecules such as ATP and NADH, that are then directly used to drive endergonic reactions in cells.

As an example, let's consider the breakdown of glucose into two molecules of pyruvate. As discussed in Chapter 7, the breakdown of glucose to pyruvate involves a catabolic pathway called glycolysis. Some of the energy released during the breakage of covalent bonds in glucose is harnessed to synthesize ATP. However, this does not occur in a single step. Rather, glycolysis involves a series of steps in which covalent bonds are broken and rearranged. This process creates molecules that can readily donate a phosphate group to ADP, thereby creating ATP. For example, phosphoenolpyruvate has a phosphate group attached to pyruvate. Due to the arrangement of bonds in phosphoenolpyruvate, this phosphate bond is easily broken. Therefore, the phosphate can be readily transferred to ADP:

$$\text{Phosphoenolpyruvate} + \text{ADP} \rightarrow \text{Pyruvate} + \text{ATP}$$

$$\Delta G = -7.5 \text{ kcal/mole}$$

This is an exergonic reaction and therefore favors the formation of products. In this step of glycolysis, the breakdown of an organic molecule, namely phosphoenolpyruvate, results in the synthesis of an energy intermediate molecule, ATP, which can then be used by a cell to drive endergonic reactions. This way of synthesizing ATP, termed **substrate-level phosphorylation**, occurs when an enzyme directly transfers a phosphate from an organic molecule to ADP, thereby making ATP. In this case, a phosphate is transferred from phosphoenolpyruvate to ADP. Another way to make ATP is via **chemiosmosis**. In this process, energy stored in an ion electrochemical gradient is used to make ATP from ADP and P_i. We will consider this mechanism in Chapter 7.

Redox Reactions Are Important in the Metabolism of Small Organic Molecules

During the breakdown of small organic molecules, **oxidation**—the removal of one or more electrons from an atom or molecule—may occur. This process is called oxidation because oxygen is frequently involved in chemical reactions that remove electrons from other molecules. By comparison, **reduction** is the addition of electrons to an atom or molecule. Reduction is

so named because the addition of a negatively charged electron reduces the net charge of a molecule.

Electrons do not exist freely in solution. When an atom or molecule is oxidized, the electron that is removed must be transferred to another atom or molecule, which becomes reduced. This type of reaction is termed a **redox reaction**, which is short for a reduction-oxidation reaction. As a generalized equation, an electron may be transferred from molecule A to molecule B as follows:

$$Ae^- + B \rightarrow A + Be^-$$
$$\text{(oxidized)} \quad \text{(reduced)}$$

As shown in the right side of this reaction, A has been oxidized (that is, had an electron removed), and B has been reduced (that is, had an electron added). In general, a substance that has been oxidized has less energy, whereas a substance that has been reduced has more energy.

During the oxidation of organic molecules such as glucose, the electrons are used to create energy intermediates such as NADH (**Figure 6.11**). In this process, an organic molecule has been oxidized, and **NAD$^+$ (nicotinamide adenine dinucleotide**) has been reduced to NADH. Cells use NADH in two common ways. First, as we will see in Chapter 7, the oxidation of NADH is a highly exergonic reaction that can be used to make ATP. Second, NADH can donate electrons to other organic molecules and thereby energize them. Such energized molecules can more readily form covalent bonds. Therefore, as described next, NADH is often needed in anabolic reactions that involve the synthesis of larger molecules through the formation of covalent bonds between smaller molecules.

Anabolic Reactions Require an Input of Energy to Make Larger Molecules

Anabolic reactions are also called **biosynthetic reactions**, because they are necessary to make larger molecules and macromolecules. We will examine the synthesis of macromolecules in several chapters of this textbook. For example, RNA and protein biosynthesis are described in Chapter 12. Cells also need to synthesize small organic molecules, such as amino acids and fats, if they are not readily available from food sources. Such molecules are made by the formation of covalent linkages between precursor molecules. For example, glutamate (an amino acid) is made by the covalent linkage between α-ketoglutarate (a product of sugar metabolism) and ammonium.

α-ketoglutarate Ammonium   Glutamate

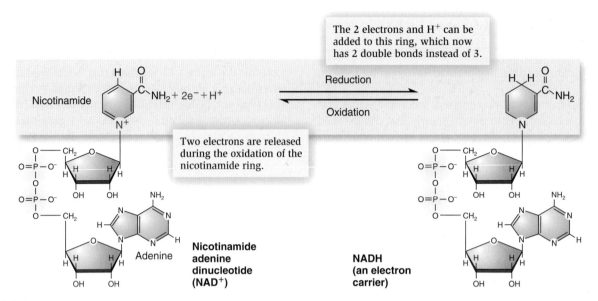

Figure 6.11 **The reduction of NAD^+ to create NADH.** NAD^+ is composed of two nucleotides, one with an adenine base and one with a nicotinamide base. The oxidation of organic molecules releases electrons that can bind to NAD^+, and along with a hydrogen ion, result in the formation of NADH. The two electrons and H^+ are incorporated into the nicotinamide ring. Note: The actual net charges of NAD^+ and NADH are minus one and minus two, respectively. They are designated NAD^+ and NADH to emphasize the net charge of the nicotinamide ring, which is involved in oxidation-reduction reactions.

Concept check: *Which is the oxidized form, NAD^+ or NADH?*

Subsequently, another amino acid, glutamine, is made from glutamate and ammonium.

$$\text{Glutamate} + NH_4^+ + ATP^{4-} + H_2O \longrightarrow \text{Glutamine} + ADP^{2-} + P_i^{2-}$$

Glutamate   Ammonium   Glutamine

In both reactions, an energy intermediate molecule such as NADH or ATP is needed to drive the reaction forward.

Genomes & Proteomes Connection

Many Proteins Use ATP as a Source of Energy

Over the past several decades, researchers have studied the functions of many types of proteins and discovered numerous examples in which a protein uses the hydrolysis of ATP to drive a cellular process (**Table 6.3**). In humans, a typical cell uses millions of ATP molecules per second. At the same time, the breakdown of food molecules to form smaller molecules releases energy that allows us to make more ATP from ADP and P_i. The turnover of ATP occurs at a remarkable pace. An average person hydrolyzes about 100 pounds of ATP per day, yet at any given time we do not have 100 pounds of ATP in our bodies. For this to happen, each ATP undergoes about

10,000 cycles of hydrolysis and resynthesis during an ordinary day (**Figure 6.12**).

By studying the structures of many proteins that use ATP, biochemists have discovered that particular amino acid sequences within proteins function as ATP-binding sites. This information has allowed researchers to predict whether a newly discovered protein uses ATP or not. When an entire genome sequence of a species has been determined, the genes that encode proteins can be analyzed to find out if the encoded proteins have ATP-binding sites in their amino acid sequences. Using this approach, researchers have been able to analyze

Table 6.3	Examples of Proteins That Use ATP for Energy
Type	**Description**
Metabolic enzymes	Many enzymes use ATP to catalyze endergonic reactions. For example, hexokinase uses ATP to attach phosphate to glucose.
Transporters	Ion pumps, such as the Na^+/K^+-ATPase, use ATP to pump ions against a gradient (see Chapter 5).
Motor proteins	Motor proteins such as myosin use ATP to facilitate cellular movement, as in muscle contraction (see Chapter 46).
Chaperones	Chaperones are proteins that use ATP to aid in the folding and unfolding of cellular proteins (see Chapter 4).
Protein kinases	Protein kinases are regulatory proteins that use ATP to attach a phosphate to proteins, thereby phosphorylating the protein and affecting its function (see Chapter 9).

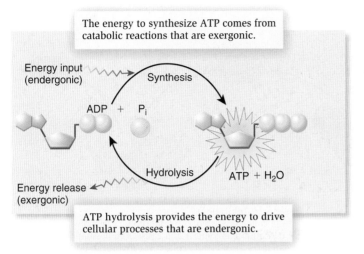

The energy to synthesize ATP comes from catabolic reactions that are exergonic.

Energy input (endergonic)

Synthesis

ADP + P_i

Hydrolysis

ATP + H_2O

Energy release (exergonic)

ATP hydrolysis provides the energy to drive cellular processes that are endergonic.

Figure 6.12   The ATP cycle.   Living cells continuously recycle ATP. The breakdown of food molecules into smaller molecules is used to synthesize ATP from ADP and P_i. The hydrolysis of ATP to ADP and P_i is used to drive many different endergonic reactions and processes that occur in cells.

Concept check: *If a large amount of ADP was broken down in the cell, how would this affect the ATP cycle?*

proteomes—all of the proteins that a given cell can make—and estimate the percentage of proteins that are able to bind ATP. This approach has been applied to the proteomes of bacteria, archaea, and eukaryotes.

On average, over 20% of all proteins bind ATP. However, this number is likely to be an underestimate of the total percentage of ATP-utilizing proteins because we may not have identified all of the types of ATP-binding sites in proteins. In humans, who have an estimated genome size of 20,000 to 25,000 different genes, a minimum of 4,000 to 5,000 of those genes encode proteins that use ATP. From these numbers, we can see the enormous importance of ATP as a source of energy for living cells.

Metabolic Pathways Are Regulated in Three General Ways

The regulation of metabolic pathways is important for a variety of reasons. Catabolic pathways are regulated so that organic molecules are broken down only when they are no longer needed or when the cell requires energy. During anabolic reactions, regulation assures that a cell synthesizes molecules only when they are needed. The regulation of catabolic and anabolic pathways occurs at the genetic, cellular, and biochemical levels.

Gene Regulation   Because enzymes in every metabolic pathway are encoded by genes, one way that cells control chemical reactions is via gene regulation. For example, if a bacterial cell is not exposed to a particular sugar in its environment, it will turn off the genes that encode the enzymes that are needed to break down that sugar. Alternatively, if the sugar becomes available, the genes are switched on. Chapter 13 examines the steps of gene regulation in detail.

Cellular Regulation   Metabolism is also coordinated at the cellular level. Cells integrate signals from their environment and adjust their chemical reactions to adapt to those signals. As discussed in Chapter 9, cell-signaling pathways often lead to the activation of protein kinases—enzymes that covalently attach a phosphate group to target proteins. For example, when people are frightened, they secrete a hormone called epinephrine into their bloodstream. This hormone binds to the surface of muscle cells and stimulates an intracellular pathway that leads to the phosphorylation of several intracellular proteins, including enzymes involved in carbohydrate metabolism. These activated enzymes promote the breakdown of carbohydrates, an event that supplies the frightened individual with more energy. Epinephrine is sometimes called the "fight-or-flight" hormone because the added energy prepares an individual to either stay and fight or run away. After a person is no longer frightened, hormone levels drop, and other enzymes called phosphatases remove the phosphate groups from enzymes, thereby restoring the original level of carbohydrate metabolism.

Another way that cells control metabolic pathways is via compartmentalization. The membrane-bound organelles of eukaryotic cells, such as the endoplasmic reticulum and mitochondria, serve to compartmentalize the cell. As discussed in Chapter 7, this allows specific metabolic pathways to occur in one compartment in the cell but not in others.

Biochemical Regulation   A third and very prominent way that metabolic pathways are controlled is at the biochemical level. In this case, the binding of a molecule to an enzyme directly regulates its function. As discussed earlier, one form of biochemical regulation involves the binding of molecules such as competitive or noncompetitive inhibitors (see Figure 6.6). An example of noncompetitive inhibition is a type of regulation called **feedback inhibition**, in which the product of a metabolic pathway inhibits an enzyme that acts early in the pathway, thus preventing the overaccumulation of the product (**Figure 6.13**).

Many metabolic pathways use feedback inhibition as a form of biochemical regulation. In such cases, the inhibited enzyme has two binding sites. One site is the active site, where the reactants are converted to products. In addition, enzymes controlled by feedback inhibition also have an allosteric site, where a molecule can bind noncovalently and affect the function of the active site. The binding of a molecule to an allosteric site causes a conformational change in the enzyme that inhibits its catalytic function. Allosteric sites are often found in the enzymes that catalyze the early steps in a metabolic pathway. Such allosteric sites typically bind molecules that are the products of the metabolic pathway. When the products bind to these sites, they inhibit the function of these enzymes and thereby prevent the formation of too much product.

Cellular and biochemical regulation are important and rapid ways to control chemical reactions in a cell. For a metabolic pathway composed of several enzymes, which enzyme in a pathway should be controlled? In many cases, a metabolic pathway has a **rate-limiting step**, which is the slowest step in a pathway. If the rate-limiting step is inhibited or enhanced, such

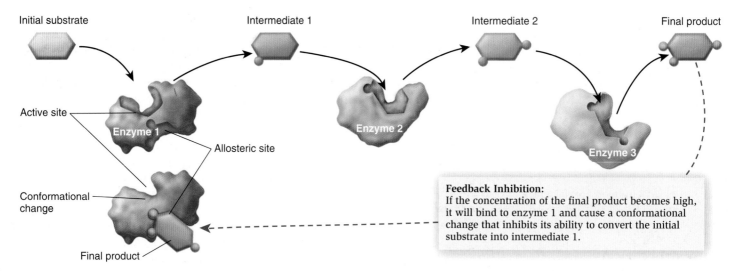

Figure 6.13 Feedback inhibition. In this process, the product of a metabolic pathway inhibits an enzyme that functions in the pathway, thereby preventing the overaccumulation of the product.

Concept check: *What would be the consequences if a mutation had no effect on the active site on enzyme 1 but altered its allosteric site so that it no longer recognized the final product?*

changes will have the greatest impact on the formation of the product of the metabolic pathway. Rather than affecting all of the enzymes in a metabolic pathway, cellular and biochemical regulation are often directed at the enzyme that catalyzes the rate-limiting step. This is an efficient and rapid way to control the amount of product of a pathway.

6.4 Recycling of Macromolecules

Except for DNA, which is stably maintained and inherited from cell to cell, other large molecules such as RNA, proteins, lipids, and polysaccharides typically exist for a relatively short period of time. Biologists often speak of the **half-life** of molecules, which is the time it takes for 50% of the molecules to be broken down and recycled. For example, a population of messenger RNA molecules in prokaryotes has an average half-life of about 5 minutes, whereas mRNAs in eukaryotes tend to exist for longer periods of time, on the order of 30 minutes to 24 hours or even several days.

Why is recycling important? To compete effectively in their native environments, all living organisms must efficiently use and recycle the organic molecules that are needed as building blocks to construct larger molecules and macromolecules. Otherwise, they would waste a great deal of energy making such building blocks. For example, organisms conserve an enormous amount of energy by re-using the amino acids that are needed to construct cellular proteins.

As discussed in Chapters 1 and 4, the characteristics of cells are controlled by the genome and the resulting proteome. The genome of every cell contains many genes that are transcribed into RNA. Most of these RNA molecules, called messenger RNA, or mRNA, encode proteins that ultimately determine the structure and function of cells. The expression of the genome is a very dynamic process, allowing cells to respond to changes in their environment. RNA and proteins are made when they are needed and then broken down when they are not. After they are broken down, the building blocks of RNA and proteins—nucleotides and amino acids—are recycled to make new RNAs and proteins. In this section, we will explore how RNAs and proteins are recycled and consider a mechanism for the recycling of materials found in an entire organelle.

Messenger RNA Molecules in Eukaryotes Are Broken Down by 5′ → 3′ Cleavage or by the Exosome

The degradation of mRNA serves two important functions. First, the proteins that are encoded by particular mRNAs may be needed only under certain conditions. A cell conserves energy by degrading mRNAs when such proteins are no longer necessary. Second, mRNAs may be faulty. For example, mistakes during mRNA synthesis can result in mRNAs that produce aberrant proteins. The degradation of faulty mRNAs is beneficial to the cell to prevent the potentially harmful effects of such aberrant proteins.

As described in Chapter 12, eukaryotic mRNAs contain a cap at their 5′ end. A tail is found at their 3′ end consisting of many adenine bases (look ahead to Figure 12.11). In most cases, degradation of mRNA begins with the removal of nucleotides in the poly A tail at the 3′ end (**Figure 6.14**). After the tail gets shorter, two mechanisms of degradation may occur.

In one mechanism, the 5′ cap is removed, and the mRNA is degraded by an **exonuclease**—an enzyme that cleaves off nucleotides, one at a time, from the end of the RNA. In this case, the exonuclease removes nucleotides starting at the 5′ end and moving toward the 3′. The nucleotides can then be used to make new RNA molecules.

The other mechanism involves mRNA being degraded by an **exosome**, a multiprotein complex discovered in 1997. Exosomes are found in eukaryotic cells and some archaea, whereas in bacteria a simpler complex called the degradosome carries out similar functions. The core of the exosome has a six-membered protein ring to which other proteins are attached (see inset to Figure 6.14). Certain proteins within the exosome are exonucleases that degrade the mRNA starting at the 3′ end and moving toward the 5′ end, thereby releasing nucleotides that can be recycled.

Proteins in Eukaryotes and Archaea Are Broken Down in the Proteasome

Cells continually degrade proteins that are faulty or no longer needed. To be degraded, proteins are recognized by **proteases**—enzymes that cleave the bonds between adjacent amino acids. The primary pathway for protein degradation in archaea and eukaryotic cells is via a protein complex called a **proteasome**. Similar to the exosome that has a central cavity surrounded by a ring of proteins, the core of the proteasome is formed from four stacked rings, each composed of seven protein subunits (**Figure 6.15a**). The proteasomes of eukaryotic cells also contain cap structures at each end that control the entry of proteins into the proteasome.

In eukaryotic cells, unwanted proteins are directed to a proteasome by the covalent attachment of a small protein called **ubiquitin**. **Figure 6.15b** describes the steps of protein degradation via eukaryotic proteasomes. First, a string of ubiquitin proteins are attached to the target protein. This event directs the protein to a proteasome cap, which has binding sites for ubiquitin. The cap also has enzymes that unfold the protein and inject it into the internal cavity of the proteasome core. The ubiquitin proteins are removed during entry and are returned to the cytosol for reuse. Inside the proteasome, proteases degrade the protein into small peptides and amino acids. The process is completed when the peptides and amino acids are recycled back into the cytosol. The amino acids can be used to make new proteins.

Ubiquitin targeting has two advantages. First, the enzymes that attach ubiquitin to its target recognize improperly folded proteins, allowing cells to identify and degrade nonfunctional proteins. Second, changes in cellular conditions may warrant the rapid breakdown of particular proteins. For example, cell division requires a series of stages called the cell cycle, which depends on the degradation of specific proteins. After these proteins perform their functions in the cycle, ubiquitin targeting directs them to the proteasome for degradation.

Autophagy Recycles the Contents of Entire Organelles

As described in Chapter 4, lysosomes contain many different types of acid hydrolases that break down proteins, carbohydrates, nucleic acids, and lipids. This enzymatic function enables lysosomes to break down complex materials. One function of lysosomes involves the digestion of substances that are taken up from outside the cell. This process, called endocytosis, is described in Chapter 5. In addition, lysosomes help digest intracellular materials. In a process known as **autophagy** (from the Greek, meaning eating one's self), cellular material, such as a worn-out organelle, becomes enclosed in a double membrane

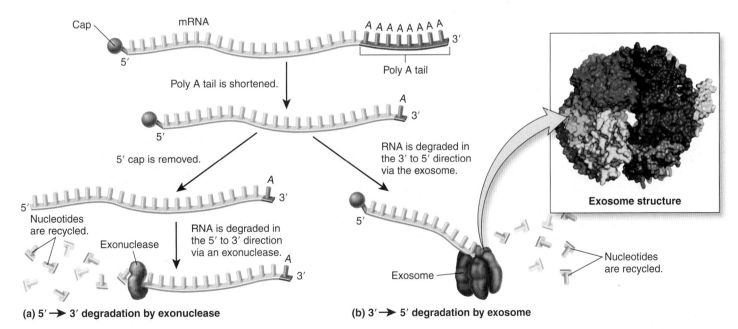

(a) 5′ → 3′ degradation by exonuclease

(b) 3′ → 5′ degradation by exosome

Figure 6.14   Two pathways for mRNA degradation in eukaryotic cells.   Degradation usually begins with a shortening of the poly A tail. After tail shortening, either **(a)** the 5′ cap is removed and the RNA degraded in a 5′ to 3′ direction by an exonuclease, or **(b)** the mRNA is degraded in the 3′ to 5′ direction via an exosome. The reason why cells have two different mechanisms for RNA degradation is not well understood.

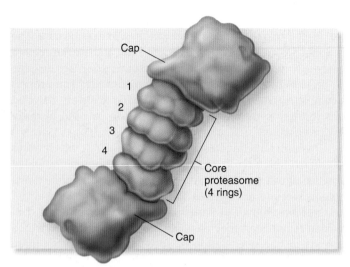

(a) Structure of the eukaryotic proteasome

Figure 6.15   Protein degradation via the proteasome.

Concept check: *What are advantages of protein degradation?*

(**Figure 6.16**). This double membrane is formed from a tubule that elongates and eventually wraps around the organelle to form an **autophagosome**. The autophagosome then fuses with a lysosome, and the material inside the autophagosome is digested. The small molecules released from this digestion are recycled back into the cytosol.

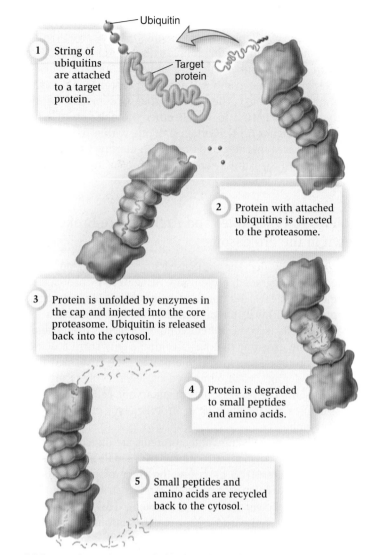

1   String of ubiquitins are attached to a target protein.

2   Protein with attached ubiquitins is directed to the proteasome.

3   Protein is unfolded by enzymes in the cap and injected into the core proteasome. Ubiquitin is released back into the cytosol.

4   Protein is degraded to small peptides and amino acids.

5   Small peptides and amino acids are recycled back to the cytosol.

(b) Steps of protein degradation in eukaryotic cells

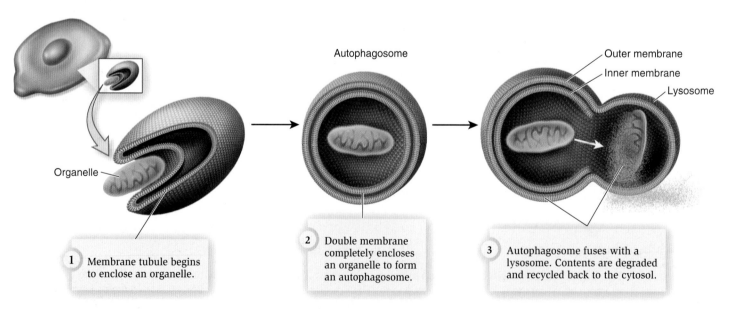

1   Membrane tubule begins to enclose an organelle.

2   Double membrane completely encloses an organelle to form an autophagosome.

3   Autophagosome fuses with a lysosome. Contents are degraded and recycled back to the cytosol.

Figure 6.16   Autophagy.

Summary of Key Concepts

6.1 Energy and Chemical Reactions

- The fate of a chemical reaction is determined by its direction and rate.

- Energy, the ability to promote change or do work, exists in many forms. According to the first law of thermodynamics, energy cannot be created or destroyed, but it can be converted from one form to another. The second law of thermodynamics states that energy interconversions involve an increase in entropy. (Figures 6.1, 6.2, Table 6.1)

- Free energy is the amount of available energy that can be used to promote change or do work. Spontaneous reactions, which release free energy, have a negative free-energy change. (Figure 6.3)

- An exergonic reaction has a negative free-energy change, whereas an endergonic reaction has a positive change. Chemical reactions proceed until they reach a state of chemical equilibrium, where the rate of formation of products equals the rate of formation of reactants.

- Exergonic reactions, such as the breakdown of ATP, are commonly coupled to cellular processes that would otherwise be endergonic.

6.2 Enzymes and Ribozymes

- Proteins that speed up the rate of a chemical reaction are called enzymes. They lower the activation energy that is needed to achieve a transition state. (Figure 6.4)

- Enzymes recognize reactants, also called substrates, with a high specificity. Conformational changes lower the activation energy for a chemical reaction. (Figure 6.5)

- Each enzyme-catalyzed reaction exhibits a maximal velocity (V_{max}). The K_M is the substrate concentration at which the velocity of the chemical reaction is half of the V_{max}. Competitive inhibitors raise the apparent K_M for the substrate, whereas noncompetitive inhibitors lower the V_{max}. (Figure 6.6)

- Enzyme function may be affected by a variety of other factors, including prosthetic groups, cofactors, coenzymes, temperature, and pH. (Figure 6.7)

- Altman and colleagues discovered that RNase P is a ribozyme—the RNA molecule within RNase P is a catalyst. Other ribozymes also play key roles in the cell. (Figures 6.8, 6.9, Table 6.2)

6.3 Overview of Metabolism

- Metabolism is the sum of the chemical reactions in a living organism. Enzymes often function in pathways that lead to the formation of a particular product. (Figure 6.10)

- Catabolic reactions involve the breakdown of larger molecules into smaller ones. These reactions regenerate small molecules that are used as building blocks to make new molecules. The small molecules are also broken down to make energy intermediates such as ATP and NADH. Such reactions are often redox reactions in which electrons are transferred from one molecule to another. (Figure 6.11)

- Anabolic reactions involve the synthesis of larger molecules and macromolecules.

- Cells continuously synthesize ATP from ADP and P_i and then hydrolyze it to drive endergonic reactions. Estimates from genome analysis indicate that over 20% of a cell's proteins use ATP. (Table 6.3, Figure 6.12)

- Metabolic pathways are controlled by gene regulation, cell signaling, compartmentalization, and feedback inhibition. (Figure 6.13)

6.4 Recycling of Macromolecules

- Large molecules in cells have a finite half-life.

- Recycling of macromolecules is important because it saves a great deal of energy for living organisms.

- Messenger RNAs in eukaryotes are degraded by 5′ to 3′ exonucleases or by the exosome. (Figure 6.14)

- Proteins in eukaryotes and archaea are degraded by the proteasome. (Figure 6.15)

- During autophagy in eukaryotes, an entire organelle is surrounded by a double membrane and then fuses with a lysosome. The internal contents are degraded, and the smaller building blocks are recycled to the cytosol. (Figure 6.16)

Assess and Discuss

Test Yourself

1. According to the second law of thermodynamics,
   a. energy cannot be created or destroyed.
   b. each energy transfer decreases the disorder of a system.
   c. energy is constant in the universe.
   d. each energy transfer increases the level of disorder in a system.
   e. chemical energy is a form of potential energy.

2. Reactions that release free energy are
   a. exergonic.
   b. spontaneous.
   c. endergonic.
   d. endothermic.
   e. both a and b.

3. Enzymes speed up reactions by
   a. providing chemical energy to fuel a reaction.
   b. lowering the activation energy necessary to initiate the reaction.
   c. causing an endergonic reaction to become an exergonic reaction.
   d. substituting for one of the reactants necessary for the reaction.
   e. none of the above.

4. Which of the following factors may alter the function of an enzyme?
   a. pH   d. all of the above
   b. temperature   e. b and c only
   c. cofactors

5. In biological systems, ATP functions by
   a. providing the energy to drive endergonic reactions.
   b. acting as an enzyme and lowering the activation energy of certain reactions.
   c. adjusting the pH of solutions to maintain optimal conditions for enzyme activity.
   d. regulating the speed at which endergonic reactions proceed.
   e. interacting with enzymes as a cofactor to stimulate chemical reactions.

6. In a chemical reaction, NADH is converted to $NAD^+ + H^+$. We would say that NADH has been
   a. reduced.
   b. phosphorylated.
   c. oxidized.
   d. decarboxylated.
   e. methylated.

7. Currently, scientists are identifying proteins that use ATP as an energy source by
   a. determining whether those proteins function in anabolic or catabolic reactions.
   b. determining if the protein has a known ATP-binding site.
   c. predicting the free energy necessary for the protein to function.
   d. determining if the protein has an ATP synthase subunit.
   e. all of the above.

8. With regard to its effects on an enzyme-catalyzed reaction, a competitive inhibitor
   a. lowers the K_M only.
   b. lowers the K_M and lowers the V_{max}.
   c. raises the K_M only.
   d. raises the K_M and lowers the V_{max}.
   e. raises the K_M and raises the V_{max}.

9. In eukaryotes, mRNAs may be degraded by
   a. a 5′ to 3′ exonuclease.
   b. the exosome.
   c. the proteasome.
   d. all of the above.
   e. a and b only.

10. Autophagy provides a way for cells to
    a. degrade entire organelles and recycle their components.
    b. automatically control the level of ATP.
    c. engulf bacterial cells.
    d. export unwanted organelles out of the cell.
    e. inhibit the first enzyme in a metabolic pathway.

Conceptual Questions

1. With regard to rate and direction, discuss the differences between endergonic and exergonic reactions.

2. Describe the mechanism and purpose of feedback inhibition in a metabolic pathway.

3. Why is recycling of amino acids and nucleotides an important metabolic function of cells? Explain how eukaryotic cells recycle amino acids found in worn-out proteins.

Collaborative Questions

1. Living cells are highly ordered units, yet the universe is heading toward higher entropy. Discuss how life can maintain its order in spite of the second law of thermodynamics. Are we defying this law?

2. What is the advantage of using ATP as a common energy source? Another way of asking this question is, Why is ATP an advantage over using a bunch of different food molecules? For example, instead of just having a Na^+/K^+-ATPase in a cell, why not have a bunch of different ion pumps each driven by a different food molecule, like a Na^+/K^+-glucosase (a pump that uses glucose), a Na^+/K^+-sucrase (a pump that uses sucrose), a Na^+/K^+-fatty acidase (a pump that uses fatty acids), and so on?

Online Resource

www.brookerbiology.com

Stay a step ahead in your studies with animations that bring concepts to life and practice tests to assess your understanding. Your instructor may also recommend the interactive ebook, individualized learning tools, and more.

Cellular Respiration, Fermentation, and Secondary Metabolism

7

Physical endurance. Conditioned athletes, like these marathon runners, have very efficient metabolism of organic molecules such as glucose.

C armen became inspired while watching the 2008 Summer Olympics and set a personal goal to run a marathon. Although she was active in volleyball and downhill skiing in high school, she had never attempted distance running. At first, running an entire mile was pure torture. She was out of breath, overheated, and unhappy, to say the least. However, she became committed to endurance training and within a few weeks discovered that running a mile was a "piece of cake." Two years later, she participated in her first marathon (42.2 kilometers or 26.2 miles) and finished with a time of 4 hours and 11 minutes—not bad for someone who had previously struggled to run a single mile!

How had Carmen's training allowed her to achieve this goal? Perhaps the biggest factor is that the training had altered the metabolism in her leg muscles. For example, the network of small blood vessels supplying oxygen to her leg muscles became more extensive, allowing the more efficient delivery of oxygen and removal of wastes. Second, her muscle cells developed more mitochondria. With these changes, Carmen's leg muscles were better able to break down organic molecules in her food and use them to make ATP.

The cells in Carmen's leg muscles had become more efficient at **cellular respiration**, which refers to the metabolic reactions that a cell uses to get energy from food molecules and release waste products. When we eat food, we are using much of that food for energy. People often speak of "burning calories." While metabolism does generate some heat, the chemical reactions that take place in the cells of living organisms are uniquely different from those that occur, say, in a fire. When wood is burned, the reaction produces enormous amounts of heat in a short period of time—the reaction lacks control. In contrast, the metabolism that occurs in living cells is extremely controlled. The food molecules from which we harvest energy give up that energy in a very restrained manner rather than all at once, as in a fire. An underlying theme in metabolism is the remarkable control that cells possess when they coordinate chemical reactions. A key emphasis of this chapter is how cells use energy that is stored within the chemical bonds of organic molecules.

We will begin by surveying a group of chemical reactions that involves the breakdown of carbohydrates, namely, the sugar glucose. As you will learn, cells carry out an intricate series of reactions so that glucose can be "burned" in a very controlled fashion when

oxygen is available. We will then examine how cells can use organic molecules in the absence of oxygen via processes known as anaerobic respiration and fermentation. Finally, we will consider secondary metabolism, which is not vital for cell survival, but produces organic molecules that serve unique and important functions.

7.1 Cellular Respiration in the Presence of Oxygen

As mentioned, cellular respiration is a process by which living cells obtain energy from organic molecules and release waste products. A primary aim of cellular respiration is to make ATP. When oxygen (O_2) is used, this process is termed **aerobic respiration**. During aerobic respiration, O_2 is used, and CO_2 is released via the oxidation of organic molecules. When we breathe, we inhale the oxygen needed for aerobic respiration and exhale the CO_2, a by-product of the process. For this reason, the term respiration has a second meaning, which is the act of breathing.

Different types of organic molecules, such as carbohydrates, proteins, and fats, can be used as energy sources to drive aerobic respiration. In this section, we will largely focus on the use of glucose as an energy source for cellular respiration.

$$C_6H_{12}O_6 + 6\,O_2 \rightarrow 6\,CO_2 + 6\,H_2O + \text{Energy intermediates} + \text{Heat}$$
Glucose

$$\Delta G = -686 \text{ kcal/mole}$$

We will examine the metabolic pathways in which glucose is broken down into carbon dioxide and water, thereby releasing a large amount of energy that is used to make many ATP molecules. In so doing, we will focus on four pathways: (1) glycolysis, (2) the breakdown of pyruvate, (3) the citric acid cycle, and (4) oxidative phosphorylation.

Distinct Metabolic Pathways Are Involved in the Breakdown of Glucose to CO_2

Let's begin our discussion of cellular respiration with an overview of the entire process. We will focus on the breakdown of glucose in a eukaryotic cell in the presence of oxygen. Certain covalent bonds within glucose store a large amount of chemical bond energy. When glucose is broken down via oxidation, ultimately to CO_2 and water, the energy within those bonds is released and used to make three types of energy intermediates: ATP, NADH, and $FADH_2$. The following is an overview of the stages that occur during the breakdown of glucose (**Figure 7.1**):

1. **Glycolysis:** In glycolysis, glucose (a compound with six carbon atoms) is broken down to two pyruvate molecules (with three carbons each), producing a net gain of two ATP molecules and two NADH molecules. The two ATP are made via **substrate-level phosphorylation**, which occurs when an enzyme directly transfers a phosphate from an organic molecule to ADP. In eukaryotes, glycolysis occurs in the cytosol.

2. **Breakdown of pyruvate to an acetyl group:** The two pyruvate molecules enter the mitochondrial matrix, where

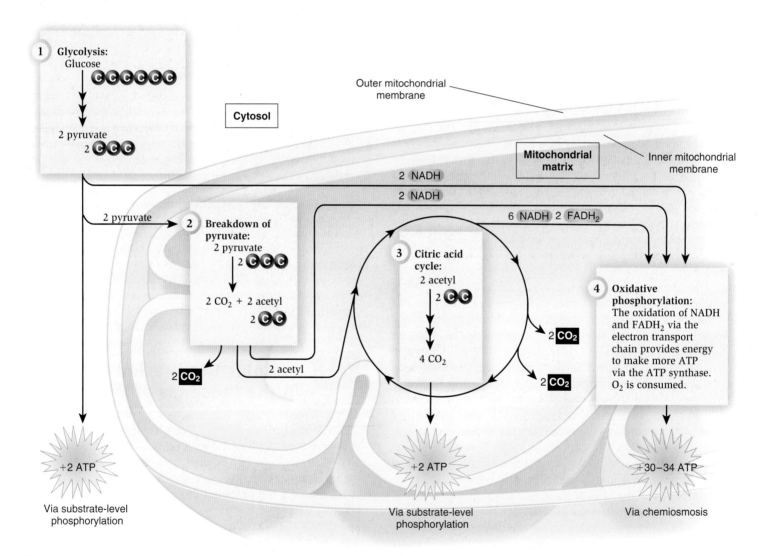

Figure 7.1 An overview of glucose metabolism.

Concept check: The breakdown of glucose produces a lot of NADH. What is this NADH mostly used for?

each one is broken down to an acetyl group (with two carbons each) and one CO_2 molecule. For each pyruvate broken down via oxidation, one NADH molecule is made by the reduction of NAD^+.

3. **Citric acid cycle:** Each acetyl group is incorporated into an organic molecule, which is later oxidized to liberate two CO_2 molecules. One ATP, three NADH, and one $FADH_2$ are made in this process. Because there are two acetyl groups (one from each pyruvate), the total yield is four CO_2, two ATP via substrate-level phosphorylation, six NADH, and two $FADH_2$. This process occurs in the mitochondrial matrix.

4. **Oxidative phosphorylation:** The NADH and $FADH_2$ made in the three previous stages contain high-energy electrons that can be readily transferred in a redox reaction to other molecules. Once removed from NADH or $FADH_2$ via oxidation, these high-energy electrons release some energy, and that energy is harnessed to produce a H^+ electrochemical gradient. In the process of **chemiosmosis**, energy stored in the H^+ electrochemical gradient is used to synthesize ATP from ADP and P_i. This process is called phosphorylation because ADP has become phosphorylated. Approximately 30 to 34 ATP molecules are made via chemiosmosis. As discussed later, oxidative phosphorylation is accomplished by two components: the electron transport chain and ATP synthase.

In eukaryotes, oxidation phosphorylation occurs along the cristae, which are invaginations of the inner mitochondrial membrane. The invaginations greatly increase the surface area of the inner membrane and thereby increase the amount of ATP that can be made. In prokaryotes, oxidative phosphorylation occurs along the plasma membrane.

Now, let's examine in detail the chemical changes that take place in each of these four stages.

Stage 1: Glycolysis Is a Metabolic Pathway That Breaks Down Glucose to Pyruvate

Glycolysis (from the Greek *glykos*, meaning sweet, and *lysis*, meaning splitting) involves the breakdown of glucose, a simple sugar. This process can occur in the presence or absence of oxygen, that is, under aerobic or anaerobic conditions. During the 1930s, the efforts of several German biochemists, including Gustav Embden, Otto Meyerhof, and Jacob Parnas, determined that glycolysis involves 10 steps, each one catalyzed by a different enzyme. The elucidation of these steps was a major achievement in the field of **biochemistry**—the study of the chemistry of living organisms. Researchers have since discovered that glycolysis is the common pathway for glucose breakdown in bacteria, archaea, and eukaryotes. Remarkably, the steps of glycolysis are virtually identical in nearly all living species, suggesting that glycolysis arose very early in the evolution of life on our planet.

The 10 steps of glycolysis can be grouped into three phases (**Figure 7.2**). The first phase (steps 1–3) involves an energy investment. Two ATP molecules are hydrolyzed, and the phosphates from those ATP molecules are attached to glucose, which is converted to fructose-1,6-bisphosphate. The energy investment phase raises the free energy of glucose and thereby allows later reactions to be exergonic. The cleavage phase (steps 4–5) breaks this six-carbon molecule into two molecules of glyceraldehyde-3-phosphate, which are three-carbon molecules. The third phase (steps 6–10) liberates energy to produce energy intermediates. In step 6, two molecules of NADH are made when two molecules of glyceraldehyde-3-phosphate

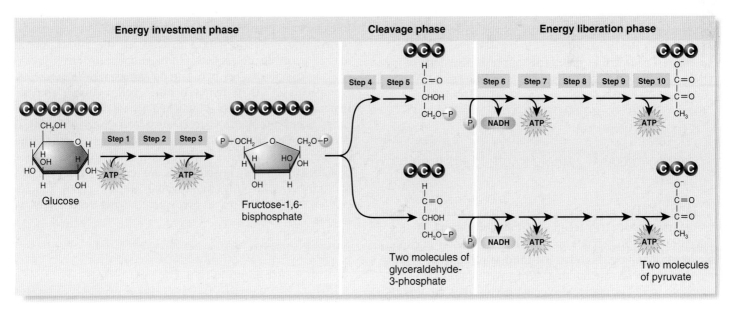

Figure 7.2   Overview of glycolysis.

Concept check: *Explain why the three phases are named the energy investment phase, the cleavage phase, and the energy liberation phase.*

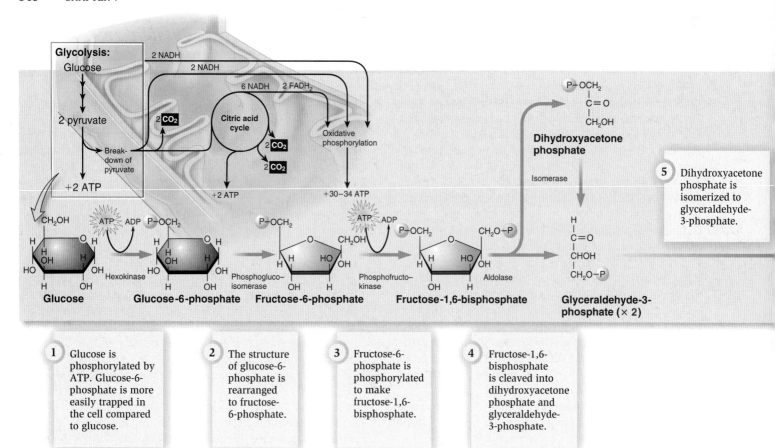

Figure 7.3 **A detailed look at the steps of glycolysis.** The pathway begins with a 6-carbon molecule (glucose) that is eventually broken down into 2 molecules that contain 3 carbons each. The notation **x 2** in the figure indicates that 2 of these 3-carbon molecules are produced from each glucose molecule.

Concept check: Which organic molecules donate a phosphate group to ADP during substrate-level phosphorylation?

are oxidized to two molecules of 1,3 bisphosphoglycerate. In steps 7 and 10, four molecules of ATP are made via substrate-level phosphorylation. Because two molecules of ATP are used in the energy investment phase, the net yield of ATP is two molecules.

Figure 7.3 describes the details of the 10 reactions of glycolysis. The net reaction of glycolysis is as follows:

$$C_6H_{12}O_6 + 2\ NAD^+ + 2\ ADP^{2-} + 2\ P_i^{2-} \rightarrow$$
Glucose

$$2\ CH_3(C{=}O)COO^- + 2\ H^+ + 2\ NADH + 2\ ATP^{4-} + 2\ H_2O$$
Pyruvate

How do cells control glycolysis? When a cell has a sufficient amount of ATP, feedback inhibition occurs. At high concentrations, ATP binds to an allosteric site in phosphofructokinase, which catalyzes the third step in glycolysis, the step thought to be rate limiting. When ATP binds to this allosteric site, a conformational change occurs that renders the enzyme functionally inactive. This prevents the further breakdown of glucose and thereby inhibits the overproduction of ATP. (Allosteric sites and rate-limiting steps are discussed in Chapter 6.)

Stage 2: Pyruvate Enters the Mitochondrion and Is Broken Down to an Acetyl Group and CO_2

In eukaryotes, pyruvate is made in the cytosol and then transported into the mitochondrion. Once in the mitochondrial matrix, pyruvate molecules are broken down (oxidized) by an enzyme complex called pyruvate dehydrogenase (**Figure 7.4**). A molecule of CO_2 is removed from each pyruvate, and the remaining acetyl group is attached to an organic molecule called coenzyme A (CoA) to create acetyl CoA. (In chemical equations, CoA is depicted as CoA—SH to emphasize how the SH group participates in the chemical reaction.) During this process, two high-energy electrons are removed from pyruvate and transferred to NAD^+ and together with H^+ create a molecule of NADH. For each pyruvate, the net reaction is as follows:

$$\overset{\displaystyle O\ \ \ O}{\underset{\text{Pyruvate}}{^-O{-}\overset{\parallel}{C}{-}\overset{\parallel}{C}{-}CH_3}} + \underset{\text{CoA}}{CoA{-}SH} + NAD^+ \rightarrow$$

$$\underset{\text{Acetyl CoA}}{CoA{-}S{-}\overset{\displaystyle O}{\overset{\parallel}{C}}{-}CH_3} + CO_2 + NADH$$

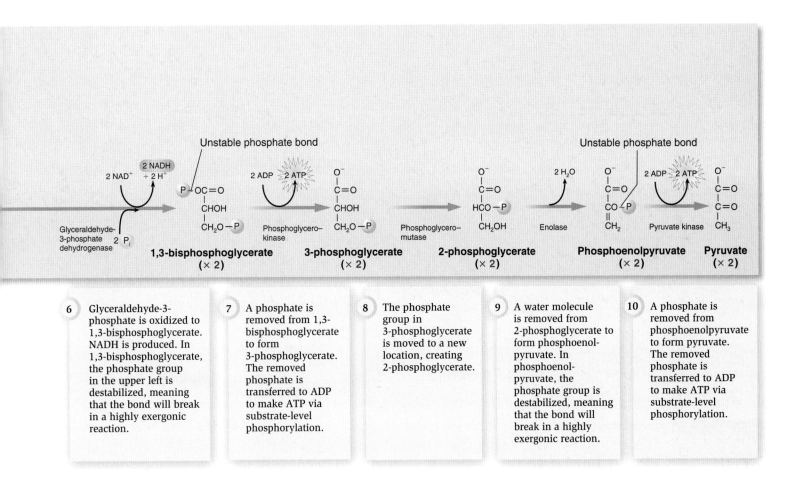

6. Glyceraldehyde-3-phosphate is oxidized to 1,3-bisphosphoglycerate. NADH is produced. In 1,3-bisphosphoglycerate, the phosphate group in the upper left is destabilized, meaning that the bond will break in a highly exergonic reaction.

7. A phosphate is removed from 1,3-bisphosphoglycerate to form 3-phosphoglycerate. The removed phosphate is transferred to ADP to make ATP via substrate-level phosphorylation.

8. The phosphate group in 3-phosphoglycerate is moved to a new location, creating 2-phosphoglycerate.

9. A water molecule is removed from 2-phosphoglycerate to form phosphoenolpyruvate. In phosphoenolpyruvate, the phosphate group is destabilized, meaning that the bond will break in a highly exergonic reaction.

10. A phosphate is removed from phosphoenolpyruvate to form pyruvate. The removed phosphate is transferred to ADP to make ATP via substrate-level phosphorylation.

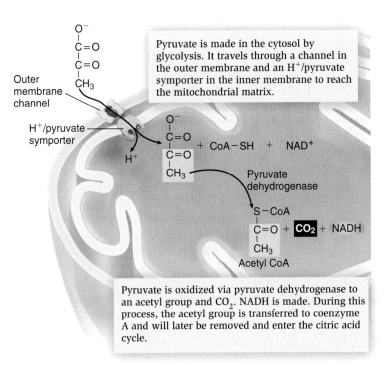

Figure 7.4 Breakdown of pyruvate and the attachment of an acetyl group to CoA.

The acetyl group is attached to CoA via a covalent bond to a sulfur atom. The hydrolysis of this bond releases a large amount of free energy, making it possible for the acetyl group to be transferred to other organic molecules. As described next, the acetyl group attached to CoA enters the citric acid cycle.

Stage 3: During the Citric Acid Cycle, an Acetyl Group Is Oxidized to Yield Two CO_2 Molecules

The third stage of sugar metabolism introduces a new concept, that of a **metabolic cycle**. During a metabolic cycle, particular molecules enter the cycle while others leave. The process is cyclical because it involves a series of organic molecules that are regenerated with each turn of the cycle. The idea of a metabolic cycle was first proposed in the early 1930s by German biochemist Hans Krebs. While studying carbohydrate metabolism in England, he analyzed cell extracts from pigeon muscle and determined that citric acid and other organic molecules participated in a cycle that resulted in the breakdown of carbohydrates to carbon dioxide. This cycle is called the **citric acid cycle**, or the Krebs cycle, in honor of Krebs, who was awarded the Nobel Prize in 1953.

An overview of the citric acid cycle is shown in Figure 7.5. In the first step of the cycle, the acetyl group (with two carbons) is removed from acetyl CoA and attached to oxaloacetate (with four carbons) to form citrate (with six carbons), also called

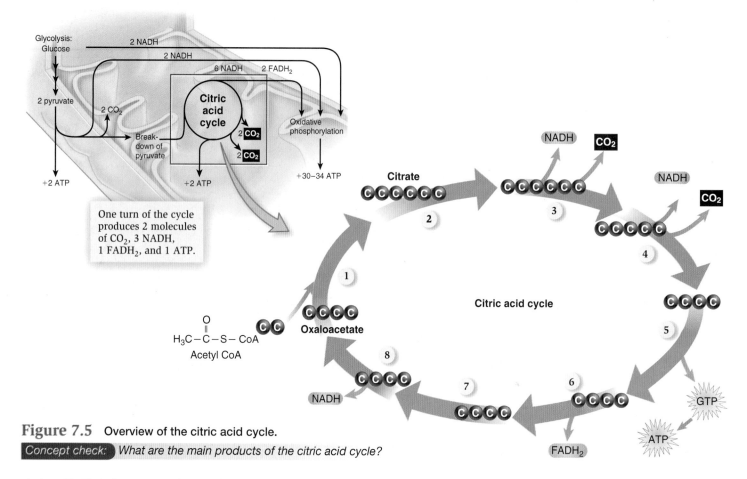

Figure 7.5 Overview of the citric acid cycle.

Concept check: *What are the main products of the citric acid cycle?*

citric acid. Then in a series of several steps, two CO_2 molecules are released. As this occurs, three molecules of NADH, one molecule of $FADH_2$, and one molecule of GTP are made. The GTP, which is made via substrate-level phosphorylation, is used to make ATP. After eight steps, oxaloacetate is regenerated so the cycle can begin again, provided acetyl CoA is available. **Figure 7.6** shows a more detailed view of the citric acid cycle. For each acetyl group attached to CoA, the net reaction of the citric acid cycle is as follows:

$$\text{Acetyl-CoA} + 2\ H_2O + 3\ NAD^+ + FAD + GDP^{2-} + P_i^{2-} \rightarrow$$
$$\text{CoA—SH} + 2\ CO_2 + 3\ NADH + FADH_2 + GTP^{4-} + 3\ H^+$$

How is the citric acid cycle controlled? One way is competitive inhibition. Oxaloacetate is a competitive inhibitor of succinate dehydrogenase, the enzyme that catalyzes step 6 of the cycle (Figure 7.6). When the oxaloacetate level becomes too high, succinate dehydrogenase is inhibited, and the citric acid cycle slows down.

Stage 4: During Oxidative Phosphorylation, NADH and $FADH_2$ Are Oxidized to Power ATP Production

Up to this point, the oxidation of glucose has yielded 6 molecules of CO_2, 4 molecules of ATP, 10 molecules of NADH, and 2 molecules of $FADH_2$. Let's now consider how high-energy electrons are removed from NADH and $FADH_2$ to make more ATP. This process is called **oxidative phosphorylation**. The

term refers to the observation that NADH and $FADH_2$ have had electrons removed and have thus become <u>oxidized</u>, and ATP is made by the <u>phosphorylation</u> of ADP (**Figure 7.7**). As described next, the oxidative process involves the electron transport chain, whereas the phosphorylation occurs via ATP synthase.

Oxidation: The Role of the Electron Transport Chain in Establishing an Electrochemical Gradient The **electron transport chain** (**ETC**) consists of a group of protein complexes and small organic molecules embedded in the inner mitochondrial membrane. These components are referred to as an electron transport chain because electrons are passed from one component to the next in a series of redox reactions (Figure 7.7). Most of the members of the ETC are protein complexes (designated I to IV) that have prosthetic groups, which are small molecules permanently attached to the surface of proteins that aid in their function. For example, cytochrome oxidase contains two prosthetic groups, each with an iron atom. The iron in each prosthetic group can readily accept and release an electron. One of the members of the electron transport chain, ubiquinone (Q), is not a protein. Rather, ubiquinone is a small organic molecule that can accept and release an electron. It is a nonpolar molecule that can diffuse through the lipid bilayer.

The red line in Figure 7.7 shows the path of electron flow. The electrons, which are originally located on NADH or $FADH_2$, are transferred to components of the ETC. The electron path is a series of redox reactions in which electrons are transferred to components with increasingly higher electronegativity. As discussed in Chapter 2, electronegativity is the ability to attract electrons. At the end of the chain is oxygen, which is the most electronegative and the final electron acceptor. The electron transport chain is also called the **respiratory chain** because the oxygen we breathe is used in this process.

NADH and $FADH_2$ donate their electrons at different points in the ETC. Two high-energy electrons from NADH are first transferred one at a time to NADH dehydrogenase (complex I). They are then transferred to ubiquinone (Q, also called coenzyme Q), cytochrome b-c_1 (complex III), cytochrome c, and cytochrome oxidase (complex IV). The final electron acceptor is O_2. By comparison, $FADH_2$ transfers electrons to succinate reductase (complex II), then to ubiquinone, and the rest of the chain.

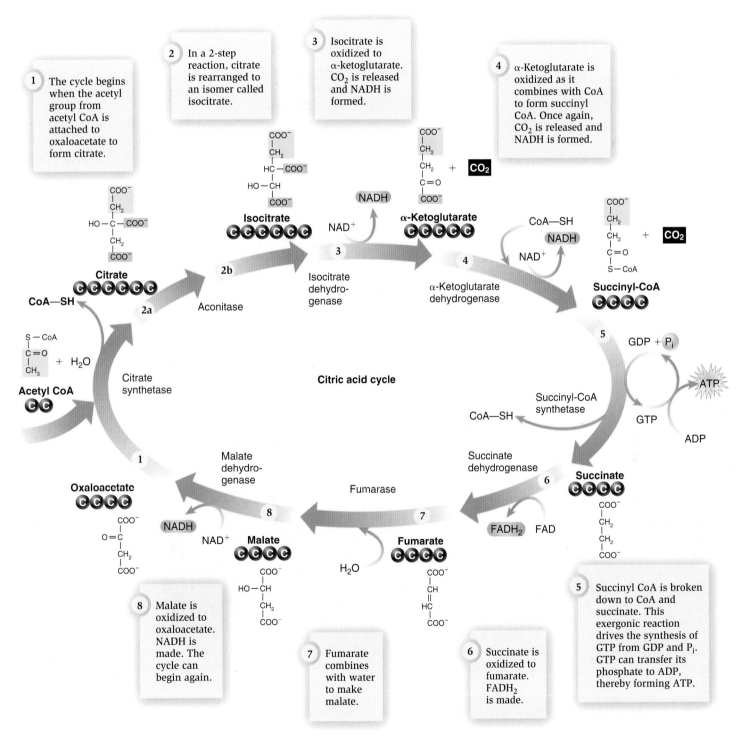

Figure 7.6 **A detailed look at the steps of the citric acid cycle.** The blue boxes indicate the location of the acetyl group, which is oxidized at step 6. (It is oxidized again in step 8.) The green boxes indicate the locations where CO_2 molecules are removed.

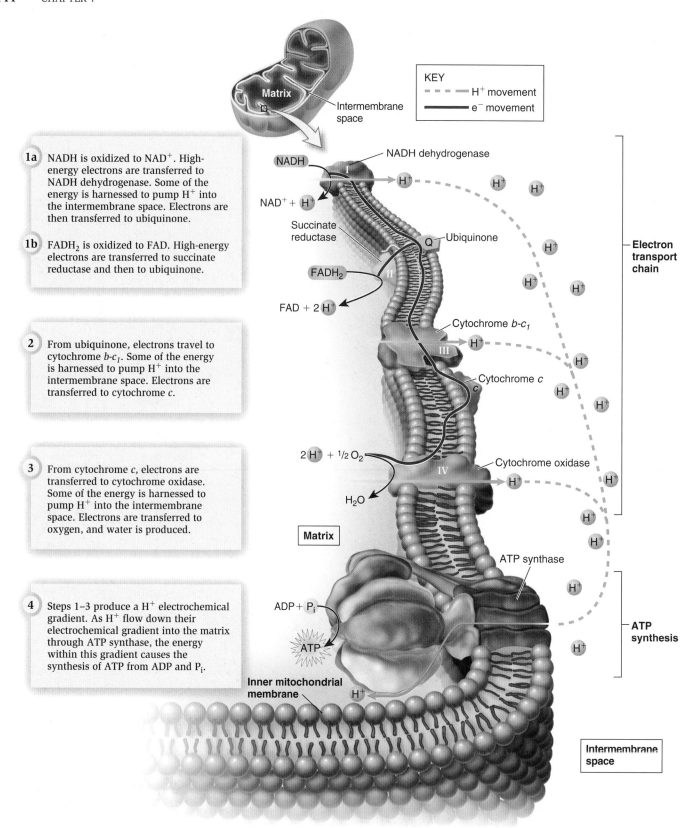

1a NADH is oxidized to NAD$^+$. High-energy electrons are transferred to NADH dehydrogenase. Some of the energy is harnessed to pump H$^+$ into the intermembrane space. Electrons are then transferred to ubiquinone.

1b FADH$_2$ is oxidized to FAD. High-energy electrons are transferred to succinate reductase and then to ubiquinone.

2 From ubiquinone, electrons travel to cytochrome b-c_1. Some of the energy is harnessed to pump H$^+$ into the intermembrane space. Electrons are transferred to cytochrome c.

3 From cytochrome c, electrons are transferred to cytochrome oxidase. Some of the energy is harnessed to pump H$^+$ into the intermembrane space. Electrons are transferred to oxygen, and water is produced.

4 Steps 1–3 produce a H$^+$ electrochemical gradient. As H$^+$ flow down their electrochemical gradient into the matrix through ATP synthase, the energy within this gradient causes the synthesis of ATP from ADP and P$_i$.

KEY
- - - H$^+$ movement
—— e$^-$ movement

Matrix
Intermembrane space

NADH — NADH dehydrogenase
NAD$^+$ + H$^+$
Succinate reductase
FADH$_2$
FAD + 2 H$^+$
Q — Ubiquinone
Cytochrome b-c_1
Cytochrome c
2 H$^+$ + ½ O$_2$
H$_2$O
Cytochrome oxidase
Matrix
ATP synthase
ADP + P$_i$
ATP
Inner mitochondrial membrane
H$^+$
Intermembrane space

— **Electron transport chain**

— **ATP synthesis**

Figure 7.7 Oxidative phosphorylation. This process consists of two distinct events involving the electron transport chain and ATP synthase. The electron transport chain oxidizes, or removes electrons from, NADH or FADH$_2$ and pumps H$^+$ across the inner mitochondrial membrane. ATP synthase uses the energy in this H$^+$ electrochemical gradient to phosphorylate ADP and thereby synthesize ATP.

Concept check: *Can you explain the name of cytochrome oxidase? Can you think of another appropriate name?*

As shown in Figure 7.7, some of the energy from this movement of electrons is used to pump H^+ across the inner mitochondrial membrane from the matrix and into the intermembrane space. This active transport establishes a large **H^+ electrochemical gradient** in which the concentration of H^+ is higher outside of the matrix than inside and an excess of positive charge exists outside the matrix. Because hydrogen ions consist of protons, the H^+ electrochemical gradient is also called the **proton-motive force**. NADH dehydrogenase, cytochrome b-c_1, and cytochrome oxidase are H^+ pumps. While traveling along the electron transport chain, electrons release free energy, and some of this energy is captured by these proteins to actively transport H^+ out of the matrix into the intermembrane space against the H^+ electrochemical gradient. Because the electrons from $FADH_2$ enter the chain at an intermediate step, they release less energy and so result in fewer hydrogen ions being pumped out of the matrix than do electrons from NADH.

Why do electrons travel from NADH or $FADH_2$ to the ETC and then to O_2? As you might expect, the answer lies in free-energy changes. The electrons found on the energy intermediates have a high amount of potential energy. As they travel along the electron transport chain, free energy is released (Figure 7.8). The movement of one electron from NADH to O_2 results in a very negative free-energy change of approximately −25 kcal/mole. That is why the process is spontaneous and proceeds in the forward direction. Because it is a highly exergonic reaction, some of the free energy can be harnessed to do cellular work. In this case, some energy is used to pump H^+ across the inner mitochondrial membrane and establish a H^+ electrochemical gradient that is then used to power ATP synthesis.

Chemicals that inhibit the flow of electrons along the ETC can have lethal effects. For example, one component of the electron transport chain, cytochrome oxidase, can be inhibited by cyanide. The deadly effects of cyanide occur because the electron transport chain is shut down, preventing cells from making enough ATP for survival.

Phosphorylation: The Role of ATP Synthase in Making ATP via Chemiosmosis

The second event of oxidative phosphorylation is the synthesis of ATP by an enzyme called **ATP synthase**. The H^+ electrochemical gradient across the inner mitochondrial membrane is a source of potential energy. How is this energy used? The passive flow of H^+ back into the matrix is an exergonic process. The lipid bilayer is relatively impermeable to H^+. However, H^+ can pass through the membrane-embedded portion of ATP synthase. This enzyme harnesses some of the free energy that is released as the ions flow through its membrane-embedded region to synthesize ATP from ADP and P_i (see Figure 7.7). This is an example of an energy conversion: Energy in the form of a H^+ gradient is converted to chemical bond energy in ATP. The synthesis of ATP that occurs as a result of pushing H^+ across a membrane is called chemiosmosis (from the Greek *osmos*, meaning to push). The theory behind it was proposed by Peter Mitchell, a British biochemist who was awarded the Nobel Prize in chemistry in 1978.

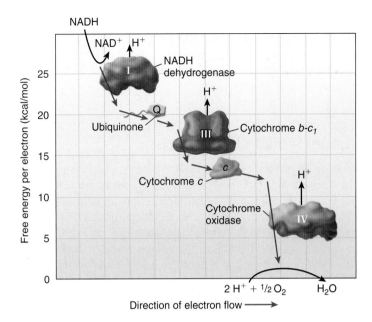

Figure 7.8 The relationship between free energy and electron movement along the electron transport chain. As electrons hop from one site to another along the electron transport chain, they release energy. Some of this energy is harnessed to pump H^+ across the inner mitochondrial membrane. The total energy released by a single electron is approximately −25 kcal/mole.

The Relationship Between NADH Oxidation and Amount of ATP Synthesis

For each molecule of NADH that is oxidized and each molecule of ATP that is made, the two chemical reactions of oxidative phosphorylation can be represented as follows:

$$NADH + H^+ + 1/2\,O_2 \rightarrow NAD^+ + H_2O$$

$$ADP^{2-} + P_i^{2-} \rightarrow ATP^{4-} + H_2O$$

The oxidation of NADH to NAD^+ results in a H^+ electrochemical gradient in which more hydrogen ions are in the intermembrane space than are in the matrix. The synthesis of one ATP molecule is thought to require the movement of three to four ions into the matrix, down their H^+ electrochemical gradient.

When we add up the maximal amount of ATP that can be made by oxidative phosphorylation, most researchers agree it is in the range of 30 to 34 ATP molecules for each glucose molecule that is broken down to CO_2 and water. However, the maximum amount of ATP is rarely achieved for two reasons. First, although 10 NADH and 2 $FADH_2$ are available to create the H^+ electrochemical gradient across the inner mitochondrial membrane, a cell may use some of these molecules for anabolic pathways. For example, NADH is used in the synthesis of organic molecules such as glycerol (a component of phospholipids) and lactate (which is secreted from muscle cells during strenuous exercise). Second, the mitochondrion may use some of the H^+ electrochemical gradient for other purposes. For example, the gradient is used for the uptake of pyruvate into the matrix via a H^+/pyruvate symporter (see Figure 7.4). Therefore, the actual amount of ATP synthesis is usually a little less than the maximum number of 30 to 34. Even so, when we compare the amount of ATP that can be made by glycolysis (2), the citric acid cycle (2), and oxidative phosphorylation (30–34), we see that oxidative phosphorylation provides a cell with a much greater capacity to make ATP.

Experiments with Purified Proteins in Membrane Vesicles Verified Chemiosmosis

To show experimentally that ATP synthase actually uses a H^+ electrochemical gradient to make ATP, researchers needed to purify the enzyme and study its function in vitro. In 1974, Ephraim Racker and Walther Stoeckenius purified ATP synthase and another protein called bacteriorhodopsin, which is found in certain species of archaea. Previous research had shown that bacteriorhodopsin is a light-driven H^+ pump. Racker and Stoeckenius took both purified proteins and inserted them into membrane vesicles (**Figure 7.9**). ATP synthase was oriented so its ATP synthesizing region was on the outside of the vesicles.

Bacteriorhodopsin was oriented so it would pump H^+ into the vesicles. They added ADP and P_i on the outside of the vesicles. In the dark, no ATP was made. However, when they shone light on the vesicles, a substantial amount of ATP was made. Because bacteriorhodopsin was already known to be a light-driven H^+ pump, these results convinced researchers that ATP synthase uses a H^+ electrochemical gradient as an energy source to make ATP.

ATP Synthase Is a Rotary Machine That Makes ATP as It Spins

The structure and function of ATP synthase are particularly intriguing and have received much attention over the past few decades (**Figure 7.10**). ATP synthase is a rotary machine. The membrane-embedded region is composed of three types of subunits called a, b, and c. Approximately 9 to 12 c subunits form a ring in the membrane. Each c subunit is a H^+ channel. One a subunit is bound to this ring, and two b subunits are attached to the a subunit and protrude from the membrane. The non-membrane-embedded subunits are designated with Greek letters. One ε and one γ subunit bind to the ring of c subunits. The γ subunit forms a long stalk that pokes into the center of another ring of three α and three β subunits. Each β subunit contains a catalytic site where ATP is made. Finally, the δ subunit forms a connection between the ring of α and β subunits and the two b subunits.

When hydrogen ions pass through a c subunit, a conformational change causes the γ subunit to turn clockwise (when viewed from the intermembrane space). Each time the γ subunit turns 120°, it changes its contacts with the three β subunits,

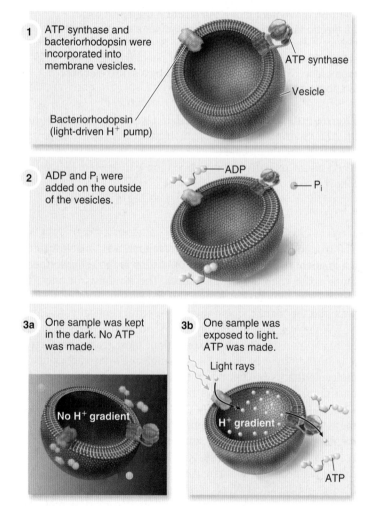

1 ATP synthase and bacteriorhodopsin were incorporated into membrane vesicles.

ATP synthase

Vesicle

Bacteriorhodopsin (light-driven H^+ pump)

2 ADP and P_i were added on the outside of the vesicles.

ADP

P_i

3a One sample was kept in the dark. No ATP was made.

No H^+ gradient

3b One sample was exposed to light. ATP was made.

Light rays

H^+ gradient

ATP

Figure 7.9 The Racker and Stoeckenius experiment showing that a H^+ electrochemical gradient drives ATP synthesis via ATP synthase.

Concept check: Is the functioning of the electron transport chain always needed to make ATP via ATP synthase?

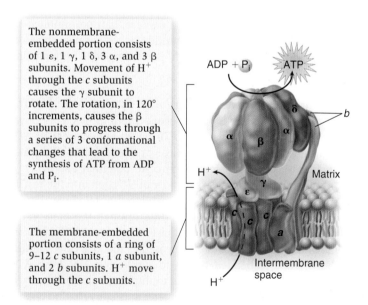

The nonmembrane-embedded portion consists of 1 ε, 1 γ, 1 δ, 3 α, and 3 β subunits. Movement of H^+ through the c subunits causes the γ subunit to rotate. The rotation, in 120° increments, causes the β subunits to progress through a series of 3 conformational changes that lead to the synthesis of ATP from ADP and P_i.

The membrane-embedded portion consists of a ring of 9–12 c subunits, 1 a subunit, and 2 b subunits. H^+ move through the c subunits.

ADP + P_i

ATP

δ

b

α α

β

H^+

γ

Matrix

ε

c c c

a

Intermembrane space

H^+

Figure 7.10 The subunit structure and function of ATP synthase.

Concept check: If the β subunit in the front center of this figure is in conformation 2, what are the conformations of the β subunit on the left and the β subunit on the back right?

which, in turn, causes the β subunits to change their conformations. How do these conformational changes promote ATP synthesis? The answer is that the conformational changes occur in a way that favors ATP synthesis and release. The conformational changes in the β subunits happen in the following order:

- Conformation 1: ADP and P_i bind with good affinity.
- Conformation 2: ADP and P_i bind so tightly that ATP is made.
- Conformation 3: ATP (and ADP and P_i) bind very weakly, and ATP is released.

Each time the γ subunit turns 120°, it causes a β subunit to change to the next conformation. After conformation 3, a 120° turn by the γ subunit returns a β subunit back to conformation 1, and the cycle of ATP synthesis can begin again. Because ATP synthase has three β subunits, each subunit is in a different conformation at any given time.

Paul Boyer proposed the concept of a rotary machine in the late 1970s. In his model, the three β subunits alternate between three conformations, as described previously. Boyer's original idea was met with great skepticism, because the concept that part of an enzyme could spin was very novel, to say the least. In 1994, John Walker and colleagues were able to determine the three-dimensional structure of the nonmembrane-embedded portion of the ATP synthase. The structure revealed that each of the three β subunits had a different conformation—one with ADP bound, one with ATP bound, and one without any nucleotide bound. This result supported Boyer's model. In 1997, Boyer and Walker shared the Nobel Prize in chemistry for their work on ATP synthase. As described next in the Feature Investigation, other researchers subsequently visualized the rotation of the γ subunit.

FEATURE INVESTIGATION

Yoshida and Kinosita Demonstrated That the γ Subunit of the ATP Synthase Spins

In 1997, Masasuke Yoshida, Kazuhiko Kinosita, and colleagues set out to experimentally visualize the rotary nature of ATP synthase (**Figure 7.11**). The membrane-embedded region of ATP synthase can be separated from the rest of the protein by treatment of mitochondrial membranes with a high concentration of salt, releasing the portion of the protein containing one γ, three α, and three β subunits. The researchers adhered the $\gamma\alpha_3\beta_3$ complex to a glass slide so the γ subunit was protruding upwards. Because the γ subunit is too small to be seen with a light microscope, the rotation of the γ subunit cannot be visualized directly. To circumvent this problem, the researchers attached a large, fluorescently labeled actin filament to the γ subunit via a linker protein. The fluorescently labeled actin filament is very long compared to the γ subunit and can be readily seen with a fluorescence microscope.

Because the membrane-embedded portion of the protein is missing, you may be wondering how the researchers could get the γ subunit to rotate. The answer is they added ATP. Although the normal function of the ATP synthase is to make ATP, it can also run backwards. In other words, ATP synthase can hydrolyze ATP. As shown in the data for Figure 7.11, when the researchers added ATP, they observed that the fluorescently labeled actin filament rotated in a counterclockwise direction, which is opposite to the direction that the γ subunit rotates when ATP is synthesized. Actin filaments were observed to rotate for more than 100 revolutions in the presence of ATP. These results convinced the scientific community that the ATP synthase is a rotary machine.

Experimental Questions

1. The components of ATP synthase are too small to be visualized by light microscopy. For the experiment of Figure 7.11, how did the researchers observe the movement of ATP synthase?

2. In the experiment of Figure 7.11, what observation did the researchers make that indicated ATP synthase is a rotary machine? What was the control of this experiment? What did it indicate?

3. Were the rotations seen by the researchers in the data of Figure 7.11 in the same direction as expected in the mitochondria during ATP synthesis? Why or why not?

Figure 7.11 Evidence that ATP synthase is a rotary machine.

HYPOTHESIS ATP synthase is a rotary machine.

KEY MATERIALS Purified complex containing 1 γ, 3 α, and 3 β subunits.

Experimental level | Conceptual level

1 Adhere the purified $\gamma\alpha_3\beta_3$ complex to a glass slide so the base of the γ subunit is protruding upwards.

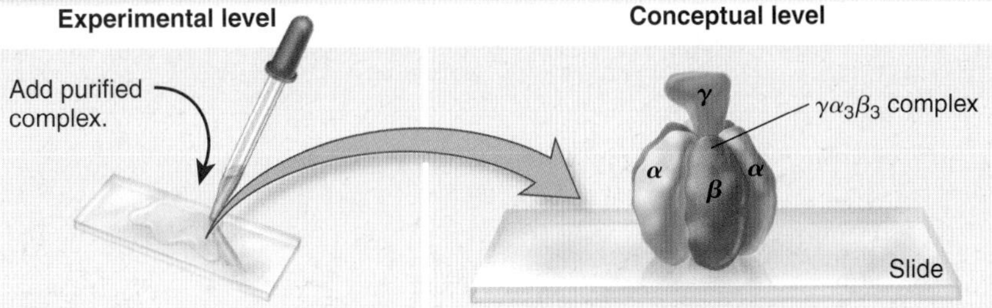

Add purified complex.

$\gamma\alpha_3\beta_3$ complex

Slide

2   Add linker proteins and fluorescently labeled actin filaments. The linker protein recognizes sites on both the γ subunit and the actin filament.

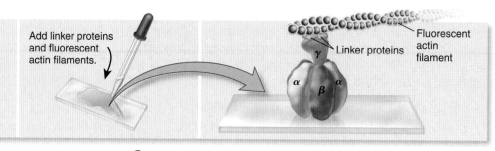

Add linker proteins and fluorescent actin filaments.

Fluorescent actin filament

Linker proteins

3   Add ATP. As a control, do not add ATP.

Add ATP

Control: No ATP

4   Observe under a fluorescence microscope. The method of fluorescence microscopy is described in Chapter 4.

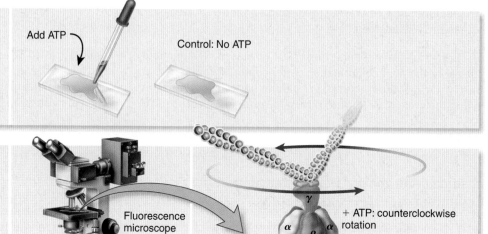

Fluorescence microscope

+ ATP: counterclockwise rotation

5   **THE DATA**

Results from step 4:

ATP	Rotation
No ATP added	No rotation observed.
ATP added	Rotation was observed as shown below. This is a time-lapse view of the rotation in action.

Row 1

Row 2

6   **CONCLUSION** The γ subunit rotates counterclockwise when ATP is hydrolyzed. It would be expected to rotate clockwise when ATP is synthesized.

7   **SOURCE** Reprinted by permission from Macmillan Publishers Ltd. Noji, H., Yasuda, R.,Yoshida, M., and Kinosita, K. 1997. Direct observation of the rotation of F_1-ATPase. *Nature* 386:299–303.

Genomes & Proteomes Connection

Cancer Cells Usually Favor Glycolysis Over Oxidative Phosphorylation

Thus far, we have examined how eukaryotic cells metabolize glucose under aerobic conditions to produce CO_2 and a large amount of ATP. This occurs in four stages, beginning with glycolysis and ending with oxidative phosphorylation. Our understanding of carbohydrate metabolism has far-reaching medical implications. Many disease conditions, including common disorders such as cancer and diabetes, are associated with alterations in carbohydrate metabolism.

In 1931, the German physiologist Otto Warburg discovered that certain cancer cells preferentially use glycolysis for ATP production while decreasing the level of oxidative phosphorylation. This phenomenon, termed the Warburg effect, is very common among different types of tumors. The Warburg effect is used to clinically diagnose cancer via a procedure called positron emission tomography (PET scan, see Chapter 3). In this technique, patients are given a radiolabeled glucose analogue called [18F]-fluorodeoxyglucose (FDG). The scanner detects regions of the body that metabolize FDG rapidly, which are visualized as bright spots on the PET scan. **Figure 7.12** shows a PET scan of a patient with lung cancer. The bright regions next to the arrows are tumors that show abnormally high levels of glycolysis.

In the past few decades, cancer biologists have analyzed the levels of proteins involved in glycolysis—the glycolytic enzymes described earlier in Figure 7.3. Glycolytic enzymes are overexpressed in approximately 80% of all types of cancer. These include lung, skin, colon, liver, pancreatic, breast, ovarian, and prostate cancer. The three enzymes of glycolysis whose overexpression is most commonly associated with cancer are glyceraldehyde-3-phosphate dehydrogenase, enolase, and pyruvate kinase (see Figure 7.3). In many cancers, all 10 glycolytic enzymes are overexpressed!

What factors cause glycolytic enzymes to be overexpressed? Both genetic and physiological factors are known to play a role. As discussed in Chapter 14, cancer is caused by mutations—changes in the DNA that affect the expression of genes. Mutations that cause cancer are generally not found in the genes that encode glycolytic enzymes themselves. Rather, cancer-causing mutations commonly occur in genes that encode regulatory proteins that control the expression of other genes. As an example, mutations in a human gene called *VHL* are associated with a disorder called von Hippel-Lindau syndrome, which is characterized by different tumor types throughout the body. The *VHL* gene mutations alter the function of the VHL regulatory protein, which then leads to an overexpression of the genes that encode glycolytic enzymes. In addition to mutations, the second factor that affects gene expression is the physiological conditions within a tumor. As a tumor grows, the internal regions of the tumor tend to become deficient in oxygen, a condition called hypoxia. The hypoxic state inside

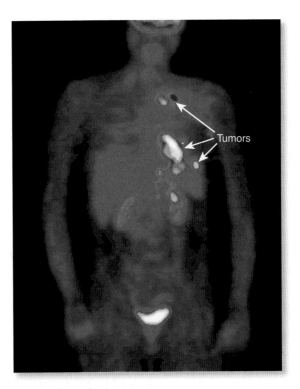

Figure 7.12   A PET scan of a patient with lung cancer.   The bright regions in the lungs are tumors (see arrows). Organs such as the brain, which are not cancerous, appear bright because they perform high levels of glucose metabolism. Also, the kidneys and bladder appear bright because they filter and accumulate FDG. (Note: FDG is taken up by cells and converted to FDG-phosphate by hexokinase, the first enzyme in glycolysis. However, because FDG lacks an —OH group, it is not metabolized further. Therefore, FDG-phosphate accumulates in metabolically active cells.)

Concept check: How might a higher level of glycolysis allow tumors to grow faster?

a tumor may also cause the overexpression of glycolytic genes and thereby lead to a higher level of glycolytic enzymes within the cancer cells. This favors glycolysis as a means to make ATP, which does not require oxygen.

How do changes in the overexpression of glycolytic enzymes affect tumor growth? While the genetic changes associated with tumor growth are complex, researchers have speculated that an increase in glycolysis may favor the growth of the tumor as it becomes hypoxic. This would provide an advantage to the cancer cells, which would otherwise have trouble making ATP via oxidative phosphorylation. Based on these findings, some current research is aimed at discovering drugs to inhibit glycolysis in cancer cells as a way to prevent their growth.

Metabolic Pathways for Carbohydrate Metabolism Are Interconnected to Pathways for Amino Acid and Fat Metabolism

Before we end our discussion of cellular respiration in the presence of oxygen, let's consider the metabolism of other organic

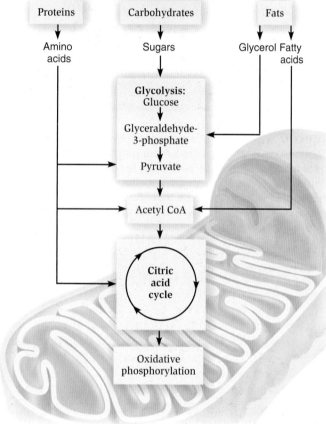

Figure 7.13   Integration of protein, carbohydrate, and fat metabolism.   Breakdown products of amino acids and fats can enter the same pathway that is used to break down carbohydrates.

Concept check: *What is a cellular advantage of integrating protein, carbohydrate, and fat metabolism?*

molecules, namely proteins and fats. When you eat a meal, it usually contains not only carbohydrates (including glucose) but also proteins and fats. These molecules are broken down by some of the same enzymes involved with glucose metabolism.

As shown in **Figure 7.13**, proteins and fats can enter into glycolysis or the citric acid cycle at different points. Proteins are first acted upon by enzymes, either in digestive juices or within cells, that cleave the bonds connecting individual amino acids. Because the 20 amino acids differ in their side chains, amino acids and their breakdown products can enter at different points in the pathway. Breakdown products of amino acids can enter at later steps of glycolysis, or an acetyl group can be removed from certain amino acids and become attached to CoA. Other amino acids can be modified and enter the citric acid cycle. Similarly, fats can be broken down to glycerol and fatty acids. Glycerol can be modified to glyceraldehyde-3-phosphate and enter glycolysis at step 5 (see Figure 7.3). Fatty acyl tails can have two carbon acetyl units removed, which bind to CoA and then enter the citric acid cycle. By using the same pathways for the breakdown of sugars, amino acids, and fats, cellular metabolism is more efficient because the same enzymes can be used for the breakdown of different starting molecules.

Likewise, carbohydrate metabolism is connected to the metabolism of other cellular components at the anabolic level. Cells may use carbohydrates to manufacture parts of amino acids, fats, and nucleotides. For example, the glucose-6-phosphate of glycolysis is used to construct the sugar and phosphate portion of nucleotides, while the oxaloacetate of the citric acid cycle can be used as a precursor for the biosynthesis of purine and pyrimidine bases. Portions of amino acids can be made from products of glycolysis (for example, pyruvate) and components of the citric acid cycle (oxaloacetate). In addition, several other catabolic and anabolic pathways are found in living cells that connect the metabolism of carbohydrates, proteins, fats, and nucleic acids.

7.2 Anaerobic Respiration and Fermentation

Thus far, we have surveyed catabolic pathways that result in the complete breakdown of glucose in the presence of oxygen. Cells also commonly metabolize organic molecules in the absence of oxygen. The term **anaerobic** is used to describe an environment that lacks oxygen. Many bacteria and archaea and some fungi exist in anaerobic environments but still have to oxidize organic molecules to obtain sufficient amounts of energy. Examples include microbes living in your intestinal tract and those living deep in the soil. Similarly, when a person exercises strenuously, the rate of oxygen consumption by muscle cells may greatly exceed the rate of oxygen delivery. Under these conditions, the muscle cells become anaerobic and must obtain sufficient energy in the absence of oxygen to maintain their level of activity.

Organisms have evolved two different strategies to metabolize organic molecules in the absence of oxygen. One mechanism is to use a substance other than O_2 as the final electron acceptor of an electron transport chain, a process called **anaerobic respiration**. A second approach is to produce ATP only via substrate-level phosphorylation. In this section, we will consider examples of both strategies.

Some Microorganisms Carry Out Anaerobic Respiration

At the end of the electron transport chain discussed earlier in Figure 7.7, cytochrome oxidase recognizes O_2 and catalyzes its reduction to H_2O. The final electron acceptor of the chain is O_2. Many species of bacteria that live under anaerobic conditions have evolved enzymes that function similarly to cytochrome oxidase but recognize molecules other than O_2 and use them as the final electron acceptor. For example, *Escherichia coli*, which is a bacterial species found in your intestinal tract, produces an enzyme called nitrate reductase under anaerobic conditions. This enzyme recognizes nitrate (NO_3^-), which is used as the final electron acceptor of an electron transport chain.

Figure 7.14 shows a simplified electron transport chain in *E. coli* in which nitrate is the final electron acceptor. In *E. coli* and other bacterial species, the electron transport chain is in the plasma membrane that surrounds the cytoplasm. Electrons travel from NADH to NADH dehydrogenase to ubiquinone (Q) to cytochrome *b* and then to nitrate reductase. At the end of

the chain, nitrate is converted to nitrite (NO_2^-). This process generates a H^+ electrochemical gradient in three ways. First, NADH dehydrogenase pumps H^+ out of the cytoplasm. Second, ubiquinone picks up H^+ in the cytoplasm and carries it to the other side of the membrane. Third, the reduction of nitrate to nitrite consumes H^+ in the cytoplasm. The generation of a H^+ gradient via these three processes allows *E. coli* cells to make ATP via chemiosmosis under anaerobic conditions.

Fermentation Is the Breakdown of Organic Molecules Without Net Oxidation

Many organisms, including animals and yeast, can use only O_2 as the final electron acceptor of their electron transport chains. When confronted with anaerobic conditions, these organisms must have a different way of producing sufficient ATP. One strategy is to make ATP via glycolysis, which can occur under anaerobic or aerobic conditions. Under anaerobic conditions, the cells do not use the citric acid cycle or the electron transport chain, but make ATP only via glycolysis.

A key issue is that glycolysis requires NAD^+ and generates NADH. Under aerobic conditions, oxygen acts as a final electron acceptor, and the high-energy electrons from NADH can be used to make more ATP. To make ATP, NADH is oxidized to NAD^+. However, this cannot occur under anaerobic conditions in yeast and animals, and, as a result, NADH builds up and NAD^+ decreases. This is a potential problem for two reasons. First, at high concentrations, NADH will haphazardly donate its electrons to other molecules and promote the formation of free radicals, highly reactive chemicals that can damage DNA and cellular proteins. For this reason, yeast and animal cells exposed to anaerobic conditions must have a way to remove the excess NADH generated from the breakdown of glucose. The second problem is the decrease in NAD^+. Cells need to regenerate NAD^+ to keep glycolysis running and make ATP via substrate-level phosphorylation.

How do muscle cells overcome these two problems? When a muscle is working strenuously and becomes anaerobic, the pyruvate from glycolysis is reduced to make lactate. (The uncharged [protonated] form is called lactic acid.) The electrons to reduce pyruvate are derived from NADH, which is oxidized to NAD^+ (**Figure 7.15a**). Therefore, this process decreases NADH and reduces its potentially harmful effects. It also increases the level of NAD^+, thereby allowing glycolysis to continue. The lactate is secreted from muscle cells. Once sufficient oxygen is restored, the lactate produced during strenuous exercise can be taken up by cells, converted back to pyruvate, and used for energy, or it may be used to make glucose by the liver and other tissues.

Yeast cells cope with anaerobic conditions differently. During wine making, a yeast cell metabolizes sugar under anaerobic conditions. The pyruvate is broken down to CO_2 and a two-carbon molecule called acetaldehyde. The acetaldehyde is then reduced to make ethanol while NADH is oxidized to NAD^+ (**Figure 7.15b**). Similar to lactate production in muscle cells, this

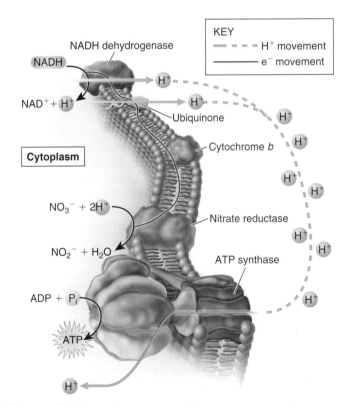

Figure 7.14 **An example of anaerobic respiration in *E. coli*.** When oxygen is absent, *E. coli* can use nitrate instead of oxygen as the final electron acceptor in an electron transport chain. This generates a H^+ electrochemical gradient that is used to make ATP via chemiosmosis. Note: As shown in this figure, ubiquinone (Q) picks up H^+ on one side of the membrane and deposits it on the other side. A similar event happens during aerobic respiration in mitochondria (described in Figure 7.7), except that ubiquinone transfers H^+ to cytochrome b-c_1, which pumps it into the intermembrane space.

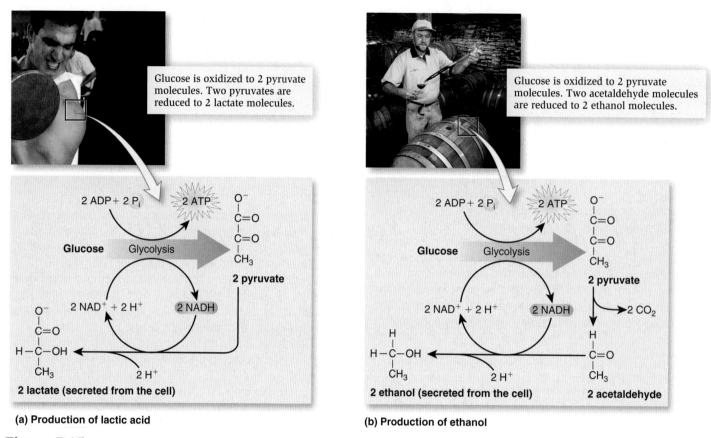

(a) Production of lactic acid

(b) Production of ethanol

Figure 7.15 **Examples of fermentation.** In these examples, NADH is produced by the oxidation of an organic molecule, and then the NADH is used up by donating electrons to a different organic molecule such as pyruvate **(a)** or acetaldehyde **(b)**.

decreases NADH and increases NAD^+, thereby preventing the harmful effects of NADH and allowing glycolysis to continue.

The term **fermentation** is used to describe the breakdown of organic molecules to harness energy without any net oxidation (that is, without any removal of electrons). The breakdown of glucose to lactate or ethanol are examples of fermentation. Although electrons are removed from an organic molecule such as glucose to make pyruvate and NADH, the electrons are donated back to an organic molecule in the production of lactate or ethanol. Therefore, there is no net removal of electrons from an organic molecule. Compared with oxidative phosphorylation, fermentation produces far less ATP for two reasons. First, glucose is not oxidized completely to CO_2 and water. Second, the NADH made during glycolysis cannot be used to make more ATP. Overall, the complete breakdown of glucose in the presence of oxygen yields 34 to 38 ATP molecules. By comparison, the anaerobic breakdown of glucose to lactate or ethanol yields only two ATP molecules.

7.3 Secondary Metabolism

Primary metabolism is the synthesis and breakdown of molecules and macromolecules that are found in all forms of life and are essential for cell structure and function. These include compounds such as sugars, amino acids, lipids, and

nucleotides, and the macromolecules that are derived from them. Cellular respiration, which we considered earlier in this chapter, is an example of primary metabolism. By comparison, **secondary metabolism** involves the synthesis of molecules— **secondary metabolites**—that are not essential for cell structure and growth. Secondary metabolites, also called secondary compounds, are commonly made in plants, bacteria, and fungi. Any given secondary metabolite is unique to one species or group of species and is not usually required for survival.

Secondary metabolites perform diverse functions for the species that produce them, often enhancing their chances of survival and reproduction. For example, many secondary metabolites taste bad. When produced in a plant, for example, such a molecule may prevent an animal from eating the plant. In some cases, secondary metabolites are toxic. Such molecules may act as a chemical weapon that inhibits the growth of nearby organisms. In addition, many secondary metabolites produce a strong smell or bright color that attracts or repels other organisms. For example, the scent from a rose is due to secondary metabolites. The scent attracts insects that aid in pollination.

Biologists have discovered thousands of different secondary metabolites, though any given species tends to produce only one or a few types. Plants are particularly diverse in the types of secondary metabolites they produce, perhaps because they have evolved defenses that are effective in stationary organisms. Bacteria and fungi also produce a large array of these compounds, whereas animals tend to produce relatively few. As you will learn, humans have put many of these compounds to practical use, from the spices we use in cooking to the antibiotics we use to treat diseases. In this section, we will survey four categories of secondary metabolites: phenolics, alkaloids, terpenoids, and polyketides.

Phenolic Compounds Are Antioxidants That Defend or Attract with Intense Flavors and Bright Colors

The **phenolic** compounds all contain a cyclic ring of carbon with three double bonds, known as a benzene ring, within their structure. When a benzene ring is covalently linked to a single hydroxyl group, the compound is known as phenol.

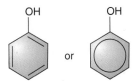

Phenol is the simplest of the phenolic compounds, though free phenol is not significantly accumulated in living organisms. However, more complex molecules that are derived from phenol are made in cells. Such phenolic compounds are synthesized using the side groups of the amino acids phenylalanine (which has a benzene ring) or tyrosine (which has a phenol ring). Common categories of phenolics are the flavonoids, tannins, and lignins.

Flavonoids are produced by many plant species and create a variety of flavors and smells. These can play a role as deterrents to eating a plant or as attractants that promote pollination. The flavors of chocolate and vanilla come largely from a mixture of flavonoid molecules. Vanilla is produced by several species of perennial vines of the genus *Vanilla*, native to Mexico and tropical America (**Figure 7.16a**). The primary source of commercial vanilla comes from *V. planifolia*. Vanilla extract is obtained from the seed capsules. Another role of flavonoids is pigmentation. Anthocyanins (from the Greek *anthos*, meaning flower, and *kyanos*, meaning blue) produce the red, blue, and purple colors of many flowers, fruits, and vegetables (**Figure 7.16b**).

Biochemists have discovered that flavonoids have remarkable antioxidant properties that prevent the formation of damaging free radicals. In plants, flavonoids are thought to act as powerful antioxidants, helping to protect plants from ultraviolet (UV) damage. In recent times, nutritionists have advocated the consumption of fruits and vegetables that have high amounts of flavonoids, such as blueberries, broccoli, and spinach. Dark chocolate is also rich in these antioxidants!

Tannins are large polymeric molecules composed of many phenolic units. They are named tannins because they combine with the protein of animal skins in the making of leather. This process, known as tanning, also imparts a tan color to the skins. Tannins are found in many plant species and typically act as a deterrent to animals, either because of a bitter taste or due to toxic effects. If consumed in large amounts, they also can

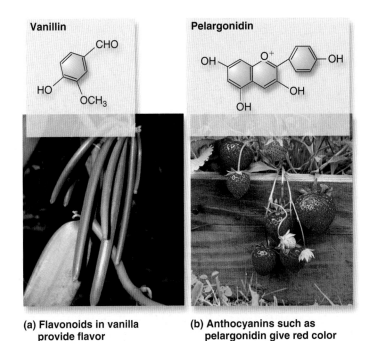

(a) Flavonoids in vanilla provide flavor

(b) Anthocyanins such as pelargonidin give red color

Figure 7.16 Phenolic compounds as secondary metabolites.   The two examples shown here are flavonoids, which are a type of phenolic compound. **(a)** The flavor of vanilla is largely produced by flavonoids, an example of which is vanillin produced by this *Vanilla planifolia* vine. **(b)** Another group of flavonoids that causes red, blue, or purple color are anthocyanins. The red color of strawberries is caused by pelargonidin, an anthocyanin.

Concept check: *Besides fruits, what other parts of plants may contain anthocyanins?*

inhibit the enzymes found in the digestive tracts of animals. Tannins are found abundantly in grape skins and play a key role in the flavor of red wine. Aging breaks down tannins, making the wine less bitter.

Lignins are also large phenolic polymers synthesized by plants. Lignins are found in plant cell walls and make up about one-quarter to one-third of the weight of dry wood. The lignins form polymers that bond with other plant wall components such as cellulose. This strengthens plant cells and enables a plant to better withstand the rigors of environmental stress. To make paper, which is much more malleable than wood, the lignins are removed.

Alkaloids Form a Large Group of Bitter-Tasting Molecules That Also Provide Defense Mechanisms

Alkaloids are a group of structurally related molecules that all contain nitrogen and usually have a cyclic, ring-like structure. More than 12,000 different alkaloids have been discovered. Their name is derived from the observation that they are basic or alkaline molecules. Alkaloids are usually synthesized from amino acid precursors. Alkaloids are commonly made in plant species and occasionally in fungi and animals (shellfish). Familiar examples include caffeine, nicotine, atropine, morphine, ergot, and quinine.

Deadly nightshade

Figure 7.17   Alkaloids as secondary metabolites.   Atropine is an alkaloid produced by the plant called deadly nightshade (*Hyoscyamus niger*). Atropine is toxic because it interferes with nerve transmission. In humans, atropine causes the heart to speed up to dangerous and possibly fatal rates.

Concept check: How does the production of atropine provide protection to deadly nightshade?

Like phenolics, many alkaloids serve a defense function in plants. Alkaloids are bitter-tasting molecules and often have an unpleasant odor. These features may prevent an animal from eating a plant or its fruit. For example, an alkaloid in chile peppers called capsaicin elicits a burning sensation. This molecule is so potent that one-millionth of a drop can be detected by the human tongue. Capsaicin may discourage mammals from eating the peppers. Interestingly, however, birds do not experience the burning sensation of capsaicin and serve to disperse the seeds.

Other alkaloids are poisonous, like atropine, a potent toxin derived from the deadly nightshade plant (**Figure 7.17**). Animals that eat this plant and consequently ingest atropine become very sick and may die. Any animal that eats deadly nightshade and survives would be unlikely to eat it a second time. Atropine acts by interfering with nerve transmission. In humans, for example, atropine causes the heart to speed up to dangerous rates, because the nerve inputs that normally keep a check on heart rate are blocked by atropine. Other alkaloids are not necessarily toxic but can cause an animal that eats them to become overstimulated (caffeine), understimulated (any of the opium alkaloids such as morphine), or simply nauseated because the compound interferes with nerves required for proper functioning of the gastrointestinal system.

Terpenoids Are Molecules with Intense Smells and Color That Have Diverse Functions

A third major class of secondary metabolites are the **terpenoids**, of which over 25,000 have been identified, more than any other family of naturally occurring products. Terpenoids are synthesized from five-carbon isoprene units (shown here) and are also called isoprenoids.

$$H_2C \diagup{}^{H}_{C}$$
$$H_3C \diagdown{}_{CH_2}^{C}$$

Isoprene units are linked to each other to form larger compounds with multiples of five-carbon atoms. In many cases, the isoprene units form cyclic structures.

Terpenoids have a wide array of functions in plants. Notably, because many terpenoids are volatile (they become gases), they are responsible for the odors emitted by many types of plants, such as menthol produced by mint. The odors of terpenoids may attract pollinators or repel animals that eat plants. In addition, terpenoids often impart an intense flavor to plant tissues. Many of the spices we use in cooking are rich in different types of terpenoids. Examples include cinnamon, fennel, cloves, cumin, caraway, and tarragon. Terpenoids are found in many traditional herbal remedies and are under medical investigation for potential pharmaceutical effects.

Other terpenoids, such as the carotenoids, are responsible for the coloration of many species. An example is β-carotene, which gives carrots their orange color. Carotenoids are also found in leaves, but their color is masked by chlorophyll, which is green. In the autumn, when chlorophyll breaks down, the color of the carotenoids becomes evident. In addition, carotenoids give color to animals such as salmon, goldfish, and flamingos (**Figure 7.18**).

Polyketides Are Often Used as Chemical Weapons to Kill Competing Organisms

Polyketides are a group of secondary metabolites that are produced by bacteria, fungi, plants, insects, dinoflagellates,

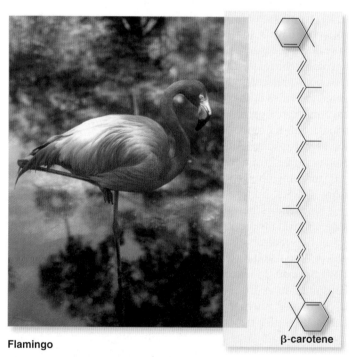

Flamingo

β-carotene

Figure 7.18   Terpenoids as secondary metabolites. Carotenoids are a type of terpenoid with bright color. The example shown here is β-carotene, which gives many organisms an orange color. Flamingos (*Phoenicopterus ruber*) receive β-carotene in their diet, primarily from eating shellfish.

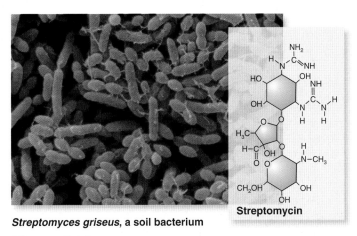

***Streptomyces griseus*, a soil bacterium**

Figure 7.19 **Polyketides as secondary metabolites.** Streptomycin, whose structure is shown here, is an antibiotic produced by *Streptomyces griseus*, a soil bacterium. The scanning electron micrograph shows *S. griseus*.

Concept check: *How does the production of streptomycin provide S. griseus with a growth advantage?*

mollusks, and sponges. They are synthesized by the polymerization of acetyl (CH_3COOH) and propionyl (CH_3CH_2COOH) groups to create a diverse collection of molecules, often with many ringed structures. During the past several decades, over 10,000 polyketides have been identified and analyzed. Familiar examples include streptomycin, erythromycin, and tetracycline.

Polyketides are usually secreted by the organism that makes them and are often highly toxic to other organisms. For example, the polyketide known as streptomycin is made by the soil bacterium *Streptomyces griseus* (**Figure 7.19**). It is secreted by this bacterium and taken up by other species, where it disrupts protein synthesis and thereby inhibits their growth. In this way, *S. griseus* is able to kill or inhibit the growth of other species in its vicinity.

The toxic effects of polyketides are often very selective, making them valuable medical tools. For example, streptomycin disrupts protein synthesis in many bacterial species, but it does not adversely affect protein synthesis in mammalian cells. Therefore, it has been used as an antibiotic to treat or prevent bacterial infections in humans and other mammals. Similarly, other polyketides inhibit the growth of fungi, parasites, and insects. More recently, researchers have even discovered that certain polyketides inhibit the growth of cancer cells. The production and sale of polyketides to treat and prevent diseases and as pesticides constitute an enormous industry, with annual sales in the U.S. at over $20 billion.

Summary of Key Concepts

7.1 Cellular Respiration in the Presence of Oxygen

- Cells obtain energy via cellular respiration, which involves the breakdown of organic molecules and the export of waste products.

- The breakdown of glucose occurs in four stages: glycolysis, pyruvate breakdown, citric acid cycle, and oxidative phosphorylation. (Figure 7.1)

- Glycolysis is the breakdown of glucose to two pyruvates, producing two net molecules of ATP and two NADH. ATP is made by substrate-level phosphorylation. (Figures 7.2, 7.3)

- Pyruvate is broken down to CO_2 and an acetyl group that becomes attached to CoA. NADH is made during this process. (Figure 7.4)

- During the citric acid cycle, each acetyl group attached to CoA is incorporated into an organic molecule, which is oxidized and releases two CO_2 molecules. Three NADH, one $FADH_2$, and one ATP are made during this process. (Figures 7.5, 7.6)

- Oxidative phosphorylation involves two events. The electron transport chain oxidizes NADH or $FADH_2$ and generates a H^+ electrochemical gradient. This gradient is used by ATP synthase to make ATP via chemiosmosis. (Figures 7.7, 7.8)

- Racker and Stoeckenius showed that ATP synthase uses a H^+ gradient by reconstituting ATP synthase with a light-driven H^+ pump. (Figure 7.9)

- ATP synthase is a rotary machine. The rotation is caused by the movement of H^+ through the *c* subunits that cause the γ subunit to spin, resulting in conformational changes in the β subunits that promote ATP synthesis. (Figure 7.10)

- Yoshida and Kinosita demonstrated rotation of the γ subunit by attaching a fluorescently labeled actin filament and watching it spin in the presence of ATP. (Figure 7.11)

- Cancer cells preferentially carry out glycolysis due to both genetic changes associated with cancer and physiological changes within the tumor itself. (Figure 7.12)

- Proteins and fats can enter into glycolysis or the citric acid cycle at different points. (Figure 7.13)

7.2 Anaerobic Respiration and Fermentation

- Anaerobic respiration occurs in the absence of oxygen. Certain microorganisms can carry out anaerobic respiration in which the final electron acceptor of the electron transport chain is a substance other than oxygen, such as nitrate. (Figure 7.14)

- During fermentation, organic molecules are broken down without any net oxidation (that is, without any net removal of electrons). Examples include lactate production in muscle cells and ethanol production in yeast. (Figure 7.15)

7.3 Secondary Metabolism

- Secondary metabolites are not usually necessary for cell structure and function, but they provide an advantage to an organism that may involve taste, smell, color, or poison. Four categories of secondary metabolites are phenolic compounds, alkaloids, terpenoids, and polyketides. (Figures 7.16, 7.17, 7.18, 7.19)

Assess and Discuss

Test Yourself

1. Which of the following pathways occurs in the cytosol?
   a. glycolysis
   b. breakdown of pyruvate to an acetyl group
   c. citric acid cycle
   d. oxidative phosphorylation
   e. all of the above

2. To break down glucose to CO_2 and H_2O, which of the following metabolic pathways is <u>not</u> involved?
   a. glycolysis
   b. breakdown of pyruvate to an acetyl group
   c. citric acid cycle
   d. photosynthesis
   e. c and d only

3. The net products of glycolysis are
   a. 6 CO_2, 4 ATP, and 2 NADH.
   b. 2 pyruvate, 2 ATP, and 2 NADH.
   c. 2 pyruvate, 4 ATP, and 2 NADH.
   d. 2 pyruvate, 2 GTP, and 2 CO_2.
   e. 2 CO_2, 2 ATP, and glucose.

4. During glycolysis, ATP is produced by
   a. oxidative phosphorylation.
   b. substrate-level phosphorylation.
   c. redox reactions.
   d. all of the above.
   e. both a and b.

5. Certain drugs act as ionophores that cause the mitochondrial membrane to be highly permeable to H^+. How would such drugs affect oxidative phosphorylation?
   a. Movement of electrons down the electron transport chain would be inhibited.
   b. ATP synthesis would be inhibited.
   c. ATP synthesis would be unaffected.
   d. ATP synthesis would be stimulated.
   e. Both a and b are correct.

6. The source of energy that <u>directly</u> drives the synthesis of ATP during oxidative phosphorylation is
   a. the oxidation of NADH.
   b. the oxidation of glucose.
   c. the oxidation of pyruvate.
   d. the H^+ gradient.
   e. the reduction of O_2.

7. Compared to oxidative phosphorylation in mitochondria, a key difference of anaerobic respiration in bacteria is
   a. more ATP is made.
   b. ATP is made only via substrate-level phosphorylation.
   c. O_2 is converted to H_2O_2 rather than H_2O.
   d. something other than O_2 acts as a final electron acceptor of the electron transport chain.
   e. b and d.

8. When a muscle becomes anaerobic during strenuous exercise, why is it necessary to convert pyruvate to lactate?
   a. to decrease NAD^+ and increase NADH
   b. to decrease NADH and increase NAD^+
   c. to increase NADH and increase NAD^+
   d. to decrease NADH and decrease NAD^+
   e. to keep oxidative phosphorylation running

9. Secondary metabolites
   a. help deter predation of certain organisms by causing the organism to taste bad.
   b. help attract pollinators by producing a pleasant smell.
   c. help organisms compete for resources by acting as a poison to competitors.
   d. provide protection from DNA damage.
   e. do all of the above.

10. Which of the following is an example of a secondary metabolite?
    a. flavonoids found in vanilla
    b. atropine found in deadly nightshade
    c. β-carotene found in carrots and flamingo feathers
    d. streptomycin made by soil bacteria
    e. all of the above

Conceptual Questions

1. The electron transport chain is so named because electrons are transported from one component to another. Describe the purpose of the electron transport chain.

2. What causes the rotation of the γ subunit of the ATP synthase? How does this rotation promote ATP synthesis?

3. During fermentation, explain why it is important to oxidize NADH to NAD^+.

Collaborative Questions

1. Discuss the advantages and disadvantages of aerobic respiration, anaerobic respiration, and fermentation.

2. Discuss the roles of secondary metabolites in biology. Such compounds have a wide variety of practical applications. If you were going to start a biotechnology company that produced secondary metabolites for sale, which type(s) would you focus on? How might you go about discovering new secondary metabolites that could be profitable?

Online Resource

www.brookerbiology.com

Stay a step ahead in your studies with animations that bring concepts to life and practice tests to assess your understanding. Your instructor may also recommend the interactive ebook, individualized learning tools, and more.

Photosynthesis

8

A tropical rain forest in the Amazon. Plant life in tropical rain forests carries out a large amount of the world's photosynthesis and supplies the atmosphere with a sizeable fraction of its oxygen.

T ake a deep breath. Nearly all of the oxygen in every breath you take is made by the abundant plant life, algae, and cyanobacteria on Earth. More than 20% of the world's oxygen is produced in the Amazon rain forest in South America alone (see chapter-opening photo). Biologists are alarmed about the rate at which such forests are being destroyed by human activities. Rain forests once covered 14% of the Earth's land surface but now occupy less than 6%. At their current rate of destruction, rain forests may be nearly eliminated in less than 40 years. Such an event may lower the level of oxygen in the atmosphere and thereby have a harmful impact on living organisms on a global scale.

In rain forests and across all of the Earth, the most visible color on land is green. The green color of plants is due to a pigment called chlorophyll. This pigment provides the starting point for the process of **photosynthesis**, in which the energy from light is captured and used to synthesize carbohydrates. Nearly all living organisms ultimately rely on photosynthesis for their nourishment, either directly or indirectly. Photosynthesis is also responsible for producing the oxygen that makes up a large portion of the Earth's atmosphere. Therefore, all aerobic organisms rely on photosynthesis for cellular respiration.

We begin this chapter with an overview of photosynthesis as it occurs in green plants and algae. We will then explore the two stages of photosynthesis in more detail. In the first stage, called the light reactions, light energy is captured by the chlorophyll pigments and converted to chemical energy in the form of two energy intermediates, ATP and NADPH. During the second stage, known as the Calvin cycle, ATP and NADPH are used to drive the synthesis of carbohydrates. We conclude with a consideration of the variations in photosynthesis that occur in plants existing in hot and dry conditions.

8.1 Overview of Photosynthesis

In the mid-1600s, a Flemish physician, Jan Baptista Van Helmont, conducted an experiment in which he transplanted the shoot of a young willow tree into a bucket of soil and allowed it to grow for 5 years. After this time, the willow tree had added 164 pounds to its original weight, but the soil had lost only 2 ounces. Van Helmont correctly concluded that the willow tree did not get most of its nutrients from the soil. He also hypothesized that the mass of the tree came from the water he had added over the 5 years. This hypothesis was partially correct, but we now know that CO_2 from the air is also a major contributor to the growth and mass of plants.

In the 1770s, Jan Ingenhousz, a Dutch physician, immersed green plants under water and discovered they released bubbles of oxygen. Ingenhousz determined that sunlight was necessary for oxygen production. During this same period, Jean Senebier, a Swiss botanist, found that CO_2 is required for plant growth. With this accumulating information, Julius von Mayer, a German physicist, proposed in 1845 that plants convert light energy from the sun into chemical energy.

For the next several decades, plant biologists studied photosynthesis in plants, algae, and bacteria. Researchers discovered that some photosynthetic bacteria could use hydrogen sulfide (H_2S) instead of water (H_2O) for photosynthesis and these organisms released sulfur instead of oxygen. In the 1930s, based on this information, Dutch-American microbiologist Cornelis van Niel proposed a general equation for photosynthesis that applies to plants, algae, and photosynthetic bacteria alike.

$$CO_2 + 2\ H_2A + \text{Light energy} \rightarrow CH_2O + A_2 + H_2O$$

where A is oxygen (O) or sulfur (S) and CH_2O is the general formula for a carbohydrate. This is a redox reaction in which CO_2 is reduced and H_2A is oxidized.

In green plants, A is oxygen and 2 A is a molecule of oxygen that is designated O_2. Therefore, this equation becomes

$$CO_2 + 2\ H_2O + \text{Light energy} \rightarrow CH_2O + O_2 + H_2O$$

When the carbohydrate produced is glucose ($C_6H_{12}O_6$), we multiply each side of the equation by six to obtain:

$$6\ CO_2 + 12\ H_2O + \text{Light energy} \rightarrow C_6H_{12}O_6 + 6\ O_2 + 6\ H_2O$$

$$\Delta G = +685\ \text{kcal/mole}$$

In this redox reaction, CO_2 is reduced during the formation of glucose, and H_2O is oxidized during the formation of O_2. Notice that the free-energy change required for the production of 1 mole of glucose from carbon dioxide and water is a whopping +685 kcal/mole! As we learned in Chapter 6, endergonic reactions are driven forward by coupling the reaction with an exergonic process that releases free energy. In this case, the energy from sunlight ultimately drives the synthesis of glucose.

In this section, we will survey the general features of photosynthesis as it occurs in green plants and algae. Later sections will examine the various steps in this process.

Photosynthesis Powers the Biosphere

The term **biosphere** describes the regions on the surface of the Earth and in the atmosphere where living organisms exist. Organisms can be categorized as heterotrophs and autotrophs. **Heterotrophs** must consume food—organic molecules from their environment—to sustain life. Heterotrophs include most species of bacteria and protists, as well as all species of fungi and animals. By comparison, **autotrophs** are organisms that make organic molecules from inorganic sources such as CO_2 and H_2O. **Photoautotrophs** are autotrophs that use light as a source of energy to make organic molecules. These include green plants, algae, and some prokaryotic species such as cyanobacteria.

Life in the biosphere is largely driven by the photosynthetic power of green plants and algae. The existence of most species relies on a key energy cycle that involves the interplay between organic molecules (such as glucose) and inorganic molecules, namely, O_2, CO_2, and H_2O (**Figure 8.1**). Photoautotrophs, such as plants, make a large proportion of the Earth's organic molecules via photosynthesis, using light energy, CO_2, and H_2O. During this process, they also produce O_2. To supply their energy needs, both photoautotrophs and heterotrophs metabolize organic molecules via cellular respiration. As described in Chapter 7, cellular respiration generates CO_2 and H_2O and is used to make ATP. The CO_2 is released into the atmosphere and can be re-used by photoautotrophs to make more organic

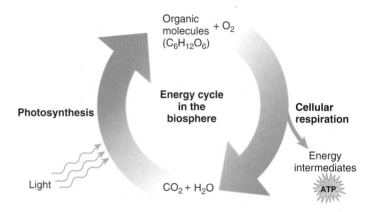

Figure 8.1 An important energy cycle between photosynthesis and cellular respiration. Photosynthesis uses light, CO_2, and H_2O to produce O_2 and organic molecules. The organic molecules can be broken down to CO_2 and H_2O via cellular respiration to supply energy in the form of ATP; O_2 is reduced to H_2O.

Concept check: *Which types of organisms carry out cellular respiration? Is it heterotrophs, autotrophs, or both?*

molecules such as glucose. In this way, an energy cycle exists between photosynthesis and cellular respiration that sustains life on our planet.

In Plants and Algae, Photosynthesis Occurs in the Chloroplast

Chloroplasts are organelles found in plant and algal cells that carry out photosynthesis. These organelles contain large quantities of **chlorophyll**, which is a pigment that gives plants their green color. All green parts of a plant contain chloroplasts and can perform photosynthesis, although the majority of photosynthesis occurs in the leaves (**Figure 8.2**). The internal part of the leaf, called the **mesophyll**, contains cells with chloroplasts that carry out the bulk of photosynthesis in plants. For photosynthesis to occur, the mesophyll cells must obtain water and carbon dioxide. The water is taken up by the roots of the plant and is transported to the leaves by small veins. Carbon dioxide gas enters the leaf, and oxygen exits via pores called **stomata** (singular, stoma or stomate; from the Greek, meaning mouth). The anatomy of leaves will be examined further in Chapter 35.

Like the mitochondrion, a chloroplast contains an outer and inner membrane, with an intermembrane space lying between the two. A third membrane, called the **thylakoid membrane**, contains pigment molecules, including chlorophyll. The thylakoid membrane forms many flattened, fluid-filled tubules called the **thylakoids**, which enclose a single, convoluted compartment known as the **thylakoid lumen**. Thylakoids stack on top of each other to form a structure called a **granum** (plural, grana). The **stroma** is the fluid-filled region of the chloroplast between the thylakoid membrane and the inner membrane (Figure 8.2).

Photosynthesis Occurs in Two Stages: Light Reactions and the Calvin Cycle

How does photosynthesis occur? The process of photosynthesis can be divided into two stages called the **light reactions** and the **Calvin cycle**. The term photosynthesis is derived from the association between these two stages: The prefix photo refers to the light reactions that capture the energy from sunlight needed for the synthesis of carbohydrates that occurs in the Calvin cycle. The light reactions take place at the thylakoid membrane, and the Calvin cycle occurs in the stroma (Figure 8.3).

The light reactions involve an amazing series of energy conversions, starting with light energy and ending with chemical energy that is stored in the form of covalent bonds. The light reactions produce three chemical products: ATP, NADPH, and O_2. ATP and NADPH are energy intermediates that provide the needed energy and electrons to drive the Calvin cycle. Like NADH, **NADPH (nicotinamide adenine dinucleotide phosphate)** is an electron carrier that can accept two electrons. Its structure differs from NADH by the presence of an additional phosphate group. The structure of NADH is described in Chapter 6 (see Figure 6.11).

Although O_2 is not needed to make carbohydrates, it is still an important product of the light reactions. As described in Chapter 7, O_2 is vital to the process of aerobic cellular respiration. Nearly all of the O_2 in the atmosphere is produced by photosynthesis from green plants and aquatic microorganisms.

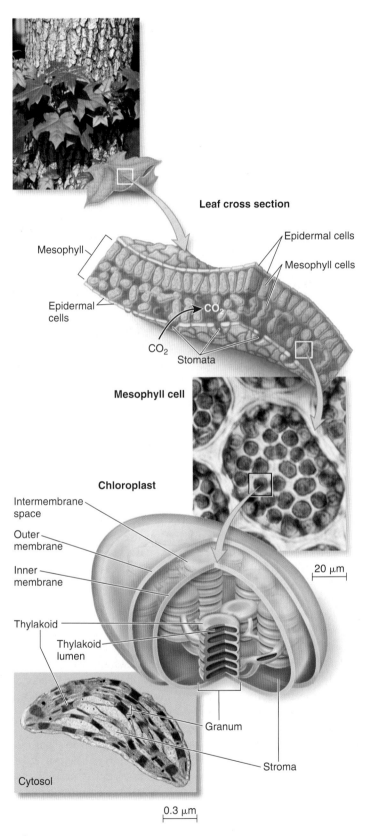

Figure 8.2 **Leaf organization.** Leaves are composed of layers of cells. The epidermal cells are on the outer surface, both top and bottom, with mesophyll cells sandwiched in the middle. The mesophyll cells contain chloroplasts and are the primary sites of photosynthesis in most plants.

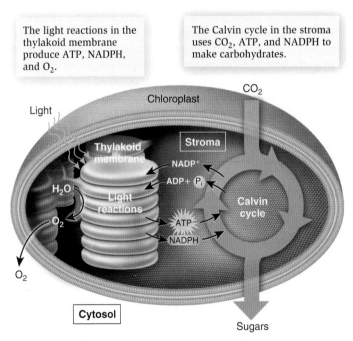

Figure 8.3 **An overview of the two stages of photosynthesis: light reactions and the Calvin cycle.** The light reactions, through which ATP, NADPH, and O_2 are made, occur at the thylakoid membrane. The Calvin cycle, in which enzymes use ATP and NADPH to incorporate CO_2 into carbohydrate, occurs in the stroma.

Concept check: *Can the Calvin cycle occur in the dark?*

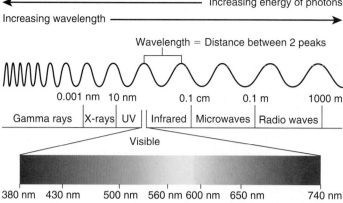

Figure 8.4 **The electromagnetic spectrum.** The bottom portion of this figure emphasizes visible light, the wavelengths of electromagnetic radiation that are visible to the human eye. Light in the visible portion of the electromagnetic spectrum drives photosynthesis.

Concept check: *Which has higher energy, gamma rays or radio waves?*

8.2 Reactions That Harness Light Energy

According to the first law of thermodynamics discussed in Chapter 6, energy cannot be created or destroyed, but it can be transferred from one place to another and transformed from one form to another. During photosynthesis, energy in the form of light is transferred from the sun, some 92 million miles away, to a pigment molecule in a photosynthetic organism such as a plant. What follows is an interesting series of energy transformations in which light energy is transformed into electrochemical energy and then into energy stored within chemical bonds.

In this section, we will explore this series of transformations, collectively called the light reactions of photosynthesis. We begin by examining the unique properties of light and then consider the features of chloroplasts that allow them to capture light energy. The rest of this section focuses on how the light reactions of photosynthesis create three important products: ATP, NADPH, and O_2.

Light Energy Is a Form of Electromagnetic Radiation

Light is essential to support life on Earth. Light is a type of electromagnetic radiation, so named because it consists of energy in the form of electric and magnetic fields. Electromagnetic radiation travels as waves caused by the oscillation of the electric and magnetic fields. The **wavelength** is the distance between the peaks in a wave pattern. The **electromagnetic spectrum** encompasses all possible wavelengths of electromagnetic radiation, from relatively short wavelengths (gamma rays) to much longer wavelengths (radio waves) (**Figure 8.4**). Visible light is the range of wavelengths detected by the human eye, commonly between 380–740 nm. As discussed later, it is this visible light that provides the energy to drive photosynthesis.

Physicists have also discovered that light has properties that are characteristic of particles. Albert Einstein formulated the photon theory of light in which he proposed that light is composed of discrete particles called **photons**—massless particles traveling in a wavelike pattern and moving at the speed of light (about 300 million meters/second). Each photon contains a specific amount of energy. An important difference between the various types of electromagnetic radiation, described in Figure 8.4, is the amount of energy found in the photons. Shorter wavelength radiation carries more energy per unit of time than longer wavelength radiation. For example, the photons of gamma rays carry more energy than those of radio waves.

The sun radiates the entire spectrum of electromagnetic radiation, but the atmosphere prevents much of this radiation from reaching the Earth's surface. For example, the ozone layer forms a thin shield in the upper atmosphere, protecting life on Earth from much of the sun's ultraviolet rays. Even so, a substantial amount of electromagnetic radiation does reach the Earth's surface. The effect of light on living organisms is critically dependent on the energy of the photons that reach them.

The photons found in gamma rays, X-rays, and UV rays have very high energy. When molecules in cells absorb such energy, the effects can be devastating. Such types of radiation can cause mutations in DNA and even lead to cancer. By comparison, the energy of photons found in visible light is much milder. Molecules can absorb this energy in a way that does not cause permanent harm. Next, we will consider how molecules in living cells absorb the energy within visible light.

Pigments Absorb Light Energy

When light strikes an object, one of three things will happen. First, light may simply pass through the object. Second, the object may change the path of light toward a different direction. A third possibility is that the object may absorb the light. The term **pigment** is used to describe a molecule that can absorb light energy. When light strikes a pigment, some of the wavelengths of light energy are absorbed, while others are reflected. For example, leaves look green to us because they reflect radiant energy of the green wavelength. Various pigments in the leaves absorb the other light energy wavelengths. At the extremes of color reflection are white and black. A white object reflects nearly all of the visible light energy falling on it, whereas a black object absorbs nearly all of the light energy. This is why it's coolest to wear white clothes on a sunny, hot day.

What do we mean when we say that light energy is absorbed? In the visible spectrum, light energy may be absorbed by boosting electrons to higher energy levels (**Figure 8.5**). Recall from Chapter 2 that electrons are located around the nucleus of an atom. The location in which an electron is likely to be found is called its orbital. Electrons in different orbitals possess different amounts of energy. For an electron to absorb light energy and be boosted to an orbital with a higher energy, it must overcome the difference in energy between the orbital it is in and the orbital to which it is going. For this to happen, an electron must absorb a photon that contains precisely that amount of energy. Different pigment molecules contain a

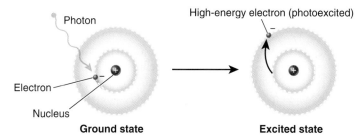

Figure 8.5 Absorption of light energy by an electron. When a photon of light of the correct amount of energy strikes an electron, the electron is boosted from the ground (unexcited) state to a higher energy level (an excited state). When this occurs, the electron occupies an orbital that is farther away from the nucleus of the atom. At this farther distance, the electron is held less firmly and is considered unstable.

Concept check: For a photoexcited electron to become more stable, describe the three things that could happen.

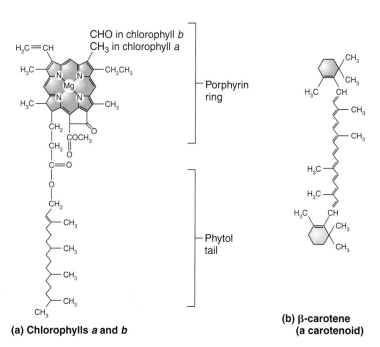

(a) Chlorophylls *a* and *b*

(b) β-carotene (a carotenoid)

Figure 8.6 Structures of pigment molecules. (a) The structure of chlorophylls *a* and *b*. As indicated, chlorophylls *a* and *b* differ only at a single site, at which chlorophyll *a* has a $-CH_3$ group and chlorophyll *b* has a $-CHO$ group. (b) The structure of β-carotene, an example of a carotenoid. The dark green and light green areas in parts (a) and (b) are the regions where a delocalized electron can hop from one atom to another.

variety of electrons that can be shifted to different energy levels. Therefore, the wavelength of light that a pigment absorbs depends on the amount of energy needed to boost an electron to a higher orbital.

After an electron absorbs energy, it is said to be in an excited state. Usually, this is an unstable condition. The electron may release the energy in different ways. First, when an excited electron drops back down to a lower energy level, it may release heat. For example, on a sunny day, the sidewalk heats up because it absorbs light energy that is released as heat. A second way that an electron can release energy is in the form of light. Certain organisms, such as jellyfish, possess molecules that make them glow. This glow is due to the release of light when electrons drop down to lower energy levels, a phenomenon called fluorescence.

In the case of photosynthetic pigments, however, a different event happens that is critical for the process of photosynthesis. Rather than releasing energy, an excited electron in a photosynthetic pigment is removed from that molecule and transferred to another molecule where the electron is more stable. When this occurs, the energy in the electron is said to be "captured," because the electron does not readily drop down to a lower energy level and release heat or light.

Plants Contain Different Types of Photosynthetic Pigments

In plants, different pigment molecules absorb the light energy used to drive photosynthesis. Two types of chlorophyll pigments, termed **chlorophyll *a*** and **chlorophyll *b***, are found in green plants and green algae. Their structure was determined in the 1930s by German chemist Hans Fischer (**Figure 8.6a**). In the chloroplast, both chlorophylls *a* and *b* are bound to integral membrane proteins in the thylakoid membrane.

The chlorophylls contain a porphyrin ring and a phytol tail. A magnesium ion (Mg^{2+}) is bound to the porphyrin ring. An electron in the porphyrin ring can follow a path in which it spends some of its time around several different atoms. Because this electron isn't restricted to a single atom, it is called a delocalized electron. The delocalized electron can absorb light energy.

The phytol tail in chlorophyll is a long hydrocarbon structure that is hydrophobic. Its function is to anchor the pigment to the surface of proteins within the thylakoid membrane.

Carotenoids are another type of pigment found in chloroplasts (**Figure 8.6b**). These pigments impart a color that ranges from yellow to orange to red. Carotenoids are often the major pigments in flowers and fruits. In leaves, the more abundant chlorophylls usually mask the colors of carotenoids. In temperate climates where the leaves change colors, the quantity of chlorophyll in the leaf declines during autumn. The carotenoids become readily visible and produce the yellows and oranges of autumn foliage.

An **absorption spectrum** is a diagram that depicts the wavelengths of electromagnetic radiation that are absorbed by a pigment. Each of the photosynthetic pigments shown in **Figure 8.7a** absorbs light in different regions of the visible spectrum. The absorption spectra of chlorophylls *a* and *b* are slightly different, though both chlorophylls absorb light most strongly in the red and violet parts of the visible spectrum and absorb green light poorly. Green light is reflected, which is why leaves appear green. Carotenoids absorb light in the blue and blue-green regions of the visible spectrum.

Why do plants have different pigments? Having different pigments allows plants to absorb light at many different wavelengths. In this way, plants are more efficient at capturing the energy in sunlight. This phenomenon is highlighted in an **action spectrum**, which shows the rate of photosynthesis plotted as a function of different wavelengths of light (**Figure 8.7b**). The

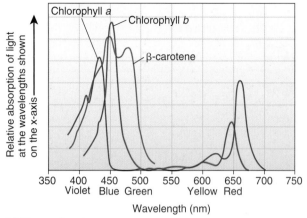

(a) Absorption spectra

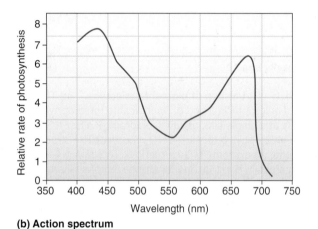

(b) Action spectrum

Figure 8.7 **Properties of pigment function: absorption and action spectra.** (a) These absorption spectra show the absorption of light by chlorophyll *a*, chlorophyll *b*, and β-carotene. (b) An action spectrum of photosynthesis depicting the relative rate of photosynthesis in green plants at different wavelengths of light.

Concept check: *What is the advantage of having different pigment molecules?*

highest rates of photosynthesis correlate with the wavelengths that are strongly absorbed by the chlorophylls and carotenoids. Photosynthesis is poor in the green region of the spectrum, because these pigments do not readily absorb this wavelength of light.

Photosystems II and I Work Together to Produce ATP and NADPH

Photosynthetic organisms have the unique ability not only to absorb light energy but also to capture that energy in a stable way. Many organic molecules can absorb light energy. For example, on a sunny day, molecules in your skin absorb light energy and release the energy as heat. The heat that is released, however, cannot be harnessed to do useful work. A key feature of photosynthesis is the ability of pigments to capture light energy and transfer it to other molecules that can hold on to

the energy in a stable fashion and ultimately produce energy intermediate molecules that can do cellular work.

Let's now consider how chloroplasts capture light energy. The thylakoid membranes of the chloroplast contain two distinct complexes of proteins and pigment molecules called **photosystem I** (**PSI**) and **photosystem II** (**PSII**) (Figure 8.8). Photosystem I was discovered before photosystem II, but photosystem II is the initial step in photosynthesis. We will consider the structure and function of PSII in greater detail later in this chapter.

As described in steps 1 and 2, light excites electrons in pigment molecules, such as chlorophylls, which are located in regions of PSII and PSI called light-harvesting complexes. Rather than releasing their energy in the form of heat, the excited electrons follow a path shown by the red arrow. Initially, the excited electrons move from a pigment molecule called P680 in PSII to other electron carriers called pheophytin (Pp), Q_A, and Q_B. The excited electrons are moved out of PSII by Q_B. PSII also oxidizes water, which generates O_2 and adds H^+ into the thylakoid lumen. The electrons released from the oxidized water molecules are used to replenish the electrons that leave PSII via Q_B.

After a pair of electrons reaches Q_B, each one enters an **electron transport chain**—a series of electron carriers—located in the thylakoid membrane. The electron transport chain functions similarly to the one found in mitochondria. From Q_B, an electron goes to a cytochrome complex; then to plastocyanin (Pc), a small protein; and then to photosystem I. Along its journey from photosystem II to photosystem I, the electron releases some of its energy at particular steps and is transferred to the next component that has a higher electronegativity. The energy released is harnessed to pump H^+ into the thylakoid lumen. One result of the electron movement is to establish a H^+ electrochemical gradient.

A key role of photosystem I is to make NADPH (Figure 8.8, step 3). When light strikes the light-harvesting complex of photosystem I, this energy is also transferred to a reaction center, where a high-energy electron is removed from a pigment molecule, designated P700, and transferred to a primary electron acceptor. A protein called ferredoxin (Fd) can accept two high-energy electrons, one at a time, from the primary electron acceptor. Fd then transfers the two electrons to the enzyme $NADP^+$ reductase. This enzyme transfers the two electrons to $NADP^+$ and together with a H^+ creates NADPH. The formation of NADPH results in fewer H^+ in the stroma and thereby contributes to the formation of a H^+ electrochemical gradient across the thylakoid membrane.

As described in step 4, the synthesis of ATP in chloroplasts is achieved by a chemiosmotic mechanism similar to that used to make ATP in mitochondria. In chloroplasts, ATP synthesis is driven by the flow of H^+ from the thylakoid lumen into the stroma via ATP synthase (Figure 8.8). A H^+ gradient is generated in three ways: (1) the splitting of water, which places H^+ in the thylakoid lumen; (2) the movement of high-energy electrons from photosystem II to photosystem I, which pumps H^+ into the thylakoid lumen; and (3) the formation of NADPH, which consumes H^+ in the stroma.

A key difference between photosystem II and photosystem I is how the pigment molecules receive electrons. As discussed

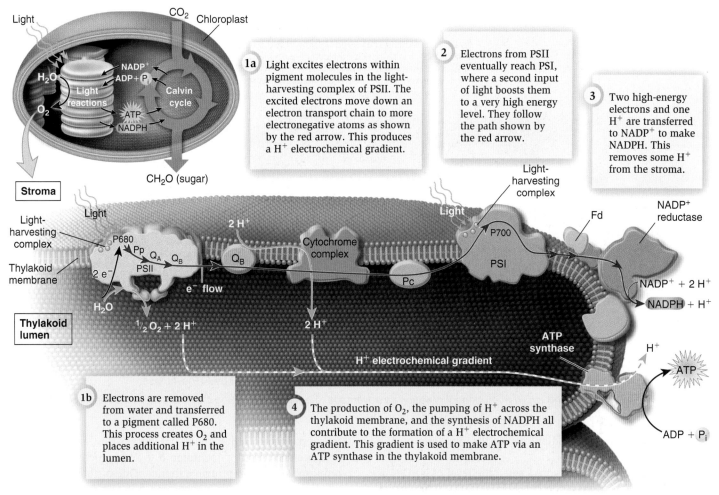

Figure 8.8   The synthesis of ATP, NADPH, and O_2 by the concerted actions of photosystems II and I.

Concept check: Are ATP, NADPH, and O_2 produced in the stroma or in the thylakoid lumen?

in more detail later, $P680^+$ receives an electron from water. By comparison, $P700^+$—the oxidized form of P700—receives an electron from Pc. Therefore, photosystem I does not need to split water to reduce $P700^+$ and does not generate oxygen.

In summary, the steps of the light reactions of photosynthesis produce three chemical products:

1. O_2 is produced in the thylakoid lumen by the oxidation of water by photosystem II. Two electrons are removed from water, which creates two H^+ and $1/2$ O_2. The two electrons are transferred to $P680^+$ molecules.
2. NADPH is produced in the stroma from high-energy electrons that start in photosystem II and are boosted a second time in photosystem I. Two high-energy electrons and one H^+ are transferred to $NADP^+$ to create NADPH.
3. ATP is produced in the stroma via ATP synthase that uses a H^+ electrochemical gradient.

The combined action of photosystem II and photosystem I is termed **noncyclic electron flow** because the electrons move linearly from PSII to PSI and ultimately reduce $NADP^+$ to NADPH.

Cyclic Electron Flow Produces Only ATP

The mechanism of harvesting light energy described in Figure 8.8 is called noncyclic electron flow because it is a linear process. This electron flow produces ATP and NADPH in roughly equal amounts. However, as we will see later, the Calvin cycle uses more ATP than NADPH. How can plant cells avoid making too much NADPH and not enough ATP? In 1959, Daniel Arnon discovered a pattern of electron flow that is cyclic and generates only ATP (**Figure 8.9**). Arnon termed the process **cyclic photophosphorylation** because (1) the path of electrons is cyclic, (2) light energizes the electrons, and (3) ATP is made via the phosphorylation of ADP. Due to the path of electrons, the mechanism is also called **cyclic electron flow**.

When light strikes photosystem I, high-energy electrons are sent to the primary electron acceptor and then to ferredoxin (Fd). The key difference in cyclic photophosphorylation is that the high-energy electrons are transferred from ferredoxin to Q_B. From Q_B, the electrons then go to the cytochrome complex, then to plastocyanin (Pc), and back to photosystem I. As the electrons travel along this cyclic route, they release energy, and some of this energy is used to transport H^+ into the thylakoid

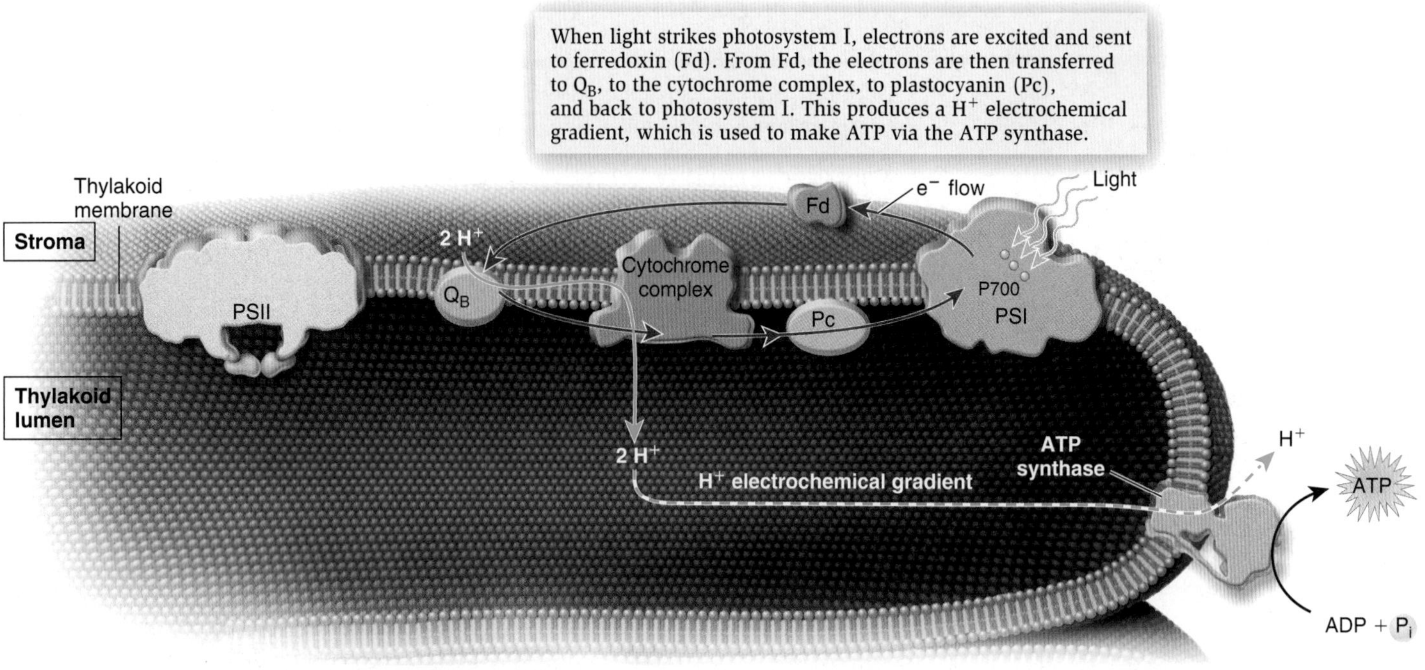

When light strikes photosystem I, electrons are excited and sent to ferredoxin (Fd). From Fd, the electrons are then transferred to Q_B, to the cytochrome complex, to plastocyanin (Pc), and back to photosystem I. This produces a H^+ electrochemical gradient, which is used to make ATP via the ATP synthase.

Figure 8.9 **Cyclic photophosphorylation.** In this process, an electron follows a cyclic path that is powered by photosystem I. This contributes to the formation of a H^+ electrochemical gradient, which is then used to make ATP by ATP synthase.

Concept check: *Why is having cyclic photophosphorylation an advantage to a plant over having only noncyclic electron flow?*

lumen. The resulting H^+ gradient drives the synthesis of ATP via ATP synthase.

Cyclic electron flow is favored when the level of $NADP^+$ is low and NADPH is high. Under these conditions, there is sufficient NADPH to run the Calvin cycle, which is described later. Alternatively, when $NADP^+$ is high and NADPH is low, noncyclic electron flow is favored, so more NADPH can be made. Cyclic electron flow is also favored when ATP levels are low.

Genomes & Proteomes Connection

The Cytochrome Complexes of Mitochondria and Chloroplasts Contain Evolutionarily Related Proteins

A recurring theme in cell biology is that evolution has resulted in groups of genes that encode proteins that play similar but specialized roles in cells—descent with modification. When two or more genes are similar because they are derived from the same ancestral gene, they are called **homologous genes**. As discussed in Chapter 23, homologous genes encode proteins that have similar amino acid sequences and may perform similar functions.

A comparison of the electron transport chains of mitochondria and chloroplasts reveals homologous genes. In particular, let's consider the cytochrome complex found in the thylakoid membrane of plants and algae, called cytochrome b_6-f (**Figure 8.10a**) and cytochrome b-c_1, which is found in the electron

transport chain of mitochondria (**Figure 8.10b**; also refer back to Figure 7.7). Both cytochrome b_6-f and cytochrome b-c_1 are composed of several protein subunits. One of those proteins is called cytochrome b_6 in cytochrome b_6-f and cytochrome b in cytochrome b-c_1.

By analyzing the sequences of the genes that encode these proteins, researchers discovered that cytochrome b_6 and cytochrome b are homologous. These proteins carry out similar functions: Both of them accept electrons from a quinone (Q_B or ubiquinone) and both donate an electron to another protein within their respective complexes (cytochrome f or cytochrome c_1). Likewise, both of these proteins function as H^+ pumps that capture some of the energy that is released from electrons to transport H^+ across the membrane. In this way, evolution has produced a family of cytochrome b-type proteins that play similar but specialized roles.

8.3 Molecular Features of Photosystems

Thus far, we have considered how chloroplasts absorb light energy and produce ATP, NADPH, and O_2. Photosystems, namely PSI and PSII, play critical roles in two aspects of photosynthesis. First, both PSI and PSII absorb light energy and capture that energy in the form of excited electrons. Second, PSII is also able to oxidize water and thereby produce O_2. In this section, we will examine how these events occur at the molecular level.

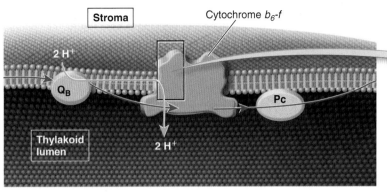

(a) Cytochrome b_6-f in the chloroplast

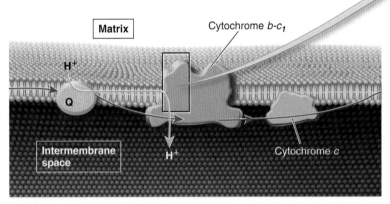

(b) Cytochrome b-c_1 in the mitochondrion

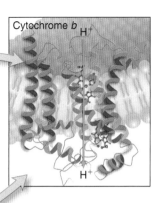

Figure 8.10 Homologous proteins in the electron transport chains of chloroplasts and mitochondria. **(a)** Cytochrome b_6-f is a complex involved in electron and H^+ transport in chloroplasts, and **(b)** cytochrome b-c_1 is a complex involved in electron and H^+ transport in mitochondria. These complexes contain homologous proteins designated cytochrome b_6 in chloroplasts and cytochrome b in mitochondria. The inset shows the three-dimensional structure of cytochrome b, which was determined by X-ray crystallography. It is an integral membrane protein with several transmembrane helices and two heme groups, which are prosthetic groups involved in electron transfer. The structure of cytochrome b_6 has also been determined and found to be very similar.

Concept check: *Explain why the three-dimensional structures of cytochrome b and cytochrome b_6 are very similar.*

Photosystem II Captures Light Energy and Produces O_2

PSI and PSII have two main components: a light-harvesting complex and a reaction center. Figure 8.11 shows how these components function in PSII. In 1932, Robert Emerson and an undergraduate student, William Arnold, originally discovered the **light-harvesting complex** in the thylakoid membrane. It is composed of several dozen pigment molecules that are anchored to transmembrane proteins. The role of the complex is to directly absorb photons of light. When a pigment molecule absorbs a photon, an electron is boosted to a higher energy level. As shown in Figure 8.11, the energy (not the electron itself) can be transferred to adjacent pigment molecules by a process called **resonance energy transfer**. The energy may be transferred among multiple pigment molecules until it is eventually transferred to a special pigment molecule designated P680, which is located within the reaction center of PSII. The P680 pigment is so named because it can directly absorb light at a wavelength of 680 nm. However, P680 is more commonly excited by resonance energy transfer from another chlorophyll pigment. In either case, when an electron in P680 is excited, it is designated P680*. The light-harvesting complex is also called the **antenna complex** because it acts like an antenna that absorbs energy from light and funnels that energy to P680 in the reaction center.

A high-energy (photoexcited) electron in a pigment molecule is relatively unstable. It may abruptly release its energy by giving off heat or light. Unlike the pigments in the antenna complex that undergo resonance energy transfer, P680* can actually release its high-energy electron and become P680$^+$.

$$P680^* \rightarrow P680^+ + e^-$$

The role of the reaction center is to quickly remove the high-energy electron from P680* and transfer it to another molecule, where the electron will be more stable. This molecule is called the **primary electron acceptor** (Figure 8.11). The transfer of the electron from P680* to the primary electron acceptor is remarkably fast. It occurs in less than a few picoseconds! (One picosecond equals one-trillionth of a second, also noted as 10^{-12} s.) Because this occurs so quickly, the excited electron does not have much time to release its energy in the form of heat or light.

After the primary electron acceptor has received this high-energy electron, the light energy has been captured and can be used to perform cellular work. As discussed earlier, the work it performs is to synthesize the energy intermediates ATP and NADPH.

Let's now consider what happens to P680$^+$, which has given up its high-energy electron. After P680$^+$ is formed, it is necessary to replace the electron so that P680 can function again. Therefore, another role of the reaction center is to replace the electron that is removed when P680* becomes P680$^+$. This missing electron of P680$^+$ is replaced with a low-energy electron from water (Figure 8.11).

$$H_2O \rightarrow 1/2\ O_2 + 2\ H^+ + 2\ e^-$$

$$2\ P680^+ + 2\ e^- \rightarrow 2\ P680$$
$$\text{(from water)}$$

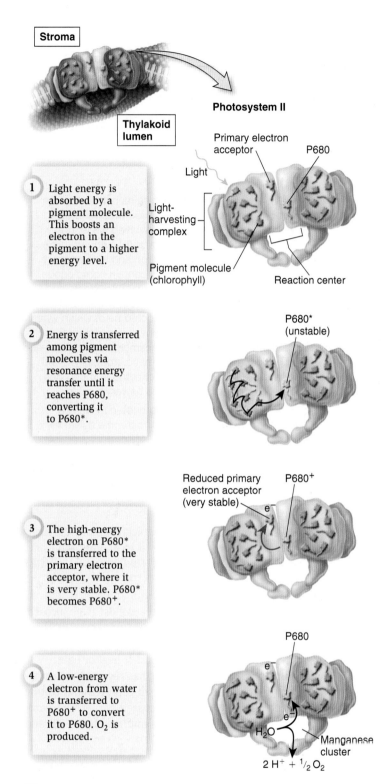

Stroma

Thylakoid lumen

Photosystem II

Primary electron acceptor

P680

Light

Light-harvesting complex

Pigment molecule (chlorophyll)

Reaction center

1 Light energy is absorbed by a pigment molecule. This boosts an electron in the pigment to a higher energy level.

2 Energy is transferred among pigment molecules via resonance energy transfer until it reaches P680, converting it to P680*.

P680* (unstable)

3 The high-energy electron on P680* is transferred to the primary electron acceptor, where it is very stable. P680* becomes P680+.

Reduced primary electron acceptor (very stable)

P680+

e^-

4 A low-energy electron from water is transferred to P680+ to convert it to P680. O_2 is produced.

P680

e^-

e^-

H_2O

Manganese cluster

$2 H^+ + \frac{1}{2} O_2$

Figure 8.11 A closer look at how PSII absorbs light energy and oxidizes water.

The oxidation of water results in the formation of oxygen gas (O_2), which is used by many organisms for cellular respiration. Photosystem II is the only known protein complex that can oxidize water, resulting in the release of O_2 into the atmosphere.

Photosystem II Is an Amazing Redox Machine

All cells rely on redox reactions to store and utilize energy and to form covalent bonds in organic molecules. Photosystem II is a particularly remarkable example of a redox machine. As we have learned, this complex of proteins removes high-energy electrons from a pigment molecule and transfers them to a primary electron acceptor. Perhaps even more remarkable is that photosystem II can remove low-energy electrons from water—a very stable molecule that holds onto its electrons tightly. The removal of electrons is how O_2 is made.

Many approaches have been used to study how photosystem II works. In recent years, much effort has been aimed at determining the biochemical composition of the protein complex and the roles of its individual components. The number of protein subunits varies somewhat from species to species and may vary due to environmental changes. Typically, photosystem II contains around 19 different protein subunits. Two subunits, designated D1 and D2, contain the reaction center that carries out the redox reactions (**Figure 8.12a**). Two other subunits, called CP43 and CP47, bind the pigment molecules that form the light-harvesting complex. Many additional subunits regulate the function of photosystem II and provide structural support.

Figure 8.12a illustrates the pathway of electron movement through photosystem II. The red arrows indicate the movement of a high-energy electron, whereas the black arrows show the path of a low-energy electron. Let's begin with a high-energy electron. When the electron on P680 becomes boosted to a higher energy level, usually by resonance energy transfer, this high-energy electron then moves to the primary electron acceptor, which is a chlorophyll molecule lacking Mg^{2+}, called pheophytin (Pp). Pheophytin is permanently bound to photosystem II and transfers the electron to a plastoquinone molecule, designated Q_A, which is also permanently bound to photosystem II. Next, the electron is transferred to another plastoquinone molecule designated Q_B, which can accept two high-energy electrons and bind two H^+. As shown earlier in Figure 8.8, Q_B can diffuse away from the reaction center.

Let's now consider the path of a low-energy electron. The oxidation of water occurs in a region called the **manganese cluster**. This site is located on the side of D1 that faces the thylakoid lumen. The manganese cluster has four Mn^{2+}, one Ca^{2+}, and one Cl^-. Two water molecules bind to this site. D1 catalyzes the removal of four low-energy electrons from the two water molecules to create four H^+ and O_2. Each low-energy electron is transferred, one at a time, to an amino acid in D1 (a tyrosine, Tyr) and then to P680+ to produce P680.

In 2004, So Iwata, James Barber, and colleagues determined the three-dimensional structure of photosystem II using a technique called **X-ray crystallography**. In this method, researchers must purify a protein or protein complex and expose it to conditions that cause the proteins to associate with each other in an ordered array. In other words, the proteins form a crystal. When a crystal is exposed to X-rays, the resulting pattern can be analyzed mathematically to determine the three-dimensional structure of the crystal's components. Major advances in this technique over the last couple of decades have enabled researchers to

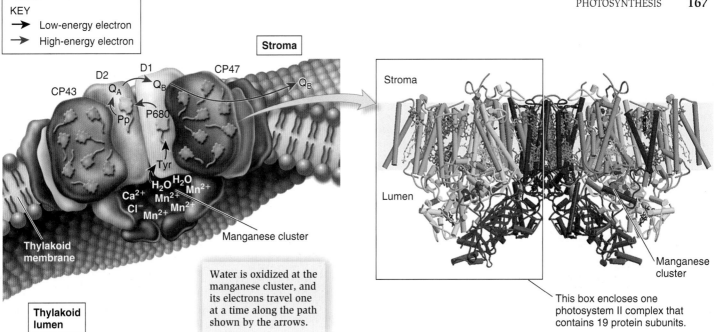

KEY

→ Low-energy electron
→ High-energy electron

Stroma

D2 · D1 · CP47

CP43

Q_A · Q_B · Q_B

Pp · P680

Tyr

H_2O H_2O

Ca^{2+} Mn^{2+} Mn^{2+}
Cl^- Mn^{2+} Mn^{2+}

Thylakoid membrane

Manganese cluster

Thylakoid lumen

Water is oxidized at the manganese cluster, and its electrons travel one at a time along the path shown by the arrows.

Stroma

Lumen

Manganese cluster

This box encloses one photosystem II complex that contains 19 protein subunits.

(a) The path of electron flow through photosystem II

(b) Three-dimensional structure of photosystem II as determined by X-ray crystallography

Figure 8.12 **The molecular structure of photosystem II.** **(a)** Schematic drawing showing the path of electron flow from water to Q_B. The CP43 and CP47 protein subunits wrap around D1 and D2 so that pigments in CP43 and CP47 can transfer energy to P680 by resonance energy transfer. **(b)** The three-dimensional structure of photosystem II as determined by X-ray crystallography. In the crystal structure, the colors are CP43 (green), D2 (orange), D1 (yellow), and CP47 (red).

Concept check: *According to this figure, how many redox reactions does photosystem II catalyze?*

determine the structures of relatively large macromolecular complexes such as photosystem II (**Figure 8.12b**). The structure shown here is a dimer; it has two PSII complexes, each with 19 protein subunits. As seen in this figure, the intricacy of the structure of photosystem II rivals the complexity of its function.

The Use of Light Flashes of Specific Wavelengths Provided Experimental Evidence for the Existence of PSII and PSI

An experimental technique that uses light flashes at particular wavelengths has been important in helping researchers to understand the function of photosystems. In this method, pioneered by Robert Emerson, a photosynthetic organism is exposed to a particular wavelength of light, after which the rate of photosynthesis is measured by the amount of CO_2 consumed or the amount of O_2 produced. In the 1950s, Emerson performed a particularly intriguing experiment that greatly stimulated photosynthesis research (**Figure 8.13**). He subjected algae to light flashes of different wavelengths and obtained a mysterious result. When he exposed algae to a wavelength of 680 nm, he observed a low rate of photosynthesis. A similarly low rate of photosynthesis occurred when he exposed algae to a wavelength of 700 nm. However, when he exposed the algae to both wavelengths of light simultaneously, the rate of photosynthesis was more than double the rate observed at only one wavelength. This phenomenon was termed the **enhancement effect**.

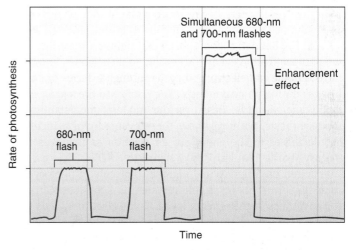

Simultaneous 680-nm and 700-nm flashes

Enhancement effect

Rate of photosynthesis

680-nm flash

700-nm flash

Time

Figure 8.13 **The enhancement effect observed by Emerson.** When photosynthetic organisms such as green plants and algae are exposed to 680-nm and 700-nm light simultaneously, the resulting rate of photosynthesis is much more than double the rate produced by each wavelength individually.

Concept check: *Would the enhancement effect be observed if two consecutive flashes of light occurred at 680 nm?*

We know now that it occurs because light of 680-nm wavelength can readily activate the pigment (P680) in the reaction center in photosystem II but is not very efficient at activating pigments in photosystem I. In contrast, light of 700-nm wavelength is optimal at activating the pigments in photosystem I

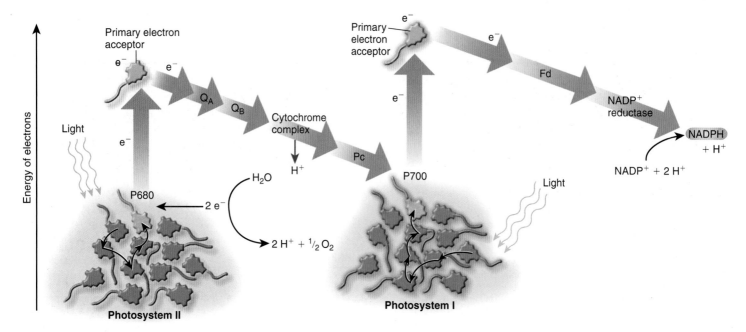

Figure 8.14 **The Z scheme, showing the energy of an electron moving from photosystem II to NADP$^+$.** The oxidation of water releases two electrons that travel one at a time from photosystem II to NADP$^+$. As seen here, the input of light boosts the energy of the electron twice. At the end of the pathway, two electrons are used to make NADPH.

Concept check: *During its journey from photosystem II to NADP$^+$, at what point does an electron have the highest amount of energy?*

but not those in photosystem II. When algae are exposed to both wavelengths, however, the pigments in both photosystems are maximally activated.

When researchers began to understand that photosynthesis results in the production of both ATP and NADPH, Robin Hill and Fay Bendall also proposed that photosynthesis involves two photoactivation events. According to their model, known as the **Z scheme**, an electron proceeds through a series of energy changes during photosynthesis. The Z refers to the zigzag shape of this energy curve. Based on our modern understanding of photosynthesis, we now know these events involve increases and decreases in the energy of an electron as it moves from photosystem II through photosystem I to NADP$^+$ (**Figure 8.14**). An electron on a nonexcited pigment molecule in photosystem II has the lowest energy. In photosystem II, light boosts an electron to a much higher energy level. As the electron travels from photosystem II to photosystem I, some of the energy is released. The input of light in photosystem I boosts the electron to an even higher energy than it attained in photosystem II. The electron releases a little energy before it is eventually transferred to NADP$^+$.

8.4 Synthesizing Carbohydrates via the Calvin Cycle

In the previous sections, we learned how the light reactions of photosynthesis produce ATP, NADPH, and O$_2$. We will now turn our attention to the second phase of photosynthesis, the Calvin cycle, in which ATP and NADPH are used to make carbohydrates. The Calvin cycle consists of a series of steps that occur in a metabolic cycle.

The Calvin cycle takes CO$_2$ from the atmosphere and incorporates the carbon into organic molecules, namely, carbohydrates. As mentioned earlier, carbohydrates are critical for two reasons. First, these organic molecules provide the precursors to make the organic molecules and macromolecules of nearly all living cells. The second key reason why the Calvin cycle is important involves the storage of energy. The Calvin cycle produces carbohydrates, which store energy. These carbohydrates are accumulated inside plant cells. When a plant is in the dark and not carrying out photosynthesis, the stored carbohydrates can be used as a source of energy. Similarly, when an animal consumes a plant, it can use the carbohydrates as an energy source.

In this section, we will examine the three phases of the Calvin cycle. We will also explore the experimental approach of Melvin Calvin and his colleagues that enabled them to elucidate the steps of this cycle.

The Calvin Cycle Incorporates CO$_2$ into Carbohydrate

The Calvin cycle, also called the Calvin-Benson cycle, was determined by chemists Melvin Calvin and Andrew Adam Benson and their colleagues in the 1940s and 1950s. This cycle requires a massive input of energy. For every 6 carbon dioxide molecules that are incorporated into a carbohydrate such as glucose (C$_6$H$_{12}$O$_6$), 18 ATP molecules are hydrolyzed and 12 NADPH molecules are oxidized.

$$6 \text{ CO}_2 + 12 \text{ H}_2\text{O} \rightarrow \text{C}_6\text{H}_{12}\text{O}_6 + 6 \text{ O}_2 + 6 \text{ H}_2\text{O}$$

$$18 \text{ ATP} + 18 \text{ H}_2\text{O} \rightarrow 18 \text{ ADP} + 18 \text{ P}_i$$

$$12 \text{ NADPH} \rightarrow 12 \text{ NADP}^+ + 12 \text{ H}^+ + 24 \text{ e}^-$$

Although biologists commonly describe glucose as a product of photosynthesis, glucose is not directly made by the Calvin cycle. Instead, molecules of glyceraldehyde-3-phosphate, which are products of the Calvin cycle, are used as starting materials for the synthesis of glucose and other molecules, including sucrose. After glucose molecules are made, they may be linked together to form a polymer of glucose called starch, which is stored in the chloroplast for later use. Alternatively, the disaccharide sucrose may be made and transported out of the leaf to other parts of the plant.

The Calvin cycle can be divided into three phases. These phases are carbon fixation, reduction and carbohydrate production, and regeneration of RuBP (Figure 8.15).

Carbon Fixation (Phase 1) In **carbon fixation**, CO_2 becomes incorporated into ribulose bisphosphate (RuBP), a five-carbon sugar. The product of the reaction is a six-carbon intermediate that immediately splits in half to form two molecules of 3-phosphoglycerate (3PG). The enzyme that catalyzes this step is named RuBP carboxylase/oxygenase, or **rubisco**. It is the most abundant protein in chloroplasts and perhaps the most abundant protein on Earth! This observation underscores the massive amount of carbon fixation that happens in the biosphere.

Reduction and Carbohydrate Production (Phase 2) In the second phase, ATP is used to convert 3PG to 1,3-bisphosphoglycerate. Next, electrons from NADPH reduce 1,3-bisphosphoglycerate to glyceraldehyde-3-phosphate (G3P). G3P is a carbohydrate with three carbon atoms. The key difference between 3PG and G3P is that G3P has a C—H bond, whereas the analogous carbon in 3PG forms a C—O bond (Figure 8.15). The C—H bond can occur because the G3P molecule has been reduced by the addition of two electrons from NADPH. Compared to 3PG, the bonds

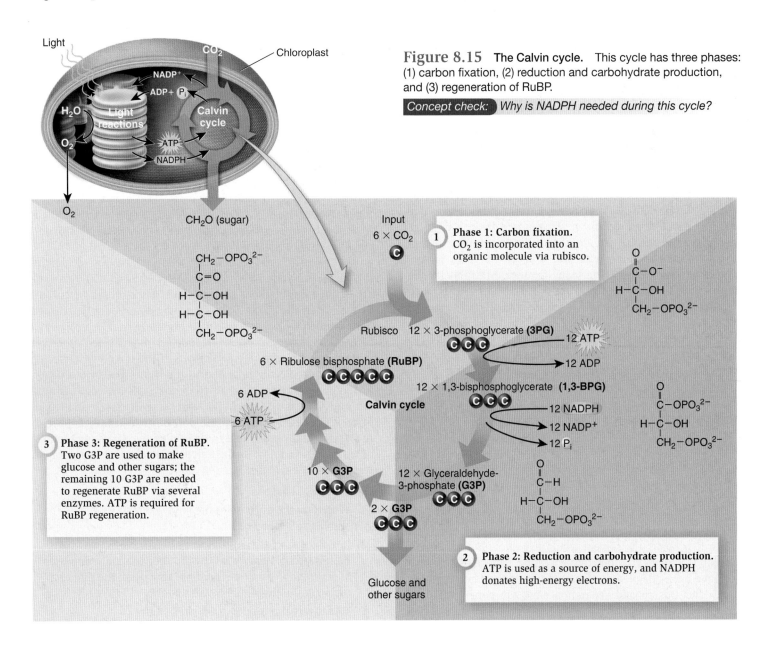

Figure 8.15 **The Calvin cycle.** This cycle has three phases: (1) carbon fixation, (2) reduction and carbohydrate production, and (3) regeneration of RuBP.

Concept check: *Why is NADPH needed during this cycle?*

in G3P store more energy and enable G3P to readily form larger organic molecules such as glucose.

As shown in Figure 8.15, only some of the G3P molecules are used to make glucose or other carbohydrates. Phase 1 begins with 6 RuBP molecules and 6 CO_2 molecules. Twelve G3P molecules are made at the end of phase 2. Two of these G3P molecules are used in carbohydrate production. As described next, the other 10 G3P molecules are needed to keep the Calvin cycle turning by regenerating RuBP.

Regeneration of RuBP (Phase 3)   In the last phase of the Calvin cycle, a series of enzymatic steps converts the 10 G3P molecules into 6 RuBP molecules, using 6 molecules of ATP. After the RuBP molecules are regenerated, they serve as acceptors for CO_2, thereby allowing the cycle to continue.

As we have just seen, the Calvin cycle begins by using carbon from an inorganic source, that is, CO_2, and ends with organic molecules that will be used by the plant to make other compounds. You may be wondering why CO_2 molecules cannot be directly linked to form these larger molecules. The answer lies in the number of electrons that orbit carbon atoms. In CO_2, the carbon atom is considered electron poor. Oxygen is a very electronegative atom that monopolizes the electrons it shares with other atoms. In a covalent bond between carbon and oxygen, the shared electrons are closer to the oxygen atom.

By comparison, in an organic molecule, the carbon atom is electron rich. During the Calvin cycle, ATP provides energy and NADPH donates high-energy electrons, so the carbon originally in CO_2 has been reduced. The Calvin cycle combines less electronegative atoms with carbon atoms so that C—H and C—C bonds are formed. This allows the eventual synthesis of larger organic molecules including glucose, amino acids, and so on. In addition, the covalent bonds within these molecules are capable of storing large amounts of energy.

FEATURE INVESTIGATION

The Calvin Cycle Was Determined by Isotope Labeling Methods

The steps in the Calvin cycle involve the conversion of one type of molecule to another, eventually regenerating the starting material, RuBP. In the 1940s and 1950s, Calvin and his colleagues used ^{14}C, a radioisotope of carbon, to label and trace molecules produced during the cycle (**Figure 8.16**). They injected ^{14}C-labeled CO_2 into cultures of the green algae *Chlorella pyrenoidosa* grown in an apparatus called a "lollipop" (because of its shape). The *Chlorella* cells were given different lengths of time to incorporate the ^{14}C-labeled carbon, ranging from fractions of a second to many minutes. After this incubation period, the cells were abruptly placed into a solution of alcohol to inhibit enzymatic reactions and thereby stop the cycle.

The researchers separated the newly made radiolabeled molecules by a variety of methods. The most commonly used method was two-dimensional paper chromatography. In this approach, a sample containing radiolabeled molecules was spotted onto a corner of the paper at a location called the origin. The edge of the paper was placed in a solvent, such as phenol-water. As the solvent rose through the paper, so did the radiolabeled molecules. The rate at which they rose depended on their structures, which determined how strongly they interacted with the paper. This step separated the mixture of molecules spotted onto the paper at the origin.

The paper was then dried, turned 90°, and then the edge was placed in a different solvent, such as butanol-propionic acid-water. Again, the solvent would rise through the paper (in a second dimension), thereby separating molecules that may not have been adequately separated during the first separation step. After this second separation step, the paper was dried and exposed to X-ray film, a procedure called autoradiography.

Radioactive emission from the ^{14}C-labeled molecules caused dark spots to appear on the film.

The pattern of spots changed depending on the length of time the cells were incubated with ^{14}C-labeled CO_2. When the incubation period was short, only molecules that were made in the first steps of the Calvin cycle were seen. Longer incubations revealed molecules synthesized in later steps. For example, after short incubations, 3-phosphoglycerate (3PG) and 1,3-bisphosphoglycerate (1,3-BPG) were observed, whereas longer incubations also showed glyceraldehyde-3-phosphate (G3P) and ribulose bisphosphate (RuBP).

A challenge for Calvin and his colleagues was to identify the chemical nature of each spot. They achieved this by a variety of chemical methods. For example, a spot could be cut out of the paper, the molecule within the paper could be washed out or eluted, and then the eluted molecule could be subjected to the same procedure that included a radiolabeled molecule whose structure was already known. If the unknown molecule and known molecule migrated to the same spot in the paper, this indicated they were likely to be the same molecule. During the late 1940s and 1950s, Calvin and his coworkers identified all of the ^{14}C-labeled spots and the order in which they appeared. In this way, they were able to determine the series of reactions of what we now know as the Calvin cycle. For this work, Calvin was awarded the Nobel Prize in 1961.

Experimental Questions

1. What was the purpose of the study conducted by Calvin and his colleagues?

2. In Calvin's experiments shown in Figure 8.15, why did the researchers use ^{14}C? Why did they examine samples at several different time periods? How were the different molecules in the samples identified?

3. What were the results of Calvin's study?

Figure 8.16   The determination of the Calvin cycle using CO_2 labeled with ^{14}C and paper chromatography.

GOAL   The incorporation of CO_2 into carbohydrate involves a biosynthetic pathway. The aim of this experiment was to identify the steps.

KEY MATERIALS   The green alga *Chlorella pyrenoidosa* and ^{14}C-labeled CO_2.

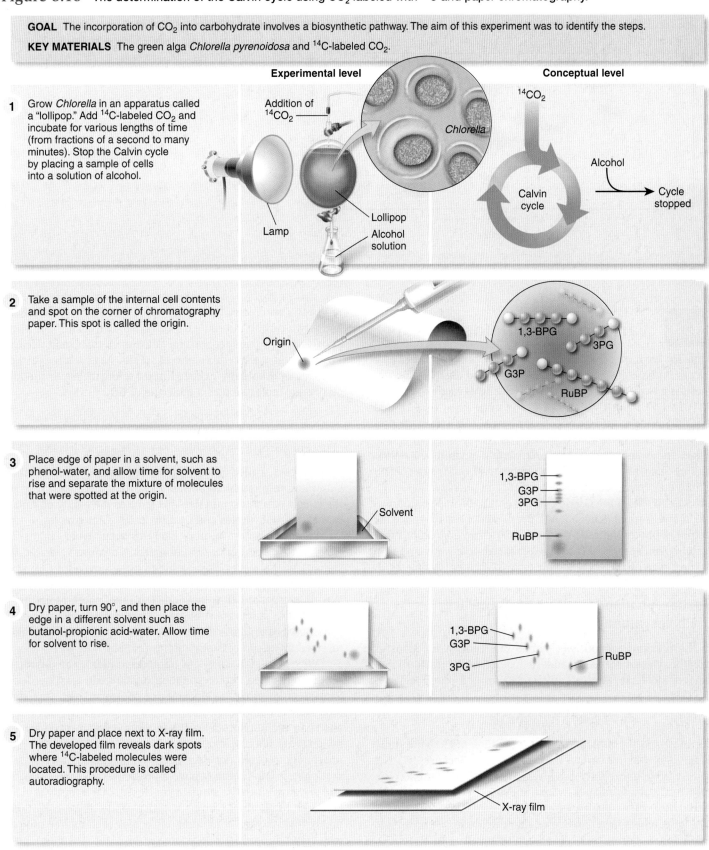

Experimental level

Conceptual level

1   Grow *Chlorella* in an apparatus called a "lollipop." Add ^{14}C-labeled CO_2 and incubate for various lengths of time (from fractions of a second to many minutes). Stop the Calvin cycle by placing a sample of cells into a solution of alcohol.

Addition of [14]CO_2

Chlorella

Lamp

Lollipop

Alcohol solution

[14]CO_2

Alcohol

Calvin cycle

Cycle stopped

2   Take a sample of the internal cell contents and spot on the corner of chromatography paper. This spot is called the origin.

Origin

1,3-BPG

3PG

G3P

RuBP

3   Place edge of paper in a solvent, such as phenol-water, and allow time for solvent to rise and separate the mixture of molecules that were spotted at the origin.

Solvent

1,3-BPG
G3P
3PG

RuBP

4   Dry paper, turn 90°, and then place the edge in a different solvent such as butanol-propionic acid-water. Allow time for solvent to rise.

1,3-BPG
G3P

3PG

RuBP

5   Dry paper and place next to X-ray film. The developed film reveals dark spots where ^{14}C-labeled molecules were located. This procedure is called autoradiography.

X-ray film

6 **THE DATA***

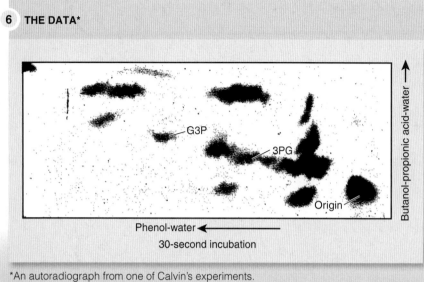

Phenol-water ←

30-second incubation

Butanol-propionic acid-water ↑

*An autoradiograph from one of Calvin's experiments.

7 **CONCLUSION** The identification of the molecules in each spot elucidated the steps of the Calvin cycle.

8 **SOURCE** Calvin, M. December 11, 1961. The path of carbon in photosynthesis. Nobel Lecture.

8.5   Variations in Photosynthesis

Thus far, we have considered the process of photosynthesis as it occurs in the chloroplasts of green plants and algae. Photosynthesis is a two-stage process in which the light reactions produce ATP, NADPH, and O_2, and the Calvin cycle uses the ATP and NADPH in the synthesis of carbohydrates. This two-stage process is a universal feature of photosynthesis in all green plants, algae, and cyanobacteria. However, certain environmental conditions such as light intensity, temperature, and water availability may influence both the efficiency of photosynthesis and the way in which the Calvin cycle operates. In this section, we begin by examining how hot and dry conditions may reduce the output of photosynthesis. We then explore two adaptations that certain plant species have evolved that conserve water and help to maximize photosynthetic efficiency in such environments.

Photorespiration Decreases the Efficiency of Photosynthesis

In the previous section, we learned that rubisco functions as a carboxylase because it adds a CO_2 molecule to RuBP, an organic molecule, to create two molecules of 3-phosphoglycerate (3PG).

$$RuBP + CO_2 \rightarrow 2 \ 3PG$$

For most species of plants, the incorporation of CO_2 into RuBP is the only way for carbon fixation to occur. Because 3PG is a three-carbon molecule, these plants are called **C_3 plants**. Examples of C_3 plants include wheat and oak trees (**Figure 8.17**). About 90% of the plant species on Earth are C_3 plants.

Researchers have discovered that the active site of rubisco can also function as an oxygenase, although its affinity for CO_2 is over 10-fold better than that for O_2. Even so, when O_2 levels are high and CO_2 levels are low, rubisco adds an O_2 molecule to RuBP. This creates only one molecule of 3-phosphoglycerate and a two-carbon molecule called phosphoglycolate. The phosphoglycolate is then dephosphorylated to glycolate and released from the chloroplast. In a series of several steps, the two-carbon glycolate is eventually oxidized in other organelles to produce an organic molecule plus a molecule of CO_2.

$$RuBP + O_2 \rightarrow \text{3-phosphoglycerate} + \text{Phosphoglycolate}$$

$$\text{Phosphoglycolate} \rightarrow \text{Glycolate} \rightarrow \rightarrow \text{Organic molecule} + CO_2$$

This process, called **photorespiration**, uses O_2 and liberates CO_2. Photorespiration is considered wasteful because it reverses the effects of photosynthesis. This reduces the ability of a plant to make carbohydrates and thereby limits plant growth.

Photorespiration is more likely to occur when plants are exposed to a hot and dry environment. To conserve water, the stomata of the leaves close, inhibiting the uptake of CO_2 from the air and trapping the O_2 that is produced by photosynthesis. When the level of CO_2 is low and O_2 is high, photorespiration is favored. If C_3 plants are subjected to hot and dry environmental conditions, as much as 25–50% of their photosynthetic work is reversed by the process of photorespiration.

Why do plants carry out photorespiration? The answer is not entirely clear. Photorespiration undoubtedly has the disadvantage of lowering the efficiency of photosynthesis. One common view is that photorespiration does not offer any advantage and is an evolutionary relic. When rubisco first evolved some 3 billion years ago, the atmospheric oxygen level was low, so photorespiration would not have been a problem. Another view is that photorespiration may have a protective advantage. On hot and dry days when the stomata are closed, CO_2 levels within the leaves will fall, and O_2 levels will rise. Under these conditions, highly toxic oxygen-containing molecules such as free radicals may be produced that could damage the plant. Therefore, plant biologists have speculated that the role of photorespiration may be to protect the plant against the harmful effects of such toxic

(a) Wheat plants

(b) Oak leaves

Figure 8.17 **Examples of C₃ plants.** The structures of **(a)** wheat and **(b)** red oak leaves are similar to that shown in Figure 8.2.

molecules by consuming O_2 and releasing CO_2. In addition, photorespiration may affect the metabolism of other compounds in plants. Recent research suggests that photorespiration may also help plants to assimilate nitrogen into organic molecules.

C₄ Plants Have Evolved a Mechanism to Minimize Photorespiration

Certain species of plants have developed an interesting way to minimize photorespiration. In the early 1960s, Hugo Kortschak

discovered that the first product of carbon fixation in sugarcane is not 3-phosphoglycerate but instead is a compound with four carbon atoms. Species such as sugarcane are called **C₄ plants** because of this four-carbon compound. Later, Marshall Hatch and Roger Slack confirmed this result and identified the compound as oxaloacetate. For this reason, the pathway is sometimes called the Hatch-Slack pathway.

Some C₄ plants employ an interesting cellular organization to avoid photorespiration (**Figure 8.18**). Unlike C₃ plants, an interior layer in the leaves of many C₄ plants has a two-cell

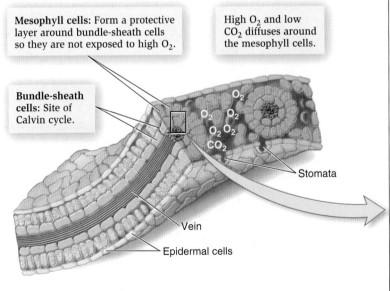

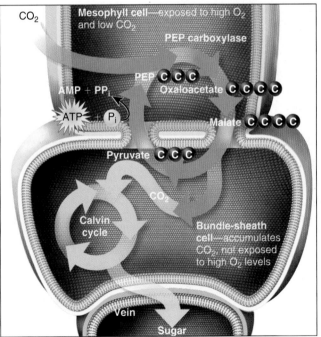

Figure 8.18 **Leaf structure and its relationship to the C₄ cycle.** C₄ plants have mesophyll cells, which initially take up CO_2, and bundle-sheath cells, where much of the carbohydrate synthesis occurs. Compare this leaf structure with the structure of C₃ leaves shown in Figure 8.2.

Concept check: How does this cellular arrangement minimize photorespiration?

organization composed of mesophyll cells and bundle-sheath cells. CO_2 from the atmosphere enters the mesophyll cells via stomata. Once inside, the enzyme **PEP carboxylase** adds CO_2 to phosphoenolpyruvate (PEP), a three-carbon molecule, to produce oxaloacetate, a four-carbon compound. PEP carboxylase does not recognize O_2. Therefore, unlike rubisco, PEP carboxylase does not promote photorespiration when CO_2 is low and O_2 is high. Instead, PEP carboxylase continues to fix CO_2.

In these types of C_4 plants, a four-carbon compound is transferred between cells. As shown in Figure 8.18, the compound oxaloacetate is converted to the four-carbon compound malate, which is transported into the bundle-sheath cell. Malate is then broken down into pyruvate and CO_2. The pyruvate returns to the mesophyll cell, where it is converted to PEP via ATP, and the cycle in the mesophyll cell can begin again. The main outcome of this C_4 cycle is that the mesophyll cell provides the bundle-sheath cell with CO_2. The Calvin cycle occurs in the chloroplasts of the bundle-sheath cell. Because the mesophyll cell supplies the bundle-sheath cell with a steady supply of CO_2, the concentration of CO_2 remains high in the bundle-sheath cell. Also, the mesophyll cells shield the bundle sheath cells from high levels of O_2. This strategy minimizes photorespiration, which requires low CO_2 and high O_2 levels to proceed.

Which is better—being a C_3 or a C_4 plant? The answer is that it depends on the environment. In warm and dry climates, C_4 plants have an advantage. During the day, they can keep their stomata partially closed to conserve water. Furthermore,

they can avoid photorespiration. C_4 plants are well adapted to habitats with high daytime temperatures and intense sunlight. Examples of C_4 plants are sugarcane, crabgrass, and corn. In cooler climates, C_3 plants have the edge because they use less energy to fix carbon dioxide. The process of carbon fixation that occurs in C_4 plants uses ATP to regenerate PEP from pyruvate (Figure 8.18), which C_3 plants do not have to expend.

CAM Plants Are C_4 Plants That Take Up CO_2 at Night

We have just learned that certain C_4 plants prevent photorespiration by providing CO_2 to the bundle-sheath cells, where the Calvin cycle occurs. This mechanism separates photosynthesis into different cells. Another strategy followed by other C_4 plants, called **CAM plants**, is to separate these processes in time. CAM stands for crassulacean acid metabolism, because the process was first studied in members of the plant family Crassulaceae. CAM plants are water-storing succulents such as cacti, bromeliads (including pineapple), and sedums. To avoid water loss, CAM plants keep their stomata closed during the day and open them at night, when it is cooler and the relative humidity is higher.

How, then, do CAM plants carry out photosynthesis? **Figure 8.19** compares CAM plants with the other type of C_4 plants we considered in Figure 8.18. Photosynthesis in CAM plants occurs entirely within mesophyll cells. During the night, the stomata

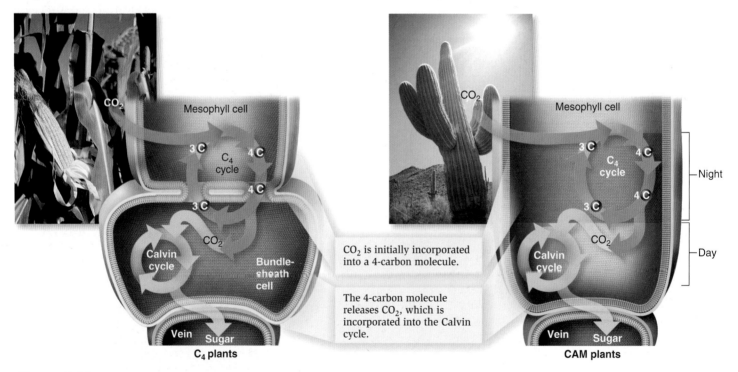

Figure 8.19 A comparison of C_4 and CAM plants.   The name C_4 plant describes those plants in which the first organic product of carbon fixation is a four-carbon compound. Using this definition, CAM plants are a type of C_4 plant. CAM plants, however, do not separate the functions of making a four-carbon molecule and the Calvin cycle into different types of cells. Instead, they make a four-carbon molecule at night and break down that molecule during the day so the CO_2 can be incorporated into the Calvin cycle.

Concept check: *What are the advantages and disadvantages among C_3, C_4, and CAM plants?*

of CAM plants open, thereby allowing the entry of CO_2 into mesophyll cells. CO_2 is joined with PEP to form the four-carbon compound oxaloacetate. This is then converted to malate, which accumulates during the night in the central vacuoles of the cells. In the morning, the stomata close to conserve moisture. The accumulated malate in the mesophyll cells leaves the vacuole and is broken down to release CO_2, which then drives the Calvin cycle during the daytime.

 # Summary of Key Concepts

- Photosynthesis is the process by which plants, algae, and cyanobacteria capture light energy to synthesize carbohydrates.

8.1 Overview of Photosynthesis

- During photosynthesis, carbon dioxide, water, and energy are used to make carbohydrates and oxygen.

- Heterotrophs must obtain organic molecules in their food, whereas autotrophs can make organic molecules from inorganic sources. Photoautotrophs use the energy from light to make organic molecules.

- An energy cycle occurs in the biosphere in which photosynthesis uses CO_2 and H_2O to make organic molecules, and the organic molecules are broken back down to CO_2 and H_2O via cellular respiration so that organisms can make energy intermediates such as ATP. (Figure 8.1)

- In plants and algae, photosynthesis occurs within chloroplasts, which have an outer membrane, inner membrane, and thylakoid membrane. The stroma is found between the thylakoid membrane and inner membrane. In plants, the leaves are the major site of photosynthesis. (Figure 8.2)

- The light reactions of photosynthesis capture light energy to make ATP, NADPH, and O_2. These reactions occur at the thylakoid membrane. Carbohydrate synthesis via the Calvin cycle happens in the stroma and uses ATP and NADPH from the light reactions. (Figure 8.3)

8.2 Reactions That Harness Light Energy

- Light is a form of electromagnetic radiation that travels in waves and is composed of photons with discrete amounts of energy. (Figure 8.4)

- Electrons can absorb light energy and be boosted to a higher energy level, an excited state. (Figure 8.5)

- Photosynthetic pigments include chlorophylls a and b and carotenoids. These pigments absorb light energy in the visible spectrum. (Figures 8.6, 8.7)

- During noncyclic electron flow, electrons from photosystem II follow a pathway along an electron transport chain in the thylakoid membrane. This pathway generates a H^+ gradient that is used to make ATP. In addition, light energy striking photosystem I boosts electrons to a very high energy level that allows the synthesis of NADPH. (Figure 8.8)

- During cyclic photophosphorylation, electrons are activated in PSI and flow through the electron transport chain back to PSI.

This cyclic electron route produces a H^+ gradient that is used to make ATP. (Figure 8.9)

- Cytochrome b_6 in chloroplasts and cytochrome b in mitochondria are homologous proteins, both of which are involved in electron transport and H^+ pumping. (Figure 8.10)

8.3 Molecular Features of Photosystems

- Pigment molecules in photosystem II absorb light energy, and that energy is transferred to the reaction center via resonance energy transfer. A high-energy electron from P680* is transferred to a primary electron acceptor. An electron from water is then used to replenish the electron that is lost from P680*. (Figures 8.11, 8.12)

- Emerson showed that, compared to single light flashes at 680 nm and 700 nm, light flashes at both wavelengths more than doubled the amount of photosynthesis, a result called the enhancement effect. This occurred because these wavelengths activate pigments in PSII and PSI, respectively. (Figure 8.13)

- Hill and Bendall proposed the Z scheme for electron activation during photosynthesis. According to this scheme, an electron absorbs light energy twice, at both PSII and PSI, and it loses some of that energy as it flows along the electron transport chain in the thylakoid membrane. (Figure 8.14)

8.4 Synthesizing Carbohydrates via the Calvin Cycle

- The Calvin cycle can be divided into three phases: carbon fixation, reduction and carbohydrate production, and regeneration of ribulose bisphosphate (RuBP). During this process, ATP is used as a source of energy, and NADPH is used as a source of high-energy electrons so that CO_2 can be incorporated into carbohydrate. (Figure 8.15)

- Calvin and Benson determined the steps in the Calvin cycle by isotope labeling methods in which products of the Calvin cycle were separated by chromatography. (Figure 8.16)

8.5 Variations in Photosynthesis

- C_3 plants can incorporate CO_2 only into RuBP to make 3PG, a three-carbon molecule. (Figure 8.17)

- Photorespiration can occur when the level of O_2 is high and CO_2 is low, which happens under hot and dry conditions. During this process, some O_2 is used and CO_2 is liberated. Photorespiration is a disadvantage because it reverses the work of photosynthesis.

- Some C_4 plants avoid photorespiration because the CO_2 is first incorporated, via PEP carboxylase, into a four-carbon molecule, which is pumped from mesophyll cells into bundle-sheath cells. This maintains a high concentration of CO_2 in the bundle-sheath cells, where the Calvin cycle occurs. The high CO_2 concentration minimizes photorespiration. (Figure 8.18)

- CAM plants, a type of C_4 plant, prevent photorespiration by fixing CO_2 into a four-carbon molecule at night and then running the Calvin cycle during the day with their stomata closed. (Figure 8.19)

Assess and Discuss

Test Yourself

1. The water necessary for photosynthesis
   a. is split into H_2 and O_2.
   b. is directly involved in the synthesis of carbohydrate.
   c. provides the electrons to replace lost electrons in photosystem II.
   d. provides H^+ needed to synthesize G3P.
   e. does none of the above.

2. The reaction center pigment differs from the other pigment molecules of the light-harvesting complex in that
   a. the reaction center pigment is a carotenoid.
   b. the reaction center pigment absorbs light energy and transfers that energy to other molecules without the transfer of electrons.
   c. the reaction center pigment transfers excited electrons to the primary electron acceptor.
   d. the reaction center pigment does not transfer excited electrons to the primary electron acceptor.
   e. the reaction center acts as an ATP synthase to produce ATP.

3. The cyclic electron flow that occurs via photosystem I produces
   a. NADPH.
   b. oxygen.
   c. ATP.
   d. all of the above.
   e. a and c only.

4. During the light reactions, the high-energy electron from P680*
   a. eventually moves to $NADP^+$.
   b. becomes incorporated in water molecules.
   c. is pumped into the thylakoid space to drive ATP production.
   d. provides the energy necessary to split water molecules.
   e. falls back to the low-energy state in photosystem II.

5. During the first phase of the Calvin cycle, carbon dioxide is incorporated into ribulose bisphosphate by
   a. oxaloacetate.
   b. rubisco.
   c. RuBP.
   d. quinone.
   e. G3P.

6. The NADPH produced during the light reactions is necessary for
   a. the carbon fixation phase, which incorporates carbon dioxide into an organic molecule of the Calvin cycle.
   b. the reduction phase, which produces carbohydrates in the Calvin cycle.
   c. the regeneration of RuBP of the Calvin cycle.
   d. all of the above.
   e. a and b only.

7. The majority of the G3P produced during the reduction and carbohydrate production phase is used to produce
   a. glucose.
   b. ATP.
   c. RuBP to continue the cycle.
   d. rubisco.
   e. all of the above.

8. Photorespiration
   a. is the process where plants use sunlight to make ATP.
   b. is an inefficient way plants can produce organic molecules and in the process use O_2 and release CO_2.
   c. is a process that plants use to convert light energy to NADPH.
   d. occurs in the thylakoid lumen.
   e. is the normal process of carbohydrate production in cool, moist environments.

9. Photorespiration is avoided in C_4 plants because
   a. these plants separate the formation of a four-carbon molecule from the rest of the Calvin cycle in different cells.
   b. these plants carry out only anaerobic respiration.
   c. the enzyme PEP functions to maintain high CO_2 concentrations in the bundle-sheath cells.
   d. all of the above.
   e. a and c only.

10. Plants commonly found in hot and dry environments that carry out carbon fixation at night are
    a. oak trees.
    b. C_3 plants.
    c. CAM plants.
    d. all of the above.
    e. a and b only.

Conceptual Questions

1. What are the two stages of photosynthesis? What are the key products of each stage?

2. What is the function of NADPH in the Calvin cycle?

3. Why is resonance energy transfer an important phenomenon to capture light energy? How do you think photosynthesis would be affected if resonance energy transfer did not occur?

Collaborative Questions

1. Discuss the advantages and disadvantages of being a heterotroph or a photoautotroph.

2. Biotechnologists are trying to genetically modify C_3 plants to convert them to C_4 or CAM plants. Why would this be useful? What genes might you add to C_3 plants to convert them to C_4 or CAM plants?

Online Resource

www.brookerbiology.com

Stay a step ahead in your studies with animations that bring concepts to life and practice tests to assess your understanding. Your instructor may also recommend the interactive ebook, individualized learning tools, and more.

Cell Communication

9

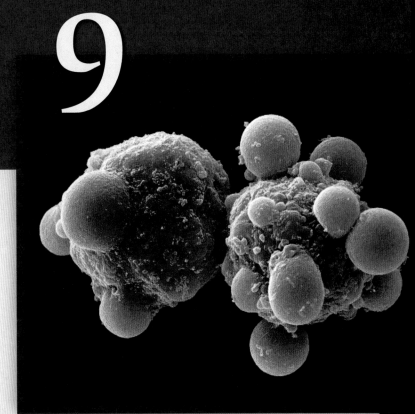

Over 2 billion cells will die in your body during the next hour. In an adult human body, approximately 50 to 70 billion cells die each day due to programmed cell death—the process in which a cell breaks apart into small fragments (see chapter-opening photo). In a year, your body produces and purposely destroys a mass of cells that is equal to your own body's weight! Though this may seem like a scary process, it's actually keeping you healthy. Programmed cell death, also called apoptosis, ensures that your body maintains a proper number of cells. It also eliminates cells that are worn out or potentially harmful, such as cancer cells. Programmed cell death can occur via signals that intentionally cause particular cells to die, or it can result from a failure of proper cell communication. It may also happen when environmental agents cause damage to a cell. Programmed cell death is one example of a response that involves **cell communication**—the process through which cells can detect and respond to signals in their environment.

In this chapter, we will examine how cells detect environmental signals and also how they produce signals so they can communicate with other cells. As you will learn, cell communication involves an amazing diversity of signaling molecules and cellular proteins that are devoted to this process.

Programmed cell death. The two cells shown here are breaking apart due to signaling molecules that initiated a pathway that programmed their death.

living organisms both respond to incoming signals and produce outgoing signals. Cell communication is a two-way street.

Communication at the cellular level involves not only receiving and sending signals but also their interpretation. For this to occur, a signal must be recognized by a cellular protein called a **receptor**. When a signal and receptor interact, the receptor changes shape, or conformation, thereby changing the way the receptor interacts with cellular factors. These interactions eventually lead to some type of response in the cell. In this section, we begin by considering why cells need to respond to signals. We will then examine various forms of signaling that are based on the distance between the cells that communicate with each other. Finally, we will examine the main steps that occur when a cell is exposed to a signal and elicits a response to it.

Cells Detect and Respond to Signals from Their Environment and from Other Cells

Before getting into the details of cell communication, let's take a general look at why cell communication is necessary. The

9.1 General Features of Cell Communication

All living cells, including bacteria, protists, fungi, plant cells, and animal cells, conduct and require cell communication to survive. This phenomenon, also known as cell signaling, involves both incoming and outgoing signals. A **signal** is an agent that can influence the properties of cells. For example, on a sunny day, cells can sense their exposure to ultraviolet (UV) light—a physical signal—and respond accordingly. In humans, UV light acts as an incoming signal to promote the synthesis of melanin, a protective pigment that helps to prevent the harmful effects of UV radiation. In addition, cells can produce outgoing signals that influence the behavior of neighboring cells. Plant cells, for example, produce hormones that influence the pattern of cell elongation so the plant grows toward light. Cells of all

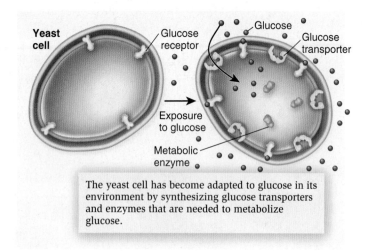

The yeast cell has become adapted to glucose in its environment by synthesizing glucose transporters and enzymes that are needed to metabolize glucose.

Figure 9.1   **Response of a yeast cell to glucose.**   When glucose is absent from the extracellular environment, the cell is not well prepared to take up and metabolize this sugar. However, when glucose is present, some of that glucose binds to receptors in the membrane, which leads to changes in the amounts and properties of intracellular and membrane proteins so the cell can readily use glucose.

Concept check: *What is the signaling molecule in this example?*

first reason is that cells need to respond to a changing environment. Changes in the environment are a persistent feature of life, and living cells are continually faced with alterations in temperature and availability of nutrients and water. A cell may even be exposed to a toxic chemical in its environment. Being able to respond to change, a phenomenon known as **adaptation**, is critical for the survival of all living organisms. Adaptation at the cellular level is called a **cellular response**.

As an example, let's consider the response of a yeast cell to glucose in its environment (**Figure 9.1**). Some of the glucose acts as a signaling molecule that binds to a receptor and causes a cellular response. In this case, the cell responds by increasing

the number of glucose transporters needed to take glucose into the cell and also by increasing the number of metabolic enzymes required to utilize glucose once it is inside. The cellular response has allowed the cell to use glucose efficiently. We could say the cell has become adapted to the presence of glucose in its environment. Note that the term adaptation also refers to more permanent changes in a species as a result of evolutionary changes. We will consider these types of adaptations in Chapter 23.

A second reason for cell signaling is the need for cells to communicate with each other—a type of cell communication also called **cell-to-cell communication**. In one of the earliest experiments demonstrating cell-to-cell communication, Charles Darwin and his son Francis Darwin studied phototropism, the phenomenon in which plants grow toward light (**Figure 9.2**). The Darwins observed that the actual bending occurs in a zone below the growing shoot tip. They concluded that a signal must be transmitted from the growing tip to cells below the tip for this to occur. Later research revealed that the signal is a molecule called auxin, which is transmitted from cell to cell. A higher amount of auxin present on the nonilluminated side of the shoot promotes cell elongation on that side of the shoot only, thereby causing the shoot to bend toward the light source.

Cell-to-Cell Communication Can Occur Between Adjacent Cells and Between Cells That Are Long Distances Apart

Researchers have determined that organisms have a variety of different mechanisms to achieve cell-to-cell communication. The mode of communication depends, in part, on the distance between the cells that need to communicate with each other. Let's first examine the various ways in which signals are transferred between cells. Later in this chapter, we will learn how such signals elicit a cellular response.

One way to categorize cell signaling is by the manner in which the signal is transmitted from one cell to another. Signals are relayed between cells in five common ways, all of

Cells in the growing shoot tip sense light and send a signal (auxin) to cells on the nonilluminated side of the shoot.

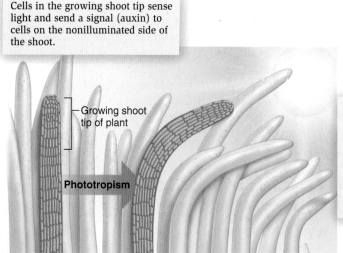

Cells located below the growing tip receive this signal and elongate, thereby causing a bend in the shoot. In this way, the tip grows toward the light.

Figure 9.2   **Phototropism in plants.**   This process involves cell-to-cell communication that leads to a shoot bending toward light just beneath its actively growing tip.

Concept check: *Below the shoot tip that is illuminated from one side, where is more auxin located? Does auxin cause cells to elongate or to shorten?*

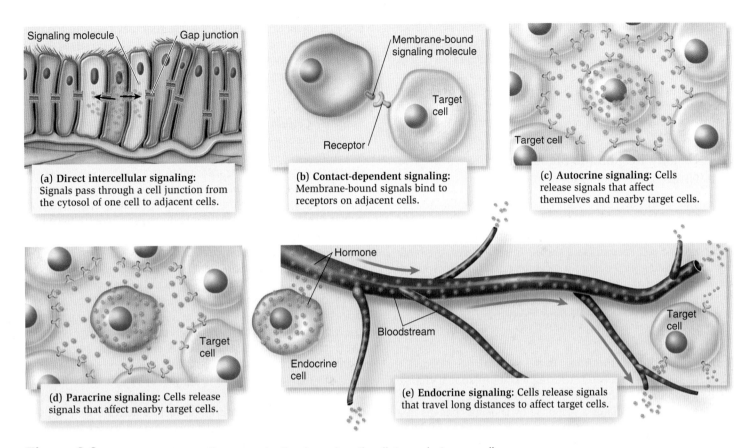

(a) Direct intercellular signaling: Signals pass through a cell junction from the cytosol of one cell to adjacent cells.

(b) Contact-dependent signaling: Membrane-bound signals bind to receptors on adjacent cells.

(c) Autocrine signaling: Cells release signals that affect themselves and nearby target cells.

(d) Paracrine signaling: Cells release signals that affect nearby target cells.

(e) Endocrine signaling: Cells release signals that travel long distances to affect target cells.

Figure 9.3   Types of cell-to-cell communication based on the distance between cells.

Concept check: *Which type of signal, paracrine or endocrine, is likely to exist for a longer period of time? Explain why this is necessary.*

which involve a cell that produces a signal and a target cell that receives the signal (**Figure 9.3**).

Direct Intercellular Signaling   In a multicellular organism, cells adjacent to each other may have contacts, called cell junctions, that enable them to pass ions, signaling molecules, and other materials between the cytosol of one cell and the cytosol of another (Figure 9.3a). For example, cardiac muscle cells, which cause your heart to beat, have intercellular connections called gap junctions that pass electrical signals needed for the coordinated contraction of cardiac muscle cells. We will examine how gap junctions work in Chapter 10.

Contact-Dependent Signaling   Not all signaling molecules can readily diffuse from one cell to another. Some molecules are bound to the surface of cells and provide a signal to other cells that make contact with the surface of that cell (Figure 9.3b). In this case, one cell has a membrane-bound signaling molecule that is recognized by a receptor on the surface of another cell. This occurs, for example, when portions of nerve cells (neurons) grow and make contact with other neurons. This is important for the formation of the proper connections between neurons.

Autocrine Signaling   In autocrine signaling, a cell secretes signaling molecules that bind to receptors on its own cell surface, stimulating a response (Figure 9.3c). In addition, the

signaling molecule can affect neighboring cells of the same cell type. What is the purpose of autocrine signaling? It is often important for groups of cells to sense cell density. When cell density is high, the concentration of autocrine signals is also high. In some cases, such signals will inhibit further cell growth and thereby prevent the cell density from becoming too high.

Paracrine Signaling   In paracrine signaling, a specific cell secretes a signaling molecule that does not affect the cell secreting the signal but instead influences the behavior of target cells in close proximity (Figure 9.3d). Paracrine signaling is typically of short duration. Usually, the signal is broken down too quickly to be carried to other parts of the body and affect distant cells. A specialized form of paracrine signaling called **synaptic signaling** occurs in the nervous system of animals (see Chapter 41). Neurotransmitters—molecules made in neurons that transmit a signal to an adjacent cell—are released at the end of the neuron and traverse a narrow space called the synapse. The neurotransmitter then binds to a receptor in a target cell.

Endocrine Signaling   In contrast to the previous mechanisms of cell signaling, endocrine signaling occurs over relatively long distances (Figure 9.3e). In both animals and plants, molecules involved in long-distance signaling are called **hormones**. They usually last longer than signaling molecules involved in autocrine and paracrine signaling. In animals, endocrine signaling involves the secretion of hormones into the bloodstream, which may affect virtually all cells of the body, including those that are far from the cells that secrete the signaling molecules. In plants, hormones move through the plant vascular system and can also move through adjacent cells. Some hormones are even gases that diffuse into the air. Ethylene, a gas given off by plants, plays a variety of roles, such as accelerating the ripening of fruit.

Cells Usually Respond to Signals by a Three-Stage Process

Up to this point, we have learned that signals influence the behavior of cells in close proximity or at long distances, interacting with receptors to elicit a cellular response. What events occur when a cell encounters a signal? In most cases, the binding of a signaling molecule to a receptor causes the receptor to activate a signal transduction pathway, which then leads to a cellular response. Figure 9.4 diagrams the three common stages of cell signaling: receptor activation, signal transduction, and a cellular response.

Stage 1: Receptor Activation   In the initial stage, a signaling molecule binds to a receptor, causing a conformational change in the receptor that activates its function. In most cases, the activated receptor initiates a response by causing changes in a series of proteins that collectively forms a signal transduction pathway, as described next.

Stage 2: Signal Transduction   During signal transduction, the initial signal is converted—or transduced—to a different signal inside the cell. This process is carried out by a group of proteins that form a **signal transduction pathway**. These proteins undergo a series of changes that may result in the production of an intracellular signaling molecule. However, some receptors are intracellular and some do not activate a signal transduction pathway. As discussed later, certain types of intracellular receptors directly cause a cellular response.

Stage 3: Cellular Response   Cells can respond to signals in several different ways. Figure 9.4 shows three common categories of proteins that are controlled by cell signaling: enzymes, structural proteins, and transcription factors.

Many signaling molecules exert their effects by altering the activity of one or more enzymes. For example, certain hormones provide a signal that the body needs energy. These hormones activate enzymes that are required for the breakdown of molecules such as carbohydrates.

Cells also respond to signals by altering the functions of structural proteins in the cell. For example, when animal cells move during embryonic development or when an amoeba moves toward food, signals play a role in the rearrangement of actin filaments, which are components of the cytoskeleton. The coordination of signaling and changes in the cytoskeleton enable cells to move in the correct direction.

Cells may also respond to signals by affecting the function of **transcription factors**—proteins that regulate the transcription of genes. Some transcription factors activate gene expression. For example, when cells are exposed to sex hormones, transcription factors can activate genes that change the properties of cells, which can lead to changes in the sexual characteristics of entire organisms. As discussed in Chapter 51, estrogens and androgens are responsible for the development of secondary sex characteristics in humans, including breast development in females and beard growth in males, respectively.

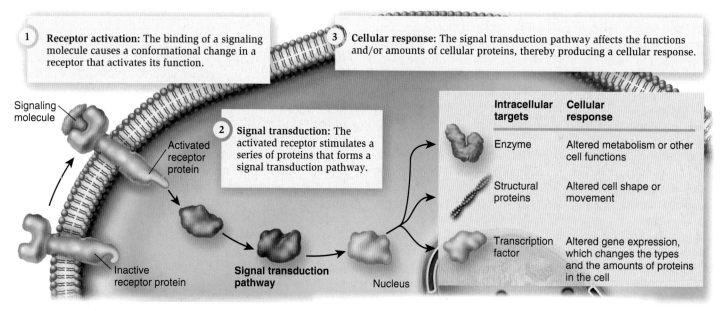

Figure 9.4   The three stages of cell signaling: receptor activation, signal transduction, and a cellular response.

Concept check: *For most signaling molecules, explain why a signal transduction pathway is necessary.*

9.2 Cellular Receptors and Their Activation

In this section, we will take a closer look at receptors and how they interact with signaling molecules. We will compare receptors based on whether they are located on the cell surface or inside the cell. In this chapter, our focus will be on receptors that respond to chemical signaling molecules. Other receptors discussed in Units VI and VII respond to mechanical motion (mechanoreceptors), temperature changes (thermoreceptors), and light (photoreceptors).

Receptors Bind to Specific Signals and Undergo Conformational Changes

The ability of cells to respond to a signal usually requires precise recognition between a signal and its receptor. In many cases, the signal is a molecule, such as a steroid or a protein, that binds to the receptor. A signaling molecule binds to a receptor in much the same way that a substrate binds to the active site of an enzyme, as described in Chapter 6. The signaling molecule, which is called a **ligand**, binds noncovalently to the receptor molecule with a high degree of specificity. The binding occurs when the ligand and receptor happen to collide in the correct orientation with enough energy to form a **ligand · receptor complex**.

$$[\text{Ligand}] + [\text{Receptor}] \underset{k_{off}}{\overset{k_{on}}{\rightleftharpoons}} [\text{Ligand} \cdot \text{Receptor complex}]$$

Brackets [ ] refer to concentration. The value k_{on} is the rate at which binding occurs. After a complex forms between the ligand and its receptor, the noncovalent interaction between a ligand and receptor remains stable for a finite period of time. The term k_{off} is the rate at which the ligand · receptor complex falls apart or dissociates.

In general, the binding and release between a ligand and its receptor are relatively rapid, and therefore an equilibrium is reached when the rate of formation of new ligand · receptor complexes equals the rate at which existing ligand · receptor complexes dissociate:

$$k_{on}[\text{Ligand}][\text{Receptor}] = k_{off}[\text{Ligand} \cdot \text{Receptor complex}]$$

Rearranging,

$$\frac{[\text{Ligand}][\text{Receptor}]}{[\text{Ligand} \cdot \text{Receptor complex}]} = \frac{k_{off}}{k_{on}} = K_d$$

K_d is called the **dissociation constant** between a ligand and its receptor. The K_d value is inversely related to the affinity between the ligand and receptor. Let's look carefully at the left side of this equation and consider what it means. At a ligand concentration where half of the receptors are bound to a ligand, the concentration of the ligand · receptor complex equals the concentration of receptor that doesn't have ligand bound. At this ligand concentration, [Receptor] and [Ligand · Receptor complex] cancel out of the equation because they are equal. Therefore, at a ligand concentration where half of the receptors have bound ligand:

$$K_d = [\text{Ligand}]$$

When the ligand concentration is above the K_d value, most of the receptors are likely to have ligand bound to them. In contrast, if the ligand concentration is substantially below the K_d value, most receptors will not be bound by their ligand. The K_d values for many different ligands and their receptors have been experimentally determined. How is this information useful? It allows researchers to predict when a signaling molecule is likely to cause a cellular response. If the concentration of a signaling molecule is far below the K_d value, a cellular response is not likely because relatively few receptors will form a complex with the signaling molecule.

Unlike enzymes, which convert their substrates into products, receptors do not usually alter the structure of their ligands. Instead, the ligands alter the structure of their receptors, causing a conformational change (Figure 9.5). In this case, the binding of the ligand to its receptor changes the receptor in a way that will activate its ability to initiate a cellular response.

Because the binding of a ligand to its receptor is a reversible process, the ligand and receptor will also dissociate. Once the ligand is released, the receptor is no longer activated.

Cells Contain a Variety of Cell Surface Receptors That Respond to Extracellular Signals

Most signaling molecules are either small hydrophilic molecules or large molecules that do not readily pass through the plasma membrane of cells. Such extracellular signals bind to **cell surface receptors**—receptors found in the plasma membrane. A typical cell is expected to contain dozens or even hundreds of different cell surface receptors that enable the cell to respond to different kinds of extracellular signaling molecules. By analyzing the functions of cell surface receptors from many different organisms, researchers have determined that most fall into one

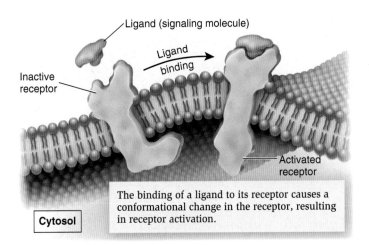

The binding of a ligand to its receptor causes a conformational change in the receptor, resulting in receptor activation.

Figure 9.5 Receptor activation.

of three categories: enzyme-linked receptors, G-protein-coupled receptors, and ligand-gated ion channels, which are described next.

Enzyme-Linked Receptors

Receptors known as **enzyme-linked receptors** are found in all living species. Many human hormones bind to this type of receptor. For example, when insulin binds to an enzyme-linked receptor in muscle cells, it enhances their ability to use glucose. Enzyme-linked receptors typically have two important domains: an extracellular domain, which binds a signaling molecule, and an intracellular domain, which has a catalytic function (**Figure 9.6a**). When a signaling molecule binds to the extracellular domain, a conformational change is transmitted through the membrane-embedded portion of the protein that affects the conformation of the intracellular catalytic domain. In most cases, this conformational change causes the catalytic domain to become functionally active.

Most types of enzyme-linked receptors function as **protein kinases**, enzymes that transfer a phosphate group from ATP to specific amino acids in a protein. For example, tyrosine kinases attach phosphate to the amino acid tyrosine, whereas serine/threonine kinases attach phosphate to the amino acids serine and threonine. In the absence of a signaling molecule, the catalytic domain of the receptor remains inactive (**Figure 9.6b**). However, when a signal binds to the extracellular domain, the catalytic domain is activated. Under these conditions, the cell surface receptor may phosphorylate itself or it may phosphorylate intracellular proteins. The attachment of a negatively charged phosphate changes the structure of a protein and thereby can alter its function. Later in this chapter, we will explore how this event leads to a cellular response, such as the activation of enzymes that affect cell function.

G-Protein-Coupled Receptors

Receptors called **G-protein-coupled receptors** (**GPCRs**) are found in the cells of all eukaryotic species and are particularly common in animals. GPCRs typically contain seven transmembrane segments that wind back and forth through the plasma membrane. The receptors interact with intracellular proteins called **G proteins**, which are so named because of their ability to bind guanosine triphosphate (GTP) and guanosine diphosphate (GDP). GTP is similar in structure to ATP except it has guanine as a base instead of adenine. In the 1970s, the existence of G proteins was first proposed by Martin Rodbell and colleagues, who found that GTP is needed for certain hormone receptors to cause an intracellular response. Later, Alfred Gilman and coworkers used genetic and biochemical techniques to identify and purify a G protein. In 1994, Rodbell and Gilman won the Nobel Prize for their pioneering work.

Figure 9.7 shows how a GPCR and a G protein interact. At the cell surface, a signaling molecule binds to a GPCR, causing a conformational change that activates the receptor. The activated receptor then causes the G protein, which is a lipid-anchored protein, to release GDP and bind GTP instead. GTP binding changes the conformation of the G protein, causing it to dissociate into an α subunit and a β/γ dimer. Later in this chapter, we will examine how the α subunit interacts with other proteins in a signal transduction pathway to elicit a cellular response. The β/γ dimer can also play a role in signal transduction. For example, it can regulate the function of ion channels in the plasma membrane.

When a signaling molecule and GPCR dissociate, the GPCR is no longer activated, and the cellular response will be reversed. For the G protein to return to the inactive state, the α subunit will first hydrolyze its bound GTP to GDP and P_i. After this occurs, the α and β/γ subunits reassociate with each other to form an inactive complex.

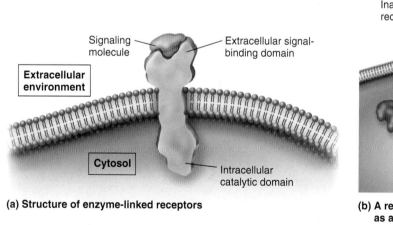

(a) **Structure of enzyme-linked receptors**

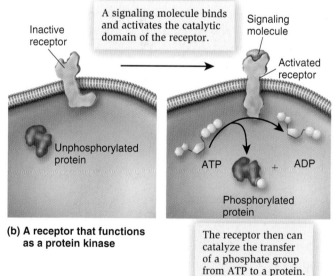

(b) **A receptor that functions as a protein kinase**

Figure 9.6 Enzyme-linked receptors.

Concept check: *Based on your understanding of ATP as an energy intermediate, is the phosphorylation of a protein via a protein kinase an exergonic or endergonic reaction? How is the energy of protein phosphorylation used—what does it accomplish?*

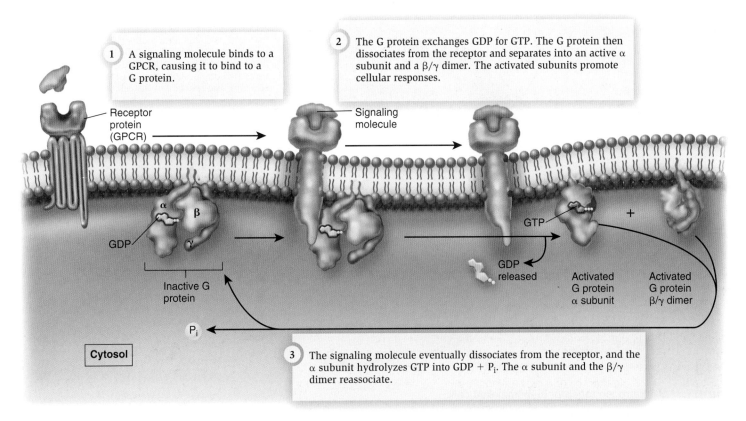

1. A signaling molecule binds to a GPCR, causing it to bind to a G protein.

2. The G protein exchanges GDP for GTP. The G protein then dissociates from the receptor and separates into an active α subunit and a β/γ dimer. The activated subunits promote cellular responses.

3. The signaling molecule eventually dissociates from the receptor, and the α subunit hydrolyzes GTP into GDP + Pi. The α subunit and the β/γ dimer reassociate.

Receptor protein (GPCR)

Signaling molecule

GDP

α   β

γ

Inactive G protein

Cytosol

Pi

GTP

GDP released

Activated G protein α subunit

Activated G protein β/γ dimer

+

Figure 9.7   **The activation of G-protein-coupled receptors and G proteins.**   Note: The left drawing of the receptor emphasizes that it has seven transmembrane segments.

Concept check: *What has to happen for the α and β/γ subunits of the G protein to reassociate with each other?*

Ligand-Gated Ion Channels   As described in Chapter 5, ion channels are proteins that allow the diffusion of ions across cellular membranes. **Ligand-gated ion channels** are a third type of cell surface receptor found in the plasma membrane of animal, plant, and fungal cells. When signaling molecules (ligands) bind to this type of receptor, the channel opens and allows the flow of ions through the membrane (**Figure 9.8**).

In animals, ligand-gated ion channels are important in the transmission of signals between nerve and muscle cells and between two nerve cells. In addition, ligand-gated ion channels in the plasma membrane allow the influx of Ca^{2+} into the cytosol. As discussed later in this chapter, changes in the cytosolic concentration of Ca^{2+} often play a role in signal transduction.

Cells Also Have Intracellular Receptors Activated by Signaling Molecules That Pass Through the Plasma Membrane

Although most receptors for signaling molecules are located in the plasma membrane, some are found inside the cell. In these cases, an extracellular signaling molecule must pass through the plasma membrane to gain access to its receptor.

In vertebrates, receptors for steroid hormones are intracellular. As discussed in Chapter 51, steroid hormones, such as estrogens and androgens, are secreted into the bloodstream from cells of endocrine glands. The behavior of estrogen is

typical of many steroid hormones (**Figure 9.9**). Because estrogen is hydrophobic, it can diffuse through the plasma membrane of a target cell and bind to a receptor in the cell. Some steroids bind to receptors in the cytosol, which then travel into the nucleus. Other steroid hormones, such as estrogen, bind to receptors already in the nucleus. After binding, the estrogen • receptor complex undergoes a conformational change that enables it to form a dimer with another estrogen • receptor complex. The dimer then binds to the DNA and activates the transcription of specific genes. The estrogen receptor is an

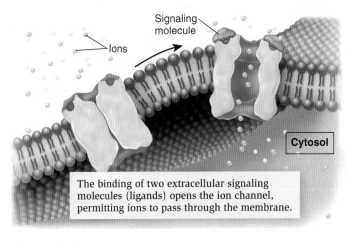

Signaling molecule

Ions

Cytosol

The binding of two extracellular signaling molecules (ligands) opens the ion channel, permitting ions to pass through the membrane.

Figure 9.8   The function of a ligand-gated ion channel.

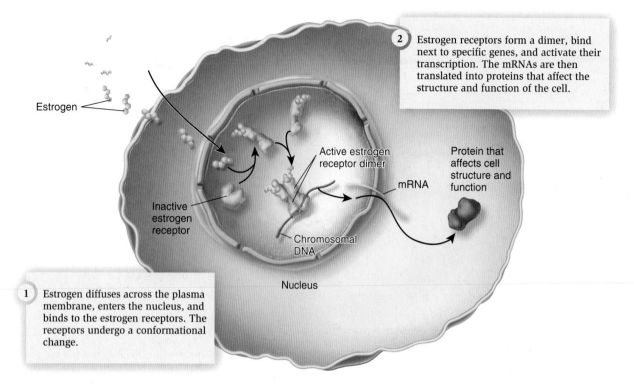

Figure 9.9 Estrogen receptor in mammalian cells.

example of a transcription factor—a protein that regulates the transcription of genes. The expression of specific genes changes cell structure and function in a way that results in a cellular response.

Signal Transduction and the Cellular Response

We now turn our attention to the intracellular events that enable a cell to respond to a signaling molecule that binds to a cell surface receptor. In most cases, the binding of a signaling molecule to its receptor stimulates a signal transduction pathway. We begin by examining a pathway that is controlled by an enzyme-linked receptor. We will then examine pathways and cellular responses that are controlled by G-protein-coupled receptors. As you will learn, these pathways sometimes involve the production of intracellular signals called second messengers.

Receptor Tyrosine Kinases Activate Signal Transduction Pathways Involving a Protein Kinase Cascade That Alters Gene Transcription

Receptor tyrosine kinases are a category of enzyme-linked receptors that are found in all animals and also in choanoflagellates, which are the protists that are most closely related to animals (see Chapter 32). However, they are not found in bacteria, archaea, or other eukaryotic species. (Bacteria do have receptor histidine kinases, and all eukaryotes have receptor serine/threonine kinases.) The human genome contains about 60 different genes that encode receptor tyrosine kinases that

recognize various types of signaling molecules such as hormones. A type of hormone called a **growth factor** is a protein ligand that acts as a signaling molecule that stimulates cell growth or division.

Figure 9.10 describes a simplified signal transduction pathway for epidermal growth factor (EGF). This protein ligand is secreted from endocrine cells, travels through the bloodstream, and binds to a receptor tyrosine kinase called the EGF receptor. EGF is responsible for stimulating epidermal cells, such as skin cells, to divide. Following receptor activation, the three general parts of the signal transduction pathway are as follows: (1) relay proteins (also called adaptor proteins) activate a protein kinase cascade; (2) the protein kinase cascade phosphorylates proteins in the cell such as transcription factors; and (3) the phosphorylated transcription factors stimulate gene transcription. Next, we will consider the details of this pathway.

EGF Receptor Activation For receptor activation to occur, two EGF receptor subunits each bind a molecule of EGF. The binding of EGF causes the subunits to dimerize and phosphorylate each other on tyrosines within the receptors themselves, which is why they are named receptor tyrosine kinases. This event is called **autophosphorylation**. Next comes the signal transduction pathway.

Relay Proteins The phosphorylated form of the EGF receptor is first recognized by a relay protein of the signal transduction pathway called Grb. This interaction changes the conformation of Grb so that it binds to another relay protein in the signal transduction pathway termed Sos, thereby changing the conformation of Sos. The activation of Sos causes a third relay protein

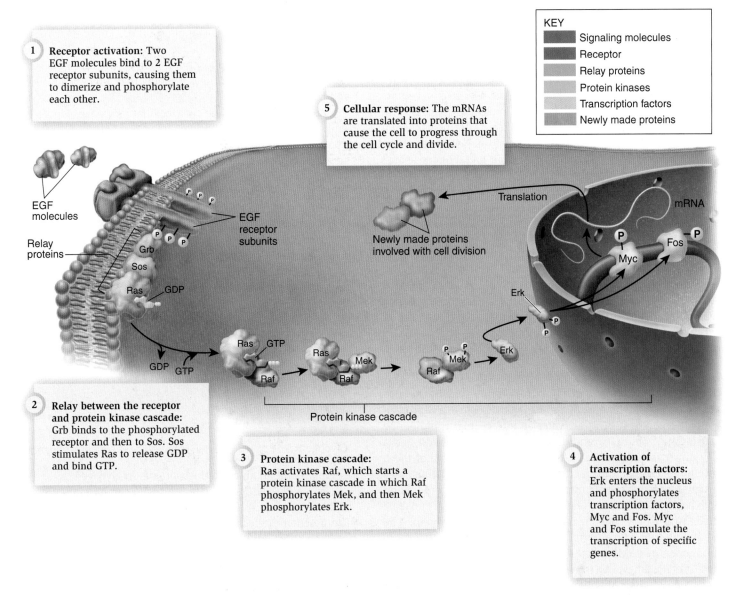

KEY
- Signaling molecules
- Receptor
- Relay proteins
- Protein kinases
- Transcription factors
- Newly made proteins

1 **Receptor activation:** Two EGF molecules bind to 2 EGF receptor subunits, causing them to dimerize and phosphorylate each other.

5 **Cellular response:** The mRNAs are translated into proteins that cause the cell to progress through the cell cycle and divide.

EGF molecules

Relay proteins

Grb

Sos

Ras   GDP

EGF receptor subunits

Newly made proteins involved with cell division

Translation

mRNA

P

Fos

Myc

P

Erk

GDP   GTP

Ras   GTP

Raf

Ras   Mek   Raf

Mek   Raf   Erk

P

Erk

P

Protein kinase cascade

2 **Relay between the receptor and protein kinase cascade:** Grb binds to the phosphorylated receptor and then to Sos. Sos stimulates Ras to release GDP and bind GTP.

3 **Protein kinase cascade:** Ras activates Raf, which starts a protein kinase cascade in which Raf phosphorylates Mek, and then Mek phosphorylates Erk.

4 **Activation of transcription factors:** Erk enters the nucleus and phosphorylates transcription factors, Myc and Fos. Myc and Fos stimulate the transcription of specific genes.

Figure 9.10 The epidermal growth factor (EGF) pathway that promotes cell division.

Concept check: *Certain mutations can alter the structure of the Ras protein so it will not hydrolyze GTP. Such mutations cause cancer. Explain why.*

called Ras to release GDP and bind GTP. The GTP form of Ras is the active form.

Protein Kinase Cascade The function of Grb, Sos, and Ras is to relay a cellular signal to additional proteins in the signal transduction pathway that form a **protein kinase cascade**. This cascade involves the sequential activation of multiple protein kinases. Activated Ras binds to Raf, the first protein kinase in the cascade. Raf then phosphorylates Mek, which becomes active and, in turn, phosphorylates Erk. Raf, Mek, and Erk, the protein kinase cascade, are all examples of <u>mitogen-activated protein kinases</u> (**MAP-kinases**). This type of protein kinase was first discovered because it is activated in the presence of mitogens—agents that cause a cell to divide.

Activation of Transcription Factors and the Cellular Response
The phosphorylated form of Erk enters the nucleus and phosphorylates transcription factors such as Myc and Fos, which then activate the transcription of genes involved in cell division. What is the cellular response? Once these transcription factors are phosphorylated, they stimulate the expression of many genes that encode proteins that promote cell division. After these proteins are made, the cell will be stimulated to divide.

Growth factors such as EGF cause a rapid increase in the expression of many genes in mammals, perhaps as many as 100. As we will discuss in Chapter 14, growth factor signaling pathways are often involved in cancer. Mutations that cause proteins in these pathways to become hyperactive result in cells that divide uncontrollably!

Second Messengers Such as Cyclic AMP Are Key Components of Many Signal Transduction Pathways

Let's now turn to examples of signal transduction pathways and cellular responses that involve G-protein-coupled receptors (GPCRs). Cell biologists call signaling molecules that bind to a cell surface receptor the first messengers. After first messengers bind to receptors such as GPCRs, many signal transduction pathways lead to the production of **second messengers**—small molecules or ions that relay signals inside the cell. The signals that result in second messenger production often act quickly, in a matter of seconds or minutes, but their duration is usually short. Therefore, such signaling is typically used when a cell needs a quick and short cellular response.

Production of cAMP Mammalian and plant cells make several different types of G protein α subunits. One type of α subunit binds to **adenylyl cyclase**, an enzyme in the plasma membrane. This interaction stimulates adenylyl cyclase to synthesize **cyclic adenosine monophosphate** (**cyclic AMP**, or **cAMP**) from ATP (**Figure 9.11**). The molecule cAMP is an example of a second messenger.

Signal Transduction Pathway Involving cAMP As discussed earlier, the binding of a signaling molecule to a G-protein-coupled receptor (GPCR) activates an intracellular G protein by causing it to bind GTP and dissociate into an α subunit and a β/γ dimer (see Figure 9.7). Let's now follow the role of the α subunit in a signal transduction pathway. **Figure 9.12** illustrates a signal transduction pathway that involves cAMP production and leads to a cellular response. First, a signaling molecule binds to a GPCR, which, in turn, activates a G protein. The α subunit then activates adenylyl cyclase, which catalyzes the production of cAMP from ATP. One effect of cAMP is to activate protein kinase A (PKA), which is composed of four subunits: two catalytic subunits that phosphorylate specific cellular proteins, and two regulatory subunits that inhibit the catalytic subunits when they are bound to each other. Cyclic AMP binds to the regulatory subunits of PKA. The binding of cAMP separates the regulatory and catalytic subunits, which allows each catalytic subunit to be active.

Cellular Response via PKA How does PKA activation lead to a cellular response? The catalytic subunit of PKA phosphorylates

specific cellular proteins such as enzymes, structural proteins, and transcription factors. The phosphorylation of enzymes and structural proteins will influence the structure and function of the cell. Likewise, the phosphorylation of transcription factors leads to the synthesis of new proteins that affect cell structure and function.

As a specific example of a cellular response, **Figure 9.13** shows how a skeletal muscle cell can respond to elevated levels of the hormone epinephrine (also called adrenaline). This hormone is sometimes called the "fight or flight" hormone. Epinephrine is produced when an individual is confronted with a stressful situation and helps the individual deal with that situation. Epinephrine binds to a GPCR, leading to an increase in cAMP, which, in turn, activates PKA. In skeletal muscle cells, PKA phosphorylates two enzymes—phosphorylase kinase and glycogen synthase. Both of these enzymes are involved with the metabolism of glycogen, which is a polymer of glucose used to store energy. When phosphorylase kinase is phosphorylated, it becomes activated. The function of phosphorylase kinase is to phosphorylate another enzyme in the cell called glycogen phosphorylase, which then becomes activated. This enzyme causes glycogen breakdown by phosphorylating glucose units at the ends of a glycogen polymer, which releases individual glucose molecules from glycogen:

$$\text{Glycogen}_n + P_i \xrightarrow{\substack{\text{Glycogen} \\ \text{phosphorylase}}} \text{Glycogen}_{n-1} + \text{Glucose-phosphate}$$

where n is the number of glucose units in glycogen.

When PKA phosphorylates glycogen synthase, the function of this enzyme is inhibited rather than activated (Figure 9.13). The function of glycogen synthase is to make glycogen. Therefore, the effect of cAMP is to prevent glycogen synthesis.

Taken together, the effects of epinephrine in skeletal muscle cells are to stimulate glycogen breakdown and inhibit glycogen synthesis. This provides these cells with more glucose molecules, which they can use for the energy needed for muscle contraction. In this way, the individual is better prepared to fight or flee.

Reversal of the Cellular Response As mentioned, signaling that involves second messengers is typically of short duration. When the signaling molecule is no longer produced and its level falls, a larger percentage of the receptors are not bound by their

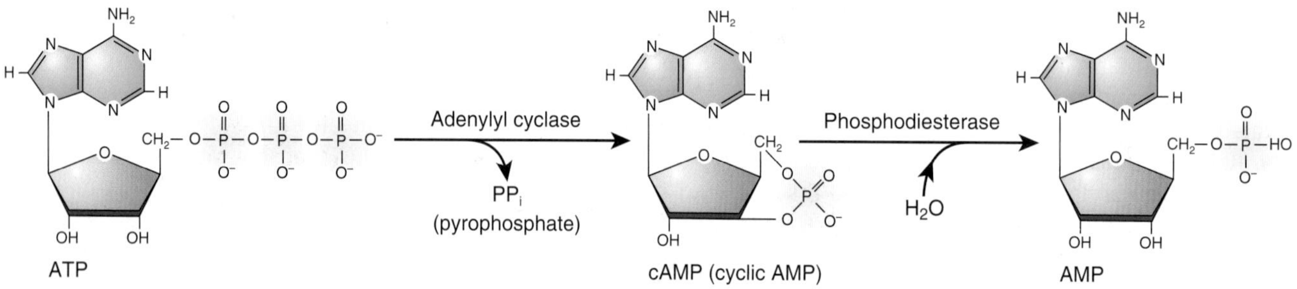

Figure 9.11 The synthesis and breakdown of cyclic AMP.

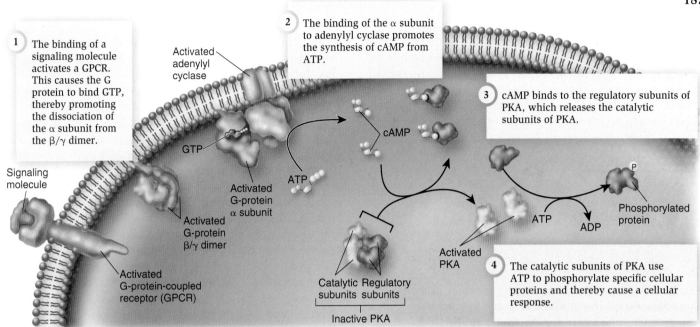

1. The binding of a signaling molecule activates a GPCR. This causes the G protein to bind GTP, thereby promoting the dissociation of the α subunit from the β/γ dimer.

2. The binding of the α subunit to adenylyl cyclase promotes the synthesis of cAMP from ATP.

3. cAMP binds to the regulatory subunits of PKA, which releases the catalytic subunits of PKA.

4. The catalytic subunits of PKA use ATP to phosphorylate specific cellular proteins and thereby cause a cellular response.

Activated adenylyl cyclase

GTP

cAMP

ATP

Signaling molecule

Activated G-protein α subunit

Activated G-protein β/γ dimer

Activated G-protein-coupled receptor (GPCR)

Catalytic subunits Regulatory subunits

Inactive PKA

Activated PKA

ATP ADP

P

Phosphorylated protein

Figure 9.12 **A signal transduction pathway involving cAMP.** The pathway leading to the formation of cAMP and subsequent activation of PKA, which is mediated by a G-protein-coupled receptor (GPCR).

Concept check: *In this figure, which part is the signal transduction pathway, and which is the cellular response?*

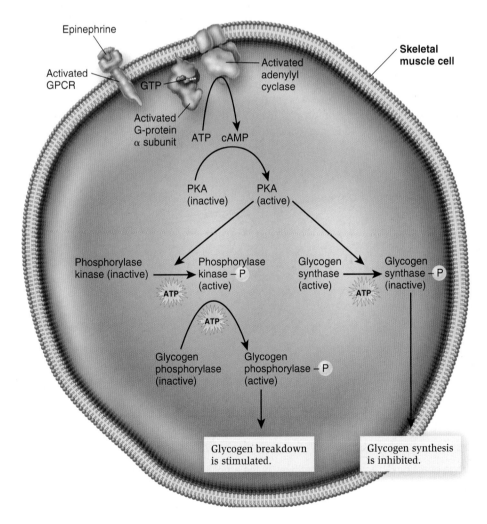

Epinephrine

Activated GPCR

GTP

Activated G-protein α subunit

Activated adenylyl cyclase

Skeletal muscle cell

ATP cAMP

PKA (inactive)

PKA (active)

Phosphorylase kinase (inactive) → Phosphorylase kinase – P (active)

ATP

Glycogen synthase (active) → Glycogen synthase – P (inactive)

ATP

Glycogen phosphorylase (inactive) → Glycogen phosphorylase – P (active)

ATP

Glycogen breakdown is stimulated.

Glycogen synthesis is inhibited.

Figure 9.13 **The cellular response of a skeletal muscle cell to epinephrine.**

Concept check: *Explain whether phosphorylation activates or inhibits enzyme function.*

ligands. When a ligand dissociates from the GPCR, the GPCR becomes deactivated. Intracellularly, the α subunit hydrolyzes its GTP to GDP, and the α subunit and β/γ dimer reassociate to form an inactive G protein (see step 3, Figure 9.7). The level of cAMP decreases due to the action of an enzyme called **phosphodiesterase**, which converts cAMP to AMP.

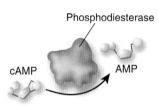

As the cAMP level falls, the regulatory subunits of PKA release cAMP, and the regulatory and catalytic subunits reassociate, thereby inhibiting PKA. Finally, enzymes called **protein phosphatases** are responsible for removing phosphate groups from proteins, which reverses the effects of PKA.

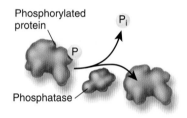

The Main Advantages of Second Messengers Are Amplification and Speed

In the 1950s, Earl Sutherland determined that many different hormones cause the formation of cAMP in a variety of cell types. This observation, for which he won the Nobel Prize in 1971, stimulated great interest in the study of signal transduction pathways. Since Sutherland's discovery, the production of second messengers such as cAMP has been found to have two important advantages: amplification and speed.

Amplification of the signal involves the synthesis of many cAMP molecules, which, in turn, activate many PKA proteins (Figure 9.14). Likewise, each PKA protein can phosphorylate many target proteins in the cell to promote a cellular response.

A second advantage of second messengers such as cAMP is speed. Because second messengers are relatively small, they can diffuse rapidly through the cytosol. For example, Brian Bacskai and colleagues studied the response of nerve cells to a signaling molecule called serotonin, which is a neurotransmitter that binds to a GPCR. In humans, serotonin is believed to play a role in depression, anxiety, and sexual drive. To monitor cAMP levels, nerve cells grown in a laboratory were injected with a fluorescent protein that changes its fluorescence when cAMP is made. As shown in the right micrograph in Figure 9.15, such cells made a substantial amount of cAMP within 20 seconds after the addition of serotonin.

Signal Transduction Pathways May Also Lead to Second Messengers, Such as Diacylglycerol and Inositol Trisphosphate, and Alter Ca²⁺ Levels

Cells use several different types of second messengers, and more than one type may be used at the same time. Let's now consider a second way that an activated G protein can influence a signal transduction pathway and produce second messengers. This pathway produces the second messengers diacylglycerol

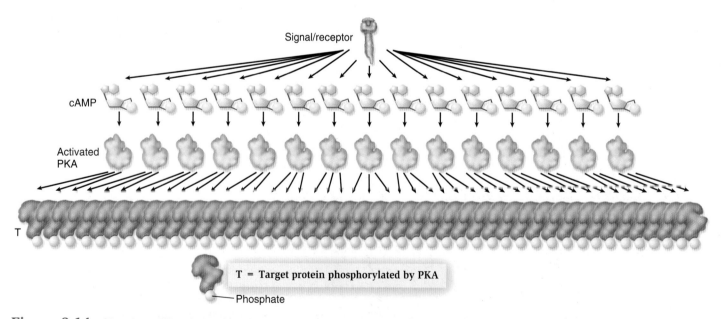

Figure 9.14   **Signal amplification.**   An advantage of a signal transduction pathway is the amplification of a signal. In this case, a single signaling molecule can lead to the phosphorylation of many, perhaps hundreds or thousands of, target proteins.

Concept check: *In the case of signaling pathways involving hormones, why is signal amplification an advantage?*

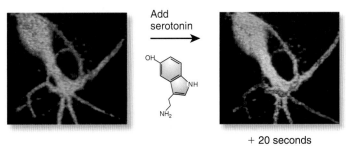

Add
serotonin

+ 20 seconds

Figure 9.15 **The rapid speed of cAMP production.** The micrograph on the left shows a nerve cell prior to its exposure to serotonin; the micrograph on the right shows the same cell 20 seconds after exposure. Blue indicates a low level of cAMP, yellow is an intermediate level, and red/purple is a high level.

(DAG) and inositol trisphosphate (IP_3) and ultimately can cause cellular effects by altering the levels of calcium in the cell.

Production of DAG and IP_3 To start this pathway, a signaling molecule binds to its GPCR, which, in turn, activates a G protein. However, rather than activating adenylate cyclase as described earlier in Figure 9.12, the α subunit of this G protein activates an enzyme called phospholipase C (**Figure 9.16**). When phospholipase C becomes active, it breaks a covalent bond in a particular plasma membrane phospholipid with an inositol head group, producing the two second messengers DAG and IP_3.

Release of Ca^{2+} into the Cytosol Due to active transport via a Ca^{2+}-ATPase, the lumen of the ER contains a very high concentration of Ca^{2+} compared to the cytosol. After IP_3 is released into the cytosol, it binds to a ligand-gated Ca^{2+} channel in the ER membrane. The binding of IP_3 causes the channel to open, releasing Ca^{2+} into the cytosol. Therefore, this pathway also involves calcium ions, which act as a second messenger. Calcium ions can elicit a cellular response in a variety of ways, two of which are shown in Figure 9.16 and described next.

Cellular Response via Protein Kinase C Ca^{2+} can bind to protein kinase C (PKC), which, in combination with DAG, activates the kinase. Once activated, PKC can phosphorylate specific cellular proteins, thereby altering their function and leading to a cellular response. In smooth muscle cells, for example, protein kinase C phosphorylates proteins that are involved with contraction.

Cellular Response via Calmodulin Ca^{2+} also can bind to a protein called calmodulin, which is a calcium-modulated protein. The Ca^{2+}-calmodulin complex can then interact with specific cellular proteins and alter their functions. For example, calmodulin regulates proteins involved in carbohydrate breakdown in liver cells.

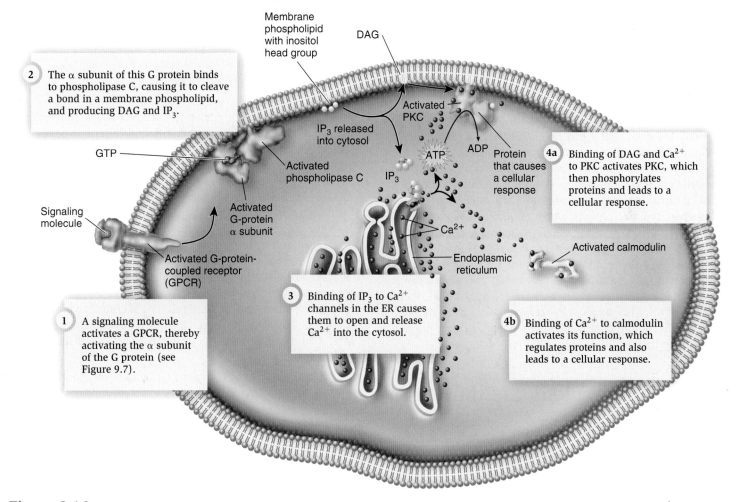

2 The α subunit of this G protein binds to phospholipase C, causing it to cleave a bond in a membrane phospholipid, and producing DAG and IP_3.

Membrane phospholipid with inositol head group

DAG

Activated PKC

IP_3 released into cytosol

GTP

Activated phospholipase C

IP_3

ATP

ADP

Protein that causes a cellular response

4a Binding of DAG and Ca^{2+} to PKC activates PKC, which then phosphorylates proteins and leads to a cellular response.

Signaling molecule

Activated G-protein α subunit

Ca^{2+}

Activated calmodulin

Activated G-protein-coupled receptor (GPCR)

Endoplasmic reticulum

1 A signaling molecule activates a GPCR, thereby activating the α subunit of the G protein (see Figure 9.7).

3 Binding of IP_3 to Ca^{2+} channels in the ER causes them to open and release Ca^{2+} into the cytosol.

4b Binding of Ca^{2+} to calmodulin activates its function, which regulates proteins and also leads to a cellular response.

Figure 9.16 A signal transduction pathway involving diacylglycerol (DAG), inositol trisphosphate (IP_3), and changing Ca^{2+} levels.

9.4 Hormonal Signaling in Multicellular Organisms

Thus far, we have considered how signaling molecules bind to particular types of receptors, thereby activating a signal transduction pathway that leads to a cellular response. In this section, we will consider the effects of signaling molecules in multicellular organisms that have a variety of cell types. As you will learn, the type of cellular response that is caused by a given signaling molecule depends on the type of cell that is responding to the signal. Each cell type responds to a particular signaling molecule in its own unique way. The variation in a cellular response is determined by the types of proteins, such as receptors and signal transduction proteins, that each cell type makes.

The Cellular Response to a Given Hormone Can Vary Among Different Cell Types

As we have seen, signaling molecules usually exert their effects on cells via signal transduction pathways that control the functions and/or synthesis of specific proteins. In multicellular organisms, one of the amazing effects of hormones is their ability to coordinate cellular activities. One example is epinephrine, which is secreted from endocrine cells. As mentioned, epinephrine is also called the fight-or-flight hormone because it quickly prepares the body for strenuous physical activity. Epinephrine is also secreted into the bloodstream when someone is exercising vigorously.

Epinephrine has different effects throughout the body (Figure 9.17). We have already discussed how it promotes the breakdown of glycogen in skeletal muscle cells. In the lungs, it relaxes the airways, allowing a person to take in more oxygen. In the heart, epinephrine stimulates heart muscle cells so the heart beats faster. Interestingly, one of the effects of caffeine can be explained by this mechanism. Caffeine inhibits phosphodiesterase, which converts cAMP to AMP. Phosphodiesterase functions to remove cAMP once a signaling molecule, such as epinephrine, is no longer present. When phosphodiesterase is inhibited by caffeine, cAMP persists for a longer period of time and thereby causes the heart to beat faster. Therefore, even low levels of signaling molecules such as epinephrine will have a greater effect. This is one of the reasons why drinks containing caffeine, including coffee and many energy drinks, provide a feeling of vitality and energy.

Genomes & Proteomes Connection

A Cell's Response to Hormones and Other Signaling Molecules Depends on the Proteins It Makes

As Figure 9.17 shows, a hormone such as epinephrine produces diverse responses throughout the body. How do we explain the

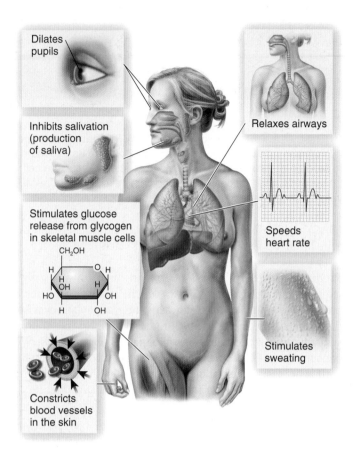

Figure 9.17 **The effects of epinephrine in humans.** This hormone prepares the body for fight or flight.

observation that various cell types can respond so differently to the same hormone? The answer lies in **differential gene regulation**. As a multicellular organism develops from a fertilized egg, the cells of the body become differentiated into particular types, such as heart and lung cells. The mechanisms that underlie this differentiation process are described in Chapter 19. Although different cell types, such as heart and lung cells, contain the same set of genes—the same genome—they are not expressed in the same pattern. Certain genes that are turned off in heart cells are turned on in lung cells, whereas some genes that are turned on in heart cells are turned off in lung cells. This causes each cell type to have its own distinct proteome. The set of proteins made in any given cell type is critical to a cell's ability to respond to signaling molecules. The following are examples of how differential gene regulation affects the cellular response:

1. *A cell may or may not express a receptor for a particular signaling molecule.* For example, not all cells of the human body express a receptor for epinephrine. These cells are not affected when epinephrine is released into the bloodstream.

2. *Different cell types have different cell surface receptors that recognize the same signaling molecule.* In humans, for example, a signaling molecule called acetylcholine has two different types of receptors. One acetylcholine receptor is a

ligand-gated ion channel that is expressed in skeletal muscle cells. Another acetylcholine receptor is a G-protein-coupled receptor (GPCR) that is expressed in heart muscle cells. Because of this, acetylcholine activates different signal transduction pathways in skeletal and heart muscle cells. Therefore, these cells respond differently to acetylcholine.

3. *Two (or more) receptors may work the same way in different cell types but have different affinities for the same signaling molecule.* For example, two different GPCRs may recognize the same hormone, but the receptor expressed in liver cells may have a higher affinity (that is, a lower K_d) for the hormone than does a receptor expressed in muscle cells. In this case, liver cells will respond to a lower hormone concentration than muscle cells will.

4. *The expression of proteins involved in intracellular signal transduction pathways may vary in different cell types.* For example, one cell type may express the proteins that are needed to activate PKA, while another cell type may not.

5. *The expression of proteins that are controlled by signal transduction pathways may vary in different cell types.* For example, the presence of epinephrine in skeletal muscle cells leads to the activation of glycogen phosphorylase, an enzyme involved in glycogen breakdown. However, this enzyme is not expressed in all cells of the body. Glycogen breakdown will only be stimulated by epinephrine if glycogen phosphorylase is expressed in that cell.

9.5 Apoptosis: Programmed Cell Death

We will end our discussion of cell communication by considering one of the most dramatic responses that eukaryotic cells exhibit—**apoptosis**, or programmed cell death. During this process, a cell orchestrates its own destruction! The cell first shrinks and forms a rounder shape due to the internal destruction of its nucleus and cytoskeleton (Figure 9.18). The plasma membrane then forms irregular extensions that eventually become blebs—small cell fragments that break away from the cell as it destroys itself. In this section, we will examine the pioneering work that led to the discovery of apoptosis and explore its molecular mechanism.

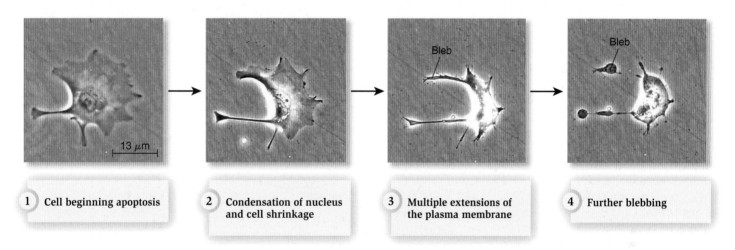

1 Cell beginning apoptosis

2 Condensation of nucleus and cell shrinkage

3 Multiple extensions of the plasma membrane

4 Further blebbing

Figure 9.18   Stages of apoptosis.

FEATURE INVESTIGATION

Kerr, Wyllie, and Currie Found That Hormones May Control Apoptosis

How was this process discovered? One line of evidence involved the microscopic examination of tissues in mammals. In the 1960s, British pathologist John Kerr microscopically examined liver tissue that was deprived of oxygen. Within hours of oxygen deprivation, he observed that some cells underwent a process that involved cell shrinkage. Around this time, similar results had been noted by other researchers, such as Scottish pathologists Andrew Wyllie and Alastair Currie, who had studied cell death in the adrenal glands. In 1973, Kerr, Wyllie, and Currie joined forces to study this process further.

Prior to their collaboration, other researchers had already established that certain hormones affect the growth of the adrenal glands, which sit atop the kidneys. Adrenocorticotropic hormone (ACTH) was known to increase the number of cells in the adrenal cortex, which is the outer layer of the adrenal glands. By contrast, prednisolone was shown to suppress the synthesis of ACTH and cause a decrease in the number of cells in the cortex. In the experiment described in Figure 9.19, Kerr, Wyllie, and Currie wanted to understand how these hormones

Figure 9.19 Discovery of apoptosis in the adrenal cortex by Kerr, Wyllie, and Currie.

HYPOTHESIS Hormones may affect cell number in the adrenal gland by controlling the rate of apoptosis.

KEY MATERIALS Laboratory rats, prednisolone, and ACTH.

	Experimental level	Conceptual level

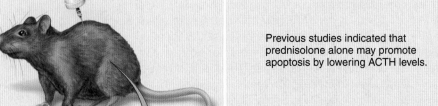

1   Inject 5 rats with saline (control). Inject 5 rats with prednisolone alone. Inject 5 rats with prednisolone plus ACTH. Inject 5 rats with ACTH alone.

Previous studies indicated that prednisolone alone may promote apoptosis by lowering ACTH levels.

2   After 2 days, obtain samples of adrenal tissue from all 20 rats.

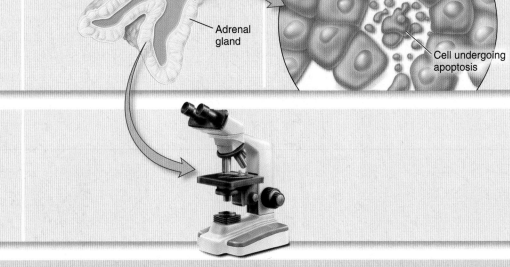

Adrenal gland

Cell undergoing apoptosis

3   Observe the samples via light microscopy, described in Chapter 4.

4   **THE DATA**

Micrograph of adrenal tissue showing occasional cells undergoing apoptosis (see arrow)

13.9 μm

Treatment	Number of animals	Glands with enhanced apoptosis*/ Total number of animals
Saline	5	0/10
Prednisolone	5	9/10
Prednisolone + ACTH	5	0/10
ACTH	5	0/10

*Samples from two adrenal glands were removed from each animal. Enhanced apoptosis means that cells undergoing apoptosis were observed in every sample under the light microscope.

5   **CONCLUSION** Prednisolone alone, which lowers ACTH levels, causes some cells to undergo apoptosis. During this process, the cells shrink and form blebs as they kill themselves. Apoptosis is controlled by hormones.

6   **SOURCE** Wyllie, A.H., Kerr, J.F.R., Macaskill, I.A.M., and Currie, A.R. 1973. Adrenocortical cell deletion: the role of ACTH. *Journal of Pathology* 111:85–94.

exert their effects. They subjected rats to four types of treatments. The control rats were injected with saline (salt water). Other rats were injected with prednisolone alone, prednisolone plus ACTH, or ACTH alone. After two days, samples of adrenal cortex were obtained from the rats and observed by light microscopy. Even in control samples, the researchers occasionally observed cell death via apoptosis (see micrograph under The Data). However, in prednisolone-treated rats, the cells in the adrenal cortex were found to undergo a dramatically higher rate of apoptosis. Multiple cells undergoing apoptosis were found in 9 out of every 10 samples observed under the light microscope. Such a high level of apoptosis was not observed in control samples or in samples obtained from rats treated with both prednisolone and ACTH or ACTH alone.

The results of Kerr, Wyllie, and Currie are important for two reasons. First, their results indicated that tissues decrease their cell number via a mechanism that involves cell shrinkage and eventually blebbing. Second, they showed that cell death could follow a program that, in this case, was induced by the presence of prednisolone (which decreases ACTH). They coined the term apoptosis to describe this process.

Experimental Questions

1. In the experiment of Figure 9.19, explain the effects on apoptosis in the control rats (saline injected) versus those injected with prednisolone alone, predinisolone + ACTH, or ACTH alone.

2. Prednisolone inhibits the production of ACTH in rats. Do you think it inhibited the ability of rats to make their own ACTH when they were injected with both prednisolone and ACTH? Explain.

3. Of the four groups—control, prednisolone alone, prednisolone + ACTH, and ACTH alone—which would you expect to have the lowest level of apoptosis? Explain.

Intrinsic and Extrinsic Signal Transduction Pathways Lead to Apoptosis

Since these early studies on apoptosis, cell biologists have discovered that apoptosis plays many important roles. During embryonic development in animals, it is needed to sculpt the tissues and organs. For example, the fingers on a human hand, which are initially webbed, become separated during embryonic development when the cells between the fingers are programmed to die (see Chapter 19, Figure 19.4). Apoptosis is also necessary in adult organisms to maintain the proper cell number in tissues and organs. This process also eliminates cells that have become worn out, infected by viruses or intracellular bacteria, or have the potential to cause cancer. In mammals, apoptosis is also important in the proper functioning of the immune system, which wards off infections. The immune system is composed of a variety of cell types, such as B cells and T cells, that can fight infectious agents and eliminate damaged cells. For this to occur, the immune system creates a large pool of B and T cells and then uses apoptosis to weed out those that are potentially damaging to the body or ineffective at fighting infection.

Apoptosis involves the activation of cell signaling pathways. One pathway, called the intrinsic or mitochondrial pathway, is stimulated by internal signals, such as DNA damage that could cause cancer. Proteins on the surface of the mitochondria play a key role in eliciting the response. Alternatively, extracellular signals can promote apoptosis. This is called the extrinsic or death receptor pathway.

Let's consider how an extracellular signal causes apoptosis. The extrinsic pathway of apoptosis begins with the activation of **death receptors** on the surface of the cell. Death receptors, such as Fas, stimulate a pathway that leads to apoptosis when they become bound to an extracellular ligand. **Figure 9.20** shows a simplified pathway for this process. In this example, the extracellular ligand is a protein composed of three identical subunits—a trimeric protein. Such trimeric ligands that promote cell death are typically produced on the surface of cells of the immune system that recognize abnormal cells and target them for destruction. For example, when a cell is infected with a virus, cells of the immune system may target the infected cell for apoptosis. The trimeric ligand binds to three death receptors, which causes them to aggregate into a trimer. This results in a conformational change that exposes the death domain in the cytosol. Once the death domain is exposed, it binds to an adaptor, such as FADD, which then binds to a procaspase. (FADD is an abbreviation for Fas-associated protein with death domain.) The complex between the death receptors, FADD, and procaspase is called the **death-inducing signaling complex** (**DISC**).

Once the procaspase, which is inactive, is part of the death-inducing signaling complex, it is converted by proteolytic cleavage to caspase, which is active. An active **caspase** functions as a protease—an enzyme that digests other proteins. After it is activated, the caspase is then released from the DISC. This caspase is called an initiator caspase because it initiates the activation of many other caspases in the cell. These other caspases are called executioner or effector caspases because they are directly responsible for digesting intracellular proteins and causing the cell to die. The executioner caspases digest a variety of intracellular proteins, including the proteins that constitute the cytoskeleton and nuclear lamina as well as proteins involved with DNA replication and repair. In this way, the executioner caspases cause the cellular changes described earlier in Figure 9.18. The caspases also activate an enzyme called DNase that chops the DNA in the cell into small fragments. This event may be particularly important for eliminating virally infected cells because it will also destroy viral genomes that are composed of DNA.

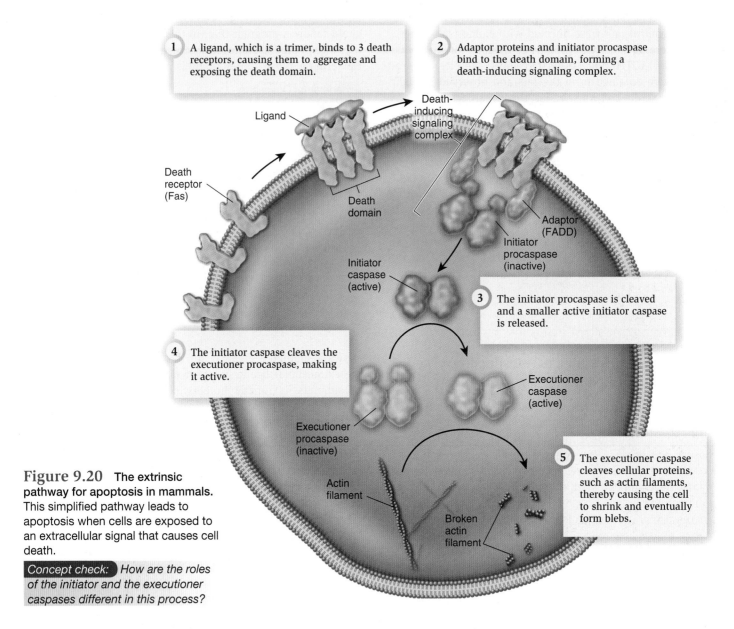

Figure 9.20 **The extrinsic pathway for apoptosis in mammals.** This simplified pathway leads to apoptosis when cells are exposed to an extracellular signal that causes cell death.

Concept check: How are the roles of the initiator and the executioner caspases different in this process?

(From figure, in order:)

1. A ligand, which is a trimer, binds to 3 death receptors, causing them to aggregate and exposing the death domain.

2. Adaptor proteins and initiator procaspase bind to the death domain, forming a death-inducing signaling complex.

3. The initiator procaspase is cleaved and a smaller active initiator caspase is released.

4. The initiator caspase cleaves the executioner procaspase, making it active.

5. The executioner caspase cleaves cellular proteins, such as actin filaments, thereby causing the cell to shrink and eventually form blebs.

Labels: Ligand; Death receptor (Fas); Death-inducing signaling complex; Death domain; Adaptor (FADD); Initiator procaspase (inactive); Initiator caspase (active); Executioner caspase (active); Executioner procaspase (inactive); Actin filament; Broken actin filament

Summary of Key Concepts

9.1   General Features of Cell Communication

- A signal is an agent that can influence the properties of cells. Cell signaling is needed so that cells can sense and respond to environmental changes and communicate with each other.

- When a cell responds to an environmental signal, it has become adapted to its environment. (Figure 9.1)

- Cell-to-cell communication also allows cells to adapt, as when plants grow toward light. (Figure 9.2)

- Cell-to-cell communication can vary in the mechanism and distance that a signal travels. Signals are relayed between cells in five common ways: direct intercellular, contact-dependent, autocrine, paracrine, and endocrine signaling. (Figure 9.3)

- Cell communication is usually a three-stage process involving receptor activation, signal transduction, and a cellular response. A signal transduction pathway is a group of proteins that convert an initial signal to a different signal inside the cell. (Figure 9.4)

9.2   Cellular Receptors and Their Activation

- A signaling molecule, also called a ligand, binds to a receptor with an affinity that is measured as a K_d value. The binding of a ligand to a receptor is usually very specific and alters the conformation of the receptor. (Figure 9.5)

- Most receptors involved in cell signaling are found on the cell surface.

- Enzyme-linked receptors have some type of catalytic function. Many of them are protein kinases that can phosphorylate proteins. (Figure 9.6)

- G-protein-coupled receptors (GPCRs) interact with G proteins to initiate a cellular response. (Figure 9.7)

- Some receptors are ligand-gated ion channels that allow the flow of ions across cellular membranes. (Figure 9.8)

- Some receptors, such as the estrogen receptor, are intracellular receptors. (Figure 9.9)

9.3   Signal Transduction and the Cellular Response

- Signaling pathways influence whether or not a cell will divide. An example is the pathway that is stimulated by epidermal growth factor, which binds to a receptor tyrosine kinase. (Figure 9.10)

- Second messengers, such as cAMP, play a key role in signal transduction pathways, such as those that occur via G-protein-coupled receptors. These pathways are reversible once the signal is degraded. (Figures 9.11, 9.12)

- An example of a pathway that uses cAMP is found in skeletal muscle cells. In these cells, epinephrine enhances the function of enzymes that increase glycogen breakdown and inhibits enzymes that cause glycogen synthesis. (Figure 9.13)

- Second messenger pathways amplify the signal and occur with great speed. (Figures 9.14, 9.15)

- Diacylglycerol (DAG), inositol trisphosphate (IP_3), and Ca^{2+} are other examples of second messengers involved in signal transduction. (Figure 9.16)

9.4   Hormonal Signaling in Multicellular Organisms

- Hormones such as epinephrine exert different effects throughout the body. (Figure 9.17)

- The way in which any particular cell responds to a signaling molecule depends on the types of proteins it makes. These include the types of receptors, proteins involved in signaling transduction pathways, and proteins that carry out the cellular response. The amounts of these proteins are controlled by differential gene regulation.

9.5   Apoptosis: Programmed Cell Death

- Apoptosis is the process of programmed cell death in which the nucleus and cytoskeleton break down, and eventually the cell breaks apart into blebs. (Figure 9.18)

- Microscopy studies of Kerr, Wyllie, and Currie, in which they studied the effects of hormones on the adrenal cortex, were instrumental in the identification of apoptosis. (Figure 9.19)

- Apoptosis plays many important roles in multicellular organisms, including the sculpting of tissues and organs during embryonic development, maintaining the proper cell number in tissues and organs, eliminating cells that have become worn out or have the potential to cause cancer, and the proper functioning of the immune system.

- Apoptosis can occur via intrinsic or extrinsic pathways. (Figure 9.20)

■ Assess and Discuss

Test Yourself

1. The ability of a cell to respond to changes in its environment is termed
   a. signaling.
   b. apoptosis.
   c. irritability.
   d. adaptation.
   e. stimulation.

2. When a cell secretes a signaling molecule that binds to receptors on neighboring cells as well as the same cell, this is called _____ signaling.
   a. direct intercellular
   b. contact-dependent
   c. autocrine
   d. paracrine
   e. endocrine

3. Which of the following does not describe a typical cellular response to signaling molecules?
   a. activation of enzymes within the cell
   b. change in the function of structural proteins, which determine cell shape
   c. alteration of levels of certain proteins in the cell by changing the level of gene expression
   d. change in a gene sequence that encodes a particular protein
   e. All of the above are examples of cellular responses.

4. A receptor has a K_d for its ligand of 50 nM. This receptor
   a. has a higher affinity for its ligand compared to a receptor with a K_d of 100 nM.
   b. has a higher affinity for its ligand compared to a receptor with a K_d of 10 nM.
   c. will be mostly bound by its ligand when the ligand concentration is 100 nM.
   d. must be an intracellular receptor.
   e. both a and c

5. _____ binds to receptors inside cells.
   a. Estrogen
   b. Epinephrine
   c. Epidermal growth factor
   d. All of the above
   e. None of the above

6. Small molecules, such as cAMP, that relay signals within the cell are called
   a. secondary metabolites.
   b. ligands.
   c. G proteins.
   d. second messengers.
   e. transcription factors.

7. The benefit of second messengers in signal transduction pathways is
   a. an increase in the speed of a cellular response.
   b. duplication of the ligands in the system.
   c. amplification of the signal.
   d. all of the above.
   e. a and c only.

8. All cells of a multicellular organism may not respond in the same way to a particular ligand (signaling molecule) that binds to a cell surface receptor. The difference in response may be due to
   a. the type of receptor for the ligand that the cell expresses.
   b the affinity of the ligand for the receptor in a given cell type.
   c. the type of signal transduction pathways that the cell expresses.
   d. the type of target proteins that the cell expresses.
   e. all of the above.

9. Apoptosis is the process of
   a. cell migration.
   b. cell signaling.
   c. signal transduction.
   d. signal amplification.
   e. programmed cell death.

10. Which statement best describes the extrinsic pathway for apoptosis?
   a. Caspases recognize an environmental signal and expose their death domain.
   b. Death receptors recognize an environmental signal which then leads to the activation of caspases.
   c. Initiator caspases digest the nuclear lamina and cytoskeleton.
   d. Executioner caspases are part of the death-inducing signaling complex (DISC).
   e. all of the above

Conceptual Questions

1. What are the two general reasons that cells need to communicate?

2. What are the three stages of cell signaling? What stage does not occur when the estrogen receptor is activated?

3. What would be some of the harmful consequences if apoptosis did not occur?

Collaborative Questions

1. Discuss and compare several different types of cell-to-cell communication. What are some advantages and disadvantages of each type?

2. How does differential gene regulation enable various cell types to respond differently to the same signaling molecule? Why is this useful to multicellular organisms?

Online Resource

www.brookerbiology.com

Stay a step ahead in your studies with animations that bring concepts to life and practice tests to assess your understanding. Your instructor may also recommend the interactive ebook, individualized learning tools, and more.

Multicellularity

10

The General Sherman tree in Sequoia National Park, a striking example of the size that multicellular organisms can reach. This tree is thought to be the largest organism (by mass) in the world.

What is the largest living organism on Earth? The size of an organism can be defined by its volume, mass, height, length, or the area it occupies. A giant fungus (*Armillaria ostoyae*), growing in the soil in the Malheur National Forest in Oregon, spans 8.9 km², or 2,200 acres, which makes it the largest single organism by area. In the Mediterranean Sea, marine biologists discovered a giant aquatic plant (*Posidonia oceanica*) that is 8 km or 4.3 miles in length, making it the longest organism. With regard to mass, the largest organism is probably a tree named the General Sherman tree that is 83.8 meters tall (275 feet), nearly the length of a football field (see chapter-opening photo). This giant sequoia tree (*Sequoiadendron giganteum*) is estimated to weigh nearly 2 million kg (over 2,000 tons)—equivalent to a herd of 400 elephants!

An organism composed of more than one cell is said to be **multicellular**. The preceding examples illustrate the amazing sizes that certain multicellular organisms have achieved. As we will discuss in Chapter 22, multicellular organisms came into being approximately 1 billion years ago. Some species of protists are multicellular, as are most species of fungi. In this chapter, we will focus on plants and animals, which are always multicellular organisms.

The main benefit of multicellularity arises from the division of labor between different types of cells in an organism. For example, the intestinal cells of animals and the root cells of plants have become specialized for nutrient uptake. Other types of cells in a multicellular organism perform different roles, such as reproduction. In animals, most of the cells of the body—somatic cells—are devoted to the growth, development, and survival of the organism, while specialized cells—gametes—function in sexual reproduction.

Multicellular species usually have much larger genomes than unicellular species. The increase in genome size is associated with an increase in proteome size—multicellular organisms produce a larger array of proteins than do unicellular species. The additional proteins play a role in three general phenomena. First, in a multicellular organism, cell communication is vital for the proper organization and functioning of cells. Many more proteins involved in cell communication are made in multicellular species. Second, both the arrangement of cells within the body and the attachment of cells to each other require a greater variety of proteins in multicellular species than in unicellular species. Finally, additional proteins play a role in cell specialization because proteins that are needed for the structure and function of one cell type may not be needed in a different cell type, and vice versa. Likewise, additional proteins are needed to regulate the expression of genes so these proteins are expressed in the proper cell types.

In this chapter, we consider characteristics specific to the cell biology of multicellular organisms. We will begin by exploring the material that is produced by animal and plant cells to form an extracellular matrix or cell wall, respectively. This material plays many important roles in the structure, organization, and functioning of cells within multicellular organisms. We will then turn our attention to cell junctions, specialized structures that enable cells to make physical contact with one another. Cells within multicellular organisms form junctions that help to make a cohesive and well-organized body. Finally, we examine the organization and function of tissues, groups of cells that have a similar structure and function. In this chapter, we will survey the general features of tissues from a cellular perspective. Units VI and VII will explore the characteristics of plant and animal tissues in greater detail.

10.1 Extracellular Matrix and Cell Walls

Organisms are not composed solely of cells. A large portion of an animal or plant consists of a network of material that is secreted from cells and forms a complex meshwork outside of cells. In animals, this is called the **extracellular matrix** (**ECM**), whereas plant cells are surrounded by a cell wall. The ECM and cell walls are a major component of certain parts of animals and plants, respectively. For example, bones and cartilage in animals and the woody portions of plants are composed largely of ECM and cell walls, respectively. Although the cells within wood eventually die, the cell walls they have produced provide a rigid structure that can support the plant for years or even centuries.

Over the past few decades, cell biologists have examined the synthesis, composition, and function of the ECM in animals and the cell walls in plants. In this section, we will begin by examining the structure and role of the ECM in animals, focusing on the functions of the major ECM components, proteins and polysaccharides. We will then explore the cell wall of plant cells and consider how it differs in structure and function from the ECM of animal cells.

The Extracellular Matrix in Animals Supports and Organizes Cells and Plays a Role in Cell Signaling

Unlike the cells of bacteria, fungi, and plants, the cells of animals are not surrounded by a rigid cell wall that provides structure and support. However, animal cells secrete materials that form an extracellular matrix that also provides support and helps to organize cells. Certain animal cells are completely embedded within an extensive ECM, whereas other cells may adhere to the ECM on only one side. Figure 10.1 illustrates the general features of the ECM and its relationship to cells. The major macromolecules of the ECM are proteins and polysaccharides. The most abundant proteins are those that form large fibers. The polysaccharides give the ECM surrounding animal cells a gel-like character.

As we will see, the ECM found in animals performs many important roles, including strength, structural support, organization, and cell signaling.

- **Strength:** The ECM is the "tough stuff" of animals' bodies. In the skin of mammals, the strength of the ECM prevents tearing. The ECM found in cartilage resists compression and provides protection to the joints. Similarly, the ECM protects the soft parts of the body, such as the internal organs.

- **Structural support:** The bones of many animals are composed primarily of ECM. Skeletons not only provide structural support but also facilitate movement via the functioning of attached muscles.

- **Organization:** The attachment of cells to the ECM plays a key role in the proper arrangement of cells throughout

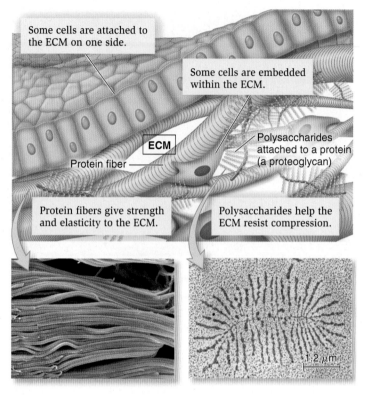

Figure 10.1 **The extracellular matrix (ECM) of animal cells.** The micrograph (SEM) at the bottom left shows collagen fibers. The micrograph (TEM) at the bottom right shows a proteoglycan.

Concept check: *What are the four functions of the ECM in animals?*

the body. In addition, the ECM binds many body parts together, such as tendons to bones.

- **Cell signaling:** A newly discovered role of the ECM is cell signaling. One way that cells in multicellular organisms sense their environment is via changes in the ECM.

Let's now consider the synthesis and structure of ECM components found in animals.

Adhesive and Structural Proteins Are Major Components of the ECM of Animals

In the 1850s, German biologist Rudolf Virchow suggested that all extracellular materials are made and secreted by cells. Around the same time, biologists realized that gelatin and glue, which are produced by the boiling of animal tissues, must contain a common fibrous substance. This substance was named **collagen** (from the Greek, meaning glue producing). Since that time, the advent of experimental techniques in chemistry, microscopy, and biophysics has enabled scientists to probe the structure of the ECM. We now understand that the ECM contains a mixture of several different components, including proteins such as collagen, that form fibers.

The proteins found in the ECM can be grouped into adhesive proteins, such as fibronectin and laminin, and structural

Labels in figure:
- Some cells are attached to the ECM on one side.
- Some cells are embedded within the ECM.
- ECM
- Protein fiber
- Polysaccharides attached to a protein (a proteoglycan)
- Protein fibers give strength and elasticity to the ECM.
- Polysaccharides help the ECM resist compression.
- 1.2 μm

Table 10.1		Proteins in the ECM of Animals
General type	**Example**	**Function**
Adhesive	Fibronectin	Connects cells to the ECM and helps to organize components in the ECM.
	Laminin	Connects cells to the ECM and helps to organize components in the basal lamina, a specialized ECM found next to epithelial cells (described in Section 10.3).
Structural	Collagen	Forms large fibers and interconnected fibrous networks in the ECM. Provides tensile strength.
	Elastin	Forms elastic fibers in the ECM that can stretch and recoil.

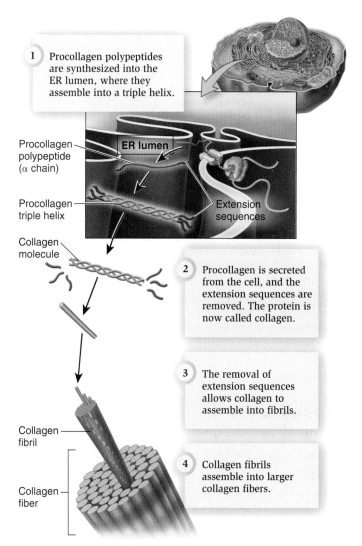

1 Procollagen polypeptides are synthesized into the ER lumen, where they assemble into a triple helix.

Procollagen polypeptide (α chain)

ER lumen

Procollagen triple helix

Extension sequences

Collagen molecule

2 Procollagen is secreted from the cell, and the extension sequences are removed. The protein is now called collagen.

3 The removal of extension sequences allows collagen to assemble into fibrils.

Collagen fibril

4 Collagen fibrils assemble into larger collagen fibers.

Collagen fiber

Figure 10.2 Formation of collagen fibers. Collagen is one type of structural protein found in the ECM of animal cells.

Concept check: *What prevents large collagen fibers from forming intracellularly?*

proteins, such as collagen and elastin (**Table 10.1**). How do adhesive proteins work? Fibronectin and laminin have multiple binding sites that bind to other components in the ECM, such as protein fibers and polysaccharides. These same proteins also have binding sites for receptors on the surfaces of cells. Therefore, adhesive proteins are so named because they adhere ECM components together and to the cell surface. They provide organization to the ECM and facilitate the attachment of cells to the ECM.

Structural proteins, such as collagen and elastin, form large fibers that give the ECM its strength and elasticity. A key function of collagen is to impart tensile strength, which is a measure of how much stretching force a material can bear without tearing apart. Collagen provides high tensile strength to many parts of the animal body. Collagen is the main protein found in bones, cartilage, tendons, and skin and is also found lining blood vessels and internal organs. In mammals, more than 25% of the total protein mass consists of collagen, much more than any other protein. Approximately 75% of the protein in mammalian skin is composed of collagen. Leather is largely a pickled and tanned form of collagen.

Figure 10.2 depicts the synthesis and assembly of collagen. As described in Chapter 4, proteins, such as collagen, that are secreted from eukaryotic cells are first directed to the endoplasmic reticulum (ER), then to the Golgi apparatus, and subsequently are secreted from the cell via vesicles that fuse with the plasma membrane. Individual procollagen polypeptides (called α chains) are synthesized into the lumen (inside) of the ER. Three procollagen polypeptides then associate with each other to form a procollagen triple helix. The amino acid sequences at both ends of the polypeptides, termed extension sequences, promote the formation of procollagen and prevent the formation of a much larger fiber. After procollagen is secreted out of the cell, extracellular enzymes remove the extension sequences. Once this occurs, the protein, now called collagen, can form larger structures. Collagen proteins assemble in a staggered way to form relatively thin collagen fibrils, which then align

and produce large collagen fibers. The many layers of these proteins give collagen fibers their tensile strength.

In addition to tensile strength, elasticity is needed in regions of the body such as the lungs and blood vessels, which regularly expand and return to their original shape. In these places, the ECM contains an abundance of elastic fibers composed primarily of the protein **elastin** (**Figure 10.3**). Elastin proteins form many covalent cross-links to make a fiber with remarkable elastic properties. In the absence of a stretching force, each protein tends to adopt a compact conformation. When subjected to a stretching force, however, the compact proteins become more linear, with the covalent cross-links holding the fiber together. When the stretching force has ended, the proteins naturally return to their compact conformation. In this way, elastic fibers behave much like a rubber band, stretching under tension and snapping back when the tension is released.

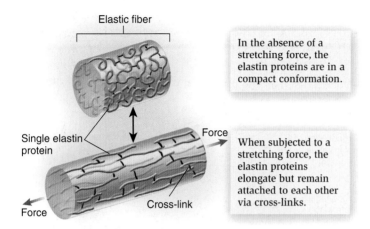

Figure 10.3   **Structure and function of elastic fibers.**
Elastic fibers are made of elastin, one type of structural protein found in the ECM surrounding animal cells.

Concept check: *Suppose you started with an unstretched elastic fiber and treated it with a chemical that breaks the cross-links between adjacent elastin proteins. What would happen when the fiber is stretched?*

Genomes & Proteomes Connection

Collagens Are a Family of Proteins That Give Animal Cells a Variety of ECM Properties

Researchers have determined that animal cells make many different types of collagen fibers. These are designated as type I, type II, and so on. At least 27 different types of collagens have been identified in humans. To make different types of collagens, the human genome, as well as the genomes of other animals, has many different genes that encode procollagen polypeptides.

Collagens have a common structure, in which three polypeptides wind around each other to form a triple helix (see Figure 10.2). Each polypeptide is an α chain. In some collagens, all three α chains are identical, while in others, the α chains may be encoded by different collagen genes. Nevertheless, the triple helix structure is common to all collagen proteins.

Why are different collagens made? Each of the many different types of collagen polypeptides has a similar yet distinctive amino acid sequence that affects the structure of not only individual collagen proteins but also the resulting collagen fibers. For example, the amino acid sequence may cause the α chains within each collagen protein to bind to each other very tightly, thereby creating rigid proteins that form a relatively stiff fiber. Such collagen fibers are found in bone and cartilage.

The amino acid sequence of the α chains also influences the interactions between the collagen proteins within a fiber. For example, the amino acid sequences of certain chains may promote a looser interaction that produces a more bendable or thin fiber. More flexible collagen fibers support the lining of your lungs and intestines. In addition, domains within the collagen polypeptide may affect the spatial arrangement of collagen proteins. The collagen shown earlier in Figure 10.2 forms fibers in which collagen proteins align themselves in parallel arrays. However, not all collagen proteins form long fibers. For example, type IV collagen proteins interact with each other in a meshwork pattern. This meshwork acts as a filtration unit around capillaries.

Differential gene regulation controls which types of collagens are made throughout the body and in what amounts they are made. Of the 27 types of collagens, **Table 10.2** considers types I to IV, each of which varies with regard to where it is primarily synthesized and its structure and function. Collagen genes are regulated, so the required type of collagen is made in the correct sites in your body. In skin cells, for example, the genes that encode the polypeptides that make up collagen types I, III, and IV are turned on, while the synthesis of type II collagen is minimal.

The regulation of collagen synthesis has received a great deal of attention due to the phenomenon of wrinkling. Many face and skin creams contain collagen as an ingredient! As we age, the amount of collagen that is synthesized in our skin significantly decreases. The underlying network of collagen fibers, which provides scaffolding for the surface of our skin, loosens and unravels. This is one of the factors that causes the skin of older people to sink, sag, and form wrinkles. Various therapeutic and cosmetic agents have been developed to prevent or reverse the appearance of wrinkles, most with limited benefits. One approach is collagen injections, in which small amounts of collagen (from cows) are injected into areas where the body's collagen has weakened, filling the depressions to the level of the surrounding skin. Because collagen is naturally broken down in the skin, the injections are not permanent and last only about 3 to 6 months.

Table 10.2	Examples of Collagen Types	
Type	**Sites of synthesis***	**Structure and function**
I	Tendons, ligaments, bones, and skin	Forms a relatively rigid and thick fiber. Very abundant, provides most of the tensile strength to the ECM.
II	Cartilage, discs between vertebrae	Forms a fairly rigid and thick fiber but is more flexible than type I. Permits smooth movements of joints.
III	Arteries, skin, internal organs, and around muscles	Forms thin fibers, often arranged in a meshwork pattern. Allows for greater elasticity in tissues.
IV	Skin, intestine, and kidneys; also found around capillaries	Does not form long fibers. Instead, the proteins are arranged in a meshwork pattern that provides organization and support to cell layers. Functions as a filter around capillaries.

*The sites of synthesis denote where a large amount of the collagen type is made.

Animal Cells Also Secrete Polysaccharides Into the ECM

In addition to proteins, polysaccharides are the second major component of the extracellular matrix of animals. As discussed in Chapter 3, polysaccharides are polymers of simple sugars. Among vertebrates, the most abundant types of polysaccharides in the ECM are **glycosaminoglycans** (**GAGs**). These molecules are long, unbranched polysaccharides containing a repeating disaccharide unit (**Figure 10.4a**). GAGs are highly negatively charged molecules that tend to attract positively charged ions and water. The majority of GAGs in the ECM are linked to core proteins, forming **proteoglycans** (**Figure 10.4b**).

Providing resistance to compression is the primary function of GAGs and proteoglycans. Once secreted from cells, these macromolecules form a gel-like component in the ECM. How is this gel-like property important? Due to its high water content, the ECM is difficult to compress and thereby serves to protect cells. GAGs and proteoglycans are found abundantly in regions of the body that are subjected to harsh mechanical forces, such as the joints of the human body. Two examples of GAGs are chondroitin sulfate, which is a major component of cartilage, and hyaluronic acid, which is found in the skin, eyes, and joint fluid.

Among many invertebrates, an important ECM component is **chitin**, a nitrogen-containing polysaccharide. Chitin forms

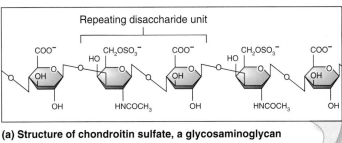

(a) Structure of chondroitin sulfate, a glycosaminoglycan

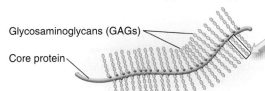

(b) General structure of a proteoglycan

Figure 10.4 **Structures of glycosaminoglycans and proteoglycans.** These large molecules are found in the ECM of animal cells. **(a)** Glycosaminoglycans (GAGs) are composed of repeating disaccharide units. They can range in length from several dozen to 25,000 disaccharide units. The GAG shown here is chondroitin sulfate, which is commonly found in cartilage. **(b)** Proteoglycans are composed of a long, linear core protein with many GAGs attached. Note that each GAG is typically 80 disaccharide units long but only a short chain of sugars is shown in this illustration.

Concept check: *What structural feature of GAGs and proteoglycans give them a gel-like character?*

the hard protective outer covering (called an exoskeleton) of insects, such as crickets and grasshoppers, and shellfish, such as lobsters and shrimp. The chitin exoskeleton is so rigid that as these animals grow, they must periodically shed this outer layer and secrete a new, larger one—a process called molting (look ahead to Figure 32.11).

The Cell Wall of Plants Provides Strength and Resistance to Compression

Let's now turn our attention to the cell walls of plants. Plants cells are surrounded by a **cell wall**, a protective layer that forms outside of the plasma membrane. Like animal cells, the cells of plants are surrounded by material that provides tensile strength and resistance to compression. The cell walls of plants, however, are usually thicker, stronger, and more rigid than the ECM found in animals. Plant cell walls provide rigidity for mechanical support and also play a role in the maintenance of cell shape and the direction of cell growth. As we learned in Chapter 5, the cell wall also prevents expansion when water enters the cell, thereby preventing osmotic lysis.

The cell walls of plants are composed of a primary cell wall and a secondary cell wall (**Figure 10.5**). These walls are named according to the timing of their synthesis—the primary cell wall is made before the secondary cell wall. During cell division, the **primary cell wall** develops between two newly made daughter cells. It is usually very flexible and allows new cells to increase in size. The main macromolecule of the plant cell wall is **cellulose**, a polysaccharide made of repeating molecules of glucose attached end to end. These glucose polymers associate with each other via hydrogen bonding to form microfibrils that provide great tensile strength (**Figure 10.6**).

Cellulose was discovered in 1838 by the French chemist Anselme Payen, who was the first scientist to try to separate wood into its component parts. After treating different types of wood with nitric acid, Payen obtained a fibrous substance that was also found in cotton and other plants. His chemical analysis revealed that the fibers were made of the carbohydrate glucose. Payen called this substance cellulose (from the Latin, meaning consisting of cells). Cellulose is probably the single most abundant organic molecule on Earth. Wood consists mostly of cellulose, and cotton and paper are almost pure cellulose. The mechanism of cellulose synthesis is described in Chapter 30.

In addition to cellulose, other components found in the primary cell wall include hemicellulose, glycans, and pectins (see Figure 10.5). Hemicellulose is another linear polysaccharide, with a structure similar to that of cellulose, but it contains sugars other than glucose in its structure and usually forms thinner microfibrils. Glycans, polysaccharides with branching structures, are also important in cell wall structure. The cross-linking glycans bind to cellulose and provide organization to the cellulose microfibrils. Pectins, which are highly negatively charged polysaccharides, attract water and have a gel-like character that provides the cell wall with the ability to resist compression.

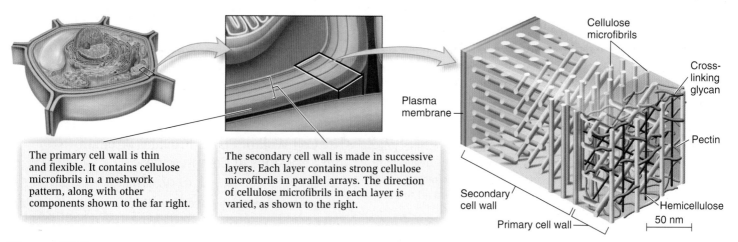

The primary cell wall is thin and flexible. It contains cellulose microfibrils in a meshwork pattern, along with other components shown to the far right.

The secondary cell wall is made in successive layers. Each layer contains strong cellulose microfibrils in parallel arrays. The direction of cellulose microfibrils in each layer is varied, as shown to the right.

Figure 10.5 **Structure of the cell wall of plant cells.** The primary cell wall is relatively thin and flexible. It contains cellulose (tan), hemicellulose (red), cross-linking glycans (blue), and pectin (green). The secondary cell wall, which is produced only by certain plant cells, is made after the primary cell wall and is synthesized in successive layers.

Concept check: *With regard to cell growth, what would happen if the secondary cell wall was made too soon?*

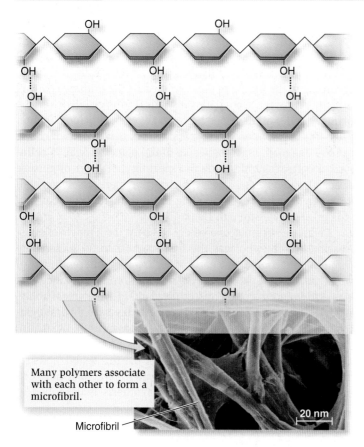

Many polymers associate with each other to form a microfibril.

Microfibril

Figure 10.6 **Structure of cellulose, the main macromolecule of the primary cell wall.** Cellulose is made of repeating glucose units linked end to end that hydrogen-bond to each other to form microfibrils (SEM).

The **secondary cell wall** is synthesized and deposited between the plasma membrane and the primary cell wall (see Figure 10.5) after a plant cell matures and has stopped increasing in size. It is made in layers by the successive deposition of cellulose microfibrils and other components. While the primary wall structure is relatively similar in nearly all cell types and species, the structure of the secondary cell wall is more variable. The secondary cell wall often contains components in addition to those found in the primary cell wall. For example, phenolic compounds called lignins are very hard and impart considerable strength to the secondary wall structure. Lignin, a type of secondary metabolite described in Chapter 7, is found in the woody parts of plants.

10.2 Cell Junctions

Thus far, we have learned that the cells of animals and plants create an extracellular matrix or cell wall that provides strength, support, and organization. For an organism to become a multicellular unit, cells within the body must be linked to each other. In animals and plants, this is accomplished by specialized structures called **cell junctions** (Table 10.3). In this section, we will examine different types of cell junctions in animal and plants.

Animal cells, which lack the structural support provided by the cell wall, have a more varied group of junctions than plant cells. In animals, junctions called anchoring junctions play a role in anchoring cells to each other or to the extracellular matrix. In other words, they hold cells in their proper place in the body. Other junctions, termed tight junctions, seal cells together to prevent small molecules from leaking across a layer of cells. Still another type of junction, known as a gap junction, allows cells to communicate directly with each other.

In plants, cellular organization is somewhat different because plant cells are surrounded by a rigid cell wall. Plant cells are connected to each other by a component called the middle lamella, which cements their cell walls together. They also have junctions termed plasmodesmata that allow adjacent cells to communicate with each other. In this section, we will examine these various types of junctions found between the cells of animals and plants.

Table 10.3	Common Types of Cell Junctions
Type	**Description**
Animals	
Anchoring junctions	Cell junctions that hold adjacent cells together or bond cells to the ECM. Anchoring junctions are mechanically strong.
Tight junctions	Junctions between adjacent cells in a layer that prevent the leakage of material between cells.
Gap junctions	Channels that permit the direct exchange of ions and small molecules between the cytosol of adjacent cells.
Plants	
Middle lamella	A polysaccharide layer that cements together the cell walls of adjacent cells.
Plasmodesmata	Passageways between the cell walls of adjacent cells that can be opened or closed. When open, they permit the direct diffusion of ions and molecules between cells.

Anchoring Junctions Link Animal Cells to Each Other and to the ECM

The advent of electron microscopy allowed researchers to explore the types of junctions that occur between cells and within the extracellular matrix. In the 1960s, Marilyn Farquhar, George Palade, and colleagues conducted several studies showing that various types of cellular junctions connect cells to each other. Over the past few decades, researchers have begun to unravel the functions and molecular structures of these types of junctions, collectively called **anchoring junctions**, which attach cells to each other and to the extracellular matrix. Anchoring junctions are particularly common in parts of the body where the cells are tightly connected and form linings. An example is the layer of cells that line the small intestine. Having anchoring junctions keeps intestinal cells tightly adhered to one another, thereby forming a strong barrier between the lumen of the intestine and the blood. A key component of anchoring junctions that form the actual connections are integral membrane proteins called **cell adhesion molecules (CAMs)**. Two types of CAMs are cadherins and integrins.

Anchoring junctions are grouped into four main categories, according to their functional roles and their connections to cellular components. **Figure 10.7** shows these junctions between cells of the mammalian small intestine.

1. **Adherens junctions** connect cells to each other via cadherins. In many cases, these junctions are organized into bands around cells. In the cytosol, adherens junctions bind to cytoskeletal filaments called actin filaments.
2. **Desmosomes** also connect cells to each other via cadherins. They are spotlike points of intercellular contact that rivet cells together. Desmosomes are connected to cytoskeletal filaments called intermediate filaments.

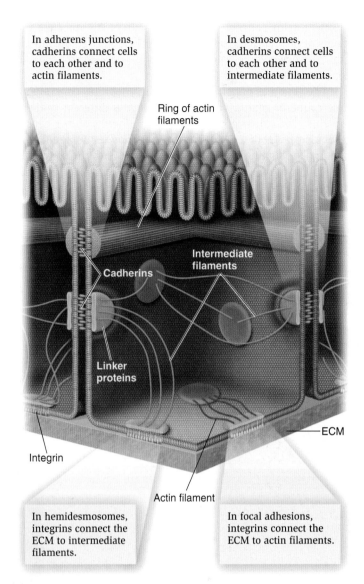

Figure 10.7 Types of anchoring junctions. This figure shows these junctions in three adjacent intestinal cells.

Concept check: Which junctions are cell-to-cell junctions and which are cell-to-ECM junctions?

3. **Hemidesmosomes** connect cells to the extracellular matrix via integrins. Like desmosomes, they interact with intermediate filaments.
4. **Focal adhesions** also connect cells to the extracellular matrix via integrins. In the cytosol, focal adhesions bind to actin filaments.

Let's now consider the molecular components of anchoring junctions. As noted, **cadherins** are CAMs that create cell-to-cell junctions (**Figure 10.8a**). The extracellular domains of two cadherin proteins, each in adjacent cells, bind to each other to promote cell-to-cell adhesion. This binding requires the presence of calcium ions, which change the conformation of the cadherin protein such that cadherins in adjacent cells bind to each other. (This calcium dependence is where cadherin gets its name—Ca^{2+} dependent adhering molecule.) On the inside of the cell, linker proteins connect cadherins to actin or intermediate filaments of the cytoskeleton. This promotes a more stable interaction between two cells because their strong cytoskeletons are connected to each other.

The genomes of vertebrates and invertebrates contain multiple cadherin genes, which encode slightly different cadherin proteins. The expression of particular cadherins allows cells to recognize each other. Dimer formation follows a homophilic, or like-to-like, binding mechanism. To understand the concept of homophilic binding, let's consider an example. One type of cadherin is called E-cadherin, and another is N-cadherin. E-cadherin in one cell will bind to E-cadherin in an adjacent cell to form a homodimer. However, E-cadherin in one cell will not bind to N-cadherin in an adjacent cell to form a heterodimer. Similarly, N-cadherin will bind to N-cadherin but not to E-cadherin in an adjacent cell. Why is such homophilic binding important? By expressing only certain types of cadherins, each cell will bind only to other cells that express the same cadherin types. This phenomenon plays a key role in the proper arrangement of cells throughout the body, particularly during development.

Integrins, a group of cell-surface receptor proteins, are a second type of CAM, one that creates connections between cells and the extracellular matrix. Integrins do not require Ca^{2+} to function. Each integrin protein is composed of two nonidentical subunits. In the example shown in **Figure 10.8b**, an integrin is bound to fibronectin, an adhesive protein in the ECM that binds to other ECM components such as collagen fibers. Like cadherins, integrins also bind to actin or intermediate filaments in the cytosol of the cell, via linker proteins, to promote a strong association between the cytoskeleton of a cell and the extracellular matrix. Thus, integrins have an extracellular domain for the binding of ECM components and an intracellular domain for the binding of cytosolic proteins.

When these CAMs were first discovered, researchers imagined that cadherins and integrins played only a mechanical role. In other words, their functions were described as holding cells together or to the ECM. More recently, however, experiments have shown that cadherins and integrins are also important in cell communication. When cell-to-cell and cell-to-ECM junctions are formed or broken, this affects signal transduction pathways within the cell. Similarly, intracellular signal transduction pathways can affect cadherins and integrins in ways that alter intercellular junctions and the binding of cells to ECM components.

Abnormalities in CAMs such as integrins are often associated with the ability of cancer cells to metastasize, that is, to move to other parts of the body. Cell adhesion molecules are critical for keeping cells in their correct locations. When they become defective due to cancer-causing mutations, cells lose their proper connections with the ECM and adjacent cells and may spread to other parts of the body. This topic is considered in more detail in Chapter 14.

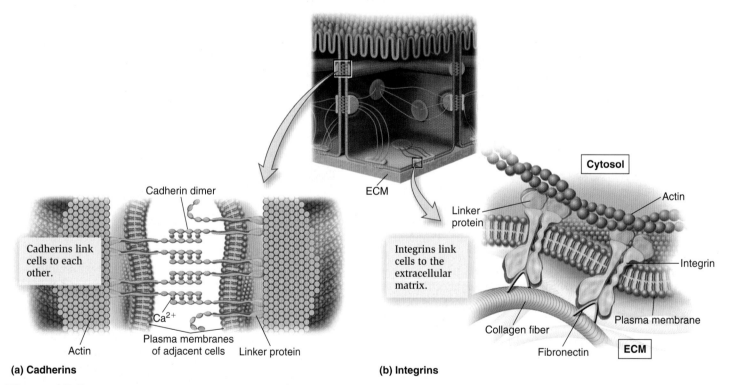

(a) Cadherins

(b) Integrins

Figure 10.8   Types of cell adhesion molecules (CAMs).   Cadherins and integrins are CAMs that form connections in anchoring junctions. **(a)** A cadherin in one cell binds to a cadherin of an identical type in an adjacent cell. This binding requires Ca^{2+}. In the cytosol, cadherins bind to actin or intermediate filaments of the cytoskeleton via linker proteins. **(b)** Integrins link cells to the extracellular matrix and form intracellular connections to actin or intermediate filaments. Each integrin protein is composed of two nonidentical subunits, a heterodimer.

Tight Junctions Prevent the Leakage of Materials Across Animal Cell Layers

In animals, **tight junctions**, or occluding junctions, are a second type of junction, one that forms a tight seal between adjacent cells and thereby prevents material from leaking between cells. As an example, let's consider the intestine. The cells that line the intestine form a sheet that is one cell thick. One side faces the intestinal lumen, and the other faces the ECM and blood vessels (Figure 10.9). Tight junctions between these cells ensure that nutrients pass through the plasma membranes of the intestinal cells before entering the blood, and also prevent the leakage of materials from the blood into the intestine.

Tight junctions are made by membrane proteins, called occludin and claudin, that form interlaced strands in the plasma membrane (see inset to Figure 10.9). These strands of proteins, each in adjacent cells, bind to each other and thereby form a tight seal between cells. Tight junctions are not mechanically strong like anchoring junctions, because they do not have strong connections with the cytoskeleton. Therefore, adjacent cells that have tight junctions also have anchoring junctions to hold the cells in place.

The amazing ability of tight junctions to prevent the leakage of material across cell layers has been demonstrated by

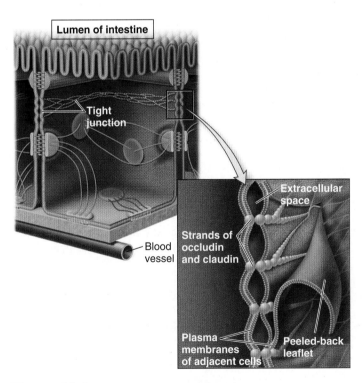

Figure 10.9 **Tight junctions between adjacent intestinal cells.** In this example, tight junctions form a seal that prevents the movement of material between cells, from the intestinal lumen into the blood, and vice versa. The inset shows the interconnected network of occludin and claudin that forms the tight junction.

Concept check: *What do you think is the role of tight junctions in the epidermal layers of your skin?*

dye-injection studies. In 1972, Daniel Friend and Norton Gilula injected lanthanum, a metallic element that is electron dense and can be visualized under the electron microscope, into the bloodstream of a rat. A few minutes later, a sample of a cell layer in the digestive tract was removed and visualized by electron microscopy. As seen in the micrograph in Figure 10.10, lanthanum diffused into the region between the cells that faces the blood, but it could not move past the tight junction to the side of the cell layer facing the lumen of the digestive tract.

Gap Junctions in Animal Cells Provide a Passageway for Intercellular Transport

A third type of junction found in animals is called a **gap junction**, because a small gap occurs between the plasma membranes of cells connected by these junctions (Figure 10.11). Gap junctions are abundant in tissues and organs where the cells need to communicate with each other. For example, cardiac muscle cells, which cause your heart to beat, are interconnected by many gap junctions. Because gap junctions allow the passage of ions, electrical changes in one cardiac muscle cell are easily transmitted to an adjacent cell that is connected via gap junctions. This is needed for the coordinated contraction of cardiac muscle cells.

In vertebrates, gap junctions are composed of an integral membrane protein called connexin. Invertebrates have a structurally similar protein called innexin. Six connexin proteins in one vertebrate cell align with six connexin proteins in an adjacent cell to form a channel called a **connexon** (see inset to Figure 10.11).

The connexons allow the passage of ions and small molecules with a molecular mass that is less than 1,000 Daltons, including amino acids, sugars, and signaling molecules such as

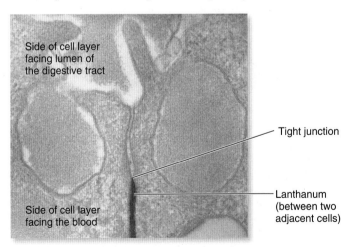

Figure 10.10 **An experiment demonstrating the function of a tight junction.** When lanthanum was injected into the bloodstream of a rat, it diffused between the cells in the region up to a tight junction but could not diffuse past the junction to the other side of the cell layer.

Concept check: *What results would you expect if a rat was fed lanthanum and then a sample of intestinal cells was observed under the EM?*

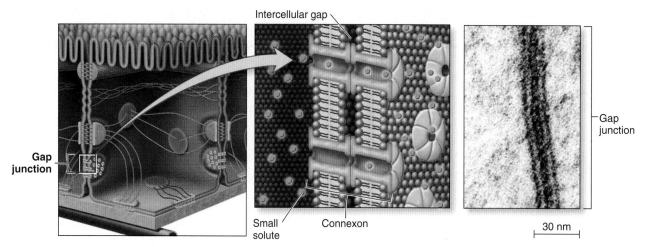

Figure 10.11   Gap junctions between adjacent cells. Gap junctions form intercellular channels that allow the passage of small solutes with masses less than 1,000 Daltons. A transmembrane channel called a connexon consists of 12 proteins called connexins, 6 in each cell. The micrograph shows a gap junction between intestinal cells.

Ca^{2+}, cAMP, and IP_3. In this way, gap junctions allow adjacent cells to share metabolites and directly signal each other. At the same time, gap-junction channels are too small to allow the passage of RNA, proteins, or polysaccharides. Therefore, cells that communicate via gap junctions still maintain their own distinctive set of macromolecules.

FEATURE INVESTIGATION

Loewenstein and Colleagues Followed the Transfer of Fluorescent Dyes to Determine the Size of Gap-Junction Channels

As mentioned, gap junctions allow the passage of small molecules, those with a mass up to about 1,000 Daltons. This property of gap junctions was determined in experiments involving the transfer of fluorescent dyes. During the 1960s, several research groups began using fluorescent dyes to study cell morphology and function. As discussed in Chapter 4, the location of fluorescent dyes within cells can be seen via fluorescence microscopy. In 1964, Werner Loewenstein and colleagues observed that a fluorescent dye could move from one cell to an adjacent cell, which prompted them to investigate this phenomenon further.

In the experiment shown in **Figure 10.12**, Loewenstein and colleagues grew rat liver cells in the laboratory, where they formed a single layer. The adjacent cells formed gap junctions. Single cells were injected with various dyes composed of fluorescently labeled amino acids or peptide molecules with different masses, and then the cell layers were observed via fluorescence microscopy. As shown in The Data, the researchers observed that dyes with a molecular mass up to 901 Daltons passed from cell to cell. Larger dyes, however, did not move intercellularly. Loewenstein and other researchers subsequently investigated dye transfer in other cell types and species. Though some variation is found when comparing different cell types and species, the researchers generally observed that molecules with a mass greater than 1,000 Daltons do not pass through gap junctions.

Figure 10.12   Use of fluorescent molecules by Loewenstein and colleagues to determine the size of gap-junction channels.

HYPOTHESIS Gap-junction channels allow the passage of ions and molecules, but there is a limit to how large the molecules can be.

KEY MATERIALS Rat liver cells grown in the laboratory, a collection of fluorescent dyes.

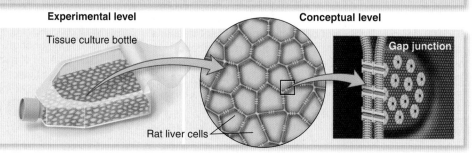

1   Grow rat liver cells in a laboratory on solid growth media until they become a single layer. At this point, adjacent cells have formed gap junctions.

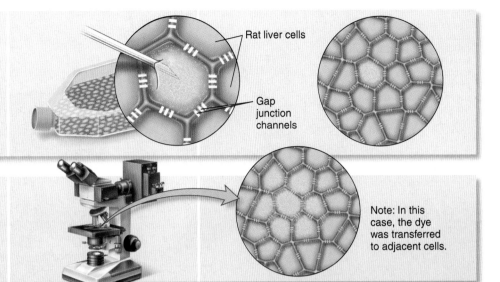

2 Inject 1 cell in the layer with fluorescently labeled amino acids or peptides. Note: Several dyes with different molecular masses were tested.

Rat liver cells

Gap junction channels

3 Incubate for various lengths of time (for example, 40–45 minutes). Observe cell layer under the fluorescence microscope to determine if the dye has moved to adjacent cells.

Note: In this case, the dye was transferred to adjacent cells.

4 **THE DATA**

Mass of dye (in Daltons)	Transfer to adjacent cells*	Mass of dye	Transfer to adjacent cells*
376	+ + + +	851**	−
464	+ + + +	901	+ + +
536	+ + +	946	−
559	+ + + +	1004	−
665	+	1158	−
688	+ + + +	1678	−
817	+ + +	1830	−

*The number of pluses indicates the relative speed of transfer. Four pluses denote fast transfer, whereas one plus is slow transfer. A minus indicates that transfer between cells did not occur. ** In some cases, molecules with less mass did not pass between cells compared to molecules with a higher mass. This may be due to differences in their structures (for example, charges) that influence whether or not they can easily penetrate the channel.

5 **CONCLUSION** Gap junctions allow the intercellular movement of molecules that have a mass of approximately 900 Daltons or less.

6 **SOURCE** Flagg-Newton, J., Simpson, I., and Loewenstein, W.R. 1979. Permeability of the Cell-to-Cell Membrane Channels in Mammalian Cell Junction. *Science* 205:404–407.

Experimental Questions

1. What was the purpose of the study conducted by Loewenstein and colleagues?

2. Explain the experimental procedure used by Loewenstein to determine the size of gap-junction channels.

3. What did the results of Figure 10.12 indicate about the size of gap-junction channels?

The Middle Lamella Cements Adjacent Plant Cell Walls Together

In animals, we have seen that cell-to-cell contact, via anchoring junctions, tight junctions, and gap junctions, involves interactions between membrane proteins in adjacent cells. In plants, cell junctions are quite different. Rather than using membrane proteins to form cell-to-cell connections, plant cells make an additional component called the **middle lamella** (plural, lamellae), which is found between most adjacent plant cells (**Figure 10.13**). When plant cells are dividing, the middle lamella is the first layer formed. The primary cell wall is then made. The middle lamella is rich in pectins, negatively charged polysaccharides that are also found in the primary cell wall (see Figure 10.5). These polymers attract water and make a hydrated gel. Ca^{2+} and Mg^{2+} interact with the negative charges in the

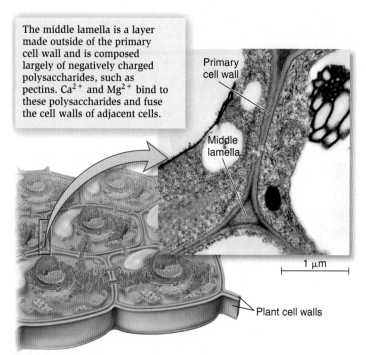

The middle lamella is a layer made outside of the primary cell wall and is composed largely of negatively charged polysaccharides, such as pectins. Ca^{2+} and Mg^{2+} bind to these polysaccharides and fuse the cell walls of adjacent cells.

Primary cell wall

Middle lamella

Plant cell walls

1 μm

Figure 10.13 Plant cell-to-cell junctions known as middle lamellae.

Concept check: *How are middle lamellae similar to the anchoring junctions and desmosomes found between animal cells? How are they different?*

polysaccharides and cement the cell walls of adjacent cells together.

The process of fruit ripening illustrates the importance of pectins in holding plant cells together. An unripened fruit, such as a green tomato, is very firm because the rigid cell walls of adjacent cells are firmly attached to each other. During ripening, the cells secrete a group of enzymes called pectinases, which digest pectins in the middle lamella as well as those in the primary cell wall. As this process continues, the attachments between cells are broken, and the cell walls become less rigid. For this reason, a red ripe tomato is much less firm than an unripe tomato.

Plasmodesmata Are Channels Connecting the Cytoplasm of Adjacent Plant Cells

In 1879, Eduard Tangl, a Russian botanist, observed intercellular connections in the seeds of the strychnine tree and hypothesized that the cytoplasm of adjacent cells is connected by ducts in the cell walls. He was the first to propose that direct cell-to-cell communication integrates the functioning of plant cells. The ducts or intercellular channels that Tangl observed are now known as **plasmodesmata** (singular, plasmodesma).

Plasmodesmata are functionally similar to gap junctions in animal cells because they allow the passage of ions and molecules between adjacent plant cells. However, the structure of plasmodesmata is quite different from that of gap junctions. As shown in **Figure 10.14**, plasmodesmata are channels in the cell walls of adjacent cells. At these sites, the plasma membrane of

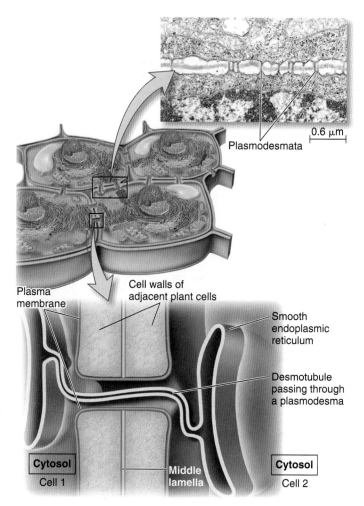

Plasmodesmata

0.6 μm

Plasma membrane

Cell walls of adjacent plant cells

Smooth endoplasmic reticulum

Desmotubule passing through a plasmodesma

Cytosol
Cell 1

Middle lamella

Cytosol
Cell 2

Figure 10.14 Structure of plasmodesmata.
Plasmodesmata are cell junctions connecting the cytosol of adjacent plant cells, allowing water, ions, and molecules to pass from cell to cell. At these sites, the plasma membrane of one cell is continuous with the plasma membrane of an adjacent cell. In addition, the ER from one cell is connected to that of the adjacent cell via a desmotubule.

one cell is continuous with the plasma membrane of the other cell, which permits the diffusion of molecules from the cytosol of one cell to the cytosol of the other. In addition to a cytosolic connection, plasmodesmata also have a central tubule, called a desmotubule, connecting the ER membranes of adjacent cells.

Plasmodesmata can change the size of their opening between closed, open, and dilated states. In the open state, they allow the passage of ions and small molecules, such as sugars and cAMP. In this state, plasmodesmata play a similar role to gap junctions between animal cells. Plasmodesmata tend to close when a large pressure difference occurs between adjacent cells. Why does this happen? One reason is related to cell damage. When a plant is wounded, damaged cells will lose their turgor pressure. (Turgor pressure is described in Chapter 5; refer back to Figure 5.17.) The closure of plasmodesmata between adjacent cells helps to prevent the loss of water and nutrients from the wound site.

Unlike gap junctions between animal cells, researchers have recently discovered that plasmodesmata can dilate to also allow the passage of macromolecules and even viruses between adjacent plant cells. Though the mechanism of dilation is not well understood, the wider opening of plasmodesmata is important for the passage of proteins and mRNA during plant development. It also provides a key mechanism whereby viruses can move from cell to cell.

10.3 Tissues

A **tissue** is a part of an animal or plant consisting of a group of cells having a similar structure and function. In this section, we will view tissues from the perspective of cell biology. Animals and plants contain many different types of cells. Humans, for example, contain over 200 different cell types, each with a specific structure and function. Even so, these cells can be grouped into a few general categories. For example, muscle cells found in your heart (cardiac muscle cells), in your biceps (skeletal muscle cells), and around your arteries (smooth muscle cells) look somewhat different under the microscope and have unique roles in the body. Yet due to structural and functional similarities, all three types can be categorized as muscle tissue. In this section, we will begin by surveying the basic processes that cells undergo to make tissues. Next, we will examine the main categories of animal and plant tissues. We will conclude by taking a more in-depth look at some differences and similarities between selected animal and plant tissues, focusing in particular on the functions of the ECM and cell junctions.

Six Basic Cell Processes Produce Tissues and Organs

A multicellular organism such as a plant or animal contains many cells. For example, an adult human has somewhere between 10 and 100 trillion cells in her or his body. Cells are organized into tissues, and tissues are organized into organs. An **organ** is a collection of two or more tissues that performs a specific function or set of functions. The heart is an organ found in the bodies of complex animals, while a leaf is an organ found in plants. We will examine the structures and functions of organs in Units VI and VII.

How are tissues and organs formed? To form tissues and organs, cells undergo six basic processes that influence their morphology, arrangement, and number: cell division, cell growth, differentiation, migration, apoptosis, and the formation of cell connections.

1. *Cell division:* As discussed in Chapter 15, eukaryotic cells progress through a cell cycle that leads to cell division.
2. *Cell growth:* Following cell division, cells take up nutrients and usually expand in volume. Cell division and cell growth are the primary mechanisms for increasing the size of tissues, organs, and organisms.
3. *Differentiation:* Due to gene regulation, cells differentiate into specialized types of cells. Cell differentiation is described in Chapter 19.
4. *Migration:* During embryonic development in animals, cells migrate to their appropriate positions within the body. Also, adults have cells that can move into regions that have become damaged. Cell migration does not occur during plant development.

5. *Apoptosis:* Cell death, also known as apoptosis (discussed in Chapter 9), is necessary to produce certain morphological features of the body. For example, during development in mammals, the formation of individual fingers and toes requires the removal, by apoptosis, of the skin cells between them.
6. *Cell connections:* In the first section of this chapter, we learned that cells produce an extracellular matrix or cell wall that provides strength and support. In animals, the ECM serves to organize cells within tissues and organs. In plants, the cell wall is largely responsible for the shapes of plant tissues. Different types of cell junctions in both animal and plant cells enable cells to make physical contact and communicate with one another.

Animals Are Composed of Epithelial, Connective, Nervous, and Muscle Tissues

The body of an animal contains four general types of tissue—epithelial, connective, nervous, and muscle—that serve very different purposes (**Figure 10.15**).

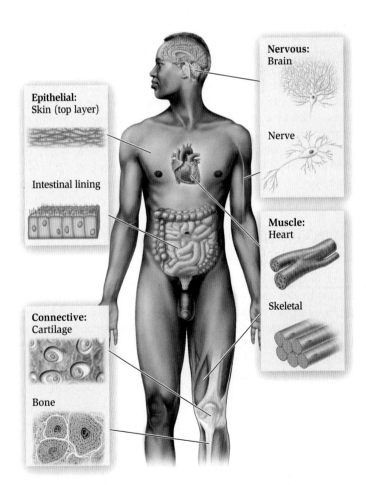

Figure 10.15 Examples of the four general types of tissues—epithelial, connective, nervous, and muscle—found in animals.

Concept check: Which of these four types of tissues would have the most extensive ECM?

Epithelial Tissue   **Epithelial tissue** is composed of cells that are joined together via tight junctions and form continuous sheets. Epithelial tissue covers or forms the lining of all internal and external body surfaces. For example, epithelial tissue lines organs such as the lungs and digestive tract. In addition, epithelial tissue forms skin, a protective surface that shields the body from the outside environment.

Connective Tissue   Most **connective tissue** provides support to the body and/or helps to connect different tissues to each other. Connective tissue is rich in extracellular matrix. In some cases, the tissue contains only a sparse population of cells that are embedded in the ECM. Examples of connective tissue include cartilage, tendons, bone, fat tissue, and the inner layers of the skin. Blood is also considered a form of connective tissue because it provides liquid connections to various regions of the body.

Nervous Tissue   **Nervous tissue** receives, generates, and conducts electrical signals throughout the body. In vertebrates, these electrical signals are integrated by nervous tissue in the brain and transmitted down the spinal cord to the rest of the body. Chapter 41 considers the cellular basis for nerve signals, and Chapters 42 and 43 examine the organization of nervous systems in animals.

Muscle Tissue   **Muscle tissue** can generate a force that facilitates movement. Muscle contraction is needed for bodily movements such as walking and running and also plays a role in the movement of materials throughout the body. For example, contraction of heart muscle propels blood through your body, and smooth muscle contractions move food through the digestive system. The properties of muscle tissue in animals are examined in Chapter 46.

Plants Contain Dermal, Ground, and Vascular Tissues

Plant biologists usually classify tissues as simple or complex. Simple tissues are usually composed of one or possibly two cell types. Complex tissues are composed of two or more cell types but lack an organization that would qualify them as organs. The bodies of most plants contain three general types of tissue—dermal, ground, and vascular—each with a different structure suited to its functions (**Figure 10.16**).

Dermal Tissue   The **dermal tissue** is a complex tissue that forms a covering on various parts of the plant. The **epidermis** refers to the newly made tissue on the surfaces of leaves, stems, and roots. Surfaces of leaves are usually coated with a waxy cuticle to prevent water loss. In addition, leaf epidermis often has hairs, or trichomes, which are specialized types of epidermal cells. Trichomes have diverse functions, including the secretion of oils and leaf protection. Epidermal cells called guard cells form pores in leaves, known as stomata, that permit gas exchange. The function of the root epidermis is the

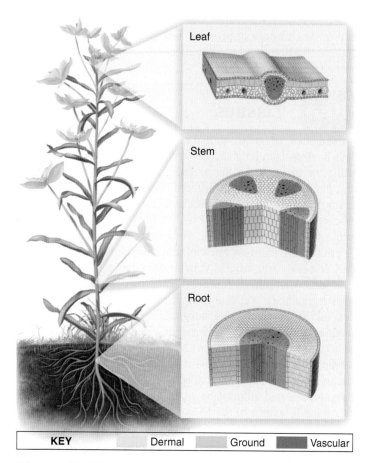

Figure 10.16   Locations of the three general types of tissues—dermal, ground, and vascular—found in plants.

Concept check: *Which of these three types of tissues would be found on the surfaces of leaves, stems, and roots?*

absorption of water and nutrients. The root epidermis does not have a waxy cuticle because such a cuticle would inhibit water and nutrient absorption.

Ground Tissue   Most of a plant's body is made of **ground tissue**, which has a variety of functions, including photosynthesis, storage of carbohydrates, and support. Ground tissue can be subdivided into three types of simple tissues: parenchyma, collenchyma, and sclerenchyma. Let's look briefly at each of these types of ground tissue.

1. Parenchyma tissue is very active metabolically. The mesophyll, the central part of the leaf that carries out the bulk of photosynthesis, is parenchyma tissue. Parenchyma tissue also functions in the storage of carbohydrates. The cells of parenchyma tissue usually lack a secondary cell wall.

2. Collenchyma tissue provides structural support to the plant body, particularly to growing regions such as the periphery of the stems and leaves. Collenchyma cells tend to have thick, secondary cell walls but do not contain much lignin. Therefore, they provide support but are also able to stretch.

3. Sclerenchyma tissue also provides structural support to the plant body, particularly to those parts that are no longer growing, such as the dense, woody parts of stems. The secondary cell walls of sclerenchyma cells tend to have large amounts of lignin and thereby provide rigid support. In many cases, sclerenchyma cells are dead at maturity, but their cell walls continue to provide structural support during the life of the plant.

Vascular Tissue Most plants living today are vascular plants. In these species, which include ferns and seed plants, the **vascular tissue** is a complex tissue composed of cells that are interconnected and form conducting vessels for water and nutrients. There are two types of vascular tissue called xylem and phloem. The xylem transports water and mineral ions from the root to the rest of the plant, while the phloem distributes the products of photosynthesis and a variety of other nutrients throughout the plant. Some types of modern plants, such as mosses, are nonvascular plants that lack conducting vessels. These plants tend to be small and live in damp, shady places.

Animal and Plant Tissues Have Striking Differences and Similarities

Because plants and animals appear strikingly different, it is not too surprising their cells and tissues show conspicuous differences. For example, the vascular tissue of plants (which transports water and nutrients) does not resemble any one tissue in animals. The blood vessels of animals (which transport blood carrying oxygen and nutrients throughout the body) are hollow tubes that contain both connective and muscle tissue. In addition, animals have two tissue types that are not found in plants: muscle and nervous tissue. Even so, plants are capable of movement and the transmission of signals via action potentials. For example, the Venus flytrap (*Dionaea muscipula*) has two modified leaves that resemble a clamshell. When an insect touches the trichomes on the surface of these leaves, an electrical signal is triggered that causes the leaves to move closer to each other, thereby trapping the unsuspecting insect.

Although cellular differences are prominent between plants and animals, certain tissues show intriguing similarities. Why are there similarities between some animal and plant tissues? The answer is that certain types of cell organization and structure provide functions that are needed by both animals and plants. For example, the epithelial tissue of animals and the dermal tissue of plants both form a protective covering over the organism. Also, the connective tissue of animals and the ground tissue of plants both play a role in structural support. Let's take a closer look at the similarities between these tissues in animals and plants.

A Comparison of Epithelial and Dermal Tissues Both the epithelial tissue in animals (also called an epithelium) and dermal tissue in plants form layers of cells. Let's begin with epithelial tissue. An epithelium can be classified according to its number of layers. Simple epithelium is one cell layer thick,

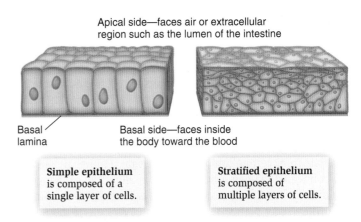

Apical side—faces air or extracellular region such as the lumen of the intestine

Basal lamina

Basal side—faces inside the body toward the blood

Simple epithelium is composed of a single layer of cells.

Stratified epithelium is composed of multiple layers of cells.

Figure 10.17 Simple and stratified epithelia in animals.

whereas stratified epithelium has several layers (**Figure 10.17**). In both cases, the epithelium has a polarity, which is due to an asymmetry to its organization. The outer, or apical, side of an epithelium is exposed to air or to a watery fluid such as the lumen of the intestine. The inner, or basal, side faces toward the blood. The basal side of the epithelium rests on some type of support, such as another type of tissue or on a form of ECM called the basal lamina.

A hallmark of epithelial cells is they form many connections with each other. For example, in the simple epithelium lining the intestine (**Figure 10.18**), adjacent cells form

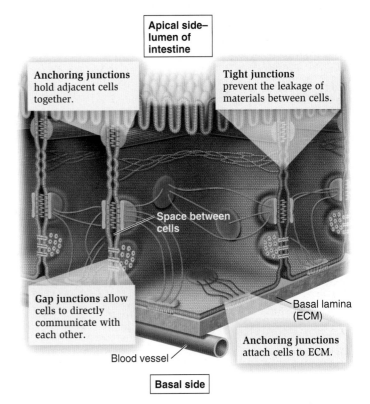

Apical side– lumen of intestine

Anchoring junctions hold adjacent cells together.

Tight junctions prevent the leakage of materials between cells.

Space between cells

Gap junctions allow cells to directly communicate with each other.

Basal lamina (ECM)

Anchoring junctions attach cells to ECM.

Blood vessel

Basal side

Figure 10.18 Connections between cells of a simple epithelium that lines the intestine. This figure emphasizes the three major types of cell junctions that are common in epithelial tissue.

anchoring junctions with each other and with the basal lamina. These anchoring junctions hold the cells firmly in place. Tight junctions, found near the apical surface, prevent the leakage of materials from the lumen of the intestine into the blood. Instead, nutrients are selectively transported from the intestinal lumen into the cytosol of the epithelial cell and then are exported across the basal side of the cell into the blood. This phenomenon, called transepithelial transport, allows the body to take up the nutrients it needs while preventing unwanted materials from getting into the bloodstream. Epithelial cells are also connected via gap junctions, which allow the exchange of nutrients and signaling molecules throughout the epithelium.

In flowering plants, the epidermis covers all of the newly made parts of a plant. For example, the upper and lower sides of leaves are covered by epidermis, which is usually a single layer of closely packed cells (Figure 10.19a). Epidermal cells have a thick primary cell wall and are tightly interlocked by their middle lamella. As a consequence, plant epidermal cells are tightly woven together, much like epithelial cell layers in animals.

As a plant ages, the epidermis may be replaced by another dermal tissue called the periderm (Figure 10.19b). In woody plants, an example of periderm is the bark on trees. Periderm

protects a plant from pathogens, prevents excessive water loss, and provides insulation. The periderm consists of interconnected cork cells, which may be several layers thick. The cork cells have extremely thick cell walls. When cork cells reach maturity, they die, but the cell walls continue to provide support.

A Comparison of Connective and Ground Tissue In contrast to epithelial tissue, which is mostly composed of cells, the connective tissue of animals is largely composed of extracellular matrix and has relatively few cells. In animal connective tissue, cell-to-cell contact is somewhat infrequent. Instead, cells are usually adhered to the ECM via integrins, as shown earlier in Figure 10.8b. In some cases, the primary function of cells within connective tissue is to synthesize the components of the ECM. For example, let's consider cartilage, a connective tissue found in joints such as your knees. The cells that synthesize cartilage, known as chondrocytes, actually represent a small proportion of the total volume of cartilage. As shown in Figure 10.20, the chondrocytes are found in small cavities within the cartilage called lacunae (singular, lacuna). In some types of cartilage, the chondrocytes represent only 1–2% of the total volume of the tissue! Chondrocytes are the only cells found in cartilage. They are solely responsible for the synthesis of protein fibers, such as collagen, as well as glycosaminoglycans and proteoglycans that are found in cartilage.

Similar to connective tissue in animals, ground tissue in plants provides structural support. Figure 10.21 shows a scanning electron micrograph of sclerenchyma cells found in *Arabidopsis thaliana*, a model plant studied by plant biologists. At maturity, the cells are dead, but the thick secondary cell walls continue to provide rigid support for the stem. However, not all cells in ground tissue have thick cell walls. For example, mesophyll cells are a type of parenchyma cell in the leaf that carry out photosynthesis. Because a thick cell wall would inhibit the transmission of light, mesophyll cells have relatively thin cell walls.

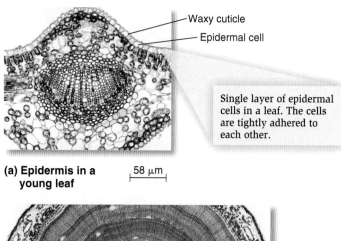

Waxy cuticle
Epidermal cell

Single layer of epidermal cells in a leaf. The cells are tightly adhered to each other.

(a) Epidermis in a young leaf   58 μm

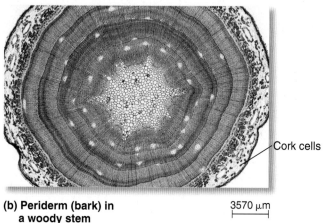

Cork cells

(b) Periderm (bark) in a woody stem   3570 μm

Figure 10.19   Dermal tissues in plants.

Concept check: Do you notice any parallels between simple epithelium and epidermis, and between stratified epithelium and periderm?

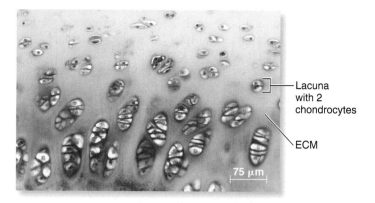

Lacuna with 2 chondrocytes

ECM

75 μm

Figure 10.20   An example of connective tissue in animals that is rich in extracellular matrix.   This micrograph of cartilage shows chondrocytes in the ECM. The chondrocytes, which are responsible for making the components of cartilage, are found in cavities called lacunae.

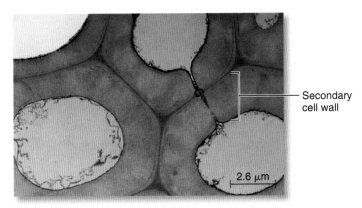

Secondary
cell wall

2.6 μm

Figure 10.21   **An example of ground tissue in plants.**
This scanning electron micrograph shows sclerenchyma cells
from *Arabidopsis thaliana*. The cells themselves are dead; only
their thick secondary cell walls remain. These cell walls provide
structural support to the plant.

Concept check: *Do you notice any parallels between ground
tissue in plants and connective tissue in animals?*

Summary of Key Concepts

10.1 Extracellular Matrix and Cell Walls

- The extracellular matrix (ECM) is a network of material that
  forms a complex meshwork outside of animal cells. Plant cells
  are surrounded by cell walls.

- In the ECM of animals, proteins and polysaccharides are
  the major constituents. These materials are involved in
  strength, structural support, organization, and cell signaling.
  (Figure 10.1)

- Adhesive proteins, such as fibronectin and laminin, help
  adhere cells to the ECM. Structural proteins form fibers.
  Collagen fibers provide tensile strength, whereas elastic
  fibers allow regions of the body to stretch. (Table 10.1,
  Figures 10.2, 10.3)

- Differential gene regulation controls where in the body
  different types of collagen fibers are made. (Table 10.2)

- Glycosaminoglycans (GAGs) are polysaccharides of repeating
  disaccharide units that give a gel-like character to the ECM of
  animals. Proteoglycans consist of a core protein with attached
  GAGs. (Figure 10.4)

- Plant cells are surrounded by a cell wall. The primary cell wall
  is made first. It is composed largely of cellulose. The secondary
  cell wall is made after the primary cell wall and is often quite
  thick and rigid. (Figures 10.5, 10.6)

10.2 Cell Junctions

- The three common types of cell junctions found in animals are
  anchoring, tight, and gap junctions. Plant junctions include
  middle lamella and plasmodesmata. (Table 10.3)

- Anchoring junctions involve cell adhesion molecules (CAMs),
  which bind cells to each other or to the ECM. The four types

are adherens junctions, desmosomes, hemidesmosomes, and
focal adhesions. (Figure 10.7)

- Two types of CAMs are cadherins and integrins. Cadherins link
  cells to each other, whereas integrins link cells to the ECM.
  In the cytosol, CAMs bind to actin or intermediate filaments.
  (Figure 10.8)

- Tight junctions between cells, composed of occludin and
  claudin, prevent the leakage of materials across a layer of cells.
  (Figures 10.9, 10.10)

- Gap junctions form channels called connexons that permit the
  direct passage of materials between adjacent cells. (Figure 10.11)

- Experiments of Loewenstein and colleagues involving the
  transfer of fluorescent dyes showed that gap junctions permit
  the passage of substances with a molecular mass of less than
  1,000 Daltons. (Figure 10.12)

- The cell walls of adjacent plant cells are cemented together
  via middle lamella. (Figure 10.13)

- Adjacent plant cells usually have direct connections called
  plasmodesmata, which are channels in the cell walls where
  the plasma membranes of adjacent cells are continuous with
  each other. The endoplasmic reticula of adjacent cells are also
  connected via plasmodesmata. (Figure 10.14)

10.3 Tissues

- A tissue is a group of cells that have a similar structure and
  function. An organ is composed of two or more tissues and
  carries out a particular function or functions.

- Six processes—cell division, cell growth, differentiation,
  migration, apoptosis, and the formation of cell connections—
  produce tissues and organs.

- The four general kinds of tissues found in animals are epithelial,
  connective, nervous, and muscle tissues. (Figure 10.15)

- The three general kinds of tissues found in plants are dermal,
  ground, and vascular tissues. (Figure 10.16)

- Epithelial and dermal tissues form layers of cells that are highly
  interconnected. These layers can be one cell thick or several
  cells thick, and they serve as protective coverings for various
  parts of animal and plant bodies. (Figures 10.17, 10.18, 10.19)

- Connective and ground tissues often play a structural role in
  animals and plants. (Figures 10.20, 10.21)

Assess and Discuss

Test Yourself

1. The function of the extracellular matrix (ECM) in animals is
   a. to provide strength.
   b. to provide structural support.
   c. to organize cells and other body parts.
   d. cell signaling.
   e. all of the above.

2. The protein found in the ECM of animals that provides strength
   and resistance to tearing when stretched is
   a. elastin.   c. collagen.   e. fibronectin.
   b. cellulose.   d. laminin.

3. The polysaccharide that forms the hard outer covering of many invertebrates is
   a. collagen.   c. chondroitin sulfate.   e. cellulose.
   b. chitin.   d. pectin.

4. The extension sequence found in procollagen polypeptides
   a. causes procollagen to be synthesized into the ER lumen.
   b. causes procollagen to form a triple helix.
   c. prevents procollagen from forming large collagen fibers.
   d. causes procollagen to be secreted from the cell.
   e. Both b and c are correct.

5. The dilated state of plasmodesmata allows the passage of
   a. water.
   b. ions.
   c. small molecules.
   d. macromolecules and viruses.
   e. all of the above.

6. The gap junctions of animal cells differ from the plasmodesmata of plant cells in that
   a. gap junctions serve as communicating junctions and plasmodesmata serve as adhesion junctions.
   b. gap junctions prevent extracellular material from moving between adjacent cells but the plasmodesmata do not.
   c. gap junctions allow for direct exchange of cellular material between cells but plasmodesmata cannot allow the same type of exchange.
   d. gap junctions are formed by specialized proteins that form channels through the membranes of adjacent cells but plasmodesmata are not formed by specialized proteins.
   e. All of the above are correct.

7. Which of the following is involved in the process of tissue and organ formation in multicellular organisms?
   a. cell division
   b. cell growth
   c. cell differentiation
   d. cell connections
   e. all of the above

8. The tissue type common to animals that functions in the conduction of electrical signals is
   a. epithelial.
   b. dermal.
   c. muscle.
   d. nervous.
   e. ground.

9. A type of tissue that is rich in ECM or has cells with a thick cell wall would be
   a. dermal tissue in plants.
   b. ground tissue in plants.
   c. nervous tissue in animals.
   d. connective tissue in animals.
   e. both b and d.

10. Which of the following is not a correct statement when comparing plant tissues to animal tissues?
    a. Nervous tissue of animals plays the same role as vascular tissue in plants.
    b. The dermal tissue of plants is similar to epithelial tissue of animals in that both provide a covering for the organism.
    c. The epithelial tissue of animals and the dermal tissue of plants have special characteristics that limit the movement of material between cell layers.
    d. The ground tissue of plants and the connective tissue of animals provide structural support for the organism.
    e. All of the above are correct comparisons between animal and plant tissues.

Conceptual Questions

1. What are key differences between the primary cell wall and the secondary cell wall of plant cells?

2. What are similarities and differences in the structures and functions of cadherins and integrins found in animal cells?

3. What are the six basic cell processes required to make tissues and organs?

Collaborative Questions

1. Discuss the similarities and differences between the extracellular matrix of animals and the cell walls of plants.

2. Cell junctions in animals are important in preventing cancer cells from metastasizing—moving to other parts of the body. Certain drugs can bind to CAMs and influence their structure and function. Some of these drugs may help to prevent the spread of cancer cells. What would you hypothesize to be the mechanism by which such drugs work? What might be some harmful side effects?

Online Resource

www.brookerbiology.com

Stay a step ahead in your studies with animations that bring concepts to life and practice tests to assess your understanding. Your instructor may also recommend the interactive ebook, individualized learning tools, and more.

Nucleic Acid Structure, DNA Replication, and Chromosome Structure

11

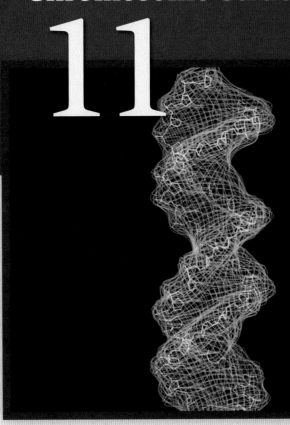

A molecular model for the structure of a DNA double helix.

O n October 17, 2001, Mario K. was set free after serving 16 years in prison. He had been convicted of sexual assault and murder. The charges were dropped because investigators discovered that another person, Edwin M., had actually committed the crime. How was Edwin M. identified as the real murderer? In 2001, he committed another crime, and his DNA was entered into a computer database. Edwin's DNA matched the DNA that had been collected from the victim in 1985, and other evidence was then gathered indicating that Edwin M. was the true murderer. Like Mario K., over 200 other inmates have been exonerated when DNA tests have shown that a different person was responsible for the crime.

Deoxyribonucleic acid, or DNA, is the genetic material that provides the blueprint to produce an individual's traits. Each person's DNA is distinct and unique. Even identical twins show minor differences in their DNA sequences. We begin our survey of genetics by examining DNA at the molecular level. Once we understand how DNA works at this level, it becomes easier to see how the function of DNA controls the properties of cells and ultimately the characteristics of unicellular and multicellular organisms. The past several decades have seen exciting advances in techniques and approaches to investigate and even to alter the genetic material. Not only have these advances greatly expanded our understanding of molecular genetics, such technologies are also widely used in related disciplines such as biochemistry, cell biology, and microbiology. Likewise, genetic techniques have many important applications in biotechnology and are used in criminal justice, including forensics, to provide evidence of guilt or innocence.

To a large extent, our understanding of genetics comes from our knowledge of the molecular structure of DNA. In this chapter, we begin by considering some classic experiments that were consistent with the theory that DNA is the genetic material. We will then survey the molecular features of DNA, which will allow us to appreciate how DNA can store information and be accurately copied. Though this chapter is largely concerned with DNA, we will also consider the components of ribonucleic acid (RNA), which bear some striking similarities to DNA. Lastly, we will examine the molecular composition of chromosomes where the DNA is found.

11.1 Biochemical Identification of the Genetic Material

DNA carries the genetic instructions for the physical characteristics of living organisms. In the case of multicellular organisms such as plants and animals, the information stored in the genetic material enables a fertilized egg to develop into an embryo and eventually into an adult organism. In addition, the genetic material allows organisms to survive in their native environments. For example, an individual's DNA provides the blueprint to produce enzymes that are needed to metabolize nutrients in food. To fulfill its role, the genetic material must meet the following key criteria:

1. **Information:** The genetic material must contain the information necessary to construct an entire organism.
2. **Replication:** The genetic material must be accurately copied.
3. **Transmission:** After it is replicated, the genetic material can be passed from parent to offspring. It also must be passed from cell to cell during the process of cell division.

4. **Variation:** Differences in the genetic material must account for the known variation within each species and among different species.

How was the genetic material discovered? The quest to identify the genetic material really began in the late 1800s, when a few scientists postulated that living organisms possess a blueprint that has a biochemical basis. In 1883, August Weismann and Karl Nägeli championed the idea that a chemical substance exists within living cells that is responsible for the transmission of traits from parents to offspring. During the next 30 years, experimentation along these lines centered on the behavior of **chromosomes**, the cellular structures that we now know contain the genetic material. Taken literally, chromosome is from the Greek words *chromo* and *soma,* meaning colored body, which refers to the observation of early microscopists that the chromosomes are easily stained by colored dyes. By studying the transmission patterns of chromosomes from cell to cell and from parent to offspring, researchers were convinced that chromosomes carry the determinants that control the outcome of traits.

Ironically, the study of chromosomes initially misled researchers regarding the biochemical identity of the genetic material. Chromosomes contain two classes of macromolecules, namely, proteins and DNA. Scientists of this era viewed proteins as being more biochemically complex because they are made from 20 different amino acids. Furthermore, biochemists already knew that proteins perform an amazingly wide range of functions, and complexity seemed an important prerequisite for the blueprint of an organism. By comparison, DNA seemed less complex, because it contains only four types of repeating units, called nucleotides, which will be described later in this chapter. In addition, the functional role of DNA in the nucleus had not been extensively investigated prior to the 1920s. Therefore, from the 1920s to the 1940s, most scientists were expecting that research studies would reveal that proteins are the genetic material. Contrary to this expectation, however, the experiments described in this section were pivotal in showing that DNA carries out this critical role.

Griffith's Bacterial Transformation Experiments Indicated the Existence of a Biochemical Genetic Material

Studies in microbiology were important in developing an experimental strategy to identify the genetic material. In the late 1920s, an English microbiologist, Frederick Griffith, studied a type of bacterium known then as pneumococci and now classified as *Streptococcus pneumoniae.* Some strains of *S. pneumoniae* secrete a polysaccharide capsule, while other strains do not. When streaked on petri plates containing solid growth media, capsule-secreting strains have a smooth colony morphology and therefore look smooth to the naked eye. Those strains unable to secrete a capsule have a colony morphology that looks rough. In mammals, smooth strains of *S. pneumo-*

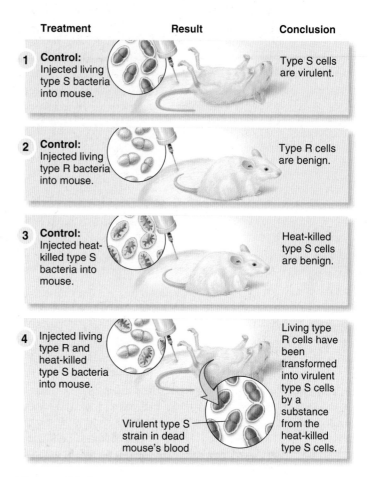

Figure 11.1 Griffith's experiments that showed the transformation of bacteria by a "transformation principle." Note: To determine if a mouse's blood contained live bacteria, a sample of blood was applied to solid growth media to determine if smooth or rough bacterial colonies would form.

Concept check: Let's suppose that the type R strain used by Griffith was resistant to killing by an antibiotic, while the type S strain lacked this trait. For the experiment described in treatment 4, would you expect the living type S bacteria found in the dead mouse's blood to be resistant to the antibiotic?

niae may cause pneumonia and other symptoms. However, in mice, such infections are often fatal.

As shown in **Figure 11.1,** Griffith injected live and/or heat-killed bacteria into mice and then observed whether or not the bacteria caused them to die. He investigated the effects of two strains of *S. pneumoniae*: type S for smooth and type R for rough. When injected into a live mouse, the type S strain killed the mouse (Figure 11.1, step 1). Such a strain is said to be virulent. The capsule present in type S strains prevents the mouse's immune system from killing the bacterial cells. Following the death of the mouse, many type S bacteria were found in the mouse's blood. By comparison, when type R bacteria were injected into a mouse, they did not kill the mouse, and after several days, living bacteria were not found in the live mouse's blood (Figure 11.1, step 2). In a follow-up to these results,

Griffith also heat-killed the smooth bacteria and then injected them into a mouse. As expected, the mouse survived (Figure 11.1, step 3).

A surprising result occurred when Griffith mixed live type R bacteria with heat-killed type S bacteria and then injected them into a mouse—the mouse died (Figure 11.1, step 4). The blood from the dead mouse contained living type S bacteria! How did Griffith explain these results? He postulated that a substance from dead type S bacteria was transforming the type R bacteria into type S bacteria. Griffith called this process **transformation**, and he termed the unidentified material responsible for this phenomenon the "transformation principle."

Now that we have examined Griffith's experiments, it's helpful if we consider what these observations mean with regard to the four criteria for the genetic material that were described previously. According to Griffith's results, the transformed bacteria had acquired the information (criterion 1) to make a capsule from the heat-killed cells. For the transformed bacteria to proliferate and thereby kill the mouse, the substance conferring the ability to make a capsule must be replicated (criterion 2) and then transmitted (criterion 3) from mother to daughter cells during cell division. Finally, Griffith already knew that variation (criterion 4) existed in the ability of his strains to produce a capsule (S strain) or not produce a capsule (R strain). Taken together, these observations are consistent with the idea that the formation of a capsule is governed by genetic material, because it meets the four criteria described at the beginning of this section. The experiment of Figure 11.1, step 4, was consistent with the idea that some genetic material from the heat-killed type S bacteria had been transferred to the living type R bacteria and provided those bacteria with a new trait. At the time of his studies, however, Griffith could not determine the biochemical composition of the transforming substance.

FEATURE INVESTIGATION

Avery, MacLeod, and McCarty Used Purification Methods to Reveal That DNA Is the Genetic Material

Exciting discoveries sometimes occur when researchers recognize that another scientist's experimental approach may be modified and then used to dig deeper into a scientific question. In the 1940s, American physician Oswald Avery and American biologists Colin MacLeod and Maclyn McCarty were also interested in the process of bacterial transformation. During the course of their studies, they realized that Griffith's observations could be used as part of an experimental strategy to biochemically identify the genetic material. They asked the question, What substance is being transferred from the dead type S bacteria to the live type R bacteria?

To answer this question, Avery, MacLeod, and McCarty needed to purify the general categories of substances found in living cells. They used established biochemical procedures to purify classes of macromolecules, such as proteins, DNA, and RNA, from the type S streptococcal strain. Initially, they discovered that only the purified DNA could convert type R bacteria into type S. To further verify that DNA is the genetic material, they performed the investigation outlined in **Figure 11.2**. They purified DNA from the type S bacteria and mixed it with type R bacteria. After allowing time for DNA uptake, they added an antibody that aggregated any nontransformed type R bacteria, which were removed by centrifugation. The remaining bacteria were incubated overnight on petri plates.

When they mixed their S strain DNA extract with type R bacteria, some of the bacteria were converted to type S bacteria (see plate B in step 5 of Figure 11.2). As a control, if no DNA extract was added, no type S bacterial colonies were observed on the petri plates (see plate A in step 5). Though this result was consistent with the idea that DNA is the genetic material, a careful biochemist could argue that the DNA extract might not be 100% pure. Realistically, any purified extract is likely to contain small traces of other substances. For this reason, the researchers realized that a small amount of contaminating material in the DNA extract could actually be the genetic material. The most likely contaminating substances in this case would be RNA or protein. To address this possibility, Avery, MacLeod, and McCarty treated the DNA extract with enzymes that digest DNA (called **DNase**), RNA (**RNase**), or protein (**protease**) (see step 2). When the DNA extracts were treated with RNase or protease, the type R bacteria were still converted into type S bacteria, suggesting that contaminating RNA or protein in the extract was not acting as the genetic material (see step 5, plates D and E). Moreover, when the extract was treated with DNase, it lost the ability to convert type R bacteria into type S bacteria (see plate C). Taken together, these results were consistent with the idea that DNA is the genetic material.

Experimental Questions

1. Avery, MacLeod, and McCarty worked with two strains of *Streptococcus pneumoniae* to determine the biochemical identity of the genetic material. Explain the characteristics of the *Streptococcus pneumoniae* strains that made them particularly well suited for such an experiment.

2. What is a DNA extract?

3. In the experiment of Avery, MacLeod, and McCarty, what was the purpose of using the protease, RNase, and DNase if only the DNA extract caused transformation?

Figure 11.2 The Avery, MacLeod, and McCarty experiments that identified DNA as Griffith's "transformation principle"—the genetic material.

HYPOTHESIS A purified macromolecule from type S bacteria, which functions as the genetic material, will be able to convert type R bacteria into type S.

KEY MATERIALS Type R and type S strains of *Streptococcus pneumoniae*.

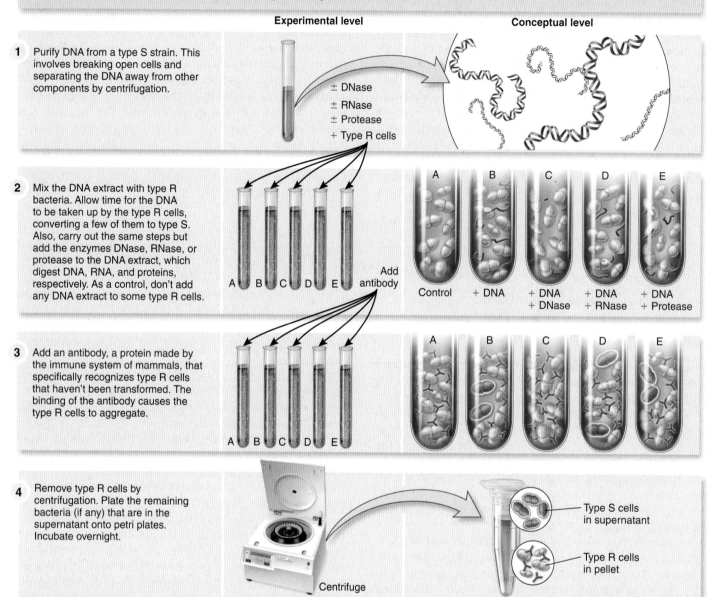

Experimental level

Conceptual level

1 Purify DNA from a type S strain. This involves breaking open cells and separating the DNA away from other components by centrifugation.

± DNase
± RNase
± Protease
+ Type R cells

2 Mix the DNA extract with type R bacteria. Allow time for the DNA to be taken up by the type R cells, converting a few of them to type S. Also, carry out the same steps but add the enzymes DNase, RNase, or protease to the DNA extract, which digest DNA, RNA, and proteins, respectively. As a control, don't add any DNA extract to some type R cells.

A B C D E

Add antibody

A   B   C   D   E

Control   + DNA   + DNA   + DNA   + DNA
                    + DNase + RNase + Protease

3 Add an antibody, a protein made by the immune system of mammals, that specifically recognizes type R cells that haven't been transformed. The binding of the antibody causes the type R cells to aggregate.

A B C D E

A   B   C   D   E

4 Remove type R cells by centrifugation. Plate the remaining bacteria (if any) that are in the supernatant onto petri plates. Incubate overnight.

Centrifuge

Type S cells in supernatant

Type R cells in pellet

5 **THE DATA**

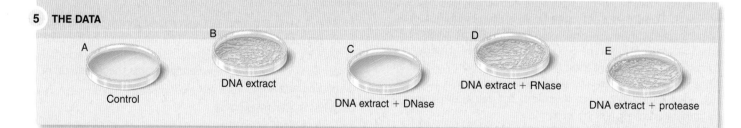

A   B   C   D   E

Control DNA extract   DNA extract + DNase   DNA extract + RNase   DNA extract + protease

6 **CONCLUSION** DNA is responsible for transforming type R cells into type S cells.

7 **SOURCE** Avery, O.T., MacLeod, C.M., and McCarty, M. 1944. Studies on the Chemical Nature of the Substance Inducing Transformation of Pneumococcal Types. *Journal of Experimental Medicine* 79:137–156.

Hershey and Chase Determined That DNA Is the Genetic Material of T2 Bacteriophage

In a second avenue of research conducted in 1952, the efforts of Alfred Hershey and Martha Chase centered on the study of a virus named T2. This virus infects bacterial cells, in this case *Escherichia coli*, and is therefore known as a **bacteriophage** or simply a **phage**. A T2 phage has an outer covering called the phage coat that contains a head (capsid), sheath, tail fibers, and base plate (**Figure 11.3**). We now know the phage coat is composed entirely of protein. DNA is found inside the head of T2. From a biochemical perspective, T2 is very simple because it is composed of only proteins and DNA.

The genetic material of T2 provides a blueprint to make new phages. To replicate, all viruses must introduce their genetic material into the cytoplasm of a living host cell. In the case of T2, this involves the attachment of its tail fibers to the bacterial cell wall and the injection of its genetic material into the cytoplasm (Figure 11.3b). However, at the time of Hershey and Chase's work, it was not known if the phage was injecting DNA or protein.

To determine if DNA is the genetic material of T2, Hershey and Chase devised a method to separate the phage coat, which is attached to the outside of the bacterium, from the genetic material, which is injected into the cytoplasm. They reasoned that the attachment of T2 on the surface of the bacterium could be disrupted if the cells were subjected to high shear forces such as those produced by a blender.

They also needed a way to distinguish T2 DNA from T2 proteins. Hershey and Chase used radioisotopes, which are described in Chapter 2, as a way to label these molecules. Sulfur atoms are found in phage proteins but not in DNA, whereas phosphorus atoms are found in DNA but not in phage proteins. They exposed T2-infected bacterial cells to ^{35}S (a radioisotope of sulfur) or to ^{32}P (a radioisotope of phosphorus). These infected cells produced phages that had incorporated ^{35}S into their proteins or ^{32}P into their DNA. The ^{35}S- or ^{32}P-labeled phages were then used in the experiment shown in **Figure 11.4**.

Let's now consider the steps in this experiment. In separate tubes, they took samples of T2 phage, one in which the proteins were labeled with ^{35}S and the other in which the DNA was labeled with ^{32}P, and mixed them with *E. coli* cells for a short period of time. This allowed the phages enough time to inject their genetic material into the bacterial cells. The samples were then subjected to a shearing force, using a blender for up to 8 minutes. This treatment removed the phage coat from the surface of the bacterial cell without causing cell lysis. Each sample was then subjected to centrifugation at a speed that caused the heavier bacterial cells to form a pellet at the bottom of the tube, while the lighter phage coats remained in the supernatant, the solution above the pellet. The amount of radioactivity in the supernatant (emitted from either ^{35}S or ^{32}P) was determined using an instrument called a Geiger counter.

As you can see in the data of Figure 11.4, most of the ^{35}S isotope (80%) was found in the supernatant. Because the shearing force removed only the phage coat, this result indicates that the empty phages contain primarily protein. In contrast, only about 35% of the ^{32}P was found in the supernatant following shearing. This indicates that most of the phage DNA was located within the bacterial cells in the pellet. Taken together, these results suggest that the phage DNA is injected into the bacterial cytoplasm during infection. This is the expected outcome if DNA is the genetic material of T2.

In other experiments, Hershey and Chase measured the amount of radioactivity incorporated into phages that were produced by the infected bacterial cells. Bacteria infected with ^{35}S-labeled phages produced new phages with a negligible amount of radioactivity, whereas bacteria infected with ^{32}P-labeled phages produced new phages with a significant amount of radioactivity. Again, this is the expected result if DNA is the genetic material.

11.2   Nucleic Acid Structure

An important principle in biology is that structure determines function. When biologists want to understand the function of a material at the molecular and cellular level, they focus some of their efforts on the investigation of its biochemical structure. In this regard, an understanding of DNA's structure has proven to be particularly exciting because the structure makes it easier for us to understand how DNA can store information, how it is replicated and then transmitted from cell to cell, and how variation in its structure can occur.

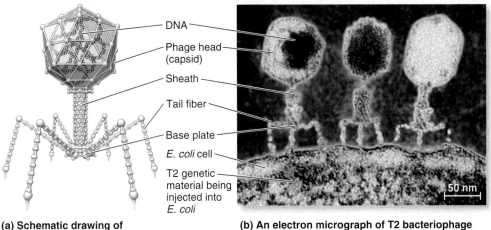

(a) **Schematic drawing of T2 bacteriophage**

DNA
Phage head (capsid)
Sheath
Tail fiber
Base plate
E. coli cell
T2 genetic material being injected into *E. coli*

(b) **An electron micrograph of T2 bacteriophage infecting *E. coli***

50 nm

Figure 11.3   The structure of **T2 bacteriophage.**   The colorized electron micrograph in part **(b)** shows T2 phages attached to an *E. coli* cell and injecting their genetic material into the cell.

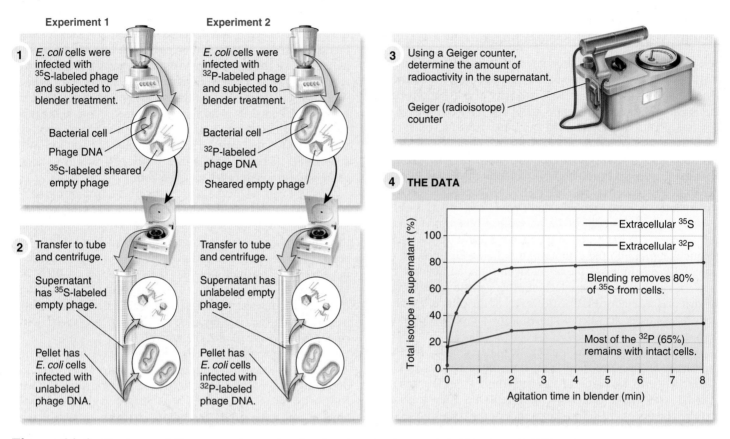

Figure 11.4   Hershey and Chase experiment showing that the genetic material of T2 phage is DNA.   Green coloring indicates radiolabeling with either ^{35}S or ^{32}P. Note: The phages and bacteria are not drawn to scale; bacteria are much larger.

Concept check: *In these experiments, what was the purpose of using two different isotopes, ^{35}S and ^{32}P?*

DNA and its molecular cousin, RNA, are known as **nucleic acids**. This term is derived from the discovery of DNA by Friedrich Miescher in 1869. He identified a novel phosphorus-containing substance from the nuclei of white blood cells found in waste surgical bandages. He named this substance nuclein. As the structure of DNA and RNA became better understood, it was found they are acidic molecules, which means they release hydrogen ions (H^+) in solution, and have a net negative charge at neutral pH. Thus, the name nucleic acid was coined.

DNA is a very large macromolecule composed of smaller building blocks. We can consider the structural features of DNA at different levels of complexity (**Figure 11.5**):

1. **Nucleotides** are the building blocks of DNA (and RNA).
2. A **strand** of DNA (or RNA) is formed by the covalent linkage of nucleotides in a linear manner.
3. Two strands of DNA can hydrogen-bond with each other to form a **double helix**. In a DNA double helix, two DNA strands are twisted together to form a structure that resembles a spiral staircase.
4. In living cells, DNA is associated with an array of different proteins to form **chromosomes**. The association of proteins with DNA organizes the long strands into a compact structure.
5. A **genome** is the complete complement of an organism's genetic material. For example, the genome of most

bacteria is a single circular chromosome, whereas eukaryotic cells have DNA in their nucleus, mitochondria, and chloroplasts.

The first three levels of complexity will be the focus of this section. Level 4 will be discussed in Section 11.5, and level 5 is examined in Chapter 21.

Nucleotides Contain a Phosphate, a Sugar, and a Base

A nucleotide has three components: a phosphate group, a pentose sugar, and a nitrogenous base. The nucleotides in DNA and RNA contain different sugars: Deoxyribose is found in DNA, and ribose is found in RNA. The base and phosphate group are attached to the sugar molecule at different sites (**Figure 11.6**).

Five different bases are found in nucleotides, although any given nucleotide contains only one base. The five bases are subdivided into two categories, the **purines** and the **pyrimidines**, due to differences in their structures (Figure 11.6). The purine bases, **adenine** (**A**) and **guanine** (**G**), have a double-ring structure; the pyrimidine bases, **thymine** (**T**), **cytosine** (**C**), and **uracil** (**U**), have a single-ring structure. Adenine, guanine, and cytosine are found in both DNA and RNA. Thymine is found only in DNA, whereas uracil is found only in RNA.

A conventional numbering system describes the locations of carbon and nitrogen atoms in the sugars and bases (**Figure 11.7**).

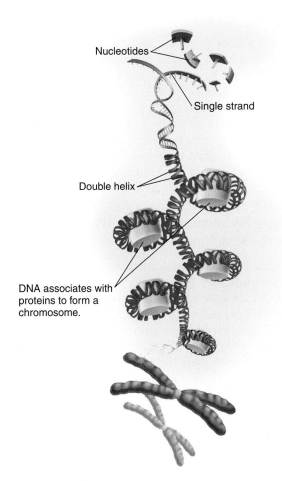

Figure 11.5   Levels of DNA structure to create a chromosome.

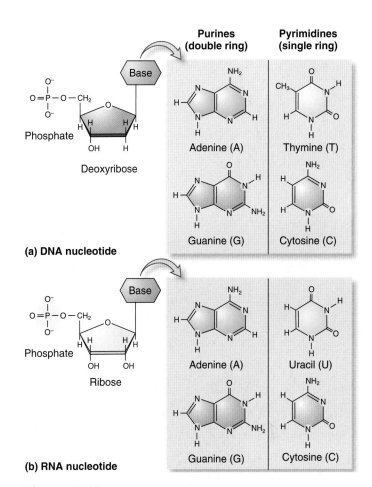

(a) DNA nucleotide

(b) RNA nucleotide

Figure 11.6   **Nucleotides and their components.**   For simplicity, the carbon atoms in the ring structures are not shown.

Concept check: *Which pyrimidine(s) is/are found in both DNA and RNA?*

In the sugar ring, carbon atoms are numbered in a clockwise direction starting with the carbon atom to the right of the ring oxygen atom. The fifth carbon is outside the ring. The prime symbol (′) is used to distinguish the numbering of carbons in the sugar. The atoms in the ring structures of the bases are not given the prime designation. The sugar carbons are designated 1′ (that is, "one prime"), 2′, 3′, 4′, and 5′. A base is attached to the 1′ carbon atom, and a phosphate group is attached at the 5′ position. Compared to ribose (see Figure 11.6), deoxyribose lacks a single oxygen atom at the 2′ position; the prefix deoxy- (meaning without oxygen) refers to this missing atom.

A Strand Is a Linear Linkage of Nucleotides with Directionality

The next level of nucleotide structure is the formation of a strand of DNA or RNA in which nucleotides are covalently attached to each other in a linear fashion. Figure 11.8 depicts a short strand of DNA with four nucleotides. The linkage is a phosphoester bond (a covalent bond between phosphorus and oxygen) involving a sugar molecule in one nucleotide and a phosphate group in the next nucleotide. Another way of viewing this linkage is to notice that a phosphate group connects

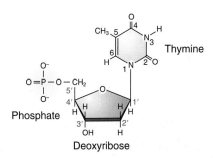

Figure 11.7   **Conventional numbering in a DNA nucleotide.** The carbons in the sugar are given a prime designation, whereas those in the base are not.

Concept check: *What is the numbering designation of the carbon atom to which the phosphate is attached?*

two sugar molecules. From this perspective, the linkage in DNA and RNA strands is called a **phosphodiester linkage**, which has two phosphoester bonds. The phosphates and sugar molecules form the **backbone** of a DNA or RNA strand, while the bases project from the backbone. The backbone is negatively charged due to the negative charges of the phosphate groups.

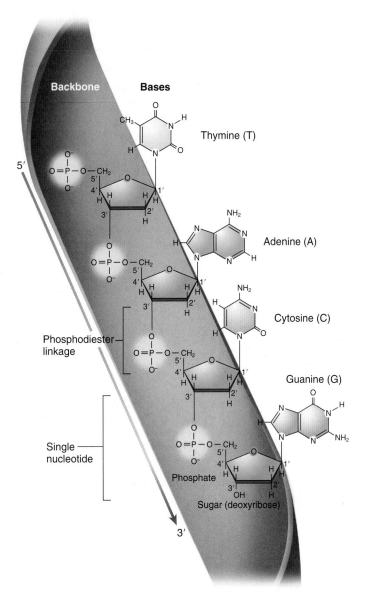

Figure 11.8 **The structure of a DNA strand.** Nucleotides are covalently bonded to each other in a linear manner. Notice the directionality of the strand and that it carries a particular sequence of bases. An RNA strand has a very similar structure, except the sugar is ribose rather than deoxyribose, and uracil is substituted for thymine.

Concept check: *What is the difference between a phosphoester bond versus a phosphodiester linkage?*

An important structural feature of a nucleic acid strand is the orientation of the nucleotides. Each phosphate in a phosphodiester linkage is covalently bonded to the 5′ carbon in one nucleotide and to the 3′ carbon in the other. In a strand, all sugar molecules are oriented in the same direction. For example, in the strand shown in Figure 11.8, all of the 5′ carbons in every sugar molecule are above the 3′ carbons. A strand has a **directionality** based on the orientation of the sugar molecules within that strand. In Figure 11.8, the direction of the strand is said to be 5′ to 3′ when going from top to bottom. The 5′ end

of a DNA strand has a phosphate group, while the 3′ end has an —OH group.

From the perspective of function, a key feature of DNA and RNA structure is that a strand contains a specific sequence of bases. In Figure 11.8, the sequence of bases is thymine—adenine—cytosine—guanine, or TACG. To indicate its directionality, the strand is abbreviated 5′–TACG–3′. Because the nucleotides within a strand are attached to each other by stable covalent bonds, the sequence of bases in a DNA strand will remain the same over time, except in rare cases when mutations occur. The sequence of bases in DNA and RNA is the critical feature that allows them to store and transmit information.

A Few Key Experiments Paved the Way to Solving the Structure of DNA

James Watson and Francis Crick wanted to determine the structure of DNA because they thought this knowledge would provide insights regarding the function of genes. Before we examine the characteristics of the double helix, let's consider the events that led to the discovery of the double helix structure.

In the early 1950s, more information was known about the structure of proteins than that of nucleic acids. Linus Pauling correctly proposed that regions of proteins can fold into a structure known as an α helix. To determine the structure of the α helix, Pauling built large models by linking together simple ball-and-stick units. In this way, he could see if atoms fit together properly in a complicated three-dimensional structure. This approach is still widely used today, except that now researchers construct three-dimensional models on computers. Watson and Crick also used a ball-and-stick approach to solve the structure of the DNA double helix.

What experimental approaches were used to analyze DNA structure? X-ray diffraction was a key experimental tool that led to the discovery of the DNA double helix. When a substance is exposed to X-rays, the atoms in the substance will cause the X-rays to be scattered (**Figure 11.9**). If the substance has a repeating structure, the pattern of scattering, known as the diffraction pattern, is mathematically related to the structural arrangement of the atoms causing the scattering. The diffraction pattern is analyzed using mathematical theory to provide information regarding the three-dimensional structure of the molecule. Rosalind Franklin, working in the 1950s in the same laboratory as Maurice Wilkins, was a gifted experimentalist who made marked advances in X-ray diffraction techniques involving DNA. The diffraction pattern of DNA fibers produced by Franklin suggested a helical structure with a diameter that is relatively uniform and too wide to be a single-stranded helix. In addition, the pattern provided information regarding the number of nucleotides per turn and was consistent with a 2-nm (nanometers) spacing between the strands in which a purine (A or G) bonds with a pyrimidine (T or C). These observations were instrumental in solving the structure of DNA.

Another piece of information that proved to be critical for the determination of the double helix structure came from the studies of Erwin Chargaff. In 1950, Chargaff analyzed the base

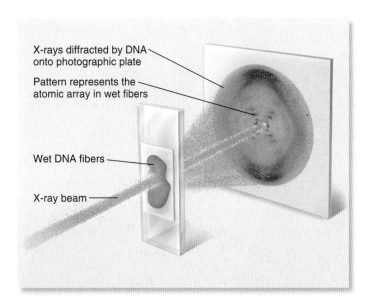

X-rays diffracted by DNA onto photographic plate

Pattern represents the atomic array in wet fibers

Wet DNA fibers

X-ray beam

Figure 11.9 Rosalind Franklin's X-ray diffraction of DNA fibers. The exposure of X-rays to DNA wet fibers causes the X-rays to be scattered.

composition of DNA that was isolated from many different species. His experiments consistently showed that the amount of adenine in each sample was similar to the amount of thymine, and the amount of cytosine was similar to the amount of guanine (**Table 11.1**). As we will see, this observation became crucial evidence that helped Watson and Crick develop the double helix model of DNA.

Watson and Crick Deduced the Double Helix Structure of DNA

Thus far, we have considered the experimental studies that led to the determination of the DNA double helix. These included the biochemical modeling approach of Pauling, the X-ray

Table 11.1	Base Content in the DNA from a Variety of Organisms as Determined by Chargaff			
	% of bases			
Organism	**Adenine**	**Thymine**	**Guanine**	**Cytosine**
Escherichia coli (bacterium)	26.0	23.9	24.9	25.2
Streptococcus pneumoniae (bacterium)	29.8	31.6	20.5	18.0
Saccharomyces cerevisiae (yeast)	31.7	32.6	18.3	17.4
Turtle	28.7	27.9	22.0	21.3
Salmon	29.7	29.1	20.8	20.4
Chicken	28.0	28.4	22.0	21.6
Human	30.3	30.3	19.5	19.9

diffraction work of Franklin, and the base composition studies of Chargaff. Watson and Crick assumed that nucleotides are linked together in a linear fashion and that the chemical linkage between two nucleotides is always the same. Along with Wilkins, they then set out to build ball-and-stick models that incorporated all of the known experimental observations.

Modeling of chemical structures involves trial and error. Watson and Crick initially considered several incorrect models. One model was a double helix in which the bases were on the outside of the helix. In another model, each base formed hydrogen bonds with the identical base in the opposite strand (A to A, T to T, G to G, and C to C). However, model-building revealed that purine-purine pairs were too wide and pyrimidine-pyrimidine pairs were too narrow to fit the uniform diameter of the double helix. Eventually, they realized that the hydrogen bonding of adenine to thymine was structurally similar to that of guanine to cytosine. In both cases, a purine base (A or G) bonds with a pyrimidine base (T or C). With an interaction between A and T and between G and C, the ball-and-stick models showed that the two strands would form a double helix structure in which all atoms would fit together properly.

Watson and Crick proposed the structure of DNA, which was published in the journal *Nature* in 1953. In 1962, Watson, Crick, and Wilkins were awarded the Nobel Prize in Physiology or Medicine. Unfortunately, Rosalind Franklin had died before this time, and the Nobel Prize is awarded only to living recipients.

DNA Has a Repeating, Antiparallel Helical Structure Formed by the Complementary Base Pairing of Nucleotides

The structure that Watson and Crick proposed is a double-stranded, helical structure with the sugar-phosphate backbone on the outside and the bases on the inside (**Figure 11.10a**). This structure is stabilized by hydrogen bonding between the bases in opposite strands to form **base pairs**. A distinguishing feature of base pairing is its specificity. An adenine (A) base in one strand forms two hydrogen bonds with a thymine (T) base in the opposite strand, or a guanine (G) base forms three hydrogen bonds with a cytosine (C) (**Figure 11.10b**). This **AT/GC rule** (also known as Chargaff's rule) is consistent with Chargaff's observation that DNA contains equal amounts of A and T, and equal amounts of G and C. According to the AT/GC rule, purines (A and G) always bond with pyrimidines (T and C) (recall that purines have a double-ring structure, whereas pyrimidines have single rings). This keeps the width of the double helix relatively constant. One complete turn of the double helix is composed of 10 base pairs.

Due to the AT/GC rule, the base sequences of two DNA strands are **complementary** to each other. That is, you can predict the sequence in one DNA strand if you know the sequence in the opposite strand. For example, if one strand has the sequence of 5′–GCGGATTT–3′, the opposite strand must be 3′–CGCCTAAA–5′. With regard to their 5′ and 3′ directionality,

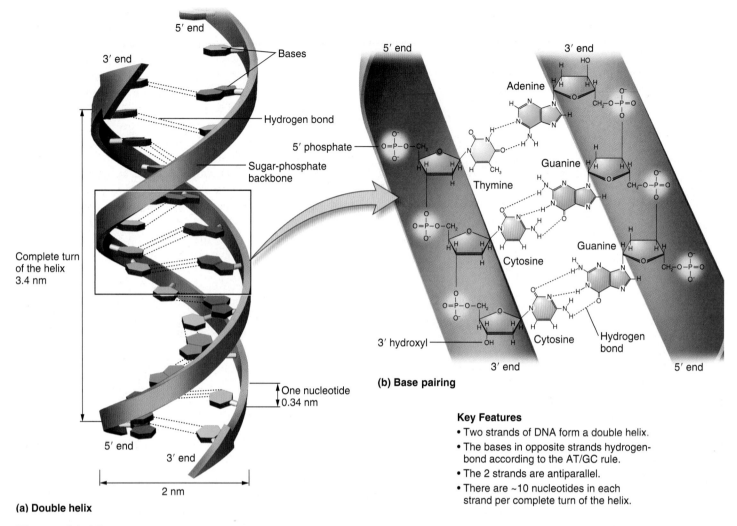

Figure 11.10 **Structure of the DNA double helix.** As seen in part **(a)**, DNA is a helix composed of two antiparallel strands. Part **(b)** shows the AT/GC base pairing that holds the strands together via hydrogen bonds.

Concept check: *If one DNA strand is 5′–GATTCGTTC–3′, what is the complementary strand?*

the two strands of a DNA double helix are **antiparallel**. If you look at Figure 11.10, one strand runs in the 5′ to 3′ direction from top to bottom, while the other strand is oriented 3′ to 5′ from top to bottom. Watson and Crick proposed an antiparallel structure in their original DNA model.

The DNA model in Figure 11.10a is called a ribbon model, which clearly shows the components of the DNA molecule. However, other models are also used to visualize DNA. The model for the DNA double helix shown in **Figure 11.11** is a space-filling model in which the atoms are depicted as spheres. Why is this model useful? This type of structural model emphasizes the surface of DNA. As you can see in this model, the sugar-phosphate backbone is on the outermost surface of the double helix; the backbone has the most direct contact with water. The atoms of the bases are more internally located within the double-stranded structure. The indentations where the atoms of the bases make contact with the surrounding water are termed **grooves**. Two grooves, called the **major groove** and the **minor groove**, spiral around the double helix. As discussed

in later chapters, the major groove provides a location where a protein can bind to a particular sequence of bases and affect the expression of a gene.

11.3 | An Overview of DNA Replication

In the previous section, we considered the structure of the genetic material. DNA is a double helix that obeys the AT/GC rule. The structure of DNA immediately suggested to Watson and Crick a mechanism by which DNA can be copied. They proposed that during this process, known as **DNA replication**, the original DNA strands are used as templates for the synthesis of new DNA strands. In this section, we will look at an early experiment that helped to determine the mechanism of DNA replication and then examine the structural characteristics that enable a double helix to be faithfully copied.

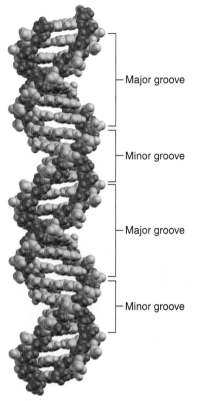

Figure 11.11

A space-filling model of the DNA double helix. In the sugar-phosphate backbone, sugar molecules are shown in blue, and phosphate groups are yellow. The backbone is on the outermost surface of the double helix. The atoms of the bases, shown in green, are more internally located within the double-stranded structure. Notice the major and minor grooves that are formed by this arrangement.

Meselson and Stahl Used Density Measurements to Investigate Three Proposed Mechanisms of DNA Replication

Researchers in the late 1950s considered three different models for the mechanism of DNA replication (**Figure 11.12**). In all of these models, the two newly made strands are called the **daughter strands**, and the original strands are the **parental strands**. The first model is a **semiconservative mechanism** (Figure 11.12a). In this model, the double-stranded DNA is half conserved following the replication process such that the new double-stranded DNA contains one parental strand and one daughter strand. This mechanism is consistent with the ideas of Watson and Crick. Even so, other models were possible and had to be ruled out. According to a second model, called a **conservative mechanism**, both parental strands of DNA remain together following DNA replication (Figure 11.12b). The original arrangement of parental strands is completely conserved, while the two newly made daughter strands are also together following replication. Finally, a third possibility, called a **dispersive mechanism**, proposed that segments of parental DNA and newly made DNA are interspersed in both strands following the replication process (Figure 11.12c).

In 1958, Matthew Meselson and Franklin Stahl devised an experimental approach to distinguish among these three mechanisms. An important feature of their research was the use of isotope labeling. Nitrogen, which is found in DNA, occurs in a common light (^{14}N) form and a rare heavy (^{15}N) form. Meselson and Stahl studied DNA replication in the bacterium *Escherichia coli*. They grew *E. coli* cells for many generations in a medium that contained only the ^{15}N form of nitrogen (**Figure 11.13**). This produced a population of bacterial cells in which all of the DNA was heavy labeled. Then they switched the bacteria to

Original double helix   First round of replication   Second round of replication

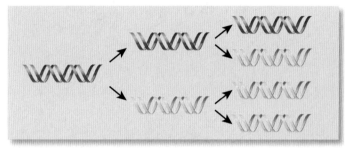

(a) Semiconservative mechanism. DNA replication produces DNA molecules with 1 parental strand and 1 newly made daughter strand.

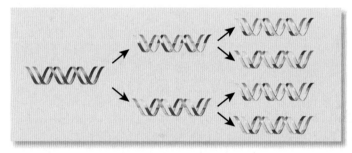

(b) Conservative mechanism. DNA replication produces 1 double helix with both parental strands and the other with 2 new daughter strands.

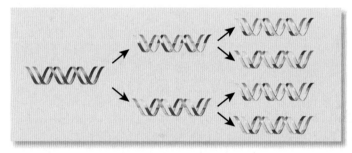

(c) Dispersive mechanism. DNA replication produces DNA strands in which segments of new DNA are interspersed with the parental DNA.

Figure 11.12   **Three proposed mechanisms for DNA replication.** The strands of the original double helix are shown in red. Two rounds of replication are illustrated with new strands shown in blue.

a medium that contained only ^{14}N as its nitrogen source. The cells were allowed to divide, and samples were collected after one generation (that is, one round of DNA replication), two generations, and so on. Because the bacteria were doubling in a medium that contained only ^{14}N, all of the newly made DNA strands would be labeled with light nitrogen, while the original strands would remain labeled with the heavy form.

How were the DNA molecules analyzed? Meselson and Stahl used centrifugation to separate DNA molecules based on differences in density. Samples were placed on the top of a solution that contained a salt gradient, in this case, cesium chloride (CsCl). A double helix containing all heavy nitrogen

1 Grow bacteria in ^{15}N media.

^{15}N medium (heavy)

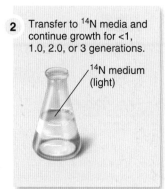

2 Transfer to ^{14}N media and continue growth for <1, 1.0, 2.0, or 3 generations.

^{14}N medium (light)

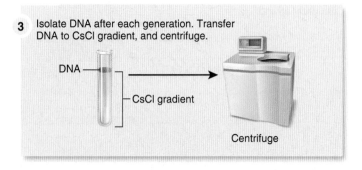

3 Isolate DNA after each generation. Transfer DNA to CsCl gradient, and centrifuge.

DNA

CsCl gradient

Centrifuge

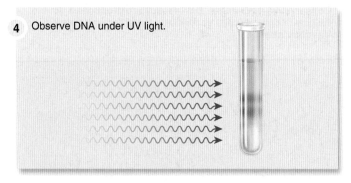

4 Observe DNA under UV light.

5 THE DATA

Approximate generations after transfer to ^{14}N medium.

< 1.0   1.0   2.0   3.0

Light
Half-heavy
Heavy

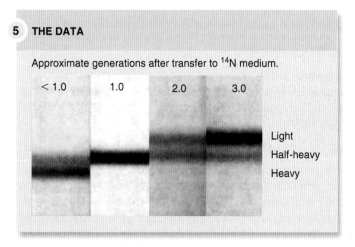

Figure 11.13 The Meselson and Stahl experiment showing that DNA replication is semiconservative.

Concept check: *If this experiment were conducted for four rounds of DNA replication (that is, four generations), what would be the expected fractions of light DNA and half-heavy DNA according to the semiconservative model?*

has a higher density and will travel closer to the bottom of the gradient. By comparison, if both DNA strands contained ^{14}N, the DNA would have a light density and remain closer to the top of the gradient. If one strand contained ^{14}N and the other strand contained ^{15}N, the DNA would be half-heavy and have an intermediate density, ending up near the middle of the gradient.

After one cell doubling (that is, one round of DNA replication), all of the DNA exhibited a density that was half-heavy (Figure 11.13, step 5). These results are consistent with both the semiconservative and dispersive models. In contrast, the conservative mechanism predicts two different DNA types: a light type and a heavy type. Because the DNA was found in a single (half-heavy) band after one doubling, the conservative model was disproved. After two cell doublings, both light DNA and half-heavy DNA were observed. This result was also predicted by the semiconservative mechanism of DNA replication, because some DNA molecules should contain all light DNA, while other molecules should be half-heavy (see Figure 11.12a). However, in the dispersive mechanism, all of the DNA strands would have been 1/4 heavy after two generations. This mechanism predicts that the heavy nitrogen would be evenly dispersed among four double helices, each strand containing 1/4 heavy nitrogen and 3/4 light nitrogen (see Figure 11.12c). This result was not obtained. Taken together, the results of the Meselson and Stahl experiment are consistent only with a semiconservative mechanism for DNA replication.

Semiconservative DNA Replication Proceeds According to the AT/GC Rule

As originally proposed by Watson and Crick, semiconservative DNA replication relies on the complementarity of DNA strands according to the AT/GC rule. During the replication process, the two complementary strands of DNA separate and serve as **template strands** (also called parental strands) for the synthesis of new daughter strands of DNA (**Figure 11.14a**). After the double helix has separated, individual nucleotides have access to the template strands in a region called the replication fork. First, individual nucleotides hydrogen-bond to the template strands according to the AT/GC rule. Next, a covalent bond is formed between the phosphate of one nucleotide and the sugar of the previous nucleotide. The end result is that two double helices are made that have the same base sequence as the original DNA molecule (**Figure 11.14b**). This is a critical feature of DNA replication, because it enables the replicated DNA molecules to retain the same information (that is, the same base sequence) as the original molecule. In this way, DNA has the remarkable ability to direct its own duplication.

11.4 Molecular Mechanism of DNA Replication

Thus far, we have considered the general mechanism of DNA replication, known as semiconservative replication, and examined how DNA synthesis obeys the AT/GC rule. In this section,

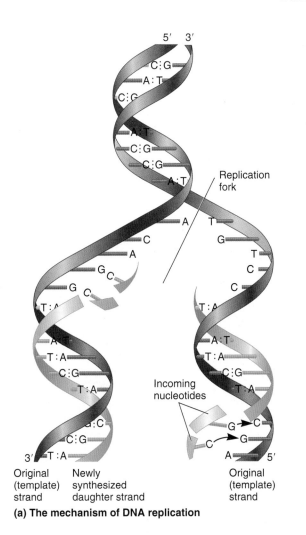

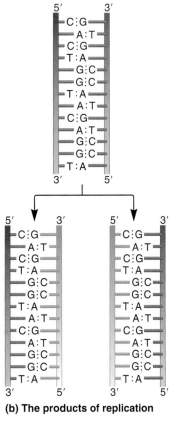

Figure 11.14 DNA replication according to the AT/GC rule. (a) The mechanism of DNA replication as originally proposed by Watson and Crick. As we will see in Section 11.4, the synthesis of one newly made strand (the leading strand on the left side) occurs in the direction toward the replication fork, whereas the synthesis of the other newly made strand (the lagging strand on the right side) occurs in small segments away from the fork. (b) DNA replication produces two copies of DNA with the same sequence as the original DNA molecule.

(a) The mechanism of DNA replication

(b) The products of replication

we will examine the details of DNA replication as it occurs inside living cells. As you will learn, several cellular proteins are needed to initiate DNA replication and allow it to proceed quickly and accurately.

DNA Replication Begins at an Origin of Replication, Where DNA Replication Forks Are Formed

Where does DNA replication begin? An **origin of replication** is a site within a chromosome that serves as a starting point for DNA replication. At the origin, the two DNA strands unwind (**Figure 11.15a**). DNA replication proceeds outward from two **replication forks**, a process termed **bidirectional replication** (Figure 11.15a). The number of origins of replication varies among different organisms. In bacteria, which have a small circular chromosome, a single origin of replication is found. Bidirectional replication starts at the origin of replication and proceeds until the new strands meet on the opposite side of the chromosome (**Figure 11.15b**). Eukaryotes have larger chromosomes that are linear. They require multiple origins of replication so the DNA can be replicated in a reasonable length of time. The newly made strands from each origin eventually make contact with each other to complete the replication process (**Figure 11.15c**).

DNA Replication Requires the Action of Several Different Proteins

Thus far, we have considered how DNA replication occurs outward from an origin of replication in a region called a DNA replication fork. In all living species, a set of several different proteins is involved in this process. An understanding of the functions of these proteins is critical to explaining the replication process at the molecular level.

Helicase, Topoisomerase, and Single-Strand Binding Proteins: Formation and Movement of the Replication Fork

To act as a template for DNA replication, the strands of a double helix must separate, and the resulting fork must move. As mentioned, an origin of replication serves as a site where this separation initially occurs. The strand separation at each fork then moves outward from the origin via the action of an enzyme called **DNA helicase**. At each fork, DNA helicase binds to one of the DNA strands and travels in the 5′ to 3′ direction toward the fork (**Figure 11.16**). It uses energy from ATP to separate the DNA strands and keeps the fork moving forward. The action of DNA helicase generates additional coiling just ahead of the replication fork that is alleviated by another enzyme called **DNA topoisomerase**.

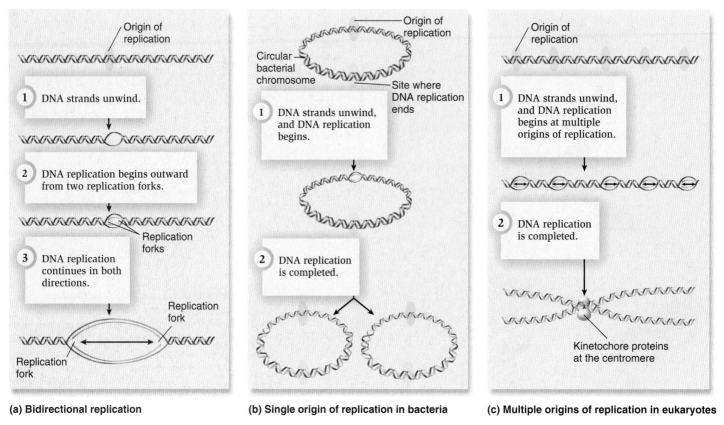

(a) Bidirectional replication

(b) Single origin of replication in bacteria

(c) Multiple origins of replication in eukaryotes

Figure 11.15 The bidirectional replication of DNA. (a) DNA replication proceeds in both directions from an origin of replication. (b) Bacterial chromosomes have a single origin of replication, whereas (c) eukaryotes have multiple origins.

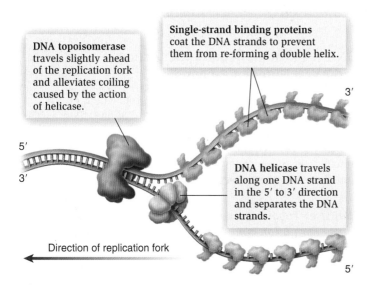

Figure 11.16 Proteins that facilitate the formation and movement of a replication fork.

After the two template DNA strands have separated, they must remain that way until the complementary daughter strands have been made. The function of **single-strand binding proteins** is to coat both of the single strands of template DNA and prevent them from re-forming a double helix. In this way, the

bases within the template strands are kept exposed so they can act as templates for the synthesis of complementary strands.

DNA Polymerase and Primase: Synthesis of DNA Strands

The enzyme **DNA polymerase** is responsible for covalently linking nucleotides together to form DNA strands. Arthur Kornberg originally identified this enzyme in the 1950s. The structure of DNA polymerase resembles a human hand with the DNA threaded through it (Figure 11.17a). As DNA polymerase slides along the DNA, free nucleotides with three phosphate groups, called **deoxynucleoside triphosphates**, hydrogen-bond to the exposed bases in the template strand according to the AT/GC rule. At the catalytic site, DNA polymerase breaks a bond between the first and second phosphate and then attaches the resulting nucleotide with one phosphate group (a deoxynucleoside monophosphate) to the 3′ end of a growing strand via a phosphoester bond. The breakage of the covalent bond that releases pyrophosphate is an exergonic reaction that provides the energy to covalently connect adjacent nucleotides (Figure 11.17b). The pyrophosphate is broken down to two phosphates. The rate of synthesis is truly remarkable. In bacteria, DNA polymerase can synthesize DNA at a rate of 500 nucleotides per second, while eukaryotic species can make DNA at a rate of about 50 nucleotides per second.

DNA polymerase has two additional enzymatic features that affect how DNA strands are made. First, DNA polymerase

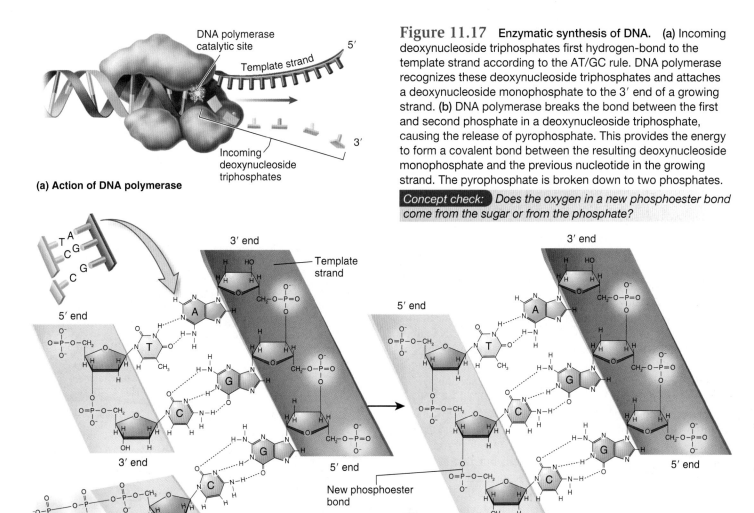

(a) Action of DNA polymerase

Figure 11.17 Enzymatic synthesis of DNA. **(a)** Incoming deoxynucleoside triphosphates first hydrogen-bond to the template strand according to the AT/GC rule. DNA polymerase recognizes these deoxynucleoside triphosphates and attaches a deoxynucleoside monophosphate to the 3′ end of a growing strand. **(b)** DNA polymerase breaks the bond between the first and second phosphate in a deoxynucleoside triphosphate, causing the release of pyrophosphate. This provides the energy to form a covalent bond between the resulting deoxynucleoside monophosphate and the previous nucleotide in the growing strand. The pyrophosphate is broken down to two phosphates.

Concept check: *Does the oxygen in a new phosphoester bond come from the sugar or from the phosphate?*

(b) Chemistry of DNA replication

is unable to begin DNA synthesis on a bare template strand. However, if a DNA or RNA strand is already attached to a template strand, DNA polymerase can elongate such a pre-existing strand by making DNA. A different enzyme called **DNA primase** is required if the template strand is bare. DNA primase makes a complementary **primer** that is actually a short segment of RNA, typically 10 to 12 nucleotides in length. These short RNA strands start, or prime, the process of DNA replication (**Figure 11.18a**). A second feature of DNA polymerase is that once synthesis has begun, it can synthesize new DNA only in a 5′ to 3′ direction (**Figure 11.18b**).

Leading and Lagging DNA Strands Are Made Differently

Let's now consider how new DNA strands are made at the replication forks. DNA replication occurs near the opening that forms each replication fork (**Figure 11.19**, step 1). The synthesis of a

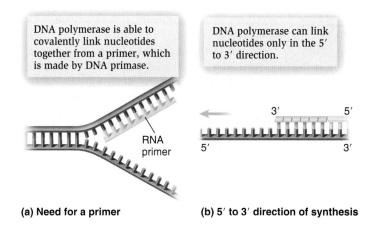

DNA polymerase is able to covalently link nucleotides together from a primer, which is made by DNA primase.

DNA polymerase can link nucleotides only in the 5′ to 3′ direction.

(a) Need for a primer

(b) 5′ to 3′ direction of synthesis

Figure 11.18 Enzymatic feature of DNA polymerase. **(a)** DNA polymerase needs a primer to begin DNA synthesis, and **(b)** it can synthesize DNA only in the 5′ to 3′ direction.

strand always begins with an RNA primer (depicted in yellow), and the new DNA is made in the 5′ to 3′ direction. The manner in which the two daughter strands are synthesized is strikingly different. One strand, called the **leading strand**, is made in the same direction that the fork is moving. The leading strand is synthesized as one long continuous molecule. By comparison, the other daughter strand, termed the **lagging strand**, is made as a series of small fragments that are subsequently connected to each other to form a continuous strand. The synthesis of these fragments occurs in the direction away from the fork. For example, the lower fragment seen in Figure 11.19, steps 2 and 3, is synthesized from left to right. These DNA fragments are known as **Okazaki fragments**, after Reiji and Tuneko Okazaki, who initially discovered them in the late 1960s. As shown in Figure 11.19, step 4, the RNA primer is eventually removed, and adjacent Okazaki fragments are connected to each other to form a continuous strand of DNA.

Figure 11.20 shows the proteins involved with the synthesis of the leading and lagging strands in *Escherichia coli*. In this bacterium, two different DNA polymerases, called DNA polymerase I and DNA polymerase III, are primarily responsible for DNA replication. In the leading strand, DNA primase makes one RNA primer at the origin, and then DNA polymerase III attaches nucleotides in a 5′ to 3′ direction as it slides toward the opening of the replication fork. DNA polymerase III has a subunit called the clamp protein that allows it to slide along the template strand without falling off. In the lagging strand, DNA is also synthesized in a 5′ to 3′ direction, but this synthesis occurs in the direction away from the replication fork. In the lagging strand, short segments of DNA are made discontinuously as a series of Okazaki fragments, each of which requires its own primer. DNA polymerase III synthesizes the remainder of the fragment.

To complete the synthesis of Okazaki fragments within the lagging strand, three additional events must occur: the removal of the RNA primers, the synthesis of DNA in the area where the primers have been removed, and the covalent joining of adjacent fragments of DNA (Figure 11.20, steps 3 and 4). The RNA primers are removed by DNA polymerase I, which digests the linkages between nucleotides in a 5′ to 3′ direction. After the RNA primer is removed, DNA polymerase I fills in the vacant region with DNA. However, once the DNA has been completely filled in, a covalent bond is missing between the last nucleotide added by DNA polymerase I and the next DNA nucleotide in the adjacent Okazaki fragment. An enzyme known as **DNA ligase** catalyzes the formation of a covalent bond between these two DNA fragments to complete the replication process in the lagging strand (Figure 11.20, step 4). **Table 11.2** provides a summary of the functions of the proteins we have discussed in this section.

DNA Replication Is Very Accurate

Although errors can happen during DNA replication, permanent mistakes are extraordinarily rare. For example, during bacterial DNA replication, only 1 mistake per 100 million nucleotides

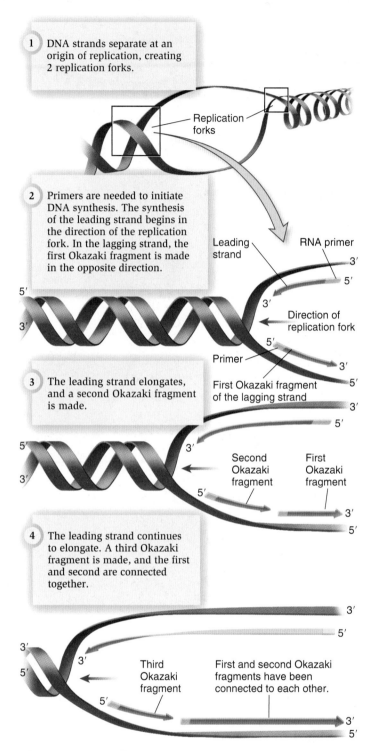

1 DNA strands separate at an origin of replication, creating 2 replication forks.

2 Primers are needed to initiate DNA synthesis. The synthesis of the leading strand begins in the direction of the replication fork. In the lagging strand, the first Okazaki fragment is made in the opposite direction.

3 The leading strand elongates, and a second Okazaki fragment is made.

4 The leading strand continues to elongate. A third Okazaki fragment is made, and the first and second are connected together.

Figure 11.19   Synthesis of new DNA strands.   The separation of DNA at the origin of replication produces two replication forks that move in opposite directions. New DNA strands are made near the opening of each fork. The leading strand is made continuously in the same direction the fork is moving. The lagging strand is made as small pieces in the opposite direction. Eventually, these small pieces are connected to each other to form a continuous lagging strand.

Concept check: *Which strand, the leading or lagging strand, is made discontinuously in the direction opposite to the movement of the replication fork?*

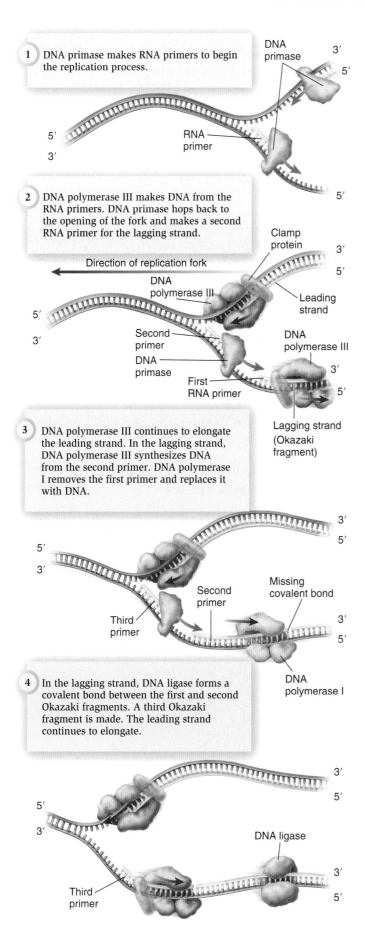

1 DNA primase makes RNA primers to begin the replication process.

2 DNA polymerase III makes DNA from the RNA primers. DNA primase hops back to the opening of the fork and makes a second RNA primer for the lagging strand.

Direction of replication fork

3 DNA polymerase III continues to elongate the leading strand. In the lagging strand, DNA polymerase III synthesizes DNA from the second primer. DNA polymerase I removes the first primer and replaces it with DNA.

4 In the lagging strand, DNA ligase forms a covalent bond between the first and second Okazaki fragments. A third Okazaki fragment is made. The leading strand continues to elongate.

Figure 11.20 Proteins involved with the synthesis of the leading and lagging strands in *E. coli*.

Concept check: *Briefly describe the movement of primase in the lagging strand in this figure. In which direction does it move when it is making a primer, from left to right or right to left? Describe how it must move after it is done making a primer and has to start making the next primer at a new location. Does it have to hop from left to right or from right to left?*

Table 11.2	Proteins Involved in DNA Replication
Common name	**Function**
DNA helicase	Separates double-stranded DNA into single strands
Single-strand binding protein	Binds to single-stranded DNA and prevents it from re-forming a double helix
Topoisomerase	Removes tightened coils ahead of the replication fork
DNA primase	Synthesizes short RNA primers
DNA polymerase	Synthesizes DNA in the leading and lagging strands, removes RNA primers, and fills in gaps
DNA ligase	Covalently attaches adjacent Okazaki fragments in the lagging strand

is made. Biologists use the term high fidelity to refer to a process that occurs with relatively few mistakes. How can we explain such a remarkably high fidelity for DNA replication? First, hydrogen bonding between A and T or between G and C is more stable than between mismatched pairs. Second, the active site of DNA polymerase is unlikely to catalyze bond formation between adjacent nucleotides if a mismatched base pair is formed. Third, DNA polymerase can identify a mismatched nucleotide and remove it from the daughter strand. This event, called **proofreading**, occurs when DNA polymerase detects a mismatch and then reverses its direction and digests the linkages between nucleotides at the end of a newly made strand in the 3′ to 5′ direction. Once it passes the mismatched base and removes it, DNA polymerase then changes direction again and continues to synthesize DNA in the 5′ to 3′ direction.

Genomes & Proteomes Connection

DNA Polymerases Are a Family of Enzymes with Specialized Functions

Thus far, we have examined the general properties of DNA replication. Three important issues are speed, fidelity, and completeness. DNA replication must proceed quickly and with great accuracy, and gaps should not be left in the newly made strands. To ensure that these three requirements are met, living species produce more than one type of DNA polymerase, each of which may differ with regard to the rate and accuracy of DNA replication and/or the ability to prevent the formation of DNA gaps. Let's first consider how evolution produced these different forms of DNA polymerase and then examine how their functions are finely tuned to the process of DNA replication.

The genomes of living species have multiple DNA polymerase genes, which were produced by random gene duplication events. During evolution, mutations have altered each gene to produce a family of DNA polymerase enzymes with more specialized functions. Natural selection has favored certain mutations that result in DNA polymerase properties that are suited to the organism in which they are found. For comparison, let's consider the bacterium *E. coli* and humans. *E. coli* has five different DNA polymerases, designated I, II, III, IV, and V. In humans, over a dozen different DNA polymerases have been identified (**Table 11.3**). Why does *E. coli* need 5 DNA polymerases, while humans need 12 or more? The answer lies in specialization and the functional needs of each species.

In *E. coli*, DNA polymerase III is responsible for most DNA replication. It is composed of multiple subunits, each with its own functional role. In addition to the catalytic subunit that synthesizes DNA, DNA polymerase III has other subunits that allow it to clamp onto the template DNA and synthesize new DNA very rapidly and with high fidelity. By comparison, DNA polymerase I is composed of a single subunit. Its role during DNA replication is to remove the RNA primers and fill in the short vacant regions with DNA. DNA polymerases II, IV, and V are involved in repairing DNA and in replicating DNA that has been damaged. DNA polymerases I and III become stalled when they encounter DNA damage and may be unable to make a complementary strand at such a site. By comparison, DNA

polymerases II, IV, and V do not stall. Although their rate of synthesis is not as rapid as DNA polymerases I and III, they ensure that DNA replication is complete.

In human cells, DNA polymerases are designated with Greek letters (Table 11.3). DNA polymerase α has its own "built-in" primase subunit. It synthesizes RNA primers followed by short DNA regions. Two other DNA polymerases, δ (delta) and ε (epsilon), then extend the DNA at a faster rate. DNA polymerase γ (gamma) functions in the mitochondria to replicate mitochondrial DNA.

Several additional DNA polymerases function as lesion-replicating enzymes. Although most abnormalities in DNA structure (lesions) are eliminated by DNA repair, some may remain. When DNA replication occurs, the general DNA polymerases (α, δ, or ε) may be unable to replicate over the lesion. If this happens, lesion-replicating polymerases are attracted to the damaged DNA. These polymerases have special properties that enable them to synthesize a complementary strand over the lesion. Each type of lesion-replicating polymerase may be able to replicate over different kinds of DNA damage.

Similarly, other human DNA polymerases play an important role in DNA repair. The need for multiple repair enzymes is rooted in the various ways that DNA can be damaged, as described in Chapter 14. Multicellular organisms must be particularly vigilant about repairing DNA or cancer may occur.

Telomerase Attaches DNA Sequences at the Ends of Eukaryotic Chromosomes

We will end our discussion of DNA replication by considering a specialized form of DNA replication that happens at the ends of eukaryotic chromosomes. This region, called the **telomere**, contains a short nucleotide sequence that is repeated a few dozen to several hundred times in a row (**Figure 11.21**). The repeat sequence shown here, 5′–GGGTTA–3′, is the sequence found in human telomeres. Other organisms have different repeat sequences. For example, the sequence found in the telomeres of maize is 5′–GGGTTTA–3′. A telomere has a region at the 3′ end that is termed a 3′ overhang, because it does not have a complementary strand.

Table 11.3	DNA Polymerases in *E. coli* and Humans

Polymerase types*	Functions
E. coli	
III	Replicates most of the DNA during cell division
I	Removes RNA primers and fills in the gaps
II, IV, and V	Repairs damaged DNA and replicates over DNA damage
Humans	
α (alpha)	Makes RNA primers and synthesizes short DNA strands
δ (delta), ε (epsilon)	Displaces DNA polymerase α and then replicates DNA at a rapid rate
γ (gamma)	Replicates the mitochondrial DNA
η (eta), κ (kappa), ι (iota), ζ (zeta)	Replicates over damaged DNA
α, β (beta), δ, ε, σ (sigma), λ (lambda), μ (mu), ϕ (phi), θ (theta)	Repairs DNA or has other functions

*Certain DNA polymerases may have more than one function.

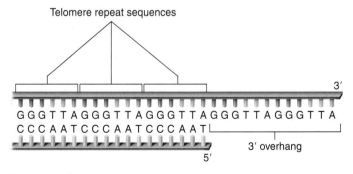

Figure 11.21   Telomere sequences at the end of a human chromosome.   The telomere sequence shown here is found in humans and other mammals. The length of the 3′ overhang is variable among different species and cell types.

As discussed previously, DNA polymerase synthesizes DNA only in a 5′ to 3′ direction and requires a primer. For these reasons, DNA polymerase cannot copy the tip of a DNA strand with a 3′ end. Therefore, if this replication problem was not overcome, a linear chromosome would become progressively shorter with each round of DNA replication.

In 1984, Carol Greider and Elizabeth Blackburn discovered an enzyme called **telomerase** that prevents chromosome shortening by attaching many copies of a DNA repeat sequence to the ends of chromosomes (**Figure 11.22**). Telomerase contains both protein and RNA. The RNA part of telomerase is a sequence that is complementary to the DNA repeat sequence. This allows telomerase to bind to the 3′ overhang region of the telomere. Following binding, the RNA sequence beyond the binding site functions as a template, allowing telomerase to synthesize a six-nucleotide sequence at the end of the DNA strand. The enzyme then moves to the new end of this DNA strand and attaches another six nucleotides to the end. This occurs many times and thereby greatly lengthens the 3′ end of the DNA in the telomeric region. This lengthening provides an upstream site for an RNA primer to be made. DNA polymerase then synthesizes the complementary DNA strand. In this way, the progressive shortening of eukaryotic chromosomes is prevented.

Researchers have discovered an interesting connection between telomeres and cellular aging. In humans and other mammals, the cells of the body have a predetermined life span. For example, if a small sample of skin is removed from a person's body and grown in the laboratory, the cells will double a finite number of times. Furthermore, the number of doublings depends on the age of the person from which the sample is taken. If a sample is from an infant, the cells will typically double about 80 times, whereas if a sample is from an older person, the cells will double only 10 to 20 times before division ceases. Cells that have doubled many times and have reached a point where they have lost the capacity to divide any further are termed **senescent**.

The progressive shortening of telomeres is correlated with cellular senescence, though the relationship between the two phenomena is not well understood. The telomerase enzyme is normally present in germ-line cells, which give rise to gametes, and also in many rapidly dividing somatic cells. However, telomerase function is typically reduced as an organism ages. In 1998, Andrea Bodnar and her colleagues inserted a gene that encodes a highly active telomerase into human cells grown in the laboratory, using techniques described in Chapter 20. The results were amazing. The expression of telomerase prevented telomere shortening and cellular senescence. The cells expressing telomerase continued to divide, just like younger, healthy cells!

Telomerase function is also associated with cancer. When cells become cancerous, they continue to divide uncontrollably. In 90% of all types of human cancers, telomerase has been found to be present at high levels in the cancerous cells. This prevents telomere shortening and may play a role in the continued growth of cancer cells. The mechanism whereby cancer cells are able to increase the function of telomerase is not well understood and is a topic of active research.

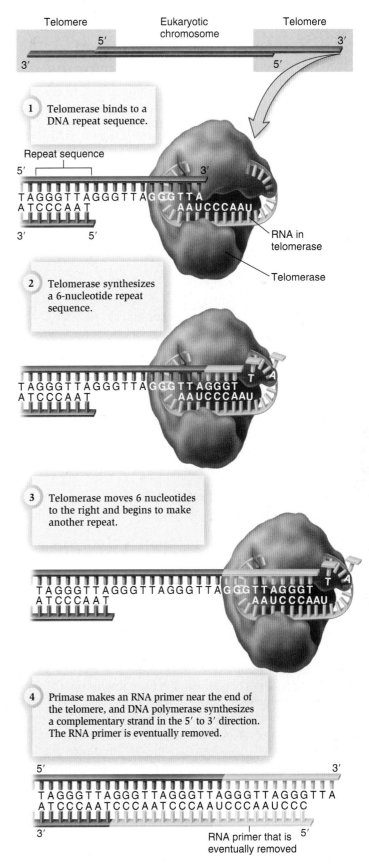

Figure 11.22   Mechanism of DNA replication by telomerase.

Concept check: What does telomerase use as a template to make DNA?

11.5 Molecular Structure of Eukaryotic Chromosomes

We now turn our attention to the structure of eukaryotic chromosomes. A typical eukaryotic chromosome contains a single, linear, double-stranded DNA molecule that may be hundreds of millions of base pairs in length. If the DNA from a single set of human chromosomes were stretched from end to end, the length would be over 1 meter! By comparison, most eukaryotic cells are only 10–100 μm (micrometers) in diameter, and the cell nucleus is only about 2–4 μm in diameter. Therefore, to fit inside the nucleus, the DNA in a eukaryotic cell must be folded and packaged by a staggering amount.

The term chromosome is used to describe a discrete unit of genetic material. For example, a human somatic cell contains 46 chromosomes. By comparison, the term chromatin has a biochemical meaning. **Chromatin** is used to describe the DNA-protein complex that makes up eukaryotic chromosomes. The chromosomes found in the nucleus are composed of chromatin, as are the highly condensed chromosomes found in dividing cells. Chromosomes are very dynamic structures that alternate between tight and loose compaction states. In this section, we will focus our attention on two issues of chromosome structure. First, we will consider how chromosomes are compacted and organized within the cell nucleus. Then, we will examine the additional compaction that is necessary to produce the highly condensed chromosomes that occur during cell division.

DNA Wraps Around Histone Proteins to Form Nucleosomes

The first way that DNA is compacted is by wrapping itself around a group of proteins called **histones**. As shown in **Figure 11.23**, a repeating structural unit of eukaryotic chromatin is the **nucleosome**, which is 11 nanometers (nm) in diameter and composed of double-stranded DNA wrapped around an octamer of histone proteins. Each octamer contains two molecules of four types of histone proteins: H2A, H2B, H3, and H4. Histone proteins are very basic proteins because they contain a large number of positively charged lysine and arginine amino acids. The negative charges found in the phosphate of DNA are attracted to the positive charges on histone proteins. The DNA lies on the surface of the histone octamer and makes 1.65 turns around it. The amount of DNA required to wrap around the histone octamer is 146 or 147 bp (base pairs). The amino terminal tail of each histone protein protrudes from the histone octamer. As discussed in Chapter 13, these tails can be covalently modified and play a key role in gene regulation.

The nucleosomes are connected by linker regions of DNA that vary in length from 20 to 100 bp, depending on the species and cell type. A particular histone named histone H1 is bound to the linker region, as are other types of proteins. The overall structure of connected nucleosomes resembles beads on a

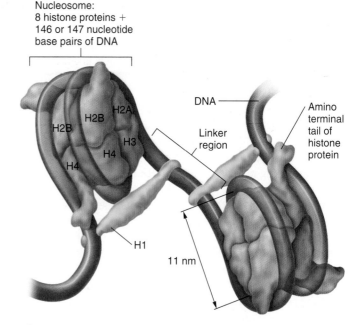

Nucleosome:
8 histone proteins +
146 or 147 nucleotide
base pairs of DNA

Figure 11.23 **Structure of a nucleosome.** A nucleosome is composed of double-stranded DNA wrapped around an octamer of histone proteins. A linker region connects two adjacent nucleosomes. Histone H1 is bound to the linker region, as are other proteins not shown in this figure.

string. This structure shortens the length of the DNA molecule about sevenfold.

Nucleosomes Form a 30-nm Fiber

Nucleosome units are organized into a more compact structure that is 30 nm in diameter, known as the **30-nm fiber** (Figure 11.24a). Histone H1 and other proteins are important in the formation of the 30-nm fiber, which shortens the nucleosome structure another sevenfold. The structure of the 30-nm fiber has proven difficult to determine because the conformation of the DNA may be substantially altered when extracted from living cells. A current model for the 30-nm fiber was proposed by Rachel Horowitz and Christopher Woodcock in the 1990s (Figure 11.24b). According to their model, linker regions in the 30-nm structure are variably bent and twisted, with little direct contact observed between nucleosomes. The 30-nm fiber forms an asymmetric, three-dimensional zigzag of nucleosomes. At this level of compaction, the overall picture of chromatin that emerges is an irregular, fluctuating structure with stable nucleosome units connected by bendable linker regions.

Chromatin Loops Are Anchored to the Nuclear Matrix

Thus far, we have examined two mechanisms that compact eukaryotic DNA: the formation of nucleosomes and their arrangement into a 30-nm fiber. Taken together, these two events shorten the folded DNA about 49-fold. A third level of

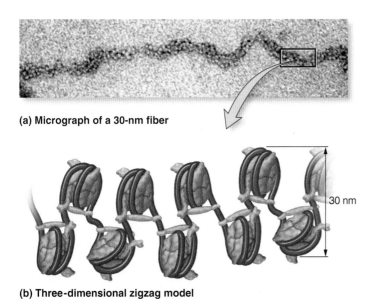

(a) Micrograph of a 30-nm fiber

30 nm

(b) Three-dimensional zigzag model

Figure 11.24 The 30-nm fiber. **(a)** A photomicrograph of the 30-nm fiber. **(b)** In this three-dimensional zigzag model, the linker DNA forms a bendable structure with little contact between adjacent nucleosomes.

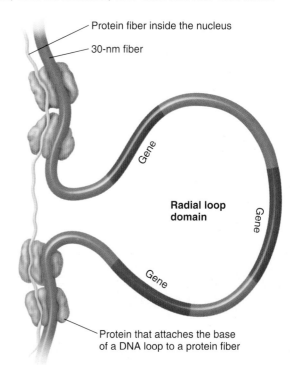

Protein fiber inside the nucleus

30-nm fiber

Gene

Radial loop domain

Gene

Gene

Protein that attaches the base of a DNA loop to a protein fiber

Figure 11.25 Attachment of the 30-nm fiber to a protein fiber to form a radial loop domain.

Concept check: *What holds the bottoms of the loops in place?*

compaction involves interactions between the 30-nm fibers and a filamentous network of proteins in the nucleus called the **nuclear matrix**. This matrix consists of the **nuclear lamina**, which is composed of protein fibers that line the inner nuclear membrane (see Chapter 4), and an internal nuclear matrix that is connected to the lamina and fills the interior of the nucleus. The internal nuclear matrix is an intricate network of irregular protein fibers plus many other proteins that bind to these fibers. The nuclear matrix is involved in the compaction of the 30-nm fiber by participating in the formation of **radial loop domains**. These loops, often 25,000 to 200,000 base pairs in size, are anchored to the nuclear matrix (**Figure 11.25**).

How are chromosomes organized within the cell nucleus? Each chromosome in the cell nucleus is located in a discrete and nonoverlapping chromosome territory, which can be experimentally viewed in nondividing cells (refer back to Chapter 4, Figure 4.16). Each chromosome in nondividing cells occupies its own discrete region in the cell nucleus that usually does not overlap with the territory of adjacent chromosomes. In other words, different chromosomes are not substantially intertwined with each other, even when they are in a noncompacted condition.

The compaction level of chromosomes in the cell nucleus is not completely uniform. This variability can be seen with a light microscope and was first observed by the German cytologist E. Heitz in 1928. He used the term **heterochromatin** to describe the highly compacted regions of chromosomes. By comparison, the less condensed regions are known as **euchromatin**. Euchromatin is the form of chromatin in which the 30-nm fiber forms radial loop domains. In heterochromatin, these radial loop domains are compacted even further. In nondividing cells,

most chromosomal regions are euchromatic, and some localized regions are heterochromatic.

During Cell Division, Chromosomes Undergo Maximum Compaction

When cells prepare to divide, the chromosomes become even more compacted or condensed. This aids in their proper alignment during metaphase, which is a stage of eukaryotic cell division described in Chapter 15. **Figure 11.26** illustrates the levels of compaction that contribute to the formation of a metaphase chromosome. DNA in the nucleus is always compacted by forming nucleosomes and condensing into a 30-nm fiber (Figure 11.26a,b,c). In euchromatin, the 30-nm fibers are arranged in radial loop domains that are relatively loose, meaning that a fair amount of space is between the 30-nm fibers (Figure 11.26d). The average width of such loops is about 300 nm.

By comparison, heterochromatin involves a much tighter packing of the loops, so little space is between the 30-nm fibers (Figure 11.26e). Heterochromatic regions tend to be wider, in the range of 700 nm. When cells prepare to divide, all of the euchromatin becomes highly compacted. The compaction of euchromatin greatly shortens the chromosomes. In a metaphase chromosome, which contains two copies of the DNA (Figure 11.26f), the width averages about 1,400 nm, but the length of a metaphase chromosome is much shorter than the same chromosome in the nucleus of a nondividing cell.

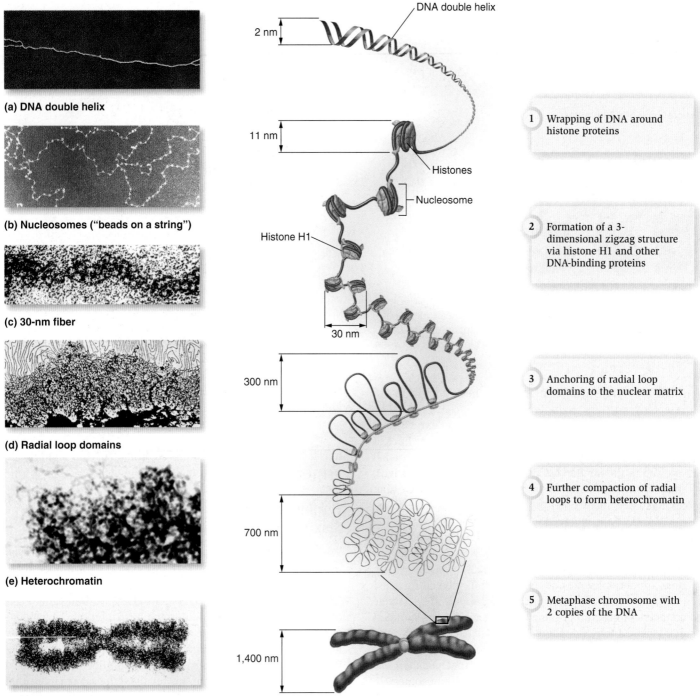

(a) DNA double helix

(b) Nucleosomes ("beads on a string")

(c) 30-nm fiber

(d) Radial loop domains

(e) Heterochromatin

(f) Metaphase chromosome

DNA double helix

2 nm

11 nm

Histones

Nucleosome

Histone H1

30 nm

300 nm

700 nm

1,400 nm

1 Wrapping of DNA around histone proteins

2 Formation of a 3-dimensional zigzag structure via histone H1 and other DNA-binding proteins

3 Anchoring of radial loop domains to the nuclear matrix

4 Further compaction of radial loops to form heterochromatin

5 Metaphase chromosome with 2 copies of the DNA

Figure 11.26 The steps in eukaryotic chromosomal compaction leading to the metaphase chromosome.

Concept check: After they have replicated and become compacted in preparation for cell division, chromosomes are often shaped like an X, as in part (f) of this figure. Which proteins are primarily responsible for this X shape?

Summary of Key Concepts

11.1 Biochemical Identification of the Genetic Material

- The genetic material carries information to produce the traits of organisms. It is replicated and transmitted from cell to cell and generation to generation, and it has differences that explain the variation among different organisms.

- Griffith's work with type S and type R bacteria was consistent with the transfer of genetic material, which he called the transformation principle. (Figure 11.1)

- Avery, MacLeod, and McCarty used biochemical methods to show that DNA is the transformation principle. (Figure 11.2)

- Hershey and Chase labeled T2 phage with ^{35}S and ^{32}P and determined that the ^{32}P-labeled DNA is the genetic material of this phage. (Figures 11.3, 11.4)

11.2 Nucleic Acid Structure

- DNA is composed of nucleotides, which covalently link to form DNA strands. Two DNA strands are held together by hydrogen bonds between the bases to form a double helix. Chromosomes are made of DNA and proteins. (Figure 11.5)

- Nucleotides are composed of a phosphate, sugar, and nitrogenous base. The sugar can be deoxyribose (DNA) or ribose (RNA). The purine bases are adenine and guanine, and the pyrimidine bases are thymine (DNA only), cytosine, and uracil (RNA only). (Figure 11.6)

- The atoms in a nucleotide are numbered in a conventional way. (Figure 11.7)

- In a strand of DNA (or RNA), the sugars are connected by covalent bonds in a 5′ to 3′ direction. (Figure 11.8)

- Watson and Crick used the X-ray diffraction data of Franklin and the biochemical data of Chargaff (that is, A = T, G = C), and constructed ball-and-stick models to reveal the double helix structure of DNA. (Figure 11.9, Table 11.1)

- DNA is a double helix in which the DNA strands are antiparallel and obey the AT/GC rule. (Figures 11.10, 11.11)

11.3 An Overview of DNA Replication

- Meselson and Stahl used ^{15}N- and ^{14}N-isotope labeling methods to show that DNA is replicated by a semiconservative mechanism in which the product of DNA replication is one original strand and one new strand. (Figures 11.12, 11.13)

- New DNA strands are made according to the AT/GC rule in which parental strands serve as templates for the synthesis of new daughter strands. The result of DNA replication is two double helices with the same base sequence. (Figure 11.14)

11.4 Molecular Mechanism of DNA Replication

- DNA synthesis occurs bidirectionally from an origin of replication. The synthesis of new DNA strands happens near each replication fork. (Figure 11.15)

- DNA helicase separates DNA strands, single-strand binding proteins keep them separated, and DNA topoisomerase alleviates coiling ahead of the fork. (Figure 11.16)

- Deoxynucleoside triphosphates bind to the template strands, and DNA polymerase catalyzes the formation of a phosphoester bond between the 3′ end of the strand and a deoxynucleoside monophosphate. (Figure 11.17)

- DNA polymerase requires a primer and can make new DNA strands only in the 5′ to 3′ direction. (Figure 11.18)

- The leading strand is made continuously, in the same direction the fork is moving. The lagging strand is made in the opposite direction as short Okazaki fragments that are connected together. (Figure 11.19)

- DNA primase makes one RNA primer in the leading strand and multiple RNA primers in the lagging strand. In *E. coli*, DNA polymerase III extends these primers with DNA, and DNA polymerase I removes the primers when they are no longer needed. DNA ligase connects adjacent Okazaki fragments in the lagging strand. (Figure 11.20, Table 11.2)

- Living organisms have several different types of DNA polymerases with specialized functions. (Table 11.3)

- The ends of linear, eukaryotic chromosomes have telomeres composed of repeat sequences. Telomerase binds to the telomere repeat sequence and synthesizes a six-nucleotide repeat. This happens many times in a row to lengthen one DNA strand of the telomere. DNA primase, DNA polymerase, and DNA ligase are needed to synthesize the complementary DNA strand. (Figures 11.21, 11.22)

11.5 Molecular Structure of Eukaryotic Chromosomes

- Chromosomes are structures in living cells that carry the genetic material. Chromatin is the name given to the DNA-protein complex that makes up chromosomes.

- In eukaryotic chromosomes, the DNA is wrapped around histone proteins to form nucleosomes. Nucleosomes are further compacted into 30-nm fibers. The linker regions are variably twisted and bent into a zigzag pattern. (Figures 11.23, 11.24)

- A third level of compaction of eukaryotic chromosomes involves the formation of radial loop domains in which the bases of 30-nm fibers are anchored to a network of proteins called the nuclear matrix. This level of compaction is called euchromatin. In heterochromatin, the loops are even more closely packed together. (Figure 11.25)

- Chromosome compaction to produce a metaphase chromosome involves the conversion of all euchromatin into heterochromatin. (Figure 11.26)

▌ Assess and Discuss

Test Yourself

1. Why did researchers initially believe the genetic material was protein?
   a. Proteins are more biochemically complex than DNA.
   b. Proteins are found only in the nucleus, but DNA is found in many areas of the cell.
   c. Proteins are much larger molecules and can store more information than DNA.
   d. all of the above
   e. both a and c

2. Considering the components of a nucleotide, what component is always different when comparing nucleotides in a DNA strand or an RNA strand?
   a. phosphate group
   b. pentose sugar
   c. nitrogenous base
   d. both b and c
   e. a, b, and c

3. Which of the following equations would be appropriate when considering DNA base composition?
   a. %A + %T = %G + %C
   b. %A = %G
   c. %A = %G = %T = %C
   d. %A + %G = %T + %C

4. If the sequence of a segment of DNA is 5′–CGCAACTAC–3′, what is the appropriate sequence for the opposite strand?
   a. 5′–GCGTTGATG–3′
   b. 3′–ATACCAGCA–5′
   c. 5′–ATACCAGCA–3′
   d. 3′–GCGTTGATG–5′

5. Of the following statements, which is correct when considering the process of DNA replication?
   a. New DNA molecules are composed of two completely new strands.
   b. New DNA molecules are composed of one strand from the old molecule and one new strand.
   c. New DNA molecules are composed of strands that are a mixture of sections from the old molecule and sections that are new.
   d. none of the above

6. Meselson and Stahl were able to demonstrate semiconservative replication in *E. coli* by
   a. using radioactive isotopes of phosphorus to label the old strand and visually determining the relationship of old and new DNA strands.
   b. using different enzymes to eliminate old strands from DNA.
   c. using isotopes of nitrogen to label the DNA and determining the relationship of old and new DNA strands by density differences of the new molecules.
   d. labeling viral DNA before it was incorporated into a bacterial cell and visually determining the location of the DNA after centrifugation.

7. During replication of a DNA molecule, the daughter strands are not produced in exactly the same manner. One strand, the leading strand, is made toward the replication fork, while the lagging strand is made in fragments in the opposite direction. This difference in the synthesis of the two strands is the result of which of the following?
   a. DNA polymerase is not efficient enough to make two "good" strands of DNA.
   b. The two template strands are antiparallel, and DNA polymerase makes DNA only in the 5′ to 3′ direction.
   c. The lagging strand is the result of DNA breakage due to UV light.
   d. The cell does not contain enough nucleotides to make two complete strands.

8. In eukaryotic cells, chromosomes consist of
   a. DNA and RNA.
   b. DNA only.
   c. RNA and proteins.
   d. DNA and proteins.
   e. RNA only.

9. A nucleosome is
   a. a dark-staining body composed of RNA and proteins found in the nucleus.
   b. a protein that helps organize the structure of chromosomes.
   c. another word for a chromosome.
   d. a structure composed of DNA wrapped around eight histones.
   e. the short arm of a chromosome.

10. The conversion of euchromatin into heterochromatin involves
    a. the formation of more nucleosomes.
    b. the formation of less nucleosomes.
    c. a greater compaction of loop domains.
    d. a lesser compaction of loop domains.
    e. both a and c.

Conceptual Questions

1. What are the four key characteristics of the genetic material? What was Frederick Griffith's contribution to the study of DNA, and why was it so important?

2. The Hershey and Chase experiment used radioactive isotopes to track the DNA and protein of phages as they infected bacterial cells. Explain how this procedure allowed them to determine that DNA is the genetic material of this particular virus.

3. Explain or describe the essential features of the Watson and Crick model of the structure of DNA.

Collaborative Questions

1. A trait that some bacterial strains exhibit is resistance to killing by antibiotics. For example, certain strains of bacteria are resistant to tetracycline, whereas other strains are sensitive to this antibiotic. Describe an experiment you would carry out to demonstrate that tetracycline resistance is an inherited trait carried in the DNA of the resistant strain.

2. How might you provide evidence that DNA is the genetic material in mice?

Online Resource

www.brookerbiology.com

Stay a step ahead in your studies with animations that bring concepts to life and practice tests to assess your understanding. Your instructor may also recommend the interactive ebook, individualized learning tools, and more.

Gene Expression at the Molecular Level

12

An electron micrograph of many ribosomes in the act of translating two mRNA molecules into many polypeptides. The short polypeptides are seen emerging from the ribosomes.

Mina, age 21, works part-time in an ice-cream shop and particularly enjoys the double-dark chocolate and chocolate fudge brownie flavors on her breaks. She exercises little and spends most of her time studying and watching television. Mina is effortlessly thin. She never worries about what or how much she eats. By comparison, her close friend, Rezzy, has struggled with her weight as long as she can remember. Compared to Mina, she feels like she must constantly deprive herself of food just to maintain her current weight—a weight she would describe as 30 pounds too much.

How do we explain the differences between Mina and Rezzy? Two fundamental factors are involved. Obesity is strongly influenced by the environment, especially a person's diet, along with social and behavioral factors. The amount and types of food we eat are correlated with weight gain. However, there is little doubt that obesity is also influenced by variation in our genes. Obesity runs in families. A similarity is observed in the degree of obesity between genetically identical twins who have been raised apart. Why has genetic variation resulted in some genes that cause certain people to gain weight? A popular hypothesis is that we have "thrifty genes" as hand-me-downs from our ancestors, who periodically faced famines and food scarcity. Such thrifty genes allow us to store body fat more easily and to use food resources more efficiently when times are lean. The negative side is that when food is abundant, unwanted weight gain can become a serious health problem.

Why do we care about our genes? Let's consider this question with regard to obesity. Researchers have identified several key genes that influence a person's predisposition to becoming obese. Dozens more are likely to play a minor role. By identifying those genes and studying the proteins specified by those genes, researchers may gain a better understanding of how genetic variation can cause certain people to gain weight more easily than others. In addition, this knowledge has led to the development of drugs that are used to combat obesity.

In this chapter, we begin to explore the inner workings of genes. We can broadly define a gene as a unit of heredity. Geneticists view gene function at different biological levels. In Chapter 16, we will examine how genes affect the traits or characteristics of individuals.

For example, we will consider how the transmission of genes from parents to offspring affects the color of the offspring's eyes and their likelihood of becoming bald. In this chapter, we will explore how genes work at the molecular level. You will learn how DNA sequences are organized to form genes and how those genes are used as a template to make RNA copies, ultimately leading to the synthesis of a functional protein. The term **gene expression** can refer to gene function either at the level of traits or at the molecular level. In reality, the two phenomena are intricately woven together. The expression of genes at the molecular level affects the structure and function of cells, which, in turn, determine the traits that an organism expresses.

We begin this chapter by considering how researchers came to realize that most genes store the information to make proteins. Then we will explore the steps of gene expression as they occur at the molecular level. These steps include the use of a gene as a template to make an RNA molecule, the processing of the RNA into a functional molecule, and the use of RNA to direct the formation of a protein.

12.1 Overview of Gene Expression

Even before DNA was known to be the genetic material, scientists had asked the question, How does the functioning of genes create the traits of living organisms? At the molecular level, a similar question can be asked. How do genes affect the composition and/or function of molecules found within living cells? An approach that was successful in answering these questions involved the study of **mutations**, which are changes in the genetic material. Mutations can affect the genetic blueprint by altering gene function. For this reason, research that focused on the effects of mutations proved instrumental in determining the molecular function of genes.

In this section, we will consider two early experiments in which researchers studied the effects of mutations in humans and in a bread mold. Both studies led to the conclusion that the role of some genes is to carry the information to produce enzymes. Then we will examine the general features of gene expression at the molecular level.

The Study of Inborn Errors of Metabolism Suggested That Some Genes Carry the Information to Make Enzymes

In 1908, Archibald Garrod, a British physician, proposed a relationship between genes and the production of enzymes. Prior to his work, biochemists had studied many metabolic pathways that consist of a series of conversions of one molecule to another, each step catalyzed by an enzyme. Figure 12.1 illustrates part of the metabolic pathway for the breakdown of phenylalanine, an amino acid commonly found in human diets. The enzyme phenylalanine hydroxylase catalyzes the conversion of phenylalanine to tyrosine, another amino acid. A different enzyme, tyrosine aminotransferase, converts tyrosine into the next molecule, called p-hydroxyphenylpyruvic acid. In each case, a specific enzyme catalyzes a single chemical reaction.

Much of Garrod's early work centered on the inherited disease alkaptonuria, in which the patient's body accumulates abnormal levels of homogentisic acid (also called alkapton). This compound, which is bluish black, results in discoloration of the skin and cartilage and causes the urine to appear black. Garrod hypothesized that the accumulation of homogentisic acid in these patients is due to a defect in an enzyme, namely, homogentisic acid oxidase (Figure 12.1). Furthermore, he already knew that alkaptonuria is an inherited condition that follows a recessive pattern of inheritance. As discussed in Chapter 16, if a disorder is recessive, an individual with the disease has inherited the mutant (defective) gene that causes the disorder from both parents.

How did Garrod explain these observations? In 1908, he proposed a relationship between the inheritance of a mutant gene and a defect in metabolism. In the case of alkaptonuria, if an individual inherited the mutant gene from both parents,

she or he would not produce any normal enzyme and would be unable to metabolize homogentisic acid. Garrod described alkaptonuria as an **inborn error of metabolism**. An inborn error refers to a mutation in a gene that is inherited from one or both parents. At the turn of the last century, this was a particularly insightful idea because the structure and function of the genetic material were completely unknown.

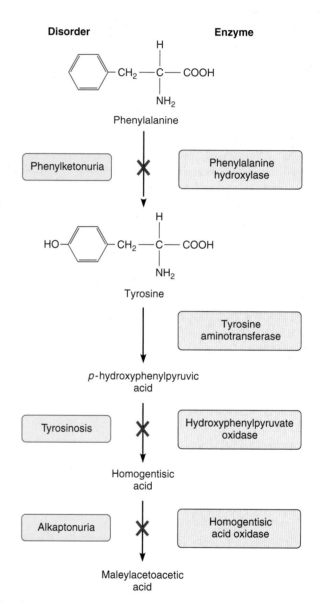

Figure 12.1 The metabolic pathway that breaks down phenylalanine and its relationship to certain genetic diseases. Each step in the pathway is catalyzed by a different enzyme, shown in the boxes on the right. If one of the enzymes is not functioning, the previous compound builds up, causing the disorders named in the boxes on the left.

Concept check: What disease would occur if a person had inherited two defective copies of the gene that encodes phenylalanine hydroxylase?

Beadle and Tatum Proposed the One Gene–One Enzyme Hypothesis

In early 1940s, George Beadle and Edward Tatum became aware of Garrod's work and were interested in the relationship between genes and enzymes. They focused their studies on *Neurospora crassa*, a common bread mold. *Neurospora* is easily grown in the laboratory and has only a few nutritional requirements: a carbon source (namely, sugar), inorganic salts, and one vitamin known as biotin. Otherwise, *Neurospora* has many different enzymes that synthesize the molecules, such as amino acids and many vitamins, that are essential for growth.

Like Garrod, Beadle and Tatum hypothesized that genes carry the information to make specific enzymes. They reasoned that a mutation, or change in a gene, might cause a defect in an enzyme required for the synthesis of an essential molecule, such as an amino acid or vitamin. A mutant *Neurospora* strain (one that carries such a mutation) would be unable to grow unless the amino acid or vitamin was supplemented in the growth medium. Strains without a mutation are called wild-type. In their original study of 1941, Beadle and Tatum exposed *Neurospora* cells to X-rays, which caused mutations to occur, and studied the resulting cells. By plating the cells on growth media with or without vitamins, they were able to identify mutant strains that required vitamins for growth. In each case, a single mutation resulted in the requirement for a single type of vitamin in the growth media.

This early study by Beadle and Tatum led to additional research by themselves and others to study enzymes involved in the synthesis of other substances, including the amino acid arginine. At that time, the pathway leading to arginine synthesis was known to involve certain precursor molecules, including ornithine and citrulline. A simplified pathway for arginine synthesis is shown in **Figure 12.2a**. Each step is catalyzed by a different enzyme.

Researchers first isolated several different mutants that required arginine for growth. They hypothesized that each mutant strain might be blocked at only a single step in the consecutive series of reactions that lead to arginine synthesis. To test this hypothesis, the mutant strains were examined for their ability to grow in the presence of ornithine, citrulline, or arginine (**Figure 12.2b**). The wild-type strain could grow on minimal growth media that did not contain ornithine, citrulline, or arginine. Based on their growth properties, the mutant strains that had been originally identified as requiring arginine for growth could be placed into three groups, designated 1, 2, and 3. Group 1 mutants were missing enzyme 1, needed for the conversion of a precursor molecule into ornithine. They could grow only if ornithine, citrulline, or arginine was added to the growth medium. Group 2 mutants were missing the second enzyme in this pathway that is needed for the conversion of ornithine into citrulline. The group 2 mutants would not grow if only ornithine was added, but could grow if citrulline or arginine was added. Finally, the group 3 mutants were missing the enzyme needed for the conversion of citrulline into arginine.

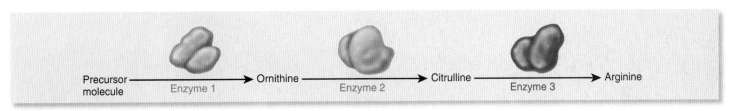

(a) Simplified pathway for arginine synthesis

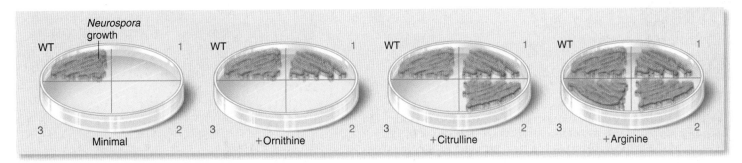

(b) Growth of strains on minimal and supplemented growth media

Figure 12.2   An experiment that supported Beadle and Tatum's one gene–one enzyme hypothesis.   (a) This simplified pathway shows three enzymes that are required for arginine synthesis. (b) Growth of wild-type (WT) and mutant *Neurospora* strains (groups 1, 2, and 3) on minimal plates or in the presence of ornithine, citrulline, or arginine.

Concept check: *What type of enzyme function is missing in group 2 mutants?*

These mutants could grow only if arginine was added. How were these results interpreted? The researchers were able to order the functions of the genes involved in arginine synthesis in the following way:

Group 1   Group 2   Group 3
Precursor ——————→ Ornithine ——————→ Citrulline ——————→ Arginine

From these results and earlier studies, Beadle and Tatum concluded that a single gene controlled the synthesis of a single enzyme. This was referred to as the **one gene–one enzyme hypothesis**.

In later decades, this idea was modified in three ways. First, the information to make all proteins is contained within genes, and many proteins do not function as enzymes. Second, some proteins are composed of two or more different polypeptides. The term **polypeptide** refers to a linear sequence of amino acids; it denotes structure. Most genes carry the information to make a particular polypeptide. By comparison, the term **protein** denotes function. Some proteins are composed of one polypeptide. In such cases, a single gene does contain the information to make a single protein. In other cases, however, a functional protein is composed of two or more different polypeptides. An example is hemoglobin, the protein that carries oxygen in red blood cells, which is composed of two α-globin and two β-globin polypeptides. In this case, the expression of two genes (that is, the α-globin and β-globin genes) is needed to create a functional protein. A third modification to the one gene–one enzyme hypothesis is that some genes encode RNAs that are not used to make polypeptides. For example, as discussed later in this chapter, some genes encode RNA molecules that form part of the structure of ribosomes.

Molecular Gene Expression Involves the Processes of Transcription and Translation

Thus far, we have considered two classic studies that led researchers to conclude that some genes carry the information to make enzymes. Let's now consider the general steps of gene expression at the molecular level. The first step, known as **transcription**, produces an RNA copy of a gene, also called an RNA transcript (**Figure 12.3**). The term transcription literally means the act of making a copy. Most genes, which are termed **structural genes**[1], produce an RNA molecule that contains the information to specify a polypeptide with a particular amino acid sequence. This type of RNA is called **messenger RNA** (abbreviated **mRNA**), because its job is to carry information from the DNA to cellular components called ribosomes. As discussed later, ribosomes play a key role in the synthesis of polypeptides. The process of synthesizing a specific polypeptide on a ribosome is called **translation**. The term translation is used because a nucleotide sequence in mRNA is "translated" into an amino acid sequence of a polypeptide.

Together, the transcription of DNA into mRNA and the translation of mRNA into a polypeptide constitute the **central dogma** of gene expression at the molecular level, which was first proposed by Francis Crick in 1958 (Figure 12.3). The

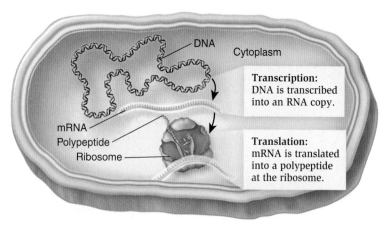

(a) Molecular gene expression in prokaryotes

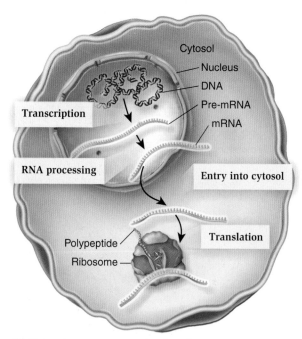

(b) Molecular gene expression in eukaryotes

Figure 12.3   The central dogma of gene expression at the molecular level.   (a) In bacteria, transcription and translation occur in the cytoplasm. (b) In eukaryotes, transcription and RNA processing occur in the nucleus, whereas translation takes place in the cytosol.

Concept check: _What is the direction of flow of genetic information?_

---

[1] Geneticists commonly use the term structural gene to describe all genes that encode polypeptides, which is how it is used in this textbook. Some geneticists, however, distinguish structural genes from regulatory genes—genes that encode proteins regulating the expression of structural genes.

central dogma applies equally to prokaryotes and eukaryotes. However, in eukaryotes, two additional steps occur between transcription and translation. During **RNA processing**, the RNA transcript, termed **pre-mRNA**, is modified in ways that make it a functionally active mRNA (Figure 12.3b). The processing events will be described later in this chapter. The mRNA is then transported into the cytosol. Though the direction of information flow—DNA → RNA → protein—is the most common pathway, exceptions do occur. For example, certain viruses can use RNA as a template to synthesize DNA. Such viruses are described in Chapter 18.

The Protein Products of Genes Determine an Organism's Characteristics

The genes that constitute the genetic material provide a blueprint for the characteristics of every organism. They contain the information necessary to create an organism and allow it to favorably interact with its environment. Each structural gene stores the information for the production of a polypeptide, which then becomes a unit within a functional protein. The activities of proteins determine the structure and function of cells. Furthermore, the characteristics of an organism are rooted in the activities of cellular proteins.

The main purpose of the genetic material is to encode the production of proteins in the correct cell, at the proper time, and in suitable amounts. This is an intricate task, because living cells make thousands of different kinds of proteins. Genetic analyses have shown that a typical bacterium can make a few thousand different proteins, and estimates for eukaryotes range from several thousand in simpler eukaryotes to tens of thousands in more complex eukaryotes like humans.

12.2   Transcription

DNA is an information storage unit. For genes to be expressed, the information in them must be accessed at the molecular level. Rather than accessing the information directly, however, a working copy of the DNA, composed of RNA, is made. This occurs by the process of transcription, in which a DNA sequence is copied into an RNA sequence. Importantly, transcription does not permanently alter the structure of DNA. Therefore, the same DNA can continue to store information even after an RNA copy has been made. In this section, we will examine the steps necessary for genes to act as transcriptional units. We will also consider some differences in these steps between prokaryotes and eukaryotes.

At the Molecular Level, a Gene Can Be Transcribed and Produces a Functional Product

What is a gene? At the molecular level, a **gene** is defined as an organized unit of DNA sequences that enables a segment of DNA to be transcribed into RNA and ultimately results in

the formation of a functional product. When a structural gene is transcribed, an mRNA is made that specifies the amino acid sequence of a polypeptide. After it is made, the polypeptide becomes a functional product. The mRNA is an intermediary in polypeptide synthesis. Among all species, most genes are structural genes. However, for some genes, the functional product is the RNA itself. The RNA from a nonstructural gene is never translated. Two important products of nonstructural genes are transfer RNA and ribosomal RNA. **Transfer RNA (tRNA)** translates the language of mRNA into that of amino acids; **ribosomal RNA (rRNA)** forms part of ribosomes, which provide the site where translation occurs. We'll learn more about these two types of RNA later in this chapter.

A gene is composed of specific base sequences organized in a way that allows the DNA to be transcribed into RNA. **Figure 12.4** shows the general organization of sequences in a structural gene. Transcription begins next to a site in the DNA called the **promoter**, whereas the **terminator** specifies the end of transcription. Therefore, transcription occurs between these two boundaries. As shown in Figure 12.4, the DNA is transcribed into mRNA from the end of the promoter through the coding sequence to the terminator. Within this transcribed region is the information that will specify the amino acid sequence of a polypeptide when the mRNA is translated.

Other DNA sequences are involved in the regulation of transcription. These **regulatory sequences** function as sites for genetic regulatory proteins. When a regulatory protein binds to a regulatory sequence, the rate of transcription is affected. Some regulatory proteins enhance the rate of transcription, while others inhibit it.

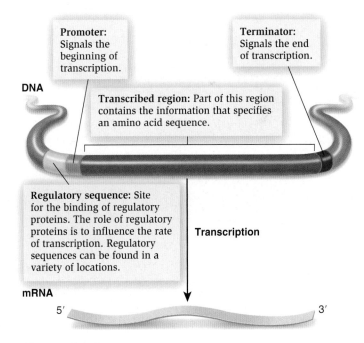

Figure 12.4   A structural gene as a transcriptional unit.

Concept check: If a terminator was removed from a gene, how would this affect transcription? Where would transcription end?

During Transcription, RNA Polymerase Uses a DNA Template to Make RNA

Transcription occurs in three stages, called initiation, elongation, and termination, during which proteins interact with DNA sequences (**Figure 12.5**). The **initiation stage** is a recognition step. In bacteria such as *E. coli*, a protein called **sigma factor** binds to **RNA polymerase**, the enzyme that synthesizes strands of RNA. Sigma factor also recognizes the base sequence of a promoter and binds there. In this way, sigma factor causes RNA polymerase to specifically bind to a promoter sequence. The initiation stage is completed when the DNA strands are separated near the promoter to form an **open complex** that is approximately 10 to 15 base pairs long.

During the **elongation stage**, RNA polymerase synthesizes the RNA transcript. For this to occur, sigma factor is released and RNA polymerase slides along the DNA in a way that maintains an open complex as it goes. The DNA strand that is used as a template for RNA synthesis is called the **template strand**. The opposite DNA strand is called the **coding strand**. The coding strand has the same sequence of bases as the mRNA, except that thymine in the DNA is substituted for uracil in the RNA. The coding strand is so named because, like mRNA, it carries the information that codes for a polypeptide.

During the elongation stage of transcription, nucleotides bind to the template strand and are covalently connected in the 5′ to 3′ direction (see inset of step 2, Figure 12.5). The complementarity rule used in this process is similar to the AT/GC rule of DNA replication, except that uracil (U) substitutes for thymine (T) in RNA. For example, an RNA with a sequence reading 5′–AUGUUACAUCGG–3′ will be transcribed from a DNA template with a sequence of 3′–TACAATGTAGCC–5′. In bacteria, the rate of RNA synthesis is about 40 nucleotides per second! Behind the open complex, the DNA rewinds back into a double helix. Eventually, RNA polymerase reaches a terminator, which causes it and the newly made RNA transcript to dissociate from the DNA. This event constitutes the **termination stage** of transcription.

The catalytic portion of RNA polymerase that is responsible for the synthesis of RNA has a similar structure in all species. The structure of a bacterial RNA polymerase is shown in **Figure 12.6**. RNA polymerase contains a cavity that allows it to slide along the DNA. The DNA strands enter at the side of the protein, and RNA is made in a 5′ to 3′ direction. Both the DNA and the newly made strand of RNA then exit from the top of the protein (see Figure 12.5).

When considering the transcription of multiple genes within a chromosome, the direction of transcription and the

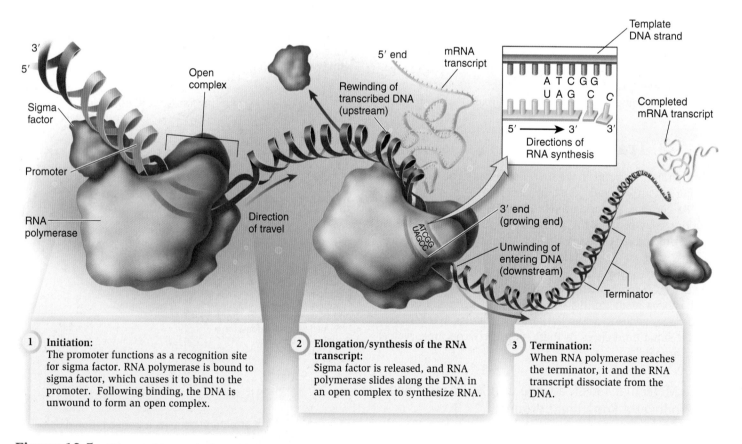

1 **Initiation:**
The promoter functions as a recognition site for sigma factor. RNA polymerase is bound to sigma factor, which causes it to bind to the promoter. Following binding, the DNA is unwound to form an open complex.

2 **Elongation/synthesis of the RNA transcript:**
Sigma factor is released, and RNA polymerase slides along the DNA in an open complex to synthesize RNA.

3 **Termination:**
When RNA polymerase reaches the terminator, it and the RNA transcript dissociate from the DNA.

Figure 12.5 **Stages of transcription.** Transcription can be divided into initiation, elongation, and termination. The inset emphasizes the direction of RNA synthesis and base pairing between the DNA template strand and RNA. Note: Some recent evidence suggests that sigma factor may not always be released during elongation.

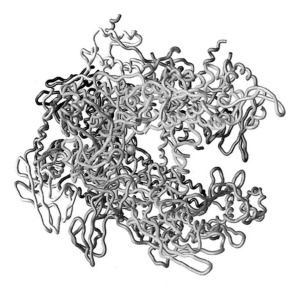

Figure 12.6 Three-dimensional structure of a bacterial RNA polymerase.

The transcription of eukaryotic genes tends to involve a greater complexity of protein components. For example, three forms of RNA polymerase are found in eukaryotes, designated I, II, and III. RNA polymerase II is responsible for transcribing the mRNA from eukaryotic structural genes, whereas RNA polymerases I and III transcribe nonstructural genes such as the genes that encode tRNAs and rRNAs. By comparison, bacteria have a single type of RNA polymerase that transcribes all genes.

The initiation stage of transcription in eukaryotes is also more complex. Recall that bacteria such as *E. coli* use a single protein, sigma factor, to recognize the promoter of genes. By comparison, RNA polymerase II of eukaryotes always requires five general transcription factors to initiate transcription. **Transcription factors** are proteins that influence the ability of RNA polymerase to transcribe genes. In addition, the regulation of gene transcription in eukaryotes typically involves the function of several different proteins. The roles of eukaryotic transcription factors are considered in Chapter 13.

DNA strand that is used as a template vary among different genes. Figure 12.7 shows three genes adjacent to each other within a chromosome. Genes A and B are transcribed from left to right, using the bottom DNA strand as the template strand. By comparison, gene C is transcribed from right to left, using the top DNA strand as a template strand. In all three cases, the synthesis of the RNA transcript begins at the promoter and occurs in a 5′ to 3′ direction. The template strand is read in the 3′ to 5′ direction.

Transcription Is Similar in Prokaryotes and Eukaryotes, Except That Eukaryotes Use More Proteins

The basic features of transcription are similar between prokaryotic and eukaryotic organisms. Eukaryotic and prokaryotic genes have promoters, and the transcription process involves the stages of initiation, elongation, and termination.

12.3 RNA Processing in Eukaryotes

During the 1960s and 1970s, the physical structure of the gene became well established based largely on studies of bacterial genes. Most bacterial mRNAs can be translated into polypeptides as soon as they are made. By comparison, eukaryotic mRNA transcripts undergo RNA processing or modification that is needed for their proper translation. In eukaryotes, transcription initially produces a longer RNA, called **pre-mRNA**, which undergoes certain processing events before it exits the nucleus. The final product is called a **mature mRNA** or simply mRNA.

In the late 1970s, when the experimental tools became available to study eukaryotic genes at the molecular level, the scientific community was astonished by the discovery that the coding sequences within many eukaryotic structural genes are

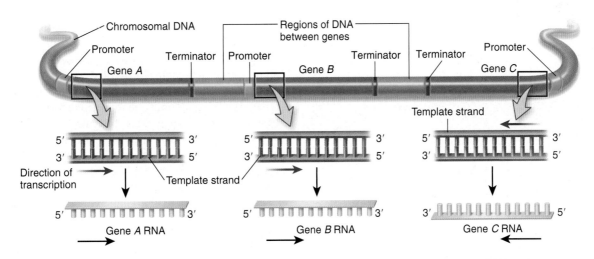

Figure 12.7 **The transcription of three different genes that are found in the same chromosome.** RNA polymerase synthesizes each RNA transcript in a 5′ to 3′ direction, sliding along a DNA template strand in a 3′ to 5′ direction. However, the use of the template strand can vary from gene to gene. For example, genes A and B use the bottom strand, while gene C uses the top strand.

separated by DNA sequences that are transcribed but not translated into protein. These intervening sequences that are not translated are called **introns**, while coding sequences are found within **exons** contained in the mature mRNA. The exons are expressed regions, whereas the introns are intervening regions that are not expressed because they are removed from the mRNA.

To create a functional mRNA, the pre-mRNA undergoes a process known as **splicing**, in which the introns are removed and the remaining exons are connected to each other (**Figure 12.8**). In addition to splicing, eukaryotic pre-mRNA transcripts are modified in other ways, including the addition of caps and tails to the ends of the mRNA. After these modifications have been completed, the mRNA leaves the nucleus and enters the cytosol, where translation occurs. In this section, we will examine the molecular mechanisms that account for these RNA processing events and consider why they are functionally important.

Splicing Involves the Removal of Introns and the Linkage of Exons

Introns are found in many eukaryotic genes. Splicing is less frequent among unicellular eukaryotic species, such as yeast, but is a widespread phenomenon among more complex eukaryotes. In many animals and flowering plants, most structural genes have one or more introns. For example, an average human gene has about 9 introns. The sizes of introns can vary from a few dozen nucleotides to over one hundred thousand! A few bacterial genes have been found to have introns, but they are rare among all prokaryotic species.

Introns are precisely removed from eukaryotic pre-mRNA by a large complex called a **spliceosome** that is composed

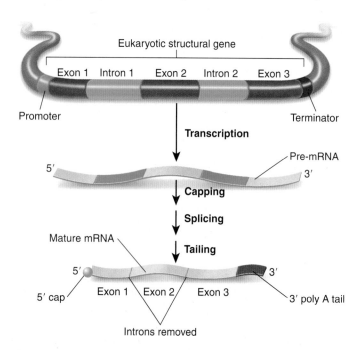

Figure 12.8   Modifications to eukaryotic pre-mRNA that are needed to create a functional (mature) mRNA molecule.

of several different subunits known as snRNPs (pronounced "snurps"). Each snRNP contains small nuclear RNA and a set of proteins. This small nuclear RNA is the product of a nonstructural gene. How are introns identified and removed? Intron RNA is defined by particular sequences within the intron and at the intron-exon boundaries (**Figure 12.9**). These include a 5′ splice site, a branch site, and a 3′ splice site. Spliceosome subunits bind to specific sequences at these three locations. This binding causes the intron to loop outward, which brings the two exons close together. The 5′ splice site is then cut, and the 5′ end of the intron becomes covalently attached to the branch site. In the final step, the 3′ splice site is cut, and then the exons are covalently attached to each other. The intron is released and eventually degraded.

In some cases, the function of the spliceosome can be regulated so the splicing of exons for a given mRNA can occur in two or more ways. This phenomenon, called **alternative splicing**, enables a single gene to encode two or more polypeptides with differences in their amino acid sequences (see Chapter 13).

Although primarily found in mRNAs, introns occasionally occur in rRNA and tRNA molecules of certain species. These introns, however, are not removed by the action of a spliceosome. Instead, such rRNAs and tRNAs are **self-splicing**, which means the RNA itself can catalyze the removal of its own intron. Portions of the RNA act like an enzyme to cleave the covalent bonds at the intron-exon boundaries and connect the exons together. An RNA molecule that catalyzes a chemical reaction is termed a **ribozyme**.

RNA Processing Also Involves Adding a 5′ Cap and a 3′ Poly A Tail to the Ends of Eukaryotic mRNAs

Mature mRNAs of eukaryotes have a modified guanosine covalently attached at the 5′ end, an event known as **capping** (**Figure 12.10a**). Capping occurs while a pre-mRNA is being made by RNA polymerase, usually when the transcript is only 20 to 25 nucleotides in length. What are the functions of the cap? The 7-methylguanosine structure, called a **5′ cap**, is recognized by cap-binding proteins, which are needed for the proper exit of mRNAs from the nucleus. After an mRNA is in the cytosol, the cap structure is recognized by other cap-binding proteins that enable the mRNA to bind to a ribosome for translation.

At the 3′ end, most mature eukaryotic mRNAs have a string of adenine nucleotides, typically 100 to 200 nucleotides in length, referred to as a **poly A tail** (**Figure 12.10b**). A long poly A tail aids in the export of mRNAs from the nucleus. It also causes a eukaryotic mRNA to be more stable and thereby exist for a longer period of time in the cytosol. The poly A tail is not encoded in the gene sequence. Instead, the tail is added enzymatically after a pre-mRNA has been completely transcribed. Interestingly, new research has shown that some bacterial mRNAs also have poly A tails attached to them. However, the poly A tail has an opposite effect in bacteria, where it causes the mRNA to be rapidly degraded. The importance of a poly A tail in bacterial mRNAs is not well understood.

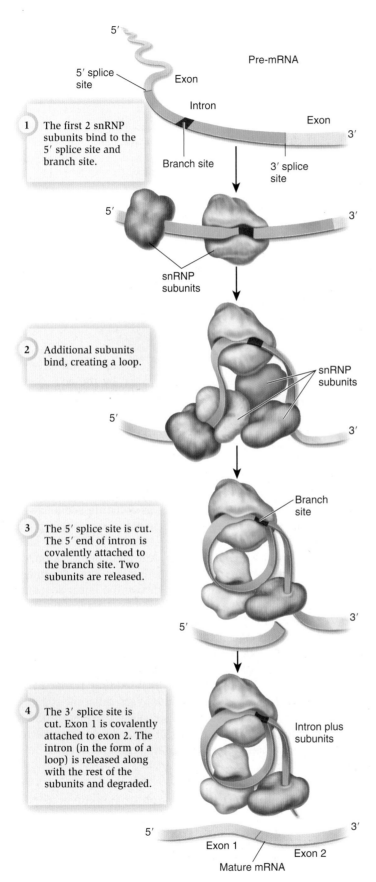

1 The first 2 snRNP subunits bind to the 5′ splice site and branch site.

2 Additional subunits bind, creating a loop.

3 The 5′ splice site is cut. The 5′ end of intron is covalently attached to the branch site. Two subunits are released.

4 The 3′ splice site is cut. Exon 1 is covalently attached to exon 2. The intron (in the form of a loop) is released along with the rest of the subunits and degraded.

Figure 12.9   The splicing of a eukaryotic pre-mRNA by a spliceosome.

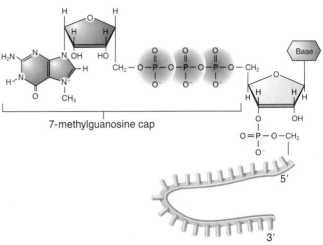

(a) Cap structure at the 5′ end of eukaryotic mRNA

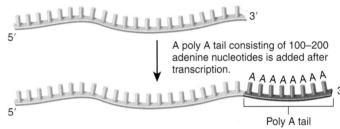

A poly A tail consisting of 100–200 adenine nucleotides is added after transcription.

(b) Addition of a poly A tail at the 3′ end of eukaryotic mRNA

Figure 12.10   Modifications that occur at the ends of mRNA in eukaryotic cells.   **(a)** A guanosine cap is attached to the 5′ end. This guanosine is modified by having a methyl group attached to it. The linkage between the cap and the mRNA is a 5′ to 5′ linkage. **(b)** A poly A tail is added to the 3′ end.

Concept check: Do the ends of structural genes have a poly T region that provides a template for the synthesis of a poly A tail in mRNA? Explain.

12.4 Translation and the Genetic Code

In the two previous sections, we considered how an RNA transcript is made and how eukaryotes process that transcript. Now we will begin to examine the next process, that of translation, at the molecular level. In 1960, Matthew Meselson and Francois Jacob found that proteins are synthesized on cellular structures known as ribosomes. One year later, Francois Jacob and Jacques Monod made an insightful hypothesis. They proposed that RNA, which is transcribed from DNA, provides the information for protein synthesis via ribosomes. This type of RNA, which they named messenger RNA (mRNA), carries information from the DNA to the ribosome, where polypeptides are made during the process called translation.

Since these early studies, much has been learned about the details of translation. To understand the process of translation, we will first examine the **genetic code**, which specifies the relationship between the sequence of nucleotides in the mRNA and the sequence of amino acids in a polypeptide.

During Translation, the Genetic Code Is Used to Make a Polypeptide with a Specific Amino Acid Sequence

The ability of mRNA to be translated into a polypeptide relies on the genetic code. The code is read in groups of three nucleotide bases known as **codons**. The genetic code consists of 64 different codons (**Table 12.1**). The sequence of three bases in most codons specifies a particular amino acid. For example, the codon CCC specifies the amino acid proline, whereas the codon GGC encodes the amino acid glycine. From the analysis of many different species, including bacteria, protists, fungi, plants, and animals, researchers have found that the genetic code is nearly universal. Only a few rare exceptions to the genetic code have been discovered.

Why are there 64 codons, as shown in Table 12.1? Because there are 20 types of amino acids, at least 20 different codons are needed so that each amino acid can be specified by a codon. With four types of bases in mRNA (U, C, A, and G), a genetic code containing two bases in a codon would not be sufficient, because only 4^2, or 16, different codons would be possible. A three-base system can specify 4^3, or 64, different codons, which is far more than the number of amino acids. The genetic code is said to be **degenerate** because more than one codon can specify the same amino acid (Table 12.1). For example, the codons GGU, GGC, GGA, and GGG all code for the amino acid glycine. In most instances, the third base in the codon is the degenerate or variable base.

Let's look at the organization of a bacterial mRNA to see how translation occurs (**Figure 12.11**). A ribosomal-binding site

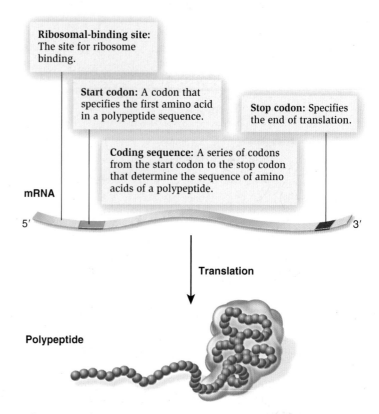

Figure 12.11 The organization of a bacterial mRNA as a translational unit.

Concept check: If a start codon was missing from a gene, how would that affect transcription, and how would it affect translation?

is located near the 5′ end of the mRNA. Beyond this site, a large portion of an mRNA functions as a **coding sequence**—a region that specifies the amino acid sequence of a polypeptide. This coding sequence consists of a series of codons. The **start codon**, which specifies the amino acid methionine, is only a few nucleotides from the ribosomal-binding site. The many codons that follow the start codon dictate the linear sequence of amino acids within a given polypeptide. A typical polypeptide is a few hundred amino acids in length. Finally, one of three **stop codons** signals the end of translation. These codons, also known as **termination codons** or **nonsense codons**, are UAA, UAG, and UGA.

The start codon also defines the **reading frame** of an mRNA. Beginning at the start codon, each adjacent codon is read as a group of three bases, also called a **triplet**, in the 5′ to 3′ direction. For example, look at the following two mRNA sequences and their corresponding amino acid sequences.

Ribosomal-binding site	Start codon

mRNA 5′–AUAAGGAGGUUACG(AUG)(CAG)(CAG)(GGC)(UUU)(ACC)–3′

Polypeptide   Met - Gln - Gln - Gly - Phe - Thr

Ribosomal-binding site	Start codon

mRNA 5′–AUAAGGAGGUUACG(AUG)(UCA)(GCA)(GGG)(CUU)(UAC)C–3′

Polypeptide   Met - Ser - Ala - Gly - Leu - Tyr

Table 12.1 The Genetic Code*

		Second position							
		U		**C**		**A**		**G**	
U	UUU UUC	Phe	UCU UCC UCA UCG	Ser	UAU UAC	Tyr	UGU UGC	Cys	U C
	UUA UUG	Leu			UAA UAG	Stop Stop	UGA UGG	Stop Trp	A G
C	CUU CUC CUA CUG	Leu	CCU CCC CCA CCG	Pro	CAU CAC	His	CGU CGC CGA CGG	Arg	U C A G
					CAA CAG	Gln			
A	AUU AUC AUA	Ile	ACU ACC ACA ACG	Thr	AAU AAC	Asn	AGU AGC	Ser	U C A G
	AUG	Met/ start			AAA AAG	Lys	AGA AGG	Arg	
G	GUU GUC GUA GUG	Val	GCU GCC GCA GCG	Ala	GAU GAC	Asp	GGU GGC GGA GGG	Gly	U C A G
					GAA GAG	Glu			

(First Position — left; Third Position — right)

*Exceptions to the genetic code are sporadically found among various species. For example, AUA encodes methionine in yeast and mammalian mitochondria.

The first sequence shows how the mRNA codons would be correctly translated into amino acids. In the second sequence, an additional U has been added to the same sequence after the start codon. This shifts the reading frame and thereby changes the codons as they occur in the 5′ to 3′ direction. The polypeptide produced from this series of codons would have a very different sequence of amino acids. From this comparison, we can also see that the reading frame is not overlapping, which means that each base functions within a single codon.

The relationships among the DNA sequence of a gene, the mRNA transcribed from the gene, and the polypeptide sequence are shown schematically in **Figure 12.12.** The coding strand of DNA corresponds to the mRNA strand, except that T in the DNA is substituted for U in the mRNA. The template strand is used to make mRNA. The 5′ end of the mRNA contains an untranslated region as does the 3′ end. The middle portion contains a series of codons that specify the amino acid sequence of a polypeptide.

To translate a nucleotide sequence of mRNA into an amino acid sequence, recognition occurs between mRNA and transfer RNA (tRNA) molecules. Transfer RNA, which is described in Section 12.5, functions as the "translator" or intermediary between an mRNA codon and an amino acid. The **anticodon** is a three-base sequence in a tRNA molecule that is complementary to a codon in mRNA. Due to this complementarity, the anticodon in the tRNA and a codon in an mRNA bind to each other. Furthermore, the anticodon in a tRNA corresponds to the amino acid that it carries. For example, if the anticodon in a tRNA is 3′–AAG–5′, it is complementary to a 5′–UUC–3′ codon. According to the genetic code, a UUC codon specifies phenylalanine (Phe). Therefore, a tRNA with a 3′–AAG–5′ anticodon must carry phenylalanine. As another example, a tRNA with a 3′–GGG–5′ anticodon is complementary to a 5′–CCC–3′ codon, which specifies proline. This tRNA must carry proline (Pro).

As seen at the bottom of Figure 12.12, the direction of polypeptide synthesis parallels the 5′ to 3′ orientation of mRNA. The first amino acid is said to be at the **N-terminus** or **amino terminus** of the polypeptide. The term N-terminus refers to the presence of a nitrogen atom (N) at this end, while amino terminus indicates the presence of an amino group (NH₂). **Peptide bonds** connect the amino acids together. These covalent bonds form between the carboxyl group of the previous amino acid and the amino group of the next amino acid. The last amino acid in a completed polypeptide does not have another amino acid attached to its carboxyl group. This last amino acid is said to be located at the **C-terminus**, or **carboxyl terminus**.

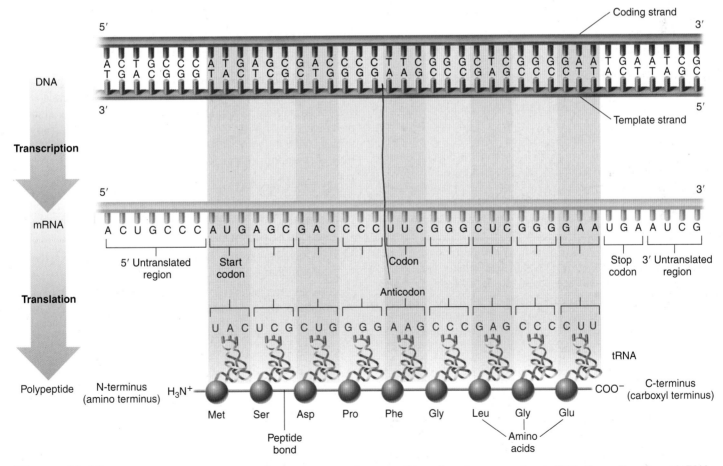

Figure 12.12   Relationships among the coding sequence of a gene, the codon sequence of an mRNA, the anticodons of tRNA, and the amino acid sequence of a polypeptide.

Concept check: *If an anticodon in a tRNA molecule has the sequence 3′–ACC–5′, which amino acid does it carry?*

A carboxyl group (COOH) is always found at this end of the polypeptide chain. Note that at neutral pH, the amino group is positively charged (NH_3^+), whereas the carboxyl group is negatively charged (COO^-).

Synthetic RNA Helped to Decipher the Genetic Code

Now let's look at some early experiments that allowed scientists to decipher the genetic code. During the early 1960s, the genetic code was determined by the collective efforts of several researchers, including Marshall Nirenberg, Severo Ochoa, and Philip Leder. Prior to their studies, other scientists had discovered that bacterial cells can be broken open and components from the cytoplasm can synthesize polypeptides. This is termed an in vitro or cell-free translation system. Nirenberg and Ochoa made synthetic RNA molecules using an enzyme that covalently connects nucleotides together. Using this synthetic mRNA, they then determined which amino acids were incorporated into polypeptides. For example, if an RNA molecule had only adenine-containing nucleotides (for example, 5′–AAAAAAAAAAAAAAAAAAAA–3′), a polypeptide was produced that contained only lysine. This result indicated that the AAA codon specifies lysine.

Another method used to decipher the genetic code involved the chemical synthesis of short RNA molecules. This method is described next in the Feature Investigation.

FEATURE INVESTIGATION

Nirenberg and Leder Found That RNA Triplets Can Promote the Binding of tRNA to Ribosomes

In 1964, Nirenberg and Leder discovered that RNA molecules containing three nucleotides (that is, a triplet) can stimulate ribosomes to bind a tRNA molecule. In other words, an RNA triplet can act like a codon within an mRNA molecule. Ribosomes bind RNA triplets, and then a tRNA with the appropriate anticodon subsequently binds to the ribosome.

To establish the relationship between triplet sequences and specific amino acids, Nirenberg and Leder made triplets with specific base sequences (**Figure 12.13**). For example, in one experiment they studied 5′–CCC–3′ triplets. A particular triplet was added to 20 different tubes. To each tube, they next added an in vitro translation system, which contained ribosomes and tRNAs that already had amino acids attached to them. However, each translation system had only one type of radiolabeled amino acid. One translation system had only proline that was radiolabeled, a second translation system had only serine that was radiolabeled, and so on.

As shown in step 2, the triplets became bound to the ribosomes just like the binding of mRNA to a ribosome. The tRNA with an anticodon that was complementary to the added triplet would bind to the triplet, which was already bound to the ribosome. For example, if the triplet was 5′–CCC–3′, a tRNA with a 3′–GGG–5′ anticodon would bind to the triplet/ribosome complex. This tRNA carries proline.

To determine which tRNA had bound, the contents from each tube were poured through a filter that trapped the large ribosomes but did not trap tRNAs that were not bound to ribosomes (see step 3). If the tRNA carrying the radiolabeled amino acid was bound to the triplet/ribosome complex, radioactivity would be trapped on the filter. Using a scintillation counter, the researchers determined the amount of radioactivity on each filter. Because only one amino acid was radiolabeled in each in vitro translation system, they could determine which triplet corresponded to which amino acid. In the example shown here, CCC corresponds to proline. Therefore, the in vitro translation system containing radiolabeled proline showed a large amount of radioactivity on the filter. As shown in the data, by studying triplets with different sequences, Nirenberg and Leder identified many codons of the genetic code.

Experimental Questions

1. Briefly explain how a triplet mimics the role of an mRNA molecule. How was this observation useful in the study done by Nirenberg and Leder?

2. What was the benefit of using radiolabeled amino acids in the Nirenberg and Leder experiment?

3. Predict the results that Nirenberg and Leder would have found for the following triplets: AUG, UAA, UAG, or UGA.

Figure 12.13 Nirenberg and Leder's use of triplet binding assays to decipher the genetic code.

HYPOTHESIS An RNA triplet can bind to a ribosome and promote the binding of the tRNA that carries the amino acid that the RNA triplet specifies.

KEY MATERIALS The researchers made 20 in vitro translation systems, which included ribosomes, tRNAs, and 20 amino acids. The 20 translation systems differed with regard to which amino acid was radiolabeled. For example, in 1 translation system, radiolabeled glycine was added, and the other 19 amino acids were unlabeled. In another system, radiolabeled proline was added, and the other 19 amino acids were unlabeled. The in vitro translation systems also contained the enzymes that attach amino acids to tRNAs.

Experimental level   **Conceptual level**

1   Mix together RNA triplets of a specific sequence and 20 in vitro translation systems. In the example shown here, the triplet is 5′–CCC–3′. Each translation system contained a different radiolabeled amino acid. (Note: Only 3 tubes are shown here.)

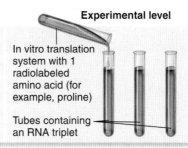 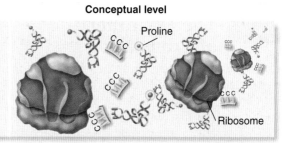

In vitro translation system with 1 radiolabeled amino acid (for example, proline)

Tubes containing an RNA triplet

Proline

Ribosome

2   Allow time for the RNA triplet to bind to the ribosome and for the appropriate tRNA to bind to the RNA triplet.

 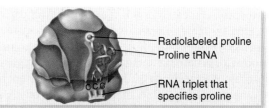

Radiolabeled proline
Proline tRNA
RNA triplet that specifies proline

3   Pour each mixture through a filter that allows the passage of unbound tRNA but does not allow the passage of ribosomes.

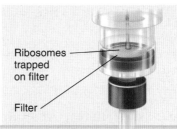 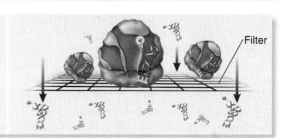

Ribosomes trapped on filter

Filter

Filter

4   Count radioactivity on the filter.

Scintillation counter

5   **THE DATA**

Triplet	Radiolabeled amino acid trapped on the filter	Triplet	Radiolabeled amino acid trapped on the filter
5′ – AAA – 3′	Lysine	5′ – GAC – 3′	Aspartic acid
5′ – ACA – 3′	Threonine	5′ – GCC – 3′	Alanine
5′ – ACC – 3′	Threonine	5′ – GGU – 3′	Glycine
5′ – AGA – 3′	Arginine	5′ – GGC – 3′	Glycine
5′ – AUA – 3′	Isoleucine	5′ – GUU – 3′	Valine
5′ – AUU – 3′	Isoleucine	5′ – UAU – 3′	Tyrosine
5′ – CCC – 3′	Proline	5′ – UGU – 3′	Cysteine
5′ – CGC – 3′	Arginine	5′ – UUG – 3′	Leucine
5′ – GAA – 3′	Glutamic acid		

6   **CONCLUSION**   This method enabled the researchers to identify many of the codons of the genetic code.

7   **SOURCE**   Leder, Philip, and Nirenberg, Marshall W. 1964. RNA Codewords and Protein Synthesis, III. On the nucleotide sequence of a cysteine and a leucine RNA codeword. *Proceedings of the National Academy of Sciences* 52:1521–1529.

12.5 The Machinery of Translation

Let's now turn our attention to the components found in living cells that are needed to use the genetic code and translate mRNA into polypeptides. Earlier in this chapter, we considered transcription, the first step in gene expression. To transcribe an RNA molecule, a pre-existing DNA template strand is used to make a complementary RNA strand. A single enzyme, RNA polymerase, can catalyze this reaction. By comparison, translation requires more components because the sequence of codons in an mRNA molecule must be translated into a sequence of amino acids according to the genetic code. A single protein cannot accomplish such a task. Instead, many different proteins and RNA molecules interact in an intricate series of steps to achieve the synthesis of a polypeptide. A cell must make many different components, including mRNAs, tRNAs, ribosomes, and translation factors, so that polypeptides can be made (**Table 12.2**).

Though the estimates vary from cell to cell and from species to species, most cells use a substantial amount of their energy to translate mRNA into polypeptides. In *E. coli*, for example, approximately 90% of the cellular energy is used for this process. This value underscores the complexity and importance of translation in living organisms. In this section, we will focus on the components of the translation machinery. The last section of the chapter will describe the steps of translation as they occur in living cells.

Transfer RNAs Share Common Structural Features

To understand how tRNAs act as carriers of the correct amino acids during translation, researchers have examined their structural characteristics. The tRNAs of both prokaryotes and eukaryotes share common features. As originally proposed by Robert Holley in 1965, the two-dimensional structure of tRNAs exhibits a cloverleaf pattern. The structure has three stem-loops and a fourth stem with a 3′ single-stranded region (**Figure**

Table 12.2	Components of the Translation Machinery
Component	**Function**
mRNA	Contains the information for a polypeptide sequence according to the genetic code.
tRNA	A molecule with two functional sites. One site, termed the anticodon, recognizes a codon in mRNA. A second site has the appropriate amino acid attached to it.
Ribosomes	Composed of many proteins and rRNA molecules. The ribosome provides a location where mRNA and tRNA molecules can properly interact with each other. The ribosome also catalyzes the formation of covalent bonds between adjacent amino acids so that a polypeptide can be made.
Translation factors	Proteins needed for the three stages of translation. Initiation factors are required for the assembly of mRNA, the first tRNA, and ribosomal subunits. Elongation factors are needed to synthesize the polypeptide. Release factors are needed to recognize the stop codon and disassemble the translation machinery. Several translation factors use GTP as an energy source to carry out their functions.

12.14a). The stems are regions where the RNA is double stranded due to complementary base pairing, whereas the loops are regions without base pairing. The anticodon is located in the loop of the second stem-loop region. The 3′ single-stranded region is called the acceptor stem because it accepts the attachment of an amino acid. The three-dimensional structure of tRNA molecules involves additional folding of the secondary structure (**Figure 12.14b**).

The cells of every organism make many different tRNA molecules, each encoded by a different gene. A tRNA is named according to the amino acid it carries. For example, tRNA^{ser} carries a serine. Because the genetic code contains six different serine codons as shown in Table 12.1, a cell produces more than one type of tRNA^{ser}.

Figure 12.14 **Structure of tRNA.**
(a) The two-dimensional or secondary structure is that of a cloverleaf. The anticodon is within the middle stem-loop structure. The 3′ single-stranded region (acceptor stem) is where an amino acid can attach. (b) The actual three-dimensional structure folds in on itself.

Concept check: *What is the function of the anticodon?*

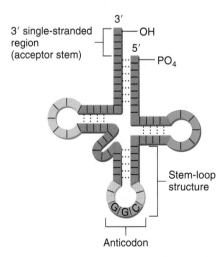

(a) Two-dimensional structure of tRNA

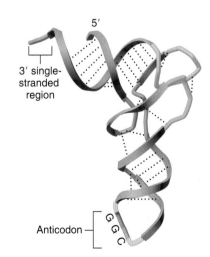

(b) Three-dimensional structure of tRNA

Aminoacyl-tRNA Synthetases Charge tRNAs by Attaching an Appropriate Amino Acid

To perform its role during translation, a tRNA must have the appropriate amino acid attached to its 3′ end. The enzymes that catalyze the attachment of amino acids to tRNA molecules are known as **aminoacyl-tRNA synthetases**. Cells make 20 distinct types of aminoacyl-tRNA synthetase enzymes; each type recognizes just one of the 20 different amino acids. Each aminoacyl-tRNA synthetase is named for the specific amino acid it attaches to tRNA. For example, alanyl-tRNA synthetase recognizes alanine and attaches this amino acid to all tRNAs with alanine anticodons.

Aminoacyl-tRNA synthetases catalyze chemical reactions involving an amino acid, a tRNA molecule, and ATP (**Figure 12.15**). First, a specific amino acid and ATP are recognized by the enzyme. Next, the amino acid is activated by the covalent attachment of an AMP molecule, and pyrophosphate is released. In a third step, the activated amino acid is covalently attached to the 3′ end of a tRNA molecule, and AMP is released. Finally, the tRNA with its attached amino acid, called a **charged tRNA** or an **aminoacyl tRNA**, is released from the enzyme.

The ability of each aminoacyl-tRNA synthetase to recognize an appropriate tRNA has been called the second genetic code. A precise recognition process is necessary to maintain the fidelity of genetic information. If the wrong amino acid was attached

to a tRNA, the amino acid sequence of the translated polypeptide would be incorrect. To prevent this from happening, aminoacyl-tRNA synthetases are amazingly accurate enzymes. The wrong amino acid is attached to a tRNA less than once in 100,000 times! The anticodon region of the tRNA is usually important for recognition by the correct aminoacyl-tRNA synthetase. In addition, the base sequences in other regions may facilitate binding to an aminoacyl-tRNA synthetase.

Ribosomes Are Assembled from rRNA and Proteins

Let's now turn our attention to the **ribosome**, which is often described as a molecular machine. The ribosome is the site where translation takes place. Bacterial cells have one type of ribosome, which translates all mRNAs in the cytoplasm. Because eukaryotic cells are compartmentalized into cellular organelles bounded by membranes, their translation machinery is more complex. Biochemically distinct ribosomes are found in different cellular compartments. The most abundant type of eukaryotic ribosome functions in the cytosol. In addition, mitochondria have ribosomes, and plant and algal cells have ribosomes in their chloroplasts. The compositions of mitochondrial and chloroplast ribosomes are more similar to bacterial ribosomes than they are to eukaryotic cytosolic ribosomes. Unless otherwise noted, the term eukaryotic ribosome refers to ribosomes in the cytosol, not to those found in organelles.

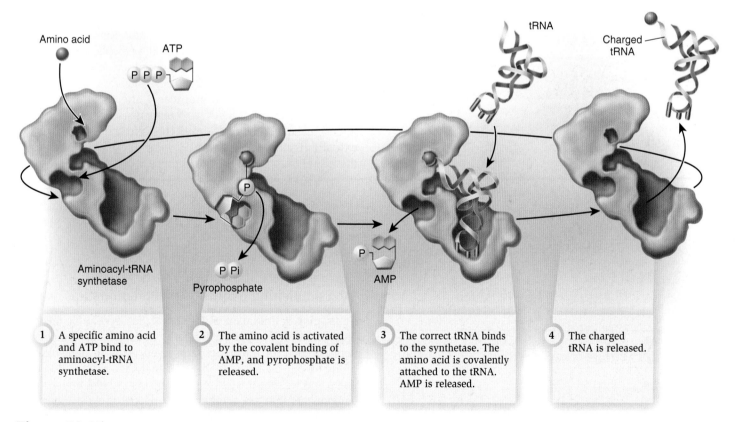

Figure 12.15 Aminoacyl-tRNA synthetase charging a tRNA.

Concept check: Why is ATP needed to charge a tRNA?

A ribosome is a large complex composed of structures called the large and small subunits. The term subunit is perhaps misleading, because each ribosomal subunit is itself assembled from many different proteins and one or more RNA molecules. In the bacterium *E. coli*, the small ribosomal subunit is called 30S, and the large subunit is 50S (**Table 12.3**). The designations 30S and 50S refer to the rate at which these subunits sediment when subjected to a centrifugal force. This rate is described as a sedimentation coefficient in Svedberg units (S) in honor of Theodor Svedberg, who invented the ultracentrifuge. The 30S subunit is formed from the assembly of 21 different ribosomal proteins and one 16S rRNA molecule. The 50S subunit contains 34 different proteins and two different rRNA molecules, called 5S and 23S. Together, the 30S and 50S subunits form a 70S ribosome. (Svedberg units don't add up linearly, because the sedimentation coefficient is a function of both size and shape.) In bacteria, ribosomal proteins and rRNA molecules are synthesized in the cytoplasm, and the ribosomal subunits are assembled there as well.

Eukaryotic ribosomes consist of subunits that are slightly larger than their bacterial counterparts (Table 12.3). In eukaryotes, 40S and 60S subunits combine to form an 80S ribosome. The 40S subunit is composed of 33 proteins and an 18S rRNA, and the 60S subunit has 49 proteins and 5S, 5.8S, and 28S rRNAs. The synthesis of eukaryotic rRNA occurs in the nucleolus, a region of the nucleus that is specialized for that purpose. The ribosomal proteins are made in the cytosol and imported into the nucleus. The rRNAs and ribosomal proteins are then assembled within the nucleolus to make the 40S and 60S subunits. The 40S and 60S subunits are exported into the cytosol, where they associate to form an 80S ribosome during translation.

Due to structural differences between bacterial and eukaryotic ribosomes, certain chemicals may bind to bacterial ribosomes but not to eukaryotic ribosomes, and vice versa. Some **antibiotics**, which are chemicals that inhibit the growth of certain microorganisms, bind only to bacterial ribosomes and inhibit translation. Examples include erythromycin and chloramphenicol. Because these chemicals do not inhibit eukaryotic ribosomes, they have been effective drugs for the treatment of bacterial infections in humans and domesticated animals.

Components of Ribosomal Subunits Form Functional Sites for Translation

To understand the structure and function of the ribosome at the molecular level, researchers have determined the locations and functional roles of individual ribosomal proteins and rRNAs. In recent years, a few research groups have succeeded in purifying ribosomes and causing them to crystallize in a test tube. Using the technique of X-ray diffraction, the crystallized ribosomes provide detailed information about ribosome structure. **Figure 12.16a** shows a model of a bacterial ribosome. The overall shape of each subunit is largely determined by the structure of the rRNAs, which constitute most of the mass of the ribosome.

During bacterial translation, the mRNA lies on the surface of the 30S subunit, within a space between the 30S and 50S subunits (**Figure 12.16b**). As a polypeptide is synthesized, it exits through a hole within the 50S subunit. Ribosomes contain discrete sites where tRNAs bind and the polypeptide is synthesized. In 1964, James Watson proposed a two-site model for tRNA binding to the ribosome. These sites are known as the **peptidyl site** (**P site**) and **aminoacyl site** (**A site**). In 1981, Knud Nierhaus and Hans-Jorg Rheinberger expanded this to a three-site model (Figure 12.16b). The third site is known as the **exit site** (**E site**). In Section 12.6, we will examine the roles of these sites in the synthesis of a polypeptide.

| Table 12.3 | Composition of Bacterial and Eukaryotic Ribosomes |

	Small subunit	Large subunit	Assembled ribosome
Bacterial			
Sedimentation coefficient	30S	50S	70S
Number of proteins	21	34	55
rRNA	16S rRNA	5S rRNA, 23S rRNA	16S rRNA, 5S rRNA, 23S rRNA
Eukaryotic			
Sedimentation coefficient	40S	60S	80S
Number of proteins	33	49	82
rRNA	18S rRNA	5S rRNA, 5.8S rRNA, 28S rRNA	18S rRNA, 5S rRNA, 5.8S rRNA, 28S rRNA

Genomes & Proteomes Connection

Comparisons of Small Subunit rRNAs Among Different Species Provide a Basis for Establishing Evolutionary Relationships

Translation is a fundamental process that is vital for the existence of all living species. Research indicates that the components needed for translation arose very early in the evolution of life on our planet in an ancestor that gave rise to all known living species. For this reason, all organisms have translational components that are evolutionarily related to each other. For example, the rRNA found in the small subunit of ribosomes is similar in all forms of life, though it is slightly larger in eukaryotic species (18S) than in bacterial species (16S). In other words,

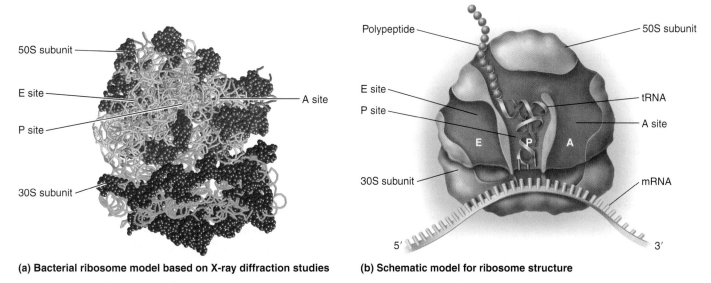

(a) Bacterial ribosome model based on X-ray diffraction studies

(b) Schematic model for ribosome structure

Figure 12.16   Ribosome structure.   **(a)** A model for the structure of a bacterial ribosome based on X-ray diffraction studies, showing the large and small subunits and the major binding sites. The rRNA is shown in gray (large subunit) and turquoise (small subunit), whereas the ribosomal proteins are magenta (large subunit) and purple (small subunit). **(b)** A schematic model emphasizing functional sites in the ribosome, and showing bound mRNA and tRNA with an attached polypeptide.

the gene for the small subunit rRNA (SSU rRNA) is found in the genomes of all organisms.

How is this observation useful? One way that geneticists explore evolutionary relationships is to compare the sequences of evolutionarily related genes. At the molecular level, gene evolution involves changes in DNA sequences. After two different species have diverged from each other during evolution, the genes of each species have an opportunity to accumulate changes, or mutations, that alter the sequences of those genes. After many generations, evolutionarily related species contain genes that are similar but not identical to each other, because each species will accumulate different mutations. In general, if a very long time has elapsed since two species diverged evolutionarily, their genes tend to be quite different. In contrast, if two species diverged relatively recently on an evolutionary time scale, their genes tend to be more similar.

Figure 12.17 compares a portion of the sequence of the small subunit rRNA gene from three mammalian and three bacterial species. The colors highlight different types of compari-

sons. The bases shaded in yellow are identical in five or six species. Sequences of bases that are very similar or identical in different species are said to be **evolutionarily conserved**. Presumably, these sequences were found in the primordial gene that gave rise to modern species. Perhaps, because these sequences may have some critical function, they have not changed over evolutionary time. Those sequences shaded in green are identical in all three mammals, but differ compared to one or more bacterial species. Actually, if you scan the mammalian species, you may notice that all three sequences are identical to each other in this region. The sequences shaded in red are identical in two or three bacterial species, but differ compared to the mammalian small subunit rRNA genes. The sequences from *Escherichia coli* and *Serratia marcescens* are more similar to each other than the sequence from *Bacillus subtilis* is to either of them. This observation suggests that *E. coli* and *S. marcescens* are more closely related evolutionarily than either of them is to *B. subtilis*.

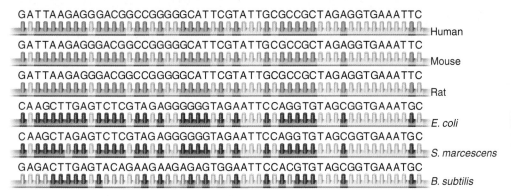

Figure 12.17   Comparison of small subunit rRNA gene sequences from three mammalian and three bacterial species.   Note the many similarities (yellow) and differences (green and red) among the sequences.

Concept check: Based on the gene sequences shown here, pick two species that are closely related evolutionarily and two that are distantly related.

12.6   The Stages of Translation

Like transcription, the process of translation occurs in three stages called initiation, elongation, and termination. **Figure 12.18** provides an overview of the process. During initiation, an mRNA, the first tRNA, and the ribosomal subunits assemble into a complex. Next, in the elongation stage, the ribosome moves in the 5′ to 3′ direction from the start codon in the mRNA toward the stop codon, synthesizing a polypeptide according to the sequence of codons in the mRNA. Finally, the process is terminated when the ribosome reaches a stop codon and the complex disassembles, releasing the completed polypeptide. In this section, we will examine the steps in this process as they occur in living cells.

Translation Is Initiated with the Assembly of mRNA, tRNA, and the Ribosomal Subunits

During the **initiation stage**, a complex is formed between an mRNA molecule, the first tRNA, and the ribosomal subunits. In all species, the assembly of this complex requires the help of proteins called **initiation factors** that facilitate the interactions between these components (see Table 12.2). The assembly also requires an input of energy. Guanosine triphosphate

(GTP) is hydrolyzed by certain initiation factors to provide the necessary energy.

In the absence of translation, the small and large ribosomal subunits exist separately. To begin assembly in bacteria, mRNA binds to the small ribosomal subunit (**Figure 12.19**). The binding of mRNA to this subunit is facilitated by a short ribosomal-binding sequence near the 5′ end of the mRNA. This sequence is complementary to a portion of the 16S rRNA within the small ribosomal subunit. For this reason, the mRNA and rRNA hydrogen-bond to each other by base pairing. The start codon is usually just a few nucleotides downstream (that is, toward the 3′ end) from the ribosomal-binding sequence. A specific tRNA, which functions as the **initiator tRNA**, recognizes the start codon in mRNA and binds to it. In eukaryotes, this tRNA carries a methionine, whereas in bacteria it carries a methionine that has been modified by the attachment of a formyl group. To complete the initiation stage, the large ribosomal subunit associates with the small subunit. At the end of this stage, the initiator tRNA is located in the P site of the ribosome.

In eukaryotic species, the initiation phase of translation differs in two ways from the process in bacteria. First, instead of a ribosomal-binding sequence, eukaryotic mRNAs have a guanosine cap at their 5′ end. This 5′ cap is recognized by cap-binding proteins that promote the binding of the mRNA to the small ribosomal subunit. Also, unlike bacteria, in which

Figure 12.18   An overview of the stages of translation.

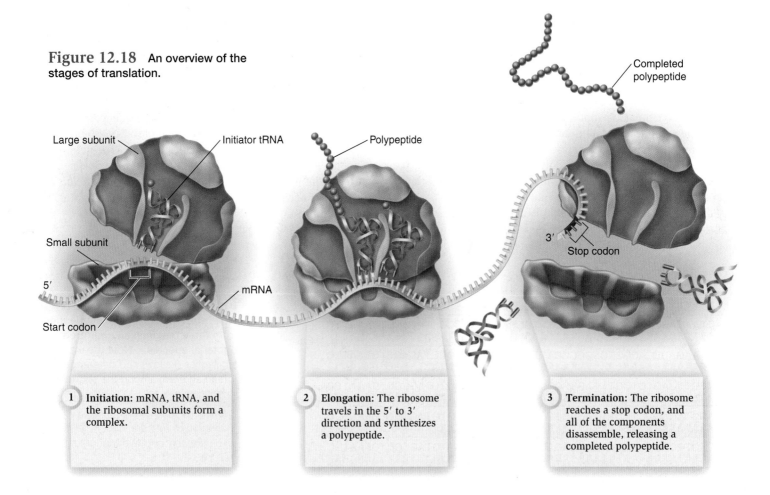

① **Initiation:** mRNA, tRNA, and the ribosomal subunits form a complex.

② **Elongation:** The ribosome travels in the 5′ to 3′ direction and synthesizes a polypeptide.

③ **Termination:** The ribosome reaches a stop codon, and all of the components disassemble, releasing a completed polypeptide.

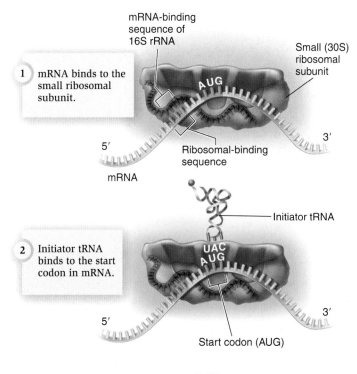

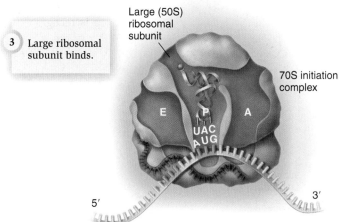

Figure 12.19 Initiation stage of translation in bacteria.

Concept check: What promotes the binding between the mRNA and the small ribosomal subunit?

the start codon is very close to a ribosomal-binding sequence, the location of start codons in eukaryotes is more variable. In 1978, Marilyn Kozak proposed that the small ribosomal subunit identifies a start codon by beginning at the 5′ end and then scanning along the mRNA in the 3′ direction in search of an AUG sequence. In many, but not all, cases the first AUG codon is used as a start codon. By analyzing the sequences of many eukaryotic mRNAs, Kozak and her colleagues discovered that the sequence around an AUG codon is important for it to be used as a start codon. The sequence for optimal start codon recognition is shown here:

Upstream of start codon	Start codon	Downstream coding region

. . . G C C (A or G) C C (**A U G**) G . . . .

Aside from an AUG codon itself, a guanine just past the start codon and the sequence of six bases directly upstream from the start codon are important for start codon selection. If the first AUG codon is within a site that deviates markedly from this optimal sequence, the small subunit may skip this codon and instead use another AUG codon farther downstream. Once the small subunit selects a start codon, an initiator tRNA binds to the start codon, and then the large ribosomal subunit associates with the small subunit to complete the assembly process.

Polypeptide Synthesis Occurs During the Elongation Stage

As its name suggests, the **elongation stage** involves the covalent bonding of amino acids to each other, one at a time, to create a polypeptide. Even though this process involves several different components, translation occurs at a remarkable rate. Under normal cellular conditions, the translation machinery can elongate a polypeptide chain at a rate of 15 to 18 amino acids per second in bacteria and 6 amino acids per second in eukaryotes!

To elongate a polypeptide by one amino acid, a tRNA brings a new amino acid to the ribosome, where it is attached to the end of a growing polypeptide chain. In step 1 of **Figure 12.20**, translation has already proceeded to a point where a short polypeptide is attached to the tRNA located in the P site of the ribosome. This is called peptidyl tRNA. In the first step of elongation, a charged tRNA carrying a single amino acid binds to the A site. This binding occurs because the anticodon in the tRNA is complementary to the codon in the mRNA. The hydrolysis of GTP by proteins that function as **elongation factors** provides the energy for the binding of the tRNA to the A site (see Table 12.2). At this stage of translation, a peptidyl tRNA is in the P site and a charged tRNA (an aminoacyl tRNA) is in the A site. This is how the P and A sites came to be named.

In the second step, a peptide bond is formed between the amino acid at the A site and the growing polypeptide chain, thereby lengthening the chain by one amino acid. As this occurs, the polypeptide is removed from the tRNA in the P site and transferred to the amino acid at the A site, an event termed a **peptidyl transfer reaction**. This reaction is catalyzed by a region of the 50S subunit known as the peptidyltransferase center, which is composed of several proteins and rRNA. Thomas Steitz, Peter Moore, and their colleagues proposed that the rRNA is responsible for catalyzing the peptide bond formation between adjacent amino acids. It is now accepted that the ribosome is a ribozyme!

After the peptidyl transfer reaction is complete, the third step involves the movement or translocation of the ribosome toward the 3′ end of the mRNA by exactly one codon. This shifts the tRNAs in the P and A sites to the E and P sites, respectively. Notice that the next codon in the mRNA is now exposed at the unoccupied A site. The uncharged tRNA exits the E site. At this point, the next charged tRNA can enter the empty A site, and the same series of steps will add the next amino acid to the polypeptide chain.

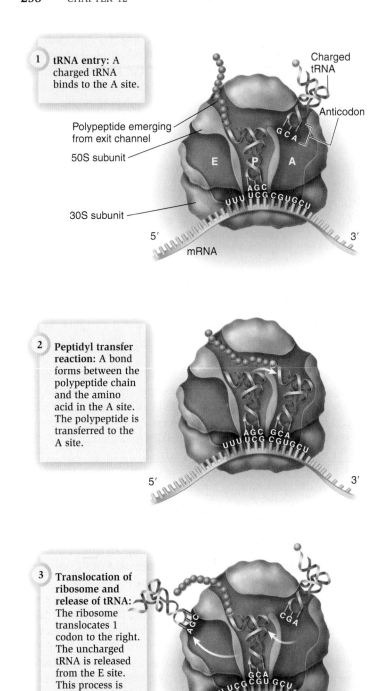

Figure 12.20   Elongation stage of translation in bacteria.

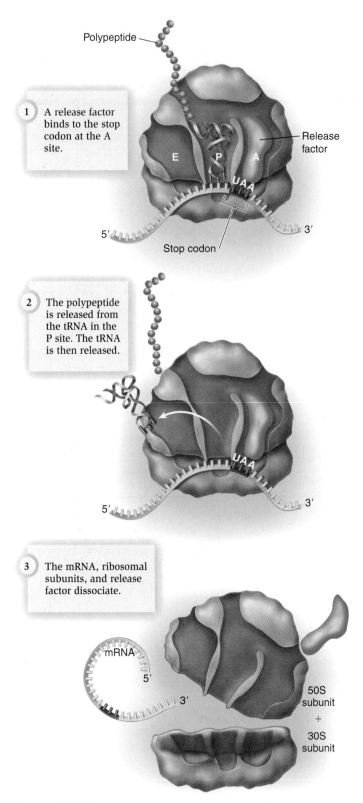

Figure 12.21   Termination stage of translation in bacteria.

Termination Occurs When a Stop Codon Is Reached in the mRNA

Elongation continues until a stop codon moves into the A site of a ribosome. The three stop codons, UAA, UAG, and UGA, are not recognized by a tRNA with a complementary sequence. Instead, they are recognized by a protein known as a **release**

factor. The three-dimensional structure of a release factor protein mimics the structure of tRNAs, which allows it to fit into the A site.

Figure 12.21 illustrates the **termination stage** of translation. In step 1 of this figure, a release factor binds to the stop codon at the A site. The completed polypeptide chain is attached to a tRNA in the P site. In the second step, the bond between

Table 12.4	Comparison of Bacterial and Eukaryotic Translation	
	Bacterial	**Eukaryotic**
Ribosome composition	70S ribosomes:	80S ribosomes:
	30S subunit- 21 proteins + 1 rRNA	40S subunit- 33 proteins + 1 rRNA
	50S subunit- 34 proteins + 2 rRNAs	60S subunit- 49 proteins + 3 rRNAs
Initiator tRNA	tRNA$^{formyl-methionine}$	tRNA^{methionine}
Initial binding of mRNA	Requires a ribosomal-binding sequence	Requires a 7-methylguanosine cap
Selection of a start codon	Just downstream from the ribosomal-binding sequence	According to Kozak's rules
Termination factors	Two factors: RF1 and RF2	One factor: eRF

the polypeptide and the tRNA is hydrolyzed, causing the polypeptide and tRNA to be released from the ribosome. In the third step, the mRNA, ribosomal subunits, and release factor dissociate. The termination stage of translation is similar in bacteria and eukaryotes except that bacteria have two different termination factors that recognize stop codons (RF1 and RF2), whereas eukaryotes have only one (eRF). **Table 12.4** compares some of the key differences between bacterial and eukaryotic translation.

Summary of Key Concepts

12.1 Overview of Gene Expression

- Based on his studies of inborn errors of metabolism, Garrod hypothesized that some genes encode enzymes. (Figure 12.1)
- By studying the nutritional requirements of bread mold, Beadle and Tatum proposed the one gene–one enzyme hypothesis. (Figure 12.2)
- A polypeptide is a unit of structure. A protein, composed of one or more polypeptides, is a unit of function.
- At the molecular level, the central dogma states that most genes are transcribed into mRNA, and then the mRNA is translated into polypeptides. Eukaryotes modify their RNA transcripts to make them functional. (Figure 12.3)
- The molecular expression of genes is fundamental to the characteristics of an organism's traits.

12.2 Transcription

- The promoter of a gene signals the beginning of transcription whereas the terminator specifies where transcription will end for a given gene. Regulatory sequences control whether a gene is turned on or off. (Figure 12.4)
- In bacteria, sigma factor binds to RNA polymerase and to a promoter, thereby promoting the initiation of transcription. The RNA transcript is made during the elongation stage due to base pairing of nucleotides to the template strand of DNA. RNA

polymerase is released from the DNA at the termination site. (Figures 12.5, 12.6)
- The genes along a chromosome are transcribed in different directions using either DNA strand as a template. RNA is always synthesized in a 5′ to 3′ direction. (Figure 12.7)

12.3 RNA Processing in Eukaryotes

- Eukaryotic mRNA is first made as a pre-mRNA that is capped, spliced, and given a poly A tail. In the process called splicing, introns are removed from eukaryotic pre-mRNA by a spliceosome. The components of a spliceosome first recognize the intron boundaries and the branch site, and then remove the intron and connect the adjacent exons. (Figures 12.8, 12.9, 12.10)

12.4 Translation and the Genetic Code

- The genetic code determines the amino acid sequences of polypeptides. Each of the 64 codons specifies a start codon (methionine), other amino acids, or a stop codon. (Table 12.1, Figure 12.11)
- The template strand of DNA is used to make mRNA with a series of codons. Recognition between mRNA and many tRNA molecules determines the amino acid sequence of a polypeptide. A polypeptide has a directionality in which the first amino acid is at the N-terminus or amino terminus, whereas the last amino acid is at the C-terminus or carboxyl terminus. (Figure 12.12)
- Nirenberg and Leder used the ability of RNA triplets to promote the binding of tRNA to ribosomes as a way to determine many of the codons of the genetic code. (Figure 12.13)

12.5 The Machinery of Translation

- Translation requires mRNA, aminoacyl tRNAs, ribosomes, and many translation factors. (Table 12.2)
- tRNA molecules have a cloverleaf structure. Two important sites are the 3′ single-stranded region, which covalently binds an amino acid, and the anticodon, which base-pairs with a codon in mRNA. (Figure 12.14)
- The enzyme aminoacyl-tRNA synthetase attaches the correct amino acid to a tRNA molecule, creating a charged tRNA. (Figure 12.15)
- Ribosomes are composed of a small and large subunit, each consisting of rRNA molecules and many proteins. Bacterial and eukaryotic ribosomes differ in their molecular composition. (Table 12.3)
- Ribosomes have three sites, the A, P, and E sites, which are locations for the binding and release of tRNA molecules. (Figure 12.16)
- The gene that encodes the small subunit rRNA (SSU rRNA) has been extensively used in the evolutionary comparisons of different species. (Figure 12.17)

12.6 The Stages of Translation

- Translation occurs in three stages, called initiation, elongation, and termination. (Figure 12.18)

- During initiation of translation, the mRNA assembles with the ribosomal subunits and the first tRNA molecule. (Figure 12.19)

- Polypeptide synthesis occurs during the elongation stage, one amino acid at a time. (Figure 12.20)

- During the termination of translation, the binding of a release factor to the stop codon causes the release of the completed polypeptide from the tRNA and the disassembly of the mRNA, ribosomal subunits, and release factor. (Figure 12.21)

- Though translation in bacteria and eukaryotes is strikingly similar, some key differences have been observed. (Table 12.4)

Assess and Discuss

Test Yourself

1. Which of the following best represents the central dogma of gene expression?
   a. During transcription, DNA codes for polypeptides.
   b. During transcription, DNA codes for mRNA, which codes for polypeptides during translation.
   c. During translation, DNA codes for mRNA, which codes for polypeptides during transcription.
   d. none of the above

2. Transcription of a gene begins at a site on DNA called _____ and ends at a site on DNA known as _____.
   a. an initiation codon, the termination codon
   b. a promoter, the termination codon
   c. an initiation codon, the terminator
   d. a promoter, the terminator
   e. an initiator, the terminator

3. The functional product of a structural gene is
   a. tRNA.
   b. mRNA.
   c. rRNA.
   d. a polypeptide.
   e. a, b, and c.

4. During eukaryotic RNA processing, the nontranslated sequences that are removed are called
   a. exons.
   b. introns.
   c. promoters.
   d. codons.
   e. ribozymes.

5. The _____ is the site where the translation process takes place.
   a. mitochondria
   b. nucleus
   c. ribosome
   d. lysosome
   e. ribozyme

6. The small subunit of a ribosome is composed of
   a. a protein.
   b. an rRNA molecule.
   c. many proteins.
   d. many rRNA molecules.
   e. many proteins and one rRNA molecule.

7. The region of the tRNA that is complementary to a codon in mRNA is
   a. the acceptor stem.
   b. the codon.
   c. the peptidyl site.
   d. the anticodon.
   e. the adaptor loop.

8. During the initiation step of translation, the first codon, ____, will enter the _____ and associate with the initiator tRNA.
   a. UAG, A site
   b. AUG, A site
   c. UAG, P site
   d. AUG, P site
   e. AUG, E site

9. The movement of the polypeptide from the tRNA in the P site to the tRNA in the A site is referred to as
   a. peptide bonding.
   b. aminoacyl binding.
   c. translation.
   d. peptidyl transfer reaction.
   e. elongation.

10. The synthesis of a polypeptide occurs during which stage of translation?
    a. initiation
    b. elongation
    c. termination
    d. splicing

Conceptual Questions

1. Describe the one gene–one enzyme hypothesis and the more modern modifications of this hypothesis. Briefly explain how studying the pathway that leads to arginine synthesis allowed Beadle and Tatum to conclude that one gene encodes one enzyme.

2. What is the function of an aminoacyl-tRNA synthetase?

3. A tRNA has an anticodon sequence 3′–GGU–5′. What amino acid does it carry?

Collaborative Questions

1. Why do you think some complexes, such as spliceosomes and ribosomes, have both protein and RNA components?

2. Discuss and make a list of the similarities and differences in the events that occur during the initiation, elongation, and termination stages of transcription and translation.

Online Resource

www.brookerbiology.com

Stay a step ahead in your studies with animations that bring concepts to life and practice tests to assess your understanding. Your instructor may also recommend the interactive ebook, individualized learning tools, and more.

Gene Regulation

13

A model for a protein that binds to DNA and regulates genes. The catabolite activator protein, shown in dark and light blue, is binding to the DNA double helix, shown in orange and white. This protein, described later in Figure 13.10, activates gene transcription.

E milio took a weight-lifting class in college and was surprised by the results. Within a few weeks, he was able to lift substantially more weight. He was inspired by this progress and continued lifting weights after the semester-long course ended. A year later, he was not only much stronger, but he could see physical changes in his body. Certain muscles, such as his biceps and triceps in his upper arms, were noticeably larger. How can we explain the increase in mass of Emilio's muscles? Unknowingly, when he was lifting weights, Emilio was affecting the regulation of his genes. Certain genes in his muscle cells were being "turned on" during his workouts, which then led to the synthesis of proteins that increased the mass of Emilio's muscles.

At the molecular level, **gene expression** is the process by which the information within a gene is made into a functional product, such as a protein or RNA molecule. The majority of genes in all species are regulated so that the proteins they specify are produced at certain times and in specific amounts. The term **gene regulation** refers to the ability of cells to control the expression of their genes. By comparison, some genes have relatively constant levels of expression in all conditions over time. These are called **constitutive genes**. Frequently, constitutive genes encode proteins that are always required for the survival of an organism, such as certain metabolic enzymes.

The importance of gene regulation is underscored by the number of genes devoted to this process in an organism. For example, in *Arabidopsis thaliana*, a plant that is studied as a model organism by plant geneticists, over 5% of its genome is involved with regulating gene transcription. This species has more than 1,500 different genes that encode proteins that regulate the transcription of other genes.

In this chapter, we will begin with an overview that emphasizes the benefits of gene regulation and the general mechanisms that achieve such regulation. Later sections will describe how bacteria regulate gene expression in the face of environmental change and the more complex nature of gene regulation in eukaryotes.

13.1 Overview of Gene Regulation

How do living organisms benefit from gene regulation? One reason is that it conserves energy. Proteins that are encoded by genes will be produced only when they are needed. For example, some proteins function in the metabolism of small molecules, such as sugars, that may or may not be present in the environment. These proteins are required only when the bacterium is exposed to such sugars. Like bacteria, eukaryotic organisms also need to adapt to changes in their environment. For example, all eukaryotic species can respond to environmental stresses such as ultraviolet (UV) radiation by turning on genes that provide protection against this harmful agent. In humans, exposure to UV radiation turns on genes that result in a tanning response.

Gene regulation also ensures that genes are expressed in the appropriate cell types and at the correct stage of development. In multicellular organisms, certain proteins are made only in particular cell types, or their amounts may vary from cell to cell. In humans, for example, some proteins are needed only in muscle cells but not in nerve cells, and vice versa. Similarly, in multicellular organisms that progress through different developmental stages (for example, fertilized egg, embryo, and adult), certain proteins are needed only at particular stages of development. In this section, we will examine a few examples that illustrate the important consequences of gene regulation. We will also survey the major points in the gene expression process at which genes are regulated in prokaryotic and eukaryotic cells.

Bacteria Regulate Genes to Respond to Nutrients in Their Environment

To fully appreciate how gene regulation helps bacteria survive in a changing environment, let's look at an example. The bacterium *Escherichia coli* can use many types of sugars as food sources, thereby increasing its chances of survival. Let's consider the process of how it uses lactose, which is the sugar found in milk. *E. coli* can use lactose because it carries genes that code for proteins that enable it to take up lactose from the environment and metabolize it.

Figure 13.1 illustrates the effects of lactose on the regulation of those genes. In order to utilize lactose, an *E. coli* cell requires a transporter, called lactose permease, that facilitates the uptake of lactose into the cell, and an enzyme, called β-galactosidase, that catalyzes the breakdown of lactose. When lactose is not present in the environment, an *E. coli* cell makes very little of these proteins. However, when lactose becomes available, the bacterium will produce many more copies of these proteins, enabling it to efficiently use lactose from its environment. Eventually, all of the lactose in the environment will be used up. At

this point, the genes encoding these proteins will be shut off, and most of the proteins will be degraded. In the case of lactose utilization, gene regulation ensures that the proteins needed for this process are made only when lactose is present in the environment.

Eukaryotic Gene Regulation Produces Different Cell Types in a Single Organism

One of the most amazing examples of gene regulation is the phenomenon of **cell differentiation**, the process by which cells become specialized into particular types. In humans, for example, cells may differentiate into muscle cells, nerve cells, skin cells, or other types. **Figure 13.2** shows micrographs of three types of cells found in humans. As seen here, their morphologies are strikingly different. Likewise, their functions within the body are also quite different. Muscle cells are important in body movements, nerve cells function in cell signaling, and skin cells form a protective outer surface to the body.

Gene regulation is responsible for creating different types of cells within a multicellular organism. The three cell types shown in Figure 13.2 contain the same **genome**, meaning they carry the same set of genes. However, their **proteomes**—the collection of proteins they make—are quite different; this is due to gene regulation. Certain proteins are found in particular cell types but not in others. Alternatively, a protein may be present in all three cell types, but the relative amounts of the protein

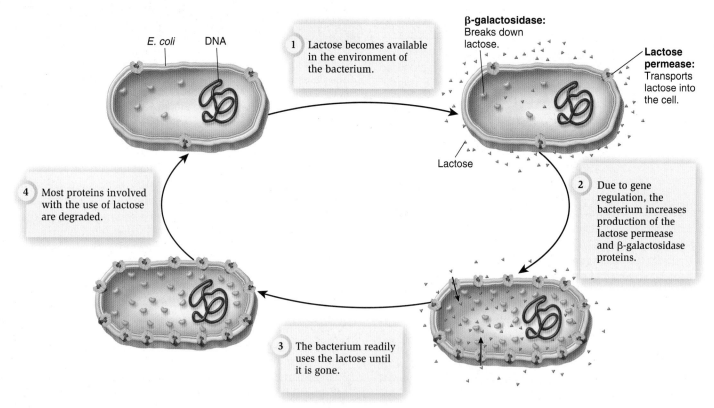

Figure 13.1   Gene regulation of lactose utilization in *E. coli.*

Concept check: What is the advantage to E. coli of regulating the genes involved with lactose utilization?

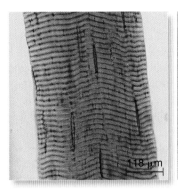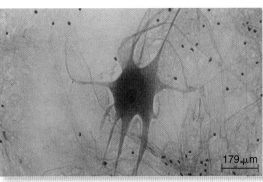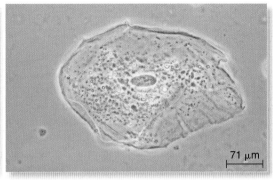

(a) Skeletal muscle cell   **(b) Nerve cell**   **(c) Skin cell**

Figure 13.2   **Examples of different cell types in humans.**   These cells have the same genetic composition. Their unique morphologies are due to differences in the proteins they make.

Concept check: *How does gene regulation underlie the different morphologies of these cells?*

may be different. The amount of a given protein depends on many factors, including how strongly the corresponding gene is turned on and how much protein is synthesized from mRNA. Gene regulation plays a major role in determining the proteome of each cell type.

Eukaryotic Gene Regulation Enables Multicellular Organisms to Progress Through Developmental Stages

In multicellular organisms that progress through developmental stages, certain genes are expressed at particular stages of development but not others. We'll discuss this topic in greater detail in Chapter 19. Let's consider an example of such developmental gene regulation in mammals. Early stages of development occur in the uterus of female mammals. Following fertilization, an embryo develops inside the uterus. In humans, the embryonic stage lasts from fertilization to 8 weeks. During this stage, major developmental changes produce the various body parts. The fetal stage occurs from 8 weeks to birth (41 weeks). This stage is characterized by continued refinement of body parts and a large increase in size.

Because of this internal development, a system has evolved to provide both the embryonic and fetal cells with the oxygen they require for cellular respiration. The oxygen demands of a rapidly growing embryo and fetus are quite different from the needs of the mother. Gene regulation plays a vital role in ensuring that an embryo and fetus get the proper amount of oxygen. Hemoglobin is the main protein that delivers oxygen to the cells of a mammal's body. The genomes of mammals carry several genes (designated with Greek letters) that encode slightly different globin polypeptides. A hemoglobin protein is composed of four globin polypeptides, two encoded by one globin gene and two encoded by another globin gene (**Figure 13.3**). During the embryonic stage of development, the epsilon (ε)-globin and zeta (ζ)-globin genes are turned on. At the fetal stage, these genes are turned off, and the alpha (α)-globin and gamma (γ)-globin genes are turned on. Finally, at birth, the γ-globin gene is turned off, and the beta (β)-globin gene is turned on.

How do the embryo and fetus acquire oxygen from their mother's bloodstream? The hemoglobin produced during the embryonic and fetal stages has a much higher binding affinity for oxygen than does the hemoglobin produced after birth. Therefore, the embryo and fetus can remove oxygen from the mother's bloodstream and use that oxygen for their own needs. This occurs across the placenta, where the mother's bloodstream is adjacent to the bloodstream of the embryo or fetus. In this way, gene regulation enables mammals to develop internally, even though the embryo and fetus are not breathing on their own. Gene regulation ensures that the correct hemoglobin protein is produced at the right time in development.

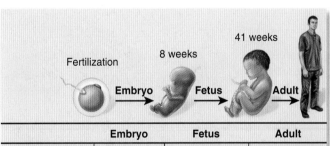

	Embryo	Fetus	Adult
Hemoglobin protein	2 ζ-globins 2 ε-globins	2 α-globins 2 γ-globins	2 α-globins 2 β-globins
Oxygen affinity	Highest	High	Moderate
Gene expression α-globin gene β-globin gene γ-globin gene ζ-globin gene ε-globin gene	Off Off Off On On	On Off On Off Off	On On Off Off Off

Figure 13.3   **Developmental regulation of human globin genes.**   Note: The delta (δ) globin gene is also expressed in the adult.

Concept check: *How does this form of gene regulation help the embryo and fetus to obtain oxygen?*

Gene Regulation Can Occur at Different Points in the Process from DNA to Protein

Thus far, we have learned that gene regulation can have a dramatic impact on the ability of organisms to respond to environmental changes, differentiate cells, and progress through developmental stages. For structural genes that encode proteins, the regulation of gene expression can occur at any of the steps that are needed to produce a functional protein.

In bacteria, gene regulation most commonly occurs at the level of transcription, which means that bacteria regulate how much mRNA is made from genes (Figure 13.4a). When geneticists say a gene is "turned off," they mean that very little or no mRNA is made from that gene, whereas a gene that is "turned on" is transcribed into mRNA. Because transcription is the first step in gene expression, transcriptional regulation is a particularly efficient way to regulate genes because cells avoid wasting energy when the product of the gene is not needed. A second way for bacteria to regulate gene expression is to control the rate at which mRNA is translated into protein. This form of gene regulation is less common in bacteria. Last, gene expression can be regulated at the protein or post-translational level.

In eukaryotes, gene regulation occurs at many levels, including transcription, RNA processing, translation, and after translation is completed (Figure 13.4b). Like their bacterial counterparts, transcriptional regulation is a prominent form of gene regulation for eukaryotes. As discussed later in this chapter, eukaryotic genes are transcriptionally regulated in several different ways, some of which are not found in bacteria. As

discussed in Chapter 12, eukaryotes process their mRNA transcripts in ways that do not commonly occur in bacteria (refer back to Figure 12.3). For example, RNA splicing is a widespread phenomenon in eukaryotes. Later in this chapter, we will examine how this process is regulated to create two or more different types of mRNA from a single gene. Eukaryotes can also regulate an mRNA after its modification. The amount of mRNA may be regulated by controlling its degradation. In addition, the translation of mRNA may be regulated by small, inhibitory RNA molecules or by RNA-binding proteins that prevent translation from occurring. As in prokaryotes, eukaryotic proteins can be regulated in a variety of ways, including feedback inhibition, post-translational modification, and protein degradation. These various types of protein regulation are best understood within the context of cell biology, so they were primarily discussed in Unit II. Post-translational modifications are summarized in Chapter 21 (look ahead to Figure 21.10).

13.2 Regulation of Transcription in Bacteria

Due to gene regulation, bacteria can respond to changes in their cellular and environmental conditions. As we have seen, when a bacterium is exposed to a particular nutrient in its environment, such as a sugar, the genes are expressed that encode proteins needed for the uptake and metabolism of that sugar. In addition, bacteria have enzymes that synthesize cellular molecules such as particular amino acids. In such cases, the control of gene expression often occurs at the level of transcription. When we say that a gene is turned on, this refers to a high rate of transcription, whereas a gene that is turned off has a very low rate, perhaps negligible. In this section, we will examine the underlying molecular mechanisms that bring about transcriptional regulation in bacteria.

Transcriptional Regulation Often Involves Regulatory Transcription Factors and Small Effector Molecules

In most cases, transcriptional regulation involves the actions of **regulatory transcription factors**, proteins that bind to DNA in the vicinity of a promoter and affect the rate of transcription of one or more nearby genes. These transcription factors can either decrease or increase the rate of transcription of a gene. **Repressors** are transcription factors that bind to DNA and inhibit transcription, whereas **activators** bind to the DNA and increase the rate of transcription. The term **negative control** refers to transcriptional regulation by repressor proteins; **positive control** refers to regulation by activator proteins (Figure 13.5a).

In conjunction with regulatory transcription factors, molecules called **small effector molecules** often play a critical role in transcriptional regulation. A small effector molecule exerts its effects by binding to a regulatory transcription factor and causing a conformational change in the protein. In many cases, the effect of the conformational change determines whether or

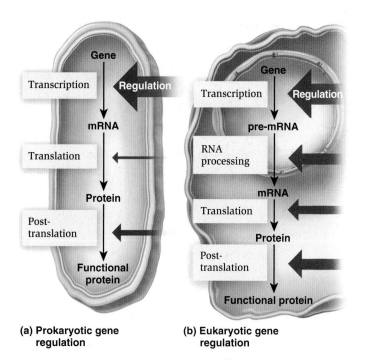

(a) Prokaryotic gene regulation

(b) Eukaryotic gene regulation

Figure 13.4   Overview of gene regulation in (a) prokaryotes and (b) eukaryotes.   The relative width of the red arrows indicates the prominence with which regulation is used to control the production of functional proteins.

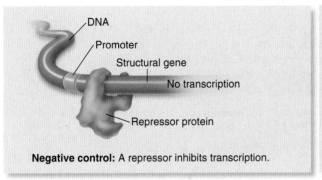
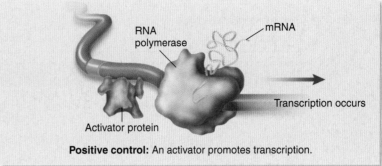

Negative control: A repressor inhibits transcription.

Positive control: An activator promotes transcription.

(a) Actions of regulatory transcription factors

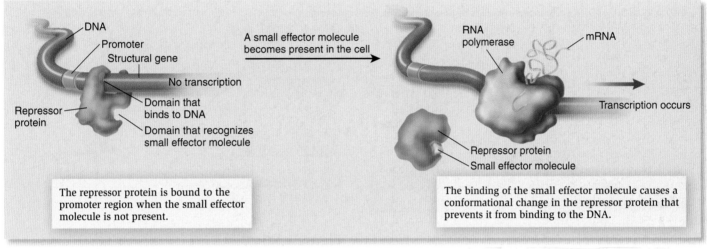

The repressor protein is bound to the promoter region when the small effector molecule is not present.

The binding of the small effector molecule causes a conformational change in the repressor protein that prevents it from binding to the DNA.

(b) Action of a small effector molecule on a repressor protein

Figure 13.5 Actions of regulatory transcription factors and small effector molecules.   (a) Regulatory transcription factors may exert negative or positive control. (b) One way that a small effector molecule may exert its effects is by preventing a repressor protein from binding to the DNA.

not the protein can bind to the DNA. **Figure 13.5b** illustrates an example. When the small effector molecule is not present in the cytoplasm, the repressor binds to the DNA and inhibits transcription. However, when the small effector molecule is subsequently found in the cytoplasm, it will bind to the repressor and cause a conformational change that inhibits the ability of the protein to bind to the DNA. The gene is turned on because the repressor is not able to bind to the DNA. Regulatory transcription factors that respond to small effector molecules have two functional regions called **domains**. One domain is a site where the protein binds to the DNA, whereas the other is the binding site for the small effector molecule.

The *lac* Operon Contains Genes That Encode Proteins Involved in Lactose Metabolism

In bacteria, structural genes are sometimes clustered together in units that are under the transcriptional control of a single promoter and have a regulatory region called an **operator**. This arrangement is known as an **operon**. The transcription of the structural genes occurs as a single unit and results in the production of a **polycistronic mRNA**, an mRNA that encodes more

than one protein. What advantage is this arrangement? An operon organization allows a bacterium to coordinately regulate a group of genes that encode proteins whose functions are used in a common pathway.

The genome of *E. coli* carries an operon, called the ***lac* operon**, that contains the genes for the proteins that allow it to metabolize lactose (see Figure 13.1). **Figure 13.6a** shows the organization of this operon as it is found in the *E. coli* chromosome, as well as the polycistronic mRNA that is transcribed from it. The *lac* operon contains a promoter, *lacP*, that is used to transcribe three structural genes: *lacZ*, *lacY*, and *lacA*. *LacZ* encodes β-galactosidase, which is an enzyme that breaks down lactose (**Figure 13.6b**). As a side reaction, β-galactosidase also converts a small percentage of lactose into allolactose, a structurally similar sugar or lactose analogue. As described later, allolactose is important in the regulation of the *lac* operon. The *lacY* gene encodes lactose permease, which is a membrane protein required for the transport of lactose into the cytoplasm of the bacterium. The *lacA* gene encodes galactoside transacetylase, which covalently modifies lactose and lactose analogues by attaching an acetyl group (—COCH$_3$). Although the functional necessity of this enzyme remains unclear, the attachment

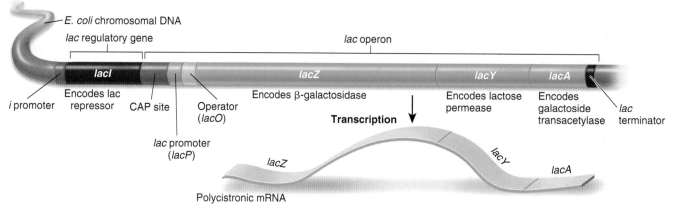

(a) Organization of DNA sequences in the *lac* region of the *E. coli* chromosome

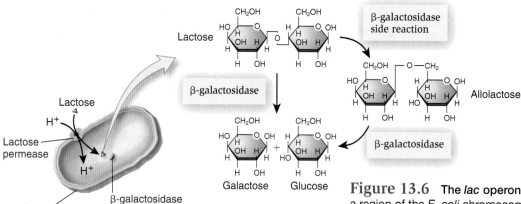

(b) Functions of lactose permease and β-galactosidase

of acetyl groups to nonmetabolizable lactose analogues may prevent their toxic buildup in the cytoplasm.

Near the *lac* promoter are two regulatory sites designated the operator and the CAP site (see Figure 13.6a). The operator, or *lacO* site, is a sequence of nucleotides that provides a binding site for a repressor protein. The **CAP site** is a DNA sequence recognized by an activator protein.

Adjacent to the *lac* operon is the *lacI* gene, which encodes the **lac repressor**. This repressor protein is important for the regulation of the *lac* operon. The *lacI* gene, which is constitutively expressed at fairly low levels, has its own promoter called the *i* promoter. It is called a **regulatory gene** because the sole function of the encoded protein is to regulate the expression of other genes. The *lacI* gene is not considered a part of the *lac* operon. Let's now take a look at how the *lac* operon is regulated by the lac repressor.

The *lac* Operon Is Under Negative Control by a Repressor Protein

In the late 1950s, the first researchers to investigate gene regulation were Francois Jacob and Jacques Monod at the Pasteur Institute in Paris, France. Their focus on gene regulation stemmed from an interest in the phenomenon known as

Figure 13.6 The *lac* operon. (a) This diagram depicts a region of the *E. coli* chromosome that contains the *lacI* regulatory gene and the adjacent *lac* operon, as well as the polycistronic mRNA transcribed from the operon. The mRNA is translated into three proteins: lactose permease, β-galactosidase, and galactoside transacetylase. (b) Lactose permease cotransports H$^+$ with lactose. Bacteria maintain an H$^+$ gradient across their cytoplasmic membrane that drives the active transport of lactose into the cytoplasm. β-galactosidase cleaves lactose into galactose and glucose. As a side reaction, it can also convert lactose into allolactose.

Concept check: *Which genes are under the control of the lac promoter?*

enzyme adaptation, which had been identified early in the 20th century. Enzyme adaptation refers to the observation that a particular enzyme appears within a living cell only after the cell has been exposed to the substrate for that enzyme. Jacob and Monod studied lactose metabolism in *E. coli* to investigate this phenomenon. When they exposed bacteria to lactose, the levels of lactose-using enzymes in the cells increased by 1,000- to 10,000-fold. After lactose was removed, the synthesis of the enzymes abruptly stopped.

The first mechanism of regulation that Jacob and Monod discovered involved the lac repressor protein, which binds to the sequence of nucleotides found at the *lac* operator site. Once bound, the lac repressor prevents RNA polymerase from transcribing the *lacZ*, *lacY*, and *lacA* genes (**Figure 13.7a**). RNA polymerase can bind to the promoter when the lac repressor is bound to the operator site, but RNA polymerase

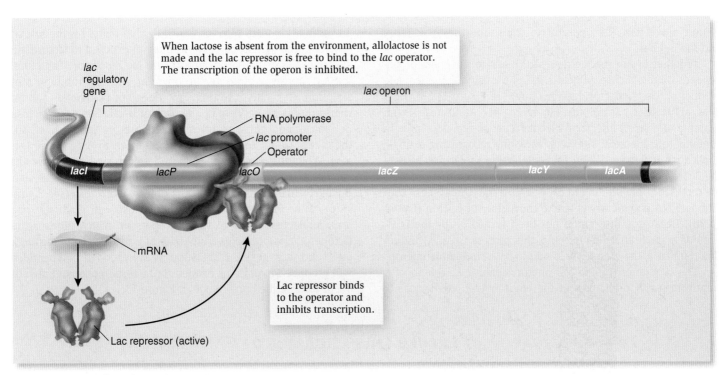

(a) Lactose absent from the environment

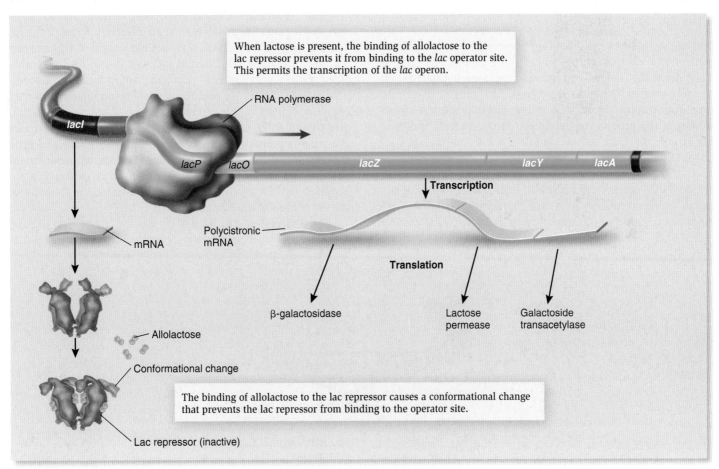

(b) Lactose present

Figure 13.7 Negative control of an inducible set of genes: function of the lac repressor in regulating the *lac* operon.

Concept check: *With regard to regulatory proteins and small effector molecules, explain the meaning of the terms "negative control" and "inducible."*

cannot move past the operator to transcribe the *lacZ*, *lacY*, and *lacA* genes.

Whether or not the lac repressor binds to the operator site depends on allolactose, which is the previously mentioned side product of the β-galactosidase enzyme (see Figure 13.6b). How does allolactose control the lac repressor? Allolactose is an example of a small effector molecule. The lac repressor protein contains four identical subunits, each one recognizing a single allolactose molecule. When four allolactose molecules bind to the lac repressor, a conformational change occurs that prevents the repressor from binding to the operator site. Under these conditions, RNA polymerase is free to transcribe the operon (**Figure 13.7b**). Because transcription has been turned on by the presence of a small effector molecule, this process is called **induction**. Similarly, the *lac* operon is said to be an **inducible operon**.

The regulation of the *lac* operon enables *E. coli* to efficiently respond to changes in the environment. Allolactose is an **inducer**, a small effector molecule that increases the rate of transcription. When the bacterium is not exposed to lactose, no allolactose is available to bind to the lac repressor. Therefore, the lac repressor binds to the operator site and inhibits transcription. In reality, the repressor does not completely inhibit transcription, so very small amounts of β-galactosidase, lactose permease, and galactoside transacetylase are made. Even so, the levels are far too low for the bacterium to readily use lactose. When the bacterium is exposed to lactose, a small amount can be transported into the cytoplasm via lactose permease, and β-galactosidase will convert some of it to allolactose (see Figure 13.6). The cytoplasmic level of allolactose will gradually rise until allolactose binds to the lac repressor, which induces the *lac* operon and promotes a high rate of transcription of the *lacZ*, *lacY*, and *lacA* genes. Translation of the encoded polypeptides will produce the proteins needed for lactose uptake and metabolism as described previously in Figure 13.1.

FEATURE INVESTIGATION

Jacob, Monod, and Pardee Studied a Constitutive Bacterial Mutant to Determine the Function of the Lac Repressor

Thus far, we have learned that the lac repressor binds to the *lac* operator site to exert its effects. Let's now take a look back at experiments that helped researchers determine the function of the lac repressor. Our understanding of *lac* operon regulation came from studies involving *E. coli* strains that showed abnormalities in the process. In the 1950s, Jacob, Monod, and their colleague Arthur Pardee had identified a few rare mutant bacteria that had abnormal lactose use. The mutants expressed the genes of the *lac* operon constitutively, meaning that the *lacZ*, *lacY*, and *lacA* genes were expressed even in the absence of lactose in the environment. The researchers discovered that some mutations that caused this abnormality had occurred in the *lacI* region. Such strains were termed *lacI⁻* (*lacI* minus) to indicate

that the *lacI* region was not functioning properly. Normal or wild-type *lacI* strains of *E. coli* are called *lacI⁺* (*lacI* plus).

The researchers initially hypothesized that the *lacI* gene encoded an enzyme that degraded an internal inducer of the *lac* operon. The *lacI⁻* mutation was thought to inhibit this enzyme and thereby allow the internal inducer to always be synthesized. In this way, the *lacI⁻* mutation would make it unnecessary for cells to be exposed to lactose for induction. However, over the course of this study and later studies, they eventually arrived at the correct hypothesis that the *lacI* gene encodes a repressor protein (**Figure 13.8**). A mutation in the *lacI* gene that eliminates the synthesis of a functional lac repressor would thereby prevent the lac repressor protein from inhibiting transcription. At the time of their work, however, the function of the lac repressor was not yet known.

To understand the nature of the *lacI⁻* mutation, Jacob, Monod, and Pardee applied a genetic approach. Although bacte-

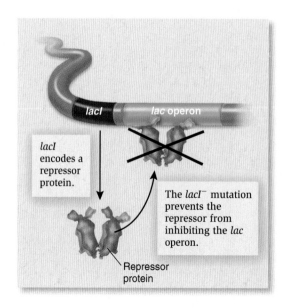

lacI encodes a repressor protein.

The *lacI⁻* mutation prevents the repressor from inhibiting the *lac* operon.

Repressor protein

Figure 13.8
A hypothesis for the function of the *lacI* gene.

rial conjugation is described in Chapter 18, let's briefly examine this process in order to understand this experiment. The earliest studies of Jacob, Monod, and Pardee in 1959 involved matings between recipient cells, termed F⁻ (F minus), and donor cells, which were called Hfr strains. Such Hfr strains were able to transfer a portion of the bacterial chromosome to a recipient cell. Later experiments in 1961 involved the transfer of circular segments of DNA known as F factors. We will consider this later type of experiment here. Sometimes an F factor also carries genes that were originally found within the bacterial chromosome. These types of F factors are called F′ factors (F prime factors). A strain of bacteria containing F′ factor genes is called a **merozygote**, or partial diploid. The production of merozygotes was instrumental in allowing Jacob, Monod, and Pardee to elucidate the function of the *lacI* gene.

As shown in **Figure 13.9**, these researchers studied the *lac* operon in a bacterial strain carrying a *lacI⁻* mutation that caused constitutive expression of the *lac* operon. In addition, the mutant strain was subjected to mating to create a merozygote that also carried a normal *lac* operon and normal *lacI⁺* gene on an F′ factor. The merozygote contained both *lacI⁺* and *lacI⁻* genes. The constitutive mutant and corresponding merozygote were allowed to grow separately in liquid media and then divided into two tubes each. In half of the tubes, the cells were incubated with lactose to determine if lactose was needed to induce the expression of the operon. In the other tubes, lactose was omitted. To monitor the expression of the *lac* operon, the cells were broken open and then tested for the amount of β-galactosidase they released by measuring the ability of any β-galactosidase present to convert a colorless compound into a yellow product.

The data table of Figure 13.9 summarizes the effects of this constitutive mutation and its analysis in a merozygote. As Jacob, Monod, and Pardee already knew, the *lacI⁻* mutant strain expressed the *lac* operon constitutively, in both the presence and absence of lactose. However, when a normal *lac* operon and *lacI⁺* gene were introduced on an F′ factor into a cell harboring the mutant *lacI⁻* gene on the chromosome, the normal *lacI⁺* gene could regulate both operons. In the absence of lactose, both operons were shut off. How did Jacob, Monod, and Pardee eventually explain these results? This occurred because a single *lacI⁺* gene on the F′ factor can produce enough repressor protein to bind to both operator sites. Furthermore, this protein is diffusible—can spread through the cytoplasm—and can bind to

Figure 13.9   The experiment performed by Jacob, Monod, and Pardee to study a constitutive *lacI⁻* mutant.

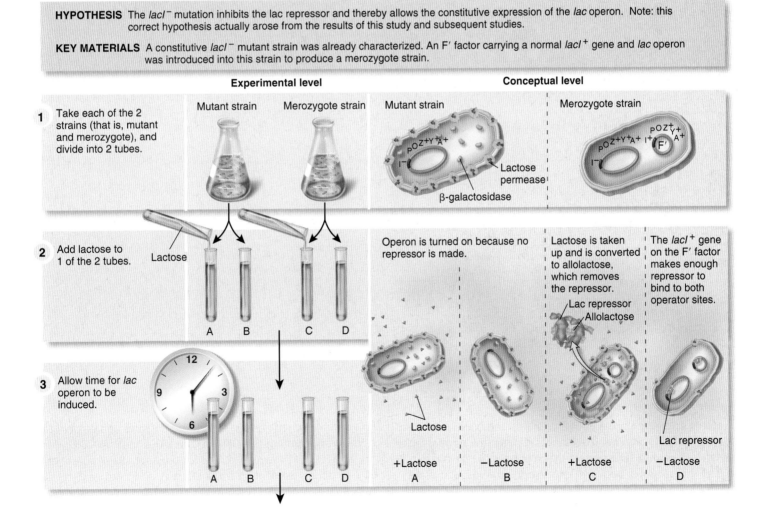

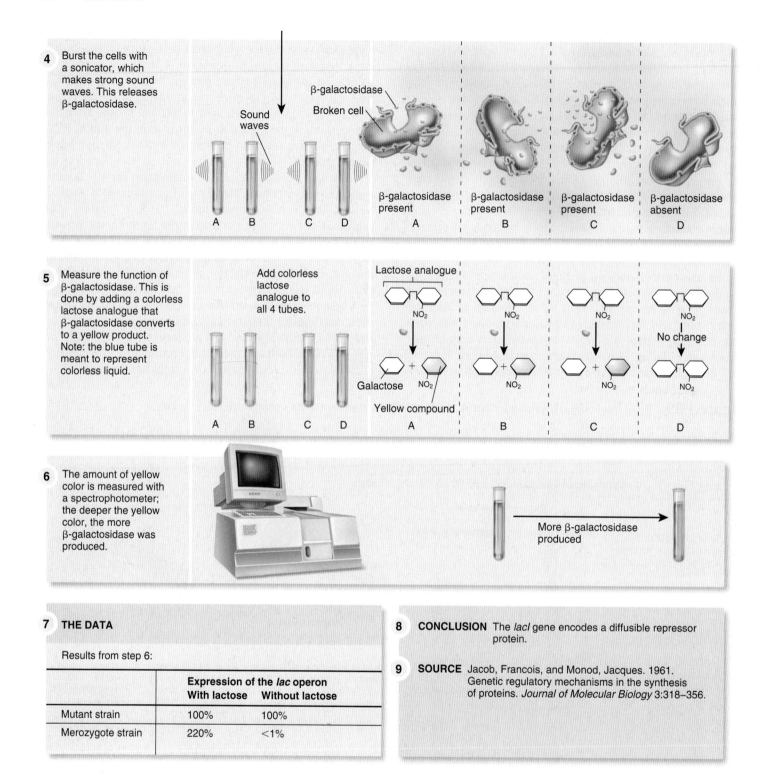

4 Burst the cells with a sonicator, which makes strong sound waves. This releases β-galactosidase.

Sound waves

β-galactosidase

Broken cell

β-galactosidase present

A

B

C

D

β-galactosidase present
A

β-galactosidase present
B

β-galactosidase present
C

β-galactosidase absent
D

5 Measure the function of β-galactosidase. This is done by adding a colorless lactose analogue that β-galactosidase converts to a yellow product. Note: the blue tube is meant to represent colorless liquid.

Add colorless lactose analogue to all 4 tubes.

Lactose analogue

NO_2

Galactose NO_2

Yellow compound

A   B   C   D

NO_2

NO_2

NO_2

No change

NO_2

A   B   C   D

6 The amount of yellow color is measured with a spectrophotometer; the deeper the yellow color, the more β-galactosidase was produced.

More β-galactosidase produced

7 THE DATA

Results from step 6:

| | Expression of the *lac* operon | |
	With lactose	Without lactose
Mutant strain	100%	100%
Merozygote strain	220%	<1%

8 CONCLUSION The *lacI* gene encodes a diffusible repressor protein.

9 SOURCE Jacob, Francois, and Monod, Jacques. 1961. Genetic regulatory mechanisms in the synthesis of proteins. *Journal of Molecular Biology* 3:318–356.

lac operons that are on the F′ factor and on the bacterial chromosome. Taken together, the data indicated that the normal *lacI* gene encodes a diffusible protein that represses the *lac* operon.

The interactions between regulatory proteins and DNA sequences illustrated in this experiment have led to the defini-tion of three genetic terms. In both prokaryotes and eukaryotes, **a *cis*-acting element** is a DNA segment that must be adjacent to the gene(s) that it regulates. The *lac* operator site is an example of a *cis*-acting element. A ***trans*-effect** is a form of gene regula-tion that can occur even though two DNA segments are not physically adjacent. The action of the lac repressor on the *lac* operon is a *trans*-effect. A ***cis*-effect** is mediated by a *cis*-acting element that binds regulatory proteins, whereas a *trans*-effect is mediated by genes that encode diffusible regulatory proteins.

Experimental Questions

1. What were the key observations made by Jacob, Monod, and Pardee that led to the development of their hypothesis regarding the *lacI* gene and the regulation of the *lac* operon?

2. What was the eventual hypothesis proposed by the researchers to explain the function of the *lacI* gene and the regulation of the *lac* operon?

3. How did Jacob, Monod, and Pardee test the hypothesis? What were the results of the experiment? How do these results support the idea that the *lacI* gene produces a repressor protein?

The *lac* Operon Is Also Under Positive Control by an Activator Protein

In addition to negative control by a repressor protein, the *lac* operon is also positively regulated by an activator protein called the **catabolite activator protein** (**CAP**). CAP is controlled by a small effector molecule, **cyclic AMP** (**cAMP**), that is produced from ATP via an enzyme known as adenylyl cyclase. Gene regulation involving CAP and cAMP is an example of positive control (**Figure 13.10**). When cAMP binds to CAP, the cAMP-CAP complex binds to the CAP site near the *lac* promoter. This causes a bend in the DNA that enhances the ability of RNA polymerase to bind to the promoter. In this way, the rate of transcription is increased.

The key functional role of CAP is to allow *E. coli* to choose between different sources of sugar. In a process known as **catabolite repression**, transcription of the *lac* operon is inhibited by the presence of glucose, which is a catabolite (it is broken down—**catabolized**—inside the cell). This gene regulation allows *E. coli* to preferentially use glucose compared to other sugars, such as lactose. How does this occur? Glucose inhibits the production of cAMP and thereby prevents the binding of CAP to the DNA. In this way, glucose blocks the activation of the *lac* operon and thereby inhibits transcription. Though it may seem puzzling, the term catabolite repression was coined before the action of the cAMP-CAP complex was understood at the molecular level. Historically, the primary observation of researchers was that glucose (a catabolite) inhibited (repressed) lactose metabolism. Further experimentation revealed that CAP is actually an activator protein.

Figure 13.11 considers the four possible environmental conditions that an *E. coli* bacterium might experience with regard to these two sugars. When both lactose and glucose levels are high, the rate of transcription of the *lac* operon is low, because CAP does not activate transcription. Under these conditions, the bacterium primarily uses glucose rather than lactose. Why is this a benefit to the bacterium? Greater efficiency is achieved if the bacterium uses one type of sugar at a time. If lactose levels are high and glucose is low, the transcription rate of the *lac* operon is very high because CAP is bound to the CAP site and the lac repressor is not bound to the operator site. Under these conditions, the bacterium metabolizes lactose. When lactose levels are low, the lac repressor prevents transcription of the *lac* operon, whether glucose levels are high or low.

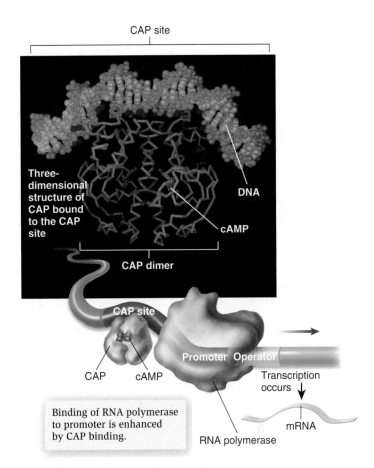

Figure 13.10 Positive regulation of the *lac* operon by the catabolite activator protein (CAP). When cAMP is bound to CAP, CAP binds to the DNA and causes it to bend. This bend facilitates the binding of RNA polymerase.

The *trp* Operon Is Also Under Negative Control by a Repressor Protein

So far in this section, we have examined the regulation of the *lac* operon. Let's now consider an example of an operon that encodes enzymes involved in biosynthesis rather than breakdown. Our example is the ***trp* operon** of *E. coli*, which encodes enzymes that are required to make the amino acid tryptophan, a building block of cellular proteins. More specifically, the *trpE*, *trpD*, *trpC*, *trpB*, and *trpA* genes encode enzymes that are involved in a pathway that leads to tryptophan synthesis.

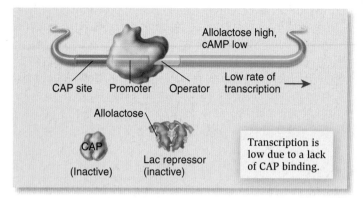

(a) Lactose high, glucose high

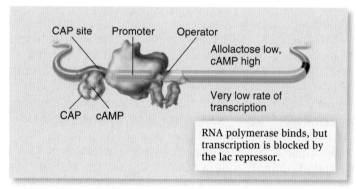

(b) Lactose high, glucose low

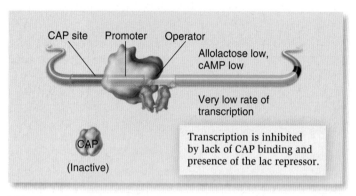

(c) Lactose low, glucose high

(d) Lactose low, glucose low

Figure 13.11   Effects of lactose and glucose on the expression of the *lac* operon.

Concept check: *What are the advantages of having both an activator and a repressor protein?*

The *trp* operon is regulated by a repressor protein that is encoded by the *trpR* gene. The binding of the repressor to the *trp* operator site inhibits transcription. The ability of the trp repressor to bind to the *trp* operator is controlled by tryptophan, which is the product of the enzymes that are encoded by the operon. When tryptophan levels within the cell are very low, the trp repressor cannot bind to the operator site. Under these conditions, RNA polymerase readily transcribes the operon (**Figure 13.12a**). In this way, the cell expresses the genes that encode enzymes that result in the synthesis of tryptophan, which is in short supply. Alternatively, when the tryptophan levels within the cell are high, tryptophan turns off the *trp* operon. Tryptophan acts as a small effector molecule, or **corepressor**, by binding to the trp repressor protein. This causes a conformational change in the repressor that allows it to bind to the *trp* operator site, inhibiting the ability of RNA polymerase to transcribe the operon (**Figure 13.12b**). Therefore, the bacterium does not waste energy making tryptophan when it is abundant.

When comparing the *lac* and *trp* operons, the actions of their small effector molecules are quite different. The lac repressor binds to its operator in the absence of its small effector molecule, whereas the trp repressor binds to its operator only in the presence of its small effector molecule. The *lac* operon is categorized as inducible because its small effector molecule, namely allolactose, induces transcription. By comparison, the *trp* operon

is considered to be a **repressible operon** because its small effector molecule, namely tryptophan, represses transcription.

Repressible Operons Usually Encode Anabolic Enzymes, and Inducible Operons Encode Catabolic Enzymes

By comparing the mechanisms of regulation among many bacterial operons, geneticists have noticed a general trend. The genes in some operons encode proteins that function in the breakdown, or **catabolism**, of a substance. In such cases, the substance to be broken down (or a related compound) often acts as the inducer. This keeps the genes turned off unless the appropriate substance is available. For example, allolactose, which is a product of lactose metabolism, acts as an inducer of the *lac* operon. An inducible form of regulation allows the bacterium to express the appropriate genes only when they are needed to metabolize lactose.

Other cellular enzymes are important for synthesizing organic molecules, a process termed **anabolism**. Because these molecules are generally needed for the functioning of the cell, the genes that encode these anabolic enzymes tend to be regulated by a repressible mechanism, allowing the genes to be transcribed unless they are turned off. The small effector molecule is commonly a product of the enzymes' biosynthetic activities.

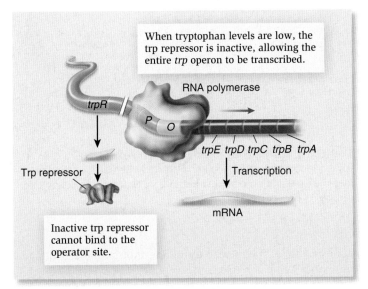

When tryptophan levels are low, the trp repressor is inactive, allowing the entire *trp* operon to be transcribed.

RNA polymerase

trpR

P   *O*

trpE trpD trpC trpB trpA

Transcription

Trp repressor

mRNA

Inactive trp repressor cannot bind to the operator site.

(a) Low tryptophan

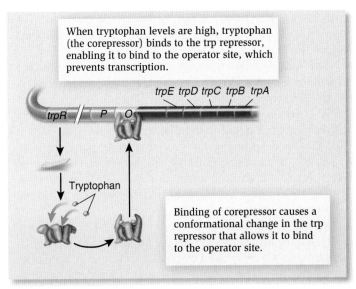

When tryptophan levels are high, tryptophan (the corepressor) binds to the trp repressor, enabling it to bind to the operator site, which prevents transcription.

trpE trpD trpC trpB trpA

trpR   *P*   *O*

Tryptophan

Binding of corepressor causes a conformational change in the trp repressor that allows it to bind to the operator site.

(b) High tryptophan

Figure 13.12   Negative control of a repressible set of genes: function of the trp repressor and corepressor in regulating the *trp* operon.

Concept check: *How are the functions of the lac repressor and trp repressor similar to each other, and how are they different?*

For example, as we learned, tryptophan is produced by the enzymes that are encoded by the *trp* operon. When enough of this amino acid has been made, tryptophan itself acts as a corepressor, turning off the genes required for tryptophan biosynthesis. Therefore, a repressible form of regulation provides the bacterium with a way to prevent the overproduction of the product of a biosynthetic pathway.

13.3   Regulation of Transcription in Eukaryotes

Transcriptional regulation in eukaryotes follows some of the same principles as those found in prokaryotes. For example, activator and repressor proteins are involved in regulating genes by influencing the ability of RNA polymerase to initiate transcription. In addition, many eukaryotic genes are regulated by small effector molecules. However, some important differences also occur. In eukaryotic species, genes are almost always organized individually, not in operons. In addition, eukaryotic gene regulation tends to be more intricate, because eukaryotes are faced with complexities that differ from their prokaryotic counterparts. For example, eukaryotes have more complicated cell structures that contain many more proteins and a variety of cell organelles. Many eukaryotes such as animals and plants are multicellular and contain different cell types. As discussed earlier in this chapter, animal cells may differentiate into nerve cells, muscle cells, and skin cells, among others. Furthermore, animals and plants progress through developmental stages that require changes in gene expression. For these reasons, gene regulation in eukaryotes requires much more coordination and integration.

By studying transcriptional regulation, researchers have discovered that most eukaryotic genes, particularly those found in multicellular species, are regulated by many factors. This phenomenon is called **combinatorial control** because the combination of many factors determines the expression of any given gene. At the level of transcription, common factors that contribute to combinatorial control include the following:

1. One or more activator proteins may stimulate the ability of RNA polymerase to initiate transcription.
2. One or more repressor proteins may inhibit the ability of RNA polymerase to initiate transcription.
3. The function of activators and repressors may be modulated in several ways, which include the binding of small effector molecules, protein–protein interactions, and covalent modifications.
4. Activator proteins are necessary to alter chromatin structure in the region where a gene is located, thereby making it easier for the gene to be recognized and transcribed by RNA polymerase.
5. DNA methylation usually inhibits transcription, either by preventing the binding of an activator protein or by recruiting proteins that inhibit transcription.

All five of these factors may contribute to the regulation of a single gene, or possibly only three or four will play a role. In most cases, transcriptional regulation is aimed at controlling the initiation of transcription at the promoter. In this section, we will survey these basic types of gene regulation in eukaryotic species.

Eukaryotic Structural Genes Have a Core Promoter and Regulatory Elements

To understand gene regulation in eukaryotes, we first need to consider the DNA sequences that are needed to initiate transcription. For eukaryotic structural genes that encode proteins, three features are common among most promoters: a **TATA box**, a **transcriptional start site**, and **regulatory elements** (Figure 13.13).

The TATA box and transcriptional start site form the **core promoter**. The transcriptional start site is the place in the DNA where transcription actually begins. The TATA box, which is a 5′–TATAAA–3′ sequence, is usually about 25 base pairs upstream from a transcriptional start site. The TATA box is important in determining the precise starting point for transcription. If it is missing from the core promoter, transcription may start at a variety of different locations. The core promoter, by itself, results in a low level of transcription that is termed **basal transcription**.

Regulatory elements (or response elements) are DNA segments that regulate eukaryotic genes. As described later, regulatory elements are recognized by regulatory transcription factors that control the ability of RNA polymerase to initiate transcription at the core promoter. Some regulatory elements, known as **enhancers**, play a role in the ability of RNA polymerase to begin transcription and thereby enhance the rate of transcription. When enhancers are not functioning, most eukaryotic genes have very low levels of basal transcription. Other regulatory elements, known as **silencers**, prevent transcription of a given gene when its expression is not needed. When these sequences function, the rate of transcription is decreased.

A common location for regulatory elements is the region that is 50 to 100 base pairs upstream from the transcriptional start site (Figure 13.13). However, the locations of regulatory elements are quite variable among different eukaryotic genes. Regulatory elements can be quite distant from the promoter, even 100,000 base pairs away, yet exert strong effects on the

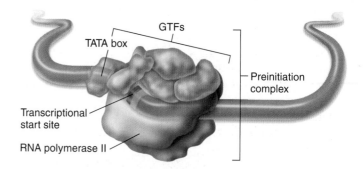

Figure 13.14   **The preinitiation complex.**   General transcription factors (GTFs) and RNA polymerase II assemble into the preinitiation complex at the core promoter in eukaryotic structural genes.

ability of RNA polymerase to initiate transcription at the core promoter! Regulatory elements were first discovered by Susumu Tonegawa and coworkers in the 1980s. While studying genes that play a role in immunity, they identified a region that was far away from the core promoter but was needed for high levels of transcription to take place.

RNA Polymerase II, General Transcription Factors, and Mediator Are Needed to Transcribe Eukaryotic Structural Genes

As discussed in Chapter 12, eukaryotes have three RNA polymerases designated I, II, and III. RNA polymerase II transcribes structural genes that encode proteins. By studying transcription in a variety of eukaryotic species, researchers have identified three types of proteins that play a role in initiating transcription at the core promoter of structural genes. These are RNA polymerase II, five different proteins called **general transcription factors** (**GTFs**), and a large protein complex called mediator. GTFs are needed for DNA binding at the core promoter and for initiation of transcription. Mediator, which is described later, is also needed for RNA polymerase to proceed to the elongation phase of transcription.

RNA polymerase II and GTFs must come together at the core promoter before transcription can be initiated. A series of interactions occurs between these proteins so that RNA polymerase II can bind to the DNA. **Figure 13.14** shows the structure of the completed assembly of RNA polymerase II and GTFs at the TATA box within the core promoter. This assembly is known as the **preinitiation complex**. In vitro, when researchers mix together RNA polymerase II, GTFs, and a DNA sequence containing a TATA box and a transcriptional start site, the DNA is transcribed into RNA. Therefore, these components are referred to as the **basal transcription apparatus**. In a living cell, however, additional components, such as regulatory transcription factors, control the assembly of RNA polymerase II and GTFs at the core promoter and are responsible for causing transcription to begin at a fast or slow rate.

A third component needed for transcription in eukaryotes is the mediator protein complex. **Mediator** is composed of several proteins that bind to each other to form an elliptical-shaped

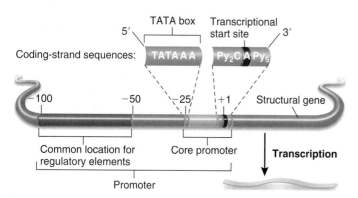

Figure 13.13   **A common organization of sequences for the promoter of a eukaryotic structural gene.**   The core promoter has a TATA box and a transcriptional start site. The TATA box sequence is 5′–TATAAA–3′. However, not all structural genes in eukaryotes have a TATA box. The A highlighted in dark blue is the transcriptional start site. This A marks the site of the first A in the RNA transcript. The sequence that flanks the A of the transcriptional start site is two pyrimidines, then C, then five pyrimidines. Py refers to pyrimidine—cytosine or thymine. Regulatory elements, such as enhancers and silencers, are usually found upstream from the core promoter.

complex that partially wraps around RNA polymerase II and the GTFs. Mediator derives its name from the observation that it mediates interactions between the preinitiation complex and regulatory transcription factors such as activators or repressors that bind to enhancers or silencers. The function of mediator is to control the rate at which RNA polymerase can begin to transcribe RNA at the transcriptional start site.

Activators and Repressors May Influence the Function of GTFs or Mediator

In eukaryotes, regulatory transcription factors called activators and repressors bind to enhancers or silencers, respectively, and regulate the rate of transcription of a nearby gene. In some cases, activator proteins interact with **coactivators**—proteins that increase the rate of transcription but do not directly bind to the DNA itself.

Activators and repressors commonly regulate the function of RNA polymerase II by binding to GTFs or mediator. As shown in **Figure 13.15**, some activators bind to an enhancer and then influence the function of GTFs. For example, an activator may improve the ability of a GTF called TFIID to initiate transcription. The function of TFIID is to recognize the TATA box and

begin the assembly process. An activator may recruit TFIID to the TATA box, thereby promoting the assembly of GTFs and RNA polymerase II into the preinitiation complex. In contrast, repressors may inhibit the function of TFIID. Certain repressors exert their effects by preventing the binding of TFIID to the TATA box or by inhibiting the ability of TFIID to assemble other GTFs and RNA polymerase II at the core promoter.

A second way that regulatory transcription factors control RNA polymerase II is via mediator (**Figure 13.16**). In this example, an activator also interacts with a coactivator. The activator/coactivator complex stimulates the function of mediator and thereby causes RNA polymerase II to proceed to the elongation phase of transcription more quickly. Alternatively, repressors have the opposite effect to those seen in Figure 13.16. When a repressor inhibits mediator, RNA polymerase II cannot progress to the elongation stage.

A third way that regulatory transcription factors influence transcription is by recruiting proteins that affect chromatin structure in the promoter region. As described in Chapter 11, the DNA found in eukaryotic chromosomes is wrapped in nucleosomes. The arrangement of nucleosomes also affects the ability of RNA polymerase II and GTFs to initiate transcription. This topic is described next.

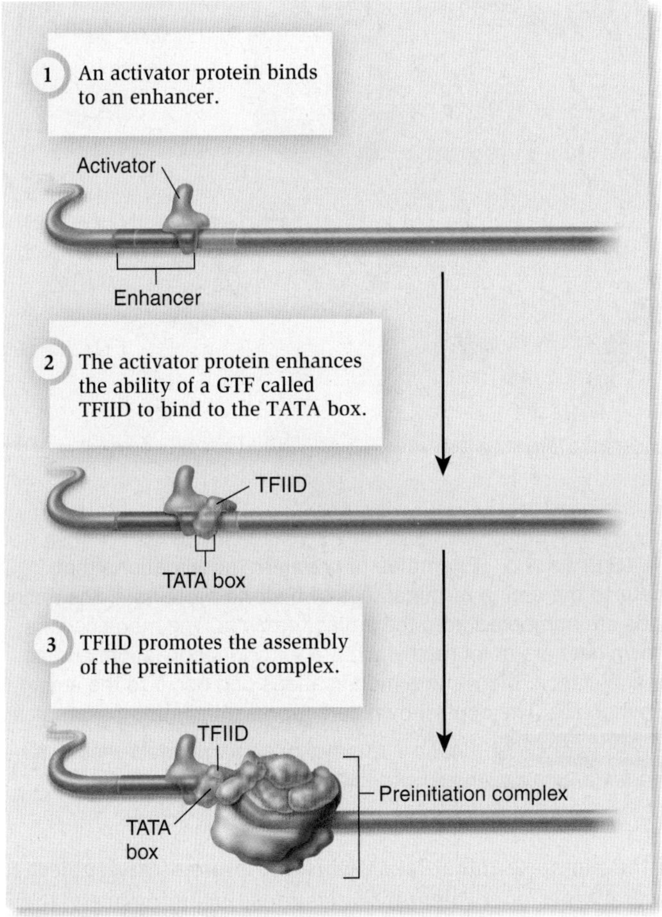

1. An activator protein binds to an enhancer.

Activator

Enhancer

2. The activator protein enhances the ability of a GTF called TFIID to bind to the TATA box.

TFIID

TATA box

3. TFIID promotes the assembly of the preinitiation complex.

TFIID

TATA box

Preinitiation complex

Figure 13.15   Effect of an activator via TFIID, a general transcription factor.

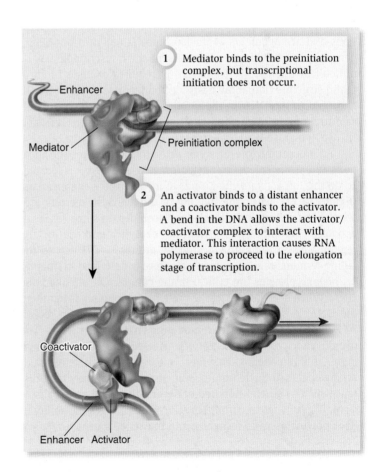

1. Mediator binds to the preinitiation complex, but transcriptional initiation does not occur.

Enhancer

Mediator

Preinitiation complex

2. An activator binds to a distant enhancer and a coactivator binds to the activator. A bend in the DNA allows the activator/coactivator complex to interact with mediator. This interaction causes RNA polymerase to proceed to the elongation stage of transcription.

Coactivator

Enhancer   Activator

Figure 13.16   Effect of an activator via mediator.

Concept check: When an activator interacts with mediator, how does this affect the function of RNA polymerase?

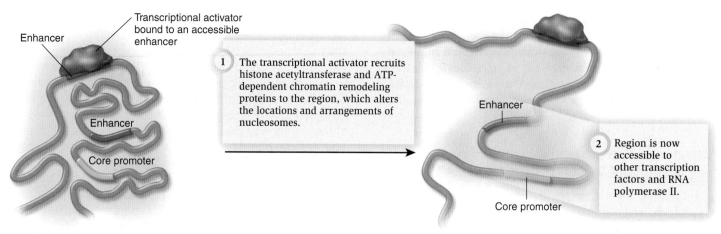

Figure 13.17   Effects of an activator on chromatin structure.

Concept check: *Why are changes in chromatin structure needed for transcription to occur?*

Transcription Is Also Controlled by Changes in Chromatin Structure

In eukaryotes, DNA is associated with proteins to form a structure called **chromatin** (see Chapter 11). How does the structure of chromatin affect gene transcription? Depending on the locations and arrangements of nucleosomes, a region containing a gene may be in a **closed conformation**, and transcription may be difficult or impossible. Transcription requires changes in chromatin structure that allow transcription factors to gain access to and bind to the DNA in the promoter region. Such chromatin, said to be in an **open conformation**, is accessible to GTFs and RNA polymerase II so that transcription can take place.

An important role of some activators is to alter the locations and arrangements of nucleosomes where a gene is located. To do this, an activator first binds to an accessible enhancer site (**Figure 13.17**). Next, the binding of the activator recruits proteins to the region that alter the nucleosomes. In some cases, an activator protein attracts **histone acetyltransferase** to the region. This enzyme attaches acetyl groups ($—COCH_3$) to the amino terminal tails of histone proteins. As described in Chapter 11, histone proteins are critical in the compaction of eukaryotic DNA. When acetylated, histone proteins do not bind as tightly to the DNA. A second effect of an activator protein is to recruit **ATP-dependent chromatin remodeling enzymes** to the site. The overall effect of histone acetyltransferase and ATP-dependent chromatin remodeling enzymes is to alter the locations and arrangements of nucleosomes, sometimes over a fairly long distance such as several hundred or several thousand base pairs of DNA. This change in chromatin structure facilitates the ability of RNA polymerase II to recognize and transcribe a gene.

The Histone Code Controls Chromatin Compaction

As described in Figure 13.17, acetylation of histone proteins can loosen the level of chromatin packing. In recent years, researchers have discovered that many different amino acids

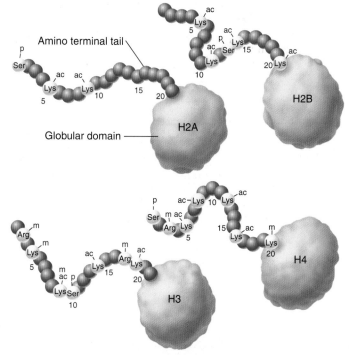

Figure 13.18   Examples of covalent modifications that occur to the amino terminal tails of histone proteins.   The amino acids are numbered from the amino terminus. The modifications shown here are m for methylation, p for phosphorylation, and ac for acetylation. Many more modifications can occur to the amino terminal tails. The ones shown here represent common examples.

Concept check: *What are the two opposing effects that histone modifications may have with regard to chromatin structure?*

in the amino terminal tails of histone proteins are subject to several types of covalent modifications, including acetylation, methylation, and phosphorylation. Over 50 different enzymes have been identified in mammals that selectively modify amino terminal tails. **Figure 13.18** shows examples of sites in the tails of histone proteins H2A, H2B, H3, and H4 that can be modified.

What are the effects of covalent modifications of histones? First, modifications may directly influence interactions between DNA and histone proteins, and between adjacent nucleosomes. Second, histone modifications provide binding sites that are recognized by other proteins. According to the **histone code hypothesis**, proposed by Brian Strahl and David Allis in 2000, the pattern of histone modification is recognized by proteins much like a language or code. For example, one pattern might involve phosphorylation of the serine at the first amino acid in H2A and acetylation of the lysines at the fifth and eighth amino acids in H4. A different pattern could involve acetylation of the fifth amino acid, a lysine, in H2B and methylation of the third amino acid in H4, which is an arginine.

The pattern of covalent modifications of amino terminal tails provides binding sites for proteins that subsequently affect chromatin structure. One pattern of histone modification may attract proteins that cause the chromatin to be less accessible to RNA polymerase and general transcription factors. This would silence the transcription of genes in the region. Alternatively, a different combination of histone modifications may attract proteins, such as chromatin remodeling enzymes, that promote gene transcription. In this way, the histone code plays a key role in accessing the information within the genomes of eukaryotic species.

Steroid Hormones Exert Their Effects by Binding to a Regulatory Transcription Factor and Controlling the Transcription of Nearby Genes

Thus far, we have considered the general ways that regulatory transcription factors control transcription. Let's now turn to a specific example that illustrates how a regulatory transcription factor functions within living cells. Our example involves a transcriptional activator that responds to steroid hormones. This factor is known as a **steroid receptor**, because it binds directly to a steroid hormone. The hormone is an example of a small effector molecule.

As discussed in Chapter 50, steroid hormones are a category of hormones that are synthesized by specialized cells of many organisms, including the endocrine glands of mammals, and then secreted into the bloodstream. The hormones are then taken up by cells that respond to the hormones in different ways. For example, glucocorticoid hormones influence nutrient metabolism in most body cells by promoting the metabolism of glucose, proteins, and fats.

The effect of glucocorticoid hormones is to activate the transcription of specific genes. Glucocorticoids are released from endocrine cells and secreted into the bloodstream when an animal is fasting and needs to regulate its blood levels of glucose, amino acids, and fats. The hormone molecules diffuse across the plasma membrane of target cells and bind to glucocorticoid receptors, which are a type of steroid receptor (**Figure 13.19**). This binding releases proteins called chaperones and thereby exposes an amino acid sequence within the receptor called a nuclear localization signal (NLS). This signal allows

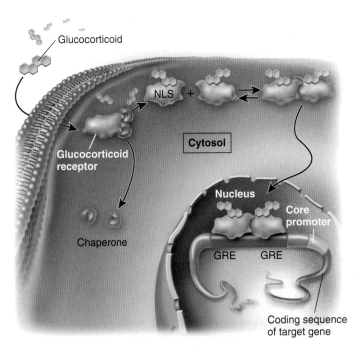

Figure 13.19 Action of the glucocorticoid receptor as a transcriptional activator.

Concept check: If a GRE next to a gene was deleted, how would that affect the regulation of the gene?

the receptor to travel into the nucleus through a nuclear pore. Two glucocorticoid receptors bind to each other noncovalently to form a dimer and then travel through the nuclear pore into the nucleus. The glucocorticoid receptor dimer binds to two adjacent glucocorticoid response elements (GREs) that are next to particular genes. The GREs function as enhancer sequences. The binding of the glucocorticoid receptor dimer to GREs activates the transcription of the adjacent gene, eventually leading to the synthesis of the encoded protein.

How do glucocorticoids affect cell function? Mammalian cells usually have a large number of glucocorticoid receptors within their cytosol. Because GREs are located near several different genes, the uptake of hormone molecules can activate many glucocorticoid receptors and thereby enhance the transcription of several different genes that encode proteins involved with the metabolism of glucose, proteins, and fats. For this reason, glucocorticoid hormones facilitate the coordinated expression of genes that play a role in nutrient metabolism.

DNA Methylation Inhibits Gene Transcription

Let's now turn our attention to a mechanism that usually silences gene expression. DNA structure can be modified by the covalent attachment of methyl groups ($-CH_3$) by an enzyme called **DNA methylase**. This modification, termed **DNA methylation**, is common in some eukaryotic species but not all. For example, yeast and *Drosophila* have little or no detectable methylation of their DNA, whereas DNA methylation in vertebrates and plants is relatively abundant. In mammals, approximately 5% of the

DNA is methylated. Eukaryotic DNA methylation occurs on the cytosine base. The sequence that is methylated is shown here:

$$
\begin{array}{c}
\text{CH}_3 \\
| \\
5'\text{—CG—}3' \\
3'\text{—GC—}5' \\
| \\
\text{CH}_3
\end{array}
$$

DNA methylation usually inhibits the transcription of eukaryotic genes, particularly when it occurs in the vicinity of the promoter. In vertebrates and flowering plants, many genes contain sequences called **CpG islands** near their promoters. CpG refers to the nucleotides of <u>C</u> and <u>G</u> in DNA that are connected by a phosphodiester linkage. A CpG island is a cluster of CpG sites. Unmethylated CpG islands are usually correlated with active genes, whereas repressed genes contain methylated CpG islands. In this way, DNA methylation may play an important role in the silencing of particular genes.

How does DNA methylation inhibit transcription? This can occur in two general ways. First, methylation of CpG islands may prevent an activator from binding to an enhancer element, thus inhibiting the initiation of transcription. A second way that methylation inhibits transcription is by converting chromatin from an open to a closed conformation. Proteins known as **methyl-CpG-binding proteins** bind methylated sequences. Once bound to the DNA, the methyl-CpG-binding protein recruits other proteins to the region that inhibit transcription. A human genetic disorder called Rett syndrome involves a defect in a methyl-CpG-binding protein that is made in nerve cells. The syndrome is primarily found in females and results in a variety of neurodevelopmental problems, including a small head, seizures, and mental impairment. These symptoms are presumably the result of improper gene regulation.

13.4 Regulation of RNA Processing and Translation in Eukaryotes

In the first three sections of this chapter, we have focused on gene regulation at the level of transcription in bacteria and eukaryotes. Eukaryotic gene expression is commonly regulated at the levels of RNA processing and translation. These added levels of regulation provide benefits that are important to eukaryotic species. First, by regulating RNA processing, eukaryotes can produce more than one mRNA transcript from a single gene. This allows a gene to encode two or more polypeptides, thereby increasing the complexity of eukaryotic proteomes. A second issue is timing. Transcriptional regulation in eukaryotes takes a fair amount of time before its effects are observed at the cellular level. During transcriptional regulation, (1) the chromatin must be converted to an open conformation, (2) the gene must be transcribed, (3) the RNA must be processed and

exported from the nucleus, and (4) the protein must be made via translation. All four steps take time, on the order of several minutes. One way to achieve faster regulation is to control steps that occur after an RNA transcript is made. In eukaryotes, translational regulation provides a faster way to regulate the levels of gene products, namely, proteins. Translation can be regulated by controlling the stability of an mRNA transcript, causing it to remain in the cytosol for a long time, or causing it to be rapidly degraded. Alternatively, small RNA molecules or RNA-binding proteins can bind to mRNAs and control whether or not a ribosome can translate the mRNA into a polypeptide.

During the past few decades, many critical advances have been made regarding our knowledge of the regulation of RNA processing and translation. Even so, molecular geneticists are still finding new forms of regulation, making this an exciting area of modern research. In this section, we will survey a few of the known mechanisms of RNA processing and translational regulation.

Alternative Splicing of Pre-mRNAs Creates Protein Diversity

In eukaryotes, a pre-mRNA transcript is processed before it becomes a mature mRNA. When a pre-mRNA has multiple introns and exons, splicing may occur in more than one way, resulting in the creation of two of more different polypeptides. Such **alternative splicing** is a form of gene regulation that allows an organism to use the same gene to make different proteins at different stages of development, in different cell types, and/or in response to a change in the environmental conditions. Alternative splicing is an important form of gene regulation in complex eukaryotes such as animals and plants.

As an example of how alternative splicing occurs, let's suppose a human pre-mRNA contains seven exons (**Figure 13.20**). In nerve cells, it is spliced to contain the following pattern of exons: 1-2-3-5-6-7. In muscle cells, it is alternatively spliced to have a different pattern: 1-2-4-5-6-7. In this example, the mRNA from nerve cells contains exon 3, while the mRNA from muscle

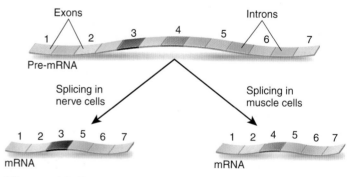

Figure 13.20 Alternative splicing. In this example, the pre-mRNA transcript can be spliced to contain exon 3 (in nerve cells) or exon 4 (in muscle cells), but not both.

Concept check: *What is the biological advantage of alternative splicing?*

cells contains exon 4. When alternative splicing occurs, proteins with significant differences in their amino acid sequences are produced.

What are the consequences of alternative splicing? In most cases, the alternative versions of a protein will have similar functions, because much of their amino acid sequences will be identical to each other. Nevertheless, alternative splicing produces differences in amino acid sequences that will provide each protein with its own unique characteristics. The alternatively spliced versions tend to be expressed in different cell types (for example, nerve versus muscle cells) or at different stages of development (for example, embryonic versus adult). This provides a way for multicellular organisms to fine-tune a given protein to function optimally in a given cell type or stage of development. The advantage of alternative splicing is that two or more different polypeptides can be derived from a single gene, thereby increasing the size of the proteome while minimizing the size of the genome. A small genome size is beneficial because less energy is spent replicating the DNA, and the DNA more easily fits within the nucleus of the cell.

Genomes & Proteomes Connection

Increases in Biological Complexity Are Correlated with Greater Sizes of Genomes and Proteomes

As we have just seen, alternative splicing can increase the proteome size without increasing the total number of genes. For organisms to become more complex, as in plants and animals, evolution has produced more complex proteomes. In the past few decades, many technical advances have improved our ability to analyze the genomes and proteomes of many different species. Researchers have been able to determine the amount of DNA from several species and estimate the total number of genes. In addition, scientists can also estimate the number of polypeptides if information is available concerning the degree of alternative splicing in a given species.

Table 13.1 compares six species: a bacterium (*Escherichia coli*), a eukaryotic single-celled organism (yeast—*Saccharomyces cerevisiae*), a small nematode worm (*Caenorhabditis elegans*), a fruit fly (*Drosophila melanogaster*), a small flowering plant (*Arabidopsis thaliana*), and a human (*Homo sapiens*). One general trend is that less complex organisms tend to have fewer genes. For example, unicellular organisms have only a few thousand genes, whereas multicellular species have tens of thousands. However, the trend is by no means a linear one. If we compare *C. elegans* and *D. melanogaster*, the fly actually has fewer genes even though it is morphologically more complex.

A second trend you can see in Table 13.1 concerns alternative splicing. This phenomenon does not occur in bacteria and is rare in *S. cerevisiae*. The frequency of alternative splicing increases from worms to flies to humans. For example, the level of alternative splicing is 10-fold higher in humans compared to *Drosophila*. This trend can partially explain the increase in complexity among these species. Even though humans have only

Table 13.1	Genome Size and Biological Complexity			
Species	**Level of complexity**	**Genome size (million bp)**	**Approximate number of genes**	**Percentage of genes alternatively spliced**
Escherichia coli	A unicellular prokaryote	4.2	4,000	0
Saccharomyces cerevisiae	A unicellular eukaryote	12	6,000	<1
Caenorhabditis elegans	A tiny worm (about 1,000 cells)	97	19,000	2
Drosophila melanogaster	An insect	137	14,000	7
Arabidopsis thaliana	A flowering plant	142	26,000	11
Homo sapiens	A complex mammal	3,000	25,000	70

about 25,000 different genes, they can make well over 100,000 different proteins because most genes are alternatively spliced in multiple ways.

RNA Interference May Inhibit mRNA by Translational Repression or mRNA Degradation

Let's now turn our attention to regulatory mechanisms that affect translation. **MicroRNAs** (**miRNAs**) and **short-interfering RNAs** (**siRNAs**) are small RNA molecules, typically 22 nucleotides in length, that silence the expression of pre-existing mRNAs. MicroRNAs are partially complementary to certain cellular mRNAs and inhibit their translation, whereas short-interfering RNAs are usually a perfect match to specific mRNAs and cause the mRNAs to be degraded.

In 1993, Victor Ambros and his colleagues, who were interested in the developmental stages that occur in the worm *C. elegans*, determined that the transcription of a particular gene produced a small RNA, now called a microRNA, that does not encode a protein. Instead, this miRNA was found to be partially complementary to an mRNA and inhibit its translation.

Insight into the mechanism of miRNA and siRNA inhibition came from the research of Andrew Fire and Craig Mello, who discovered the mechanism of action of miRNA (**Figure 13.21**). MiRNAs and siRNAs are first synthesized as a single-stranded molecule that folds back on itself to form a hairpin structure. This double-stranded region is trimmed to a 22-base pair sequence by an enzyme called dicer. One of the strands becomes part of a complex called the **RNA-induced silencing complex** (**RISC**), which also includes several proteins. The miRNA or siRNA in the complex then binds to a target mRNA with a complementary sequence. Upon binding, two different

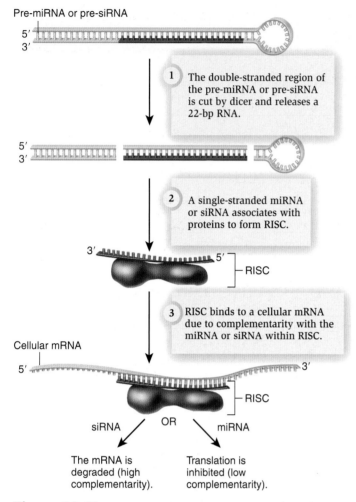

Figure 13.21   Mechanism of action of microRNA (miRNA).

things may happen. In some cases, the mRNA is degraded. This occurs when the siRNA and mRNA are a perfect match or highly complementary. Alternatively, the RISC may inhibit translation. This occurs when the miRNA and mRNA are not a perfect match or are only partially complementary. In either case, the expression of the mRNA is silenced. Fire and Mello called this **RNA interference** (**RNAi**), because the miRNA or siRNA interferes with the proper expression of an mRNA.

Since this study, researchers have discovered that genes encoding miRNAs and siRNAs are widely found in animals and plants. In humans, for example, approximately 200 different genes encode miRNAs. MiRNAs and siRNAs represent an important mechanism of gene regulation that results in mRNA silencing. In 2006, Fire and Mello were awarded the Nobel Prize for their studies of RNA interference.

The Prevention of Iron Toxicity in Mammals Involves the Regulation of Translation

Another way to regulate translation involves RNA-binding proteins that directly affect translational initiation. The regulation of iron absorption provides a well-studied example. While iron is a vital cofactor for many cellular enzymes, it is toxic at high

levels. To prevent toxicity, mammalian cells synthesize a protein called ferritin, which forms a hollow, spherical complex that can store excess iron.

The mRNA that encodes ferritin is controlled by an RNA-binding protein known as the **iron regulatory protein** (**IRP**). When iron levels in the cytosol are low and more ferritin is not needed, IRP binds to a regulatory element within the ferritin mRNA known as the **iron regulatory element** (**IRE**). The IRE is located between the 5′-cap, where the ribosome binds, and the start codon where translation begins. This region is called the 5′-untranslated region (5′-UTR). Due to base pairing, it forms a stem-loop structure. The binding of IRP to the IRE inhibits translation of the ferritin mRNA (**Figure 13.22a**). However, when iron is abundant in the cytosol, the iron binds directly to IRP and prevents it from binding to the IRE. Under these conditions, the ferritin mRNA is translated to make more ferritin protein (**Figure 13.22b**).

Why is translational regulation of ferritin mRNA an advantage over transcriptional regulation of the ferritin gene? This mechanism of translational control allows cells to rapidly respond to changes in their environment. When cells are confronted with high levels of iron, they can quickly make more

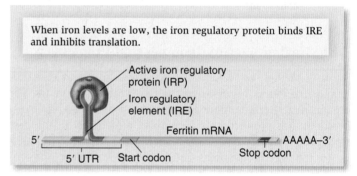

(a) Low iron levels

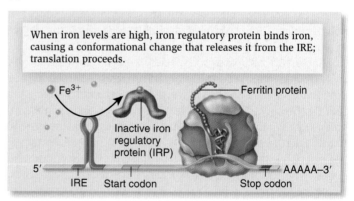

(b) High iron levels

Figure 13.22   Translational regulation of ferritin mRNA by the iron regulatory protein (IRP).

Concept check: Poisoning may occur when a young child finds a bottle of vitamins, such as those that taste like candy, and eats a large number of them. One of the toxic effects involves the ingestion of too much iron. How does the IRP protect people from the toxic effects of too much iron?

ferritin protein to prevent the toxic buildup of iron. This mechanism is faster than transcriptional regulation, which would require the activation of the ferritin gene and the transcription of ferritin mRNA prior to the synthesis of more ferritin protein.

 Summary of Key Concepts

13.1 Overview of Gene Regulation

- Most genes are regulated so the levels of gene expression can vary under different conditions. By comparison, constitutive genes are expressed at constant levels.

- Organisms regulate genes so gene products are made only when they are needed. An example is the synthesis of the gene products needed for lactose utilization in bacteria. (Figure 13.1)

- Multicellular eukaryotes regulate genes to produce different cell types, such as muscle, nerve, and skin cells. (Figure 13.2)

- Eukaryotes also regulate genes so the gene products are produced at different developmental stages. An example is the group of globin genes in mammals. (Figure 13.3)

- All organisms regulate gene expression at a variety of levels, including transcription, translation, and post-translation. Eukaryotes also regulate RNA processing. (Figure 13.4)

13.2 Regulation of Transcription in Bacteria

- Repressors and activators are regulatory proteins that bind to the DNA and regulate the transcription of genes. Small effector molecules control the ability of regulatory proteins to bind to DNA. (Figure 13.5)

- The *lac* operon found in *E. coli* is an arrangement of three structural genes controlled by a single promoter. The operon is transcribed into a polycistronic mRNA. The operator and CAP site are involved with gene regulation via the lac repressor and CAP, respectively. (Figure 13.6)

- The lac repressor binds to the operator site and prevents RNA polymerase from transcribing the operon. When allolactose binds to the repressor, a conformational change occurs that prevents the repressor from binding to the operator site so transcription can proceed. (Figure 13.7)

- By constructing a merozygote, Jacob, Monod, and Pardee determined that *lacI* encodes a diffusible protein that represses the *lac* operon. (Figures 13.8, 13.9)

- The catabolite activator protein (CAP) binds to the CAP site in the presence of cAMP. This causes a bend in the DNA, which promotes the binding of RNA polymerase to the promoter. (Figure 13.10)

- Glucose inhibits cAMP production. This inhibits the expression of the *lac* operon because CAP cannot bind to the CAP site. This form of regulation provides bacteria with a more efficient utilization of their resources because the bacteria use one sugar at a time. (Figure 13.11)

- The *trp* operon is repressible. The presence of tryptophan causes the trp repressor to bind to the *trp* operator and stop transcription. This prevents the excessive buildup of tryptophan in the cell, which would be a waste of energy. (Figure 13.12)

13.3 Regulation of Transcription in Eukaryotes

- Eukaryotic genes exhibit combinatorial control, meaning that many factors control the expression of a single gene. (See list on p. 273.)

- Eukaryotic promoters consist of a core promoter and regulatory elements, such as enhancers or silencers, that regulate the rate of transcription. (Figure 13.13)

- General transcription factors (GTFs) are needed for RNA polymerase II to bind to the core promoter. (Figure 13.14)

- Activators and repressors may regulate RNA polymerase II by interacting with GTFs, such as TFIID, or via mediator, a protein complex that wraps around RNA polymerase II. (Figures 13.15, 13.16)

- A change in chromatin structure is needed for eukaryotic genes to be transcribed. (Figure 13.17)

- The pattern of covalent modification of the amino terminal tails of histone proteins, also called the histone code, is one way to control the level of transcription. (Figure 13.18)

- Steroid hormones bind to receptors that function as transcriptional activators. (Figure 13.19)

- DNA methylation, which occurs at CpG islands near promoters, usually inhibits transcription by preventing the binding of activator proteins or by promoting the binding of proteins that inhibit transcription.

13.4 Regulation of RNA Processing and Translation in Eukaryotes

- Alternative splicing occurs when a single type of pre-mRNA can be spliced in more than one way, producing polypeptides with somewhat different sequences. This is a common way for complex eukaryotes to increase the size of their proteomes. (Figure 13.20, Table 13.1)

- MicroRNAs (miRNAs) and short-interfering RNAs (siRNAs) inhibit mRNAs, either by inhibiting translation or by promoting the degradation of mRNAs, respectively. (Figure 13.21)

- RNA-binding proteins can regulate the translation of specific mRNAs. An example is the iron regulatory protein (IRP), which regulates the translation of ferritin mRNA. (Figure 13.22)

Assess and Discuss

Test Yourself

1. Genes that are expressed at all times at relatively constant levels are known as ____ genes.
   a. inducible
   b. repressible
   c. positive
   d. constitutive
   e. structural

2. Which of the following is not considered a common level of gene regulation in prokaryotes?
   a. transcriptional
   b. RNA processing
   c. translational

  d. post-translational
  e. All of the above are levels at which prokaryotes are able to regulate gene expression.

3. Transcription factors that bind to DNA and stimulate transcription are
  a. repressors.
  b. small effector molecules.
  c. activators.
  d. promoters.
  e. operators.

4. In prokaryotes, the unit of DNA that contains multiple structural genes under the control of a single promoter is called _____. The mRNA produced from this unit is referred to as _____ mRNA.
  a. an operator, a polycistronic
  b. a template, a structural
  c. an operon, a polycistronic
  d. an operon, a monocistronic
  e. a template, a monocistronic

5. In the *lac* operon, what would be the expected effects of a mutation in the operator site that prevented the binding of the repressor protein?
  a. The operon would always be turned on.
  b. The operon would always be turned off.
  c. The operon would always be turned on, except when glucose is present.
  d. The operon would be turned on only in the presence of lactose.
  e. The operon would be turned on only in the presence of lactose and the absence of glucose.

6. The presence of _____ in the medium prevents the CAP from binding to the DNA, resulting in _____ in transcription of the *lac* operon.
  a. lactose, an increase
  b. glucose, an increase
  c. cAMP, a decrease
  d. glucose, a decrease
  e. lactose, a decrease

7. The *trp* operon is considered _____ operon because the structural genes necessary for tryptophan synthesis are not expressed when the levels of tryptophan in the cell are high.
  a. an inducible
  b. a positive
  c. a repressible
  d. a negative
  e. Both c and d are correct.

8. Regulatory elements that function to increase transcription levels in eukaryotes are called
  a. promoters.
  b. silencers.
  c. enhancers.
  d. transcriptional start sites.
  e. activators.

9. DNA methylation in many eukaryotic organisms usually causes
  a. increased translation levels.
  b. introns that will be removed.
  c. regions of DNA that do not contain structural genes.
  d. decreased transcription levels.
  e. regulatory elements that are not necessary for transcription.

10. _____ refers to the phenomenon where a single type of pre-mRNA may give rise to multiple types of mRNAs due to different patterns of intron and exon removal.
  a. Spliceosomes
  b. Variable expression
  c. Alternative splicing
  d. Polycistronic mRNA
  e. Induced silencing

Conceptual Questions

1. What is the difference between inducible and repressible operons?

2. Transcriptional regulation often involves a regulatory protein that binds to a segment of DNA and a small effector molecule that binds to the regulatory protein. Do the following terms apply to a regulatory protein, a segment of DNA, or a small effector molecule? a. repressor; b. inducer; c. operator site; d. corepressor; e. activator

3. What are two general ways that DNA methylation inhibits transcription?

Collaborative Questions

1. Discuss the advantages and disadvantages of genetic regulation at the different levels described in Figure 13.4.

2. Let's suppose that a mutation in the glucocorticoid receptor gene does not prevent the binding of the hormone to the mutant glucocorticoid receptor protein but does prevent the ability of the protein to activate transcription. Make a list of all the possible defects that may explain why transcription cannot be activated.

Online Resource

www.brookerbiology.com

Stay a step ahead in your studies with animations that bring concepts to life and practice tests to assess your understanding. Your instructor may also recommend the interactive ebook, individualized learning tools, and more.

Mutation, DNA Repair, and Cancer

14

During the past two decades, over 25% of the beluga whales in Canada's St. Lawrence Seaway have died of cancer. Biologists speculate that these deaths are caused by cancer-causing pollutants, such as polycystic aromatic hydrocarbons (PAHs).

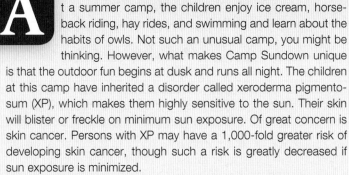

A t a summer camp, the children enjoy ice cream, horseback riding, hay rides, and swimming and learn about the habits of owls. Not such an unusual camp, you might be thinking. However, what makes Camp Sundown unique is that the outdoor fun begins at dusk and runs all night. The children at this camp have inherited a disorder called xeroderma pigmentosum (XP), which makes them highly sensitive to the sun. Their skin will blister or freckle on minimum sun exposure. Of great concern is skin cancer. Persons with XP may have a 1,000-fold greater risk of developing skin cancer, though such a risk is greatly decreased if sun exposure is minimized.

What explains the symptoms of xeroderma pigmentosum? XP individuals are highly susceptible to **mutation**, which is defined as a heritable change in the genetic material. When a mutation occurs, the order of nucleotide bases in a DNA molecule, its base sequence, is changed permanently, and this alteration can be passed from mother to daughter cells during cell division. Mutations that lead to cancer cause particular genes to be expressed in an abnormal way. For example, a mutation could affect the transcription of a gene, or it could alter the functional properties of the polypeptide that is specified by a gene.

Should we be afraid of mutations? Yes and no. On the positive side, mutations are essential to the long-term continuity of life. They supply the variation that enables species to evolve and become better adapted to their environments. Mutations provide the foundation for evolutionary change. On the negative side, however, new mutations are more likely to be harmful than beneficial to the individual. The genes within modern species are the products of billions of years of evolution and have evolved to work properly. Random mutations are more likely to disrupt genes rather than enhance their function. As we will see in this chapter, mutations can cause cancer. In addition, many forms of inherited diseases, such as xeroderma pigmentosum and cystic fibrosis, are caused by gene mutations. For these and many other reasons, understanding the molecular nature of mutations is a compelling area of research.

Because mutations can be harmful, all species have evolved several ways to repair damaged DNA. Such **DNA repair systems** reverse DNA damage before a permanent mutation can occur. DNA repair systems are vital to the survival of all organisms. If these systems did not exist, mutations would be so prevalent that few species, if any, would survive. Persons with XP have an impaired DNA repair system, which is the underlying cause of their disorder. DNA damage from sunlight is normally corrected by DNA repair systems. In people with XP, damaged DNA remains unrepaired, which can lead to cancer. In this chapter, we will examine how such DNA repair systems operate. But first, let's explore the molecular basis of mutation.

14.1 Mutation

How do mutations affect traits? To answer this question at the molecular level, we must understand how changes in DNA structure can ultimately affect DNA function. Most of our understanding of mutation has come from the study of experimental organisms, such as bacteria and *Drosophila*. Researchers can expose these organisms to environmental agents that cause mutations and then study the consequences of the mutations that arise. In addition, because these organisms have a short generation time, researchers can investigate the effects of mutations when they are passed from parent to offspring over many generations.

The structure and amount of genetic material can be altered in a variety of ways. For example, chromosome structure and number can change. We will examine these types of genetic changes in Chapter 15. In this section, we will focus our attention on **gene mutations**, which are relatively small changes in DNA structure that alter a particular gene. We will also consider how the timing of new mutations during an organism's development has important consequences. Finally, we will explore how environmental agents may bring about mutations and examine a testing method that can determine if an agent causes mutations.

Gene Mutations Alter the DNA Sequence of a Gene

Mutations can cause two basic types of changes to a gene: (1) the base sequence within a gene can be changed; and (2) one or more nucleotides can be added to or removed from a gene. A **point mutation** affects only a single base pair within the DNA. For example, the DNA sequence shown here has been altered by a **base substitution** in which a T (in the top strand) has been replaced by a G:

5′–CCCGCTAGATA–3′   ⟶   5′–CCCGCGAGATA–3′
3′–GGGCGATCTAT–5′   3′–GGGCGCTCTAT–5′

A point mutation could also involve the addition or deletion of a single base pair to a DNA sequence. For example, in the following sequence, a single base pair has been added to the DNA:

5′–GGCGCTAGATC–3′   ⟶   5′–GGCAGCTAGATC–3′
3′–CCGCGATCTAG–5′   3′–CCGTCGATCTAG–5′

Though point mutations may seem like small changes to a DNA sequence, they can have important consequences when genes are expressed. This topic is discussed next.

Gene Mutations May Affect the Amino Acid Sequence of a Polypeptide

If a mutation occurs within the region of a structural gene that specifies the amino acid sequence, such a mutation may alter that sequence in a variety of ways. **Table 14.1** considers the potential effects of point mutations. **Silent mutations** do not alter the amino acid sequence of the polypeptide, even though the nucleotide sequence has changed. As discussed in Chapter 12, the genetic code is degenerate, that is, more than one codon can specify the same amino acid. Silent mutations can occur in the third base of many codons without changing the type of amino acid it encodes.

A **missense mutation** is a base substitution that changes a single amino acid in a polypeptide sequence. A missense mutation may not alter protein function because it changes only a single amino acid within a polypeptide that is typically hundreds of amino acids in length. A missense mutation that substitutes

Table 14.1 Consequences of Point Mutations Within the Coding Sequence of a Structural Gene

Mutation in the DNA	Effect on polypeptide	Example*
None	None	ATGGCCGGCCCGAAAGAGACC — Met Ala Gly Pro Lys Glu Thr
Base substitution	Silent—causes no change	ATGGCCGGCCCCAAAGAGACC — Met Ala Gly Pro Lys Glu Thr
Base substitution	Missense—changes one amino acid	ATGCCCGGCCCGAAAGAGACC — Met Pro Gly Pro Lys Glu Thr
Base substitution	Nonsense—changes to a stop codon	ATGGCCGGCCCGTAAGAGACC — Met Ala Gly Pro-STOP
Addition (or deletion) of single base	Frameshift—produces a different amino acid sequence	ATGGCCGGCACCGAAAGAGACC — Met Ala Gly Thr Glu Arg Asp

*DNA sequence in the coding strand. This sequence is the same as the mRNA sequence except that RNA contains uracil (U) instead of thymine (T).

an amino acid with a chemistry similar to the original amino acid is less likely to alter protein function. For example, a missense mutation that substitutes a glutamic acid for an aspartic acid may not alter protein function because both amino acids are negatively charged and have similar side chain structures (refer back to Chapter 3).

Alternatively, some missense mutations have a dramatic effect on protein function. A striking example occurs in the human disease known as **sickle-cell disease**. This disease involves a missense mutation in the β-globin gene, which encodes one of the polypeptide subunits that make up hemoglobin, the oxygen-carrying protein in red blood cells. In the most common form of this disease, a missense mutation alters the polypeptide sequence such that the sixth amino acid is changed from a glutamic acid to a valine (**Figure 14.1**). Because glutamic acid is hydrophilic but valine is hydrophobic, this single amino acid substitution alters the structure and function of the hemoglobin protein. The mutant hemoglobin subunits tend to stick to one another when the oxygen concentration is low. The aggregated proteins form fiber-like structures within red blood cells, which causes the cells to lose their normal disk-shaped morphology and become sickle-shaped. It seems amazing that a single amino acid substitution could have such a profound effect on the structure of cells.

Two other types of point mutations cause more dramatic changes to a polypeptide sequence. A **nonsense mutation** involves a change from a normal codon to a stop or termination codon. This causes translation to be terminated earlier than expected, producing a truncated polypeptide (see Table 14.1). Compared to a normal polypeptide, such a shorter polypeptide is much less likely to function properly. Finally, a **frameshift**

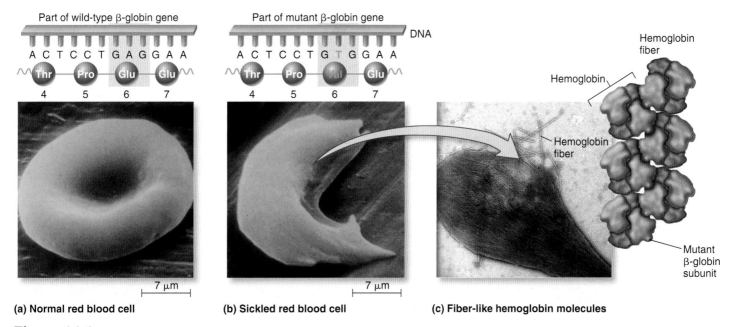

Part of wild-type β-globin gene

Part of mutant β-globin gene

DNA

(a) Normal red blood cell

(b) Sickled red blood cell

(c) Fiber-like hemoglobin molecules

Figure 14.1   A missense mutation that causes red blood cells to sickle in sickle-cell disease.   Scanning electron micrographs of (a) normal red blood cells and (b) sickled red blood cells. As shown above the micrographs, a missense mutation in the β-globin gene (which codes for a subunit of hemoglobin) changes the sixth amino acid in the β-globin polypeptide from a glutamic acid to a valine. (c) This micrograph shows how this alteration to the structure of β-globin causes the formation of abnormal fiber-like structures. In normal cells, hemoglobin proteins do not form fibers.

Concept check: *Based on the fiber-like structures seen in part (c), what aspect of hemoglobin structure does a glutamic acid at the sixth position in normal β-globin prevent? Speculate on how the charge of this amino acid may play a role.*

mutation involves the addition or deletion of nucleotides that are not in multiples of three nucleotides. For example, a frameshift mutation could involve the addition or deletion of one, two, four, or five nucleotides. Because the codons are read in multiples of three, these types of insertions or deletions shift the reading frame so that a completely different amino acid sequence occurs downstream from the mutation (see Table 14.1). Such a large change in polypeptide structure is likely to inhibit protein function.

Except for silent mutations, new mutations are more likely to produce polypeptides that have reduced rather than enhanced function. However, mutations can occasionally produce a polypeptide that has a better ability to function. Changes in protein function may affect the ability of an organism to survive and to reproduce. Such mutations may change in frequency in a population over the course of many generations due to natural selection. This topic is discussed in Chapter 24.

Gene Mutations Can Occur Outside of Coding Sequences and Influence Gene Expression

Thus far, we have focused our attention on mutations in the coding regions of structural genes. In Chapters 12 and 13, we learned how other DNA sequences play important roles during gene expression. A mutation can occur within noncoding sequences and affect gene expression (**Table 14.2**). For example, a mutation may alter the sequence within the promoter of a gene and thereby affect the rate of transcription. A mutation

that improves the ability of transcriptional activators to bind to the DNA may enhance transcription, whereas other mutations may block their binding and thereby inhibit transcription.

Mutations in regulatory elements or operator sites can alter the regulation of gene transcription. For example, in Chapter 13, we considered the roles of regulatory elements such as the *lac* operator site in *E. coli*, which is recognized by the lac repressor protein (refer back to Figure 13.7). Mutations in the *lac* operator site can disrupt the proper regulation of the *lac* operon. An operator mutation may change the DNA sequence so that the lac repressor protein does not bind to it. This mutation would cause the operon to be constitutively expressed.

Table 14.2	Effects of Mutations Outside of the Coding Sequence of a Gene
Sequence	**Effect of mutation**
Promoter	May increase or decrease the rate of transcription
Transcriptional regulatory element/ operator site	May alter the regulation of transcription
Splice junctions	May alter the ability of pre-mRNA to be properly spliced
Translational regulatory element	May alter the ability of mRNA to be translationally regulated
Intergenic region	Not as likely to have an effect on gene expression

FEATURE INVESTIGATION

The Lederbergs Used Replica Plating to Show That Mutations Are Random Events

Mutations can affect the expression of genes in a variety of ways. Let's now consider the following question: Do mutations that affect the traits of an individual occur as a result of pre-existing circumstances, or are they random events that may happen in any gene of any individual? In the 19th century, French naturalist Jean Baptiste Lamarck proposed that physiological events (such as use or disuse) determine whether traits are passed along to offspring. For example, his hypothesis sug-

gested that an individual who practiced and became adept at a physical activity, such as the long jump, would pass that quality on to his or her offspring. Alternatively, geneticists in the early 1900s suggested that genetic variation occurs as a matter of chance. According to this view, those individuals whose genes happen to contain beneficial mutations are more likely to survive and pass those genes to their offspring.

These opposing views were tested in bacterial studies in the 1940s and 1950s. One such study, by Joshua and Esther Lederberg, focused on the occurrence of mutations in bacteria (**Figure 14.2**). First, they placed a large number of *E. coli* bac-

Figure 14.2   The experiment performed by the Lederbergs showing that mutations are random events.

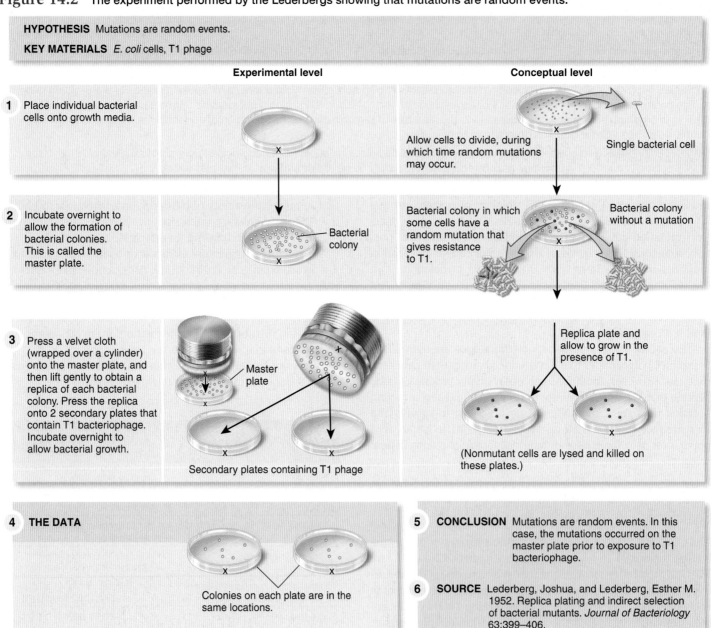

HYPOTHESIS Mutations are random events.

KEY MATERIALS *E. coli* cells, T1 phage

Experimental level   **Conceptual level**

1 Place individual bacterial cells onto growth media.

Allow cells to divide, during which time random mutations may occur.

Single bacterial cell

2 Incubate overnight to allow the formation of bacterial colonies. This is called the master plate.

Bacterial colony

Bacterial colony in which some cells have a random mutation that gives resistance to T1.

Bacterial colony without a mutation

3 Press a velvet cloth (wrapped over a cylinder) onto the master plate, and then lift gently to obtain a replica of each bacterial colony. Press the replica onto 2 secondary plates that contain T1 bacteriophage. Incubate overnight to allow bacterial growth.

Master plate

Secondary plates containing T1 phage

Replica plate and allow to grow in the presence of T1.

(Nonmutant cells are lysed and killed on these plates.)

4 **THE DATA**

Colonies on each plate are in the same locations.

5 **CONCLUSION** Mutations are random events. In this case, the mutations occurred on the master plate prior to exposure to T1 bacteriophage.

6 **SOURCE** Lederberg, Joshua, and Lederberg, Esther M. 1952. Replica plating and indirect selection of bacterial mutants. *Journal of Bacteriology* 63:399–406.

teria onto a master plate that was incubated overnight, so each bacterial cell divided many times to form a bacterial colony composed of millions of cells. Using a technique known as **replica plating**, a sterile piece of velvet cloth was lightly touched to this plate to pick up a few bacterial cells from each colony on the master plate. They then transferred this replica to two secondary plates containing an agent that selected for the growth of bacterial cells with a particular mutation.

In the example shown in Figure 14.2, the secondary plates contained T1 bacteriophages, which are viruses that infect bacteria and cause them to lyse. On these plates, only those rare cells that had acquired a mutation conferring resistance to T1, termed *ton^r*, could grow. All other cells were lysed by the proliferation of bacteriophages in the bacteria. Therefore, only a few colonies were observed on the secondary plates. Strikingly, these colonies occupied the same locations on each plate. How

did the Lederbergs interpret these results? The data indicated that the *ton^r* mutations occurred randomly while the bacterial cells were forming colonies on the nonselective master plate. The presence of T1 bacteriophages in the secondary plates did not cause the mutations to develop. Rather, the T1 bacteriophages simply selected for the growth of *ton^r* mutants that were already in the population. These results supported the idea that mutations are random events.

Experimental Questions

1. Explain the opposing views of mutation prior to the Lederbergs' study.
2. What hypothesis was being tested by the Lederbergs? What were the results of the experiment?
3. How did the results of the Lederbergs support or falsify the hypothesis?

Mutations Can Occur in Germ-Line or Somatic Cells

Let's now consider how the timing of a mutation may have an important impact on its potential effects. Multicellular organisms typically begin their lives as a single fertilized egg cell that divides many times to produce all the cells of an adult organism. A mutation can occur in any cell of the body, either very early in life, such as in a gamete (eggs or sperm) or a fertilized egg, or later in life, such as in the embryonic or adult stages. The number and location of cells with a mutation are critical both to the severity of the genetic effect and to whether the mutation can be passed on to offspring.

Geneticists classify the cells of animals into two types: germ-line and somatic cells. The term **germ line** refers to cells that give rise to gametes, such as egg and sperm cells. A germ-line mutation can occur directly in an egg or sperm cell, or it can occur in a precursor cell that produces the gametes. If a mutant human gamete participates in fertilization, all the cells of the resulting offspring will contain the mutation, as indicated by the red color in **Figure 14.3a**. Likewise, when such an individual produces gametes, the mutation may be transmitted to future generations of offspring. Because humans carry two copies of most genes, a new mutation in a single gene has a 50% chance of being transmitted from parent to offspring.

The **somatic cells** constitute all cells of the body excluding the germ-line cells. Examples include skin cells and muscle cells. Mutations can also occur within somatic cells at early or late stages of development. What are the consequences of a mutation that happens during the embryonic stage? As shown in **Figure 14.3b**, a mutation occurred within a single embryonic cell. This single somatic cell was the precursor for many cells of the adult. Therefore, in the adult, a patch of tissue contains cells that carry the mutation. The size of any patch depends on the timing of a new mutation. In general, the earlier a mutation occurs during development, the larger the patch. An individual

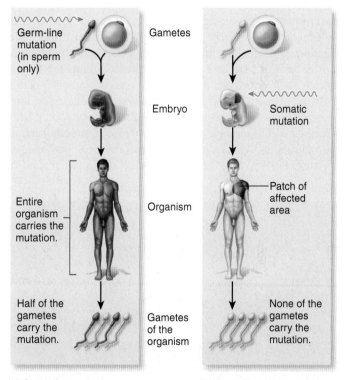

(a) Germ-line mutation **(b) Somatic cell mutation**

Figure 14.3 The effects of germ-line versus somatic cell mutations. The red color indicates which cells carry the mutation. (a) If a mutation is passed via gametes, such germ-line mutations occur in every cell of the body. Because humans have two copies of most genes, a germ-line mutation in one of those two copies will be transmitted to only half of the gametes. (b) Somatic mutations affect a limited area of the body and are not transmitted to offspring.

Concept check: Why are somatic mutations unable to be transmitted to offspring?

with somatic regions that are genetically different from each other is called a **mosaic**.

Figure 14.4 illustrates a woman who probably had a somatic mutation during an early stage of development. In this case, the woman has a patch of white hair while the rest of her hair is black. Presumably, this individual initially had a single mutation happen in an embryonic cell that ultimately gave rise to the patch that produced the white hair.

Although a change in hair color is not a harmful consequence, mutations during early stages of life can be quite harmful, especially if they disrupt essential developmental processes. Even though it is sensible to avoid environmental agents that cause mutations at any stage of life, the possibility of somatic mutations is a compelling reason to avoid such agents during the early stages of life such as embryonic and fetal development, infancy, and early childhood.

Mutations May Be Spontaneous or Induced

Biologists categorize the causes of mutation as spontaneous or induced. **Spontaneous mutations** result from abnormalities in biological processes (**Table 14.3**). Spontaneous mutations reflect the observation that biology isn't perfect. Enzymes, for example, can function abnormally. In Chapter 11, we learned that DNA polymerase can make a mistake during DNA replication by putting the wrong base in a newly synthesized daughter strand. Though such errors are rare due to the proofreading function of DNA polymerase and DNA repair systems (discussed later in the chapter), they do occur. In addition, normal metabolic processes within the cell may produce toxic chemicals such as free radicals that can react directly with the DNA and alter its structure. Finally, the structure of nucleotides is not absolutely

Table 14.3	Some Common Causes of Gene Mutations
Common causes of mutations	**Description**
Spontaneous:	
Errors in DNA replication	A mistake by DNA polymerase may cause a point mutation.
Toxic metabolic products	The products of normal metabolic processes may be reactive chemicals such as free radicals that can alter the structure of DNA.
Changes in nucleotide structure	On rare occasions, the linkage between purines and deoxyribose can spontaneously break. Changes in base structure (isomerization) may cause mispairing during DNA replication.
Transposons	As discussed in Chapter 21, transposons are small segments of DNA that can insert at various sites in the genome. If they insert into a gene, they may inactivate the gene.
Induced:	
Chemical agents	Chemical substances, such as benzo(a) pyrene, a chemical found in cigarette smoke, may cause changes in the structure of DNA.
Physical agents	Physical agents such as UV (ultraviolet) light and X-rays can damage the DNA.

stable. On occasion, the structure of a base may spontaneously change, and such a change may cause a mutation if it occurs immediately prior to DNA replication.

The rates of spontaneous mutations vary from species to species and from gene to gene. Larger genes are usually more likely to incur a mutation than are smaller genes. A common rate of spontaneous mutation among various species is approximately 1 mutation for every 1 million genes per cell division, which equals 1 in 10^6, or simply 10^{-6}. This is the expected rate of spontaneous mutation, which creates the variation that is the raw material of evolution.

Induced mutations are caused by environmental agents that enter the cell and alter the structure of DNA. They cause the mutation rate to be higher than the spontaneous mutation rate. Agents that cause mutation are called **mutagens**. Mutagenic agents can be categorized as **chemical** or **physical mutagens** (**Table 14.4**). We will consider their effects next.

Mutagens Alter DNA Structure in Different Ways

Researchers have discovered that an enormous array of agents can act as mutagens. We often hear in the news media that we should avoid these agents in our foods and living environments. We even use products such as sunscreens that help us avoid the mutagenic effects of ultraviolet (UV) light from the sun. The public is often concerned about mutagens for two important reasons. First, mutagenic agents are usually involved in the development of human cancers. Second, because new mutations may be deleterious, people want to avoid mutagens

Figure 14.4 Example of a somatic mutation.   This woman has a patch of white hair. This is likely to have occurred because a somatic mutation occurred in a single cell during embryonic development that caused white pigmentation of the hair. This cell continued to divide to produce a patch of white hair.

Concept check: *Can this woman with a patch of white hair transmit this trait to her offspring?*

Table 14.4	Examples of Mutagens
Mutagen	**Effect(s) on DNA structure**
Chemical:	
Nitrous acid	Deaminates bases
5-bromouracil	Acts as a base analogue
2-aminopurine	Acts as a base analogue
Nitrogen mustard	Alkylates bases
Ethyl methanesulfonate (EMS)	Alkylates bases
Benzopyrene	Its metabolic product inserts next to bases in the DNA double helix and causes additions or deletions
Physical:	
X-rays	Causes base deletions, single nicks in DNA strands, cross-linking, and chromosomal breaks
UV light	Promotes pyrimidine dimer formation, which involves covalent bonds between adjacent pyrimidines (C or T)

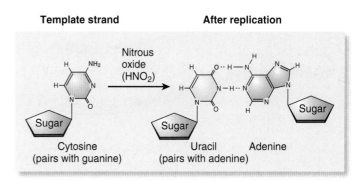

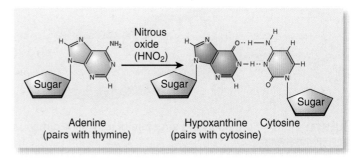

Figure 14.5 **Deamination and mispairing of modified bases by a chemical mutagen.**   Nitrous acid changes cytosine to uracil and adenine to hypoxanthine by replacing NH₂ with an oxygen. During DNA replication, uracil will pair with adenine, and hypoxanthine will pair with cytosine. These incorrect bases will create mutations in the newly replicated strand.

to prevent mutations that may have harmful effects in their future offspring.

How do mutagens affect DNA structure? Some chemical mutagens act by covalently modifying the structure of nucleotides. For example, nitrous acid (HNO_2) deaminates bases by replacing amino groups with keto groups ($-NH_2$ to $=O$). This can change cytosine to uracil, and adenine to a base called hypoxanthine. When this altered DNA replicates, the modified bases do not pair with the appropriate nucleotides in the newly made strand. Instead, uracil pairs with adenine, and hypoxanthine pairs with cytosine (**Figure 14.5**).

Similarly, 5-bromouracil and 2-aminopurine, which are called base analogues, have structures that are similar to particular bases in DNA. When incorporated into DNA, they also cause errors in DNA replication. Other chemical mutagens can disrupt the appropriate pairing between nucleotides by alkylating bases within the DNA. During alkylation, methyl or ethyl groups are covalently attached to the bases. Examples of alkylating agents include nitrogen mustards (used as a chemical weapon during World War I) and ethyl methanesulfonate (EMS).

Some chemical mutagens exert their effects by interfering with DNA replication. For example, benzopyrene, which is found in automobile exhaust and charbroiled food, is metabolized to a compound (benzopyrene diol epoxide) that inserts in between the bases of the double helix, thereby distorting the helical structure. When DNA containing these mutagens is replicated, single nucleotide additions and/or deletions can be incorporated into the newly made strands.

DNA molecules are also sensitive to physical agents such as radiation. In particular, radiation of short wavelength and high energy, known as ionizing radiation, is known to alter DNA structure. Ionizing radiation includes X-rays and gamma rays. This type of radiation can penetrate deeply into biological materials, where it creates free radicals. These molecules can alter the structure of DNA in a variety of ways. Exposure to high

doses of ionizing radiation can cause base deletions, breaks in one DNA strand, or even a break in both DNA strands.

Nonionizing radiation, such as UV light, contains less energy, and so it penetrates only the surface of biological materials, such as the skin. Nevertheless, UV light is known to cause DNA mutations. For example, UV light can cause the formation of a **thymine dimer**, which is a site where two adjacent thymine bases become covalently cross-linked to each other (**Figure 14.6**).

Thymine dimers are typically repaired before or during DNA replication. However, if such repair fails to occur, a thymine dimer may cause a mutation when that DNA strand is replicated. When DNA polymerase attempts to replicate over a thymine dimer, proper base pairing does not occur between the template strand and the incoming nucleotides. This mispairing can cause gaps in the newly made strand or the incorporation of incorrect bases. Plants, in particular, must have effective ways to prevent UV damage because they are exposed to sunlight throughout the day.

Testing Methods Can Determine If an Agent Is a Mutagen

Because mutagens are harmful, researchers have developed testing methods to evaluate the ability of a substance to cause mutation. One commonly used test is the **Ames test**, which was developed by Bruce Ames in the 1970s. This test uses a strain of a bacterium, *Salmonella typhimurium*, that cannot

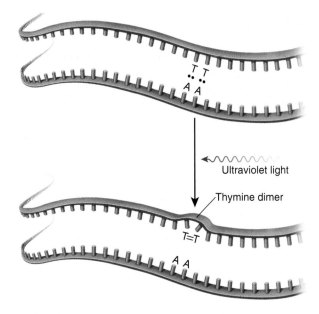

Figure 14.6   Formation and structure of a thymine dimer.

Concept check: *Why is a thymine dimer harmful?*

synthesize the amino acid histidine. This strain contains a point mutation within a gene that encodes an enzyme required for histidine biosynthesis. The mutation renders the enzyme inactive. The bacteria cannot grow unless histidine has been added to the growth medium. However, a second mutation may correct the first mutation and thereby restore the ability to synthesize histidine. The Ames test monitors the rate at which this

second mutation occurs and thereby indicates whether an agent increases the mutation rate above the spontaneous rate.

Figure 14.7 outlines the steps in the Ames test. The suspected mutagen is mixed with a rat liver extract and the bacterial strain of *S. typhimurium* that cannot synthesize histidine. Because some potential mutagens may require activation by cellular enzymes, the rat liver extract provides a mixture of enzymes that may cause such activation. This step improves the ability to identify agents that may cause mutations in mammals. As a control, bacteria that have not been exposed to the mutagen are also tested. After an incubation period in which mutations may occur, a large number of bacteria are plated on a growth medium that does not contain histidine. The *S. typhimurium* strain is not expected to grow on these plates. However, if a mutation has occurred that allows a cell to synthesize histidine, the bacterium harboring this second mutation will proliferate during an overnight incubation period to form a visible bacterial colony.

To estimate the mutation rate, the colonies that grow in the absence of histidine are counted and compared with the total number of bacterial cells that were originally placed on the plate for both the suspected-mutagen sample and the control. The control condition is a measure of the spontaneous mutation rate, whereas the other sample measures the rate of mutation in the presence of the suspected mutagen. As an example, let's suppose that 2 million bacteria were plated from both the suspected-mutagen and control tubes. In the control experiment, 2 bacterial colonies were observed. The spontaneous mutation rate is calculated by dividing 2 (the number of mutants) by

Figure 14.7   **The Ames test for mutagenicity.**   In this example, 2 million bacterial cells were placed on plates lacking histidine. Two colonies were observed in the control sample, whereas 44 were observed in the sample exposed to a suspected mutagen.

Concept check: *Based on the results seen in this figure, what is the rate of mutation that is caused by the suspected mutagen?*

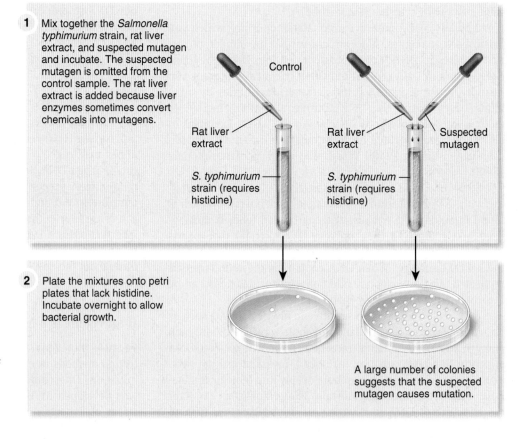

1   Mix together the *Salmonella typhimurium* strain, rat liver extract, and suspected mutagen and incubate. The suspected mutagen is omitted from the control sample. The rat liver extract is added because liver enzymes sometimes convert chemicals into mutagens.

Control

Rat liver extract

S. typhimurium strain (requires histidine)

Rat liver extract

Suspected mutagen

S. typhimurium strain (requires histidine)

2   Plate the mixtures onto petri plates that lack histidine. Incubate overnight to allow bacterial growth.

A large number of colonies suggests that the suspected mutagen causes mutation.

2 million (the number of original cells). This equals 1 in 1 million, or 1×10^{-6}. By comparison, 44 colonies were observed in the suspected-mutagen sample (Figure 14.7). In this case, the mutation rate would be 44 divided by 2 million, which equals 2.2×10^{-5}. The mutation rate in the presence of the mutagen is over 20 times higher than the spontaneous mutation rate.

How do we judge if an agent is a mutagen? Researchers compare the mutation rate in the presence and absence of the suspected mutagen. The experimental approach shown in Figure 14.7 is conducted several times. If statistics reveal that the mutation rate in the suspected-mutagen sample is significantly higher than the control sample, they may tentatively conclude that the agent is a mutagen. Interestingly, many studies have used the Ames test to compare the urine from cigarette smokers to that from nonsmokers. This research has shown that urine from smokers contains much higher levels of mutagens.

14.2   DNA Repair

In the previous section, we considered the causes and consequences of mutation. As we have seen, mutations are random events that often have negative consequences. To minimize mutation, all living organisms must have the ability to repair changes that occur in the structure of DNA. Such DNA repair systems have been studied extensively in many organisms, particularly *E. coli*, yeast, mammals, and plants. The diverse ways of repairing DNA underscore the necessity for the structure of DNA to be maintained properly. The importance of these systems becomes evident when they are missing. For example, as discussed at the beginning of this chapter, persons with xeroderma pigmentosum are highly susceptible to the harmful effects of sunlight because they are missing a single DNA repair system.

How do organisms minimize the occurrence of mutations? Cells contain several DNA repair systems that can fix different types of DNA alterations (**Table 14.5**). Each repair system is composed of one or more proteins that play specific roles in the repair mechanism. DNA repair requires two coordinated events. In the first step, one or more proteins in the repair system detect an irregularity in DNA structure. In the second step, the abnormality is repaired. In some cases, the change in DNA structure can be directly repaired. For example, DNA may be modified by the attachment of an alkyl group, such as —CH_2CH_3, to a base. In **direct repair**, an enzyme removes this alkyl group, thereby restoring the structure of the original base. More commonly, however, the altered DNA is removed, and a new segment of DNA is synthesized. In this section, we will examine nucleotide excision repair as an example of how such systems operate. This system, which is found in all species, is an important mechanism of DNA repair.

Nucleotide Excision Repair Removes Segments of Damaged DNA

In **nucleotide excision repair** (**NER**), a region encompassing several nucleotides in the damaged strand is removed from the

Table 14.5	Common Types of DNA Repair Systems
System	**Description**
Direct repair	A repair enzyme recognizes an incorrect structure in the DNA and directly converts it back to a correct structure.
Base excision and nucleotide excision repair	An abnormal base or nucleotide is recognized, and a portion of the strand containing the abnormality is removed. The complementary DNA strand is then used as a template to synthesize a normal DNA strand.
Methyl-directed mismatch repair	Similar to excision repair except that the DNA defect is a base pair mismatch in the DNA, not an abnormal nucleotide. The mismatch is recognized, and a strand of DNA in this region is removed. The complementary strand is used to synthesize a normal strand of DNA.

*Other types of repair systems exist; these are common examples.

DNA, and the intact undamaged strand is used as a template for the resynthesis of a normal complementary strand. NER can fix many different types of DNA damage, including UV-induced damage, chemically modified bases, missing bases, and various types of cross-links (such as thymine dimers). The system is found in all prokaryotes and eukaryotes, although its molecular mechanism is better understood in prokaryotic species.

In *E. coli*, the NER system is composed of four key proteins: UvrA, UvrB, UvrC, and UvrD. They are named Uvr because they are involved in <u>u</u>ltra<u>v</u>iolet light <u>r</u>epair of thymine dimers, although these proteins are also important in repairing chemically damaged DNA. In addition, DNA polymerase and DNA ligase are required to complete the repair process.

How does the NER system work? Two UvrA proteins and one UvrB protein form a complex that tracks along the DNA in search of a damaged site (**Figure 14.8**). Such DNA will have a distorted double helix, which is sensed by the UvrA-UvrB complex. When the complex identifies a damaged site, the two UvrA proteins are released, and UvrC binds to UvrB at the site. The UvrC protein makes incisions in one DNA strand on both sides of the damaged site. After this incision process, UvrC is released. UvrD, which is a helicase, binds to UvrB. UvrD then begins to separate the DNA strands, and UvrB is released. The action of UvrD unravels the DNA, which removes a short DNA strand that contains the damaged region. UvrD is released. After the damaged DNA strand is removed, a gap is left in the double helix. DNA polymerase fills in the gap using the undamaged strand as a template. Finally, DNA ligase makes the final covalent connection between the newly made DNA and the original DNA strand.

Human Genetic Diseases Occur When a Component of the NER System Is Missing

Thus far, we have considered the NER system in *E. coli*. In humans, NER systems were discovered by the analysis of genetic diseases that affect DNA repair. These include xeroderma

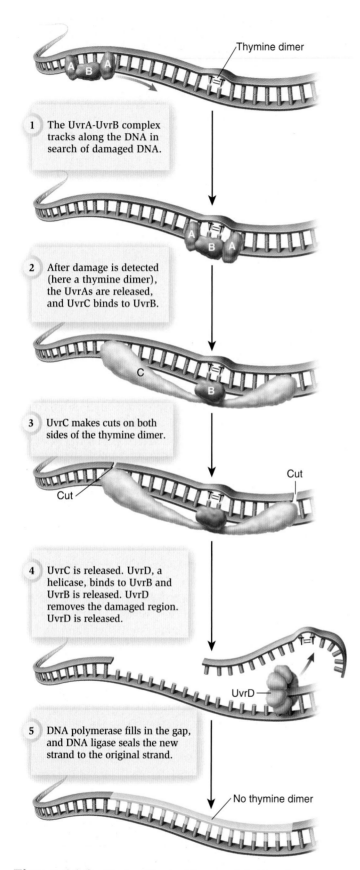

1 The UvrA-UvrB complex tracks along the DNA in search of damaged DNA.

2 After damage is detected (here a thymine dimer), the UvrAs are released, and UvrC binds to UvrB.

3 UvrC makes cuts on both sides of the thymine dimer.

4 UvrC is released. UvrD, a helicase, binds to UvrB and UvrB is released. UvrD removes the damaged region. UvrD is released.

5 DNA polymerase fills in the gap, and DNA ligase seals the new strand to the original strand.

Figure 14.8 Nucleotide excision repair in *E. coli.*

Concept check: Which components of NER are responsible for removing the damaged DNA?

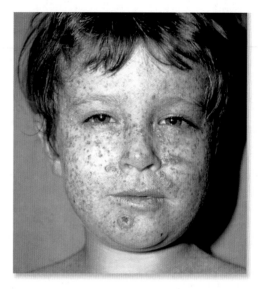

Figure 14.9 An individual affected by xeroderma pigmentosum.

Concept check: Why is this person so sensitive to the sun?

pigmentosum (XP), which was discussed at the beginning of this chapter, and also Cockayne's syndrome (CS) and PIBIDS. (PIBIDS is an acronym for a syndrome with symptoms that include photosensitivity [increased sensitivity to sunlight], ichthyosis [a skin abnormality], brittle hair, impaired intelligence, decreased fertility, and short stature.) Photosensitivity is a common characteristic in all three syndromes because of an inability to repair UV-induced lesions. Therefore, people with any of these syndromes must avoid prolonged exposure to sunlight as do the children at Camp Sundown. Figure 14.9 shows a photograph of a person with XP who has had significant sun exposure. Such individuals may have pigmentation abnormalities, many precancerous lesions, and a high predisposition to developing skin cancer.

14.3 Cancer

Cancer is a disease of multicellular organisms characterized by uncontrolled cell division. Worldwide, cancer is the second leading cause of death in humans, exceeded only by heart disease. In the United States, approximately 1.5 million people are diagnosed with cancer each year; over 0.5 million will die from the disease. Overall, about one in four Americans will die from cancer.

In about 10% of cancers, a higher predisposition to develop the disease is an inherited trait. Most cancers, though, perhaps 90%, do not involve genetic changes that are passed from parent to offspring. Rather, cancer is usually an acquired condition that typically occurs later in life. At least 80% of all human cancers are related to exposure to **carcinogens**, agents that increase the likelihood of developing cancer. Most carcinogens, such as UV light and certain chemicals in cigarette smoke, are mutagens that promote genetic changes in somatic cells. These DNA alterations can lead to effects on gene expression that

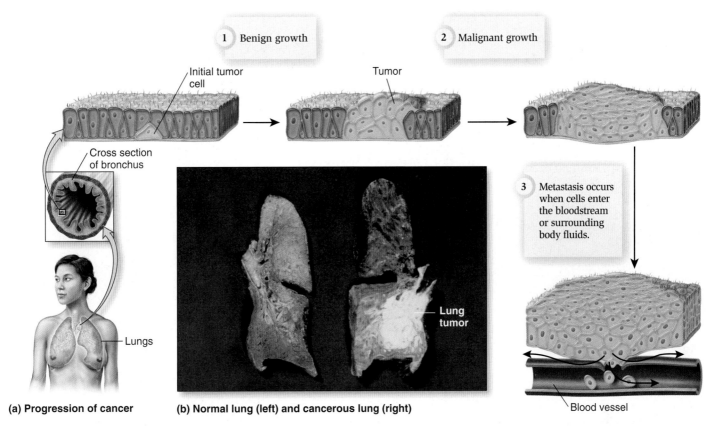

Figure 14.10   Cancer: its progression and effects.   (a) In a healthy individual, an initial mutation converts a normal cell into a tumor cell. This cell divides to produce a benign tumor. Additional genetic changes in the tumor cells may occur, leading to a malignant tumor. At a later stage in malignancy, the tumor cells will invade surrounding tissues, and some malignant cells may metastasize by traveling through the bloodstream to other parts of the body. (b) On the left of the photo is a human lung that was obtained from a healthy nonsmoker. The lung shown on the right has been ravaged by lung cancer. This lung was taken from a person who was a heavy smoker.

ultimately affect cell division and thereby lead to cancer. In this section, we will explore such genetic abnormalities.

How does cancer occur? In most cases, the development of cancer is a multistep process (**Figure 14.10**). Cancers originate from a single cell. This single cell and its lineage of daughter cells undergo a series of mutations that causes the cells to grow abnormally. At an early stage, the cells form a **tumor**, which is an overgrowth of cells. For most types of cancer, a tumor begins as a precancerous or **benign** growth. Such tumors do not invade adjacent tissues and do not spread throughout the body. This may be followed by additional mutations that cause some cells in the tumor to lose their normal growth regulation and become **malignant**. At this stage, the individual has cancer. Cancerous tumors invade healthy tissues and may spread through the bloodstream or surrounding body fluids, a process called **metastasis**. If left untreated, malignant cells will cause the death of the organism.

Over the past few decades, researchers have identified many genes that promote cancer when they are mutant. By comparing the function of each mutant gene with the corresponding nonmutant gene found in healthy cells, these genes have been placed into two categories. In some cases, a mutation causes a gene to be overactive—have an abnormally high level of expression. This overactivity contributes to the uncontrolled cell growth that is observed in cancer cells. This type of mutant gene is called an **oncogene**. Alternatively, when a **tumor-suppressor gene** is normal (that is, not mutant), it encodes a protein that helps to prevents cancer. However, when a mutation eliminates its function, cancer may occur. Thus, the two categories of cancer-causing genes are based on the effects of mutations. Oncogenes are the result of mutations that cause overactivity, whereas cancer-causing mutations in tumor-suppressor genes are due to a loss of activity. In this section, we will begin with a discussion of oncogenes and then consider tumor-suppressor genes.

Oncogenes Cause the Overactivity of Proteins That Promote Cell Division

Over the past four decades, researchers have identified many oncogenes. A large number of oncogenes encode proteins that function in cell growth signaling pathways. Cell division is regulated, in part, by growth factors, which are a type of hormone that regulates cell division. A growth factor binds to a receptor, which results in receptor activation (**Figure 14.11**). This stimulates an intracellular signal transduction pathway that activates

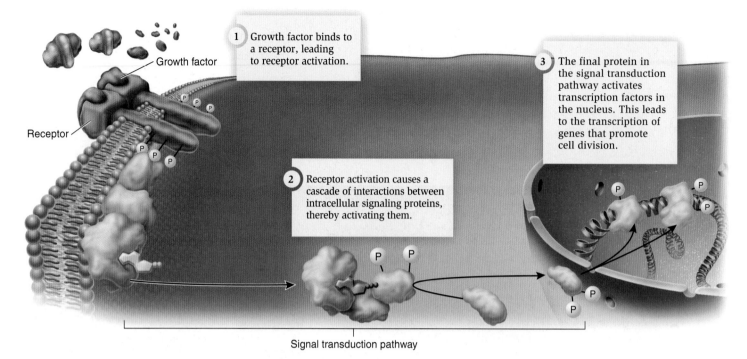

Figure 14.11   **General features of a growth factor signaling pathway that promotes cell division.**   A detailed description of this pathway is found in Chapter 9 (Figure 9.10).

Concept check:) *How does the presence of a growth factor ultimately affect the function of the cell?*

transcription factors. In this way, the transcription of specific genes is activated in response to a growth factor. After they are made, the gene products promote cell division.

Eukaryotic species produce many different growth factors that play a role in cell division. Likewise, cells have several different types of signal transduction pathways that respond to these molecules and promote cell division. Mutations in the genes that produce these signaling proteins can change them into oncogenes (**Table 14.6**). Oncogenes result in an abnormally high level of activity in these proteins, which can include growth factor receptors, intracellular signaling proteins, and transcription factors.

How can an oncogene promote cancer? In some cases, an oncogene may keep the cell division signaling pathway in a permanent "on" position. One way oncogenes can keep cell division turned on is by producing a functionally overactive protein. As a specific example, let's consider how a mutation can alter an intracellular signaling protein called Ras, which is discussed in Chapter 9 (refer back to Figure 9.10). The Ras protein is a GTPase that hydrolyzes GTP to GDP + P_i (**Figure 14.12**). When a signal transduction pathway is activated, the Ras protein exchanges GDP for GTP. When GTP is bound, the activated Ras protein promotes cell division. The Ras protein returns to its inactive state by hydrolyzing its bound GTP, and

Table 14.6	Examples of Genes Encoding Proteins of Growth Factor Signaling Pathways That Can Mutate to Become Oncogenes
Gene*	**Cellular function**
erbB	Growth factor receptor for EGF (epidermal growth factor)
ras	Intracellular signaling protein
raf	Intracellular signaling protein
src	Intracellular signaling protein
fos	Transcription factor
jun	Transcription factor

*The genes described in this table are found in humans as well as other vertebrate species. Most of the genes have been given three-letter names that are abbreviations for the type of cancer the oncogene causes or the type of virus in which the gene was first identified.

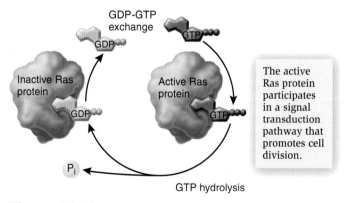

Figure 14.12   **The function of Ras, a protein that is part of signal transduction pathways.**   When GTP is bound, the activated Ras protein promotes cell division. When GTP is hydrolyzed to GDP and P_i, Ras is inactivated, and cell division is inhibited.

cell division is inhibited. Mutations that convert the normal *ras* gene into an oncogenic *ras* either decrease the ability of Ras protein to hydrolyze GTP or increase the rate of exchange of bound GDP for GTP. Both of these functional changes result in a greater amount of the active GTP-bound form of the Ras protein. In this way, these mutations keep the signaling pathway turned on when it should not be.

Mutations in Proto-Oncogenes Convert Them to Oncogenes

Thus far, we have examined the functions of proteins that cause cancer when they become overactive. Such overactivity promotes uncontrolled cell division. Let's now consider the common types of genetic changes that create such oncogenes. A **proto-oncogene** is a normal gene that, if mutated, can become an oncogene. Several types of genetic changes may convert a proto-oncogene into an oncogene. **Figure 14.13** describes four common types: missense mutations, gene amplifications, chromosomal translocations, and retroviral insertions.

Missense Mutation   A missense mutation (Figure 14.13a) can alter the function of an encoded protein in a way that promotes cancer. This type of mutation is responsible for the conversion of the *ras* gene into an oncogene. An example is a mutation in the *ras* gene that changes a specific glycine to a valine in the Ras protein. This mutation decreases the ability of the Ras protein to hydrolyze GTP, which promotes cell division (see Figure 14.12). Experimentally, chemical mutagens have been shown to cause this missense mutation and thereby lead to cancer.

Gene Amplification   Another genetic event that occurs in cancer cells is **gene amplification**, in this case an increase in the number of copies of a proto-oncogene (Figure 14.13b). An abnormal increase in the number of genes results in too much of the encoded protein. In 1982, Mark Groudine discovered that the *myc* gene, which encodes a transcription factor, was amplified in a human leukemia. Many human cancers are associated with the amplification of particular proto-oncogenes.

Chromosomal Translocation   A third type of genetic alteration that can lead to cancer is a chromosomal translocation (Figure 14.13c). This occurs when one segment of a chromosome becomes attached to a different chromosome. In 1960, Peter Nowell discovered that a form of leukemia called chronic myelogenous leukemia—a type of cancer involving blood cells—was correlated with the presence of a shortened version of a human chromosome, which he called the Philadelphia chromosome, after the city where it was discovered. This shortened chromosome is the result of a chromosome translocation in which pieces of two different chromosomes, chromosomes 9 and 22, fuse with each other. This activates a proto-oncogene, *abl*, in an unusual way (**Figure 14.14**). In healthy individuals, the *bcr* gene and the *abl* gene are located on different chromosomes. In chronic myelogenous leukemia, these chromosomes break and rejoin in a way that causes the promoter and the first part of *bcr*

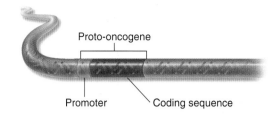

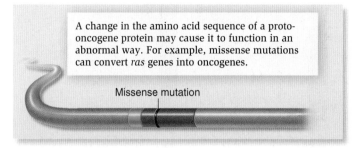

(a) Missense mutation

A change in the amino acid sequence of a proto-oncogene protein may cause it to function in an abnormal way. For example, missense mutations can convert *ras* genes into oncogenes.

Missense mutation

(a) Missense mutation

The copy number of a proto-oncogene may be increased by gene duplication. *Myc* genes have been amplified in human leukemias; breast, stomach, lung, and colon carcinomas; and brain cancers such as neuroblastomas and glioblastomas.

Three gene copies instead of one

(b) Gene amplification

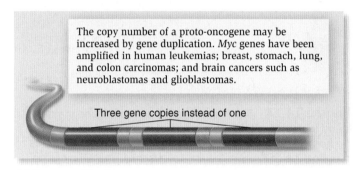

A piece of chromosome may be translocated to another chromosome and affect the expression of genes at the breakpoint site. In one form of leukemia, for example, a translocation causes parts of the *bcr* and *abl* genes to fuse, thereby creating a chimeric oncogene.

Fused, chimeric gene

(c) Chromosomal translocation

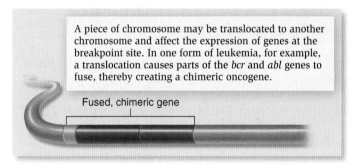

When a virus integrates into the chromosome, viral regulatory elements may enhance the expression of a nearby proto-oncogene, converting it to an oncogene.

Viral regulatory sequences

Inserted retroviral genome

(d) Retroviral insertion

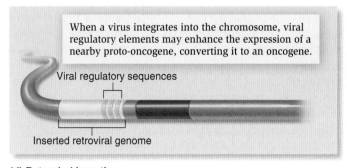

Figure 14.13 Genetic changes that convert proto-oncogenes to oncogenes.   In addition to these four, other types of genetic changes may also convert proto-oncogenes into oncogenes.

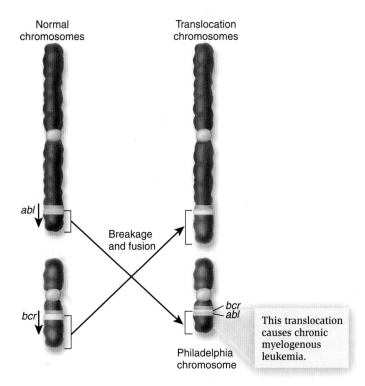

Normal chromosomes · Translocation chromosomes · abl · Breakage and fusion · bcr · bcr abl · Philadelphia chromosome · This translocation causes chronic myelogenous leukemia.

Figure 14.14 **The formation of a chimeric gene that is found in people with certain forms of leukemia.** The fusion of the *bcr* and *abl* genes creates a chimeric gene that encodes an abnormal fusion protein, leading to leukemia. The blue regions are the promoters for the *bcr* and *abl* genes.

Concept check: The *bcr* gene is normally expressed in blood cells. Explain how this observation is related to the type of cancer that the translocation causes.

to fuse with part of *abl*. This abnormal fusion event creates a **chimeric gene** composed of two gene fragments. This chimeric gene acts as an oncogene that encodes an abnormal fusion protein whose functional overactivity leads to leukemia.

Retroviral Insertion   Finally, certain types of viruses can convert proto-oncogenes into oncogenes during the viral replication cycle (see Figure 14.13d). Retroviruses insert their DNA into the chromosomal DNA of the host cell. The viral genome contains promoter and regulatory elements that cause a high level of expression of viral genes. On occasion, the viral DNA may insert into a host chromosome in such a way that a viral promoter and regulatory elements are next to a proto-oncogene. This may result in the overexpression of the proto-oncogene, thereby promoting cancer. This is one way for a virus to cause cancer. Alternatively, a virus may cause cancer because it carries an oncogene in the viral genome. This phenomenon is described next.

Some Types of Cancer Are Caused by Viruses

The great majority of cancers are caused by mutagens that alter the structure and expression of genes that are found in somatic cells. A few viruses, however, are known to cause cancer in plants, animals, and humans (**Table 14.7**).

Table 14.7   Examples of Viruses That Cause Cancer

Virus	Description
Rous sarcoma virus	Causes sarcomas in chickens
Simian sarcoma virus	Causes sarcomas in monkeys
Abelson leukemia virus	Causes leukemia in mice
Hardy-Zuckerman-4 feline sarcoma virus	Causes sarcomas in cats
Hepatitis B	Causes liver cancer in several species, including humans
Papillomavirus	Causes benign tumors and malignant carcinomas in several species, including humans; causes cervical cancer in humans
Epstein-Barr virus	Causes Burkitt's lymphoma, which primarily occurs in immunosuppressed individuals such as AIDS patients

In 1911, the first cancer-causing virus to be discovered was isolated from chicken sarcomas by Peyton Rous. A **sarcoma** is a tumor of connective tissue such as bone or cartilage. The virus was named the Rous sarcoma virus (RSV). In the 1970s, research involving RSV led to the identification of a viral gene that acts as an oncogene. Researchers investigated RSV by using it to infect chicken cells grown in the laboratory. This causes the chicken cells to grow like cancer cells, continuously and in an uncontrolled manner. Researchers identified mutant RSV strains that infected and proliferated within chicken cells without transforming them into malignant cells. These RSV strains were missing a gene that is found in the form of the virus that does cause cancer. This gene was called the *src* gene because it causes sarcoma.

Harold Varmus and Michael Bishop, in collaboration with Peter Vogt, later discovered that normal (nonviral-infected) cells also contain a copy of the *src* gene in their chromosomes. It is a proto-oncogene. When the *src* gene is incorporated into a viral genome, it is overexpressed because it is transcribed from a very active viral promoter. This ultimately produces too much of the Src protein in infected cells and promotes uncontrolled cell division.

Tumor-Suppressor Genes Prevent Mutation or Cell Proliferation

Thus far, we have examined one category of genes that can promote cancer, namely oncogenes. We now turn our attention to the second category of genes, those called tumor-suppressor genes. The functioning of a normal (nonmutant) tumor-suppressor gene prevents cancerous growth. The proteins encoded by tumor-suppressor genes usually have one of two functions—maintenance of genome integrity or negative regulation of cell division (**Table 14.8**).

Maintenance of Genome Integrity   Some tumor-suppressor genes encode proteins that maintain the integrity of the genome. Such proteins monitor and/or repair alterations in the genome. The proteins encoded by these genes are vital for the prevention of abnormalities such as gene mutations, DNA breaks, and improperly segregated chromosomes. Therefore, when these

Table 14.8	Functions of Selected Tumor-Suppressor Genes
Gene	Function of encoded protein
Maintenance of genome integrity	
p53	p53 is a transcription factor that acts as a sensor of DNA damage. It can promote DNA repair, prevent the progression through the cell cycle, and promote apoptosis.
BRCA-1 *BRCA-2*	BRCA-1 and BRCA-2 proteins are both involved in the cellular defense against DNA damage. They may play a role in sensing DNA damage or act to facilitate DNA repair. These genes are mutant in persons with certain inherited forms of breast cancer.
XPD	This represents one of several different genes whose products function in DNA repair. These genes are defective in patients with xeroderma pigmentosum.
Negative regulation of cell division	
Rb	The Rb protein is a negative regulator that represses the transcription of genes required for DNA replication and cell division.
NF1	The NF1 protein stimulates Ras to hydrolyze its GTP to GDP. Loss of NF1 function causes the Ras protein to be overactive, which promotes cell division.
p16	The p16 protein is a negative regulator of cyclin-dependent protein kinase.

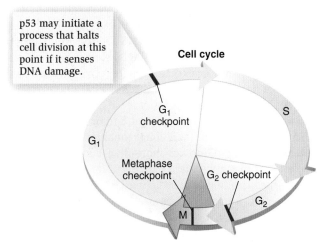

Figure 14.15 **The cell cycle and checkpoints.** As discussed in Chapter 15, eukaryotic cells progress through a cell cycle composed of G₁, S, G₂, and M phases (look ahead to Figure 15.2). The red bars indicate common checkpoints that will stop the cell cycle if genetic abnormalities are detected. The p53 protein will stop a cell at the G₁ checkpoint if it senses DNA damage.

Concept check: Why is it an advantage for an organism to have checkpoints that can stop the cell cycle?

proteins are functioning properly, they minimize the chance that a cancer-causing mutation will occur. In some cases, the proteins encoded by tumor-suppressor genes will prevent a cell from progressing through the cell cycle if an abnormality is detected. These are termed **checkpoint proteins** because their role is to <u>check</u> the integrity of the genome and prevent a cell from progressing past a certain <u>point</u> in the cell cycle. Checkpoint proteins are not usually required to regulate normal, healthy cell division, but they can stop cell division if an abnormality is detected.

Proteins called cyclins and cyclin-dependent protein kinases (cdks) are responsible for advancing a cell through the four phases of the cell cycle (see Chapter 15). The formation of activated cyclin/cdk complexes can be stopped by checkpoint proteins. A specific example of a tumor-suppressor gene that encodes a checkpoint protein is *p53*, discovered in 1979 by Arnold Levine. Its name refers to the molecular mass of the p53 protein, which is <u>53</u> kDa (kilodaltons). About 50% of all human cancers are associated with mutations in this gene, including malignant tumors of the lung, breast, esophagus, liver, bladder, and brain, as well as leukemias and lymphomas (cancer of the lymphatic system).

As shown in **Figure 14.15**, p53 is a G₁ checkpoint protein. The expression of the *p53* gene is induced when DNA is damaged. The p53 protein is a regulatory transcription factor that activates several different genes, leading to the synthesis of proteins that stop the cell cycle and other proteins that repair the DNA. When p53 is activated, a cell cannot progress from G₁ to the S, or synthesis, phase of the cell cycle. If the DNA is eventually repaired, a cell may later proceed through the cell cycle.

Alternatively, if the DNA damage is too severe, the p53 protein will also activate other genes that promote programmed cell death. This process, called **apoptosis**, involves cell shrinkage

and DNA degradation. As described in Chapter 9, enzymes known as **caspases** are activated during apoptosis (refer back to Figure 9.20). They function as proteases that are sometimes called the "executioners" of the cell. Caspases digest selected cellular proteins such as microfilaments, which are components of the cytoskeleton. This causes the cell to break down into small vesicles that are eventually phagocytized by cells of the immune system. It is beneficial for a multicellular organism to kill an occasional cell with cancer-causing potential.

When checkpoint genes such as *p53* are rendered inactive by mutation, the division of normal healthy cells may not be adversely affected. For example, mice that are missing the *p53* gene are born healthy. This indicates that checkpoint proteins such as p53 are not necessary for normal cell growth and division. However, these mice are very sensitive to mutagens such as UV light and easily develop cancer. The loss of p53 function makes it more likely that undesirable genetic changes will occur that could cause cancerous growth.

Negative Regulation of Cell Division A second category of tumor-suppressor genes encodes proteins that are negative regulators or inhibitors of cell division. Their function is necessary to properly halt cell division. If their function is lost, cell division is abnormally accelerated.

An example of such a tumor-suppressor gene is the *Rb* gene. It was the first tumor-suppressor gene to be identified in humans by studying patients with a disease called retinoblastoma, a cancerous tumor that occurs in the retina of the eye. Some people have an inherited predisposition to develop this disease within the first few years of life. By comparison, the noninherited form of retinoblastoma, which is caused by environmental agents, is more likely to occur later in life.

Based on these differences, in 1971, Alfred Knudson proposed a two-hit hypothesis for retinoblastoma. According to this hypothesis, retinoblastoma requires two mutations to occur. People have two copies of the *Rb* gene, one from each parent. Individuals with the inherited form of the disease already have received one mutant gene from one of their parents. They need only one additional mutation to develop the disease. Because the retina has more than 1 million cells, it is relatively likely that a mutation may occur in one of these cells at an early age, leading to the disease. However, people with the noninherited form of the disease must have two *Rb* mutations in the same retinal cell to cause the disease. Because two mutations are less likely than a single mutation, the noninherited form of this disease is expected to occur much later in life, and only rarely. Since Knudson's original work, molecular studies have confirmed the two-hit hypothesis for retinoblastoma.

The Rb protein negatively controls a regulatory transcription factor called E2F that activates genes required for cell cycle progression from G_1 to S phase. The binding of the Rb protein to E2F inhibits its activity and prevents cell division (**Figure 14.16**). When a normal cell is supposed to divide, cyclins bind to cyclin-dependent protein kinases. This binding activates the kinases, which then leads to the phosphorylation of the Rb protein. The phosphorylated form of the Rb protein is released from E2F, thereby allowing E2F to activate genes needed to progress through the cell cycle. By comparison, we can imagine how the cell cycle becomes unregulated without a functional Rb protein. When both copies of Rb are defective, the E2F protein is always active. This explains why uncontrolled cell division occurs in retinoblastoma.

Gene Mutations, Chromosome Loss, and DNA Methylation Can Inhibit the Expression of Tumor-Suppressor Genes

Cancer biologists would also like to understand how tumor-suppressor genes are inactivated, because this knowledge may ultimately help them to prevent or combat cancer. How are tumor-suppressor genes silenced? The function of tumor-suppressor genes is lost in three common ways. First, a mutation can occur within a tumor-suppressor gene to inactivate its function. For example, a mutation could abolish the function of the promoter for a tumor-suppressor gene or introduce an early stop codon in its coding sequence. Either of these would prevent the expression of a functional protein.

Chromosome loss is a second way that the function of a tumor-suppressor gene is lost. Chromosome loss may contribute to the progression of cancer if the missing chromosome carries one or more tumor-suppressor genes.

Recently, researchers have discovered a third way that these genes may be inactivated. Tumor-suppressor genes found in cancer cells are sometimes abnormally methylated. As discussed in Chapter 13, transcription is inhibited when CpG islands near a promoter region are methylated. Such DNA

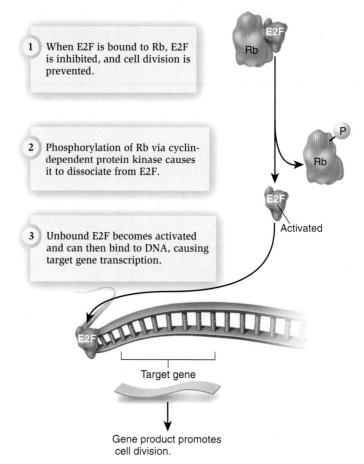

1. When E2F is bound to Rb, E2F is inhibited, and cell division is prevented.

2. Phosphorylation of Rb via cyclin-dependent protein kinase causes it to dissociate from E2F.

3. Unbound E2F becomes activated and can then bind to DNA, causing target gene transcription.

Target gene

Gene product promotes cell division.

Figure 14.16 **Function of the Rb protein.** The Rb protein inhibits the function of E2F, which turns on genes that cause a cell to divide. When cells are supposed to divide, Rb is phosphorylated by cyclin-dependent protein kinase, which allows E2F to function. If Rb protein is not properly made due to a mutation, E2F will always be active, and the cell will be stimulated to divide uncontrollably.

Concept check: Would cancer occur if both copies of the Rb gene and both copies of the E2F gene were rendered inactive due to mutations?

methylation near the promoters of tumor-suppressor genes has been found in many types of tumors, suggesting that this form of gene inactivation plays an important role in the formation and/or progression of malignancy.

Most Forms of Cancer Are Caused by a Series of Genetic Changes That Progressively Alter the Growth Properties of Cells

The discovery of oncogenes and tumor-suppressor genes has allowed researchers to study the progression of certain forms of cancer at the molecular level. Cancer usually requires multiple genetic changes to the same cell lineage, perhaps in the range of 10 or more. Many cancers begin with a benign genetic alteration that, over time and with additional mutations, leads to malignancy. Furthermore, a malignancy can continue to accumulate genetic changes that make it even more difficult to treat because the cells divide faster or invade surrounding tissues more readily.

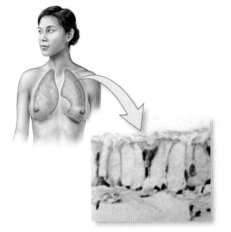

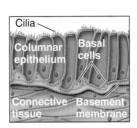

Normal lung epithelium

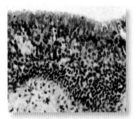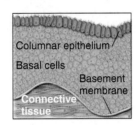

Hyperplasia

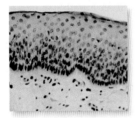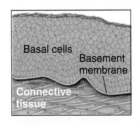

Loss of ciliated cells

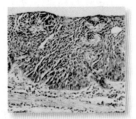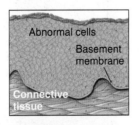

Dysplasia (initially precancerous, then cancerous)

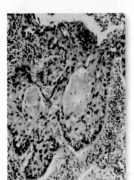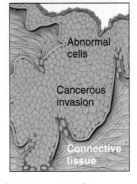

Invasive cancerous cells that can metastasize

(a) Cellular changes

Genes that are commonly mutated in lung cancer include

Oncogenes	**Tumor-suppressor genes**
erbB – epidermal growth factor receptor	*p53* – checkpoint
ras – cell signaling	*XPD* – DNA repair
myc – transcription factor	*Rb* – negative regulator
Cyclin D1 – promotes the cell cycle	*p16* – negative regulator

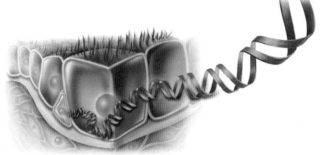

(b) Genetic changes

Figure 14.17 **Progression of changes leading to lung cancer.** Lung tissue is largely composed of different types of connective tissue and epithelial cells, including columnar and basal cells. **(a)** A progression of cellular changes in basal cells, caused by the accumulation of mutations, leads to basal cell carcinoma, a common type of lung cancer. **(b)** Mutations in several different genes can contribute to lung cancer.

Lung cancer progresses through different stages of abnormal cell proliferation. Lung cancer is diagnosed in approximately 170,000 men and women each year in the U.S. Worldwide, more than 1.2 million cases are diagnosed. Nearly 90% of these cases are caused by smoking and are thus preventable. Unlike other cancers for which early diagnosis is possible, lung cancer is usually detected only after it has become advanced and is difficult if not impossible to cure. The five-year survival rate for lung cancer patients is approximately 15%.

What is the cellular basis for lung cancer? Most cancers in the lung are **carcinomas**—cancers of epithelial cells (**Figure 14.17a**). Epithelial cells are described in Chapter 10. The top images in this figure show the normal epithelium found in a healthy lung. The rest of the figure shows the progression of cancer that is due to mutations in basal cells, a type of epithelial cell. Keep in mind that cancer occurs due to the accumulation of mutations in a cell lineage, beginning with an initial mutant cell that then divides multiple times to produce a population of many daughter cells (refer back to Figure 14.10). As mutations accumulate in a lineage of basal cells, their numbers increase dramatically. This causes a thickening of the epithelium, a condition called hyperplasia. The proliferation of such basal cells causes the loss of the ciliated, columnar epithelial cells that normally line the airways. As additional mutations accumulate in this cell lineage, the basal cells develop more abnormal morphologies, a condition known as dysplasia. In the early stages of dysplasia, the abnormal basal cells are precancerous. If the source of chronic irritation (usually cigarette smoke) is eliminated, the abnormal cells are likely to disappear. Alternatively, if smoking continues, these abnormal cells may accumulate additional genetic changes and lose the ability to stop dividing. Such cells have become cancerous—the person has basal cell carcinoma.

The basement membrane is a sheetlike layer of extracellular matrix that provides a barrier between the lung cells and the bloodstream. If the cancer cells have not yet penetrated the basement membrane, they will not have metastasized, that is, spread into the blood and to other parts of the body. If the entire tumor is removed at this stage, the patient should be cured. The lower images in Figure 14.17a show a tumor that has broken through the basement membrane. The metastasis of these cells to other parts of the body will likely kill the patient, usually within a year of diagnosis.

The cellular changes that lead to lung cancer are correlated with genetic changes (**Figure 14.17b**). These include the occurrence of mutations that create oncogenes and inhibit tumor-suppressor genes. The order of mutations is not absolute. It takes time for multiple changes to accumulate, so cancer is usually a disease of older people. Reducing your exposure to mutagens such as cigarette smoke throughout your lifetime will minimize the risk of mutations to your genes that could promote cancer.

Genomes & Proteomes Connection

Chromosomal Changes and Mutations in Approximately 300 Human Genes May Promote Cancer

Researchers have identified a large number of genes that are mutated in cancer cells. Though not all of these mutant genes have been directly shown to affect the growth rate of cells, such mutations are likely to be found in tumors because they provide some type of growth advantage for the cell population from which the cancer developed. For example, certain mutations may enable cells to metastasize to neighboring locations. These mutations may not affect growth rate, but they provide the growth advantage that cancer cells are not limited to growing in a particular location. They can migrate to new locations.

How many genes can contribute to cancer when they become mutant? Researchers have estimated that about 300 different genes may play a role in the development of human cancer. With an approximate genome size of 20,000 to 25,000 genes, this observation indicates that over 1% of our genes have the potential to promote cancer if their function is altered by a mutation.

In addition to mutations within specific genes, another common genetic change associated with cancer is abnormalities in chromosome structure and number. **Figure 14.18** compares the chromosome composition of a normal male cell and a tumor cell taken from the same person. The normal composition for this person is 22 pairs of chromosomes plus two sex chromosomes (X and Y). By comparison, the chromosome composition of the tumor cell is quite bizarre, including the observation that the tumor cell has two X chromosomes, which is characteristic of females. The tumor cells are also missing several chromosomes. If tumor-suppressor genes were located on these missing chromosomes, their function is lost as well. Figure 14.18 also shows a few cases of extra chromosomes. If these chromosomes contain proto-oncogenes, the expression of those genes may be overactive. Finally, tumor cells often contain chromosomes that have translocations. Such translocations may create chimeric genes (as in the case of the Philadelphia chromosome discussed earlier in this chapter), or they may place a gene next to the regulatory sequences of another gene.

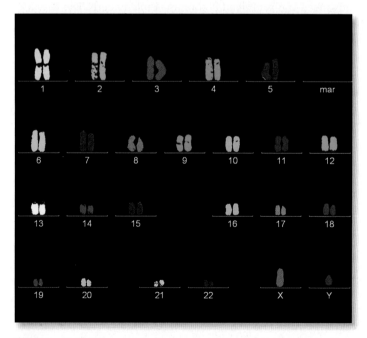 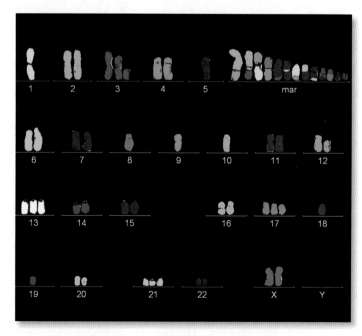

Figure 14.18   A comparison between chromosomes found in a normal human cell (left) and a cancer cell (right) from the same person.   The set found in the cancer cell on the right is highly abnormal, with extra copies of some chromosomes and lost copies of others. Chromosomes made of fused pieces of chromosomes (designated mar in this figure) are also common in cancer cells.

Concept check: How might these changes in chromosome structure and number contribute to cancer?

Summary of Key Concepts

14.1 Mutation

- A mutation is a heritable change in the genetic material.
- Point mutations, which affect a single base pair, can alter the coding sequence of genes in several ways. These include silent, missense, nonsense, and frameshift mutations. (Table 14.1)
- Sickle-cell disease is caused by a missense mutation that changes a single amino acid in β-globin. (Figure 14.1)
- Gene mutations can also alter gene function by changing DNA sequences that are not within the coding region. (Table 14.2)
- The Lederbergs used replica plating to show that mutations conferring resistance to T1 occur randomly. (Figure 14.2)
- Germ-line mutations affect gametes, whereas somatic mutations affect only a part of the body and cannot be passed to offspring. (Figures 14.3, 14.4)
- Spontaneous mutations are the result of errors in natural biological processes. Induced mutations are due to agents in the environment that cause changes in DNA structure. (Table 14.3)
- Mutagens are chemical or physical agents that lead to mutations in DNA. (Table 14.4, Figures 14.5, 14.6)
- Testing methods, such as the Ames test, can determine whether an agent is a mutagen. (Figure 14.7)

14.2 DNA Repair

- DNA repair systems involve proteins that sense DNA damage and repair it before a mutation occurs. (Table 14.5)
- Nucleotide excision repair (NER) systems recognize various types of DNA damage, such as thymine dimers. In this type of system, the damaged strand is excised, and a new strand is made. (Figure 14.8)
- Certain inherited diseases in humans, such as xeroderma pigmentosum, are due to defects in NER. (Figure 14.9)

14.3 Cancer

- Cancer is due to the accumulation of mutations in a lineage of cells that leads to uncontrolled cell growth. (Figure 14.10)
- Mutations in proto-oncogenes that result in overactivity produce cancer-causing genes called oncogenes.
- Oncogenes often encode proteins involved in cell-signaling pathways that promote cell division. (Figures 14.11, 14.12, Table 14.6)
- Four common types of genetic changes, namely, missense mutations, gene amplifications, chromosomal translocations, and retroviral insertions, can change proto-oncogenes into oncogenes. (Figure 14.13)
- A chromosome translocation that fuses parts of the *bcr* gene and the *abl* gene creates an oncogene that causes leukemia. (Figure 14.14)
- Some types of cancer are caused by viruses. (Table 14.7)
- The normal function of tumor-suppressor genes is to prevent cancer. Loss-of-function mutations in such genes can promote cancer. Tumor-suppressor genes often encode proteins that

maintain the integrity of the genome or function as negative regulators of cell division. (Table 14.8)
- Checkpoint proteins, such as p53, monitor the integrity of the genome and prevent the cell from progressing through the cell cycle if abnormalities are detected. (Figure 14.15)
- The Rb protein is a negative regulator of cell division because it inhibits E2F, a transcription factor that promotes cell division. (Figure 14.16)
- Gene mutations, chromosome loss, and DNA methylation are common ways that tumor-suppressor genes are inactivated.
- Most forms of cancer, such as lung cancer, involve multiple genetic changes that lead to malignancy. (Figure 14.17)
- Over 300 human genes are known to be associated with cancer when they become mutant. In addition, changes in chromosome number and structure are commonly found in cancer cells. (Figure 14.18)

Assess and Discuss

Test Yourself

1. Point mutations that do not alter the amino acid sequence of the resulting gene product are called _____ mutations.
   a. frameshift
   b. natural
   c. silent
   d. nonsense
   e. missense

2. Some point mutations will lead to an mRNA that produces a shorter polypeptide. This type of mutation is known as a _____ mutation.
   a. neutral
   b. silent
   c. missense
   d. nonsense
   e. chromosomal

3. A mutation in which of the following regions is least likely to affect gene function?
   a. promoter
   b. coding region
   c. splice junction
   d. intergenic region
   e. regulatory site

4. Mutagens can cause mutations by
   a. chemically altering DNA nucleotides.
   b. disrupting DNA replication.
   c. altering the genetic code of an organism.
   d. all of the above.
   e. a and b only.

5. The mutagenic effect of UV light is
   a. the alteration of cytosine bases to adenine bases.
   b. the formation of adenine dimers that interfere with genetic expression.
   c. the breaking of the sugar-phosphate backbone of the DNA molecule.
   d. the formation of thymine dimers that disrupt DNA replication.
   e. the deletion of thymine bases along the DNA molecule.

6. The Ames test
   a. provides a way to determine if any type of cell has experienced a mutation.
   b. provides a way to determine if an agent is a mutagen.
   c. allows researchers to experimentally disrupt gene activity by causing a mutation in a specific gene.
   d. provides a way to repair mutations in bacterial cells.
   e. does all of the above.

7. Xeroderma pigmentosum
   a. is a genetic disorder that results in uncontrolled cell growth.
   b. is a genetic disorder where the NER system is not fully functional.
   c. is a genetic disorder that results in the loss of pigment in certain patches of skin.
   d. results from the lack of DNA polymerase proofreading.
   e. is both b and d.

8. If a mutation eliminated the function of UvrC, which aspect of nucleotide excision repair would not work?
   a. sensing a damaged DNA site
   b. endonuclease cleavage of the damaged strand
   c. removal of the damaged strand
   d. synthesis of a new strand, using the undamaged strand as a template
   e. none of the above

9. Cancer cells are said to be metastatic when they
   a. begin to divide uncontrollably.
   b. invade healthy tissue.
   c. migrate to other parts of the body.
   d. cause mutations in other healthy cells.
   e. do all of the above.

10. Oncogenes can be caused by
    a. missense mutations.
    b. gene amplification.
    c. chromosomal translocation.
    d. retroviral insertion.
    e. all of the above.

Conceptual Questions

1. Is a random mutation more likely to be beneficial or harmful? Explain your answer.

2. Distinguish between spontaneous and induced mutations. Which are more harmful? Which are avoidable?

3. In the treatment of cancer, the basis for many types of chemotherapy and radiation therapy is that mutagens are more effective at killing dividing cells compared to nondividing cells. Explain why. What are possible harmful side effects of chemotherapy and radiation therapy?

Collaborative Questions

1. Discuss the pros and cons of mutation.

2. A large amount of research is aimed at studying mutation. However, there is not an infinite amount of research dollars. Where would you put your money for mutation research?
   a. testing of potential mutagens
   b. investigating molecular effects of mutagens
   c. investigating DNA repair mechanisms
   d. or some other place

Online Resource

www.brookerbiology.com

Stay a step ahead in your studies with animations that bring concepts to life and practice tests to assess your understanding. Your instructor may also recommend the interactive ebook, individualized learning tools, and more.

The Eukaryotic Cell Cycle, Mitosis, and Meiosis

15

A scanning electron micrograph of human chromosomes. These chromosomes are highly compacted and found in a dividing cell.

Over 10,000,000,000,000! Researchers estimate the adult human body contains somewhere between 10 trillion to 50 trillion cells. It is almost an incomprehensible number. Even more amazing is the accuracy of the process that produces these cells. After a human sperm and egg unite, the fertilized egg goes through a long series of cell divisions to produce an adult with over 10 trillion cells. Let's suppose you randomly removed a cell from your arm and compared it to a cell from your foot. If you examined the chromosomes found in both cells under the microscope, they would look identical. Likewise, the DNA sequences along those chromosomes would also be the same, barring rare mutations. Similar comparisons could be made among the trillions of cells in your body. When you consider how many cell divisions are needed to produce an adult human, the precision of cell division is truly remarkable.

What accounts for this high level of accuracy? As we will examine in this chapter, **cell division**, the reproduction of cells, is a highly regulated process that monitors the integrity of the genetic material. The eukaryotic cell cycle is a series of phases that are needed for cell division. The cells of eukaryotic species may follow one of two different sorting processes so that new daughter cells will receive the correct number and types of chromosomes. The first sorting process we will explore, called mitosis, is needed so that daughter cells will receive the same amount of genetic material as the mother cell that produced them. We will then examine another sorting process, called meiosis, which is needed for sexual reproduction. In meiosis, cells that have two sets of chromosomes produce daughter cells with a single set of chromosomes. Lastly, we will explore variation in the structure and number of chromosomes. As you will see, a variety of mechanisms that alter chromosome structure and number can have important consequences for the organisms that carry them.

15.1 The Eukaryotic Cell Cycle

Life is a continuum in which new living cells are formed by the division of pre-existing cells. The Latin axiom *Omnis cellula e cellula*, meaning "Every cell from a cell," was first proposed in 1858 by a German pathologist, Rudolf Virchow. From an evolutionary perspective, cell division has a very ancient origin. All living organisms, from unicellular bacteria to multicellular plants and animals, have been produced by a series of repeated rounds of cell growth and division extending back to the beginnings of life nearly 4 billion years ago. We now know that cell division is a process that involves remarkable accuracy and precise timing. A cell must be able to sense when conditions are appropriate for division to occur and then orchestrate a series of events that will ensure the production of healthy new cells. A key issue is that the chromosomes must be properly replicated and sorted to new daughter cells. In this section, we will examine the phases of the eukaryotic cell cycle and see how the cell cycle is controlled by proteins that carefully monitor the division process to ensure its accuracy. But first, we need to consider some general features of chromosomes in eukaryotic species.

Eukaryotic Chromosomes Are Inherited in Sets and Occur in Homologous Pairs

To understand the chromosomal composition of cells and the behavior of chromosomes during cell division, scientists observe cells and chromosomes with the use of microscopes.

Cytogenetics is the field of genetics that involves the microscopic examination of chromosomes and cell division. When a cell prepares to divide, the chromosomes become more tightly compacted, a process that decreases their apparent length and increases their diameter. A consequence of this compaction is that distinctive shapes and numbers of chromosomes become visible with a light microscope.

Microscopic Examination of Chromosomes   Figure 15.1 shows the general procedure for preparing and viewing chromosomes from a eukaryotic cell. In this example, the cells are obtained from a sample of human blood. Specifically, the chromosomes within leukocytes (white blood cells) are examined. A sample of the blood cells is obtained and treated with drugs that stimulate the cells to divide. The actively dividing cells are centrifuged to concentrate them and then mixed with a hypotonic solution that makes the cells swell. The expansion of the cell causes the chromosomes to spread out from each other, making it easier to see each individual chromosome.

Next, the cells are concentrated by a second centrifugation and treated with a fixative, which chemically fixes them in place so that the chromosomes will no longer move around. The cells are then exposed to a chemical dye, such as Giemsa, that binds to the chromosomes and stains them. This gives chromosomes a distinctive banding pattern that greatly enhances their contrast and ability to be uniquely identified. The cells are then placed on a slide and viewed with a light microscope. In a cytogenetics laboratory, the microscopes are equipped with an electronic camera to photograph the chromosomes. On a computer screen, the chromosomes can be organized in a standard way, usually from largest to smallest. A photographic representation of the chromosomes, as in the photo in step 5 of Figure 15.1, is called a **karyotype**. A karyotype reveals the number, size, and form of chromosomes found within an actively dividing cell. It

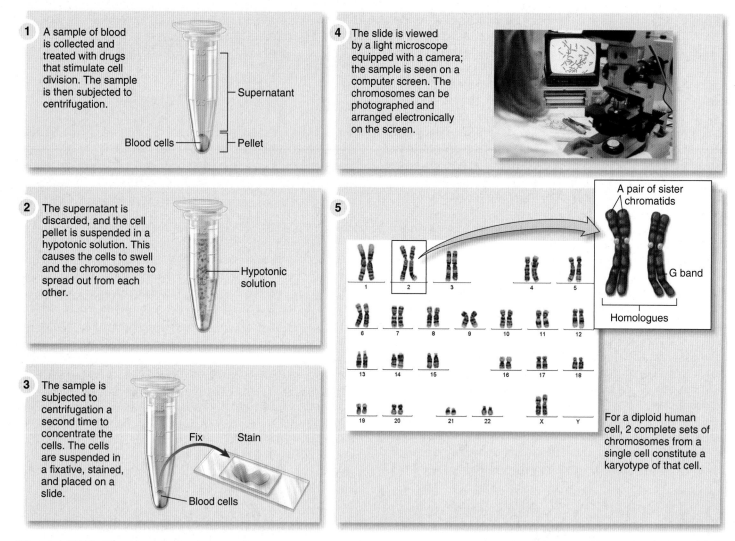

1 A sample of blood is collected and treated with drugs that stimulate cell division. The sample is then subjected to centrifugation.

Supernatant
Blood cells
Pellet

2 The supernatant is discarded, and the cell pellet is suspended in a hypotonic solution. This causes the cells to swell and the chromosomes to spread out from each other.

Hypotonic solution

3 The sample is subjected to centrifugation a second time to concentrate the cells. The cells are suspended in a fixative, stained, and placed on a slide.

Fix   Stain
Blood cells

4 The slide is viewed by a light microscope equipped with a camera; the sample is seen on a computer screen. The chromosomes can be photographed and arranged electronically on the screen.

5

A pair of sister chromatids
G band
Homologues

For a diploid human cell, 2 complete sets of chromosomes from a single cell constitute a karyotype of that cell.

Figure 15.1   **The procedure for making a karyotype.**   In this example, the chromosomes were treated with the dye Giemsa, and the resulting bands are called G bands.

Concept check: *Researchers usually treat cells with drugs that stimulate them to divide prior to the procedure for making a karyotype. Why is this useful?*

should also be noted that the chromosomes that are viewed in actively dividing cells have already replicated to form sister chromatids (see inset to Figure 15.1). We will discuss the formation of sister chromatids later in this section.

Sets of Chromosomes   What type of information is learned from a karyotype? By studying the karyotypes of many species, scientists have discovered that eukaryotic chromosomes occur in sets. Each set is composed of several different types of chromosomes. For example, one set of human chromosomes contains 23 different types of chromosomes (see Figure 15.1). By convention, the chromosomes are numbered according to size, with the largest chromosomes having the smallest numbers. For example, human chromosomes 1, 2, and 3 are relatively large, whereas 21 and 22 are the two smallest. This numbering system does not apply to the **sex chromosomes**, which determine the sex of the individual. Sex chromosomes in humans are designated with the letters X and Y. The chromosomes that are not sex chromosomes are called **autosomes**. Humans have 22 different types of autosomes.

A second feature of many eukaryotic species is that most cells contain two sets of chromosomes. The karyotype shown in Figure 15.1 contains two sets of chromosomes, with 23 different chromosomes in each set. Therefore, this human cell contains a total of 46 chromosomes. A person's cells have 46 chromosomes each because the individual inherited one set from the father and one set from the mother. When the cells of an organism carry two sets of chromosomes, that organism is said to be **diploid**. Geneticists use the letter n to represent a set of chromosomes, so diploid organisms are referred to as $2n$. For example, humans are $2n$, where $n = 23$. Most human cells are diploid. An exception involves **gametes**, namely, sperm and egg cells. Gametes are **haploid**, or $1n$, which means they contain one set of chromosomes.

Homologous Pairs of Chromosomes   When an organism is diploid, the members of a pair of chromosomes are called **homologues** (see inset to Figure 15.1). The term **homology** refers to any similarity that is due to common ancestry. Pairs of homologous chromosomes are evolutionarily derived from the same chromosome. However, homologous chromosomes are not usually identical to each other because over many generations they have accumulated some genetic changes that make them distinct.

How similar are homologous chromosomes to each other? Each of the two chromosomes in a homologous pair is nearly identical in size and contains a very similar composition of genetic material. A particular gene found on one copy of a chromosome is also found on the homologue. Because one homologue is received from each parent, the two homologues may vary with regard to the way that a gene affects an organism's traits. As an example, let's consider a gene in humans called *OCA2*, which plays a major role in determining eye color. The *OCA2* gene is found on chromosome 15. One copy of chromosome 15 might carry the form of this eye color gene that confers brown eyes, whereas the gene on the homologue could confer blue eyes. The topic of how genes affect an organism's traits will be considered in Chapter 16.

The DNA sequences on homologous chromosomes are very similar. In most cases, the sequence of bases on one homologue differs by less than 1% from the sequence on the other homologue. For example, the DNA sequence of chromosome 1 that you inherited from your mother is likely to be more than 99% identical to the DNA sequence of chromosome 1 that you inherited from your father. Nevertheless, keep in mind that the sequences are not identical. The slight differences in DNA sequence provide important variation in gene function. Again, if we use the eye color gene *OCA2* as an example, a minor difference in DNA sequence distinguishes two forms of the gene, brown versus blue.

The striking similarity between homologous chromosomes does not apply to pairs of sex chromosomes (for example, X and Y). These chromosomes differ in size and genetic composition. Certain genes found on the X chromosome are not found on the Y chromosome, and vice versa. The X and Y chromosomes are not considered homologous chromosomes, although they do have short regions of homology.

The Cell Cycle Is a Series of Phases That Lead to Cell Division

Eukaryotic cells that are destined to divide progress through the **cell cycle**, a sequence of growth, replication, and division that produces new cells. Figure 15.2 provides an overview of the cell cycle. In this diagram, the mother cell has three pairs of chromosomes, for a total of six individual chromosomes. Such a cell is diploid $(2n)$ and contains three chromosomes per set $(n = 3)$. The paternal set is shown in blue, and the homologous maternal set is shown in red.

The phases of the cell cycle are G_1 (first gap), **S** (synthesis of DNA, the genetic material), G_2 (second gap), and **M phase** (mitosis and cytokinesis). The G_1 and G_2 phases were originally described as gap phases to indicate a pause in activity between DNA synthesis and mitosis. However, we now know these are critical phases of the cell cycle. In actively dividing cells, the G_1, S, and G_2 phases are collectively known as **interphase**. During interphase, the cell grows and copies its chromosomes in preparation for cell division. Alternatively, cells may exit the cell cycle and remain for long periods of time in a phase called G_0 (G zero). The G_0 phase is an alternative to proceeding through G_1. A cell in the G_0 phase has postponed making a decision to divide or, in the case of terminally differentiated cells (such as nerve cells in an adult animal), has made a decision to never divide again. G_0 is a nondividing phase.

G_1 Phase   The G_1 phase is a period in a cell's life when it may become committed to divide. Depending on the environmental conditions and the presence of signaling molecules, a cell in the G_1 phase may accumulate molecular changes that cause it to progress through the rest of the cell cycle. Cell growth typically occurs during the G_1 phase.

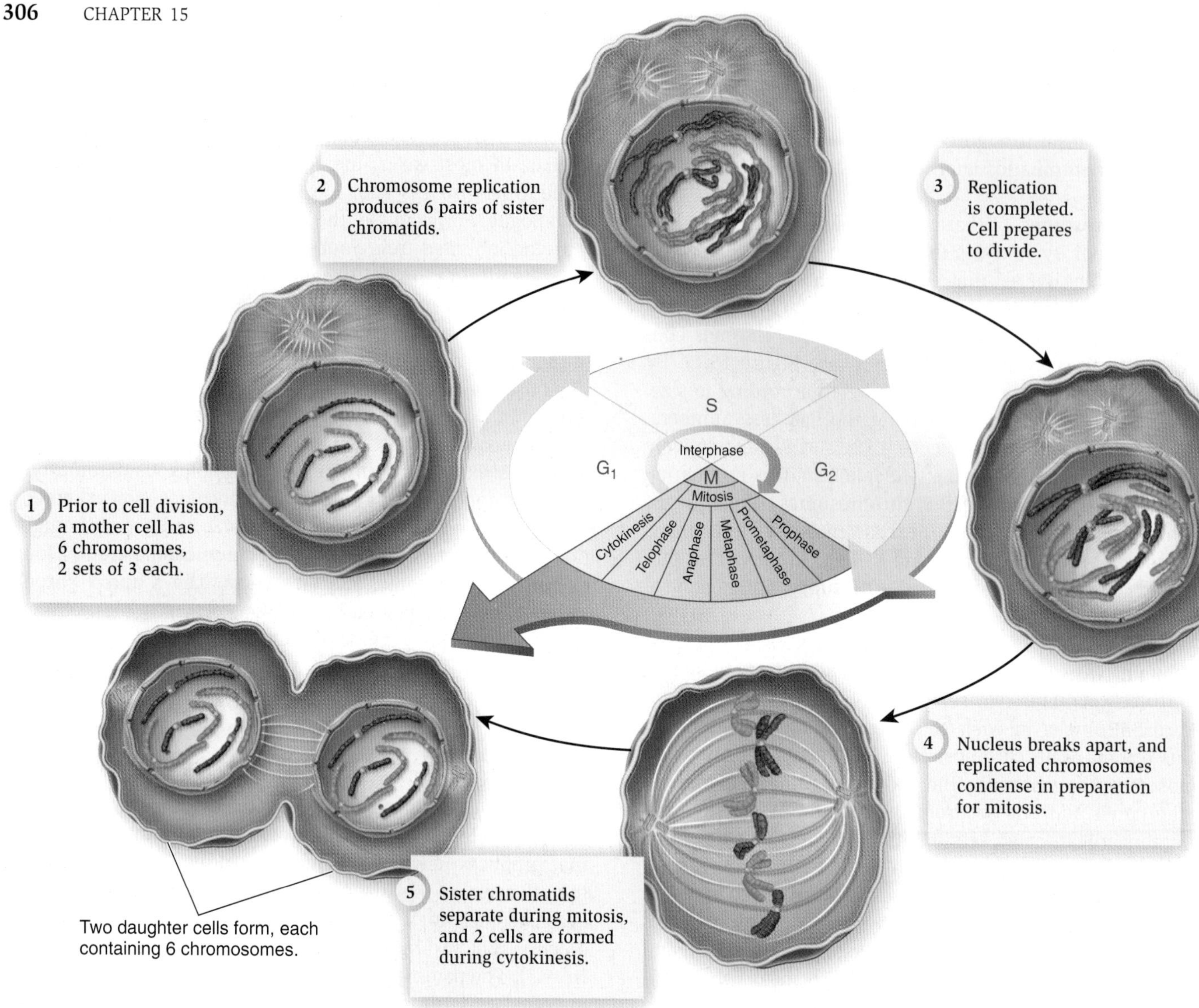

2 Chromosome replication produces 6 pairs of sister chromatids.

3 Replication is completed. Cell prepares to divide.

1 Prior to cell division, a mother cell has 6 chromosomes, 2 sets of 3 each.

4 Nucleus breaks apart, and replicated chromosomes condense in preparation for mitosis.

Two daughter cells form, each containing 6 chromosomes.

5 Sister chromatids separate during mitosis, and 2 cells are formed during cytokinesis.

Figure 15.2 **The eukaryotic cell cycle.** Dividing cells progress through a series of phases denoted G_1, S, G_2, and M. This diagram shows the progression of a cell through the cell cycle to produce two daughter cells. The original diploid cell had three pairs of chromosomes, for a total of six individual chromosomes. During S phase, these have replicated to yield 12 chromatids. After mitosis is complete, two daughter cells each contain six chromosomes. The width of the phases shown in this figure is not meant to reflect their actual length. G_1 is typically the longest phase of the cell cycle, whereas M phase is relatively short.

Concept check: *Which phases make up interphase?*

S Phase During the S phase, the chromosomes are replicated, which is discussed in Chapter 11. After replication, the two copies are still joined to each other and referred to as a pair of **sister chromatids** (Figure 15.3). When S phase is completed, a cell actually has twice as many chromatids as the number of chromosomes in the G_1 phase. For example, a human cell in the G_1 phase has 46 distinct chromosomes, whereas the same cell in G_2 would have 46 pairs of sister chromatids, for a total of 92 chromatids.

G_2 Phase During the G_2 phase, a cell synthesizes proteins that are necessary for chromosome sorting and cell division. This prepares the cell for the last phase of the cell cycle. Some cell growth may occur.

M Phase The first part of M phase is **mitosis**. The purpose of mitosis is to divide one cell nucleus into two nuclei, distributing the duplicated chromosomes so that each daughter cell will receive the same complement of chromosomes. As noted previously, a human cell in the G_2 phase has 92 chromatids, which are found in 46 pairs. During mitosis, these pairs of chromatids are separated and sorted so that each daughter cell will receive 46 chromosomes. Mitosis is the name given to this sorting process. In most cases, mitosis is followed by **cytokinesis**, which is the division of the cytoplasm to produce two distinct daughter cells.

The length of the cell cycle varies considerably among different cell types, ranging from several minutes in quickly growing embryos to several months in slow-growing adult cells.

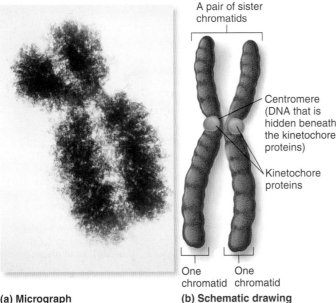

A pair of sister chromatids

Centromere (DNA that is hidden beneath the kinetochore proteins)

Kinetochore proteins

One chromatid   One chromatid

(a) Micrograph   **(b) Schematic drawing**

Figure 15.3 Sister chromatids. (a) After a chromosome replicates, the two copies remain attached to each other and are called sister chromatids. Sister chromatids are formed during S phase, but they do not become microscopically visible until later, when they become more compact during M phase. This micrograph shows a pair of sister chromatids during metaphase, which is a part of M phase. (b) A schematic drawing of sister chromatids. This structure has two chromatids that lie side-by-side. The two chromatids are held together by cohesin proteins (not shown in this drawing). The kinetochore is a group of proteins that are attached to the centromere and play a role during chromosome sorting.

Concept check: *In a human cell, how many total chromatids would you expect to find during metaphase?*

For fast-dividing mammalian cells in adults, the length of the cycle is typically 24 hours. The various phases within the cell cycle also vary in length. G_1 is often the longest and also the most variable phase, and M phase is the shortest. For a cell that divides in 24 hours, the following lengths of time for each phase are typical:

- G_1 phase: 11 hours
- S phase: 8 hours
- G_2 phase: 4 hours
- M phase: 1 hour

What factors determine whether or not a cell will divide? First, the determination to divide is based on external factors, such as environmental conditions and signaling molecules. The effects of growth factors on cell division are discussed in Chapter 9 (refer back to Figure 9.10). Second, internal controls affect cell division. These include cell cycle control molecules and checkpoints, as we will discuss next.

The Cell Cycle Is Controlled by Checkpoint Proteins

The progression through the cell cycle is a process that is highly regulated to ensure that the nuclear genome is intact and that the conditions are appropriate for a cell to divide. This is necessary to minimize the occurrence of mutations, which could have harmful effects and potentially lead to cancer. Proteins called **cyclins** and **cyclin-dependent kinases** (**cdks**) are responsible for advancing a cell through the phases of the cell cycle. Cyclins are so named because their amount varies throughout the cell cycle. To be active, the kinases controlling the cell cycle must bind to (are dependent on) a cyclin. The number of different types of cyclins and cdks varies from species to species.

Figure 15.4 gives a simplified description of how cyclins and cdks work together to advance a cell through G_1 and mitosis. During G_1, the amount of a particular cyclin termed G_1 cyclin increases. The G_1 cyclin binds to a cdk to form an activated G_1 cyclin/cdk complex. Once activated, cdk functions as a protein kinase that phosphorylates other proteins that are needed to advance the cell to the next phase in the cell cycle. For example, certain proteins involved with DNA synthesis are phosphorylated and activated, thereby allowing the cell to carry on events in S phase. When the cell passes into the S phase, G_1 cyclin is degraded. Similar events advance the cell through other phases of the cell cycle. A different cyclin, called mitotic cyclin, accumulates late in G_2. It binds to a cdk to form an activated mitotic cyclin/cdk complex. This complex phosphorylates proteins that are needed to advance into M phase.

Three critical regulatory points called **checkpoints** are found in the cell cycle of eukaryotic cells (Figure 15.4). At these checkpoints, a variety of proteins, referred to as checkpoint proteins, act as sensors to determine if a cell is in the proper condition to divide. The G_1 checkpoint, also called the **restriction point**, determines if conditions are favorable for cell division. In addition, G_1-checkpoint proteins can sense if the DNA has incurred damage. What happens if DNA damage is detected? The checkpoint proteins will prevent the formation of active cyclin/cdk complexes and thereby stop the progression of the cell cycle.

A second checkpoint exists in G_2. This checkpoint also checks the DNA for damage and ensures that all of the DNA has been replicated. In addition, the G_2 checkpoint monitors the levels of proteins that are needed to progress through M phase. A third checkpoint, called the metaphase checkpoint, senses the integrity of the spindle apparatus. As we will see later, the spindle apparatus is involved in chromosome sorting. Metaphase is a step in mitosis during which all of the chromosomes should be attached to the spindle apparatus. If a chromosome is not correctly attached, the metaphase checkpoint will stop the cell cycle. This checkpoint prevents cells from incorrectly sorting their chromosomes during division.

Checkpoint proteins delay the cell cycle until problems are fixed, or they even prevent cell division when problems cannot be fixed. A primary aim of checkpoint proteins is to prevent the division of a cell that may have incurred DNA damage or harbors abnormalities in chromosome number. As discussed in Chapter 14, when the functions of checkpoint genes are lost due to mutation, this increases the likelihood that undesirable genetic changes will occur that can cause additional mutations and cancerous growth.

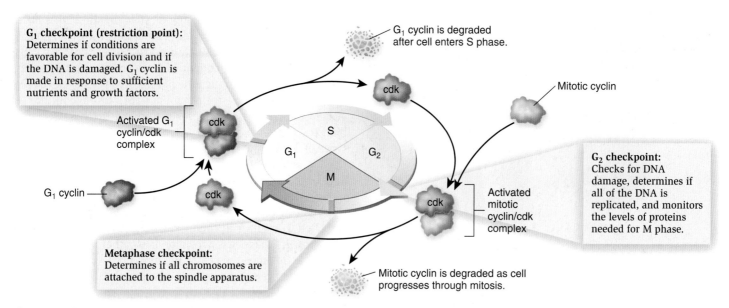

G₁ checkpoint (restriction point): Determines if conditions are favorable for cell division and if the DNA is damaged. G₁ cyclin is made in response to sufficient nutrients and growth factors.

G₁ cyclin is degraded after cell enters S phase.

Mitotic cyclin

Activated G₁ cyclin/cdk complex

G₁ cyclin

G₂ checkpoint: Checks for DNA damage, determines if all of the DNA is replicated, and monitors the levels of proteins needed for M phase.

Activated mitotic cyclin/cdk complex

Metaphase checkpoint: Determines if all chromosomes are attached to the spindle apparatus.

Mitotic cyclin is degraded as cell progresses through mitosis.

Figure 15.4 **Checkpoints in the cell cycle.** This is a general diagram of the eukaryotic cell cycle. Progression through the cell cycle requires the formation of activated cyclin/cdk complexes. Cells make different types of cyclin proteins, which are typically degraded after the cell has progressed to the next phase. The formation of activated cyclin/cdk complexes is regulated by checkpoint proteins.

Concept check: *Why is it beneficial for cells to have checkpoint proteins?*

FEATURE INVESTIGATION

Masui and Markert's Study of Oocyte Maturation Led to the Identification of Cyclins and Cyclin-Dependent Kinases

During the 1960s, researchers were intensely searching for the factors that promote cell division. In 1971, Yoshio Masui and Clement Markert developed a way to test whether a substance causes a cell to progress from one phase of the cell cycle to the next. They chose to study frog oocytes—cells that mature into egg cells. At the time of their work, researchers had already determined that frog oocytes naturally become dormant in the G₂ phase of the cell cycle for up to eight months (**Figure 15.5**). During mating season, female frogs produce a hormone called progesterone. After progesterone binds to receptors in dormant egg cells, they progress from G₂ to the beginning of M phase, where the chromosomes condense and become visible under the microscope. This phenomenon is called maturation. When a sperm fertilizes the egg, M phase is completed, and the zygote continues to undergo cellular divisions.

Because progesterone is a signaling molecule, Masui and Markert speculated that this hormone affects the functions and/or amounts of proteins that trigger the oocyte to progress through the cell cycle. To test this hypothesis, they developed the procedure described in **Figure 15.6**, using the oocytes of the leopard frog (*Rana pipiens*). They began by exposing oocytes to progesterone in vitro and then incubating these oocytes for 2 hours or 12 hours. As a control, they also used oocytes that had not been exposed to progesterone. These three types of cells were called the donor oocytes.

Next, they used a micropipette to transfer a small amount of cytosol from the three types of donor oocytes to recipient oocytes that had not been exposed to progesterone. As seen in the data, the recipient oocytes that had been injected with cytosol from the control donor oocytes or from oocytes that had been incubated with progesterone for only 2 hours did not progress to M phase. However, cytosol from donor oocytes that had been incubated with progesterone for 12 hours caused the recipient oocytes to advance to M phase. Masui and Markert concluded that a cytosolic factor, which required more than 2 hours to be synthesized after progesterone treatment, had been

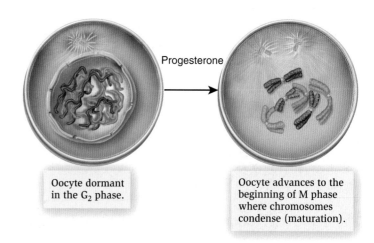

Progesterone

Oocyte dormant in the G₂ phase.

Oocyte advances to the beginning of M phase where chromosomes condense (maturation).

Figure 15.5 **Oocyte maturation in certain species of frogs.**

Figure 15.6   The experimental approach of Masui and Markert to identify cyclin and cyclin-dependent kinase (cdk).

HYPOTHESIS Progesterone induces the synthesis of a factor(s) that advances frog oocytes through the cell cycle from G_2 to M phase.

KEY MATERIALS Oocytes from *Rana pipiens*.

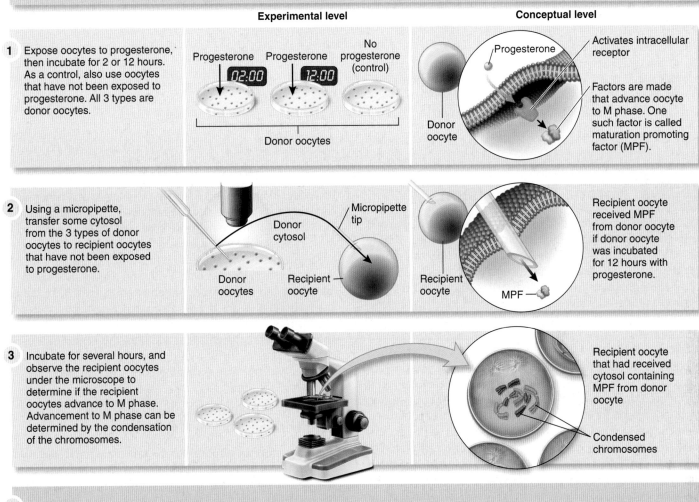

Experimental level   **Conceptual level**

1 Expose oocytes to progesterone, then incubate for 2 or 12 hours. As a control, also use oocytes that have not been exposed to progesterone. All 3 types are donor oocytes.

Progesterone   Progesterone   No progesterone (control)
02:00   12:00

Donor oocytes

Progesterone
Donor oocyte

Activates intracellular receptor

Factors are made that advance oocyte to M phase. One such factor is called maturation promoting factor (MPF).

2 Using a micropipette, transfer some cytosol from the 3 types of donor oocytes to recipient oocytes that have not been exposed to progesterone.

Donor cytosol
Micropipette tip
Donor oocytes   Recipient oocyte

Recipient oocyte   MPF

Recipient oocyte received MPF from donor oocyte if donor oocyte was incubated for 12 hours with progesterone.

3 Incubate for several hours, and observe the recipient oocytes under the microscope to determine if the recipient oocytes advance to M phase. Advancement to M phase can be determined by the condensation of the chromosomes.

Recipient oocyte that had received cytosol containing MPF from donor oocyte

Condensed chromosomes

4 THE DATA

Donor oocytes	Recipient oocytes proceeded to M phase?
Control, no progesterone exposure	No
Progesterone exposure, incubation for 2 hours	No
Progesterone exposure, incubation for 12 hours	Yes

5 CONCLUSION Exposure of oocytes to progesterone for 12 hours results in the synthesis of a factor(s) that advances frog oocytes through the cell cycle from G_2 to M phase.

6 SOURCE Masui, Y., and Markert, C.L. 1971. Cytoplasmic control of nuclear behavior during meiotic maturation of frog oocytes. *Journal of Experimental Zoology* 177:129–145.

transferred to the recipient oocytes and induced maturation. The factor that caused the oocytes to progress (or mature) from G_2 to M phase was originally called the **maturation promoting factor** (**MPF**).

After MPF was discovered in frogs, it was found in all eukaryotic species that researchers studied. MPF is important in the division of all types of cells, not just oocytes. It took another 17 years before Manfred Lohka, Marianne Hayes, and

James Maller were able to purify the components that make up MPF. This was a difficult undertaking because these components are found in very small amounts in the cytosol, and they are easily degraded during purification procedures. We now know that MPF is a complex made of a mitotic cyclin and a cyclin-dependent kinase (cdk), as described in Figure 15.4.

Experimental Questions

1. At the time of Masui and Markert's study shown in Figure 15.6, what was known about the effects of progesterone on oocytes?

2. What hypothesis did Masui and Markert propose to explain the function of progesterone? Explain the procedure used to test the hypothesis.

3. How did the researchers explain the difference between the results using 2-hour-exposed donor oocytes versus 12-hour-exposed donor oocytes?

15.2   Mitotic Cell Division

We now turn our attention to a mechanism of cell division and its relationship to chromosome replication and sorting. During the process of **mitotic cell division**, a cell divides to produce two new cells (the daughter cells) that are genetically identical to the original cell (the mother cell). Mitotic cell division involves mitosis—the division of one nucleus into two nuclei—and then cytokinesis in which the mother cell divides into two daughter cells.

Why is mitotic cell division important? One purpose is **asexual reproduction**. Certain unicellular eukaryotic organisms, such as baker's yeast (*Saccharomyces cerevisiae*) and the amoeba, increase their numbers in this manner. A second important reason for mitotic cell division is the production and maintenance of multicellularity. Organisms such as plants, animals, and most fungi are derived from a single cell that subsequently undergoes repeated cellular divisions to become a multicellular organism. Humans, for example, begin as a single fertilized egg and repeated mitotic cell divisions produce an adult with 10 to 50 trillion cells. As you might imagine, the precise transmission of chromosomes is critical during every cell division so that all cells of the body receive the correct amount of genetic material.

In this section, we will explore how the process of cell division requires the replication, organization, and sorting of chromosomes. We will also examine how a single cell is separated into two distinct cells by cytokinesis.

In Preparation for Cell Division, Eukaryotic Chromosomes Are Replicated and Compacted to Produce Pairs Called Sister Chromatids

As discussed earlier in Figure 15.1, eukaryotic chromosomes are found in sets, and many eukaryotic species are diploid. We will now turn our attention to how those chromosomes are replicated and sorted during cell division. Let's begin with the process of chromosome replication. In Chapter 11, we examined the molecular process of DNA replication. Figure 15.7 describes the process at the chromosomal level. Prior to DNA replication, the DNA of each eukaryotic chromosome consists of a linear DNA double helix that is found in the nucleus and is not highly compacted. When the DNA is replicated, two identical copies of the original double helix are produced. As discussed earlier, these copies, along with associated proteins, lie side-by-side and are termed sister chromatids. When a cell prepares to divide, the sister chromatids become highly compacted and readily visible under the microscope. As shown in Figure 15.7b, the two sister chromatids are tightly associated at a region called the **centromere**. A protein called cohesin is necessary to hold the sister chromatids together. In addition, the centromere serves as an attachment site for a group of proteins that form the **kinetochore**, which is necessary for sorting each chromosome.

The Mitotic Spindle Organizes and Sorts Chromosomes During Cell Division

What structure is responsible for organizing and sorting the chromosomes during cell division? The answer is the mitotic spindle apparatus, also known simply as the **mitotic spindle** (**Figure 15.8**). It is composed of microtubules—protein fibers that are components of the cytoskeleton (refer back to Table 4.1). In animal cells, microtubule growth and organization starts at two **centrosomes**, regions that are also referred to as microtubule organizing centers (MTOCs). A single centrosome duplicates during interphase. After they separate from each other during mitosis, each centrosome defines a **pole** of the spindle apparatus, one within each of the future daughter cells. The centrosome in animal cells has a pair of **centrioles**. However, centrioles are not found in many other eukaryotic species, such as plants, and are not required for spindle formation.

Each centrosome organizes the construction of the microtubules by rapidly polymerizing tubulin proteins. The three types of spindle microtubules are termed astral, polar, and kinetochore microtubules. The astral microtubules, which extend away from the chromosomes, are important for positioning the spindle apparatus within the cell. The polar microtubules, also called interpolar microtubules, project into the region between the two poles. Polar microtubules that overlap with each other play a role in the separation of the two poles. Finally, the

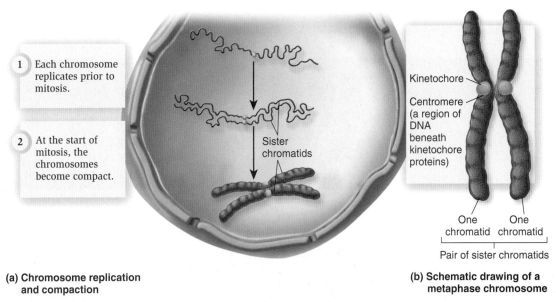

(a) Chromosome replication and compaction

(b) Schematic drawing of a metaphase chromosome

Figure 15.7 Replication and compaction of chromosomes into pairs of sister chromatids. (a) Chromosomal replication producing a pair of sister chromatids. While the chromosomes are elongated, they are replicated to produce two copies that are connected and lie parallel to each other. This is a pair of sister chromatids. Later, when the cell is preparing to divide, the sister chromatids condense into more compact structures that are easily seen with a light microscope. (b) A schematic drawing of a metaphase chromosome. This structure has two chromatids that lie side-by-side. The two chromatids are held together by cohesin proteins (not shown in this drawing). The kinetochore is a group of proteins that are attached to the centromere and play a role during chromosome sorting.

Concept check: *Look back at the karyotype in Figure 15.1. In this micrograph, is each of the 46 objects a pair of sister chromatids?*

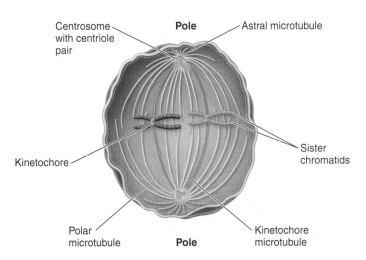

Figure 15.8 The structure of the mitotic spindle. The mitotic spindle in animal cells is formed by the centrosomes, which produce three types of microtubules. The astral microtubules emanate away from the region between the poles. The polar microtubules project into the region between the two poles. The kinetochore microtubules are attached to the kinetochores of sister chromatids. Note: For simplicity, this diagram just shows one pair of homologous chromosomes. Eukaryotic species typically have multiple chromosomes per set.

Concept check: *What are the functions of the three types of microtubules?*

kinetochore microtubules are attached to kinetochores, which are bound to the centromere of each chromosome.

The Transmission of Chromosomes Requires a Sorting Process Known as Mitosis

Mitosis is the sorting process to divide one cell nucleus into two nuclei. The duplicated chromosomes are distributed so that each daughter cell will receive the same complement of chromosomes. Mitosis was first observed microscopically in the 1870s by a German biologist, Walter Flemming, who coined the term mitosis (from the Greek *mitos*, meaning thread). He studied the large, transparent skin cells of salamander larvae as they were dividing and noticed that chromosomes are constructed of "threads" that are doubled in appearance along their length. These double threads divided and moved apart, one going to each of the two daughter nuclei. By this mechanism, Flemming pointed out, the two daughter cells receive an identical group of threads, the same as the number of threads in the mother cell.

Figure 15.9 depicts the process of mitosis in an animal cell, though the process is quite similar in a plant cell. Mitosis occurs as a continuum of phases known as prophase, prometaphase, metaphase, anaphase, and telophase. In the simplified diagrams shown along the bottom of Figure 15.9, the original mother cell contains six chromosomes. One set of chromosomes is depicted in red, whereas the homologous set is blue. These different colors represent maternal and paternal chromosomes.

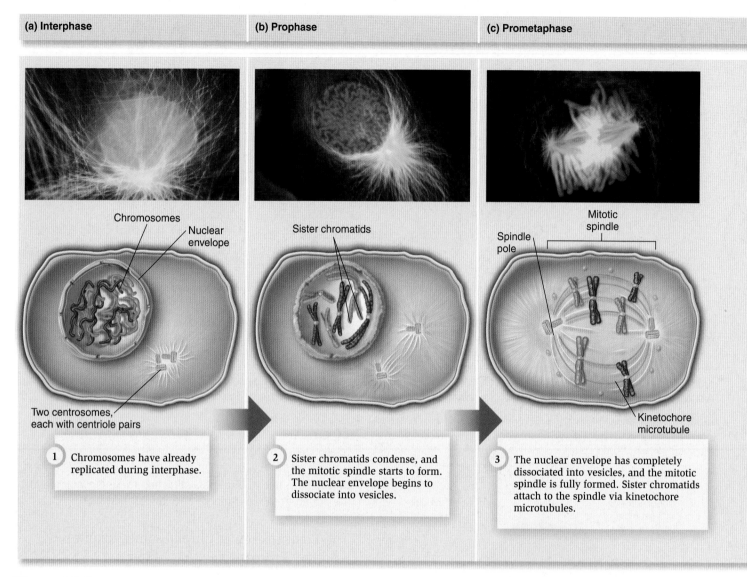

| (a) Interphase | (b) Prophase | (c) Prometaphase |

Figure 15.9 **The process of mitosis in an animal cell.** The top panels illustrate the cells of a newt progressing through mitosis. The bottom panels are schematic drawings that emphasize the sorting and separation of the chromosomes in which the diploid mother cell had six chromosomes (three in each set). At the start of mitosis, these have already replicated into 12 chromatids. The final result is two daughter cells, each containing six chromosomes.

Concept check: With regard to chromosome composition, how does the mother cell compare to the two daughter cells?

Interphase Prior to mitosis, the cells are in **interphase**. As discussed earlier, interphase includes the G_1, S, and G_2 phases of the cell cycle. During interphase, the chromosomes are decondensed and found in the nucleus (Figure 15.9a).

Prophase At the start of mitosis, in **prophase**, the chromosomes have already replicated to produce 12 chromatids, joined as six pairs of sister chromatids (Figure 15.9b). As prophase proceeds, the nuclear envelope begins to dissociate into small vesicles. At the same time, the chromatids condense into highly compacted structures that are readily visible by light microscopy.

Prometaphase The nuclear envelope completely fragments into small vesicles, and the mitotic spindle is fully formed

during **prometaphase** (Figure 15.9c). As mitosis progresses, the centrosomes move apart and demarcate the two poles. Once the nuclear envelope has dissociated, the spindle fibers can interact with the sister chromatids. How do the sister chromatids become attached to the spindle apparatus? Initially, microtubules are rapidly formed and can be seen under a microscope growing out from the two poles. As it grows, if a microtubule happens to make contact with a kinetochore, it is said to be "captured" and remains firmly attached to the kinetochore. Alternatively, if a microtubule does not collide with a kinetochore, the microtubule will eventually depolymerize and retract to the centrosome. This random process is how sister chromatids become attached to kinetochore microtubules. As the end of prometaphase nears, the two kinetochores on each pair of sister chromatids are attached to kinetochore microtubules

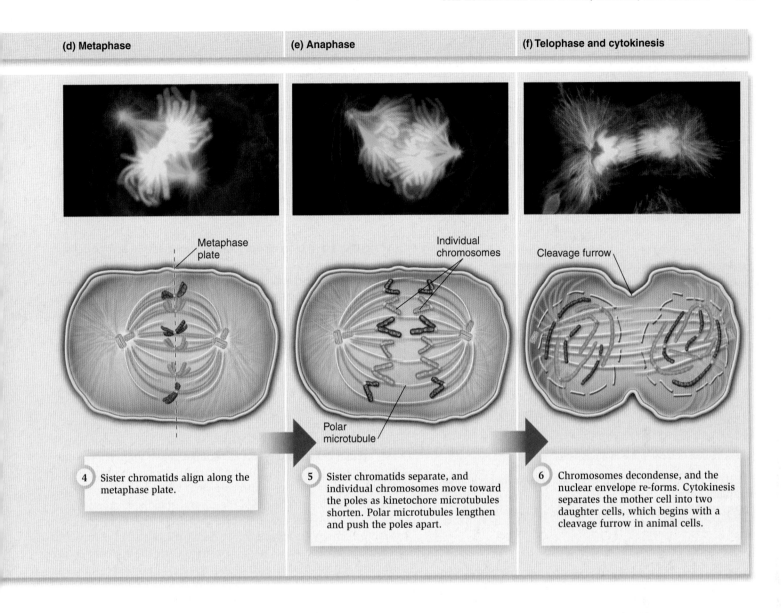

(d) Metaphase

(e) Anaphase

(f) Telophase and cytokinesis

Metaphase plate

Individual chromosomes

Cleavage furrow

Polar microtubule

4 Sister chromatids align along the metaphase plate.

5 Sister chromatids separate, and individual chromosomes move toward the poles as kinetochore microtubules shorten. Polar microtubules lengthen and push the poles apart.

6 Chromosomes decondense, and the nuclear envelope re-forms. Cytokinesis separates the mother cell into two daughter cells, which begins with a cleavage furrow in animal cells.

from opposite poles. As these events are occurring, the sister chromatids are seen under the microscope to undergo jerky movements as they are tugged, back and forth, between the two poles by the kinetochore microtubules.

Metaphase Eventually, the pairs of sister chromatids are aligned in a single row along the **metaphase plate**, a plane half-way between the poles. When this alignment is complete, the cell is in **metaphase** of mitosis (Figure 15.9d). The chromatids can then be equally distributed into two daughter cells.

Anaphase The next step in the sorting process occurs during **anaphase** (Figure 15.9e). At this phase, the connections between the pairs of sister chromatids are broken. Each chromatid, now an individual chromosome, is linked to only one of the two poles by one or more kinetochore microtubules. As anaphase proceeds, the kinetochore microtubules shorten, pulling the chromosomes toward the pole to which they are attached. In addition, the two poles move farther away from each other. This occurs because the overlapping polar micro-

tubules lengthen and push against each other, thereby pushing the poles farther apart.

Telophase During **telophase**, the chromosomes have reached their respective poles and decondense. The nuclear envelope now re-forms to produce two separate nuclei. In Figure 15.9f, two nuclei are being produced that contain six chromosomes each.

Cytokinesis In most cases, mitosis is quickly followed by cytokinesis, in which the two nuclei are segregated into separate daughter cells. While the phases of mitosis are similar between plant and animal cells, the process of cytokinesis is quite different. In animal cells, cytokinesis involves the formation of a **cleavage furrow**, which constricts like a drawstring to separate the cells (Figure 15.10a). In plants, vesicles from the Golgi apparatus move along microtubules to the center of the cell and coalesce to form a **cell plate** (Figure 15.10b), which then forms a cell wall between the two daughter cells.

What are the results of mitosis and cytokinesis? These processes ultimately produce two daughter cells having the same

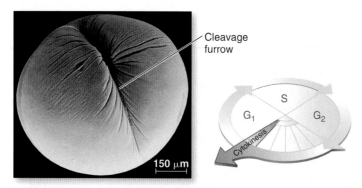

(a) Cleavage of an animal cell

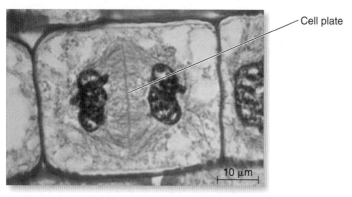

(b) Formation of a cell plate in a plant cell

Figure 15.10   Micrographs showing cytokinesis in animal and plant cells.

Concept check: *What are the similarities and differences between cytokinesis in animal and plant cells?*

number of chromosomes as the mother cell. Barring rare mutations, the two daughter cells are genetically identical to each other and to the mother cell from which they were derived. Thus, the critical consequence of this sorting process is to ensure genetic consistency from one cell to the next. The development of multicellularity relies on the repeated process of mitosis and cytokinesis. For diploid organisms that are multicellular, most of the somatic cells are diploid and genetically identical to each other.

Genomes & Proteomes Connection

The Genomes of Diverse Animal Species Encode Approximately 20 Proteins That Are Involved in Cytokinesis

To understand how a process works at the molecular and cellular level, researchers often try to identify the genes within a given species that encode proteins necessary for the process. Cytokinesis has been analyzed in this way. By comparing the results from vertebrates, insects, and worms, researchers have

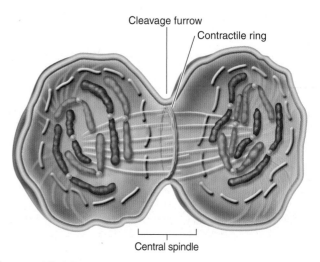

Figure 15.11   A closer look at cytokinesis in animal cells.

identified approximately 20 proteins that are involved with cytokinesis in nearly all animal cells. In any given species, cytokinesis may also involve additional proteins beyond these 20, but these other proteins are not needed among all animal species. Evolutionary biologists would say the 20 proteins that are common to all animals are highly conserved, meaning their structure and function has been retained during the evolution of animals. The 20 conserved proteins are likely to play the most fundamental roles in the process of cytokinesis.

What are the functions of these 20 proteins? To appreciate their functions, we need to take a closer look at cytokinesis in animal cells (**Figure 15.11**). Animal cells produce a contractile ring that is attached to the plasma membrane to create the cleavage furrow. The contractile ring, which encircles a region of the mitotic spindle called the central spindle, is a network of actin (a cytoskeletal protein) and myosin (a motor protein). The motor activity of myosin moves actin filaments in a way that causes the contractile ring to constrict. Once the contractile ring becomes very small, membrane vesicles are inserted into the constricted site to achieve division of the plasma membranes in the two resulting cells.

The 20 conserved proteins perform one of four possible functions.

1. Contractile ring: Seven proteins, including actin, myosin, and other proteins that regulate actin and myosin function, are necessary for the formation of the contractile ring.

2. Central spindle: Eight proteins are known to be components that bind to the central spindle and are necessary for cytokinesis.

3. Cell separation via membrane insertion: Two proteins are needed for the final separation of the two daughter cells.

4. RhoA pathway: Five proteins are components of a cell signal transduction pathway called the RhoA pathway. This pathway initiates the formation of the contractile ring.

The 20 conserved proteins should be considered a minimum estimate. As we gain a deeper understanding of cytokinesis at the molecular level, it is likely that additional proteins may be discovered.

15.3 Meiosis and Sexual Reproduction

We now turn our attention to sexual reproduction. As discussed earlier, a diploid cell contains two homologous sets of chromosomes, whereas a haploid cell contains a single set. For example, a diploid human cell contains 46 chromosomes, but a human gamete—sperm or egg cell—is a haploid cell that contains only 23 chromosomes, one from each of the 23 pairs. **Sexual reproduction** requires a **fertilization** event in which two haploid gametes unite to form a diploid cell called a **zygote**. For multicellular species such as animals and plants, the zygote then grows and divides by mitotic cell divisions into a multicellular organism with many diploid cells.

Meiosis is the process by which haploid cells are produced from a cell that was originally diploid. The term meiosis, which means "to make smaller," refers to the fewer chromosomes found in cells following this process. For this to occur, the chromosomes must be correctly sorted and distributed in a way that reduces the chromosome number to half its original diploid value. In the case of human gametes, for example, each gamete must receive half the total number of chromosomes, but not just any 23 chromosomes will do. A gamete must receive one chromosome from each of the 23 pairs. For this to happen, two rounds of divisions are necessary, termed meiosis I and meiosis II (**Figure 15.12**). When a cell begins meiosis, it contains chromosomes that are found in homologous pairs. When meiosis is completed, a single diploid cell with homologous pairs of chromosomes has produced four haploid cells.

In this section, we will examine the cellular events of meiosis that reduce the chromosome number from diploid to haploid. In addition, we will briefly consider how this process plays a role in the life cycles of animals, plants, fungi, and protists.

Bivalent Formation and Crossing Over Occurs at the Beginning of Meiosis

Like mitosis, meiosis begins after a cell has progressed through the G_1, S, and G_2 phases of the cell cycle. However, two key events occur at the beginning of meiosis that do not occur in mitosis. First, homologous pairs of sister chromatids associate with each other, lying side by side to form a **bivalent**, also called a **tetrad** (**Figure 15.13**). The process of forming a bivalent is termed **synapsis**. In most eukaryotic species, a protein structure called the synaptonemal complex connects homologous chromosomes during a portion of meiosis. However, the synaptonemal complex is not required for the pairing of homologous chromosomes because some species of fungi completely lack such a complex, yet their chromosomes associate with each other correctly. At present, the precise role of the synaptonemal complex is not clearly understood.

The second event that occurs at the beginning of meiosis, but not usually during mitosis, is **crossing over**, which involves a physical exchange between chromosome segments of the bivalent (Figure 15.13). As discussed in Chapter 17, crossing over

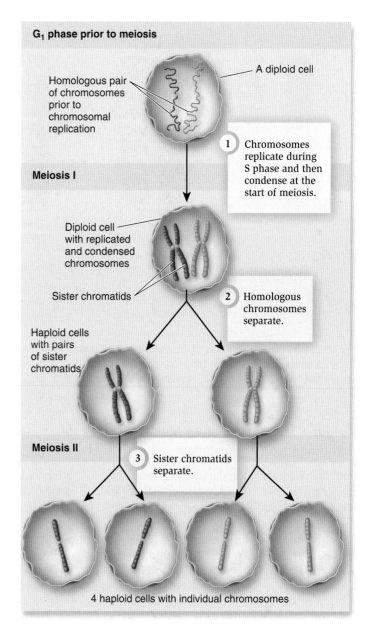

Figure 15.12 How the process of meiosis reduces chromosome number.   This simplified diagram emphasizes the reduction in chromosome number as a diploid cell divides by meiosis to produce four haploid cells.

may increase the genetic variation of a species. After crossing over occurs, the arms of the chromosomes tend to separate but remain adhered at a crossover site. This connection is called a **chiasma** (plural, chiasmata), because it physically resembles the Greek letter chi, χ. The number of crossovers is carefully controlled by cells and depends on the size of the chromosome and the species. The range of crossovers for eukaryotic chromosomes is typically one or two to a couple dozen. During the formation of sperm in humans, for example, an average chromosome undergoes slightly more than two crossovers, whereas chromosomes in certain plant species may undergo 20 or more crossovers.

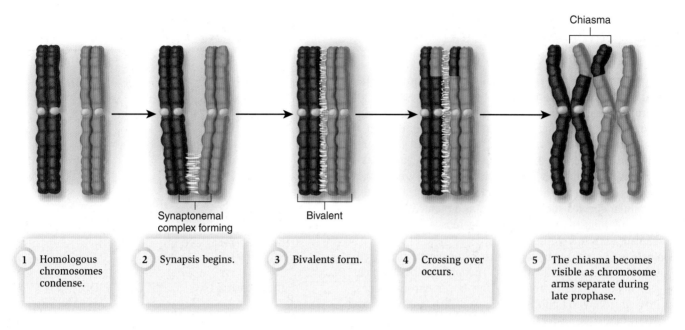

Chiasma

Synaptonemal
complex forming

Bivalent

| 1 | Homologous chromosomes condense. | 2 | Synapsis begins. | 3 | Bivalents form. | 4 | Crossing over occurs. | 5 | The chiasma becomes visible as chromosome arms separate during late prophase. |

Figure 15.13 **Formation of a bivalent and crossing over during meiosis I.** At the beginning of meiosis, homologous chromosomes pair with each other to form a bivalent, usually with a synaptonemal complex between them. Crossing over then occurs between homologous chromatids within the bivalent. During this process, homologues exchange segments of chromosomes.

The First Meiotic Division, Meiosis I, Separates Homologous Chromosomes

Now that we have an understanding of bivalent formation and crossing over, we are ready to consider the phases of meiosis (**Figure 15.14**, look two pages ahead to pp. 318 and 319). These simplified diagrams depict a diploid cell (2*n*) that contains a total of six chromosomes (as in our look at mitosis in Figure 15.9). Prior to meiosis, the chromosomes are replicated in S phase to produce pairs of sister chromatids. This single replication event is then followed by the sequential divisions called meiosis I and II. Like mitosis, each of these is a continuous series of stages called prophase, prometaphase, metaphase, anaphase, and telophase. The sorting that occurs during **meiosis I** separates homologues from each other (Figure 15.14).

Prophase I In prophase I, the replicated chromosomes condense, the homologous chromosomes form bivalents, and crossing over occurs. The nuclear envelope then starts to fragment into small vesicles.

Prometaphase I In prometaphase I, the nuclear envelope is completely broken down into vesicles, and the spindle apparatus is entirely formed. The sister chromatids are attached to kinetochore microtubules. However, a key difference occurs between mitosis and meiosis. In mitosis, a pair of sister chromatids is attached to both poles (see Figure 15.9c). In meiosis, a pair of sister chromatids is attached to just one pole via kinetochore microtubules (Figure 15.14b).

Metaphase I At metaphase I, the bivalents are organized along the metaphase plate. Notice how this pattern of alignment is strikingly different from that observed during mitosis (see Figure 15.9d). In particular, the sister chromatids are aligned in a double row rather than a single row (as in mitosis). Furthermore, the arrangement of sister chromatids within this double row is random with regard to the (red and blue) homologues. In Figure 15.14c, one of the red homologues is to the left of the metaphase plate, and the other two are to the right, while two of the blue homologues are to the left of the metaphase plate and the other one is to the right. In other cells, homologues could be arranged differently along the metaphase plate (for example, three blues to the left and none to the right, or none to the left and three to the right).

Because eukaryotic species typically have many chromosomes per set, homologues can be randomly aligned along the metaphase plate in a variety of ways. For example, consider that humans have 23 chromosomes per set. The possible number of different, random alignments equals 2^n, where n equals the number of chromosomes per set. Thus, in humans, this equals 2^{23}, or over 8 million possibilities. Because the homologues are genetically similar but not identical, we see from this calculation that the random alignment of homologous chromosomes provides a mechanism to promote a vast amount of genetic diversity among the resulting haploid cells. When meiosis is complete, it is very unlikely that any two human gametes will have the same combination of homologous chromosomes.

Anaphase I The segregation of homologues occurs during anaphase I (Figure 15.14d). The connections between bivalents break, but not the connections that hold sister chromatids together. Each joined pair of chromatids migrates to one pole, and the homologous pair of chromatids moves to the opposite pole, both pulled by kinetochore microtubules.

Telophase I At telophase I, the sister chromatids have reached their respective poles, and they then decondense. The nuclear envelope now re-forms to produce two separate nuclei.

If we consider the end result of meiosis I, we see that two nuclei are produced, each with three pairs of sister chromatids; this is called a reduction division. The original diploid cell had its chromosomes in homologous pairs, whereas the two cells produced as a result of meiosis I and cytokinesis are considered haploid—they do not have pairs of homologous chromosomes.

The Second Meiotic Division, Meiosis II, Separates Sister Chromatids

Meiosis I is followed by cytokinesis and then **meiosis II** (see Figure 15.14). An S phase does not occur between meiosis I and meiosis II. The sorting events of meiosis II are similar to those of mitosis, but the starting point is different. For a diploid cell with six chromosomes, mitosis begins with 12 chromatids that are joined as six pairs of sister chromatids (see Figure 15.9). By comparison, the two cells that begin meiosis II each have six chromatids that are joined as three pairs of sister chromatids. Otherwise, the steps that occur during prophase, prometaphase, metaphase, anaphase, and telophase of meiosis II are analogous to a mitotic division. Sister chromatids are separated during anaphase II, unlike anaphase I in which bivalents are separated.

Changes in a Few Key Steps in Mitosis and Meiosis Account for the Different Outcomes of These Two Processes

How are the outcomes of mitosis and meiosis different from each other? Mitosis produces two diploid daughter cells that are genetically identical. In our example shown in Figure 15.9, the

starting cell had six chromosomes (three homologous pairs of chromosomes), and both daughter cells had copies of the same six chromosomes. By comparison, meiosis reduces the number of sets of chromosomes. In the example shown in Figure 15.14, the starting cell also had six chromosomes, whereas the four daughter cells had only three chromosomes. However, the daughter cells did not contain a random mix of three chromosomes. Each haploid daughter cell contained one complete set of chromosomes, whereas the original diploid mother cell had two complete sets.

How do we explain the different outcomes of mitosis and meiosis? **Table 15.1** emphasizes the differences between certain key steps in mitosis and meiosis that account for the different outcomes of these two processes. During prophase of meiosis I, the homologues synapse to form bivalents. This explains why crossing over occurs commonly during meiosis, but rarely during mitosis. During prometaphase of mitosis and meiosis II, pairs of sister chromatids are attached to both poles. In contrast, during meiosis I, each pair of sister chromatids (within a bivalent) is attached to a single pole. This affects their alignment during metaphase. Bivalents align along the metaphase plate during metaphase of meiosis I, whereas sister chromatids align along the metaphase plate during metaphase of mitosis and meiosis II. At anaphase of meiosis I, the homologous chromosomes separate, while the sister chromatids remain together. In contrast, sister chromatid separation occurs during anaphase of mitosis and meiosis II. Taken together, the steps of mitosis produce two diploid cells, whereas the steps of meiosis involve two sequential cell divisions that produce four haploid cells.

Sexually Reproducing Species Produce Haploid and Diploid Cells at Different Times in Their Life Cycles

Let's now turn our attention to the relationship between mitosis, meiosis, and sexual reproduction in animals, plants, fungi, and protists. For any given species, the sequence of events that produces another generation of organisms is known as a **life cycle**. For sexually reproducing organisms, this usually involves

Table 15.1	A Comparison of Mitosis, Meiosis I, and Meiosis II		
Event	**Mitosis**	**Meiosis I**	**Meiosis II**
Synapsis during prophase:	No	Yes, bivalents are formed.	No
Crossing over during prophase:	Rarely	Commonly	Rarely
Attachment to poles at prometaphase:	A pair of sister chromatids is attached to kinetochore microtubules from both poles.	A pair of sister chromatids is attached to kinetochore microtubules from just one pole.	A pair of sister chromatids is attached to kinetochore microtubules from both poles.
Alignment along the metaphase plate:	Sister chromatids align.	Bivalents align.	Sister chromatids align.
Type of separation at anaphase:	Sister chromatids separate. A single chromatid, now called a chromosome, moves to each pole.	Homologous chromosomes separate. A pair of sister chromatids moves to each pole.	Sister chromatids separate. A single chromatid, now called a chromosome, moves to each pole.
End result when the mother cell is diploid:	Two daughter cells that are diploid	—	Four daughter cells that are haploid

Meiosis I

(a) Prophase I	(b) Prometaphase I	(c) Metaphase I

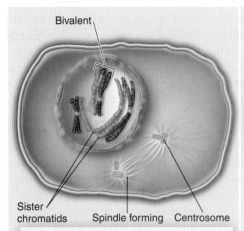 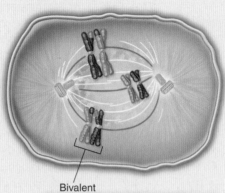 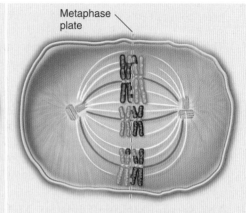

Bivalent

Sister chromatids   Spindle forming   Centrosome

Bivalent

Metaphase plate

1 Homologous chromosomes synapse to form bivalents, and crossing over occurs. Chromosomes condense, and the nuclear envelope begins to dissociate into vesicles.

2 The nuclear envelope completely dissociates into vesicles, and bivalents become attached to kinetochore microtubules.

3 Bivalents randomly align along the metaphase plate.

Meiosis II

(f) Prophase II	(g) Prometaphase II	(h) Metaphase II

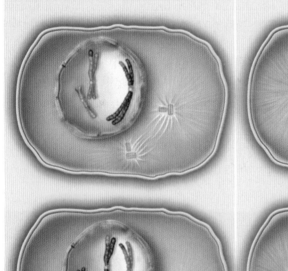 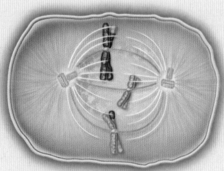 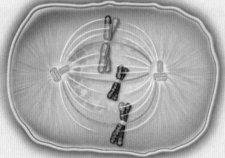

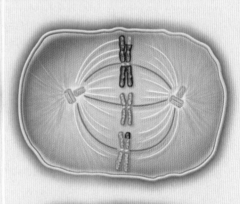 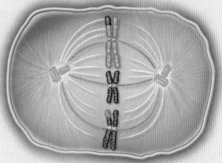

6 Sister chromatids condense, and the spindle starts to form. The nuclear envelope begins to dissociate into vesicles.

7 The nuclear envelope completely dissociates into vesicles. Sister chromatids attach to the spindle via kinetochore microtubules.

8 Sister chromatids align along the metaphase plate.

(d) Anaphase I

4 Homologous chromosomes separate and move toward opposite poles.

(e) Telophase I **and cytokinesis**

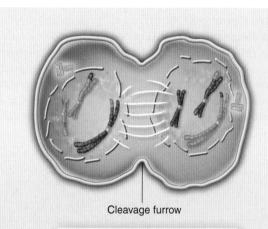

Cleavage furrow

5 The chromosomes decondense, and the nuclear envelope re-forms. The 2 daughter cells are separated by a cleavage furrow.

(i) Anaphase II

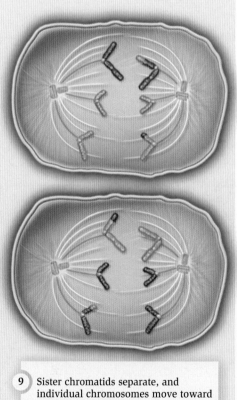

9 Sister chromatids separate, and individual chromosomes move toward the poles as kinetochore microtubules shorten. Polar microtubules lengthen and push the poles apart.

(j) Telophase II **and cytokinesis**

Four haploid cells

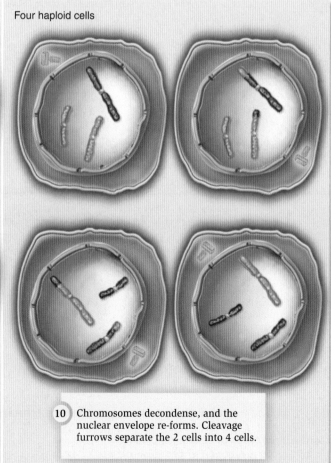

10 Chromosomes decondense, and the nuclear envelope re-forms. Cleavage furrows separate the 2 cells into 4 cells.

Figure 15.14 The phases of meiosis in an animal cell.

Concept check:
Relative to the original mother cell, what is the end result of meiosis?

an alternation between haploid cells or organisms and diploid cells or organisms (Figure 15.15).

Most species of animals are diploid, and their haploid gametes are considered to be a specialized type of cell. For this reason, animals are viewed as **diploid-dominant species** (Figure 15.15a). Certain diploid cells in the testes or ovaries undergo meiosis to produce haploid sperm or eggs, respectively. During fertilization, sperm and egg unite to form a diploid zygote, which then undergoes repeated mitotic cell divisions to produce a diploid multicellular organism.

By comparison, most fungi and some protists are just the opposite; they are **haploid-dominant species** (Figure 15.15b). In fungi, the multicellular organism is haploid ($1n$). Haploid fungal cells are most commonly produced by mitosis. During sexual reproduction, haploid cells unite to form a diploid zygote, which then immediately proceeds through meiosis to produce four haploid cells called spores. Each spore goes through mitotic cellular divisions to produce a haploid multicellular organism.

Plants and some algae have life cycles that are intermediate between the extreme cases of diploid or haploid dominance. Such

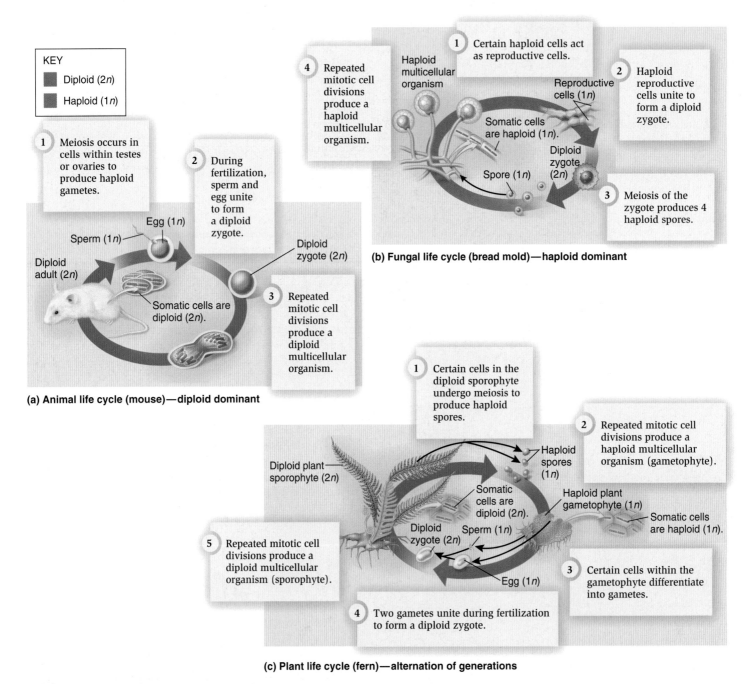

(a) Animal life cycle (mouse)—diploid dominant

(b) Fungal life cycle (bread mold)—haploid dominant

(c) Plant life cycle (fern)—alternation of generations

Figure 15.15 A comparison of three types of sexual life cycles.

Concept check: *What is the main reason for meiosis in animals? What is the main reason for mitosis in animals?*

species exhibit an **alternation of generations** (Figure 15.15c). The species alternate between diploid multicellular organisms called **sporophytes**, and haploid multicellular organisms called **gametophytes**. Meiosis in certain cells within the sporophyte produces haploid spores, which divide by mitosis to produce the gametophyte. Particular cells within the gametophyte differentiate into haploid gametes. Fertilization occurs between two gametes, producing a diploid zygote that then undergoes repeated mitotic cell divisions to produce a sporophyte.

Among different plant species, the relative sizes of the haploid and diploid organisms vary greatly. In mosses, the haploid gametophyte is a visible multicellular organism, whereas the diploid sporophyte is smaller and survives within the haploid organism. In other plants, such as ferns (Figure 15.15c), both the diploid sporophyte and haploid gametophyte can grow independently. The sporophyte is considerably larger and is the organism we commonly think of as a fern. In seed-bearing plants, such as roses and oak trees, the diploid sporophyte is the large multicellular plant, whereas the gametophyte is composed of only a few cells and is formed within the sporophyte.

When comparing animals, plants, and fungi, it's interesting to consider how gametes are made. Animals produce gametes by meiosis. In contrast, plants and fungi produce reproductive cells by mitosis. The gametophyte of plants is a haploid multicellular organism that is created by mitotic cellular divisions of a haploid spore. Within the multicellular gametophyte, certain cells become specialized as gametes.

15.4 Variation in Chromosome Structure and Number

In the previous sections of this chapter, we have examined two important features of chromosomes. First, we considered how chromosomes occur in sets, and second, we explored two sorting processes that determine the chromosome number following cell division. In this section, we will examine how the structures and numbers of chromosomes can vary between different species and within the same species.

Why is the study of chromosomal variation important? First, geneticists have discovered that variations in chromosome structure and number can have major effects on the characteristics of an organism. For example, we now know that several human genetic diseases are caused by such changes. In addition, changes in chromosome structure and number have been an important force in the evolution of new species, which is a topic we will consider in Chapter 25.

Chromosome variation can be viewed in two ways. On relatively rare occasions, the structure or number of chromosomes changes so that an individual is different from most other members of the same species. This is generally viewed as an abnormality. Alternatively, the structure and number of chromosomes among different species tend to show wide variation, which is normal. In this section, we will examine both abnormal and normal types of variation. Let's begin with natural (normal) variation.

Natural Variation Exists in Chromosome Structure and Number

Before we begin to examine chromosome variation, we need to have a reference point for a normal set of chromosomes. To determine what the normal chromosomes of a species look like, a cytogeneticist microscopically examines the chromosomes from several members of the species. Chromosome composition within a given species tends to remain relatively constant. In most cases, normal individuals of the same species will have the same number and types of chromosomes. For example, as mentioned previously, the normal chromosome composition of human cells is two sets of 23 chromosomes, for a total of 46. Other diploid species may have different numbers of chromosomes. The dog has 78 chromosomes (39 per set), the fruit fly has 8 chromosomes (4 per set), and the tomato has 24 chromosomes (12 per set). When comparing distantly related species, such as humans and fruit flies, major differences in chromosomal composition are observed.

The chromosomes of a given species can also vary considerably in size and shape. Cytogeneticists have various ways to classify and identify chromosomes in their metaphase form. The three most commonly used features are size, location of the centromere, and banding patterns that are revealed when the chromosomes are treated with stains. Based on centromere location, each chromosome is classified as **metacentric** (near the middle), **submetacentric** (off center), **acrocentric** (near one end), or **telocentric** (at the end) (Figure 15.16). Because the centromere is not exactly in the center of a chromosome, each chromosome has a short arm and a long arm. The short arm is designated with the letter p (for the French *petite*), while the long arm is designated with the letter q. In the case of telocentric chromosomes, the short arm may be nearly nonexistent. When preparing a karyotype, the chromosomes are aligned with the short arms on top and the long arms on the bottom.

Because different chromosomes often have similar sizes and centromeric locations, cytogeneticists must use additional methods to accurately identify each type of chromosome within a karyotype. For detailed identification, chromosomes are treated with stains to produce characteristic banding patterns. Cytogeneticists use several different staining procedures to identify specific chromosomes. An example is Giemsa stain, which produces G banding (see Figure 15.1). The alternating pattern of G bands is unique for each type of chromosome.

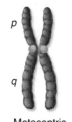
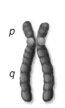

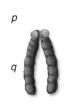

Metacentric   Submetacentric   Acrocentric   Telocentric

Figure 15.16 A comparison of centromeric locations among metaphase chromosomes.

The banding pattern of eukaryotic chromosomes is useful in two ways. First, individual chromosomes can be distinguished from each other, even if they have similar sizes and centromeric locations. Also, banding patterns are used to detect changes in chromosome structure that occur as a result of mutation.

Mutations Can Alter Chromosome Structure

Let's now consider how the structures of chromosomes can be modified by a mutation, a heritable change in the genetic material. Chromosomal mutations are categorized as deletions, duplications, inversions, and translocations (**Figure 15.17**).

Deletions and duplications are changes in the total amount of genetic material in a single chromosome. When a **deletion** occurs, a segment of chromosomal material is missing. In other words, the affected chromosome is deficient in a significant amount of genetic material. In a **duplication**, a section of a chromosome occurs two or more times in a row.

What are the consequences of a deletion or duplication? Their possible effects depend on their size and whether they include genes or portions of genes that are vital to the development of the organism. When deletions or duplications have an effect, they are usually detrimental. Larger changes in the amount of genetic material tend to be more harmful because more genes are missing or duplicated.

Inversions and translocations are chromosomal rearrangements. An **inversion** is a change in the direction of the genetic material along a single chromosome. When a segment of one chromosome has been inverted, the order of G bands is opposite to that of a normal chromosome (see Figure 15.17c). A **translocation** occurs when one segment of a chromosome becomes attached to a different chromosome. In a **simple translocation**, a single piece of chromosome is attached to another chromosome. In a **reciprocal translocation**, two different types of chromosomes exchange pieces, thereby producing two abnormal chromosomes carrying translocations (see Figure 15.17d).

Variation Occurs in the Number of Chromosome Sets and the Number of Individual Chromosomes

Variations in chromosome number can be categorized in two ways: variation in the number of sets of chromosomes and variation in the number of particular chromosomes within a set. The suffix -ploid or -ploidy refers to a complete set of chromosomes. Organisms that are **euploid** (the prefix eu- means true) have chromosomes that occur in one or more complete sets. For example, in a species that is diploid, a euploid organism would have two sets of chromosomes in its somatic cells. In *Drosophila melanogaster*, for example, a normal individual has eight chromosomes. The species is diploid, having two sets of four chromosomes each (**Figure 15.18a**). Organisms can vary with regard to the number of sets of chromosomes they have. For example, on rare occasions, an abnormal fruit fly can be produced with 12 chromosomes, containing three sets of 4 chromosomes each (**Figure 15.18b**). Organisms with three or more sets of chromosomes are called **polyploid**. A diploid

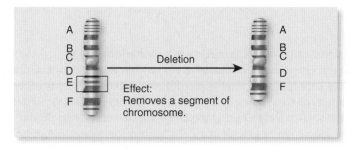

(a) Deletion

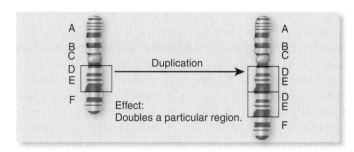

(b) Duplication

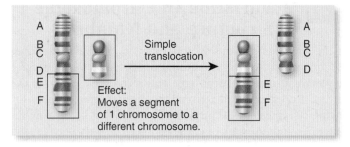

(c) Inversion

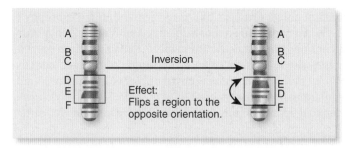

(d) Simple translocation

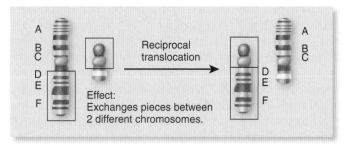

(e) Reciprocal translocation

Figure 15.17 Types of changes in chromosome structure. The letters alongside the chromosomes are placed there as frames of reference.

Concept check: *Which types of changes shown here do not affect the total amount of genetic material?*

organism is referred to as $2n$, a **triploid** organism as $3n$, a **tetraploid** organism as $4n$, and so forth. All such organisms are euploid.

A second way that chromosome number can vary is a phenomenon called **aneuploidy**. This refers to an alteration in the number of particular chromosomes, so the total number of chromosomes is not an exact multiple of a set. For example, an abnormal fruit fly could contain nine chromosomes instead of eight because it had three copies of chromosome 2 instead of the normal two copies (**Figure 15.18c**). Such an animal is said to have trisomy 2 or to be **trisomic**. Instead of being perfectly diploid, a trisomic animal is $2n + 1$. By comparison, a fruit fly could be lacking a single chromosome, such as chromosome 3, and contain a total of seven chromosomes ($2n - 1$). This animal is **monosomic** and would be described as having monosomy 3.

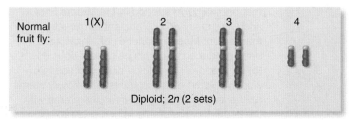

(a) Normal fruit fly chromosome composition

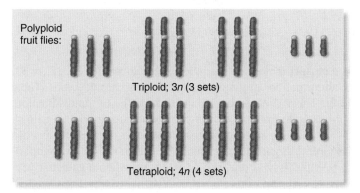

(b) Polyploidy

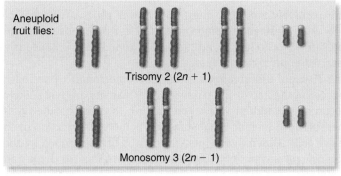

(c) Aneuploidy

Figure 15.18 Types of variation in chromosome number.
(a) The normal diploid number of chromosomes in *Drosophila*. The X chromosome is also called chromosome 1. Examples of chromosomes of **(b)** polyploid flies and **(c)** aneuploid flies.

Variations in chromosome number are fairly widespread and have a significant impact on the characteristics of plants and animals. For these reasons, researchers have wanted to understand the mechanisms that cause these variations. In some cases, a change in chromosome number is the result of the abnormal sorting of chromosomes during cell division. The term **nondisjunction** refers to an event in which the chromosomes do not separate properly during cell division. Nondisjunction can occur during meiosis I or meiosis II and produces haploid cells that have too many or too few chromosomes. If such a cell becomes a gamete that fuses with a another gamete during fertilization, the zygote and the resulting organism will have an abnormal number of chromosomes in all of its cells.

Changes in Chromosome Number Have Important Consequences

How do changes in chromosome number affect the characteristics of animals and plants? In many cases, animals do not tolerate deviations from diploidy well. For example, polyploidy in mammals is generally a lethal condition. However, a few cases of naturally occurring variations from diploidy do occur in animals. Male bees, which are called drones, contain a single set of chromosomes and are therefore haploid. They are produced from unfertilized eggs. By comparison, fertilized eggs become female bees, which are diploid. A few examples of vertebrate polyploid animals have been discovered. Interestingly, on rare occasions, animals that are morphologically very similar to each other can be found as a diploid species as well as a separate polyploid species. This situation occurs among certain amphibians and reptiles. **Figure 15.19** shows photographs of a diploid and a tetraploid frog. As you can see, they look very similar to each other. Their differences in chromosome number can be revealed only by a microscopic examination of the chromosomes in the somatic cells of the animals.

In contrast to animals, plants commonly exhibit polyploidy. Among ferns and flowering plants, about 30–35% of species are polyploid. Polyploidy is also important in agriculture. In many instances, polyploid strains of plants display characteristics that are helpful to humans. They are often larger in size and more robust. These traits are clearly advantageous in the production of food. Many of the fruits and grains we eat are produced from polyploid plants. For example, the species of wheat that we use to make bread, *Triticum aestivum*, is a hexaploid (containing six sets of chromosomes) that arose from the union of diploid genomes from three closely related species (**Figure 15.20a**). During the course of its cultivation, two diploid species must have interbred to produce a tetraploid, and then a third species interbred with the tetraploid to produce a hexaploid. Plant polyploids tend to exhibit a greater adaptability, which allows them to withstand harsher environmental conditions. Polyploid ornamental plants commonly produce larger flowers than their diploid counterparts (**Figure 15.20b**).

Although polyploidy is often beneficial in plants, aneuploidy in all eukaryotic species usually has detrimental consequences on the characteristics of an organism. Why is aneuploidy usually

(a) *Hyla chrysoscelis* (diploid)

(b) *Hyla versicolor* (tetraploid)

Figure 15.19 Differences in chromosome number in two closely related frog species. The frog in **(a)** is diploid, whereas the frog in **(b)** is tetraploid. These frogs are in the act of performing their mating calls, which is why the skin under their mouths is protruding as a large bubble.

(a) Wheat, *Triticum aestivum* (hexaploid)

(b) Diploid daylily (left) and tetraploid daylily (right)

Figure 15.20 Examples of polyploid plants. **(a)** Cultivated wheat, *Triticum aestivum*, is a hexaploid. It was derived from three different diploid species of grasses that originally were found in the Middle East and were cultivated by ancient farmers in that region. Modern varieties of wheat have been produced from this hexaploid species. **(b)** Differences in euploidy exist in these two closely related daylily species. The flower stems on the left are diploid, whereas the stems with the larger flowers on the right are tetraploid.

detrimental? To answer this question, we need to consider the relationship between gene expression and chromosome number. For many, but not all genes, the level of gene expression is correlated with the number of genes per cell. Compared to a diploid cell, if a gene is carried on a chromosome that is present in three copies instead of two, approximately 150% of the normal amount of gene product will be made. Alternatively, if only one copy of that gene is present due to a missing chromosome, only 50% of the gene product is usually made. For some genes, producing too much or too little of the gene product may not have adverse effects. However, for other genes, the over- or underexpression may interfere with the proper functioning of cells.

One important reason that geneticists are so interested in aneuploidy is its relationship to certain inherited disorders in humans. Even though most people are born with a normal number of chromosomes, alterations in chromosome number occur at a surprising frequency during gamete formation. About 5–10% of all fertilized human eggs result in an embryo with an abnormality in chromosome number. In most cases, these abnormal embryos do not develop properly and result in a spontaneous abortion very early in pregnancy. Approximately 50% of all spontaneous abortions are due to alterations in chromosome number.

In some cases, an abnormality in chromosome number produces an offspring that can survive. Several human disorders are the result of abnormalities in chromosome number.

The most common are trisomies of chromosomes 21, 18, or 13, or abnormalities in the number of the sex chromosomes (**Table 15.2**). These syndromes are most likely due to nondisjunction. For example, Turner syndrome (XO) may occur when a gamete that is lacking a sex chromosome due to nondisjunction has fused with a gamete carrying an X chromosome. By comparison, Triple X syndrome (XXX) can occur when a gamete carrying two X chromosomes fuses with a gamete carrying a single X chromosome.

Most of the known trisomies involve chromosomes that are relatively small, so they carry fewer genes. Trisomies of the other human chromosomes and most monosomies are presumed to be lethal and have been found in spontaneously aborted embryos and fetuses.

Human abnormalities in chromosome number are influenced by the age of the parents. Older parents are more likely to produce children with abnormalities in chromosome number, because meiotic nondisjunction is more likely to occur in older cells. **Down syndrome**, which was first described by the English physician John Langdon Down in 1866, provides an example. This disorder is caused by the inheritance of three copies of chromosome 21 (Table 15.2). The incidence of Down syndrome rises with the age of either parent. In males, however, the rise occurs relatively late in life, usually past the age when most men have children. By comparison, the likelihood of having a child with Down syndrome rises dramatically during the later reproductive ages of women.

Table 15.2		Aneuploid Conditions in Humans	
Condition	Frequency (# of live births)	Syndrome	Characteristics
Autosomal			
Trisomy 21	1/800	Down	Mental impairment, abnormal pattern of palm creases, slanted eyes, flattened face, short stature
Trisomy 18	1/6,000	Edward	Mental and physical impairment, facial abnormalities, extreme muscle tone, early death
Trisomy 13	1/15,000	Patau	Mental and physical impairment, wide variety of defects in organs, large triangular nose, early death
Sex chromosomal			
XXY	1/1,000 (males)	Klinefelter	Sexual immaturity (no sperm), breast swelling (males)
XYY	1/1,000 (males)	Jacobs	Tall
XXX	1/1,500 (females)	Triple X	Tall and thin, menstrual irregularity
XO	1/5,000 (females)	Turner	Short stature, webbed neck, sexually undeveloped

▌ Summary of Key Concepts

15.1 The Eukaryotic Cell Cycle

- Cytogeneticists examine cells microscopically to determine their chromosome composition. A micrograph that shows the alignment of chromosomes from a given cell is called a karyotype. Eukaryotic chromosomes are inherited in sets. A diploid cell has two sets of chromosomes. The members of each pair are called homologues. (Figure 15.1)

- Haploid cells, such as sperm and egg, have one set of chromosomes.

- The eukaryotic cell cycle consists of four phases called G_1 (first gap), S (synthesis of DNA), G_2 (second gap), and M phase (mitosis and cytokinesis). The G_1, S, and G_2 phases are collectively known as interphase. (Figure 15.2)

- Once a cell passes a restriction point in G_1, it is destined to replicate its DNA and to divide. During S phase, chromosomes are replicated and form pairs of sister chromatids. (Figure 15.3)

- An interaction between cyclin and cyclin-dependent kinase is necessary for cells to progress through the cell cycle. Checkpoint proteins sense the environmental conditions and the integrity of the genome and control whether or not the cell progresses through the cell cycle. (Figure 15.4)

- Masui and Markert studied the maturation of frog oocytes to identify a substance that was necessary for oocytes to progress through the cell cycle. This substance was initially called maturation promoting factor (MPF) and was later identified as a complex of mitotic cyclin and cyclin-dependent kinase. (Figures 15.5, 15.6)

15.2 Mitotic Cell Division

- The process of mitosis involves the sorting of chromosomes to produce two nuclei with the same number and types of chromosomes.

- During S phase, eukaryotic chromosomes are replicated to produce a pair of identical sister chromatids that remain attached to each other. (Figure 15.7)

- The mitotic spindle is composed of astral, kinetochore, and polar microtubules. The spindle organizes the process of cell division and plays a central role in chromosome sorting. (Figure 15.8)

- Mitosis occurs in five phases called prophase, prometaphase, metaphase, anaphase, and telophase. During prophase, the chromosomes condense, and the nuclear envelope begins to dissociate. The spindle apparatus is completely formed by the end of prometaphase. During metaphase, the chromosomes are aligned in a single row along the metaphase plate. At anaphase, the sister chromatids separate from each other and move to opposite poles; the poles themselves also move farther apart. During telophase, the chromosomes decondense, and the nuclear envelope re-forms. (Figure 15.9)

- Cytokinesis, which occurs after mitosis, is the division of the cytoplasm to produce two distinct daughter cells. In animal cells, cytokinesis involves the formation of a cleavage furrow. In plant cells, two separate cells are produced by the formation of a cell plate. Among all animals, 20 different proteins are required for cytokinesis to occur. (Figures 15.10, 15.11)

15.3 Meiosis and Sexual Reproduction

- The process of meiosis begins with a diploid cell and produces four haploid cells with one set of chromosomes each. (Figure 15.12)

- During prophase of meiosis, homologous pairs of sister chromosomes synapse, and crossing over occurs. After crossing over, chiasmata—the site where crossing over occurs—become visible. (Figure 15.13)

- Meiosis consists of two divisions, meiosis I and II, each composed of prophase, prometaphase, metaphase, anaphase, and telophase. During meiosis I, the homologues are separated to different cells, and during meiosis II, the sister chromatids are separated to different cells. (Figure 15.14, Table 15.1)

- The life cycle of animals is diploid dominant, whereas most fungi and some protists show a haploid-dominant life cycle. Plants alternate between diploid and haploid forms. (Figure 15.15)

15.4 Variation in Chromosome Structure and Number

- Chromosomes are named metacentric, submetacentric, acrocentric, and telocentric, according to their centromere location. Each type of chromosome can be uniquely identified by its banding pattern after staining. (Figure 15.16)

- Deletions, duplications, inversions, and translocations are different ways in which mutations alter chromosome structure. (Figure 15.17)

- A euploid organism has chromosomes that occur in complete sets. A polyploid organism has three or more sets of chromosomes. An organism that has one too many (trisomy) or one too few (monosomy) chromosomes is termed aneuploid. (Figure 15.18)

- Polyploid animals are relatively rare, but polyploid plants are common and tend to be more robust than their diploid counterparts. (Figures 15.19, 15.20)

- Aneuploidy in humans is responsible for several types of human genetic diseases, including Down syndrome. (Table 15.2)

Assess and Discuss

Test Yourself

1. In which phase of the cell cycle are chromosomes replicated?
   a. G_1 phase
   b. S phase
   c. M phase
   d. G_2 phase
   e. none of the above

2. If two chromosomes are homologous, they
   a. look similar under the microscope.
   b. have very similar DNA sequences.
   c. carry the same types of genes.
   d. may carry different versions of the same gene.
   e. are all of the above.

3. Checkpoints during the cell cycle are important because they
   a. allow the organelle activity to catch up to cellular demands.
   b. ensure the integrity of the cell's DNA.
   c. allow the cell to generate sufficient ATP for cellular division.
   d. are the only time DNA replication can occur.
   e. do all of the above.

4. Which of the following is a reason for mitotic cell division?
   a. asexual reproduction
   b. gamete formation in animals
   c. multicellularity
   d. all of the above
   e. both a and c

5. A replicated chromosome is composed of
   a. two homologous chromosomes held together at the centromere.
   b. four sister chromatids held together at the centromere.
   c. two sister chromatids held together at the centromere.
   d. four homologous chromosomes held together at the centromere.
   e. one chromosome with a centromere.

6. Which of the following is not an event of anaphase of mitosis?
   a. The nuclear envelope breaks down.
   b. Sister chromatids separate.
   c. Kinetochore microtubules shorten, pulling the chromosomes to the pole.
   d. Polar microtubules push against each other, moving the poles farther apart.
   e. All of the above occur during anaphase.

7. A student is looking at cells under the microscope. The cells are from an organism that has a diploid number of 14. In one particular case, the cell has seven replicated chromosomes (sister chromatids) aligned at the metaphase plate of the cell. Which of the following statements accurately describes this particular cell?
   a. The cell is in metaphase of mitosis.
   b. The cell is in metaphase of meiosis I.
   c. The cell is in metaphase of meiosis II.
   d. All of the above are correct.
   e. Both b and c are correct.

8. Which of the following statements accurately describes a difference between mitosis and meiosis?
   a. Mitosis may produce diploid cells, whereas meiosis produces haploid cells.
   b. Homologous chromosomes synapse during meiosis but do not synapse during mitosis.
   c. Crossing over commonly occurs during meiosis, but it does not commonly occur during mitosis.
   d. All of the above are correct.
   e. Both a and c are correct.

9. During crossing over in meiosis I,
   a. homologous chromosomes are not altered.
   b. homologous chromosomes exchange genetic material.
   c. chromosomal damage occurs.
   d. genetic information is lost.
   e. cytokinesis occurs.

10. Aneuploidy may be the result of
    a. duplication of a region of a chromosome.
    b. inversion of a region of a chromosome.
    c. nondisjunction during meiosis.
    d. interspecies breeding.
    e. all of the above.

Conceptual Questions

1. Distinguish between homologous chromosomes and sister chromatids.

2. The *Oca2* gene, which influences eye color in humans, is found on chromosome 15. How many copies of this gene are found in the karyotype of Figure 15.1? Is it one, two, or four?

3. A diploid cell carries four chromosomes per set. During meiosis I, it undergoes nondisjunction such that one cell receives two copies of chromosome 3 while the other cell receives zero. At the end of meiosis, how many total chromosomes will be found in each of the four resulting cells?

Collaborative Questions

1. Why is it necessary that the chromosomes condense during mitosis and meiosis? What do you think might happen if the chromosomes were not condensed?

2. A diploid eukaryotic cell has 10 chromosomes (five per set). As a group, take turns having one student draw the cell as it would look during a phase of mitosis, meiosis I, or meiosis II; then have the other students guess which phase it is.

Online Resource

www.brookerbiology.com

Stay a step ahead in your studies with animations that bring concepts to life and practice tests to assess your understanding. Your instructor may also recommend the interactive ebook, individualized learning tools, and more.

Simple Patterns of Inheritance

16

Ntombi knew she looked different as long as she can remember. Born in Nigeria in 1991, she has accepted her appearance, though she still finds the occasional stare from strangers to be disturbing. Ntombi has albinism, a disorder characterized by a total or a partial lack of pigmentation of the skin, hair, and eyes. As a result, she has very fair skin, blond hair, and blue eyes.[1] In contrast, her parents and three brothers have dark skin, black hair, and brown eyes, as do most of her relatives and most of the people in the city where she lives. Ntombi is very close to her aunt, who also has albinism.

Cases like Ntombi's have intrigued people for many centuries. How do we explain the traits that are found in people, plants, and other organisms? Can we predict what types of offspring that two parents will produce? To answer such questions, researchers have studied the traits among related individuals and tried to make some sense of the data. Their goal is to understand **inheritance**—the acquisition of traits by their transmission from parent to offspring.

The first systematic attempt to understand inheritance was carried out by the plant breeder Joseph Kolreuter between 1761 and 1766. In crosses between two strains of tobacco plants, Kolreuter found that the offspring were usually intermediate in appearance between the two parents. He concluded that parents make equal genetic contributions to their offspring and that their genetic material blends together as it is passed to the next generation. This interpretation was consistent with the concept known as **blending inheritance**, which was widely accepted at that time. In the late 1700s, Jean Baptiste Lamarck, a French naturalist, hypothesized that physiological events (such as use or disuse) could modify traits and such modified traits would be inherited by offspring. For example, an individual who became adept at archery would pass that skill to his or her offspring. Overall, the prevailing view prior to the 1800s was that hereditary traits were rather malleable and could change and blend over the course of one or two generations.

In contrast, microscopic observations of chromosome transmission during mitosis and meiosis in the second half of the 19th century provided compelling evidence for **particulate inheritance**—the idea that the determinants of hereditary traits are transmitted in

An African girl with albinism. This condition results in very light skin and hair color.

discrete units or particles from one generation to the next. Remarkably, this idea was first put forward in the 1860s by a researcher who knew nothing about chromosomes (**Figure 16.1**). Gregor Mendel, remembered today as the "father of genetics," used statistical

Figure 16.1 Gregor Johann Mendel, the father of genetics.

---

[1] In contrast to popular belief, most people with albinism have blue eyes, not pink eyes. This is particularly the case among Africans with albinism.

analysis of carefully designed breeding experiments to arrive at the concept of a gene, which is broadly defined as a unit of heredity. Forty years later, through the convergence of Mendel's work and that of cell biologists, this concept became the foundation of the modern science of genetics.

In this chapter, we will consider inheritance patterns and how the transmission of genes is related to the transmission of chromosomes. We will first consider the fundamental genetic patterns known as Mendelian inheritance and the relationship of these patterns to the behavior of chromosomes during meiosis. We will then examine the distinctive inheritance patterns of genes located on the X chromosome, paying special attention to the work of Thomas Hunt Morgan, whose investigation of these patterns confirmed that genes are on chromosomes. Finally, we will discuss the molecular basis of Mendelian inheritance and its variations, and consider how probability calculations can be used to predict the outcome of crosses.

16.1 Mendel's Laws of Inheritance

Gregor Johann Mendel grew up on a small farm in northern Moravia, then a part of the Austrian Empire and now in the Czech Republic. At the age of 21, he entered the Augustinian monastery of St. Thomas in Brno, and was ordained a priest in 1847. Mendel then worked for a short time as a substitute teacher, but to continue teaching he needed a license. Surprisingly, he failed the licensing exam due to poor answers in physics and natural history, so he enrolled at the University of Vienna to expand his knowledge in these two areas. Mendel's training in physics and mathematics taught him to perceive the world as an orderly place, governed by natural laws that could be stated as simple mathematical relationships.

In 1856, Mendel began his historic studies on pea plants. For 8 years, he analyzed thousands of pea plants that he grew on a small plot in his monastery garden. He published his work, entitled "Experiments on Plant Hybrids," in 1866. This paper was largely ignored by scientists at that time, partly because of its title and because it was published in a rather obscure journal (*The Proceedings of the Brünn Society of Natural History*). Also, Mendel was clearly ahead of his time. During this period, biology had not become a quantitative, experimental science. In addition, the behavior of chromosomes during mitosis and meiosis, which provides a framework for understanding inheritance patterns, had yet to be studied. Prior to his death in 1884, Mendel reflected, "My scientific work has brought me a great deal of satisfaction and I am convinced it will be appreciated before long by the whole world." Sixteen years later, in 1900, Mendel's work was independently rediscovered by three biologists with an interest in plant genetics: Hugo de Vries of Holland, Carl Correns of Germany, and Erich von Tschermak of Austria. Within a few years, the impact of Mendel's studies was felt around the world.

In this section, we will examine Mendel's experiments and how they led to the formulation of the basic genetic principles known as Mendel's laws. We will see that these principles apply not only to the pea plants Mendel studied, but also to a wide variety of sexually reproducing organisms, including humans.

Mendel Chose the Garden Pea to Study Inheritance

When two individuals with different characteristics are mated or crossed to each other, this is called a **hybridization** experiment, and the offspring are referred to as hybrids. For example, a hybridization experiment could involve a cross between a purple-flowered plant and a white-flowered plant. Mendel was particularly intrigued by the consistency with which offspring of such crosses showed characteristics of one or the other parent in successive generations. His intellectual foundation in physics and the natural sciences led him to consider that this regularity might be rooted in natural laws that could be expressed mathematically. To uncover these laws, he carried out quantitative experiments in which he carefully analyzed the numbers of offspring carrying specific traits.

Mendel chose the garden pea, *Pisum sativum*, to investigate the natural laws that govern inheritance. Why did he choose this species? Several properties of the garden pea were particularly advantageous for studying inheritance. First, it was available in many varieties that differed in characteristics, such as the appearance of seeds, pods, flowers, and stems. Such general features of an organism are called **characters**. Figure 16.2 illustrates the seven characters that Mendel eventually chose to follow in his breeding experiments. Each of these characters was found in two discrete variants. For example, one character he followed was height, which had the variants known as tall and dwarf. Another was seed color, which had the variants yellow and green. A **trait** is an identifiable characteristic of an organism. The term trait usually refers to a variant.* For example, yellow seed color is a trait.

A second important feature of garden peas is they are normally self-fertilizing. In **self-fertilization**, a female gamete is fertilized by a male gamete from the same plant. Like many flowering plants, peas have male and female sex organs in the same flower (Figure 16.3). Male gametes (sperm cells) are produced within pollen grains, which are formed in structures called stamens. Female gametes (egg cells) are produced in structures called ovules, which form within an organ called an ovary. For fertilization to occur, a pollen grain must land on the receptacle called a stigma, enabling a sperm to migrate to an ovule and fuse with an egg cell. In peas, the stamens and the ovaries are enclosed by a modified petal, an arrangement that greatly favors self-fertilization. Self-fertilization makes it easy to produce plants that breed true for a given trait, meaning the trait does not vary from generation to generation. For example, if a pea plant with yellow seeds breeds true for seed color, all the plants that grow from these seeds will also produce yellow seeds. A variety that continues to exhibit the same trait after several generations of self-fertilization is called a **true-breeding line**. Prior to conducting the studies described in this chapter, Mendel had already established that the seven characters he

---

* Geneticists may also use the term trait to refer to a character.

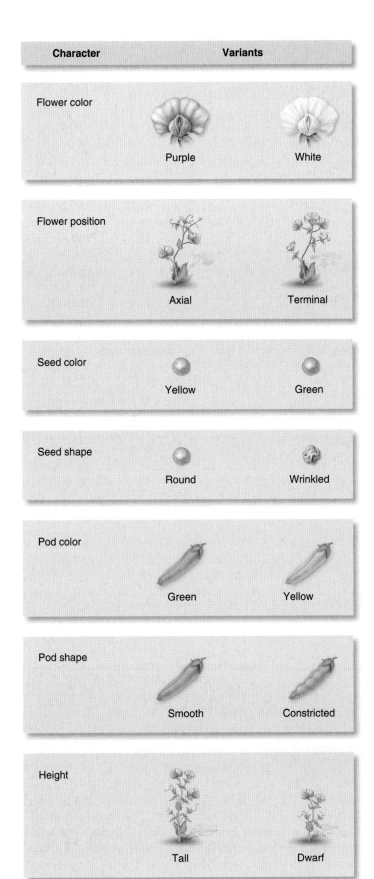

Character	Variants	
Flower color	Purple	White
Flower position	Axial	Terminal
Seed color	Yellow	Green
Seed shape	Round	Wrinkled
Pod color	Green	Yellow
Pod shape	Smooth	Constricted
Height	Tall	Dwarf

Figure 16.2 The seven characters that Mendel studied.

Concept check: Is having blue eyes a character, a variant, or both?

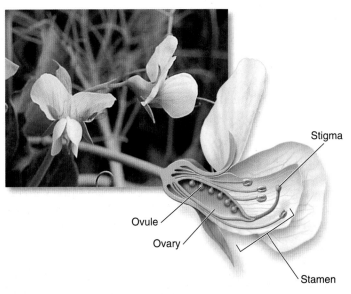

Figure 16.3 **Flower structure in pea plants.** The pea flower produces both male and female gametes. Sperm form in the pollen produced within the stamens; egg cells form in ovules within the ovary. A modified petal encloses the stamens and stigma, encouraging self-fertilization.

chose to study were true-breeding in the strains of pea plants he had obtained.

A third reason for using garden peas in hybridization experiments is the ease of making crosses: The flowers are quite large and easy to manipulate. In some cases, Mendel wanted his pea plants to self-fertilize, but in others, he did not want his plants to self-fertilize. Rather, he wanted to cross plants that differed with respect to some character, a process called hybridization, or **cross-fertilization**. In garden peas, cross-fertilization requires placing pollen from one plant onto the stigma of a flower on a different plant. Mendel's cross-fertilization procedure is shown in Figure 16.4. He would pry open an immature flower and remove the stamens before they produced pollen, so the flower could not self-fertilize. He then used a paintbrush to

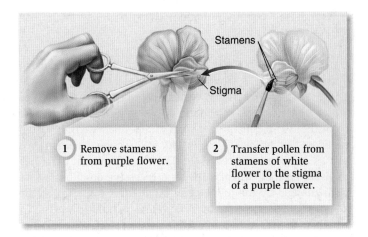

1 Remove stamens from purple flower.

2 Transfer pollen from stamens of white flower to the stigma of a purple flower.

Figure 16.4 A procedure for cross-fertilizing pea plants.

Concept check: Why are the stamens removed from the purple flower?

transfer pollen from another plant to the stigma of the flower that had its stamens removed. In this way, Mendel was able to cross-fertilize any two of his true-breeding pea plants and obtain any type of hybrid he wanted.

By Following the Inheritance Pattern of Single Traits, Mendel's Work Revealed the Law of Segregation

Mendel began his investigations by studying the inheritance patterns of pea plants that differed with regard to a single character. A cross in which an experimenter follows the variants of only one character is called a **monohybrid cross**, or **single-factor cross**. As an example, we will consider a monohybrid cross in which Mendel followed the tall and dwarf variants for height (**Figure 16.5**). The left-hand side of Figure 16.5a shows his experimental approach. The true-breeding parents are termed the **P generation** (parental generation), and a cross of these plants is called a P cross. The first-generation offspring of a P cross constitute the **F₁ generation** (first filial generation, from the Latin *filius*, meaning son). When the true-breeding parents differ with regard to a single character, their F₁ offspring are called single-trait hybrids, or **monohybrids**. When Mendel crossed true-breeding tall and dwarf plants, he observed that all plants of the F₁ generation were tall.

Next, Mendel followed the transmission of this character for a second generation. To do so, he allowed the F₁ monohybrids to self-fertilize, producing a generation called the **F₂ generation** (second filial generation). The dwarf trait reappeared in the F₂ offspring: Three-fourths of the plants were tall and one-fourth were dwarf. Mendel obtained similar results for each of the seven characters he studied, as shown in the data of Figure 16.5b. A quantitative analysis of his data allowed Mendel to postulate three important ideas regarding the properties and transmission of these traits from parents to offspring: (1) traits exist in two forms: dominant and recessive; (2) an individual carries two genes for a given character, and genes have variant forms, which are called alleles; and (3) the two alleles of a gene separate during gamete formation so that each sperm and egg receives only one allele.

Dominant and Recessive Traits   Perhaps the most surprising outcome of Mendel's work was that the data argued strongly against the prevailing notion of blending inheritance. In each of the seven cases, the F₁ generation displayed a trait distinctly like one of the two parents rather than an intermediate trait. Using genetic terms that Mendel originated, we describe the alternative traits as dominant and recessive. The term **dominant** describes the displayed trait, whereas the term **recessive** describes a trait that is masked by the presence of a dominant trait. Tall stems and purple flowers are examples of dominant traits; dwarf stems and white flowers are examples of recessive traits. We say that tall is dominant over dwarf, and purple is dominant over white.

Genes and Alleles   Mendel's results were consistent with particulate inheritance, in which the determinants of traits

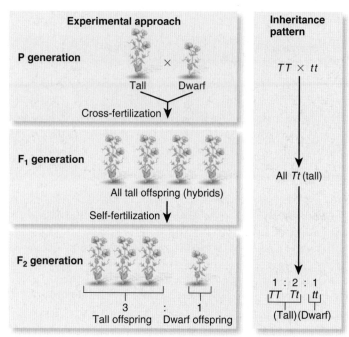

(a) **Mendel's protocol for making monohybrid crosses**

THE DATA			
P cross	**F₁ generation**	**F₂ generation**	**Ratio**
Purple × white flowers	All purple	705 purple, 224 white	3.15:1
Axial × terminal flowers	All axial	651 axial, 207 terminal	3.14:1
Yellow × green seeds	All yellow	6,022 yellow, 2,001 green	3.01:1
Round × wrinkled seeds	All round	5,474 round, 1,850 wrinkled	2.96:1
Green × yellow pods	All green	428 green, 152 yellow	2.82:1
Smooth × constricted pods	All smooth	882 smooth, 299 constricted	2.95:1
Tall × dwarf stem	All tall	787 tall, 277 dwarf	2.84:1
Total	**All dominant**	**14,949 dominant, 5,010 recessive**	**2.98:1**

(b) **Mendel's observed data for all 7 traits**

Figure 16.5   Mendel's analyses of monohybrid crosses.

Concept check: *Why do offspring of the F₁ generation exhibit only one variant of each character?*

are inherited as unchanging, discrete units. In all seven cases, the recessive trait reappeared in the F₂ generation: Some F₂ plants displayed the dominant trait, while a smaller proportion showed the recessive trait. This observation led Mendel to conclude that the genetic determinants of traits are "unit factors" that are passed intact from generation to generation. These unit factors are what we now call **genes** (from the Greek *genos*, meaning birth), a term coined by the Danish botanist Wilhelm Johannsen in 1909. Mendel postulated that every individual carries two genes for a given character and that the gene for each character in his pea plant exists in two variant forms, which we now call **alleles**. For example, the gene controlling height in Mendel's pea plants occurs in two variants, called the tall allele and the dwarf allele. The right-hand side of Figure 16.5a shows Mendel's conclusions, using genetic symbols (letters) that were adopted later. The letters T and t represent the alleles of the gene for plant height. By convention, the uppercase letter represents the dominant allele (in this case, tall), and the same letter in lowercase represents the recessive allele (dwarf).

Segregation of Alleles   When Mendel compared the numbers of F_2 offspring exhibiting dominant and recessive traits, he noticed a recurring pattern. Although some experimental variation occurred, he always observed an approximately 3:1 ratio between the dominant and the recessive trait (Figure 16.5b). How did Mendel interpret this ratio? He concluded that each parent carries two versions (alleles) of a gene and that the two alleles carried by an F_1 plant will **segregate** (separate) from each other during gamete formation, so each sperm or egg carries only one allele. The diagram in **Figure 16.6** shows that the segregation of the F_1 alleles should result in equal numbers of gametes carrying the dominant allele (T) and the recessive allele (t). If these gametes combine with one another randomly at fertilization, as shown in the figure, this would account for the 3:1 ratio of the F_2 generation. Note that a Tt individual can be produced by two different combinations of alleles—the T allele can come from the male gamete and the t allele from the female gamete, or vice versa. This accounts for the observation that the Tt genotype is produced twice as often as either TT or tt. The idea that *the two alleles of a gene separate (segregate) during the formation of eggs and sperm so that every gamete receives only one allele* is known today as Mendel's **law of segregation**.

Genotype Describes an Organism's Genetic Makeup, Whereas Phenotype Describes Its Characteristics

To continue our discussion of Mendel's results, we need to introduce a few more genetic terms. The term **genotype** refers to the genetic composition of an individual. In the example shown in Figure 16.5a, TT and tt are the genotypes of the P generation, and Tt is the genotype of the F_1 generation. In the P generation, both parents are true-breeding plants, which means that each have identical copies of the allele of the gene for height. An individual with two identical alleles of a gene is said to be **homozygous** with respect to that gene. In the specific P cross we are considering, the tall plant is homozygous for T, and the dwarf plant is homozygous for t. In contrast, a **heterozygous** individual carries two different alleles of a gene. Plants of the F_1 generation are heterozygous, with the genotype Tt, because every individual carries one copy of the tall allele (T) and one copy of the dwarf allele (t). The F_2 generation includes both homozygous individuals (homozygotes) and heterozygous individuals (heterozygotes).

The term **phenotype** refers to the characteristics of an organism that are the result of the expression of its genes. In

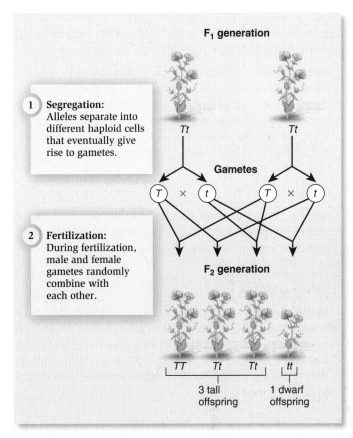

Figure 16.6   How the law of segregation explains Mendel's observed ratios.   The segregation of alleles in the F_1 generation gives rise to gametes that carry just one of the two alleles. These gametes combine randomly during fertilization, producing the allele combinations TT, Tt, and tt in the F_2 offspring. The combination Tt occurs twice as often as either of the other two combinations because it can be produced in two different ways. The TT and Tt offspring are tall, whereas the tt offspring are dwarf.

Concept check: *What is ratio of the T allele to the t allele in the F_2 generation? Does this ratio differ from the 3:1 phenotype ratio? If so, explain why.*

the example in Figure 16.5a, one of the parent plants is phenotypically tall, and the other is phenotypically dwarf. Although the F_1 offspring are heterozygous (Tt), they are phenotypically tall because each of them has a copy of the dominant tall allele. In contrast, the F_2 plants display both phenotypes in a ratio of 3:1. Later in the chapter, we will examine the underlying molecular mechanisms that produce phenotypes, but in our discussion of Mendel's results, the term simply refers to a visible characteristic such as flower color or height.

A Punnett Square Can Be Used to Predict the Outcome of Crosses

A common way to predict the outcome of simple genetic crosses is to make a **Punnett square**, a method originally proposed by the British geneticist Reginald Punnett. To construct a

Punnett square, you must know the genotypes of the parents. What follows is a step-by-step description of the Punnett square approach, using a cross of heterozygous tall plants.

Step 1. *Write down the genotypes of both parents.* In this example, a heterozygous tall plant is crossed to another heterozygous tall plant. The plant providing the pollen is considered the male parent and the plant providing the eggs, the female parent. (In self-pollination, a single individual produces both types of gametes.)

Male parent: *Tt*
Female parent: *Tt*

Step 2. *Write down the possible gametes that each parent can make.* Remember the law of segregation tells us that a gamete contains only one copy of each allele.

Male gametes: *T* or *t*
Female gametes: *T* or *t*

Step 3. *Create an empty Punnett square.* The number of columns equals the number of male gametes, and the number of rows equals the number of female gametes. Our example has two rows and two columns. Place the male gametes across the top of the Punnett square and the female gametes along the side.

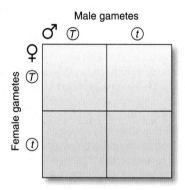

Step 4. *Fill in the possible genotypes of the offspring by combining the alleles of the gametes in the empty boxes.*

Male gametes

Step 5. *Determine the relative proportions of genotypes and phenotypes of the offspring.* The genotypes are obtained directly from the Punnett square. In this example, the genotypic ratios are 1*TT* : 2*Tt* : 1*tt*. To determine the phenotypes,

you must know which allele is dominant. For plant height, *T* (tall) is dominant to *t* (dwarf). The genotypes *TT* and *Tt* are tall, whereas the genotype *tt* is dwarf. Therefore, our Punnett square shows us that the phenotypic ratio is expected to be 3 tall : 1 dwarf. Keep in mind, however, these are predicted ratios for large numbers of offspring. If only a few offspring are produced, the observed ratios could deviate significantly from the predicted ratios. We will examine the topics of sample size and genetic prediction later in this chapter.

A Testcross Can Be Used to Determine an Individual's Genotype

When a character has two variants, one of which is dominant over the other, we know that an individual with a recessive phenotype is homozygous for the recessive allele. A dwarf pea plant, for example, must have the genotype *tt*. But an individual with a dominant phenotype may be either homozygous or heterozygous—a tall pea plant may have the genotype *TT* or *Tt*. How can we distinguish between these two possibilities? Mendel devised a method called a **testcross** to address this question. In a testcross, the researcher crosses the individual of interest to a homozygous recessive individual and observes the phenotypes of the offspring.

Figure 16.7 shows how this procedure can be used to determine the genotype of a tall pea plant. If the testcross produces some dwarf offspring, as shown in the Punnett square on the right side, these offspring must have two copies of the recessive allele, one inherited from each parent. Therefore, the tall parent must be a heterozygote, with the genotype *Tt*. Alternatively, if all of the offspring are tall, as shown in the Punnett square on the left, the tall parent is likely to be a homozygote, with the genotype *TT*.

Analyzing the Inheritance Pattern of Two Characters Demonstrated the Law of Independent Assortment

Mendel's analysis of single-factor crosses suggested that traits are inherited as discrete units and that the alleles for a given gene segregate during the formation of haploid cells. To obtain additional insights into how genes are transmitted from parents to offspring, Mendel conducted crosses in which he simultaneously followed the inheritance of two different characters. A cross of this type is called a **dihybrid cross**, or a **two-factor cross**. We will examine a two-factor cross in which Mendel simultaneously followed the inheritance of seed color and seed shape (Figure 16.8). He began by crossing strains of pea plants that bred true for both characters. The plants of one strain had yellow, round seeds, and plants of the other strain had green, wrinkled seeds. He then allowed the F₁ offspring to self-fertilize and observed the phenotypes of the F₂ generation.

What are the possible patterns of inheritance for two characters? One possibility is that the two genes are linked in some way, so variants that occur together in the parents are always

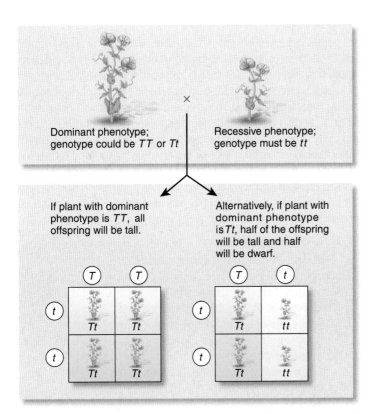

Figure 16.7 **A testcross.** The purpose of this experiment is to determine if the organism with the dominant phenotype, in this case a tall pea plant, is a homozygote (*TT*) or a heterozygote (*Tt*).

Concept check: *Let's suppose you had a plant with purple flowers and unknown genotype and conducted a testcross to determine its genotype. You obtained 41 plants, 20 with white flowers and 21 with purple flowers. What was the genotype of the original purple-flowered plant?*

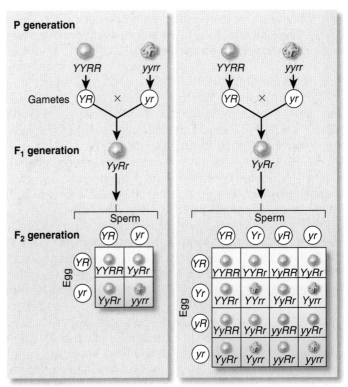

(a) Hypothesis: linked assortment

(b) Hypothesis: independent assortment

P cross	F₁ generation	F₂ generation
Yellow, round seeds × Green, wrinkled seeds	Yellow, round seeds	315 yellow, round seeds
		101 yellow, wrinkled seeds
		108 green, round seeds
		32 green, wrinkled seeds

(c) The data observed by Mendel

Figure 16.8 **Two hypotheses for the assortment of two different genes.** In a cross between two true-breeding pea plants, one with yellow, round seeds and one with green, wrinkled seeds, all of the F₁ offspring have yellow, round seeds. When the F₁ offspring self-fertilize, the two hypotheses predict different phenotypes in the F₂ generation. **(a)** The linkage hypothesis proposes that the parental alleles for the two characters stay associated with each other. In this case, all of the F₂ offspring will have either yellow, round seeds or green, wrinkled seeds. **(b)** The independent assortment hypothesis proposes that each allele assorts independently. In this case, the F₂ generation will display four different phenotypes. **(c)** Mendel's observations supported the independent assortment hypothesis.

Concept check: *What ratio of offspring phenotypes would have occurred if the linked hypothesis had been correct?*

inherited as a unit. In our example, the allele for yellow seeds (*Y*) would always be inherited with the allele for round seeds (*R*), and the alleles for green seeds (*y*) would always be inherited with the allele for wrinkled seeds (*r*), as shown in Figure 16.8a. A second possibility is that the two genes are independent of one another, so their alleles are randomly distributed into gametes (Figure 16.8b). By following the transmission pattern of two characters simultaneously, Mendel could determine whether the genes that determine seed shape and seed color assort (are distributed) together as a unit or independently of each other.

What experimental results could Mendel predict for each of these two models? The two homozygous plants of the P generation can produce only two kinds of gametes, *YR* and *yr*, so in either case the F₁ offspring would be heterozygous for both genes; that is, they would have the genotypes *YyRr*. Because Mendel knew from his earlier experiments that yellow was dominant over green and round over wrinkled, he could predict that all the F₁ plants would have yellow, round seeds. In contrast, as shown in Figure 16.8, the ratios he obtained in the F₂ generation would depend on whether the alleles of both genes assort together or independently.

If the parental genes are linked, as in Figure 16.8a, the F₁ plants could produce gametes that are only *YR* or *yr*. These

gametes would combine to create offspring with the genotypes *YYRR* (yellow, round), *YyRr* (yellow, round), or *yyrr* (green, wrinkled). The ratio of phenotypes would be 3 yellow, round to 1 green, wrinkled. Every F₂ plant would be phenotypically like one P-generation parent or the other. None would display a new combination of the parental traits. However, if the alleles assort independently, the F_2 generation would show a wider range of genotypes and phenotypes, as shown by the large Punnett square in Figure 16.8b. In this case, each F_1 parent produces four kinds of gametes—*YR*, *Yr*, *yR*, and *yr*—instead of two, so the square is constructed with four rows on each side and shows 16 possible genotypes. The F_2 generation includes plants with yellow, round seeds; yellow, wrinkled seeds; green, round seeds; and green, wrinkled seeds, in a ratio of 9:3:3:1.

The actual results of this two-factor cross are shown in Figure 16.8c. Crossing the true-breeding parents produced **dihybrid** offspring—offspring that are hybrids with respect to both traits. These F_1 dihybrids all had yellow, round seeds, confirming that yellow and round are dominant traits. This result was consistent with either hypothesis. However, the data for the F_2 generation were consistent only with the independent assortment hypothesis. Mendel observed four phenotypically different types of F_2 offspring, in a ratio that was reasonably close to 9:3:3:1.

In his original studies, Mendel reported that he had obtained similar results for every pair of characters he analyzed. His work supported the idea, now called the **law of independent assortment**, that *the alleles of different genes assort independently of each other during gamete formation*. Independent assortment means that a specific allele for one gene may be found in a gamete regardless of which allele for a different gene is found in the same gamete. In our example, the yellow and green alleles assort independently of the round and wrinkled alleles. The union of gametes from F_1 plants carrying these alleles produces the F_2 genotype and phenotype ratios shown in Figure 16.8b.

As we will see in Chapter 17, not all dihybrid crosses exhibit independent assortment. In some cases, the alleles of two genes that are physically located near each other on the same chromosome do not assort independently.

16.2 The Chromosome Theory of Inheritance

Mendel's studies with pea plants led to the concept of a gene, which is the foundation for our understanding of inheritance. However, at the time of Mendel's work, the physical nature and location of genes were a complete mystery. The idea that inheritance has a physical basis was not even addressed until 1883, when the German biologist August Weismann and the Swiss botanist Carl Nägeli championed the idea that a substance in living cells is responsible for the transmission of hereditary traits. This idea challenged other researchers to identify the genetic material. Several scientists, including the German biologists Eduard Strasburger and Walter Flemming, observed dividing cells under the microscope and suggested that the chromosomes are the carriers of the genetic material. As we now know, the genetic material is the DNA within chromosomes.

In the early 1900s, the idea that chromosomes carry the genetic material dramatically unfolded as researchers continued to study the processes of mitosis, meiosis, and fertilization. It became increasingly clear that the characteristics of organisms are rooted in the continuity of cells during the life of an organism and from one generation to the next. Several scientists noted striking parallels between the segregation and assortment of traits noted by Mendel and the behavior of chromosomes during meiosis. Among these scientists were the German biologist Theodor Boveri and the American biologist Walter Sutton, who independently proposed the chromosome theory of inheritance. According to this theory, the inheritance patterns of traits can be explained by the transmission of chromosomes during meiosis and fertilization.

A modern view of the **chromosome theory of inheritance** consists of a few fundamental principles:

1. Chromosomes contain DNA, which is the genetic material. Genes are found in the chromosomes.
2. Chromosomes are replicated and passed from parent to offspring. They are also passed from cell to cell during the development of a multicellular organism.
3. The nucleus of a diploid cell contains two sets of chromosomes, which are found in homologous pairs. The maternal and paternal sets of homologous chromosomes are functionally equivalent; each set carries a full complement of genes.
4. At meiosis, one member of each chromosome pair segregates into one daughter nucleus, and its homologue segregates into the other daughter nucleus. During the formation of haploid cells, the members of different chromosome pairs segregate independently of each other.
5. Gametes are haploid cells that combine to form a diploid cell during fertilization, with each gamete transmitting one set of chromosomes to the offspring.

In this section, we will relate the chromosome theory of inheritance to Mendel's laws of inheritance.

Mendel's Law of Segregation Is Explained by the Segregation of Homologous Chromosomes During Meiosis

Now that you have an understanding of the basic tenets of the chromosome theory of inheritance, let's relate these ideas to Mendel's laws of inheritance. To do so, it will be helpful to introduce another genetic term. The physical location of a gene on a chromosome is called the gene's **locus** (plural, loci). As shown in **Figure 16.9**, each member of a homologous chromosome pair carries an allele of the same gene at the same locus. The individual in this example is heterozygous (*Tt*), so each homologue has a different allele.

How can we relate the chromosome theory of inheritance to Mendel's law of segregation? **Figure 16.10** follows a homologous chromosome pair through the events of meiosis. This example involves a pea plant, heterozygous for height, *Tt*. The top of Figure 16.10 shows the two homologues prior to DNA replication. When a cell prepares to divide, the homologues replicate to produce pairs of sister chromatids. Each chromatid carries a copy of the allele found on the original homologue, either *T* or *t*. During meiosis I, the homologues, each consisting

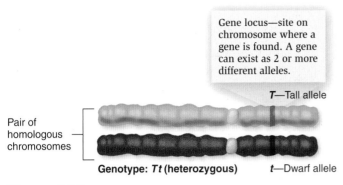

Gene locus—site on chromosome where a gene is found. A gene can exist as 2 or more different alleles.

T—Tall allele

Pair of homologous chromosomes

Genotype: *Tt* (heterozygous)   *t*—Dwarf allele

Figure 16.9   A gene locus.   The locus (location) of a gene is the same for each member of a homologous pair, whether the individual is homozygous or heterozygous for that gene. This individual is heterozygous (*Tt*) for a gene for plant height in peas.

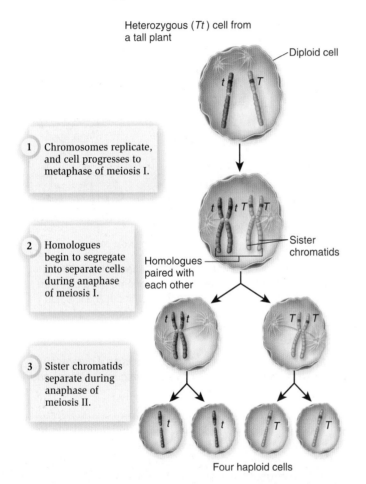

Heterozygous (*Tt*) cell from a tall plant

Diploid cell

1   Chromosomes replicate, and cell progresses to metaphase of meiosis I.

Homologues paired with each other

Sister chromatids

2   Homologues begin to segregate into separate cells during anaphase of meiosis I.

3   Sister chromatids separate during anaphase of meiosis II.

Four haploid cells

Figure 16.10   The chromosomal basis of allele segregation. This example shows a pair of homologous chromosomes in a cell of a pea plant. The blue chromosome was inherited from the male parent, and the red chromosome was inherited from the female parent. This individual is heterozygous (*Tt*) for a height gene. The two homologues segregate from each other during meiosis, leading to segregation of the tall allele (*T*) and the dwarf allele (*t*) into different haploid cells. Note: For simplicity, this diagram shows a single pair of homologous chromosomes, though eukaryotic cells typically have several different pairs of homologous chromosomes.

Concept check: *When we say that alleles segregate, what does the word segregate mean? How is this related to meiosis, described in Chapter 15?*

of two sister chromatids, pair up and then segregate into two daughter cells. One of these cells has two copies of the *T* allele, and the other has two copies of the *t* allele. The sister chromatids separate during meiosis II, which produces four haploid cells. The end result of meiosis is that each haploid cell has a copy of just one of the two original homologues. Two of the cells have a chromosome carrying the *T* allele, while the other two have a chromosome carrying the *t* allele at the same locus. If the haploid cells shown at the bottom of Figure 16.10 combine randomly during fertilization, they produce diploid offspring with the genotypic and phenotypic ratios shown earlier in Figure 16.6.

Mendel's Law of Independent Assortment Is Explained by the Independent Alignment of Different Chromosomes During Meiosis

How can we relate the chromosome theory of inheritance to Mendel's law of independent assortment? **Figure 16.11** shows the alignment and segregation of two pairs of chromosomes in a pea plant. One pair carries the gene for seed color: The yellow allele (*Y*) is on one chromosome, and the green allele (*y*) is on its homologue. The other pair of chromosomes carries the gene for seed shape: One member of the pair has the round allele (*R*), whereas its homologue carries the wrinkled allele (*r*). Thus, this individual is heterozygous for both genes, with the genotype *YyRr*.

When meiosis begins, each of the chromosomes has already replicated and consists of two sister chromatids. At metaphase I of meiosis, the two pairs of chromosomes randomly align themselves along the metaphase plate. This alignment can occur in two equally probable ways, shown on the two sides of the figure. On the left, the chromosome carrying the *y* allele is aligned on the same side of the metaphase plate as the chromosome carrying the *R* allele; *Y* is aligned with *r*. On the right, the opposite has occurred: *Y* is aligned with *R*, and *y* is with *r*. In each case, the chromosomes that aligned on the same side of the metaphase plate segregate into the same daughter cell. In this way, the random alignment of chromosome pairs during meiosis I leads to the independent assortment of alleles found on different chromosomes. For two loci found on different chromosomes, each with two variant alleles, meiosis produces four allele combinations in equal numbers, as seen at the bottom of the figure.

If a *YyRr* (dihybrid) plant undergoes self-fertilization, any two gametes can combine randomly during fertilization. Because four kinds of gametes are made, this allows for 16 possible allele combinations in the offspring. These genotypes, in turn, produce four phenotypes in a 9:3:3:1 ratio, as seen earlier in Figure 16.8. This ratio is the expected outcome when a heterozygote for two genes on different chromosomes undergoes self-fertilization.

But what if two different genes are located on the same chromosome? In this case, the transmission pattern may not conform to the law of independent assortment. We will discuss this phenomenon, known as linkage, in Chapter 17.

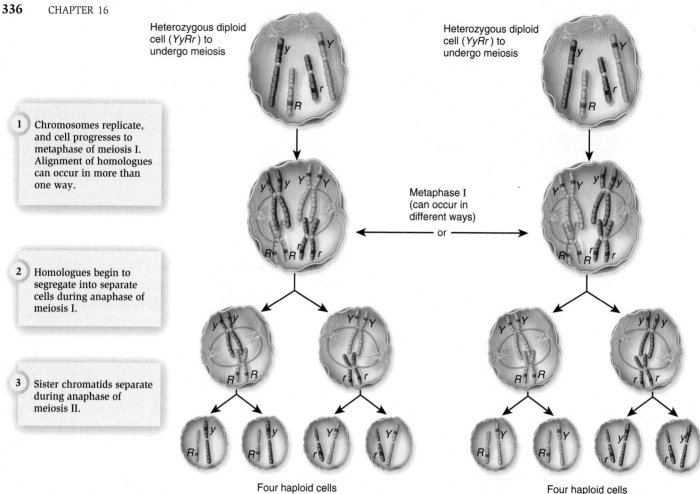

Figure 16.11   The chromosomal basis of independent assortment.   The genes for seed color (*Y* or *y*) and seed shape (*R* or *r*) in peas are on different chromosomes. During metaphase of meiosis I, different arrangements of the two chromosome pairs can lead to different combinations of the alleles in the resulting haploid cells. On the left, the chromosome carrying the dominant *R* allele has segregated with the chromosome carrying the recessive *y* allele. On the right, the two chromosomes carrying the dominant alleles (*R* and *Y*) have segregated together. Note: For simplicity, this diagram shows only two pairs of homologous chromosomes, though eukaryotic cells typically have several different pairs of homologous chromosomes.

Concept check: *Let's suppose that a cell is heterozygous for three different genes (AaBbCc) and that each gene is on a different chromosome. How many different ways can these three pairs of homologous chromosomes align themselves during metaphase I, and how many different types of gametes can be produced?*

16.3   Pedigree Analysis of Human Traits

As we have seen, Mendel conducted experiments by making selective crosses of pea plants and analyzing large numbers of offspring. Later geneticists also relied on crosses of experimental organisms, especially fruit flies. However, geneticists studying human traits cannot use this approach, for ethical and practical reasons. Instead, human geneticists must rely on information from family trees, or pedigrees. In this approach, called **pedigree analysis**, an inherited trait is analyzed over the course of a few generations in one family. The results of this method may be less definitive than the results of breeding experiments because the small size of human families may lead to large sampling errors. Nevertheless, a pedigree analysis can often provide important clues concerning human inheritance.

Pedigree analysis has been used to understand the inheritance of human genetic diseases that follow simple Mendelian patterns. Many genes that play a role in disease exist in two forms—the normal allele and an abnormal allele that has arisen by mutation. The disease symptoms are associated with the mutant allele. Pedigree analysis allows us to determine whether the mutant allele is dominant or recessive and to predict the likelihood of an individual being affected.

Let's consider a recessive condition to illustrate pedigree analysis. The pedigree in **Figure 16.12** concerns a human genetic disease known as cystic fibrosis (CF). Approximately 3% of Americans of European descent are heterozygous carriers of the recessive *CF* allele. Carriers are usually phenotypically normal. Individuals who are homozygous for the *CF* allele exhibit the disease symptoms, which include abnormalities of the pancreas, intestine, sweat glands, and lungs. A human pedigree, like the one in Figure 16.12, shows the oldest generation

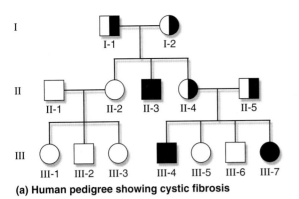

(a) Human pedigree showing cystic fibrosis

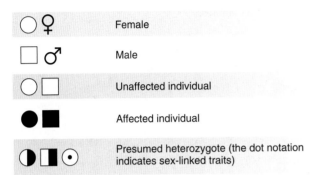

Female

Male

Unaffected individual

Affected individual

Presumed heterozygote (the dot notation indicates sex-linked traits)

(b) Symbols used in a human pedigree

Figure 16.12 A family pedigree for a recessive trait. Some members of the family in this pedigree are affected with cystic fibrosis. Phenotypically normal individuals I-1, I-2, II-4, and II-5 are presumed to be heterozygotes because they have produced affected offspring.

Concept check: Let's suppose a genetic disease is caused by a mutant allele. If two affected parents produce an unaffected offspring, can the mutant allele be recessive?

(designated by the Roman numeral I) at the top, with later generations (II and III) below it. A woman (represented by a circle) and a man (represented by a square) who produce offspring are connected by a horizontal line; a vertical line connects parents with their offspring. Siblings (brothers and sisters) are denoted by downward projections from a single horizontal line, from left to right in the order of their birth. For example, individuals I-1 and I-2 are the parents of individuals II-2, II-3, and II-4, who are all siblings. Individuals affected by the disease, such as individual II-3, are depicted by filled symbols.

Why does this pedigree indicate a recessive pattern of inheritance for CF? The answer is that two unaffected individuals can produce an affected offspring. Such individuals are presumed to be heterozygotes (designated by a half-filled symbol). However, the same unaffected parents can also produce unaffected offspring, because an individual must inherit two copies of the mutant allele to exhibit the disease. A recessive mode of inheritance is also characterized by the observation that all of the offspring of two affected individuals will be affected. However, for genetic diseases like CF that limit survival or fertility, there may rarely or never be cases where two affected individuals produce offspring.

Although many of the alleles causing human genetic diseases are recessive, some are known to be dominant. Figure

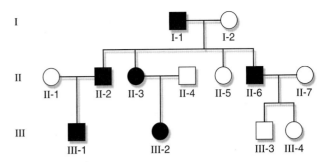

Figure 16.13 A family pedigree for a dominant trait. Huntington disease is caused by a dominant allele. Note that each affected offspring in this pedigree has an affected parent.

Concept check: What observation in a pedigree suggests a dominant pattern of inheritance?

16.13 shows a family pedigree involving Huntington disease, a condition that causes the degeneration of brain cells involved in emotions, intellect, and movement. If you examine this pedigree, you will see that every affected individual has one affected parent. This pattern is characteristic of most dominant disorders. However, affected parents do not always produce affected offspring. For example, II-6 is a heterozygote that has passed the normal allele to his offspring and thereby produced unaffected offspring (III-3 and III-4).

The symptoms of Huntington disease, which usually begin to appear when people are 30 to 50 years old, include uncontrollable jerking movements of the limbs, trunk, and face; progressive loss of mental abilities; and the development of psychiatric problems. In 1993, researchers identified the gene involved in this disorder. The gene encodes a protein called huntingtin, which functions in nerve cells. The mutant allele encodes an abnormal form of the protein, which aggregates within nerve cells in the brain. Further research is needed to determine how this aggregation contributes to the disease.

Most human genes are found on the paired chromosomes known as **autosomes**, which are the same in both sexes. Mendelian inheritance patterns involving these autosomal genes are described as autosomal inheritance patterns. Huntington disease is an example of a trait with an autosomal dominant inheritance pattern, whereas cystic fibrosis displays an autosomal recessive pattern. However, some human genes are located on sex chromosomes, which are different in males and females. These genes have their own characteristic inheritance patterns, which we will consider next.

16.4 Sex Chromosomes and X-Linked Inheritance Patterns

In the first part of this chapter, we discussed Mendel's experiments that established the basis for understanding how traits are transmitted from parents to offspring. We also examined the chromosome theory of inheritance, which provided a framework for explaining Mendel's observations. Mendelian patterns of gene transmission are observed for most genes located on autosomes in a wide variety of eukaryotic species.

We will now turn our attention to genes located on **sex chromosomes**. As you learned in Chapter 15, this term refers to a distinctive pair of chromosomes that are different in males and females. Sex chromosomes are found in many but not all species with two sexes. The study of sex chromosomes proved pivotal in confirming the chromosome theory of inheritance. The distinctive transmission patterns of genes on sex chromosomes helped early geneticists show that particular genes are located on particular chromosomes. Later, other researchers became interested in these genes because some of them were found to cause inherited diseases in humans.

In this section, we will consider several mechanisms by which sex chromosomes in various species determines an individual's sex. We will then examine some of the early research involving sex chromosomes that provided convincing evidence for the chromosome theory of inheritance. Finally, we will consider the inheritance patterns of genes on sex chromosomes and why recessive alleles are expressed more frequently in males than in females.

In Many Species, Sex Differences Are Due to the Presence of Sex Chromosomes

Some early evidence supporting the chromosome theory of inheritance involved a consideration of sex determination. In 1901, the American biologist C. E. McClung suggested that the inheritance of particular chromosomes is responsible for determining sex in fruit flies. Following McClung's initial observations, several mechanisms of sex determination were found in different species of animals. Some examples are described in **Figure 16.14**. All of these mechanisms involve chromosomal differences between the sexes, and most involve a difference in a single pair of sex chromosomes.

In the X-Y system of sex determination, which operates in mammals, the somatic cells of males have one X and one Y chromosome, whereas female somatic cells contain two X chromosomes (Figure 16.14a). For example, the 46 chromosomes carried by human cells consist of 22 pairs of autosomes and one pair of sex chromosomes (either XY or XX). Which chromosome, the X or Y, determines sex? In mammals, the presence of the Y chromosome causes maleness. This is known from the analysis of rare individuals who carry chromosomal abnormalities. For example, mistakes that occasionally occur during meiosis may produce an individual who carries two X chromosomes and one Y chromosome. Such an individual develops into a male. A gene called the *SRY* gene located on the Y chromosome of mammals plays a key role in the developmental pathway that leads to maleness.

The X-O system operates in many insects (Figure 16.14b). Unlike the X-Y system in mammals, the presence of the Y chromosome in the X-O system does not determine maleness. Females in this system have a pair of sex chromosomes and are designated XX. In some insect species that follow the X-O system, the male has only one sex chromosome, the X. In other

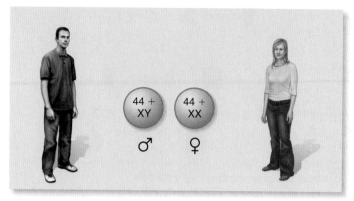

(a) The X-Y system in mammals

(b) The X-O system in certain insects

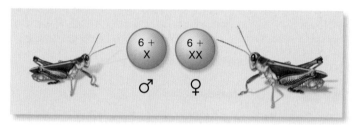

(c) The Z-W system in birds

(d) The haplodiploid system in bees

Figure 16.14 **Different mechanisms of sex determination in animals.** The numbers shown in the circles indicate the numbers of autosomes.

Concept check: If a person is born with only one X chromosome and no Y chromosome, would you expect that person to be a male or a female? Explain your answer.

X-O insect species, such as *Drosophila melanogaster*, the male has both an X chromosome and a Y chromosome. The insect's sex is determined by the ratio between its X chromosomes and its sets of autosomes. If a fly has one X chromosome and is diploid for the autosomes (2n), this ratio is 1/2, or 0.5. This fly will become a male whether or not it receives a Y chromosome. On the other hand, if a diploid fly receives two X chromosomes, the ratio is 2/2, or 1.0, and the fly becomes a female.

Thus far, we have considered examples where females have two similar copies of a sex chromosome, the X. However, in some animal species, such as birds and some fish, the male carries two similar chromosomes (Figure 16.14c). This is called the Z-W system to distinguish it from the X-Y system found in mammals. The male is ZZ, and the female is ZW.

Not all chromosomal mechanisms of sex determination involve a special pair of sex chromosomes. An interesting mechanism known as the haplodiploid system is found in bees (Figure 16.14d). The male bee, or drone, is produced from an unfertilized haploid egg. Thus, male bees are haploid individuals. Females, both worker bees and queen bees, are produced from fertilized eggs and therefore are diploid.

Although sex in many species of animals is determined by chromosomes, other mechanisms are also known. In certain reptiles and fish, sex is controlled by environmental factors such as temperature. For example, in the American alligator (*Alligator mississippiensis*), temperature controls sex development. When eggs of this alligator are incubated at 33°C, nearly all of them produce male individuals. When the eggs are incubated at a temperature significantly below 33°C, they produce nearly all females, whereas at a temperature above 33°C, they produce a mixture of males and females.

Most species of flowering plants, including pea plants, have a single type of diploid plant, or sporophyte, that makes both male and female gametophytes. However, the sporophytes of some species have two sexually distinct types of individuals, one with flowers that produce male gametophytes, and the other with flowers that produce female gametophytes. Examples include hollies, willows, poplars, and date palms. Sex chromosomes, designated X and Y, are responsible for sex determination in many such species. The male plant is XY, whereas the female plant is XX. However, in some plant species with separate sexes, microscopic examination of the chromosomes does not reveal distinct types of sex chromosomes.

In Humans, Recessive X-Linked Traits Are More Likely to Occur in Males

In humans, the X chromosome is rather large and carries over 1,000 genes, whereas the Y chromosome is quite small and has less than 100 genes. Therefore, many genes are found on the X chromosome but not on the Y; these are known as **X-linked genes**. By comparison, fewer genes are known to be Y linked, meaning they are found on the Y chromosome but not on the X. The term **sex linked** refers to genes found on one sex chromosome but not on the other. Because fewer genes are found on the Y chromosome, the term usually refers to X-linked genes. In mammals, a male cannot be described as being homozygous

or heterozygous for an X-linked gene, because these terms apply to genes that are present in two copies. Instead, the term **hemizygous** is used to describe an individual with only one copy of a particular gene. A male mammal is said to be hemizygous for an X-linked gene.

Many recessive X-linked alleles cause diseases in humans, and these diseases occur more frequently in males than in females. As an example, let's consider the X-linked recessive disorder called classical hemophilia (hemophilia A). In individuals with hemophilia, blood does not clot normally, and a minor cut may bleed for a long time. Small bumps can lead to large bruises because broken capillaries may leak blood profusely into surrounding tissues before the capillaries are repaired. Common accidental injuries pose a threat of severe internal or external bleeding for hemophiliacs. Hemophilia A is caused by a recessive X-linked allele that encodes a defective form of a clotting protein. If a mother is a heterozygous carrier of hemophilia A, each of her children has a 50% chance of inheriting the recessive allele. The following Punnett square shows a cross between an unaffected father and a heterozygous mother. X^H designates an X chromosome carrying the normal allele, and $X^{h\text{-}A}$ is the X chromosome that carries the recessive allele for hemophilia A.

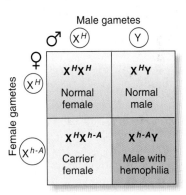

Although each child has a 50% chance of inheriting the hemophilia allele from the mother, only 1/2 of the sons will exhibit the disorder. Because a son inherits only one X chromosome, a son who inherits the abnormal allele from his mother will have hemophilia. However, a daughter inherits an X chromosome from both her mother and her father. In this example, a daughter who inherits the hemophilia allele from her mother will also inherit a normal allele from her father. This daughter will have a normal phenotype, but if she passes the abnormal allele to her sons, they will have hemophilia.

FEATURE INVESTIGATION

Morgan's Experiments Showed a Correlation Between a Genetic Trait and the Inheritance of a Sex Chromosome in *Drosophila*

The distinctive inheritance pattern of X-linked alleles provides a way of demonstrating that a specific gene is on an X chromosome. An X-linked gene was the first gene to be located on a specific chromosome. In 1910, the American geneticist Thomas Hunt Morgan began work on a project in which he reared large populations of fruit flies, *Drosophila melanogaster*, in the dark to determine if their eyes would atrophy from disuse and disappear in future generations. Even after

Figure 16.15 Morgan's crosses of red-eyed and white-eyed *Drosophila*.

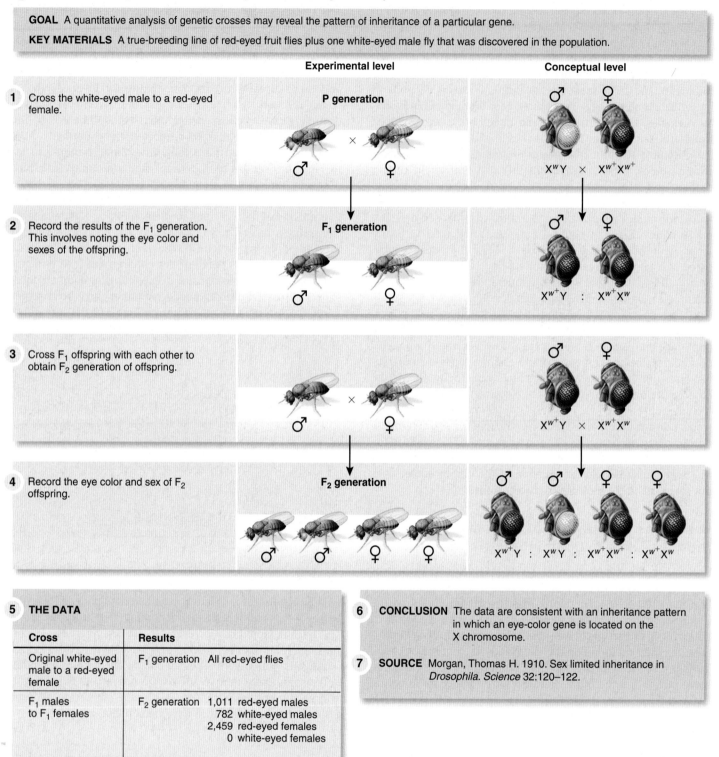

GOAL A quantitative analysis of genetic crosses may reveal the pattern of inheritance of a particular gene.

KEY MATERIALS A true-breeding line of red-eyed fruit flies plus one white-eyed male fly that was discovered in the population.

Experimental level   Conceptual level

1 Cross the white-eyed male to a red-eyed female.

P generation

$X^w Y \times X^{w^+} X^{w^+}$

2 Record the results of the F_1 generation. This involves noting the eye color and sexes of the offspring.

F_1 generation

$X^{w^+} Y \; : \; X^{w^+} X^w$

3 Cross F_1 offspring with each other to obtain F_2 generation of offspring.

$X^{w^+} Y \times X^{w^+} X^w$

4 Record the eye color and sex of F_2 offspring.

F_2 generation

$X^{w^+} Y \; : \; X^w Y \; : \; X^{w^+} X^{w^+} \; : \; X^{w^+} X^w$

5 **THE DATA**

Cross	Results
Original white-eyed male to a red-eyed female	F_1 generation All red-eyed flies
F_1 males to F_1 females	F_2 generation 1,011 red-eyed males 782 white-eyed males 2,459 red-eyed females 0 white-eyed females

6 **CONCLUSION** The data are consistent with an inheritance pattern in which an eye-color gene is located on the X chromosome.

7 **SOURCE** Morgan, Thomas H. 1910. Sex limited inheritance in *Drosophila*. *Science* 32:120–122.

many consecutive generations, the flies showed no noticeable changes. After 2 years of looking at many flies, Morgan happened to discover a male fly with white eyes rather than the normal red eyes. The white-eye trait must have arisen from a new mutation that converted a red-eye allele into a white-eye allele.

To study the inheritance of the white-eye trait, Morgan followed an approach similar to Mendel's in which he made crosses and quantitatively analyzed their outcome. In the experiment described in **Figure 16.15**, Morgan crossed his white-eyed male to a red-eyed female. All of the F_1 offspring had red eyes, indicating that red is dominant to white. The F_1 offspring were then mated to each other to obtain an F_2 generation. As seen in the data table, this cross produced 1,011 red-eyed males, 782 white-eyed males, and 2,459 red-eyed females. Surprisingly, no white-eyed females were observed in the F_2 generation.

How did Morgan interpret these results? The results suggested a connection between the alleles for eye color and the sex of the offspring. As shown in the conceptual column of Figure 16.15 and in the Punnett square below, his data were consistent with the idea that the eye-color alleles in *Drosophila* are located on the X chromosome. X^{w+} is the chromosome carrying the normal allele for red eyes, and X^w is the chromosome with the mutant allele for white eyes.

F_1 male is $X^{w+}Y$
F_1 female is $X^{w+}X^w$

The Punnett square predicts that the F_2 generation will not have any white-eyed females. This prediction was confirmed by Morgan's experimental data. However, it should also be pointed out that the experimental ratio of red eyes to white eyes in the F_2 generation is $(2{,}459 + 1{,}011) : 782$, which equals $4.4 : 1$. This ratio deviates significantly from the ratio of $3 : 1$ predicted in the Punnett square. The lower than expected number of white-eyed flies is explained by a decreased survival of white-eyed flies.

Following this initial discovery, Morgan carried out many experimental crosses that located specific genes on the *Drosophila* X chromosome. This research provided some of the most persuasive evidence for Mendel's laws and the chromosome theory of inheritance, which are the foundations of modern genetics. In 1933, Morgan became the first geneticist to receive a Nobel Prize.

Experimental Questions

1. Prior to the Feature Investigation, what was the original purpose of Morgan's experiments with *Drosophila*?

2. What results led Morgan to conclude that eye color was associated with the sex of the individual?

3. What crosses between fruit flies could yield female offspring with white eyes?

16.5 Variations in Inheritance Patterns and Their Molecular Basis

The term **Mendelian inheritance** describes the inheritance patterns of genes that segregate and assort independently. In the first section of this chapter, we considered the inheritance pattern of traits affected by a single gene that is found in two variants, one of which is dominant over the other. This pattern is called **simple Mendelian inheritance**, because the phenotypic ratios in the offspring clearly demonstrate Mendel's laws. In the previous section, we examined **X-linked inheritance**, the pattern displayed by pairs of dominant and recessive alleles located on X chromosomes. Early geneticists observed these Mendelian inheritance patterns without knowing why one trait was dominant over another.

In this section, we will discuss the molecular basis of dominant and recessive traits and see how the molecular expression of a gene can have widespread effects on an organism's phenotype. In addition, we will examine the inheritance patterns of genes that segregate and assort independently but do not display a simple dominant/recessive relationship. The transmission of these genes from parents to offspring does not usually produce the ratios of phenotypes we would expect on the basis of Mendel's observations. This does not mean that Mendel was

wrong. Rather, the inheritance patterns of many traits are more intricate and interesting than the simple patterns he chose to study. As described in **Table 16.1**, our understanding of gene function at the molecular level explains both simple Mendelian inheritance and other, more complex, inheritance patterns that conform to Mendel's laws. This modern knowledge also sheds light on the role of the environment in producing an organism's phenotype, which we will discuss at the end of the section.

Protein Function Explains the Phenomenon of Dominance

As we discussed at the beginning of this chapter, Mendel studied seven characters that were found in two variants each (see Figure 16.2). The dominant variants are caused by the common alleles for these traits in pea plants. For any given gene, geneticists refer to a prevalent allele in a population as a **wild-type allele**. In most cases, a wild-type allele encodes a protein that is made in the proper amount and functions normally. By comparison, alleles that have been altered by mutation are called **mutant alleles**; these tend to be rare in natural populations. In the case of Mendel's seven characters, the recessive alleles are due to rare mutations.

How do we explain why one allele is dominant while another allele is recessive? By studying genes and their gene products at the molecular level, researchers have discovered

Table 16.1   Different Types of Mendelian Inheritance Patterns and Their Molecular Basis

Type	Description
Simple Mendelian inheritance	**Inheritance pattern:** Pattern of traits determined by a pair of alleles that display a dominant/recessive relationship and are located on an autosome. The presence of the dominant allele masks the presence of the recessive allele. **Molecular basis:** In many cases, the recessive allele is nonfunctional. Though a heterozygote may produce 50% of the functional protein compared to a dominant homozygote, this is sufficient to produce the dominant trait.
X-linked inheritance	**Inheritance pattern:** Pattern of traits determined by genes that display a dominant/recessive relationship and are located on the X chromosome. In mammals and fruit flies, males are hemizygous for X-linked genes. In these species, X-linked recessive traits occur more frequently in males than in females. **Molecular basis:** In a female with one recessive X-linked allele (a heterozygote), the protein encoded by the dominant allele is sufficient to produce the dominant trait. A male with a recessive X-linked allele (a hemizygote) does not have a dominant allele and does not make any of the functional protein.
Incomplete dominance	**Inheritance pattern:** Pattern that occurs when the heterozygote has a phenotype intermediate to the phenotypes of the homozygotes, as when a cross between red-flowered and white-flowered plants produces pink-flowered offspring. **Molecular basis:** 50% of the protein encoded by the functional (wild-type) allele is not sufficient to produce the normal trait.
Codominance	**Inheritance pattern:** Pattern that occurs when the heterozygote expresses both alleles simultaneously. For example, a human carrying the A and B alleles for the ABO antigens of red blood cells produces both the A and the B antigens (has an AB blood type). **Molecular basis:** The codominant alleles encode proteins that function slightly differently from each other. In a heterozygote, the function of each protein affects the phenotype uniquely.
Sex-influenced inheritance	**Inheritance pattern:** Pattern that occurs when an allele is dominant in one sex and recessive in the other, as in pattern baldness in humans. **Molecular basis:** Sex hormones affect the molecular expression of genes, which can have an impact on the phenotype.

that a recessive allele is often defective in its ability to express a functional protein. In other words, mutations that produce recessive alleles are likely to decrease or eliminate the synthesis or functional activity of a protein. These are called loss-of-function alleles. To understand why many loss-of-function alleles are recessive, we need to take a quantitative look at protein function.

In a simple dominant/recessive relationship, the recessive allele does not affect the phenotype of the heterozygote. In this type of relationship, a single copy of the dominant (wild-type) allele is sufficient to mask the effects of the recessive allele. How do we explain the dominant phenotype of the heterozygote? **Figure 16.16** considers the example of flower color in a pea plant. The gene encodes an enzyme that is needed to make a purple pigment. The *P* allele is dominant because one *P* allele encodes enough of the functional protein—50% of the amount found in a normal homozygote—to provide a normal phenotype. Thus, the *PP* homozygote and the *Pp* heterozygote both make enough of the purple pigment to yield purple flowers. The *pp* homozygote cannot make any of the functional protein required for pigment synthesis, so its flowers are white.

The explanation—50% of the normal protein is enough—is true for many dominant alleles. In such cases, the normal homozygote is making much more of the protein than necessary, so if the amount is reduced to 50%, as it is in the heterozygote, the individual still has plenty of this protein to accomplish whatever cellular function it performs. In other cases, however, an allele may be dominant because the heterozygote actually

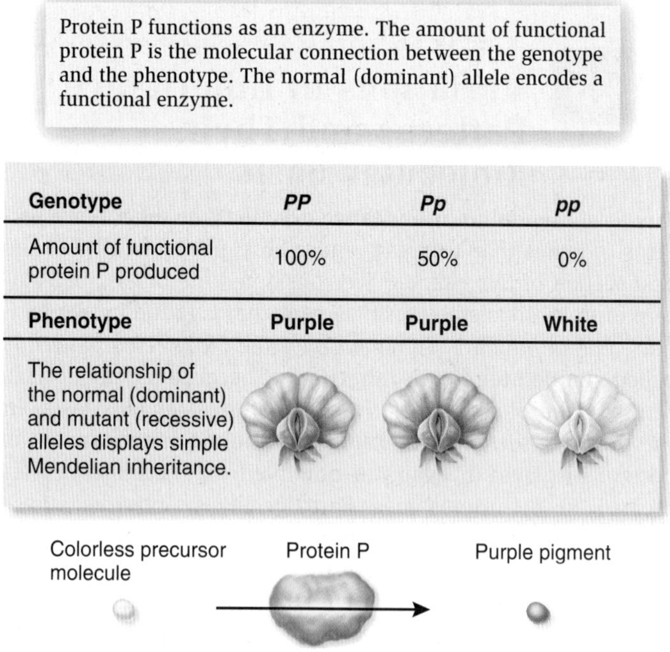

Protein P functions as an enzyme. The amount of functional protein P is the molecular connection between the genotype and the phenotype. The normal (dominant) allele encodes a functional enzyme.

Genotype	*PP*	*Pp*	*pp*
Amount of functional protein P produced	100%	50%	0%
Phenotype	**Purple**	**Purple**	**White**
The relationship of the normal (dominant) and mutant (recessive) alleles displays simple Mendelian inheritance.			

Colorless precursor molecule   Protein P   Purple pigment

Figure 16.16   How genes give rise to traits during simple Mendelian inheritance. In many cases, the amount of protein encoded by a single dominant allele is sufficient to produce the normal phenotype. In this example, a plant with one or two copies of the normal allele produces enough pigment to produce purple flowers. In a *pp* homozygote, the complete lack of the normal protein results in white flowers.

produces more than 50% of the normal amount of functional protein. This increased production is due to the phenomenon of gene regulation, which is discussed in Chapter 13. The normal gene is "up-regulated" in the heterozygote to compensate for the lack of function of the defective allele.

Genomes & Proteomes Connection

Single-Gene Mutations Cause Many Inherited Diseases and Have Pleiotropic Effects

The idea that recessive alleles usually cause a substantial decrease in the expression of a functional protein is supported by analyses of many human genetic diseases. Keep in mind that many genetic diseases are caused by rare mutant alleles. **Table 16.2** lists several examples of human genetic diseases in which a recessive allele fails to produce a specific cellular protein in its active form.

Over 7,000 human disorders are caused by mutations in single genes. With a human genome size of 20,000 to 25,000 genes, this means that roughly one-third of our genes are known to cause some kind of abnormality when mutations alter the expression or functionality of their gene product. Any particular single-gene disorder is relatively rare. But taken together, about one individual in 100 has a disorder that is due to a single-gene mutation. Such diseases generally have simple inheritance patterns in family pedigrees. Although the majority of these diseases follow a recessive inheritance pattern, some are known to be dominant. We have already discussed Huntington disease as an example of a dominant human disorder (see Figure 16.13). Other examples of diseases caused by dominant alleles include achondroplasia (a form of dwarfism) and osteogenesis imperfecta (brittle bone disease).

Single-gene disorders also illustrate the phenomenon of **pleiotropy**, which means that a mutation in a single gene can have multiple effects on an individual's phenotype. Pleiotropy occurs for several reasons, including the following:

1. The expression of a single gene can affect cell function in more than one way. For example, a defect in a microtubule protein may affect cell division and cell movement.

2. A gene may be expressed in different cell types in a multicellular organism.

3. A gene may be expressed at different stages of development.

In this genetics unit, we tend to discuss genes as they affect a single trait. This educational approach allows us to appreciate how genes function and how they are transmitted from parents to offspring. However, this focus may also obscure how amazing genes really are. In all or nearly all cases, the expression of a gene is pleiotropic with regard to the characteristics of an organism. The expression of any given gene influences the expression of many other genes in the genome, and vice

versa. Pleiotropy is revealed when researchers study the effects of gene mutations.

As an example of a pleiotropic mutation, let's consider cystic fibrosis (CF), which we discussed earlier as an example of a recessive human disorder (see Figure 16.12). In the late 1980s, the gene for CF was identified. The normal allele encodes a protein called the cystic fibrosis transmembrane conductance regulator (CFTR), which regulates ionic balance by allowing the transport of chloride ions (Cl^-) across epithelial-cell membranes. The mutation that causes CF diminishes the function of this Cl^- transporter, affecting several parts of the body in different ways. Because the movement of Cl^- affects water transport across membranes, the most severe symptom of CF is the production of thick mucus in the lungs, which occurs because of a water imbalance. In sweat glands, the normal Cl^- transporter has the function of recycling salt out of the glands and back into the skin before it can be lost to the outside world. Persons with CF have excessively salty sweat due to their inability to recycle salt back into their skin cells. A common test for CF is the measurement of salt on the skin. Another effect is seen in the reproductive systems of males who are homozygous for

Table 16.2 Examples of Recessive Human Genetic Diseases

Disease	Protein produced by the normal gene*	Description
Phenylketonuria	Phenylalanine hydroxylase	Inability to metabolize phenylalanine. Can lead to severe mental retardation and physical degeneration. The disease can be prevented by following a phenylalanine-free diet beginning early in life.
Cystic fibrosis	A chloride-ion transporter	Inability to regulate ion balance in epithelial cells. Leads to a variety of abnormalities, including production of thick lung mucus and chronic lung infections.
Tay-Sachs disease	Hexosaminidase A	Defect in lipid metabolism. Leads to paralysis, blindness, and early death.
Alpha-1 antitrypsin deficiency	Alpha-1 antitrypsin	Inability to prevent the activity of protease enzymes. Leads to a buildup of certain proteins that cause liver damage and emphysema.
Hemophilia A	Coagulation factor VIII	A defect in blood clotting due to a missing clotting factor. An accident may cause excessive bleeding or internal hemorrhaging.

*Individuals who exhibit the disease are homozygous (or hemizygous) for a recessive allele that results in a defect in the amount or function of the normal protein.

the mutant allele. Some males with CF are infertile because the vas deferens, the tubules that transport sperm from the testes, are absent or undeveloped. Presumably, a normally functioning Cl⁻ transporter is needed for the proper development of the vas deferens in the embryo. Taken together, we can see that a defect in CFTR has multiple effects throughout the body.

Incomplete Dominance Results in an Intermediate Phenotype

We will now turn our attention to examples in which the alleles for a given gene do not show a simple dominant/recessive relationship. In some cases, a heterozygote that carries two different alleles exhibits a phenotype that is intermediate between the corresponding homozygous individuals. This phenomenon is known as **incomplete dominance**.

In 1905, Carl Correns discovered this pattern of inheritance for alleles affecting flower color in the four-o'clock plant (*Mirabilis jalapa*). **Figure 16.17** shows a cross between two four-o'clock plants, a red-flowered homozygote and a white-flowered homozygote. The allele for red flower color is designated C^R, and the white allele is C^W. These alleles are designated with superscripts rather than upper- and lowercase letters because neither allele is dominant. The offspring of this cross have pink flowers—they are C^RC^W heterozygotes with an intermediate phenotype. If these F_1 offspring are allowed to self-fertilize, the F_2 generation has 1/4 red-flowered plants, 1/2 pink-flowered plants, and 1/4 white-flowered plants. This is a 1:2:1 phenotypic ratio rather than the 3:1 ratio observed for simple Mendelian inheritance. What is the molecular explanation for this ratio? In this case, the red allele encodes a functional protein needed to produce a red pigment, whereas the white allele is a mutant allele that is nonfunctional. In the C^RC^W heterozygote, 50% of the protein encoded by the C^R allele is not sufficient to produce the red-flower phenotype, but it does provide enough pigment to give pink flowers.

The degree to which we judge an allele to exhibit incomplete dominance may depend on how closely we examine an individual's phenotype. An example is an inherited human disease called phenylketonuria (PKU). This disorder is caused by a rare mutation in a gene that encodes an enzyme called phenylalanine hydroxylase. This enzyme is needed to metabolize the amino acid phenylalanine, which is found in milk, eggs, and other protein-rich foods. If left untreated, phenylalanine builds up, affecting various systems in the body. Homozygotes carrying the mutant allele suffer severe symptoms, including mental retardation, seizures, microcephaly (small head), poor development of tooth enamel, and decreased body growth. By comparison, heterozygotes appear phenotypically normal. For this reason, geneticists consider PKU to be a recessive disorder. However, biochemical analysis of the blood of heterozygotes shows they typically have a phenylalanine blood level double that of an individual carrying two normal copies of the gene.

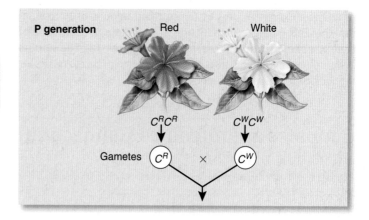

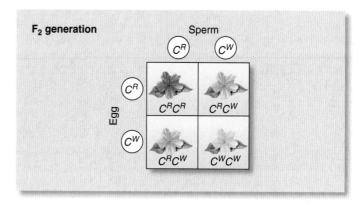

Figure 16.17 Incomplete dominance in the four-o'clock plant.   When red-flowered and white-flowered homozygotes (C^RC^R and C^WC^W) are crossed, the resulting heterozygote (C^RC^W) has an intermediate phenotype of pink flowers.

Individuals with PKU (homozygous recessive) typically have phenylalanine blood levels 30 times higher than normal. Therefore, at this closer level of examination, heterozygotes exhibit an intermediate phenotype in comparison to the homozygous dominant and recessive individuals. At this closer level of inspection, the relationship between the normal and mutant alleles would be defined as incomplete dominance.

ABO Blood Type Is an Example of Multiple Alleles and Codominance

Although diploid individuals have only two copies of most genes, the majority of genes have three or more variants in natural populations. We describe such genes as occurring in **multiple alleles**. Particular phenotypes depend on which two alleles each individual inherits. ABO blood types in humans are an example of phenotypes produced by multiple alleles.

As shown in **Table 16.3**, human red blood cells have structures on their plasma membrane known as surface antigens, which are constructed from several sugar molecules that are connected to form a carbohydrate tree. The carbohydrate tree is attached to lipids or membrane proteins to form glycolipids or glycoproteins, which are described in Chapter 5.

Antigens are substances (in this case, carbohydrates) that may be recognized as foreign material when introduced into the body of an animal. Let's consider two types of surface antigens, known as A and B, which may be found on red blood cells. The synthesis of these antigens is determined by enzymes that are encoded by a gene that exists in three alleles, designated I^A, I^B, and i, respectively. The i allele is recessive to both I^A and I^B. A person who is ii homozygous will not produce surface antigen A or B and will have blood type O. The red blood cells of an I^AI^A homozygous or I^Ai heterozygous individual will have surface antigen A (blood type A). Similarly, a homozygous I^BI^B or heterozygous I^Bi individual will produce surface antigen B (blood type B). A person who is I^AI^B heterozygous makes both antigens, A and B, on every red blood cell (blood type AB). The phenomenon in which a single individual expresses both alleles is called **codominance**.

What is the molecular explanation for codominance? Biochemists have analyzed the carbohydrate tree produced in people of differing blood types. The differences are shown schematically in Table 16.3. In type O, the carbohydrate tree is smaller than in type A or type B because a sugar has not been attached to a specific site on the tree. People with blood type O have a loss-of-function mutation in the gene that encodes the enzyme that attaches a sugar at this site. This enzyme, called a glycosyl transferase, is inactive in type O individuals. In contrast, the type A and type B antigens have sugars attached to this site, but each of them has a different sugar. This difference occurs because the enzymes encoded by the I^A allele and the I^B allele have slightly different active sites.

As a result, the enzyme encoded by the I^A allele attaches a sugar called N-acetylgalactosamine to the carbohydrate tree, whereas the enzyme encoded by the I^B allele attaches galactose. N-acetylgalactosamine is represented by an orange hexagon in Table 16.3, and galactose by a green triangle.

Blood type is a critical issue for a blood transfusion between a donor and a recipient. Surface antigens A and B have different molecular structures. Such differences allow antibodies, which are produced by the immune system, to recognize and bind very specifically to these antigens. The blood of type A individuals has antibodies that bind to the B antigen. Similarly, type B individuals produce antibodies against the A antigen. Type O individuals produce both kinds of antibodies, and type AB individuals produce neither. (The structure that exists in the absence of added galactose or galactosamine is called the H antigen. Because everyone makes this portion of the carbohydrate tree, no antibodies are formed against it.) When a person receives a blood transfusion, the donor's blood must be an appropriate match with the recipient's blood to avoid a dangerous antigen-antibody reaction. For example, if a person with type O blood is given type A blood, the recipient's anti-A antibodies will react with the donated blood cells and cause them to agglutinate (clump together). This situation is life-threatening because it will cause the blood vessels to clog. Identification of the donor and recipient blood types, called blood typing, is essential for safe transfusions.

The Expression of Certain Traits Is Influenced by the Sex of the Individual

Certain autosomal genes are expressed differently in heterozygous males and females. The term **sex-influenced inheritance** refers to the phenomenon in which an allele is dominant in one sex but recessive in the other. A particular form of baldness, called androgenetic alopecia, or pattern baldness, is an example of a sex-influenced trait in humans. This trait is characterized by a pattern in which hair loss occurs on the front and top but not on the sides (**Figure 16.18**). A male who is heterozygous for the pattern-baldness allele (designated B) will exhibit hair loss,

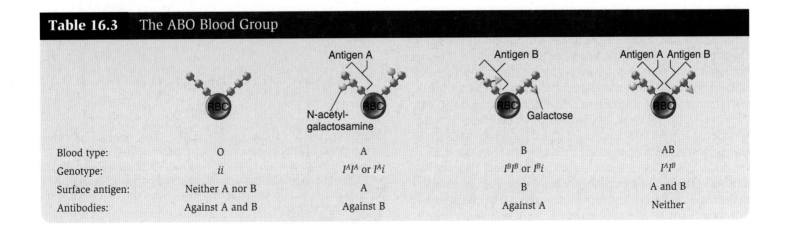

Table 16.3   The ABO Blood Group

	O	A	B	AB
Blood type:	O	A	B	AB
Genotype:	ii	I^AI^A or I^Ai	I^BI^B or I^Bi	I^AI^B
Surface antigen:	Neither A nor B	A	B	A and B
Antibodies:	Against A and B	Against B	Against A	Neither

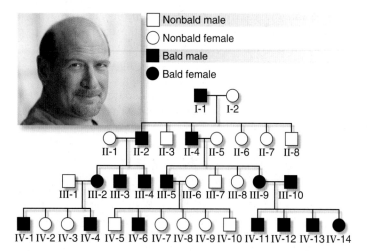

Figure 16.18 A family pedigree showing sex-influenced inheritance. Pattern baldness, shown in an adult male in the photograph, is an example of sex-influenced inheritance of an autosomal gene. Bald individuals are represented by filled symbols in the pedigree.

Concept check: Let's suppose two nonbald parents produce a bald son. What are the genotypes of the parents and the son?

but a heterozygous female will not. In other words, the baldness allele is dominant in males but recessive in females:

Genotype	Phenotype	
	Females	*Males*
BB	bald	bald
Bb	nonbald	bald
bb	nonbald	nonbald

A woman who is homozygous for the baldness allele may develop the trait, although in women it is usually characterized by a significant thinning of the hair that occurs relatively late in life.

As you can see from the pedigree in Figure 16.18, a bald male may have inherited the baldness allele from either parent. Thus, a striking observation is that fathers with pattern baldness can pass this trait to their sons. This could not occur if the trait was X-linked, because fathers transmit only Y chromosomes to their sons.

The sex-influenced nature of pattern baldness is related to the production of the male sex hormone testosterone. Though other genes may influence baldness, the gene that plays a primary role in pattern baldness encodes an enzyme called 5α-reductase, which converts testosterone to 5α-dihydrotestosterone (DHT). This gene is not X-linked. It is located on chromosome 5, which is an autosome. DHT binds to cellular receptors and affects the expression of many genes, including those in the cells of the scalp. The allele that causes pattern baldness results in an overexpression of this enzyme. Because mature males normally make more testosterone than females, this allele has a greater phenotypic impact in males. However, a rare tumor of the adrenal gland can cause the secretion of abnormally large amounts

of testosterone in females. If this occurs in a woman who is heterozygous *Bb*, she will become bald. If the tumor is removed surgically, her hair will return to its normal condition.

The Environment Plays a Vital Role in the Making of a Phenotype

In this chapter, we have been mainly concerned with the effects of genes on phenotypes. In addition, phenotypes are shaped by an organism's environment. An organism cannot exist without its genes or without an environment in which to live. Both are indispensable for life. An organism's genotype provides the plan to create a phenotype, while the environment provides nutrients and energy so that plan can be executed.

The term **norm of reaction** refers to the effects of environmental variation on a phenotype. Specifically, it is the phenotypic range seen in individuals with a particular genotype. To evaluate the norm of reaction, researchers study members of true-breeding strains that have the same genotypes and subject them to different environmental conditions. For example, **Figure 16.19** shows the norm of reaction for genetically identical plants raised at different temperatures. As shown in the figure, these plants attain a maximal height when raised at 75°F. At 50°F and 85°F, the plants are substantially shorter. Growth cannot occur below 40°F or above 95°F.

The norm of reaction can be quite dramatic when we consider environmental influences on certain inherited diseases. A striking example is the human genetic disease phenylketonuria (PKU). As we discussed earlier in the chapter, this disorder is caused by a rare mutation in the gene that encodes the enzyme phenylalanine hydroxylase, which is needed to metabolize the amino acid phenylalanine. People with one or two functional

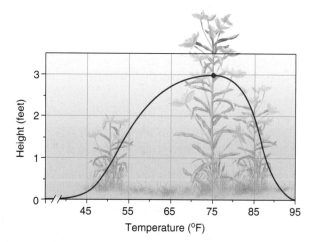

Figure 16.19 The norm of reaction. The norm of reaction is the range of phenotypes that an organism with a particular genotype exhibits under different environmental conditions. In this example, genetically identical plants were grown at different temperatures in a greenhouse and then measured for height.

Concept check: Could you study the norm of reaction in a wild population of squirrels?

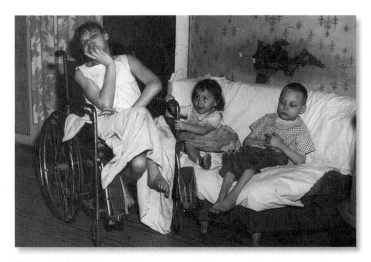

Figure 16.20 Environmental influences on the expression of PKU within a single family.   All three children in this photo have inherited the alleles that cause PKU. The child in the middle was raised on a phenylalanine-free diet and developed normally. The other two children, born before the benefits of such a diet were known, were raised on diets containing phenylalanine. These two children have symptoms of PKU, including mental impairment.

copies of the gene can eat foods containing the amino acid phenylalanine and metabolize it correctly. However, individuals with two copies of the mutant gene cannot metabolize phenylalanine. When these individuals eat a standard diet containing phenylalanine, this amino acid accumulates within their bodies and becomes highly toxic. Under these conditions, PKU homozygotes manifest a variety of detrimental symptoms, including mental impairment, underdeveloped teeth, and foul-smelling urine. In contrast, when these individuals are identified at birth and given a restricted diet that is free of phenylalanine, they develop normally (**Figure 16.20**). This is a dramatic example of how genes and the environment can interact to determine an individual's phenotype. In the U.S., most newborns are tested for PKU, which occurs in about 1 in 10,000 babies. A newborn who is found to have this disorder can be raised on a phenylalanine-free diet and develop normally.

16.6   Genetics and Probability

As we have seen throughout this chapter, Mendel's laws of inheritance can be used to predict the outcome of genetic crosses. How is this useful? In agriculture, plant and animal breeders use predictions about the types and relative numbers of offspring their crosses will produce in order to develop commercially important crops and livestock. Also, people are often interested in the potential characteristics of their future children. This has particular importance to individuals who may carry alleles that cause inherited diseases. Of course, no one can see into the future and definitively predict what will happen. Nevertheless, genetic counselors can often help couples predict the likelihood of having an affected child. This probability is one factor that may influence a couple's decision about whether to have children.

Earlier in this chapter, we considered how a Punnett square can be used to predict the outcome of simple genetic crosses. In addition to Punnett squares, we can apply the tools of mathematics and probability to solve more complex genetic problems. In this section, we will examine a couple of ways to calculate the outcomes of genetic crosses using these tools.

Genetic Predictions Are Based on the Mathematical Rules of Probability

The chance that an event will have a particular outcome is called the **probability** of that outcome. The probability of a given outcome depends on the number of possible outcomes. For example, if you draw a card at random from a 52-card deck, the probability that you will get the jack of diamonds is 1 in 52, because there are 52 possible outcomes for the draw. In contrast, only two outcomes are possible when you flip a coin, so the probability is one in two (1/2, or 0.5, or 50%) that the heads side will be showing when the coin lands. The general formula for the probability (P) that a random event will have a specific outcome is

$$P = \frac{\text{Number of times an event occurs}}{\text{Total number of possible outcomes}}$$

Thus, for a single coin toss, the chance of getting heads is

$$P_{\text{heads}} = \frac{1 \text{ heads}}{(1 \text{ heads} + 1 \text{ tails})} = \frac{1}{2}$$

Earlier in this chapter, we used Punnett squares to predict the fractions of offspring with a given genotype or phenotype. In a cross between two pea plants that were heterozygous for the height gene (Tt), our Punnett square predicted that one-fourth of the offspring would be dwarf. We can make the same prediction by using a probability calculation.

$$P_{\text{dwarf}} = \frac{1 \text{ } tt}{(1 \text{ } TT + 2 \text{ } Tt + 1 \text{ } tt)} = \frac{1}{4} = 25\%$$

A probability calculation allows us to predict the likelihood that a future event will have a specific outcome. However, the accuracy of this prediction depends to a great extent on the number of events we observe—in other words, on the size of our sample. For example, if we toss a coin six times, the calculation we just presented for P_{heads} suggests we should get heads three times and tails three times. However, each coin toss is an independent event, meaning that every time we toss the coin there is a random chance that it will come up heads or tails, regardless of the outcome of the previous toss. With only six tosses, we would not be too surprised if we got four heads and two tails instead of the expected three heads and three tails. The deviation between the observed and expected outcomes is called the **random sampling error**. With a small sample, the random sampling error may cause the observed data to be quite different from the expected outcome. By comparison, if we flipped a coin 1,000 times, the percentage of heads would be fairly close to the predicted 50%. With a larger sample, we expect the sampling error to be smaller.

The Product Rule Is Used to Predict the Outcome of Independent Events

Punnett squares allow us to predict the likelihood that a genetic cross will produce an offspring with a particular genotype or phenotype. To predict the likelihood of producing multiple offspring with particular genotypes or phenotypes, we can use the **product rule**, which states that *the probability that two or more independent events will occur is equal to the product of their individual probabilities.* As we have already discussed, events are independent if the outcome of one event does not affect the outcome of another. In our previous coin-toss example, each toss is an independent event—if one toss comes up heads, another toss still has an equal chance of coming up either heads or tails. If we toss a coin twice, what is the probability that we will get heads both times? The product rule says that it is equal to the probability of getting heads on the first toss (1/2) times the probability of getting heads on the second toss (1/2), or one in four (1/2 × 1/2 = 1/4).

To see how the product rule can be applied to a genetics problem, let's consider a rare recessive human trait known as congenital analgesia. (Congenital refers to a condition present at birth; analgesia means insensitivity to pain.) People with this trait can distinguish between sensations such as sharp and dull, or hot and cold, but they do not perceive extremes of sensation as painful. The first known case of congenital analgesia, described in 1932, was a man who made his living entertaining the public as a "human pincushion." For a phenotypically normal couple, each heterozygous for the recessive allele causing congenital analgesia, we can ask, What is the probability that their first three offspring will have the disorder? To answer this question, we must first determine the probability of a single offspring having the abnormal phenotype. By using a Punnett square, we would find that the probability of an individual offspring being homozygous recessive is 1/4. Thus, each of this couple's children has a one in four chance of having the disorder.

We can now use the product rule to calculate the probability of this couple having three affected offspring in a row. The phenotypes of the first, second, and third offspring are independent events; that is, the phenotype of the first offspring does not affect the phenotype of the second or third offspring. The product rule tells us that the probability of all three children having the abnormal phenotype is

$$\frac{1}{4} \times \frac{1}{4} \times \frac{1}{4} = \frac{1}{64} = 0.016$$

The probability of the first three offspring having the disorder is 0.016, or 1.6%. In other words, we can say that this couple's chance of having three children in a row with congenital analgesia is very small—only 1.6 out of 100. The phenotypes of the first, second, and third child are independent of each other.

The product rule can also be used to predict the outcome of a cross involving two or more genes. Let's suppose a pea plant with the genotype *TtYy* was crossed to a plant with the genotype *Ttyy*. We could ask the question, What is the probability that an offspring will have the genotype *ttYy*? If the two genes independently assort, the probability of inheriting alleles for one gene is independent of the other gene. Therefore, we can separately calculate the probability of the desired outcome for each gene. By constructing two small Punnett squares, we can determine the probability of genotypes for each gene individually, as shown below.

Cross: *TtYy* × *Ttyy*

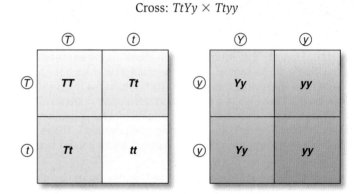

Probability that an offspring will be *tt* is 1/4, or 0.25.

Probability that an offspring will be *Yy* is 1/2, or 0.5

We can now use the product rule to determine the probability that an offspring will be *ttYy*;

$$P = (0.25)(0.5) = 0.125, \text{ or } 12.5\%$$

The Sum Rule Is Used to Predict the Outcome of Mutually Exclusive Events

Let's now consider a second way to predict the outcome of particular crosses. In a cross between two heterozygous (*Tt*) pea plants, we may want to know the probability of a particular offspring being a homozygote. In this case we are asking, What is the chance that this individual will be either homozygous *TT* or homozygous *tt*? To answer an "either/or" question, we use the sum rule, which applies to events with mutually exclusive outcomes. When we say that outcomes are mutually exclusive, we mean they cannot occur at the same time. A pea plant can be tall or dwarf, but not both at the same time. The tall and dwarf phenotypes are mutually exclusive. Similarly, a plant with the genotype *TT* cannot be *Tt* or *tt*. Each of these genotypes is mutually exclusive with the other two. According to the **sum rule**, *the probability that one of two or more mutually exclusive outcomes will occur is the sum of the probabilities of the individual outcomes.*

To find the probability that an offspring will be either homozygous *TT* or homozygous *tt*, we add together the probability that it will be *TT* and the probability that it will be *tt*. If we constructed a Punnett square, we would find that the probability for each of these genotypes is one in four. We can now use the sum rule to determine the probability of an individual having one of these genotypes.

$$\frac{1}{4} + \frac{1}{4} = \frac{1}{2}$$

(probability of *TT*)   (probability of *tt*)   (probability of either *TT* or *tt*)

This calculation predicts that in crosses of two *Tt* parents, half of the offspring will be homozygotes—either *TT* or *tt*.

Summary of Key Concepts

16.1 Mendel's Laws of Inheritance

- Mendel studied seven characters found in garden peas that existed in two variants each. (Figures 16.1, 16.2)
- Mendel allowed his peas to self-fertilize, or he carried out cross-fertilization, also known as hybridization. (Figures 16.3, 16.4)
- By following the inheritance pattern of a single character (a monohybrid cross) for two generations, Mendel determined the law of segregation. This law tells us that two alleles of a gene segregate during the formation of eggs and sperm so that every gamete receives only one allele. (Figures 16.5, 16.6)
- The genotype is the genetic makeup of an organism. Alleles are alternative versions of the same gene. Phenotype is a description of the traits that an organism displays.
- A Punnett square can be constructed to predict the outcome of crosses.
- A testcross can be conducted to determine if an individual displaying a dominant trait is a homozygote or a heterozygote. (Figure 16.7)
- By conducting a dihybrid cross, Mendel determined the law of independent assortment, which states that the alleles of different genes assort independently of each other during gamete formation. In a dihybrid cross, this yields a 9:3:3:1 ratio in the F_2 generation. (Figure 16.8)

16.2 The Chromosome Theory of Inheritance

- The chromosome theory of inheritance explains how the steps of meiosis account for Mendel's laws of inheritance. Each gene is located at a particular locus on a chromosome. (Figures 16.9, 16.10, 16.11)

16.3 Pedigree Analysis of Human Traits

- The inheritance patterns in humans are determined from a pedigree analysis. (Figures 16.12, 16.13)

16.4 Sex Chromosomes and X-Linked Inheritance Patterns

- Many species of animals and some species of plants have separate male and female sexes. In many cases, sex is determined by differences in sex chromosomes. (Figure 16.14)
- In mammals, recessive X-linked traits such as hemophilia are more likely to occur in males.

- Morgan's experiments showed that an eye-color gene in *Drosophila* is located on the X chromosome. (Figure 16.15)

16.5 Variations in Inheritance Patterns and Their Molecular Basis

- Several inheritance patterns have been discovered that obey Mendel's laws but yield differing ratios of offspring compared to Mendel's crosses. (Table 16.1)
- Recessive inheritance is often due to a loss-of-function mutation. In many simple dominant/recessive relationships, the heterozygote has a dominant phenotype because 50% of the normal protein is sufficient to produce that phenotype. (Figure 16.16)
- Mutant genes are responsible for many inherited diseases in humans. In many cases, the effects of a mutant gene are pleiotropic, meaning the gene affects several different aspects of bodily structure and function. (Table 16.2)
- Incomplete dominance occurs when a heterozygote has a phenotype that is intermediate between either homozygote. This occurs because 50% of the functional protein is not enough to produce the same phenotype as a homozygote. (Figure 16.17)
- ABO blood type is an example of multiple alleles in which a gene exists in three alleles in a population. The I^A and I^B alleles show codominance, which means that both are expressed in the same individual. These alleles encode enzymes with different specificities for attaching sugar molecules to make antigens. (Table 16.3)
- Pattern baldness in people is a sex-influenced trait that is dominant in males and recessive in females. This pattern occurs because sex hormones influence the expression of certain genes. (Figure 16.18)
- Phenotypes are influenced by an organism's environment as well its genes. The norm of reaction is a description of how a phenotype may change depending on the environmental conditions. (Figures 16.19, 16.20)

16.6 Genetics and Probability

- Probability is the likelihood that an event will occur in the future. Random sampling error is the deviation between observed and expected values.
- The product rule states that the probability of two or more independent events occurring is equal to the product of their individual probabilities. The sum rule states that the probability that two or more mutually exclusive events occurring is the sum of the individual probabilities.

Assess and Discuss

Test Yourself

1. Based on Mendel's experimental crosses, what is the expected F_2 phenotypic ratio of a monohybrid cross?
   a. 1:2:1   c. 3:1   e. 4:1
   b. 2:1   d. 9:3:3:1

2. During which phase of cellular division does Mendel's law of segregation physically occur?
   a. mitosis
   b. meiosis I
   c. meiosis II
   d. all of the above
   e. b and c only

3. An individual that has two different alleles of a particular gene is said to be
   a. dihybrid.
   b. recessive.
   c. homozygous.
   d. heterozygous.
   e. hemizygous.

4. Which of Mendel's laws cannot be observed in a monohybrid cross?
   a. segregation
   b. dominance/recessiveness
   c. independent assortment
   d. codominance
   e. All of the above can be observed in a monohybrid cross.

5. During a _____ cross, an individual with the dominant phenotype and unknown genotype is crossed with a _____ individual to determine the unknown genotype.
   a. monohybrid, homozygous recessive
   b. dihybrid, heterozygous
   c. test, homozygous dominant
   d. monohybrid, homozygous dominant
   e. test, homozygous recessive

6. A woman is heterozygous for an X-linked trait, hemophilia A. If she has a child with a man without hemophilia A, what is the probability that the child will be a male with hemophilia A? (Note: The child could be a male or female.)
   a. 100%
   b. 75%
   c. 50%
   d. 25%
   e. 0%

7. A gene that affects more than one phenotypic trait is said to be
   a. dominant.
   b. wild type.
   c. dihybrid.
   d. pleiotropic.
   e. heterozygous.

8. A hypothetical flowering plant species produces red, pink, and white flowers. To determine the inheritance pattern, the following crosses were conducted with the results indicated:
   red × red → all red
   white × white → all white
   red × white → all pink
   What type of inheritance pattern does this represent?
   a. dominance/recessiveness
   b. X-linked
   c. codominance
   d. incomplete dominance
   e. pleiotropy

9. Genes located on a sex chromosome are said to be
   a. X-linked.
   b. dominant.
   c. hemizygous.
   d. sex linked.
   e. sex influenced.

10. A nonbald male has an offspring with a woman who is homozygous for the pattern baldness allele. What is the probability that the offspring will become bald?
    a. 100%
    b. 75%
    c. 50%
    d. 25%
    e. 0%

Conceptual Questions

1. Describe one observation in a human pedigree that would rule out a recessive pattern of inheritance. Describe an observation that would rule out a dominant pattern.

2. A cross is made between individuals of the following genotypes: *AaBbCCDd* and *AabbCcdd*. What is the probability that an offspring will be *AAbbCCDd*? Hint: Don't waste your time making a really large Punnett square. Make four small Punnett squares instead and use the product rule.

3. Explain why recessive X-linked traits in humans are more likely to occur in males.

Collaborative Questions

1. Discuss the principles of the chromosome theory of inheritance. Which principles do you think were deduced via light microscopy, and which were deduced from crosses? What modern techniques could be used to support the chromosome theory of inheritance?

2. When examining a human pedigree, what observations do you look for to distinguish between X-linked recessive inheritance versus autosomal recessive inheritance? How would you distinguish X-linked dominant inheritance from autosomal dominant inheritance from an analysis of a human pedigree?

Online Resource

www.brookerbiology.com

Stay a step ahead in your studies with animations that bring concepts to life and practice tests to assess your understanding. Your instructor may also recommend the interactive ebook, individualized learning tools, and more.

Complex Patterns of Inheritance

17

Darren was invited to a Friday night party at Emily's apartment. Darren took his roommate, Chris, with him. While at the party, Chris noticed that Emily had a cat with a calico coat pattern, in which patches of orange fur are mixed with patches of black fur (see chapter-opening photo). Chris said to Darren, "I'll bet you ten to one that Emily's cat is a female." Since Darren knew that Chris had never met Emily before and certainly had not seen her cat before, Darren said, "You're on." So he walked up to Emily and asked, "What's your cat's name?" "Her name is Patches," Emily replied. "Isn't she cute?" Hmmmm. . . . thought Darren, maybe I shouldn't have made that bet.

How did Chris know that Emily's cat was a female? The answer is that the calico coat pattern almost always occurs in females. It is an example of a complex pattern of inheritance, one that could not have been predicted from Mendel's laws.

In this chapter, we will explore inheritance patterns that would be difficult if not impossible to predict based solely on Mendel's laws of inheritance, which we discussed in Chapter 16. Some of them even violate the law of segregation or the law of independent assortment. Studies of complex inheritance patterns have helped us appreciate more fully how genes influence phenotypes. Such research has revealed an astounding variety of ways that inheritance occurs. The

Photo of a calico cat. This female cat is heterozygous for X-linked alleles that confer orange or black patches of fur.

picture that emerges is of a wonderful web of diverse mechanisms by which genes give rise to phenotypes. **Table 17.1** provides a summary of Mendelian inheritance and the types of inheritance patterns we will consider in this chapter.

Table 17.1	Different Types of Inheritance Patterns
Type	**Description**
Mendelian	Inheritance patterns in which a single gene affects a single trait and the alleles obey the law of segregation. These patterns include simple dominant/recessive traits, X-linked traits, incomplete dominance, codominance, and sex-influenced traits (refer back to Table 16.1).
Epistasis	A type of gene interaction in which the alleles of one gene mask the effects of a dominant allele of another gene.
Continuous variation	Inheritance pattern in which the offspring display a continuous range of phenotypes. This pattern is produced by the additive interactions of several genes, along with environmental influences.
Linkage	Inheritance pattern involving two or more genes that are close together on the same chromosome. Linked genes do not assort independently.
Extranuclear inheritance	Inheritance pattern of genes found in the genomes of mitochondria or chloroplasts. Usually these genes are inherited from the mother.
X inactivation	Phenomenon of female mammals in which one X chromosome is inactivated in every somatic cell, producing a mosaic phenotype.
Genomic imprinting	Inheritance pattern in which an allele from one parent is silenced in the somatic cells of the offspring, whereas the allele from the other parent is expressed.
Maternal effect	Inheritance pattern in which the genotype of the mother determines the phenotype of the offspring. This occurs because the mother provides the gene products from maternal effect genes to developing egg cells.

17.1 Gene Interaction

The study of single genes was pivotal in establishing the science of genetics. This focus allowed Mendel to formulate the basic laws of inheritance for traits with a simple dominant/recessive inheritance pattern. Likewise, this approach helped later researchers understand inheritance patterns involving incomplete dominance and codominance, as well as traits that are influenced by an individual's sex. However, all or nearly all traits are influenced by many genes. For example, in both plants and animals, height is affected by genes that encode proteins involved in the production of growth hormones, cell division, the uptake of nutrients, metabolism, and many other functions. Variation in any of the genes involved in these processes is likely to have an impact on an individual's height.

If height is controlled by many genes, how was Mendel able to study the effects of a single gene that produced tall or dwarf pea plants? The answer lies in the genotypes of his strains. Although many genes affect the height of pea plants, Mendel chose true-breeding strains that differed with regard to only one of those genes. As a hypothetical example, let's suppose that pea plants have 10 genes affecting height, which we will call K, L, M, N, O, P, Q, R, S, and T. The genotypes of two hypothetical strains of pea plants may be:

Tall strain: *KK LL MM NN OO PP QQ RR SS TT*

Dwarf strain: *KK LL MM NN OO PP QQ RR SS tt*

In this example, the tall and dwarf strains differ at only a single locus. One strain is *TT* and the other is *tt*, and this accounts for the difference in their height. If we make crosses of tall and dwarf plants, the genotypes of the F_2 offspring will differ with regard to only one gene; the other nine genes will be identical in all of them. This approach allows a researcher to study the effects of a single gene even though many genes may affect a single character.

In this section, we will examine situations in which a single character is controlled by two or more genes, each of which has two or more alleles. This phenomenon is called **gene interaction**. As you will see, allelic variation at two or more loci may affect the outcome of traits in different ways. First we will look at a gene interaction in which an allele of one gene prevents the phenotypic expression of an allele of a different gene. Then we will discuss an interaction in which multiple genes have additive effects on a single character. These additive effects, together with environmental influences, account for the continuous phenotypic variation that we see for most traits.

In an Epistatic Gene Interaction, the Allele of One Gene Masks the Phenotypic Effects of a Different Gene

In some gene interactions, the alleles of one gene mask the expression of the alleles of another gene. This phenomenon is called **epistasis** (from the Greek *ephistanai*, meaning stopping). An example is the unexpected gene interaction discovered by William Bateson and Reginald Punnett in the early 1900s, when they were studying crosses involving the sweet pea, *Lathyrus odoratus*. A cross between a true-breeding purple-flowered plant and a true-breeding white-flowered plant produced an F_1 generation with all purple-flowered plants and an F_2 generation with a 3:1 ratio of purple- to white-flowered plants. Mendel's laws predicted this result. The surprise came when the researchers crossed two different true-breeding varieties of white-flowered sweet peas (**Figure 17.1**). All of the F_1 generation plants had purple flowers! When these plants were allowed to self-fertilize, the F_2 generation had purple-flowered and white-flowered plants in a 9:7 ratio. From these results, Bateson and Punnett deduced that two different genes were involved. To have purple flowers, a plant must have one or two dominant alleles for each of these genes. The relationships among the alleles are as follows:

C (one allele for purple) is dominant to *c* (white)

P (an allele of a different gene for purple) is dominant to *p* (white)

cc masks *P*, or *pp* masks *C*, in either case producing white flowers

A plant that was homozygous for either *c* or *p* would have white flowers even if it had a dominant purple-producing allele at the other locus.

How do we explain these results at the molecular and cellular level? Epistatic interactions often arise because two or more different proteins are involved in a single cellular function. For example, two or more proteins may be part of an enzymatic pathway leading to the formation of a single product. This is the case for the formation of a purple pigment in the sweet pea strains we have been discussing:

Colorless precursor $\xrightarrow{\text{Enzyme C}}$ Colorless intermediate $\xrightarrow{\text{Enzyme P}}$ Purple pigment

In this example, a colorless precursor molecule must be acted on by two different enzymes to produce the purple pigment. Gene *C* encodes a functional protein called enzyme C that converts the colorless precursor into a colorless intermediate. The recessive *c* allele results in a lack of production of enzyme C in the homozygote. Gene *P* encodes the functional enzyme P, which converts the colorless intermediate into the purple pigment. Like the *c* allele, the *p* allele results in an inability to produce a functional enzyme. A plant homozygous for either of the recessive alleles will not make any functional enzyme C or enzyme P. When either of these enzymes is missing, the plant cannot make the purple pigment and has white flowers. Note that the results observed in Figure 17.1 do not conflict with Mendel's laws of segregation or independent assortment. Mendel investigated the effects of only a single gene on a given

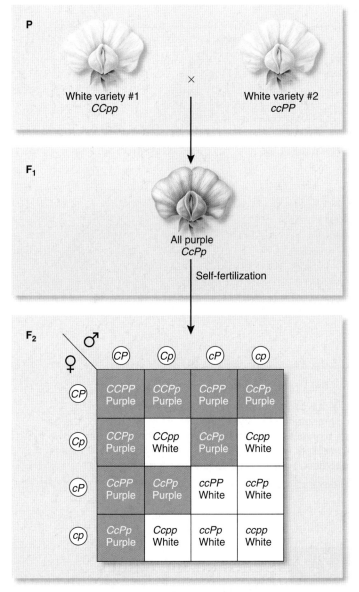

Figure 17.1 **Epistasis in the sweet pea.** The color of the sweet pea flower is controlled by two genes, each with a dominant and a recessive allele. Each of the dominant alleles (*C* and *P*) encodes an enzyme required for the synthesis of purple pigment. A plant that is homozygous recessive for either gene (*cc* or *pp*) cannot synthesize the pigment and will have white flowers.

Concept check: *In a Ccpp individual, which functional enzyme is missing? Is it the enzyme encoded by the C or P gene?*

character. The 9:7 ratio is due to a gene interaction in which two genes affect a single character.

Polygenic Inheritance and Environmental Influences Produce Continuous Phenotypic Variation

Until now, we have discussed the inheritance of characters with clearly defined phenotypic variants, such as red or white

eyes in fruit flies. These are known as **discrete traits**, because the phenotypes do not overlap. For most traits, however, the phenotypes cannot be sorted into discrete categories. Traits that show continuous variation over a range of phenotypes are called **quantitative traits**. In humans, quantitative traits include height, weight, skin color, metabolic rate, and heart size. In the case of domestic animals and plant crops, many of the traits that people consider desirable are quantitative in nature, such as the number of eggs a chicken lays, the amount of milk a cow produces, and the number of apples on an apple tree. Consequently, much of our modern understanding of quantitative traits comes from agricultural research.

Quantitative traits are usually **polygenic**, which means that several or many genes contribute to the outcome of the trait. For many polygenic traits, genes contribute to the phenotype in an additive way. As a hypothetical example, let's suppose that three different genes (*W1*, *W2*, and *W3*) affect weight in turkeys; each gene can occur in heavy (*W*) and light (*w*) alleles. A heavy allele contributes an extra pound to an individual's weight compared to a light allele. A turkey homozygous for all the heavy alleles (*W1W1 W2W2 W3W3*) would weigh 6 pounds more than an individual homozygous for all the light alleles (*w1w1 w2w2 w3w3*). A turkey heterozygous for all three genes (*W1w1 W2w2 W3w3*) would have an intermediate weight that would be 3 pounds lighter than the homozygous turkey carrying all of the heavy alleles, because the heterozygote carries 3 light alleles.

Another important factor regarding quantitative traits is the environment that an individual experiences. As we learned in Chapter 16, the environment plays a vital role in the phenotypic expression of genes. Environmental factors often have a major impact on quantitative traits. For example, an animal's diet affects its weight, and the amount of rain and sunlight that fall on an apple tree affect how many apples it produces.

Because quantitative traits are polygenic and greatly influenced by environmental conditions, the phenotypes among different individuals may vary substantially in any given population. As an example, let's consider skin pigmentation in humans. This character is influenced by several genes that tend to interact in an additive way. As a simplified example, let's consider a population in which skin pigmentation in people is controlled by three genes, which we will designate *A*, *B*, and *C*. Each gene may exist as a dark allele, designated A^D, B^D, or C^D, or a light allele, designated A^L, B^L, or C^L, respectively. All of the alleles encode enzymes that cause the synthesis of skin pigment, but the enzymes encoded by dark alleles cause more pigment synthesis than the enzymes encoded by light alleles. Figure 17.2 considers a hypothetical case in which people who were heterozygous for all three genes produced a large population of offspring. The bar graph shows the genotypes of the offspring, grouped according to the total number of light and dark alleles. As shown by the shading of the figure, skin pigmentation increases as the number of dark alleles increases. Offspring who have all light alleles or who have all dark alleles—that

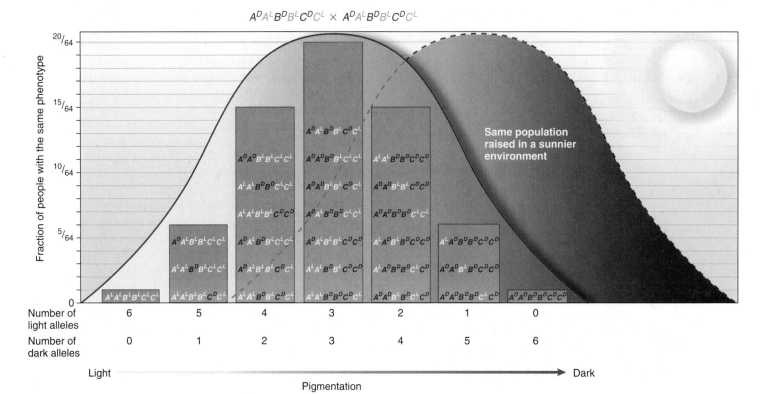

$A^D A^L B^D B^L C^D C^L \times A^D A^L B^D B^L C^D C^L$

Figure 17.2 **Continuous variation in a polygenic trait.** Skin color is a polygenic character that displays a continuum of phenotypes. The bell curve on the left (solid line) shows the range of skin pigmentation in a hypothetical human population. The bar graphs below the curve show the additive effects of three genes that affect pigment production in this population; each bar shows the fraction of people with a particular number of dark alleles (A^D, B^D, and C^D) and light alleles (A^L, B^L, and C^L). The bell curve on the right (dashed line) represents the expected range of phenotypes if the same population was raised in a sunnier environment.

Concept check: What are the main reasons the pigmentation phenotype displays a continuous distribution?

is, those who are homozygous for all three genes—are fewer in number than those with some combination of light and dark alleles. As seen in the bell-shaped curve above the bar graph, the phenotypes of the offspring fall along a continuum. This continuous phenotypic variation, which is typical of quantitative traits, is produced by genotypic differences together with environmental effects. A second bell-shaped curve (the dashed line) depicts the expected phenotypic range if the same population of offspring had been raised in a sunnier environment, which increases pigment production. This curve illustrates how the environment can also have a significant influence on the range of phenotypes.

In our discussion of genetics, we tend to focus on discrete traits because this makes it easier to relate a specific genotype with a phenotype. This is usually not possible for continuous traits. For example, as depicted in the middle bar of Figure 17.2, seven different genotypes can produce individuals with a medium amount of pigmentation. It is important to emphasize that the majority of traits in all organisms are continuous, not discrete. Most traits are influenced by multiple genes, and the environment has an important impact on the phenotypic outcome.

17.2 Genes on the Same Chromosome: Linkage, Recombination, and Mapping

In the inheritance patterns we have examined so far, the alleles segregate and assort independently as predicted by Mendel's laws. As we have just seen, phenotypes can be influenced by a variety of factors, including gene interactions and environmental effects, which make it difficult to relate a specific genotype to a specific phenotype. Even so, if we understand all of these factors and take them into account, we can see that each of the genes is transmitted according to Mendel's laws.

In this section, we will focus on inheritance patterns that do not conform to the law of independent assortment. We will begin by examining the first experimental cross that demonstrated such a pattern. This pattern was subsequently explained by Thomas Hunt Morgan, who proposed that different genes located close to each other on the same chromosome tend to be inherited together. Finally, we will see how crossing over between such genes provided the first method of mapping genes on chromosomes.

FEATURE INVESTIGATION

Bateson and Punnett's Crosses of Sweet Peas Showed That Genes Do Not Always Assort Independently

In Chapter 16, we learned that the independent assortment of alleles is due to the random alignment of homologous chromosomes during meiosis (refer back to Figure 16.11). But what happens when the alleles of different genes are on the same chromosome? A typical chromosome contains many hundreds or even a few thousand different genes. When two genes are close together on the same chromosome, they tend to be transmitted as a unit, a phenomenon known as **linkage**. A group of genes that usually stay together during meiosis is called a **linkage group**, and the genes in the group are said to be linked. The genes on a single chromosome can be considered to consti-

tute a linkage group. In a two-factor cross, linked genes that are close together on the same chromosome do not follow the law of independent assortment.

The first study showing linkage between two different genes was a cross of sweet peas carried out by William Bateson and Reginald Punnett in 1905. A surprising result occurred when they conducted a two-factor cross involving flower color and pollen shape (**Figure 17.3**). One of the parent plants had purple flowers (*PP*) and long pollen (*LL*); the other had red flowers (*pp*) and round pollen (*ll*). As Bateson and Punnett expected, the F_1 plants all had purple flowers and long pollen (*PpLl*). The unexpected result came in the F_2 generation.

Although the F_2 offspring displayed the four phenotypes predicted by Mendel's laws, the observed numbers of offspring did not conform to the predicted 9:3:3:1 ratio (refer back to

Figure 17.3   A cross of sweet peas showing that independent assortment does not always occur.

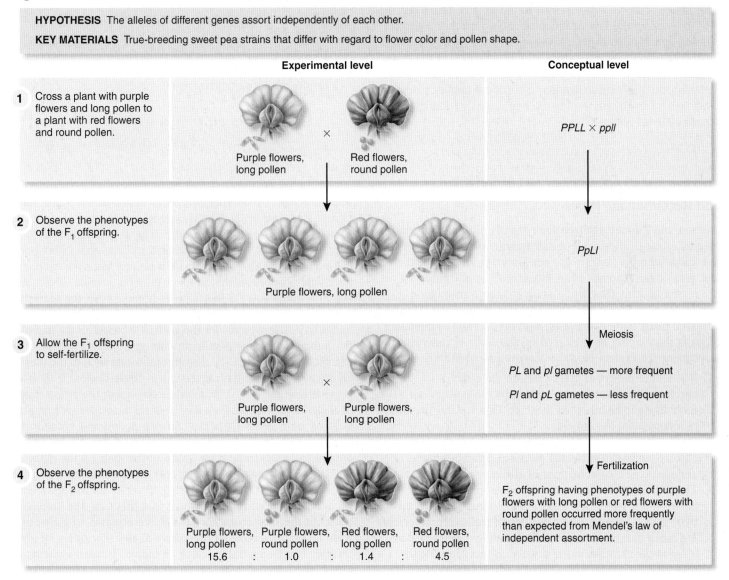

HYPOTHESIS The alleles of different genes assort independently of each other.

KEY MATERIALS True-breeding sweet pea strains that differ with regard to flower color and pollen shape.

| Experimental level | Conceptual level |

1 Cross a plant with purple flowers and long pollen to a plant with red flowers and round pollen.

Purple flowers, long pollen × Red flowers, round pollen

$PPLL \times ppll$

2 Observe the phenotypes of the F_1 offspring.

Purple flowers, long pollen

PpLl

3 Allow the F_1 offspring to self-fertilize.

Purple flowers, long pollen × Purple flowers, long pollen

Meiosis

PL and *pl* gametes — more frequent

Pl and *pL* gametes — less frequent

4 Observe the phenotypes of the F_2 offspring.

Purple flowers, long pollen : Purple flowers, round pollen : Red flowers, long pollen : Red flowers, round pollen
15.6 : 1.0 : 1.4 : 4.5

Fertilization

F_2 offspring having phenotypes of purple flowers with long pollen or red flowers with round pollen occurred more frequently than expected from Mendel's law of independent assortment.

5   THE DATA

Phenotypes of F₂ offspring	Observed number	Observed ratio	Expected number	Expected ratio
Purple flowers, long pollen	296	15.6	240	9
Purple flowers, round pollen	19	1.0	80	3
Red flowers, long pollen	27	1.4	80	3
Red flowers, round pollen	85	4.5	27	1

6   CONCLUSION   The data are not consistent with the law of independent assortment.

7   SOURCE   Bateson, William, and Punnett, Reginald C. 1911. On the inter-relations of genetic factors. *Proceedings of the Royal Society of London, Series B,* 84:3–8.

Figure 16.8). Rather, as seen in the data in Figure 17.3, the F₂ generation had a much higher proportion of the two phenotypes found in the parental generation: purple flowers with long pollen, and red flowers with round pollen. These results did not support the law of independent assortment. How did Bateson and Punnett explain these results? They suggested that the transmission of flower color and pollen shape was somehow coupled, so these traits did not always assort independently. Although the law of independent assortment applies to many other genes, in this example, the hypothesis of independent assortment was rejected.

Experimental Questions

1. What hypothesis were Bateson and Punnett testing when conducting the crosses in the sweet pea?

2. What were the expected results of Bateson and Punnett's cross?

3. How did the observed results differ from the expected results? What did Bateson and Punnett conclude about the results of this particular cross?

Linkage and Crossing Over Produce Parental and Recombinant Types

Bateson and Punnett realized their results did not conform to Mendel's law of independent assortment. However, they did not know why the genes were not assorting independently. A few years later, Thomas Hunt Morgan obtained similar ratios in crosses of fruit flies while studying the transmission pattern of genes in *Drosophila*. Like Bateson and Punnett, Morgan observed many more F₂ offspring with the parental combination of traits than would be predicted on the basis of independent assortment. To explain his data, Morgan proposed three ideas:

1. When different genes are located on the same chromosome, the traits determined by those genes are more likely to be inherited together. This violates the law of independent assortment.

2. Due to crossing over during meiosis, homologous chromosomes can exchange pieces of chromosomes and create new combinations of alleles.

3. The likelihood of a crossover occurring in the region between two genes depends on the distance between the two genes. Crossovers between homologous chromosomes are much more likely to occur between two genes farther apart in the chromosome compared to two genes closer together.

To illustrate the first two ideas, **Figure 17.4** considers a series of crosses involving two genes linked on the same chromosome in *Drosophila*. The two genes are located on an autosome, not on a sex chromosome. The P generation cross is between flies that are homozygous for alleles that affect body color and wing shape. The female is homozygous for the dominant wild-type alleles that produce gray body color (b^+b^+) and straight wings (c^+c^+); the male is homozygous for recessive mutant alleles that produce black body color (bb) and curved wings (cc). The symbols for the genes are based on the name of the mutant allele; the dominant wild-type allele is indicated by a superscript plus sign ($^+$). The chromosomes next to the flies in Figure 17.4 show the arrangement of these alleles. If the two genes are on the same chromosome, we know the arrangement of alleles in the P generation flies because these flies are homozygous for both genes ($b^+b^+c^+c^+$ for one parent and $bbcc$ for the other parent). In the P generation female on the left, b^+ and c^+ are linked, while b and c are linked in the male on the right.

Let's now look at the outcome of the crosses in Figure 17.4. As expected, the F₁ offspring (b^+bc^+c) all had gray bodies and straight wings, confirming that these are the dominant traits. In the next cross, F₁ females were mated to males that were homozygous for both recessive alleles ($bbcc$). Recall from Chapter 16 that a cross in which an individual with a dominant phenotype is mated with a homozygous recessive individual is

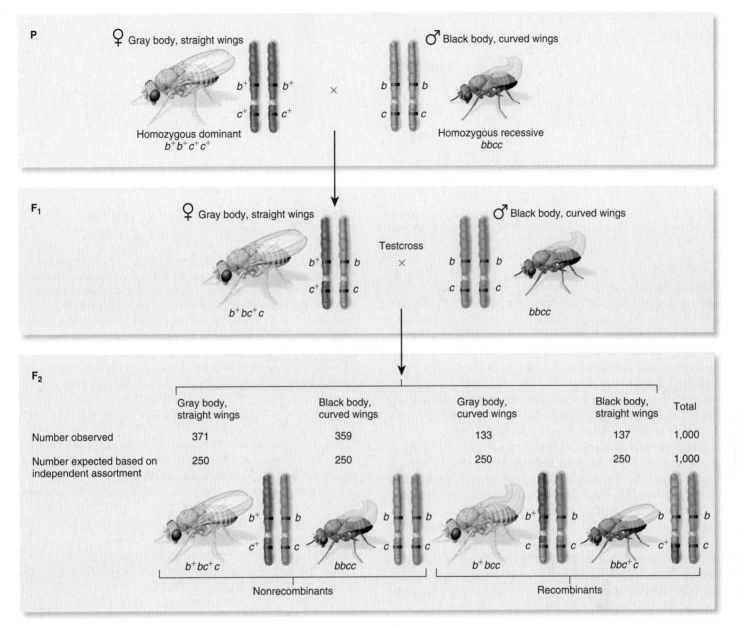

Figure 17.4 **Linkage and recombination of alleles.**   An experimenter crossed $b^+b^+c^+c^+$ and $bbcc$ flies to produce F_1 heterozygotes. F_1 females were then testcrossed to $bbcc$ males. The large number of parental phenotypes in the F_2 generation suggests that the two genes are linked on the same chromosome. F_2 recombinant phenotypes occur because the alleles can be rearranged by crossing over. Note: The b^+ and c^+ alleles are dominant and the b and c alleles are recessive.

Concept check: *In which fly or flies did crossing over occur to produce the recombinant offspring of the F_2 generation?*

called a **testcross**. However, in the crosses we are discussing here, the purpose of the testcross is to determine whether the genes for body color and wing shape are linked. If the genes are on different chromosomes and assort independently, this testcross will produce equal numbers of F_2 offspring with the four possible phenotypes. The observed numbers clearly conflict with this prediction, which is based on independent assortment. The two most abundant phenotypes are those with the combinations of characteristics in the P generation: gray bodies and straight wings or black bodies and curved wings. These offspring are termed **nonrecombinants**, or parental types, because

their combination of traits has not changed from the parental generation. The smaller number of offspring that have a combination of traits not found in the parental generation—gray bodies and curved wings or black bodies and straight wings—are called **recombinants**.

How do we explain the occurrence of recombinants when genes are linked on the same chromosome? As shown beside the flies of the F_2 generation in Figure 17.4, each recombinant individual has a chromosome that is the product of a crossover. The crossover occurred while the F_1 female fly was making egg cells.

As shown below, four different egg cells are possible:

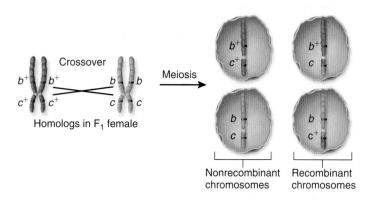

Due to crossing over, two of the four egg cells produced by meiosis have recombinant chromosomes. What happens when eggs containing such chromosomes are fertilized in the testcross? Each of the male fly's sperm cells carries a chromosome with the two recessive alleles. If the egg contains the recombinant chromosome carrying the b^+ and c alleles, the testcross will produce an F_2 offspring with a gray body and curved wings. If the egg contains the recombinant chromosome carrying the b and c^+ alleles, F_2 offspring will have a black body and straight wings. Therefore, crossing over in the F_1 female can explain the occurrence of both types of F_2 recombinant offspring.

Morgan's ideas about linkage and crossing over were based on similar data, derived from his studies of genes on the X chromosome. The idea that linked genes tend to be inherited together explained the high frequency of parental combinations of traits in certain crosses. The proposal that crossing over produces chromosomes with new allele combinations accounted for the occurrence of recombinant phenotypes. Morgan's third idea regarding linkage was that the frequency of crossing over between linked genes depends on the distance between them. This suggested a method for determining the relative positions of genes on a chromosome, as we will discuss next.

Recombination Frequencies Provide a Method for Mapping Genes Along Chromosomes

The study of the arrangement of genes in a species' genome is called **genetic mapping**. As depicted in Figure 17.5, the linear order of genes that are linked to each other along the same chromosome is shown in a chart known as a **genetic map**. Each gene has its own unique locus at a particular site within a chromosome. For example, the gene for black body color (b) that we discussed earlier is located near the middle of the chromosome, whereas the gene for curved wings (c) is closer to one end. The first genetic map, showing five genes on the *Drosophila* X chromosome, was constructed in 1911 by Alfred Sturtevant, an undergraduate student who studied in Morgan's laboratory.

Genetic mapping allows us to estimate the relative distances between linked genes based on the likelihood that a crossover will occur between them. This likelihood is proportional to the

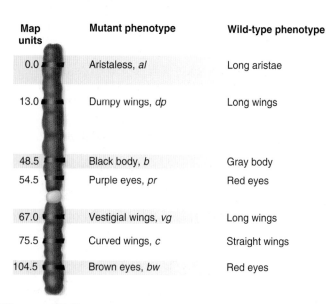

Map units	Mutant phenotype	Wild-type phenotype
0.0	Aristaless, *al*	Long aristae
13.0	Dumpy wings, *dp*	Long wings
48.5	Black body, *b*	Gray body
54.5	Purple eyes, *pr*	Red eyes
67.0	Vestigial wings, *vg*	Long wings
75.5	Curved wings, *c*	Straight wings
104.5	Brown eyes, *bw*	Red eyes

Figure 17.5   A simplified genetic map. This map shows the relative locations of a few genes along chromosome number 2 in *Drosophila melanogaster*. The name of each gene is based on the mutant phenotype. The numbers on the left are map units (mu). The distance between two genes, in map units, corresponds to their recombination frequency in testcrosses.

Concept check: *How would you set up a testcross to determine the distance between the al and dp genes? What would be the genotypes of the P, F₁, and F₂ generations?*

distance between the genes, as Morgan first proposed. If the genes are very close together, a crossover is unlikely to begin in the region between them. However, if the genes are very far apart, a crossover is more likely to be initiated between them and thereby recombine their alleles. Therefore, in a testcross involving two genes on the same chromosome, the percentage of recombinant offspring is correlated with the distance between the genes. This correlation provides the experimental basis for gene mapping. If a two-factor testcross produces many recombinants, the experimenter concludes that the two genes are far apart. If very few recombinants are observed, the two genes must be close together.

To find the distance between two genes, the experimenter must determine the frequency of crossing over between them, called their **recombination frequency**. This is accomplished by conducting a testcross. As an example, let's refer back to the *Drosophila* testcross described in Figure 17.4. As we discussed, the genes for body color and wing shape are on the same chromosome; the recombinants are the result of crossing over during egg formation in the F_1 female. We can use the data from the testcross shown in Figure 17.4 to estimate the distance between these two genes. The **map distance** between two linked genes is defined as the number of recombinants divided by the total number of offspring times 100.

$$\text{Map distance} = \frac{\text{Number of recombinants}}{\text{Total number of offspring}} \times 100$$

$$= \frac{133 + 137}{371 + 359 + 133 + 137} \times 100$$

$$= 27.0 \text{ map units}$$

The units of distance are called **map units** (**mu**), or sometimes **centiMorgans** (**cM**) in honor of Thomas Hunt Morgan. One map unit is equivalent to a 1% recombination frequency. In this example, 270 out of 1,000 offspring are recombinants, so the recombination frequency is 27%, and the two genes are 27.0 mu apart.

Genetic mapping has been useful for analyzing the genes of organisms that are easily crossed and produce many offspring in a short time. It has been used to map the genes of several plant species and of certain species of animals, such as *Drosophila*. However, for most organisms, including humans, genetic mapping via crosses is impractical due to long generation times or the inability to carry out experimental crosses. Fortunately, many alternative methods of gene mapping have been developed in the past few decades that are faster and do not depend on crosses. These newer cytological and molecular approaches, which we will discuss in Chapter 20, are also used to map genes in a wide variety of organisms.

17.3 Extranuclear Inheritance: Organelle Genomes

In the previous section, we examined the inheritance patterns of linked genes that violate the law of independent assortment. In this section, we will explore inheritance patterns that violate the law of segregation. The segregation of genes is explained by the pairing and segregation of homologous chromosomes during meiosis. However, some genes are not found on the chromosomes in the cell nucleus, and these genes do not segregate in the same way. The transmission of genes located outside the cell nucleus is called **extranuclear inheritance**. Two important types of extranuclear inheritance patterns involve genes found in mitochondria and chloroplasts. Extranuclear inheritance is also called **cytoplasmic inheritance** because these organelles are in the cytoplasm of the cell. In this section, we will examine the transmission patterns observed for genes found in the chloroplast and mitochondrial genomes and consider how mutations in these genes may affect an individual's traits.

Genomes & Proteomes Connection

Chloroplast and Mitochondrial Genomes Are Relatively Small, but Contain Genes That Encode Important Proteins

As we discussed in Chapter 4, mitochondria and chloroplasts are found in eukaryotic cells because of an ancient endosymbiotic relationship. They contain their own genetic material, called the mitochondrial genome and chloroplast genome, respectively (**Figure 17.6**). Mitochondrial and chloroplast genomes are composed of a single, circular DNA molecule. The mitochondrial genome of many mammalian species has been analyzed and usually contains a total of 37 genes. Twenty-four genes encode tRNAs and rRNAs, which are needed for translation inside the

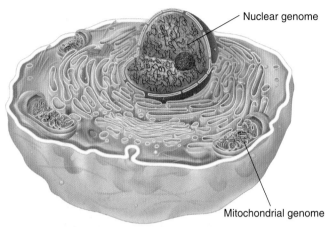

(a) An animal cell

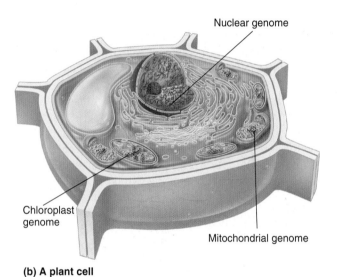

(b) A plant cell

Figure 17.6   The locations of genetic material in animal and plant cells.   The chromosomes in the cell nucleus are collectively known as the nuclear genome. Mitochondria and chloroplasts have small circular chromosomes called the mitochondrial and chloroplast genomes, respectively.

Concept check: *What is the evolutionary origin of mitochondria and chloroplasts in eukaryotic cells?*

mitochondrion, and 13 genes encode proteins that are involved in oxidative phosphorylation. As discussed in Chapter 7, the primary function of the mitochondrion is the synthesis of ATP via oxidative phosphorylation. Among different species of plants, chloroplast genomes typically contain about 110 to 120 genes. Many of these genes encode proteins that are vital to the process of photosynthesis, which we discussed in Chapter 8.

Chloroplast Genomes Are Often Maternally Inherited

One of the first experiments showing an extranuclear inheritance pattern was carried out by German botanist Carl Correns in 1909. Correns discovered that leaf pigmentation in the four-o'clock plant (*Mirabilis jalapa*) follows a pattern of inheritance that does not obey Mendel's law of segregation. Four-o'clock leaves may be green, white, or variegated. Correns observed that the pigmentation of the offspring depended solely on the pigmentation of the female parent, a phenomenon called **maternal inheritance** (**Figure 17.7**). If the female parent had white leaves, all of the offspring had white leaves. Similarly, if the female was green, so were all of the offspring. The offspring of a variegated female parent could be green, white, or variegated.

What accounts for maternal inheritance? At the time, Correns did not understand that chloroplasts contain genetic material. Subsequent research identified DNA present in chloroplasts as responsible for the unusual inheritance pattern observed. We now know that the pigmentation of four-o'clock leaves can be explained by the occurrence of genetically different types of chloroplasts in the leaf cells. As discussed in Chapter 8, chloroplasts are the site of photosynthesis, and their green color is due to the presence of the pigment called chlorophyll. Certain genes required for chlorophyll synthesis are found within the chloroplast DNA. The green phenotype is due to the presence of chloroplasts that have normal genes and synthesize the usual quantity of chlorophyll. The white phenotype is caused by a mutation in a gene within the chloroplast DNA that prevents the synthesis of most of the chlorophyll. (Enough chlorophyll is made for the plant to survive.) The variegated phenotype occurs in leaves that have a mixture of the two types of chloroplasts.

Leaf pigmentation follows a maternal inheritance pattern because the chloroplasts in four-o'clocks are transmitted only through the cytoplasm of the egg (**Figure 17.8**). Recall from Chapter 4 that chloroplasts are derived from proplastids. In four-o'clocks, the egg cell contains several proplastids that are inherited by the offspring. The sperm cell does not contribute any proplastids. For this reason, the phenotype of a four-o'clock plant reflects the types of proplastids it inherits from the maternal parent. If the maternal parent transmits only normal proplastids, all offspring will have green leaves (Figure 17.8a). Alternatively, if the maternal parent transmits only mutant proplastids, all offspring will have white leaves (Figure 17.8b). Because an egg cell contains several proplastids, an offspring from a variegated maternal parent may inherit only normal proplastids, only mutant proplastids, or a mixture of normal and mutant proplastids. Consequently, the offspring of a variegated maternal parent can be green, white, or variegated individuals (Figure 17.8c).

How do we explain the variegated phenotype at the cellular level? This phenotype is due to events that occur after fertilization. As a zygote containing both types of proplastids grows via cellular division to produce a multicellular plant, some cells may receive mostly those that develop into normal chloroplasts. Further division of these cells gives rise to a patch of green tissue. Alternatively, as a matter of chance, other cells may receive all or mostly mutant chloroplasts that are defective in chlorophyll synthesis. The result is a patch of white tissue.

In most species of plants, the egg cell provides most of the zygote's cytoplasm, whereas the much smaller male gamete often provides little more than a nucleus. Therefore,

Correns' crosses

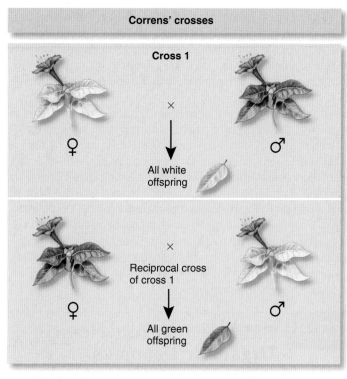

Cross 1

♀ × ♂

All white offspring

♀ × ♂

Reciprocal cross of cross 1

All green offspring

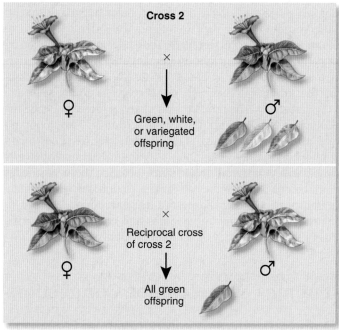

Cross 2

♀ × ♂

Green, white, or variegated offspring

♀ × ♂

Reciprocal cross of cross 2

All green offspring

Figure 17.7   **Maternal inheritance in the four-o'clock plant.** Genes for green pigment synthesis in plants are found in the chloroplast genome. The white phenotype in four-o'clocks is due to chloroplasts with a mutant allele that greatly reduces green pigment production. The variegated phenotype is due to a mixture of normal and mutant chloroplasts. In four-o'clocks, the egg contains all of the plastids that are inherited by the offspring, so the phenotype of the offspring is determined by the female parent.

Concept check: *In this example, where is the gene located that causes the green color of four-o'clock leaves? How is this gene transmitted from parent to offspring?*

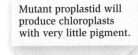
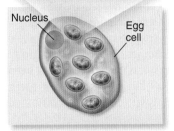

Normal proplastid will produce chloroplasts with a normal amount of green pigment.

Mutant proplastid will produce chloroplasts with very little pigment.

Nucleus

Egg cell

(a) Egg cell from a maternal parent with green leaves

(b) Egg cell from a maternal parent with white leaves

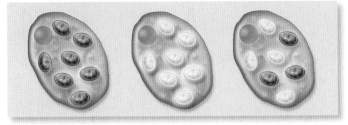

(c) Possible egg cells from a maternal parent with variegated leaves

Figure 17.8 **Plastid composition of egg cells from green, white, and variegated four-o'clock plants.** In this drawing of four-o'clock egg cells, normal proplastids are represented as green and mutant proplastids as white. (Note: This drawing is schematic. Proplastids do not differentiate into chloroplasts in egg cells, and they are not actually green.) **(a)** A green plant produces eggs carrying normal proplastids. **(b)** A white plant produces eggs carrying mutant proplastids. **(c)** A variegated plant produces eggs that may contain either or both types of proplastids.

chloroplasts are most often inherited via the egg. In seed-bearing plants, maternal inheritance of chloroplasts is the most common transmission pattern. However, certain species exhibit a pattern called **biparental inheritance**, in which both the pollen and the egg contribute chloroplasts to the offspring. Others exhibit **paternal inheritance**, in which only the pollen contributes these organelles. For example, most types of pine trees show paternal inheritance of chloroplasts.

Mitochondrial Genomes Are Maternally Inherited in Humans and Most Other Species

Mitochondria are found in nearly all eukaryotic species. As with the transmission of chloroplasts in plants, maternal inheritance is the most common pattern of mitochondrial transmission in eukaryotic species, although some species do exhibit biparental or paternal inheritance.

In humans, mitochondria are maternally inherited. Researchers have discovered that mutations in human mitochondrial genes can cause a variety of rare diseases (**Table 17.2**). These

Table 17.2	Examples of Human Mitochondrial Diseases
Disease	**Causes and symptoms**
Leber's hereditary optic neuropathy	A mutation in one of several mitochondrial genes that encode electron transport proteins. The main symptom is loss of vision.
Neurogenic muscle weakness	A mutation in a mitochondrial gene that encodes a subunit of mitochondrial ATP synthase, which is required for ATP synthesis. Symptoms involve abnormalities in the nervous system that affect the muscles and eyes.
Maternal myopathy and cardiomyopathy	A mutation in a mitochondrial gene that encodes a tRNA for leucine. The primary symptoms involve muscle abnormalities, most notably in the heart.
Myoclonic epilepsy and ragged-red muscle fibers	A mutation in a mitochondrial gene that encodes a tRNA for lysine. Symptoms include epilepsy, dementia, blindness, deafness, and heart and kidney malfunctions.

are usually chronic degenerative disorders that affect organs and cells that require high levels of ATP such as the brain, eyes, heart, muscle, kidney, and endocrine glands. For example, Leber's hereditary optic neuropathy (LHON) affects the optic nerve and can lead to the progressive loss of vision in one or both eyes. LHON can be caused by a mutation in one of several different mitochondrial genes.

17.4 X Inactivation, Genomic Imprinting, and Maternal Effect

We will end our discussion of complex inheritance patterns by considering examples in which the timing and control of gene expression create inheritance patterns that are determined by the sex of the individual or by the sex of the parents. The first two patterns, called X inactivation and genomic imprinting, are types of **epigenetic inheritance**. In epigenetic inheritance, modification of a gene or chromosome during egg formation, sperm formation, or early stages of embryo growth alters gene expression in a way that is fixed during an individual's lifetime. Epigenetic changes permanently affect the phenotype of the individual, but they are not permanent over the course of two or more generations, and they do not change the actual DNA sequence. For example, a gene may undergo an epigenetic change that inactivates the gene for an individual's entire life, so it is never expressed in that individual. However, when the same individual produces gametes, the gene may become activated and remain active during the lifetime of an offspring that inherits the gene.

At the end of this section, we will also consider genes that exhibit an intriguing inheritance pattern called the **maternal effect**, in which the genotype of the mother directly determines the phenotype of her offspring. Surprisingly, for maternal effect genes, the genotypes of the father and of the offspring themselves do not affect the offspring's phenotype.

In Female Mammals, One X Chromosome Is Inactivated in Each Somatic Cell

In 1961, the British geneticist Mary Lyon proposed the phenomenon of **X inactivation**, in which one X chromosome in the somatic cells of female mammals is inactivated, meaning that its genes are not expressed. X inactivation is based on two lines of evidence. The first evidence came from microscopic studies of mammalian cells. In 1949, Murray Barr and Ewart Bertram identified a highly condensed structure in the cells of female cats that was not found in the cells of male cats. This structure was named a **Barr body** after one of its discoverers (**Figure 17.9**). In 1960, Susumu Ohno correctly proposed that a Barr body is a highly condensed X chromosome. Lyon's second line of evidence was the inheritance pattern of variegated coat colors in certain female mammals. A classic case is the calico cat, which has randomly distributed patches of black and orange fur (see chapter-opening photo).

How do we explain this patchwork phenotype? According to Lyon's hypothesis, the calico pattern is due to the permanent inactivation of one X chromosome in each cell that forms a patch of the cat's skin, as shown in **Figure 17.10**. The gene involved is an X-linked gene that occurs as an orange allele, X^O, and a black allele, X^B. A female cat heterozygous for this gene will be calico. (The cat's white underside is due to a dominant allele of a different autosomal gene.) At an early stage

of embryonic development, one of the two X chromosomes is randomly inactivated in each of the cat's somatic cells, including those that will give rise to the hair-producing skin cells. As the embryo grows and matures, the pattern of X inactivation is maintained during subsequent cell divisions. For example, skin cells derived from a single embryonic cell in which the X^B-carrying chromosome has been inactivated will produce a patch of orange fur, because they express only the X^O allele that is carried on the active chromosome. Alternatively, a group of skin cells in which the chromosome carrying X^O has been inactivated will express only the X^B allele, producing a patch of black fur. The result is an animal with randomly distributed patches of black and orange fur.

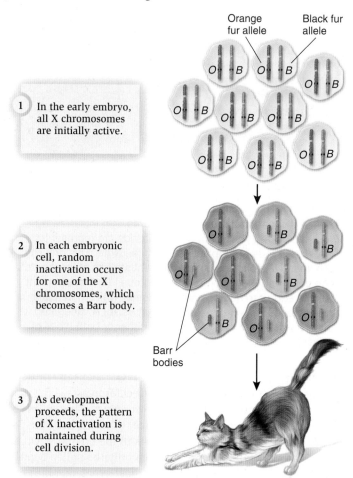

1 In the early embryo, all X chromosomes are initially active.

2 In each embryonic cell, random inactivation occurs for one of the X chromosomes, which becomes a Barr body.

Barr bodies

3 As development proceeds, the pattern of X inactivation is maintained during cell division.

Figure 17.10 Random X-chromosome inactivation in a calico cat. The calico pattern is due to random X-chromosome inactivation in a female that is heterozygous for an X-linked gene with black and orange alleles. The cells at the top of this figure represent a small mass of cells making up the very early embryo. In these cells, both X chromosomes are active. At an early stage of embryonic development, one X chromosome is randomly inactivated in each cell. The initial inactivation pattern is maintained in the descendents of each cell as the embryo matures into an adult. The pattern of orange and black fur in the adult cat reflects the pattern of X inactivation in the embryo.

Concept check: On rare occasions, a phenotypically male cat is calico. How is this possible?

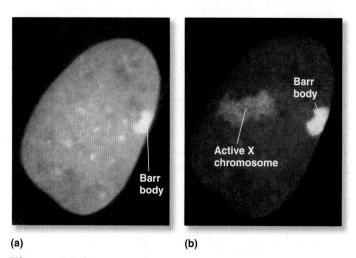

(a)   (b)

Figure 17.9 X-chromosome inactivation in female mammals. (a) A Barr body is seen on the periphery of a human nucleus (during interphase) after staining with a DNA-specific dye. Because it is compact, the Barr body is the most brightly stained. (b) The same nucleus was labeled using a yellow fluorescent probe that recognizes the X chromosome. The Barr body is more compact compared to the active X chromosome, which is to the left of the Barr body.

Concept check: How is the Barr body different from the other X chromosome in this cell?

In female mammals that are heterozygous for X-linked genes, approximately half of their somatic cells will express one allele, whereas the rest of their somatic cells will express the other allele. These heterozygotes are called **mosaics** because they are composed of two types of cells. The phenomenon of mosaicism is readily apparent in calico cats, in which the alleles affect fur color.

For many X-linked traits in humans, females who are heterozygous for recessive X-linked alleles usually show the dominant trait because the expression of the dominant allele in 50% of their cells is sufficient to produce the dominant phenotype. For example, let's consider the recessive X-linked form of hemophilia that we discussed in Chapter 16. This type of hemophilia is caused by a defect in a gene that encodes a blood-clotting protein, called factor VIII, that is made by cells in the liver and secreted into the bloodstream. In a heterozygous female, approximately half of her liver cells will make and secrete this clotting factor, which is sufficient to prevent hemophilia. Therefore, she will exhibit the dominant trait of normal blood clotting.

On rare occasions, a female who is heterozygous may show mild or even severe disease symptoms. How is this possible? X inactivation in humans occurs when an embryo is 10 days old. At this stage, the liver contains only about a dozen cells. In most females who are heterozygous for the normal and hemophilia alleles, roughly half of their liver cells will express the normal allele. However, on rare occasions, all or most of the dozen embryonic liver cells may inactivate the X chromosome carrying the dominant normal allele. Following growth and development, such a female will have a very low level of factor VIII and as a result will show symptoms of hemophilia.

Why does X inactivation occur? Researchers have proposed that X inactivation achieves **dosage compensation**, a process that equalizes the expression of X-linked genes in male and female mammals. The X chromosome carries many genes, whereas the Y chromosome has relatively few. The inactivation of one X chromosome in the female reduces the number of expressed copies (doses) of X-linked genes from two to one. As a result, the expression of X-linked genes in females and males is roughly equal.

The X Chromosome Has an X Inactivation Center That Controls Compaction into a Barr Body

After Lyon's hypothesis was confirmed, researchers became interested in the genetic control of X inactivation. The cells of humans and other mammals have the ability to count their X chromosomes and allow only one of them to remain active. Additional X chromosomes are converted to Barr bodies. In normal females, two X chromosomes are counted and one is inactivated. In normal males, one X chromosome is counted and none inactivated.

On rare occasions, people are born with abnormalities in the number of their sex chromosomes. In the disorders known as Turner syndrome, triple X syndrome, and Klinefelter syndrome, the cells inactivate the number of X chromosomes necessary to leave a single active chromosome. For example, in triple X syndrome, two X chromosomes convert to Barr bodies.

Phenotype	Chromosome composition	Number of Barr bodies	Number of active X chromosomes
Normal female	XX	1	1
Normal male	XY	0	1
Turner syndrome (female)	XO	0	1
Triple X syndrome (female)	XXX	2	1
Klinefelter syndrome (male)	XXY	1	1

In spite of X inactivation, people with these three syndromes do exhibit some phenotypic abnormalities. The symptoms associated with these disorders may be due to effects that occur prior to X inactivation or because not all of the genes on the Barr body are completely silenced.

Although the genetic control of inactivation is not entirely understood at the molecular level, a short region on the X chromosome called the **X inactivation center** (**Xic**) is known to play a critical role. Eeva Therman and Klaus Patau determined that X inactivation is accomplished by counting the number of Xics and inactivating all X chromosomes except for one. In cells with two X chromosomes, if one of them is missing its Xic due to a chromosome mutation, neither X chromosome will be inactivated, because only one Xic is counted. Having two active X chromosomes is a lethal condition for a human female embryo.

The expression of a specific gene within the X inactivation center is required for compaction of the X chromosome into a Barr body. This gene, discovered in 1991, is named *Xist* (for X inactive specific transcript). The *Xist* gene product is a long RNA molecule that does not encode a protein. Instead, the role of *Xist* RNA is to coat one of the two X chromosomes during the process of X inactivation. After coating, proteins associate with the *Xist* RNA and promote compaction of the chromosome into a Barr body. The *Xist* gene on the Barr body continues to be expressed after other genes on this chromosome have been silenced. The expression of the *Xist* gene also maintains a chromosome as a Barr body during cell division. Whenever a somatic cell divides in a female mammal, the Barr body is replicated to produce two Barr bodies.

The Transcription of an Imprinted Gene Depends on the Sex of the Parent

As we have seen, X inactivation is a type of epigenetic inheritance in which a chromosome is modified in the early embryo, permanently altering gene expression in that individual. Other types of epigenetic inheritance occur in which genes or chromosomes are modified in the gametes of a parent, permanently altering gene expression in the offspring. **Genomic imprinting**, which was discovered in the early 1980s, refers to an inheritance pattern in which a segment of DNA is imprinted or marked so that gene expression occurs only from the genetic material inherited from one parent. It occurs in numerous species, including insects, plants, and mammals.

Genomic imprinting may involve a single gene, a part of a chromosome, an entire chromosome, or even all of the chromosomes inherited from one parent. It is permanent in the somatic cells of a given individual, but the marking of the DNA is altered from generation to generation. Imprinted genes do not follow a Mendelian pattern of inheritance because imprinting causes the offspring to distinguish between maternally and paternally inherited alleles. Depending on how a particular gene is marked by each parent, the offspring will express either the maternal or the paternal allele, but not both.

One of the first imprinted genes to be identified is a gene called *Igf2* that is found in mice and other mammals. This gene encodes a growth hormone called insulin-like growth factor 2 (Igf2) that is needed for proper growth. If a normal copy of this gene is not expressed, a mouse will be dwarf. The *Igf2* gene is known to be located on an autosome, not on a sex chromosome. Because mice are diploid, they have two copies of this gene, one from each parent.

Researchers have discovered mutations in the *Igf2* gene that block the function of the Igf2 hormone. When mice carrying normal or mutant alleles are crossed to each other, a bizarre result is obtained (**Figure 17.11**). If the male parent is homozygous for the normal allele and the female is homozygous for the mutant allele, all the offspring grow to a normal size. In contrast, if the male is homozygous for the mutant allele and the female is homozygous for the normal allele, all the

offspring are dwarf. The reason this result is so surprising is that the normal and dwarf offspring have the same genotype but different phenotypes! These phenotypes are not the result of any external influence on the offspring's development. Rather, the allele that is expressed in their somatic cells is dependent upon its parental origin. In mice, the *Igf2* gene is imprinted in such a way that only the paternal gene is expressed, which means it is transcribed into mRNA. The maternal gene is not transcribed.

The baby mice shown on the left side of the photograph of Figure 17.11 are normal because they express a functional paternal gene. In contrast, the baby mice on the right are dwarf because the paternal gene is a mutant allele that results in a nonfunctional hormone.

Why is the maternal gene encoding Igf2 not transcribed into mRNA? To answer this question we need to consider the regulation of gene transcription in eukaryotes. As discussed in Chapter 13, the attachment of methyl ($-CH_3$) groups to the bases of DNA can alter gene transcription. In most genes, DNA methylation silences gene expression by inhibiting the initiation of transcription or by causing the chromatin in a region to become more compact. In contrast, for a few imprinted genes, methylation may enhance gene expression by attracting activator proteins to the promoter or by preventing the binding of repressor proteins. Researchers have discovered that DNA methylation is the marking process that occurs during the imprinting of certain genes, including the *Igf2* gene.

Figure 17.12 shows the imprinting process in which a maternal gene is methylated. The left side of the figure follows the marking process during the life of a female individual; the

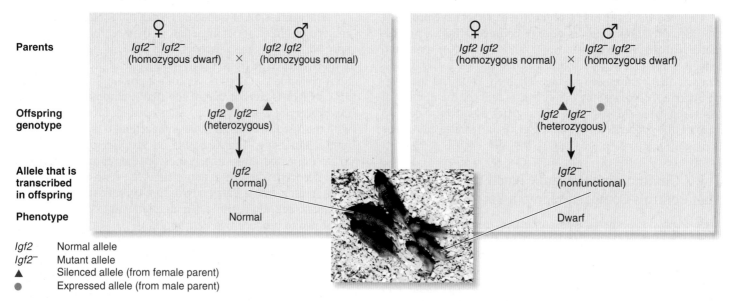

Figure 17.11 **An example of genomic imprinting in the mouse.** In the cross on the left, a homozygous male with the normal *Igf2* allele is crossed to a homozygous female carrying a defective allele, *Igf2⁻*. Offspring are phenotypically normal because the paternal allele is expressed. In the cross on the right, a homozygous male carrying the defective allele is crossed to a homozygous normal female. In this case, offspring are dwarf because the paternal allele is defective and the maternal allele is not expressed. The photograph shows normal-size (left) and dwarf littermates (right) derived from a cross between a wild-type female and a heterozygous male carrying a loss-of-function *Igf2* allele (courtesy of A. Efstratiadis). The loss-of-function allele was created using methods described in Chapter 20.

Concept check: *If you cross an Igf2 Igf2⁻ male mouse to an Igf2 Igf2 female mouse, what would be the expected results?*

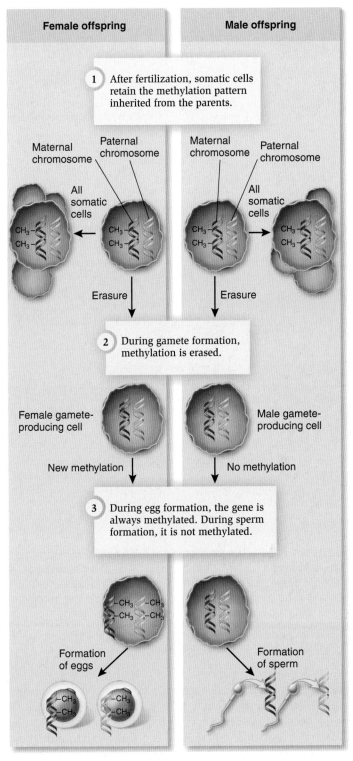

Female offspring | **Male offspring**

1. After fertilization, somatic cells retain the methylation pattern inherited from the parents.

Maternal chromosome / Paternal chromosome

All somatic cells

Maternal chromosome / Paternal chromosome

All somatic cells

CH₃ CH₃ | CH₃ CH₃ | CH₃ CH₃ | CH₃ CH₃

Erasure | Erasure

2. During gamete formation, methylation is erased.

Female gamete-producing cell | Male gamete-producing cell

New methylation | No methylation

3. During egg formation, the gene is always methylated. During sperm formation, it is not methylated.

Formation of eggs | Formation of sperm

Figure 17.12 Genomic imprinting via DNA methylation.
The cells at the top of this figure have a methylated gene inherited from the mother and a nonmethylated version of the same gene inherited from the father. This pattern of methylation is the same in male and female offspring and is maintained in their somatic cells. The methylation is erased during gamete formation, but in females, the gene is methylated again at a later stage in the formation of eggs. Therefore, females always transmit a methylated, transcriptionally silent copy of this gene, whereas males transmit a nonmethylated, transcriptionally active copy.

right side follows the same process in a male. Both individuals received a methylated gene from their mother and a nonmethylated copy of the same gene from their father. Via cell division, the zygote develops into a multicellular organism. Each time a somatic cell divides, enzymes in the cell maintain the methylation of the maternal gene, while the paternal gene remains unmethylated. If methylation inhibits transcription of this gene, only the paternal copy will be expressed in the somatic cells of both the male and female offspring.

The methylation state of an imprinted gene may be altered when individuals make gametes. First, the methylation is erased (Figure 17.12, step 2). Next, the gene may be methylated again, but that depends on whether the individual is a female or male. In females making eggs, both copies of the gene are methylated; in males making sperm, neither copy is methylated. When we consider the effects of methylation over the course of two or more generations, we can see how this phenomenon creates an epigenetic transmission pattern. The male in Figure 17.12 has inherited a methylated gene from his mother that is transcriptionally silenced in his somatic cells. Although he does not express this gene during his lifetime, he can pass on an active, nonmethylated copy of this exact same gene to his offspring.

Genomic imprinting is a recently discovered phenomenon that has been shown to occur for a few genes in mammals. For some genes, such as *Igf2*, the maternal allele is silenced, but for other genes, the paternal allele is silenced. While several hypotheses have been advanced, biologists are still trying to understand the reason for this curious marking process.

For Maternal Effect Genes, the Genotype of the Mother Determines the Phenotype of the Offspring

In epigenetic inheritance, genes are altered in ways that affect their expression in an individual or the individual's offspring. As we have seen, some of these alterations produce unusual inheritance patterns in which organisms with the same genotype have different phenotypes. Another inheritance pattern, with a very different mode of action, involves a category of genes called **maternal effect genes**. Surprisingly, for maternal effect genes, the genotypes of the father and of the offspring themselves do not affect the offspring's phenotype.

Inheritance patterns due to maternal effect genes were first identified in the 1920s by A. E. Boycott, in his studies of the freshwater snail *Lymnaea peregra*. In this species, the shell and internal organs can be arranged in either a right-handed (dextral) or a left-handed (sinistral) direction (**Figure 17.13**). The dextral orientation is dominant to the sinistral orientation. Whether a snail's body curves in a dextral or a sinistral direction depends on the pattern of cell division immediately following fertilization. Boycott crossed true-breeding strains of snails with either a dextral or a sinistral orientation (**Figure 17.14**). When a dextral female (*DD*) was crossed to a sinistral male (*dd*), all of the offspring were dextral. However, crossing a sinistral female (*dd*) to a dextral male (*DD*) produced the opposite result: All of the offspring were sinistral. These seemingly contradictory outcomes could not be explained in terms of Mendelian inheritance.

Figure 17.13 Snail shells (*Lymnaea peregra*) that coil to the right or left. The larger shell on the right is coiling to the right.

Alfred Sturtevant later suggested that snail coiling is due to a maternal effect gene that exists as a dextral (*D*) and a sinistral (*d*) allele. In the cross shown on the upper left in Figure 17.14, the P generation female is dextral (*DD*), and the male is sinistral (*dd*). In the cross on the right, the female is sinistral (*dd*), and the male is dextral (*DD*). All F$_1$ offspring are *Dd*, but their phenotype depends on their mother's genotype.

When the F$_1$ individuals from these two crosses are mated to each other, a genotypic ratio of 1 *DD* : 2 *Dd* : 1 *dd* is predicted for the F$_2$ generation. Because the *D* allele is dominant to the *d* allele, a Mendelian inheritance pattern would produce a 3:1 phenotypic ratio of dextral to sinistral snails. Instead, the snails of the F$_2$ generation were all dextral. How did Sturtevant explain this result? He proposed that the phenotype of the F$_2$ offspring depended solely on the genotype of the F$_1$ mother. Because the F$_1$ mothers were *Dd* and the *D* allele is dominant, the F$_2$ offspring were dextral even if their genotype was *dd*!

Sturtevant's hypothesis is also supported by the ratio of phenotypes seen in the F$_3$ generation. When members of the F$_2$ generation were crossed, the F$_3$ generation exhibited a 3:1 ratio of dextral to sinistral snails. These F$_3$ phenotypes reflect the genotypes of the F$_2$ mothers. The ratio of genotypes for the F$_2$ females was 1 *DD* : 2 *Dd* : 1 *dd*. The *DD* and *Dd* females produced dextral offspring, whereas the *dd* females produced sinistral offspring. This is consistent with the 3:1 phenotypic ratio in the F$_3$ generation.

The peculiar inheritance pattern of maternal effect genes can be explained by the process of egg maturation in female animals (**Figure 17.15**). Maternal cells called nurse cells surround a developing egg cell and provide it with nutrients. Within these diploid nurse cells, both copies of a maternal effect gene are activated to produce their gene products. The gene products are transported into the egg, where they persist for a significant time during embryonic development. The *D*

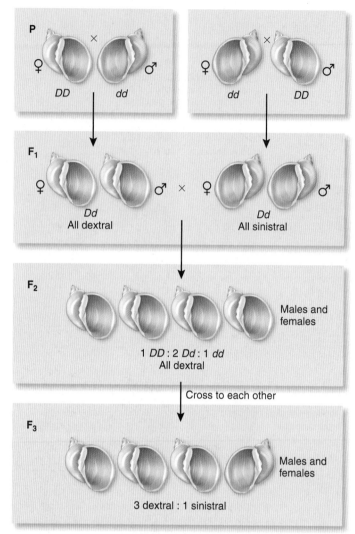

Figure 17.14 The inheritance of snail-coiling direction as an example of a maternal effect gene. The direction of body coiling is controlled by a single pair of genes. *D* (dextral, or right-handed) is dominant to *d* (sinistral, or left-handed). The genotype of the mother determines the phenotype of the offspring.

Concept check: An offspring has a genotype of *Dd* and coils to the left. What is the genotype of its mother?

and *d* gene products influence the pattern of cell division during the early stages of the snail's embryonic development. If an egg receives only the *D* gene product, the snail will develop a dextral orientation, whereas an egg that receives only the *d* gene product will produce a snail with a sinistral orientation. If an egg receives both *D* and *d* gene products, the snail will be dextral because the *D* gene product is dominant over *d*. In this way, the gene products of nurse cells, which are determined by the mother's genotype, influence the development of the offspring.

Several dozen maternal effect genes have been identified in experimental organisms, such as *Drosophila*. Recently, they have also been found in mice and humans. As we will discuss in Chapter 19, the products of maternal effect genes are critically important in the early stages of animal development.

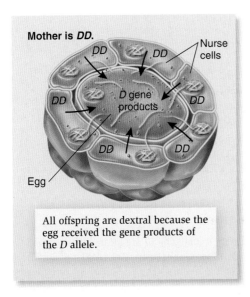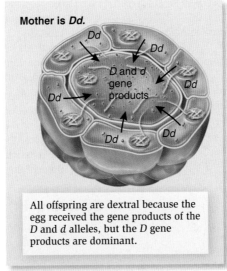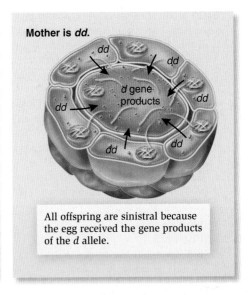

Mother is *DD*.

Nurse cells

DD *DD*

D gene products

DD *DD*

DD

Egg

DD *DD*

All offspring are dextral because the egg received the gene products of the *D* allele.

Mother is *Dd*.

Dd *Dd*

D and *d* gene products

Dd *Dd*

Dd *Dd*

All offspring are dextral because the egg received the gene products of the *D* and *d* alleles, but the *D* gene products are dominant.

Mother is *dd*.

dd *dd*

d gene products

dd *dd*

dd *dd*

All offspring are sinistral because the egg received the gene products of the *d* allele.

Figure 17.15 **The mechanism of maternal effect in snail coiling.** In this simplified diagram, the mother's diploid nurse cells transfer gene products to the egg as it matures. These gene products persist after fertilization, affecting development of the early embryo.

Concept check: Can a haploid egg cell that carries a D allele in its genome result in an offspring (following fertilization) that coils to the left? Can a haploid egg that carries a d allele in its genome result in an offspring that coils to the right? Explain your answers.

Summary of Key Concepts

- A variety of inheritance patterns are more complex than Mendel had realized. Many of these do not obey one or both of his laws of inheritance. (Table 17.1)

17.1 Gene Interaction

- Epistasis is a gene interaction that occurs when the alleles of one gene mask the effects of the alleles of a different gene. (Figure 17.1)

- Quantitative traits such as height and weight are polygenic, which means that several genes govern the trait. Often, the alleles of such genes contribute in an additive way to the phenotype. This produces continuous variation in the trait, which is graphed as a bell-shaped curve. (Figure 17.2)

17.2 Genes on the Same Chromosome: Linkage, Recombination, and Mapping

- When two different genes are on the same chromosome, they are said to be linked. Linked genes tend to be inherited as a unit, unless crossing over separates them. (Figures 17.3, 17.4)

- The percentage of offspring produced in a two-factor testcross can be used to create a genetic map, which shows the relative locations of genes along a chromosome. (Figure 17.5)

17.3 Extranuclear Inheritance: Organelle Genomes

- Mitochondria and chloroplasts carry a small number of genes. The inheritance of such genes is called extranuclear inheritance. (Figure 17.6)

- Chloroplasts in the four-o'clock plant are transmitted via the egg, a pattern called maternal inheritance. (Figures 17.7, 17.8)

- Several human diseases are known to be caused by mutations in mitochondrial genes, which follow a maternal inheritance pattern. (Table 17.2)

17.4 X Inactivation, Genomic Imprinting, and Maternal Effect

- Epigenetic inheritance refers to patterns in which a gene is inactivated during the life of an organism, but not over the course of two or more generations.

- X inactivation in female mammals occurs when one X chromosome in every somatic cell is randomly inactivated. If the female is heterozygous for an X-linked gene, this can lead to a mosaic phenotype, with half of the somatic cells expressing one allele and half expressing the other. (Figures 17.9, 17.10)

- Imprinted genes are inactivated by one parent but not both. The offspring expresses only one of the two alleles. During gamete formation, methylation of a gene from one parent is a mechanism to achieve imprinting. (Figures 17.11, 17.12)

- In inheritance patterns due to maternal effect genes, the genotype of the mother determines the phenotype of the offspring. This is explained by the phenomenon that the mother's nurse cells contribute gene products to egg cells that are needed for early stages of development. (Figures 17.13, 17.14, 17.15)

Assess and Discuss

Test Yourself

1. When two genes are located on the same chromosome they are said to be
   a. homologous.
   b. allelic.
   c. epistatic.
   d. linked.
   e. polygenic.

2. Based on the ideas proposed by Morgan, which of the following statements concerning linkage is <u>not</u> true?
   a. Traits determined by genes located on the same chromosome are likely to be inherited together.
   b. Crossing over between homologous chromosomes can create new gene combinations.
   c. A crossover is more likely to occur in a region between two genes that are close together compared to a region between two genes that are farther apart.
   d. The probability of crossing over depends on the distance between the genes.
   e. Genes that tend to be transmitted together are physically located on the same chromosome.

3. In genetic linkage mapping, 1 map unit is equivalent to
   a. 100 base pairs.
   b. 1 base pair.
   c. 10% recombination frequency.
   d. 1% recombination frequency.
   e. 1% the length of the chromosome.

4. Extranuclear (cytoplasmic) inheritance occurs because
   a. certain genes are found on the X chromosome.
   b. chromosomes in the nucleus may be transferred to the cytoplasm.
   c. some organelles contain DNA.
   d. the nuclear membrane breaks down during cell division.
   e. both a and c.

5. In many organisms, organelles such as the mitochondria are contributed only by the egg. This phenomenon is known as
   a. biparental inheritance.
   b. paternal inheritance.
   c. maternal effect.
   d. maternal inheritance.
   e. both c and d.

6. Modification of a gene during gamete formation or early development that alters the way the gene is expressed during the individual's lifetime is called
   a. maternal inheritance.
   b. epigenetic inheritance.
   c. epistasis.
   d. multiple allelism.
   e. alternative splicing.

7. A male mouse that is homozygous for the normal allele of the *Igf2* gene is mated to a female that is heterozygous, carrying one normal copy and one defective copy of the gene. What would be the expected outcome of this cross?
   a. all normal offspring
   b. 1/2 normal and 1/2 dwarf
   c. all dwarf
   d. 3/4 normal and 1/4 dwarf
   e. none of the above

8. When a gene is inactivated during gamete formation and that gene is maintained in an inactivated state in the somatic cells of offspring, such an inheritance pattern is called
   a. linkage.
   b. X inactivation.
   c. maternal effect.
   d. genomic imprinting.
   e. polygenic inheritance.

9. Calico coat pattern in cats is the result of
   a. X inactivation.
   b. epistasis.
   c. organelle heredity.
   d. genomic imprinting.
   e. maternal inheritance.

10. Maternal effect inheritance can be explained by
    a. gene products that are given to an egg by the nurse cells.
    b. the methylation of genes during gamete formation.
    c. the spreading of X inactivation from the Xic locus.
    d. the inheritance of alleles that contribute additively to a trait.
    e. none of the above.

Conceptual Questions

1. Two genes (called gene *A* and gene *B*) are located on the same chromosome and are 12 map units apart. An *AABB* individual was crossed to an *aabb* individual. The F_1 (*AaBb*) offspring were crossed to *aabb* individuals. What percentage of the F_2 offspring would you expect to be *Aabb*?

2. Certain forms of human color blindness are inherited as X-linked recessive traits. Heterozygous females are not usually color blind, but on rare occasions, a female may exhibit partial color blindness or may be color blind in just one eye. Explain how this could happen.

3. A maternal effect gene in flies affects head size. The dominant allele (*N*) produces a normal head size, whereas a recessive, mutant allele (*n*) causes a smaller head. A female with a small head produces all offspring with normal heads. What are all the possible genotypes of the mother, father, and offspring?

Collaborative Questions

1. As discussed in Chapter 16, Mendel studied seven traits in pea plants, and the garden pea happens to have seven different chromosomes. It has been pointed out that Mendel was very lucky not to have conducted crosses involving two traits that are closely linked on the same chromosome because the results would have confounded his theory of independent assortment. It has even been suggested that Mendel may not have published data involving traits that were linked. An article by Blixt ("Why Didn't Gregor Mendel Find Linkage?" *Nature* 256:206) considers this issue. Look up this article and discuss why Mendel did not find linkage.

2. Discuss the similarities and differences between X inactivation and genomic imprinting.

Online Resource

www.brookerbiology.com

Stay a step ahead in your studies with animations that bring concepts to life and practice tests to assess your understanding. Your instructor may also recommend the interactive ebook, individualized learning tools, and more.

Genetics of Viruses and Bacteria

18

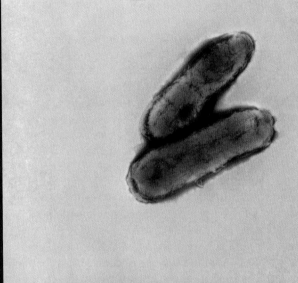

A colorized micrograph of *Haemophilus influenzae*, type b. This bacterium is a common cause of meningitis—a serious infection of the fluid in the spinal cord and the fluid that surrounds the brain.

While studying for his calculus test, Jason was having trouble concentrating due to a severe headache and fever. He thought he must be coming down with a cold. Though he had taken some aspirin, it didn't seem to be working. As he was eating some potato chips, one dropped in his lap. When he tried to look down to see where the chip had fallen, he realized that his neck was extremely stiff; he could barely move his head to look downward. Also, the brightness of his desk light seemed freakishly painful to his eyes. Over the course of that evening, Jason became confused and lethargic, and his roommate urged him to see a doctor. Fortunately, Jason took his advice and went to the college clinic. The diagnosis was bacterial meningitis—an inflammation of the protective membranes that cover the brain and spinal cord, collectively called the meninges. Although a relatively rare disease, bacterial meningitis is up to six times more common among people living in close quarters such as college dormitories. Because Jason sought help early enough, his disease could be treated with antibiotics. Had he not gotten help, the disease could have progressed to the point of causing severe brain damage and even death.

Jason's story highlights a primary reason why biologists are so interested in viruses and bacteria. Infectious diseases caused by viruses and bacteria are a leading cause of human suffering and death, accounting for one-quarter to one-third of deaths worldwide. The spread of infectious diseases results from human behavior, and in recent times, it has been accelerated by changes in land-use patterns, increased trade and travel, and the inappropriate use of antibiotic drugs. Although the incidence of fatal infectious diseases in the U.S. is low compared to the worldwide average, an alarming increase in more deadly strains of viruses and bacteria has occurred over the past few decades. Since 1980, the number of deaths in the U.S. due to infectious diseases has approximately doubled.

In this chapter, we turn our attention to the genetic analyses of viruses and bacteria. We will begin by examining viruses and other nonliving particles that infect living cells. All organisms are susceptible to infection by one or more types of viruses, which use the host's cellular machinery to replicate their own genome. Once a cell is infected, the genetic material of a virus orchestrates a series of events that ultimately leads to the production of new virus particles. We will consider the biological complexity of viruses and explore viral reproductive cycles. We will also examine some of the simplest and smallest infectious agents, called viroids and prions.

In the remaining sections of this chapter, we will examine the bacterial genome and the methods used in its investigation. Like their eukaryotic counterparts, bacteria have genetic differences that affect their cellular traits, and the techniques of modern microbiology make many of these differences, such as sensitivity to antibiotics and differences in nutritional requirements, easy to detect. Although bacteria reproduce asexually by cell division, their genetic variety is enhanced by the phenomenon called gene transfer, in which genes are passed from one bacterial cell to another. Like sexual reproduction in eukaryotes, gene transfer enhances the genetic diversity observed among bacterial species. In this chapter, we will explore three interesting ways that bacteria can transfer genetic material.

18.1 Genetic Properties of Viruses

In earlier chapters, we examined the replication and expression of eukaryotic and prokaryotic genes. Because all living organisms are either eukaryotes or prokaryotes, you may be thinking that we have considered every type of genome. However, certain nonliving things also have genomes. Viruses are nonliving particles with nucleic acid genomes. Why are viruses considered nonliving? They do not exhibit all seven properties associated with living organisms (refer back to Figure 1.5). Viruses are not composed of cells, and by themselves, they do not carry out metabolism, use energy, maintain homeostasis, or even reproduce. A virus or its genetic material must be taken up by a living cell to replicate.

The first virus to be discovered was tobacco mosaic virus (TMV). This virus infects several species of plants and causes mosaic-like patterns in which normal-colored patches are interspersed with light green or yellowish patches on the leaves (Figure 18.1). TMV damages leaves, flowers, and fruit but almost never kills the plant. In 1883, the German scientist Adolf Mayer determined that this disease could be spread by spraying the sap from one plant onto another. By subjecting this sap to filtration, the Russian scientist Dmitri Ivanovski demonstrated that the disease-causing agent was not a bacterium. Sap that had been passed through filters with pores small enough to prevent the passage of bacterial cells was still able to spread the disease. At first, some researchers suggested the agent was a chemical toxin. However, the Dutch botanist Martinus Beijerinck ruled out this possibility by showing that sap could continue to transmit the disease after many plant generations. A toxin would have been diluted after many generations, but Beijerinck's results indicated the disease agent was multiplying in the plant. Around the same time, animal viruses were discovered in connection with a disease of cattle called foot-and-mouth disease. In 1900, the first human virus, the virus that causes yellow fever, was identified.

Since these early studies, microbiologists, geneticists, and molecular biologists have taken a great interest in the structure,

Figure 18.1   A plant infected with tobacco mosaic virus.

genetic composition, and replication of viruses. In this section, we will discuss the structure of viruses and examine viral reproductive cycles in detail, paying particular attention to human immunodeficiency virus (HIV), the virus that causes acquired immunodeficiency syndrome (AIDS) in humans.

Viruses Are Remarkably Varied, Despite Their Simple Structure

A **virus** is a small infectious particle that consists of nucleic acid enclosed in a protein coat. Researchers have identified and studied over 4,000 different types of viruses. Although all viruses share some similarities, such as small size and the reliance on a living cell for replication, they vary greatly in their characteristics, including their host range, structure, and genome composition. Some of the major differences are described next, and characteristics of selected viruses are shown in **Table 18.1**.

Table 18.1	Hosts and Characteristics of Selected Viruses					
Virus or group of viruses	**Host**	**Effect on host**		**Nucleic acid***	**Genome size (kb)[†]**	**Number of genes[†]**
Phage fd	E. coli	Slows growth		ssDNA	6.4	10
Phage λ	E. coli	Can exist harmlessly in the host cell or cause lysis		dsDNA	48.5	71
Phage T4	E. coli	Causes lysis		dsDNA	169	288
Phage Qβ	E. coli	Slows growth		ssRNA	4.2	4
Tobacco mosaic virus (TMV)	Many plants	Causes mottling and necrosis of leaves and other plant parts		ssRNA	6.4	6
Baculoviruses	Insects	Most baculoviruses are species specific; they usually kill the insect		dsDNA	133.9	154
Parvovirus	Mammals	Causes respiratory, flulike symptoms		ssDNA	5.0	5
Influenza virus	Mammals	Causes classical "flu," with fever, cough, sore throat, and headache		ssRNA	13.5	11
Epstein-Barr virus	Humans	Causes mononucleosis, with fever, sore throat, and fatigue		dsDNA	172	80
Adenovirus	Humans	Causes respiratory symptoms and diarrhea		dsDNA	34	35
Herpes simplex type II	Humans	Causes blistering sores around the genital region		dsDNA	158.4	77
HIV (type I)	Humans	Causes AIDS, an immunodeficiency syndrome eventually leading to death		ssRNA	9.7	9

*The abbreviations ss and ds refer to single stranded and double stranded, respectively.
[†]Several of the viruses listed in this table are found in different strains that show variation with regard to genome size and number of genes. The numbers reported in this table are typical values. The abbreviation kb refers to kilobase, which equals 1,000 bases.

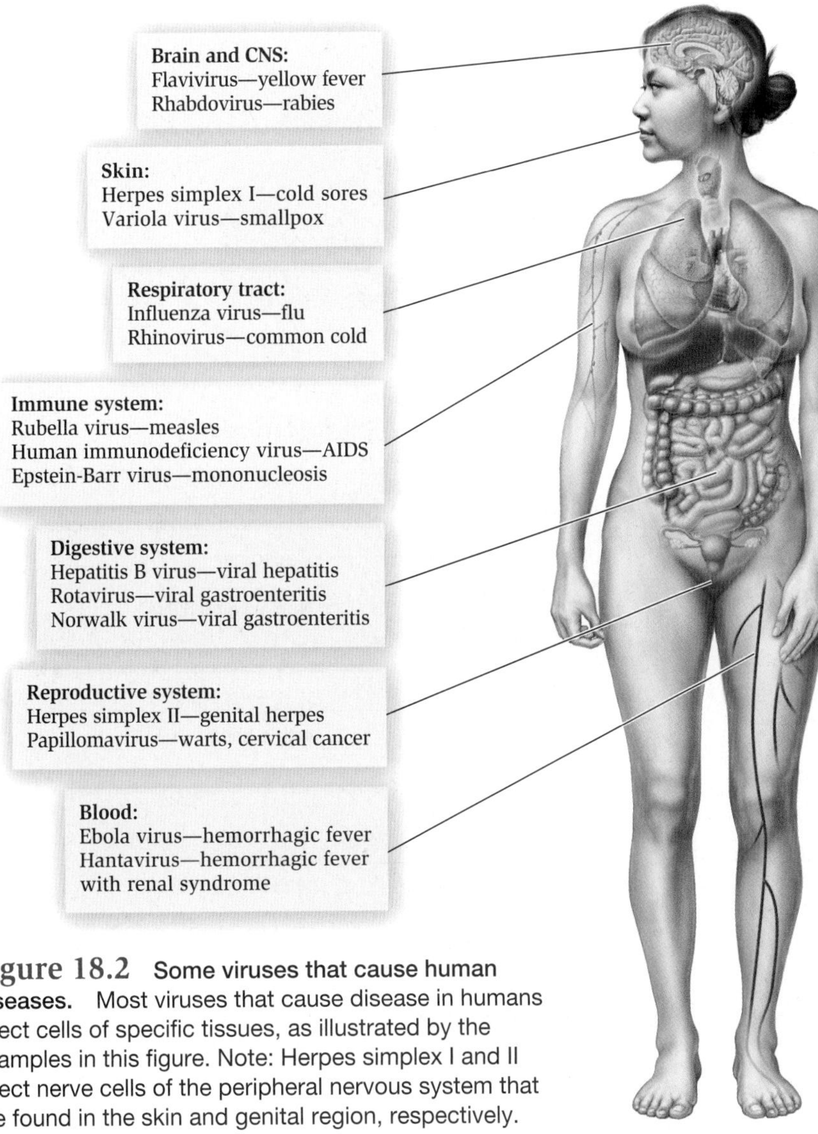

Brain and CNS:
Flavivirus—yellow fever
Rhabdovirus—rabies

Skin:
Herpes simplex I—cold sores
Variola virus—smallpox

Respiratory tract:
Influenza virus—flu
Rhinovirus—common cold

Immune system:
Rubella virus—measles
Human immunodeficiency virus—AIDS
Epstein-Barr virus—mononucleosis

Digestive system:
Hepatitis B virus—viral hepatitis
Rotavirus—viral gastroenteritis
Norwalk virus—viral gastroenteritis

Reproductive system:
Herpes simplex II—genital herpes
Papillomavirus—warts, cervical cancer

Blood:
Ebola virus—hemorrhagic fever
Hantavirus—hemorrhagic fever
with renal syndrome

Figure 18.2   **Some viruses that cause human diseases.**   Most viruses that cause disease in humans infect cells of specific tissues, as illustrated by the examples in this figure. Note: Herpes simplex I and II infect nerve cells of the peripheral nervous system that are found in the skin and genital region, respectively.

Differences in Host Range   A cell that is infected by a virus is called a **host cell**, and a species that can be infected by a specific virus is called a host species for that virus. Viruses differ greatly in their **host range**—the number of species and cell types they can infect. Table 18.1 lists a few examples of viruses with widely different ranges of host species. Tobacco mosaic virus, which we discussed earlier, has a broad host range. TMV is known to infect over 150 different species of plants. By comparison, other viruses have a narrow host range, with some infecting only a single species. Furthermore, a virus may infect only a specific cell type in a host species. **Figure 18.2** shows some viruses that infect particular human cells and cause disease.

Structural Differences   Although the existence of viruses was postulated in the 1890s, viruses were not observed until the 1930s, when the electron microscope was invented. Viruses cannot be resolved by even the best light microscope. Most of them are smaller than the wavelength of visible light. Viruses range in size from about 20–400 nm in diameter (1 nanometer = 10^{-9} meters). For comparison, a typical bacterium is

1,000 nm in diameter, and the diameter of most eukaryotic cells is 10 to 1,000 times that of a bacterium. Adenoviruses, which cause infections of the respiratory and gastrointestinal tracts, have an average diameter of 75 nm. Over 50 million adenoviruses could fit into an average-sized human cell.

What are the common structural features of all viruses? As shown in **Figure 18.3**, all viruses have a protein coat called a **capsid** that encloses a genome consisting of one or more molecules of nucleic acid. Capsids are composed of one or several different protein subunits called capsomers. Capsids have a variety of shapes, including helical and polyhedral. Figure 18.3a shows the structure of TMV, which has a helical capsid made of identical capsomers. Figure 18.3b shows an adenovirus, which has a polyhedral capsid. Protein fibers with a terminal knob are located at the corners of the polyhedral capsid. Many viruses that infect animal cells, such as the influenza virus shown in Figure 18.3c, have a **viral envelope** enclosing the capsid. The envelope consists of a lipid bilayer that is derived from the plasma membrane of the host cell and is embedded with virally encoded spike glycoproteins, also called spikes or peplomers.

In addition to encasing and protecting the genetic material, the capsid and envelope enable viruses to infect their hosts. In many viruses, the capsids or envelopes have specialized proteins, including protein fibers with a knob (Figure 18.3b) and spike glycoproteins (Figure 18.3c), that help them bind to the surface of a host cell. Viruses that infect bacteria, called **bacteriophages**, or **phages**, may have more complex protein coats, with accessory structures used for anchoring the virus to a host cell and injecting the viral nucleic acid (Figure 18.3d). As discussed later, the tail fibers of such bacteriophages are needed to attach the virus to the bacterial cell wall.

Genome Differences   The genetic material in a virus is called a **viral genome**. The composition of viral genomes varies markedly among different types of viruses, as suggested by the examples in Table 18.1. The nucleic acid of some viruses is DNA, whereas in others it is RNA. These are referred to as DNA viruses and RNA viruses, respectively. It is striking that some viruses use RNA for their genome, whereas all living organisms use DNA. In some viruses, the nucleic acid is single stranded, whereas in others, it is double stranded. The genome can be linear or circular, depending on the type of virus. Some kinds of viruses have more than one copy of the genome.

Viral genomes also vary considerably in size, ranging from a few thousand to more than a hundred thousand nucleotides in length (see Table 18.1). For example, the genomes of some

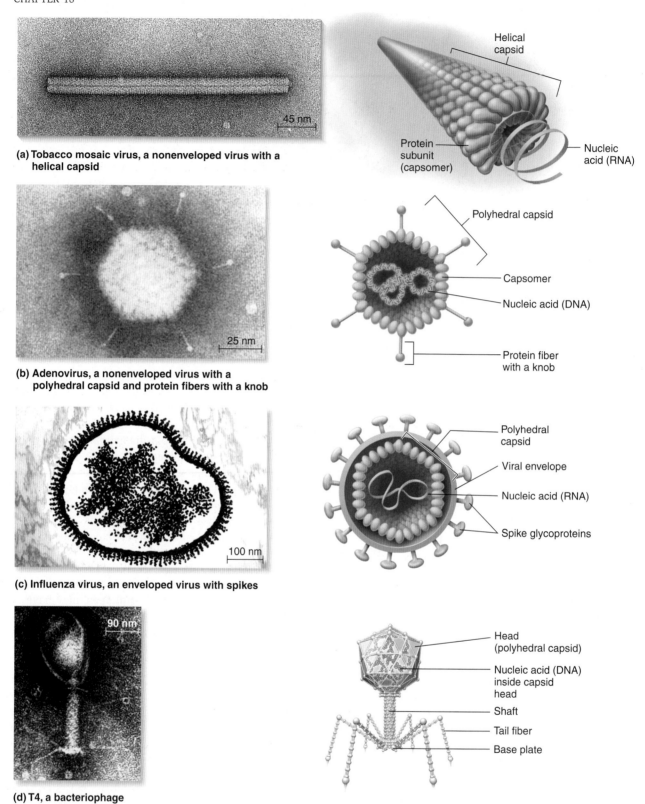

(a) Tobacco mosaic virus, a nonenveloped virus with a helical capsid

Helical capsid

Protein subunit (capsomer)

Nucleic acid (RNA)

(b) Adenovirus, a nonenveloped virus with a polyhedral capsid and protein fibers with a knob

Polyhedral capsid

Capsomer

Nucleic acid (DNA)

Protein fiber with a knob

(c) Influenza virus, an enveloped virus with spikes

Polyhedral capsid

Viral envelope

Nucleic acid (RNA)

Spike glycoproteins

(d) T4, a bacteriophage

Head (polyhedral capsid)

Nucleic acid (DNA) inside capsid head

Shaft

Tail fiber

Base plate

Figure 18.3 Variations in the structure of viruses, as shown by transmission electron microscopy. All viruses contain nucleic acid (DNA or RNA) surrounded by a protein capsid. They may or may not have an outer envelope surrounding the capsid. **(a)** Tobacco mosaic virus (TMV) has a capsid made of 2,130 identical protein subunits, helically arranged around a strand of RNA. **(b)** Adenoviruses have polyhedral capsids containing protein fibers with a knob. **(c)** Many animal viruses, including the influenza virus, have an envelope composed of a lipid bilayer and spike glycoproteins. The lipid bilayer is obtained from the host cell when the virus buds from the plasma membrane. **(d)** Some bacteriophages, such as T4, have protein coats with accessory structures that facilitate invasion of a bacterial cell.

Concept check: *What features vary among different types of viruses?*

simple viruses, such as phage Qβ, are only a few thousand nucleotides in length and contain only a few genes. Other viruses, particularly those with a complex structure, such as phage T4, contain many more genes. These extra genes encode many different proteins that are involved in the formation of the elaborate structure shown in Figure 18.3d.

Viruses Reproduce by Mobilizing Their Host Cells to Produce New Viruses

When a virus infects a host cell, the expression of viral genes leads to a series of steps, called a **viral reproductive cycle**, that results in the production of new viruses. The details of the steps may be quite different among various types of viruses, and even the same virus may have the capacity to follow alternative cycles. Even so, by studying the reproductive cycles of hundreds of different viruses, researchers have determined that the viral reproductive cycle consists of five or six basic steps.

To illustrate the general features of viral reproductive cycles, Figure 18.4 considers these steps for two types of viruses. Figure 18.4a shows the cycle of phage λ (lambda), a bacteriophage with double-stranded DNA as its genome, and Figure 18.4b depicts the cycle of HIV, an enveloped animal virus containing single-stranded RNA. The descriptions that follow compare the reproductive cycles of these two very different viruses.

Step 1: Attachment   In the first step of a viral reproductive cycle, the virus must attach to the surface of a host cell. This attachment is usually specific for one or just a few types of cells because proteins in the virus recognize and bind to specific molecules on the cell surface. In the case of phage λ, the phage tail fibers bind to proteins in the outer bacterial cell membrane of *E. coli* cells. In the case of HIV, spike glycoproteins in the viral envelope bind to protein receptors in the plasma membrane of human blood cells called helper T cells.

Step 2: Entry   After attachment, the viral genome enters the host cell. Attachment of phage λ stimulates a conformational change in the phage coat proteins, so the shaft (also called the sheath) contracts, and the phage injects its DNA into the bacterial cytoplasm. In contrast, the envelope of HIV fuses with the plasma membrane of the host cell, so both the capsid and its contents are released into the cytosol. Some of the HIV capsid proteins are then removed by host cell enzymes, a process called uncoating. This releases two copies of the viral RNA and two molecules of an enzyme called reverse transcriptase into the cytosol. As discussed shortly, reverse transcriptase is needed for step 3.

Once a viral genome has entered the cell, one or several viral genes are expressed immediately due to the action of host cell enzymes and ribosomes. Expression of these key genes leads quickly to either step 3 or step 4 of the reproductive cycle, depending on the specific virus. The genome of some viruses, including both phage λ and HIV, can integrate into a chromosome of the host cell. For such viruses, the cycle may proceed from step 2 to step 3 as described next, delaying the production of new viruses. Alternatively, the cycle may proceed directly from step 2 to step 4 and quickly lead to the production of new viruses.

Step 3: Integration   Viruses capable of integration carry a gene that encodes an enzyme called **integrase**. For integration to occur, this gene is expressed soon after entry so that integrase protein is made. Integrase cuts the host's chromosomal DNA and inserts the viral genome into the chromosome. In the case of phage λ, the double-stranded DNA that entered the cell can be directly integrated into the double-stranded DNA of the chromosome. Once integrated, the phage DNA in a bacterium is called a **prophage**. While it exists as a prophage, this type of viral reproductive cycle is called the **lysogenic cycle**. As discussed later, new phages are not made during the lysogenic cycle, and the host cell is not destroyed. On occasion, a prophage can be excised from the bacterial chromosome and proceed to step 4.

How can an RNA virus integrate its genome into the host cell's DNA? For this to occur, the viral genome must be copied into DNA. HIV accomplishes this by means of a viral enzyme called **reverse transcriptase**, which is carried within the capsid and released into the host cell along with the viral RNA. Reverse transcriptase uses the viral RNA strand to make a complementary copy of DNA, and it then uses the DNA strand as a template to make double-stranded viral DNA. This process is called reverse transcription because it is the reverse of the usual transcription process, in which a DNA strand is used to make a complementary strand of RNA. The viral double-stranded DNA enters the host cell nucleus and is inserted into a host chromosome via integrase. Once integrated, the viral DNA in a eukaryotic cell is called a **provirus**. Viruses that follow this mechanism are called **retroviruses**.

Step 4: Synthesis of Viral Components   The production of new viruses by a host cell involves the replication of the viral genome and the synthesis of viral proteins that make up the protein coat. In the case of a bacteriophage that has been integrated into the host chromosome, the prophage must be excised as described in step 3 before synthesis of new viral components can occur. An enzyme called excisionase is required for this process. Following excision, host cell enzymes make many copies of the phage DNA and transcribe the genes within these copies into mRNA. Host cell ribosomes translate this viral mRNA into viral proteins. The expression of phage genes also leads to the degradation of the host chromosomal DNA.

In the case of HIV, the DNA provirus is not excised from the host chromosome. Instead, it is transcribed in the nucleus to produce many copies of viral RNA. These viral RNA molecules enter the cytosol, where they are used to make viral proteins and serve as the genome for new viral particles.

Step 5: Viral Assembly   After all of the necessary components have been synthesized, they must be assembled into new viruses. Some viruses with a simple structure self-assemble, meaning that viral components spontaneously bind to each other to form a complete virus particle. An example of a self-assembling

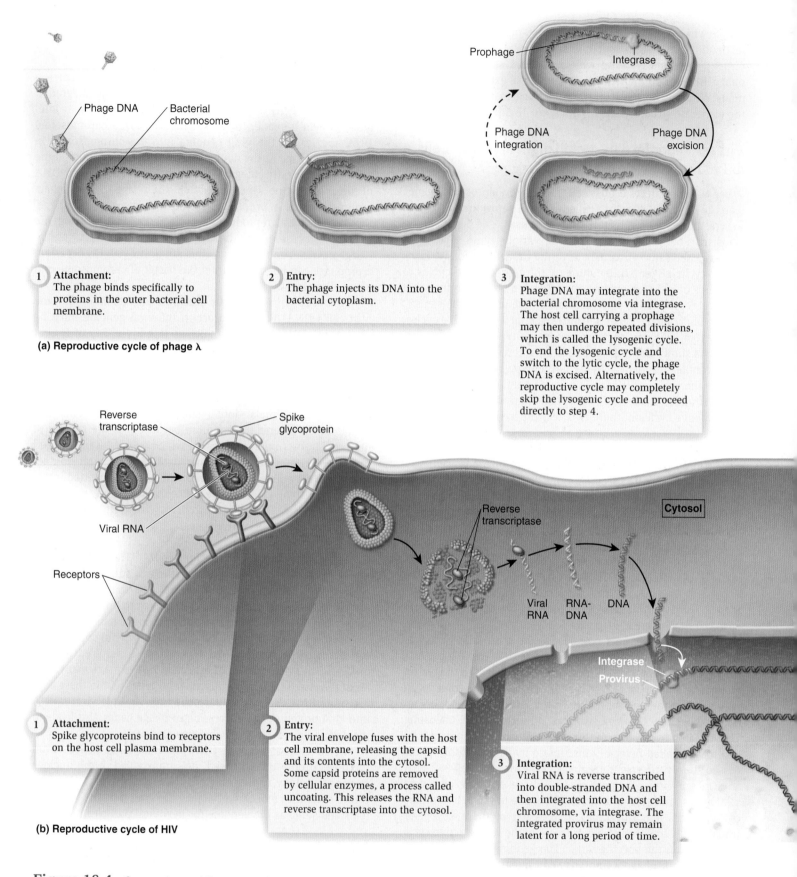

(a) Reproductive cycle of phage λ

1 **Attachment:**
The phage binds specifically to proteins in the outer bacterial cell membrane.

2 **Entry:**
The phage injects its DNA into the bacterial cytoplasm.

3 **Integration:**
Phage DNA may integrate into the bacterial chromosome via integrase. The host cell carrying a prophage may then undergo repeated divisions, which is called the lysogenic cycle. To end the lysogenic cycle and switch to the lytic cycle, the phage DNA is excised. Alternatively, the reproductive cycle may completely skip the lysogenic cycle and proceed directly to step 4.

(b) Reproductive cycle of HIV

1 **Attachment:**
Spike glycoproteins bind to receptors on the host cell plasma membrane.

2 **Entry:**
The viral envelope fuses with the host cell membrane, releasing the capsid and its contents into the cytosol. Some capsid proteins are removed by cellular enzymes, a process called uncoating. This releases the RNA and reverse transcriptase into the cytosol.

3 **Integration:**
Viral RNA is reverse transcribed into double-stranded DNA and then integrated into the host cell chromosome, via integrase. The integrated provirus may remain latent for a long period of time.

Figure 18.4 **Comparison of the steps of two viral reproductive cycles.** **(a)** The reproductive cycle of phage λ, a bacteriophage with a double-stranded DNA genome. **(b)** The reproductive cycle of HIV, an enveloped animal virus with a single-stranded RNA genome.

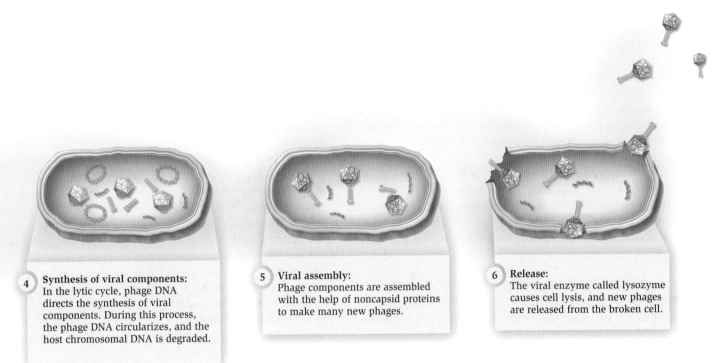

4 **Synthesis of viral components:**
In the lytic cycle, phage DNA directs the synthesis of viral components. During this process, the phage DNA circularizes, and the host chromosomal DNA is degraded.

5 **Viral assembly:**
Phage components are assembled with the help of noncapsid proteins to make many new phages.

6 **Release:**
The viral enzyme called lysozyme causes cell lysis, and new phages are released from the broken cell.

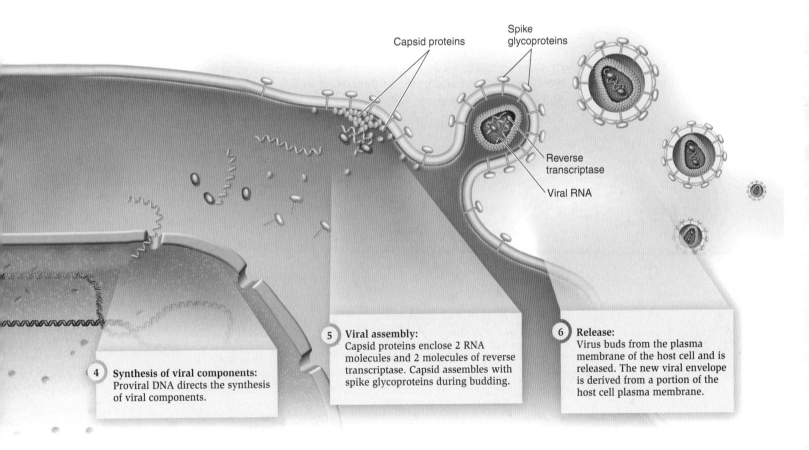

Capsid proteins

Spike glycoproteins

Reverse transcriptase

Viral RNA

4 **Synthesis of viral components:**
Proviral DNA directs the synthesis of viral components.

5 **Viral assembly:**
Capsid proteins enclose 2 RNA molecules and 2 molecules of reverse transcriptase. Capsid assembles with spike glycoproteins during budding.

6 **Release:**
Virus buds from the plasma membrane of the host cell and is released. The new viral envelope is derived from a portion of the host cell plasma membrane.

virus is TMV, which we examined earlier (see Figure 18.3a). TMV capsid proteins assemble around a TMV RNA molecule, which becomes trapped inside the hollow capsid.

Other viruses, including the two shown in Figure 18.4, do not self-assemble. The correct assembly of phage λ requires the help of noncapsid proteins not found in the completed phage particle. Some of these noncapsid proteins function as enzymes that modify capsid proteins, while others serve as scaffolding for the assembly of the capsid.

The assembly of an HIV virus occurs in two stages. First, capsid proteins assemble around two molecules of HIV RNA and two molecules of reverse transcriptase. Next, the newly formed capsid acquires its outer envelope in a budding process. This second phase of assembly occurs during step 6, as the virus is released from the cell.

Step 6: Release The last step of a viral reproductive cycle is the release of new viruses from the host cell. The release of bacteriophages is a dramatic event. Because bacteria are surrounded by a rigid cell wall, the phages must burst, or lyse, their host cell in order to escape. After the phages have been assembled, a phage-encoded enzyme called lysozyme digests the bacterial cell wall, causing the cell to burst. Lysis releases many new phages into the environment, where they can infect other bacteria and begin the cycle again. Collectively, steps 1, 2, 4, 5, and 6 are called the **lytic cycle** because they lead to cell lysis.

The release of enveloped viruses from an animal cell is far less dramatic. This type of virus escapes by a mechanism called budding that does not lyse the cell. In the case of HIV, a newly assembled virus particle associates with a portion of the plasma membrane containing HIV spike glycoproteins. The membrane enfolds the viral capsid and eventually buds from the surface of the cell. This is how the virus acquires its envelope, which is a piece of host cell membrane studded with viral glycoproteins.

Latency in Bacteriophages As we saw in step 3, viruses can integrate their genomes into a host chromosome. In some cases, the prophage or provirus may remain inactive, or **latent**, for a long time. Most of the viral genes are silent during latency, and the viral reproductive cycle does not progress to step 4.

Latency in bacteriophages is also called lysogeny. When this occurs, both the prophage and its host cell are said to be lysogenic. When a lysogenic bacterium prepares to divide, it copies the prophage DNA along with its own DNA, so each daughter cell inherits a copy of the prophage. A prophage can be replicated repeatedly in this way without killing the host cell or producing new phage particles. As mentioned earlier, this is called the lysogenic cycle.

Many bacteriophages can alternate between lysogenic and lytic cycles (**Figure 18.5**). A bacteriophage that may spend some of its time in the lysogenic cycle is called a **temperate phage**. Phage λ is an example of a temperate phage. Upon infection, it can either enter the lysogenic cycle or proceed directly to the lytic cycle. Other phages, called **virulent phages**, have only lytic cycles. The genome of a virulent phage is not capable of integration into a host chromosome. Phage T2, which we

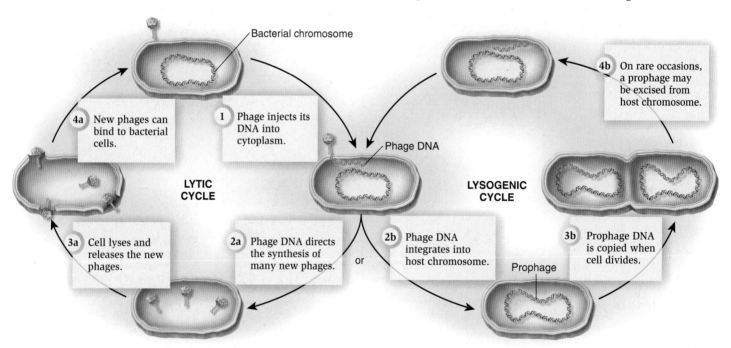

Figure 18.5 Lytic and lysogenic cycles of bacteriophages. Some phages, such as phage λ, may follow either a lytic or a lysogenic reproductive cycle. During the lytic cycle, new phages are made, and the bacterial cell is destroyed. During the lysogenic cycle, the integrated phage DNA, or prophage, is replicated along with the DNA of the host cell. Environmental conditions influence how long the phage remains in the lysogenic cycle. Other phages, such as T2, follow only lytic cycles.

Concept check: *From the perspective of the virus, what are the primary advantages of the lytic and lysogenic cycles?*

examined in Chapter 11, is a virulent phage that infects *E. coli*. Unlike phage λ, which may coexist harmlessly with *E. coli*, T2 always lyses the infected cell.

For phages such as λ that can follow either cycle, environmental conditions influence whether or not viral DNA is integrated into a host chromosome and how long the virus remains in the lysogenic cycle. If nutrients are readily available, phage λ usually proceeds directly to the lytic cycle after its DNA enters the cell. Alternatively, if nutrients are in short supply, the lysogenic cycle is often favored because sufficient material may not be available to make new viruses. If more nutrients become available later, this may cause the prophage to become activated. At this point, the viral reproductive cycle will switch to the lytic cycle, and new viruses will be made and released.

Latency in Human Viruses   Latency among human viruses can occur in two different ways. For HIV, latency occurs because the virus has integrated into the host genome and may remain dormant for long periods of time. In addition, the genomes of other viruses can exist as an **episome**—a genetic element that can replicate independently of the chromosomal DNA but also can occasionally integrate into chromosomal DNA. Examples of viral genomes that can exist as episomes include different types of herpesviruses that cause cold sores (herpes simplex type I), genital herpes (herpes simplex type II), and chickenpox (varicella zoster). A person infected with a given type of herpesvirus may have periodic outbreaks of disease symptoms when the virus switches from the latent, episomal form to the active form that produces new virus particles.

As an example, let's consider the herpesvirus called varicella zoster. The initial infection by this virus causes chickenpox, after which the virus may remain latent for many years as an episome. The disease called shingles occurs when varicella zoster switches from the latent state and starts making new virus particles. Shingles begins as a painful rash that eventually erupts into blisters. The blisters follow the path of the nerve cells that carry the latent varicella zoster virus. The blisters often form a ring around the back of the patient's body, which is why the disease is called shingles—the pattern of blisters line up like the shingles on a house.

Emerging Viruses, Such as HIV, Have Arisen Recently and May Rapidly Spread Through a Population

A primary reason researchers have been interested in viral reproductive cycles is the ability of many viruses to cause diseases in humans and other hosts. Some examples of human disease-causing viruses were presented earlier in Figure 18.2. **Emerging viruses** are viruses that have arisen recently, or are likely to have a greater probability of causing infection. Such viruses often cause public alarm and may lead to a significant loss of human life. New strains of influenza virus arise fairly regularly due to new mutations. An example is the strain H1N1, also called swine flu. In the U.S., despite attempts to minimize influenza deaths by vaccination, over 30,000 people die annually from this disease.

Another emerging virus causes a potentially life-threatening illness called severe acute respiratory syndrome (SARS). This RNA virus was first identified by researchers in Hong Kong, the U.S., and Germany in 2003. The type of virus causing SARS is called a coronavirus. The SARS coronavirus is believed to have originated in bats and acquired the ability to infect humans and livestock.

During the past few decades, the most devastating example of an emerging virus has been **human immunodeficiency virus (HIV)**, the causative agent of **acquired immune deficiency syndrome (AIDS)**. AIDS is primarily spread by sexual contact between infected and uninfected individuals, but it can also be spread by the transfusion of HIV-infected blood, by the sharing of needles among drug users, and from infected mother to unborn child. The total number of AIDS deaths between 1981 and the end of 2006 was over 25 million; more than 0.5 million of these deaths occurred in the U.S. During 2008, around 3 million adults and children became infected with HIV. Worldwide, nearly 1 in every 100 adults between ages 15 and 49 is infected. In the U.S., about 55,000 new HIV infections occur each year, 70% of which are in men and 30% in women.

The devastating effects of AIDS result from viral destruction of helper T cells, a type of white blood cell that plays an essential role in the immune system of mammals. **Figure 18.6** shows HIV virus particles invading a helper T cell. As described in Chapter 53, helper T cells interact with other cells of the immune system to facilitate the production of antibodies and other molecules that target and kill foreign invaders of the body. When large numbers of helper T cells are destroyed by HIV, the function of the immune system is seriously compromised, and the individual becomes susceptible to infectious diseases called opportunistic infections that would not normally occur in a healthy person. For example, *Pneumocystis jiroveci*, a fungus that causes pneumonia, is easily destroyed by a normal immune system. However, in people with AIDS, infection by this fungus can be fatal.

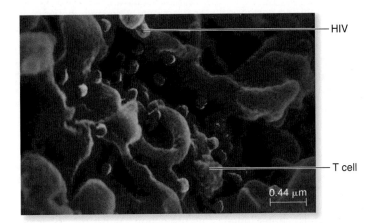

Figure 18.6   **Micrograph of HIV invading a human helper T cell.**   This is a colorized scanning electron micrograph. The surface of the T cell is purple, and HIV particles are red.

An insidious feature of HIV replication, described earlier in Figure 18.4b, is that reverse transcriptase, the enzyme that copies the RNA genome into DNA, lacks a proofreading function. In Chapter 11, we learned that DNA polymerase can identify and remove mismatched nucleotides in newly synthesized DNA. Because reverse transcriptase lacks this function, it makes more errors and thereby tends to create mutant strains of HIV. This undermines the ability of the body to combat HIV because mutant strains may be resistant to the body's defenses. In addition, mutant strains of HIV may be resistant to antiviral drugs, as described next.

Drugs Have Been Developed to Combat the Proliferation of HIV

A compelling reason to understand the reproductive cycle of HIV and other disease-causing viruses is that such knowledge may be used to develop drugs that stop viral proliferation. For example, in the U.S., the estimated annual number of AIDS-related deaths fell approximately 14% from 1998 to 2002, owing in part to the use of new antiviral drugs. These drugs inhibit viral proliferation, though they cannot eliminate the virus from the body.

One approach to the design of antiviral treatments has been to create drugs that specifically bind to proteins encoded by the viral genome. For example, azidothymidine (AZT) mimics the structure of a normal nucleotide and can bind to reverse transcriptase. In this way, AZT inhibits reverse transcription, thereby inhibiting viral replication. Another way to combat HIV involves the use of antiviral drugs that inhibit proteases, enzymes that are needed during the assembly of the HIV capsid. Certain proteases cut capsid proteins, which makes them smaller and able to assemble into a capsid structure. If the proteases do not function, the capsid will not assemble, and new HIV particles will not be made. Several drugs known as protease inhibitors have been developed that bind to HIV proteases and inhibit their function.

A major challenge in AIDS research is to discover drugs that inhibit viral proteins without also binding to host cell proteins and inhibiting normal cellular functions. A second challenge is to develop drugs to which mutant strains will not become resistant. As mentioned, HIV readily accumulates mutations during viral replication. A current strategy is to treat HIV patients with a cocktail of three or more HIV drugs, making it less likely that any mutant strain will overcome all of the inhibitory effects.

Another approach to fighting HIV and other infectious diseases is vaccination—inoculation with a substance or group of substances that causes the immune system to respond to and destroy infectious agents such as bacteria or viruses. Vaccinations have been successful in the prevention of other viral diseases, such as influenza. In the case of HIV, the ideal vaccine should be both inexpensive and easy to store and administer, and it must confer long-lasting protection against HIV infection by sexual contact or by exposure to infected blood. Importantly, due to the high mutation rate of HIV, the vaccine must protect against exposure to many different strains of the virus.

Several Hypotheses Have Been Proposed to Explain the Origin of Viruses

Because viruses are such small particles, there is no fossil record of their evolution. Researchers must rely on analyses of modern viruses to develop hypotheses about their origin. Viral genomes follow the same rules of gene expression as the genomes of their host cells. Viral genes have promoter sequences similar to those of their host cells, and the translation of viral proteins relies on the genetic code. Viruses depend entirely on host cells for their proliferation. No known virus makes its own ribosomes or generates the energy it requires to make new viruses. Therefore, many biologists have argued that cells must have evolved before viruses.

How did viruses come into existence? A common hypothesis for the origin of viruses is they evolved from macromolecules inside living cells. The precursors of the first viruses may have been plasmids—small, circular DNA molecules that exist independently of chromosomal DNA. (Plasmids are described later in this chapter.) Biologists have hypothesized that such DNA molecules may have acquired genes that code for proteins that facilitate their own replication. Though many biologists favor the idea that viruses originated from primitive plasmids or other chromosomal elements, some have suggested they are an example of regressive evolution—the reduction of a trait or traits over time. This hypothesis proposes that viruses are degenerate cells that have retained the minimal genetic information essential for reproduction.

A new and interesting hypothesis is that viruses did not evolve from living cells but instead evolved in parallel with cellular organisms. As discussed in Chapter 22, the precursors of cellular DNA genomes may have been RNA molecules that could replicate independently of cells. This stage of evolution, termed the RNA world, could have involved the parallel evolution of both viruses and cellular organisms.

18.2 Viroids and Prions

Some nonliving infectious agents are even simpler then viruses. Viroids are composed solely of RNA, and prions are composed solely of protein. In this section, we will begin by examining viroids, infectious agents that cause diseases in plants. Next, we will discuss infectious proteins known as prions, which cause devastating neurological diseases in humans and other mammals. Unlike other agents of infection, prions have no genes and cannot be copied by the replication machinery of a cell. Instead, they increase their numbers by inducing changes in other protein molecules within living cells.

Viroids Are RNA Particles That Infect Plant Cells

In 1971, Theodor Diener discovered that the agent of potato spindle tuber disease is a small RNA molecule devoid of any protein. He coined the term **viroid** for this newly discovered infectious particle. Viroids are composed solely of a single-stranded circular RNA molecule that is a few hundred nucleotides in length.

Viroids infect plant cells, where they depend entirely on host enzymes for their replication. Some viroids are replicated in the host cell nucleus, others in the chloroplast. In contrast to viral genomes, the RNA genomes of viroids do not code for any proteins. How do viroids affect plant cells? The RNA of some viroids is known to possess ribozyme activity, and some researchers think this activity may damage plants by interfering with the function of host cell molecules. However, the mechanism by which viroids induce disease is not well understood.

Since Diener's initial discovery, many more viroids have been characterized as the agents of diseases affecting many economically important plants, including potato, tomato, cucumber, orange, coconut, grape, avocado, peach, apple, pear, and plum. Some viroids have devastating effects, as illustrated by the case of the coconut cadang-cadang viroid, which has killed more than 20 million coconut trees in Southeast Asia and New Guinea (**Figure 18.7**). Other viroids produce less severe damage, causing necrosis on leaves, shortening of stems, bark

Figure 18.7 Effects of a viroid. This palm tree in Papua, New Guinea, has been infected with the coconut cadang-cadang viroid.

cracking, and delays in foliation, flowering, and fruit ripening. A few viroids induce mild symptoms or no symptoms at all.

Prions Are Infectious Proteins That Cause Neurodegenerative Diseases

Before we end our discussion of nonliving, infectious particles, let's consider an unusual mechanism in which agents known as **prions** cause a group of rare, fatal brain diseases affecting humans and other mammals. Until the 1980s, biologists thought that any infectious agent, whether living or nonliving, must have genetic material. It seemed logical that genetic material is needed to store the information to create new infectious particles.

In the 1960s, British researchers Tikvah Alper and John Stanley Griffith discovered that preparations from animals with certain neurodegenerative diseases remained infectious even after exposure to radiation that would destroy any DNA or RNA. They suggested that the infectious agent was a protein. In the early 1970s, Stanley Prusiner, moved by the death of a patient from such a neurodegenerative disease, began to search for the causative agent. In 1982, Prusiner isolated a disease-causing particle composed entirely of protein, which he called a prion. The term was based on his characterization of the particle as a proteinaceous infectious agent. In 1997, Prusiner was awarded the Nobel Prize in Physiology or Medicine for his work on prions.

Prion diseases arise from the ability of the prion protein to induce abnormal folding in normal protein molecules (**Figure 18.8**). The prion protein exists in a disease-causing conformation designated PrP^{Sc}. The superscript Sc refers to scrapie, an example of a prion disease. A normal conformation of this same protein, which does not cause disease, is termed PrP^{C}. The superscript C stands for cellular. The normal protein is encoded by an individual's genome, and the protein is expressed at low levels in certain types of nerve cells.

How does someone contract a prion disease? A healthy person may become "infected" with the abnormal protein by eating meat of an animal with the disease. Unlike most other proteins in the diet, the prion protein escapes digestion in the stomach and small intestine and is absorbed into the bloodstream. After being taken up by nerve cells, the prion protein gradually converts the cell's normal proteins to the abnormal conformation. As a prion disease progresses, the PrP^{Sc} proteins are deposited as dense aggregates that form tough fibrils in the cells of the brain and peripheral nervous tissues, causing the disease symptoms. Some of the abnormal prion proteins are also excreted from infected cells, where they travel through the bloodstream. In this way, a prion disease can spread through the body like many viral diseases.

Prions are now known to cause several types of fatal neurodegenerative diseases affecting humans, livestock, and wildlife (**Table 18.2**). Prion diseases are termed transmissible spongiform encephalopathies (TSE). The postmortem examination of the brains of affected individuals reveals a substantial destruction of brain tissue. The brain has a spongy appearance.

Table 18.2	Examples of Neurodegenerative Diseases Caused by Infectious Prions
Disease	**Description**
Scrapie	A disease of sheep and pigs characterized by intense itching. The animals tend to scrape themselves against trees or other objects, followed by neurodegeneration.
Mad cow disease	Begins with changes in posture and temperament, followed by loss of coordination and neurodegeneration.
Chronic wasting disease	A disease of deer (genus *Odocoileus*) and Rocky Mountain elk (*Cervus elaphus*). A consistent symptom is weight loss over time. The disease is progressive and fatal.

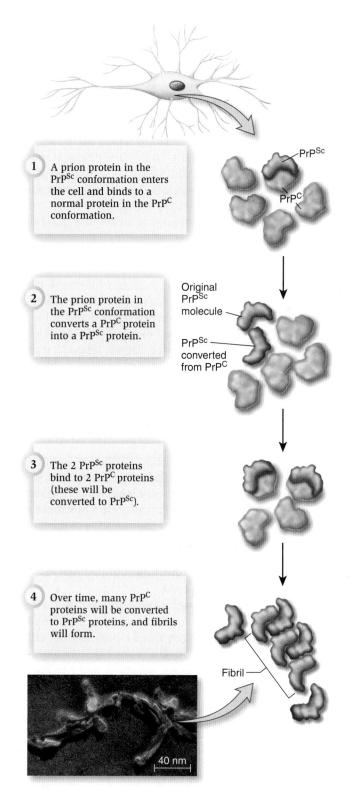

1. A prion protein in the PrP^Sc conformation enters the cell and binds to a normal protein in the PrP^C conformation.

2. The prion protein in the PrP^Sc conformation converts a PrP^C protein into a PrP^Sc protein.

3. The 2 PrP^Sc proteins bind to 2 PrP^C proteins (these will be converted to PrP^Sc).

4. Over time, many PrP^C proteins will be converted to PrP^Sc proteins, and fibrils will form.

PrP^Sc

PrP^C

Original PrP^Sc molecule

PrP^Sc converted from PrP^C

Fibril

40 nm

Figure 18.8 **A proposed molecular mechanism of prion diseases.** A healthy neuron normally contains only the PrP^C conformation of the prion protein. The abnormal PrP^Sc conformation catalyzes the conversion of PrP^C proteins into PrP^Sc proteins, thereby causing the symptoms of prion diseases.

Concept check: *Researchers are trying to discover drugs that prevent prion diseases. What are possible effects of a drug that would prevent the spread of the disease?*

Most prion diseases progress fairly slowly. Over the course of a few years, symptoms proceed from a loss of motor control to dementia, paralysis, wasting, and eventually death. These symptoms are correlated with an increase in the level of prion protein in the nerve cells of infected individuals. No current treatment can halt the progression of any of the TSEs. For this reason, great public alarm occurs when an outbreak of a TSE is reported. For example, in 2003, a single report of bovine spongiform encephalitis, also known as mad cow disease, in the U.S. prompted several countries to restrict the import of American beef.

18.3 | Genetic Properties of Bacteria

Bacteria and archaea, collectively referred to as prokaryotes, are usually unicellular organisms. Individual cells may exist as single units or remain associated with each other after cell division, forming pairs, chains, or clumps. Bacteria are widespread on Earth, and numerous species are known to cause various types of infectious diseases. Many species of archaea are also known. In this chapter, we will focus on bacteria. The genomes of bacteria, archaea, and eukaryotes are compared in Chapter 21.

We begin this section by exploring the structure and replication of the bacterial genome and the organization of DNA sequences along a bacterial chromosome. We then examine how the chromosome is compacted to fit inside a bacterium and how it is transmitted during asexual reproduction.

Bacteria Typically Have Circular Chromosomes That Carry a Few Thousand Genes

The genes of bacteria are found within structures known as bacterial chromosomes. Although a bacterial cell usually has a single type of chromosome, it may have more than one copy of that chromosome. The number of copies depends on the bacterial species and on growth conditions, but a bacterium typically has one to four identical chromosomes. Each bacterial chromosome is tightly packed within a distinct **nucleoid region** of the cell (**Figure 18.9**). Unlike the eukaryotic nucleus, the bacterial

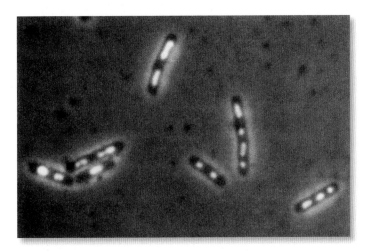

Figure 18.9 Nucleoid regions within the bacterium *Bacillus subtilis.* In the light micrograph shown here, the nucleoid regions are fluorescently labeled and seen as bright, oval-shaped areas within the bacterial cytoplasm. Two or more nucleoid regions are usually found within each cell.

Concept check: How many nucleoid regions are in the bacterial cell to the far right?

nucleoid region is not a separate cellular compartment bounded by a membrane. The DNA in the nucleoid region is in direct contact with the cytoplasm of the cell.

Like eukaryotic chromosomes, bacterial chromosomes contain molecules of double-stranded DNA along with many different proteins. Unlike eukaryotic chromosomes, however, bacterial chromosomes are usually circular and tend to be much shorter, typically only a few million base pairs (bp) long. For example, the chromosome of *Escherichia coli* has approximately 4.6 million bp, and the *Hemophilus influenzae* chromosome has roughly 1.8 million bp. By comparison, an average human chromosome is over 100 million bp in length.

A typical bacterial chromosome contains a few thousand unique genes that are found throughout the chromosome (**Figure 18.10**). Structural gene sequences, nucleotide sequences that encode proteins, account for the largest part of bacterial DNA. Other nucleotide sequences in the chromosome influence DNA replication, gene expression, and chromosome structure. One of these sequences is the origin of replication, which is a few hundred bp long. Bacterial chromosomes have a single origin of replication that functions as an initiation site for the assembly of several proteins that are required for DNA replication (refer back to Figure 11.15b).

The Formation of Chromosomal Loops and DNA Supercoiling Makes the Bacterial Chromosome Compact

Bacterial cells are much smaller than most eukaryotic cells (refer back to Figure 4.1). *E. coli* cells, for example, are approximately 1 μm wide and 2 μm long. To fit within a bacterial cell, the DNA of a typical bacterial chromosome must be compacted about 1,000-fold. How does this occur? The compaction of a bacterial chromosome, shown in **Figure 18.11**, occurs by two processes: the formation of loops and by the supercoiling of the looped DNA.

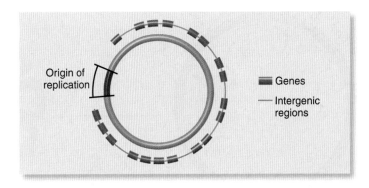

Key features

- Most, but not all, bacterial species contain circular chromosomal DNA.

- A typical chromosome is a few million base pairs in length.

- Most bacterial species contain a single type of chromosome, but it may be present in multiple copies.

- Several thousand different genes are interspersed throughout the chromosome.

- One origin of replication is required to initiate DNA replication.

Figure 18.10 The organization of nucleotide sequences in bacterial chromosomal DNA.

Unlike eukaryotic DNA, bacterial DNA is not wound around histone proteins to form nucleosomes. However, the binding of proteins to bacterial DNA is important in the formation of **loop domains**—chromosomal segments that are folded into loops. As seen in Figure 18.11, DNA-binding proteins anchor the bases of the loops in place. The number of loops varies according to the size of a bacterial chromosome and the species. The *E. coli* chromosome has 50 to 100 loop domains, each with about 40,000 to 80,000 bp. This looping compacts the circular chromosome about 10-fold. A similar process of loop-domain formation occurs in eukaryotic chromatin compaction, which is described in Chapter 11.

DNA supercoiling is a second important way to compact the bacterial chromosome. Because DNA is a long, thin molecule, twisting can dramatically change its conformation. This compaction is similar to what happens to a rubber band if you twist it in one direction. Because the two strands of DNA already coil around each other, the formation of additional coils due to twisting is referred to as supercoiling. Bacterial enzymes called topoisomerases twist the DNA and control the degree of DNA supercoiling.

Plasmids Are Small Pieces of Extrachromosomal DNA

In addition to chromosomal DNA, bacterial cells commonly contain **plasmids**, small, circular pieces of DNA that exist separate from the bacterial chromosome (**Figure 18.12**). Plasmids

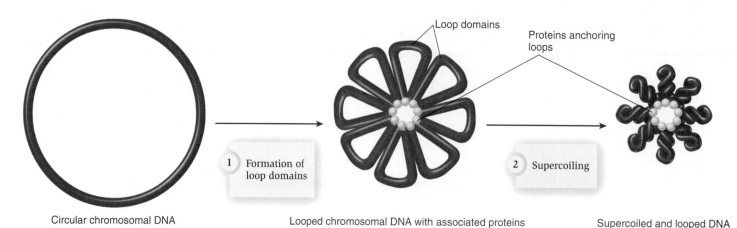

Figure 18.11   **The compaction of a bacterial chromosome.**   As a way to compact the large, circular chromosome, segments are organized into smaller loop domains by binding to proteins at the bases of the loops. These loops are made more compact by DNA supercoiling.

Concept check: *Describe how the loop domains are held in place.*

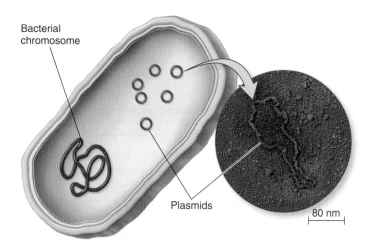

Figure 18.12   **Plasmids in a bacterial cell.**   Plasmids are small, circular DNA molecules that exist independently of the bacterial chromosome.

Concept check: *Describe the similarities and differences between a bacterial chromosome and a plasmid.*

occur naturally in many strains of bacteria and in a few types of eukaryotic cells, such as yeast. The smallest plasmids consist of just a few thousand base pairs and carry only a gene or two. The largest are in the range of 100,000 to 500,000 bp and carry several dozen or even hundreds of genes. A plasmid has its own origin of replication that allows it to be replicated independently of the bacterial chromosome. The DNA sequence of the origin of replication influences how many copies of the plasmid are found within a cell. Some origins are said to be very strong because they result in many copies of the plasmid, perhaps as many as 100 per cell. Other origins of replication have sequences that are much weaker, so the number of copies is relatively low, such as one or two per cell.

Why do bacteria have plasmids? Certain genes within a plasmid usually provide some type of growth advantage to the cell or may aid in survival under certain conditions. By studying plasmids in many different species, researchers have discovered that most plasmids fall into five different categories:

1. Resistance plasmids, also known as R factors, contain genes that confer resistance against antibiotics and other types of toxins.
2. Degradative plasmids carry genes that enable the bacterium to digest and utilize an unusual substance. For example, a degradative plasmid may carry genes that allow a bacterium to digest an organic solvent such as toluene.
3. Col-plasmids contain genes that encode colicins, which are proteins that kill other bacteria.
4. Virulence plasmids carry genes that turn a bacterium into a pathogenic strain.
5. Fertility plasmids, also known as F factors, allow bacteria to mate with each other, a topic described later in this chapter.

On occasion, a plasmid may integrate into the bacterial chromosome. Plasmids that can integrate or remain independent of the chromosome are also termed episomes.

Bacteria Reproduce Asexually by Binary Fission

Thus far, we have considered the genetic material of bacteria and how the bacterial chromosome is compacted to fit inside the cell. Let's now turn our attention to the process of cell division. The capacity of bacteria to divide is really quite astounding. The cells of some species, such as *E. coli*, can divide every 20–30 minutes. When placed on a solid growth medium in a petri dish, an *E. coli* cell and its daughter cells will undergo repeated cellular divisions and form a clone of genetically identical cells called a **bacterial colony** (Figure 18.13). Starting with a single cell that is invisible to the naked eye, a visible bacterial colony containing 10 to 100 million cells will form in less than a day!

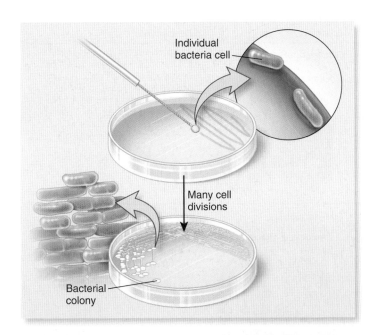

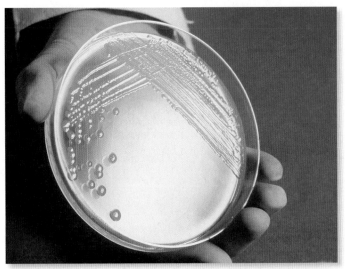

Figure 18.13 **Growth of a bacterial colony.** Through successive cell divisions, a single bacterial cell of *E. coli* forms a genetically identical group of cells called a bacterial colony.

Concept check: *Let's suppose a bacterial strain divides every 30 minutes. If a single cell is placed on a plate, how many cells will be in the colony after 16 hours?*

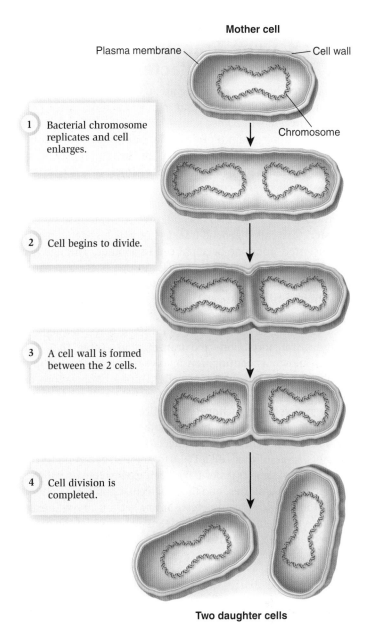

Mother cell

Plasma membrane — Cell wall

Chromosome

1 Bacterial chromosome replicates and cell enlarges.

2 Cell begins to divide.

3 A cell wall is formed between the 2 cells.

4 Cell division is completed.

Two daughter cells

Figure 18.14 **Bacterial cell division.** Bacteria reproduce by a type of cell division called binary fission. Before a bacterium divides, the bacterial chromosome is replicated to produce two identical copies. These two copies segregate from each other during cell division, with one copy going to each daughter cell.

As described in Chapter 15, the division of eukaryotic cells requires a sorting process called mitosis, because eukaryotic chromosomes occur in sets and each daughter cell must receive the correct number and types of chromosomes. By comparison, a bacterial cell usually has only a single type of chromosome. Cell division occurs by a much simpler process called **binary fission**, during which a cell divides into two daughter cells. Figure 18.14 shows this process for a cell with a single chromosome. Before it divides, the cell replicates its DNA. This produces two identical copies of the chromosome. Next, the cell's plasma membrane is drawn inward and deposits new cell-wall

material, separating the two daughter cells. Each daughter cell receives one of the copies of the original chromosome. Therefore, except when a mutation occurs, each daughter cell contains an identical copy of the mother cell's genetic material. Like other types of asexual reproduction, binary fission does not involve genetic contributions from two different parents.

If a bacterial cell contains plasmids, these will replicate independently of the bacterial chromosome. During binary fission, the plasmids are distributed to daughter cells so that each daughter cell usually receives one or more copies of the plasmid.

18.4   Gene Transfer Between Bacteria

Even though bacteria reproduce asexually, they exhibit a great deal of genetic diversity. Within a given bacterial species, the term **strain** refers to a lineage that has genetic differences compared to another strain. For example, one strain of *E. coli* may be resistant to an antibiotic, whereas another strain may be sensitive to the same antibiotic. How does genetic diversity arise in an asexual species? It comes primarily from two sources. First, mutations can occur that alter the bacterial genome and affect the traits of bacterial cells. Second, diversity can arise by **gene transfer**, also called genetic transfer, in which genetic material is transferred from one bacterial cell to another. Through gene transfer, genetic variation that arises in one bacterium can be spread to new strains and even to other species. For example, an antibiotic-resistance gene may be transferred from a resistant strain to a sensitive strain.

Gene transfer occurs in three different ways, termed conjugation, transformation, and transduction (**Table 18.3**). The process known as **conjugation** involves a direct physical interaction between two bacterial cells. During conjugation, one bacterium acts as a donor and transfers DNA to a recipient cell. In the process of **transformation**, DNA that is released into the environment is taken up by another bacterial cell. **Transduction** occurs when a virus infects a bacterial cell and then transfers some of that cell's DNA to another bacterium. These three types of gene transfer have been extensively investigated in research laboratories, and their molecular pathways continue to be studied with great interest. In this section, we will examine these mechanisms in greater detail and consider the experiments that led to their discovery.

Table 18.3   Mechanisms of Gene Transfer Between Bacterial Cells

Mechanism	Description
Conjugation: 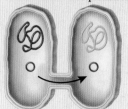	Requires direct contact between a donor and a recipient cell. The donor cell transfers a strand of DNA to the recipient. In the example shown here, DNA from a plasmid is transferred to the recipient cell. Both donor and recipient cells end up with a plasmid.
Transformation: 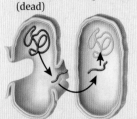	A fragment of its DNA from a donor cell is released into the environment. This may happen when a bacterial cell dies. This DNA fragment is taken up by a recipient cell, which incorporates the DNA into its chromosome.
Transduction: 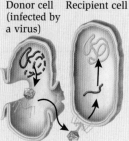	When a virus infects a donor cell, it causes the bacterial chromosome of the donor cell to break up into fragments. A fragment of bacterial chromosomal DNA is incorporated into a newly made virus particle. The virus then transfers this fragment of DNA to a recipient cell.

FEATURE INVESTIGATION

Lederberg and Tatum's Work with *E. coli* Demonstrated Gene Transfer Between Bacteria and Led to the Discovery of Conjugation

In 1946 and 1947, Joshua Lederberg and Edward Tatum carried out the first experiments that clearly demonstrated gene transfer from one bacterial strain to another (**Figure 18.15**). The researchers had been studying strains of *E. coli* that had different nutritional requirements for growth. They designated one strain *met⁻bio⁻thr⁺pro⁺* because its growth required that the amino acid methionine (met) and the vitamin biotin (bio) be added to the growth medium. This strain did not require the amino acids threonine (thr) or proline (pro) for growth. Another strain, designated *met⁺bio⁺thr⁻pro⁻*, had just the opposite requirement. It needed threonine and proline in its growth medium, but not methionine or biotin. These differences in nutritional requirements correspond to allelic differences between the two strains. The *met⁻bio⁻thr⁺pro⁺* strain had defective genes encoding enzymes necessary for methionine and biotin synthesis, whereas the *met⁺bio⁺thr⁻pro⁻* strain had defective genes for the enzymes required to make threonine and proline.

Figure 18.15 compares the results of mixing the two *E. coli* strains with the results when they were not mixed. The tube shown on the left contained only *met⁻bio⁻thr⁺pro⁺* cells, and the tube on the right had only *met⁺bio⁺thr⁻pro⁻* cells. The middle tube contained a mixture of the two kinds of cells. In each case, the researchers applied about 100 million (10^8) cells to plates containing a growth medium lacking amino acids and the vitamin biotin. When the unmixed strains were applied to these plates, no colonies were observed to grow. This result was expected because the plates did not contain the methionine and biotin that the *met⁻bio⁻thr⁺pro⁺* cells needed for growth or the threonine and proline that the *met⁺bio⁺thr⁻pro⁻* cells required. The striking result occurred when the researchers plated 10^8

Figure 18.15   Experiment of Lederberg and Tatum demonstrating gene transfer in *E. coli*.

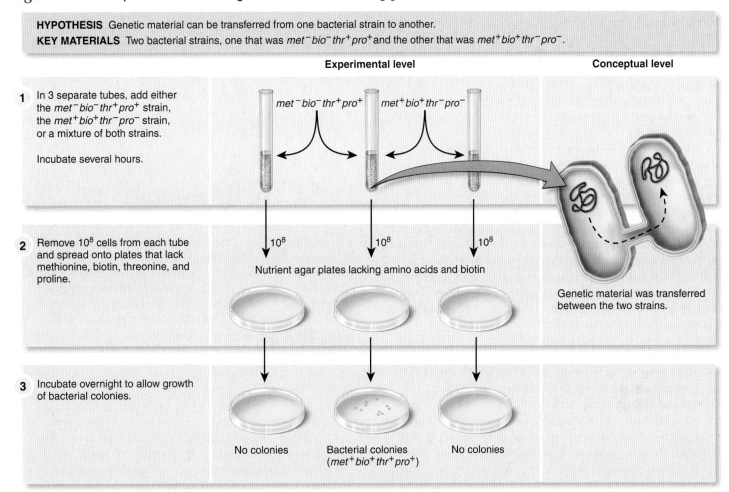

HYPOTHESIS Genetic material can be transferred from one bacterial strain to another.

KEY MATERIALS Two bacterial strains, one that was $met^- bio^- thr^+ pro^+$ and the other that was $met^+ bio^+ thr^- pro^-$.

Experimental level   **Conceptual level**

1 In 3 separate tubes, add either the $met^- bio^- thr^+ pro^+$ strain, the $met^+ bio^+ thr^- pro^-$ strain, or a mixture of both strains.

Incubate several hours.

$met^- bio^- thr^+ pro^+$ $met^+ bio^+ thr^- pro^-$

2 Remove 10^8 cells from each tube and spread onto plates that lack methionine, biotin, threonine, and proline.

10^8 10^8 10^8

Nutrient agar plates lacking amino acids and biotin

Genetic material was transferred between the two strains.

3 Incubate overnight to allow growth of bacterial colonies.

No colonies   Bacterial colonies ($met^+ bio^+ thr^+ pro^+$)   No colonies

4 **THE DATA**

Strain	Number of colonies after overnight growth
$met^- bio^- thr^+ pro^+$	0
$met^+ bio^+ thr^- pro^-$	0
Both strains together	~10

5 **CONCLUSION** Gene transfer has occurred from one bacterial strain to another.

6 **SOURCE** Lederberg, Joshua, and Tatum, Edward L. 1946. Novel genotypes in mixed cultures of biochemical mutants of bacteria. *Cold Spring Harbor Symposia on Quantitative Biology* 11:113–114.

Tatum, Edward L., and Lederberg, Joshua. 1947. Genetic recombination in the bacterium *Escherichia coli*. *Journal of Bacteriology* 53:673–684.

cells from the tube containing the mixture of the two strains. In this case, approximately 10 cells multiplied and formed visible bacterial colonies on the plates. Because these cells were able to reproduce without supplemental amino acids or vitamins, their genotype must have been $met^+ bio^+ thr^+ pro^+$. Mutation cannot account for the occurrence of this new genotype because colonies were not observed on the other two plates, which had the same number of cells and also could have incurred mutations.

To explain the results of their experiment, Lederberg and Tatum hypothesized that some genetic material had been transferred between the two strains when they were mixed. This transfer could have occurred in two ways. One possibility is that the genes providing the ability to synthesize threonine and pro-

line ($thr^+ pro^+$) were transferred to the $met^+ bio^+ thr^- pro^-$ strain. Alternatively, the genes providing the ability to synthesize methionine and biotin ($met^+ bio^+$) may have been transferred to the $met^- bio^- thr^+ pro^+$ cells. The experimental results cannot distinguish between these two possibilities, but they provide compelling evidence that at least one of them occurred.

How did the bacteria in Lederberg and Tatum's experiment transfer genes between strains? Two mechanisms seemed plausible. Either genetic material was released from one strain and taken up by the other, or cells of the two different strains made contact with each other and directly transferred genetic material. To distinguish these two scenarios, Bernard Davis conducted experiments using the same two strains of *E. coli*.

The apparatus he used, known as a U-tube, is shown in **Figure 18.16**. The tube had a filter with pores big enough for pieces of DNA to pass through, but too small to permit the passage of bacteria. After filling the tube with a liquid medium, Davis added $met^-bio^-thr^+pro^+$ bacteria on one side of the filter and $met^+bio^+thr^-pro^-$ bacteria on the other. The application of pressure or suction promoted the movement of liquid through the pores. Although the two kinds of bacteria could not mix, any genetic material released by one of them would be available to the other.

After allowing the bacteria to incubate in the U-tube, Davis placed cells from each side of the tube on growth plates lacking methionine, biotin, threonine, and proline. No bacterial colonies grew on these plates. How did Davis interpret these results? He proposed that without physical contact, the two *E. coli* strains could not transfer genetic material from one to the other. The conceptual level of Figure 18.15, step 1, shows the physical connection that explains Lederberg and Tatum's results. Conjugation is the process of gene transfer that requires direct cell-to-cell contact. It has been subsequently observed in other species of bacteria. Many, but not all, species of bacteria can conjugate.

Experimental Questions

1. What was the hypothesis tested by Lederberg and Tatum?

2. During the Lederberg and Tatum experiment, the researchers compared the growth of mutant strains under two scenarios: mixed strains or unmixed strains. When the unmixed strains were plated on the experimental growth medium, why were no colonies observed to grow? When the mixed strains were plated on the experimental growth medium, a number of colonies were seen to grow. What was the significance of the growth of these colonies?

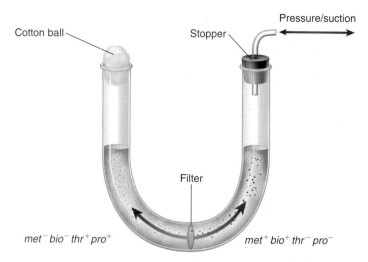

Figure 18.16   A U-tube apparatus like the one used by Bernard Davis.   Bacteria of two different strains were suspended in the liquid in the tube and separated by a filter. The liquid was forced through the filter by alternating suction and pressure. The pores in the filter were too small for the passage of bacteria, but they allowed the passage of DNA.

Concept check: *Would the results have been different if the pore size was larger and allowed the passage of bacterial cells?*

3. The gene transfer seen in the Lederberg and Tatum experiment could have occurred in one of two ways: taking up DNA released into the environment or contact between two bacterial cells allowing for direct transfer. Bernard Davis conducted an experiment to determine the correct process. Explain how his results indicated the correct gene transfer process.

During Conjugation, DNA Is Transferred from a Donor Cell to a Recipient Cell

In the early 1950s, Joshua and Esther Lederberg, William Hayes, and Luca Cavalli-Sforza independently discovered that only certain bacterial strains can donate genetic material during conjugation. For example, only about 5% of *E. coli* strains found in nature can act as donor strains. Further research showed that a strain that is incapable of acting as a donor can acquire this ability after being mixed with a donor strain. Hayes correctly proposed that donor strains contain a type of plasmid called a fertility factor, or **F factor**, that can be transferred to recipient strains. Also, other donor *E. coli* strains were later identified that can transfer portions of the bacterial chromosome at high frequencies. After a segment of the chromosome is transferred, it then inserts, or recombines, into the chromosome of the recipient cell. Such donor strains were named Hfr (for High frequency of recombination). In our discussion, we will focus on donor strains that carry F factors.

The micrograph in **Figure 18.17a** shows two conjugating *E. coli* cells. The cell on the left is designated F^+, meaning that it has an F factor. This donor cell is transferring genetic material

to the recipient cell on the right, which lacks an F factor and is designated F^-. F factors carry several genes that are required for conjugation and also may carry genes that confer a growth advantage for the bacterium.

Figure 18.17b describes the events that occur during conjugation in *E. coli*. The process is similar in other bacteria that are capable of conjugating, although the details vary somewhat from one species to another. Contact between donor and recipient cells is often a key step that initiates the conjugation process. Recall from Chapter 4 that many bacteria have appendages called pili that allow them to attach to surfaces and to each other. **Sex pili** are made by F^+ cells that bind specifically to F^- cells. They are so named because conjugation has sometimes been called bacterial mating or bacterial sex. However, these terms are a bit misleading because the process does not involve equal genetic contributions from two gametes and it does not produce offspring. Instead, bacterial mating is a form of gene transfer that alters the genetic composition of the recipient cell. Donor strains have genes responsible for the formation of sex pili. In F^+ strains, the genes are located on the F factor. In *E. coli* and some other species, F^+ cells make very long pili that attempt to make contact with nearby F^- cells. Once contact is

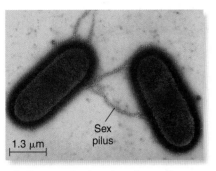

(a) Micrograph of conjugating cells

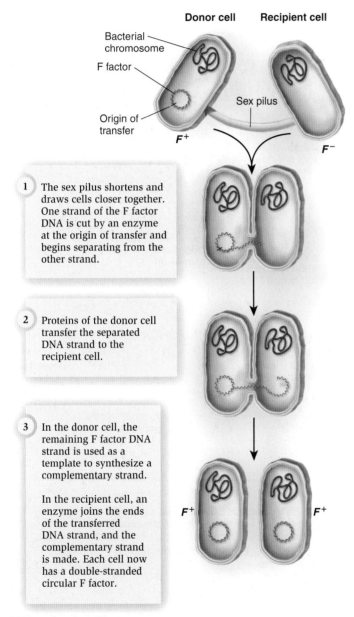

Donor cell   Recipient cell

Bacterial chromosome

F factor

Origin of transfer   Sex pilus

F^+ F^-

1 The sex pilus shortens and draws cells closer together. One strand of the F factor DNA is cut by an enzyme at the origin of transfer and begins separating from the other strand.

2 Proteins of the donor cell transfer the separated DNA strand to the recipient cell.

3 In the donor cell, the remaining F factor DNA strand is used as a template to synthesize a complementary strand.

In the recipient cell, an enzyme joins the ends of the transferred DNA strand, and the complementary strand is made. Each cell now has a double-stranded circular F factor.

F^+ F^+

(b) Transfer of an F factor

Figure 18.17   Bacterial conjugation.   (a) A micrograph of two *E. coli* cells that are conjugating. The cell on the left, designated F^+, is the donor; the cell on the right, designated F^-, is the recipient. The two cells make contact via sex pili made by the F^+ cell. (b) The transfer of an F factor during conjugation. At the end of conjugation, both the donor cell and the recipient cell are F^+.

Concept check: *If a donor cell has only one F factor, explain how the donor and recipient cell both contain one F factor following the transfer of an F factor during conjugation.*

made, the pili shorten, drawing the donor and recipient cells closer together.

Successful contact stimulates the donor cell to begin the transfer process. Genes within the F factor encode proteins that promote the transfer of one strand of F factor DNA. This DNA strand is cut at the origin of transfer, and then the strand travels into the recipient cell. The other strand remains in the donor cell, and the complementary strand is synthesized, thereby restoring the F factor DNA to its original double-stranded condition. In the recipient cell, the two ends of the newly acquired F factor DNA strand are joined to form a circular molecule, and its complementary strand is synthesized to produce a double-stranded F factor. The end result of conjugation is that the recipient cell has acquired an F factor, converting it from an F^- to an F^+ cell. The genetic composition of the donor strain has not been changed.

In Transformation, Bacteria Take Up DNA from the Environment

In contrast to conjugation, the process of gene transfer known as bacterial transformation does not require direct contact between bacterial cells. Frederick Griffith first discovered this process in 1928 while working with strains of *Streptococcus pneumoniae*. We discussed early experiments involving transformation in Chapter 11 (refer back to Figures 11.1 and 11.2).

How does a bacterial cell become transformed? First, it imports a strand of DNA from the environment. This DNA strand, which is typically derived from a dead bacterial cell, may then insert or recombine into the bacterial chromosome. The live bacterium is now carrying genes from the dead bacterium—the live bacterium has been transformed. Not all bacterial strains have the ability to take up DNA. Those that do have this ability are described as naturally **competent**, and they have genes that encode proteins called competence factors. Competence factors facilitate the binding of DNA fragments to the bacterial cell surface, the uptake of DNA into the cytoplasm, and the incorporation of the imported DNA into the bacterial chromosome. Temperature, ionic conditions, and the availability of nutrients also affect whether or not a bacterium will be competent to take up genetic material.

In recent years, biologists have unraveled some of the steps that occur when competent bacterial cells are transformed by taking up genetic material from the environment. In the example shown in **Figure 18.18**, the DNA released from a dead bacterium carries a gene, tet^R, that confers resistance to the antibiotic tetracycline. First, a large fragment of the DNA binds to a surface receptor on the outside of a bacterial cell that is sensitive to tetracycline. Enzymes secreted by the bacterium cut this large fragment into fragments small enough to enter the cell. The next step is for a small DNA fragment to begin its entry into the bacterial cytoplasm. One of the two DNA strands of this fragment is degraded. The other strand enters the bacterial cytoplasm via a DNA uptake system that transports the DNA across the plasma membrane. Finally, the imported DNA strand is incorporated into the bacterial chromosome, and the complementary strand is synthesized. Following transformation, the

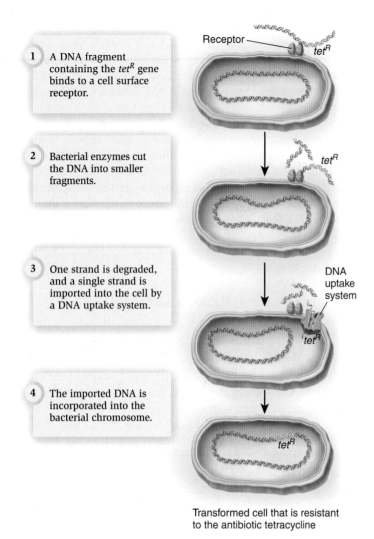

1   A DNA fragment containing the *tet*^R gene binds to a cell surface receptor.

2   Bacterial enzymes cut the DNA into smaller fragments.

3   One strand is degraded, and a single strand is imported into the cell by a DNA uptake system.

4   The imported DNA is incorporated into the bacterial chromosome.

Transformed cell that is resistant to the antibiotic tetracycline

Figure 18.18   The steps of bacterial transformation.   This process has transformed a bacterium that was sensitive to the antibiotic tetracycline into one that can grow in the presence of this antibiotic.

recipient cell has been transformed from a tetracycline-sensitive cell to a tetracycline-resistant cell.

In Transduction, Viruses Transfer Genetic Material from One Bacterium to Another

Perhaps the most curious method of gene transfer is transduction, in which bacteriophages transfer bacterial genes from one bacterium to another. As discussed earlier in this chapter, a bacteriophage (or simply phage) is a virus that uses the cellular machinery of a bacterium for its own replication. The new viral particles made in this way usually contain only viral genes. On rare occasions, however, a phage may pick up a piece of DNA from the bacterial chromosome. When a phage carrying a segment of bacterial DNA infects another bacterium, it transfers this segment into the chromosome of its new bacterial host.

Transduction is actually an error in a phage lytic cycle, as shown in **Figure 18.19**. In this example, a phage called P1 infects an *E. coli* cell that has a gene (*his*^+) for histidine

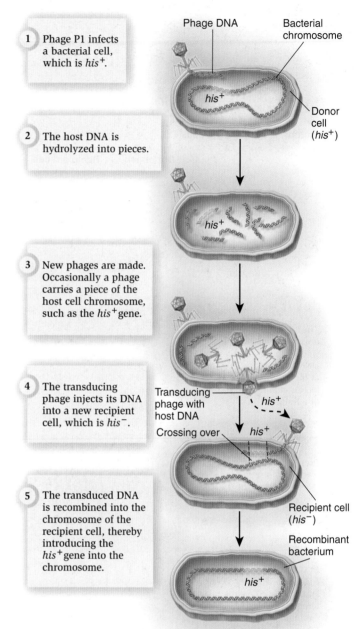

1   Phage P1 infects a bacterial cell, which is *his*^+.

2   The host DNA is hydrolyzed into pieces.

3   New phages are made. Occasionally a phage carries a piece of the host cell chromosome, such as the *his*^+ gene.

4   The transducing phage injects its DNA into a new recipient cell, which is *his*^-.

5   The transduced DNA is recombined into the chromosome of the recipient cell, thereby introducing the *his*^+ gene into the chromosome.

The recombinant bacterium has a genotype (*his*^+) that is different from the original recipient bacterial cell (*his*^-).

Figure 18.19   Bacterial transduction by P1 phage.

Concept check: *Is transduction a normal part of the phage life cycle? Explain.*

synthesis. Phage P1 causes the host cell chromosome to degrade into small pieces. When new phages are assembled, coat proteins may enclose a piece of host DNA that carries this gene. This produces a phage carrying bacterial chromosomal DNA. In the example shown in Figure 18.19, this transducing phage is released and binds to an *E. coli* cell that lacks the *his*^+ gene. It inserts the bacterial DNA fragment into the recipient cell, which then incorporates this fragment into its own chromosome by recombination. In this case, gene transfer by transduction converts a *his*^- strain of *E. coli* to a *his*^+ strain.

Genomes & Proteomes Connection

Horizontal Gene Transfer Is the Transfer of Genes Between the Same or Different Species

So far we have considered gene transfer from one bacterial strain to another strain of the same species. In addition, conjugation, transformation, and transduction occasionally occur between cells of different bacterial species. The term **horizontal gene transfer** refers to a process in which an organism incorporates genetic material from another organism without being the offspring of that organism. Conjugation, transformation, and transduction are examples of horizontal gene transfer. In contrast, vertical gene transfer occurs when genes are passed from one generation to the next—from parents to offspring and from mother cells to daughter cells.

Why is horizontal gene transfer important? In recent years, analyses of bacterial genomes have shown that a sizeable fraction of bacterial genes are derived from horizontal gene transfer. For example, roughly 17% of the genes of *E. coli* and of *Salmonella typhimurium* have been acquired from other species by horizontal transfer during the past 100 million years. Many of these acquired genes are for traits that give cells a selective advantage, including genes that confer antibiotic resistance, the ability to degrade toxic compounds, and the ability to withstand extreme environments. Some horizontally transferred genes confer pathogenicity, turning a harmless bacterial strain into one that can cause disease. Geneticists have suggested that horizontal gene transfer has played a major role in the evolution of different bacterial species. In many cases, the acquisition of new genes allows a bacterium to survive in a new type of environment and can eventually lead to the formation of a new species.

A second reason why horizontal gene transfer is important is its medical relevance. Let's consider the topic of antibiotic resistance. Antibiotics are widely prescribed to treat bacterial infections in humans. They are also used in agriculture to control bacterial diseases. Unfortunately, the widespread use of antibiotics has greatly increased the prevalence of antibiotic resistant strains of bacteria, strains that have a selective advantage over those that are susceptible to antibiotics. Resistant strains carry genes that counteract the action of antibiotics in various ways. A resistance gene may encode a protein that breaks down the drug, pumps it out of the cell, or prevents it from inhibiting cellular processes.

The term **acquired antibiotic resistance** refers to the common phenomenon of a previously susceptible strain becoming resistant to a specific antibiotic. This change may result from genetic alterations in the bacteria's own genome, but it is often due to the horizontal transfer of resistance genes from a resistant strain. As often mentioned in the news media, antibiotic resistance has increased dramatically worldwide over the past few decades, with resistant strains reported in almost all pathogenic strains of bacteria. For example, the most common cause of pneumonia is infection by *Streptococcus pneumoniae*. In many countries, nearly 50% of all *S. pneumoniae* strains are now penicillin resistant, with resistance to other drugs increasing

as well. Some of the most severe antibiotic resistance problems occur in hospitals. Resistant strains of *Klebsiella pneumoniae* and *Enterococcus faecium* are significant causes of infection and death among critically ill patients in intensive care units.

▮ Summary of Key Concepts

18.1 Genetic Properties of Viruses

- Tobacco mosaic virus (TMV) was the first virus to be discovered. It infects many species of plants. (Figure 18.1)
- Viruses vary with regard to their host range, structure, and genome composition. (Table 18.1, Figures 18.2, 18.3)
- The viral reproductive cycle consists of five or six basic steps, including attachment, entry, integration, synthesis, assembly, and release. (Figure 18.4)
- Some bacteriophages can alternate between two reproductive cycles: the lytic cycle and lysogenic cycle. (Figure 18.5)
- The disease AIDS is caused by a virus called human immunodeficiency virus (HIV). The virus is a retrovirus whose reproductive cycle involves the integration of the viral genome into a chromosome in the host cell. (Figure 18.6)
- Drugs to combat viral proliferation are often created specifically to inhibit viral proteins.

18.2 Viroids and Prions

- Viroids are RNA molecules that infect plant cells. (Figure 18.7)
- Prions are proteins that exist in an abnormal conformation that can cause disease. (Figure 18.8, Table 18.2)

18.3 Genetic Properties of Bacteria

- Bacteria typically have a single type of circular chromosome found in the nucleoid region of the cell. The chromosome contains many genes and one origin of replication. (Figures 18.9, 18.10)
- The bacterial chromosome is made more compact by the formation of loops and by DNA supercoiling. (Figure 18.11)
- Plasmids are small, circular DNA molecules that exist independently of the bacterial chromosome. Examples are resistance, degradative, col-, virulence, and fertility plasmids. (Figure 18.12)
- When placed on solid growth media, a single bacterial cell will divide many times to produce a colony composed of many cells. (Figure 18.13)
- Bacterial cells reproduce by a process called binary fission, during which a cell divides to form two daughter cells. (Figure 18.14)

18.4 Gene Transfer Between Bacteria

- Three common modes of gene transfer among bacteria are conjugation, transformation, and transduction. (Table 18.3)
- Lederberg and Tatum's work demonstrated the transfer of bacterial genes between different strains of *E. coli* by

conjugation. Davis showed that direct contact was needed for this type of gene transfer. (Figures 18.15, 18.16)

- During the mechanism of conjugation, a strand of DNA from an F factor is transferred from a donor to a recipient cell. (Figure 18.17)

- Transformation is the process in which a segment of DNA from the environment is taken up by a competent cell and incorporated into the bacterial chromosome. (Figure 18.18)

- Bacterial transduction is a form of gene transfer in which a bacteriophage transfers a segment of bacterial chromosomal DNA to another cell. (Figure 18.19)

- Horizontal gene transfer is a process in which an organism incorporates genetic material from another organism without being the offspring of that organism.

Assess and Discuss

Test Yourself

1. The _____ is the protein coat of a virus that surrounds the genetic material.
   a. host
   b. prion
   c. capsid
   d. viroid
   e. capsule

2. Among the viruses identified, the characteristics of their genomes show many variations. Which of the following does not describe a typical characteristic of viral genomes?
   a. The genetic material may be DNA or RNA.
   b. The nucleic acid may be single stranded or double stranded.
   c. The genome may carry just a few genes or several dozen.
   d. The number of copies of the genome may vary.
   e. All of the above describe typical variation in viral genomes.

3. During viral infection, attachment is usually specific to a particular cell type because
   a. the virus is attracted to the appropriate host cells by proteins secreted into the extracellular fluid.
   b. the virus recognizes and binds to specific molecules in the cytoplasm of the host cell.
   c. the virus recognizes and binds to specific molecules on the surface of the host cell.
   d. the host cell produces channel proteins that provide passageways for viruses to enter the cytoplasm.
   e. the virus releases specific proteins that make holes in the membrane large enough for the virus to enter.

4. HIV, a retrovirus, has a high mutation rate because
   a. the DNA of the viral genome is less stable than other viral genomes.
   b. the viral enzyme reverse transcriptase has a high likelihood of making replication errors.
   c. the viral genome is altered every time it is incorporated into the host genome.
   d. antibodies produced by the host cell mutate the viral genome when infection occurs.
   e. all of the above.

5. A _____ is an infectious agent composed solely of RNA, whereas a _____ is an infectious agent composed solely of protein.
   a. retrovirus, bacteriophage
   b. viroid, virus
   c. prion, virus
   d. retrovirus, prion
   e. viroid, prion

6. Genetic diversity is maintained in bacterial populations by all of the following except
   a. binary fission.
   b. mutation.
   c. transformation.
   d. transduction.
   e. conjugation.

7. Bacterial cells divide by a process known as
   a. mitosis.
   b. cytokinesis.
   c. meiosis.
   d. binary fission.
   e. glycolysis.

8. Gene transfer, whereby a bacterial cell takes up bacterial DNA from the environment, is
   a. conjugation.
   b. binary fission.
   c. recombination.
   d. transformation.
   e. transduction.

9. A bacterial cell can donate DNA during conjugation when it
   a. produces competence factors.
   b. contains an F factor.
   c. is virulent.
   d. has been infected by a bacteriophage.
   e. all of the above.

10. A bacterial species that becomes resistant to certain antibiotics may have acquired the resistance genes from another bacterial species. The phenomenon of acquiring genes from another organism without being the offspring of that organism is known as
    a. hybridization.
    b. integration.
    c. horizontal gene transfer.
    d. vertical gene transfer.
    e. competence.

Conceptual Questions

1. How are viruses similar to living cells, and how are they different?

2. What are three mechanisms of gene transfer in bacteria? Discuss the evolutionary and medical significance of horizontal gene transfer.

3. If you mix together an equal number of F^+ and F^- cells, how would you expect the proportions to change over time? Do you expect an increase in the relative proportions of F^+ and F^- cells? Explain your answer.

Collaborative Questions

1. Discuss the possible origin of viruses. Which idea(s) do you think is (are) the most likely?

2. Conjugation is sometimes called "bacterial mating." Discuss how conjugation is similar to sexual reproduction in eukaryotes and how it is different.

Online Resource

www.brookerbiology.com

Stay a step ahead in your studies with animations that bring concepts to life and practice tests to assess your understanding. Your instructor may also recommend the interactive ebook, individualized learning tools, and more.

Developmental Genetics

19

A child with aniridia. The nature of this disease, which involves a defect in iris development, is described at the beginning of the chapter.

T ake a close look at the child in the chapter-opening photo. Do you notice anything unusual? Though it may not be immediately apparent, this child has a disorder called aniridia, in which the iris in each eye does not develop properly. The iris is the part of the eye, usually blue, green, or brown, that regulates the amount of light entering the eye. In aniridia, the place where each iris should be located appears black, giving the appearance of very large pupils. People with aniridia cannot adjust the amount of light entering their eyes, which results in a decreased quality of vision and leads to eye diseases such as glaucoma and cataracts. In addition, other structures within the eye, such as the retina and optic nerve, may not develop correctly. What is the underlying cause of aniridia? It is due to a mutation in a gene called *Pax6*, which is responsible for the development of the eye. People with aniridia are heterozygotes, having one normal copy of the *Pax6* gene and one defective copy. The proper development of the eye requires two normal copies of the *Pax6* gene. This disorder illustrates how genes play a key role in the development of our bodies.

In biology, the term **development** refers to a series of changes in the state of a cell, tissue, organ, or organism. Development is the underlying process that gives rise to the structures and functions of living organisms. The structure or form of an organism is called its **morphology**. As we have learned throughout this textbook, an important paradigm in biology is that structure (morphology) determines function.

Biologists came to realize that animals and plants undergo amazing changes in development that create the structures and functions found in adult organisms. How do these developmental changes occur? Since the 1940s, the genetic makeup of an organism has emerged as the fundamental force behind development. The science of **developmental genetics** is concerned with understanding how gene expression controls the process of development.

In this chapter, we will learn how the sequential actions of genes provide a program for the development of an organism from a fertilized egg to an adult. Utilizing a few experimental organisms, such as the fruit fly, a nematode worm, the mouse, and the plant *Arabidopsis*, scientists are working toward the identification and characterization of the genes required for running their developmental programs. Researchers are now exploring how proteins encoded by these genes control the course of development in these organisms. In this

chapter, we will begin with an overview that emphasizes the general principles of development. We will then examine specific examples of development in animals and plants, focusing on the role of genes in embryonic development. Chapters 39 and 52 also consider plant and animal development, respectively, with an emphasis on structure and function.

19.1 General Themes in Development

Animals and plants begin to develop when a sperm and an egg unite to produce a **zygote**, a diploid cell that divides and develops into a multicellular **embryo**, and eventually into an adult organism. During the early stages of development, cells divide and begin to arrange themselves into ordered units. As this occurs, each cell also becomes **determined**, which means it is committed to become a particular cell type, such as a muscle or intestinal cell. The commitment to become a specific cell type occurs long before a cell becomes differentiated. During the process of **cell differentiation**, a cell's morphology and function have changed, usually permanently, into a highly specialized cell type. In an adult, each cell type plays its own particular role. In animals, for example, muscle cells allow an organism to move, while intestinal cells facilitate the absorption of nutrients. This division of labor among various cells of an organism works collectively to promote its survival.

The genomes of living organisms contain a set of genes that constitute a program of development. In unicellular species, the program controls the structure and function of the cell. In multicellular species such as animals and plants, the program not only controls cellular features but also determines the arrangement of cells in the organisms. In this section, we will examine some of the general issues associated with the development of multicellular species.

Developmental Biologists Have Chosen a Few Model Organisms to Study Development

The development of even a simple multicellular organism involves many types of changes in form and function. For this reason, the research community has focused its efforts on only a few **model organisms**—organisms studied by many different researchers so they can compare their results and determine scientific principles that apply more broadly to other species.

With regard to animal development, the two organisms that have been the most extensively investigated are two invertebrate species: the fruit fly *Drosophila melanogaster* and *Caenorhabditis elegans* (**Figure 19.1a,b**). *C. elegans* is a small, nematode worm, about 1 mm in length, which lives in temperate soils. Why have these two organisms been chosen as models to investigate development? *Drosophila* has been studied for a variety of reasons.

First, researchers have exposed this organism to mutagens and identified many mutant organisms with altered developmental pathways. Second, in all of its life stages, *Drosophila* has distinct morphological features and is large enough to easily identify the effects of mutations. *C. elegans* is used by developmental geneticists for its simplicity. The adult organism is a small transparent worm composed of only about 1,000 somatic cells. Starting with a fertilized egg, the pattern of cell division and the fate of each cell within the embryo are completely known. This pattern is essentially identical from one worm to another, which allows researchers to predict cell fates in this organism.

Embryologists have also studied the morphological features of development in vertebrate species. Historically, amphibians and birds have been studied extensively, because their eggs are rather large and easy to manipulate. From a morphological point of view, the developmental stages of the chicken (*Gallus gallus*) and the African clawed frog (*Xenopus laevis*) have been described in great detail. More recently, a few vertebrate species have been the subject of genetic studies of development. These include the house mouse (*Mus musculus*) and the small aquarium zebrafish (*Danio rerio*) (**Figure 19.1c,d**).

In the study of plant development, the model organism for genetic analysis is a small flowering plant known as thale cress (*Arabidopsis thaliana*), which is typically called *Arabidopsis* by researchers (**Figure 19.1e**). *Arabidopsis* is an annual weed that belongs to the wild mustard family. It occurs naturally throughout temperate regions of the world. *Arabidopsis* has a short generation time of about 6 weeks and a small genome size of 12×10^7 bp, which is similar in size to that of *Drosophila* and *C. elegans*. A flowering *Arabidopsis* plant is small enough to be grown in the laboratory and produces a large number of seeds.

(a) *Drosophila melanogaster*

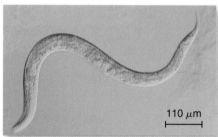

110 μm

(b) *Caenorhabditis elegans*

(c) *Mus musculus*

(d) *Danio rerio*

(e) *Arabidopsis thaliana*

Figure 19.1 Model organisms used to study developmental genetics.

Concept check: *Why do most researchers focus their efforts on just a few model organisms?*

Both Animals and Plants Develop by Pattern Formation

Development in animals and plants produces a body plan or pattern. At the cellular level, the body pattern is due to the arrangement of cells and their differentiation. The process, called **pattern formation**, gives rise to the formation of a body with a particular morphology. Pattern formation in animals is usually organized along three axes: the **dorsoventral axis**, the **anteroposterior axis**, and the **left-right axis** (Figure 19.2a). In addition, many animal bodies are then segmented into separate sections containing specific body parts such as wings or legs.

By comparison, pattern formation in plants is quite different, being organized along a **root-shoot axis** and in a **radial pattern** (Figure 19.2b). The root-shoot axis is determined at the first division of the fertilized egg, and growth occurs in a radial pattern around this axis. As we'll see later, the identification of mutant alleles that disrupt development has permitted great insight into the genes controlling pattern formation.

Pattern Formation Depends on Positional Information

Before we examine how genes affect pattern formation, let's consider a central concept in developmental biology—**positional information**. For an organism to develop the correct morphological features or pattern, each cell of the body must become the appropriate cell type based on its position relative to other cells. How does this occur? At appropriate times during development, cells receive positional information that provides them with cues regarding their location relative to other cells of the body. Later in this chapter, we will examine how the expression of genes at the correct times provides this information.

A cell may respond to positional information in one of four ways: cell division, cell migration, cell differentiation, and cell death (Figure 19.3). First, positional information may stimulate a cell to divide. Second, positional information in animals may cause the migration of a cell or group of cells in a particular direction from one region of the embryo to another. Cell

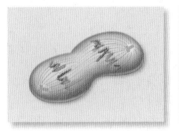

(a) Cell division

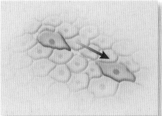

(b) Cell migration

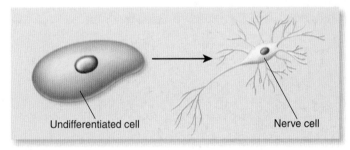

(c) Cell differentiation

Undifferentiated cell   Nerve cell

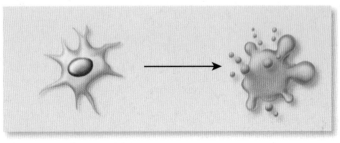

(d) Cell death (apoptosis)

Figure 19.3 Four types of cellular responses to positional information in animals.

Concept check: *Which of these four responses do you expect to be more prevalent in the early stages of development, and which would become more prevalent in later stages?*

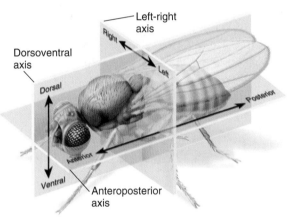

Left-right axis

Right

Left

Dorsoventral axis

Dorsal

Posterior

Ventral

Anterior

Anteroposterior axis

(a) Body plan found in many animals

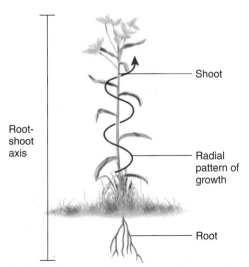

Root-shoot axis

Shoot

Radial pattern of growth

Root

(b) Body plan found in many seed-bearing plants

Figure 19.2 Body plan axes in animals and plants.

migration does not occur during development in plants. Third, it may cause a cell to differentiate into a specific cell type such as a nerve cell. Finally, positional information may promote cell death. This process, known as **apoptosis**, is a necessary event during normal animal development. Apoptosis is known to play a key role in sculpting the bodies of animals. In plants, programmed cell death is also important during development. For example, cells within xylem tissue undergo programmed cell death to form tracheids that function in water transport (see Chapter 38).

As an example of how the coordination of these four processes is required for pattern formation, Figure 19.4 shows the growth and development of a human arm during the embryonic stage. Cell division with accompanying cell growth increases the size of the limb. Cell migration is also important in this process. For example, embryonic cells that eventually form muscles in the arm and hand must migrate long distances to reach their correct location within the limb. As development proceeds, cell differentiation produces the various tissues that will eventually be found in the fully developed limb. Some cells will become nerve cells, others will be muscle cells, and still others will form the outer layer of skin. Finally, apoptosis is important in the formation of fingers. If apoptosis did not occur, a human hand would have webbed fingers.

Morphogens and Cell-to-Cell Contacts Convey Positional Information

How does positional information lead to the development of a body plan? Though the details of pattern formation vary widely among different species, two main molecular mechanisms are commonly used to communicate positional information. One of these mechanisms involves molecules called morphogens. **Morphogens** impart positional information and

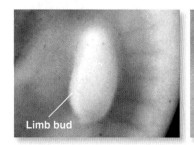
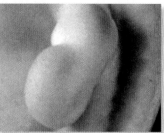

(a) Limb development in a human embryo

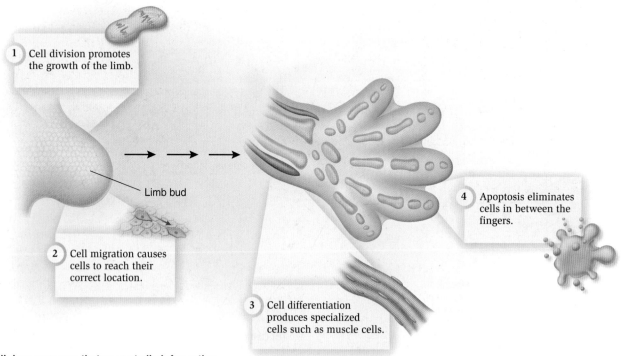

1 Cell division promotes the growth of the limb.

Limb bud

2 Cell migration causes cells to reach their correct location.

3 Cell differentiation produces specialized cells such as muscle cells.

4 Apoptosis eliminates cells in between the fingers.

(b) Four cellular processes that promote limb formation

Figure 19.4 Limb development in humans. (a) Photographs of limb development in human embryos. The limb begins as a protrusion called a limb bud that eventually forms an arm and hand. (b) The development of a human limb from an embryonic limb bud.

Concept check: How would finger formation be affected if apoptosis did not occur?

promote developmental changes at the cellular level. A morphogen influences the fate of a cell by promoting cell division, cell migration, cell differentiation, or apoptosis. A key feature of morphogens is they act in a concentration-dependent manner. At a high concentration, a morphogen will restrict a cell into a particular developmental pathway, whereas at a lower concentration, it will not. There is often a critical **threshold concentration** above which the morphogen will exert its effects.

Morphogens typically are distributed asymmetrically along a concentration gradient. Morphogenic gradients may be established in the oocyte (**Figure 19.5a**). In addition, a morphogenic gradient can be established in the embryo by secretion and diffusion (**Figure 19.5b**). A certain cell or group of cells may synthesize and secrete a morphogen at a specific stage of development. After secretion, the morphogen may diffuse to neighboring cells, as in Figure 19.5b, or it may be transported to cells that are distant from the cells that secrete the morphogen. The morphogen may then influence the developmental fate of cells exposed to it. The process by which a cell or group of cells governs the developmental fate of other cells is known as **induction**.

Another mechanism used to convey positional information involves **cell adhesion** (**Figure 19.5c**). Each animal cell makes its own collection of surface receptors that enable it to adhere to other cells and to the extracellular matrix (ECM). Such receptors, known as **cell adhesion molecules** (**CAMs**), are described in Chapter 10 (refer back to Figure 10.8). The positioning of a cell within a multicellular organism is strongly influenced by the combination of contacts it makes with other cells and with the ECM.

The phenomenon of cell adhesion and its role in multicellular development was first recognized by Henry Wilson in 1907. He took multicellular sponges and passed them through a sieve, dissociating them into individual cells. Remarkably, the cells actively migrated until they adhered to one another to form a new sponge, complete with the chambers and canals that characterize a sponge's internal structure! When sponge cells from different species were mixed, they sorted themselves properly, adhering only to cells of the same species. Overall, these results indicate that cells possess specific CAMs, which are critical in cell-to-cell recognition. Cell adhesion plays an important role in governing the position that an animal cell will adopt during development.

A Hierarchy of Transcription Factors Orchestrates a Program of Development

The formation of a body, in both animals and plants, occurs in a series of organizational phases that overlap with each other. As an overview of this process, let's consider four general phases of pattern formation in an animal (**Figure 19.6**). The first phase organizes the body along major axes. The anteroposterior axis determines the organization from head to tail, the dorsoventral axis governs the structure from back (dorsal) to front/abdomen (ventral), and the left-right axis provides organization from side to side. During the second phase, the body becomes organized into smaller regions that will eventually contain organs and other structures such as legs. In insects, these regions form well-defined segments. In mammals, some segmentation of the body is apparent during embryonic development, but defined boundaries are lost as the embryo proceeds to the fetal and adult stages. In the third phase, the cells within the segments organize themselves in ways that will produce particular body parts. Finally, during the fourth phase, the cells themselves change their morphologies and become differentiated. This final phase of development produces an organism with many types of tissues, organs, and other body parts with specialized functions.

How does genetics underlie the phases of animal development? Geneticists have discovered a parallel between the expression of specific transcription factors and the four major phases of animal development. As diagrammed in Figure 19.6, a hierarchy of transcription factors control whether or not certain genes are expressed at a specific phase of development in a particular cell type, a phenomenon called **differential gene regulation**.

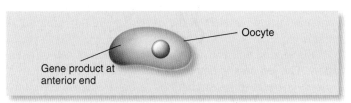

(a) Asymmetric distribution of morphogens in the oocyte

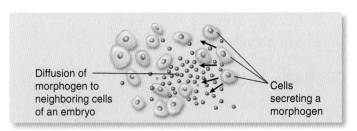

(b) Induction: Asymmetric synthesis and extracellular distribution of a morphogen

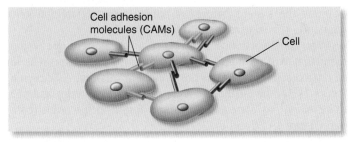

(c) Cell adhesion: Cell-to-cell contact conveys positional information

Figure 19.5   Molecular mechanisms that convey positional information.   Asymmetric distribution of a morphogen in the **(a)** oocyte or **(b)** embryo. **(c)** Positional information may also be obtained by cell-to-cell contact.

Concept check: Why is positional information important during development?

Many morphogens, particularly those that act at an early phase of development, function as transcription factors. Such transcription factors regulate the expression of genes in a way that controls the formation of the body axes. Next, these early

Hierarchy of transcription factors

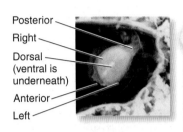

Posterior
Right
Dorsal
(ventral is
underneath)
Anterior
Left

1 **Phase 1:**
Transcription factors determine the formation of the body axes and control the expression of transcription factors of phase 2.

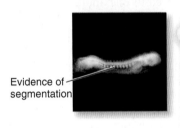

Evidence of segmentation

2 **Phase 2:**
Transcription factors cause the embryo to become subdivided into regions that have properties of individual segments. They also control transcription factors of phase 3.

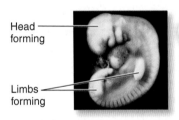

Head forming

Limbs forming

3 **Phase 3:**
Transcription factors cause each segment and groups of segments to develop specific characteristics. They also control transcription factors of phase 4.

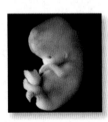

4 **Phase 4:**
Transcription factors cause cells to differentiate into specific cell types such as skin, nerve, and muscle cells.

Figure 19.6 **Pattern formation in a human embryo.** As shown here, pattern formation in animals occurs in four phases that are controlled by a hierarchy of transcription factors. The example shown here involves human development, although research suggests that pattern formation in all complex animals follows a similar plan. The ideas in this scenario are based largely on analogies between pattern formation in *Drosophila* and mammals. Many of the transcription factors that are likely to control the early phases of pattern formation in mammals have yet to be identified.

Concept check: *During which of the four phases of development would you expect cell division and cell migration to be the most prevalent?*

transcription factors cause the expression of other transcription factors that direct the segmented body plan. After the body plan has been segmented, a third category of transcription factors controls what structures will be made within each segment. Finally, a fourth category of transcription factors controls the differentiation of each cell type. Also, note that the phases of development are overlapping. For example, cell differentiation begins to occur as the cells are adopting their correct locations.

19.2 Development in Animals

In this section, we will begin by examining the general stages of *Drosophila* development and then focus our attention on its embryonic stage. During this stage, the overall body plan is determined. We will see how the differential expression of particular genes and the localization of positional information within the embryo control pattern formation. While the roles of genes in the organization of mammalian embryos are not as well understood as they are in *Drosophila*, the analysis of the genomes of mammals and many other species has revealed many interesting parallels in the developmental program of all animals.

This section will end with an examination of cell differentiation. This process is better understood in mammals than in *Drosophila* because researchers have been extensively studying mammalian cells in the laboratory for many decades. To explore cell differentiation, we will consider mammals as our primary example.

Embryonic Development Determines the Pattern of Structures in the Adult: The Development of *Drosophila*

As a way to appreciate the phases of pattern formation in animals, we will largely focus on development in *Drosophila*. However, as described in Chapter 52, animal development is quite varied among different species. **Figure 19.7** illustrates a simplified sequence of events in *Drosophila* development. Let's examine these steps before we consider the differential gene regulation that causes them to happen.

The oocyte is critical to establishing the pattern of development that will ultimately produce an adult organism. It is an elongated cell that contains positional information. As shown in Figure 19.7a, the fertilized oocyte already has anterior and posterior ends that correspond to those found in the adult (compare Figure 19.7a and e).

A key process in *Drosophila* embryonic development is the formation of a segmented body pattern. The embryo is subdivided into visible units. In *Drosophila*, the segments can be grouped into three general areas: the head, the thorax, and the abdomen. Figure 19.7b shows the segmented pattern of a *Drosophila* embryo about 10 hours after fertilization. Later in this section, we will explore how the coordination of gene expression underlies the formation of these segments.

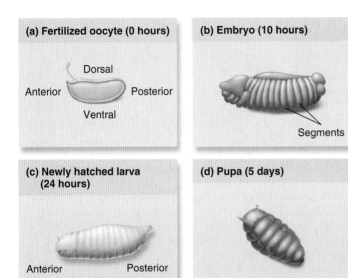

(a) Fertilized oocyte (0 hours)

Dorsal

Anterior — Posterior

Ventral

(b) Embryo (10 hours)

Segments

(c) Newly hatched larva (24 hours)

Anterior   Posterior

(d) Pupa (5 days)

(e) Adult (10 days)

Figure 19.7
Developmental stages of the
fruit fly *Drosophila*.

As an example of one morphogen that plays a role in axis formation, let's consider the product of a gene in *Drosophila* called *bicoid*. Its name is derived from the observation that a mutation that inactivates the gene results in a larva with two posterior ends (**Figure 19.8**). During normal oocyte development, the *bicoid* gene product accumulates in the anterior region of the oocyte. This gene product later acts as a morphogen to cause the development of the anterior end of the embryo.

How does the *bicoid* gene product accumulate in the anterior region of the oocyte? The answer involves specialized nurse cells that are found next to the oocyte, which matures in a follicle within the ovary of a female fly. As discussed in Chapter 17, nurse cells supply the products (for example, mRNA) of maternal effect genes to the developing oocyte. These genes cause an unusual pattern of inheritance called maternal effect (refer back to Figure 17.14). In *Drosophila*, the *bicoid* gene is transcribed in the nurse cells, and *bicoid* mRNA is then transported into the anterior end of the oocyte and trapped there (**Figure 19.9a**). Prior to fertilization, the *bicoid* mRNA is highly concentrated near the anterior end of the oocyte (**Figure 19.9b**). After fertilization, the *bicoid* mRNA is translated, and a gradient of Bicoid protein is established across the zygote (**Figure 19.9c**). This gradient starts a progression of developmental events that will provide the positional information that causes the end of the zygote with a high Bicoid protein concentration to become the anterior region of the embryo.

The Bicoid protein is a morphogen that functions as a transcription factor to activate particular genes at specific times. The ability of Bicoid to activate a given gene depends

A *Drosophila* embryo then develops into a **larva** (Figure 19.7c), which is a free-living organism that is morphologically very different from the adult. Many animal species do not have larval stages. *Drosophila* undergoes three successive larval stages. After the third larval stage, the organism becomes a **pupa** (Figure 19.7d), a transitional stage between the larva and the adult. Through a process known as **metamorphosis**, the organism transforms into a mature adult and emerges from the pupal case (Figure 19.7e). Each segment in the adult develops its own characteristic structures. For example, the wings are on a thoracic segment. From beginning to end, this process takes about 10 days.

Phase 1 Pattern Formation: Maternal Effect Genes Promote the Formation of the Main Body Axes

The first phase in *Drosophila* pattern formation is the establishment of the body axes, which occurs before the embryo becomes segmented. The morphogens necessary to establish these axes are distributed prior to fertilization. In most invertebrates and some vertebrates, certain morphogens, which are important in early developmental stages, are deposited asymmetrically within the egg as it develops. Later, after the egg has been fertilized and development begins, these morphogens will initiate developmental programs that govern the formation of the body axes of the embryo.

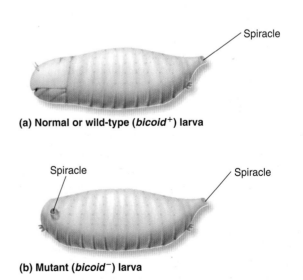

Spiracle

(a) Normal or wild-type (*bicoid*⁺) larva

Spiracle   Spiracle

(b) Mutant (*bicoid*⁻) larva

Figure 19.8 **The bicoid mutation in *Drosophila*.** (a) A normal *bicoid*⁺ larva. (b) A *bicoid*⁻ larva, in which both ends of the larva develop posterior structures. For example, both ends develop a spiracle, a small pore that normally is found only at the posterior end.

Concept check: *What would you expect to be the phenotype of a larva in which the bicoid gene was expressed in both the anterior region and the posterior region of the oocyte?*

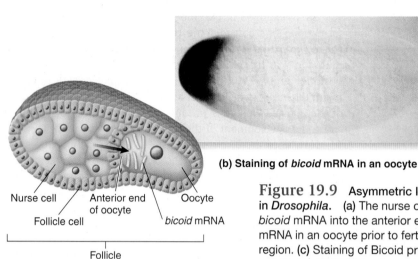

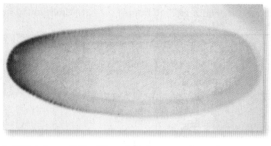

(b) Staining of *bicoid* mRNA in an oocyte   **(c) Staining of Bicoid protein in an early embryo**

Nurse cell   Anterior end   Oocyte
of oocyte
Follicle cell   *bicoid* mRNA

Follicle

(a) Transport of maternal effect gene products (*bicoid* mRNA) into the oocyte

Figure 19.9   Asymmetric localization of gene products during egg development in *Drosophila*.   **(a)** The nurse cells transport maternal effect gene products such as *bicoid* mRNA into the anterior end of the developing oocyte. **(b)** Staining of *bicoid* mRNA in an oocyte prior to fertilization. The *bicoid* mRNA is trapped at the anterior region. **(c)** Staining of Bicoid protein after fertilization. The Bicoid protein forms a gradient, with its highest concentration near the anterior end.

Concept check: *What is the function of the Bicoid protein? After fertilization, in which part of the resulting zygote would its function be highest?*

on its concentration. Due to its asymmetric distribution, the Bicoid protein will activate genes only in certain regions of the embryo. For example, a high concentration of Bicoid stimulates the expression of a gene called *hunchback* (that also encodes a transcription factor) in the anterior half of the embryo, but its concentration is too low in the posterior half to activate the *hunchback* gene. The ability of Bicoid to activate genes in certain regions but not others plays a role in the second phase of pattern formation, which is segmentation.

The Study of *Drosophila* Mutants Has Identified Genes That Control the Development of Segments

As described earlier in Figure 19.6, the second phase of pattern formation is the development of segments. The normal *Drosophila* embryo is subdivided into 15 segments: three head segments, three thoracic segments, and nine abdominal segments (**Figure 19.10**). Each segment of the embryo will give rise to unique morphological features in the adult. For example, the second thoracic segment (T2) produces a pair of legs and a pair of wings.

In the 1970s, Christiane Nüsslein-Volhard and Eric Wieschaus undertook a systematic search for *Drosophila* mutants with disrupted development. They focused their search on **segmentation genes**, genes that alter the segmentation pattern of the *Drosophila* embryo and larva. Based on the characteristics of abnormal larva, they identified three classes of segmentation genes: gap genes, pair-rule genes, and segment-polarity genes. When a mutation inactivates a **gap gene**, several adjacent segments are missing in the larva—a gap occurs. A defect in a **pair-rule gene** may cause alternating segments or parts of segments to be absent. Finally, **segment-polarity gene** mutations cause portions of segments to be missing and cause adjacent regions to become mirror images of each other. The role of these segmentation genes during normal *Drosophila* development is described next.

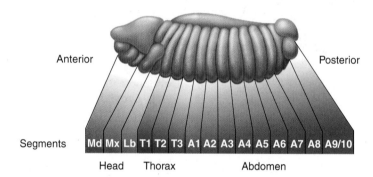

Anterior   Posterior

Segments | Md | Mx | Lb | T1 | T2 | T3 | A1 | A2 | A3 | A4 | A5 | A6 | A7 | A8 | A9/10 |

Head   Thorax   Abdomen

Figure 19.10   The organization of segments in the *Drosophila* embryo.

Phase 2 Pattern Formation: Segmentation Genes Act Sequentially to Divide the *Drosophila* Embryo into Segments

The study of segmentation genes has revealed how segments are formed. To make a segment, particular genes act sequentially to govern the fate of a given region of the body. A simplified scheme of gene expression that leads to a segmented pattern in the *Drosophila* embryo is shown in **Figure 19.11**. Many more genes are actually involved in this process.

In general, the products of maternal effect genes such as *bicoid*, which promote the formation of body axes, activate gap genes. This activation is seen as broad bands of gap proteins in the embryo (Figure 19.11, step 2). Next, products from the gap genes and maternal effect genes function as transcription factors to activate the pair-rule genes in alternating stripes in the embryo (Figure 19.11, step 3). Once the pair-rule genes are activated, their gene products then regulate the segment-polarity genes. As you follow the progression from maternal effect genes to segment-polarity genes, notice that a body pattern is emerging in the embryo that matches the segmentation pattern found in the larva and adult animal. As you can see in step 4 of Figure

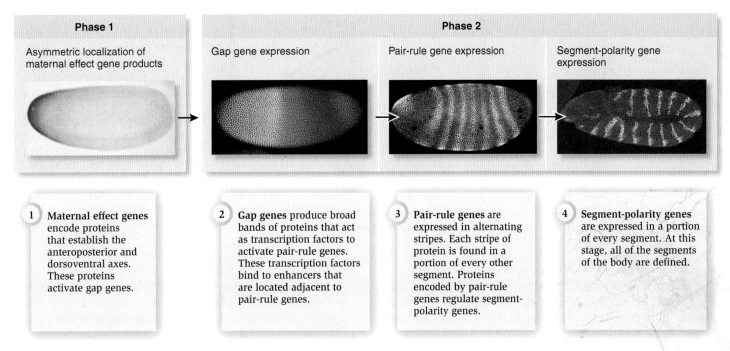

Phase 1	Phase 2		
Asymmetric localization of maternal effect gene products	Gap gene expression	Pair-rule gene expression	Segment-polarity gene expression

1 Maternal effect genes encode proteins that establish the anteroposterior and dorsoventral axes. These proteins activate gap genes.

2 Gap genes produce broad bands of proteins that act as transcription factors to activate pair-rule genes. These transcription factors bind to enhancers that are located adjacent to pair-rule genes.

3 Pair-rule genes are expressed in alternating stripes. Each stripe of protein is found in a portion of every other segment. Proteins encoded by pair-rule genes regulate segment-polarity genes.

4 Segment-polarity genes are expressed in a portion of every segment. At this stage, all of the segments of the body are defined.

Figure 19.11   **Overview of segmentation in *Drosophila*.**   The micrographs depict the progression of *Drosophila* development during the first few hours following fertilization. The micrographs also show the expression of protein products of a maternal effect gene (step 1) or segmentation genes (steps 2–4). In step 1, the protein is stained brown and is found in the left side of the early embryo, which is the anterior end. The rest of the embryo is counterstained in yellow. In step 2, one protein encoded by a gap gene is stained in green and another is stained in red. The yellow region is where the two different gap proteins overlap. In step 3, a protein encoded by a pair-rule gene is stained in light blue. In step 4, a protein encoded by a segment-polarity gene is stained pink. When comparing steps 3 and 4, note that the embryo has undergone a 180° turn, folding back on itself.

Concept check: *How many pink stripes can you count in the embryo in step 4? How does this number compare to the number of segments in the embryo in Figure 19.10?*

19.12, the locations of the expression of a segment-polarity gene correspond to portions of segments in the adult fly. To appreciate this phenomenon, notice that the embryo at this stage is curled up and folded back on itself. If you imagine that the embryo was stretched out linearly, the 15 stripes seen in this embryo correspond to portions of the 15 segments of an adult fly.

Phase 3 Pattern Formation: Homeotic Genes Control the Development of Segment Characteristics

Thus far, we have considered how the *Drosophila* embryo becomes organized along axes and then into a segmented body pattern. During the third phase of pattern formation, each segment begins to develop its own unique characteristics (see Figure 19.6). Geneticists use the term **fate** to describe the ultimate morphological features that a cell or group of cells will adopt. For example, the fate of cells in segment T2 in *Drosophila* is to develop into a thoracic segment containing two legs and two wings. In *Drosophila*, the cells in each segment of the body have their fate determined at a very early stage of embryonic development, long before the morphological features become apparent.

Our understanding of developmental fate has been greatly aided by the identification of mutant genes that alter cell fates.

In animals, the first mutant of this type was described by the German entomologist G. Kraatz in 1876. He observed a sawfly (*Cimbex axillaris*) in which part of an antenna was replaced with a leg. During the late 19th century, the English zoologist William Bateson collected many of these types of observations and published them in a book. He coined the term homeotic to describe changes in which one body part is replaced by another. We now know these are caused by mutant alleles of what we call **homeotic genes**. Each homeotic gene specifies the fate of a particular segment or region of the body.

As an example of a homeotic mutation, **Figure 19.12** shows a normal fly and one with mutations in a complex of genes called the *bithorax* complex. In a normal fly, two wings are found on the second thoracic segment, and two halteres, which together function as a balancing organ that resembles a pair of miniature wings, are found on the third thoracic segment. In this mutant fly, the third thoracic segment has the characteristics of the second, so the fly has no halteres and four wings. The term *bithorax* refers to the duplicated characteristics of the second thoracic segment. Edward Lewis, a pioneer in the genetic study of development, became interested in the bithorax phenotype and began investigating it in 1946. He discovered that the mutant chromosomal region actually contains a complex of three genes that play a role in the third phase of development.

(a) Normal fly with two wings

(b) Mutant fly with four wings

Figure 19.12   **The bithorax mutation in *Drosophila*.** **(a)** A normal fly has two wings on the second thoracic segment, and two halteres on the third thoracic segment. **(b)** This fly contains mutations in a complex of genes called the *bithorax* complex. In this fly, the third thoracic segment has the same characteristics as the second thoracic segment, thereby producing a fly with four wings instead of two.

Drosophila has eight homeotic genes that are found in two clusters called the *Antennapedia* complex and the *bithorax* complex (**Figure 19.13**). Both of these complexes are located on the same chromosome, but a long stretch of DNA separates them. As you can see in Figure 19.13, the order of homeotic genes along the chromosome correlates with their expression along the anteroposterior axis of the body. This phenomenon is called the **colinearity rule**. For example, *lab* (for labial) is expressed in the anterior segment and governs the formation of mouth structures. The *Antp* (for antennapedia) gene is expressed in the thoracic region during embryonic development and controls the formation of thoracic structures.

As we have seen in Figure 19.12, the role of homeotic genes in determining the identity of particular segments has been revealed by mutations that alter their function. As a second example, a mutation in the *Antp* gene has been identified in which the gene is incorrectly expressed in an anterior segment (**Figure 19.14**). A fly with this mutation has the bizarre trait in which it develops legs where antennae are normally found!

How do homeotic genes work at the molecular level? Homeotic genes encode homeotic proteins that function as transcription factors. The coding sequence of homeotic genes contains a 180-bp sequence known as a **homeobox** (**Figure 19.15a**). This sequence was first discovered in the *Antp* and *Ubx* genes, and it has since been found in many *Drosophila* homeotic genes. The homeobox is also found in other genes affecting pattern formation. The homeobox encodes a region of the protein called a **homeodomain**, which can bind to DNA (**Figure 19.15b**). The arrangement of α helices in the homeodomain promotes the binding of the protein to the DNA.

The primary function of homeotic proteins is to activate the transcription of specific genes that promote developmental changes in the animal. The homeodomain protein binds to DNA

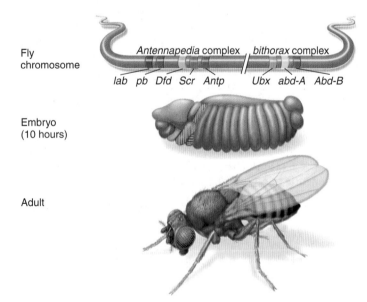

Fly chromosome

Antennapedia complex   *bithorax* complex

lab pb Dfd Scr Antp   Ubx abd-A Abd-B

Embryo (10 hours)

Adult

Figure 19.13   **Expression pattern of homeotic genes in *Drosophila*.** The order of homeotic genes, *labial (lab)*, *proboscipedia (pb)*, *deformed (Dfd)*, *sex combs reduced (Scr)*, *antennapedia (Antp)*, *ultrabithorax (Ubx)*, *abdominal A (abd-A)*, and *abdominal B (Abd-B)*, correlates with their spatial order of expression in the embryo. (Note: These genes were discovered and named by different researchers and the capitalization of the names is not consistent.)

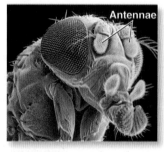

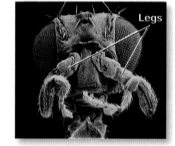

Antennae

Legs

(a) Normal fly

(b) Mutant fly

Figure 19.14   **The Antennapedia mutation in *Drosophila*.** **(a)** A normal fly with antennae. **(b)** This fly has a mutation in which the *Antp* gene is expressed in the embryonic segment that normally gives rise to antennae. The abnormal expression of *Antp* causes this region to have legs rather than antennae.

Concept check: *What phenotype would you expect if the Antp gene was expressed where abd-A is supposed to be expressed?*

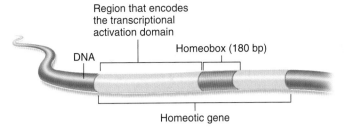

(a) Homeotic gene containing homeobox

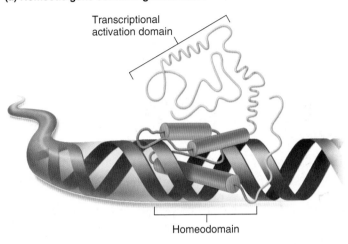

(b) Homeodomain binding to DNA

Figure 19.15 Molecular features of homeotic genes and proteins. **(a)** A homeotic gene (shown mostly in green) contains a 180-bp sequence called the homeobox (shown in blue). **(b)** Homeotic genes encode proteins that function as transcription factors. The homeobox encodes a region of the protein called a homeodomain, which binds to the DNA at a regulatory site such as an enhancer. The transcriptional activation domain activates RNA polymerase to begin transcription.

sequences called enhancers, which are described in Chapter 13. These enhancers are found in the vicinity of specific genes that control development. Most homeotic proteins also contain a transcriptional activation domain (Figure 19.15b). After the homeodomain binds an enhancer, the transcriptional activation domain of the homeotic protein activates RNA polymerase to begin transcription. Some homeotic proteins also function as repressors of certain genes.

Genomes & Proteomes Connection

A Homologous Group of Homeotic Genes Is Found in All Animals

Homologous genes are evolutionarily derived from the same ancestral gene and have similar DNA sequences. Researchers have found that homeotic genes in vertebrate species are homologous to genes that control development in simpler organisms such as *Drosophila*. For example, in the mouse and other mammals, including humans, homeotic genes are organized into four clusters, designated *HoxA*, *HoxB*, *HoxC*, and *HoxD*. Homeotic genes in vertebrates are called ***Hox*** **genes**, an abbreviation for homeobox-containing genes. Thirty-eight genes are found in the four clusters, which represent 13 different gene types. As shown

in **Figure 19.16**, several *Hox* genes in fruit flies and the mouse and other mammals are evolutionarily related. Among the first six types of *Hox* genes in the mouse, five of them are homologous to genes found in the *Antennapedia* complex of *Drosophila*. Among the last seven (genes numbered 7–13), three are homologous to the genes of the *bithorax* complex.

Like the *Antennapedia* and *bithorax* complexes in *Drosophila*, the arrangement of *Hox* genes along the mouse chromosome follows the colinearity rule, reflecting their pattern of expression from the anterior to the posterior end (**Figure 19.17**). Research has shown that the *Hox* genes play a role in determining the fates of regions along the anteroposterior axis. Nevertheless, additional research will be necessary to understand the individual role that each of the 38 *Hox* genes plays during embryonic development.

How widespread are *Hox* genes? They are present in all animals, but in different numbers. Sponges, which are simple animals with no true tissues, have a single *Hox* gene. As noted previously, humans have 38 *Hox* genes organized in four clusters. The study of *Hox* genes in many different animal species has shown that the *Hox* cluster, with its colinear expression and its role of determining the anteroposterior axis, originated very early in the evolution of animals. At the level of genetics, fundamental similarities are observed in the ways that animals, such as worms, fruit flies, and mammals, undergo embryonic development. Researchers have suggested there is a universal body plan for animal development and that a portion of the

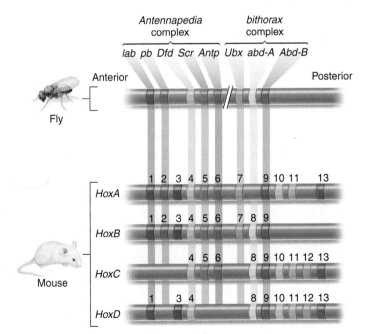

Figure 19.16 A comparison of homeotic genes in *Drosophila* and the mouse. The mouse and other mammals have four gene complexes, *HoxA–D*, that correspond to certain homeotic genes found in *Drosophila*. Thirteen different types of homeotic genes are found in the mouse, although each *Hox* complex does not contain all 13 genes. In this drawing, homologous genes are aligned in columns. For example, *lab* is the homologue to *HoxA-1*, *HoxB-1*, and *HoxD-1*.

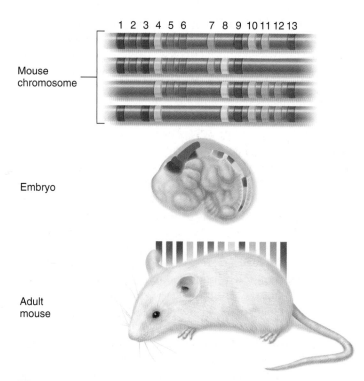

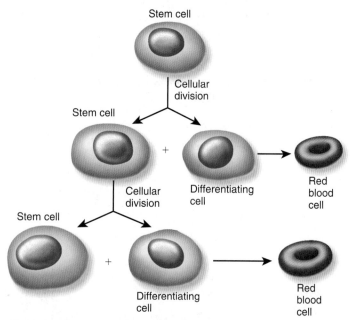

Figure 19.18 Growth pattern of stem cells. When a stem cell divides, one of the two daughter cells may remain a stem cell, while the other cell can differentiate into a specialized cell type, such as the red blood cells shown here.

Concept check: What are the two key features of stem cells?

Figure 19.17 Expression pattern of *Hox* genes in the mouse. A schematic illustration of *Hox* gene expression in the embryo and the corresponding regions in the adult. The order of *Hox* gene expression, from anterior to posterior, parallels the order of genes along the chromosome.

genome of all animals is devoted to the execution of this plan. The biological diversity that we see among animals is due to genetic variation from this common plan. The role of *Hox* genes in the evolution of animal body plans is also discussed in Chapter 25 (look ahead to Figure 25.15).

Phase 4 Pattern Formation: Stem Cells Can Divide and Differentiate into Specialized Cell Types

Thus far we have focused our attention on patterns of gene expression that occur during the early stages of development. These genes control the basic body plan of the organism. During the fourth phase of pattern formation, the emphasis shifts to cell differentiation (see Figure 19.6).

Although invertebrates have been instrumental in our understanding of pattern formation in animals, cell differentiation has been studied more extensively in mammals. One reason is because researchers have been able to grow mammalian cells in the laboratory for many decades. The availability of laboratory-grown cells makes it much easier to analyze the process of cell differentiation.

By studying mammalian cells in the laboratory, geneticists have determined that the profound morphological differences between two different types of differentiated cells, such as muscle and nerve cells, arise through gene regulation. Though muscle and nerve cells contain the same set of genes, they regulate the expression of their genes in very different ways. Certain

genes that are transcriptionally active in muscle cells are inactive in nerve cells, and vice versa. Therefore, muscle and nerve cells express different proteins that affect the characteristics of the respective cells in distinct ways. In this manner, differential gene expression underlies cell differentiation.

General Properties of Stem Cells To understand the process of cell differentiation in a multicellular organism, we need to consider the special properties of **stem cells**, undifferentiated cells that divide and supply the cells that constitute the bodies of all animals and plants. Stem cells have two common characteristics. First, they have the capacity to divide, and second, their daughter cells can differentiate into one or more specialized cell types. The two daughter cells that are produced from the division of a stem cell can have different fates (**Figure 19.18**). One of the cells may remain an undifferentiated stem cell, and the other daughter cell can differentiate into a specialized cell type. With this asymmetric division/differentiation pattern, stem cells can both continue dividing throughout life and generate a population of specialized cells. For example, in mammals, this mechanism is needed to replenish cells that have a finite life span, such as skin cells and red blood cells.

Stem Cells During Development In mammals, stem cells are commonly categorized according to their developmental stage and their ability to differentiate (**Figure 19.19**). The ultimate stem cell is the fertilized egg, which, via multiple cellular divisions, can give rise to an entire organism. A fertilized egg is considered to be **totipotent** because it can produce all of the cell types in the adult organism. The early mammalian embryo, or blastocyst, contains **embryonic stem cells** (**ES cells**), which are found in the inner cell mass. Embryonic stem cells are **pluripotent**, which means they can also differentiate into every or

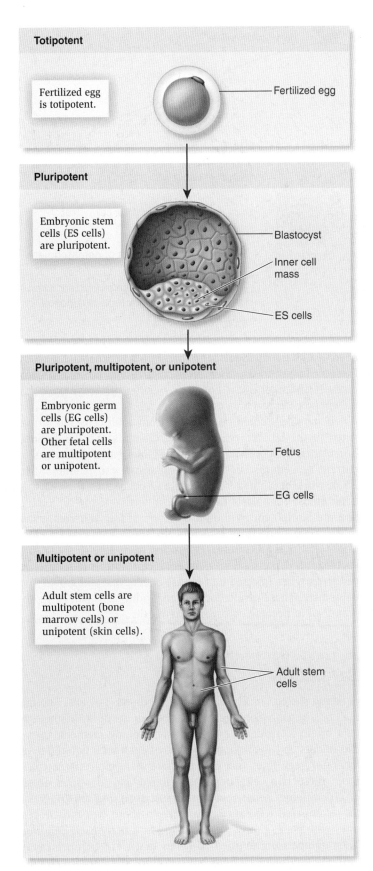

Figure 19.19 Occurrence of stem cells at different stages of mammalian development.

Within the figure:

Totipotent

Fertilized egg is totipotent.

Fertilized egg

Pluripotent

Embryonic stem cells (ES cells) are pluripotent.

Blastocyst

Inner cell mass

ES cells

Pluripotent, multipotent, or unipotent

Embryonic germ cells (EG cells) are pluripotent. Other fetal cells are multipotent or unipotent.

Fetus

EG cells

Multipotent or unipotent

Adult stem cells are multipotent (bone marrow cells) or unipotent (skin cells).

Adult stem cells

---

nearly every cell type of the body. However, a single embryonic stem cell by itself has lost the ability to produce an entire, intact individual. At an early fetal stage of development, the cells that later give rise to sperm or eggs cells, known as the **embryonic germ cells** (**EG cells**), also are pluripotent.

During the embryonic and fetal stages of development, cells lose their ability to differentiate into a wide variety of cell types. Adults have multipotent and unipotent stem cells. A **multipotent** stem cell can differentiate into several cell types, but far fewer than an embryonic stem cell. For example, hematopoietic stem cells (HSCs) found in the bone marrow give rise to multiple blood cell types (**Figure 19.20**). Multipotent HSCs can follow a pathway in which cell division produces a myeloid cell, which then differentiates into various cells of the blood and immune systems. Alternatively, an HSC can follow a path in which it becomes a lymphoid cell that develops into different blood cell types. A **unipotent** stem cell produces daughter cells that differentiate into only one cell type. For example, stem cells in the skin produce daughter cells that develop into skin cells.

Stem Cells in Medicine Why are researchers so interested in stem cells? A compelling medical reason is their potential to treat human diseases or injuries that cause cell and tissue damage. This application has already become a reality in certain cases. For example, bone marrow transplants are used to treat patients with certain forms of cancer, such as leukemia. When bone marrow from a healthy person is injected into the body of a patient who has had her/his immune system wiped out via radiation, the stem cells within the transplanted marrow have the ability to proliferate and differentiate into various types of blood cells within the body of the patient.

Renewed interest in the use of stem cells in the potential treatment of many other diseases has been fostered by studies in 1998 in which researchers obtained ES cells from blastocysts and EG cells from aborted fetuses and successfully propagated them in the laboratory. Because ES and EG cells are pluripotent, they could potentially be used to treat a wide variety of diseases associated with cell and tissue damage (**Table 19.1**). Much progress has been made in testing the use of stem cells in animal models. However, more research will need to be done before the use of stem cells to treat such diseases in humans is realized.

From an ethical perspective, the primary issue that raises debate is the source of stem cells for research and potential treatments. Most ES cells have been derived from human embryos that were produced from in vitro fertilization, a method of assisted conception in which fertilization occurs outside of the mother's body and a limited number of the resulting embryos are transferred to the uterus. Most EG cells are obtained from aborted fetuses, either those that were spontaneously aborted or those in which the decision to abort was not related to donating the fetal tissue to research. Some feel that it is morally wrong to use such tissue in research and/or the treatment of disease. Furthermore, some people fear this technology could lead to intentional abortions for the sole purpose of obtaining fetal tissues for transplantation. Others feel the embryos and fetuses that have been the sources of ES and EG cells were not going to

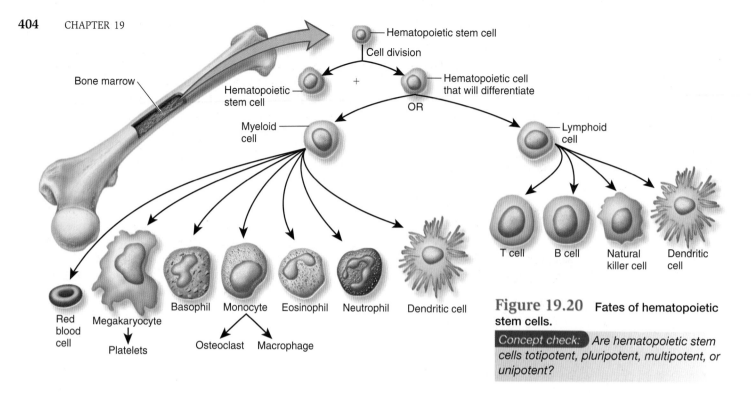

Figure 19.20 Fates of hematopoietic stem cells.

Concept check: Are hematopoietic stem cells totipotent, pluripotent, multipotent, or unipotent?

Table 19.1	Some Potential Uses of Stem Cells to Treat Diseases
Cell/tissue type	**Disease treatment**
Nerve	Implantation of cells into the brain to treat Parkinson disease; treatment of spinal cord injuries
Skin	Treatment of burns and skin disorders
Cardiac	Repair of heart damage associated with heart attacks
Cartilage	Repair of joints damaged by injury or arthritis
Bone	Repair or replacement of damaged bone
Liver	Repair or replacement of liver tissue damaged by injury or disease
Skeletal muscle	Repair or replacement of damaged muscle

become living individuals, and therefore it is beneficial to study these cells and to use them in a positive way to treat human diseases and injury. It is not clear whether these two opposing viewpoints can reach a common ground.

If stem cells could be obtained from adult cells and propagated in the laboratory, an ethical dilemma may be avoided because most people do not have serious moral objections to current procedures such as bone marrow transplantation. In 2006, work by Shinya Yamanaka and colleagues showed that adult mouse fibroblasts (a type of connective tissue cell) could become pluripotent by the introduction of four different genes that encode transcription factors. In 2007, Yamanaka's laboratory and two other research groups were able to show that such induced pluripotent stem cells can differentiate into all cell types when injected into mouse blastocysts and grown into baby mice. These results indicate that adult cells can be reprogrammed to become embryonic stem cells.

FEATURE INVESTIGATION

Davis, Weintraub, and Lassar Identified Genes That Promote Muscle Cell Differentiation

A key question regarding the study of stem cells is, What causes a stem cell to differentiate into a particular cell type? Researchers have discovered that certain proteins function as "master transcription factors" that can cause cells to differentiate into a particular cell type. The investigation described here was one of the first studies to reveal this phenomenon.

In 1987, Robert Davis, Harold Weintraub, and Andrew Lassar conducted a study to identify genes that promote skeletal muscle cell differentiation. The initial strategy for their experiments was to identify genes that are expressed only in differ-

entiating skeletal muscle cells, not in nonmuscle cells. Though methods of gene cloning are described in detail in Chapter 20, let's briefly consider these scientists' cloning methods so we can understand their approach. They began with two different laboratory cell lines that could differentiate into muscle cells. From these two cell lines, they cloned and identified about 10,000 different genes that were transcribed into mRNA. Next, they compared the expressed genes in these two muscle cell lines with genes that were expressed in a nonmuscle cell line. Their comparison revealed 26 genes that were expressed only in the two muscle cell lines but not in the nonmuscle cell line. To narrow their search further, they compared these 26 genes with other nonmuscle cell lines they had available. Among the

26, only 3 of them were expressed exclusively in the two muscle cell lines, which they termed *MyoA*, *MyoD*, and *MyoH*.

In the experiment shown in **Figure 19.21**, the scientists' goal was to determine if any of these three genes could cause nonmuscle cells to differentiate into muscle cells. Using techniques described in Chapter 20, the coding sequence of each cloned gene was placed next to an active promoter that caused a high level of transcription, and then the genes were introduced into fibroblasts, which are a type of cell that normally differentiates into osteoblasts (bone cells), chondrocytes (cartilage cells), adipocytes (fat cells), and smooth muscle cells, but never differentiates into skeletal muscle cells in vivo. However, when the cloned *MyoD* gene was expressed in fibroblast cells in a laboratory, the fibroblasts differentiated into skeletal muscle cells. These cells contained large amounts of myosin, which is a protein expressed in muscle cells. The other two cloned genes (*MyoA* and *MyoH*) did not cause muscle cell differentiation or promote myosin production.

Since this initial discovery, researchers have found that *MyoD* belongs to a small group of genes termed myogenic

bHLH genes that initiate muscle cell development. Myogenic bHLH genes encode transcription factors that contain two functional regions or domains: a basic domain and a helix-loop-helix domain (bHLH). They are found in all vertebrates, and they have been identified in several invertebrates, such as *Drosophila* and *C. elegans*. In all cases, myogenic bHLH genes are activated during skeletal muscle cell development.

Experimental Questions

1. What was the goal of the research conducted by Davis, Weintraub, and Lassar?

2. How did Davis, Weintraub, and Lassar's research identify the candidate genes for muscle differentiation?

3. Once the researchers identified the candidate genes for muscle differentiation, how did they test the effect of each gene on cell differentiation? What were the results of the study?

Figure 19.21   Davis, Weintraub, and Lassar and the promotion of skeletal muscle cell differentiation in fibroblasts by the expression of *MyoD.*

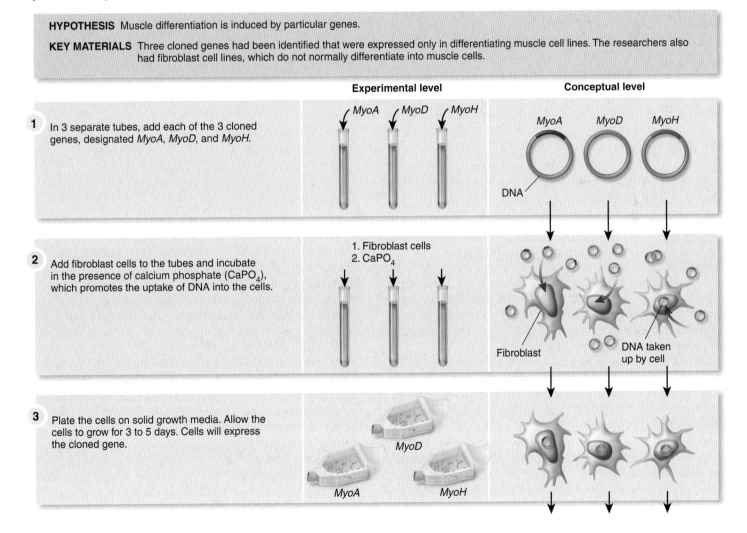

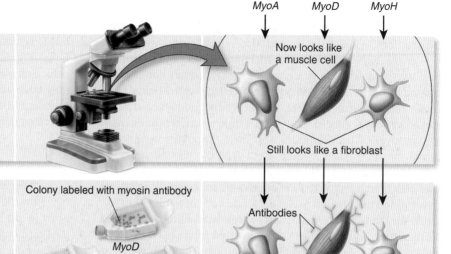

4   Examine the cells under a microscope to determine if they have the morphology of differentiating muscle cells.

Now looks like a muscle cell

Still looks like a fibroblast

5   Also, determine if the cells are synthesizing myosin, which is a protein that is abundantly made in muscle cells. This is done by adding a labeled antibody that recognizes myosin and determining the amounts of antibody that bind.

Colony labeled with myosin antibody

Antibodies

MyoD

MyoA   MyoH

6   **THE DATA**

Results from step 4:

DNA added	Microscopic morphology of cells
MyoA	Fibroblasts
MyoD	Muscle cells
MyoH	Fibroblasts

Results from step 5:

DNA added	Colonies labeled with antibody that binds to myosin?
MyoA	No
MyoD	Yes
MyoH	No

7   **CONCLUSION** The *MyoD* gene encodes a protein that causes cells to differentiate into skeletal muscle cells.

8   **SOURCE** Davis, Robert L., Weintraub, Harold, and Lassar, Andrew B. 1987. Expression of a single transfected cDNA converts fibroblasts to myoblasts. *Cell* 51:987–1000.

19.3   Development in Plants

Because all eukaryotic organisms evolved from a common ancestor, animals and plants share many common features, including the types of events that occur during development. However, the general morphology of plants is quite different from animals. Plant morphology exhibits two key features (see Figure 19.2b). The first is the root-shoot axis. Most plant growth occurs via cell division near the tips of the shoots and the bottoms of the roots. Second, this growth occurs in a well-defined radial pattern. For example, early in *Arabidopsis* growth, a rosette of leaves is produced from leaf buds that emanate in a spiral pattern directly from the main shoot (**Figure 19.22**). Later, the shoot generates branches that produce leaf buds as they grow. Overall, the radial pattern in which a plant shoot generates buds is an important mechanism that determines much of the general morphology of the plant.

At the cellular level too, plant development shows some differences from animal development. For example, cell migration does not occur during plant development. In addition, the development of a plant does not rely on morphogens that are deposited in the oocyte, as in many animals. In plants, an entirely new individual can be regenerated from many types of somatic cells—cells that do not give rise to gametes. Such somatic cells of plants are totipotent.

In spite of these apparent differences, the underlying molecular mechanisms of pattern formation in plants still share striking similarities with those in animals. Like animals, plants use the mechanism of differential gene regulation to coordinate the development of a body plan. Like their animal counterparts, a plant's developmental program relies on the use of transcription factors, determining when and how much gene product is made. In this section, we will consider pattern formation in plants and examine how transcription factors play a key role in plant development.

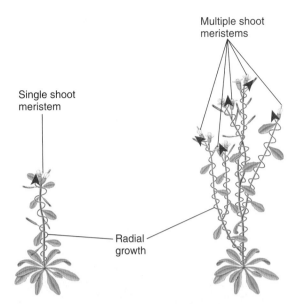

Figure 19.22 **Radial pattern of shoot growth in plants.**
Early in development, as shown here in *Arabidopsis*, a single
shoot promotes the formation of early leaves on the plant.
Later, buds will form from this main shoot that will go on to form
branches. The buds that produce the branches and the leaves
that form on the branches are also produced in a radial manner.

Plant Development Occurs from Meristems That Are Formed in the Embryo

How does pattern formation occur in plants? **Figure 19.23** illustrates a common sequence of events that takes place in the embryonic development of flowering plants such as *Arabidopsis*. After fertilization, the first cellular division is asymmetrical and produces a smaller apical cell and a larger basal cell (Figure 19.23a). In 2009, Martin Bayer and colleagues conducted experiments indicating that the sperm carries mRNA molecules that are critical for this asymmetric cell division. The apical cell will give rise to most of the embryo and later develop into the shoot of the plant. In *Arabidopsis*, the basal cell will give rise to the root, along with a structure called the suspensor, which will channel nutrients from the parent plant to the embryo (Figure 19.23b).

At the heart stage, which is composed of only about 100 cells, the basic organization of the plant has been established (Figure 19.23c). Plants have organized groups of actively dividing stem cells called **meristems**. As discussed earlier, stem cells retain the ability both to divide and to differentiate into multiple cell types. The meristem produces offshoots of proliferating and differentiating cells. The **root meristem** gives rise only to

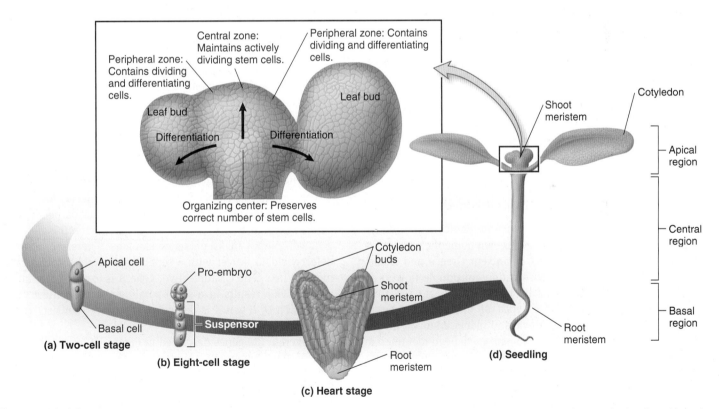

Figure 19.23 **Developmental steps in the formation of a plant embryo.** (a) The two-cell stage consists of the apical cell and basal cell. (b) The eight-cell stage consists of a pro-embryo and a suspensor. The suspensor gives rise to extra embryonic tissue that is needed for seed formation. (c) At the heart stage, all of the plant tissues have begun to form. The shoot meristem is located between the future cotyledons, and the root meristem is on the opposite side. (d) A seedling showing apical, central, and basal regions. The inset shows the organization of the shoot meristem. Note: The steps shown in parts (a), (b), and (c) occur during seed formation, and the embryo would be enclosed within a seed.

Concept check: Where are stem cells found in a growing plant?

the root, whereas the **shoot meristem** produces all aerial parts of the plant, which include the stem as well as lateral structures such as leaves and flowers.

The heart stage then progresses to the formation of a seedling that has two cotyledons, which are embryonic leaves that store nutrients for the developing embryo and seedling. In the seedling shown in Figure 19.23d, you can see three main regions. The **apical region** produces the leaves and flowers of the plant. The **central region** creates the stem. The radial pattern of cells in the central region causes the radial growth observed in plants. Finally, the **basal region** produces the roots. Each of these three regions develops differently, as indicated by their unique cell division patterns and distinct morphologies.

As seen in the inset to Figure 19.23d, the shoot meristem is organized into three areas: the organizing center, the central zone, and the peripheral zone. The **organizing center** ensures the proper organization of the meristem and preserves the correct number of actively dividing stem cells. The **central zone** is an area where undifferentiated stem cells are always maintained. The **peripheral zone** contains dividing cells that will eventually differentiate into plant structures. For example, the peripheral zone may form a bud that will produce a leaf or flower.

By analyzing mutations that disrupt the developmental process, researchers have discovered that the apical, central, and basal regions of a growing plant express different sets of genes. Gerd Jürgens and his colleagues began a search to identify a category of genes, known as **apical-basal-patterning genes**, that are important in early stages of plant development. A few examples are described in **Table 19.2**. Defects in apical-basal-patterning genes cause dramatic effects in one of these three regions. For example, the *Aintegumenta* gene is necessary for apical development. When it is defective, the growth of lateral buds is defective.

Plant Homeotic Genes Control Flower Development

Although William Bateson coined the term homeotic to describe such mutations in animals, the first known homeotic genes were described in plants. Naturalists in ancient Greece and Rome, for example, recorded their observations of double flowers in which stamens were replaced by petals. In current research, geneticists are studying these types of mutations to better understand developmental pathways in plants. Many homeotic mutations affecting flower development have been identified in *Arabidopsis* and also in the snapdragon (*Antirrhinum majus*).

A normal *Arabidopsis* flower is composed of four concentric whorls of structures (**Figure 19.24a**). The first, outer whorl contains four **sepals**, which protect the flower bud before it opens. The second whorl is composed of four **petals**, and the third whorl contains six **stamens**, structures that make the male gametophyte, pollen. Finally, the fourth, innermost whorl contains two carpels that are fused together. The **carpels** produce, enclose, and nurture the female gametophytes.

By analyzing the effects of many different homeotic mutations in *Arabidopsis*, Enrico Coen and Elliot Meyerowitz

Table 19.2 Examples of *Arabidopsis* Apical-Basal-Patterning Genes

Region: Gene	Description
Apical: *Aintegumenta*	Encodes a transcription factor that is expressed in the peripheral zone. Its expression maintains the growth of lateral buds.
Central: *Scarecrow*	Encodes a transcription factor that plays a role in the asymmetric division that produces the radial pattern of growth in the stem. Note: The Scarecrow protein also affects cell division patterns in roots and plays a role in sensing gravity.
Basal: *Monopterous*	Encodes a transcription factor. When the *monopterous* gene is defective, the plant embryo cannot initiate the formation of root structures, although root structures can be formed post-embryonically. This gene seems to be required for organizing root formation in the embryo.

proposed the ABC model for flower development in 1991. In this model, three classes of genes, called *A*, *B*, and *C*, govern the formation of sepals, petals, stamens, and carpels. More recently, a fourth category of genes, called the *E* genes, was found to also be required for this process. Figure 19.24a illustrates how these genes affect normal flower development in *Arabidopsis*. In whorl 1, gene *A* product is made. This promotes sepal formation. In whorl 2, *A*, *B*, and *E* gene products are made, which promotes petal formation. In whorl 3, the expression of genes *B*, *C*, and *E* causes stamens to be made. Finally, in whorl 4, the products of *C* and *E* genes promote carpel formation.

What happens in certain homeotic mutants that undergo transformations of particular whorls? According to the original ABC model, genes *A* and *C* repress each other's expression, and gene *B* functions independently. In a mutant defective in gene *A* expression, gene *C* will also be expressed in whorls 1 and 2. This produces a carpel-stamen-stamen-carpel arrangement in which the sepals have been transformed into carpels and the petals into stamens (**Figure 19.24b**). When gene *B* is defective, a flower cannot make petals or stamens. Therefore, a gene *B* defect yields a flower with a sepal-sepal-carpel-carpel arrangement. When gene *C* is defective, gene *A* is expressed in all four whorls. This results in a sepal-petal-petal-sepal pattern. If the expression of *E* genes is defective, the flower consists entirely of sepals.

Overall, the genes described in Figure 19.24 promote a pattern of development that leads to sepal, petal, stamen, or carpel structures. But what happens if genes *A*, *B*, and *C* are all defective? This produces a flower composed entirely of leaves (**Figure 19.24c**). These results indicate that the leaf structure is the default pathway and that the *A*, *B*, and *C* genes cause development to deviate from a leaf structure in order to make something else. In this regard, the sepals, petals, stamens, and carpels of plants can be viewed as modified leaves. With astonishing insight, Johann Wolfgang von Goethe, a German poet, novelist, playwright, and natural philosopher, originally proposed this idea over 200 years ago!

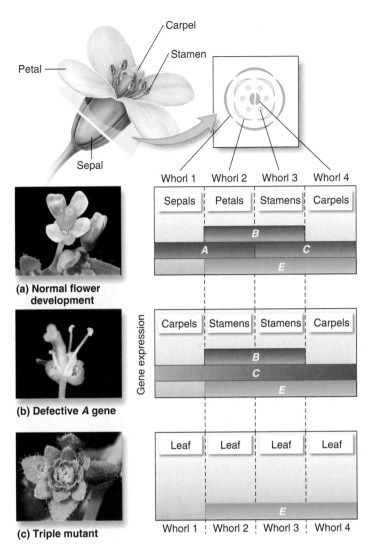

Figure 19.24 Normal and mutant homeotic gene action in *Arabidopsis.* **(a)** A normal flower composed of four concentric whorls of structures: sepals, petals, stamens, and carpels. To the right is the ABC model of homeotic gene action in *Arabidopsis.* This is a revised model based on the recent identification of *E* genes. **(b)** A homeotic mutant defective in gene *A* in which the sepals have been transformed into carpels and the petals have been transformed into stamens. **(c)** A triple mutant defective in the *A*, *B*, and *C* genes, producing a flower with all leaves.

Concept check: *What pattern would you expect if the B gene was expressed in whorls 2, 3, and 4?*

Like the *Drosophila* homeotic genes, plant homeotic genes are part of a hierarchy of gene regulation. All of these plant homeotic genes encode transcription factor proteins that contain a DNA-binding domain, called a MADS domain, and a dimerization domain. However, the *Arabidopsis* homeotic genes do not contain a sequence similar to the homeobox found in animal homeotic genes.

Summary of Key Concepts

- Development refers to a series of changes in the state of a cell, tissue, organ, or organism. Developmental genetics seeks to understand how gene expression controls the development process.

19.1 General Themes in Development

- A cell that is determined has a particular developmental fate. A cell that is differentiated has a specialized morphology and function.

- *Drosophila, C. elegans*, mice, zebrafish, and *Arabidopsis* are model organisms studied by developmental geneticists. (Figure 19.1)

- The process that gives rise to an animal or plant with a particular body structure is called pattern formation. (Figure 19.2)

- Four responses to positional information are cell division, cell migration, cell differentiation, and apoptosis. Cell migration does not occur in plants. (Figures 19.3, 19.4)

- Morphogens and cell adhesion are ways that cells obtain positional information. (Figure 19.5)

- Transcription factors control the program of development in animals and plants. In animals, pattern formation occurs in four general phases. (Figure 19.6)

19.2 Development in Animals

- Embryonic development in *Drosophila* occurs in a series of steps, starting with a fertilized oocyte, then an embryo, larvae, pupa, and an adult. The basic body plan is established in the embryo. (Figure 19.7)

- Maternal effect genes control the formation of body axes, the first phase in *Drosophila* pattern formation. (Figures 19.8, 19.9)

- The second phase of pattern formation is the development of segmentation. The sequential expression of three categories of segmentation genes divides the embryo into segments. Mutations that alter *Drosophila* development have allowed scientists to understand the normal process. (Figures 19.10, 19.11)

- During the third phase of pattern formation, each segment begins to develop its own unique characteristics. Homeotic genes control the development of a particular segment or group of segments. (Figures 19.12, 19.13, 19.14, 19.15)

- Invertebrates, such as *Drosophila*, and vertebrates, such as the mouse, both have a homologous set of homeotic genes. In vertebrates, these are called the *Hox* genes. (Figures 19.16, 19.17)

- Stem cells can divide and then one of the daughter cells can remain a stem cell while the other differentiates. (Figure 19.18)

- In mammals, a fertilized egg is totipotent, certain embryonic and fetal cells are pluripotent, and stem cells in the adult are multipotent or unipotent. (Figures 19.19, 19.20)

- Stem cells have the potential to be used to treat a variety of human disorders. (Table 19.1)

- The fourth phase of pattern formation involves cell differentiation. The differentiation of cell types within certain tissues or organs are controlled by master transcription factors. An example is *MyoD*, a gene that initiates skeletal muscle cell development. (Figure 19.21)

19.3 Development in Plants

- Plants grow in a radial pattern along a root-shoot axis. (Figure 19.22)

- Plant meristems contain dividing cells that promote the development of plant structures such as roots, stems, leaves, and flowers. (Figure 19.23)
- Several types of genes have been identified in plants that influence pattern formation. (Table 19.2)
- Four classes of homeotic genes in plants, *A*, *B*, *C*, and *E*, control flower formation and patterning. (Figure 19.24)

Assess and Discuss

Test Yourself

1. The process whereby a cell's morphology and function have changed is called
   a. determination.
   b. cell fate.
   c. differentiation.
   d. genetic engineering.
   e. both a and c.

2. Pattern formation in plants is along the _____ axis.
   a. dorsoventral
   b. anteroposterior
   c. left-right
   d. root-shoot
   e. All of the above are correct.

3. Positional information is important in determining the fate of a cell in a multicellular organism. Animal cells respond to positional information by
   a. dividing.
   b. migrating.
   c. differentiating.
   d. undergoing apoptosis.
   e. all of the above.

4. Morphogens are
   a. molecules that disrupt normal development.
   b. molecules that convey positional information.
   c. mutagenic agents that cause apoptosis.
   d. receptors that allow cells to adhere to the extracellular matrix.
   e. both a and c.

5. What group of proteins plays a key role in controlling the program of developmental changes?
   a. motor proteins
   b. transporters
   c. transcription factors
   d. restriction endonucleases
   e. cyclins

6. Using the following list of events, determine the proper sequence for the events of animal development:
   1. Tissues, organs, and other body structures in each segment are formed.
   2. Axes of the entire animal are determined.
   3. Cells become differentiated.
   4. The entire animal is divided into segments.
   a. 2, 3, 4, 1
   b. 1, 2, 4, 3
   c. 2, 4, 3, 1
   d. 3, 2, 4, 1
   e. 2, 4, 1, 3

7. The homeotic genes in *Drosophila*
   a. determine the structural and functional characteristics of different segments of the developing fly.
   b. encode motor proteins that transport morphogens throughout the embryo.
   c. are dispersed apparently randomly throughout the genome.
   d. are expressed in similar levels in all parts of the developing embryo.
   e. Both a and c are correct.

8. Which of the following genes do not play a role in the process whereby segments are formed in the fruit fly embryo?
   a. homeotic genes
   b. gap genes
   c. pair-rule genes
   d. segment-polarity genes
   e. All of the above play a role in segmentation.

9. An embryonic stem cell that can give rise to any type of cell of an adult organism but cannot produce an entire, intact individual is called
   a. totipotent.
   b. pluripotent.
   c. multipotent.
   d. unipotent.
   e. antipotent.

10. During plant development, the leaves and the flowers of the plant are derived from
    a. the central region.
    b. the basal region.
    c. the suspensor.
    d. the apical region.
    e. both a and d.

Conceptual Questions

1. If you observed fruit flies with the following developmental abnormalities, would you guess that a mutation has occurred in a segmentation gene or a homeotic gene? Explain your guess.
   a. Three abdominal segments were missing.
   b. One abdominal segment had legs.

2. The *myoD* gene in mammals plays a role in muscle cell differentiation. The *Hox* genes are homeotic genes that play a role in the differentiation of particular regions of the body. Explain how the functions of these genes are similar and different.

3. What is a meristem? Explain the role of meristems in plant development.

Collaborative Questions

1. It seems that developmental genetics boils down to a complex network of gene regulation. Starting with maternal effect genes and ending with master transcription factors, try to draw/describe how this network is structured for *Drosophila*. How many genes do you think are necessary to describe a complete developmental network for the fruit fly? How many genes do you think are needed for a network to specify one segment?

2. Is it possible for a phenotypically normal female fly to be homozygous for a loss-of-function allele in the *bicoid* gene? What would be the phenotype of the offspring that such a fly would produce if it were mated to a male that was homozygous for the normal *bicoid* allele?

Online Resource

www.brookerbiology.com

Stay a step ahead in your studies with animations that bring concepts to life and practice tests to assess your understanding. Your instructor may also recommend the interactive ebook, individualized learning tools, and more.

Genetic Technology

20

acob was diagnosed with type I diabetes, also called insulin-dependent diabetes mellitus, when he was 13 years old. Since then, he's been taking regular injections of insulin, a protein hormone that is normally made by cells in the pancreas. Jacob's pancreas fails to make enough of this hormone. His insulin prescription says Humulin® on the bottle, which stands for <u>hum</u>an in<u>sulin</u>. However, you might be surprised to discover that his insulin is not made by human cells. It's actually made by a laboratory strain of the bacterium *Escherichia coli* that has been genetically modified to synthesize a hormone that is identical in structure to human insulin. This is just one example of how researchers have been able to apply **recombinant DNA technology**—the use of laboratory techniques to isolate and manipulate fragments of DNA—to benefit humans. Such technology produces recombinant DNA, which refers to any DNA molecule that has been manipulated so it contains DNA from two or more sources.

In the early 1970s, the first successes in making recombinant DNA molecules were accomplished independently by two groups at Stanford University: David Jackson, Robert Symons, and Paul Berg; and Peter Lobban and A. Dale Kaiser. Both groups were able to isolate and purify pieces of DNA in a test tube and then covalently link two or more DNA fragments. Shortly thereafter, these recombinant DNA molecules were introduced into living cells. Once inside a host cell, the recombinant molecules are replicated to produce many identical copies. Because such recombinant molecules usually contain a particular gene of interest, this process is known as **gene cloning**. In the first part of the chapter, we will explore recombinant DNA technology and gene cloning, techniques that have enabled geneticists to probe relationships between gene sequences and phenotypic consequences. Such studies have been fundamental to our understanding of gene structure and function.

In the second part of this chapter, we will consider the topic of **genomics**—the molecular analysis of the entire genome of a species. In recent years, molecular techniques have progressed to the point where researchers can study the structure and function of many genes as large integrated networks. For example, the expression of all genes in a genome can be compared between normal and cancerous cells. This information can help us to understand how changes in gene expression can cause uncontrolled cell growth.

The first cloned pet. In 2002, the cat shown here called CC (for carbon copy) or copy cat was produced by reproductive cloning, a procedure described later in this chapter.

In the last section of this chapter, we will explore the topic of **biotechnology**—the use of living organisms or the products of living organisms for human benefit. We will learn that **genetic engineering**, the direct manipulation of genes for practical applications, is playing an ever-increasing role in the production of strains of microorganisms, plants, and animals with characteristics that are useful to people. These include bacteria that make hormones such as human insulin, crops that produce their own insecticides, and farm animals that make human medicines.

20.1 Gene Cloning

As mentioned, the term gene cloning refers to procedures that lead to the formation of many copies of a particular gene. Why is gene cloning useful? **Figure 20.1** provides an overview of the steps and goals of gene cloning. The process is usually done with one of two goals in mind. One goal would be that a researcher or clinician wants many copies of the gene, perhaps to study the DNA directly or to use the DNA as a tool. For example, geneticists may want to obtain the sequence of a gene from a person with a disease to see if the gene carries a mutation. Alternatively, the goal may be to obtain a large amount of the gene product—mRNA or protein. Along these lines, biochemists use gene cloning to obtain large amounts of proteins to study their structure and function. In modern molecular biology, the many uses for gene cloning are remarkable. Gene cloning has provided the foundation for critical technical advances in a variety of disciplines, including molecular biology, genetics, cell biology, biochemistry, and medicine. In this section, we will examine the procedures that are used to copy genes.

Step 1: Vector DNA and Chromosomal DNA Are the Starting Materials to Clone a Gene

In the first step of gene cloning, a key material is a type of DNA known as a **vector** (from the Latin, for one who carries) (Figure 20.1). Vector DNA acts as a carrier of the DNA segment that is to be cloned. In cloning experiments, a vector may carry a small segment of chromosomal DNA, perhaps only a single gene. By comparison, a chromosome carries up to a few thousand genes. When a vector is introduced into a living cell, it can replicate, and so the DNA that it carries is also replicated. This produces many identical copies of the inserted gene.

The vectors commonly used in gene cloning experiments were originally derived from two natural sources, plasmids or viruses. As discussed in Chapter 18, **plasmids** are small circular pieces of DNA that exist independently of the bacterial chromosome. They are found naturally in many strains of bacteria and also occasionally in eukaryotic cells. Commercially available plasmids have been genetically engineered for effective use in cloning experiments. They contain unique sites into which geneticists can easily insert pieces of DNA. An alternative type of vector used in cloning experiments is a **viral vector**. Viruses can infect living cells and propagate themselves by taking control of the host cell's metabolic machinery. When a chromosomal gene is inserted into a viral vector, the gene will be replicated whenever the viral DNA is replicated. Therefore, viruses can be used as vectors to carry other pieces of DNA.

Another material that is needed to clone a gene is the gene itself, which we will call the gene of interest. If a scientist wants to clone a particular gene, the source of the gene is the chromosomal DNA that carries that gene. The preparation of chromosomal DNA involves breaking open cells and extracting and purifying the DNA using biochemical separation techniques such as chromatography and centrifugation.

Step 2: Cutting Chromosomal and Vector DNA into Pieces and Linking Them Together Produces Recombinant Vectors

The second step in a gene cloning experiment is the insertion of chromosomal DNA into a plasmid or viral vector (Figure 20.1). How is this accomplished? DNA molecules must be cut and pasted to produce recombinant vectors. To cut DNA, researchers use enzymes known as **restriction enzymes** or restriction endonucleases. These enzymes, which were discovered

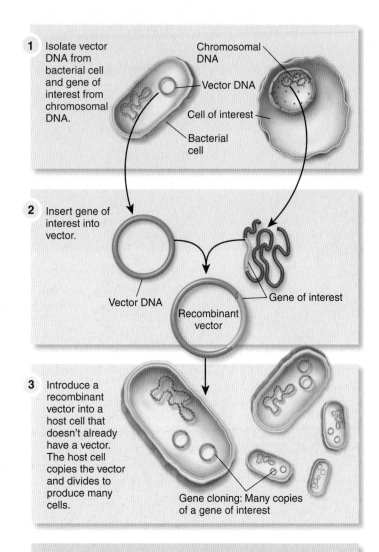

1 Isolate vector DNA from bacterial cell and gene of interest from chromosomal DNA.

Chromosomal DNA

Vector DNA

Cell of interest

Bacterial cell

2 Insert gene of interest into vector.

Vector DNA

Gene of interest

Recombinant vector

3 Introduce a recombinant vector into a host cell that doesn't already have a vector. The host cell copies the vector and divides to produce many cells.

Gene cloning: Many copies of a gene of interest

4 **Gene cloning is done to achieve one of two main goals:**

Producing large amounts of DNA of a specific gene	Expressing the cloned gene to produce the encoded protein
Examples	*Examples*
• Cloned genes provide enough DNA for DNA sequencing. The sequence of a gene can help us understand how a gene works and identify mutations that cause diseases.	• Large amounts of the protein can be purified to study its structure and function.
• Cloned DNA can be used as a probe to identify the same gene or similar genes in other organisms.	• Cloned genes can be introduced into bacteria or livestock to make pharmaceutical products such as insulin.
	• Cloned genes can be introduced into plants and animals to alter their traits.
	• Cloned genes can be used to treat diseases—a clinical approach called gene therapy.

Figure 20.1 **Gene cloning.** The process of gene cloning is used to produce large amounts of a gene or its protein product.

by Werner Arber, Hamilton Smith, and Daniel Nathans in the 1960s and 1970s, are made naturally by many different species of bacteria. Restriction enzymes protect bacterial cells from invasion by viruses by degrading the viral DNA into small fragments. Currently, several hundred different restriction enzymes from various bacterial species have been identified and are available commercially to molecular biologists.

The restriction enzymes used in cloning experiments bind to a specific base sequence and then cleave the DNA backbone at two defined locations, one in each strand. The sequences recognized by restriction enzymes are called **restriction sites**. Most restriction enzymes recognize sequences that are palindromic, which means the sequence is identical when read in the opposite direction in the complementary strand (**Table 20.1**). For example, the sequence recognized by the restriction enzyme *Eco*RI is 5′–GAATTC–3′ in the top strand. Read in the opposite direction in the bottom strand, this sequence is also 5′–GAATTC–3′. Certain restriction enzymes are useful in cloning because they digest DNA into fragments with **sticky ends**. Such DNA fragments have single-stranded ends that will hydrogen-bond to other DNA fragments that are cut with the same enzyme due to their complementary sequences.

Figure 20.2 shows the action of a restriction enzyme and the insertion of a gene into a vector. This vector carries the *amp*^R and *lacZ* genes, whose useful functions will be discussed later. The restriction enzyme binds to specific sequences in both the chromosomal and vector DNA. It then cleaves the DNA backbones, producing DNA fragments with sticky ends. The complementary single-stranded ends of fragments from the chromosomal and vector DNA hydrogen-bond with each other (Figure 20.2, step 2). However, this interaction is not stable, because it involves only a few hydrogen bonds between complementary bases. To establish a permanent connection between two DNA fragments, the sugar-phosphate backbones within the DNA strands must be covalently linked together. This linkage is catalyzed by DNA ligase (Figure 20.2, step 3). Recall from Chapter 11 that DNA ligase is an enzyme that

catalyzes the formation of a covalent bond between adjacent DNA fragments.

In some cases, the two ends of the vector will simply ligate back together, restoring it to its original circular structure; this

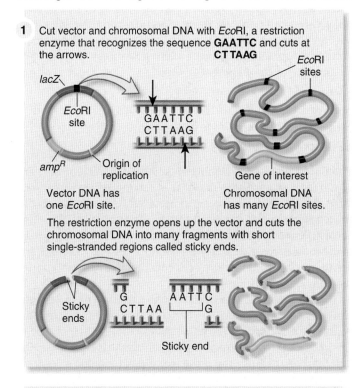

1 Cut vector and chromosomal DNA with *Eco*RI, a restriction enzyme that recognizes the sequence **GAATTC** and cuts at the arrows. **CTTAAG**

lacZ

*Eco*RI site

amp^R

Origin of replication

Vector DNA has one *Eco*RI site.

```
GAATTC
CTTAAG
```

*Eco*RI sites

Gene of interest

Chromosomal DNA has many *Eco*RI sites.

The restriction enzyme opens up the vector and cuts the chromosomal DNA into many fragments with short single-stranded regions called sticky ends.

Sticky ends

```
G          AATTC
CTTAA          G
```

Sticky end

2 Allow sticky ends to hydrogen-bond with each other due to complementary sequences.

Gene of interest
Gap   Gap
Gap
Gap   Gap
Gap
```
GAATTC
CTTAAG
```
Gap

In this example, a fragment of DNA carrying the gene of interest has hydrogen-bonded to the vector. Four gaps are found where covalent bonds in the DNA backbone are missing.

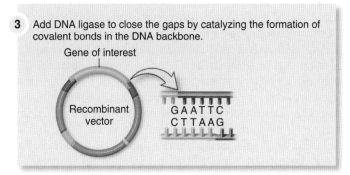

3 Add DNA ligase to close the gaps by catalyzing the formation of covalent bonds in the DNA backbone.

Gene of interest

Recombinant vector

```
GAATTC
CTTAAG
```

Figure 20.2 Step 2 of gene cloning: The actions of a restriction enzyme and DNA ligase produce a recombinant vector.

Concept check: *In the procedure shown in this figure, has the gene of interest been cloned?*

Table 20.1	Examples of Restriction Enzymes Used in Gene Cloning	
Restriction enzyme*	**Bacterial source**	**Sequence recognized†**
*Eco*RI	*Escherichia coli* (strain RY13)	↓ 5′–GAATTC–3′ 3′–CTTAAG–5′ ↑
*Sac*I	*Streptomyces achromogenes*	↓ 5′–GAGCTC–3′ 3′–CTCGAG–5′ ↑

*Restriction enzymes are named according to the species in which they are found. The first three letters are italicized because they indicate the genus and species names. Because a species may produce more than one restriction enzyme, the enzymes are designated I, II, III, etc., to indicate the order in which they were discovered in a given species.

†The arrows show the locations in the upper and lower DNA strands where the restriction enzymes cleave the DNA backbone.

forms what is called a recircularized vector. In other cases, a fragment of chromosomal DNA may become ligated to both ends of the vector. When this happens, a segment of chromosomal DNA has been inserted into the vector. The result is a vector containing a piece of chromosomal DNA, which is called a **recombinant vector** or a hybrid vector. We then have a recombinant vector that is ready to be cloned. A recombinant vector may contain the gene of interest, or it may contain a different piece of chromosomal DNA.

Step 3: Putting Recombinant Vectors into Host Cells and Allowing Those Cells to Propagate Achieves Gene Cloning

The third step in gene cloning is the actual cloning of the gene of interest. In this step, the goal is for the recombinant vector carrying the desired gene to be taken up by bacterial cells treated with agents that render them permeable to DNA molecules (**Figure 20.3**). Some bacterial cells take up a single plasmid, whereas most cells fail to take up a plasmid. The bacteria are then streaked on petri plates containing a bacterial growth medium and ampicillin.

In the experiment shown here, the bacterial cells were originally sensitive to ampicillin. The plasmid carries an antibiotic-resistance gene, called the amp^R gene. What is the purpose of this gene in a cloning experiment? Such a gene is called a **selectable marker** because the presence of the antibiotic selects for the growth of cells expressing the amp^R gene. The amp^R gene encodes an enzyme known as β-lactamase that degrades the antibiotic ampicillin, which normally kills bacteria. Bacteria that have not taken up a plasmid will be killed by the antibiotic. In contrast, any bacterium that has taken up a plasmid carrying the amp^R gene will grow and divide many times to form a bacterial colony containing tens of millions of cells. Because each cell in a single colony is derived from the same original cell that took up a single plasmid, all cells within a colony contain the same type of plasmid DNA.

In the experiment shown in Figure 20.3, the experimenter can also distinguish bacterial colonies that contain cells with a recombinant vector from those containing cells with a recircularized vector. In a recombinant vector, a piece of chromosomal DNA has been inserted into a region of the vector that contains the *lacZ* gene, which encodes the enzyme β-galactosidase. The insertion of chromosomal DNA into the vector disrupts the *lacZ* gene and thereby prevents the expression of β-galactosidase. By comparison, a recircularized vector has a functional *lacZ* gene. The functionality of *lacZ* can be determined by providing the growth medium with a colorless compound, X-Gal, which is cleaved by β-galactosidase into a blue dye. Bacteria grown in the presence of X-Gal will form blue colonies if they have a functional β-galactosidase enzyme and will form white colonies if they do not. In this experiment, therefore, bacterial colonies containing recircularized vectors will form blue colonies, whereas colonies containing recombinant vectors carrying a segment of chromosomal DNA will be white.

After a bacterial cell has taken up a recombinant vector, two subsequent events lead to the production of many copies of

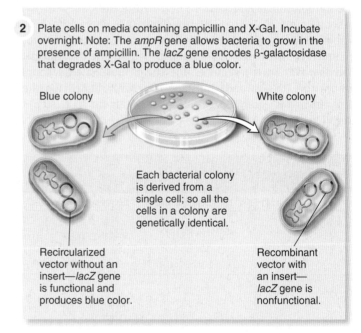

Figure 20.3 Step 3 of gene cloning: introduction of a recombinant vector into a host cell. For cloning to occur, a recombinant vector is introduced into a host cell, which copies the vector and divides to produce many cells. This produces many copies of the gene of interest.

Concept check: In this cloning experiment, what is the purpose of having the lacZ gene in the vector?

that vector. First, when the vector has a highly active origin of replication, the bacterial host cell produces many copies of the recombinant vector per cell. Second, the bacterial cells divide approximately every 20 minutes. Following overnight growth, a population of many millions of bacteria will be obtained from a single cell. Each of these bacterial cells will contain many copies of the cloned gene. For example, a bacterial colony may comprise 10 million cells, with each cell containing 50 copies of the recombinant vector. Therefore, this bacterial colony would have 500 million copies of the cloned gene!

A DNA Library Is a Collection of Many Different Cloned Genes

In a typical cloning experiment, such as the one described in Figures 20.2 and 20.3, the treatment of chromosomal DNA with restriction enzymes actually yields tens of thousands of different DNA fragments. Therefore, after the DNA fragments are ligated individually to vectors, a researcher has a collection of many recombinant vectors, with each vector containing a particular fragment of chromosomal DNA. This collection of vectors, usually within bacterial cells, is known as a **DNA library** (**Figure 20.4**). Researchers make DNA libraries using the methods shown in Figures 20.2 and 20.3 and then use those libraries to obtain clones of genes in which they are interested.

Two types of DNA libraries are commonly made. The library is called a **genomic library** when the inserts are derived from chromosomal DNA. Alternatively, researchers can isolate mRNA and use the enzyme reverse transcriptase, which is described in Chapter 18, to make DNA molecules using mRNA as a starting material. Such DNA is called **complementary DNA**, or **cDNA**. A **cDNA library** is a collection of recombinant vectors that have cDNA inserts. From a research perspective, an important advantage of cDNA is that it lacks introns. Because introns can be quite large, it is much simpler for researchers to insert cDNAs into vectors rather than work from chromosomal DNA if they want to focus their attention on the coding sequence of a gene.

Gel Electrophoresis Can Separate Macromolecules, Such as DNA

Gel electrophoresis is a technique that is used to separate macromolecules, such as DNA and proteins, on a gel. This method is often used to evaluate the results of a cloning experiment. For example, gel electrophoresis can be used to determine the sizes of DNA fragments that have been inserted into recombinant vectors.

Gel electrophoresis can separate molecules based on their charge, size/length, and mass. In the example shown in Figure 20.5, gel electrophoresis was used to separate different fragments of chromosomal DNA based on their masses. The gel is a flat semisolid gel with depressions at the top called wells where samples are added. An electric field is applied to the gel, which causes charged molecules, either proteins or nucleic acids, to migrate from the top of the gel toward the bottom—a process called electrophoresis. DNA is negatively charged and moves toward the positive end of the gel, which is at the bottom in this

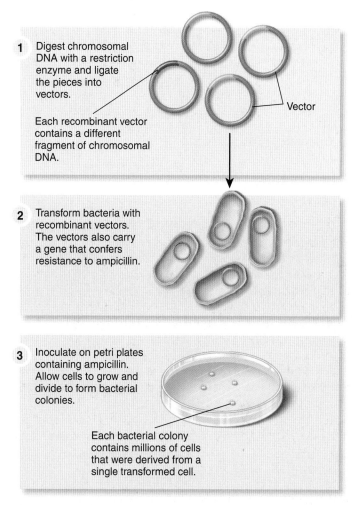

1 Digest chromosomal DNA with a restriction enzyme and ligate the pieces into vectors.

Vector

Each recombinant vector contains a different fragment of chromosomal DNA.

2 Transform bacteria with recombinant vectors. The vectors also carry a gene that confers resistance to ampicillin.

3 Inoculate on petri plates containing ampicillin. Allow cells to grow and divide to form bacterial colonies.

Each bacterial colony contains millions of cells that were derived from a single transformed cell.

Figure 20.4 **A DNA library.** Each colony in a DNA library contains a vector with a different piece of chromosomal DNA.

figure. Smaller DNA fragments move more quickly through the gel polymer and therefore are located closer to the bottom of the gel compared to larger ones. As the slab gel runs, the fragments are separated into bands within the gel. The fragments in each band can then be stained with a dye for identification.

Polymerase Chain Reaction (PCR) Can Also Be Used to Make Many Copies of DNA

As we have seen, one method of cloning involves an approach in which the gene of interest is inserted into a vector and then introduced into a host cell. Another technique to copy DNA without the aid of vectors and host cells is **polymerase chain reaction** (**PCR**), which was developed by Kary Mullis in 1985 (**Figure 20.6**). The goal of PCR is to make many copies of DNA in a defined region, perhaps encompassing a gene or part of a gene. Several reagents are required for the synthesis of DNA. First, two different primers are needed that are complementary to sequences at each end of the DNA region to be amplified. These primers are usually about 20 nucleotides long. One primer is called the forward primer, and the other is the reverse primer. PCR also requires all four deoxynucleoside triphosphates (dNTPs) and a heat-stable form of DNA polymerase called *Taq*

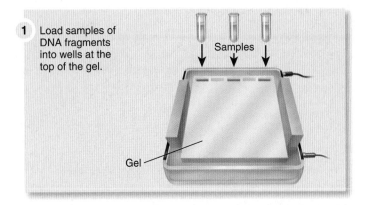

1 Load samples of DNA fragments into wells at the top of the gel.

Samples

Gel

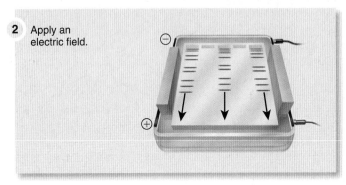

2 Apply an electric field.

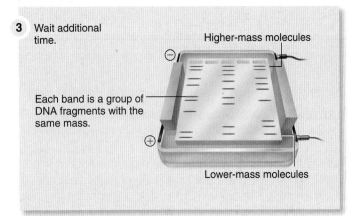

3 Wait additional time.

Higher-mass molecules

Each band is a group of DNA fragments with the same mass.

Lower-mass molecules

Figure 20.5 **Separation of molecules by gel electrophoresis.** In this example, samples containing many fragments of DNA are loaded into wells at the top of the gel and then subjected to an electric field that causes the fragments to move toward the bottom of the gel. This primarily separates the fragments according to their masses, with the smaller DNA fragments near the bottom of the gel.

Concept check: *One DNA fragment contains 600 bp and another has 1,300 bp. Following electrophoresis, which would be closer to the bottom of a gel?*

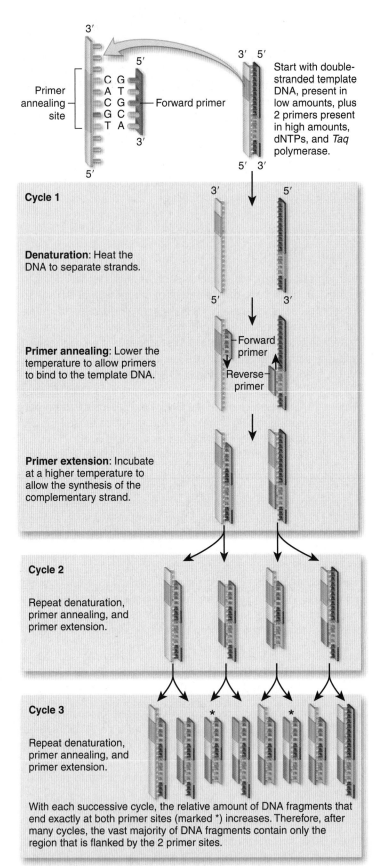

Primer annealing site — C G / A T / C G / G C / T A — Forward primer

Start with double-stranded template DNA, present in low amounts, plus 2 primers present in high amounts, dNTPs, and *Taq* polymerase.

Cycle 1

Denaturation: Heat the DNA to separate strands.

Primer annealing: Lower the temperature to allow primers to bind to the template DNA.

Forward primer

Reverse primer

Primer extension: Incubate at a higher temperature to allow the synthesis of the complementary strand.

Cycle 2

Repeat denaturation, primer annealing, and primer extension.

Cycle 3

Repeat denaturation, primer annealing, and primer extension.

With each successive cycle, the relative amount of DNA fragments that end exactly at both primer sites (marked *) increases. Therefore, after many cycles, the vast majority of DNA fragments contain only the region that is flanked by the 2 primer sites.

Figure 20.6 **Polymerase chain reaction (PCR).** During each PCR cycle, the steps of denaturation, primer annealing, and primer extension take place. The net result of PCR is the synthesis of many copies of DNA in the region that is flanked by the two primers. To conduct this type of PCR experiment, the researcher must have prior knowledge about the base sequence of the template DNA in order to design primers with base sequences that are complementary to the ends of the template DNA.

Concept check: *Why do the PCR primers bind specifically to the primer annealing sites (shown in green)?*

polymerase. *Taq* polymerase is isolated from the bacterium *Thermus aquaticus*, which lives in hot springs and can tolerate temperatures up to 95°C. A heat-stable form of DNA polymerase is necessary because PCR involves heating steps that would inactivate most other natural forms of DNA polymerase.

To make copies, a sample of chromosomal DNA, called the double-stranded template DNA, is denatured into single-stranded molecules by heat treatment. Then the primers bind to the DNA as the temperature is lowered (Figure 20.6). The binding of the primers to the specific sites in the template DNA is called annealing. After the primers have annealed, the temperature is slightly raised and *Taq* polymerase uses dNTPs to catalyze the synthesis of complementary DNA strands, thereby doubling the amount of DNA in the region that is flanked by the primers. This step is called primer extension because the length of the primers is extended by the synthesis of DNA. The sequential process of denaturation—primer annealing—primer extension is then repeated many times in a row. This method is called a chain reaction because the products of each previous step are used as reactants in subsequent steps. A device that controls the temperature and automates the timing of each step, known as a thermocycler, is used to carry out PCR. The PCR technique can amplify the amount of DNA by a staggering amount. After 30 cycles of denaturation, primer annealing, and primer extension, a DNA sample will increase 2^{30}-fold, which is approximately a billionfold!

20.2   Genomics

As discussed throughout Unit III, the genome is the complete genetic composition of an organism. As genetic technology has progressed over the past few decades, researchers have gained an increasing ability to analyze the composition of genomes as a whole unit. The term genomics refers to the molecular analysis of the entire genome of a species. Segments of chromosomes are cloned and analyzed in progressively smaller pieces, the locations of which are known on the intact chromosomes. This is the mapping phase of genomics. The mapping of a genome ultimately progresses to the determination of the complete DNA sequence, which provides the most detailed description available of an organism's genome at the molecular level. By comparison, **functional genomics** studies the expression of a genome. For example, functional genomics can be used to analyze which genes are turned on or off in normal versus cancer cells. In this section, we will consider a few of the methods that are used in genomics and functional genomics.

BAC Cloning Vectors Are Used to Make Contigs of Chromosomes to Map a Genome

A common goal of genomics research is to clone and analyze the entire genome of a species. For large eukaryotic genomes, which may contain over 1 billion bp (base pairs), cloning an entire genome is much easier when a cloning vector can accept very large chromosomal DNA inserts. In general, most plasmid and viral vectors can accommodate inserts only a few

thousand to perhaps tens of thousands of nucleotides in length. If a plasmid or viral vector has a DNA insert that is too large, it will have difficulty with DNA replication and is likely to suffer deletions in the insert. By comparison, a type of cloning vector known as a **bacterial artificial chromosome** (**BAC**) can reliably contain much larger inserted DNA fragments. BACs are derived from large plasmids called F factors (see Chapter 18). They can typically contain inserts up to 500,000 bp. BACs are used in genomic research in the same way as other types of vectors. Similarly, yeast artificial chromosomes (YACs) are used as vectors in yeast. An insert in a YAC can be several hundred thousand to perhaps 2 million bp in length.

The term **mapping** refers to the process of determining the relative locations of genes or other DNA segments along a chromosome. After many large fragments of chromosomal DNA have been inserted into BACs or YACs, the first step of mapping is to determine the relative locations of the inserted chromosomal pieces as they would occur in an intact chromosome. This is called physical mapping. To obtain a complete physical map of a chromosome, researchers need a series of clones that contain overlapping pieces of chromosomal DNA. Such a collection of clones, known as a **contig**, contains a contiguous region of a chromosome that is found as overlapping regions within a group of vectors (**Figure 20.7**). Overlapping regions carry the same genetic material between adjacent clones. For example, clones 7 and 8 both carry gene *K*. These overlapping regions allow researchers to identify the order of the clones along the chromosome.

The Dideoxy Chain-Termination Method Is Used to Determine the Base Sequence of DNA

Once researchers have cloned DNA into vectors and obtained a physical map, the next phase of genomic research is **DNA sequencing**, which is a method to determine the base sequence of DNA. Scientists can learn a great deal of information about the function of a gene if its nucleotide sequence is known. For example, the investigation of genetic sequences has been vital in our understanding of the genetic basis of human diseases.

The most commonly used method for DNA sequencing, developed in 1977 by Frederick Sanger and colleagues, is known as the **dideoxy chain-termination method**, or more simply, dideoxy sequencing. Dideoxy sequencing is based on our knowledge of DNA replication. As described in Chapter 11, DNA polymerase connects adjacent deoxynucleoside triphosphates (dNTPs) by catalyzing a covalent linkage between the 5′-phosphate on one nucleotide and the 3′—OH group on the previous nucleotide. Chemists, however, can synthesize nucleotides, called dideoxynucleoside triphosphates (ddNTPs), that are missing the —OH group at the 3′ position (**Figure 20.8**, step 1). What happens if a dideoxynucleotide is incorporated during DNA replication? Sanger reasoned that if a dideoxynucleotide ddNTP is added to a growing DNA strand, the strand can no longer grow because the 3′—OH group, the site of attachment for the next nucleotide, is missing. This ending of DNA synthesis is called chain termination.

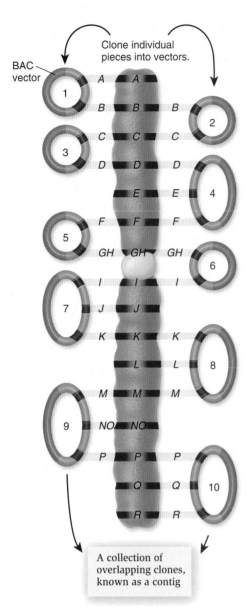

Clone individual pieces into vectors.

A collection of overlapping clones, known as a contig

Figure 20.7 **A contig.** As shown here, a contig is a collection of clones that have overlapping pieces of DNA from a particular chromosome. The numbers denote the order of the members of the contig. The chromosome is labeled with letters that denote the locations of particular genes. The members of the contig have overlapping regions that have the same genes, which allows you to order them.

Concept check: *What does it mean when we say that two members of a contig have overlapping regions?*

Before describing the steps of this DNA sequencing protocol, let's first consider the DNA segment that is analyzed in a sequencing experiment. The segment of DNA to be sequenced, the target DNA, must be obtained in large amounts by using the cloning techniques that were described earlier in this chapter. In Figure 20.8, the target DNA was inserted into a vector next to a primer-annealing site, the site where a primer will bind. The target DNA is initially double stranded, but Figure 20.8a,

step 1, shows the DNA after it has been denatured into a single strand by heat treatment.

Let's now examine the steps involved in DNA sequencing. Many copies of this single-stranded DNA are placed into four tubes and mixed with primers that bind to the primer-annealing site. DNA polymerase and all four types of regular dNTPs are also added to each tube. Finally, each of the four tubes has a low concentration of just one of the four possible dideoxynucleoside triphosphates: ddGTP, ddATP, ddTTP, or ddCTP. The tubes are then incubated to allow DNA polymerase to make strands that are complementary to the target DNA sequence. However, the ddNTPs will occasionally cause DNA synthesis to terminate early. For example, let's consider the third tube, which contains ddTTP. Synthesis of new DNA strands will occasionally stop at the sixth or thirteenth position after the annealing site if a ddTTP, instead of a dTTP, is incorporated into the growing DNA strand. This means the target DNA has a complementary A at the sixth and thirteenth positions.

Within the four tubes, mixtures of DNA strands of different lengths are made. These DNA strands are separated according to their lengths by subjecting them to gel electrophoresis. The shorter strands move to the bottom of the gel more quickly than the longer strands. To detect the newly made DNA strands, the dNTPs that were added to each reaction are radiolabeled. This enables the strands to be visualized as bands when the gel is exposed to X-ray film. In Figure 20.8a, step 2, the DNA strands in the four tubes were run in separate lanes on a gel. Because we know which ddNTP was added to each tube, we also know which base is at the very end of each DNA strand separated on this gel, because ddNTPs cause chain termination. Therefore, we can determine the DNA sequence by reading which base is at the end of every DNA strand and matching this sequence with the length of the strand.

Dideoxy sequencing can now be done much more quickly with automated sequencing. Instead of having four separate tubes with a single type of ddNTP in each tube, automated sequencing uses one tube containing all four ddNTPs, each of which has a different-colored fluorescent label attached. After incubating the template DNA with DNA polymerase, primers, dNTPs, and the four types of fluorescent ddNTPs, the sample is then loaded into a single lane of a gel, and the fragments are separated by gel electrophoresis. Electrophoresis is continued until each band emerges from the bottom of the gel, where a laser excites the fluorescent dye. A fluorescence detector records the amount of fluorescence emission at four wavelengths, corresponding to the four dyes. An example of a printout from a fluorescence detector is shown in Figure 20.8b. The peaks of fluorescence correspond to the DNA sequence that is complementary to the target DNA. The height of the fluorescent peaks is not always the same because ddNTPs get incorporated at certain sites more readily than at other sites.

Researchers are also developing alternative methods to the dideoxy chain termination in order to sequence DNA. For example, pyrosequencing is a new method of DNA sequencing that is based on the detection of released pyrophosphate (PP_i) during DNA synthesis.

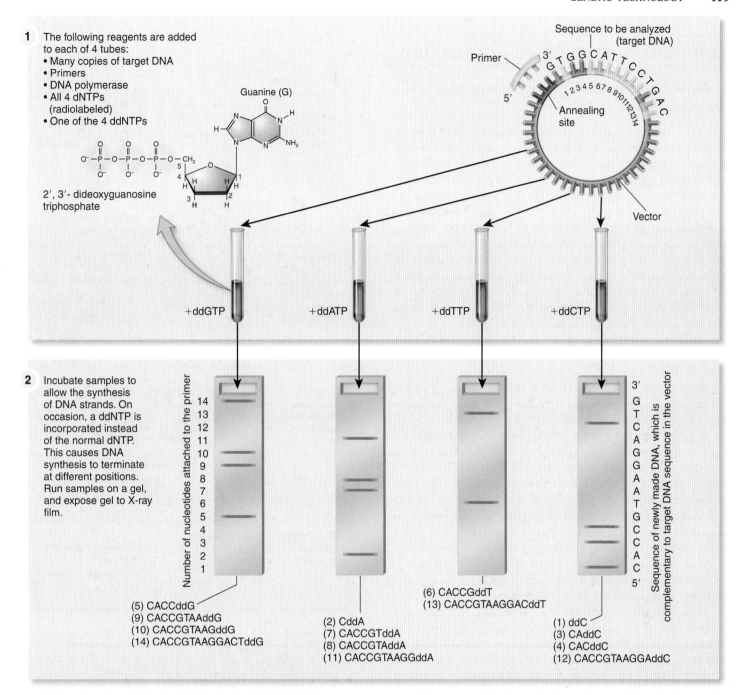

1 The following reagents are added to each of 4 tubes:
- Many copies of target DNA
- Primers
- DNA polymerase
- All 4 dNTPs (radiolabeled)
- One of the 4 ddNTPs

Guanine (G)

2′, 3′- dideoxyguanosine triphosphate

Sequence to be analyzed (target DNA)

Primer

3′ G T G G C A T T C C T G A C 5′

1 2 3 4 5 6 7 8 9 10 11 12 13 14

Annealing site

Vector

+ddGTP   +ddATP   +ddTTP   +ddCTP

2 Incubate samples to allow the synthesis of DNA strands. On occasion, a ddNTP is incorporated instead of the normal dNTP. This causes DNA synthesis to terminate at different positions. Run samples on a gel, and expose gel to X-ray film.

Number of nucleotides attached to the primer

14 13 12 11 10 9 8 7 6 5 4 3 2 1

3′ G T C A G G A A T G C C A C 5′

Sequence of newly made DNA, which is complementary to target DNA sequence in the vector

(5) CACCddG
(9) CACCGTAAddG
(10) CACCGTAAGddG
(14) CACCGTAAGGACTddG

(2) CddA
(7) CACCGTddA
(8) CACCGTAddA
(11) CACCGTAAGGddA

(6) CACCGddT
(13) CACCGTAAGGACddT

(1) ddC
(3) CAddC
(4) CACddC
(12) CACCGTAAGGAddC

(a) The procedure used in traditional dideoxy sequencing

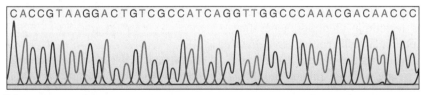

C A C C G T A A G G A C T G T C G C C A T C A G G T T G G C C C A A A C G A C A A C C C

(b) Output from automated dideoxy sequencing

Figure 20.8 **DNA sequencing by the dideoxy method.** (a) Traditional dideoxy sequencing used a mixture of radiolabeled dNTPs and nonlabeled ddNTPs. Following electrophoresis, the bands were detected by autoradiography. Step 1 shows the structure of dideoxyguanosine triphosphate, abbreviated ddGTP. It has a hydrogen, shown in red, instead of a hydroxyl group at the 3′ position. The prefix, dideoxy-, means it has two (di) missing (de) oxygens (oxy) compared with ribose, which has —OH groups at both the 2′ and 3′ positions. **(b)** Automated sequencing uses a fluorescence detector that measures the four kinds of ddNTPs as they emerge from the gel.

Concept check: What happens when a ddNTP is incorporated into a growing DNA strand?

Genomes & Proteomes Connection

A Microarray Can Identify Which Genes Are Transcribed by a Cell

Let's now turn our attention to functional genomics. Researchers have developed an exciting new technology, called a **DNA microarray** (or gene chip), that is used to monitor the expression of thousands of genes simultaneously. A DNA microarray is a small silica, glass, or plastic slide that is dotted with many different sequences of single-stranded DNA, each corresponding to a short sequence within a known gene. Each spot contains multiple copies of a known DNA sequence. For example, one spot in a microarray may correspond to a sequence within the β-globin gene, while another spot might correspond to a different gene, such as a gene that encodes a glucose transporter. A single slide contains tens of thousands of different spots in an area the size of a postage stamp. These microarrays are typically produced using a technology that "prints" spots of DNA sequences onto a slide similar to the way that an inkjet printer deposits ink on paper.

What is the purpose of using a DNA microarray? In the experiment shown in **Figure 20.9**, the goal is to determine which genes are transcribed into mRNA from a particular sample of cells. In other words, which genes in the genome are expressed? To conduct this experiment, the mRNA was isolated from the cells and then used to make fluorescently labeled cDNA. The labeled cDNAs were then incubated with a DNA microarray. The DNA in the microarray is single stranded and corresponds to the sense strand—the strand that has a sequence like mRNA. Those cDNAs that are complementary to the DNAs in the microarray will hybridize and thereby remain bound to the microarray. The array is then washed and placed in a microscope equipped with a computer that scans each spot and generates an image of the spots' relative fluorescence.

If the fluorescence intensity in a spot is high, a large amount of cDNA was in the sample that hybridized to the DNA at this location. For example, if the β-globin gene was expressed in the cells being tested, a large amount of cDNA for this gene would be made, and the fluorescence intensity for that spot would be high. Because the DNA sequence of each spot is already known, a fluorescent spot identifies cDNAs that are complementary to those DNA sequences. Furthermore, because the cDNA was generated from mRNA, this technique identifies genes that have been transcribed in a particular cell type under a given set of conditions. However, the amount of protein encoded by an mRNA may not always correlate with the amount of mRNA due to variation in the rates of mRNA translation and protein degradation.

Thus far, the most common use of microarrays is to study gene expression patterns. In addition, the technology of DNA microarrays has found several other important uses (**Table 20.2**).

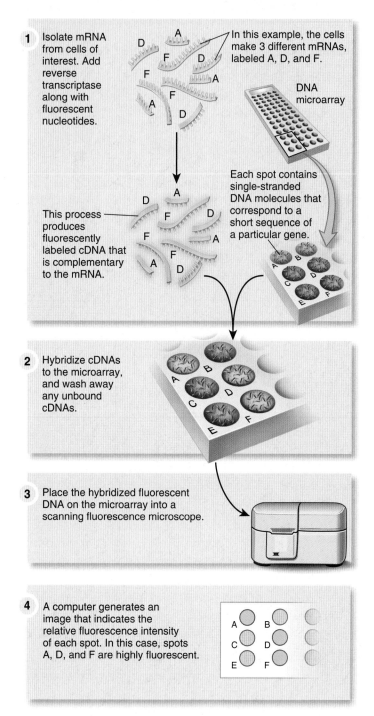

Figure 20.9   Identifying transcribed genes within a DNA microarray.   In this simplified example, only three cDNAs specifically hybridize to spots on the microarray. Those genes were expressed in the cells from which the mRNA was isolated. In an actual experiment, there are typically hundreds or thousands of different cDNAs and tens of thousands of different spots on the array.

Concept check: *If a fluorescent spot appears on a microarray, what information does this provide regarding gene expression?*

Table 20.2   Applications of DNA Microarrays

Application	Description
Cell-specific gene expression	A comparison of microarray data using cDNAs derived from mRNA of different cell types can identify genes that are expressed in a cell-specific manner.
Gene regulation	Because environmental conditions play an important role in gene regulation, a comparison of microarray data using cDNA derived from mRNA from cells exposed to two different environmental conditions may reveal genes that are induced under one set of conditions and repressed under another set.
Elucidation of metabolic pathways	Genes that encode proteins that participate in a common metabolic pathway are often expressed in a parallel manner and can be revealed from a microarray analysis.
Tumor profiling	Different types of cancer cells exhibit striking differences in their profiles of gene expression, which can be revealed by a DNA microarray analysis. This approach is gaining widespread use to classify tumors that are sometimes morphologically indistinguishable.
Genetic variation	A mutant allele may not hybridize to a spot on a microarray as well as a wild-type allele. Therefore, microarrays are gaining widespread use as a tool to detect genetic variation. This application has been used to identify disease-causing alleles in humans and to identify mutations that contribute to quantitative traits in plants and other species.
Microbial strain identification	Microarrays can distinguish between closely related bacterial species and subspecies.

20.3   Biotechnology

Biotechnology is defined as the use of living organisms, or products from living organisms, as a way to benefit humans. Although the term has become associated with molecular genetics, biotechnology is not a new topic. Its use began about 12,000 years ago, when humans began to domesticate animals and plants for the production of food. Since that time, many species of microorganisms, plants, and animals have become routinely used by people. Beginning in the 1970s, genetic engineering has provided new ways to make use of living organisms to benefit humans.

In this section, we will consider the applications of biotechnology that involve the genetic engineering of microorganisms, plants, and animals. We will also examine several topics that you often hear about in the news, such as the cloning of mammals, DNA fingerprinting, and gene therapy.

Important Medicines Are Produced by Recombinant Microorganisms

Several important medicines are now produced by recombinant organisms. These include tissue plasminogen activator (TPA), used to dissolve blood clots in heart attack patients; factor VIII, used to treat people with hemophilia; and insulin, used to treat people with diabetes. In 1982, the U.S. Food and Drug Administration approved the sale of human insulin made by recombinant bacteria. In healthy individuals, insulin is produced by the beta cells of the pancreas. Insulin functions to regulate several physiological processes, including the uptake of glucose into muscle cells. Persons with insulin-dependent diabetes cannot synthesize an adequate amount of insulin due to a defect in their beta cells. Today, people like Jacob, who was introduced at the beginning of the chapter, are usually treated with human insulin that is made by genetically engineered bacteria. Prior to 1982, insulin was isolated from pancreases removed from cattle and pigs. Unfortunately, in some cases, diabetic individuals using cow and pig insulin developed allergic responses. These patients had to use expensive combinations of insulin from human cadavers and other animals. Now, they can use human insulin made by recombinant bacteria.

Insulin is a hormone composed of two polypeptides, the A and B chains, that are held together with disulfide bonds. To make this hormone, the coding sequence of the A or B chains is inserted into a plasmid vector next to the coding sequence of the *E. coli* protein, β-galactosidase (**Figure 20.10**). After such vectors are introduced into bacteria, the cells produce many copies of a fusion protein comprising β-galactosidase and the A or B chain. Why is this step done? The reason is because the A and B chains are rapidly degraded when expressed in bacterial cells by themselves. The fusion proteins, however, are not. These fusion proteins are then extracted from the bacterial cells and treated with a chemical, cyanogen bromide (CNBr), which cleaves a peptide bond at a methionine that is found at the end of the β-galactosidase sequence, thereby separating β-galactosidase from the A or B chain. The A and B chains are purified and mixed together under conditions in which they will fold and associate with each other via disulfide bonds to form a functional insulin hormone molecule.

Microorganisms Can Reduce Pollutants

Bioremediation is the use of living organisms, typically microorganisms or plants, to detoxify pollutants in the environment. As its name suggests, it is a biological remedy for pollution. During microbial bioremediation, enzymes produced by a microorganism modify a toxic pollutant by altering or transforming its structure. In many cases, the toxic pollutant is degraded, yielding less complex, nontoxic metabolites.

Since the early 1900s, microorganisms have been used in sewage treatment plants to degrade sewage. More recently, the field of bioremediation has expanded into the treatment of hazardous and refractory chemical wastes—chemicals that are difficult to degrade and that are usually associated with industrial activity. These pollutants include heavy metals, petroleum hydrocarbons, and halogenated organic compounds such as those with chlorine atoms, as well as pesticides, herbicides, and organic solvents. Many new applications are being tested that use microorganisms to degrade these pollutants. The field of bioremediation has been fostered by better knowledge of how pollutants are degraded by microorganisms, the identification of

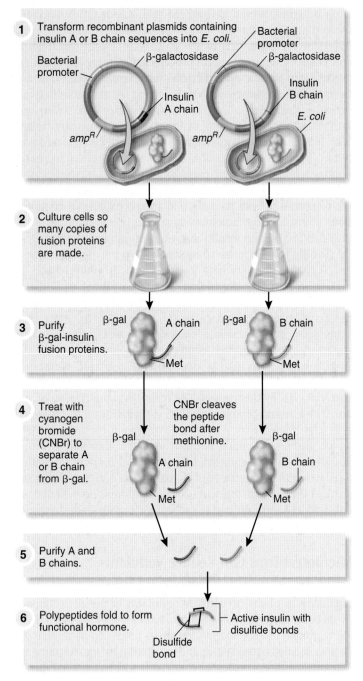

Figure 20.10 The use of bacteria to make human insulin.

Concept check: Why are the A and B chains made as fusion proteins with β-galactosidase?

new and useful strains of microbes, and the ability to enhance bioremediation through genetic engineering.

In 1980, in a landmark case (*Diamond v. Chakrabarty*), the U.S. Supreme Court ruled that a live, recombinant microorganism is patentable as a "manufacture or composition of matter." The first recombinant microorganism to be patented was an "oil-eating" bacterium that contained a laboratory-constructed plasmid. This strain can oxidize the hydrocarbons commonly found in petroleum. It grew faster on crude oil than did any

of the natural strains that were tested. Was it a commercial success? The answer is "No," because this recombinant strain metabolizes only a limited number of toxic compounds. Unfortunately, the strain did not degrade many higher-molecular-weight compounds that tend to persist in the environment.

Bioremediation is a developing industry. Recombinant microorganisms can provide an effective way to decrease the levels of toxic chemicals within our environment. This approach requires careful studies to demonstrate that recombinant organisms are effective at reducing pollutants and safe when released into the environment.

Gene Replacements and Knockouts in Mice Can Be Used to Understand Gene Function and Human Disease

Let's now turn our attention to the genetic engineering of animals. Researchers can introduce a cloned gene into an oocyte, a fertilized egg, or embryonic cells to produce animals that carry the cloned gene. The term **transgenic** is used to describe an organism that carries genes that were introduced using molecular techniques such as gene cloning. Transgenic organisms are also called **genetically modified organisms** (**GMOs**). Such GMOs are typically made in two ways. In some cases, the cloned gene will insert randomly into the genome and result in **gene addition**—the insertion of cloned gene into the genome.

Alternatively, a cloned gene may recombine with the normal gene on a chromosome, a phenomenon called **gene replacement**. For eukaryotic species that are diploid, only one of the two copies is initially replaced. In other words, the initial gene replacement produces a heterozygote carrying one normal copy of the gene and one copy that has been replaced with a cloned gene. Heterozygotes can be crossed to each other to obtain homozygotes, which carry both copies of the cloned gene. If the cloned gene carries a mutation that inactivates the normal gene's function, such a homozygote is said to have undergone a **gene knockout**. The inactive cloned gene has replaced both copies of the normal gene, and the normal gene's function is said to be knocked out. Gene replacements and gene knockouts have become powerful tools for understanding gene function.

A particularly exciting avenue of gene replacement research is its application in the study of human disease. As an example, let's consider the disease cystic fibrosis (CF), which is one of the most common and severe inherited human disorders. In humans, the defective gene that causes CF has been identified. Likewise, the homologous gene in mice was later identified. Using the technique of gene replacement, researchers have produced mice that are homozygous for the same type of mutation that is found in humans with CF. Such mice exhibit disease symptoms resembling those found in humans, namely, respiratory infections and digestive abnormalities. Why is this approach useful? These mice can be used as model organisms to study this human disease. Furthermore, these mice models have been used to test the effects of various therapies in the treatment of the disease.

Biotechnology Holds Promise in Producing Transgenic Livestock

The technology of creating transgenic mice has been extended to other animals, and much research is under way to develop transgenic species of livestock, including fish, sheep, pigs, goats, and cattle. A novel avenue of research involves the production of medically important proteins in the mammary glands of livestock. This approach is sometimes called **molecular pharming**. (The word pharming refers to the use of genetically engineered farm animals or crops to make pharmaceuticals.) Several human proteins have been successfully produced in the milk of domestic livestock such as sheep, goats, and cattle. These include Factor IX to treat a certain type of hemophilia, tissue plasminogen activator (TPA) to dissolve blood clots, and α-1-antitrypsin for the treatment of emphysema.

How are human proteins, such as hormones, made in such a way that they are produced in the milk of livestock? As we learned in Chapter 13, gene regulation may promote the expression of genes in certain cell types. Researchers have identified specific genes that are transcribed only in lactating mammary cells. One example is the gene that encodes β-lactoglobulin, a protein that is found in the milk of sheep and cows. One strategy to produce a human hormone in the milk of livestock is to clone the human hormone gene into a plasmid vector next to the β-lactoglobulin promoter (**Figure 20.11**). The plasmid is then injected into an oocyte, such as a sheep oocyte, where it integrates into the genome. The egg is then fertilized by exposure to sperm and implanted into the uterus of a female sheep. The resulting offspring carries the cloned gene. If the offspring is a female, the protein encoded by the human gene will be expressed within the mammary gland and secreted into the milk. The milk is then obtained from the animal, and the human protein isolated and purified.

Compared with the production of proteins in bacteria, one advantage of molecular pharming is that certain proteins are more likely to function properly when expressed in mammals. This may be due to post-translational modifications of proteins that occur in mammals but not in bacteria. In addition, certain proteins may be degraded rapidly or folded improperly when expressed in bacteria. Furthermore, the yield of recombinant proteins in milk can be quite large. Each dairy cow, for example, produces about 10,000 liters of milk per year. In some cases, a transgenic cow can produce approximately 1 g/L of the transgenic protein in its milk.

Agrobacterium tumefaciens Can Be Used to Make Transgenic Plants

The production of transgenic plants is somewhat easier than producing transgenic animals because many cells from plants are totipotent, which means that an entire organism can be regenerated from somatic cells. Therefore, a transgenic plant can be made by the introduction of cloned genes into somatic tissue, such as the tissue of a leaf. After the cells of a leaf have become transgenic, an entire plant can be regenerated by

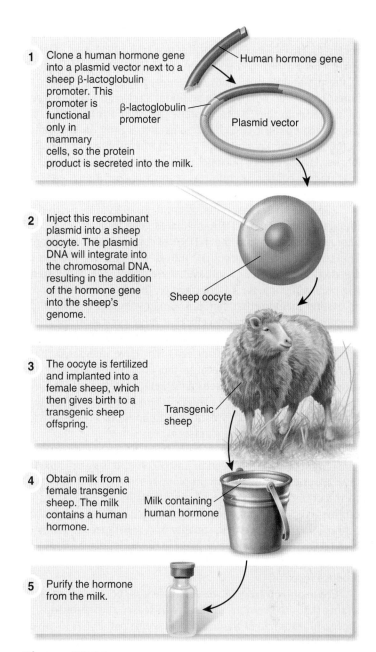

1 Clone a human hormone gene into a plasmid vector next to a sheep β-lactoglobulin promoter. This promoter is functional only in mammary cells, so the protein product is secreted into the milk.

Human hormone gene
β-lactoglobulin promoter
Plasmid vector

2 Inject this recombinant plasmid into a sheep oocyte. The plasmid DNA will integrate into the chromosomal DNA, resulting in the addition of the hormone gene into the sheep's genome.

Sheep oocyte

3 The oocyte is fertilized and implanted into a female sheep, which then gives birth to a transgenic sheep offspring.

Transgenic sheep

4 Obtain milk from a female transgenic sheep. The milk contains a human hormone.

Milk containing human hormone

5 Purify the hormone from the milk.

Figure 20.11 Molecular pharming.

treating the leaf with plant growth hormones that cause it to form roots and shoots. The result is a separate plant that is transgenic.

Molecular biologists often use the bacterium *Agrobacterium tumefaciens*, which naturally infects plant cells and causes tumors, to produce transgenic plants. This bacterium contains a plasmid known as the **Ti plasmid**, for tumor-inducing plasmid. The plasmid has a region called the T DNA (for transferred DNA) that is transferred from the bacterium to the plant cell. The T DNA from the Ti plasmid becomes integrated into the chromosomal DNA of the plant cell. After this occurs, genes within the T DNA are expressed that cause uncontrolled plant cell growth. This produces a crown gall tumor, a bulbous growth on the plant.

Researchers have modified the Ti plasmid to use it as a vector to introduce a gene of interest into plant cells. This is achieved by inserting a gene into the T DNA of the Ti plasmid. In the modified Ti plasmid, the genes that cause a crown gall tumor have been removed. In addition, a selectable marker gene is inserted into the T DNA to allow selection of plant cells that have taken up the T DNA. *Kan^R*, a gene that provides resistance to the antibiotic kanamycin, is commonly used as a selectable marker. Last, the Ti plasmid used in cloning experiments is modified to contain unique restriction sites for the convenient insertion of any gene of interest.

Figure 20.12 shows the general strategy for producing transgenic plants via T DNA–mediated gene transfer. A gene of interest is inserted into the T DNA of a genetically engineered Ti plasmid and then introduced into *A. tumefaciens*. Plant cells are then exposed to *A. tumefaciens* carrying the Ti plasmid. After allowing time for T DNA transfer, the plant cells are grown on a solid medium that contains kanamycin and carbenicillin. Kanamycin kills any plant cells that have not taken up the T DNA, and carbenicillin kills *A. tumefaciens*. Therefore, the only surviving cells are those plant cells that have integrated the T DNA into their genome. Because the T DNA also contains the gene of interest, the selected plant cells are expected to have received this gene as well. The cells are then transferred to a medium that contains the plant growth hormones necessary for the regeneration of entire plants.

Many transgenic plants have been approved for human consumption. Their production has become routine practice for several agriculturally important plant species, including alfalfa, corn, cotton, soybean, tobacco, and tomato. Transgenic plants can be given characteristics that are agriculturally useful, such as those that improve plant quality and resistance. In terms of quality, gene additions have been made to improve the nutritional value of some plants, such as making the canola grain produce more oil.

Frequently, transgenic research has sought to produce plant strains that are resistant to insects, disease, and herbicides. A successful example of the use of transgenic plants has involved the introduction of genes from *Bacillus thuringiensis* (Bt). This bacterium produces toxins that kill certain types of caterpillars and beetles and has been widely used as an insecticide for several decades. These toxins are proteins that are encoded in the genome of *B. thuringiensis*. Researchers have succeeded in cloning toxin genes from *B. thuringiensis* and transferring those genes into plants. Such Bt varieties of plants produce the toxins themselves and therefore are resistant to many types of caterpillars and beetles. Examples of commercialized crops include Bt corn (Figure 20.13a) and Bt cotton. Since their introduction in 1996, the commercial use of these two Bt crops has steadily increased (Figure 20.13b).

The use of transgenic agricultural plants has been strongly opposed by some people. What are the perceived risks? One potential risk is that transgenes in commercial crops could endanger native species. For example, Bt crops may kill pollinators of native species. Another concern is that the planting of transgenic crops could lead to the evolution of resistant insects that would render Bt ineffective. To prevent this from

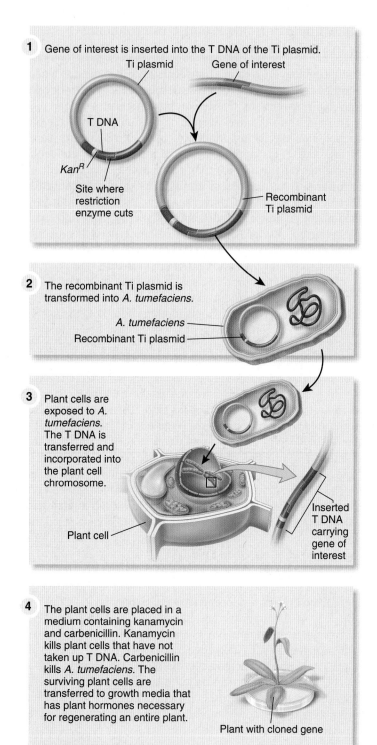

1 Gene of interest is inserted into the T DNA of the Ti plasmid.

Ti plasmid
Gene of interest
T DNA
Kan^R
Site where restriction enzyme cuts
Recombinant Ti plasmid

2 The recombinant Ti plasmid is transformed into *A. tumefaciens*.

A. tumefaciens
Recombinant Ti plasmid

3 Plant cells are exposed to *A. tumefaciens*. The T DNA is transferred and incorporated into the plant cell chromosome.

Plant cell
Inserted T DNA carrying gene of interest

4 The plant cells are placed in a medium containing kanamycin and carbenicillin. Kanamycin kills plant cells that have not taken up T DNA. Carbenicillin kills *A. tumefaciens*. The surviving plant cells are transferred to growth media that has plant hormones necessary for regenerating an entire plant.

Plant with cloned gene

Figure 20.12 Using the Ti plasmid and *Agrobacterium tumefaciens* to create transgenic plants.

Concept check: *Which region of the Ti plasmid is transferred to the plant cell?*

happening, researchers are producing transgenic strains that carry more than one toxin gene, which makes it more difficult for insect resistance to arise. A third concern is the potential for transgenic plants to elicit allergic reactions. Despite these and other concerns, many farmers are embracing transgenic crops, and their use continues to rise.

(a) A field of Bt corn

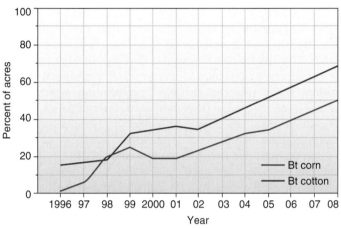

(b) Bt corn and Bt cotton usage since 1996

Figure 20.13   **The production of Bt crops.**   (a) A field of Bt corn. These corn plants carry a toxin gene from *Bacillus thuringiensis* that provides them with resistance to insects such as corn borers, which are a major pest of corn plants. (b) A graph showing the increase in usage of Bt corn and Bt cotton in the U.S. since their commercial introduction in 1996.

Researchers Have Succeeded in Cloning Mammals from Somatic Cells

We now turn our attention to cloning as a way to genetically manipulate plants and animals. The term cloning has several different meanings. At the beginning of this chapter we discussed gene cloning, which involves methods that produce many copies of a gene. The cloning of a multicellular organism, called **reproductive cloning**, is a different matter. By accident, this happens in nature. Identical twins are genetic clones that began from the same fertilized egg. Similarly, researchers can take mammalian embryos at an early stage of development (for example, the two- to eight-cell stage), separate the cells, implant them into the uterus of a female, and obtain multiple births of genetically identical individuals.

As previously noted, the reproductive cloning of new individuals is relatively easy in the case of plants, which can be cloned from somatic cells. Until recently, this approach had not been possible with mammals. Scientists believed that chromosomes within the somatic cells of mammals had incurred irreversible genetic changes that rendered them unsuitable for

reproductive cloning. However, this hypothesis has proven to be incorrect. In 1996, Ian Wilmut and his colleagues created clones of sheep using the genetic material from somatic cells. As you may have heard, they named the first cloned lamb Dolly.

How was Dolly created? As shown in **Figure 20.14**, the researchers removed mammary cells from an adult female

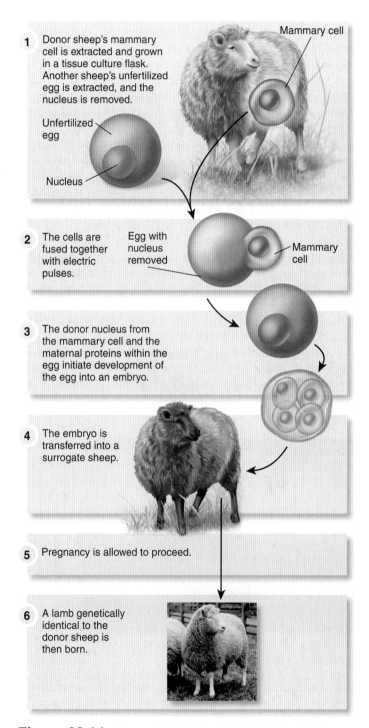

1   Donor sheep's mammary cell is extracted and grown in a tissue culture flask. Another sheep's unfertilized egg is extracted, and the nucleus is removed.

2   The cells are fused together with electric pulses.

3   The donor nucleus from the mammary cell and the maternal proteins within the egg initiate development of the egg into an embryo.

4   The embryo is transferred into a surrogate sheep.

5   Pregnancy is allowed to proceed.

6   A lamb genetically identical to the donor sheep is then born.

Figure 20.14   **Protocol for the successful cloning of sheep.** In this procedure, the genetic material from a somatic cell is used to make a cloned mammal, in this case the sheep Dolly.

Concept check: *Did all of Dolly's DNA come from a mammary cell? Explain.*

sheep and grew them in the laboratory. The researchers then extracted the nucleus from a sheep oocyte and fused the diploid mammary cell with the enucleated oocyte cell. Fusion was promoted by electric pulses. After fusion, the zygote was implanted into the uterus of an adult sheep. One hundred and forty-eight days later, Dolly was born.

Dolly was (almost) genetically identical to the sheep that donated the mammary cell. Dolly and the donor sheep were (almost) genetically identical in the same way that identical twins are. They carry the same set of genes and look remarkably similar. The reason that they may not be completely identical is that Dolly and her somatic cell donor may have some minor genetic differences due to possible differences in their mitochondrial DNA and may exhibit some phenotypic differences due to maternal effect genes.

Mammalian reproductive cloning is still at an early stage of development. Nevertheless, creating Dolly was a breakthrough that showed it is technically possible. In recent years, cloning using somatic cells has been achieved in several mammalian species, including sheep, cows, mice, goats, pigs, and cats. In 2002, the first pet was cloned, which was named CC for carbon copy (see chapter-opening photo). The cloning of mammals provides the potential for many practical applications. With regard to livestock, cloning would enable farmers to use the somatic cells from their best animals to create genetically homogeneous herds. This could be advantageous in terms of agricultural yield, although such a genetically homogeneous herd may be more susceptible to certain diseases.

Although reproductive cloning may have practical uses in the field of agriculture, our society has become greatly concerned with the possibility of human cloning. This prospect has raised serious ethical questions. Some people feel it is morally wrong and threatens the basic fabric of parenthood and family. Others feel it is a modern technology that offers a new avenue for reproduction, one that could be offered to infertile couples, for example. Human cloning is a complex subject with many more viewpoints than these two. In the public sector, the sentiment toward human cloning has been generally negative. Many countries have issued a complete ban on human cloning, whereas others permit limited research in this area. In the future, our society will have to wrestle with the legal and ethical aspects of cloning as it applies not only to animals but also to people.

DNA Fingerprinting Is Used for Identification and Relationship Testing

DNA fingerprinting is a technology that can identify and distinguish among individuals based on variations in their DNA. Like the human fingerprint, the DNA of each individual is a distinctive characteristic that provides a means of identification. When subjected to DNA fingerprinting, selected fragments of chromosomal DNA produce a series of bands on a gel (Figure 20.15a). The unique pattern of these bands is usually a distinguishing feature of each individual.

In the past two decades, the technique of DNA fingerprinting has become automated, much like the automation that changed the procedure of DNA sequencing described earlier in this chapter. DNA fingerprinting is now done using PCR, which amplifies **short tandem repeat sequences** (**STRs**)—short DNA sequences that are repeated many times in a row. Such tandem repeat sequences, which are noncoding regions of chromosomal DNA, are found at specific locations in the genomes of all species. The number of repeats at each location tends to vary from

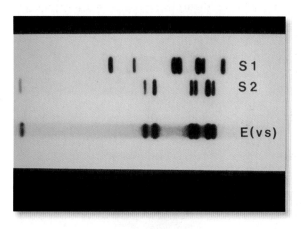

(a) Traditional DNA fingerprinting

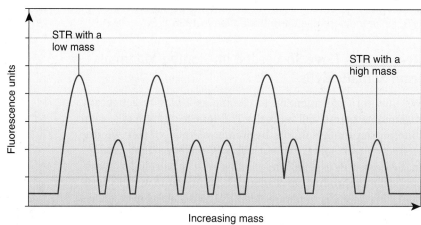

(b) Automated DNA fingerprinting

Figure 20.15   **DNA fingerprinting.**   (a) Chromosomal DNA from two different individuals was subjected to traditional DNA fingerprinting. Their DNA appears as a series of bands on a gel. The dissimilarities in the patterns of these bands distinguish different individuals, much as the differences in physical fingerprint patterns can be used for identification. DNA evidence at a crime scene (E) is compared to DNA from suspect 1 (S1) and suspect 2 (S2). (b) Automated DNA fingerprinting measures the masses of fluorescently labeled DNA segments called short tandem repeat sequences (STRs) from a selected individual. A printout from the fluorescence detector is shown here. Two individuals are almost always different in the pattern of peaks they exhibit.

Concept check: *Which suspect's DNA fingerprint (S1 or S2) matches the DNA evidence collected at a crime scene?*

one individual to the next. Using primers that are complementary to DNA sequences that flank each STR, the STRs from a sample of DNA are amplified by PCR and then separated by gel electrophoresis according to their molecular masses. As in automated DNA sequencing, the amplified STR fragments are fluorescently labeled. A laser excites the fluorescent molecule within an STR, and a detector records the amount of fluorescence emission for each STR. The DNA fingerprint yields a series of peaks, each peak having a characteristic molecular mass (**Figure 20.15b**). In this automated approach, the pattern of peaks is an individual's DNA fingerprint.

What are the uses of DNA fingerprinting? First, DNA fingerprinting has gained acceptance as a precise method of identification. In medicine, it is used to identify different species of bacteria and fungi, and it can even distinguish among closely related strains of the same species. This is useful so that clinicians can treat patients with the appropriate antibiotic or fungicide.

A second common use is forensics—providing evidence in a criminal case. DNA fingerprinting can be used as evidence that an individual was at a crime scene. Forensic DNA was first used in the U.S. court system in 1986. When a DNA sample taken from a crime scene matches the DNA fingerprint of an individual, the probability that a match could occur simply by chance can be calculated. Each STR size is given a probability score based on its observed frequency within a reference human population (Caucasian, Asian, and so on). An automated DNA fingerprint contains many peaks, and the probability scores for each peak are multiplied together to arrive at the likelihood that a particular pattern of peaks would be observed. For example, if a DNA fingerprint contains 20 fluorescent peaks, and the probability of an individual having each peak is 1/4, then the likelihood of having that pattern would be $(1/4)^{20}$, or roughly 1 in 1 trillion. Therefore, a match between two samples is rarely a matter of random chance.

Another important use of DNA fingerprinting is to establish paternity and other family relationships. Persons who are related genetically will have some peaks in common. The number they share depends on the closeness of their genetic relationship. For example, offspring are expected to receive half of their peaks from one parent and half from the other. Therefore, DNA fingerprinting can be used as evidence in paternity cases.

FEATURE INVESTIGATION

Blaese and Colleagues Performed the First Gene Therapy to Treat ADA Deficiency

Gene therapy is the introduction of cloned genes into living cells in an attempt to cure disease. Many current research efforts in gene therapy are aimed at alleviating inherited human diseases. More than 4,000 human genetic diseases involve a single gene abnormality. Common examples include cystic fibrosis and sickle-cell disease. Many inherited diseases have been investigated as potential targets for gene therapy. These include metabolic diseases, such as phenylketonuria, and blood disorders, such as hemophilia and severe combined immunodeficiency. Human gene therapy is still at an early stage of development. Relatively few patients have been successfully treated with gene therapy in spite of a large research effort. In addition, experimental gene therapy in humans has been associated with adverse reactions. In 1999, a patient even died from a reaction to a gene therapy treatment.

Adenosine deaminase (ADA) deficiency is an autosomal recessive disorder due to a lack of the enzyme adenosine deaminase. When present, adenosine deaminase deaminates the nucleoside deoxyadenosine. This is an important step in the proper metabolism of nucleosides. If both copies of the *ADA* gene are defective, however, deoxyadenosine will accumulate within the cells of the individual. At high concentration, deoxyadenosine is particularly toxic to lymphocytes in the immune system, namely, T cells and B cells. In individuals with ADA deficiency, the destruction of T and B cells leads to severe combined immunodeficiency disease (SCID). If left untreated, SCID is typically fatal at an early age (generally 1 to 2 years old),

because the compromised immune system of these individuals cannot fight infections.

Three approaches are used to treat ADA deficiency. In some cases, a bone marrow transplant is received from a compatible donor. A second method is to treat SCID patients with purified ADA enzyme that is coupled to polyethylene glycol (PEG). This PEG-ADA is taken up by lymphocytes and can correct the ADA deficiency. Unfortunately, these two approaches are not always available and/or successful. A third, more recent approach is to treat ADA patients with gene therapy.

On September 14, 1990, the first human gene therapy was approved for a young girl suffering from ADA deficiency. This work was carried out by a large team of researchers including R. Michael Blaese, Kenneth Culver, W. French Anderson, and several collaborators at the National Institutes of Health (NIH). Prior to this clinical trial, the normal gene for ADA had been cloned into a retroviral vector. The retroviral vector also contained mutations that prevented it from causing a viral disease, yet it still enabled the virus to infect human cells. The general aim of this therapy was to remove lymphocytes from the blood of the girl with SCID, introduce the normal *ADA* gene into the cells via the retrovirus, and then return them to her bloodstream.

Figure 20.16 outlines the protocol for the experimental treatment. The researchers removed lymphocytes from the girl and cultured them in a laboratory. The lymphocytes were then infected with a recombinant retrovirus that contained the normal *ADA* gene. During the reproductive cycle of the retrovirus, the retroviral genetic material was inserted into the host cell's DNA. Therefore, because this retrovirus contained the normal *ADA* gene, this gene also was inserted into the chromosomal

Figure 20.16 The first human gene therapy for adenosine deaminase (ADA) deficiency by Blaese and colleagues.

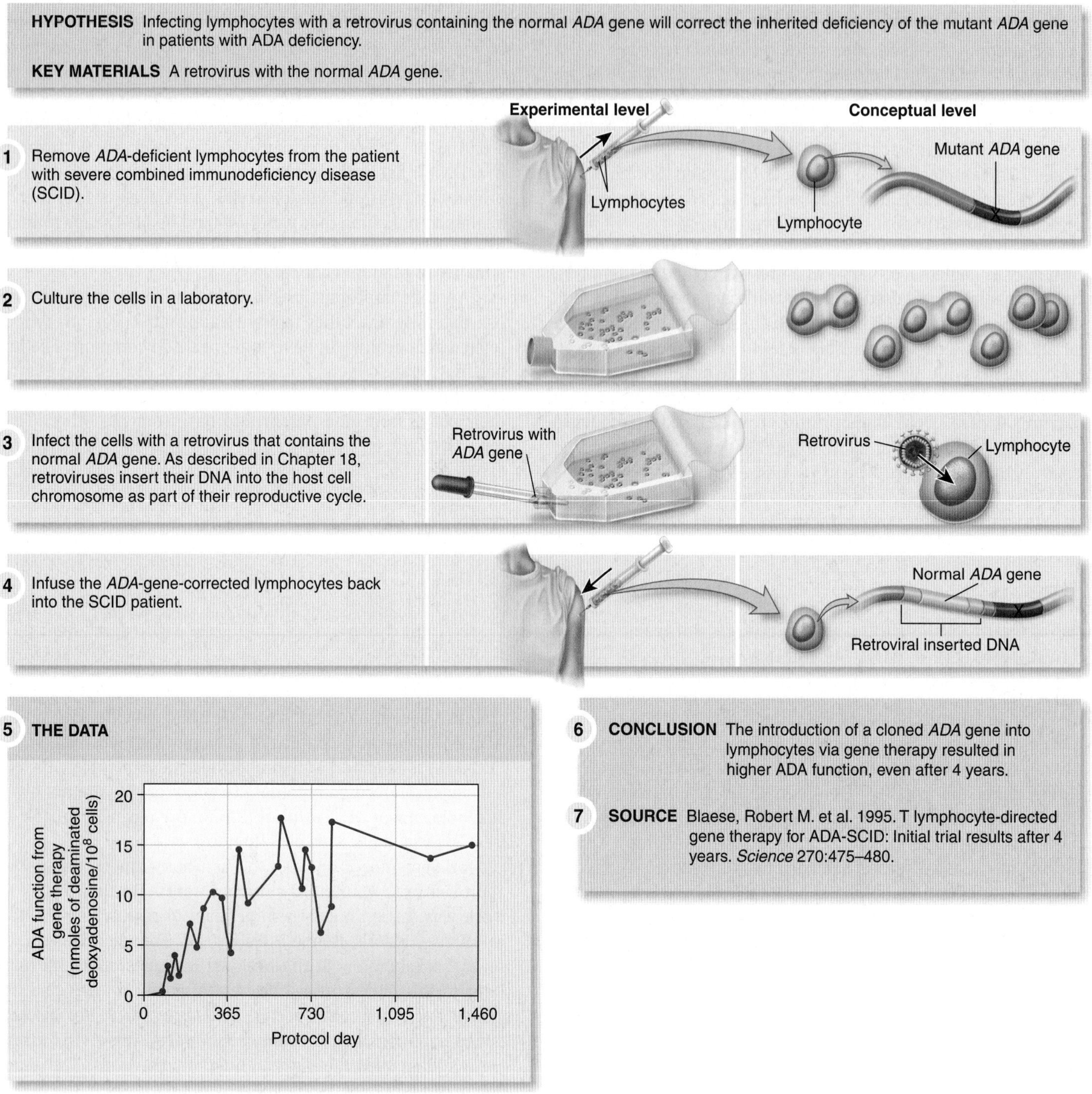
HYPOTHESIS Infecting lymphocytes with a retrovirus containing the normal *ADA* gene will correct the inherited deficiency of the mutant *ADA* gene in patients with ADA deficiency.
KEY MATERIALS A retrovirus with the normal *ADA* gene.
Experimental level
Conceptual level
1 Remove *ADA*-deficient lymphocytes from the patient with severe combined immunodeficiency disease (SCID).
Lymphocytes
Lymphocyte
Mutant *ADA* gene
2 Culture the cells in a laboratory.
3 Infect the cells with a retrovirus that contains the normal *ADA* gene. As described in Chapter 18, retroviruses insert their DNA into the host cell chromosome as part of their reproductive cycle.
Retrovirus with *ADA* gene
Retrovirus
Lymphocyte
4 Infuse the *ADA*-gene-corrected lymphocytes back into the SCID patient.
Normal *ADA* gene
Retroviral inserted DNA
5 THE DATA
ADA function from gene therapy (nmoles of deaminated deoxyadenosine/10^8 cells)
0
5
10
15
20
0
365
730
1,095
1,460
Protocol day
6 CONCLUSION The introduction of a cloned *ADA* gene into lymphocytes via gene therapy resulted in higher ADA function, even after 4 years.
7 SOURCE Blaese, Robert M. et al. 1995. T lymphocyte-directed gene therapy for ADA-SCID: Initial trial results after 4 years. *Science* 270:475–480.

DNA of the girl's lymphocytes, thereby correcting the defect in ADA. After this occurred in the laboratory, the cells were reintroduced back into the patient.

In this clinical trial, two U.S. patients were enrolled, and a third patient was later treated in Japan. The data in Figure 20.16 show the results of this trial for one of the three patients. Over the course of 2 years, this patient was given 11 infusions of lymphocytes that had been corrected with the normal *ADA* gene. Even after 4 years, this patient's lymphocytes were still making ADA. These results suggest that this first gene therapy trial may offer some benefit. However, the patients in this study were also treated with PEG-ADA as an additional therapy to prevent the adverse symptoms of SCID. Therefore, the researchers could not determine whether gene transfer into T cells was of significant clinical benefit.

Another form of SCID, termed SCID-X1, is inherited as an X-linked trait. SCID-X1 is characterized by a block in T cell growth and differentiation. This block is caused by mutations in the gene encoding the γ_c cytokine receptor, which plays a key role in the recognition of signals that are needed to promote the growth, survival, and differentiation of T cells. A gene therapy trial for SCID-X1 similar to the trial shown in Figure 20.16 was initiated in 2000. A normal γ_c cytokine receptor gene was cloned into a retroviral vector and then introduced into SCID-X1 patients' lymphocytes. The lymphocytes were then reintroduced back into their bodies. At a 10-month follow-up, T cells expressing the normal γ_c cytokine receptor were detected in two patients. Most importantly, the T cell counts in these two patients had risen to levels that were comparable to normal individuals.

This clinical trial was the first clear demonstration that gene therapy can offer clinical benefits, providing in these cases what seemed to be a complete correction of the disease phenotype.

However, in a French study involving 10 SCID-X1 patients, an unexpected and serious side effect occurred. Within 3 years of gene therapy treatment, 3 out of the 10 treated children developed leukemia—a form of cancer involving the proliferation of white blood cells. In these cases, the disease was caused by the integration of the retroviral vector next to an oncogene, a gene that promotes cancer, in the patients' genome. The development of leukemia in these patients has halted many clinical trials involving gene therapy.

Experimental Questions

1. What is gene therapy? What is ADA deficiency?

2. In the investigation of Figure 20.16, how did the researchers treat ADA deficiency?

3. How successful was the gene therapy for ADA deficiency?

Summary of Key Concepts

20.1 Gene Cloning

- Recombinant DNA technology is the use of laboratory techniques to isolate and manipulate fragments of DNA.

- Gene cloning, the process of making multiple copies of a gene, is used to obtain large amounts of the DNA that encodes a particular gene or to obtain large amounts of the gene product. (Figure 20.1)

- Plasmid and viral vectors are used in gene cloning. To obtain recombinant DNA, a vector and chromosomal DNA are cut with restriction enzymes. The DNA fragments bind to each other at their sticky ends, and the pieces are linked together via DNA ligase. (Figure 20.2, Table 20.1)

- When a recombinant vector is introduced into a bacterial cell, the cell replicates the vector and also divides to produce many cells. This achieves gene cloning. (Figure 20.3)

- A collection of recombinant vectors, each with a particular piece of chromosomal DNA, is introduced into bacterial cells to produce a DNA library. If the DNA inserts are derived from cDNA, which is made from mRNA, this is a cDNA library. (Figure 20.4)

- Gel electrophoresis is used to separate macromolecules by using an electric field that causes them to pass through a gel matrix. Gel electrophoresis typically separates molecules according to their charges, sizes, and masses. (Figure 20.5)

- Polymerase chain reaction (PCR) is another common technique to make many copies of a gene. Primers are used that flank the region of DNA to be amplified. (Figure 20.6)

20.2 Genomics

- Genomics is the study of genomes as whole units.

- For genomics, large fragments of chromosomal DNA are cloned into vectors such as BACs. One goal of genomics is to make a contig, which is a collection of clones that cover a contiguous region of a chromosome. This is a type of mapping—determining the relative locations of genes or other DNA segments along a chromosome. (Figure 20.7)

- The dideoxy method of DNA sequencing uses ddNTPs to determine the base sequence of a segment of DNA. (Figure 20.8)

- Functional genomics is aimed at studying the expression of a genome. An important technique used in functional genomics is a DNA microarray that contains a group of spots, each with a specific type of DNA. It is used as a hybridization tool to study which genes are transcribed into mRNA from a particular sample of cells. (Figure 20.9, Table 20.2)

20.3 Biotechnology

- Biotechnology is the use of living organisms, or the products of living organisms, for human benefit. For example, microorganisms can be genetically engineered to produce human products such as insulin. (Figure 20.10)

- Microorganisms are also used to reduce pollutants in the environment, a phenomenon called bioremediation.

- Transgenic organisms, also called genetically modified organisms, are made via gene replacement or gene addition. Transgenic livestock can be genetically engineered to produce human hormones in their milk. (Figure 20.11)

- The Ti plasmid in *Agrobacterium tumefaciens* has been used to produce transgenic plants such as Bt corn, which produces its own insecticide. (Figures 20.12, 20.13)

- The cloning of mammals has been achieved by fusing a somatic cell with an egg that has had its nucleus removed. (Figure 20.14)

- DNA fingerprinting is a method of identification based on the occurrence of segments of DNA in the genomes of all individuals, called STRs, that are variable in length among different individuals. (Figure 20.15)

- Gene therapy is a method to treat human diseases by the introduction of cloned genes into cells. The first gene therapy involved a disease called severe combined immunodeficiency syndrome (SCID). (Figure 20.16)

Assess and Discuss

Test Yourself

1. Vectors used to clone genes were derived originally from
   a. proteins.
   b. plasmids.
   c. viruses.
   d. all of the above.
   e. b and c only.

2. Restriction enzymes used in most cloning experiments
   a. are used to cut DNA into pieces for gene cloning.
   b. are naturally produced by bacteria cells to prevent viral infection.
   c. produce sticky ends on DNA fragments.
   d. All of the above are correct.
   e. a and c only are correct.

3. DNA ligase is needed in a cloning experiment
   a. to promote hydrogen bonding between sticky ends.
   b. to catalyze the covalent attachment of the backbone of DNA strands.
   c. to digest the chromosomal DNA into small pieces.
   d. a and b only are correct.
   e. a, b, and c are correct.

4. Let's suppose you followed the protocols described in Figures 20.2 and 20.3. Which sequence of experiments would you follow to confirm that a white colony really contained a recombinant vector with an insert?
   a. Pick a bacterial colony and restreak on plates containing X-Gal to confirm that the cells really form white colonies.
   b. Pick a bacterial colony, isolate plasmid DNA, digest the plasmid DNA with a restriction enzyme, and then run the DNA on a gel.
   c. Pick a bacterial colony and test it to see if β-galactosidase is functional within the bacterial cells.
   d. Pick a bacterial colony and retest it on ampicillin-containing plates to double-check that the cells are really ampicillin resistant.
   e. c and d should both be conducted.

5. Why is *Taq* polymerase used in PCR rather than other DNA polymerases?
   a. *Taq* polymerase is a synthetic enzyme that produces DNA strands at a faster rate than natural polymerases.
   b. *Taq* polymerase is a heat-stable form of DNA polymerase that can function after exposure to the high temperatures that are necessary for PCR.
   c. *Taq* polymerase is easier to isolate than other DNA polymerases.
   d. *Taq* polymerase is the DNA polymerase commonly produced by most eukaryotic cells.
   e. All of the above are correct.

6. Let's suppose you want to clone a gene that has never been analyzed before by DNA sequencing. Which of the following statements do you agree with the most?
   a. Do PCR to clone the gene because it's much faster.
   b. Do PCR to clone the gene because it is very specific and gives a high yield.
   c. You can't do PCR because you can't make forward and reverse primers.
   d. Do cloning by insertion into a vector because it will give you a higher yield.
   e. Do cloning by insertion into a vector because it is easier than PCR.

7. The method of determining the base sequence of DNA is
   a. PCR.
   b. gene cloning.
   c. DNA fingerprinting.
   d. DNA sequencing.
   e. gene mapping.

8. During bioremediation, microorganisms are used to
   a. clone genes from eukaryotic organisms.
   b. introduce correct genes into individuals with genetic diseases.
   c. decrease pollutants in the environment.
   d. produce useful products such as insulin.
   e. do all of the above.

9. Organisms that carry genes that were introduced using molecular techniques are called
   a. transgenics.
   b. recombinant DNA.
   c. mutants.
   d. genetically modified organisms.
   e. both a and d.

10. DNA fingerprinting is used
    a. to provide a means of precise identification of an organism, such as the identification of specific strains of bacteria.
    b. as a forensics tool to provide evidence in a criminal case.
    c. to determine genetic relationships between individuals.
    d. to determine the identity of an individual.
    e. for all of the above.

Conceptual Questions

1. Explain how using one restriction enzyme to cut both a plasmid and a gene of interest will allow the gene to be inserted into the plasmid.

2. Explain and draw the structural feature of a dideoxyribonucleotide that causes chain termination.

3. What is a mouse model for a human disease? Why is such a model useful?

Collaborative Questions

1. Discuss three important advances that have resulted from gene cloning.

2. Discuss the ethical issues associated with genetic engineering, stem cell research, and the cloning of mammals.

Online Resource

www.brookerbiology.com

Stay a step ahead in your studies with animations that bring concepts to life and practice tests to assess your understanding. Your instructor may also recommend the interactive ebook, individualized learning tools, and more.

Genomes, Proteomes, and Bioinformatics

21

I magine a book that is incredibly long and has taken billions of years to write. Such an analogy applies to the human genome, which is written in only four letters—A, T, G, and C—and is over 3 billion base pairs long. If the entire human genome were typed in a textbook like this, with about 3,000 letters per page, it would be over 1 million pages long! Our genome contains many unsolved mysteries that researchers are trying to unravel, such as: What are the functions of every gene in the genome? How do gene mutations cause disease? How are humans evolutionarily related to other species? As you will learn, genomes are full of surprises. For example, did you know that most of your DNA has no known function?

The unifying theme of biology is evolution. The genome of every living species is the product of approximately 4 billion years of evolution. We can understand the unity of modern organisms by realizing that all species evolved from an interrelated group of ancestors. Throughout this textbook, a recurring theme is a series of "Genomes and Proteomes" topics to highlight the evolutionary connections among all forms of life and underscore how the genetic material produces the form and function of living organisms. By now, you may feel familiar with the concept of a **genome**, which is the complete genetic composition of a cell or a species. The genome of each species is critical to its existence in several ways:

- The genome stores information in the form of genes, which provide a genetic blueprint to produce the characteristics of organisms.

- The genome is copied and transmitted from generation to generation.

- The accumulation of genetic changes (mutations) over the course of many generations produces the evolutionary changes that alter species and produce new species.

An extension of genome analysis is the study of proteomes. The term **proteome** refers to the entire complement of proteins that a cell or organism can make. The function of most genes is to encode proteins, which are the key determinants of cell structure and function. Analyzing the proteomes of organisms allows researchers to understand many aspects of biology, including the structure and

Genomes and computer technology. The amount of data derived from the analyses of genomes is so staggering in size and complexity that researchers have turned to the use of computers to unravel the amazing information that genomes contain.

function of cells, the complexity of multicellular organisms, and the interactions between organisms and their environment.

In the first two sections of this chapter, we will consider genome characteristics of prokaryotic and eukaryotic species, respectively. We will then turn our attention to proteomes and examine the roles of the proteins that a species can make. From a molecular perspective, genomes and proteomes contain extensive and complex information, which is studied using computer technology. In the last section of this chapter, we will consider how the field of **bioinformatics**, which employs computers and statistical techniques to analyze biological information, is critical to the study of genomes and proteomes.

21.1 Bacterial and Archaeal Genomes

The past decade has seen remarkable advances in our overall understanding of the entire genome of many species. As genetic technology has progressed, researchers have gained an increasing ability to analyze the composition of genomes as a whole unit. For many species, we now know their complete DNA sequence, which provides the most detailed description available of an organism's genome at the molecular level. In this section, we will survey the sizes and composition of the genomes in selected prokaryotic species, which includes both bacteria and archaea.

Prokaryotic Genomes Often Contain a Circular Chromosome with a Few Thousand Genes

Geneticists have made great progress in the study of bacterial and archaeal genomes. Some of the key features of prokaryotic chromosomes are described in Chapter 18 (refer back to Figure 18.10). Why are researchers interested in the genomes of prokaryotic species? First, bacteria cause many different diseases that affect humans and other animals, as well as plants. Studying the genomes of bacteria reveals important clues about the process of infection and also may help us find ways to combat bacterial infection. A second reason for studying prokaryotic genomes is that the information we learn about these microscopic organisms often applies to larger and more complex organisms. For example, basic genetic mechanisms, such as DNA replication and gene regulation, were first understood in the bacterium *Escherichia coli*. That knowledge provided a critical foundation to understand how these processes work in humans and other eukaryotic species. A third reason is evolution. The origin of the first eukaryotic cell probably involved a union between an archaeal and a bacterial cell, as we will explore in Chapter 22. The study of prokaryotic genomes helps us understand how all living species evolved. Finally, another reason to study the genomes of bacteria is because we use them as tools in research and biotechnology, which was discussed in Chapter 20.

As of 2009, the genomes of over 700 prokaryotic species have been completely sequenced and analyzed. The chromosomes of prokaryotes are usually a few million base pairs in length. Genomic researchers refer to 1 million base pairs as 1 megabase pair, abbreviated Mb. Most prokaryotes contain a single type of chromosome, though multiple copies may be present in a single cell. However, some prokaryotes are known to have different chromosomes. For example, *Vibrio cholerae*, the bacterium that causes the diarrheal disease known as cholera, has two different chromosomes in each cell, one 2.9 Mb and the other 1.1 Mb.

Bacterial chromosomes are often circular. For example, the two chromosomes in *V. cholerae* are circular, as is the single type of chromosome found in *E. coli*. However, linear chromosomes are found in some prokaryotic species, such as *Borrelia burgdorferi*, which is the bacterium that causes Lyme disease, the most common tick-borne disease in the U.S. Certain bacterial species may even contain both linear and circular chromosomes. *Agrobacterium tumefaciens*, which infects plants

and causes a disorder called crown gall disease, has one linear chromosome (2.1 Mb) and one circular chromosome (3.0 Mb).

Table 21.1 compares the sequenced genomes from several prokaryotic species. They range in size from 1.7 to 5.2 Mb. The total number of genes is correlated with the total genome size. Roughly 1,000 genes are found for every Mb of DNA. Compared to eukaryotic genomes, prokaryotic genomes are less complex. Prokaryotic chromosomes lack centromeres and telomeres and have a single origin of replication. Also, prokaryotic chromosomes have relatively little repetitive DNA, a feature typically found in eukaryotic genomes.

In addition to one or more chromosomes, prokaryotes often have plasmids, circular pieces of DNA that exist independently of the bacterial chromosome. Plasmids are typically small, in the range of a few thousand to tens of thousands of base pairs in length, though some can be quite large, even hundreds of thousands of base pairs. The various functions of plasmids are described in Chapter 18, and their use as vectors in genetic engineering is discussed in Chapter 20.

Table 21.1	Examples of Prokaryotic Genomes That Have Been Sequenced*		
Species	**Genome size (Mb)†**	**Number of genes‡**	**Description**
Methanobacterium thermoautotrophicum	1.7	1,869	An archaeon that produces methane
Haemophilus influenzae	1.8	1,753	One of several different bacterial species that causes respiratory illness and meningitis
Sulfolobus solfataricus	3.0	3,032	An archaeon that metabolizes sulfur
Lactobacillus plantarum	3.3	3,052	A type of lactic acid bacterium used in the production of cheese and yogurt
Mycobacterium tuberculosis	4.4	4,294	The bacterium that causes the respiratory disease tuberculosis
Escherichia coli	4.6	4,289	A naturally occurring intestinal bacterium; certain strains can cause human illness
Bacillus anthracis	5.2	5,439	The bacterium that causes the disease anthrax

*Prokaryotic species often exist in different strains that may differ slightly in their genome size and number of genes. The data are from common strains of the indicated species. The species shown in this table have only one type of chromosome.

†Mb equals 1 million base pairs.

‡The number of genes is an estimate based on the analysis of genome sequences.

FEATURE INVESTIGATION

Venter, Smith, and Colleagues Sequenced the First Genome in 1995

The first genome to be entirely sequenced was that of the bacterium *Haemophilus influenzae*. This bacterium causes a variety of diseases in humans, including respiratory illnesses and bacterial meningitis. *H. influenzae* has a relatively small genome consisting of approximately 1.8 Mb of DNA in a single circular chromosome.

Scientists can follow different strategies when tackling a genome-sequencing project. One strategy, which has been used for larger eukaryotic genomes, requires extensive mapping. This means that the genome is cut into large pieces of DNA whose locations are known within a given chromosome. These large pieces are then cut into smaller and smaller pieces, whose relative locations are known within the larger pieces. Once small DNA pieces have been mapped throughout the whole genome, their DNA sequences are determined by the dideoxy sequencing method, which is described in Figure 20.8.

An alternative strategy for sequencing an entire genome is called **shotgun DNA sequencing**. In this approach, researchers use the technique of dideoxy sequencing to randomly sequence many DNA fragments from the genome. As a matter of chance, some of the fragments are overlapping—the end of one fragment will contain the same DNA region as the beginning of another fragment. Computers are used to align the overlapping regions and assemble the DNA fragments into a contiguous sequence identical to that found in the intact chromosome. The advantage of shotgun DNA sequencing is that it does not require extensive mapping, a process that can be time-consuming. A disadvantage is that researchers may waste time sequencing the same region of DNA more times than necessary in order to assemble the sequence correctly.

To obtain a complete sequence of a genome with the shotgun approach, how do researchers decide how many fragments to sequence? We can calculate the probability that a base will not be sequenced (P) using this equation:

$$P = e^{-m}$$

where e is the base of the natural logarithm ($e = 2.72$), and m is the number of sequenced bases divided by the total genome size. For example, in the case of *H. influenzae*, with a genome size of 1.8 Mb, if researchers sequenced 9.0 Mb, $m = 5$ (that is, 9.0 Mb divided by 1.8 Mb):

$$P = e^{-m} = e^{-5} = 0.0067, \text{ or } 0.67\%.$$

This means that if we randomly sequence 9.0 Mb, which is five times the length of a single genome, we are likely to miss only 0.67% of the genome. With a genome size of 1.8 Mb, we would miss about 12,000 nucleotides out of approximately 1.8 million. Such missed sequences are typically on small DNA fragments that, as a matter of random chance, did not happen to be sequenced. The missing links in the genome can be sequenced later using mapping methods.

The general protocol conducted by Craig Venter, Hamilton Smith, and colleagues in this discovery-based investigation is described in **Figure 21.1**. This is a shotgun DNA sequencing approach. The researchers isolated chromosomal DNA from *H. influenzae* and used sound waves to break the DNA into small fragments of approximately 2,000 bp in length. These fragments were randomly inserted into vectors, allowing the DNA to be propagated in *E. coli*. Each *E. coli* clone carried a vector with a different piece of DNA from *H. influenzae*. The complete

Figure 21.1   Determination of the complete genome sequence of *Haemophilus influenzae* by Venter, Smith, and colleagues.

GOAL The goal is to obtain the entire genome sequence of *Haemophilus influenzae*. This information will reveal its genome size and also which genes the organism has.

KEY MATERIALS A strain of *H. influenzae*.

Experimental level   Conceptual level

1   Purify DNA from a strain of *H. influenzae*. This involves breaking the cells open by adding phenol and chloroform. Most protein and lipid components go into the phenol-chloroform phase. DNA remains in the aqueous (water) phase.

DNA in aqueous (water) phase
Proteins and lipids in phenol-chloroform phase

H. influenzae chromosomal DNA

2   Sonicate the DNA to break it into small fragments of about 2,000 bp in length.

Sound waves

DNA fragments in aqueous phase

Sound waves

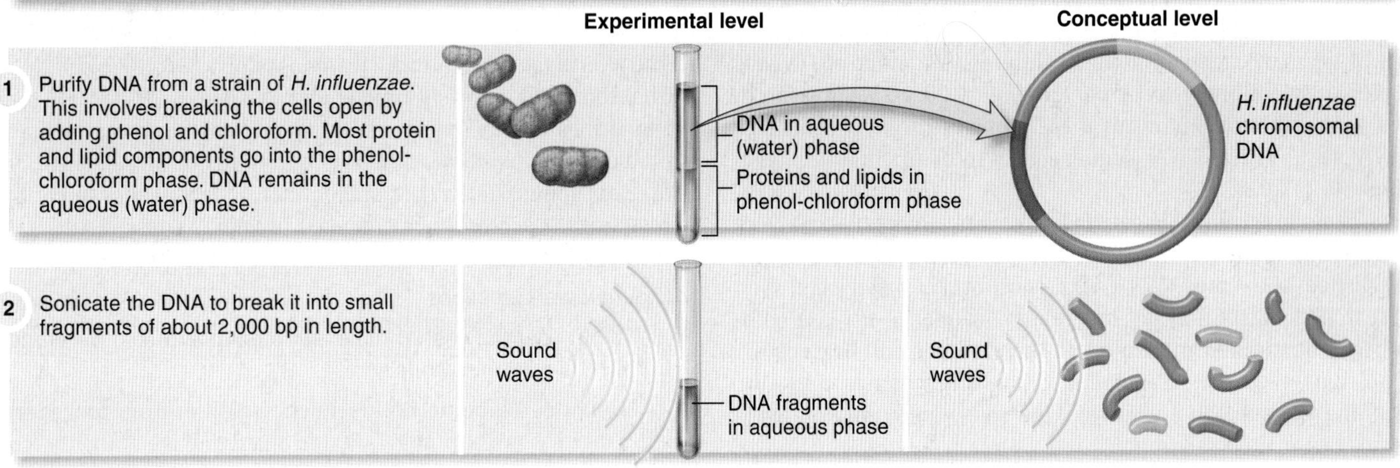

3 Clone the DNA fragments into vectors. The procedures for cloning are described in Chapter 20. This produces a DNA library.

Refer back to Figures 20.2 and 20.3.

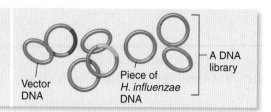

Vector DNA

Piece of H. influenzae DNA

A DNA library

4 Subject many clones to the procedure of dideoxy DNA sequencing, also described in Chapter 20. A total of 10.8 Mb was sequenced.

Refer back to Figure 20.8.

Produces a large number of overlapping sequences.

...CCAGTCCCATGCCATGGCCCAGTCCC

5 Use tools of bioinformatics, described in the last section of this chapter, to identify various types of genes in the genome.

CCATGCCATGGCCCCCATGC

Explores the genome sequence and identifies and characterizes genes.

6 THE DATA

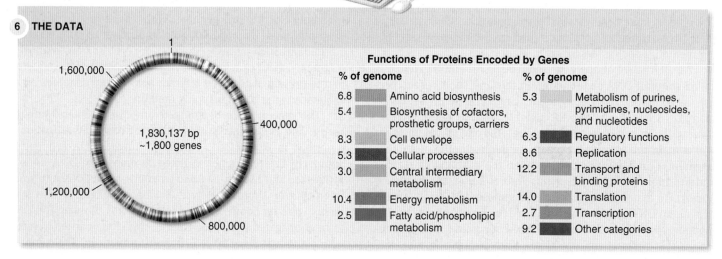

1,830,137 bp ~1,800 genes

Functions of Proteins Encoded by Genes

% of genome			% of genome	
6.8	Amino acid biosynthesis		5.3	Metabolism of purines, pyrimidines, nucleosides, and nucleotides
5.4	Biosynthesis of cofactors, prosthetic groups, carriers			
8.3	Cell envelope		6.3	Regulatory functions
5.3	Cellular processes		8.6	Replication
3.0	Central intermediary metabolism		12.2	Transport and binding proteins
10.4	Energy metabolism		14.0	Translation
2.5	Fatty acid/phospholipid metabolism		2.7	Transcription
			9.2	Other categories

7 **CONCLUSION** *H. influenzae* has a genome size of 1.83 Mb with approximately 1,800 genes. The functions of many of those genes could be inferred by comparing them to genes in other species.

8 **SOURCE** Fleischmann et al. 1995. Whole-genome random sequencing and assembly of *Haemophilus influenzae* Rd. *Science* 269:496–512.

set of vectors, each containing a different fragment of DNA, is called a **DNA library** (refer back to Figure 20.4). The researchers then subjected many of these clones to the procedure of DNA sequencing. They sequenced a total of approximately 10.8 Mb of DNA.

The outcome of this genome-sequencing project was a very long DNA sequence. In 1995, Venter, Smith, and colleagues published the entire DNA sequence of *H. influenzae*. The researchers then analyzed the genome sequence using a computer to obtain information about the properties of the genome. Questions they asked included, How many genes does the genome contain, and what are the likely functions of those genes? Later in this chapter, we will learn how scientists can answer such questions with the use of computers. The data in Figure 21.1 summarize the results that the researchers obtained.

The *H. influenzae* genome is composed of 1,830,137 bp of DNA. The computer analysis predicted 1,743 genes. Based on their similarities to known genes in other species, the researchers also predicted the functions of nearly two-thirds of these genes. The diagram shown in the data of Figure 21.1 places genes in various categories based on their predicted function. These results gave the first comprehensive "genome picture" of a living organism!

Experimental Questions

1. What was the goal of the experiment conducted by Venter, Smith, and their colleagues?

2. How does shotgun DNA sequencing differ from procedures that involve mapping? What is an advantage and a disadvantage of the shotgun DNA sequencing approach?

3. What were the results of the study described in Figure 21.1?

21.2 Eukaryotic Genomes

Thus far, we have examined the size and composition of bacterial and archaeal genomes. In this section, we turn to eukaryotes, which include protists, fungi, animals, and plants. As you will learn, their genomes are larger and more complex than their prokaryotic counterparts. In addition to genes, eukaryotic genomes often have abundant amounts of noncoding sequences. For example, eukaryotic genomes typically have a substantial amount of short repeated sequences called repetitive DNA. We will learn how certain types of repetitive DNA sequences are formed by a process called transposition. We will also examine how the duplication of genes can lead to families of related genes.

The Nuclear Genomes of Eukaryotes Are Sets of Linear Chromosomes That Vary Greatly in Size and Composition Among Different Species

As discussed in Chapter 15, the genome found in the nucleus of eukaryotic species is usually found in sets of linear chromosomes. In humans, for example, one set contains 23 linear chromosomes—22 autosomes and one sex chromosome, X or Y. In addition, certain organelles in eukaryotic cells contain a small amount of their own DNA. These include the mitochondrion, which plays a role in ATP synthesis, and the chloroplast found in plants and algae, which carries out photosynthesis. The genetic material found in these organelles is referred to as the mitochondrial or the chloroplast genome to distinguish it from the nuclear genome, which is found in the cell nucleus. In this chapter, we will focus on the nuclear genome of eukaryotes.

Nuclear Genomes In the past decade or so, the DNA sequence of entire nuclear genomes has been determined for nearly 100 eukaryotic species, including more than two dozen mammalian genomes. Examples are shown in **Table 21.2**.

Motivation to sequence these genomes comes from four main sources. First, the availability of genome sequences makes it easier for researchers to identify and characterize the genes of model organisms. This has been the impetus for genome projects involving baker's yeast (*Saccharomyces cerevisiae*), the fruit fly (*Drosophila melanogaster*), a nematode worm (*Caenorhabditis elegans*), the simple plant called thale cress (*Arabidopsis thaliana*), and the mouse (*Mus musculus*). A second reason for genome sequencing is to gather more information to identify and treat human diseases, which is an important aim for sequencing the human genome. Researchers hope that knowing the DNA sequence of the human genome will help to identify genes in which mutation plays a role in disease. Third, by sequencing the genomes of agriculturally important species, new strains of livestock and plant species with improved traits can be developed. Fourth, biologists are increasingly relying on genome sequences as a way to establish evolutionary relationships.

Genome Sizes and Repetitive Sequences Eukaryotic genomes are generally larger than prokaryotic genomes in terms of both

Table 21.2 Examples of Eukaryotic Nuclear Genomes That Have Been Sequenced

Species	Nuclear genome size (Mb)	Number of genes	Description
Saccharomyces cerevisiae (baker's yeast)	12.1	6,294	One of the simplest eukaryotic species; it has been extensively studied by researchers to understand eukaryotic cell biology and other molecular mechanisms.
Caenorhabditis elegans (nematode worm)	100	~19,000	A model organism used to study animal development.
Drosophila melanogaster (fruit fly)	180	~14,000	A model organism used to study many genetic phenomena, including development.
Arabidopsis thaliana (thale cress)	120	~26,000	A model organism studied by plant biologists.
Oryza sativa (rice)	440	~40,000	A cereal grain with a relatively small genome; it is very important worldwide as a food crop.
Mus musculus (Mouse)	2,500	~20,000–25,000	A model mammalian organism used to study genetics, cell biology, and development.
Homo sapiens (humans)	3,200	~20,000–25,000	Our own genome; the sequencing of the human genome will help to elucidate our understanding of inherited traits and may aid in the identification and treatment of diseases.

Note: The genome size refers to the number of megabase pairs in one set of chromosomes. For species with sex chromosomes, it would include both sex chromosomes.

the number of genes and genome size. The genomes of simpler eukaryotes, such as yeast, carry several thousand different genes, whereas the genomes of more complex eukaryotes contain tens of thousands of genes (Table 21.2). Note that the number of genes is not the same as genome size. When we speak of genome size, this means the total amount of DNA, often measured in megabase pairs. The relative sizes of nuclear genomes vary dramatically among different eukaryotic species (**Figure 21.2a**). In general, increases in the amount of DNA are correlated with increases in cell size, cell complexity, and body complexity. For example, yeast have smaller genomes than animals. However, major variations in genome sizes are observed among organisms that are similar in form and function. For example, the total amount of DNA found within different species of amphibians can vary over 100-fold.

The DNA content of closely related species can also vary. As an example, let's consider two closely related species of the plant called the globe thistle, *Echinops bannaticus* and *Echinops nanus* (**Figure 21.2b,c**). These species have similar numbers of chromosomes, but *E. bannaticus* has nearly double the amount of DNA as *E. nanus*. What is the explanation for the larger genome of *E. bannaticus*? The genome of *E. bannaticus* is not likely to contain

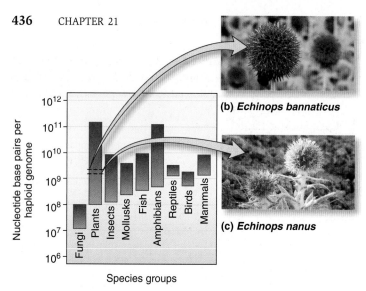

(b) Echinops bannaticus

(c) Echinops nanus

(a) Genome size

Figure 21.2 Genome sizes among selected groups of eukaryotes. (a) Genome sizes among various groups of eukaryotes are shown on a log scale. As an example for comparison, two closely related species of globe thistle are pictured. These species have similar characteristics, but *Echinops bannaticus* (b) has nearly double the amount of DNA as *E. nanus* (c) due to the accumulation of repetitive DNA sequences.

Concept check: What are two reasons why the groups of species shown in (a) have variation in their total amount of DNA?

twice as many genes. Rather, its genome composition includes many **repetitive sequences**, which are short DNA sequences that are present in many copies throughout the genome. Repetitive sequences are often abundant in eukaryotic species.

Types of Repetitive Sequences The repetitive sequences that are found in genomes fall into two broad categories, moderately and highly repetitive. Sequences found in a few hundred to several thousand copies are called **moderately repetitive sequences**. In some cases, these sequences are multiple copies of the same gene. For example, the genes that encode ribosomal RNA (rRNA) are found in many copies. The cell needs a large amount of rRNA for its cellular ribosomes. This is accomplished by having and expressing multiple copies of the genes that encode rRNA. In addition, other types of functionally important sequences can be moderately repetitive. For example, multiple copies of origins of replication are found in eukaryotic chromosomes. Other moderately repetitive sequences may play a role in the regulation of gene transcription and translation.

Highly repetitive sequences are those that are found in tens of thousands to millions of copies throughout the genome. Each copy of a highly repetitive sequence is relatively short, ranging from a few nucleotides to several hundred nucleotides in length. Most of these sequences have no known function, and whether they benefit the organism is a matter of debate. A widely studied example is the *Alu* family of sequences found in humans and other primates. The *Alu* sequence is approximately 300 bp long. This sequence derives its name from the observation that it contains a site for cleavage by a restriction enzyme known as *Alu*I. It represents about 10% of the total human

DNA and occurs (on average) approximately every 5,000–6,000 bases. Evolutionary studies suggest that the *Alu* sequence arose 65 million years ago from a section of a single ancestral gene known as the 7SL RNA gene. Remarkably, over the course of 65 million years, the *Alu* sequence has been copied and inserted into the human genome so often that it now appears more than 1 million times! The mechanism for the proliferation of *Alu* sequences will be described later.

Some highly repetitive sequences, like the *Alu* family, are interspersed throughout the genome. However, other highly repetitive sequences are clustered together in a tandem array in which a very short nucleotide sequence is repeated many times in a row. In *Drosophila*, for example, 19% of the chromosomal DNA is highly repetitive DNA found in tandem arrays. An example is shown here:

```
AATATAATATAATATAATATAATATAT
TTATATTATATTATATTATATTATATA
```

In this particular tandem array, two related sequences, AATAT and AATATAT, are repeated many times. Highly repetitive sequences, which contain tandem arrays of short sequences, can be quite long, sometimes more than 1 million bp in length!

Figure 21.3 shows the composition of the relative classes of DNA sequences that are found in the nuclear genome of humans. Surprisingly, exons, the coding regions of structural genes, and the genes that give rise to rRNA and tRNA make up only about 2% of our genome! The other 98% is composed of noncoding sequences. Though we often think of genomes as being the repository of sequences that code for proteins, most eukaryotic genomes are largely composed of other types of sequences. Intron DNA comprises the second most common portion of the genome at 24%. Unique noncoding DNA, whose function is largely unknown, constitutes 15%. Repetitive DNA makes up

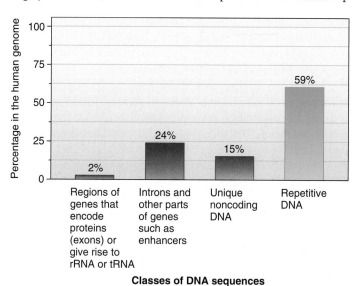

Classes of DNA sequences

Figure 21.3 The composition of DNA sequences that are found in the nuclear genome of humans. Only about 2% of our genome codes for proteins. Most of our genome is made up of repetitive sequences.

Concept check: Do these results seem surprising to you?

59% of the DNA in the genome. Much of the repetitive DNA is derived from transposable elements, stretches of DNA that can move from one location to another, which are described next.

Transposable Elements Can Move from One Chromosomal Location to Another

During a process called **transposition**, a short segment of DNA moves from its original site to a new site in the genome. Such segments are known as **transposable elements** (**TEs**). They range from a few hundred to several thousand bp in length. TEs have sometimes been referred to as "jumping genes," because they are inherently mobile. Barbara McClintock first identified transposable elements in the late 1940s from her studies with corn plants (**Figure 21.4**). She identified a segment of DNA that could move into and out of a gene that affected the color of corn kernels, producing a speckled appearance. Since that time, biologists have discovered many different types of TEs in nearly all species examined.

Though McClintock identified TEs in corn in the late 1940s, her work was met with great skepticism because many researchers had trouble believing that DNA segments could be mobile. The advent of molecular technology in the 1960s and 1970s allowed scientists to understand more about the characteristics of TEs that enable their movement. Most notably, research involving bacterial TEs eventually progressed to a molecular understanding of the transposition process. In 1983, over 30 years after her initial discovery, McClintock was awarded the Nobel Prize in Physiology or Medicine.

DNA Transposons Researchers have studied TEs from many species, including prokaryotes and eukaryotes. They have found that DNA sequences within transposable elements are organized in several different ways, and they can move by different molecular mechanisms. Let's first begin with transposable elements in which the DNA itself moves from one location to another. These are also called **DNA transposons** because they move via a DNA molecule. Both ends of DNA transposons usually have inverted repeats (IRs)—DNA sequences that are identical (or very similar) but run in opposite directions (**Figure 21.5a**), such as the following:

$$5'-\text{CTGACTCTT}-3' \quad \text{and} \quad 5'-\text{AAGAGTCAG}-3'$$
$$3'-\text{GACTGAGAA}-5' \qquad\qquad 3'-\text{TTCTCAGTC}-5'$$

Depending on the particular transposable element, inverted repeats range from 9 to 40 base pairs in length. In addition, DNA transposons may contain a central region that encodes **transposase**, an enzyme that facilitates transposition.

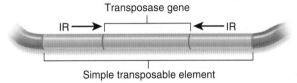

(a) Organization of a simple transposable element

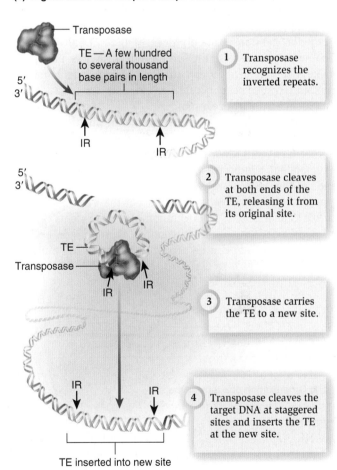

(b) Cut-and-paste mechanism of transposition

Figure 21.5 DNA transposons and their mechanism of transposition. (a) DNA transposons contain inverted repeat (IR) sequences at each end and a gene that encodes transposase in the middle. (b) Transposition occurs by a cut-and-paste mechanism.

Concept check: *What is the role of the inverted repeats in the mechanism of transposition?*

(a) Barbara McClintock

(b) Speckled corn kernels caused by transposable elements

Figure 21.4 Barbara McClintock, who discovered transposable elements. As shown in part **(b)**, when a transposable element is found within a pigment gene in corn, its frequent movement disrupts the gene, causing the kernel color to be speckled.

As shown in **Figure 21.5b**, transposition of DNA transposons occurs by a cut-and-paste mechanism. Transposase first recognizes the inverted repeats in the TE and then removes the TE from its original site. Next, the transposase/TE complex moves to a new location, where transposase cleaves the target DNA and inserts the TE into the site. Transposition may occur when a cell is in the process of DNA replication. If a transposable element is removed from a site that has already replicated and is inserted into a chromosomal site that has not yet replicated, the TE will increase in number after DNA replication is complete. This is one way for TEs to become more prevalent in a genome.

Retroelements Another category of transposable elements moves via an RNA intermediate. This form of transposition is very common but is found only in eukaryotic species. These types of elements are known as **retroelements** or retrotransposons. The *Alu* sequence in the human genome is an example of a retroelement. Some retroelements contain genes that encode the enzymes reverse transcriptase and integrase, which are needed in the transposition process (**Figure 21.6a**). Recall from Chapter 18 that reverse transcriptase uses RNA as a template to make a complementary copy of DNA. Retroelements may also contain repeated sequences called terminal repeats at each end that facilitate their recognition.

The mechanism of retroelement movement is shown in **Figure 21.6b**. First, the enzyme RNA polymerase transcribes the retroelement into RNA. Reverse transcriptase uses this RNA as a template to synthesize a double-stranded DNA molecule. The ends of the double-stranded DNA are then recognized by integrase, which catalyzes the insertion of the DNA into the host chromosomal DNA. The integration of retroelements can occur at many locations within the genome. Furthermore, because a single retroelement can be copied into many RNA transcripts,

retroelements may accumulate rapidly within a genome. This explains how the *Alu* element in the human genome was able to proliferate and constitute 10% of our genome.

Role of Transposable Elements What is the biological significance of TEs? The question is not resolved. According to the **selfish DNA hypothesis**, TEs exist solely because they have characteristics that allow them to insert themselves into the host cell DNA. In other words, they resemble parasites in the sense that they inhabit the host without offering any advantage. They can proliferate within the host as long as they do not harm the host to the extent that they significantly disrupt survival. However, TEs can do harm. For example, if they jump into the middle of an important gene and thereby disrupt its function, this may have a negative impact on the phenotype of an organism.

Other biologists have argued that TEs may provide benefits to a given species. For example, bacterial TEs often carry an antibiotic-resistance gene that provides the organism with a survival advantage. In addition, TEs may cause greater genetic variability by promoting chromosomal rearrangements. As discussed next, such rearrangements can cause a misaligned crossover during meiosis and promote the formation of a gene family.

Gene Duplications Provide Additional Material for Genome Evolution, Sometimes Leading to the Formation of Gene Families

Let's now turn our attention to a way that the number of genes in a genome can increase. These gene duplications are important because they provide raw material for the addition of more genes into a species' genome. Such duplications can produce **homologous genes**, two or more genes that are derived from the same ancestral gene (**Figure 21.7a**). Over the course of

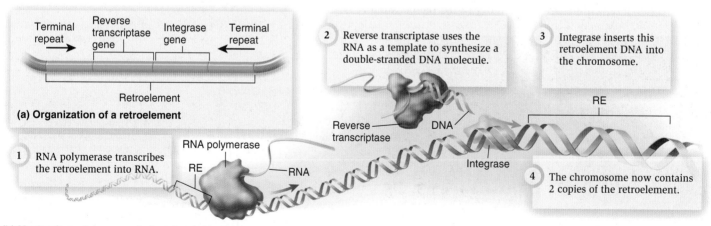

(a) Organization of a retroelement

(b) Mechanism of movement of a retroelement

Figure 21.6 **Retroelements and their mechanism of transposition.** Retroelements are found only in eukaryotic species. **(a)** Some retroelements contain terminal repeats and genes that encode the enzymes reverse transcriptase and integrase, which are needed in the transposition process. **(b)** The process that adds a copy of a retroelement into a host chromosome.

Concept check: *Based on their mechanism of movement, which type of TEs do you think would proliferate more rapidly in a genome, DNA transposons (see Figure 21.5b) or retroelements?*

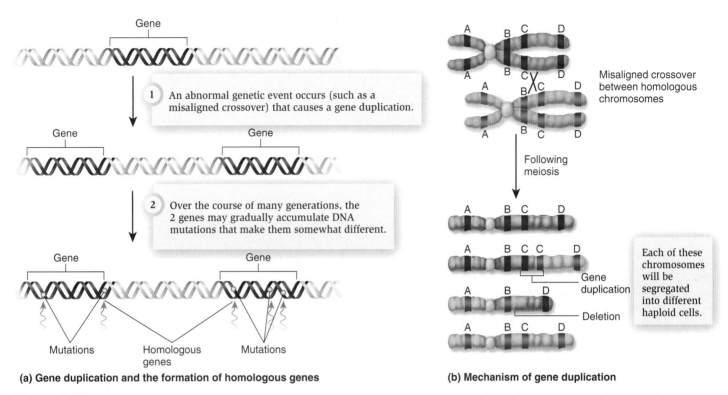

(a) Gene duplication and the formation of homologous genes

(b) Mechanism of gene duplication

Figure 21.7   Gene duplication and the evolution of homologous genes.   **(a)** A gene duplication produces two copies of the same gene. Over time, these copies accumulate different random mutations, which results in homologous genes with similar but not identical DNA sequences. **(b)** Mechanism of gene duplication. If two homologous chromosomes misalign during meiosis, a crossover will produce a chromosome with a gene duplication.

many generations, each version of the gene accumulates different mutations, resulting in genes with similar but not identical DNA sequences.

How do gene duplications occur? One mechanism that produces gene duplications is a misaligned crossover (**Figure 21.7b**). In this example, two homologous chromosomes have paired with each other during meiosis, but the homologues are misaligned. If a crossover occurs, this produces one chromosome with a gene duplication, one with a deletion, and two normal chromosomes. Each of these chromosomes will be segregated into different haploid cells. If a haploid cell carrying the chromosome with the gene duplication participates in fertilization with another gamete, an offspring with a gene duplication is produced. In this way, gene duplications can form and be transmitted to future generations. The presence of multiple copies of the same transposable element in a genome can foster this process because the chromosomes may misalign while attempting to align TEs that are at different locations in the same chromosome.

During evolution, gene duplications can occur several times. Two or more homologous genes within a single species are also called **paralogs** or paralogous genes. Multiple gene duplication followed by sequence divergence can result in a **gene family** composed of two or more paralogous genes that carry out related functions. A well-studied example is the globin gene family found in animals. The globin genes encode polypeptides that are subunits of proteins that function in oxygen binding. Hemoglobin, which is made in red blood cells, carries oxygen throughout the body. In humans, the globin gene family is composed of 14 paralogs that were originally derived from a single ancestral globin gene (**Figure 21.8**). According to an evolutionary analysis, the ancestral globin gene duplicated about 500 million years ago. Since that time, additional duplication events and chromosomal rearrangements have occurred to produce the current number of 14 genes on three different human chromosomes. Four of these are pseudogenes, which are genes that have been produced by gene duplication but have accumulated mutations that make them nonfunctional, so they are not transcribed into RNA.

Gene families have been important in the evolution of complex traits. Even though all of the globin polypeptides are subunits of proteins that play a role in oxygen binding, the accumulation of different mutations in the various family members has produced globins that are more specialized in their function. For example, myoglobin binds and stores oxygen in muscle cells, whereas the hemoglobins bind and transport oxygen via red blood cells. Also, different globin genes are expressed during different stages of human development. The zeta (ζ)-globin and epsilon (ε)-globin genes are expressed very early in embryonic life. During the second trimester of gestation, the alpha (α)-globin and gamma (γ)-globin genes are turned on. Following birth, the γ-globin genes are turned off, and the β-globin gene is turned on. These differences in the expression of the globin genes reflect the differences in the

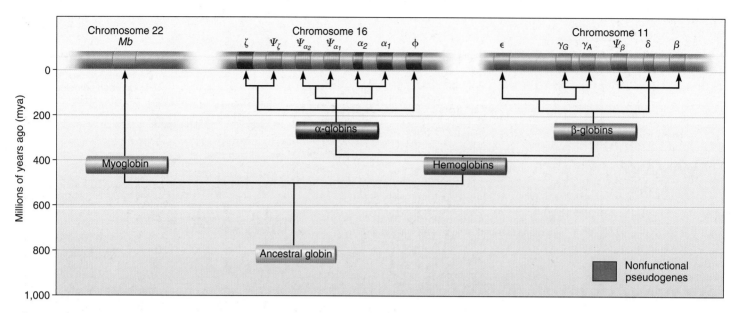

Figure 21.8 **The evolution of the globin gene family in humans.** The globin gene family evolved from a single ancestral globin gene. The first gene duplication produced two genes that accumulated mutations and became the genes encoding myoglobin and the various hemoglobins. The modern myoglobin gene is found on chromosome 22. An ancestral hemoglobin gene duplicated to produce the α- and β-globins. Further duplications of ancestral α-globin and β-globin genes produced several paralogous genes on chromosomes 16 and 11, respectively. The four genes shown in gray are nonfunctional pseudogenes.

Concept check: *What is the biological advantage of a gene family?*

oxygen transport needs of humans during the embryonic, fetal, and postpartum stages of life (refer back to Figure 13.3).

The Human Genome Project Has Stimulated Genomic Research

Before ending our discussion of genomes, let's consider the **Human Genome Project**, a research effort to identify and map all human genes. Scientists had been discussing how to undertake this project since the mid-1980s. In 1988, the National Institutes of Health in Bethesda, Maryland, established an Office of Human Genome Research with James Watson as its first director. The Human Genome Project officially began on October 1, 1990, and was largely finished by the end of 2003. It was an international consortium that included research institutions in the U.S., U.K., France, Germany, Japan, and China. From its outset, the Human Genome Project had the following goals:

1. *To identify all human genes.* This involved mapping the locations of genes throughout the entire genome. The data from the Human Genome Project suggest that humans have about 20,000 to 25,000 different genes.
2. *To obtain the DNA sequence of the entire human genome.* The first draft of a nearly completed DNA sequence was published in February 2001, and a second draft was published in 2003. The entire genome is approximately 3.2 billion base pairs in length.
3. *To develop technology for the generation and management of human genome information.* Some of the efforts of the Human Genome Project have involved improvements in

molecular genetic technology, such as gene cloning, DNA sequencing, and so forth. The Human Genome Project has also developed computer tools to allow scientists to easily access up-to-date information from the project and analytical tools to interpret genomic information.
4. *To analyze the genomes of model organisms.* These include *E. coli, S. cerevisiae, D. melanogaster, C. elegans, A. thaliana,* and *M. musculus.*
5. *To develop programs focused on understanding and addressing the ethical, legal, and social implications of the results obtained from the Human Genome Project.* Who should have access to genetic information? Should employers, insurance companies, law enforcement agencies, and schools have access to our genetic makeup? The answers to these questions are complex and will require discussion among many groups. Another controversial topic is gene patenting. In the U.S., genes can be patented for a variety of reasons. For example, the patenting of genes has been associated with the commercial development of diagnostic tests for genetic diseases. Some argue that patenting fosters greater investment into research and development; others say it can impede basic research and scientific innovation.

Some current and potential applications of the Human Genome Project include the improved diagnosis and treatment of genetic diseases such as cystic fibrosis, Huntington disease, and Duchenne muscular dystrophy. The project may also enable researchers to identify the genetic basis of common disorders such as cancer, diabetes, and heart disease, which involve alterations in several genes.

21.3 Proteomes

Thus far in this chapter, we have considered the genome characteristics of many different species, including humans. Because most genes encode proteins, a logical next step is to examine the functional roles of the proteins that a species can make. As mentioned, the entire collection of proteins that a cell or organism produces is called a proteome. As we move through the 21st century, a key challenge facing molecular biologists is the study of proteomes. Much like the study of genomes, this will require the collective contributions of many scientists, as well as improvements in technologies to investigate the complexities of the proteome. In this section, we will begin by considering the functional categories of proteins, and then examine their relative abundance in the proteome. We also will explore the molecular mechanisms that cause an organism's proteome to be much larger than its genome.

The Proteome Is a Diverse Array of Proteins with Many Kinds of Functions

The genomes of simple, unicellular organisms such as bacteria and yeast contain thousands of structural genes, whereas the genomes of complex, multicellular organisms contain tens of thousands. Such genome sizes can produce proteomes with tens of thousands to hundreds of thousands of different proteins. To bring some order to this large amount of complex information, researchers often organize proteins into different categories based on their functions. **Table 21.3** describes some general categories of protein function and provides examples of each type. Many approaches are used to categorize proteins. Table 21.3 shows just one of the more general ways to categorize protein function. For example, the data of Figure 21.1 describe the functions of proteins encoded by genes in a different, more detailed way.

The relative abundance of proteins can be viewed at two levels. First, we can consider abundance in the genome—the numbers of genes in the genome that encode a particular type or category of protein. For example, if an entire genome encodes 10,000 different types of proteins and 1,500 of these are different types of transporters, we would say that 15% of the genome is composed of transporters. However, such an analysis ignores the phenomenon that genes are expressed at different levels. In other words, various proteins are made in different amounts. Therefore, a second way to view protein abundance is to consider abundance in the cell—the amount of a given protein or protein category that is actually made by a living cell. For example, less than 1% of human genes encode proteins, such as collagen, that are found in the extracellular matrix. Even so, these genes are highly expressed in certain cells, so a large amount of this type of protein is made compared to other types.

Figure 21.9 is a general comparison of protein abundance in two cell types in humans, liver and muscle cells. Liver cells play a key role in metabolism, whereas muscle cells are involved in bodily movements. Both liver and muscle cells have the same

Table 21.3	Categories of Proteins Found in the Proteome

Function	Examples
Metabolic enzymes—accelerate chemical reactions in the cell.	Hexokinase: phosphorylates glucose during the first step in glycolysis. Glycogen synthetase: uses glucose to synthesize a large carbohydrate known as glycogen.
Structural proteins—provide shape and protection to cells.	Tubulin: forms cytoskeletal structures known as microtubules. Collagen: found abundantly in the extracellular matrix of animals.
Motor proteins—facilitate intracellular movements and the movements of whole cells.	Myosin: involved in muscle cell contraction. Kinesin: involved in the movement of chromosomes during cell division.
Cell-signaling proteins—allow cells to respond to environmental signals and send signals to each other.	Insulin: influences target cell metabolism and growth. Insulin receptor: recognizes insulin and initiates a cellular response.
Transport proteins—involved in the transport of ions and molecules across membranes and throughout the body. 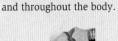	Lactose permease: transports lactose across the bacterial cell membrane. Hemoglobin: found in red blood cells and transports oxygen throughout the body.
Gene expression and regulatory proteins—involved in transcription, mRNA modification, translation, and gene regulation.	Transcription factors: regulate the expression of genes. Ribosomal proteins: components of ribosomes, which are needed for the synthesis of new proteins.
Protective proteins—help cells and organisms to survive environmental stress.	Antibodies: fight viral and bacterial infections in vertebrate species. Heat shock proteins (chaperones): play a role in protein folding and thereby help cells cope with abrupt increases in temperature.

genes. Therefore, at the level of the genome, the percentages of the different protein categories are identical. However, at the cellular level, the relative abundance of certain protein categories is quite different. Liver cells make a large number of different enzymes that play a role in the metabolism of fats, proteins, and carbohydrates. By comparison, their level of structural and motor proteins is relatively small. In contrast, muscle cells

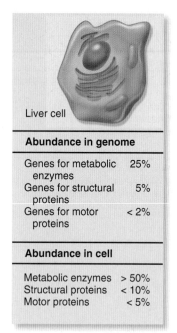

Liver cell			Skeletal muscle cell		
Abundance in genome			**Abundance in genome**		
Genes for metabolic enzymes	25%		Genes for metabolic enzymes	25%	
Genes for structural proteins	5%		Genes for structural proteins	5%	
Genes for motor proteins	< 2%		Genes for motor proteins	< 2%	
Abundance in cell			**Abundance in cell**		
Metabolic enzymes	> 50%		Metabolic enzymes	< 10%	
Structural proteins	< 10%		Structural proteins	20–30%	
Motor proteins	< 5%		Motor proteins	25–40%	

Figure 21.9 A comparison of the proteomes in human liver and skeletal muscle cells. Because all cells of the human body carry the same genome, the percentages of proteins that are encoded in the genome are the same in each cell type. However, the relative amounts of proteins that are made in different cell types can be vastly different, as is the case between liver and skeletal muscle cells.

Concept check: What genetic process explains the differences in protein abundance in liver cells versus muscle cells?

have fairly low levels of enzymes but make a high percentage of structural and motor proteins. These differences in protein composition between liver and muscle cells are largely due to differential gene regulation.

The Number of Different Proteins in a Species' Proteome Is Larger Than the Number of Genes in Its Genome

From the sequencing and analysis of genomes, researchers can identify all or nearly all of the genes that a given species has. For example, the human genome is predicted to contain between 20,000 and 25,000 different genes that encode proteins. Even so, humans can make many more than 25,000 different types of proteins. How is this possible? The larger size of the proteome relative to the genome is primarily due to two types of cellular processes, as described next.

Alternative Splicing Changes in pre-mRNA structure may ultimately affect the resulting amino acid sequence of a protein. The most important alteration that commonly occurs in eukaryotic species is **alternative splicing**, which is also described in Chapter 13. For many genes, a single pre-mRNA can be spliced in more than one way, resulting in the creation of two or more different proteins (**Figure 21.10a**). The splicing is often cell specific or may be related to environmental conditions. Alternative

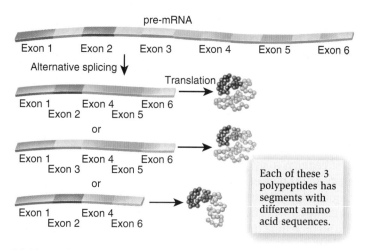

Each of these 3 polypeptides has segments with different amino acid sequences.

(a) Alternative splicing

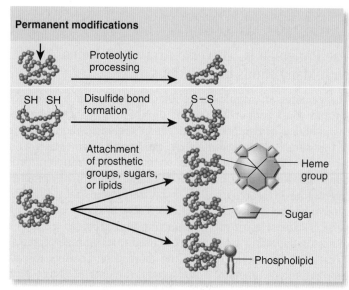

Permanent modifications

Proteolytic processing

Disulfide bond formation

Attachment of prosthetic groups, sugars, or lipids — Heme group — Sugar — Phospholipid

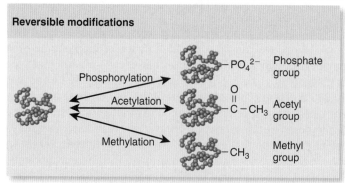

Reversible modifications

Phosphorylation — PO_4^{2-} Phosphate group

Acetylation — $\overset{O}{\overset{\|}{C}} - CH_3$ Acetyl group

Methylation — CH_3 Methyl group

(b) Post-translational covalent modification

Figure 21.10 Cellular mechanisms that increase protein diversity. (a) Following alternative splicing, the pattern of exons in the resulting mature mRNA can be different, creating multiple types of transcripts from the same gene. (b) In post-translational covalent modification, after a protein is made, it can be modified in a variety of ways, some of which are permanent and some reversible.

Concept check: Think back to the Cell unit. What is the advantage of reversible post-translational covalent modifications?

splicing is widespread, particularly among more complex eukaryotes (refer back to Table 13.1). It can lead to the production of several or perhaps dozens of different polypeptide sequences from the same pre-mRNA. This greatly increases the number of proteins in a species' proteome, while minimizing the size of the genome.

Post-translational Covalent Modification   A second process that greatly diversifies the composition of a proteome is the phenomenon of **post-translational covalent modification**, the modification of the structure of a protein after its translation (**Figure 21.10b**). Such modifications can be permanent or reversible. Permanent modifications are often involved with the assembly and construction of functional proteins. These alterations include proteolytic processing (the cleavage of a polypeptide to a smaller unit), disulfide bond formation, and the attachment of prosthetic groups, sugars, or lipids. In Chapter 6, we also considered the attachment of ubiquitin to a protein, which targets it for degradation. By comparison, reversible modifications, such as phosphorylation, acetylation, and methylation, often transiently affect the function of a protein (Figure 21.10b). Molecules are covalently attached and later removed by cellular enzymes. Because a given type of protein may be subjected to several different types of modifications, this can greatly increase the forms of a particular protein that are found in a cell at any given time.

21.4   Bioinformatics

In the previous sections, we have learned that the number of genes in a genome and the number of proteins that are made by a given cell type are extremely large. In the 1960s and 1970s, when the tools of molecular biology first became available, researchers tended to focus on the study of just one or a few genes and proteins at a time. While this is a useful approach, scientists came to realize that certain properties of life arise by complex interactions involving the expression of many genes and the functioning of many different proteins. Such an awareness challenged researchers to invent new tools to study many genes and proteins at the same time. These tools involved experimental procedures that allowed researchers to simultaneously investigate the various parts of a biological system. Studying such complex interactions is called **systems biology**. To analyze and manage the huge amounts of data produced by these studies, researchers turned to the use of computers.

As a very general definition, **bioinformatics** describes the use of computers, mathematical tools, and statistical techniques to record, store, and analyze biological information. We often think of bioinformatics in the context of examining genetic data, such as DNA sequences. Even so, bioinformatics can also be applied to information from various sources, such as patient statistics and scientific literature. This rapidly developing branch of biology is highly interdisciplinary, incorporating principles from mathematics, statistics, information science, chemistry, and physics.

Why do we need bioinformatics? Simply put, the main issues are size and speed. Earlier in this chapter, we learned

that the human genome has been sequenced and that it is approximately 3.2 billion base pairs long. A single person, or even a group of talented mathematicians, cannot, in a reasonable length of time, analyze such an enormous amount of data. Instead, the data are put into computers, and then scientists devise computational procedures to study and evaluate it.

In this section, we will consider the branch of bioinformatics that focuses on using molecular information to study biology. This area, also called **computational molecular biology**, uses computers to characterize the molecular components of living things. Molecular genetic data, which comes in the form of DNA, RNA, or protein sequences, are particularly amenable to computer analysis. In this section, we will first survey the fundamental concepts that underlie the analysis of genetic sequences. We will then consider how these methods are used to provide knowledge about how biology works at the molecular level.

Sequence Files Are Stored and Analyzed by Computers

The first steps in bioinformatics are to collect and store data in a computer. As an example, let's consider a gene sequence as a type of data. The gene sequence must first be determined experimentally using the technique of DNA sequencing. After the sequence is obtained, the next step is to put that data into a file on a computer. Typically, genetic sequence data are entered into a computer file by laboratory instruments that can read experimental data—such as data from a DNA-sequencing experiment—and enter the sequence directly into a computer.

Genetic sequence data in a computer data file can then be investigated in many different ways, corresponding to the many questions a researcher might ask about the sequence and its functional significance, including the following:

1. Does a sequence contain a gene?
2. Does a gene sequence contain a mutation that might cause a disease?
3. Where are functional sequences, such as promoters, regulatory sites, and splice sites, located within a particular gene?
4. From the sequence of a structural gene, what is the amino acid sequence of the polypeptide encoded by that gene?
5. Is there an evolutionary relationship between two or more genetic sequences?

To answer these and many other questions, computer programs have been written to analyze genetic sequences in particular ways. As an example, let's consider a computer program aimed at translating a DNA sequence into an amino acid sequence. **Figure 21.11** shows a short computer data file of a DNA sequence that is presumed to be part of the coding sequence of a structural gene. In this figure, only the coding strand of DNA is shown. A computer program can analyze this sequence and print out the possible amino acid sequences that this DNA sequence would encode. The program relies on the genetic code (refer back to Table 12.1). In the example shown in Figure 21.11, the computer program shows the results for all three possible reading frames, beginning at nucleotide 1, 2, or 3, respectively. In a newly obtained DNA sequence, a researcher would not know the proper reading frame—the series of codons read in groups of three, which starts with the start codon. Therefore, the computer program provides all three. If you look at the results, reading frames 1 and 2 include several stop codons, whereas reading frame 3 does not. From these results, reading frame 3 is likely to be the correct one. Also, for a new DNA sequence, a researcher may not know which DNA strand is the coding strand. Therefore, the sequence of the other DNA strand, which is not shown in this figure, would also be analyzed by this computer program.

The Scientific Community Has Collected Computer Data Files and Stored Them in Large Computer Databases

Over the past several decades, the amount of genetic information generated by researchers and clinicians has become enormous. The Human Genome Project alone has produced more data than any other undertaking in the history of biology. With these advances, scientists have realized that another critical use of computers is to store the staggering amount of data produced from genetic research.

When a large amount of data is collected, stored in a single location, and organized for rapid search and retrieval, this collection is called a **database**. The files within databases are often annotated, which means they contain a concise description of each gene sequence, the name of the organism from which the sequence was obtained, and the function of the encoded protein, if it is known. The file may also provide a published reference that contains the sequence.

The research community has collected genetic information from thousands of research laboratories and created several large databases. **Table 21.4** describes examples of the major genetic databases in use worldwide, all of which can be accessed online. These databases enable researchers to access and compare genetic sequences that are obtained by many laboratories. Later in this chapter, we will learn how researchers can use databases to analyze genetic sequences.

Many programs are freely available over the Internet to utilize the information within databases. For example, the National Center for Biotechnology Information (NCBI), which is a part of the U.S. National Institutes of Health, manages a website called "Tools for Data Mining," where anyone can run various types of programs that are used to analyze genetic sequences (www.ncbi.nlm.nih.gov/Tools). Like conventional mining, in which a precious mineral is extracted from a large area of land, **data mining** is the extraction of useful information and often previously unknown relationships from sequence files and large databases.

Computer Programs Can Identify Homologous Sequences

Let's now turn our attention to genes that are evolutionarily related. Organisms that are closely related evolutionarily tend to have genes with similar DNA sequences. As an example, let's consider the gene that encodes β-globin. As discussed

Computer DNA sequence file

```
5' GTGTCCACGC  GGTCCTGGAA  AACCCAGGCT  TGGGCAGGAA
   ACTCTCTGAC  TTTGGACAGG  AAACAAGCTA  TATTGAAGAC
   AACTGCAATC  AAAATGGTGC  CATATCACTG  ATCTTCTCAC
   TCAAAGAAGA  AGTTGGTGCA  TTGGCCAAAG  TATTGCGCTT
   ATTTGAGGAG  AATGATGTAA  ACCTGACCCA  CATTGAATCT
   AGACCTTCTC  GTTTAAAGAA  AGATGAGTAT  GAATTTTTCA
   CCCATTTGGA  TAAACGTAGC  CTGCCTGCTC  TGACAAACAT
   CATCAAGATC  TTGAGGCATG  ACATTGGTGC  CACTGTCCAT
   GAGCTTTCAC  GAGATAAGAA  GAAAGACACA  GTGCCCTGGT
   TTCCCAAG 3'
```

Run a computer program that translates this DNA sequence into an amino acid sequence in all 3 reading frames.

Possible amino acid sequences

5' → 3' Frame 1

Val Ser Thr Arg Ser Trp Lys Thr Gln Ala Trp Ala Gly Asn Ser Leu Thr Leu Asp Arg Lys Gln Ala Ile Leu Lys Thr Thr Ala Ile Lys Met Val Pro Tyr His **STOP** Ser Ser His Ser Lys Lys Lys Leu Val His Trp Pro Lys Tyr Cys Ala Tyr Leu Arg Arg Met Met **STOP** Thr **STOP** Pro Thr Leu Asn Leu Asp Leu Leu Val **STOP** Arg Lys Met Ser Met Asn Phe Ser Pro Ile Trp Ile Asn Val Ala Cys Leu Leu **STOP** Gln Thr Ser Ser Arg Ser **STOP** Gly Met Thr Leu Val Pro Leu Ser Met Ser Phe His Glu Ile Arg Arg Lys Thr Gln Cys Pro Gly Ser Gln

5' → 3' Frame 2

Cys Pro Arg Gly Pro Gly Lys Pro Arg Leu Gly Gln Glu Thr Leu **STOP** Leu Trp Thr Gly Asn Lys Leu Tyr **STOP** Arg Gln Leu Gln Ser Lys Trp Cys His Ile Thr Asp Leu Leu Thr Gln Arg Arg Ser Trp Cys Ile Gly Gln Ser Ile Ala Leu Ile **STOP** Gly Glu **STOP** Cys Lys Pro Asp Pro His **STOP** Ile **STOP** Thr Phe Ser Phe Lys Glu Arg **STOP** Val **STOP** Ile Phe His Pro Phe Gly **STOP** Thr **STOP** Pro Ala Cys Ser Asp Lys His His Gln Asp Leu Glu Ala **STOP** His Trp Cys His Cys Pro **STOP** Ala Phe Thr Arg **STOP** Glu Glu Arg His Ser Ala Leu Val Pro Lys

5' → 3' Frame 3

Val His Ala Val Leu Glu Asn Pro Gly Leu Gly Arg Lys Leu Ser Asp Phe Gly Gln Glu Thr Ser Tyr Ile Glu Asp Asn Cys Asn Gln Asn Gly Ala Ile Ser Leu Ile Phe Ser Leu Lys Glu Glu Val Gly Ala Leu Ala Lys Val Leu Arg Leu Phe Glu Glu Asn Asp Val Asn Leu Thr His Ile Glu Ser Arg Pro Ser Arg Leu Lys Lys Asp Glu Tyr Glu Phe Phe Thr His Leu Asp Lys Arg Ser Leu Pro Ala Leu Thr Asn Ile Ile Lys Ile Leu Arg His Asp Ile Gly Ala Thr Val His Glu Leu Ser Arg Asp Lys Lys Lys Asp Thr Val Pro Trp Phe Pro

Figure 21.11 **The use of a computer program to translate a DNA sequence into an amino acid sequence.** The top part of this figure shows the sequence of a segment of the coding strand of a structural gene (artificially divided into groups of 10 nucleotide bases for ease of reading). A computer program translates the DNA sequence into an amino acid sequence based on the genetic code. The program produces three different amino acid sequences, as shown at the bottom of the figure. In this example, reading frame 3 is likely to be the correct reading frame because it does not contain any stop codons.

Concept check: Why is it helpful to use a computer program to translate a genetic sequence rather than doing it by hand?

Table 21.4	Examples of Major Computer Databases
Nucleotide sequence	DNA sequence data are collected into three internationally collaborating databases: GenBank (a U.S. database), EMBL (European Molecular Biology Laboratory Nucleotide Sequence Database), and DDBJ (DNA Data Bank of Japan). These databases receive sequence and sequence annotation data from genome projects, sequencing centers, individual scientists, and patent offices. New and updated entries are exchanged daily.
Amino acid sequence	Protein sequence data are collected into a few international databases, including Swiss-Prot (Swiss protein database), PIR (Protein Information Resource), TrEMBL (translated sequences from the EMBL database), and Genpept (translated peptide sequences from the GenBank database).
Three-dimensional structure	PDB (Protein Data Bank) collects the three-dimensional structures of biological macromolecules with an emphasis on protein structure. These are primarily structures that have been determined by X-ray crystallography and nuclear magnetic resonance (NMR), but some models are included in the database.

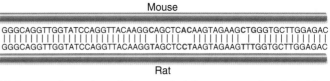

Mouse

GGGCAGGTTGGTATCCAGGTTACAAGGCAGCTCACAAGTAGAAGCTGGGTGCTTGGAGAC
GGGCAGGTTGGTATCCAGGTTACAAGGTAGCTCCTAAGTAGAAGTTTGGTGCTTGGAGAC

Rat

(a) A comparison of one DNA strand of the mouse and rat β-globin genes

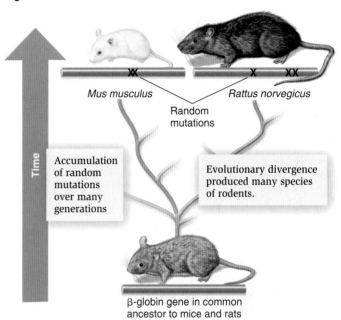

(b) The formation of homologous β-globin genes during evolution of mice and rats

Figure 21.12 Structure and formation of the homologous β-globin genes in mice and rats. **(a)** A comparison of a short region of the gene that encodes β-globin in laboratory mice (*Mus musculus*) and rats (*Rattus norvegicus*). Only one DNA strand is shown. Bases that are identical between the two sequences are connected by a vertical line. **(b)** The formation of these homologous β-globin genes during evolution. An ancestral β-globin gene was found in a rodent species that was a common ancestor to both mice and rats. This ancestral species later diverged into different species, which gave rise to modern rodent species, such as mice and rats. During this process, the β-globin genes accumulated different random mutations, resulting in DNA sequences that are slightly different from each other.

Concept check: *Is it possible for orthologs from two different species to have exactly the same DNA sequence? Explain.*

earlier, β-globin is a polypeptide found in hemoglobin, which carries oxygen in red blood cells. The β-globin gene is found in humans and other vertebrates.

Figure 21.12a compares a short region of this gene from the laboratory mouse (*Mus musculus*) and laboratory rat (*Rattus norvegicus*). As you can see, the gene sequences are similar but not identical. In this 60-nucleotide sequence, five differences are observed. The reason for the sequence similarity is that the genes are derived from the same ancestral gene. This idea is shown schematically in Figure 21.12b. An ancestral gene was found in a rodent species that was a common ancestor to both mice and rats. During evolution, this ancestral species diverged into different species, which eventually gave rise to several modern rodent species, including mice and rats. Following divergence, the β-globin genes accumulated distinct mutations that produced somewhat different base sequences for this gene. Therefore, in mice and rats, the β-globin genes have homologous sequences—sequences that are similar because they are derived from the same ancestral gene, but not identical because each species has accumulated a few different random mutations. Homologous genes in different species are also called orthologous genes or **orthologs**. Analyzing genes that are homologous to each other helps biologists understand the evolutionary relationships among modern species, a topic that we will consider in more detail in Units IV and V.

How do researchers, with the aid of computers, determine if two genes are homologous to each other? To evaluate the similarity between two sequences, a matrix can be constructed. Figure 21.13 illustrates the use of a simplified dot matrix to evaluate two sequences. In Figure 21.13a, the word BIOLOGY is compared with itself. Each point in the grid corresponds to one position of each sequence. The matrix allows all such pairs to

be compared simultaneously. Dots are placed where the same letter occurs at the two corresponding positions. Sequences that are alike produce a diagonal line on the matrix. Figure 21.13b compares two similar but different sequences: BIOLOGY and ECOLOGY. This comparison produces only a partial diagonal line. Overall, the key observation is that regions of similarity are distinguished by the occurrence of many dots along a diagonal line within the matrix. This same concept holds true when homologous gene sequences are compared with each other.

To relate orthologous genes in different species, researchers must compare relatively long DNA sequences. For such long sequences, a dot matrix approach is not adequate. Instead, dynamic computer programming methods are used to identify

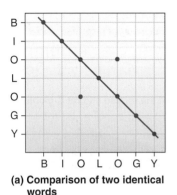
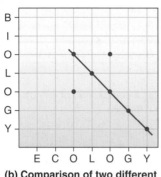

(a) Comparison of two identical words

(b) Comparison of two different words

Figure 21.13 **The use of a simple dot matrix.** In these comparisons, a diagonal line indicates sequence similarity. **(a)** The word BIOLOGY is compared with itself. Dots are placed where the same letter occurs at the two corresponding positions. Notice the diagonal line that is formed. **(b)** Two similar but different sequences, BIOLOGY and ECOLOGY, are compared with each other. Notice that only a partial line is formed by this comparison.

similarities between genetic sequences. This approach was first proposed by Saul Needleman and Christian Wunsch in 1970. Dynamic programming methods are theoretically similar to a dot matrix, but they involve mathematical operations that are beyond the scope of this textbook. In their original work, Needleman and Wunsch demonstrated that whale myoglobin and human β-globin genes have similar sequences.

A Database Can Be Searched to Identify Similar Sequences and Thereby Infer Homology and Gene Function

Why is it useful to identify homology between different genes? Because they are derived from the same ancestral gene, homologous genes usually carry out similar or identical functions. In many cases, the first way to identify the function of a newly determined gene sequence is to find a homologous gene whose function is already known. An example is the gene that is altered in cystic fibrosis patients. After this gene was identified in humans, bioinformatic methods revealed that it is homologous to several genes found in other species. A few of the homologous genes were already known to encode proteins that function in the transport of ions and small molecules across the plasma membrane. This observation provided an important clue that cystic fibrosis involves a defect in membrane transport.

The ability of computer programs to identify homology between genetic sequences provides a powerful tool for predicting the function of genetic sequences. In 1990, Stephen Altschul, David Lipman, and their colleagues developed a program called **BLAST** (for basic local alignment search tool). The BLAST program has been described by many biologists as the single most important tool in computational molecular biology. This computer program can start with a particular genetic sequence—either a nucleotide or an amino acid sequence—and then locate homologous sequences within a large database.

As an example of how the BLAST program works, let's consider the human enzyme phenylalanine hydroxylase, which functions in the metabolism of phenylalanine, an amino acid. Recessive mutations in the gene that encodes this enzyme are responsible for the disease called phenylketonuria (PKU). The computational experiment shown in **Table 21.5** started with the amino acid sequence of this protein and used the BLAST program to search the Swiss-Prot database, which contains hundreds of thousands of different protein sequences. The BLAST program can determine which sequences in the Swiss-Prot database are the closest matches to the amino acid sequence of human phenylalanine hydroxylase. Table 21.5 shows some of the results, which includes 10 of the matches to human phenylalanine hydroxylase that were identified by the program. Because this enzyme is found in nearly all eukaryotic species, the program identified phenylalanine hydroxylase from many different species. The column to the right of the match number shows the percentage of amino acids that are identical between the species indicated and the human sequence. Because the human phenylalanine hydroxylase sequence is already in the Swiss-Prot database, the closest match of human phenylalanine hydroxylase is to itself. The next nine sequences are in order of similarity. The next most similar sequence is from the orangutan, a close relative of humans. This is followed by two mammals, the mouse and rat, and then five vertebrates that

Table 21.5		Results from a BLAST Program Comparing Human Phenylalanine Hydroxylase with Database Sequences	
Match	Percentage of identical* amino acids	Species	Function of sequence†
1	100	Human (*Homo sapiens*)	Phenylalanine hydroxylase
2	99	Orangutan (*Pongo pygmaeus*)	Phenylalanine hydroxylase
3	95	Mouse (*Mus musculus*)	Phenylalanine hydroxylase
4	95	Rat (*Rattus norvegicus*)	Phenylalanine hydroxylase
5	89	Chicken (*Gallus gallus*)	Phenylalanine hydroxylase
6	82	Pipid frog (*Xenopus tropicalis*)	Phenylalanine hydroxylase
7	82	Green pufferfish (*Tetraodon nigroviridis*)	Phenylalanine hydroxylase
8	82	Zebrafish (*Danio rerio*)	Phenylalanine hydroxylase
9	80	Japanese pufferfish (*Takifugu rubripes*)	Phenylalanine hydroxylase
10	75	Fruit fly (*Drosophila melanogaster*)	Phenylalanine hydroxylase

*The number indicates the percentage of amino acids that are identical with the amino acid sequence of human phenylalanine hydroxylase. Note: These matches were randomly selected from a long list of matches.

†In some cases, the function of the sequence was determined by biochemical assay. In other cases, the function was inferred due to the high degree of sequence similarity with other species.

are not mammals. The 10th best match is from *Drosophila*, an invertebrate.

As you may have noticed, the order of the matches follows the evolutionary relatedness of the various species to humans. The similarity between any two sequences is related to the time that has passed since they diverged from a common ancestor. Among the species listed in this table, humans are most similar to themselves, followed by the orangutan, other mammals, other vertebrates, and finally invertebrates.

Overall, Table 21.5 is an example of the remarkable computational abilities of current computer technology. In less than a minute, the amino acid sequence of human phenylalanine hydroxylase can be compared with hundreds of thousands of different sequences to yield the data shown in this table! The main power of the BLAST program is its use with newly identified sequences, in which a researcher does not know the function of a gene or an encoded protein. When the BLAST program identifies a match to a sequence whose function is already known, it is likely that the newly identified sequence has an identical or similar function.

Summary of Key Concepts

21.1 Bacterial and Archaeal Genomes

- The genome is the complete genetic makeup of a cell or organism.

- Prokaryotic genomes are typically a single circular chromosome that has a few million base pairs of DNA. Such genomes usually have a few thousand different genes. (Table 21.1)

- Venter, Smith, and colleagues used a whole-genome shotgun sequencing strategy to determine the sequence of a prokaryotic genome, that of *Haemophilus influenzae.* (Figure 21.1)

21.2 Eukaryotic Genomes

- The nuclear genomes of eukaryotic species are composed of sets of linear chromosomes with a total length of several million to billions of base pairs. They typically contain several thousand to tens of thousands of genes. (Table 21.2)

- Genome sizes vary among eukaryotic species. In many cases, this variation is due to the accumulation of noncoding regions of DNA, particularly repetitive DNA sequences. (Figures 21.2, 21.3)

- Much of the repetitive DNA is derived from transposable elements, segments of DNA that can move from one site to another through a process called transposition. (Figure 21.4)

- DNA sequences within transposable elements can move by two different molecular mechanisms. The enzyme transposase mediates the movement of DNA transposons by a cut-and-paste mechanism. Retroelements move to new sites in the genome via RNA intermediates. (Figures 21.5, 21.6)

- Gene duplication may occur by a misaligned crossover during meiosis. This is one mechanism that can create a gene family, two or more homologous genes in a species that have related functions. (Figures 21.7, 21.8)

- The Human Genome Project, an international effort to map and sequence the entire human genome, was completed in 2003.

21.3 Proteomes

- A proteome is the collection of proteins that a given cell or species makes.

- Proteins are often placed into broad categories based on their functions. These include metabolic enzymes, structural proteins, motor proteins, cell-signaling proteins, transport proteins, proteins involved with gene expression and regulation, and those involved with protection. (Table 21.3)

- Protein abundance can refer to the relative abundance of proteins encoded in the genome or produced in the cell. (Figure 21.9)

- Protein diversity can increase via mechanisms such as alternative splicing and post-translational covalent modifications. (Figure 21.10)

21.4 Bioinformatics

- Bioinformatics involves the use of computers, mathematical tools, and statistical techniques to record, store, and analyze biological information, particularly genetic data such as DNA and protein sequences.

- Genetic information is stored in data files that can be analyzed using computer programs. The research community has collected genetic information and created several large databases. (Figure 21.11, Table 21.4)

- Homologous genes are derived from the same ancestral gene and have accumulated random mutations that make their sequences slightly different. (Figure 21.12)

- A simple dot matrix illustrates the approach of identifying regions of similarity between two sequences. (Figure 21.13)

- Computer programs, such as BLAST, can identify homologous genes that are found in a database. (Table 21.5)

Assess and Discuss

Test Yourself

1. The entire collection of proteins produced by a cell or organism is
   a. a genome.   d. a gene family.
   b. bioinformatics.   e. a protein family.
   c. a proteome.

2. Important reasons for studying the genomes of prokaryotes include all of the following except
   a. it may provide information that helps us understand how prokaryotes infect other organisms.
   b. it may provide a basic understanding of cellular processes that allow us to determine eukaryotic cellular function.
   c. it may provide the means to understand evolutionary processes.
   d. it will reveal the approximate number of genes that an organism has in its genome.
   e. All of the above are important reasons.

3. The enzyme that allows short segments of DNA to move within a cell from one location in the genome to another is

a. transposase.

b. DNA polymerase.

c. protease.

d. restriction endonuclease.

e. DNA ligase.

4. A gene family includes

a. one specific gene found in several different species.

b. all of the genes on the same chromosome.

c. two or more homologous genes found within a single species.

d. genes that code for structural proteins.

e. both a and c.

5. Which of the following was <u>not</u> a goal of the Human Genome Project?

a. identify all human genes

b. sequence the entire human genome

c. address the legal and ethical implications resulting from the project

d. develop programs to manage the information gathered from the project

e. clone a human

6. Bioinformatics is

a. the analysis of DNA by molecular techniques.

b. the use of computers to analyze and store biological information.

c. a collection of gene sequences from a single individual.

d. cloning.

e. all of the above.

7. Using bioinformatics, evolutionary relationships among species can be characterized by identifying and analyzing

a. phenotypes of selected organisms.

b. homologous DNA sequences from different organisms.

c. fossils of ancestral species.

d. all of the above.

e. a and b only.

8. Repetitive sequences

a. are short DNA sequences that are found many times throughout the genome.

b. may be multiple copies of the same gene found in the genome.

c. are more common in eukaryotes.

d. all of the above

e. a and c only

9. The BLAST program is a tool for

a. inserting many DNA fragments into a cell at the same time.

b. translating a DNA sequence into an amino acid sequence.

c. identifying homology between a selected sequence and genetic sequences in large databases.

d. all of the above.

e. both b and c.

10. Let's suppose you used the BLAST program beginning with a DNA sequence from a *Drosophila* hexokinase gene. (Hexokinase is an enzyme involved with glucose metabolism.) Which of the following choices would you expect to be the closest match?

a. a *Drosophila* globin gene

b. a human hexokinase gene

c. a housefly hexokinase gene

d. an *Arabidopsis* hexokinase gene

e. an amoeba hexokinase gene

Conceptual Questions

1. Briefly describe whether or not each of the following could be appropriately described as a genome.

a. the *E. coli* chromosome

b. human chromosome 11

c. a complete set of 10 chromosomes in corn

d. a copy of the single-stranded RNA packaged into human immunodeficiency virus (HIV)

2. Describe two main reasons why the proteomes of eukaryotes species are usually much larger than their genomes.

3. Why is it useful to search a database to identify sequences that are homologous to a newly determined sequence?

Collaborative Questions

1. Compare and contrast the genomes of prokaryotic and eukaryotic organisms.

2. Below is a DNA sequence from one strand of a gene. Go to the NCBI website (www.ncbi.nlm.nih.gov/Tools) and run the BLAST program to determine which gene it is and in which species it is found.

```
gtgaaggctc  atggcaagaa  agtgctcggt  gcctttagtg
atggcctggc  tcacctggac  aacctcaagg  gcacctttgc
cacactgagt  gagctgcact  gtgacaagct  gcacgtggat
cctgagaact  tcagggtgag  tctatgggac  gcttgatgtt
ttctttcccc  ttctttttcta tggttaagtt  catgtcatag
gaaggggata  agtaacaggg  tacagtttag  aatgggaaac
agacgaatga  ttgcatcagt  gtggaagtct  caggatcgtt
ttagtttctt  ttatttgctg  ttcataacaa  ttgttttctt
ttgtttaatt  cttgctttct  ttttttttct  tctccgcaat
```

Online Resource

www.brookerbiology.com

Stay a step ahead in your studies with animations that bring concepts to life and practice tests to assess your understanding. Your instructor may also recommend the interactive ebook, individualized learning tools, and more.

BIOLOGY

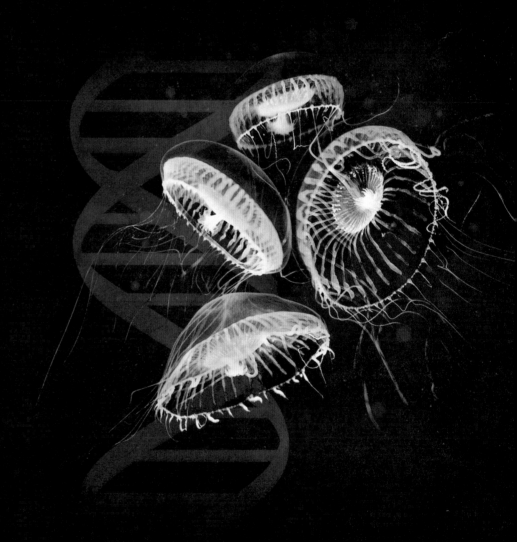

Periodic Table of the Elements

Legend:
- Metals (main-group)
- Metals (transition)
- Metals (inner transition)
- Metalloids
- Nonmetals

MAIN–GROUP ELEMENTS

TRANSITION ELEMENTS

1A (1)																	8A (18)
1 **H** 1.008	2A (2)											3A (13)	4A (14)	5A (15)	6A (16)	7A (17)	2 **He** 4.003
3 **Li** 6.941	4 **Be** 9.012											5 **B** 10.81	6 **C** 12.01	7 **N** 14.01	8 **O** 16.00	9 **F** 19.00	10 **Ne** 20.18
11 **Na** 22.99	12 **Mg** 24.31	3B (3)	4B (4)	5B (5)	6B (6)	7B (7)	8B (8)	(9)	(10)	1B (11)	2B (12)	13 **Al** 26.98	14 **Si** 28.09	15 **P** 30.97	16 **S** 32.07	17 **Cl** 35.45	18 **Ar** 39.95
19 **K** 39.10	20 **Ca** 40.08	21 **Sc** 44.96	22 **Ti** 47.88	23 **V** 50.94	24 **Cr** 52.00	25 **Mn** 54.94	26 **Fe** 55.85	27 **Co** 58.93	28 **Ni** 58.69	29 **Cu** 63.55	30 **Zn** 65.41	31 **Ga** 69.72	32 **Ge** 72.61	33 **As** 74.92	34 **Se** 78.96	35 **Br** 79.90	36 **Kr** 83.80
37 **Rb** 85.47	38 **Sr** 87.62	39 **Y** 88.91	40 **Zr** 91.22	41 **Nb** 92.91	42 **Mo** 95.94	43 **Tc** (98)	44 **Ru** 101.1	45 **Rh** 102.9	46 **Pd** 106.4	47 **Ag** 107.9	48 **Cd** 112.4	49 **In** 114.8	50 **Sn** 118.7	51 **Sb** 121.8	52 **Te** 127.6	53 **I** 126.9	54 **Xe** 131.3
55 **Cs** 132.9	56 **Ba** 137.3	57 **La** 138.9	72 **Hf** 178.5	73 **Ta** 180.9	74 **W** 183.9	75 **Re** 186.2	76 **Os** 190.2	77 **Ir** 192.2	78 **Pt** 195.1	79 **Au** 197.0	80 **Hg** 200.6	81 **Tl** 204.4	82 **Pb** 207.2	83 **Bi** 209.0	84 **Po** (209)	85 **At** (210)	86 **Rn** (222)
87 **Fr** (223)	88 **Ra** (226)	89 **Ac** (227)	104 **Rf** (263)	105 **Db** (262)	106 **Sg** (266)	107 **Bh** (267)	108 **Hs** (277)	109 **Mt** (268)	110 **Ds** (281)	111 **Rg** (272)	112 **Uub** (285)	113 **Uut** (?)	114 **Uuq** (291?)	115 **Uup** (288)	116 **Uuh** (289?)	117 **Uus** (291)	118 **Uuo** (?)

INNER TRANSITION ELEMENTS

6 Lanthanides	58 **Ce** 140.1	59 **Pr** 140.9	60 **Nd** 144.2	61 **Pm** (145)	62 **Sm** 150.4	63 **Eu** 152.0	64 **Gd** 157.3	65 **Tb** 158.9	66 **Dy** 162.5	67 **Ho** 164.9	68 **Er** 167.3	69 **Tm** 168.9	70 **Yb** 173.0	71 **Lu** 175.0
7 Actinides	90 **Th** 232.0	91 **Pa** (231)	92 **U** 238.0	93 **Np** (237)	94 **Pu** (242)	95 **Am** (243)	96 **Cm** (247)	97 **Bk** (247)	98 **Cf** (251)	99 **Es** (252)	100 **Fm** (257)	101 **Md** (258)	102 **No** (259)	103 **Lr** (260)

The complete Periodic Table of the Elements. Group numbers are different in some cases from those presented in Figure 2.5, because of the inclusion of transition elements. In some cases, the average atomic mass has been rounded to one or two decimal places, and in others only an estimate is given in parentheses due to the short-lived nature or rarity of those elements. The symbols and names of elements 112–118 are temporary until the chemical characteristics of these elements become better defined. Element 117 is currently not confirmed as a true element, and little is known about element 118. The International Union of Pure and Applied Chemistry (IUPAC) has recently proposed adopting the name copernicium (Cp) for element 112 in honor of scientist and astronomer Nicolaus Copernicus.

APPENDIX B

Answer Key

Answers to Collaborative Questions can be found on the website.

Chapter 1

Concept Checks

Figure 1.4 It benefits humans in many different ways. Discoveries in biology are important in the fields of medicine, research, agriculture, biotechnology, and many other disciplines. Most of the medicines we take were developed by biologists.

Figure 1.6 It would be at the population level.

Figure 1.8 In monkeys, the tail has been modified to grasp onto things, such as tree branches. In skunks, the tail is modified with a bright stripe; the tail can stick up and act as a warning signal to potential predators. In cattle, the tail has long hairs and is used to swat insects. Many more examples are possible.

Figure 1.9 Natural selection is the process that causes evolution to happen.

Figure 1.11 A tree of life suggests that all living organisms evolved from a single ancestor by vertical evolution with mutation. A web of life assumes that both vertical evolution with mutation and horizontal gene transfer were important mechanisms in the evolution of new species.

Figure 1.13 Taxonomy helps us to appreciate the unity and diversity of life. Organisms that are closely related evolutionarily are placed in smaller groups.

Figure 1.14 The genome stores the information to make an organism's proteins. In and of itself, the genome is merely DNA. The traits of cells and organisms are largely determined by the structures and functions of the hundreds or thousands of different proteins they make.

Figure 1.17 Discovery-based science does not require a preconceived hypothesis in order to carry out an experiment.

Figure 1.18 A researcher can compare the results in the experimental group and control group to determine if a single variable is causing a particular outcome in the experimental group.

Figure 1.19 After the *CF* gene was identified by discovery-based science, researchers realized that the *CF* gene was similar to other genes that encoded proteins that were already known to be transporters. This provided an important clue that the *CF* gene also encodes a transporter protein.

Feature Investigation Questions

1. In discovery-based science, a researcher does not need to have a preconceived hypothesis. Experimentation is conducted in the hope that it may have practical applications or may provide new information that will lead to a hypothesis. By comparison, hypothesis testing occurs when a researcher forms a hypothesis that makes certain predictions. Experiments are conducted to see if those predictions are correct. In this way, the hypothesis may be accepted or rejected.

2. This strategy may be described as a five-stage process:
   1. Observations are made regarding natural phenomena.
   2. These observations lead to a hypothesis that tries to explain the phenomena. A useful hypothesis is one that is testable because it makes specific predictions.
   3. Experimentation is conducted to determine if the predictions are correct.
   4. The data from the experiment are analyzed.
   5. The hypothesis is accepted or rejected.

3. In an ideal experiment, the control and experimental groups differ by only one factor. Biologists apply statistical analyses to their data to determine if the control and experimental groups are likely to be different from each other because of the single variable that is different between the two groups. This provides an objective way to accept or reject a hypothesis.

Test Yourself

1. d 2. a 3. c 4. c 5. d 6. b 7. d 8. d 9. a 10. b

Conceptual Questions

1. Cells and organization—All living organisms consist of cells; organisms maintain an internal order that is separated from the environment.
   - Energy use and metabolism—All living organisms acquire energy from the environment and use that energy to maintain their internal order. An organism's chemical reactions are collectively known as metabolism.
   - Response to environmental changes—Living organisms respond to environmental changes. These responses are adaptations.
   - Regulation and homeostasis—Living organisms maintain relatively stable internal conditions, homeostasis.
   - Growth and development—Growth produces more or larger cells; development produces organisms with a defined set of characteristics.
   - Reproduction—To sustain life, organisms must produce others like themselves; the genetic material maintains continuity over the generations.
   - Biological evolution—Populations of organisms change over the course of many generations.

2. The unity among different species occurs because modern species have evolved from a group of related ancestors. Some of the traits in those ancestors are also found in modern species and thereby unites them. The diversity is due to the variety of environments on the Earth. Each species has evolved to occupy its own unique environment. For every species, many traits are evolutionary adaptations to survival in a specific environment. For this reason, evolution also promotes diversity.

3. Domains and kingdoms are very diverse, being composed of hundreds of thousands or even millions of different species. The least-diverse groups are genera and species. A species is composed of just one type of organism, and a genus is typically composed of several or several dozen different species, though some genera are quite large.

Chapter 2

Concept Checks

Figure 2.4 An energy shell is a region outside the nucleus of an atom occupied by electrons of a given energy level. More than one orbital can be found within an electron shell. An orbital may be spherical or dumbbell-shaped and contains up to two electrons.

Figure 2.9 The octet rule states that atoms are stable when they have eight electrons in their outermost shell. Oxygen has six electrons in its outer shell. When two oxygen atoms share two pairs of electrons, each atom has eight electrons in its outer shell, at least part of the time.

Figure 2.11 Strand separation requires energy, because the DNA strands are held together by a large number of hydrogen bonds. Although each hydrogen bond is weak, collectively the vast number of such bonds in a molecule of DNA adds up to a considerable strength.

Figure 2.17 The oil would be in the center of the soap micelles.

Figure 2.19 Due to the colligative properties of water, the solutes in blood lower its freezing point. Human blood, for example, freezes at a temperature that is about half a degree Celsius lower than that of pure water.

Figure 2.21 It is 10^{-6} M. Because $[H^+][OH^-]$ always equals 10^{-14} M, if $[H^+]$ = 10^{-8} M (i.e., pH 8.0), then $[OH^-]$ must be 10^{-6} M.

Feature Investigation Questions

1. Scientists were aware that atoms contained charged particles. Many believed that the positive charges and mass were evenly distributed throughout the atom.

2. Rutherford was testing the hypothesis that atoms are composed of positive charges evenly distributed throughout the atom. Based on this model of the structure of the atom, alpha particles, which are positively charged nuclei of helium atoms, should be deflected as they pass through the foil, due to the presence of positive charges spread throughout the gold foil.

3. Instead of detecting slight deflection of most alpha particles as they passed through the gold foil, the majority, 98%, of the alpha particles passed directly through the gold foil without deflection. A much smaller percentage either deflected or bounced back from the gold foil. Rutherford suggested that since most of the alpha particles passed unimpeded through the gold foil, most of the volume of atoms is empty space. Rutherford also proposed that the bouncing back of some of the alpha particles indicated that most of the positively charged particles were concentrated in a compact area. These results were counter to the hypothesized model.

Test Yourself

1. b 2. b 3. b 4. d 5. e 6. e 7. e 8. c 9. e 10. b

Conceptual Questions

1. Covalent bonds are bonds in which atoms share electrons. A hydrogen bond is a weak polar covalent bond that forms when a hydrogen atom from one polar molecule becomes electrically attracted to an electronegative atom. A nonpolar covalent bond is one between two atoms of similar electronegativities, such as two carbon atoms. The van der Waal forces are temporary, weak bonds, resulting from random electrical forces generated by the changing distributions of electrons in the outer shells of nearby atoms. The strong attraction between two oppositely charged atoms forms an ionic bond.

2. Hydrophobic: "Water-fearing"—molecules that are not attracted to water molecules. Hydrophilic: "Water-loving"—generally, ions and molecules that contain polar covalent bonds will dissolve in water and are said to be hydrophilic.

3. Within limits, bonds within molecules can rotate and thereby change the shape of a molecule. This is important because it is the shape of a molecule that determines, in part, the ability of that molecule to interact with other molecules. Also, when two molecules do interact through such forces as hydrogen bonds, the shape of one or both molecules may change as a consequence. The change in shape is often part of the mechanism by which signals are sent within and between cells.

Chapter 3

Concept Checks

Figure 3.1 Due to the fact that he had earlier purified urea from urine and then formed urea crystals, he already knew what urea crystals looked like. As seen in this figure, they are quite distinctive looking. Therefore, when he reacted ammonia and cyanic acid and got a compound that formed crystals, the distinctive look of the crystals made him realize that he had synthesized urea.

Figure 3.6 One reason is that the binding of a molecule to an enzyme depends on the spatial arrangements of the atoms in that molecule. Enantiomers have different spatial relationships that are mirror images of each other. Therefore, one may bind very tightly to an enzyme while the other may not be recognized at all.

Figure 3.7 Recall from Figure 3.5 that the reverse of a dehydration reaction is called a hydrolysis reaction, in which a molecule of water is added to the molecule being broken down, resulting in the formation of monomers.

Figure 3.11 Hydrogenation is adding hydrogens to double-bonded carbon atoms, changing them from unsaturated to saturated. This causes them to be solid at room temperature.

Figure 3.12 The phospholipids would be oriented such that their polar regions dissolved in the water layer and the nonpolar regions dissolved in the oil. Thus, the phospholipids would form a layer at the interface between the water and oil.

Figure 3.15 71; one less than the number of amino acids in the polypeptide

Figure 3.19 If the primary structure of Protein 1 were altered in some way, this would, in turn, most likely alter the secondary and tertiary structures of Protein 1. Therefore, it is possible that the precise fit between Proteins 1 and 2 would be lost and that the two proteins would lose the ability to interact.

Figure 3.24 Yes. The opposite strand must be the mirror image of the first strand, because pairs can form only between A and T, and G and C. For instance, if a portion of the first strand is AATGCA, the opposite strand along that region would be TTACGT.

Feature Investigation Questions

1. Many scientists assumed that protein folding was directed by some cellular factor, meaning some other molecule in the cytoplasm, and therefore, protein folding could not occur spontaneously. Others assumed that protein folding was determined somehow by the ribosome, because this organelle is primarily responsible for synthesizing proteins.

2. Anfinsen was testing the hypothesis that the information necessary for determining the three-dimensional shape of a protein is contained within the protein itself. In other words, the chemical characteristics of the amino acids that make up a protein will determine the three-dimensional shape.

3. The urea disrupts hydrogen bonds and ionic interactions that are necessary for protein folding. The mercaptoethanol disrupted the S—S bonds that also form between certain amino acids of the same polypeptide chains. Both substances essentially allow the polypeptide chain to unfold, disrupting the three-dimensional shape. Anfinsen removed the urea and mercaptoethanol from the protein solution by size-exclusion chromatography. After removing the urea and mercaptoethanol, Anfinsen discovered that the protein refolded into its proper three-dimensional shape and became functional again. This was important because the solution contained only the protein and lacked any other cellular material that could possibly assist in protein folding. This demonstrated that the protein could refold into the functional conformation.

Test Yourself

1. b 2. b 3. e 4. b 5. c 6. b 7. b 8. d 9. b 10. b

Conceptual Questions

1. Isomers are two structures with an identical molecular formula but with different structures and arrangements of atoms within the molecule. There are two major types of isomers: structural and stereoisomers. Because many chemical reactions in biology depend upon the actions of enzymes, which are often highly specific for the spatial arrangement of atoms in a molecule, one isomer of a pair may have biological functions, and the other may not.

2. a. Carbohydrates—energy storage and structural support

   b. Lipids—energy storage and components of cellular membranes

   c. Proteins—many functions, including enzymes, defense, transport, structure, contraction

   d. Nucleic acids—information storage, gene expression

3. Saturated fatty acids are saturated with hydrogen and have only single (C—C) bonds, whereas unsaturated fatty acids have one or more double (C=C) bonds. The double bonds in unsaturated fatty acids alters their shape, resulting in a kink in the structure. Saturated fatty acids are unkinked and are better able to stack tightly together. Fats containing saturated fatty acids have a higher melting point than those containing mostly unsaturated fatty acids; consequently, saturated fats tend to be solids at room temperatures, and unsaturated fatty acids are usually liquids at room temperature.

Chapter 4

Concept Checks

Figure 4.1 You would use transmission electron microscopy. The other methods do not have good enough resolution.

Figure 4.3 The primary advantage is that it gives an image of the 3-D surface of a material.

Figure 4.6   They have different proteomes.

Figure 4.7   Centrioles: Not found in plant cells; their role is not entirely clear, but they are found in the centrosome, which is where microtubules are anchored.

Chloroplasts: Not found in animal cells; function in photosynthesis.

Cell wall: Not found in animal cells; important in cell shape.

Figure 4.12   Both dynein and microtubules are anchored in place. Using ATP as a source of energy, dynein tugs on microtubules. Because the microtubules are anchored, they bend in response to the force exerted by dynein.

Figure 4.15   The nuclear lamina organizes the nuclear envelope and also helps to organize/anchor the chromosomes. The nuclear matrix is inside the nucleus and helps to organize the chromosomes into chromosome territories.

Figure 4.18   The protein begins its synthesis in the cytosol and then is further synthesized into the ER. It travels via vesicles to the *cis-*, *medial-*, and *trans-*Golgi and then is secreted.

Figure 4.22   Of these three choices, membrane transport is probably the most important because it regulates which molecules can enter the cell and participate in metabolism and which products of metabolism are exported from the cell. Cell signaling may affect metabolism, but its overall effect is probably less important than membrane transport.

Figure 4.24   It increases the surface area where ATP synthesis takes place and thereby makes it possible to increase the amount of ATP synthesis.

Figure 4.27   Bacteria and mitochondria are similar in size; they both have circular chromosomes; they both divide by binary fission; and they both make ATP. Bacterial chromosomes are larger, and they make all of their cellular proteins. Mitochondria chromosomes are smaller, and they import most of their proteins from the cytosol.

Figure 4.29   The signal sequence of an ER protein is recognized by SRP, which halts translation. The emerging protein and its ribosome are then transferred to the ER membrane, where translation resumes.

Figure 4.31   If chaperone proteins were not found in the cytosol, the mitochondrial matrix protein would start to fold, which might prevent it from being able to pass through the channel in the outer and inner mitochondrial membrane. Normally, a protein is threaded through this channel in an unfolded state.

Feature Investigation Questions

1. In a pulse-chase experiment, radioactive material is provided to cells. This is referred to as the pulse, or single administration of the radioactive material to the cells. After a few minutes, a large amount of nonradioactive material is provided to the cells to remove or "chase away" any of the remaining radioactive material.

   The researchers were attempting to determine the movement of proteins through the different compartments of a cell. Radioactive amino acids were used to label the proteins and enable the researchers to visualize where the proteins were at different times.

2. Pancreatic cells produce large numbers of proteins that are secreted from the cell. The number and final location of the proteins would allow the researchers an ideal system for studying protein movement through the cell.

3. Using electron microscopy, the researchers found that the proteins, indicated by radioactivity, were first found in the endoplasmic reticulum of the cells. Later the radioactivity moved to the Golgi and then into vesicles near the plasma membrane.

   The researchers were able to conclude that secreted proteins moved through several cellular compartments before they were secreted from the cell. Also, the movement of proteins through these compartments was not random but followed a particular pathway: ER, Golgi, secretory vesicles, plasma membrane, and, finally, secreted.

Test Yourself

1. d   2. d   3. b   4. c   5. e   6. a   7. e   8. e   9. a It would go there first, because targeting to the ER occurs cotranslationally.   10. c It is true they carry out metabolism, but so do eukaryotic cells.

Conceptual Questions

1. There are a lot of possibilities. The interactions between a motor protein (dynein) and cytoskeletal filaments (microtubules) cause a flagellum to

bend. The interaction between v-snares and t-snares causes a vesicle to fuse with the correct target membrane.

2. If the motor is bound to a cargo and the motor can walk along a filament that is fixed in place, this will cause the movement of the cargo when the motor is activated. If the motor is fixed in place and the filament is free to move, this will cause the filament to move when the motor is activated. If both the motor and filament are fixed in place, the activation of the motor will cause the filament to bend.

3. The Golgi apparatus performs three overlapping functions: (1) processing of proteins and lipids, (2) protein sorting, and (3) secretion.

Chapter 5
Concept Checks

Figure 5.3   More double bonds and shorter fatty acyl tails make the membrane more fluid. Changing the cholesterol concentration can also affect fluidity, but that depends on the starting level of cholesterol. If cholesterol was at a level that maximized stability, increasing the cholesterol concentration would probably increase fluidity.

Figure 5.4   The low temperature prevents lateral diffusion of membrane proteins. Therefore, after fusion, all of the mouse proteins would stay on one side of the fused cell, and all of the human proteins would remain on the other.

Figure 5.6   In animal cells, the glycocalyx primarily plays a protective function. It protects proteins in the plasma membrane.

Figure 5.7   Probably not. The hydrophobic tails of both leaflets touch each other, so the heavy metal would probably show a single, thick dark line. Osmium tetroxide shows two parallel lines because it labels the polar head groups, which are separated by the hydrophobic interior of the membrane.

Figure 5.8   Lipids are transferred to the other leaflet of the ER via enzymes called flippases.

Figure 5.9   The most common way for a transmembrane segment to form is that it contains a stretch (about 20) of amino acids that mostly have hydrophobic (nonpolar) side chains.

Figure 5.12   Leucine would more readily cross a membrane because its side chain is nonpolar. The side chain of lysine is positively charged.

Figure 5.13   Although both of these molecules penetrate the bilayer fairly quickly, methanol has a polar —OH group and therefore crosses a bilayer more slowly than methane.

Figure 5.16   Water will move from outside to inside, from the hypotonic medium into the hypertonic medium.

Figure 5.18   Freshwater protists live in a hypotonic environment, which causes them to continually take in water. To avoid bursting, they use contractile vacuoles that regularly expel the water. Note that such protists lack a cell wall.

Figure 5.21   The purpose of gating is to regulate the function of channels.

Figure 5.25   The Na^+/K^+-ATPase could reach the point where the protein was covalently phosphorylated and Na^+ was released on the outside. At that stage, the reaction would stop, because it needs K^+ to proceed through the rest of the cycle.

Figure 5.26   The protein coat is needed for the membrane to bud from its site and form a vesicle.

Feature Investigation Questions

1. Most cells allow movement of water across the cell membrane by passive diffusion. However, it was noted that certain cell types had a much higher rate of water movement, indicating that something different was occurring in these cells.

2. The researchers identified water channels by characterizing proteins that are present in red blood cells and kidney cells but not other types of cells. Red blood cells and kidney cells have a faster rate of water movement across the membrane than other cell types. These cells are more likely to have water channels. By identifying proteins that are found in both of these types of cells but not in other cells, the researchers were identifying possible candidate proteins that function as water channels. In addition, CHIP28 had a structure that resembled other known channel proteins.

   Agre and his associates experimentally created multiple copies of the gene that produces the CHIP28 protein and then artificially transcribed the genes to produce many mRNAs. The mRNAs were injected into frog oocytes where they could be translated to make the CHIP28 proteins. After altering the frog oocytes by introducing the CHIP28 mRNAs, they compared the rate of water transport in the altered oocytes versus normal frog oocytes. This procedure allowed them to introduce the candidate protein to a cell type that normally does not have the protein present.

3. After artificially introducing the candidate protein into the frog oocytes, the researchers found that the experimental oocytes took up water at a much faster rate in a hypotonic solution as compared to the control oocytes. The results indicated that the presence of the CHIP28 protein did increase water transport into cells.

Test Yourself

1. c   2. c   3. b   4. d   5. b   6. e   7. d   8. e   9. e   10. c

Conceptual Questions

1. See Figure 5.1 for the type of drawing you should have made. The membrane is considered a mosaic of lipid, protein, and carbohydrate molecules. The membrane exhibits properties that resemble a fluid because lipids and proteins can move relative to each other within the membrane.

2. Integral membrane proteins can contain transmembrane segments that cross the membrane, or they may contain lipid anchors. Peripheral membrane proteins are noncovalently bound to integral membrane proteins or to the polar heads of phospholipids.

3. A solute would touch the tails of the phospholipids in the process of diffusion. For facilitated diffusion and active transport, it would avoid touching the tails because it would be moving through a protein. For exocytosis and endocytosis, the membrane vesicles fuse with the plasma membrane, and the solute never really crosses through a membrane.

Chapter 6

Concept Checks

Figure 6.2 The solution of dissolved Na^+ and Cl^- has more entropy. A salt crystal is very ordered, whereas the ions in solution are much more disordered.

Figure 6.3 The negative ΔG value tells that the direction will proceed from reactants to products. It does not tell us anything about the rate.

Figure 6.4 It speeds up the rate. When the activation energy is lower, it takes less time for reactants to reach a transition state where a chemical reaction can occur. It does not affect the direction of a reaction.

Figure 6.5 The activation energy is lowered during the second step when the substrates undergo induced fit.

Figure 6.6 At a substrate concentration of 0.5 mM, enzyme A would have a higher velocity. Enzyme A would be very near its V_{max}, whereas enzyme B would be well below its V_{max}.

Figure 6.11 The oxidized form is NAD^+.

Figure 6.12 The breakdown of ADP would have an adverse effect. Usually, ATP is made by the covalent attachment of pre-existing phosphate and ADP. If there was insufficient ADP, a cell would have to make more ADP to make ATP. This would take a lot of energy.

Figure 6.13 The metabolic pathway would not be controlled by feedback inhibition. This may result in an overaccumulation of the product of the pathway.

Figure 6.15 Protein degradation eliminates proteins that are worn out, misfolded, or no longer needed by the cell. Such proteins could interfere with normal cell function. In addition, the recycling of amino acids saves the cell energy.

Feature Investigation Questions

1. RNase P has both a protein and RNA subunit. To determine which subunit has catalytic function, it was necessary to purify them individually and then see which one is able to cleave ptRNA.

2. The experimental strategy was to incubate RNase P or subunits of RNase P with ptRNA and then run a gel to determine if ptRNA had been cleaved to a mature tRNA and a 5' fragment. The control without protein

was to determine if the RNA alone could catalyze the cleavage. The control without RNA was to determine if some other factor in the experiment (e.g., Mg^{2+} or protein) was able to cleave the ptRNA.

3. The critical results occurred when the researchers incubated the purified RNA subunit at high Mg^{2+} concentrations with the ptRNA. Under these conditions, the ptRNA was cleaved. These results indicate that the RNA subunit has catalytic activity. A high Mg^{2+} concentration is needed to keep it catalytically active in the absence of a protein subunit.

Test Yourself

1. d   2. e   3. b   4. d   5. a   6. c   7. b   8. c   9. e   10. a

Conceptual Questions

1. Exergonic reactions are spontaneous. They proceed in a particular direction. An exergonic reaction could be slow or fast. By comparison, an endergonic reaction is not spontaneous. It will not proceed in a particular direction unless free energy is supplied. An endergonic reaction can be fast or slow.

2. During feedback inhibition, the product of a metabolic pathway binds to an allosteric site on an enzyme that acts earlier in the pathway. The product inhibits this enzyme and thereby prevents the overaccumulation of the product.

3. Recycling of amino acids and nucleotides is important because it conserves a great deal of energy. Cells don't have to remake these building blocks, which would require a large amount of energy. Eukaryotes primarily use the proteasome to recycle proteins.

Chapter 7

Concept Checks

Figure 7.1 Most of the NADH is oxidized to make ATP during oxidative phosphorylation.

Figure 7.2 The first phase is named the energy investment phase because some ATP is used up. The second phase is called the cleavage phase because a 6-carbon molecule is broken down into two 3-carbon molecules. The energy liberation phase is so named because NADH and ATP are made.

Figure 7.3 The molecules that donate phosphates are 1,3-bisphosphoglycerate and phosphoenolpyruvate.

Figure 7.5 For each acetyl group that is oxidized, the main products are 2 CO_2, 3 NADH, 1 $FADH_2$, and 1 GTP.

Figure 7.7 It is called cytochrome oxidase because it removes electrons from (oxidizes) cytochrome c. Another possible name would be oxygen reductase because it reduces oxygen.

Figure 7.9 No. The role of the electron transport chain is to make an H^+ electrochemical gradient. It is the H^+ electrochemical gradient that drives ATP synthase. If the H^+ electrochemical is made another way, such as by bacteriorhodopsin, the ATP synthase still makes ATP.

Figure 7.10 The gamma subunit turns clockwise, when viewed from the intermembrane space. The β subunit in the back right is in conformation 3 and the one on the left is in conformation 1.

Figure 7.12 Tumors often become hypoxic and therefore have trouble making ATP via oxidative phosphorylation. Being able to carry out a higher level of glycolysis, which doesn't require oxygen, allows them to make ATP even if they're hypoxic.

Figure 7.13 The advantage is that the cell can use the same enzymes to metabolize different kinds of organic molecules. This saves the cell energy because it is costly to make a lot of different enzymes, which are composed of proteins.

Figure 7.16 Depending on the species, almost any part of a plant may contain anthocyanins. They are most common in fruits, vegetables, and flowers, but they may also be found in stems and even in leaves. For example, the red color found in many leaves in the autumn is due, in part, to anthocyanins.

Figure 7.17 Animals that eat this plant and ingest atropine become very sick and may die. Any animal that eats deadly nightshade and survives would be unlikely to eat it a second time.

Figure 7.19 The advantage of making streptomycin is that it kills other bacterial species in the soil that might compete with *S. griseus* for the same resources.

Feature Investigation Questions

1. The researchers attached an actin filament to the γ subunit of ATP synthase. The actin filament was fluorescently labeled so the researchers could determine if the actin filament moved when viewed under the fluorescence microscope.

2. When functioning in the hydrolysis of ATP, the actin filament was seen to rotate. The actin filament was attached to the γ subunit of ATP synthase. The rotational movement of the filament was the result of the rotational movement of the enzyme. In the control experiment, no ATP was added to stimulate enzyme activity. In the absence of ATP, no movement was observed.

3. No, the observation of counterclockwise rotation is the opposite of what would be expected inside the mitochondria. During the experiment, the enzyme was not functioning in ATP synthesis but instead was running backwards and hydrolyzing ATP.

Test Yourself

1. a 2. d 3. b 4. b 5. b 6. d 7. d 8. b 9. e 10. e

Conceptual Questions

1. The purpose of the electron transport chain is to pump H^+ across the inner mitochondrial membrane to establish a H^+ electrochemical gradient. When the H^+ flows back across the membrane through ATP synthase, ATP is synthesized.

2. The movement of H^+ through the c subunits causes the γ subunit to rotate. As it rotates, it sequentially alters the conformation of the subunits, where ATP is made. This causes: (1) ADP and P_i to bind with moderate affinity, (2) ADP and P_i to bind very tightly such that ATP is made, and (3) ATP to be released.

3. There are two main reasons. First, NADH can be toxic at high levels because it haphazardly donates electrons and may generate free radicals. Second, the oxidation of NADH to NAD^+ is necessary to keep glycolysis running so that ATP can be made.

Chapter 8

Concept Checks

Figure 8.1 Both heterotrophs and autotrophs carry out cellular respiration.

Figure 8.3 The Calvin cycle can occur in the dark as long as there is sufficient CO_2, ATP, and NADPH.

Figure 8.4 Gamma rays have higher energy than radio waves.

Figure 8.5 To drop down to a lower orbital at a lower energy level, an electron could release energy in the form of heat, release energy in the form of light, or transfer energy to another electron by resonance energy transfer.

Figure 8.7 By having different pigment molecules, plants can absorb a wider range of wavelengths of light.

Figure 8.8 ATP and NADPH are made in the stroma. O_2 is made in the thylakoid lumen.

Figure 8.9 Noncyclic electron flow produces equal amounts of ATP and NADPH. However, plants usually need more ATP than NADPH. Cyclic photophosphorylation allows plants to make just ATP and thereby increases the relative amount of ATP.

Figure 8.10 Because these two proteins are homologous, this means that the genes that encode them were derived from the same ancestral gene. Therefore, the amino acid sequences of these two proteins are expected to be very similar, though not identical to each other. Because the amino acid sequence of a protein determines its structure, two proteins with similar amino acid sequences would be expected to have similar structures.

Figure 8.12 The answer is five. It catalyzes the following electron transfers.

1. H_2O to tyrosine (Tyr).
2. Tyr to P680.
3. P680 to pheophytin (Pp).
4. Pp to Q_A.
5. Q_A to Q_B.

Figure 8.13 No. The enhancement effect occurs because the flashes activate both photosystem II and photosystem I. Light at 700 nm is needed to activate P700 in photosystem I.

Figure 8.14 An electron has its highest amount of energy just after it has been boosted by light in PSI.

Figure 8.15 NADPH reduces organic molecules and makes them more able to form C—C and C—H bonds.

Figure 8.18 The arrangement of cells in C_4 plants makes the level of CO_2 high and the level of O_2 low in the bundle sheath cells.

Figure 8.19 When there is plenty of moisture and it is not too hot, C_3 plants are more efficient. However, under hot and dry conditions, C_4 and CAM plants have the advantage because they lose less water and avoid photorespiration.

Feature Investigation Questions

1. The researchers were attempting to determine the biochemical pathway of the process of carbohydrate synthesis in plants. The researchers wanted to identify different molecules produced in plants over time to determine the steps of the biochemical pathway.

2. The purpose for using ^{14}C was to label the different carbon molecules produced during the biochemical pathway. The researchers could "follow" the carbon molecules from CO_2 that were incorporated into the organic molecules during photosynthesis. The radioactive isotope provided the researchers with a method of labeling the different molecules.

   The purpose of the experiment was to determine the steps in the biochemical pathway of photosynthesis. By examining samples from different times after the introduction of the labeled carbon source, the researchers would be able to determine which molecules were produced first and, thus, products of the earlier steps of the pathway versus products of later steps of the pathway.

   The researchers used two-dimensional paper chromatography to separate the different molecules from each other. Afterwards, the different molecules were identified by different chemical methods. The text describes the method of comparing two-dimensional paper chromatography results of unknown molecules to known molecules and identifying the unknown with the known molecule it matched.

3. The researchers were able to determine the biochemical process that plants use to incorporate CO_2 into organic molecules. The researchers were able to identify the biochemical steps and the molecules produced at these steps in what is now called the Calvin cycle.

Test Yourself

1. c 2. c 3. c 4. a 5. b 6. b 7. c 8. b 9. e 10. c

Conceptual Questions

1. The two stages of photosynthesis are the light reactions and the Calvin cycle. The key products of the light reactions are ATP, NADPH, and O_2. The key product of the Calvin cycle is carbohydrate. The initial product is G3P, which is used to make sugars and other organic molecules.

2. NADPH is used during the reduction phase of the Calvin cycle. It donates its electrons to 1,3 BPG.

3. After one pigment molecule absorbs energy, resonance energy transfer allows that energy to be transferred among many pigment molecules, eventually reaching the reaction center. If resonance energy transfer did not occur, the light energy would have to be absorbed directly by the pigment in the reaction center, which is either P680 or P700. In contrast, the light-harvesting complex is composed of many pigment molecules of different types (chlorophylls and carotenoids), which can absorb light at different wavelengths and transfer that energy to the reaction center. The light-harvesting complex makes it easier for plants to absorb light energy.

Chapter 9

Concept Checks

Figure 9.1 It is glucose.

Figure 9.2 Auxin causes cells to elongate. Therefore, cells on the nonilluminated side grow faster, causing the plant to bend toward the light.

Figure 9.3 Endocrine signals are more likely to exist for a longer period of time. This is necessary because endocrine signals called hormones travel relatively long distances to reach their target cells. Therefore, the hormone must exist long enough to reach its target cells.

Figure 9.4   The effect of a signaling molecule is to cause a cellular response. Most signaling molecules do not enter the cell. Therefore, to exert an effect, they must alter the conformation of a receptor protein, which, in turn, stimulates an intracellular signal transduction pathway that leads to a cellular response.

Figure 9.6   Phosphorylation of a protein via a kinase involves ATP hydrolysis, which is an exergonic reaction. The energy from this reaction usually alters the conformation of the phosphorylated protein and thereby influences its function. Phosphorylation is used to regulate protein function.

Figure 9.7   The α subunit has to hydrolyze its GTP to GDP. This changes the conformation of the α subunit so that it can reassociate with the β/γ subunits.

Figure 9.10   The GTP-bound form of Ras is active and promotes cell division. To turn the pathway off, Ras hydrolyzes GTP to GDP. If this cannot occur due to a mutation, the pathway will be continuously on, and uncontrolled cell division will result.

Figure 9.12   The signal transduction pathway begins with the G protein and ends with protein kinase A being activated. The cellular response involves the phosphorylation of target proteins. The phosphorylation of target proteins will change their function in some way, which is how the cell is responding.

Figure 9.13   Depending on the protein involved, phosphorylation can activate or inhibit protein function. Phosphorylation of phosphorylase kinase and glycogen phosphorylase activates their function, whereas it inhibits glycogen synthase.

Figure 9.14   Signal amplification allows a single signaling molecule to affect many proteins within a cell and thereby amplify a cellular response.

Figure 9.20   The initiator caspase is part of the death-inducing signaling complex. It is directly activated when a cell receives a death signal. The initiator caspase then activates the executioner caspases, which degrade various cellular proteins and thereby cause the destruction of the cell.

Feature Investigation Questions

1. Compared to control rats, those injected with prednisolone alone would be expected to have a decrease in the number of cells because it suppresses ACTH synthesis. Therefore, apoptosis would be higher. By comparison, prednisolone + ACTH would have a normal number of cells because the addition of ACTH would compensate for effects of prednisolone. ACTH alone would be expected to have a greater number of cells; apoptosis would be inhibited.

2. Yes, when injected with ACTH, prednisolone probably inhibited the ability of the rats to make their own ACTH. Even so, they were given ACTH by injection, so they didn't need to make their own ACTH to prevent apoptosis.

3. The lowest level of apoptosis would occur in the ACTH alone group, because they could make their own ACTH plus they were given ACTH. With such high levels of ACTH, they probably had the lowest level of apoptosis; it was already known that ACTH promotes cell division.

Test Yourself

1. d   2. c   3. d   4. e   5. a   6. d   7. e   8. e   9. e   10. b

Conceptual Questions

1. Cells need to respond to a changing environment, and cells need to communicate with each other.

2. In the first stage, a signaling molecule binds to a receptor, causing receptor activation. In the second stage, one type of signal is transduced or converted to a different signal inside the cell. In the third stage, the cell responds in some way to the signal, possibly by altering the activity of enzymes, structural proteins, or transcription factors. When the estrogen receptor is activated, the second stage, signal transduction, is not needed because the estrogen receptor is an intracellular receptor that directly activates the transcription of genes to elicit a cellular response.

3. If apoptosis did not occur, embryonic development would not occur properly, and adults would not maintain a correct number of cells. Also, cells that are worn out, infected by viruses or intracellular bacteria, or have the potential to cause cancer, would not be eliminated. In mammals, the immune system would not function properly because apoptosis is needed to eliminate B and T cells that are ineffective or potentially damaging to the body.

Chapter 10
Concept Checks

Figure 10.1   The four functions of the ECM in animals are strength, structural support, organization, and cell signaling.

Figure 10.2   The extension sequences of procollagen prevent fibers from forming intracellularly.

Figure 10.3   The proteins would become more linear, and the fiber would come apart.

Figure 10.4   GAGs are highly negatively charged molecules that tend to attract positively charged ions and water. Their high water content gives GAGs a gel-like character, which makes them difficult to compress.

Figure 10.5   Because the secondary cell wall is usually rigid, it prevents cell growth. If it were made too soon, it might prevent a cell from attaining its proper size.

Figure 10.7   Adherens junctions and desmosomes are cell-to-cell junctions, whereas hemidesomosomes and focal adhesions are cell-to-ECM junctions.

Figure 10.9   Tight junctions in your skin prevent harmful things like toxins and viruses from entering your body. They also prevent materials like nutrients from leaking out of your body.

Figure 10.10   As opposed to the results shown in Figure 10.10, the dye would be in the side of the cell layer facing the intestinal tract. You would see dye up to the tight junction on this side of the cells, but not on the side of the tight junction facing the blood.

Figure 10.13   Middle lamellae are similar to anchoring junctions and desmosomes in that they all function in cell-to-cell adhesion. However, their structures are quite different. Middle lamellae are composed primarily of carbohydrates that involve linkages between negatively charged carbohydrates and divalent cations. By comparison, anchoring junctions and desmosomes hold cells together via proteins such as cadherins and integrins.

Figure 10.15   Connective tissue would have the most extensive ECM.

Figure 10.16   Dermal tissue would be found on the surfaces of leaves, stems, and roots.

Figure 10.19   Simple epithelium and epidermis are one cell layer thick, whereas stratified epithelium and periderm are several cell layers thick.

Figure 10.21   Both ground tissue in plants and connective tissue in animals are important in supporting the organism. These tissues have a large amount of ECM that provides structural support.

Feature Investigation Questions

1. The purpose of this study was to determine the sizes of molecules that can move through gap junctions from one cell to another.

2. The researchers used fluorescent dyes to visibly monitor the movement of material from one cell to an adjacent cell through the gap junctions. First, single layers of rat liver cells were cultured. Next, fluorescent dyes with molecules of various masses were injected into particular cells. The researchers then used fluorescence microscopy to determine whether or not the dyes were transferred from one cell to the next.

3. The researchers found that molecules of masses less than 1,000 daltons could pass through the gap junction channels. Molecules of masses larger than 1,000 daltons could not pass through the gap junctions. Further experimentation revealed variation in gap junction channel size of different cell types. However, the upper limit of the gap junction channel size was determined to usually be around 1,000 daltons.

Test Yourself

1. e   2. c   3. b   4. e   5. e   6. d   7. e   8. d   9. e   10. a

Conceptual Questions

1. The primary cell wall is synthesized first between the two newly made daughter cells. It is relatively thin and allows cells to expand and grow. The secondary cell wall is made in layers by the deposition of cellulose fibrils and other components. In many cell types, it is relatively thick.

2. Cadherins and integrins are both membrane proteins that function as cell adhesion molecules. They also can function in cell signaling. Cadherins bind one cell to another cell, whereas integrins bind a cell to

the extracellular matrix. Cadherins require calcium ions to function, but integrins do not.

3. To create tissues and organs, cells must undergo six basic processes that influence their shape, arrangement, and number:

- Cell division—Many cells are needed to make tissues and organs. These arise via cell division.
- Cell growth—After a cell divides, it needs to grow to reach its correct size.
- Differentiation—Due to the expression of different genes, cells can differentiate into specialized cells based on what cells are needed at that particular time in the tissue or organ.
- Migration—During embryonic development in animals, cells migrate to their appropriate position within the body. This event doesn't occur in plants.
- Apoptosis—Apoptosis is also known as programmed cell death. During development, organs and tissues need to be shaped to form their correct structure. For example, during the development of fingers and toes, the cells between the digits must be removed. This cell removal is done through the process of apoptosis.
- Cell connections—For tissues and organs to work properly, the cells must be held together in a specific arrangement. This is achieved through the different types of cell-to-cell connections.

Chapter 11
Concept Checks

Figure 11.1 Yes, they would be resistant to killing. These bacteria are derived from the type R bacteria, so they would have this trait. In addition, they have become type S because they obtained genetic material from the dead type S bacteria.

Figure 11.4 ^{35}S was used to label phage proteins, whereas ^{32}P was used to label phage DNA.

Figure 11.6 Cytosine is found in both DNA and RNA.

Figure 11.7 The phosphate is attached to the number 5′ carbon in a single nucleotide. In a DNA strand, it is attached to both the 5′ carbon and 3′ carbon.

Figure 11.8 A phosphoester bond is a single covalent bond between a phosphorus atom and an oxygen atom. A phosphodiester linkage involves two phosphoester bonds. This linkage occurs along the backbone of DNA and RNA strands.

Figure 11.10 Because it is antiparallel and obeys the AT/GC rule, it would be 3′–CTAAGCAAG–5′.

Figure 11.13 It would be 1/8 half-heavy and 7/8 light.

Figure 11.17 The oxygen in a new phosphoester bond comes from the sugar.

Figure 11.19 The lagging strand is made discontinuously in the direction opposite to the movement of the replication fork.

Figure 11.20 When primase is synthesizing a primer in the lagging strand, it moves from left to right in this figure. After it is done making a primer, it needs to hop to the opening of the replication fork to make a new primer. This movement is from right to left in this figure.

Figure 11.22 Telomerase uses a short strand of RNA as template to make the DNA repeat sequence.

Figure 11.25 Proteins hold the bottoms of the loops in place.

Figure 11.26 Proteins that compact the radial loop domains are primarily responsible for the X shape.

Feature Investigation Questions

1. Previous studies had indicated that mixing different strains could lead to transformation or the changing of a strain into a different one. Griffith had shown that mixing heat-killed type S with living type R would result in the transformation of the type R to type S. Though mutations could cause the changing of the identity of certain strains, the type R to type S transformation was not due to mutation but was more likely due to the transmission of a biochemical substance between the two strains. Griffith recognized this and referred to the biochemical substance as the "transformation principle." If Avery, MacCleod, and McCarty could determine the biochemical identity of this "transformation principle," they could identify the genetic material for this organism.

2. A DNA extract contains DNA that has been purified from a sample of cells.

3. The researchers could not verify that the DNA extract was completely pure and did not have small amounts of contaminating molecules, such as proteins and RNA. The researchers were able to treat the extract with enzymes to remove proteins (using protease), RNA (using RNase), or DNA (using DNase). Removing the proteins or RNA did not alter the transformation of the type R to type S strains. Only the enzymatic removal of DNA disrupted the transformation, indicating that DNA is the genetic material.

Test Yourself

1. a   2. b   3. d   4. d   5. b   6. c   7. b   8. d   9. d   10. c

Conceptual Questions

1. The genetic material must contain the information necessary to construct an entire organism. The genetic material must be accurately copied and transmitted from parent to offspring and from cell to cell during cell division in multicellular organisms. The genetic material must contain variation that can account for the known variation within each species and among different species.

   Griffith discovered something called the transformation principle, and his experiments showed the existence of biochemical genetic information. In addition, he showed that this genetic information can move from one individual to another of the same species. In his experiments, Griffith took heat-killed type S bacteria and mixed them with living type R bacteria and injected them into a live mouse, which died after the injection. By themselves, these two strains would not kill the mouse, but when they were put together, the genetic information from the heat-killed type S bacteria was transferred into the living type R bacteria, thus transforming the type R bacteria into type S.

2. In the case of the Hershey and Chase experiment, a radioactive isotope of sulfur was used to label the protein in the viral protein coat. The DNA was labeled using a radioactive isotope of phosphorus. This was an ideal way of labeling the different components, because sulfur is found in proteins but not DNA, and phosphorus is found in DNA but not proteins. By labeling the two candidate molecules with the radioactive isotopes, Hershey and Chase could determine the genetic material by seeing which isotope entered the bacterial cells.

3. Two long chains of nucleotides are coiled around a central axis forming a helix. The two chains run in opposite directions or are antiparallel. Hydrogen bonds between the bases in opposite strands stabilize the structure. Adenine always pairs with thymine, and cytosine always pairs with guanine. The width of the double helix is relatively constant. One complete turn of the double helix is composed of 10 base pairs.

Chapter 12
Concept Checks

Figure 12.1 A person with two defective copies of phenylalanine hydroxylase would have phenylketonuria.

Figure 12.2 The ability to convert ornithine into citrulline is missing.

Figure 12.3 The usual direction of flow of genetic information is from DNA to RNA to protein, though exceptions occur.

Figure 12.4 If a terminator was removed, transcription would occur beyond the normal stopping point. Eventually, RNA polymerase would encounter a terminator from an adjacent gene, and transcription would end.

Figure 12.10 The ends of structural genes do not have a poly T region that acts as a template for the synthesis of a poly A tail. Instead, the poly A tail is added after the pre-mRNA is made by an enzyme that attaches many adenine nucleotides in a row.

Figure 12.11 A structural gene would still be transcribed into RNA if the start codon was missing. However, it would not be translated properly into a polypeptide.

Figure 12.12 It would bind to a 5′–UGG–3′codon, and it would carry tryptophan.

Figure 12.14 The function of the anticodon in tRNA is to recognize a codon in an mRNA.

Figure 12.15 The attachment of an amino acid to a tRNA is an endergonic reaction. ATP provides the energy to catalyze this reaction.

Figure 12.17   Each mammal is closely related to the other mammals, and *E. coli* and *S. marcescens* are also closely related. The mammals are relatively distantly related to the bacterial species.

Figure 12.19   A region near the 5′ end of the mRNA is complementary to a region of rRNA in the small subunit. These complementary regions hydrogen-bond with each other to promote the binding of the mRNA to the small ribosomal subunit.

Feature Investigation Questions

1. A triplet mimics mRNA because it can cause a specific tRNA to bind to the ribosome. This was useful to Nirenberg and Leder because it allowed them to correlate the binding of a tRNA carrying a specific amino acid with a triplet sequence.

2. The researchers were attempting to match codons with appropriate amino acids. By labeling one amino acid in each of the 20 tubes for each codon, the researchers were able to identify the correct relationship by detecting which tube resulted in radioactivity on the filter.

3. The AUG triplet would have shown radioactivity in the methionine test tube. Even though AUG acts as the start codon, it also codes for the amino acid methionine. The other three codons act as stop codons and do not code for an amino acid. In these cases, the researchers would not have found radioactivity trapped on filters.

Test Yourself

1. b   2. d   3. d   4. b   5. c   6. e   7. d   8. d   9. d   10. b

Conceptual Questions

1. Beadle and Tatum had the insight from their studies that a single gene controlled the synthesis of a single enzyme. In later years, it became apparent that genes code for all proteins and that some proteins consist of more than one polypeptide chain. So the modern statement is one gene codes for each polypeptide.

   Confirmation of their hypothesis came from studies involving arginine biosynthesis. Biochemists had already established that particular enzymes are involved in a pathway to produce arginine. Intermediates in this pathway are ornithine and citrulline. Mutants in single genes disrupted the ability of cells to catalyze just one reaction in this pathway, thereby suggesting that a single gene encodes a single enzyme.

2. Each of these 20 enzymes catalyzes the attachment of a specific amino acid to a specific tRNA molecule.

3. It would be complementary to the 5′–CCA–3′ codon. This tRNA should carry proline.

Chapter 13
Concept Checks

Figure 13.1   The advantage is energy savings. The bacterium saves energy by making these proteins only when they are needed for lactose uptake and breakdown.

Figure 13.2   Gene regulation causes each cell type to express its own unique set of proteins, which, in turn, are largely responsible for the morphologies and functions of cells.

Figure 13.3   The embryonic and fetal forms of hemoglobin have a higher affinity for oxygen. This allows the embryo and fetus to obtain oxygen from their mother's bloodstream.

Figure 13.6   The *lacZ, lacY,* and *lacA* genes are under the control of the *lac* promoter.

Figure 13.7   Negative control refers to the action of a repressor protein, which inhibits transcription when it binds to the DNA. Inducible refers to the action of a small effector molecule. When it is present, it promotes transcription.

Figure 13.11   In this case, the repressor keeps the *lac* operon turned off unless lactose is present in the environment. The activator allows the bacterium to choose between glucose and lactose.

Figure 13.12   Both proteins are similar in that they repress transcription. They prevent RNA polymerase from transcribing the operons. They are different with regard to the effects of their small effector molecules. For the lac repressor, the binding of allolactose causes a conformational change that

prevents the repressor from binding to its operator site. In contrast, the binding of tryptophan to the trp repressor allows it to bind to its operator site. Another difference is that the lac repressor binds to the DNA sequence found in the *lac* operator site, whereas the trp repressor recognizes a different DNA sequence that is found in the *trp* operator site.

Figure 13.16   When an activator interacts with mediator, it causes RNA polymerase to proceed to the elongation phase of transcription.

Figure 13.17   The common state of euchromatin, the 30-nm fiber, is too compact to be transcribed. This level of compaction must be loosened up so that transcription can occur.

Figure 13.18   Some histone modifications may promote a loosening of chromatin structure, whereas others cause the chromatin to become more compact.

Figure 13.19   The gene could not be activated in the presence of glucocorticoid hormone.

Figure 13.20   The advantage of alternative splicing is that it allows a single gene to encode two or more polypeptides. This enables organisms to have smaller genomes, which is more efficient and easier to package into a cell.

Figure 13.22   When iron levels rise in the cell, the iron binds to IRP and removes it from the mRNA that encodes ferritin. This results in the rapid translation of ferritin protein, which can store excess iron. Unfortunately, ferritin storage does have limits, so iron poisoning can occur if too much is ingested.

Feature Investigation Questions

1. The first observation was the identification of rare bacterial strains that had constitutive expression of the *lac* operon. Normally, the genes are expressed only when lactose is present. These mutant strains expressed the genes all the time. The researchers also observed that some of these strains had mutations in the *lacI* gene. These two observations were key to the development of hypotheses explaining the relationship between the *lacI* gene and the regulation of the *lac* operon.

2. The correct hypothesis is that the *lacI* gene encodes a repressor protein that inhibits the operon.

3. The researchers used an F′ factor to introduce the wild-type *lacI* gene into the cell. In this case, the cells that contained the F′ factor had both a mutant copy of the gene and a normal copy of the gene. By creating a merozygote with an F′ factor with a normal copy of the *lacI* gene, regulation of the *lac* operon was restored. The researchers concluded that the normal *lacI* gene produced adequate amounts of a diffusible protein that could interact with the operator on the chromosomal DNA as well as the F′ factor DNA and regulate transcription.

Test Yourself

1. d   2. b   3. c   4. c   5. c   6. d   7. c   8. c   9. d   10. c

Conceptual Questions

1. In an inducible operon, the presence of a small effector molecule causes transcription to occur. In repressible operons, a small effector molecule inhibits transcription. The effects of these small molecules are mediated through regulatory proteins that bind to the DNA. Repressible operons usually encode anabolic enzymes, and inducible operons encode catabolic enzymes.

2. a. regulatory protein; b. small effector molecule; c. segment of DNA; d. small effector molecule; and e. regulatory protein

3. The addition of methyl groups to CpG islands, especially near the promoters of eukaryotic genes, may prevent an activator from binding to an enhancer element or may convert chromatin from an open to a closed conformation.

Chapter 14
Concept Checks

Figure 14.1   At neutral pH, glutamic acid is negatively charged. Perhaps the negative charges repel each other and prevent hemoglobin proteins from aggregating into fiber-like structures.

Figure 14.3   Only germ-line cells give rise to gametes (sperm or egg cells). A somatic cell cannot give rise to a gamete and therefore cannot be passed to offspring.

Figure 14.4 This is a mutation in a somatic cell, so it cannot be transmitted to an offspring.

Figure 14.6 A thymine dimer is harmful because it can cause errors in DNA replication.

Figure 14.7 If we divide 44 by 2 million, the rate is 2.2×10^{-5}.

Figure 14.8 UvrC and UvrD are responsible for removing the damaged DNA. UvrC makes cuts on both sides of the damage, and then UvrD removes the damaged region.

Figure 14.9 The sun has UV rays and other harmful radiation that could damage the DNA. This person has a defect in the nucleotide excision repair pathway. Therefore, his DNA is more likely to suffer mutations, which cause growths on the skin.

Figure 14.11 Growth factors turn on a signaling pathway that ultimately leads to cell division.

Figure 14.14 The type of cancer associated with this fusion is leukemia, which is a cancer of blood cells. The gene fusion produces a chimeric gene that is expressed in blood cells because it has the *bcr* promoter. The abnormal fusion protein promotes cancer in these cells.

Figure 14.15 Checkpoints prevent cell division if a genetic abnormality is detected. This helps to properly maintain the genome, thereby minimizing the possibility that a cell harboring a mutation will divide to produce two daughter cells.

Figure 14.16 Cancer would not occur if both copies of the *Rb* gene and both copies of the *E2F* gene were rendered inactive due to mutations. An active copy of the *E2F* gene is needed to promote cell division.

Figure 14.18 Translocations could create oncogenes as in the *bcr/abl* fusion example found in the Philadelphia chromosome. Chromosome loss could result in the loss of tumor suppressor genes. Increases in chromosome number could contribute to cancer if the extra chromosomes carry proto-oncogenes.

Feature Investigation Questions

1. Some individuals believed that heritable traits may be altered by physiological events. This suggests that mutations may be stimulated by certain needs of the organism. Others believed that mutations were random. If a mutation had a beneficial effect that improved survival and/reproductive success, these mutations would be maintained in the population through natural selection.

2. The Lederbergs were testing the hypothesis that mutations are random events. By subjecting the bacteria to some type of environmental stress, the bacteriophage, the researchers would be able to see if the stress induced mutations or if mutations occurred randomly.

3. When looking at the number and location of colonies that were resistant to viral infection, the pattern was consistent among the secondary plates. This indicates that the mutation that allowed the colonies to be resistant to viral infection occurred on the master plate. The secondary plates introduced the selective agent that allowed the resistant bacteria colonies to survive and reproduce while the other colonies were destroyed. Thus, mutations occurred randomly in the absence of any selective agent.

Test Yourself

1. c   2. d   3. d   4. e   5. d   6. b   7. b   8. b   9. c   10. e

Conceptual Questions

1. Random mutations are more likely to be harmful than beneficial. The genes within each species have evolved to work properly. They have functional promoters, coding sequences, terminators, and so on, that allow the genes to be expressed. Mutations are more likely to disrupt these sequences. For example, mutations within the coding sequence may produce early stop codons, frameshift mutations, and missense mutations that result in a nonfunctional polypeptide. On rare occasions, however, mutations are beneficial; they may produce a gene that is expressed better than the original gene or produce a polypeptide that functions better.

2. A spontaneous mutation originates within a living cell. It may be due to spontaneous changes in nucleotide structure, errors in DNA replication, or products of normal metabolism that may alter the structure of DNA. The causes of induced mutations originate from outside the cell. They may be physical agents, such as UV light or X-rays, or chemicals that

act as mutagens. Both spontaneous and induced mutations may cause a harmful phenotype such as a cancer. In many cases, induced mutations are avoidable if the individual can prevent exposure to the environmental agent that acts as a mutagen.

3. The effects of mutations are cumulative. If one mutation occurs in a cell, this mutation will be passed to the daughter cells. If a mutation occurs in the daughter cell, now there will be two mutations. These two mutations will be passed to the next generation of daughter cells, and so forth. The accumulation of many mutations eventually kills the cells. That is why mutagens are more effective at killing dividing cells compared to nondividing cells. It is because the number of mutations accumulates to a lethal level.

There are two main side effects to this treatment. First, some normal (noncancerous) cells of the body, particularly skin cells and intestinal cells, are actively dividing. These cells are also killed by chemotherapy and radiation therapy. Second, it is possible that the therapy may produce mutations that will cause noncancerous cells to become cancerous. For these reasons, there is a maximal dose of chemotherapy or radiation therapy that is recommended.

Chapter 15
Concept Checks

Figure 15.1 Chromosomes are readily seen when they are compacted in a dividing cell. By adding such a drug, you increase the percentage of cells that are actively dividing.

Figure 15.2 Interphase consists of the G_1, S, and G_2 phases of the cell cycle.

Figure 15.3 You would find 92 chromatids in a human cell at metaphase. These are attached to form 46 pairs of sister chromatids.

Figure 15.4 Checkpoint proteins monitor conditions and prevent cell division if the conditions are not appropriate. They also sense if there is DNA damage, incompletely replicated chromosomes, and chromosomes not attached to the spindle. If such abnormalities are detected, cell division is halted. This maintains the integrity of the genome.

Figure 15.7 As shown in the inset, each object is a pair of sister chromatids.

Figure 15.8 The astral microtubules, which extend away from the chromosomes, are important for positioning the spindle apparatus within the cell. The polar microtubules project into the region between the two poles. Polar microtubules that overlap with each other play a role in the separation of the two poles. Kinetochore microtubules are attached to kinetochores at the centromeres and are needed to sort the chromosomes.

Figure 15.9 The mother cell (in G_1 phase) and the daughter cells have the same chromosome composition. They are genetically identical.

Figure 15.10 Micrographs showing cytokinesis in animal and plant cells. Cytokinesis in both animal and plant cells separates a mother cell into two daughter cells. In animal cells, cytokinesis involves the formation of a cleavage furrow, which constricts like a drawstring to separate the cells. In plants, the two daughter cells are separated by the formation of a cell plate, which forms a cell wall between the two daughter cells.

Figure 15.14 The mother cell is diploid with two sets of chromosomes, whereas the four resulting cells are haploid with one set of chromosomes.

Figure 15.15 The reason for meiosis in animals is to produce gametes. These gametes combine during fertilization to produce a diploid organism. Following fertilization, the purpose of mitosis is to produce a multicellular organism.

Figure 15.17 Inversions and the translocations shown here do not affect the total amount of genetic material.

Feature Investigation Questions

1. Researchers had demonstrated that the binding of progesterone to receptors in oocytes caused the cells to progress from the G_2 phase of the cell cycle to mitosis. It appeared that progesterone acted as a signaling molecule for the progression through the cell cycle.

2. The researchers proposed that progesterone acted as a signaling molecule that led to the synthesis of molecules that cause the cell to progress through the cell cycle. These changes led to the maturation of the oocyte.

To test their hypothesis, donor eggs were exposed to progesterone for either 2 or 12 hours. Control donor oocytes were not exposed to progesterone. Cytosol from each treatment was then transferred to recipient oocytes. The researchers recorded whether or not the recipient oocytes underwent maturation.

3. The oocytes that were exposed to the progesterone for only 2 hours did not induce maturation in the recipient oocytes, whereas the oocytes that were exposed to progesterone for 12 hours did induce maturation in the recipient oocytes. The researchers suggested that a time span greater than 2 hours is needed to accumulate the proteins that are necessary to promote maturation.

Test Yourself

1. b   2. e   3. b   4. e   5. c   6. a   7. c   8. d   9. b   10. c

Conceptual Questions

1. In diploid species, chromosomes are present in pairs, one from each parent, and contain similar gene arrangements. Such chromosomes are homologous. When DNA is replicated, two identical copies are created, and these are sister chromatids.

2. There are four copies. A karyotype shows homologous chromosomes that come in pairs. Each member of the pair has replicated to form a pair of sister chromatids. Therefore, four copies of each gene are present. See the inset to Figure 15.1.

3. Two cells would have five chromosomes (one copy of each chromosome plus an extra copy of chromosome 3), and the other two cells would have only three chromosomes because they would be missing a chromosome (chromosome 3).

Chapter 16
Concept Checks

Figure 16.2   Having blue eyes is a variant (also called a trait). A character is a more general term, which in this case would refer to eye color.

Figure 16.4   In this procedure, stamens are removed from the purple flower to prevent self-fertilization.

Figure 16.5   The reason why offspring of the F_1 generation exhibit only one variant of each character is because one trait is dominant over the other.

Figure 16.6   The ratio of alleles (T to t) is 1:1. The reason why the phenotypic ratio is 3:1 is because T is dominant to t.

Figure 16.7   It was Pp. To produce white offspring, which are pp, the original plant had to have at least one copy of the p allele. Because it had purple flowers, it also had to have one copy of the P allele. So, its genotype must be Pp.

Figure 16.8   If the linked hypothesis had been correct, the ratio would have been 3 round, yellow : 1 wrinkled, green.

Figure 16.10   The word segregate means that alleles are separated into different places. In this case, the alleles are segregated into different cells during the process of meiosis. Alleles are located on chromosomes. A diploid cell has two copies of each allele. During meiosis, a diploid cell divides twice to produce four haploid cells that each have only one copy of an allele.

Figure 16.11   There would be four possible ways of aligning the chromosomes, and eight different types of gametes (ABC, abc, ABc, abC, Abc, aBC, AbC, aBc) could be produced.

Figure 16.12   No. If two parents are affected with the disease, they must be homozygous for the mutant allele if it's recessive. Two homozygous parents would have to produce all affected offspring. If they don't, then the inheritance pattern is not recessive.

Figure 16.13   When all affected offspring have at least one affected parent, this suggests a dominant pattern of inheritance.

Figure 16.14   The person would be a female. In mammals, the presence of the Y chromosome causes maleness. Therefore, without a Y chromosome, a person with a single X chromosome would develop into a female.

Figure 16.18   The mother is Bb, and the father is bb. Both of these parents would not be bald. The son is Bb and is bald because B is dominant in males.

Figure 16.19   No. You need a genetically homogenous population to study the norm of reaction. A wild population of squirrels is not genetically homogenous, so it could not be used.

Feature Investigation Questions

1. Morgan was testing the hypothesis of use and disuse. This hypothesis suggests that if a structure is not used, over time, it will diminish and/or disappear. In Morgan's experiments, originally he was testing to see if flies reared in the dark would lose some level of eye development.

2. When the F_1 individuals were crossed, only male F_2 offspring expressed the white eye color. At this time, Morgan was aware of sex chromosome differences between male and female flies. He realized that since males only possess one copy of X-linked genes, this would explain why only F_2 males exhibited the recessive trait.

3. In a cross between a white-eyed male and a female that is heterozygous for the white and red alleles, 1/2 of the female offspring would have white eyes. Also, a cross between a white-eyed male and a white-eyed female would yield all offspring with white eyes.

Test Yourself

1. c   2. b Mendel's law of segregation refers to the separation of the two alleles into separate cells. Meiosis is the cellular division process that produces haploid cells. During the first meiotic division, a diploid cell divides to produce haploid cells. This is the phase in which the two alleles segregate, or separate, from each other.   3. d   4. c   5. e   6. d   7. d   8. d   9. d   10. c

Conceptual Questions

1. If two affected parents had an unaffected offspring, that would rule out recessive inheritance. If two unaffected parents had an affected offspring, that would rule out dominant inheritance. However, it should be noted that this answer assumes that no new mutations are happening. In rare cases, a new mutation could cause or alter these results. For recessive inheritance, two affected parents could have an unaffected offspring if the offspring had a new mutation that converted the recessive allele to the dominant allele. Similarly for dominant inheritance, two unaffected parents could have an affected offspring if the offspring inherited a new mutation that was dominant. Note: New mutations are expected to be relatively rare.

2. The individual probabilities are as follows: $AA = 0.25$; $bb = 0.5$; $CC = 0.5$; and $Dd = 0.5$. These are determined by making small Punnett squares. We use the product rule to calculate the probability of $AAbbCCDd = (0.25)(0.5)(0.5)(0.5) = 0.03125$, or 3.125%.

3. Because males are hemizygous, they may display a recessive trait that is masked by the dominant allele in a heterozygous female. It only takes one recessive allele for the male to display the trait.

Chapter 17
Concept Checks

Figure 17.1   The recessive allele is the result of a loss-of-function mutation. In a $Ccpp$ individual, the enzyme encoded by the P gene is defective.

Figure 17.2   The pigmentation phenotype displays a continuous distribution because it is polygenic and because environmental variation has a big impact. This creates genotypes that result in a range of phenotypes that overlap.

Figure 17.4   Crossing over occurred during oogenesis in the heterozygous female of the F_1 generation to produce the recombinant offspring of the F_2 generation.

Figure 17.5   One strategy would be to begin with two true-breeding parental strains: $alal\ dpdp$ and $al^+al^+\ dp^+dp^+$ and cross them together to get F_1 heterozygotes $al^+al\ dp^+dp$. Then testcross female F_1 heterozygotes to male $alal\ dpdp$ homozygotes. In the F_2 generation, the recombinant offspring would be $al^+al\ dpdp$ and $alal\ dp^+dp$, and the nonrecombinants would be $al^+al\ dp^+dp$, and $alal\ dpdp$.

Figure 17.6   The evolutionary origin of these organelles is an ancient endosymbiotic relationship. Mitochondria are derived from purple bacteria, and chloroplasts are derived from cyanobacteria.

Figure 17.7   The gene is located in the chloroplast DNA. In this species, chloroplasts are transmitted from parent to offspring via eggs but not via sperm.

Figure 17.9   The Barr body is much more compact than the other X chromosome in the cell. This compaction prevents most of the genes on the Barr body from being expressed.

Figure 17.10 On rare occasions, a cat can be XXY. Because it carries a Y chromosome, it will be a male. If it is heterozygous for the orange and black coat-color alleles that are X-linked, it will be a calico male.

Figure 17.11 Only the male genes are transcriptionally active in the offspring. In this case, half the offspring would be normal, and half would be dwarf. The dwarf offspring would have inherited the *Igf-2* allele from their father.

Figure 17.14 Its mother must be *dd*. The genotype of the mother determines the phenotype of the offspring. A *dd* mother produces offspring that coil to the left.

Figure 17.15 A haploid egg that carries a *D* allele cannot produce an offspring that coils to the left. Such an egg would have to come from a mother that carried at least one *D* allele. The nurse cells would supply this egg with the *D* gene product, and the offspring would coil to the right because the *D* gene product is dominant. On the other hand, an egg that carries the *d* allele could possibly produce an offspring that coils to the right. Such an egg could be from a mother that is *Dd*. The nurse cells from such a mother would supply the egg with both gene products. Because the *D* gene product is dominant, such an offspring would coil to the right.

Feature Investigation Questions

1. Bateson and Punnett were testing the hypothesis that the gene pairs that influence flower color and pollen shape would assort independently of each other. The two traits were expected to show a pattern consistent with Mendel's law of independent assortment.

2. The expected results were a phenotypic ratio of 9:3:3:1. The researchers expected 9/16 of the offspring would have purple flowers and long pollen, 3/16 of the offspring would have purple flowers and round pollen, 3/16 of the offspring would have red flowers and long pollen, and 1/16 of the offspring would have red flowers and round pollen.

3. Though all four of the expected phenotype groups were seen, they were not in the predicted ratio of 9:3:3:1. The number of individuals with the phenotypes found in the parental generation (purple flowers and long pollen or red flowers and round pollen) was much higher than expected. Bateson and Punnett suggested that the gene controlling flower color was somehow coupled with the gene that controls pollen shape. This would explain why these traits did not always assort independently.

Test Yourself

1. d   2. c   3. d   4. c   5. d   6. b   7. a   8. d   9. a   10. a

Conceptual Questions

1. The correct answer is 6%. Individuals that are *Aabb* are recombinants that occurred as a result of crossing over. Because the genes are 12 map units apart, we expect that 12% will be recombinants. However, there are two types of recombinants: *Aabb* and *aaBb*, which would occur in equal amounts. Therefore, we expect 6% to be *Aabb*.

2. This may happen due to X inactivation. As a matter of bad luck, a female embryo may preferentially inactivate the X chromosome carrying the normal allele in the embryonic cells that will give rise to the eyes. If the X chromosome carrying the color-blind allele is preferentially expressed, one or both eyes may show color blindness to some degree.

3. The mother is *Nn*; the father and offspring could be any genotype. The mother has a small head, so her mother must have been *nn*. Because the mother with the small head also had offspring with normal heads, she also must carry the *N* allele. Therefore, the mother must be *Nn*.

Chapter 18
Concept Checks

Figure 18.3 Viruses vary with regard to their structure and their genomes. Genome variation is described in Table 18.1.

Figure 18.5 The advantage of the lytic cycle is that the virus can make many copies of itself and proliferate. However, sometimes the growth conditions may not be favorable to make new viruses. The advantage of the lysogenic cycle is that the virus can remain latent until conditions become favorable to make new viruses.

Figure 18.8 Here are four possible effects of a drug: 1. A drug could specifically recognize the PrP^{Sc} conformation and prevent it from binding to PrP^C.

2. It could convert PrP^{Sc} back to PrP^C. 3. It could recognize PrP^C and prevent the binding of PrP^{Sc}. 4. It could bind to PrP^C and stabilize its conformation, thereby preventing PrP^{Sc} from changing it to the abnormal conformation. You may also think of other interesting possibilities.

Figure 18.9 There appears to be three nucleoids in the bacterial cell to the far right.

Figure 18.11 The loop domains are held in place by proteins that bind to the DNA at the bases of the loops. The proteins also bind to each other.

Figure 18.12 Bacterial chromosomes and plasmids are similar in that they typically contain circular DNA molecules. However, bacterial chromosomes are usually much longer than plasmids and carry many more genes. Also, bacterial chromosomes tend to be more compacted due to the formation of loop domains and supercoiling.

Figure 18.13 16 hours is the same as 32 doublings. So, 2^{32} = 4,294,967,296. (The actual number would be much less because the cells would deplete the growth media and grow more slowly than the maximal rate.)

Figure 18.16 Yes. The two strains would have mixed together, allowing them to conjugate. Therefore, there would have been colonies on the plates.

Figure 18.17 During conjugation, only one strand of the DNA from an F factor is transferred from the donor to the recipient cell. The single-stranded DNA in both cells is then used as a template to create double-stranded F factor DNA in both cells.

Figure 18.19 Transduction is not a normal part of the phage life cycle. It is a mistake in which a piece of the bacterial chromosome is packaged into a phage coat and is then transferred to another bacterial cell.

Feature Investigation Questions

1. Lederberg and Tatum were testing the hypothesis that genetic material could be transferred from one bacterial strain to another.

2. The experimental growth medium lacked particular amino acids and biotin. The mutant strains were unable to synthesize these particular amino acids or biotin. Therefore, they were unable to grow due to the lack of the necessary nutrients. The two strains used in the experiment each lacked the ability to make two essential nutrients necessary for growth. The appearance of colonies growing on the experimental growth medium indicated that some bacterial cells had acquired the normal genes for the two mutations they carried. By acquiring these normal genes, the ability to synthesize the essential nutrients was restored.

3. Bernard Davis placed samples of the two bacterial strains in different arms of a U-tube. A filter allowed the free movement of the liquid in which the bacterial cells were suspended, but prevented the actual contact between the bacterial cells. After incubating the strains in this environment, Davis found that genetic transfer did not take place. He concluded that physical contact between cells of the two strains was required for genetic transfer.

Test Yourself

1. c   2. e   3. c   4. b   5. e   6. a   7. d   8. d   9. b   10. c

Conceptual Questions

1. Viruses are similar to living cells in that they contain a genetic material that provides a blueprint to make new viruses. However, viruses are not composed of cells, and by themselves, they do not carry out metabolism, use energy, maintain homeostasis, or even reproduce. A virus or its genetic material must be taken up by a living cell to replicate.

2. Conjugation—The process involves a direct physical contact between two bacterial cells in which a donor cell transfers a strand of DNA to a recipient cell.

   • Transformation—This occurs when a living bacteria takes up genetic information that has been released from a dead bacteria.
   • Transduction—When a virus infects a donor cell, it incorporates a fragment of bacterial chromosomal DNA into a newly made virus particle. The virus then transfers this fragment of DNA to a recipient cell.
   • Horizontal gene transfer is the transfer of genes from another organism without being the offspring of that organism. These acquired genes sometimes increase survival and therefore may have an evolutionary advantage. Such genes may even promote the formation of new species. From a medical perspective, an important example of horizontal gene transfer is when one bacterium acquires

antibiotic resistance from another bacterium and then itself becomes resistant to that antibiotic. This phenomenon is making it increasingly difficult to treat a wide variety of bacterial diseases.

3. If neither cell has a selective growth advantage, we would expect that the F^+ cells would eventually overrun the population. This is because a mating starts with an F^+ and F^- cell and ends with two F^+ cells. Therefore, F^+ cells can convert F^- cells into F^+ cells, but the opposite cannot occur.

Chapter 19

Concept Checks

Figure 19.1   Model organisms are studied by many different researchers so they can compare their results and determine scientific principles that apply more broadly to other species.

Figure 19.3   Cell division and cell migration are common in the earliest stages of development, whereas cell differentiation and apoptosis are more common as tissues and organs start to form.

Figure 19.4   If apoptosis did not occur, the fingers would be webbed.

Figure 19.5   During development, positional information may a cause a cell to respond in one of four ways: cell division, cell migration, cell differentiation, and cell death.

Figure 19.6   Cell division and migration would be the most prevalent in the early phases of development, such as phase 1 and 2.

Figure 19.8   The larva would have anterior structures at both ends and would lack posterior structures such as a spiracle.

Figure 19.9   The Bicoid protein functions as a transcription factor. Its function is highest in the anterior end of the zygote.

Figure 19.11   There are 15 pink stripes in this embryo. Each stripe corresponds to a portion of the 15 segments in the embryo.

Figure 19.14   The last abdominal segment would have legs!

Figure 19.18   Stem cells can divide, and they can differentiate into specific cell types.

Figure 19.20   Hematopoietic stem cells are multipotent.

Figure 19.23   Most stem cells in plants are found in meristems, which are located at the tips of roots and shoots.

Figure 19.24   The pattern would be sepal, petal, stamen, stamen.

Feature Investigation Questions

1. The researchers were interested in the factors that cause cells to differentiate. For this particular study, the researchers were attempting to identify genes involved in the differentiation of muscle cells.

2. Using genetic technology, the researcher compared the gene expression in cells that could differentiate into muscle cells to the gene expression in cells that could not differentiate into muscle cells. Though many genes were expressed in both, the researchers were able to isolate three genes that were expressed in muscle cell lines that were not expressed in the nonmuscle cell lines.

3. Again, using genetic technology, each of the candidate genes was introduced into a cell that normally did not give rise to skeletal muscle. This procedure was used to test whether or not these genes played a key role in muscle cell differentiation. If the genetically engineered cell gave rise to muscle cells, the researchers would have evidence that a particular candidate gene was involved in muscle cell differentiation. Of the three candidate genes, only one was shown to be involved in muscle cell differentiation. When the *MyoD* gene was expressed in fibroblasts, these cells differentiated into skeletal muscle cells.

Test Yourself

1. c   2. d   3. e   4. b   5. c   6. e   7. a   8. a   9. b   10. d

Conceptual Questions

1. a. This would be consistent with a defect in a segmentation gene, such as a gap gene.

   b. This would be consistent with a mutation in a homeotic gene because the characteristics of a particular segment have been changed.

2. Both types of genes encode transcription factors that bind to the DNA and regulate the expression of other genes. The effects of *Hox* genes are to determine the characteristics of certain regions of the body, whereas the *myoD* gene is cell specific—it causes a cell to become a skeletal muscle cell.

3. In plants, there are organized groups of cells that are very active with respect to cell division and producing stem cells. These areas are called meristems. At these areas, cells divide and retain the ability to differentiate into several different types of cells. In plants, there are two major places where these meristems are found. First, meristem tissue found in the roots is called the root meristem, which gives rise to the roots and tissue associated with the roots. The second is the shoot meristem, which produces all of the aerial parts of the plant, such as stems, leaves and flowers.

Chapter 20

Concept Checks

Figure 20.2   No. A recombinant vector has been made, but it has not been cloned. In other words, many copies of the recombinant vector have not been made yet.

Figure 20.3   The insertion of chromosomal DNA into the vector disrupts the *lacZ* gene and thereby prevents the expression of β-galactosidase. The functionality of *lacZ* can be determined by providing the growth medium with a colorless compound, X-Gal, which is cleaved by β-galactosidase into a blue dye. Bacterial colonies containing recircularized vectors will form blue colonies, whereas colonies containing recombinant vectors carrying a segment of chromosomal DNA will be white.

Figure 20.5   The 600 bp piece would be closer to the bottom. Smaller pieces travel faster through the gel.

Figure 20.6   The primers are complementary to sequences at each end of the DNA region to be amplified.

Figure 20.7   It means that part of their inserts are exactly the same, but other regions are not.

Figure 20.8   If a dideoxynucleotide ddNTP is added to a growing DNA strand, the strand can no longer grow because the 3′—OH group, the site of attachment for the next nucleotide, is missing.

Figure 20.9   A fluorescent spot identifies a cDNA that is complementary to a particular DNA sequence. Because the cDNA was generated from mRNA, this technique identifies a gene that has been transcribed in a particular cell type under a given set of conditions.

Figure 20.10   The reason why the A and B chains are made as fusion proteins is because the A and B chains are rapidly degraded when expressed in bacterial cells by themselves. The fusion proteins, however, are not.

Figure 20.12   Only the T DNA within the Ti plasmid is transferred to a plant cell.

Figure 20.14   Not all of Dolly's DNA came from a mammary cell. Her mitochondrial DNA came from the oocyte donor.

Figure 20.15   The bands match suspect 2.

Feature Investigation Questions

1. Gene therapy is the introduction of cloned genes into living cells to correct genetic mutations. The hope is that the cloned genes will correct or restore the normal gene function and thereby eliminate the clinical effects of the disease.

   ADA deficiency is a recessive genetic disorder in which an enzyme, adenosine deaminase, is not functional. The absence of this enzyme causes a buildup of deoxyadenosine, which is toxic to lymphocytes. When lymphocytes are destroyed, a person's immune system begins to fail, leading to a severe combined immunodeficiency disease, or SCID.

2. The researchers introduced normal copies of the ADA gene into lymphocytes, restoring normal cell metabolism. The researchers isolated lymphocytes from the patient and used a viral vector to introduce the gene into the lymphocytes. These lymphocytes were then reintroduced back into the patient.

3. Following several rounds of treatment with gene therapy, researchers were able to document continued production of the correct enzyme by the lymphocytes over the course of 4 years. However, because the

patients were also receiving other forms of treatment, it was not possible to determine if the gene therapy reduced the negative effects of the genetic disease.

Test Yourself

1. e   2. d   3. b   4. b   5. b   6. c   7. d   8. c   9. e   10. e

Conceptual Questions

1. The restriction enzyme cuts the plasmid at a specific site, leaving sticky ends. The gene of interest, cut with the same enzyme, will have complementary sticky ends that allow hydrogen bonding between the gene of interest and the plasmid. The connections are then made permanent, using DNA ligase that connects the DNA backbones.

2. A ddNTP is missing an oxygen at the 3′ position. These prevents the further growth of a DNA strand and thereby causes chain termination.

3. A mouse model is a strain of mice that carries a mutation that is analogous to a mutation that causes a human disease. Such mice exhibit disease symptoms resembling those found in humans. These mice can be used as model organisms to study a human disease. Such mice models have also been used to test the effects of various therapies in the treatment of human diseases.

Chapter 21

Concept Checks

Figure 21.2   One reason is that more complex species tend to have more genes. A second reason is that species vary with regard to the amount of repetitive DNA that is found in their genome.

Figure 21.3   The answer is a matter of opinion. Many people find it surprising that the vast majority of DNA is not part of genes or the coding region of genes.

Figure 21.5   For DNA transposons, inverted repeats are recognized by transposase, which cleaves the DNA and inserts the transposon into a new location.

Figure 21.6   Retroelements. A single retroelement can be transcribed into multiple copies of RNA, which can be converted to DNA by reverse transcriptase, and inserted into multiple sites in the genome.

Figure 21.8   The overall advantage is specialization. When multiple copies of a gene are found in the genome, each copy can become specialized to suit the needs of particular cell types or particular stages of development.

Figure 21.9   Differential gene regulation. Genes that encode metabolic enzymes are highly expressed in liver cells, whereas those same genes are expressed in lower amounts in muscle cells. Conversely, genes that encode cytoskeletal and motor proteins are highly expressed in muscle cells, but less so in liver cells.

Figure 21.10   Reversible post-translation covalent modifications provide a way to modulate protein function. Certain types can turn off protein function, whereas others can turn on protein function. These modifications provide a rapid way for a cell to control protein function.

Figure 21.11   The two main advantages of having a computer program translate a genetic sequence is that it's faster and probably more accurate.

Figure 21.12   It is possible for orthologs to have exactly the same DNA sequence if neither of them has accumulated any new mutations that would cause their sequences to become different. This is likely only for closely related species that have diverged relatively recently from each other.

Feature Investigation Questions

1. The goal of the experiment was to sequence the entire genome of *Haemophilus influenzae.* By conducting this experiment, the researchers would have information about genome size and the types of genes the bacterium has.

2. One strategy requires mapping the genome prior to sequencing. After mapping is completed, each region of the genome is then sequenced. The shotgun approach does not require mapping of the genome prior to sequencing. Instead, many fragments are randomly sequenced.

   The advantage of the shotgun approach is the speed at which the sequencing can be conducted because the researchers do not have to spend time mapping the genome first. The disadvantage is that because

the researchers are sequencing random fragments, some fragments may be sequenced more than necessary.

3. The researchers were successful in sequencing the entire genome of the bacterium. The genome size was determined to be 1,830,137 base pairs, with a predicted 1,743 structural genes. The researchers were also able to predict the function of many of these genes. More importantly, the results were the first complete genomic sequence of a living organism.

Test Yourself

1. c   2. e   3. a   4. c   5. e   6. b   7. b   8. d   9. c   10. c

Conceptual Questions

1. a. yes

   b. No, it's only one chromosome in the nuclear genome.

   c. yes

   d. yes

2. The two main reasons why the proteomes of eukaryote species are usually much larger than their genomes are alternative splicing and post-translational covalent modifications. During alternative splicing, a pre-mRNA is spliced in two or more different ways to yield two or more different polypeptides. Post-translational covalent modifications can affect protein structure in a variety of ways, including proteolytic processing; disulfide bond formation; the attachment of prosthetic group, sugars, or lipids; phosphorylation; acetylation; and methylation.

3. Because they are derived from the same ancestral gene, homologous genes usually carry out similar or identical functions. In many cases, the first way to identify the function of a newly determined gene sequence is to find a homologous gene whose function is already known.

Chapter 22

Concept Checks

Figure 22.2   Organic molecules form the chemical foundation for the structure and function of living organisms. Modern organisms can synthesize organic molecules. However, to explain how life got started, biologists need to explain how organic molecules were made prior to the existence of living cells.

Figure 22.3   These vents release hot gaseous substances from the interior of the Earth. Organic molecules can form in the temperature gradient between the extremely hot vent water and the cold water that surrounds the vent.

Figure 22.4   A liposome is more similar to real cells, which are surrounded by a membrane that is composed of a phospholipid bilayer.

Figure 22.5   Certain chemicals, such as RNA molecules, may have properties that provide advantages and therefore cause them to increase in number compared to other molecules.

Figure 22.7   In a sedimentary rock formation, the layer at the bottom is usually the oldest.

Figure 22.8   For this time frame, you would analyze the relative amounts of the rubidium-87 and strontium-87 isotopes.

Figure 22.12   In part (a) at the top, the two cells are associating with each other, but one cell is not inside of the other cell, as in part (b).

Figure 22.13   The number of cells increases, and parts (c) and (d) have two cell types (somatic and reproductive). When comparing (c) and (d), the number of somatic cells increases relative to the number of reproductive cells.

Figure 22.14   Most animal species exhibit bilateral symmetry, including fruit flies, fishes, and humans.

Feature Investigation Questions

1. Chemical selection occurs when a particular chemical in a mixture has advantageous properties that allow it to increase in number compared to the other chemicals in the mixture. Bartel and Szostak hypothesized that variation in the catalytic abilities of RNA molecules would allow for chemical selection in the laboratory. Bartel and Szostak proposed to select for RNA molecules with higher catalytic abilities.

2. The short RNA molecules allowed the researchers to physically separate the mixture of longer RNA molecules based on catalytic properties. Long RNA molecules with catalytic abilities would covalently bond

with the short RNA molecules. The short RNA molecules had a specific region that caused them to be attracted to column beads in the experimental apparatus. The long RNA molecules that did not have catalytic abilities passed through the column and therefore could be separated from the ones that had catalytic activity and became bound to the column beads.

3. The researchers found that with each round of selection, the enzymatic activity of the selected pool of RNA molecules increased. These results provided evidence that chemical selection could improve the functional characteristics of a group of molecules. Much of the explanation of the evolution of life on Earth is theoretical, meaning it is based on scientific principles but has not been experimentally verified. Researchers are attempting to develop laboratory experiments that test the explanations of the evolution of life. The experiment conducted by Bartel and Szostak provided experimental data to support the hypothesis of chemical selection as a possible mechanism for the early evolutionary process that led to living cells.

Test Yourself

1. b   2. e   3. b   4. c   5. e   6. a   7. d   8. c   9. b   10. d

Conceptual Questions

1. Nucleotides and amino acids were produced prior to the existence of cells.

   Nucleotides and amino acids became polymerized to form DNA, RNA, and proteins.

   Polymers became enclosed in membranes.

   Polymers enclosed in membranes evolved cellular properties.

2. The relative ages of fossils can be determined by the locations in sedimentary rock formation. Older fossils are found in lower layers. A common way to determine the ages of fossils is via radioisotope dating, which is often conducted on igneous rock in the vicinity of the fossil. A radioisotope is an unstable isotope of an element that decays spontaneously, releasing radiation at a constant rate. The half-life is the length of time required for a radioisotope to decay to exactly one-half of its initial value. To determine the age of a rock (and that of a nearby fossil), scientists can measure the amount of a given radioisotope as well as the amount of the decay product.

3. The Cambrian period lasted from 543 million years ago to 490 million years ago. The Cambrian explosion was an abrupt increase on a geological scale in the diversity of animal species. During the Cambrian period, all of the existing major types of marine invertebrates arose as well as many other major animal groups. The basic body types of all modern animal species are based on body types that arose during the Cambrian.

Chapter 23

Concept Checks

Figure 23.2 A single organism does not evolve. Populations may evolve from one generation to the next.

Figure 23.7 Due to a changing global climate, the island fox became isolated from the mainland species. Over time, natural selection resulted in adaptations for the population on the island and eventually resulted in a new species with characteristics that are somewhat different from the mainland species.

Figure 23.8 Many answers are possible. One example is the wing of a bird and the wing of a bat.

Figure 23.11 The relative sizes of traits are changing. For example, in dogs, the lengths of legs, body size, etc., are quite different. Artificial selection is often aimed at changing the relative sizes of body parts.

Figure 23.13 Rhesus and green monkeys = 0, Congo puffer fish and European flounder = 2, and Rhesus monkey and Congo puffer fish = 10. Pairs that are closely related evolutionarily have fewer differences than do pairs that are more distantly related.

Figure 23.14 Orthologs have similar gene sequences because they are derived from the same ancestral gene. The sequences are not identical because after the species diverged, each one accumulated different random mutations that changed their sequences.

Figure 23.15 It creates multifunctional proteins that may have new properties that can be acted upon by natural selection.

Figure 23.17 Humans have one large chromosome 2, but this chromosome is divided into two separate chromosomes in the other three species. In chromosome 3, the banding patterns among humans, chimpanzees, and gorillas are very similar, but the orangutan has a large inversion that flips the arrangement of bands in the centromeric region.

Feature Investigation Questions

1. The island has a moderate level of isolation but is located near enough to the mainland to have some migrants. The island is an undisturbed habitat, so the researchers would not have to consider the effects of human activity on the study. Finally, the island had an existing population of ground finches that would serve as the study organism over many generations.

2. First, the researchers were able to show that beak depth is a genetic trait that has variation in the population. Second, the depth of the beak is an indicator of the types of seeds the birds can eat. The birds with larger beaks can eat larger and drier seeds; therefore, changes in the types of seeds available could act as a selective force on the bird population.

   During the study period, there were annual changes in rainfall. This had an impact on the seed sizes produced by the plants on the island. In the drier year, fewer small seeds were produced, so the birds would have to eat larger, drier seeds.

3. The researchers found that following the drought in 1978, the average beak depth in the finch population increased. This indicated that birds with larger beaks were better able to adapt to the environmental changes due to the drought and produce more offspring. This is direct evidence of the phenomenon of natural selection.

Test Yourself

1. d   2. d   3. b   4. b   5. b   6. d   7. c   8. b   9. d   10. e

Conceptual Questions

1. Some random mutations result in a phenotype with greater reproductive success. If so, natural selection results in a greater proportion of such individuals in succeeding generations. These individuals are more likely to survive and reproduce, which means they have evolved to be better adapted to their environment.

2. The process of convergent evolution produces two different species from different lineages that show similar characteristics because they occupy similar environments. An example is the long snout and tongue of both the giant anteater, found in South America, and the echidna, found in Australia. This enables these animals to feed on ants, but the two structures evolved independently. These observations support the idea that evolution results in adaptations to particular environments.

3. Homologous structures are two or more structures that are similar because they are derived from a common ancestor. An example is the same set of bones that is found in the human arm, turtle arm, bat wing, and whale flipper. The forearms in these species have been modified to perform different functions. This supports the idea that all of these animals evolved from a common ancestor.

Chapter 24

Concept Checks

Figure 24.2 If C^R is 0.4, then C^W must be 0.6, because the allele frequencies add up to 1.0. The heterozygote ($2pq$) equals $2(0.4)(0.6)$, which equals 0.48, or 48%.

Figure 24.3 Over the short run, alleles that confer better fitness would be favored and increase in frequency, perhaps enhancing diversity. Over the long run, however, an allele that confers high fitness in the homozygous state may become monomorphic, thereby reducing genetic diversity.

Figure 24.4 Stabilizing selection eliminates alleles that give phenotypes that deviate significantly from the average phenotype. For this reason, it tends to decrease genetic diversity.

Figure 24.6 If malaria was eradicated, there would be no selective advantage for the heterozygote. The H^S allele would eventually be eliminated because the H^SH^S homozygote has a lower fitness. Directional selection would occur.

Figure 24.7   This is likely to be a form of intersexual selection. Such traits are likely to be involved in mate choice.

Figure 24.11   The bottleneck effect decreases genetic diversity. This may eliminate adaptations that promote survival and reproductive success. Therefore, the bottleneck effect makes it more difficult for a population to survive.

Figure 24.12   There are several possibilities. Two examples would be changing the DNA sequence within an intron or changing the DNA sequencing in a chromosomal region where a gene is not found.

Figure 24.13   Gene flow tends to make the allele frequencies in neighboring populations more similar to each other. It also promotes genetic diversity by introducing new alleles into populations.

Figure 24.14   Inbreeding favors homozygotes. If a homozygote has a higher Darwinian fitness, inbreeding would accelerate the prevalence of the allele in the population. Alternatively, if a homozygote has a lower fitness, inbreeding would accelerate the elimination of the allele from the population.

Feature Investigation Questions

1. The two species of cichlids used in the experiment are distinguishable by coloration, and the researchers were testing the hypothesis that the females make mate choices based on this variable.

2. Individual females were placed in tanks that contained one male from each species. The males were held in small glass tanks to limit their movement but allowed the female to see each of the males. The researchers recorded the courtship behavior between the female and males and the number of positive encounters between the female and each of the different males. This procedure was conducted under normal lighting and under monochromatic lighting that obscured the coloration differences between the two species. Comparing the behavior of the females under normal light conditions and monochromatic light conditions allowed the researchers to determine the importance of coloration in mate choice.

3. The researchers found that the female was more likely to select a mate from her own species in normal light conditions. However, under monochromatic light conditions, the species-specific mate choice was not observed. Females were as likely to choose males of the other species as they were males of their own species. This indicated that coloration is an important factor in mate choice in these species of fish.

Test Yourself

1. d   2. c   3. c   4. e   5. b   6. c   7. b   8. d   9. b   10. a

Conceptual Questions

1. The frequency of the disease is a genotype frequency because it represents individuals with the disease. If we let q^2 represent the genotype frequency, then q equals the square root of 0.04, which is 0.2. If $q = 0.2$, then $p = 1 - q$, which is 0.8. The frequency of heterozygous carriers is $2pq$, which is $2(0.8)(0.2) = 0.32$, or 32%.

2. Directional selection—This is when natural selection favors an extreme phenotype that makes the organism better suited to survive and reproduce in its environment. As a result, the extreme phenotype will become predominant in the population. This can occur either through new mutation or through a prolonged environmental change. In addition to selecting for a certain phenotype, the opposite end of the extreme is removed from the gene pool.

   • Stabilizing selection—In this type of selection, natural selection favors individuals with intermediate phenotypes, whereas organisms with extreme phenotypes are less likely to reproduce. This selection tends to prevent major changes in the phenotypes of populations.

   • Disruptive selection—This type of selection favors both extremes and removes the intermediate phenotype. It is also known as diversifying selection.

   • Balancing selection—This type of selection results in a balanced polymorphism in which two or more alleles are stably maintained in a population. Examples include heterozygote advantage, as in the sickle-cell allele, and negative frequency-dependent selection, as in certain prey.

   • Sexual selection—This is a type of natural selection that is directly aimed at reproductive success. It can occur by any of the previous four mechanisms. Male coloration in African cichlids is an example.

3. The founder effect occurs when a small group of individuals separates from a larger population and establishes a colony in a new location. Genetic drift can occur for two reasons. First, the founding population, which is relatively small, may have less genetic variation and different allele frequencies than the larger, original population from which it was derived. Second, as a matter of chance, the allele frequencies in the founding population will drift substantially while the population is small.

Chapter 25
Concept Checks

Figure 25.1   There are a lot of possibilities. Certain grass species look quite similar. Elephant species look very similar. And so on.

Figure 25.3   Temporal isolation is an example of a prezygotic isolating mechanism. Because the species breed at different times of the year, hybrid zygotes are not formed between the two species.

Figure 25.5   Hybrid sterility is a type of postzygotic isolating mechanism. A hybrid forms between the two species, but it is sterile.

Figure 25.7   The Hawaiian Islands have many different ecological niches that can be occupied by birds. The first founding bird inhabitants evolved to occupy those niches and thereby evolved into many different species.

Figure 25.11   The offspring would inherit 16 chromosomes from *G. tetrahit*, and from the hybrid, it would inherit anywhere from 8 to 16. So the answer is 24 to 32. The hybrid parent would always pass the 8 chromosomes that are found in pairs. With regard to the 8 chromosomes not found in pairs, it could pass 0 to 8 of them.

Figure 25.12   The insects on different host plants would tend to breed with each other, and natural selection would favor the development of traits that are an advantage for feeding on that host. Over time, the accumulation of genetic changes may lead to reproductive isolation between the populations of insects.

Figure 25.14   If the *Gremlin* gene was underexpressed, this would cause less Gremlin protein to be produced. Because Gremlin protein inhibits apoptosis, more cell death would occur, and the result would probably be smaller feet, and maybe they would not be webbed.

Figure 25.15   By comparing the number of *Hox* genes in many different animal species, a general trend is observed that animals with more complex body structures have a greater number of *Hox* genes.

Figure 25.17   The tip of the mouse's tail would have a mouse eye!

Feature Investigation Questions

1. Podos hypothesized that the morphological changes in the beak would also affect the birds' songs. A bird's song is an important component for mate choice. If changes in the beak alter the song of the bird, this would impact reproductive ability. Podos suggested that changes in the beak morphology could thus lead to reproductive isolation among the birds.

2. Podos first caught male birds in the field and collected data on beak size. The birds were banded for identification and released. Later, the banded birds' songs were recorded and analyzed for range of frequencies and trill rates. The results were then compared to similar data from other species of birds to determine if beak size constrained the frequency range and trill rate of the song.

3. The results of the study did indicate that natural selection on beak size due to changes in diet could lead to changes in song. Considering the importance of bird song to mate choice, the changes in the song could also lead to reproductive isolation.

   The phrase "by-product of adaptation" refers to changes in the phenotype that are not directly acted on by natural selection. In the case of the Galápagos finches, the changes in beak size were directly related to diet; however, as a consequence of that selection, the song pattern was also altered. The change in song pattern was a by-product.

Test Yourself

1. b   2. b   3. e   4. d   5. c   6. a   7. b   8. d   9. c   10. c

Conceptual Questions

1. Prezygotic isolating mechanisms prevent the formation of the zygote. An example is mechanical isolation, the incompatibility of genitalia. Postzygotic isolating mechanisms act after the formation of the zygote.

An example is inviability of the hybrid that is formed. (Other examples shown in Figure 25.2 would also be correct.) Postzygotic mechanisms are more costly because some energy is spent in the formation of a zygote and its subsequent growth.

2. The concept of gradualism suggests that each new species evolves continuously over long spans of time (Figure 25.13a). The principal idea is that large phenotypic differences that produce new species are due to the accumulation of many small genetic changes. According to the punctuated equilibrium model, species exist relatively unchanged for many generations. During this period, the species is in equilibrium with its environment. These long periods of equilibrium are punctuated by relatively short periods during which evolution occurs at a far more rapid rate. This rapid evolution is caused by relatively few genetic changes.

3. One example involves the *Hox* genes, which control morphological features along the anteroposterior axis in animals. An increase in the number of *Hox* genes during evolution is associated with an increase in body complexity and may have spawned many different animal species.

Chapter 26

Concept Checks

Figure 26.2   A phylum is broader than a family.

Figure 26.3   Yes. They can have many common ancestors, depending on how far back you go in the tree. For example, dogs and cats have a common ancestor that gave rise to mammals, and an older common ancestor that gave rise to vertebrates. The most recent common ancestor is the point at which two species diverged from each other.

Figure 26.4   An order is a smaller taxa that would have a more recent common ancestor.

Figure 26.9   A hinged jaw is the character common to the salmon, lizard, and rabbit, but not to the lamprey.

Figure 26.10   Changing the second G to an A is common to species A, B, and C, but not to species G.

Figure 26.12   The pair with a 3% difference would have an older common ancestor. A higher difference (3% compared to 1%) has occurred because the common ancestor is older and there has been more time to accumulate mutations.

Figure 26.13   Gorillas and humans would be expected to have fewer genetic differences because their common ancestor (named C) is more recent than that of orangutans and gorillas, which is ancestor B.

Figure 26.15   The kiwis are found in New Zealand. Even so, the kiwis are more closely related to Australian and African flightless birds than they are to the moas, which were found in New Zealand.

Figure 26.16   Monophyletic groups are based on the concept that a particular group of species descended from a common ancestor. When horizontal gene transfer occurs, not all of the genes in a species were inherited from the common ancestor, so this muddles the concept of monophyletic groups.

Feature Investigation Questions

1. Molecular paleontology is the sequencing and analysis of DNA obtained from extinct species. Tissue samples from specimens of extinct species may contain DNA molecules that can be extracted, amplified, and sequenced. The DNA sequences can then be compared to living species to study evolutionary relationships between modern and extinct species.

   The researchers extracted DNA from tissue samples of moas, extinct flightless birds that lived in New Zealand. The DNA sequences from the moas were compared to the DNA sequences of modern species of flightless birds to determine the evolutionary relationships of this particular group of organisms.

2. The researchers compared the DNA sequences of the extinct moas and modern kiwis of New Zealand to the emu and cassowary of Australia and New Guinea, the ostrich of Africa, and rheas of South America. All of the birds are flightless birds. With the birds selected, the researchers could look for similarities between birds over a large geographic area.

3. The sequences were very similar among the different species of flightless birds. Interestingly, the sequences of the kiwis of New Zealand were more similar to those of the modern species of flightless birds found on other land masses than they were to those of the moas found in New Zealand.

The researchers constructed a new evolutionary tree that suggests that kiwis are more closely related to the emu, cassowary, and ostrich. Also, based on the results of this study, the researchers suggested that New Zealand was colonized twice by ancestors of flightless birds. The first ancestor gave rise to the now-extinct moas. The second ancestor gave rise to the kiwis.

Test Yourself

1. c   2. d   3. e   4. d   5. b   6. d   7. b   8. b   9. c   10. e

Conceptual Questions

1. The scientific name of every species has two parts, which are the genus name and the species epithet. The genus name is always capitalized, whereas the species name is not. Both names are italicized. An example is *Canis lupus.*

2. Morphological analysis focuses on morphological features of extinct and modern species. Many traits are analyzed to obtain a comprehensive picture of two species' relatedness. Convergent evolution leads to similar traits that arise independently in different species as they adapt to similar environments. Convergent evolution can, therefore, cause errors if a researcher assumes that a particular trait arose only once and that all species having the trait have the same common ancestor.

3. If neutral mutations occur at a relatively constant rate, they act as a molecular clock on which to measure evolutionary time. Genetic diversity between species that is due to neutral mutation gives an estimate of the time elapsed since the last common ancestor. A molecular clock can provide a timescale to a phylogenetic tree.

Chapter 27

Concept Checks

Figure 27.2   The red color arises from rhodopsins, pigment-protein complexes located in the cell membranes of the halophytic archaea growing abundantly in these salty ponds.

Figure 27.5   The cell will tend to float because it is full of intact gas vesicles.

Figure 27.11   The fluorescence staining process may be faster but requires the use of a fluorescence microscope, which is more expensive and complex than a simple compound microscope. The Gram stain can be assessed with a simple compound microscope of the type often found in biology class laboratories.

Figure 27.12   The motion of the stiff filament of a prokaryotic flagellum is more like that of a propeller shaft than the flexible arms of a human swimmer.

Figure 27.14   Cells having pili tend to move with a twitching or gliding motion.

Figure 27.15   When DNA sequencing studies show that samples contain many uncultured bacterial species, the fluorescence method is preferred, though it requires the use of a fluorescence microscope. Under such conditions, the culture method will give an underestimate of bacterial numbers. But when the goal is to estimate numbers of bacteria whose culture preferences are known, the culture method may provide good estimates.

Figure 27.16   Endospores allow bacterial cells to survive treatments and environmental conditions that would kill ordinary cells.

Figure 27.18   The transition point for both genes occurs around dusk.

Figure 27.19   Structural similarities to bacterial flagella and pili indicate that these types of attack systems evolved from these structures.

Feature Investigation Questions

1. *Deinococcus radiodurans* has the ability to survive levels of ionizing radiation that would kill most other organisms, and for periods of time that are not tolerated by other organisms. Investigators wanted to know why *D. radiodurans* was so resistant to radiation.

2. Daly and associates suggested that cellular levels of manganese ion might play a role in radiation resistance.

3. Bacteria that had been grown on media containing higher levels of manganese ion were better able to resist radiation than those grown on media containing lower levels of manganese ion.

Test Yourself

1. c   2. b   3. c   4. e   5. a   6. a   7. b   8. e   9. d   10. d

Conceptual Questions

1. Small cell size and simple division processes allow many bacteria to divide much more rapidly than eukaryotes. This helps to explain why food can spoil so quickly and why infections can spread very rapidly within the body. Other factors also influence these rates.

2. Pathogen populations naturally display genetic variation in their susceptibility to antibiotics. When such populations are exposed to antibiotics, even if initially only a few cells are resistant, the numbers of resistant cells will eventually increase and could come to dominate natural populations.

3. Humans. Only when humans pollute natural waters with high levels of fertilizers originating from sewage effluent or crop field runoff are cyanobacterial populations able to grow large enough to produce harmful blooms.

Chapter 28
Concept Checks

Figure 28.1   Diatoms are algal protists, meaning that they are typically photosynthetic and produce organic compounds. These organic compounds can be digested and respired as food by heterotrophic protists.

Figure 28.6   After particles are ingested via feeding grooves, particles are enclosed by membrane vesicles and then digested by enzymes.

Figure 28.7   The intestinal parasite *Giardia lamblia* is transmitted from one person to another via fecal wastes, whereas the urogenital parasite *Trichomonas vaginalis* can be transmitted by sexual activity.

Figure 28.14   The nucleomorph encodes some of the materials needed for plastid function.

Figure 28.16   The sail-like portions of the dinoflagellate cell wall help keep the cells afloat.

Figure 28.17   Flagellar hairs function like oars, helping to pull cells through the water.

Figure 28.18   Kelps are harvested for the production of industrially useful materials. In addition, they nurture fishes and other wildlife of economic importance.

Figure 28.21   Genes that encode cell adhesion and extracellular matrix proteins are likely essential to modern choanoflagellates' ability to attach to surfaces, where they feed. Similar proteins are involved in the formation of multicellular tissues in animals. Evolutionary biologists would say that ancient choanoflagellates were preadapted for the later evolution of multicellular tissues in early animals.

Figure 28.24   Cysts allow protists to survive conditions that are not suitable for growth. One such condition would be the dry or cold environment outside a parasitic protist's warm, moist host tissues.

Figure 28.29   Gametes of *Plasmodium falciparum* undergo fusion to produce zygotes while in the mosquito host.

Feature Investigation Questions

1. One strain had earlier been reported to be toxic to fishes, while the other had been reported to be nontoxic, a difference that could be attributed to differing experimental conditions. The investigators wanted to determine the degree of toxicity of the two strains when grown under the same conditions.

2. Producing toxins requires considerable ATP and other resources, so many organisms produce such compounds only when needed. In the case of *Pfiesteria shumwayae*, this might be when a major food source, fish, was present, but not when they fed primarily upon algal cells. The investigators needed to know if this dinoflagellate produces toxin even when feeding on algae alone (which would not require toxin production) or only when exposed to fishes.

3. The team knew that fishermen and scientists had suffered amnesia and other neurological impairments when they were near water containing large populations of the genus *Pfiesteria*. These observations suggested that the toxin was volatile or suspended in water droplets that people could inhale. As a precaution, they used the biohazard containment system to avoid personal harm. The use of biohazard containment systems is generally recommended for scientists who work with hazardous or potentially hazardous biological materials.

Test Yourself

1. c   2. a   3. b   4. b   5. e   6. b   7. e   8. d   9. b   10. c

Conceptual Questions

1. Protists are amazingly diverse, reflecting the occurrence of extensive adaptive radiation after the origin of eukaryotic cells, widespread occurrence of endosymbiosis, and adaptation to many types of moist habitats, including the tissues of animals and plants. As a result of this extensive diversity, protists cannot be classified into a single kingdom or phylum.

2. Several protists, including the apicomplexans *Cryptosporidium parvum* and *Plasmodium falciparum* and the kinetoplastids *Leishmania major* and *Trypanosoma brucei*, cause many cases of illness around the world, but few treatments are available, and organisms often evolve drug resistance. Genomic data allow researchers to identify metabolic features of these parasites that are not present in humans and are therefore good targets for development of new drugs. An example is provided by metabolic pathways of the apicoplast, a reduced plastid that is present in cells of the genus *Plasmodium*. Because the apicoplast plays essential metabolic roles in the protist but is absent from humans, drugs that disable apicoplast metabolism would kill the parasite without harming the human host.

3. Most protist cells cannot survive outside moist environments, but cysts have tough walls and dormant cytoplasm that allow them to persist in habitats that are unfavorable for growth. While cysts play important roles in the asexual reproduction and survival of many protists, they also allow protist parasites such as *Entamoeba histolytica* (the cause of amoebic dysentery) to spread to human hosts who consume food or water that have been contaminated with cysts. Widespread contamination can sicken thousands of people at a time.

Chapter 29
Concept Checks

Figure 29.3   Liverworts grow very close to surfaces such as soil or tree trunks. Raising their sporophytes off the surface helps to disperse spores into air currents.

Figure 29.4   Wind speed varies, so if the moss released all the spores at the same time into a weak air current, the spores would not travel very far and might have to compete with the parent plant for scarce resources. By releasing spores gradually, some spores may enter strong gusts of wind that carry them long distances, reducing competition with the parent.

Figure 29.8   Larger sporophytes are able to capture more resources for use in producing larger numbers of progeny and therefore have greater fitness than do smaller sporophytes.

Figure 29.14   The capacity to produce both wood and seeds are key features of lignophytes.

Figure 29.16   The polyester cutin found in cuticle, sporopollenin on spore walls, and lignin on water-conducting tracheids of vascular tissues are resistant to decay and thus help plants fossilize.

Figure 29.17   During the Carboniferous (Coal Age), atmospheric oxygen levels reached historic high levels that were able to supply the large needs of giant insects, which obtain oxygen by diffusion.

Figure 29.20   Increase in the surface area of placental transfer cells provides room for increased numbers of transport proteins. The greater the number of transport proteins per cell, the more rapidly solutes can be transferred from one cell to another.

Figure 29.22   Because the veins of fern leaves reflect the vascular systems of branched stem systems, you might infer that leaves evolved from more highly branched stem systems would be more-densely veined, that is, have more veins per unit area than fern leaves.

Figure 29.23   Although some angiosperm seeds, such as those of corn and coconut, contain abundant endosperm, many angiosperm embryos consume most or all of the nutritive endosperm during their development.

Figure 29.25   Because the lacy integument of *Runcaria* does not completely enclose the megasporangium, it probably did not function to protect the megasporangium before fertilization nor as an effective seed coat after fertilization, as do the integuments of modern seed plants. However, the lacy integument of *Runcaria* might have retained the megasporangium on the parent sporophyte during the period of time when nutrients flowed from parent to developing ovule and seed. That function would prevent megasporangia from dropping off the parent plant before fertilization occurred, allow the parent plant to provide nutrients needed during embryo development, and allow seeds time to absorb and store more nutrients from the parent. Such a function would illustrate how one mutation having a positive reproductive benefit can lay the foundation for subsequent mutations that confer additional fitness. *Runcaria* illustrates a first step in the multistage evolutionary process that gave rise to modern seeds.

Feature Investigation Questions

1. The experimental goals were to determine the rate at which organic molecules produced by gametophyte photosynthesis were able to move into sporophytes and to investigate the effect of sporophyte size on the amount of organic molecules transferred from the gametophyte.

2. The investigators shaded sporophytes with black glass covers to ensure that all of the radioactive organic molecules detected in sporophytes at the end of the experiment came originally from the gametophyte.

3. The investigators measured the amount of radioactivity in gametophytes and sporophytes, and in sporophytes of different sizes. These measurements indicated the relative amounts of labeled organic compounds that were present in different plant tissues.

Test Yourself

1. c   2. d   3. d   4. e   5. b   6. a   7. c   8. e   9. c   10. b

Conceptual Questions

1. Charophycean algae, particularly the complex genera *Chara* and *Coleochaete*, share many features of structure, reproduction, and biochemistry with land plants. Examples include cell division similarities and plasmodesmata and sexual reproduction by means of flagellate sperm and eggs.

2. Bryophytes are well adapted for sexual reproduction when water is available for fertilization. Their green gametophytes efficiently transfer nutrients to developing embryos, enhancing their growth into sporophytes. Their sporophytes are able to produce many genetically diverse spores as the result of meiosis and effectively disperse these spores by means of wind.

3. Vascular tissues allow tracheophytes to effectively conduct water from roots to stems and to leaves. Waxy cuticle helps prevent loss of water by evaporation through plant surfaces. Stomata allow plants to achieve gas exchange under moist conditions and help them avoid losing excess water under arid conditions.

Chapter 30

Concept Checks

Figure 30.3 People should not eat cycad seeds and other plant parts because they typically contain toxic compounds.

Figure 30.4 The nitrogen-fixing cyanobacteria that often occur within the coralloid roots of cycads are photosynthetic organisms that require light. If coralloid roots occurred underground, symbiotic cyanobacteria would not receive enough light to survive.

Figure 30.9 In the dry or cold conditions in which conifers live, air bubbles may form in tracheids; these air bubbles can interfere with water flow if they spread from one tracheid to another. When such bubbles form, the torus seals off connections to other tracheids, thereby helping to maintain water flow.

Figure 30.10 Ways in which conifer leaves are adapted to resist water loss include low surface area/volume needle- or scale-shape, thick surface coating of waxy cuticle, and stomata that are sunken into the leaf and are therefore less exposed to drying winds.

Figure 30.12 Wide vessels are commonly present in the water transport tissues of angiosperms and much less commonly in other plants. The vessels occasionally found in nonangiosperms are thought to have evolved independently from those of angiosperms.

Figure 30.20 A large, showy perianth would not be useful to grass plants because they are wind pollinated; such a perianth would interfere with

pollination in grasses. By not producing a showy perianth, grasses increase the chances of successful pollination and save resources that would otherwise be consumed during perianth development.

Figure 30.24 The flower characteristics of *Brighhamia insignis* shown in this figure (white color and deep, narrow nectar tubes) are consistent with pollination by a moth (see Table 30.1).

Figure 30.26 Importantly, ears of modern *Zea mays* do not readily shatter when the fruits are mature, as do those of teosinte. This feature fosters human ability to harvest the fruits.

Feature Investigation Questions

1. The investigators obtained many samples from around the world because they wanted to increase their chances of finding as many species as possible.

2. The researchers grew plants in a greenhouse under consistent environmental conditions because they wanted to reduce possible impact of environmental variation on the ratio of cannabinoids produced.

3. Although cannabinoids are produced in glandular hairs that cover the plant surface, these compounds are most abundant on leaves near the flowers. Collecting such leaves reduces the chances that compounds might be missed by the analysis.

Test Yourself

1. d   2. a   3. e   4. e   5. b   6. d   7. e   8. c   9. d   10. e

Conceptual Questions

1. Humans should generally not consume food products made from cycads because these plants typically produce toxins that protect against herbivory. At least some cycads harbor cyanobacterial symbionts that are known to produce an unusual amino acid (BMAA) that is associated with dementia in humans.

2. Apple, strawberry, and cherry plants coevolved with animals that use the fleshy, sweet portion of the fruits as food and excrete the seeds, thereby dispersing them. Humans have sensory systems similar to those of the target animals and likewise are attracted by the same colors, odors, and tastes.

3. A sunflower is not a single flower, but rather is an inflorescence, a group of flowers.

Chapter 31

Concept Checks

Figure 31.3 Fungal hyphae growing into a substrate having much higher solute concentration will tend to lose cell water to the substrate, a process that could inhibit fungal growth. This process explains how salting or drying foods helps to protect them from fungal degradation and thus are common preservation techniques.

Figure 31.6 You might filter the air entering the patient's room and limit the entry of visitors and materials that could introduce fungal spores from the outside environment.

Figure 31.8 Early-diverging fungi that are adapted to live and reproduce in the water would not display the reproductive features shown.

Figure 31.11 The toxin amanitin could kill eukaryotic cells by interfering with transcription, thus stopping gene expression.

Figure 31.16 Compounds that interfere with the function of histidine kinase would not harm humans (because we lack such proteins) but would prevent dimorphic fungi from producing the yeast form that spreads so readily in the body by means of budding.

Figure 31.18 Modern AM (arbuscular mycorrhizal fungi), also known as Glomeromycota, do not occur separately from plant hosts, as far as is known.

Figure 31.19 Ectomycorrhizal fungi provide their plant partners with water and minerals absorbed from a much larger area of soil than plant roots can exploit on their own.

Figure 31.22 Lichens do not necessarily contain the same algae as the soredia from which the lichens develop, because lichens often switch algal partners.

Feature Investigation Questions

1. Plants growing on soils up to 65°C would be expected to have fungal endophytes that aid in heat stress tolerance.

2. The investigators cured some of their *C. protuberata* cultures of an associated virus; then they compared the survival of plants infected with fungal endophytes that had virus versus endophytes lacking virus under conditions of heat stress. Only plants having fungal endophytes that possessed the virus were able to survive growth on soils of high temperature.

3. The fungus *C. protuberata* might be used to confer heat stress tolerance to crop plants, as the investigators demonstrated in tomato.

Test Yourself

1. c 2. b 3. e 4. b 5. a 6. d 7. e 8. b 9. e 10. a

Conceptual Questions

1. Fungi are like animals in being heterotrophic, having absorptive nutrition, and storing surplus organic compounds in their cells as glycogen. Fungi are like plants in having rigid cell walls and reproducing by means of walled spores that are dispersed by wind, water, or animals.

2. Toxic or hallucinogenic compounds likely help to protect the fungi from organisms that would consume them.

3. Some fungi partner with algae or cyanobacteria to form lichens. Some fungi associate with plant roots to form mycorrhizae. Some fungi grow as endophytes within the bodies of plants. In all cases, the heterotrophic fungi receive photosynthetic products from the autotrophic partner.

Chapter 32

Concept Checks

Figure 32.2   Simple choanoflagellates are single-celled organisms. Only later, when such organisms become colonial and groups of cells acquire specialized functions, as in sponges, can we consider them early animals.

Figure 32.5   The coelom functions as a hydrostatic skeleton, which aids in movement. This feature permitted increased burrowing activity and contributed to the development of a profusion of wormlike body shapes.

Figure 32.10   Molecular analysis splits the protostomes into two distinct clades—the Lophotrochozoa and the Ecdysozoa—whereas the traditional phylogeny does not.

Figure 32.11   The sister group to the deuterostomes is the protostomes, but in the body plan phylogeny, the sister group is a more loosely defined part of the protostomes, the coelomate protostomes, including mollusks, annelids, and arthropods.

Figure 32.12   The main members of the Ecdysozoa are the arthropods (insects, spiders, and crustaceans) and the nematodes.

Feature Investigation Questions

1. The researchers sequenced the complete gene that encodes small subunit rRNA from a variety of representative taxa of animals to determine their phylogenetic relationships, particularly the relationships of arthropods to other animal taxa.

2. The results indicated a monophyletic clade containing arthropods and nematodes, plus several other smaller phyla. This clade was called the Ecdysozoa. The results of this study indicated that nematodes were more closely related to the arthropods than previously believed.

3. The fruit fly, *Drosophila melanogaster,* and the nematode, *Caenorhabditis elegans,* have been widely studied to understand early development. Under the traditional phylogeny, these two species were not considered to be closely related, so similarities in development were assumed to have arisen early in animal evolution. With the closer relationship indicated by this study, these similarities may have evolved after the divergence of the Ecdysozoan clade. This puts into question the applicability of studies of these organisms to the understanding of human biology.

Test Yourself

1. b 2. c 3. e 4. c 5. c 6. e 7. d 8. d 9. b 10. e

Conceptual Questions

1. (1) Absence or existence of different tissue types. (2) Type of body symmetry. (3) Presence or absence of a true body cavity. (4) Patterns of embryonic development.

2. Radially symmetric animals can be divided equally by a longitudinal plane passing through the central axis. Bilaterally symmetric animals can be divided along a vertical plane at the midline to create two halves; thus, a bilateral animal has a left side and a right side, which are mirror images.

3. Sea urchins are deuterostomes. Deuterostomes have indeterminate cleavage, and all cells have the ability to develop into a complete embryo. Humans are also deuterostomes, so sea urchin embryos can be used as a model for human development.

Chapter 33

Concept Checks

Figure 33.2   Sponges aren't eaten by other organisms because they produce toxic chemicals and contain needle-like silica spicules that are hard to digest.

Figure 33.4   The dominant life stages are jellyfish: medusa; sea anemone: polyp; Portuguese man-of-war: polyp (in a large floating colony).

Figure 33.7   Having no specialized respiratory or circulatory system, flatworms obtain oxygen by diffusion. A flattened shape ensures no cells are too far from the body surface.

Figure 33.11   (1) A ciliary feeding device, and (2) a respiratory device are the two main functions of the lophophore.

Figure 33.12   Technically, most mollusks pump hemolymph into vessels and then into tissues. The hemolymph collects in open, fluid-filled cavities called sinuses, which flow into the gills and then back to the heart. This is known as an open circulatory system. Only closed circulatory systems pump blood, as occurs in the cephalopods.

Figure 33.17   Some advantages of segmentation are organ duplication, minimization of body distortion during movement, and specialization of some segments.

Figure 33.20   Other parasitic nematodes in humans are roundworms, *Ascaris lumbricoides;* hookworms, *Necator americanus;* and pinworms, *Enterobius vermicularis.*

Figure 33.25   All arachnids have a body consisting of two tagmata: a cephalothorax and an abdomen. Insects have three tagmata: a head, thorax, and abdomen.

Figure 33.27   Two key insect adaptations are the development of wings and an exoskeleton that reduced water loss and aided in the colonization of land.

Figure 33.33   In embryonic development, deuterostomes have radial cleavage, indeterminate cleavage, and the blastopore becomes the anus. (In protostomes, cleavage is spiral and determinate, and the blastopore becomes the mouth.)

Figure 33.34   Two unique features of an echinoderm are an internal skeleton of calcified plates and a water vascular system.

Feature Investigation Questions

1. The researchers tested the hypothesis that an octopus can learn by observing the behavior of another octopus.

2. The results indicated that the observer learned by watching the training of the other octopus. The observer was much more likely to choose the same color ball that the demonstrator was trained to attack. These results seem to support the hypothesis that octopuses can learn by observing the behavior of others.

3. The untrained octopuses had no prior exposure to the demonstrators. The results indicated that these octopuses were as likely to attack the white ball as the red ball. No preference for either color was indicated. The untrained octopuses acted as a control. This is an important factor to ensure the results from the trials using observers indicate response to learning and not an existing preference for a certain color.

Test Yourself

1. b 2. d 3. d 4. d 5. b 6. c 7. b 8. a 9. c 10. a

Conceptual Questions

1. The five main feeding methods used by animals are (1) suspension feeding, (2) decomposition, (3) herbivory, (4) predation, and (5) parasitism. Suspension feeding is usually used to filter out food particles from the water column. A great many phyla are filter feeders, including sponges, rotifers, lophophorates, some mollusks and echinoderms and tunicates. Decomposers usually feed on dead material such as animal carcasses or dead leaves. For example, many fly and beetle larvae feed on dead animals, and earthworms consume dead leaves from the surface of the Earth. Earthworms and crabs also sift through soil or mud, eating the substrate and digesting the soil-dwelling bacteria, protists, and dead organic material. Herbivores eat plants or algae and are especially common in the arthropoda. Adult moths and butterflies also consume nectar. Snails are also common plant feeders. Predators feed on other animals, killing their prey, and may be active hunters or sit-and-wait predators. Many scorpions and spiders actively pursue their prey, whereas web-spinning spiders ambush their prey using webs. Parasites also feed on other animals but do not normally kill their hosts. Endoparasites live inside their hosts and include flukes, tapeworms, and nematodes. Ectoparasites live on the outside of their hosts and include ticks and lice.

2. The nematocyst is a powerful capsule with an inverted coiled and barbed thread that functions to immobilize small prey so they can be passed to the mouth and ingested. It is a unique and characteristic feature of the cnidarians.

3. Complete metamorphosis has four stages: egg, larva, pupa, and adult. The larval stage is often spent in an entirely different habitat from that of the adult, and larval and adult forms utilize different food sources. Incomplete metamorphosis has only three stages: egg, nymph, and adult. Young insects, called nymphs, look like miniature adults when they hatch from their eggs.

Chapter 34

Concept Checks

Figure 34.1   Vertebrates (but not invertebrates) usually possess a (1) notochord; (2) dorsal hollow nerve chord; (3) pharyngeal slits; (4) postanal tail, exhibited by all chordates; (5) cranium; (6) neural crest, exhibited by all craniates; (7) vertebral column; (8) endoskeleton of cartilage or bone; and (9) diversity of internal organs.

Figure 34.2   The hagfish is not a true fish because it does not possess vertebrae.

Figure 34.7   Ray-finned fishes (but not sharks) have a (1) bony skeleton; (2) mucus-covered skin; (3) swim bladder; and (4) operculum covering the gills.

Figure 34.11   The advantages to animals that moved onto land included an oxygen-rich environment and a bonanza of food in the form of terrestrial plants and the insects that fed on them.

Figure 34.14   No. Caecilians and some salamanders give birth to live young.

Figure 34.15   Besides the amniotic egg, other critical innovations in amniotes are thoracic breathing; internal fertilization; a thicker, less permeable skin; and more efficient kidneys.

Figure 34.18   Both classes have four-chambered hearts and care for their young.

Figure 34.21   Adaptations in birds to reduce body weight for flight include a lightweight skull; reduction of organ size; and a reduction of organs outside of breeding season. Also female birds have one ovary and relatively few eggs, and no urinary bladder.

Figure 34.28   Defining features of primates are grasping hands; eyes situated on the front of the head to facilitate binocular vision; a large brain; and digits with flat nails instead of claws.

Feature Investigation Questions

1. The researchers were interested in determining the method in which *Hox* genes controlled limb development.

2. The researchers bred mice that were homozygous for certain mutations in specific *Hox* genes. This allowed the researchers to determine the function of individual genes.

3. The researchers found that homozygous mutants would develop limbs of shorter lengths compared to the wild-type mice. The reduced length was due to the lack of development of particular bones in the limb, specifically, the radius, ulna, and some carpels. These results indicated that simple mutations in a few genes could lead to dramatic changes in limb development.

Test Yourself

1. e   2. d   3. a   4. d   5. d   6. c   7. c   8. a   9. c   10. d

Conceptual Questions

1. Both taxa have external limbs that move when the attached muscles contract or relax. The difference is that arthropods have external skeletons with the muscles attached internally, whereas vertebrates have internal skeletons with the muscles attached externally.

2. The sensors of the lateral line pick up pressure waves and send nervous signals to the brain. The operculum is a protective flap that covers the gills.

3. 1. The amnion, the innermost membrane, protects the developing embryo in a fluid-filled sac.
   2. The yolk sac provides a stockpile of nutrients.
   3. The allantois functions as a disposal sac for metabolic wastes.
   4. The chorion allows gas exchange between the embryo and the surrounding air.

Chapter 35

Concept Checks

Figure 35.3   Because organ systems are defined as structures that are composed of more than one organ, roots lack organ systems.

Figure 35.5   As in the case of shoots, the capacity to divide the root into two equal pieces by means of a line drawn from the circular edges through the center would indicate that a root has superficial radial symmetry. In order to determine that an organ has radial symmetry at the cellular level, you would have to compare the microscopic views of randomly chosen, wedge-shaped pieces of cross-slices. If the structure of the wedges is similar, the organ has radial symmetry at the microscopic level.

Figure 35.8   Locating stomata on the darker and cooler lower leaf surface helps reduce water loss from the leaf.

Figure 35.12   A twig having five sets of bud scale scars is likely to be approximately 6 years old.

Figure 35.17   Cactus stems are green and photosynthetic, playing the role served by the leaves of most plants.

Figure 35.22   A woody stem builds up a thicker layer of wood than inner bark in part because older tracheids and vessel element walls are not lost during shedding of bark, which is the case for secondary phloem. In addition, plants typically produce a greater volume of xylem than phloem tissue per year, in part because vessel elements are relatively wide. A large volume of water-conducting tissue helps plants maintain a large amount of internal water.

Figure 35.26   Lateral roots are produced from internal meristematic tissue because roots do not produce axillary buds like those from which shoot branches develop. Internal production of branch roots helps to prevent them from shearing off as the root tip grows through abrasive soil.

Feature Investigation Questions

1. The advantages of using natural plants include the opportunity to avoid influencing plants with unnatural environmental factors, such as artificial light, and the exposure of all experimental plants to similar growth conditions. In addition, the investigators studied the leaves of some large trees, which would be hard to accommodate in a greenhouse.

2. Pinnately veined leaves were splinted to prevent their breaking, since they were cut at the single main vein, which has both support and conducting functions.

3. Sack and associates measured leaf water conduction at two or more places on each leaf because the effect of cutting a vein might have affected some portions of leaves more than others.

Test Yourself

1. d   2. c   3. b   4. a   5. c   6. a   7. d   8. e   9. 6   10. d

Conceptual Questions

1. If overall plant architecture were bilaterally symmetrical, plants would be shaped like higher animals, with a distinct front (ventral surface) and back (dorsal surface). By comparison to radially symmetrical organisms, bilaterally symmetrical plants would have reduced ability to deploy branches and leaves in a way that would fill available lighted space and would thus not be able to take optimal photosynthetic advantage of their habitats.

2. If leaves were generally radially symmetrical (shaped like spheres or cylinders), leaves would not have maximal ability to absorb sunlight, and they would not be able to optimally disperse excess heat from their surfaces.

3. Although tall herbaceous plants exist (palms and bamboo are examples), the additional support and water-conducting capacity that are provided by secondary xylem allow woody plants to grow tall.

Chapter 36

Concept Checks

Figure 36.4 Auxin efflux carriers could be located on the upper sides of root cells, thereby allowing auxin to move upward in roots.

Figure 36.6 Once a callus has been established from a single plant having desirable characteristics using plant tissue culture, the callus can be divided into many small calluses. A grower could transfer these to separate containers having the appropriate hormone mixtures to induce root and shoot growth, then transplant the young plant clones to soil. This would allow the grower to produce many identical plants.

Figure 36.9 The triple response that dicot seedlings show in response to internally produced ethylene allows them to protect the delicate apical meristem from damage as the seedling emerges through the soil.

Figure 36.10 The active conformation of phytochrome absorbs far-red light. Such absorption causes the active conformation of phytochrome to change

to the inactive conformation and to move out of the nucleus and into the cytosol.

Figure 36.11 The inactive conformation of phytochrome would absorb the red portion of sunlight, thereby converting phytochrome into the active conformation.

Figure 36.12 Exposing plants to brief periods of darkness during the daytime will have no effect on flowering because flowering is determined by night length.

Figure 36.14 Yes, just as shoots exhibit negative gravitropism in upward growth, roots are capable of using negative phototropism to grow downward, because light decreases with depth in the soil.

Figure 36.16 In some plants, aerenchyma development is genetically determined and occurs even in the absence of flooding. In other cases, aerenchyma develops only under flooding conditions as a result of controlled cell death.

Figure 36.17 Predators are more likely to be able to find their prey if the latter are concentrated and exposed while feeding on plants. Plants benefit when predation removes herbivores, a process that lessens damage to plants.

Figure 36.19 Similar suites of protective plant hormones, such as jasmonic acid, are used in both types of defenses.

Feature Investigation Questions

1. The following experiment by Briggs falsified the hypothesis that light destroys auxin:

2. Hypothetically, auxin enhances the rate at which cell membrane proton pumps acidify the plant cell wall, thereby allowing cells to extend. Although the evidence for acid effects on cell wall extension is strong, the molecular basis of possible auxin effects on proton pumps is not as yet clear.

3. A small number of seedling tips could display atypical responses for a variety of reasons. The investigators actually performed the experiment with many replicate seedling tips (coleoptiles), in order to gain confidence that the responses are general.

Test Yourself

1. c   2. c   3. a   4. e   5. d   6. d   7. c   8. d   9. d   10. d

---

(b) Briggs experiment 1

HYPOTHESIS Light destroys auxin on lit side of shoot tips, causing unequal auxin distribution. Unlit side should grow more than lit side.

STARTING MATERIALS Corn seedlings.

	Experimental level	Conceptual level

1 Collect auxin into agar blocks from:
   A dark-grown tips
   B tips grown with directional light

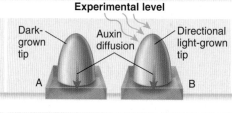

Dark-grown tip — Auxin diffusion — Directional light-grown tip

A   B

If light destroys auxin on one side, less auxin will enter the block.

2 Place agar blocks on right side of decapitated shoots.

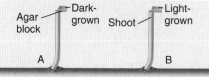

Agar block — Dark-grown — Shoot — Light-grown

A   B

If the block on the right side has less auxin, it will cause less bending.

3 **THE DATA**

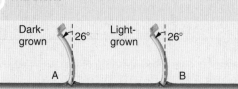

Dark-grown   26°   Light-grown   26°

A   B

4 **CONCLUSION**

Similar bending demonstrates that light did not destroy auxin in the directionally lit shoot tip. If it had, less auxin would have been present in the agar block in B, and the degree of bending would have been less. The hypothesis described under conceptual level (above) is incorrect.

Conceptual Questions

1. Behavior is defined as the responses of living things to a stimulus. Therefore, because plants display many kinds of responses to diverse stimuli, they display behavior.

2. Many kinds of disease-causing bacteria and fungi occur in nature, and these organisms evolve very quickly, producing diverse elicitors. Thus, plants must maintain a stock of resistance genes, each having many alleles.

3. Talking implies a conversation with "listeners" who detect a message and respond to it. Thus, plants that exude volatile compounds that attract enemies of herbivores could be interpreted as "talking" to those enemies. The message is "Hey, you guys, there's food for you over here." In addition, research has revealed that some plants near those under attack respond to volatile compounds by building up defenses. "Talking" to other plants does not enhance the "talker's" fitness. But the ability to "listen" enhances the "listener's" fitness, because it can take preemptive actions to prevent attack.

Chapter 37

Concept Checks

Figure 37.4 Plants adapted to deep shade may have green and photosynthetic plastids in their epidermal cells, whereas the epidermal cells of most plants have plastids that lack chlorophyll.

Figure 37.5 Plastids that occur in a cluster near the nucleus would have more rubisco than plastids at the periphery.

Figure 37.6 Chlorosis is not always a sign of iron deficiency; it can be a deficiency symptom for several mineral nutrients, including zinc in corn.

Figure 37.10 Mineral leaching occurs more readily from sandy soils than from clay soils.

Figure 37.11 Tropical soils are often acidic, as are those of higher latitude regions that are impacted by acid rain resulting from air pollution.

Figure 37.12 The list could include chlorophyll, carotenoids, ATP, NADP, rubisco, and many other enzymes.

Figure 37.13 Soil crusts containing nitrogen-fixing cyanobacteria increase soil fertility, fostering the growth of larger plants that stabilize soils against erosion and provide forage for animals.

Figure 37.14 Oxygen, which makes up 21% of Earth's present atmosphere, can bind to the active site of nitrogenase, thereby inactivating it.

Figure 37.16 Acidic conditions cause soil aluminum ions to become more mobile and thus to enter plants more easily. Hydrangea stores aluminum ions in the cell vacuole, a protective adaptation that prevents aluminum from damaging other cell components. The aluminum causes pigments that are also located in the vacuoles of sepals to change from pink to blue.

Feature Investigation Questions

1. During this period of time, the amount of phosphorus in plant tissues had significantly decreased, but plant growth had not yet been affected. Thus, a monitoring system based on gene expression changes occurring during this time would allow farmers time to apply fertilizer in order to prevent crop losses resulting from nutrient deficiency.

2. *SDQ1* expression is induced by phosphorus deficiency. This gene fosters replacement of plastid phospholipids with sulfur-containing lipids, thereby reducing the plant's phosphorus requirement.

3. They used genetic engineering techniques to place a reporter gene under the control of the *SQD1* promoter, so that when *SQD1* was expressed, the reporter gene was expressed also. After growing plants in nutrient solutions containing various levels of phosphorus, they removed sample leaves and treated them with a compound that turns blue when the reporter gene is expressed. When they saw blue leaves, the investigators could infer (1) that the plants from which those leaves had been taken were beginning to experience phosphorus deficiency, and (2) that application of fertilizer at this point could prevent damage to the plants.

Test Yourself

1. e   2. a   3. c   4. b   5. e   6. c   7. d   8. d   9. a   10. b

Conceptual Questions

1. Agricultural experts are concerned that adding excess fertilizer to crop fields increases the costs of crop production. Ecologists are concerned that excess fertilizers will wash from crop fields into natural waters and cause harmful overgrowths of cyanobacteria, algae, and aquatic plants. Methods for closely monitoring crop nutrient needs so that only the appropriate amount of fertilizer is applied would help to allay both groups' concerns.

2. Boron deficiency induces the expression of a gene that encodes a membrane transporter protein that moves boron from living root cells into root xylem for transport throughout the plant. This action helps to reduce boron deficiency in plant tissues. When plants are exposed to too much boron, the transporter protein is removed from root cell membranes, with the result that boron cannot move into the xylem and the rest of the plant. This action protects the plant from boron toxicity.

3. Use Figure 37.10 as a reference. A first arrow could be drawn from a root to rhizobia in the soil, and the arrow labeled "flavonoids." A second arrow could be drawn from rhizobia to roots and labeled "Nod factors." A third arrow from rhizobia to roots could be labeled "infection proteins." A fourth arrow from roots to rhizobia could be labeled "nodulins" and the resulting nodule environmental conditions, which influence the formation of bacteroids. A fifth arrow could represent the flow of fixed nitrogen from bacterioids to plant. A sixth arrow could represent the flow of organic compounds from plant to bacteroids.

Chapter 38

Concept Checks

Figure 38.5 When placed in pure water, a turgid cell having a water potential of 1.0 will lose water, because 1 is greater than 0. When placed in pure water, a plasmolyzed cell having a water potential of -1.0 MPa will gain water. When placed in pure water, a flaccid cell having a water potential of -0.5 MPa will gain water. This is because water moves from a region of higher water potential to a region of lower water potential, and 0 is greater than -0.5.

Figure 38.8 In most plants, most Al^{3+} will remain in the roots, because the ions can move through outer root tissues but cannot cross the endodermis. However, some aluminum may be able to get into root vascular tissues by seeping into root tips where the endodermis has not yet formed or at places where the endodermis has been broken by the emergence of branch roots. These processes, together with the fact that aluminum ions are very abundant in soils, explain why plant tissues may contain some aluminum even though it is not a plant nutrient.

Figure 38.11 You would likely see stained rings or helical ribbons extending up the insides of the long walls of extensible tracheids. You would not see staining at the ends of tracheids, where they connect to form cell files.

Figure 38.12 The large perforations in vessel element end walls allow an air bubble to extend from one element to another, thereby clogging vessels and preventing water flow through them. In contrast, the much smaller pores in the end walls of tracheids do not allow water to flow as efficiently as it does through vessels, but these smaller pores also retard the movement of air bubbles. As a result, air bubbles are confined to a single tracheid where they do little harm.

Figure 38.13 Root pressure can help to reverse embolism, thereby aiding water flow through xylem.

Figure 38.16 The evaporation of water has a powerful cooling effect because it disperses heat so effectively. Water has the highest heat of vaporization of any known liquid.

Figure 38.17 You could model a stomatal guard cell with an elongate balloon by partially inflating it, then attaching thick tape along one side to represent thickened inner walls and circles of string or thin tape to represent radial cellulose, then adding more air to the balloon. The balloon should curve as it expands, just as a guard cell does when the stomatal pore opens. Two such balloons could be used to model both guard cells and the stomatal pore.

Figure 38.19 In its desert habitat, times of drought and contrasting availability of water sufficient to support the development and photosynthetic function of leaves do not occur at predictable times, as is the case for temperate forests. For this reason, ocotillo leaf abscission is not amenable to the evolution of genetic mechanisms that allow leaf drop to be precisely timed in anticipation of the onset of drought.

Figure 38.25   You could note the relatively few genes that are plotted along the middle left side of the triangle, then try to localize the encoded proteins within the tissues of very young stem tissue, using microscopy.

Feature Investigation Questions

1. This design allowed investigators to compensate for variation among plants, which might have influenced the results had they used separate plants for experiments and controls.

2. Transpiration! Water evaporating from the surfaces of leaves exerted a tension on the water column of the xylem, pulling sap and water through it.

3. The effects of ions on sap flow rates did not directly depend on a biological process, so xylem sap of the same ionic concentration moved through dead plants at the same rate as in living plants.

Test Yourself

1. c   2. b   3. e   4. d   5. a   6. d   7. d   8. e   9. a   10. c

Conceptual Questions

1. In the case of plant fertilizers, more is not better, because the ion concentration of overfertilized soil may become so high as to draw water from plant cells. In this case, the cells would be bathed in a hypertonic solution and would likely lose water to the solution. If plant cells lose too much water, they will die.

2. When the natural vegetation is removed, transpiration stops, so water is not transported from the ground to the atmosphere, where it may be an important contributor to local rainfall. Extensive removal of plants actually changes local climates in ways that reduce agricultural productivity and human survival.

3. You cannot assume that an ocotillo plant lacking leaves is dead, because this plant responds to drought by shedding its leaves, and living plants can produce new leaves when the drought stress is relieved. However, if the ocotillo plants do not produce new leaves after normal rainstorms, you might suspect that they have died.

Chapter 39

Concept Checks

Figure 39.2   Because gametophytes are haploid, they lack the potential for allele variation at each gene locus that is present in diploid sporophytes. Hence, gametophytes are more vulnerable to environmental stresses. By living within the diploid tissues of flowers, flowering plant gametophytes are protected to some extent, and the plant does not lose its gamete-producing life cycle stage.

Figure 39.3   Some flowers lack some of the major flower parts.

Figure 39.4   By clustering its stamens around the pistil, the hibiscus flower increases the chance that a pollinator will both pick up pollen and deliver pollen from another hibiscus flower on the same trip.

Figure 39.7   The absence of showy petals often correlates with wind pollination, because large petals would interfere with the shedding of pollen in the wind.

Figure 39.10   The rim flowers of *Gerbera* inflorescences have bilateral symmetry, conferred by expression of a *CYCLOIDEA*-like gene. Rim flowers also possess showy petals that attract pollinators, but lack pollen-producing stamens. By contrast, central flowers display radial symmetry, lack showy petals, and possess pollen-producing stamens.

Figure 39.11   The maximum number of cells in a mature male gametophyte of a flowering plant is three: a tube cell and two sperm cells.

Figure 39.12   Female gametophytes are not photosynthetic and cannot produce their own food. Enclosed within ovules, female gametophytes lack direct access to the outside environment. Carpels contain veins of vascular tissue that bring nutrients from sporophytic tissue to ovules.

Figure 39.17   An embryo in which the TOPLESS genes were nonfunctional would have two roots and no shoots.

Figure 39.18   During their maturation, the cotyledons of eudicot seeds absorb the nutrients originally present in endosperm.

Feature Investigation Questions

1. Plant gametes, particularly egg cells, are produced by microscopic gametophytes enclosed by sporophytic flower tissues and were thus difficult to isolate.

2. The investigators used a pulse of electricity to stimulate cell fusion. This process is similar to electroporation, the use of electrical discharges to cause small pores to appear in the membranes of cells prior to their transformation during genetic engineering.

3. Investigators obtained egg cells and sperm cells from parents that differed in the color of stigmas and stigma hairs. They demonstrated that progeny plants were hybrids that had stigmas that were colored the same as one parent and stigma hairs that were colored the same as the other parent.

Test Yourself

1. a   2. b   3. d   4. b   5. d   6. e   7. b   8. c   9. d   10. c

Conceptual Questions

1. Pollen grains are vulnerable to mechanical damage and microbial attack during the journey through the air from the anthers of a flower to a stigma. Sporopollenin is an extremely tough polymer that helps to protect pollen cells from these dangers. The function of the beautiful sculptured patterns of sporopollenin on pollen surfaces is unclear.

2. The embryos within seeds are vulnerable to mechanical damage and microbial attack after they are dispersed. Seed coats protect embryos from these dangers and also help to prevent seeds from germinating until conditions are favorable for seedling survival and growth.

3. Flower diversity is an evolutionary response to diverse pollination circumstances. For example, plants such as oak and corn that are wind-pollinated produce flowers having a poorly developed perianth. If such wind-pollinated flowers had large, showy perianths, they would get in the way of pollen dispersal or acquisition. On the other hand, flowers that are pollinated by animals often have diverse shapes and attractive petals of differing colors or fragrances that have coevolved with different types of animal pollinators.

Chapter 40

Concept Checks

Figure 40.2   Locomotion is the movement of an animal's body from one place to another. This is achieved by the actions of skeletal muscle. However, smooth muscle contraction promotes movement of internal structures, like those of the digestive system, and contraction of cardiac muscle causes movement (beating) of the heart.

Figure 40.6   No. The brain, for example, does not contain muscle tissue (although the blood vessels supplying the brain do contain smooth muscle).

Figure 40.7   Blood, including plasma and blood cells, would leak out of the blood vessel into the interstitial space. The fluid level of the bloodstream would decrease, and that of the interstitial space near the site of the injury would increase. Eventually the blood that entered the interstitial space would be degraded by enzymes, resulting in the characteristic skin appearance of a bruise. If the injury were very severe, the fluid level in the blood could decrease to a point where the various tissues and organs of the body would not receive sufficient nutrients and oxygen to function normally.

Figure 40.8   A decrease in intracellular fluid volume, like that shown in the cell in this figure, would result in an increase in intracellular solute concentration (likewise, an increase in intracellular fluid volume would decrease intracellular solute concentrations). This may have drastic consequences on cell function. For example, some solutes, like Ca^{2+} and certain other ions, are toxic to cells at high concentrations.

Figure 40.10   Surface area is important to any living organism that needs to exchange materials with the environment. A good example of a high surface area/volume ratio is that of most tree leaves. This makes leaves ideally suited for such processes as light absorption (required for photosynthesis; see Chapter 8) and the exchange of gases and water with the environment.

Figure 40.12   No, not necessarily. Body temperature, for example, is maintained at different set points in birds and mammals. Other vertebrates and most invertebrates do not have temperature set points; their body temperature simply conforms close to that of the environment. As another example, a giraffe has a set point for blood pressure that is higher than that of a human being, because a giraffe's circulatory system must generate enough pressure to pump blood up its long neck.

Figure 40.15   In nature, an animal such as a horse would have the same type of responses shown here if threatened by a predator. Upon sensing the presence of the predator, the horse's respiratory and circulatory systems would begin increasing their activities in preparation for the possibility that the horse might have to flee or defend itself. This would occur even before the horse began to flee.

Feature Investigation Questions

1. Pavlov studied feedforward regulation of saliva production that occurs in hungry dogs even before they receive food. He hypothesized that the feedforward response could be conditioned to other, nonrelevant stimuli such as sounds, as long as the sounds were presented simultaneously with food.

2. Pavlov remained outside the room where the dog was housed when the conditioning stimulus—a metronome—was started. In addition, the room was carefully sealed to prevent any other stimuli, including smells, sights, and sounds, from interfering with the conditioning response.

3. He measured the amount of saliva secreted by salivary glands in the dog's mouth by collecting the saliva through a tube and funnel, and then recording the number of drops. He discovered that once a dog had become conditioned to hearing the sound of the metronome whenever presented with food, the sound itself was sufficient to stimulate the feedforward response of salivation. This experiment revealed that feedforward processes could be modulated by experience and learning.

Test Yourself

1. d   2. c   3. d   4. b   5. c   6. c   7. d   8. b   9. d   10. e

Conceptual Questions

1. Anatomy is the study of structure (form), and physiology is the study of function. For example, an anatomist might be interested in the arrangement of cells and tissues in an organ such as the heart, while a physiologist might be interested in the mechanisms by which heart cells contract to produce a heartbeat.

2. Structure and function are related in that the function of a given organ, for example, depends in part on the organ's size, shape, and cellular and tissue arrangement. Clues about a physical structure's function can often be obtained by examining the structure's form. For example, the extensive surface area of a moth's antennae suggests that the antennae are important in detecting the presence of airborne chemicals. Likewise, any structure that contains a large surface area for its volume is likely involved in some aspect of signal detection, cell-cell communication, or transport of materials within the animal or between the animal and the environment. Surface area increases by a power of 2, and volume increases by a power of 3 as an object enlarges; this means that in order to greatly increase surface area of a structure such as an antenna, without occupying enormous volumes, specializations must be present (such as folds) to package the structure in a small space.

3. Homeostasis is the ability of animals to maintain a stable internal environment by adjusting physiological processes, despite changes in the external environment. Examples include maintenance of salt and water balance, pH of body fluids, and body temperature. Some animals conform to their external environment to achieve homeostasis, but others regulate their internal environment themselves.

Chapter 41

Concept Checks

Figure 41.1   This is an example of a feedforward response, most famously demonstrated by the conditioning experiments of Ivan Pavlov. In this case, the peripheral and central nervous systems interact to prepare the hyena for feeding.

Figure 41.4   Many reflexes, such as the knee-jerk reflex, cannot be prevented once started. Others, however, can be controlled to an extent. Open your eyes widely and gently touch your eyelashes. A reflex that protects your eye will tend to make you close your eyelid. However, you can overcome this reflex with a bit of difficulty if you need to, for example, when you are putting in contact lenses.

Figure 41.5   The squid axon is not coated in myelin sheaths. This is another feature of the squid giant axon that makes it a convenient model for conducting in vitro experiments such as the one depicted in this figure.

Figure 41.7   Yes, the flow of K^+ down its chemical gradient does create an electrical gradient because K^+ is electrically charged. The net flow of K^+ will stop when the chemical gradient balances the electrical gradient. This occurs at the equilibrium potential.

Figure 41.10   When the K^+ channels open (at 1 msec), the Na^+ channels would still be opened, so the part of the curve that slopes downward would not occur as rapidly, and perhaps the cell would not be able to restore its resting potential.

Figure 41.12   The action potential can move faster down an axon. This is especially important for long axons, such as those that carry signals from the spinal cord to distant muscles.

Figure 41.14   In the absence of such enzymes, neurotransmitters would remain in the synapse for too long, and the postsynaptic cell could become overstimulated. In addition, the ability of the postsynaptic cell to respond to multiple, discrete inputs from the presynaptic cell would be compromised.

Feature Investigation Questions

1. Loewi was aware that electrical stimulation of the vagus nerve associated with heart muscle would slow down the rate of heart contractions in a frog. Also, he knew that electrical stimulation of other nerves associated with the frog heart produced opposite results. If the effects of the different nerves on heart muscle were mediated directly by electrical activity only, the heart muscle cells would have no way to distinguish between stimulatory and inhibitory signals. Loewi hypothesized that nerves released chemicals onto heart muscle cells and that it was these different chemicals that produced the varied effects on the heart.

2. Loewi placed two hearts in separate chambers, one heart with its vagus nerve intact and the other with its vagus nerve removed. He electrically stimulated the vagus nerve of the first heart, then removed some of the saline solution surrounding the heart and transferred it to the second heart. He then observed whether or not the second heart responded as if its vagus nerve had been intact and had been stimulated.

3. When fluid from the saline solution around the stimulated heart was added to the saline solution of the second, unstimulated heart, the rate of contraction in the second heart was decreased just as if its own vagus nerve had been intact and was stimulated. This suggested that chemicals were released into the saline solution of the first heart following the electrical stimulation of its vagus nerve, and that it was these chemicals that caused the cardiac muscle to slow its rate of contraction. The results did support Loewi's hypothesis.

Test Yourself

1. c   2. d   3. e   4. e   5. b   6. d   7. b   8. e   9. a   10. e

Conceptual Questions

1. Neurons are highly specialized, electrically excitable cells that communicate with another cell of its kind and with other types of cells by electrical or chemical signals.

   Glia are cells that surround the neurons; they are a major class of cells in nervous systems that perform various functions.

   Schwann cells are glial cells that form myelin around axons in the peripheral nervous system.

2. In a graded potential, a weak stimulus causes a small change in the membrane potential while a strong stimulus produces a greater change. Graded potentials occur along the dendrites and cell body. If a graded potential reaches the threshold potential at the axon hillock, this results in an action potential. This is a change in the membrane potential that is of a constant value and is propagated from the axon hillock to the axon terminal.

3. An increase in extracellular Na^+ concentration would slightly depolarize neurons, thereby changing the resting membrane potential. This effect would be minimal, however, because the resting membrane is not very permeable to Na^+. However, the shape of the action potentials in such neurons would be a little steeper, and the peak a little higher, because the electrochemical gradient favoring Na^+ entry into the cell through voltage-gated channels would be greater.

Chapter 42

Concept Checks

Figure 42.4   Not necessarily. Brain mass is not the sole determinant of intelligence or the ability to perform complex tasks. The degree of folding of the cerebral cortex is also important.

Figure 42.6   A spinal nerve is composed of both afferent and efferent neurons.

Figure 42.7   The major symptom experienced by patients undergoing a lumbar puncture is headache, in part because the brain is no longer cushioned adequately by CSF. Within 24–48 hours, however, the CSF is replenished to normal levels.

Figure 42.9   Damage to the cerebellum would result in loss of balance and a lack of fine motor control, such as picking up fine objects or making graceful, smooth movements.

Figure 42.12   It was in her right hand.

Figure 42.15   Thinking requires energy! Even daydreaming requires energy; imagine how much energy the brain uses when you concentrate for 60 minutes on a difficult exam. In fact, you just expended energy thinking about this question!

Feature Investigation Questions

1. Gaser and Schlaug hypothesized that repeated exposure to musical training would increase the size of certain areas of the brain associated with motor, auditory, and visual skills. All three skills are commonly used in reading and performing musical pieces.

2. The researchers used MRI to examine the areas of the brain associated with motor, auditory, and visual skills in three groups of individuals: professional musicians, amateur musicians, and nonmusicians. The researchers found that certain areas of the brain were larger in the professional musicians compared to the other groups, and larger in the amateur musicians compared to the nonmusicians.

3. Schmithorst and Holland found that, when exposed to music, certain regions of the brains of musicians were activated differently compared to nonmusicians. This study supports the hypothesis that there is a difference in the brains of musicians compared to nonmusicians.

   The experiment conducted by Gaser and Schlaug compared the size of certain regions of the brain among professional musicians, amateur musicians, and nonmusicians. Schmithorst and Holland, however, were also able to detect functional differences between musicians and nonmusicians.

Test Yourself

1. b   2. a   3. e   4. c   5. c   6. b   7. e   8. b   9. a   10. d

Conceptual Questions

1. All animals with nervous systems have reflexes, which allow rapid behavioral responses to changes in the environment. When a cnidarian senses a tactile stimulus, its nerve net responds immediately and the animal reflexively contracts nearly all of its muscles, making the animal a smaller target. This behavior protects the animal from predators. When you hear a loud, unexpected, and frightening sound (such as a firecracker), you hunch your shoulders and slightly lower your head; this reflex protects you from danger by minimizing exposure of your neck and head to danger. Dilation of the pupils of the eyes in darkness, and constriction of the pupils in bright light, are reflexes that help us see in the dark and protect our retinas in bright light. Reflexes are particularly adaptive because they occur rapidly, typically with very few synapses involved, and without the need for conscious thought.

2. White matter consists of the myelinated axons that are bundled together in large tracts in the central nervous system and which connect different CNS regions. The lipid-rich myelin gives the tracts a whitish appearance. It is distinguished from gray matter, which are the cell bodies, dendrites, and some unmyelinated axons of neurons in the CNS.

3. The sympathetic division is responsible for rapidly activating "fight-or-flight" systems that provide beneficial responses to stress or danger. For example, activation of the sympathetic division results in increased heart rate, increased breathing rate, and increased energy production.

   The parasympathetic system is involved in "rest-or-digest" processes that stimulate digestion of food, slow the heart rate, and decrease energy production.

Chapter 43

Concept Checks

Figure 43.1   The term sensory receptor refers to a type of cell that can respond to a specific type of stimulus. The term membrane receptor refers to a protein within a cell membrane that binds a ligand and thereby generates signals that initiate a cellular response.

Figure 43.3   To think about what types of touch you are aware of, let's take the example of sitting in a chair reading this textbook while holding it on your lap. You are aware of the constant weight of the book, the brush of the pages on your fingertips as you turn a page, a gentle breeze that may be circulating in your environment, the deep pressure from regularly adjusting your posture in your chair, an itch you may have on your skin, and the heat or cold of the room. Even a simple exercise such as this one is filled with stimuli of numerous types and durations.

Figure 43.11   This orientation permits animals to detect circular or angular movement of the head in three different planes. The fluid in a canal that is oriented in the same plane as the plane of movement will respond maximally to the movement. For example, the canal that is oriented horizontally would respond greatest to horizontal movements, while the other two canals would not. Overall, by comparing the signals from the three canals, the brain can interpret the motion in three dimensions.

Figure 43.18   The discs of photoreceptors are an example of increasing surface area without greatly expanding the volume of a structure. The greater surface area allows for more rhodopsin molecules per photoreceptor and thus a greater likelihood of capturing even low levels of light.

Figure 43.19   Because red-green color blindness is a sex-linked recessive gene, males require only a single defective allele on an X chromosome, whereas females require two defective alleles, one on each X chromosome.

Figure 43.27   Salt is a vital nutrient needed to maintain plasma membrane potentials and fluid balance in animals' bodies. Sugar provides glucose and other monosaccharides, important energy-yielding compounds. Sour (acidic) foods, like citrus fruits, provide nutrients and important antioxidants (vitamin C, for example) that protect against disease. Bitter substances are often toxic, and their bad taste discourages animals from eating them.

Feature Investigation Questions

1. One possibility is that many different types of odor molecules might bind to one or just a few types of receptor proteins, with the brain responding differently depending on the number or distribution of the activated receptors. The second hypothesis is that organisms can make a large number of receptor proteins, each type binding a particular odor molecule or group of odor molecules. According to this hypothesis, it is the *type* of receptor protein, and not the number or distribution of receptors, that is important for olfactory sensing.

   The researchers extracted RNA molecules from the olfactory receptor cells of the nasal epithelium. They then used this RNA to identify genes that encoded G-protein-coupled receptor proteins.

2. In their study, they identified 18 different genes that encoded different G-protein-coupled receptor proteins.

3. The results of the experiment conducted by Buck and Axel support the hypothesis that animals discriminate between different odors based on having a variety of receptor proteins that recognize different odor molecules. Current research suggests that each olfactory receptor cell has a single type of receptor protein that is specific to particular odor molecules. Because most odors are due to multiple chemicals that activate many different types of odor receptor proteins, the brain detects odors based on the combination of the activated receptor proteins. Odor seems to be discriminated by many olfactory receptor proteins, which are in the membrane of separate olfactory receptor cells.

Test Yourself

1. d   2. d   3. a   4. c   5. e   6. d   7. b   8. b   9. d   10. b

Conceptual Questions

1. Sensory transduction—The process by which incoming stimuli are converted into neural signals. An example would be the signals generated in the retina when a photon of light strikes a photoreceptor.

   Perception—An awareness of the sensations that are experienced. An example would be an awareness of what a particular visual image is.

2. The organ of Corti contains the hair cells and sensory neurons that initiate signaling. The hair cells sit on top of the basilar membrane, and their stereocilia are embedded in the tectorial membrane at the top of the organ of Corti. Pressure waves of different frequencies cause the basilar membrane to vibrate at particular sites. This bends the stereocilia of hair cells back and forth, sending oscillating signals to the sensory neurons. Consequently, the sensory neurons send intermittent action potentials to the CNS via the auditory nerve. Hair cells at the end of the basilar membrane closest to the oval window respond to high-pitched sounds, and lower-pitched sounds trigger hair cell movement further along the basilar membrane.

3. Animals that have both eyes located at the front of the head facing forward have a large degree of binocular vision, because the overlapping images coming into both eyes are processed together to form one perception. Binocular vision provides excellent depth perception. Predators depend on binocular vision to locate prey precisely. In contrast, animals with eyes toward the side of the head have reduced binocular vision, but a wide visual field, which allows them to see a wide area at one time. Most prey animals benefit from a wide visual field, which allows them to detect the presence of predators even, in some cases, if a predator is behind the prey.

Chapter 44
Concept Checks

Figure 44.1 Yes. In addition to not having a requirement to shed their skeletons periodically, animals with endoskeletons can use their skin as an efficient means of heat transfer (and, to an extent in amphibians, water transfer). In addition, the body surface of such animals is often a highly sensitive sensory organ.

Figure 44.3 If a tendon is torn, its ability to link a muscle to bone is reduced or lost. Therefore, when a muscle such as the one shown in this illustration contracts, it will not be able to move the bone to which the tendon has become dislodged.

Figure 44.8 The ATP concentration in cells becomes depleted after death, because oxygen and nutrients are not being provided to cells. Consequently, the cross-bridge cycle becomes locked before Step 3. Without ATP, the cross-bridges cannot dissociate until many hours later, when the muscle tissue sufficiently decomposes.

Figure 44.11 Na^+ enters the muscle cell because all cells have an electrochemical gradient for Na^+ that favors diffusion of Na^+ from extracellular to intracellular fluid (see Chapter 41). This is because cells have a negative membrane potential and because Na^+ concentrations are higher in the extracellular fluid. The acetylcholine receptor on skeletal muscle cells is also a ligand-gated ion channel; when acetylcholine binds the receptor, it induces a shape change that opens the channel. This allows the entry of Na^+ into the cell.

Figure 44.14 No. The data are expressed as "per kg"; this means that when normalized to a standard body mass (1 kg), the amount of energy expended for any type of locomotion by a small animal tends to be greater than that of a larger animal. However, these are *relative* values. For example, the *absolute* amount of energy expended by a tiny minnow is much less than that of a large tuna over any given distance.

Feature Investigation Questions

1. PPAR-δ is a nuclear receptor that regulates the expression of genes that enable cells to more efficiently burn fat instead of glucose for energy.

2. Evans suggested that if PPAR-δ were highly activated in mice, the mice would lose weight because of the high level of fat metabolism.

3. They developed transgenic mice with highly activated PPAR-δ. Then they fed the transgenic mice and a strain of normal mice high-fat diets. They then compared the weights of the two strains of mice to determine if the change in PPAR-δ activity affected weight. The weights of the transgenic mice were considerably lower than those of the normal mice. These results supported the hypothesis that highly activated PPAR-δ would lead to lower weight gain due to fat metabolism. Interestingly, the researchers also discovered that the transgenic mice could perform prolonged exercise for a much longer time than the normal mice. The muscle tissue of the transgenic mice was more specialized for long-term exercise.

Test Yourself

1. c 2. e 3. d 4. c 5. e 6. c 7. a 8. e 9. c 10. e

Conceptual Questions

1. Locomotion is the ability of an animal to move from place to place. Examples include swimming, walking or running, jumping, flying, crawling, and sliding.

2. Exoskeletons are on the outside of an animal's body, and endoskeletons are inside the body. Both function in support and protection, but only exoskeletons protect an animal's outer surface. Exoskeletons must be shed when an animal grows, whereas endoskeletons grow with an animal.

3. a. The cycle begins with the binding of an energized myosin cross-bridge to an actin molecule on a thin filament.

   b. The cross-bridge moves, and the thin filaments slide past the thick filaments.

   c. The ATP binds to myosin, causing the cross-bridge to detach.

   d. The ATP bound to myosin is hydrolyzed by ATPase, re-forming the energized state of myosin.

Chapter 45
Concept Checks

Figure 45.4 After a large blood meal, the body mass of a flying blood-sucking animal increases sufficiently as to make it nearly impossible to fly. The problem is solved, however, by a unique adaptation that allows such animals to concentrate the nutrients from blood and excrete most of the water portion of blood as soon as they begin eating. By the time the meal is finished, much of the water they consumed has already been excreted.

Figure 45.7 Sauropod dinosaurs were herbivores that probably contained a gizzard-type stomach in which stones helped to grind coarse vegetation. Such stones would have become smooth after months or even years of rumbling around in the gizzard. Some of these sauropods are known to have lacked the sort of grinding teeth characteristic of modern mammalian herbivores, and thus a gizzard would have aided in their digestion much as it does in modern birds.

Figure 45.10 By having bile stored in a gallbladder, bile can be released precisely when needed in response to a meal; this is particularly useful for animals that consume large or infrequent meals. In the absence of a gallbladder, bile flows into the intestine continuously and cannot be increased to match the amount or timing of food intake.

Figure 45.11 Secondary active transport requires energy provided by ATP. Thus, absorption of nutrients by this mechanism is an energy-requiring event, and some portion of an animal's regular nutrient consumption is used to provide the energy required to absorb the nutrients.

Figure 45.13 CCK inhibits stomach activity. This is an example of negative feedback. The arrival of chyme in the small intestine stimulates CCK, which promotes digestion as shown in the figure. At the same time, CCK inhibits contraction of the smooth muscles of the stomach so that the entry of chyme into the small intestine is slowed down. This allows time for controlled digestion and absorption of nutrients in the intestine, without the intestine becoming overfilled with chyme. Simultaneously, CCK inhibits acid production by the stomach so that the pH of the intestine does not become dangerously low before bicarbonate ions are able to neutralize it.

Feature Investigation Questions

1. The researchers severed the nerves that connected to the small intestine in a dog. Following the removal of the nerves, the researchers introduced an acidic solution directly into the intestine of the dog. The introduction of the acid into the intestine caused pancreatic secretion. This suggested that non-neural factors must have mediated communication between the digestive tract and the secretory cells of the pancreas.

2. Other researchers were not convinced that all the nerves were dissected from the intestine, because of the technical difficulty in performing such a procedure. To provide more conclusive evidence of other regulatory factors that were produced by the intestine, the researchers conducted a second experiment. First, they dissected a portion of a small intestine from a dog, treated it with acid, ground it up to produce a mash, and then filtered the mash to obtain an extract. The extract—which was expected to contain any secretions of the intestine that occurred following acid exposure—was then injected into the circulatory system of a second dog. The results indicated that the second dog had pancreatic secretion following the injection.

3. The results suggested that factors were secreted by the small intestine following exposure of the intestine to acid, as would occur when chyme enters the intestine from the stomach. These factors probably reached the pancreas through the bloodstream. The researchers called these factors hormones. Thus, the digestive system was regulated not only by the nervous system, but also by chemical secretions, and different parts of the digestive system were able to communicate with each other via hormones.

Test Yourself

1. d   2. e   3. e   4. b   5. c   6. b   7. d   8. c   9. a   10. e

Conceptual Questions

1. Digestion is the breakdown of large molecules into smaller ones by the action of enzymes and acid. Absorption is the transport of digested molecules and small molecules that do not require digestion, across the epithelial cells of the alimentary canal and from there into the extracellular fluid of an animal.

2. Carnivores eat live animal flesh and/or fluids or may scavenge dead animals. Carnivores' teeth are adapted for seizing, grasping, piercing, biting, slicing, tearing, or holding prey; they generally do not chew their food extensively, but may chew to facilitate swallowing. Herbivores have powerful jaw muscles and large, broad molars for grinding tough, fibrous plant material; they may also have incisors adapted for nipping grass or other vegetation. Simply examining the type of teeth an animal has is often sufficient to determine whether that animal eats vegetation, animals, or both.

3. The crop is a dilation of the esophagus, which stores and softens food. The gizzard contains swallowed pebbles that help pulverize food. Both of these functions are adaptations that assist digestion in birds, who do not have teeth and therefore do not chew food. Humans, like many animals, can chew food before swallowing.

Chapter 46

Concept Checks

Figure 46.3   The time required for the vesicles to move to the plasma membrane and fuse with it is much shorter than the time required for new GLUTs to be synthesized by activation of GLUT genes. Thus, the action of insulin on cells is very quick, because the GLUTs are already synthesized.

Figure 46.4   The glycerol and fatty acids used to make glucose are the breakdown products of triglycerides that were stored in adipose tissue during the absorptive period. The amino acids used to make glucose are derived from the breakdown of protein in muscle and other tissue.

Figure 46.6   Even though the goose was resting, sampling the air from the mask would be only a rough estimate of BMR. That is because the artificial setting and the placement of the mask would be enough of a stimulus to affect the activity and behavior of the goose and thereby increase its metabolism.

Figure 46.7   As shown in Figure 46.7, for humans exercise is a voluntary activity. In nature, however, "exercise" is often a component of the fight-or-flight reaction, such as when an animal attempts to escape danger. During such times, digestion and absorption of food are less important than providing as much blood flow, oxygen, and nutrients as possible to skeletal muscle. The gut, therefore, temporarily reduces its activity and requires less blood flow.

Figure 46.8   Nearly all animals today show a similar relationship between body mass and metabolic rate, and there is no reason why it should not always have been true. Thus, the tiny 1-foot-tall ancestral horse *Eohippus* most likely had a higher BMR than do today's larger horses.

Figure 46.11   Humans are homeothermic endotherms. We maintain our body temperature within a very narrow range, and we supply our own body heat.

Feature Investigation Questions

1. Scientists were interested in knowing why animals seemed to regulate their body mass around a particular level, even though many animals experience changes in food supply throughout the year. This seemed to indicate that a mechanism existed within the body that monitored when fuel stores were higher or lower than normal, and that initiated changes in behavior and metabolism to compensate.

2. Coleman hypothesized that communication regarding energy status must take place between the brain and the rest of the body. He suggested that chemical signals were transported through the blood from outside the brain to feeding or satiety centers within the brain, where they regulated appetite and thus regulated body weight. He tested this by linking the blood circulations of normal mice and genetically obese mice and then monitoring the mice for changes in body weight.

3. In most cases, the obese mice lost weight and ate less during the experimental procedure. This confirmed that something in the bloodstream of the wild-type mice was regulating body weight but was missing in the obese mice. When the unknown factor crossed into the bloodstream of the obese mice, it caused them to lose weight. In another group of parabiosed mice, however, the wild-type mice lost weight, but the obese mice did not. Coleman concluded that these obese mice were not able to respond to the chemical signal that regulates body weight, even though they made the signal themselves and it was active in their parabiosed wild-type partners.

Test Yourself

1. c   2. a   3. d   4. c   5. a   6. e   7. e   8. c   9. c   10. e

Conceptual Questions

1. Insulin acts on adipose and skeletal muscle cells to facilitate the diffusion of glucose from extracellular fluid into the cell cytosol. This is accomplished by increasing the translocation of glucose-transporter (GLUT) proteins from the cytosol to sites within the plasma membrane of insulin-sensitive cells. Insulin also inhibits glycogenolysis and gluconeogenesis in the liver, which decreases the amount of glucose secreted into the blood by the liver. Insulin is required for glucose transport because like many other polar molecules, glucose cannot move across the lipid bilayer of a plasma membrane by simple diffusion. The inhibitory effects of insulin on liver function help to ensure that liver glycogen stores will be spared for the postabsorptive period.

2. Appetite is controlled by a satiety center in the brain that receives signals from the stretched stomach and intestines after a meal. When digestion and absorption are complete, the stomach and intestines return to their original size, and the brain no longer senses that an animal feels "full." In addition, appetite is controlled by leptin, a hormone secreted by adipose cells in direct proportion to the amount of fat stored in an animal's body. When leptin levels in the blood are high, appetite is suppressed. When leptin levels are low, as occurs when an animal is losing weight, appetite is increased. The presence of a hormone that is released into the blood in proportion to fat mass in the body allows the brain to monitor the amount of energy stored in the body. A decrease in the concentration of leptin in the blood, for example, is the mechanism that communicates to the brain that fat stores are lower than normal. This initiates the sensation of hunger, which encourages an animal to seek food.

3. Countercurrent heat exchange is a mechanism for retaining body heat. As warm blood travels through arteries down a bird's leg, for example, heat moves by conduction from the artery to adjacent veins carrying cooler blood in the other direction, toward the heart. By the time the arterial blood reaches the tip of the leg, its temperature has dropped considerably, reducing the amount of heat loss to the environment, while the heat is returned to the body's core via the warmed veins.

Chapter 47

Concept Checks

Figure 47.2   Open circulatory systems evolved prior to closed systems. However, this does not mean that open systems are in some way inferior to closed circulatory systems. It is better to think of open systems as being ideally suited to the needs of those animals that have them. Arthropods are an incredibly successful order of animals, with the greatest number of species, and inhabiting virtually every ecological niche on the planet. Clearly, their type of circulatory system has not prevented arthropods from achieving their great success.

Figure 47.4   Keeping oxygenated and deoxygenated blood fully separate allows the arterial blood of birds and mammals to provide the maximum amount of oxygen to tissues. This means that those tissues can achieve higher metabolisms and be more active at all times.

Figure 47.6 Each hemoglobin molecule contains four subunits, each of which has an iron atom at its core. Each iron binds one oxygen molecule (O_2); therefore, a total of eight oxygen atoms can bind to one hemoglobin molecule.

Figure 47.11 Body fluids, both extracellular and intracellular, contain large amounts of charged ions, which are capable of conducting electricity. The slight electric currents generated by the beating heart muscle cells are conducted through the surrounding body fluids by the movements of ions in those fluids. This is recorded by the surface electrodes and amplified by the recording machine.

Figure 47.14 When the animal is active, the arterioles of its leg muscle would dilate, bringing more blood and, consequently, nutrients and oxygen to the active muscle tissue.

Figure 47.17 The valves open toward the heart. When the head is upright, the valves are open, and blood drains from the head to the right atrium by gravity. When the giraffe lowers its head to drink, however, gravity would prevent the venous blood from reaching the heart; instead, blood would pool in the head and could raise pressure in the head and brain. The valves in the neck veins work the same way as those in the legs of other animals, helping to propel blood against gravity to the heart.

Figure 47.20 Baroreceptors are mechanoreceptors. Like all mechanoreceptors (e.g., those in distensible or deformable structures such as the urinary bladder and stomach), their ion channels are opened by physical deformation or stretching of the plasma membrane. They are, therefore, mechanically gated ion channels.

Feature Investigation Questions

1. Furchgott noted that acetylcholine had different effects on the rabbit aorta depending on the manner in which the aorta was isolated and prepared. When applied to flattened strips of the aorta, acetylcholine caused contraction of the aorta smooth muscle; however, when applied to circular rings of the aorta, acetylcholine caused relaxation. Furchgott suggested that the difference was due to the absence of the endothelial layer of tissue in the flattened strips of aorta.

2. Furchgott hypothesized that acetylcholine stimulated the endothelial cells to secrete a substance that functioned as a vasodilator, causing the muscle layer to relax. Furchgott performed several experiments to test his hypothesis. He compared the effects of acetylcholine on circular rings of aorta that either had the endothelial layer intact or experimentally removed. The results of this experiment demonstrated that when the endothelial layer was present, relaxation occurred in the presence of acetylcholine. Removal of the endothelial layer, however, resulted in contraction of muscle in the presence of acetylcholine. In a second experiment, a strip of the aorta with the endothelial layer removed was put in contact with a strip of aorta with an intact endothelial layer. When this "sandwiched" treatment was exposed to acetylcholine, both muscle layers relaxed.

3. Furchgott concluded that the endothelial layer produced a vasodilator in the presence of acetylcholine. The vasodilator diffused from the intact strip of muscle to the denuded strip and caused the muscle layer to relax.

Test Yourself

1. b 2. a 3. c 4. b 5. a 6. d 7. c 8. d 9. c 10. d

Conceptual Questions

1. The three main components of a circulatory system are (1) blood or hemolymph, an internal body fluid containing dissolved solutes; (2) blood vessels, a system of hollow tubes within the body through which blood travels; and (3) one or more hearts, muscular structures that pump blood through the blood vessels.

2. *Closed circulatory system*—In a closed circulatory system, the blood and interstitial fluid are contained within tubes called blood vessels and are transported by a pump called the heart. All of the nutrients and oxygen that tissues require are delivered directly to them by the blood vessels. Advantages of closed circulatory systems are that different parts of an animal's body can receive blood flow in proportion to that body part's metabolic requirements at any given time. Due to its efficiency, a closed circulatory system allows organisms to become larger.

   Open circulatory system—In an open circulatory system, the organs are bathed in hemolymph that ebbs and flows into and out of the heart(s) and body cavity, rather than blood being directed to all cells. Like a closed circulatory system, there are a pump and blood vessels, but these two structures are less developed and less complex compared to a closed circulatory system. Partly as a result, organisms such as mollusks and arthropods are generally limited to being relatively small, although exceptions do exist.

3. The cardiac cycle can be divided into two phases. The first is diastole, during which the ventricles fill with blood coming from the atria through the open AV valves. This is followed by systole, the contraction of the ventricles that ejects blood through the open semilunar valves. Valves must be one-directional because if, for example, the AV valves opened in both directions, then blood would flow from the ventricles into the atria whenever the ventricles contracted. This would reduce the amount of blood flowing into the arteries, and consequently, cardiac output and blood pressure would decrease to dangerously low levels.

Chapter 48
Concept Checks

Figure 48.2 Regardless of whether the atmosphere is measured on Mt. Everest or at sea level, the percentage of gas molecules that are oxygen remains close to 21%. However, the pressure exerted by those gas molecules decreases as one ascends in elevation.

Figure 48.3 If a lungless salamander were to dry out, its capacity for gas exchange would be greatly reduced. Gases diffuse into and out of the body of the salamander by dissolving in the moist fluid layer on the skin.

Figure 48.5 Imagine holding several thin sheets of a wet substance, such as paper. If you wave them in the air, what happens? The sheets stick to one another because of surface tension and other properties of moist surfaces. This is what happens to the lamellae in gills when they are in air. When the lamellae stick to each other, this reduces the surface area available for gas exchange, and the fish suffocates.

Figure 48.7 There are probably several factors that limit insect body size, but the respiratory system most likely is one such factor. If an insect grew to the size of a human, for example, the trachea and tracheoles would be so large and extensive that there would be little room for any other internal organs in the body! Also, the mass of the animal's body and the forces generated during locomotion would probably collapse the tracheoles. Finally, diffusion of oxygen from the surface of the body to the deepest regions of a human-sized insect would take far too long to support the metabolic demands of internal structures.

Figure 48.12 Because fishes have the most efficient means of extracting oxygen from their environment, one might conclude that this is an adaptation to cope with low environmental oxygen. Based on that logic, you would conclude that the oxygen content of water was less than that of air, which is indeed correct.

Figure 48.15 The waters off the coast of Antarctica are extremely cold, rarely warmer than 0.30°C. As we saw earlier in this chapter, more oxygen dissolves in cold water than in warm water, and therefore icefish have the potential to obtain more oxygen across their gills. Cold temperatures also decrease the metabolic rate of the animals, because all chemical reactions slow down at low temperature. Thus, the oxygen demands of icefish are lower than those of warm-water fish. Several other adaptations have evolved to enable these animals to live without hemoglobin. Large gills with exceptionally high surface area facilitate diffusion of oxygen into the animal's blood. In addition, cardiovascular adaptations evolved to help increase the total amount of oxygen in the blood and its ability to be pumped to all body tissues. For example, icefish have larger blood volumes and a larger heart than warmwater fish of a similar size. Also, the absence of red blood cells makes the blood less viscous (makes it "thinner") and therefore easier to pump through the body.

Figure 48.16 An increase in the blood concentration of HCO_3^- would favor the reaction $HCO_3^- + H^+ \rightarrow H_2CO_3 \rightarrow CO_2 + H_2O$. This would reduce the hydrogen ion concentration of the blood, thereby raising the pH; the CO_2 formed as a result would be exhaled. These changes would shift the hemoglobin curve to the left of the usual position.

Feature Investigation Questions

1. The study conducted by Schmidt-Neilsen intended to determine the route of air through the avian respiratory system. This would provide a better understanding of the functions of the air sacs and the process of gas exchange in birds.

2. The first experiment by Schmidt-Neilsen compared the composition of air between the posterior and anterior air sacs. Oxygen content was high in the posterior sacs but low in the anterior sacs. Carbon dioxide levels, however, were low in the posterior sacs but high in the anterior sacs. The researchers concluded that when inhaled, the air moves first to the posterior sacs; then to the lungs where oxygen diffuses into the blood and carbon dioxide diffuses into the lungs; and, finally, to the anterior sacs before being exhaled.

3. The second experiment by Schmidt-Neilsen was conducted to verify the pathway of air through the respiratory system of the bird. In this experiment, the researcher monitored oxygen levels by surgically implanting oxygen probes in the anterior and posterior air sacs. The bird was fitted with a face mask and allowed to take one breath of pure oxygen. The researcher was then able to track the movement of this oxygen through the respiratory tract. Schmidt-Neilsen concluded that it takes two complete breaths for air to move from the environment through the lungs and back out again to the environment. The two breaths are required to move the air from the posterior air sacs through the lungs and, finally, to the anterior air sacs before exiting the body.

Test Yourself

1. a 2. e 3. c 4. c 5. a 6. b 7. e 8. e 9. d 10. b

Conceptual Questions

1. Countercurrent exchange maximizes the amount of oxygen that can be obtained from the water in fishes. Oxygenated water flows across the lamellae of a fish gill in the opposite direction in which deoxygenated blood flows through the capillaries of the lamellae. In this way, a diffusion gradient for oxygen is maintained along the entire length of the lamellae, facilitating diffusion of oxygen even when much of it has already entered the blood.

2. The avian respiratory system is unique among vertebrates in that it is supplemented with air sacs, which do not participate in gas exchange. They do, however, create a unidirectional flow of air through the respiratory system. Air enters the trachea and flows into the two bronchi and then into a series of sacs and parallel tubes called parabronchi, which comprise the avian lungs. Air moves through the system in two cycles. In the first inhalation, air flows into the posterior air sacs. On exhalation, air exits the posterior air sacs and flows through the parabronchi from the back to the front of the lungs. During the next inhalation, air flows from the anterior area of the lungs into the anterior air sacs, which serve as a holding chamber, while fresh air enters the posterior sacs again. The efficiency of this avian flow-through system is a major reason why birds can fly at altitudes with extremely low atmospheric pressure and, consequently, low partial pressures of oxygen.

3. Animals that live at high altitudes face the special challenge of obtaining oxygen where the atmospheric pressure is low. When atmospheric pressure is low, the partial pressure of oxygen in the air is also low. This means that there is less of a driving force for the diffusion of oxygen from the air into the body of the animal. Several adaptations have arisen that help animals cope with such habitats. For example, many high-altitude animals have more red blood cells and have hemoglobin with a higher affinity for oxygen than that of sea-level animals. This means their hemoglobin can bind oxygen even at the low partial pressures of high altitudes and thereby saturate their blood with oxygen. In addition, such animals generally have larger hearts and lungs for their body size than animals that live at lower altitudes. Animals that move to high altitude show increases in the number of red blood cells in their circulation and in respiratory rates. The number of capillaries in skeletal muscle increases to facilitate oxygen diffusion into the muscle cells. Myoglobin content of muscle cells also increases, expanding the reservoir of oxygen in the cytosol.

Chapter 49

Concept Checks

Figure 49.1 No, obligatory exchanges must always occur, but animals can minimize obligatory losses through modifications in behavior. For example, terrestrial animals that seek shade on a hot, sunny day reduce evaporative water loss. As another example, reducing activity minimizes water loss due to respiration.

Figure 49.4 Humans cannot survive by drinking seawater because we do not possess specialized salt glands to rid ourselves of the excess sodium and other ions ingested with seawater. The human kidneys cannot eliminate that much salt. The high blood levels of sodium and other ions would cause changes in cellular membrane potentials, disrupting vital functions of electrically excitable tissue such as cardiac muscle and nerve tissue.

Figure 49.6 Secretion of substances into excretory organ tubules is advantageous because it increases the amount of a substance that gets removed from the body by the excretory organs. This is important, because many substances that get secreted are potentially toxic. Filtration, though efficient, is limited by the volume of fluid that can leave the capillaries and enter the excretory tubule.

Figure 49.12 A brush border composed of microvilli is also present along the epithelial cell layer of the vertebrate small intestine (see Chapter 45). In the intestine, the brush border serves to increase the absorption of nutrients. In both the intestine and the proximal tubule of nephrons, therefore, a brush border provides extensive surface area for the transport of substances between a lumen and the epithelial cells (and from there to extracellular fluid).

Figure 49.14 Epithelial cells like those in the kidney tubules can distribute proteins between the luminal and basolateral sides of the plasma membrane. In this way, the Na^+/K^+-ATPase pumps that are stimulated by aldosterone are present and active only on one side of the cell, the basolateral surfaces. If the pumps were activated on the luminal surface of the cell, aldosterone would not be able to promote reabsorption of Na^+ and water, because Na^+ would also be transported from the cell into the tubule lumen.

Feature Investigation Questions

1. Symptoms of prolonged, heavy exercise include fatigue, muscle cramps, and even occasionally seizures. Fatigue results from the reduction in blood flow to muscles and other organs. Muscle cramps and seizures are the results of imbalances in plasma electrolyte levels. Cade and his colleagues hypothesized that maintaining proper water and electrolyte levels would prevent these problems, and that if water and electrolyte levels were maintained, athletic performance should not decrease as rapidly with prolonged exercise.

2. To test their hypothesis, the researchers created a drink that would restore the correct proportions of lost water and electrolytes within the athletes. If the athletes consumed the drink during exercise, they should not experience as much fatigue or muscle cramping, and thus their performance should be enhanced compared to a control group of athletes that drank only water.

3. The performance of a group of exercising athletes given the electrolyte-containing drink was better than that of the control group that drank only water during exercise. This could be attributed to the replacement of normal electrolyte levels by the drink.

Test Yourself

1. e 2. e 3. d 4. c 5. a 6. c 7. e 8. d 9. a 10. b

Conceptual Questions

1. Nitrogenous wastes are the breakdown products of the metabolism of proteins and nucleic acids. They consist of ammonia, ammonium ions, urea, and uric acid. The predominant type of waste excreted depends in part on an animal's environment. For example, aquatic animals typically excrete ammonia and ammonium ions, whereas many terrestrial animals excrete primarily urea and uric acid. Urea and uric acid are less toxic than the other types but require energy to be synthesized. Urea and uric acid also result in less water excreted, an adaptation that is especially useful for organisms that must conserve water, such as many terrestrial species.

2. Salt glands contain a network of secretory tubules that actively transport NaCl from the extracellular fluid into the tubule lumen. This solution then moves through a central duct and to the outside environment through pores in the nose, around the eyes, and in other locations. The ability to remove salt from body fluids is an adaptation for many marine reptiles and birds, which do not have ready access to fresh water and would otherwise run the risk of having very high levels of salts in their blood and other body fluids.

3. In filtration, an organ acts like a sieve or filter, removing some of the water and its small solutes from the blood, interstitial fluid, or

hemolymph, while retaining blood cells and large solutes such as proteins. Reabsorption is the process whereby epithelial cells of an excretory organ recapture useful solutes that were filtered. Secretion is the process whereby epithelial cells of an excretory organ transport unneeded or harmful solutes from the blood to the excretory tubules for elimination. Some substances such as glucose and amino acids are reabsorbed but not secreted, while some other substances such as toxic compounds are not reabsorbed and are secreted. Still other substances, namely proteins, are not filtered at all.

Chapter 50

Concept Checks

Figure 50.4   When dopamine is secreted from an axon terminal into a synapse where it diffuses to a postsynaptic cell, it is considered a neurotransmitter. When it is secreted from an axon terminal into the extracellular fluid, from where it diffuses into the blood, it is considered a hormone.

Figure 50.7   In addition to the pancreas, certain other organs in an animal's body may contain both exocrine and endocrine tissue or cells. For example, you learned in Chapters 45 and 46 that the vertebrate alimentary canal is composed of several types of secretory cells. Some of these cells release hormones into the blood that regulate the activities of the pancreas and other structures, such as the gallbladder. Other cells of the alimentary canal secrete exocrine products such as acids or mucus into the gut lumen that directly aid in digestion or act as a protective coating, respectively.

Figure 50.10   Not all mammals use the energy of sunlight to synthesize vitamin D. There are many animals, such as those that inhabit caves or that are strictly nocturnal, that rarely are exposed to sunlight. Some of these animals get their vitamin D from dietary sources. How others maintain calcium balance without dietary or sunlight-derived active vitamin D remains uncertain.

Figure 50.12   Sodium and potassium ion balance is of vital importance for most animals because of the critical role these ions play in nervous system and muscle function. It is more the rule than the exception that such important physiological variables are under multiple layers of control. This grants a high degree of fine-tuning capability such that these ions—and other similarly important molecules—rarely exceed or fall below the normal range of concentrations for a given animal.

Figure 50.13   The great height of the twin on the left in Figure 50.13 clearly indicates that his condition arose prior to puberty. The enlarged bones further suggest that the disease continued for a time after puberty, when further linear bone growth was no longer possible.

Figure 50.15   Because 20-hydroxyecdysone is a steroid hormone, you would predict that its receptor would be intracellular. All steroid hormones interact with receptors located either in the cytosol or, more commonly, in the nucleus. The hormone : receptor complex then acts to promote or inhibit transcription of one or more genes. The receptor for 20-hydroxyecdysone is indeed found in cell nuclei.

Feature Investigation Questions

1. Banting and Best based their procedure on a medical condition that results when pancreatic ducts are blocked. The exocrine cells will deteriorate in a pancreas that has obstructed ducts; however, the islet cells are not affected. The researchers proposed to experimentally replicate the condition to isolate the cells suspected of secreting the glucose-lowering factor. From these cells, they assumed they would be able to extract the substance of interest without contamination or degradation due to exocrine products.

2. The extracts obtained by Banting and Best did contain insulin, the glucose-lowering factor, but were of low strength and purity. Collip developed a procedure to obtain a more purified extract with higher concentrations of insulin.

3. The researchers chose to use bovine pancreases as their starting material for preparing the extracts. Because of the large size of these animals and their availability at local slaughterhouses, the researchers were able to obtain great yields of insulin. Second, Collip developed a highly sensitive assay for monitoring changes in blood glucose levels after injection of insulin. This allowed the researchers to better estimate how much insulin was in a preparation and how much was necessary to give to a patient.

Test Yourself

1. b 2. e 3. b 4. e 5. b 6. e 7. c 8. d 9. b 10. d

Conceptual Questions

1. Leptin acts in the hypothalamus to reduce appetite and increase metabolic rate. Because adipose tissue is typically the most important and abundant source of stored energy in an animal's body, the ability to relay information to the appetite and metabolism centers of the brain about the amount of available adipose tissue is a major benefit. In this way, the brain's centers can indirectly monitor the minute-to-minute energy status in the body. A decrease in leptin, for example, would indicate that a decrease in adipose tissue existed—as might occur during a fast. Removal of the leptin signal would cause appetite to increase and metabolism to decrease, thereby conserving energy. The presence of an appetite and the subjective sensations associated with hunger is a motivation that drives an animal to seek food at the expense of other activities, such as seeking shelter, finding a mate, and so on.

2. Insulin acts to lower blood glucose concentrations, for example, after a meal, whereas glucagon elevates blood glucose, for example, during fasting. Insulin acts by stimulating the insertion of glucose transporter proteins into the cell membrane of muscle and fat cells. Glucagon acts by stimulating glycogenolysis in the liver. If a high dose of glucagon were injected into an animal, including humans, the blood concentration of glucagon would increase rapidly. This would stimulate increased glycogenolysis, resulting in blood glucose concentrations that were above normal.

3. Type 1 DM is characterized by insufficient production of insulin due to the immune system destroying the insulin-producing cells of the pancreas. In type 2 DM, insulin is still produced by the pancreas, but adipose and muscle cells do not respond normally to insulin.

Chapter 51

Concept Checks

Figure 51.4   Aquatic environments in which the water is stagnant or only gently moving, as shown in this figure, are generally best for external fertilization. Fast-moving bodies of water reduce the likelihood of a sperm contacting an egg and increase the chances that gametes will be washed away in the current. Many river-dwelling fishes lay eggs in gently moving streams, and many marine fishes do so in relatively shallow waters.

Figure 51.7   The elevated testosterone levels would inhibit LH and FSH production through negative feedback. This would result in reduced spermatogenesis and possibly even infertility (an inability to produce sufficient sperm to cause a pregnancy).

Figure 51.10   FSH and LH concentrations do not surge in males, but instead remain fairly steady, because the testes do not show cyclical activity. Sperm production in males is constant throughout life after puberty.

Figure 51.11   In addition to its other functions, the placenta must serve the function of the lungs for the fetus, because its real lungs are not breathing air during this time. Arteries always carry blood away from the heart; veins carry blood to the heart. Consequently, blood leaving the heart of the fetus and traveling through arteries to the placenta is deoxygenated. As blood leaves the placenta and returns to the heart, the blood has become oxygenated as oxygen diffuses from the maternal blood into fetal blood. That oxygenated blood then gets pumped from the fetal heart through other arteries to the rest of the fetus' body.

Figure 51.14   Pregnancy and subsequent lactation require considerable energy and, therefore, nutrient ingestion. Consuming the placenta provides the female with a rich source of protein and other important nutrients.

Feature Investigation Questions

1. Using *Daphnia*, Paland and Lynch compared the accumulation of mitochondrial mutations between sexually reproducing populations and asexually reproducing populations.

2. The results—that sexually reproducing populations had a lower rate of deleterious mutations compared to asexually reproducing populations—indicate that sexual reproduction does decrease the accumulation of deleterious mutations, at least in this species.

3. Sexual reproduction allows for mixing of the different alleles of genes with each generation, thereby increasing genetic variation within the population. This could prevent the accumulation of deleterious alleles in the population.

Test Yourself

1. d 2. c 3. e 4. a 5. b 6. c 7. b 8. c 9. b 10. c

Conceptual Questions

1. In viviparity, most of embryonic development occurs within the mother, and the animal is born alive, as occurs in most mammals. If all or most of embryonic development occurs outside the mother and the embryo depends exclusively on yolk from an egg for nourishment, the process is called oviparity; this occurs in most vertebrates and in insects. In ovoviviparity, which occurs in some reptiles, sharks and some invertebrates, fertilized eggs covered with a very thin shell hatch inside the mother's body, but the offspring receive no nourishment from the mother. Humans are viviparous. An advantage of viviparity is that the embryo and fetus develop in a protected environment.

2. Sexual reproduction requires that males and females of a species produce different gametes and that these gametes come into contact with each other. This requires males and females to expend energy to locate mates. It also may require specialized organs for copulation and in some cases requires the production of very large numbers of gametes to increase the likelihood that the eggs are fertilized. These costs are outweighed by the genetic diversity afforded by sexual reproduction.

3. Cells of the hypothalamus produce two important hormones that regulate reproduction. GnRH stimulates the anterior pituitary gland to release two gonadotropic hormones, LH and FSH. These two hormones regulate the production of gonadal hormones and development of gametes in both sexes. In addition, increased secretion of GnRH contributes to the initiation of puberty. The hypothalamus also produces oxytocin, a hormone that is stored in the posterior pituitary gland and that acts to stimulate milk release during lactation. Finally, changes in neuroendocrine activity in the hypothalamus are linked to seasonal changes in day length and therefore contribute to seasonal breeding in certain mammals.

Chapter 52

Concept Checks

Figure 52.1 The process by which a tadpole develops into an adult frog is called metamorphosis. This process is widespread in animals and occurs in many arthropods, certain fishes, numerous marine invertebrates such as gastropods, and amphibia.

Figure 52.5 No, all vertebrates do not use internal fertilization. External fertilization is common in fishes and amphibia; these animals lay unfertilized eggs, over which males deposit sperm (see Chapter 51).

Figure 52.14 Different concentrations of a signaling protein can exert different effects on cells when, for example, different cells express different isoforms of a plasma membrane receptor for the protein. If one cell expresses a high-affinity receptor and another cell a low-affinity receptor, the two cells would respond to the signaling protein at different concentrations. Likewise, the different receptors may be linked with different second messenger molecules generated within the cell. These messengers, such as camp and Ca^{2+}, may have different effects on cell function.

Feature Investigation Questions

1. Knowing the genes expressed in this region of a developing embryo would provide important information about the control of the patterning of embryonic tissues and structures.

2. Harland and colleagues tested the hypothesis that cells within the Spemann organizer expressed certain genes important in the development of dorsal structures, such as the notochord.

3. The scientists used a procedure called expression cloning. In this process, they isolated the various mRNAs that were present in the tissue of the dorsal lip of the embryo. After purifying these mRNAs, they produced a cDNA library. This library contained all the genes expressed in the particular tissue at that particular time of development. The scientists then transcribed the different genes in the cDNA library into

mRNAs and injected these into UV-damaged eggs, which were subsequently fertilized. UV-damaged fertilized eggs fail to develop dorsal structures. The scientists were interested in any mRNA that "rescued" the developing embryo and restored some level of normal development. One protein, noggin, was found to rescue the embryos and acted as a morphogen.

Test Yourself

1. a 2. c 3. c 4. d 5. b 6. c 7. b 8. e 9. e 10. e

Conceptual Questions

1. Embryonic development is the process by which a fertilized egg is transformed into an organism with distinct physiological systems and body parts. Cell differentiation is the process by which different cells within a developing organism acquire specialized forms and functions, due to the expression of cell-specific genes. Growth is the enlargement of an embryo, as cells divide and/or enlarge.

2. The timing of the final development of an embryo's organs is typically linked with the requirement for that organ's function. In mammals, for example, the heart is required early in development to pump blood through the embryonic and fetal circulation, thereby delivering nutrients and removing wastes. Fully functional lungs, however, are not required until the animal is born and begins breathing air for the first time.

3. Autonomous specification results from the asymmetrical distribution of intracellular proteins and mRNAs during the cleavage events of embryonic development. The resulting daughter cells will contain different amounts of these cytoplasmic determinants, and this will direct these cells into different developmental fates. Conditional specification results from the interactions of proteins on the extracellular surface of the cell membranes of different cells or from proteins secreted from one cell and acting on another cell. This type of specification determines where a cell ends up within the embryo and what type of cell develops.

Chapter 53

Concept Checks

Figure 53.2 Although swelling is one of the most obvious manifestations of inflammation, it has no significant adaptive value of its own. It is a consequence of fluid leaking out of blood vessels into the interstitial space. It can, however, contribute to pain sensations, because the buildup of fluid may cause distortion of connective tissue structures such as tendons and ligaments. Pain, while obviously unpleasant, is an important signal that alerts many animals to the injury and serves as a reminder to protect the injured site.

Figure 53.3 Recall from Chapter 47 that as blood circulates, a portion of the plasma—the fluid part of blood—exits venules and capillaries and enters the interstitial fluid. Most of the plasma is reabsorbed back into the capillaries, but a portion gets left behind. That excess fluid is drained away by lymph vessels and becomes lymph. Without lymph vessels, fluid would accumulate outside of the blood, in the interstitial fluid.

Figure 53.12 Because an animal may encounter the same type of pathogen many times during its life, having a secondary immune response means that future infections will be fought off much more efficiently.

Figure 53.13 Although social insects live in colonies that may reach enormous numbers of individuals, many other insect species inhabit densely populated colonies, as do many species of vertebrates. The free-tailed bat *Tamarind brasiliensis,* for example, lives in caves that contain as many as 10–20 million individuals! It is highly likely that all such species have evolved immune defense mechanisms that enable them to ward off infections that might devastate the entire population.

Feature Investigation Questions

1. Termites produce and line their nests with antimicrobial secretions that reduce the probability that an infection can spread. Termites also practice social grooming that removes foreign objects and possible pathogens from nest mates. Sick or dead termites are also removed from the nest, thus decreasing the likelihood of disease transmission.

2. The researchers tested the hypothesis that social interaction among termites promotes disease resistance. That is, termites that had contact with nest mates that had previously been exposed to a pathogen were

subsequently less likely to become infected with that pathogen than termites that lacked prior contact with nest mates. The researchers regarded this as social immunity.

3. The researchers formed two groups of termites. The experimental group was exposed to a microbial pathogen, whereas the control group was not. After 1 week, the control group was divided into two groups. One control subgroup was introduced to the group of termites previously exposed to the pathogen, whereas the other control subgroup was kept isolated from the exposed termites. Finally, the researchers challenged both groups with a lethal concentration of the same microbial pathogen. The researchers then evaluated the effect of social interaction on survival. The results indicated that the termites that previously had been introduced to the exposed termites had higher survival rates compared to the control group that was not introduced to exposed termites. The researchers concluded that the interaction with the exposed termites allowed the control termites to acquire immunity to the microbial pathogen.

Test Yourself

1. e 2. b 3. c 4. c 5. a 6. d 7. b 8. a 9. d 10. b

Conceptual Questions

1. Nonspecific immunity is present at birth and is found in all animals. These defenses recognize general, conserved features common to a wide array of pathogens and include external barriers, such as the skin, and internal defenses involving phagocytes and other cells. Specific immunity develops *after* an animal has been exposed to a *particular* antigen. The responses include humoral and cell-mediated defenses. Specific immunity appears to be largely restricted to vertebrates. Unlike nonspecific immunity, in specific immunity, the response to an antigen is greatly increased if an animal is exposed to that antigen again at some future time.

2. Cytotoxic T cells are "attack" cells that are responsible for cell-mediated immunity. Once activated, they migrate to the location of their targets, bind to the targets by combining with an antigen on them, and directly kill the targets via secreted chemicals.

3. Each immunoglobulin molecule is Y shaped and composed of four inter-linked polypeptide chains: two long heavy chains and two short light chains. The chains within the Y have complex looplike structures due to disulfide bonds within and between the chains. This accounts for the characteristic tertiary (three-dimensional) structure of immunoglobulins. At one region of immunoglobulins, the amino acid sequence is highly variable; this accounts for the specificity of binding of immunoglobulins to particular antigens.

Chapter 54

Concept Checks

Figure 54.5   Higher predation would occur where locust numbers are highest. This means that predators would be responding to an increase in prey density by eating more individuals.

Figure 54.7   Cold water suppresses the ability of the coral-building organisms to secrete their calcium carbonate shell.

Figure 54.10   In some areas when fire is prevented, fuel, in the form of old leaves and branches, can accumulate. When a fire eventually occurs, it can be so large and hot that it destroys everything in its path, even reaching high into the tree canopy.

Figure 54.17   Acid soils are low in essential plant and animal nutrients such as calcium and nitrogen and are lethal to some soil microorganisms that are important in decomposition and nutrient cycling.

Figure 54.19   This occurs because increasing cloudiness and rain at the tropics maintain fairly constant temperatures across a wide latitudinal range.

Figure 54.24   Soil conditions can also influence biome type. Nutrient-poor soils, for example, may support vegetation different than that of the surrounding area.

Feature Investigation Questions

1. Most believe that invasive species succeed in new environments due to the lack of natural enemies and that diseases and predators present in

the original environment controlled the growth of the population. When these organisms are introduced into a novel environment, the natural enemies are usually absent. This allows for an unchecked increase in the population of the invasive species.

2. Callaway and Aschehoug were able to demonstrate through a controlled experiment that the presence of *Centaurea*, an invasive species, reduced the biomass of three other native species of grasses by releasing allelochemicals. Similar experiments using species of grasses that are found in the native region of *Centaurea* indicate that these species have evolved defenses against the allelochemicals.

3. The activated charcoal helps to remove the allelochemical from the soil. The researchers conducted this experiment to provide further evidence that the chemical released by the *Centaurea* was reducing the biomass of the native Montana grasses. With the removal of the chemicals by the addition of the charcoal, the researchers showed an increase in biomass of the native Montana grasses compared to the experiments lacking the charcoal.

Test Yourself

1. b 2. e 3. a 4. b 5. a 6. a 7. d 8. d 9. a 10. a

Conceptual Questions

1. Mountains are cooler than valleys because of adiabatic cooling. Air at higher altitudes expands because of decreased pressure. As it expands, air cools, at a rate of 10°C for every 1,000 m in elevation. As a result, mountain tops can be much cooler than the plains or valleys that surround them.

2. Solar radiation in the form of short-wave energy passes through the atmosphere to heat the Earth's surface. This energy is then radiated back to the atmosphere in the form of infrared radiation. Much of this radiation is absorbed by atmospheric gases and reradiated toward Earth, causing an increase in temperature.

3. Florida is a peninsula that is surrounded by the Atlantic Ocean and the Gulf of Mexico. Differential heating between the land and the sea creates onshore sea breezes on both the east and west coasts. These breezes often drift across the whole peninsula, bringing heavy rain.

Chapter 55

Concept Checks

Figure 55.3   In classical conditioning, an involuntary response comes to be associated with a stimulus that did not originally elicit the response, as with Pavlov's dogs salivating at the sound of a metronome.

Figure 55.5   The ability to sing the same distinctive song must be considered innate behavior because the cuckoo has had no opportunity to learn its song from its parents.

Figure 55.7   Tinbergen manipulated pinecones, but not all digger wasp nests are surrounded by pinecones. You could manipulate branches, twigs, stones, and leaves to determine the necessary size and dimensions of objects that digger wasps use as landmarks.

Figure 55.8   This is an unusual example because the return trip involves several different generations to complete: One generation overwinters in Mexico, but these individuals lay eggs and die on the return journey, and their offspring continue the return trip.

Figure 55.14   The individuals in the center of the group are less likely to be attacked than those on the edge of the group. This is referred to as the geometry of the selfish herd.

Figure 55.16   Because of the genetic benefit, the answer is nine cousins. Consider Hamilton's rule, expressed in the formula $rB > C$. Using cousins, $B = 9$, $r = 0.125$, and $C = 1$, and $1.125 > 1$. Using sisters, $B = 2$, $r = 0.5$, and $C = 1$. Because rB would not be greater than C, there would be no net genetic benefit in self-sacrifice.

Figure 55.17   All the larvae in the group are likely to be the progeny of one egg mass from one adult female moth. The death of the one caterpillar teaches a predator to avoid the pattern and benefits the caterpillar's close kin.

Figure 55.21   Because sperm are cheaper to produce than eggs, males try to maximize their fitness through attracting multiple females, whereas female fitness is maximized by choosing a mate with good genetic quality and parenting skills. Colorful plumage and elaborate adornments are thus signals of the male's overall health.

Figure 55.22 The males aren't careful because it is likely the pups were fathered in the previous year by a different male. Being a harem master is demanding, and males may often only perform this role for a year or two.

Feature Investigation Questions

1. Tinbergen observed the activity of digger wasps as they prepared to leave the nest. Each time, the wasp hovered and flew around the nest for a period of time before leaving. Tinbergen suggested that during this time, the wasp was making a mental map of the nest site. He hypothesized that the wasp was using characteristics of the nest site, particularly landmarks, to help relocate it.

2. Tinbergen placed pinecones around the nest of the wasps. When the wasps left the nest, he removed the pinecones from the nest site and set them up in the same pattern a distance away, constructing a sham nest. For each trial, the wasps would go directly to the sham nest, which had the pinecones around it. This indicated to Tinbergen that the wasps identified the nest based on the pinecone landmarks.

3. No. Tinbergen also conducted an experiment to determine if the wasps were responding to the visual cue of the pinecones or the chemical cue of the pinecone scent. The results of this experiment indicated that the wasps responded to the visual cue of the pinecones and not their scent.

Test Yourself

1. d   2. d   3. d   4. c   5. c   6. d   7. b   8. c   9. a   10. c

Conceptual Questions

1. Ethology is the scientific study of animal behavior that focuses on the specific genetic and physiological mechanisms of behavior.

2. Certainty of paternity influences degree of parental care. With internal fertilization, certainty of paternity is relatively low. With external fertilization, eggs and sperm are deposited together, and paternity is more certain. This explains why males of some species, such as mouth-breeding cichlid fish, are more likely to engage in parental care.

3. In monogamy, each individual mates exclusively with one partner for at least one breeding cycle. In polygamy, individuals mate with more than one individual during a breeding cycle. There are two types of polygamy. In polygyny, one male mates with more than one female, and in polyandry, females mate with more than one male.

Chapter 56

Concept Checks

Figure 56.2 The total population size, N, would be estimated to be $110 \times 100/20$, or 550.

Figure 56.3 In a half-empty classroom, the distribution is often clumped because friends sit together.

Figure 56.7 (a) type III, (b) type II

Figure 56.11 $dN/dt = 0.1 \times 200\ (300)/500 = 12$.

Figure 56.13 Only density-dependent factors operate in this way.

Figure 56.19 There were very few juveniles in the population and many mature adults. The population would be in decline.

Figure 56.22 Many different ecological footprint calculators are available on the Web. Does altering inputs such as type of transportation, amount of meat eaten, or amount of waste generated make a difference?

Feature Investigation Questions

1. It became apparent that the sheep population was declining. Some individuals felt that the decline in the population was due to increased wolf predation having a negative effect on population growth. This led to the suggestion of culling the wolf population to reduce the level of predation on the sheep population.

2. The survivorship curve is very similar to a typical type I survivorship curve. This suggests that survival is high among young and reproductively active members of the population and that mortality rates are higher for older members of the population. One difference between the actual survivorship curve and a typical type I curve is that the mortality

rate of very young sheep was higher in the actual curve, and then it leveled off after the second year. This suggests that very young and older sheep are more at risk for predation.

3. It was concluded that wolf predation was not the primary reason for the drop in the sheep population. It appeared that wolves prey on the vulnerable members of the population and not on the healthy, reproductively active members. The Park Service determined that several cold winters may have had a more important impact on the sheep population than wolf predation did. Based on these conclusions, the Park Service ended a wolf population control program.

Test Yourself

1. b   2. e   3. b   4. c   5. c   6. b   7. c   8. d   9. c   10. c

Conceptual Questions

1. A population can be defined as a group of interbreeding individuals occupying the same habitat at the same time. Population ecology is the study of how populations grow and what promotes and limits growth.

2. Population biologists first capture and tag the animals. The tagged animals are freed and assumed to mix freely with unmarked individuals in the population. When the population is resampled, the numbers of marked and unmarked individuals are recorded. The assumption is that the ratio of marked to unmarked individuals in the second sample is the same as the ratio of marked to unmarked individuals in the first sample, and in this way, an estimate of population size is obtained.

3. In promiscuity each female mates with a different male every year or breeding cycle. At medium values of N, $(K - N)/K$ is closer to a value of 1, and population growth is relatively large. If $K = 1,000$, $N = 500$, and $r = 0.1$, then

$$\frac{dN}{dt} = (0.1)(500) \times \frac{(1,000 - 500)}{1,000}$$

$$\frac{dN}{dt} = 25$$

However, if population sizes are low ($N = 100$), $(K - N)/K$ is so small that growth is low.

$$\frac{dN}{dt} = (0.1)(100) \times \frac{(1,000 - 100)}{1,000}$$

$$\frac{dN}{dt} = 9$$

By comparing these two examples with that shown in Section 56.3, we see that growth is small at high and low values of N and is greatest at immediate values of N. Growth is greatest when $N = K/2$. However, when expressed as a percentage, growth is greatest at low population sizes. Where $N = 100$, percentage growth = $9/100 = 9\%$. Where $N = 500$, percentage growth = $25/500 = 5\%$, and where $N = 900$, percentage growth = $9/100 = 1\%$.

Chapter 57

Concept Checks

Figure 57.2 Individual vultures often fight one another over small carcasses. These interactions would constitute intraspecific interference competition.

Figure 57.5 There would be 10 possible pairings (AB, AC, AD, AE, BC, BD, BC, CD, CE, DE), of which only neighboring species (AB, BC, CD, DE) competed. Therefore, competition would be expected in 4/10 pairings, or 40% of the cases.

Figure 57.8 A 1974 review by Tom Schoener examined segregation in a more wide-ranging literature review of over 80 species, including slime molds, mollusks, and insects, as well as birds. He found segregation by habitat occurred in the majority of the examples, 55%. The other most common form of segregation was by food type, 40%.

Figure 57.9 Omnivores, such as bears, can feed on both plant material, such as berries, and animals, such as salmon. As such, omnivores may act as both predators and herbivores depending on what they are feeding on.

APPENDIX B

Figure 57.10 Batesian mimicry has a positive effect for the mimic, and the model is unaffected, so it is a +/0 relationship, like commensalism. Müllerian mimicry has a positive effect on both species, so it is a +/+ relationship, like mutualism.

Figure 57.12 Because there is no evolutionary history between invasive predators and native prey, the native prey often have no defenses against these predators and are very easily caught and eaten.

Figure 57.14 Invertebrate herbivores can eat around mechanical defenses; therefore, chemical defenses are probably most effective against invertebrate herbivores.

Figure 57.20 It's an example of facultative mutualism, because in this case, both species can live without the other.

Figure 57.23 Fertilizer increases plant quality and hence herbivore density, which, in turn, increases the density of spiders. This is a bottom-up effect.

Feature Investigation Questions

1. The two species of barnacles can be found in the same intertidal zone, but there is a distinct difference in niche of each species. *Chthamalus stellatus* is found only in the upper intertidal zone. *Semibalanus balanoides* is found only in the lower tidal zone.

2. Connell moved rocks with young *Chthamalus* from the upper intertidal zone into the lower intertidal zone to allow *Semibalanus* to colonize the rocks. After the rocks were colonized by *Semibalanus*, he removed *Semibalanus* from one side of each rock and returned the rocks to the lower intertidal zone. This allowed Connell to observe the growth of *Chthamalus* in the presence and the absence of *Semibalanus*.

3. Connell observed that *Chthamalus* was more resistant to desiccation compared to *Semibalanus*. Though *Semibalanus* was the better competitor in the lower intertidal zone, the species was at a disadvantage in the upper intertidal zone when water levels were low. This allowed *Chthamalus* to flourish and outcompete *Semibalanus* in a different region of the intertidal zone.

Test Yourself

1. d 2. c 3. b 4. d 5. c 6. b 7. d 8. b 9. b 10. c

Conceptual Questions

1. The hypothesis states that two species with exactly the same requirements cannot live together in the same place and use the same resources, that is, occupy the same niche.

2. In Müllerian mimicry, many unpalatable species evolve to look the same, reinforcing the distasteful design; in Batesian mimicry, a palatable species mimics an unpalatable one.

3. There are at least three reasons why we don't see more herbivory in nature. First, plants possess an array of defensive chemicals, including alkaloids, phenolics, and terpenes. Second, many herbivore populations are reduced by the action of natural enemies. We see evidence for this in the world of biological control. Third, the low nutritive value of plants ensures herbivore populations remain low and unlikely to impact plant populations.

Chapter 58

Concept Checks

Figure 58.5 Species richness of trees doesn't increase because rainfall in the western United States is low compared to that in the east.

Figure 58.6 Hurricanes, tropical storms, heavy rainfall, and mudslides are disturbances that maintain a mosaic of disturbed and undisturbed habitats, favoring high species richness in the tropics.

Figure 58.10 As we walk forward from the edge of the glacier to the mouth of the inlet, we are walking backward in ecological time to communities that originated hundreds of years ago.

Figure 58.11 No, competition is also important. For example, the shade from later-arriving species, such as spruce trees, causes competitive exclusion of some of the original understory species.

Figure 58.13 Competition features more prominently. Although early colonists tend to make the habitat more favorable for later colonists, it is the later colonists who outcompete the earlier ones, and this fuels species change.

Figure 58.14 If a small island was extremely close to the mainland, it could continually receive migrating species from the source pool. Even though these species could not complete their life cycle on such a small island, extinctions would rarely be recorded because of this continual immigration.

Figure 58.15 At first glance, the change looks small, but the data are plotted on a log scale. On this scale, an increase in bird richness from 1.2 to 1.6 equals an increase from 16 to 40 species, a change of over 100%.

Feature Investigation Questions

1. Simberloff and Wilson were testing the three predictions of the theory of island biogeography. One prediction suggested that the number of species should increase with increasing island size. Another prediction suggested that the number of species should decrease with increasing distance of the island from the source pool. Finally, the researchers were testing the prediction that the turnover of species on islands should be considerable.

2. Simberloff and Wilson used the information gathered from the species survey to determine whether the same types of species recolonized the islands or if colonizing species were random.

3. The data suggested that species richness did increase with island size. Also, the researchers found that in all but one of the islands, the number of species was similar to the number of species before fumigation.

Test Yourself

1. c 2. c 3. d 4. b 5. c 6. d 7. a 8. d 9. b 10. c

Conceptual Questions

1. A community is an assemblage of many populations living in the same place at the same time. Community ecology studies how groups of species interact and form functional communities.

2.

Disturbance	Frequency	Severity of effects
Forest fire	Low to high, depending on lightning frequency	High to low, depending on frequency
Hurricane	Low	Severe
Tornado	Very low	Severe
Floods	Medium to high in riparian areas	Fairly low; many communities can recover quickly
Disease epidemics	Low	High; may cause catastrophic losses of species
Droughts	Low	Potentially severe
High winds	High	May kill large trees and create light gaps
Hard freezes	Low	May cause deaths to tropical species, such as mangroves

3. A community is in equilibrium when no change can be detected in the number of species and their population sizes over a given period of time.

Chapter 59

Concept Checks

Figure 59.3 It depends on the trophic level of their food, whether dead vegetation or dead animals. Many decomposers feed at multiple trophic levels.

Figure 59.6 The production efficiency is $(16/823) \times 100$, or 1.9%.

Figure 59.13 On a population level, plant secondary metabolites can deter herbivores from feeding. However, on an ecosystem level, these effects are not as important because higher primary production tends to result in higher secondary production.

Figure 59.17 The greatest stores are in rocks and fossil fuels.

Figure 59.18 It fluctuates because less CO_2 is emitted from vegetation in the summer and more is emitted in the winter. This pattern is driven by the large land masses of the Northern Hemisphere relative to the smaller land masses of the Southern Hemisphere.

Figure 59.23 High levels occurred because prevailing westerly winds carried acid rain from the industrial areas of the Midwest, where it was produced, to areas of the U.S. northeast.

Feature Investigation Questions

1. The researchers were testing the effects of increased carbon dioxide levels on the forest ecosystem. The researchers were testing the effects of increased carbon dioxide levels on primary production as well as other trophic levels in the ecosystem.

2. By increasing the carbon dioxide levels in only half of the chambers, the researchers were maintaining the control treatments necessary for all scientific studies. By maintaining equal numbers of control and experimental treatments, the researchers could compare data to determine what effects the experimental treatment had on the ecosystem.

3. The increased carbon dioxide levels led to an increase in primary productivity, as expected. Since photosynthetic rate is limited by carbon dioxide levels, increases in the available carbon dioxide should increase photosynthetic rates. Interestingly, though, the increase in primary productivity did not lead to an increase in herbivory. The results indicated that herbivory actually decreased with increased carbon dioxide levels.

Test Yourself

1. d 2. d 3. d 4. a 5. d 6. a 7. a 8. b 9. c 10. d

Conceptual Questions

1. Autotrophs harvest light or chemical energy and store that energy in carbon compounds. Heterotrophs obtain their nutrition by eating other organisms.

2. Chain lengths are short in food webs because there is low production efficiency and only a 10% rate of energy transfer from one level to another, so only a few links can be supported.

3. The phosphorous cycle is a local cycle with no capacity for long-distance transport. Both the carbon and nitrogen cycles are global cycles with biological, geological, and atmospheric pools.

Chapter 60

Concept Checks

Figure 60.4 It is possible that the results are driven by what is known as a sampling effect. As the numbers of species in the community increase, so does the likelihood of including a "superspecies," a species with exceptionally large individuals that would use up resources. In communities with higher diversity, care has to be taken that increased diversity is driving the results, not the increased likelihood of including a superspecies.

Figure 60.6 The extinction rate could increase because an increasing human population requires more space to live, work, and grow food, resulting in less available habitat and resources for other species.

Figure 60.8 No, some species, such as self-fertilizing flowers, appear to be less affected by inbreeding.

Figure 60.9 The effective population size (N_e) would be = $(4 \times 125 \times 500)$ / $(125 + 500)$, or 400.

Figure 60.12 Corridors might also promote the movement of invasive species or the spread of fire between areas.

Figure 60.13 They act as habitat corridors because they permit movement of species between forest fragments.

Feature Investigation Questions

1. The researchers hoped to replicate terrestrial communities that differed only in their level of biodiversity. This would allow the researchers to determine the relationship between biodiversity and ecological function.

2. The hypothesis was that ecological function was directly related to biodiversity. If biodiversity increased, the hypothesis suggested that ecological function should increase.

3. The researchers tested for ecosystem function by monitoring community respiration, decomposition, nutrient retention rates, and productivity. All of these indicate the efficiency of nutrient production and use in the ecosystem.

Test Yourself

1. d 2. e 3. a 4. c 5. c 6. e 7. e 8. a 9. c 10. b

Conceptual Questions

1. The first level is genetic diversity; the second is species diversity; and the third is ecosystem diversity.

2. The most vulnerable are those with small population sizes, low rates of population growth, K-selected (Chapter 56), with inbreeding and possible harem mating structure, tame and unafraid of humans, possibly limited to islands, flightless, possibly valuable to humans as timber, a source of meat or fur, or desirable by collectors (Chapter 60).

3. An umbrella species is a species whose habitat requirements are so large that protecting it would also protect many other species existing in the same habitat. A flagship species is a single large or instantly recognizable species typically chosen because it is attractive and thus more readily engenders support for its conservation. A keystone species is a species within the community that has a role out of proportion to its abundance.

Glossary

A

A band A wide, dark band in a myofibril produced by the orderly parallel arrangement of the thick filaments in the middle of each sarcomere.

abiotic The term used to describe interactions between organisms and their nonliving environment.

abortion A procedure or circumstance that causes the death of an embryo or fetus after implantation.

abscisic acid One of several plant hormones that help a plant cope with environmental stress.

absolute refractory period The period during an action potential when the inactivation gate of the voltage-gated sodium channel is closed; during this time, it is impossible to generate another action potential.

absorption The process in which digested nutrients are transported from the digestive cavity into an animal's circulatory system.

absorption spectrum A diagram that depicts the wavelengths of electromagnetic radiation that are absorbed by a pigment.

absorptive nutrition The process whereby an organism uses enzymes to digest organic materials and absorbs the resulting small food molecules into its cells.

absorptive state One of two alternating phases in the utilization of nutrients; occurs when ingested nutrients enter the blood from the gastrointestinal tract. The other phase is the postabsorptive state.

acclimatization A long-term and persistent physiological adaptation to an extreme environment.

accommodation In the vertebrate eye, the process in which contraction and relaxation of the ciliary muscles adjust the lens according to the angle at which light enters the eye.

acetylcholinesterase An enzyme located on membranes of muscle fibers in a neuromuscular junction; breaks down excess acetylcholine released into the synaptic cleft.

acid A molecule that releases hydrogen ions in solution.

acid hydrolase A hydrolytic enzyme found in lysosomes that functions at acidic pH and uses a molecule of water to break a covalent bond.

acid rain Precipitation with a pH of less than 5.6; results from the burning of fossil fuels.

acidic A solution that has a pH below 7.

acoelomate An animal that lacks a fluid-filled body cavity.

acquired antibiotic resistance The common phenomenon of a previously susceptible strain of bacteria becoming resistant to a specific antibiotic.

acquired immune deficiency syndrome (AIDS) A disease caused by the human immunodeficiency virus (HIV) that leads to a defect in the immune system of infected individuals.

acrocentric A chromosome in which the centromere is near one end.

acromegaly A condition in which a person's growth hormone level is abnormally elevated after puberty, causing many bones to thicken and enlarge.

acrosomal reaction An event in fertilization in which enzymes released from a sperm's acrosome break down the outer layers of an egg cell, allowing the entry of the sperm cell's nucleus into the egg cell.

acrosome A special structure at the tip of a sperm's head containing proteolytic enzymes that break down the protective outer layers of the egg cell at fertilization.

actin A cytoskeletal protein.

actin filament A thin type of protein filament composed of actin proteins that forms part of the cytoskeleton and supports the plasma membrane; plays a key role in cell strength, shape, and movement.

action potential An electrical signal along a cell's plasma membrane; occurs in animal neuron axons muscle cells and some plant cells.

action spectrum The rate of photosynthesis plotted as a function of different wavelengths of light.

activation energy An initial input of energy in a chemical reaction that allows the molecules to get close enough to cause a rearrangement of bonds.

activator A transcription factor that binds to DNA and increases the rate of transcription.

active immunity An animal's ability to fight off a pathogen to which it has been previously exposed. Active immunity can develop as a result of natural infection or artificial immunization.

active site The location in an enzyme where a chemical reaction takes place.

active transport The transport of a solute across a membrane against its gradient (from a region of low concentration to a region of higher concentration). Active transport requires an input of energy.

adaptations The processes and structures by which organisms adjust to changes in their environment.

adaptive radiation The process whereby a single ancestral species evolves into a wide array of descendant species that differ greatly in their habitat, form, or behavior.

adenine (A) A purine base found in DNA and RNA.

adenosine triphosphate (ATP) A molecule that is a common energy source for all cells.

adenylyl cyclase An enzyme in the plasma membrane that synthesizes cAMP from ATP.

adherens junction A mechanically strong cell junction between animal cells that typically occurs in bands. The cells are connected to each other via cadherins, and the cadherins are linked to actin filaments on the inside of the cells.

adhesion The ability of two different substances to cling to each other; the ability of water to be attracted to, and thereby adhere to, a surface that is not electrically neutral.

adiabatic cooling The process in which increasing elevation leads to a decrease in air temperature.

adventitious root A root that is produced on the surfaces of stems (and sometimes leaves) of vascular plants; also, roots that develop at the bases of stem cuttings.

aerenchyma Spongy plant tissue with large air spaces.

aerobic respiration A type of cellular respiration in which O_2 is consumed and CO_2 is released.

aerotolerant anaerobe A microorganism that does not use oxygen but is not poisoned by it either.

afferent arterioles Blood vessels that provide a pathway for blood into the glomeruli of the vertebrate kidney.

affinity The degree of attraction between an enzyme and its substrate.

aflatoxins Fungal toxins that cause liver cancer and are a major health concern worldwide.

age-specific fertility rate The rate of offspring production for females of a certain age; used to calculate how a population grows.

age structure The relative numbers of individuals of each defined age group in a population.

AIDS *See* acquired immune deficiency syndrome.

air sac A component of the avian respiratory system; air sacs—not lungs—expand when a bird inhales and shrink when it exhales. They do not participate in gas exchange, but help direct air through the lungs.

akinete A thick-walled, food-filled cell produced by certain bacteria or protists that enables them to survive unfavorable conditions in a dormant state.

aldosterone A steroid hormone made by the adrenal glands that regulates salt and water balance in vertebrates.

algae (singular, **alga**) A term that applies to about 10 phyla of protists that include both photosynthetic and nonphotosynthetic species; often also includes cyanobacteria.

alimentary canal In animals, the single elongated tube of a digestive system, with an opening at either end through which food and eventually wastes pass from one end to the other.

alkaline A solution that has a pH above 7.

alkaloids A group of secondary metabolites that contain nitrogen and usually have a cyclic, ringlike structure. Examples include caffeine and nicotine.

allantois One of the four extraembryonic membranes in the amniotic egg. It serves as a disposal sac for metabolic wastes.

Allee effect The phenomenon that some individuals will fail to mate successfully purely by chance, for example, because of the failure to find a mate.

allele A variant form of a gene.

allele frequency The number of copies of a particular allele in a population divided by the total number of alleles in that population.

allelochemical A powerful plant chemical, often a root exudate, that kills other plant species.

allelopathy The suppressed growth of one species due to the release of toxic chemicals by another species.

allopatric The term used to describe species occurring in different geographic areas.

allopatric speciation A form of speciation that occurs when a population becomes geographically isolated from other populations and evolves into one or more new species.

alloploid An organism having at least one set of chromosomes from two or more different species.

allosteric site A site on an enzyme where a molecule can bind noncovalently and affect the function of the active site.

alpha (α) helix A type of protein secondary structure in which a polypeptide forms a repeating helical structure stabilized by hydrogen bonds.

alternation of generations The phenomenon that occurs in plants and some protists in which the life cycle alternates between multicellular diploid organisms, called sporophytes, and multicellular haploid organisms, called gametophytes.

alternative splicing The splicing of pre-mRNA in more than one way to create two or more different polypeptides.

altruism Behavior that appears to benefit others at a cost to oneself.

alveoli 1. Saclike structures in the lungs where gas exchange occurs. 2. Saclike cellular features of the protists known as alveolates.

Alzheimer disease (AD) The leading worldwide cause of dementia; characterized by a loss of memory and intellectual and emotional function (formerly called Alzheimer's disease).

AM fungi A phylum of fungi that forms mycorrhizal associations with plants.

amensalism One-sided competition between species, where the interaction is detrimental to one species but not to the other.

Ames test A test that helps ascertain whether or not an agent is a mutagen by using a strain of a bacterium, *Salmonella typhimurium*.

amino acid The building block of proteins. Amino acids have a common structure in which a carbon atom, called the α-carbon, is linked to an amino group (NH$_2$) and a carboxyl group (COOH). The α-carbon also is linked to a hydrogen atom and a particular side chain.

aminoacyl site (A site) One of three sites for tRNA binding in the ribosome during translation; the other two are the peptidyl site (P site) and the exit site (E site). The A site is where incoming tRNA molecules bind to the mRNA (except for the initiator tRNA).

aminoacyl tRNA *See* charged tRNA.

aminoacyl-tRNA synthetase An enzyme that catalyzes the attachment of amino acids to tRNA molecules.

amino terminus *See* N-terminus.

ammonia (NH$_3$) A highly toxic nitrogenous waste typically produced by many aquatic animal species.

ammonification The conversion of organic nitrogen to NH$_3$ and NH$_4^+$ during the nitrogen cycle.

amnion The innermost of the four extraembryonic membranes in the amniotic egg. It protects the developing embryo in a fluid-filled sac called the amniotic cavity.

amniotes A group of tetrapods with amniotic eggs that includes turtles, lizards, snakes, crocodiles, birds, and mammals.

amniotic egg A type of egg produced by amniotic animals that contains the developing embryo and the four separate extraembryonic membranes that it produces: the amnion, the yolk sac, the allantois, and the chorion.

amoeba (plural, amoebae) A protist that moves by pseudopodia, which involves extending cytoplasm into filaments or lobes.

amoebocyte A mobile cell within a sponge's mesophyl that absorbs food from choanocytes, digests it, and carries the nutrients to other cells.

amphibian An ectothermic, vertebrate animal that metamorphoses from a water-breathing to an air-breathing form but must return to the water to reproduce.

amphipathic Molecules containing a hydrophobic (water-fearing) region and a hydrophilic (water-loving) region.

ampulla (plural, ampullae) 1. A muscular sac at the base of each tube foot of a echinoderm; used to store water. 2. A bulge in the walls of the semicircular canals of the mammalian inner ear; important for sensing circular motions of the head.

amygdala An area of the vertebrate forebrain known to be critical for understanding and remembering emotional situations.

amylase A digestive enzyme in saliva and the pancreas involved in the digestion of starch.

anabolic reaction A metabolic pathway that involves the synthesis of larger molecules from smaller precursor molecules. Such reactions usually require an input of energy.

anabolism A metabolic pathway that results in the synthesis of cellular molecules and macromolecules; requires an input of energy.

anaerobic Refers to a process that occurs in the absence of oxygen; a form of metabolism that does not require oxygen.

anaerobic respiration The breakdown of organic molecules in the absence of oxygen.

anagenesis The pattern of speciation in which a single species is transformed into a different species over the course of many generations.

analogous structure A structure that is the result of convergent evolution. Such structures have arisen independently, two or more times, because species have occupied similar types of environments on Earth.

anaphase The phase of mitosis during which the sister chromatids separate from each other and move to opposite poles; the poles themselves also move farther apart.

anatomy The study of the morphology of organisms, such as plants and animals.

anchoring junction A type of junction between animal cells that attaches cells to each other and to the extracellular matrix (ECM).

androecium The aggregate of stamens that forms the third whorl of a flower.

androgens Steroid hormones produced by the male testes (and, to a lesser extent, the adrenal glands) that affect most aspects of male reproduction.

anemia A condition characterized by lower than normal levels of hemoglobin, which reduces the amount of oxygen that can be stored in the blood.

aneuploidy An alteration in the number of particular chromosomes so that the total number of chromosomes is not an exact multiple of a set.

angina pectoris Chest pain during exertion due to the heart being deprived of oxygen.

angiosperm A flowering plant. The term means enclosed seed, which reflects the presence of seeds within fruits.

animal cap assay A type of experiment used to identify proteins secreted by embryonic cells that induce cells in the animal pole to differentiate into mesoderm.

animal pole In triploblast organisms, the pole of the egg with less yolk and more cytoplasm.

Animalia A eukaryotic kingdom of the domain Eukarya.

animals Multicellular heterotrophs with cells that lack cell walls. Most animals have nerves, muscles, the capacity to move at some point in their life cycle, and the ability to reproduce sexually, with sperm fusing directly with eggs.

anion An ion that has a net negative charge.

annual A plant that dies after producing seed during its first year of life.

antagonist A muscle or group of muscles that produces oppositely directed movements at a joint.

antenna complex *See* light-harvesting complex.

anterior Refers to the end of an animal where the head is found.

anteroposterior axis In bilateral animals, one of the three axes along which the adult body pattern is organized; the others are the dorsoventral axis and the right-left axis.

anther The uppermost part of a flower stamen, consisting of a cluster of microsporangia that produce and release pollen.

antheridia Round or elongate gametangia that produce sperm in plants.

anthropoidea A member of a group of primates that includes the monkeys and the hominoidea; these species are larger-brained and diurnal.

antibiotic A chemical, usually made by microorganisms, that inhibits the growth of certain other microorganisms.

antibody A protein secreted by plasma cells that is part of the immune response; antibodies travel all over the body to reach antigens identical to those that stimulated their production, combine with these antigens, then guide an attack that eliminates the antigens or the cells bearing them.

anticodon A three-nucleotide sequence in tRNA that is complementary to a codon in mRNA.

antidiuretic hormone (ADH) A hormone secreted by the posterior pituitary gland that acts on kidney cells to decrease urine production.

antigen Any foreign molecule that the host does not recognize as self and that triggers a specific immune response.

antigen-presenting cells (APCs) Cells bearing fragments of antigen, called antigenic determinants or epitopes, complexed with the cell's major histocompatibility complex (MHC) proteins.

antiparallel The arrangement in DNA where one strand runs in the 5′ to 3′ direction while the other strand is oriented in the 3′ to 5′ direction.

antiporter A type of transporter that binds two or more ions or molecules and transports them in opposite directions across a membrane.

anus In mammals, the final portion of the rectum through which feces are expelled.

aorta In vertebrates, a large blood vessel that exits a ventricle of the heart and leads to the systemic circulation.

apical-basal-patterning genes A category of genes that are important in early stages of plant development during which the apical and basal axes are formed.

apical-basal polarity An architectural feature of plants in which they display an upper, apical pole and a lower, basal pole; shoot apical meristem occurs at the apical pole, and root apical meristem occurs at the basal pole.

apical constriction A cellular process during gastrulation that occurs in bottle cells, where a reduction in the diameter of the actin rings connected to the adherens junctions causes the cells to elongate toward their basal end.

apical meristem In plants, a group of actively dividing cells at a growing tip.

apical region The region of a plant seedling that produces the leaves and flowers.

apomixis A natural asexual reproductive process in which plant fruits and seeds are produced in the absence of fertilization.

apoplast The continuum of water-soaked cell walls and intercellular spaces in a plant.

apoplastic transport The movement of solutes through cell walls and the spaces between cells.

apoptosis Programmed cell death.

aposematic coloration Warning coloration that advertises an organism's unpalatable taste.

aquaporin A transport protein in the form of a channel that allows the rapid diffusion of water across the cell membrane.

aqueous humor A thin liquid in the anterior cavity behind the cornea of the vertebrate eye.

aqueous solution A solution made with water.

aquifer An underground water supply.

arbuscular mycorrhizae Symbiotic associations between AM fungi and the roots of vascular plants.

Archaea One of the three domains of life; the other two are Bacteria and Eukarya.

archaea When not capitalized, refers to a cell or species within the domain Archaea.

archegonia Flask-shaped plant gametangia that enclose an egg cell.

archenteron A cavity formed in an animal embryo during gastrulation that will become the organism's digestive tract.

area hypothesis The proposal that larger areas contain more species than smaller areas because they can support larger populations and a greater range of habitats.

arteriole A single-celled layer of endothelium surrounded by one or two layers of smooth muscle and connective tissue that delivers blood to the capillaries and distributes blood to regions of the body in proportion to metabolic demands.

artery A blood vessel that carries blood away from the heart.

artificial selection *See* selective breeding.

asci Fungal sporangia shaped like sacs that produce and release sexual ascospores.

ascocarp The type of fruiting body produced by ascomycete fungi.

ascomycetes A phylum of fungi that produce sexual spores in saclike asci located at the surfaces of fruiting bodies known as ascocarps.

ascospore The type of sexual spore produced by the ascomycete fungi.

aseptate The condition of not being partitioned into smaller cells; usually refers to fungal cells.

asexual reproduction A reproductive strategy that occurs when offspring are produced from a single parent, without the fusion of gametes from two parents. The offspring are therefore clones of the parent.

A site *See* aminoacyl site.

assimilation During the nitrogen cycle, the process by which plants and animals incorporate the ammonia and NO_3^- formed through nitrogen fixation and nitrification.

associative learning A change in behavior due to an association between a stimulus and a response.

asthma A disease in which the smooth muscles around the bronchioles contract more than usual, decreasing airflow in the lungs.

AT/GC rule Refers to the phenomenon that an A in one DNA strand always hydrogen-bonds with a T in the opposite strand, and a G in one strand always bonds with a C.

atherosclerosis The condition in which large plaques may occlude (block) the lumen of an artery.

atmospheric (barometric) pressure The pressure exerted by the gases in air on the body surfaces of animals.

atom The smallest functional unit of matter that forms all chemical substances and cannot be further broken down into other substances by ordinary chemical or physical means.

atomic mass An atom's mass relative to the mass of other atoms. By convention, the most common form of carbon, which has six protons and six neutrons, is assigned an atomic mass of exactly 12.

atomic nucleus The center of an atom; contains protons and neutrons.

atomic number The number of protons in an atom.

ATP *See* adenosine triphosphate.

ATP-dependent chromatin remodeling enzyme An enzyme that catalyzes a change in the positions of nucleosomes.

ATP synthase An enzyme that utilizes the energy stored in a H^+ electrochemical gradient for the synthesis of ATP via chemiosmosis.

atrial natriuretic peptide (ANP) A peptide secreted from the atria of the heart whenever blood levels of sodium increase; ANP causes a natriuresis by decreasing sodium reabsorption in the kidney tubules.

atrioventricular (AV) node Specialized cardiac cells in most vertebrates that sit near the junction of the atria and ventricles and conduct the electrical events from the atria to the ventricles.

atrioventricular (AV) valve A one-way valve into the ventricles of the vertebrate heart through which blood moves from the atria.

atrium In the heart, a chamber to collect blood from the tissues.

atrophy A reduction in the size of a structure, such as a muscle.

audition The ability to detect and interpret sound waves; present in vertebrates and arthropods.

autoimmune disease In humans and many other vertebrates, a disorder in which the body's normal state of immune tolerance breaks down, with the result that attacks are directed against the body's own cells and tissues.

autonomic nervous system The division of the peripheral nervous system that regulates homeostasis and organ function.

autonomous specification The unequal acquisition of cytoplasmic factors during cell division in a developing vertebrate embryo.

autophagosome A double-membrane structure enclosing cellular material destined to be degraded; produced by the process of autophagy.

autophagy A process whereby cellular material, such as a worn-out organelle, becomes enclosed in a double membrane and is degraded.

autosomes All of the chromosomes found in the cell nucleus of eukaryotes except for the sex chromosomes.

autotomy In echinoderms, the ability to detach a body part, such as a limb, that will later regenerate.

autotroph An organism that has metabolic pathways that use energy from either inorganic molecules or light to make organic molecules.

auxin One of several types of hormones considered to be "master" plant hormones because they influence plant structure, development, and behavior in many ways.

auxin efflux carrier One of several types of PIN proteins, which transport auxin out of plant cells.

auxin influx carrier A plasma membrane protein that transports auxin into plant cells.

auxin-response genes Plant genes that are regulated by the hormone auxin.

avirulence gene (*Avr* gene) A gene in a plant pathogen that encodes a virulence-enhancing elicitor, which causes plant disease.

Avogadro's number As first described by Italian physicist Amedeo Avogadro, 1 mole of any element contains the same number of atoms— 6.022×10^{23}.

axillary bud A bud that occurs in the axil, the upper angle where a twig or leaf emerges from a stem.

axillary meristem A meristem produced in the axil, the upper angle where a twig or leaf emerges from a stem. Axillary meristems generate axillary buds, which can produce flowers or branches.

axon An extension of the plasma membrane of a neuron that is involved in sending signals to neighboring cells.

axon hillock The part of the axon closest to the cell body; typically where an action potential begins.

axon terminal The end of the axon that sends electrical or chemical messages to other cells.

axoneme The internal structure of eukaryotic flagella and cilia consisting of microtubules, the motor protein dynein, and linking proteins.

B

bacilli Rod-shaped prokaryotic cells.

backbone The linear arrangement of phosphates and sugar molecules in a DNA or RNA strand.

Bacteria One of the three domains of life; the other two are Archaea and Eukarya.

bacteria (singular, **bacterium**) When not capitalized, refers to a cell or species within the domain Bacteria.

bacterial artificial chromosome (BAC) A cloning vector derived from F factors that can contain large DNA inserts.

bacterial colony A clone of genetically identical cells formed from a single cell.

bacteriophage A virus that infects bacteria.

bacteroid A modified bacterial cell of the type known as rhizobia present in mature root nodules of some plants.

balanced polymorphism The phenomenon in which two or more alleles are kept in balance and maintained in a population over the course of many generations.

balancing selection A type of natural selection that maintains genetic diversity in a population.

balloon angioplasty A common treatment to restore blood flow through a blood vessel. A thin tube with a tiny, inflatable balloon at its tip is threaded through the artery to the diseased area; inflating the balloon compresses the plaque against the arterial wall, widening the lumen.

barometric pressure *See* atmospheric pressure.

baroreceptor A pressure-sensitive region within the walls of certain arteries that contains the endings of nerve cells; these regions sense and help to maintain blood pressure in the normal range for an animal.

Barr body A highly condensed X chromosome present in female mammals.

basal body A site at the base of flagella or cilia from which microtubules grow. Basal bodies are anchored on the cytosolic side of the plasma membrane.

basal metabolic rate (BMR) The metabolic rate of an animal under resting conditions, in a postabsorptive state, and at a standard temperature.

basal nuclei Clusters of neuronal cell bodies in the vertebrate forebrain that surround the thalamus and lie beneath the cerebral cortex; involved in planning and learning movements.

basal region The region of a plant seedling that produces the roots.

basal transcription A low level of transcription resulting from just the core promoter.

basal transcription apparatus In a eukaryotic structural gene, refers to the complex of RNA polymerase II, GTFs, and a DNA sequence containing a TATA box.

base 1. A molecule that when dissolved in water lowers the H$^+$ concentration. 2. A component of nucleotides that is a single or double ring of carbon and nitrogen atoms.

base pair The structure in which two bases in opposite strands of DNA hydrogen-bond with each other.

base substitution A mutation that involves the substitution of a single base in the DNA for another base.

basic local alignment search tool (BLAST) *See* BLAST.

basidia Club-shaped cells that produce sexual spores in basidiomycete fungi.

basidiocarp The type of fruiting body produced by basidiomycete fungi.

basidiomycetes A phylum of fungi whose sexual spores are produced on the surfaces of club-shaped structures (basidia).

basidiospore A sexual spore of the basidiomycete fungi.

basilar membrane A component of the mammalian ear that vibrates back and forth in response to sound and bends the stereocilia in one direction and then the other.

basophil A type of leukocyte that secretes the anticlotting factor heparin at the site of an infection, which helps flush out the infected site; basophils also secrete histamine, which attracts infection-fighting cells and proteins.

Batesian mimicry The mimicry of an unpalatable species (the model) by a palatable one (the mimic).

Bayesion method One method used to evaluate a phylogenetic tree based on an evolutionary model.

B cell A type of lymphocyte responsible for specific immunity.

behavior The observable response of organisms to external or internal stimuli.

behavioral ecology A subdiscipline of organismal ecology that focuses on how the behavior of an individual organism contributes to its survival and reproductive success, which, in turn, eventually affects the population density of the species.

benign tumor A precancerous mass of abnormal cells.

beta (β) pleated sheet A type of protein secondary structure in which regions of a polypeptide lie parallel to each other and are held together by hydrogen bonds to form a repeating zigzag shape.

bidirectional replication The process in which DNA replication proceeds outward from the origin in opposite directions.

biennial A plant that does not reproduce during the first year of life but may reproduce within the following year.

bilateral symmetry An architectural feature in which the body or organ of an organism can be divided along a vertical plane at the midline to create two halves.

Bilateria Bilaterally symmetric animals.

bile A substance produced by the liver that contains bicarbonate ions, cholesterol, phospholipids, a number of organic wastes, and a group of substances collectively termed bile salts.

bile salts A group of substances produced in the liver that solubilize dietary fat and increase its accessibility to digestive enzymes.

binary fission The process of cell division in bacteria and archaea in which one cell divides into two cells.

binocular vision A type of vision in animals having two eyes located at the front of the head; the overlapping images coming into both eyes are processed together in the brain to form one perception.

binomial nomenclature The standard method for naming species. Each species has a genus name and species epithet.

biochemistry The study of the chemistry of living organisms.

biodiversity The diversity of life forms in a given location.

biodiversity crisis The idea that there is currently an elevated loss of species on Earth, far beyond the normal extinction rate of species.

biofilm An aggregation of microorganisms that secrete adhesive mucilage, thereby gluing themselves to surfaces.

biogeochemical cycle The continuous movement of nutrients such as nitrogen, carbon, sulfur, and phosphorus from the physical environment to organisms and back.

biogeography The study of the geographic distribution of extinct and modern species.

bioinformatics A field of study that uses computers to study biological information.

biological control The use of an introduced species' natural enemies to control its proliferation.

biological nitrogen fixation Nitrogen fixation that is performed in nature by certain prokaryotes.

biological species concept An approach used to distinguish species, which states that a species is a group of individuals whose members have the potential to interbreed with one another in nature to produce viable, fertile offspring but cannot successfully interbreed with members of other species.

biology The study of life.

bioluminescence A phenomenon in living organisms in which chemical reactions give off light rather than heat.

biomagnification The increase in the concentration of a substance in living organisms from lower to higher trophic levels in a food web.

biomass A quantitative estimate of the total mass of living matter in a given area, usually measured in grams or kilograms per square meter.

biome A major type of habitat characterized by distinctive plant and animal life.

bioremediation The use of living organisms, usually microbes or plants, to detoxify polluted habitats such as dump sites or oil spills.

biosphere The regions on the surface of the Earth and in the atmosphere where living organisms exist.

biosynthetic reaction Also called an anabolic reaction; a chemical reaction in which small molecules are used to synthesize larger molecules.

biotechnology The use of living organisms or the products of living organisms for human benefit.

biotic The term used to describe interactions among organisms.

biparental inheritance An inheritance pattern in which both the male and female gametes contribute organellar genes to the offspring.

bipedal Having the ability to walk on two feet.

bipolar cells Cells in the vertebrate eye that make synapses with photoreceptors and relay responses to the ganglion cells.

bipolar disorder A neurological disorder characterized by alternating periods of euphoria and depression, resulting from an imbalance in neurotransmitter levels in the brain.

bivalent Homologous pairs of sister chromatids associated with each other, lying side by side.

blade The flattened portion of a leaf.

BLAST A computer program that can identify homologous genes that are found in a database.

blastocoel A cavity formed in a cleavage-stage vertebrate embryo (blastula); provides a space into which cells of the future digestive tract will migrate.

blastocyst The mammalian counterpart of a blastula.

blastoderm A flattened disc of dividing cells in the embryo of animals that undergo incomplete cleavage; occurs in birds and some fishes.

blastomeres The two half-size daughter cells produced by each cell division during cleavage.

blastopore A small opening created when a band of tissue invaginates during gastrulation. It forms the primary opening of the archenteron to the outside.

blastula An animal embryo at the stage when it forms an outer epithelial layer and an inner cavity.

blending inheritance An early hypothesis of inheritance that stated that the genetic material that dictates hereditary traits blends together from generation to generation, and the blended traits are then passed to the next generation.

blood A fluid connective tissue in animals consisting of cells and (in mammals) cell fragments suspended in a solution of water containing dissolved nutrients, proteins, gases, and other molecules.

blood-doping An example of hormone misuse in which the number of red blood cells in the circulation is boosted to increase the oxygen-carrying capacity of the blood.

blood pressure The force exerted by blood on the walls of blood vessels; blood pressure is responsible for moving blood through the vessels.

body mass index (BMI) A method of assessing body fat and health risk that involves calculating the ratio of weight compared to height; weight in kilograms is divided by the square of the height in meters.

body plan The organization of cells, tissues, and organs within a multicellular organism; also known as a body pattern.

bone A relatively hard component of the vertebrate skeleton; a living, dynamic tissue composed of organic molecules and minerals.

bottleneck effect A situation in which a population size is dramatically reduced and then rebounds. While the population is small, genetic drift may rapidly reduce the genetic diversity of the population.

Bowman's capsule A saclike structure that houses the glomerulus at the beginning of the tubular component of a nephron in the mammalian kidney.

brain Organ of the central nervous system of animals that functions to process and integrate information.

brainstem The part of the vertebrate brain composed of the medulla oblongata, the pons, and the midbrain.

brassinosteroid One of several plant hormones that help a plant to cope with environmental stress.

bronchi (singular, **bronchus**) Tubes branching from the trachea and leading into the lungs.

bronchiole A thin-walled, small tube branching from the bronchi and leading to the alveoli in mammalian lungs.

bronchodilator A compound that binds to the muscles of the bronchioles of the lung and causes them to relax, thereby widening the bronchioles.

brown adipose tissue A specialized tissue in small mammals such as hibernating bats, small rodents living in cold environments, and many newborn mammals, including humans, that can help to generate heat and maintain body temperature.

brush border The collective name for the microvilli in the vertebrate small intestine.

bryophytes Liverworts, mosses, and hornworts, the modern nonvascular land plants.

buccal pumping A form of breathing in which animals take in water or air into their mouths, then raise the floor of the mouth, creating a positive pressure that pumps water or air across the gills or into the lungs; found in fishes and amphibians.

bud A miniature plant shoot having a dormant shoot apical meristem.

budding A form of asexual reproduction in which a portion of the parent organism pinches off to form a complete new individual.

buffer A compound that acts to minimize pH fluctuations in the fluids of living organisms. Buffer systems can raise or lower pH as needed.

bulbourethral glands Paired accessory glands in the human male reproductive system that secrete an alkaline mucus that protects sperm by neutralizing the acidity in the urethra.

bulk feeders Animals that eat food in large pieces.

bulk flow The mass movement of liquid in a plant caused by pressure, gravity, or both.

C

C₃ plant A plant that incorporates CO_2 into organic molecules via RuBP to make 3PG, a three-carbon molecule.

C₄ plant A plant that uses PEP carboxylase to initially fix CO_2 into a four-carbon molecule and later uses rubisco to fix CO_2 into simple sugars; an adaptation to hot, dry environments.

cadherin A cell adhesion molecule found in animal cells that promotes cell-to-cell adhesion.

calcitonin A hormone that plays a role in Ca^{2+} homeostasis in some vertebrates.

calcium wave A brief increase in cytosolic Ca^{2+} concentrations in an egg that has been penetrated by a sperm cell; the change in Ca^{2+} moves through the cell and contributes to the slow block to polyspermy.

callose A carbohydrate that plays crucial roles in plant development and plugging wounds in plant phloem.

calorie The amount of heat required to raise the temperature of 1 gram of water 1 degree Celsius.

Calvin cycle The second stage in the process of photosynthesis. During this cycle, ATP is used as a source of energy, and NADPH is used as a source of high-energy electrons so that CO_2 can be incorporated into carbohydrate.

calyx The sepals that form the outermost whorl of a flower.

Cambrian explosion An event during the Cambrian period (543 to 490 mya) in which there was an abrupt increase (on a geological scale) in the diversity of animal species.

cAMP *See* cyclic adenosine monophosphate.

CAM plants C₄ plants that open their stomata at night to take up carbon dioxide.

cancer A disease caused by gene mutations that lead to uncontrolled cell growth.

canopy The uppermost layer of tree foliage.

capillary A tiny thin-walled vessel that is the site of gas and nutrient exchange between the blood and interstitial fluid.

capping The process in which a 7-methylguanosine is covalently attached at the 5′ end of mature mRNAs of eukaryotes.

capsid A protein coat enclosing a virus's genome.

CAP site One of two regulatory sites near the *lac* promoter; this site is a DNA sequence recognized by the catabolite activator protein (CAP).

capsule A very thick, gelatinous glycocalyx produced by certain strains of bacteria that may help them avoid being destroyed by an animal's immune (defense) system.

carapace The hard protective cuticle covering the cephalothorax of a crustacean.

carbohydrate An organic molecule often with the general formula, $C(H_2O)$; a carbon-containing compound that includes starches, sugars, and cellulose.

carbon fixation A process in which carbon from inorganic CO_2 is incorporated into an organic molecule such as a carbohydrate.

carboxyl terminus *See* C-terminus.

carcinogen An agent that increases the likelihood of developing cancer, usually a mutagen.

carcinoma A cancer of epithelial cells.

cardiac cycle The events that produce a single heartbeat, which can be divided into two phases, diastole and systole.

cardiac muscle A type of muscle tissue found only in hearts in which physical and electrical connections between individual cells enable many of the cells to contract simultaneously.

cardiac output (CO) The amount of blood the heart pumps per unit time, usually expressed in units of L/min.

cardiovascular disease Diseases affecting the heart and blood vessels.

cardiovascular system A system containing three components: blood or hemolymph, blood vessels, and one or more hearts.

carnivore An animal that consumes animal flesh or fluids.

carotenoid A type of photosynthetic or protective pigment found in plastids that imparts a color that ranges from yellow to orange to red.

carpel A flower shoot organ that produces ovules that contain female gametophytes.

carrier *See* transporter.

carrying capacity (K) The upper boundary for a population size.

Casparian strips Suberin ribbons on the walls of endodermal cells of plant roots; prevent apoplastic transport of ions into vascular tissues.

caspase An enzyme that is activated during apoptosis.

catabolic reaction A metabolic pathway in which a molecule is broken down into smaller components, usually releasing energy.

catabolism A metabolic pathway that results in the breakdown of larger molecules into smaller molecules. Such reactions are often exergonic.

catabolite activator protein (CAP) An activator protein for the *lac* operon.

catabolite repression In bacteria, a process whereby transcriptional regulation is influenced by the presence of glucose.

catalase An enzyme within peroxisomes that breaks down hydrogen peroxide to water and oxygen gas.

catalyst An agent that speeds up the rate of a chemical reaction without being consumed during the reaction.

cataract An accumulation of protein in the lens of the eye; causes blurring and poor night vision.

cation An ion that has a net positive charge.

cation exchange With regard to soil, the process in which hydrogen ions are able to replace mineral cations on the surfaces of humus or clay particles.

cDNA *See* complementary DNA.

cDNA library A type of DNA library in which the inserts are derived from cDNA.

cecum The first portion of a vertebrate's large intestine.

cell The simplest unit of a living organism.

cell adhesion A vital function of the cell membrane that allows cells to bind to each other. Cell adhesion is critical in the formation of multicellular organisms and provides a way to convey positional information between neighboring cells.

cell adhesion molecule (CAM) A membrane protein found in animal cells that promotes cell adhesion.

cell biology The study of individual cells and their interactions with each other.

cell body A part of a neuron that contains the cell nucleus and other organelles.

cell coat Also called the glycocalyx, the carbohydrate-rich zone on the surface of animal cells that shields the cell from mechanical and physical damage.

cell communication The process through which cells can detect and respond to signals in their extracellular environment. In multicellular organisms, cell communication is also needed to coordinate cellular activities within the whole organism.

cell cycle The series of phases a eukaryotic cell progresses through from its origin until it divides by mitosis.

cell differentiation The phenomenon by which cells become specialized into particular cell types.

cell division The process in which one cell divides into two cells.

cell doctrine *See* cell theory.

cell junctions Specialized structures that adhere cells to each other and to the ECM.

cell-mediated immunity A type of specific immunity in which cytotoxic T cells directly attack and destroy infected body cells, cancer cells, or transplanted cells.

cell nucleus The membrane-bound area of a eukaryotic cell in which the genetic material is found.

cell plate In plant cells, a structure that forms a cell wall between the two daughter cells during cytokinesis.

cell signaling A vital function of the plasma membrane that involves cells sensing changes in their environment and communicating with each other.

cell surface receptor A receptor found in the plasma membrane that enables a cell to respond to different kinds of signaling molecules.

cell theory A theory that states that all organisms are made of cells, cells are the smallest units of living organisms, and new cells come from pre-existing cells by cell division.

GLOSSARY

cell-to-cell communication A form of cell communication that occurs between two different cells.

cellular differentiation The process by which different cells within a developing organism acquire specialized forms and functions due to the expression of cell-specific genes.

cellular respiration A process by which living cells obtain energy from organic molecules and release waste products.

cellular response Adaptation at the cellular level that involves a cell responding to signals in its environment.

cellulose The main macromolecule of the primary cell wall of plants and many algae; a polymer made of repeating molecules of glucose attached end to end.

cell wall A relatively rigid, porous structure located outside the plasma membrane of prokaryotic, plant, fungal, and certain protist cells; provides support and protection.

centiMorgan (cM) *See* map unit (mu).

central cell In the female gametophyte of a flowering plant, a large cell that contains two nuclei; after double fertilization, it forms the first cell of the nutritive endosperm tissue.

central dogma Refers to the steps of gene expression at the molecular level. DNA is transcribed into mRNA, and mRNA is translated into a polypeptide.

central nervous system (CNS) In vertebrates, the brain and spinal cord.

central region The region of a plant seedling that produces stem tissue.

central vacuole An organelle that often occupies 80% or more of the cell volume of plant cells and stores a large amount of water, enzymes, and inorganic ions.

central zone The area of a plant shoot meristem where undifferentiated stem cells are maintained.

centrioles A pair of structures within the centrosome of animal cells. Most plant cells and many protists lack centrioles.

centromere The region where the two sister chromatids are tightly associated; the centromere is an attachment site for kinetochore proteins.

centrosome A single structure often near the cell nucleus of eukaryotic cells that forms a nucleating site for the growth of microtubules; also called the microtubule-organizing center.

cephalization The localization of a brain and sensory structures at the anterior end of the body of animals.

cephalothorax The fused head and thorax structure in species of the class Arachnida and Crustacea.

cerebellum The part of the vertebrate hindbrain, along with the pons, responsible for monitoring and coordinating body movements.

cerebral cortex The surface layer of gray matter that forms the outer part of the cerebrum of the vertebrate brain.

cerebral ganglia A paired structure in the head of invertebrates that receives input from sensory cells and controls motor output.

cerebrospinal fluid Fluid that exists in ventricles within the central nervous system and surrounds the exterior of the brain and spinal cord; it absorbs physical shocks to the brain resulting from sudden movements or blows to the head.

cerebrum A region of the vertebrate forebrain that is responsible for the higher functions of conscious thought, planning, and emotion, as well as control of motor function.

cervix A fibrous structure at the end of the female vagina that forms the opening to the uterus.

channel A transmembrane protein that forms an open passageway for the direct diffusion of ions or molecules across a membrane.

chaperone A protein that keeps other proteins in an unfolded state during the process of post-translational sorting.

character A characteristic of an organism, such as the appearance of seeds, pods, flowers, or stems.

character displacement The tendency for two species to diverge in morphology and thus resource use because of competition.

character state A particular variant of a given trait.

charged tRNA A tRNA with its attached amino acid; also called aminoacyl tRNA.

charophyceans The lineages of freshwater green algae that are most closely related to the land plants.

checkpoint One of three critical regulatory points found in the cell cycle of eukaryotic cells. At these checkpoints, a variety of proteins act as sensors to determine if a cell is in the proper condition to divide.

checkpoint protein A protein that senses if a cell is in the proper condition to divide and prevents a cell from progressing through the cell cycle if it is not.

chemical energy The potential energy contained within covalent bonds in molecules.

chemical equilibrium A state in a chemical reaction in which the rate of formation of products equals the rate of formation of reactants.

chemical mutagen A chemical that causes mutations.

chemical reaction The formation and breaking of chemical bonds, resulting in a change in the composition of substances.

chemical selection Occurs when a chemical within a mixture has special properties or advantages that cause it to increase in amount. May have played a key role in the formation of an RNA world.

chemical synapse A synapse in which a chemical called a neurotransmitter is released from the axon terminal of a neuron and acts as a signal from the presynaptic to the postsynaptic cell.

chemiosmosis A process for making ATP in which energy stored in an ion electrochemical gradient is used to make ATP from ADP and P_i.

chemoautotroph An organism able to use energy obtained by chemical modifications of inorganic compounds to synthesize organic compounds.

chemoheterotroph An organism that must obtain organic molecules both for energy and as a carbon source.

chemoreceptor A sensory receptor in animals that responds to specific chemical compounds.

chiasma The connection at a crossover site of two chromosomes.

chimeric gene A gene formed from the fusion of two gene fragments to each other.

chitin A tough, nitrogen-containing polysaccharide that forms the external skeleton of many insects and the cell walls of fungi.

chlorophyll A photosynthetic green pigment found in the chloroplasts of plants, algae, and some bacteria.

chlorophyll *a* A type of chlorophyll pigment found in plants, algae, and cyanobacteria.

chlorophyll *b* A type of chlorophyll pigment found in plants, green algae, and some other photosynthetic organisms.

chloroplast A semiautonomous organelle found in plant and algal cells that carries out photosynthesis.

chloroplast genome The chromosome found in chloroplasts.

chlorosis The yellowing of plant leaves caused by various types of mineral deficiencies.

choanocyte A specialized cell of sponges that functions to trap and eat small particles.

chondrichthyans Members of the class Chondrichthyes, including sharks, skates, and rays.

chordate An organism that has or at some point in its life has had a notochord and a hollow dorsal nerve cord; includes all vertebrates and some invertebrates.

chorion One of the four extraembryonic membranes in the amniotic egg. It exchanges gases between the embryo and the surrounding air.

chorionic gonadotropin (CG) An LH-like hormone made by the blastocyst that maintains the corpus luteum.

chromatin Refers to the biochemical composition of chromosomes, which contain DNA and many types of proteins.

chromosome A discrete unit of genetic material composed of DNA and associated proteins. Eukaryotes have chromosomes in their cell nuclei and in plastids and mitochondria.

chromosome territory A distinct, nonoverlapping area where each chromosome is located within the cell nucleus of eukaryotic cells.

chromosome theory of inheritance An explanation of how the steps of meiosis account for the inheritance patterns observed by Mendel.

chylomicrons Large fat droplets coated with amphipathic proteins that perform an emulsifying function similar to that of bile salts; chylomicrons are formed in intestinal epithelial cells from absorbed fats in the diet.

chyme A solution of water and partially digested food particles in the stomach and small intestine.

chymotrypsin A protease involved in the breakdown of proteins in the small intestine.

chytrids Simple, early-diverging phyla of fungi; commonly found in aquatic habitats and moist soil, where they produce flagellate reproductive cells.

cilia (singular, **cilium**) Cell appendages that have the same internal structure as flagella and function like flagella to facilitate cell movement; cilia are shorter and more numerous on cells than are flagella.

ciliate A protist that moves by means of cilia, which are tiny hairlike extensions that occur on the outsides of cells and have the same internal structure as flagella.

circulatory system A system that transports necessary materials to all cells of an animal's body and transports waste products away from cells. Three basic types are gastrovascular cavities, open systems, and closed systems.

***cis*-acting element** *See cis*-effect.

***cis*-effect** A DNA segment that must be adjacent to the gene(s) that it regulates. The *lac* operator site is an example of a *cis*-acting element.

cisternae Flattened, fluid-filled tubules of the endoplasmic reticulum.

***cis/trans* isomers** Organic molecules with the same chemical composition but existing in two different configurations determined by the positions of hydrogen atoms on the two carbons of a C=C double bond. When the hydrogen atoms are on the same side of the double bond, it is called a *cis* isomer; when on the opposite sides of the double bond, it is a *trans* isomer.

citric acid cycle A cycle that results in the breakdown of carbohydrates to carbon dioxide; also known as the Krebs cycle.

clade A group of species derived from a single common ancestor.

cladistic approach An approach used to construct a phylogenetic tree by comparing primitive and shared derived characters.

cladogenesis A pattern of speciation in which a species is divided into two or more species.

cladogram A phylogenetic tree constructed by using a cladistic approach.

clamp connection In basidiomycete fungi, a structure that helps distribute nuclei during cell division.

clasper An extension of the pelvic fin of a chondrichthyan, used by the male to transfer sperm to the female.

class In taxonomy, a subdivision of a phylum.

classical conditioning A type of associative learning in which an involuntary response comes to be associated positively or negatively with a stimulus that did not originally elicit the response.

cleavage A succession of rapid cell divisions with no significant growth that produces a hollow sphere of cells called a blastula.

cleavage furrow In animal cells, an area that constricts like a drawstring to separate the cells during cytokinesis.

climate The prevailing weather pattern of a given region.

climax community A distinct end point of succession.

clitoris Located at the anterior part of the labia minora, erectile tissue that becomes engorged with blood during sexual arousal and is very sensitive to sexual stimulation.

clonal deletion One of two mechanisms that explain why normal individuals lack active lymphocytes that respond to self components; T cells with receptors capable of binding self proteins are destroyed by apoptosis.

clonal inactivation One of two mechanisms that explain why normal individuals lack active lymphocytes that respond to self components; the process occurs outside the thymus and causes potentially self-reacting T cells to become nonresponsive.

clonal selection The process by which an antigen-stimulated lymphocyte divides and forms a clone of cells, each of which recognizes that particular antigen.

cloning Making many copies of something such as a DNA molecule.

closed circulatory system A circulatory system in which blood flows throughout an animal entirely within a series of vessels and is kept separate from the interstitial fluid.

closed conformation Tightly packed chromatin that cannot be transcribed into RNA.

clumped The most common pattern of dispersion within a population, in which individuals are gathered in small groups.

cnidocil On the surface of a cnidocyte, a hairlike trigger that detects stimuli.

cnidocyte A characteristic feature of cnidarians; a stinging cell that functions in defense or the capture of prey.

coacervates Droplets that form spontaneously from the association of charged polymers such as proteins, carbohydrates, or nucleic acids surrounded by water.

coactivator A protein that increases the rate of transcription but does not directly bind to the DNA itself.

coat protein A protein that surrounds a membrane vesicle and facilitates vesicle formation.

cocci Sphere-shaped prokaryotic cells.

cochlea A coiled structure in the inner ear of mammals that contains the auditory receptors (organ of Corti).

coding sequence The region of a gene or a DNA molecule that encodes the information for the amino acid sequence of a polypeptide.

coding strand The DNA strand opposite to the template (or noncoding strand).

codominance The phenomenon in which a single individual expresses two alleles.

codon A sequence of three nucleotide bases that specifies a particular amino acid or a stop codon; codons function during translation.

coefficient of relatedness (r) The probability that any two individuals will share a copy of a particular gene.

coelom A fluid-filled body cavity in an animal.

coelomate An animal with a true coelom.

coenzyme An organic molecule that participates in a chemical reaction with an enzyme but is left unchanged after the reaction is completed.

coevolution The process by which two or more species of organisms influence each other's evolutionary pathway.

cofactor Usually an inorganic ion that temporarily binds to the surface of an enzyme and promotes a chemical reaction.

cognitive learning The ability to solve problems with conscious thought and without direct environmental feedback.

cohesion The ability of like molecules to noncovalently bind to each other; the attraction of water molecules for each other.

cohesion-tension theory The explanation for long-distance water transport as the combined effect of the cohesive forces of water and evaporative tension.

cohort A group of organisms of the same age.

coleoptile A protective sheath that encloses the first bud of the epicotyl in a mature monocot embryo.

coleorhiza A protective envelope that encloses the young root of a monocot.

colinearity rule The phenomenon whereby the order of homeotic genes along the chromosome correlates with their expression along the anteroposterior axis of the body.

collagen A protein secreted from animal cells that forms large fibers in the extracellular matrix.

collecting duct A tubule in the mammalian kidney that collects urine from nephrons.

collenchyma cells Flexible cells that make up collenchyma tissue.

collenchyma tissue A plant ground tissue that provides support to plant organs.

colligative property A property of a solution that depends only on the concentration of solute molecules.

colloid A gel-like substance in the follicles of the thyroid gland.

colon A part of a vertebrate's large intestine consisting of three relatively straight segments—the ascending, transverse, and descending portions. The terminal portion of the descending colon is S-shaped, forming the sigmoid colon, which empties into the rectum.

colony hybridization A method that uses a labeled probe to identify bacterial colonies that contain a desired gene.

combinatorial control The phenomenon whereby a combination of many factors determines the expression of any given gene.

commensalism An interaction that benefits one species and leaves the other unaffected.

communication The use of specially designed visual, chemical, auditory, or tactile signals to modify the behavior of others.

community An assemblage of populations of different species that live in the same place at the same time.

community ecology The study of how populations of species interact and form functional communities.

compartmentalization A characteristic of eukaryotic cells in which many organelles separate the cell into different regions. Cellular compartmentalization allows a cell to carry out specialized chemical reactions in different places.

competent The term used to describe bacterial strains that have the ability to take up DNA from the environment.

competition An interaction that affects two or more species negatively, as they compete over food or other resources.

competitive exclusion hypothesis The proposal that two species with the same resource requirements cannot occupy the same niche.

competitive inhibitor A molecule that binds to the active site of an enzyme and inhibits the ability of the substrate to bind.

complement The family of plasma proteins that provides a means for extracellular killing of microbes without prior phagocytosis.

complementary Describes the specific base pairing that occurs between strands of nucleic acids; A pairs only with T (in DNA) or U (in RNA), and G pairs only with C.

complementary DNA (cDNA) DNA molecules that are made from mRNA as a starting material.

complete flower A flower that possesses all four types of flower organs.

complete metamorphosis During development in the majority of insects, a dramatic change in body form from larva to a very different looking adult.

compound A molecule composed of two or more different elements.

compound eyes Image-forming eyes in arthropods and some annelids consisting of several hundred to several thousand light detectors called ommatidia.

computational molecular biology An area of study that uses computers to characterize the molecular components of living things.

concentration The amount of a solute dissolved in a unit volume of solution.

condensation reaction A chemical reaction in which two or more molecules are combined into one larger molecule by covalent bonding, with the loss of a small molecule.

conditional specification The acquisition by cells of specific properties through a variety of cell-to-cell signaling mechanisms in a developing vertebrate embryo.

conditioned response The learned response that is elicited by a newly conditioned stimulus.

conditioned stimulus A new stimulus that is delivered at the same time as an old stimulus, and that over time, is sufficient to elicit the same response.

condom   A sheathlike membrane worn over the penis; in addition to their contraceptive function, condoms significantly reduce the risk of sexually transmitted diseases.

conduction   The process in which the body surface loses or gains heat through direct contact with cooler or warmer substances.

cone pigments   The several types of visual pigments found in the cones of the vertebrate eye.

cones   1. Photoreceptors found in the vertebrate eye; they are less sensitive to low levels of light but can detect color. 2. The reproductive structures of coniferous plants.

congenital hypothyroidism   A condition characterized by poor differentiation of the central nervous system due to a failure of neurons to become myelinated in fetal development; results in profound mental defects.

congestive heart failure   The condition resulting from the failure of the heart to pump blood normally; results in fluid buildup in the lungs (congestion).

conidia   A type of asexual reproductive cell produced by many fungi.

conifers   A phylum of gymnosperm plants, Coniferophyta.

conjugation   A type of genetic transfer between bacteria that involves a direct physical interaction between two bacterial cells.

connective tissue   Clusters of cells that connect, anchor, and support the structures of an animal's body; includes blood, adipose (fat-storing) tissue, bone, cartilage, loose connective tissue, and dense connective tissue.

connexon   A channel that forms gap junctions consisting of six connexin proteins in one cell aligned with six connexin proteins in an adjacent cell.

conservation biology   The study that uses principles and knowledge from molecular biology, genetics, and ecology to protect the biological diversity of life.

conservative mechanism   In this incorrect model for DNA replication, both parental strands of DNA remain together (are conserved) following DNA replication. The two newly made daughter strands also occur together.

consortia   A community of many microbial species.

constant regions   The portions of amino acid sequences in the heavy and light chains that are identical for all immunoglobulins of a given class.

constitutive gene   An unregulated gene that has constant levels of expression in all conditions over time.

contig   A series of clones that contain overlapping pieces of chromosomal DNA.

continental drift   The process by which, over the course of billions of years, the major landmasses, known as the continents, have shifted their positions, changed their shapes, and, in some cases, have become separated from each other.

contraception   The use of birth control procedures to prevent fertilization or implantation of a fertilized egg.

contractile vacuole   A small, membrane enclosed, water-filled compartment that eliminates excess liquid from the cells of certain protists.

contrast   In microscopy, relative differences in the lightness, darkness, or color between adjacent regions in a sample.

control group   The sample in an experiment that is treated just like an experimental group except that it is not subjected to one particular variable.

convection   The transfer of heat by the movement of air or water next to the body.

convergent evolution   The process whereby two different species from different lineages show similar characteristics because they occupy similar environments.

convergent extension   A cellular process during gastrulation that is crucial to development; two rows of cells merge to form a single elongated layer.

convergent trait   *See* analogous structure.

coprophagy   The practice of certain birds and mammals in which feces are consumed to maximize absorption of water and nutrients.

copulation   The process of sperm being deposited within the reproductive tract of the female.

coral reef   A type of aquatic biome found in warm, marine environments.

corepressor   A small effector molecule that binds to a repressor protein to inhibit transcription.

core promoter   Refers to the TATA box and the transcriptional start site of a eukaryotic structural gene.

Coriolis effect   The effect of the Earth's rotation on the surface flow of wind.

cork cambium   A secondary meristem in a plant that produces cork tissue.

cornea   A thin, clear layer on the front of the vertebrate eye.

corolla   The petals of a flower, which occur in the whorl to the inside of the calyx and the outside of the stamens.

corona   The ciliated crown of members of the phylum Rotifera.

coronary artery   An artery that carries oxygen and nutrients to the heart muscle.

coronary artery bypass   A common treatment to restore blood flow through a coronary artery. A small piece of healthy blood vessel is removed from one part of the body and surgically grafted onto the coronary circulation in order to bypass the diseased artery.

coronary artery disease   A condition that occurs when plaques form in the coronary arteries.

corpus callosum   The major tract that connects the two hemispheres of the cerebrum.

corpus luteum   A structure that develops from a ruptured follicle following ovulation; it is responsible for secreting hormones that stimulate the development of the uterus during pregnancy.

correlation   A meaningful relationship between two variables.

cortex   The area of a plant stem or root beneath the epidermis that is largely composed of parenchyma tissue.

cortical reaction   An event in fertilization in which IP_3 and calcium signaling produces barriers to more than one sperm cell binding to and uniting with an egg; called the slow block to polyspermy.

cortisol   A steroid hormone made by the adrenal cortex.

cotranslational sorting   The sorting process in which the synthesis of certain eukaryotic proteins begins in the cytosol and then halts temporarily until the ribosome has become bound to the ER membrane.

cotransporter   *See* symporter.

cotyledon   An embryonic seed leaf.

countercurrent exchange mechanism   An arrangement of water and blood flow in which water enters a fish's mouth and flows between the lamellae of the gills in the opposite direction to blood flowing through the lamellar capillaries.

countercurrent heat exchange   A method of regulating heat loss to the environment; many animals conserve heat by returning it to the body's core and keeping the core much warmer than the extremities.

covalent bond   A chemical bond in which two atoms share a pair of electrons.

CpG island   A cluster of CpG sites. CG refers to the nucleotides of C and G in DNA, and p refers to a phosphodiester linkage.

cranial nerve   A nerve in the peripheral nervous system that is directly connected to the brain.

craniate   A chordate that has a brain encased in a skull and possesses a neural crest.

cranium   A protective bony or cartilaginous housing that encases the brain of a craniate.

crenation   The process of cell shrinkage that occurs if animal cells are placed in a hypertonic medium.

cristae   Projections of the highly invaginated inner membrane of a mitochondrion.

critical innovations   New features that foster the diversification of phyla.

critical period   A limited period of time in which many animals develop species-specific patterns of behavior.

crop   A storage organ that is a dilation of the lower esophagus; found in most birds and many invertebrates, including insects and some worms.

cross-bridge   A region of myosin molecules that extend from the surface of the thick filaments toward the thin filaments in skeletal muscle.

cross-bridge cycle   During muscle contraction, the sequence of events that occurs between the time when a cross-bridge binds to a thin filament and when it is set to repeat the process.

cross-fertilization   Fertilization that involves the union of a female gamete and a male gamete from different individuals.

crossing over   The exchange of genetic material between homologous chromosomes during meiosis; allows for increased variation in the genetic information that each parent may pass to the offspring.

cross-pollination   The process in which a stigma receives pollen from a different plant of the same species.

cryptic coloration   The blending of an organism with the background color of its habitat; also known as camouflage.

cryptochrome   A type of blue-light receptor in plants and protists.

C-terminus   The location of the last amino acid in a polypeptide; also known as the carboxyl terminus.

CT scan   Computerized tomography, which is an X-ray technique used to examine the structure and activity level of the brain without anesthesia or surgery.

cupula   A gelatinous structure within the lateral line organ of fishes that detects changes in water movement.

cuticle   A coating of wax and cutin that helps to reduce water loss from plant surfaces. Also, a nonliving covering that serves to both support and protect an animal.

cycads   A phylum of gymnosperm plants, Cycadophyta.

cyclic adenosine monophosphate (cAMP)   A small effector molecule that acts as a second messenger and is produced from ATP.

cyclic AMP (cAMP) *See* cyclic adenosine monophosphate.

cyclic electron flow *See* cyclic photophosphorylation.

cyclic photophosphorylation During photosynthesis, a pattern of electron flow in the thylakoid membrane that is cyclic and generates ATP alone.

cyclin A protein responsible for advancing a cell through the phases of the cell cycle by binding to a cyclin-dependent kinase.

cyclin-dependent kinase (cdk) A protein responsible for advancing a cell through the phases of the cell cycle. Its function is dependent on the binding of a cyclin.

cyst A one-to-few celled structure that often has a thick, protective wall and can remain dormant through periods of unfavorable climate or low food availability.

cytogenetics The field of genetics that involves the microscopic examination of chromosomes.

cytokines A family of proteins that function in both nonspecific and specific immune defenses by providing a chemical communication network that synchronizes the components of the immune response.

cytokinesis The division of the cytoplasm to produce two distinct daughter cells.

cytokinin A type of plant hormone that promotes cell division.

cytoplasm The region of the cell that is contained within the plasma membrane.

cytoplasmic inheritance *See* extranuclear inheritance.

cytosine (C) A pyrimidine base found in DNA and RNA.

cytoskeleton In eukaryotes, a network of three different types of protein filaments in the cytosol called microtubules, intermediate filaments, and actin filaments.

cytosol The region of a eukaryotic cell that is inside the plasma membrane and outside the organelles.

cytotoxic T cell A type of lymphocyte that travels to the location of its target, binds to the target by combining with an antigen on it, and directly kills the target via secreted chemicals.

D

dalton (Da) A measure of atomic mass. One dalton equals one-twelfth the mass of a carbon atom.

data mining The extraction of useful information and often previously unknown relationships from sequence files and large databases.

database A large number of computer data files that are collected, stored in a single location, and organized for rapid search and retrieval.

daughter strand The newly made strand in DNA replication.

day-neutral plant A plant that flowers regardless of the night length, as long as day length meets the minimal requirements for plant growth.

deafness Hearing loss, usually caused by damage to the hair cells within the cochlea.

death-inducing signaling complex (DISC) A complex consisting of death receptors, FADD, and procaspase that initiates apoptosis via the extrinsic pathway.

death receptor A type of receptor found in the plasma membrane of eukaryotic cells that can promote apoptosis when it becomes activated.

decomposer A consumer that gets its energy from the remains and waste products of other organisms.

defecation The expulsion of feces that occurs through the anus of an animal's digestive canal.

defensive mutualism A mutually beneficial interaction often involving an animal defending a plant or herbivore in return for food or shelter.

deforestation The conversion of forested areas by humans to nonforested land.

degenerate In the genetic code, the observation that more than one codon can specify the same amino acid.

dehydration A reduction in the amount of water in the body.

dehydration reaction A type of condensation reaction in which a molecule of water is lost.

delayed implantation A reproductive cycle in which a fertilized egg reaches the uterus but does not implant until later, when environmental conditions are more favorable for the newly produced young.

delayed ovulation A reproductive cycle in which the ovarian cycle in females is halted before ovulation and sperm are stored and nourished in the female's uterus over the winter. Upon arousal from hibernation in the spring, the female ovulates one or more eggs, which are fertilized by the stored sperm.

deletion A type of mutation in which a segment of genetic material is missing.

demographic transition The shift in birth and death rates accompanying human societal development.

demography The study of birth rates, death rates, age distributions, and the sizes of populations.

dendrite A treelike extension of the plasma membrane of a neuron that receives electrical signals from other neurons.

dendritic cell A type of cell derived from bone marrow stem cells that plays an important role in nonspecific immunity; these cells are scattered throughout most tissues, where they perform various macrophage functions.

denitrification The reduction of nitrate to gaseous nitrogen.

density In the context of populations, the numbers of organisms in a given unit area.

density-dependent factor A mortality factor whose influence increases with the density of the population.

density-independent factor A mortality factor whose influence is not affected by changes in population density.

deoxynucleoside triphosphates Individual nucleotides with three phosphate groups.

deoxyribonucleic acid (DNA) One of two classes of nucleic acids; the other is ribonucleic acid (RNA). A DNA molecule consists of two strands of nucleotides coiled around each other to form a double helix, held together by hydrogen bonds according to the AT/GC rule.

deoxyribose A five-carbon sugar found in DNA.

depolarization The change in the membrane potential that occurs when a cell becomes less polarized, that is, less negative relative to the surrounding fluid.

dermal tissue The covering on various parts of a plant.

descent with modification Darwin's theory that existing life-forms on our planet are the product of the modification of pre-existing life-forms.

desertification The overstocking of land with domestic animals that can greatly reduce grass coverage through overgrazing, turning the area more desert-like.

desmosome A mechanically strong cell junction between animal cells that typically occurs in spotlike rivets.

determinate cleavage In animals, a characteristic of protostome development in which the fate of each embryonic cell is determined very early.

determinate growth A type of growth in plants that is of limited duration, such as the growth of flowers.

determined The term used to describe a cell that is destined to differentiate into a particular cell type.

detritivore *See* decomposer.

detritus Unconsumed plants that die and decompose, along with the dead remains of animals and animal waste products.

deuterostome An animal whose development exhibits radial, indeterminate cleavage and in which the blastopore becomes the anus; includes echinoderms and vertebrates.

development In biology, a series of changes in the state of a cell, tissue, organ, or organism; the underlying process that gives rise to the structure and function of living organisms.

developmental genetics A field of study aimed at understanding how gene expression controls the process of development.

diaphragm A large muscle that subdivides the thoracic cavity from the abdomen in mammals; contraction of the diaphragm enlarges the thoracic cavity during inhalation.

diastole The phase of the cardiac cycle in which the ventricles fill with blood coming from the atria through the open AV valves.

diazotroph A bacterium that fixes nitrogen.

dideoxy chain-termination method The most common method of DNA sequencing; utilizes dideoxynucleotides as a reagent.

differential gene regulation The phenomenon in which the expression of genes differs under various environmental conditions and in specialized cell types.

diffusion In a solution, the process that occurs when a solute moves from a region of high concentration to a region of lower concentration.

digestion The process of breaking down nutrients in food into smaller molecules that can be absorbed across the intestinal epithelia and directly used by cells.

digestive system In animals, the long tube through which food is processed. In a vertebrate, this system consists of the alimentary canal plus several associated structures.

dihybrid An offspring that is a hybrid with respect to two traits.

dihybrid cross A cross in which the inheritance of two different traits is followed.

dikaryotic The occurrence of two genetically distinct nuclei in the cells of fungal hyphae after mating has occurred.

dimorphic fungi Fungi that can exist in two different morphological forms.

dinosaur A term, meaning "terrible lizard," used to describe some of the extinct fossil reptiles.

dioecious The term to describe plants that produce staminate and carpellate flowers on separate plants.

diploblastic Having two distinct germ layers— ectoderm and endoderm but not mesoderm.

diploid Refers to cells containing two sets of chromosomes; designated as $2n$.

diploid-dominant species Species in which the diploid organism is the prevalent organism in the life cycle. Animals are an example.

direct calorimetry   A method of determining basal metabolic rate that involves quantifying the amount of heat generated by the animal.

direct repair   Refers to a DNA repair system in which an enzyme finds an incorrect structure in the DNA and directly converts it back to the correct structure.

directionality   In a DNA or RNA strand, refers to the orientation of the sugar molecules within that strand. Can be 5′ to 3′ or 3′ to 5′.

directional selection   A pattern of natural selection that favors individuals at one extreme of a phenotypic distribution.

disaccharide   A carbohydrate composed of two monosaccharides.

discovery-based science   The collection and analysis of data without the need for a preconceived hypothesis; also called discovery science.

discrete trait   A trait with clearly defined phenotypic variants.

dispersion   A pattern of spacing in which individuals in a population are clustered together or spread out to varying degrees.

dispersive mechanism   In this incorrect model for DNA replication, segments of parental DNA and newly made DNA are interspersed in both strands following the replication process.

dispersive mutualism   A mutually beneficial interaction often involving plants and pollinators that disperse their pollen, and plants and fruit eaters that disperse the plant's seeds.

dissociation constant   An equilibrium constant between a ligand and a protein, such as a receptor or an enzyme.

distal convoluted tubule   The segment of the tubule of the nephron through which fluid flows into one of the many collecting ducts in the kidney.

diversifying selection   A pattern of natural selection that favors the survival of two or more different genotypes that produce different phenotypes.

diversity-stability hypothesis   The proposal that species-rich communities are more stable than those with fewer species.

DNA (deoxyribonucleic acid)   The genetic material that provides a blueprint for the organization, development, and function of living things.

DNA fingerprinting   A technology that identifies particular individuals using properties of their DNA.

DNA helicase   An enzyme that uses ATP to separate DNA strands during DNA replication.

DNA library   A collection of recombinant vectors, each containing a particular fragment of chromosomal DNA (cDNA).

DNA ligase   An enzyme that catalyzes the formation of a covalent bond between nucleotides in adjacent DNA fragments to complete the replication process.

DNA methylase   An enzyme that attaches methyl groups to bases in DNA.

DNA methylation   A process in which methyl groups are attached to bases in DNA.

DNA microarray   A technology used to monitor the expression of thousands of genes simultaneously.

DNA polymerase   An enzyme responsible for covalently linking nucleotides together during DNA replication.

DNA primase   An enzyme that synthesizes a primer for DNA replication.

DNA repair systems   One of several systems to reverse DNA damage before a permanent mutation can occur.

DNA replication   The process by which DNA is copied.

DNase   An enzyme that digests DNA.

DNA sequencing   A method to determine the base sequence of DNA.

DNA supercoiling   A method of compacting chromosomes through the formation of additional coils around the long, thin DNA molecule.

DNA topoisomerase   An enzyme that alleviates DNA supercoiling during DNA replication.

DNA transposon   A type of transposable element that moves as a DNA molecule.

domain   1. A defined region of a protein with a distinct structure and function. 2. One of the three major categories of life: Bacteria, Archaea, and Eukarya.

domestication   A process that involves artificial selection of plants or animals for traits desirable to humans.

dominant   A term that describes the displayed trait in a heterozygote.

dominant species   A species that has a large effect in a community because of its high abundance or high biomass.

dormancy   A phase of metabolic slowdown in a plant.

dorsal   Refers to the upper side of an animal.

dorsoventral axis   In bilateral animals, one of the three axes along which the adult body pattern is organized; the others are the anteroposterior axis and the right-left axis.

dosage compensation   The phenomenon that gene dosage is compensated between males and females. In mammals, the inactivation of one X chromosome in the female reduces the number of expressed copies (doses) of X-linked genes from two to one.

double bond   A bond that occurs when the atoms of a molecule share two pairs of electrons.

double fertilization   In angiosperms, the process in which two different fertilization events occur, producing both a zygote and the first cell of a nutritive endosperm tissue.

double helix   Two strands of DNA hydrogen-bonded with each other. In a DNA double helix, two DNA strands are twisted together to form a structure that resembles a spiral staircase.

Down syndrome   A human disorder caused by the inheritance of three copies of chromosome 21.

duplication   A type of mutation in which a section of a chromosome occurs two or more times.

dynamic instability   The oscillation of a single microtubule between growing and shortening phases; important in many cellular activities, including the sorting of chromosomes during cell division.

E

Ecdysozoa   A clade of molting animals that encompasses primarily the arthropods and nematodes.

echolocation   The phenomenon in which certain species listen for echoes of high-frequency sound waves in order to determine the distance and location of an object.

ECM   See extracellular matrix.

ecological footprint   The amount of productive land needed to support each person on Earth.

ecological species concept   An approach used to distinguish species; considers a species within its native environment and states that each species occupies its own ecological niche.

ecology   The study of interactions among organisms and between organisms and their environments.

ecosystem   The biotic community of organisms in an area as well as the abiotic environment affecting that community.

ecosystem engineer   A keystone species that creates, modifies, and maintains habitats.

ecosystems ecology   The study of the flow of energy and cycling of nutrients among organisms within a community and between organisms and the environment.

ecotypes   Genetically distinct populations adapted to their local environments.

ectoderm   In animals, the outermost layer of cells formed during gastrulation that covers the surface of the embryo and differentiates into the epidermis and nervous system.

ectomycorrhizae   Beneficial interactions between temperate forest trees and soil fungi.

ectoparasite   A parasite that lives on the outside of the host's body.

ectotherm   An animal whose body temperature changes with the environmental temperature.

edge effect   A special physical condition that exists at the boundary or edge of an area.

effective population size   The number of individuals that contribute genes to future populations, often smaller than the actual population size.

effector   A molecule that directly influences cellular responses.

effector cell   A cloned lymphocyte that carries out the attack response during specific immunity.

efferent arteriole   A blood vessel that carries blood away from a glomerulus of the vertebrate kidney.

egg cell   The female gamete; also called an ovum.

ejaculation   The movement of semen through the urethra by contraction of muscles at the base of the penis.

ejaculatory duct   The structure in the male reproductive system through which sperm leave the vas deferens and enter the urethra.

elastin   A protein that makes up elastic fibers in the extracellular matrix of animals.

electrical synapse   A synapse that directly passes electric current from the presynaptic to the postsynaptic cell via gap junctions.

electrocardiogram (ECG or EKG)   A record of the electrical impulses generated by the cells of the heart during the cardiac cycle.

electrochemical gradient   The combined effect of both an electrical and chemical gradient across a membrane; determines the direction that an ion will move.

electrogenic pump   A pump that generates an electrical gradient across a membrane.

electromagnetic receptor   A sensory receptor in animals that detects radiation within a wide range of the electromagnetic spectrum, including visible, ultraviolet, and infrared light, as well as electrical and magnetic fields in some animals.

electromagnetic spectrum   All possible wavelengths of electromagnetic radiation, from relatively short wavelengths (gamma rays) to much longer wavelengths (radio waves).

electron   A negatively charged particle found in orbitals around an atomic nucleus.

electron microscope   A microscope that uses an electron beam for illumination.

electron transport chain (ETC)   A group of protein complexes and small organic molecules within the inner membranes of mitochondria and chloroplasts and the plasma membrane of prokaryotes. The components accept and donate electrons to each other in a linear manner and produce a H⁺ electrochemical gradient.

electronegativity   A measure of an atom's ability to attract electrons to its outer shell from another atom.

element   A substance composed of specific types of atoms that cannot be further broken down by ordinary chemical or physical means.

elicitor   A compound produced by bacterial and fungal pathogens that promotes virulence.

elimination   In animals, the process of undigested material passing out of the body.

elongation factor   A protein that is needed for the growth of a polypeptide during translation.

elongation stage   The second step in transcription or translation where RNA strands or polypeptides are made, respectively.

embryo   The early stages of development in a multicellular organism during which the organization of the organism is largely formed.

embryogenesis   The process by which embryos develop from single-celled zygotes by mitotic divisions.

embryonic development   The process by which a fertilized egg is transformed into an organism with distinct physiological systems and body parts.

embryonic germ cell (EG cell)   A cell in the early mammalian embryo that later gives rise to sperm or egg cells. These cells are pluripotent.

embryonic stem cell (ES cell)   A cell in the early mammalian embryo that can differentiate into almost every cell type of the body. These cells are pluripotent.

embryophyte   A synonym for the land plants.

emerging virus   A newly arising virus.

emphysema   A progressive disease characterized by a loss of elastic recoil ability of the lungs, usually resulting from chronic tobacco smoking.

empirical thought   Thought that relies on observation to form an idea or hypothesis, rather than trying to understand life from a nonphysical or spiritual point of view.

emulsification   A process during digestion that disrupts large lipid droplets into many tiny droplets, thereby increasing their total surface area and exposure to lipase action.

enantiomer   One of a pair of stereoisomers that exist as mirror images.

endangered species   Those species that are in danger of extinction throughout all or a significant portion of their range.

endemic   The term to describe organisms that are naturally found only in a particular location.

endergonic   Refers to chemical reactions that require an addition of free energy and do not proceed spontaneously.

endocrine disruptor   A chemical found in polluted water and soil that resembles a natural hormone; a common example are chemicals that resemble estrogen and can bind to estrogen receptors in animals.

endocrine gland   A structure that contains epithelial cells that secrete hormone molecules into the bloodstream, where they circulate throughout the body.

endocrine system   All the endocrine glands and other organs containing hormone-secreting cells.

endocytosis   A process in which the plasma membrane invaginates, or folds inward, to form a vesicle that brings substances into the cell.

endoderm   In animals, the innermost layer of cells formed during gastrulation; lines the gut and gives rise to many internal organs.

endodermis   In vascular plants, a thin cylinder of root tissue that forms a barrier between the root cortex and the central core of vascular tissue.

endomembrane system   A network of membranes that includes the nuclear envelope, the endoplasmic reticulum, Golgi apparatus, lysosomes, vacuoles, and plasma membrane.

endomycorrhizae   Partnerships between plants and fungi in which the fungal hyphae grow into the spaces between root cell walls and plasma membranes.

endoparasite   A parasite that lives inside the host's body.

endophyte   A mutualistic fungus that lives compatibly within the tissues of various types of plants.

endoplasmic reticulum (ER)   A convoluted network of membranes in a cell's cytoplasm that forms flattened, fluid-filled tubules or cisternae.

endoskeleton   An internal hard skeleton covered by soft tissue; present in echinoderms and vertebrates.

endosperm   A nutritive tissue that increases the efficiency with which food is stored and used in the seeds of flowering plants.

endospore   A cell with a tough coat that is produced in certain bacteria and then released when the enclosing bacterial cell dies and breaks down.

endosporic gametophyte   A plant gametophyte that grows within the confines of microspore or megaspore walls.

endosymbiont   A smaller species that lives within a larger species in a symbiotic relationship.

endosymbiosis   A symbiotic relationship in which the smaller species—the symbiont—lives inside the larger species.

endosymbiosis theory   A theory that mitochondria and chloroplasts originated from bacteria that took up residence within a primordial eukaryotic cell.

endosymbiotic   Describes a relationship in which one organism lives inside the other.

endothelium   The single-celled inner layer of a blood vessel; forms a smooth lining in contact with the blood.

endotherm   An animal that generates its own internal heat and maintains a relatively stable body temperature independent of the environment.

endothermic   A term to describe the ability of an organism to generate and retain body heat through its metabolism.

energy   The ability to promote change or to do work.

energy expenditure   The amount of energy an animal uses in a given period of time to power all of its metabolic requirements.

energy flow   The movement of energy through an ecosystem.

energy intermediate   A molecule such as ATP or NADH that stores energy and is used to drive endergonic reactions in cells.

energy shell   In an atom, an energy level of electrons occupied by one or more orbitals; each energy level is a characteristic distance from the nucleus, with outer shells having more energy than inner shells.

enhancement effect   The phenomenon in which maximal activation of the pigments in photosystems I and II is achieved when organisms are exposed to two wavelengths of light.

enhancer   A response element in eukaryotes that increases the rate of transcription.

enthalpy (*H*)   The total energy of a system.

entomology   The study of insects.

entropy   The degree of disorder of a system.

environmental science   The application of ecology to real-world problems.

enzyme   A protein that acts as a catalyst to speed up a chemical reaction in a cell.

enzyme-linked receptor   A receptor found in all living species that typically has two important domains: an extracellular domain, which binds a signaling molecule, and an intracellular domain, which has a catalytic function.

enzyme-substrate complex   The binding between an enzyme and its substrate.

eosinophil   A type of phagocyte found in large numbers in mucosal surfaces lining the gastrointestinal, respiratory, and urinary tracts, where they fight off parasitic infections.

epicotyl   The portion of an embryonic plant stem with two tiny leaves in a first bud; located above the point of attachment of the cotyledons.

epidermis   A layer of dermal tissue that helps protect a plant from damage.

epididymis   A coiled, tubular structure located on the surface of the testis in which sperm complete their differentiation.

epigenetic inheritance   An inheritance pattern in which modification of a gene or chromosome during egg formation, sperm formation, or early stages of embryonic growth alters gene expression in a way that is fixed during an individual's lifetime.

epinephrine   A hormone secreted by the adrenal glands; also known as adrenaline.

episome   A plasmid that can integrate into a bacterial chromosome.

epistasis   A gene interaction in which the alleles of one gene mask the expression of the alleles of another gene.

epithalamus   A region of the vertebrate forebrain that includes the pineal gland.

epithelial tissue   In animals, a sheet of densely packed cells that covers the body, covers individual organs, and lines the walls of various cavities inside the body.

epitopes   Antigenic determinants; the peptide fragments of an antigen that are complexed to MHC proteins and presented to a helper T cell.

equilibrium   1. In a chemical reaction, occurs when the rate of the forward reaction is balanced by the rate of the reverse reaction. 2. In a population, the situation in which the population size stays the same.

equilibrium model of island biogeography   A model to explain the process of succession on new islands; states that the number of species on an island tends toward an equilibrium number that is determined by the balance between immigration rates and extinction rates.

equilibrium potential   In membrane physiology, the membrane potential at which the flow of an ion is at equilibrium, with no net movement in either direction.

ER lumen   A single compartment enclosed by the ER membrane.

ER signal sequence   A sorting signal in a polypeptide usually located near the amino terminus that is recognized by SRP (signal recognition particle) and directs the polypeptide to the ER membrane.

erythrocyte   A cell that serves the critical function of transporting oxygen throughout an animal's body; also known as a red blood cell.

erythropoietin (EPO) A hormone made by the liver and kidneys in response to any situation where additional red blood cells are required.

E site *See* exit site.

esophagus In animals, the tubular structure that forms a pathway from the throat to the stomach.

essential amino acids Those amino acids that are required in the diet of particular organisms.

essential fatty acid A polyunsaturated fatty acid, such as linoleic acid, that cannot be synthesized by animal cells and must therefore be consumed in the diet.

essential nutrient In animals, a compound that cannot be synthesized from any ingested or stored precursor molecule and so must be obtained in the diet in its complete form. In plants, those substances needed to complete reproduction while avoiding the symptoms of nutrient deficiency.

estradiol The major estrogen in many vertebrates, including humans.

estrogens Steroid hormones produced by the ovaries that affect most aspects of female reproduction.

ethology Scientific studies of animal behavior.

ethylene A plant hormone that is particularly important in coordinating plant developmental and stress responses.

euchromatin The less condensed regions of a chromosome; areas that are capable of gene transcription.

eudicots One of the two largest lineages of flowering plants in which the embryo possesses two seed leaves.

Eukarya One of the three domains of life; the other two are Bacteria and Archaea.

eukaryote One of the two categories into which all forms of life can be placed. The distinguishing feature of eukaryotes is cell compartmentalization, including a cell nucleus; includes protists, fungi, plants, and animals.

eukaryotic Refers to organisms having cells with internal compartments that serve various functions; includes all members of the domain Eukarya.

Eumetazoa A subgroup of animals having more than one type of tissue and, for the most part, different types of organs.

euphyll A leaf with branched veins.

euphyllophytes The clade that includes pteridophytes and seed plants.

euploid An organism that has a chromosome number that is a multiple of a chromosome set (1*n*, 2*n*, 3*n*, etc.).

eusociality An extreme form of altruism in social insects in which the vast majority of females, known as workers, do not reproduce. Instead, they help one reproductive female (the queen) raise offspring.

Eustachian tube In mammals, a connection from the middle ear to the pharynx; maintains the pressure in the middle ear at atmospheric pressure.

eustele In plants, a ring of vascular tissue arranged around a central pith of nonvascular tissue; typical of progymnosperms, gymnosperms, and angiosperms.

eutherian A placental mammal and member of the subclass Eutheria.

eutrophic Waters that contain relatively high levels of nutrients such as phosphate or nitrogen and typically exhibit high levels of primary productivity and low levels of biodiversity.

eutrophication The process by which elevated nutrient levels in a body of water lead to an overgrowth of algae or aquatic plants and a subsequent depletion of water oxygen levels when these photosynthesizers decay.

evaporation The transformation of water from the liquid to the gaseous state at normal temperatures. Animals use evaporation as a means of losing excess body heat.

evapotranspiration rate The rate at which water moves into the atmosphere through the processes of evaporation from the soil and transpiration of plants.

evolution The phenomenon that populations of organisms change over the course of many generations. As a result, some organisms become more successful at survival and reproduction.

evolutionarily conserved The term used to describe homologous DNA sequences that are very similar or identical between different species.

evolutionary developmental biology (evo-devo) A field of biology that compares the development of different organisms in an attempt to understand ancestral relationships between organisms and the developmental mechanisms that bring about evolutionary change.

evolutionary lineage concept An approach used to distinguish species; states that a species is derived from a single distinct lineage and has its own evolutionary tendencies and historical fate.

excitable cell The term used to describe neurons and muscle cells because they have the capacity to generate electrical signals.

excitation-contraction coupling The sequence of events by which an action potential in the plasma membrane of a muscle fiber leads to cross-bridge activity.

excitatory postsynaptic potential (EPSP) The response from an excitatory neurotransmitter that depolarizes the postsynaptic membrane; the depolarization brings the membrane potential closer to the threshold potential that would trigger an action potential.

excretion In animals, the process of expelling waste or harmful materials from the body.

exercise Any physical activity that increases an animal's metabolic rate.

exergonic Refers to chemical reactions that release free energy and occur spontaneously.

exit site (E site) One of three sites for tRNA binding in the ribosome during translation; the other two are the peptidyl site (P site) and the aminoacyl site (A site). The uncharged tRNA exits from the E site.

exocrine gland A gland in which epithelial cells secrete chemicals into a duct, which carries those molecules directly to another structure or to the outside surface of the body.

exocytosis A process in which material inside a cell is packaged into vesicles and excreted into the extracellular medium.

exon A portion of RNA that is found in the mature mRNA molecule after splicing is finished.

exon shuffling A form of mutation in which exons and their flanking introns are inserted into genes and thereby create proteins with additional functional domains.

exonuclease An enzyme that cleaves off nucleotides, one at a time, from the end of a DNA or RNA molecule.

exoskeleton An external skeleton made of chitin and protein that surrounds and protects most of the body surface of animals such as insects.

exosome A multiprotein complex that degrades mRNA.

expansin A protein that occurs in the plant cell wall and fosters cell enlargement.

experimental group The sample in an experiment that is subjected to some type of variation that does not occur for the control group.

exploitation competition Competition in which organisms compete indirectly through the consumption of a limited resource.

exponential growth Rapid population growth that occurs when the per capita growth rate remains above zero.

extensor A muscle that straightens a limb at a joint.

external fertilization Fertilization that occurs in aquatic environments, when eggs and sperm are released into the water in close enough proximity for fertilization to occur.

external intercostal muscles Muscles of the rib cage that contract during inhalation, thereby expanding the chest.

extinction The end of the existence of a species or a group of species.

extinction vortex A downward spiral toward extinction from which a species cannot naturally recover.

extracellular fluid The fluid in an organism's body that is outside of the cells.

extracellular matrix (ECM) A network of material that is secreted from animal cells and forms a complex meshwork outside of cells. The ECM provides strength, support, and organization.

extranuclear inheritance In eukaryotes, the transmission of genes that are located outside the cell nucleus.

extremophile An organism that occurs primarily in extreme habitats.

eye The visual organ in animals that detects light and sends signals to the brain.

eyecup An eye in planaria that detects light and its direction but which does not form an image.

F

facilitated diffusion A method of passive transport that involves the aid of a transport protein.

facilitation A mechanism for succession in which a species facilitates or makes the environment more suitable for subsequent species.

facultative anaerobe A microorganism that can use oxygen in aerobic respiration, obtain energy via anaerobic fermentation, or use inorganic chemical reactions to obtain energy.

facultative mutualism An interaction between mutualistic species that is beneficial but not essential to the survival and reproduction of either species.

family In taxonomy, a subdivision of an order.

fast block to polyspermy A depolarization of the egg that blocks other sperm from binding to the egg membrane proteins.

fast fiber A skeletal muscle fiber containing myosin with a high rate of ATP hydrolysis.

fast-glycolytic fiber A skeletal muscle fiber that has high myosin ATPase activity but cannot make as much ATP as oxidative fibers because its source of ATP is glycolysis; best suited for rapid, intense actions.

fast-oxidative fiber A skeletal muscle fiber that has high myosin ATPase activity and can make large amounts of ATP; used for long-term activities.

fate The ultimate morphological features that a cell or a group of cells will adopt.

fate mapping A technique in which a small population of cells within an embryo is specifically labeled with a harmless dye, and the fate of these labeled cells is followed to a later stage of embryonic development.

feedback inhibition A form of regulation in which the product of a metabolic pathway inhibits an enzyme that acts early in the pathway, thus preventing the overaccumulation of the product.

feedforward regulation The process by which an animal's body begins preparing for a change in some variable before it even occurs.

female-enforced monogamy hypothesis The hypothesis that a male is monogamous due to various actions employed by his female mate.

female gametophyte A haploid multicellular plant generation that produces one or more eggs but does not produce sperm cells.

fermentation The breakdown of organic molecules to produce energy without any net oxidation of an organic molecule.

Ferrell cell The middle cell in the three-cell model of atmospheric circulation.

fertilization The union of two gametes, such as an egg cell with a sperm cell, to form a zygote.

fertilizer A soil addition that enhances plant growth by providing essential elements.

fetus The maturing embryo after the eighth week of gestation in humans.

fever An increase in an animal's temperature due to infection.

F factor A type of bacterial plasmid called a fertility factor that plays a role in bacterial conjugation.

F_1 generation The first filial generation in a genetic cross.

F_2 generation The second filial generation in a genetic cross.

fiber A type of tough-walled plant cell that provides support.

fibrin A protein that forms a meshwork of threadlike fibers that wrap around and between platelets and blood cells, enlarging and thickening a blood clot.

fibrous root system The root system of monocots, which consists of multiple adventitious roots that grow from the stem base.

fight-or-flight The response of vertebrates to real or perceived danger; associated with increased activity of the sympathetic branch of the autonomic nervous system.

filament 1. The elongate portion of a flower's stamen; contains vascular tissue that delivers nutrients from parental sporophytes to anthers. 2. In fishes, a part of the gills.

filtrate In the process of filtration in an excretory system, the material that passes through the filter and enters the excretory organ for either further processing or excretion.

filtration The passive removal of water and small solutes from the blood during the production of urine.

finite rate of increase In ecology, the ratio of a population size from one year to the next.

first law of thermodynamics States that energy cannot be created or destroyed; also called the law of conservation of energy.

fitness The relative likelihood that a genotype will contribute to the gene pool of the next generation as compared with other genotypes.

5′ cap The 7-methylguanosine cap structure at the 5′ end of most mature mRNAs in eukaryotes.

fixed action pattern (FAP) An animal behavior that, once initiated, will continue until completed.

fixed nitrogen Atmospheric nitrogen that has been combined with other elements into a form of nitrogen that can be used by plants. An example is ammonia, NH_3.

flagella (singular, **flagellum**) Relatively long cell appendages that facilitate cellular movement or the movement of extracellular fluids.

flagellate A protist that uses one or more flagella to move in water or cause water motions useful in feeding.

flagship species A single large or instantly recognizable species.

flame cell A cell that exists primarily to maintain osmotic balance between an organism's body and surrounding fluids; present in flatworms.

flavonoid A type of phenolic secondary metabolite that provides plants with protection from UV damage or imparts color to flowers.

flexor A muscle that bends a limb at a joint.

florigen The hypothesized flowering hormone, now identified as the FT (flowering time) protein that moves from leaves, where it is produced, into the shoot apex.

flower A reproductive shoot; a short stem that produces reproductive organs instead of leaves.

flowering plants The angiosperms, which produce ovules within the protective ovaries of flowers. The ovules develop into seeds, and the ovaries develop into fruits, which function in seed dispersal.

flow-through system The method of ventilation in fishes in which water moves unidirectionally such that the gills are constantly in contact with fresh, oxygenated water. Buccal pumping and ram ventilation are examples.

fluid-feeder An animal that licks or sucks fluid from plants or animals and does not need teeth except to puncture an animal's skin.

fluidity A property of biomembranes in which individual molecules remain in close association yet have the ability to move rotationally or laterally within the plane of the membrane. Membranes are semifluid.

fluid-mosaic model The accepted model of the plasma membrane; its basic framework is the semifluid phospholipid bilayer with a mosaic of proteins. Carbohydrates may be attached to the lipids or proteins.

fMRI See functional magnetic resonance imaging.

focal adhesion A mechanically strong cell junction that connects an animal cell to the extracellular matrix (ECM).

follicle A structure within an animal ovary where each ovum undergoes growth and development before it is released.

follicle-stimulating hormone (FSH) A gonadotropin that stimulates follicle development.

food chain A linear depiction of energy flow between organisms, with each organism feeding on and deriving energy from the preceding organism.

food-induced thermogenesis A rise in metabolic rate for a few hours after eating that produces heat.

food vacuole See phagocytic vacuole.

food web A complex model of interconnected food chains in which there are multiple links between species.

foot In mollusks, a muscular structure usually used for movement.

forebrain One of three major divisions of the vertebrate brain; the other two divisions are the midbrain and hindbrain.

fossil Recognizable preserved remains of past life on Earth.

fossil fuel A fuel formed in the Earth from protist, plant, or animal remains, such as coal, petroleum, and natural gas.

founder effect Genetic drift that occurs when a small group of individuals separates from a larger population and establishes a colony in a new location.

fovea A small area on the retina directly behind the lens, where an image is most sharply focused.

frameshift mutation A mutation that involves the addition or deletion of a number of nucleotides that are not in multiples of three.

free energy (G) In living organisms, the amount of available energy that can be used to do work.

free radical A molecule containing an atom with a single, unpaired electron in its outer shell. A free radical is unstable and interacts with other molecules by removing electrons from their atoms.

frequency In regard to sound, the number of complete wavelengths that occur in 1 second, measured in hertz (Hz).

frontal lobe One of four lobes of the cerebral cortex of the human brain; important in a variety of functions, including judgment and conscious thought.

fruit A structure that develops from flower organs, encloses seeds, and fosters seed dispersal in the environment.

fruiting bodies The visible fungal reproductive structures that are composed of densely packed hyphae that typically grow out of the substrate.

functional genomics Genomic methods aimed at studying the expression of a genome.

functional group A group of atoms with chemical features that are functionally important. Each functional group exhibits the same properties in all molecules in which it occurs.

functional magnetic resonance imaging (fMRI) A technique used to determine changes in brain activity while a person is performing specific tasks.

Fungi A eukaryotic kingdom of the domain Eukarya.

fungus-like protists Heterotrophic protists that often resemble true fungi in having threadlike, filamentous bodies and absorbing nutrients from their environment.

G

G_0 A phase in which cells exit the cell cycle and postpone making the decision to divide.

G_1 The first gap phase of the cell cycle.

G_2 The second gap phase of the cell cycle.

gallbladder In many vertebrates, a small sac underneath the liver that is a storage site for bile; allows the release of large amounts of bile to be precisely timed to the consumption of fats.

gametangia Specialized structures produced by many land plants in which developing gametes are protected by a jacket of tissue.

gamete A haploid cell that is involved with sexual reproduction, such as a sperm or egg cell.

gametic life cycle A type of life cycle where all cells except the gametes are diploid, and gametes are produced by meiosis.

gametogenesis The formation of gametes.

gametophyte In plants and many multicellular protists, the haploid stage that produces gametes by mitosis.

ganglion A group of neuronal cell bodies in the peripheral nervous system that are involved in a similar function.

ganglion cells Cells in the vertebrate eye that send their axons into the optic nerve.

gap gene A type of segmentation gene; a mutation in this type of gene may cause several adjacent segments to be missing in the larva.

gap junction A type of junction between animal cells that provides a passageway for intercellular transport.

gas exchange The process of moving oxygen and carbon dioxide in opposite directions between the environment and blood and between blood and cells.

gas vesicle A cytoplasmic structure used to adjust buoyancy in cyanobacteria and certain other bacteria that live in aquatic habitats.

gastrovascular cavity In certain invertebrates such as cnidarians, a body cavity with a single opening to the outside; it functions as both a digestive system and circulatory system.

gastrula A stage of an animal embryo that is the result of gastrulation and has three cellular layers: the ectoderm, endoderm, and mesoderm.

gastrulation In animals, a process in which an area in the blastula invaginates and folds inward, creating different embryonic cell layers called germ layers.

gated A property of many channels that allows them to open and close to control the diffusion of solutes through a membrane.

gel electrophoresis A technique used to separate macromolecules by using an electric field that causes them to pass through a gel matrix.

gene A unit of heredity that contributes to the characteristics or traits of an organism. At the molecular level, a gene is composed of organized sequences of DNA.

gene addition The insertion of a cloned gene into the genome of an organism.

gene amplification An increase in the copy number of a gene.

gene cloning The process of making multiple copies of a gene of interest.

gene expression Gene function both at the level of traits and at the molecular level.

gene family A group of homologous genes within a single species.

gene flow Occurs when individuals migrate between different populations and results in changes in the genetic composition of the resulting populations.

gene interaction A situation in which a single trait is controlled by two or more genes.

gene knockout An organism in which both copies of a functional gene have been replaced with nonfunctional copies. Experimentally, this can occur via gene replacement.

gene mutation A relatively small change in DNA structure that alters a particular gene.

gene pool All of the genes in a population.

genera (singular, **genus**) In taxonomy, a subdivision of a family.

general lineage concept A widely accepted approach used to distinguish species; states that each species is a population of an independently evolving lineage.

general transcription factors (GTFs) Five different proteins that play a role in initiating transcription at the core promoter of structural genes in eukaryotes.

generative cell In a seed plant, one of the cells resulting from the division of a microspore; a generative cell divides to produce two sperm cells.

gene regulation The ability of cells to control their level of gene expression.

gene replacement The phenomenon in which a cloned gene recombines with the normal gene on a chromosome and replaces it.

gene therapy The introduction of cloned genes into living cells in an attempt to cure disease.

genetic code A code that specifies the relationship between the sequence of nucleotides in the codons found in mRNA and the sequence of amino acids in a polypeptide.

genetic drift The random change in a population's allele frequencies from one generation to the next that is attributable to chance. It occurs more quickly in small populations.

genetic engineering The direct manipulation of genes for practical purposes.

genetic map A chart that shows the linear arrangement of genes along a chromosome.

genetic mapping The use of genetic crosses to determine the linear order of genes that are linked to each other along the same chromosome.

genetically modified organisms (GMOs) *See* transgenic.

gene transfer The process by which genetic material is transferred from one bacterial cell to another.

genome The complete genetic composition of a cell or a species.

genomic imprinting A phenomenon in which a segment of DNA is imprinted, or marked, in a way that affects gene expression throughout the life of the individual who inherits that DNA.

genomic library A type of DNA library in which the inserts are derived from chromosomal DNA.

genomics Techniques that are used in the molecular analysis of the entire genome of a species.

genotype The genetic composition of an individual.

genotype frequency In a population, the number of individuals with a given genotype divided by the total number of individuals.

geological timescale A time line of the Earth's history from its origin about 4.55 billion years ago to the present.

germination In plants, the process in which an embryo absorbs water, becomes metabolically active, and grows out of the seed coat, producing a seedling.

germ layer An embryonic cell layer such as ectoderm, mesoderm, or endoderm.

germ line Cells that give rise to gametes such as egg and sperm cells.

germ plasm Cytoplasmic determinants that help define and specify the primordial germ cells in the gastrula stage of animal development.

gestation *See* pregnancy.

giant axon A very large axon in certain species such as squids that facilitates high-speed neuronal conduction and rapid responses to stimuli.

gibberellic acid A type of gibberellin.

gibberellin A plant hormone that stimulates both cell division and cell elongation.

gills Specialized filamentous organs in aquatic animals that are used to obtain oxygen and eliminate carbon dioxide.

ginkgos A phylum of gymnosperms; Ginkgophyta.

gizzard The muscular portion of the stomach of birds and some reptiles that is capable of grinding food into smaller fragments.

glaucoma A condition in which drainage of aqueous humor in the eye becomes blocked and the pressure inside the eye increases. If untreated, this pressure damages cells in the retina and leads to irreversible loss of vision.

glia Cells that surround the neurons; a major class of cells in nervous systems that perform various functions.

global warming A gradual elevation of the Earth's surface temperature caused by an increasing greenhouse effect.

glomerular filtration rate (GFR) The rate at which a filtrate of plasma is formed in all the glomeruli of the vertebrate kidneys.

glomerulus A cluster of interconnected, fenestrated capillaries in the renal corpuscle of the kidney; the site of filtration in the kidney.

glucagon A hormone found in animals that stimulates the processes of glycogenolysis, gluconeogenesis, and the synthesis of ketones in the liver.

glucocorticoid A steroid hormone that regulates glucose balance and helps prepare the body for stress situations.

gluconeogenesis A mechanism for maintaining blood glucose level; enzymes in the liver convert noncarbohydrate precursors into glucose, which is then secreted into the blood.

glucose sparing A metabolic adjustment that reserves the glucose produced by the liver for use by the nervous system.

glycocalyx 1. An outer viscous covering surrounding a bacterium that traps water and helps protect bacteria from drying out. 2. A carbohydrate-rich zone on the surface of animal cells; also called a cell coat.

glycogen A polysaccharide found in animal cells (especially liver and skeletal muscle) and sometimes called animal starch; also, the major carbohydrate storage of fungi.

glycogenolysis A mechanism for maintaining blood glucose level; stored glycogen can be broken down into molecules of glucose which are then secreted into the blood.

glycolipid A lipid that has carbohydrate attached to it.

glycolysis A metabolic pathway that breaks down glucose to pyruvate.

glycolytic fiber A skeletal muscle fiber that has few mitochondria but possesses both a high concentration of glycolytic enzymes and large stores of glycogen.

glycoprotein A protein that has carbohydrate attached to it.

glycosaminoglycan (GAG) The most abundant type of polysaccharide in the extracellular matrix (ECM) of animals, consisting of repeating disaccharide units that give a gel-like character to the ECM of animals.

glycosidic bond A bond formed between two sugar molecules.

glycosylation The attachment of carbohydrate to a protein or lipid, producing a glycoprotein or glycolipid.

glyoxysome A specialized organelle within plant seeds that contains enzymes needed to convert fats to sugars.

gnathostomes All vertebrate species that possess jaws.

gnetophytes A phylum of gymnosperms; Gnetophyta.

Golgi apparatus A stack of flattened, membrane-bound compartments that performs three overlapping functions: secretion, processing, and protein sorting.

gonadotropins Hormones secreted by the anterior pituitary gland that are the same in both sexes; gonadotropins influence the ability of the testes and ovaries to produce the sex steroids.

gonads The testes in males and the ovaries in females, where the gametes are formed.

G protein An intracellular protein that binds guanosine triphosphate (GTP) and guanosine diphosphate (GDP) and participates in intracellular signaling pathways.

G-protein-coupled receptors (GPCRs) A common type of receptor found in the cells of eukaryotic species that interacts with G proteins to initiate a cellular response.

graded potential A depolarization or hyperpolarization in a neuron that varies with the strength of a stimulus.

gradualism A concept suggesting that species evolve continuously over long spans of time.

grain The characteristic single-seeded fruit of cereal grasses such as rice, corn, barley, and wheat.

Gram stain A staining process that can help to identify bacteria and predict their responses to antibiotics.

granum A structure composed of stacked membrane-bound thylakoids within a chloroplast.

gravitropism Plant growth in response to the force of gravity.

gray matter Brain tissue that consists of neuronal cell bodies, dendrites, and some unmyelinated axons.

greenhouse effect The process in which short-wave solar radiation passes through the atmosphere to warm the Earth but is radiated back to space as long-wave infrared radiation. Much of this radiation is reflected by atmospheric gases back to Earth's surface, causing its temperature to rise.

groove In the DNA double helix, an indentation where the atoms of the bases make contact with the surrounding water.

gross primary production (GPP) The measure of biomass production by photosynthetic organisms; equivalent to the carbon fixed during photosynthesis.

ground meristem In plants, a type of primary plant tissue meristem that gives rise to ground tissue.

ground tissue Most of the body of a plant, which has a variety of functions, including photosynthesis, storage of carbohydrates, and support. Ground tissue can be subdivided into three types: parenchyma, collenchyma, and sclerenchyma.

group selection A premise that attempts to explain altruism. States that natural selection produces outcomes beneficial for the whole group or species rather than for individuals.

growth An increase in weight or size.

growth factors Proteins in animals that stimulate certain cells to grow and divide.

growth hormone (GH) A hormone produced in vertebrates by the anterior pituitary gland; GH acts on the liver to produce insulin-like growth factor-1 (IGF-1).

guanine (G) A purine base found in DNA and RNA.

guard cell A specialized plant cell that allows epidermal pores (stomata) to close when conditions are too dry and to open under moist conditions, allowing the entry of CO_2 needed for photosynthesis.

gustation The sense of taste.

gut The gastrointestinal (GI) tract of an animal.

guttation Droplets of water at the edges of leaves that are the result of root pressure.

gymnosperm A plant that produces seeds that are exposed rather than seeds enclosed in fruits.

gynoecium The aggregate of carpels that forms the innermost whorl of a flower.

H

habituation The form of nonassociative learning in which an organism learns to ignore a repeated stimulus.

Hadley cell The most prominent of the three cells in the three-cell model of atmospheric circulation; the cell nearest to the equator.

hair cell A mechanoreceptor in animals that is a specialized epithelial cell with deformable stereocilia.

half-life 1. In the case of organic molecules in a cell, refers to the time it takes for 50% of the molecules to be broken down and recycled. 2. In the case of radioisotopes, the time it takes for 50% of the molecules to decay and emit radiation.

halophile A bacterium or archaeon that can live in an extremely salty environment.

halophyte A plant that can tolerate higher than normal salt concentrations and can occupy coastal salt marshes or saline deserts.

Hamilton's rule The proposal that an altruistic gene will be favored by natural selection when $rB > C$, where r is the coefficient of relatedness of the donor (the altruist) to the recipient, B is the benefit received by the recipient, and C is the cost incurred by the donor.

haplodiploid system A genetic system in which females develop from fertilized eggs and are diploid but males develop from unfertilized eggs and are haploid.

haploid Containing one set of chromosomes; designated as $1n$.

haploid-dominant species Species in which the haploid organism is the prevalent organism in the life cycle. Examples include fungi and some protists.

haplorrhini Larger-brained diurnal species of primates; includes monkeys, gibbons, orangutans, gorillas, chimpanzees, and humans.

Hardy-Weinberg equation An equation ($p^2 + 2pq + q^2 = 1$) that relates allele and genotype frequencies; the equation predicts an equilibrium if no new mutations are formed, no natural selection occurs, the population size is very large, the population does not migrate, and mating is random.

heart A muscular structure that pumps blood through blood vessels.

heart attack See myocardial infarction (MI).

heat of fusion The amount of heat energy that must be withdrawn or released from a substance to cause it to change from the liquid to the solid state.

heat of vaporization The heat required to vaporize 1 mole of any substance at its boiling point under standard pressure.

heavy chain A part of an immunoglobulin molecule.

H^+ electrochemical gradient A transmembrane gradient for H^+ composed of both a membrane potential and a concentration difference for H^+ across a membrane.

helper T cell A type of lymphocyte that assists in the activation and function of B cells and cytotoxic T cells.

hematocrit The volume of blood that is composed of red blood cells, usually between 40 and 65% in vertebrates.

hemidesmosome A mechanically strong cell junction that connects an animal cell to the extracellular matrix (ECM).

hemiparasite A parasitic organism that photosynthesizes, but lacks a root system to draw water and thus depends on its host for that function.

hemispheres The two halves of the cerebrum.

hemizygous The term used to describe the single copy of an X-linked gene in a male.

hemocyanin A copper-containing pigment that binds oxygen and gives blood or hemolymph a bluish tint.

hemodialysis A medical procedure used to artificially perform the kidneys' function.

hemoglobin An iron-containing protein that binds oxygen and is found within the cytosol of red blood cells.

hemolymph Blood and interstitial fluid combined in one fluid compartment; present in many invertebrates.

hemophilia An inherited disorder characterized by the deficiency of a specific blood clotting factor.

hemorrhage A loss of blood from a ruptured blood vessel.

herbaceous plant A plant that produces little or no wood and is composed mostly of primary vascular tissues.

herbivore An animal that eats only plants.

herbivory Refers to herbivores feeding on plants.

hermaphrodite In animals, an individual that can produce both sperm and eggs.

hermaphroditism A form of sexual reproduction in which individuals have both male and female reproductive systems.

heterochromatin The highly compacted regions of chromosomes that are usually transcriptionally inactive because of their tight conformation.

heterochrony Evolutionary changes in the rate or timing of developmental events.

heterocyst A specialized cell of some cyanobacteria in which nitrogen fixation occurs.

heterospory In plants, the formation of two different types of spores: microspores and megaspores; microspores produce male gametophytes, and megaspores produce female gametophytes.

heterotherm An animal that has a body temperature that is not constant; both exotherms and endotherms may be heterotherms.

heterotroph Organisms that cannot produce their own organic molecules and thus must obtain organic food from other organisms.

heterotrophic Requiring organic food from the environment.

heterozygote advantage A phenomenon in which a heterozygote has a higher Darwinian fitness than either corresponding homozygote.

heterozygous An individual with two different alleles of the same gene.

hibernation The state of torpor in an animal that can last for months.

highly repetitive sequence A DNA sequence found tens of thousands or even millions of times throughout a genome.

hindbrain One of three major divisions of the vertebrate brain; the other two divisions are the midbrain and forebrain.

hippocampus The area of the vertebrate forebrain that functions in establishing memories for spatial locations, facts, and the sequence of events.

histone acetyltransferase An enzyme that loosens the compaction of chromatin by attaching acetyl groups to histone proteins.

histone code hypothesis Refers to the pattern of histone modification recognized by particular proteins. The pattern of covalent modifications of amino terminus tails provides binding sites for proteins that subsequently affect the degree of chromatin compaction.

histones   A group of proteins involved in the formation of nucleosomes that aid in the compaction of eukaryotic DNA.

HIV   *See* human immunodeficiency virus.

holoblastic cleavage   A complete type of cell cleavage in certain animals in which the entire zygote is bisected into two equal-sized blastomeres.

holoparasite   A parasitic organism that lacks chlorophyll and is totally dependent on a host plant for its water and nutrients.

homeobox   A 180-bp sequence within the coding sequence of homeotic genes.

homeodomain   A region of a homeotic protein that functions in binding to the DNA.

homeostasis   The process whereby living organisms regulate their cells and bodies to maintain relatively stable internal conditions.

homeostatic control system   A system designed to regulate particular variables in an animal's body, such as body temperature; consists of a set point, sensor, integrator, and effectors.

homeotherm   An animal that maintains its body temperature within a narrow range.

homeotic gene   A gene that controls the developmental fate of particular segments or regions of an animal's body.

hominin   Either an extinct or modern species of humans.

hominoidea (hominoid)   A member of a group of primates that includes gibbons, orangutans, gorillas, chimpanzees, and humans.

homologous genes   Genes derived from the same ancestral gene that have accumulated random mutations that make their sequences slightly different.

homologous structures   Structures that are similar to each other because they are derived from the same ancestral structure.

homologue   A member of a pair of chromosomes in a diploid organism.

homology   A fundamental similarity that occurs due to descent from a common ancestor.

homozygous   An individual with two identical copies of an allele.

horizontal gene transfer   A process in which an organism incorporates genetic material from another organism without being the offspring of that organism.

hormone   A chemical messenger that is produced in a gland or other structure and acts on distant target cells in one or more parts of an animal or plant.

hornworts   A phylum of bryophytes; Anthocerophyta.

host   The prey organism in a parasitic association.

host cell   1. A cell that is infected by a virus, fungus, or a bacterium. 2. A eukaryotic cell that contains photosynthetic or nonphotosynthetic endosymbionts.

host plant resistance   The ability of plants to prevent herbivory.

host range   The number of species and cell types that a virus or bacterium can infect.

hot spot   A human-impacted geographic area with a large number of endemic species. To qualify as a hot spot, a region must contain at least 1,500 species of endemic vascular plants and have lost at least 70% of its original habitat.

Hox **genes**   In animals, a class of genes involved in pattern formation in early embryos.

Human Genome Project   A 13-year international effort coordinated by the U.S. Department of Energy and the National Institutes of Health that characterized and sequenced the entire human genome.

human immunodeficiency virus (HIV)   A retrovirus that is the causative agent of acquired immune deficiency syndrome (AIDS).

humoral immunity   A type of specific immunity in which plasma cells secrete antibodies that bind to antigens.

humus   A collective term for the organic constituents of soils.

hybridization   A situation in which two individuals with different characteristics are mated or crossed to each other; the offspring are referred to as hybrids.

hybrid zone   An area where two populations can interbreed.

hydrocarbon   Molecules with predominantly hydrogen–carbon bonds.

hydrogen bond   A weak chemical attraction between a partially positive hydrogen atom of a polar molecule and a partially negative atom of another polar molecule.

hydrolysis reaction   A chemical reaction that utilizes water to break apart molecules.

hydrophilic   Refers to ions and molecules that contain polar covalent bonds and will dissolve in water.

hydrophobic   Refers to molecules that do not have partial charges and therefore are not attracted to water molecules. Such molecules are composed predominantly of carbon and hydrogen and are relatively insoluble in water.

hydrostatic skeleton   A fluid-filled body cavity in certain soft-bodied invertebrates that is surrounded by muscles and provides support and shape.

hydroxide ion   An anion with the formula, OH^-.

hypermutation   A process that primarily involves numerous C to T point mutations that are crucial to enabling lymphocytes to produce a diverse array of immunoglobulins capable of recognizing many different antigens.

hyperpolarization   The change in the membrane potential that occurs when the cell becomes more polarized.

hypersensitive response (HR)   A plant's local defensive response to pathogen attack.

hyperthermophile   An organism that thrives in extremely hot temperatures.

hyperthyroidism   A medical condition resulting from a hyperactive thyroid gland.

hypertonic   Any solution that causes a cell to shrink due to osmosis of water out of the cell.

hypha   A microscopic, branched filament of the body of a fungus.

hypocotyl   The portion of an embryonic plant stem located below the point of attachment of the cotyledons.

hypothalamus   A part of the vertebrate brain located below the thalamus; it controls functions of the gastrointestinal and reproductive systems, among others, and regulates many basic behaviors such as eating and drinking.

hypothesis   In biology, a proposed explanation for a natural phenomenon based on previous observations or experimental studies.

hypothesis testing   Also known as the scientific method, a strategy for testing the validity of a hypothesis.

hypothyroidism   A medical condition resulting from an underactive thyroid gland.

hypotonic   Any solution that causes a cell to swell when placed in that solution.

H zone   In a myofibril, a narrow, light region in the center of the A band that corresponds to the space between the two sets of thin filaments in each sarcomere.

I

I band   In a myofibril, a light band that lies between the A bands of two adjacent sarcomeres.

immune system   The cells and organs within an animal's body that contribute to immune defenses.

immune tolerance   The process by which the body distinguishes between self and nonself components.

immunity   The ability of an animal to ward off internal threats, including harmful microorganisms, foreign molecules, and abnormal cells such as cancer cells.

immunoglobulin   A Y-shaped protein with two heavy chains and two light chains that provides immunity to foreign substances; antibodies are a type of immunoglobulin.

immunological memory   The immune system's ability to produce a secondary immune response.

imperfect flower   A flower that lacks either stamens or carpels.

implantation   The first event of pregnancy, when the blastocyst embeds within the uterine endometrium.

imprinting   1. The development of a species-specific pattern of behavior that occurs during a critical period; a form of learning, with a large innate component. 2. In genetics, the marking of DNA that occurs differently between males and females.

inactivation gate   A string of amino acids that juts out from a channel protein into the cytosol and blocks the movement of ions through the channel.

inborn error of metabolism   A genetic defect in the ability to metabolize certain compounds.

inbreeding   Mating among genetically related relatives.

inbreeding depression   The phenomenon whereby inbreeding produces homozygotes that are less fit, thereby decreasing the reproductive success of a population.

inclusive fitness   The term used to designate the total number of copies of genes passed on through one's relatives, as well as one's own reproductive output.

incomplete dominance   The phenomenon in which a heterozygote that carries two different alleles exhibits a phenotype that is intermediate between the corresponding homozygous individuals.

incomplete flower   A flower that lacks one or more of the four flower organ types.

incomplete metamorphosis   During development in some insects, a gradual change in body form from a nymph into an adult.

incurrent siphon   A structure in a tunicate used to draw water through the mouth.

indeterminate cleavage   In animals, a characteristic of deuterostome development in which each cell produced by early cleavage retains the ability to develop into a complete embryo.

indeterminate growth   Growth in which plant shoot apical meristems continuously produce new stem tissues and leaves, as long as conditions remain favorable.

indicator species   A species whose status provides information on the overall health of an ecosystem.

indirect calorimetry   A method of determining basal metabolic rate in which the rate at which an animal uses oxygen is measured.

individualistic model   A view of the nature of a community that considers it to be an assemblage of species coexisting primarily because of similarities in their physiological requirements and tolerances.

individual selection   The proposal that adaptive traits generally are selected for because they benefit the survival and reproduction of the individual rather than the group.

induced fit   Occurs when a substrate(s) binds to an enzyme and the enzyme undergoes a conformational change that causes the substrate(s) to bind more tightly to the enzyme.

induced mutation   A mutation brought about by environmental agents that enter the cell and then alter the structure of DNA.

inducer   In transcription, a small effector molecule that increases the rate of transcription.

inducible operon   In this type of operon, the presence of a small effector molecule causes transcription to occur.

induction   1. In development, the process by which a cell or group of cells governs the developmental fate of neighboring cells. 2. In molecular genetics, refers to the process by which transcription has been turned on by the presence of a small effector molecule.

industrial nitrogen fixation   The human activity of producing nitrogen fertilizers.

infertility   The inability to produce viable offspring.

inflammation   An innate local response to infection or injury characterized by local redness, swelling, heat, and pain.

inflorescence   A cluster of flowers on a plant.

infundibular stalk   The structure that physically connects the hypothalamus to the pituitary gland.

ingestion   In animals, the act of taking food into the body.

ingroup   In a cladogram, a group of interest.

inheritance   The acquisition of traits by their transmission from parent to offspring.

inheritance of acquired characteristics   Jean-Baptiste Lamarck's incorrect hypothesis that species change over the course of many generations by adapting to new environments.

inhibition   A mechanism for succession in which early colonists exclude subsequent colonists.

inhibitory postsynaptic potential (IPSP)   The response from an inhibitory neurotransmitter that hyperpolarizes the postsynaptic membrane; this hyperpolarization reduces the likelihood of an action potential.

initiation factor   A protein that facilitates the interactions between mRNA, the first tRNA, and the ribosomal subunits during the initiation stage of translation.

initiation stage   The first step in the process of transcription or translation.

initiator tRNA   A specific tRNA that recognizes the start codon AUG in mRNA and binds to it, initiating translation.

innate   The term used to describe behaviors that seem to be genetically programmed.

inner bark   The thin layer of secondary phloem that carries out most of the sugar transport in a woody stem.

inner ear   One of the three main compartments of the mammalian ear. The inner ear is composed of the bony cochlea and the vestibular system, which plays a role in balance.

inner segment   The part of the vertebrate photoreceptors (rods and cones) that contains the cell nucleus and cytoplasmic organelles.

inorganic chemistry   The study of the nature of atoms and molecules, with the exception of those that contain rings or chains of carbon.

insulin   A hormone found in animals that regulates metabolism in several ways, primarily by regulating the blood glucose concentration.

insulin-like growth factor-1 (IGF-1)   A hormone in mammals that stimulates the elongation of bones, especially during puberty.

integral membrane protein   A protein that cannot be released from the membrane unless it is dissolved with an organic solvent or detergent. Includes transmembrane proteins and lipid-anchored proteins.

integrase   An enzyme, sometimes encoded by viruses, that catalyzes the integration of the viral genome into a host-cell chromosome.

integrin   A cell adhesion molecule found in animal cells that connects cells to the extracellular matrix.

integument   In plants, a structure that encloses the megasporangium to form an ovule.

interference competition   Competition in which organisms interact directly with one another by physical force or intimidation.

interferon   A protein that generally inhibits viral replication inside host cells.

intermediate-disturbance hypothesis   The proposal that moderately disturbed communities are more diverse than undisturbed or highly disturbed communities.

intermediate filament   A type of protein filament of the cytoskeleton that helps maintain cell shape and rigidity.

internal fertilization   Fertilization that occurs in terrestrial animals in which sperm are deposited within the reproductive tract of the female during copulation.

interneuron   A type of neuron that forms interconnections between other neurons.

internode   The region of a plant stem between adjacent nodes.

interphase   The G_1, S, and G_2 phases of the cell cycle. It is the portion of the cell cycle during which the chromosomes are decondensed and found in the nucleus.

intersexual selection   Sexual selection between members of the opposite sex.

interspecies hybrid   The offspring resulting from the mating of two different species.

interspecific competition   Competition between individuals of different species.

interstitial fluid   The fluid that surrounds cells.

intertidal zone   The area where the land meets the sea, which is alternately submerged and exposed by the daily cycle of tides.

intracellular fluid   The fluid inside cells.

intranuclear spindle   A spindle that forms within an intact nuclear envelope during nuclear division in fungi and some protists.

intrasexual selection   Sexual selection between members of the same sex.

intraspecific competition   Competition between individuals of the same species.

intrauterine device (IUD)   A small object that is placed in the uterus and interferes with the endometrial preparation required for acceptance of the blastocyst; used as a form of contraception.

intrinsic rate of increase   The situation in which conditions are optimal for a population and the per capita growth rate is at its maximum rate.

introduced species   A species moved by humans from a native location to another location.

intron   Intervening DNA sequences that are found in between the coding sequences of genes.

invagination   The act of pinching inward, as during early embryonic development in animals.

invasive cell   A cancer cell that can invade healthy tissues.

invasive species   Introduced species that spread on their own, often outcompeting native species for space and resources.

inverse density-dependent factor   A mortality factor whose influence decreases as population size or density increases.

inversion   A type of mutation that involves a change in the direction of the genetic material along a single chromosome.

invertebrate   An animal that lacks vertebrae.

in vitro   Meaning, "in glass." An alternative to studying a process in living cells that involves isolating and purifying cellular components and studying their functions outside the cell.

in vivo   Meaning, "in life." Studying a process in living cells or organisms.

involution   During embryogenesis, the folding back of sheets of surface cells into the interior of an embryo.

iodine-deficient goiter   An overgrown thyroid gland that is incapable of making thyroid hormone due to a lack of dietary iodine.

ion   An atom or molecule that gains or loses one or more electrons and acquires a net electric charge.

ion electrochemical gradient   A dual gradient for an ion that is composed of both an electrical gradient and a chemical gradient for that ion.

ionic bond   The bond that occurs when a cation binds to an anion.

ionotropic receptor   One of two types of postsynaptic receptors, the other being a metabotropic receptor. Consists of a ligand-gated ion channel that opens in response to binding of a neurotransmitter.

iris   The circle of pigmented smooth muscle and connective tissue that is responsible for eye color.

iron regulatory element (IRE)   A response element within the ferritin mRNA to which the iron regulatory protein binds.

iron regulatory protein (IRP)   An RNA-binding protein that regulates the translation of the mRNA that encodes ferritin.

islets of Langerhans   Spherical clusters of endocrine cells that are scattered throughout the pancreas; the cells secrete insulin or glucagon, among other hormones.

isomers   Two structures with an identical molecular formula but different structures and characteristics.

isotonic   Condition in which the solute concentrations on both sides of a plasma membrane are equal, which does not cause a cell to shrink or swell.

isotope   An element that exists in multiple forms that differ in the number of neutrons they contain.

iteroparity   The pattern of repeated reproduction at intervals throughout an organism's life cycle.

J

joint   The juncture where two or more bones of a vertebrate endoskeleton come together.

juvenile hormone   A hormone made in arthropods that inhibits maturation from a larva into a pupa.

K

karyogamy   The process of nuclear fusion.

karyotype   A photographic representation of the chromosomes in an actively dividing cell.

K_d   The dissociation constant between a ligand and its receptor.

ketones Small compounds generated from fatty acids. Ketones are made in the liver and released into the blood to provide an important energy source during prolonged fasting for many tissues, including the brain.

keystone species A species within a community that has a role out of proportion to its abundance.

kidney The major excretory organ found in all vertebrates.

kilocalorie (kcal) One thousand calories; the amount of heat energy required to raise the temperature of 1 kg of water by 1 degree Celsius.

kinesis A movement in response to a stimulus, but one that is not directed toward or away from the source of the stimulus.

kinetic energy Energy associated with movement.

kinetic skull A characteristic of lizards and snakes in which the joints between various parts of the skull are extremely mobile.

kinetochore A group of proteins that bind to a centromere and are necessary for sorting each chromosome.

kingdom A taxonomic group; the second largest division after domain.

kin selection Selection for behavior that lowers an individual's own fitness but enhances the reproductive success of a relative.

K_M The substrate concentration at which an enzyme-catalyzed reaction is half of its maximal value.

knowledge The awareness and understanding of information.

Koch's postulates A series of steps used to determine whether a particular organism causes a specific disease.

K-selected species A type of life history strategy where species have a low rate of per capita population growth but good competitive ability.

K/T event An ancient cataclysm that involved at least one large meteorite or comet that crashed into the Earth near the present-day Yucatán Peninsula in Mexico about 65 million years ago.

L

labia majora In the female genitalia, large outer folds that surround the external opening of the reproductive tract.

labia minora In the female genitalia, smaller, inner folds near the external opening of the reproductive tract.

labor The strong rhythmic contractions of the uterus that serve to deliver a fetus during childbirth.

lac operon An operon in the genome of *E. coli* that contains the genes for the enzymes that allow it to metabolize lactose.

lac repressor A repressor protein that regulates the *lac* operon.

lactation In mammals, a period after birth in which the young are nurtured by milk produced by the mother.

lacteal A lymphatic vessel in the center of each intestinal villus; lipids are absorbed by the lacteals, which eventually empty into the circulatory system.

lagging strand During DNA replication, a DNA strand made as a series of small Okazaki fragments that are eventually connected to each other to form a continuous strand.

lamellae Platelike structures in the internal gills of fishes that branch from structures called filaments; gas exchange occurs here.

larva A free-living organism that is morphologically very different from the embryo and adult.

larynx The segment of the respiratory tract that contains the vocal cords.

latent The term used to describe a prophage or provirus that remains inactive for a long time.

lateral line system Microscopic sensory organs in fishes and some toads that allows them to detect movement in surrounding water.

lateral meristem *See* secondary meristem.

law of independent assortment States that the alleles of different genes assort independently of each other during gamete formation.

law of segregation States that two copies of a gene segregate from each other during gamete formation and during transmission from parent to offspring.

leaching The dissolution and removal of inorganic ions as water percolates through materials such as soil.

leading strand During DNA replication, a DNA strand made in the same direction that the replication fork is moving. The strand is synthesized as one long continuous molecule.

leaf abscission The process by which a leaf drops after the formation of an abscission zone.

leaflet 1. Half of a phospholipid bilayer. 2. A portion of a compound leaf.

leaf primordia Small outgrowths that occur at the sides of a shoot apical meristem and develop into young leaves.

leaf vein In plants, a bundle of vascular tissue in a leaf.

learning The ability of an animal to make modifications to a behavior based on previous experience; the process by which new information is acquired.

leaves Flattened plant organs that emerge from stems and function in photosynthesis.

leghemoglobin A protein found in legume plants that helps to regulate local oxygen concentrations around rhizobial bacteroids in root nodules.

legume A member of the pea (bean) family; also their distinctive fruits.

lek A designated communal courting area.

lens 1. A structure of the eye that focuses light. 2. The glass components of a light microscope or the electromagnetic parts of an electron microscope that allow the production of magnified images of microscopic structures.

lentic Refers to a freshwater habitat characterized by standing water.

leptin A hormone produced by adipose cells in proportion to fat mass; controls appetite and metabolic rate.

leukocyte A cell that develops from the marrow of certain bones of vertebrates; all leukocytes (also known as white blood cells) perform vital functions that defend the body against infection and disease.

lichens The mutualistic association between particular fungi and certain photosynthetic green algae or cyanobacteria. This association results in a body form distinctive from that of either partner alone.

Liebig's law of the minimum States that species' biomass or abundance is limited by the scarcest factor.

life cycle The sequence of events that characterize the steps of development of the individuals of a given species.

life table A table that provides data on the number of living individuals in a population in particular age classes.

ligand An ion or molecule that binds to a protein, such as an enzyme or a receptor.

ligand-gated ion channel A type of cell surface receptor that binds a ligand and functions as an ion channel. Ligand binding either opens or closes a channel.

ligand•receptor complex The structure formed when a ligand and its receptor noncovalently bind.

light chain 1. A part of an immunoglobulin molecule. 2. Two of the polypeptides that comprise each myosin molecule.

light-harvesting complex A component of photosystem II and photosystem I composed of several dozen pigment molecules that are anchored to proteins in the thylakoid membranes of a chloroplast. The role of these complexes is to absorb photons of light.

light microscope A microscope that utilizes light for illumination.

light reactions The first of two stages in the process of photosynthesis. During the light reactions, photosystem II and photosystem I absorb light energy and produce ATP, NADPH, and O_2.

lignin A tough polymer that adds strength and decay resistance to cell walls of tracheids, vessel elements, and other cells of plants.

lignophytes Modern and fossil seed plants and seedless ancestors that produced wood.

limbic system In the vertebrate forebrain, the areas involved in the formation and expression of emotions; also plays a role in learning, memory, and the perception of smells.

limiting factor A factor whose amount or concentration limits the rate of a biological process or a chemical reaction.

lineage A progression of changes in a series of ancestors.

line transect A sampling technique used by plant ecologists in which the number of plants located along a length of string are counted.

linkage The phenomenon that two genes close together on the same chromosome are transmitted as a unit.

linkage group A group of genes that usually stay together during meiosis.

lipase The major fat-digesting enzyme from the pancreas.

lipid A molecule composed predominantly of hydrogen and carbon atoms. Lipids are nonpolar and therefore very insoluble in water. They include fats (triglycerides), phospholipids, and steroids.

lipid-anchored protein A type of integral membrane protein that is attached to the membrane via a lipid molecule.

lipid-exchange protein A protein that extracts a lipid from one membrane, diffuses through the cell, and inserts the lipid into another membrane.

lipid raft In a membrane, a group of lipids and proteins that float together as a unit in a larger sea of lipids.

lipopolysaccharides Lipids with covalently bound carbohydrates; prevalent in the thin, outer envelope that encloses the cell walls of Gram-negative bacteria.

liposome A vesicle surrounded by a lipid bilayer.

liver An organ in vertebrates that performs diverse metabolic functions and is the site of bile production.

liverworts A phylum of bryophytes; formally called Hepatophyta.

lobe fins The Actinistia (coelacanths), Dipnoi (lungfishes), and tetrapods; also called Sarcopterygii.

lobe-finned fishes Fishes in which the fins are part of the body; the fins are supported by skeletal extensions of the pectoral and pelvic areas.

locomotion   The movement of an animal from place to place.

locus   The physical location of a gene on a chromosome.

logistic growth   The pattern in which the growth of a population typically slows down as it approaches the carrying capacity.

long-day plant   A plant that flowers in spring or early summer, when the night period is shorter (and thus the day length is longer) than a defined period.

long-term potentiation (LTP)   The long-lasting strengthening of the connection between neurons that is believed to be part of the mechanism of learning and memory.

loop domain   In bacteria, a chromosomal segment that is folded into loops by the attachment to proteins; a method of compacting bacterial chromosomes.

loop of Henle   A segment of the tubule of the nephron of the kidney containing a sharp hairpin-like loop that contributes to reabsorption of ions and water. It consists of a descending limb coming from the proximal tubule and an ascending limb leading to the distal tubule.

lophophore   A horseshoe-shaped crown of tentacles used for feeding in several invertebrate species.

Lophotrochozoa   A clade of animals that encompasses the mollusks, annelids, and several other phyla; they are distinguished by two morphological features—the lophophore, a crown of tentacles used for feeding, and the trochophore larva, a distinct larval stage.

lotic   Refers to a freshwater habitat characterized by running water.

lumen   The internal space of an organelle.

lungfishes   The Dipnoi; fish with primitive lungs that live in oxygen-poor freshwater swamps and ponds.

lungs   In terrestrial vertebrates, internal paired structures used to bring oxygen into the circulatory system and remove carbon dioxide.

luteinizing hormone (LH)   A gonadotropin that controls the production of sex steroids in both males and females.

lycophyll   A relatively small leaf having a single unbranched vein; produced by lycophytes.

lycophytes   Members of a phylum of vascular land plants whose leaves are lycophylls; Lycopodiophyta.

lymphatic system   A system of vessels along with a group of organs and tissues where most leukocytes reside. The lymphatic vessels collect excess interstitial fluid and return it to the blood.

lymphocytes   A type of leukocyte that is responsible for specific immunity; the two types are B cells and T cells.

lysogenic cycle   The growth cycle of a bacteriophage consisting of integration, prophage replication, and excision.

lysosome   A small organelle found in animal cells that contains acid hydrolases that degrade macromolecules.

lytic cycle   The growth cycle of a bacteriophage in which the production and release of new viruses lyses the host cell.

M

macroalgae   Photosynthetic protists that can be seen with the unaided eye; also known as seaweeds.

macroevolution   Evolutionary changes that create new species and groups of species.

macromolecule   Many molecules bonded together to form a polymer. Carbohydrates, proteins, and nucleic acids (for example, DNA and RNA) are important macromolecules found in living organisms.

macronutrient   An element required by plants in amounts of at least 1 g/kg of plant dry matter.

macroparasite   A parasite that lives in a host but releases infective juvenile stages outside the host's body.

macrophage   A type of phagocyte capable of engulfing viruses and bacteria.

macular degeneration   An eye condition in which photoreceptor cells in and around the fovea of the retina are lost; one of the leading causes of blindness in the U.S.

madreporite   A sievelike plate on the surface of an echinoderm where water enters the water vascular system.

magnetic resonance imaging (MRI)   An imaging method that relies on the use of magnetic fields and radio waves to visualize the internal structure of an organism's body.

magnification   The ratio between the size of an image produced by a microscope and a sample's actual size.

major depressive disorder   A neurological disorder characterized by feelings of despair and sadness, resulting from an imbalance in neurotransmitter levels in the brain.

major groove   A groove that spirals around the DNA double helix; provides a location where a protein can bind to a particular sequence of bases and affect the expression of a gene.

major histocompatibility complex (MHC)   A gene family that encodes the plasma membrane self proteins that must be complexed with an antigen for T-cell recognition to occur.

male-assistance hypothesis   A hypothesis to explain the existence of monogamy that maintains that males remain with females to help them rear their offspring.

male gametophyte   A haploid multicellular plant life cycle stage that produces sperm.

malignant tumor   A growth of cells that has progressed to the cancerous stage.

Malpighian tubules   Delicate projections from the digestive tract of insects and some other taxa that function as an excretory organ.

mammal   A vertebrate that is a member of the class Mammalia that nourishes its young with milk secreted by mammary glands. Another distinguishing feature is hair.

mammary gland   A gland in female mammals that secretes milk.

manganese cluster   A site where the oxidation of water occurs in photosystem II during photosynthesis.

mantle   In mollusks, a fold of skin draped over the visceral mass that secretes a shell in those species that form shells.

mantle cavity   The chamber in a mollusk mantle that houses delicate gills.

many-eyes hypothesis   The idea that increased group size decreases predators' success because of increased detection of predators.

map distance   The distance between genes along chromosomes, which is calculated as the number of recombinant offspring divided by the total number of offspring times 100.

mapping   The process of determining the relative locations of genes or other DNA segments along a chromosome.

map unit (mu)   A unit of distance on a chromosome equivalent to a 1% recombination frequency.

mark-recapture technique   The capture and tagging of animals so they can be released and recaptured, allowing an estimate of population size.

marsupial   A member of a group of seven mammalian orders and about 280 species found in the subclass Metatheria.

mass extinction   When many species become extinct at the same time.

mass-specific BMR   The amount of energy expended per gram of body mass.

mastax   The circular muscular pharynx in the mouth of rotifers.

mast cell   A type of cell derived from bone marrow stem cells that plays an important role in nonspecific immunity.

masting   The synchronous production of many progeny by all individuals in a population; serves to satiate predators and thereby allow some progeny to survive.

mate-guarding hypothesis   The hypothesis that a male is monogamous to prevent his mate from being fertilized by other males.

maternal effect   An inheritance pattern in which the genotype of the mother determines the phenotype of her offspring.

maternal effect gene   A gene that follows a maternal effect inheritance pattern.

maternal inheritance   A phenomenon in which offspring inherit particular genes only from the female parent (through the egg).

matrotrophy   In plants, the phenomenon in which zygotes remain enclosed within gametophyte tissues, where they are sheltered and fed.

matter   Anything that has mass and takes up space.

maturation promoting factor (MPF)   A factor, now known to be a complex of cyclin and cyclin-dependent kinase, important in the division of all types of eukaryotic cells.

mature mRNA   In eukaryotes, transcription produces a long RNA, pre-mRNA, which undergoes certain processing events before it exits the nucleus; mature mRNA is the final functional product.

maximum likelihood   One method used to evaluate a phylogenetic tree based on an evolutionary model.

mean fitness of the population   The average reproductive success of members of a population.

mechanoreceptor   A sensory receptor in animals that transduces mechanical energy such as pressure, touch, stretch, movement, and sound.

mediator   A large protein complex that plays a role in initiating transcription at the core promoter of structural genes in eukaryotes.

medulla oblongata   The part of the vertebrate hindbrain that coordinates many basic reflexes and bodily functions, such as breathing.

medusa   A type of cnidarian body form that is motile and usually floats mouth down.

megadiversity country   Those countries with the greatest numbers of species; used in targeting areas for conservation.

megaspore   In seed plants and some seedless plants, a large spore that produces a female gametophyte within the spore wall.

meiosis   The process by which haploid cells are produced from a cell that was originally diploid.

meiosis I   The first division of meiosis in which the homologues are separated into different cells.

meiosis II   The second division of meiosis in which sister chromatids are separated into different cells.

Meissner's corpuscles   Structures that sense touch and light pressure and lie just beneath the skin surface of an animal.

melatonin   A hormone produced by the pineal gland of vertebrates; plays a role in light-dependent behaviors such as seasonal reproduction and daily rhythms.

membrane attack complex (MAC) A multiunit protein formed by the activation of complement proteins; the complex creates water channels in the microbial plasma membrane and causes the microbe to swell and burst.

membrane potential The difference between the electric charges outside and inside a cell; also called a potential difference (or voltage).

membrane transport The movement of ions or molecules across a cell membrane.

memory The retention of information over time.

memory cells A cloned lymphocyte that remains poised to recognize a returning antigen; a component of specific immunity.

Mendelian inheritance The inheritance patterns of genes that segregate and assort independently.

meninges Three layers of sheathlike membranes that cover and protect the brain and spinal cord.

meningitis A potentially life-threatening infectious disease in which the meninges become inflamed.

menopause The event during which a woman permanently stops having ovarian cycles.

menstrual cycle The cyclical changes that occur in the uterus in parallel with the ovarian cycle in a female mammal. Also called the uterine cycle.

menstruation A period of bleeding at the beginning of the menstrual cycle in a female mammal.

meristem In plants, an organized tissue that includes actively dividing cells and a reservoir of stem cells.

meroblastic cleavage An incomplete type of cell cleavage in which only the region of the egg containing cytoplasm at the animal pole undergoes cell division. Occurs in birds and some fishes.

merozygote A strain of bacteria containing an F′ factor.

mesoderm In animals, a layer of cells formed during gastrulation that develops between the ectoderm and endoderm; gives rise to the skeleton, muscles, and much of the circulatory system.

mesoglea A gelatinous substance between the epidermis and the gastrodermis in the Radiata.

mesohyl A gelatinous, protein-rich matrix in between the choanocytes and the epithelial cells of a sponge.

mesophyll The internal tissue of a plant leaf; the site of photosynthesis.

messenger RNA (mRNA) RNA that contains the information to specify a polypeptide with a particular amino acid sequence.

metabolic cycle A biochemical cycle in which particular molecules enter while others leave; the process is cyclical because it involves a series of organic molecules that are regenerated with each turn of the cycle.

metabolic pathway In living cells, a series of chemical reactions in which each step is catalyzed by a specific enzyme.

metabolic rate The total energy expenditure of an organism per unit of time.

metabolism The sum total of all chemical reactions that occur within an organism. Also, a specific set of chemical reactions occurring at the cellular level.

metabotropic receptor A G-protein-coupled receptor that initiates a signaling pathway in response to a neurotransmitter. One of two types of postsynaptic receptors, the other being an ionotropic receptor.

metacentric A chromosome in which the centromere is near the middle.

metagenomics A field of study that seeks to identify and analyze the collective microbial genomes contained in a community of organisms, including those not easily cultured in the laboratory.

metamorphosis The process in which a pupal or juvenile organism changes into a mature adult with very different characteristics.

metanephridia Excretory organs found in a variety of invertebrates.

metanephridial system The filtration system used by annelids to filter out wastes and excess water.

metaphase The phase of mitosis during which the chromosomes are aligned along the metaphase plate.

metaphase plate A plane halfway between the poles of the spindle apparatus on which the sister chromatids align during the metaphase stage of mitosis.

metastasis The process by which cancer cells spread from their original location to distant parts of the body.

Metazoa The collective term for animals.

methanogens Several groups of anaerobic archaea that convert CO_2, methyl groups, or acetate to methane, and release it from their cells.

methanotroph An aerobic bacterium that consumes methane.

methyl-CpG-binding protein A protein that binds methylated sequences and inhibits transcription.

micelle The sphere formed by long amphipathic molecules when they are mixed with water. In animals, micelles aid in the absorption of poorly soluble products during digestion.

microbiome All of the microorganisms in a particular environment.

microclimate Local variations of the climate within a given area.

microevolution Changes in a population's gene pool from generation to generation.

microfilament *See* actin filament.

micrograph An image taken with the aid of a microscope.

micronutrient An element required by plants in amounts at, or less than, 0.1 g/kg of plant dry matter; also known as a trace element.

microparasite A parasite that multiplies within its host, usually within the cells.

micropyle A small opening in the integument of a seed plant ovule through which a pollen tube grows.

microRNAs (miRNAs) Small RNA molecules, typically 22 nucleotides in length, that silence the expression of specific mRNAs by inhibiting translation.

microscope A magnification tool that enables researchers to study very small structures such as cells.

microspore In seed plants and some seedless plants, a relatively small spore that produces a male gametophyte within the spore wall.

microtubule A type of hollow protein filament composed of tubulin proteins that is part of the cytoskeleton and is important for cell shape, organization, and movement.

microtubule-organizing center *See* centrosome.

microvilli Small projections in the surface membranes of epithelial cells in the small intestine and many other absorptive cells.

midbrain One of three major divisions of the vertebrate brain; the other two divisions are the hindbrain and the forebrain.

middle ear One of the three main compartments of the mammalian ear; contains three small bones

called ossicles that connect the eardrum with the oval window.

middle lamella An extracellular layer in plants composed primarily of carbohydrate; cements adjacent plant cell walls together.

migration Long-range seasonal movement among animals in order to feed or breed.

mimicry The resemblance of an organism (the mimic) to another organism (the model).

mineral An inorganic ion or inorganic molecule required by a living organism.

mineralization The general process by which phosphorus, nitrogen, CO_2, and other minerals are released from organic compounds.

mineralocorticoid A steroid hormone such as aldosterone that regulates the balance of sodium and potassium ions in the body.

minor groove A smaller groove that spirals around the DNA double helix.

miRNA *See* microRNAs.

missense mutation A base substitution that changes a single amino acid in a polypeptide sequence.

mitochondrial genome The chromosome found in mitochondria.

mitochondrial matrix A compartment inside the inner membrane of a mitochondrion.

mitochondrion A semiautonomous organelle found in eukaryotic cells that supplies most of a cell's ATP.

mitogen-activated protein kinase (MAP kinase) A type of protein kinase that is involved with promoting cell division.

mitosis In eukaryotes, the process in which nuclear division results in two nuclei, each of which receives the same complement of chromosomes.

mitotic cell division A process whereby a eukaryotic cell divides to produce two new cells that are genetically identical to the original cell.

mitotic spindle The structure responsible for organizing and sorting the chromosomes during mitosis; also called the mitotic spindle apparatus.

mixotroph An organism that is able to use autotrophy as well as phagotrophy or osmotrophy to obtain organic nutrients.

M line In a myofibril, a narrow, dark band in the center of the H zone where proteins link the central regions of adjacent thick filaments.

model organism An organism studied by many different researchers so they can compare their results and determine scientific principles that apply more broadly to other species.

moderately repetitive sequence A DNA sequence found a few hundred to several thousand times in a genome.

molar A term used to describe a solution's molarity; a 1 molar solution contains 1 mole of a solute in 1 L of water.

molarity The number of moles of a solute dissolved in 1 L of water.

mole The amount of any substance that contains the same number of particles as there are atoms in exactly 12 g of carbon.

molecular biology A field of study spawned largely by genetic technology that looks at the structure and function of the molecules of life.

molecular clock A method for estimating evolutionary time; based on the observation that neutral mutations occur at a relatively constant rate.

molecular evolution The molecular changes in genetic material that underlie the phenotypic changes associated with evolution.

molecular formula A representation of a molecule that consists of the chemical symbols for all of the atoms present and subscripts that indicate how many of those atoms are present.

molecular homologies Similarities at the molecular level that indicate that living species evolved from a common ancestor or interrelated group of common ancestors.

molecular mass The sum of the atomic masses of all the atoms in a molecule.

molecular pharming An avenue of research that involves the production of medically important proteins in agricultural crops or animals.

molecular systematics A field of study that involves the analysis of genetic data, such as DNA sequences, to identify and study genetic homology and construct phylogenetic trees.

molecule Two or more atoms that are connected by chemical bonds.

monoclonal antibodies Antibodies of a specific type that are derived from a single clone of cells.

monocots One of the two largest lineages of flowering plants in which the embryo produces a single seed leaf.

monocular vision A type of vision in animals that have eyes on the sides of the head; the animal sees a wide area at one time, though depth perception is reduced.

monocyte A type of phagocyte that circulates in the blood for only a few days, after which it takes up permanent residence in various organs as a macrophage.

monoecious The term to describe plants that produce carpellate and staminate flowers on the same plant.

monogamy A mating system in which one male mates with one female, and most individuals have mates.

monohybrid The F_1 offspring, also called single-trait hybrids, of true-breeding parents that differ with regard to a single trait.

monohybrid cross A cross in which the inheritance of only one trait is followed.

monomer An organic molecule that can be used to form larger molecules (polymers) consisting of many repeating units of the monomer.

monomorphic gene A gene that exists predominantly as a single allele in a population.

monophagous The term used to describe parasites that feed on one or a few closely related species.

monophyletic group A group of species, a taxon, consisting of the most recent common ancestor and all of its descendants.

monosaccharide A simple sugar.

monosomic An aneuploid organism that has one too few chromosomes.

monotreme A member of the mammalian order Monotremata, which consists of three species found in Australia and New Guinea: the duck-billed platypus and two species of echidna.

morphogen A molecule that imparts positional information and promotes developmental changes at the cellular level.

morphogenesis The process that creates morphology.

morphology The structure or form of a body part or an entire organism.

morula An early stage in a mammalian embryo in which physical contact between cells is maximized by compaction.

mosaic An individual with somatic cells that are genetically different from each other.

mosses A phylum of bryophytes; Bryophyta.

motor end plate The region of a skeletal muscle cell that lies beneath an axon terminal at the neuromuscular junction.

motor neuron A neuron that sends signals away from the central nervous system and elicits some type of response.

motor protein A category of cellular proteins that uses ATP as a source of energy to promote movement; consists of three domains called the head, hinge, and tail.

movement corridor Thin strips of habitat that may permit the movement of individuals between larger habitat patches.

M phase The sequential events of mitosis and cytokinesis.

mRNA *See* messenger RNA.

Müllerian mimicry A type of mimicry in which many noxious species converge to look the same, thus reinforcing the basic distasteful design.

multicellular Describes an organism consisting of more than one cell, particularly when cell-to-cell adherence and signaling processes and cellular specialization can be demonstrated.

multimeric protein A protein with more than one polypeptide chain; also said to have a quarternary structure.

multiple alleles Refers to the occurrence of a gene that exists as three or more alleles in a population.

multiple sclerosis (MS) A disease in which the patient's own body attacks and destroys myelin as if it were a foreign substance; impairs the function of myelinated neurons that control movement, speech, memory, and emotion.

multipotent A term used to describe a stem cell that can differentiate into several cell types, but far fewer than pluripotent cells.

muscle A grouping of muscle cells (fibers) bound together by a succession of connective tissue layers.

muscle fibers Individual cells within a muscle.

muscle tissue Bundles of muscle fibers that are specialized to contract when stimulated.

muscular dystrophy A group of diseases associated with progressive degeneration of skeletal and cardiac muscle fibers.

mutagen An agent known to cause mutation.

mutant allele An allele that has been altered by mutation.

mutation A heritable change in the genetic material of an organism.

mutualism A symbiotic interaction in which both species benefit.

myasthenia gravis A disease characterized by loss of ACh receptors on skeletal muscle, due to the body's own immune system destroying the receptors.

mycelium A fungal body composed of microscopic branched filaments known as hyphae.

mycorrhizae Associations between the hyphae of certain fungi and the roots of plants.

myelin sheath In the nervous system, an insulating layer made up of specialized glial cells wrapped around the axons.

myocardial infarction (MI) The death of cardiac muscle cells, which can occur if a region of the heart is deprived of blood for an extended time.

myofibrils Individual muscle cells within a muscle, each of which contains thick and thin filaments.

myogenic heart A heart in which the signaling mechanism that initiates contraction resides within the cardiac muscle itself.

myoglobin An oxygen-binding protein that provides an intracellular reservoir of oxygen for muscle fibers.

myosin A motor protein found abundantly in muscle cells and also in other cell types.

N

NAD$^+$ Nicotinamide adenine dinucleotide; a dinucleotide that functions as an energy intermediate molecule. It combines with two electrons and H$^+$ to form NADH.

NADPH Nicotinamide adenine dinucleotide phosphate; an energy intermediate that provides the energy and electrons to drive the Calvin cycle during photosynthesis.

natural killer (NK) cells A type of leukocyte that participates in both nonspecific and specific immunity; recognizes general features on the surface of cancer cells or any virus-infected cells.

natural selection The process that eliminates those individuals that are less likely to survive and reproduce in a particular environment, while allowing other individuals with traits that confer greater reproductive success to increase in numbers.

nauplius The first larval stage in a crustacean.

navigation A mechanism of migration that involves the ability not only to follow a compass bearing but also to set or adjust it.

negative control Transcriptional regulation by repressor proteins.

negative feedback loop A homeostatic system in animals in which a change in the variable being regulated brings about responses that move the variable in the opposite direction.

negative frequency-dependent selection A pattern of natural selection in which the fitness of a genotype decreases when its frequency becomes higher; the result is a balanced polymorphism.

negative pressure filling The mechanism by which reptiles, birds, and mammals ventilate their lungs.

nekton Free-swimming animals in the open ocean that can swim against currents to locate food.

nematocyst In a cnidarian, a powerful capsule with an inverted coiled and barbed thread that functions to immobilize small prey.

neocortex The layer of the brain that evolved most recently in mammals.

nephron One of several million single-cell-thick tubules that are the functional units of the mammalian kidney.

Nernst equation The formula that gives the equilibrium potential for an ion at any given concentration gradient.

nerve A structure found in the peripheral nervous system that is composed of multiple myelinated neurons bound by connective tissue; carries information to or from the central nervous system.

nerve cord In many invertebrates, a ventral structure that extends from the anterior end of the animal to the tail; a dorsal nerve cord is found in chordates.

nerve net Interconnected neurons with no central control organ.

nervous system Groups of cells that sense internal and environmental changes and transmit signals that enable an animal to respond in an appropriate way.

nervous tissue Clusters of cells that initiate and conduct electrical signals from one part of an animal's body to another part.

net primary production (NPP) Gross primary production minus the energy lost in plant cellular respiration.

net reproductive rate The population growth rate per generation.

neural crest In vertebrates, a group of embryonic cells derived from ectoderm that disperse throughout the embryo and contribute to the development of the skeleton and other structures, including peripheral nerves.

neural tube In chordates, a structure formed from ectoderm located dorsal to the notochord; all neurons and their supporting cells in the central nervous system originate from neural precursor cells derived from the neural tube.

neurogenesis The production of new neurons by cell division.

neurogenic heart A heart that will not beat unless it receives regular electrical impulses from the nervous system.

neurohormone A hormone made in and secreted by neurons whose cell bodies are in the hypothalamus.

neuromodulator Another term for a neuropeptide, which is a neurotransmitter that can alter or modulate the response of a postsynaptic neuron to other neurotransmitters.

neuromuscular junction The junction between a motor neuron's axon and a skeletal or cardiac muscle fiber.

neuron A highly specialized cell found in nervous systems of animals that communicates with other cells by electrical or chemical signals.

neuroscience The scientific study of nervous systems.

neurotransmitter A small signaling molecule that is released from an axon terminal and diffuses to a postsynaptic cell where it elicits a response.

neurulation The embryological process responsible for initiating central nervous system formation.

neutral theory of evolution States that most genetic variation is due to the accumulation of neutral mutations that have attained high frequencies in a population via genetic drift.

neutral variation Genetic variation in which natural selection does not favor any particular genotype.

neutralism The phenomenon in which two species occur together but do not interact in any measurable way.

neutron A neutral particle found in the center of an atom.

neutrophil A type of phagocyte and the most abundant type of leukocyte. Neutrophils engulf bacteria by endocytosis.

nitrification The conversion by soil bacteria of NH_3 or NH_4^+ to nitrate (NO_3^-), a form of nitrogen commonly used by plants.

nitrogen fixation A specialized metabolic process in which certain prokaryotes use the enzyme nitrogenase to convert inert atmospheric nitrogen gas into ammonia; also, the industrial process by which humans produce ammonia fertilizer from nitrogen gas.

nitrogenase An enzyme used in the biological process of fixing nitrogen.

nitrogen-limitation hypothesis The proposal that organisms select food based on its nitrogen content.

nitrogenous wastes Degradation products of proteins and nucleic acids that are toxic at high concentrations and must be eliminated from the body.

nociceptor A sensory receptor in animals that responds to extreme heat, cold, and pressure, as well as to certain molecules such as acids; also known as a pain receptor.

nocturnal enuresis Bed-wetting.

node The region of a plant stem from which one or more leaves, branches, or buds emerge.

nodes of Ranvier Exposed areas in the axons of myelinated neurons that contain many voltage-gated Na^+ channels and are the sites of regeneration of action potentials.

Nod factor Nodulation factor; a substance produced by nitrogen-fixing bacteria in response to flavonoids secreted from the roots of potential host plants. Nod factors bind to receptors in plant root membranes, starting a process that allows the bacteria to invade roots.

nodule A small swelling on a plant root that contains nitrogen-fixing bacteria.

nodulin One of several plant proteins that foster root nodule development.

noncoding strand *See* template strand.

noncompetitive inhibitor A molecule that binds to an enzyme at a location that is outside the active site and inhibits the enzyme's function.

noncyclic electron flow The combined action of photosystem II and photosystem I in which electrons flow in a linear manner to produce NADPH.

non-Darwinian evolution The idea that much of the modern variation in gene sequences is explained by neutral variation rather than adaptive variation.

nondisjunction An event in which the chromosomes do not sort properly during cell division.

nonpolar covalent bond A strong bond formed between two atoms of similar electronegativities in which electrons are shared between the atoms.

nonpolar molecule A molecule composed predominantly of nonpolar bonds.

nonrandom mating The phenomenon that individuals choose their mates based on their genotypes or phenotypes.

nonrecombinant An offspring whose combination of traits has not changed from the parental generation.

nonsense codon *See* stop codon.

nonsense mutation A mutation that changes a normal codon into a stop codon; this causes translation to be terminated earlier than expected, producing a truncated polypeptide.

nonshivering thermogenesis An increase in an animal's metabolic rate that is not due to increased muscle activity; occurs primarily in brown adipose tissue.

nonspecific (innate) immunity The body's defenses that are present at birth and act against foreign materials in much the same way regardless of their specific identity; includes the skin and mucous membranes, plus various cellular and chemical defenses.

nonvascular plant A plant that does not produce lignified vascular tissue; includes the bryophytes.

norepinephrine A type of neurotransmitter; also known as noradrenaline.

norm of reaction A description of how a trait may change depending on environmental conditions.

notochord A defining characteristic of all chordate embryos; consists of a flexible rod that lies between the digestive tract and the nerve cord.

N-terminus The location of the first amino acid in a polypeptide; also known as the amino terminus.

nuclear envelope A double-membrane structure that encloses the cell's nucleus.

nuclear genome The chromosomes found in the nucleus of a eukaryotic cell.

nuclear lamina A collection of filamentous proteins that line the inner nuclear membrane; part of the nuclear matrix.

nuclear matrix A filamentous network of proteins that is found inside the nucleus and lines the inner nuclear membrane. The nuclear matrix serves to organize the chromosomes.

nuclear pore A passageway for the movement of molecules and macromolecules into and out of the nucleus; formed where the inner and outer nuclear membranes make contact with each other.

nucleic acid An organic molecule composed of nucleotides. The two types of nucleic acids are deoxyribonucleic acid (DNA) and ribonucleic acid (RNA).

nucleoid region A site in a bacterial cell where the genetic material (DNA) is located.

nucleolus A prominent region in the nucleus of nondividing cells where ribosome assembly occurs.

nucleosome A structural unit of eukaryotic chromosomes composed of an octamer of histones (eight histone proteins) wrapped with DNA.

nucleotide An organic molecule having three components: one or more phosphate groups, a five-carbon sugar (either deoxyribose or ribose), and a single or double ring of carbon and nitrogen atoms known as a base.

nucleotide excision repair (NER) A common type of DNA repair system that removes (excises) and repairs a region of the DNA where damage has occurred.

nucleus (plural, **nuclei**) 1. In cell biology, an organelle found in eukaryotic cells that contains most of the cell's genetic material. 2. In chemistry, the region of an atom that contains protons and neutrons. 3. In neurobiology, a group of neuronal cell bodies in the brain that are devoted to a particular function.

nutrient Any substance taken up by a living organism that is needed for survival, growth, development, repair, or reproduction.

O

obese According to current National Institutes of Health guidelines, a person having a body mass index (BMI) of 30 kg/m² or more.

obligate aerobes Microorganisms that require oxygen.

obligate anaerobes Microorganisms that are poisoned by oxygen.

obligatory mutualism An interaction in which two mutualistic species cannot live without each other.

occipital lobe One of four lobes of the cerebral cortex of the human brain; controls aspects of vision and color recognition.

ocelli Photosensitive organs in some animal species.

octet rule The phenomenon that some atoms are most stable when their outer shell is full with eight electrons.

Okazaki fragments Short segments of DNA synthesized in the lagging strand during DNA replication.

olfaction The sense of smell.

olfactory bulbs Part of the limbic system of the forebrain of vertebrates; the olfactory bulbs carry information about odors to the brain.

oligodendrocytes Glial cells that produce the myelin sheath around neurons in the central nervous system.

oligotrophic The term used to describe aquatic systems that are low in nutrients such as phosphate and combined nitrogen and are consequently low in primary productivity and biomass, but typically high in species diversity.

ommatidium An independent visual unit in the eye of insects that functions as a separate photoreceptor capable of forming an independent image.

omnivore An animal that has the ability to eat and survive on both plant and animal products.

oncogene A type of mutant gene derived from a proto-oncogene. An oncogene is overactive, thus contributing to uncontrolled cell growth and promoting cancer.

one gene–one enzyme hypothesis An early hypothesis by Beadle and Tatum that suggested that one gene encodes one enzyme. It was later modified to the one gene–one polypeptide theory.

one gene–one polypeptide theory The concept that one structural gene codes for one polypeptide.

oogenesis Gametogenesis in a female animal resulting in the production of an egg cell.

oogonia (singular, **oogonium**) In animals, diploid germ cells that give rise to the female gametes, the eggs.

open circulatory system In animals, a circulatory system in which hemolymph, which is not different than the interstitial fluid, flows throughout the body and is not confined to special vessels.

open complex Also called the transcription bubble; a small bubble-like structure between two DNA strands that occurs during transcription.

open conformation Loosely packed chromatin that can be transcribed into RNA.

operant conditioning A form of behavior modification; a type of associative learning in which an animal's behavior is reinforced by a consequence, either a reward or a punishment.

operator A DNA sequence in bacteria that is recognized by activator or repressor proteins that regulate the level of gene transcription.

operculum A protective flap that covers the gills of a bony fish.

operon An arrangement of two or more genes in bacteria that are under the transcriptional control of a single promoter.

opposable thumb A thumb that can be placed opposite the fingers of the same hand; gives animals a precision grip that enables the manipulation of small objects.

opsin A protein that is a component of visual pigments in the vertebrate eye.

opsonization The process by which an antibody binds to a pathogen and provides a means to link the pathogen with a phagocyte.

optic disc In vertebrates, the point on the retina where the optic nerve leaves the eye.

optic nerve A structure of the vertebrate eye that carries electrical signals to the brain.

optimal foraging The concept that in a given circumstance, an animal seeks to obtain the most energy possible with the least expenditure of energy.

optimality theory The theory that predicts an animal should behave in a way that maximizes the benefits of a behavior minus its costs.

orbital The region surrounding the nucleus of an atom where the probability is high of finding a particular electron.

order In taxonomy, a subdivision of a class.

organ Two or more types of tissue combined to perform a common function.

organelle A subcellular structure or membrane-bound compartment with its own unique structure and function.

organic chemistry The study of carbon-containing molecules.

organic farming The production of crops without the use of commercial inorganic fertilizers, growth substances, and pesticides.

organic molecule A carbon-containing molecule, so named because they are found in living organisms.

organism A living thing that maintains an internal order that is separated from the environment.

organismal ecology The investigation of how adaptations and choices by individuals affect their reproduction and survival.

organismic model A view of the nature of a community that considers it to be equivalent to a superorganism; individuals, populations, and communities have a relationship to each other that resembles the associations found between cells, tissues, and organs.

organizing center A group of cells in a plant shoot meristem that ensures the proper organization of the meristem and preserves the correct number of actively dividing stem cells.

organogenesis The developmental stage during which cells and tissues form organs in animal embryos.

organ system Different organs that work together to perform an overall function in an organism.

orientation A mechanism of migration in which animals have the ability to follow a compass bearing and travel in a straight line.

origin of replication A site within a chromosome that serves as a starting point for DNA replication.

ortholog A homologous gene in different species.

osmoconformer An animal whose osmolarity conforms to that of its environment.

osmolarity The solute concentration of a solution of water, expressed as milliosmoles/liter (mOsm/L).

osmoregulator An animal that maintains stable internal salt concentrations and osmolarities, even when living in water with very different osmolarities than its body fluids.

osmosis The movement of water across membranes to balance solute concentrations. Water diffuses from a solution that is hypotonic (lower solute concentration) into a solution that is hypertonic (higher solute concentration).

osmotic adjustment The process by which a plant modifies the solute concentration of its cytosol.

osmotic lysis Occurs when a cell in a hypotonic environment takes up so much water that it ruptures.

osmotic pressure The hydrostatic pressure required to stop the net flow of water across a membrane due to osmosis.

osmotroph An organism that relies on osmotrophy (uptake of small organic molecules) as a form of nutrition.

osteomalacia Bone deformation in adults due to inadequate mineral intake or absorption from the intestines.

osteoporosis A disease in which the mineral and organic components of bone are reduced.

otoliths Granules of calcium carbonate found in the gelatinous substance that embeds hair cells in the vertebrate ear.

outer bark Protective layers of mostly dead cork cells that cover the outside of woody stems and roots.

outer ear One of the three main compartments of the mammalian ear; consists of the external ear, or pinna, and the auditory canal.

outer segment The highly convoluted plasma membranes found in the rods and cones of the eye.

outgroup In a cladogram, a species or group of species that does not exhibit one or more shared derived characters found in the ingroup.

ovarian cycle The events beginning with the development of an ovarian follicle, followed by release of a secondary oocyte, and concluding with formation and subsequent degeneration of a corpus luteum.

ovaries (singular, **ovary**) 1. In animals, the female gonads where eggs are formed. 2. In plants, the lowermost portion of the pistil that encloses and protects the ovules.

overweight According to current National Institutes of Health guidelines, a person having a body mass index (BMI) of 25 kg/m^2 or more.

oviduct A thin tube with undulating fimbriae (fingerlike structures) that is connected to the uterus and extends out to the ovary; also called the fallopian tube.

oviparity Development of an embryo outside the mother, usually in a protective shell or other structure from which the young hatch.

oviparous An animal whose young hatch from eggs laid outside the mother's body.

ovoviparous An animal that retains fertilized eggs covered by a protective sheath or other structure within the body, where the young hatch.

ovoviviparity Development of an embryo involving aspects of both viviparity and oviparity; fertilized eggs covered with a protective sheath are produced and hatch inside the mother's body, but the offspring receive no nourishment from the mother.

ovulation The process by which a mature oocyte is released from an ovary.

ovule In a seed plant, a megaspore-producing megasporangium and enclosing tissues known as integuments.

ovum (plural, **ova**) *See* egg.

oxidation A process that involves the removal of electrons; occurs during the breakdown of small organic molecules.

oxidative fiber A skeletal muscle fiber that contains numerous mitochondria and has a high capacity for oxidative phosphorylation.

oxidative phosphorylation A process during which NADH and FADH$_2$ are oxidized to make more ATP via the phosphorylation of ADP.

oxygen-hemoglobin dissociation curve A curve that represents the relationship between the partial pressure of oxygen and the binding of oxygen to hemoglobin proteins.

oxytocin A hormone secreted by the posterior pituitary gland that stimulates contractions of the smooth muscles in the uterus of a pregnant mammal, facilitating the birth process; after birth, it is important in milk secretion.

P

pacemaker *See* sinoatrial (SA) node.

Pacinian corpuscles Structures located deep beneath the surface of an animal's skin that respond to deep pressure or vibration.

paedomorphosis The retention of juvenile traits in an adult organism.

pair-rule gene A type of segmentation gene; a mutation in this gene may cause alternating segments or parts of segments to be deleted.

paleontologist A scientist who studies fossils.

palisade parenchyma Photosynthetic ground tissue of the plant leaf mesophyll that consists of closely packed, elongate cells adapted to efficiently absorb sunlight.

palmate A type of leaf vein pattern in which veins radiate outward, resembling an open hand.

pancreas   In vertebrates, an elongated gland located behind the stomach that secretes digestive enzymes and a fluid rich in bicarbonate ions.

parabronchi   In birds, a series of parallel air tubes that make up the lungs and are the regions of gas exchange.

paracrine   Refers to a type of cellular communication in which molecules are released into the interstitial fluid and act on nearby cells.

paralogs   Homologous genes within a single species.

paraphyletic group   A group of organisms that contains a common ancestor and some, but not all, of its descendants.

parapodia   Fleshy, footlike structures in the polychaetes that are pushed into the substrate to provide traction during movement.

parasite   A predatory organism that feeds off another organism but does not normally kill it.

parasitism   A symbiotic association in which one organism feeds off another but does not normally kill it.

parasympathetic division   The division of the autonomic nervous system that is involved in maintaining and restoring body functions.

parathyroid hormone (PTH)   A hormone that acts on bone to stimulate the activity of cells that dissolve the mineral part of bone.

Parazoa   A subgroup of animals lacking specialized tissue types or organs, although they may have several distinct types of cells; the one phylum in this group is the Porifera (sponges).

parenchyma cell   A type of plant cell that is thin-walled and alive at maturity.

parenchyma tissue   A plant ground tissue that is composed of parenchyma cells.

parental strand   The original strand in DNA replication.

parietal lobe   One of four lobes of the cerebral cortex of the human brain; receives and interprets sensory input from visual and somatic pathways.

parthenogenesis   An asexual process in which an offspring develops from an unfertilized egg.

partial pressure   The individual pressure of each gas in the air; the sum of these pressures is known as atmospheric pressure.

particulate inheritance   The idea that the determinants of hereditary traits are transmitted intact from one generation to the next.

parturition   The birth of an organism.

passive diffusion   Diffusion through a membrane without the aid of a transport protein.

passive immunity   A type of acquired immunity that confers protection against disease through the direct transfer of antibodies from one individual to another.

passive transport   The diffusion of a solute across a membrane in a process that is energetically favorable and does not require an input of energy.

paternal inheritance   A pattern in which only the male gamete contributes particular genes to the offspring.

pathogen   A microorganism that causes disease symptoms in its host.

pattern formation   The process that gives rise to a plant or animal with a particular body structure.

pedal glands   Glands in the foot of a rotifer that secrete a sticky substance that aids in attachment to the substrate.

pedicel   1. A flower stalk. 2. A narrow, waistlike point of attachment between the body parts of spiders and some insects.

pedigree analysis   An examination of the inheritance of human traits in families.

pedipalps   In spiders, a pair of appendages that have various sensory, predatory, or reproductive functions.

peer-review process   A procedure in which experts in a particular area evaluate papers submitted to scientific journals.

pelagic zone   The open ocean, where the water depth averages 4,000 m and nutrient concentrations are typically low.

penis   A male external accessory sex organ found in many animals that is involved in copulation.

pentadactyl limb   A limb ending in five digits.

PEP carboxylase   An enzyme in C_4 plants that adds CO_2 to phosphoenolpyruvate (PEP) to produce the four-carbon compound oxaloacetate.

pepsin   An active enzyme in the stomach that begins the digestion of protein.

peptide bond   The covalent bond that links amino acids in a polypeptide.

peptidoglycan   A polymer composed of carbohydrates cross-linked with peptides that is an important component of the cell walls of most bacteria.

peptidyl site (P site)   One of three sites for tRNA binding in the ribosome during translation; the other two are the aminoacyl site (A site) and the exit site (E site). The P site holds the tRNA carrying the growing polypeptide chain.

peptidyl transfer reaction   During translation, the transfer of the polypeptide from the tRNA in the P site to the amino acid at the A site.

per capita growth rate   The per capita birth rate minus the per capita death rate; the rate that determines how populations grow over any time period.

perception   An awareness of the sensations that are experienced.

perennial   A plant that lives for more than 2 years, often producing seeds each year after it reaches reproductive maturity.

perfect flower   A flower that has both stamens and carpels.

perianth   The term that refers to flower petals and sepals collectively.

pericarp   The wall of a plant's fruit.

pericycle   A cylinder of plant tissue having cell division (meristematic) capacity that encloses the root vascular tissue.

peripheral membrane protein   A protein that is noncovalently bound to regions of integral membrane proteins that project out from the membrane, or they are noncovalently bound to the polar head groups of phospholipids.

peripheral nervous system (PNS)   In vertebrates, all nerves and ganglia outside the brain and spinal cord.

peripheral zone   The area of a plant shoot meristem that contains dividing cells that will eventually differentiate into plant structures.

periphyton   Communities of microorganisms that are attached by mucilage to underwater surfaces such as rocks, sand, and plants.

peristalsis   In animals, the rhythmic, spontaneous waves of muscle contractions that propel food through the digestive system.

peritubular capillaries   Capillaries near the junction of the cortex and medulla that surround the nephron of the mammalian kidney.

permafrost   A layer of permanently frozen soil found in tundra.

peroxisome   A relatively small organelle found in all eukaryotic cells that catalyzes detoxifying reactions.

personalized medicine   A medical practice in which information about a patient's genotype is used to individualize their medical care.

petal   A flower organ that usually serves to attract insects or other animals for pollen transport.

petiole   A stalk that connects a leaf to the stem of a plant.

P generation   The parental generation in a genetic cross.

pH   The mathematical expression of a solution's hydrogen ion concentration, defined as the negative logarithm to the base 10 of the H^+ concentration.

phage   See bacteriophage.

phagocyte   A cell capable of phagocytosis; phagocytes provide nonspecific defense against pathogens that enter the body.

phagocytic vacuole   A vacuole that functions in the degradation of food particles or bacteria; also called a food vacuole.

phagocytosis   A form of endocytosis that involves the formation of a membrane vesicle, called a phagocytic vacuole, which engulfs a particle such as a bacterium.

phagotroph   An organism that specializes in phagotrophy (particle feeding) by means of phagocytosis as a form of nutrition.

pharyngeal slit   A defining characteristic of all chordate embryos. In early-diverging chordates, pharyngeal slits develop into a filter-feeding device, and in some advanced chordates, they form gills.

pharynx   A portion of the vertebrate alimentary canal; also known as the throat.

phenolics   A group of secondary metabolites that contain a benzene ring covalently linked to a single hydroxyl group. Includes tannins, lignins, and flavonoids.

phenotype   The characteristics of an organism that are the result of the expression of its genes.

pheromone   A powerful chemical attractant used to manipulate the behavior of others.

phloem   A specialized conducting tissue in a plant's stem.

phloem loading   The process of conveying sugars to sieve-tube elements for long-distance transport.

phoresy   A form of commensalism in which individuals of one species use individuals of a second species for transportation.

phosphodiesterase   An enzyme that breaks down cAMP into AMP.

phosphodiester linkage   Refers to a double linkage (two phosphoester bonds) that holds together adjacent nucleotides in DNA and RNA strands.

phospholipid   A class of lipids that are similar in structure to triglycerides, but the third hydroxyl group of glycerol is linked to a phosphate group instead of a fatty acid; a key component of biological membranes.

phospholipid bilayer   The basic framework of the cellular membrane, consisting of two layers of lipids.

phosphorylation   The attachment of a phosphate to a molecule.

photic zone   A fairly narrow zone close to the surface of an aquatic environment, where light is sufficient to allow photosynthesis to exceed respiration.

photoautotroph   An organism that uses the energy from light to make organic molecules from inorganic sources.

photoheterotroph   An organism that is able to use light energy to generate ATP but must take in organic compounds from the environment.

photon   A discrete particle that makes up light. A photon is massless and travels in a wavelike pattern.

photoperiodism   A plant's ability to measure and respond to amounts of light; used as a way of detecting seasonal change.

photoreceptor   A specialized cell in an animal that responds to visible light energy.

photorespiration   The metabolic process occurring in C_3 plants that occurs when the enzyme rubisco combines with oxygen instead of carbon dioxide and produces only one molecule of 3PG instead of two, thereby reducing photosynthetic efficiency.

photosynthesis   The process whereby light energy is captured by plant, algal, or bacterial cells and is used to synthesize organic molecules from CO_2 and H_2O (or H_2S).

photosystem I (PSI)   A distinct complex of proteins and pigment molecules in chloroplasts that absorbs light during the light reactions of photosynthesis.

photosystem II (PSII)   A distinct complex of proteins and pigment molecules in chloroplasts that generates oxygen from water during the light reactions of photosynthesis.

phototropin   The main blue-light sensor involved in phototropism in plants.

phototropism   The tendency of a plant to grow toward a light source.

phylogenetic tree   A diagram that describes a phylogeny; such a tree is a hypothesis of the evolutionary relationships among various species, based on the information available to and gathered by systematists.

phylogeny   The evolutionary history of a species or group of species.

phylum (plural, **phyla**)   In taxonomy, a subdivision of a kingdom.

physical mutagen   A physical agent, such as UV light, that causes mutations.

physiological ecology   A subdiscipline of organismal ecology that investigates how organisms are physiologically adapted to their environment and how the environment impacts the distribution of species.

physiology   The study of the functions of cells and body parts of living organisms.

phytochrome   A red and far-red-light receptor in plants.

phytoplankton   Microscopic photosynthetic protists that float in the water column or actively move through water.

phytoremediation   The process of removing harmful metals from soils by growing hyperaccumulator plants on metal-contaminated soils, then harvesting and burning the plants to ashes for disposal and/or metal recovery.

pigment   A molecule that can absorb light energy.

pili (singular, **pilus**)   Threadlike surface appendages that allow prokaryotes to attach to each other during mating or to move across surfaces.

piloting   A mechanism of migration in which an animal moves from one familiar landmark to the next.

pinnate   A type of leaf vein pattern in which veins appear feather-like.

pinocytosis   A form of endocytosis that involves the formation of membrane vesicles from the plasma membrane as a way for cells to internalize the extracellular fluid.

pistil   A flower structure that may consist of a single carpel or multiple, fused carpels and is differentiated into stigma, style, and ovary.

pit   A thin-walled circular area in a plant cell wall where secondary wall materials such as lignin are absent and through which water moves.

pitch   The tone of a sound wave that depends on its length and frequency.

pituitary dwarfism   A condition in which a person's anterior pituitary gland fails to make adequate amounts of GH during childhood; results in stunted growth. The currently accepted name is short stature.

pituitary giant   A person who has a tumor of the GH-secreting cells of the anterior pituitary gland and thus produces excess GH during childhood and, if untreated, during adulthood; the person can grow very tall before growth ceases after puberty.

pituitary gland   A multilobed endocrine gland sitting directly below the hypothalamus of the brain.

placenta   A structure through which humans and other eutherian mammals retain and nourish their young within the uterus via the transfer of nutrients and gases.

placental transfer tissue   In plants, a nutritive tissue that aids in the transfer of nutrients from maternal parent to embryo.

plant   A multicellular eukaryotic organism that is photosynthetic, generally lives on land, and is adapted in many ways to cope with the environmental stresses of life on land.

Plantae   A eukaryotic kingdom of the domain Eukarya.

plant tissue culture   A laboratory process to produce thousands of identical plants having the same desirable characteristics.

plaque   1. A deposit of lipids, fibrous tissue, and smooth muscle cells that may develop inside arterial walls. 2. A bacterial biofilm that may form on the surfaces of teeth.

plasma   The fluid part of blood that contains water and dissolved solutes.

plasma cell   A cell that synthesizes and secretes antibodies.

plasma membrane   The biomembrane that separates the internal contents of a cell from its external environment.

plasmid   A small circular piece of DNA found naturally in many strains of bacteria and occasionally in eukaryotic cells; can be used as a vector in cloning experiments.

plasmodesma (plural, **plasmodesmata**)   A membrane-lined, ER-containing channel that connects the cytoplasm of adjacent plant cells.

plasmogamy   The fusion of the cytoplasm between two gametes.

plasmolysis   The shrinkage of algal or plant cytoplasm that occurs when water leaves the cell by osmosis, with the result that the plasma membrane no longer presses on the cell wall.

plastid   A general name given to organelles found in plant and algal cells that are bound by two membranes and contain DNA and large amounts of either chlorophyll (in chloroplasts), carotenoids (in chromoplasts), or starch (in amyloplasts).

platelets   Cell fragments in the blood of mammals that play a crucial role in the formation of blood clots.

pleiotropy   The phenomenon in which a mutation in a single gene can have multiple effects on an individual's phenotype.

pleural sac   A double layer of moist sheathlike membranes that encases each lung.

pluripotent   Refers to the ability of embryonic stem cells to differentiate into almost every cell type of the body.

point mutation   A mutation that affects only a single base pair within DNA or that involves the addition or deletion of a single base pair to a DNA sequence.

polar cell   The highest latitude cell in the three-cell model of atmospheric circulation.

polar covalent bond   A covalent bond between two atoms that have different electronegativities; the shared electrons are closer to the atom of higher electronegativity than the atom of lower electronegativity. This distribution of electrons around the atoms creates a polarity, or difference in electric charge, across the molecule.

polarized   1. In cell biology, refers to cells that have different sides, such as the apical and basal sides of epithelial cells. 2. In neuroscience, refers to the electrical gradient across a neuron's plasma membrane.

polar molecule   A molecule containing significant numbers of polar bonds.

polar transport   The process whereby auxin flows primarily downward in shoots.

pole   A structure of the spindle apparatus defined by each centrosome.

pollen   In seed plants, tiny male gametophytes enclosed by sporopollenin-containing microspore walls.

pollen coat   A layer of material that covers the sporopollenin-rich pollen wall.

pollen grain   The immature male gametophyte of a seed plant.

pollen tube   In seed plants, a long, thin tube produced by a pollen grain that delivers sperm to the ovule.

pollen wall   A tough, sporopollenin wall at the surface of a pollen grain.

pollination   The process in which pollen grains are transported to an angiosperm flower or a gymnosperm cone primarily by means of wind or animal pollinators.

pollination syndromes   The pattern of coevolved traits between particular types of flowers and their specific pollinators.

pollinator   An animal that carries pollen between angiosperm flowers or cones of gymnosperms.

polyandry   A mating system in which one female mates with several males, but males mate with only one female.

poly A tail   A string of adenine nucleotides at the 3' end of most mature mRNAs in eukaryotes.

polycistronic mRNA   An mRNA that contains the coding sequences for two or more structural genes.

polycythemia   A condition of increased hemoglobin due to increased hematocrit.

polygenic   A trait in which several or many genes contribute to the outcome of the trait.

polygyny   A mating system in which one male mates with several females in a single breeding season, but females mate with only one male.

polyketides   A group of secondary metabolites produced by diverse organisms. Examples include streptomycin, erythromycin, and tetracycline.

polymer   A large molecule formed by linking many smaller molecules called monomers.

polymerase chain reaction (PCR)   A technique to make many copies of a gene in vitro; primers are used that flank the region of DNA to be amplified.

polymorphic gene   A gene that commonly exists as two or more alleles in a population.

polymorphism   The phenomenon that many traits or genes may display variation within a population.

polyp A type of cnidarian body form that is sessile and occurs mouth up.

polypeptide A linear sequence of amino acids; the term denotes structure.

polyphagous Parasites that feed on many host species.

polyphyletic group A group of organisms that consists of members of several evolutionary lines and does not include the most recent common ancestor of the included lineages.

polyploid An organism that has three or more sets of chromosomes.

polyploidy In an organism, the state of having three or more sets of chromosomes.

polysaccharide Many monosaccharides linked to form long polymers.

pons The part of the vertebrate hindbrain, along with the cerebellum, responsible for monitoring and coordinating body movements.

population A group of individuals of the same species that occupy the same environment and can interbreed with one another.

population ecology The study of how populations grow and what factors promote or limit growth.

population genetics The study of genes and genotypes in a population.

portal vein A vein that not only collects blood from capillaries—like all veins—but also forms another set of capillaries, as opposed to returning the blood directly to the heart.

positional information Molecules that are provided to a cell that allow it to determine its position relative to other cells.

positive control Transcriptional regulation by activator proteins.

positive feedback loop In animals, the acceleration of a process, leading to what is sometimes called an explosive system.

positive pressure filling The method by which amphibians ventilate their lungs. The animals gulp air and force it under pressure into the lungs, as if inflating a balloon.

postabsorptive state One of two alternating phases in the utilization of nutrients; occurs when the gastrointestinal tract is empty of nutrients and the body's own stores must supply energy. The other phase is the absorptive state.

postanal tail A defining characteristic of all chordate embryos; consists of a tail of variable length that extends posterior to the anal opening.

posterior Refers to the rear (tail-end) of an animal.

postsynaptic cell The cell that receives the electrical or chemical signal sent from a neuron.

post-translational covalent modification A process of changing the structure of a protein, usually by covalently attaching functional groups; this process greatly increases the diversity of the proteome.

post-translational sorting The uptake of proteins into the nucleus, mitochondria, chloroplasts, or peroxisomes that occurs after the protein is completely made in the cytosol (that is, completely translated).

postzygotic isolating mechanism A mechanism that prevents interbreeding by blocking the development of a viable and fertile individual after fertilization has taken place.

potential energy The stored energy that a substance possesses due to its structure or location.

power stroke In muscle, a conformation change in the myosin cross-bridge that results in binding between myosin and actin and the movement of the actin filament.

P protein Phloem protein; the proteinaceous material used by plant phloem as a response to wounding.

prebiotic soup The medium formed by the slow accumulation of organic molecules in the early oceans over a long period of time prior to the existence of life.

predation An interaction in which the action of a predator results in the death of its prey.

predator An animal that kills its prey.

prediction An expected outcome based on a hypothesis that can be shown to be correct or incorrect through observation or experimentation.

pregnancy The time during which a developing embryo and fetus grows within the uterus of the mother. The period of pregnancy is also known as gestation.

preinitiation complex The structure of the completed assembly of RNA polymerase II and GTFs at the TATA box prior to transcription of eukaryotic structural genes.

pre-mRNA In eukaryotes, the mRNA transcript prior to any processing.

pressure-flow hypothesis Explains sugar translocation in plants as a process driven by differences in turgor pressure between cells of a sugar source, where sugar is produced, and cells of a sugar sink, where sugar is consumed.

pressure potential (P) The component of water potential due to hydrostatic pressure.

presynaptic cell The neuron that sends an electrical or chemical signal to another cell.

prezygotic isolating mechanism A mechanism that stops interbreeding by preventing the formation of a zygote.

primary active transport A type of transport that involves pumps that directly use energy to transport a solute against a gradient.

primary cell wall In plants, a relatively thin and flexible cell wall that is synthesized first between two newly made daughter cells.

primary consumer An organism that obtains its food by eating primary producers; also called a herbivore.

primary electron acceptor The molecule to which a high-energy electron from an excited pigment molecule such as P680* is transferred during photosynthesis.

primary endosymbiosis The process by which a eukaryotic host cell acquires prokaryotic endosymbionts. Mitochondria and the plastids of green and red algae are examples of organelles that originated with primary endosymbiosis.

primary growth Plant growth that occurs from primary meristems and produces primary tissues and organs of diverse types.

primary immune response The response to an initial exposure to an antigen.

primary meristem A meristematic tissue that increases plant length and produces new organs.

primary metabolism The synthesis and breakdown of molecules and macromolecules that are found in all forms of life and are essential for cell structure and function.

primary oocytes In animals, cells that undergo meiosis to begin the process of egg production.

primary plastid A plastid that originated from a prokaryote as the result of primary endosymbiosis.

primary producer An autotroph, which typically harvests light energy from the sun; located at the base of the food chain.

primary spermatocytes In animals, cells that undergo meiosis to begin the process of sperm production.

primary structure The linear sequence of amino acids of a polypeptide; one of four levels of protein structure.

primary succession Succession on newly exposed sites that were not previously occupied by soil and vegetation.

primary vascular tissue Plant tissue composed of primary xylem and phloem, which is the conducting tissue of nonwoody plants.

primer A short segment of RNA, typically 10 to 12 nucleotides in length, that is needed to begin DNA replication.

primordial germ cells (PGCs) In animals, the embryonic cells that eventually give rise to gametes.

principle of parsimony The concept that the preferred hypothesis is the one that is the simplest.

principle of species individuality A view of the nature of a community in which each species is distributed according to its physiological needs and population dynamics; most communities intergrade continuously, and competition does not create distinct vegetational zones.

prion An infectious protein that causes disease by inducing the abnormal folding of other protein molecules.

probability The chance that an event will have a particular outcome.

proboscis The coiled tongue of a butterfly or moth, which can be uncoiled, enabling it to drink nectar from flowers.

procambium In plants, a type of primary tissue meristem that produces vascular tissue.

producer An organism that synthesizes the organic compounds used by other organisms for food.

product The end result of a chemical reaction.

production efficiency The percentage of energy assimilated by an organism that becomes incorporated into new biomass.

productivity hypothesis The proposal that greater production by plants results in greater overall species richness.

product rule The probability that two or more independent events will occur is equal to the product of their individual probabilities.

progesterone A hormone secreted by the female ovaries that plays a key role in pregnancy.

progymnosperms An extinct group of plants having wood but not seeds, which evolved before the gymnosperms.

prokaryote One of the two categories into which all forms of life can be placed. Prokaryotes lack a nucleus and include bacteria and archaea.

prokaryotic Refers to organisms having cells lacking a membrane-enclosed nucleus and cell compartmentalization; includes all members of the domains Bacteria and Archaea.

prometaphase The phase of mitosis during which the mitotic spindle is completely formed.

promiscuous In ecology, a term for animals that have different sexual mates every year or breeding season.

promoter The site in the DNA where transcription begins.

proofreading The ability of DNA polymerase to identify a mismatched nucleotide and remove it from the daughter strand.

prophage Refers to the DNA of a phage that has become integrated into a bacterial chromosome.

prophase The phase of mitosis during which the chromosomes condense and the nuclear membrane begins to vesiculate.

proplastid Unspecialized structures that form plastids.

prostate gland   A structure in the male reproductive system that secretes a thin fluid that protects sperm once they are deposited within the female reproductive tract.

prosthetic group   Small molecules that are permanently attached to the surface of an enzyme and aid in catalysis.

protease   An enzyme that cuts proteins into smaller polypeptides.

proteasome   A molecular machine that is the primary pathway for protein degradation in archaea and eukaryotic cells.

protein   A functional unit composed of one or more polypeptides. Each polypeptide is composed of a linear sequence of amino acids.

protein kinase   An enzyme that transfers phosphate groups from ATP to a protein.

protein kinase cascade   The sequential activation of multiple protein kinases.

protein phosphatase   An enzyme responsible for removing phosphate groups from proteins.

protein-protein interactions   The specific interactions between proteins that occur during many critical cellular processes.

protein subunit   An individual polypeptide within a functional protein; most functional proteins are composed of two or more polypeptides.

proteoglycan   A glycosaminoglycan in the extracellular matrix linked to a core protein.

proteolysis   A processing event within a cell in which enzymes called proteases cut proteins into smaller polypeptides.

proteome   The complete complement of proteins that a cell or organism can make.

proteomics   Techniques used to identify and study groups of proteins.

prothoracicotropic hormone (PTTH)   A hormone produced in certain invertebrates that stimulates a pair of endocrine glands called the prothoracic glands.

protist   A eukaryotic organism that is not a member of the animal, plant, or fungal kingdoms; lives in moist habitats and is typically microscopic in size.

Protista   Formerly a eukaryotic kingdom. Most protists can be placed into seven eukaryotic supergroups.

protobiont   The term used to describe the first nonliving structures that evolved into living cells.

protoderm   In plants, a type of primary tissue meristem that generates the outermost dermal tissue.

proton   A positively charged particle found in the nucleus of an atom. The number of protons in an atom is called the atomic number and defines each type of element.

protonephridia   Simple excretory organs found in flatworms that are used to filter out wastes and excess water.

proton-motive force   *See* H^+ electrochemical gradient.

proto-oncogene   A normal gene that, if mutated, can become an oncogene.

protostome   An animal whose development exhibits spiral determinate cleavage and in which the blastopore becomes the mouth; includes mollusks, annelid worms, and arthropods.

protozoa   A term commonly used to describe diverse heterotrophic protists.

proventriculus   The glandular portion of the stomach of a bird.

provirus   Refers to viral DNA that has become incorporated into a eukaryotic chromosome.

proximal convoluted tubule   The segment of the tubule of the nephron in the kidney that drains Bowman's capsule.

proximate cause   A specific genetic and physiological mechanism of behavior.

pseudocoelomate   An animal with a pseudocoelom.

P site   *See* peptidyl site.

pteridophytes   A phylum of vascular plants having euphylls, but not seeds; Pteridophyta.

pulmocutaneous circulation   The routing of blood from the heart to the gas exchange organs (lungs and skin) of frogs and some other amphibians.

pulmonary circulation   The pumping of blood from the right side of the heart to the lungs to pick up oxygen from the atmosphere and release carbon dioxide.

pulmonary hypertension   A condition that usually results from a diseased or damaged left ventricle that fails to pump out the usual amount of blood with each beat of the heart. This causes blood to back up in the pulmonary vessels, raising their pressure.

pulse-chase experiment   A procedure in which researchers administer a pulse of radioactively labeled materials to cells so that they make radioactive products. This is followed by the addition of nonlabeled materials called a chase.

pump   A transporter that directly couples its conformational changes to an energy source, such as ATP hydrolysis.

punctuated equilibrium   A concept that suggests that the tempo of evolution is more sporadic than gradual. Species rapidly evolve into new species followed by long periods of equilibrium with little evolutionary change.

Punnett square   A common method for predicting the outcome of simple genetic crosses.

pupa   A developmental stage in some insects that undergo metamorphosis; occurs between the larval and adult stages.

pupil   A small opening in the eye of a vertebrate that transmits different patterns of light emitted from images in the animal's field of view.

purine   The bases adenine (A) and guanine (G), with double rings of carbon and nitrogen atoms.

pyramid of biomass   A measure of trophic-level transfer efficiency in which the organisms at each trophic level are weighed.

pyramid of energy   A measure of trophic-level transfer efficiency in which rates of energy production are used rather than biomass.

pyramid of numbers   An expression of trophic-level transfer efficiency in which the number of individuals decreases at each trophic level, with a huge number of individuals at the base and fewer individuals at the top.

pyrimidine   The bases thymine (T), cytosine (C), and uracil (U) with a single ring of carbon and nitrogen atoms.

Q

quadrat   A sampling device used by plant ecologists consisting of a square frame that often encloses 0.25 m^2.

quantitative trait   A trait that shows continuous variation over a range of phenotypes.

quaternary structure   The association of two or more polypeptides to form a protein; one of four levels of protein structure.

quorum sensing   A mechanism by which prokaryotic cells are able to communicate by chemical means when they reach a critical population size.

R

radial cleavage   A mechanism of animal development in which the cleavage planes are either parallel or perpendicular to the vertical axis of the embryo.

radial loop domain   A loop of chromatin, often 25,000 to 200,000 base pairs in size, that is anchored to the nuclear matrix.

radial pattern   A characteristic of the body pattern of plants.

radial symmetry   1. In plants, an architectural feature in which embryos display a cylindrical shape, which is retained in the stems and roots of seedlings and mature plants. In addition, new leaves or flower parts are produced in circular whorls, or spirals, around shoot tips. 2. In animals, an architectural feature in which the body can be divided into symmetrical halves by many different longitudinal planes along a central axis.

Radiata   Radially symmetric animals; includes cnidarians and ctenophores.

radiation   The emission of electromagnetic waves by the surfaces of objects; a method of heat exchange in animals.

radicle   An embryonic root, which extends from the plant hypocotyl.

radioisotope   An isotope found in nature that is inherently unstable and usually does not exist for long periods of time. Such isotopes decay and emit energy in the form of radiation.

radioisotope dating   A common way to estimate the age of a fossil by analyzing the elemental isotopes within the accompanying rock.

radula   A unique, protrusible, tonguelike organ in a mollusk that has many teeth and is used to eat plants, scrape food particles off of rocks, or bore into shells of other species.

rain shadow   An area on the side of a mountain that is sheltered from the wind and experiences less precipitation.

ram ventilation   A mechanism used by fishes to ventilate their gills; fishes swim or face upstream with their mouths open, allowing water to enter into their buccal cavity and across their gills.

random   The rarest pattern of dispersion within a population, in which the location of individuals lacks a pattern.

random sampling error   The deviation between the observed and the expected outcomes.

rate-limiting step   The slowest step in a pathway.

ray-finned fishes   The Actinopterygii, which includes all bony fishes except the coelacanths and lungfishes.

reabsorption   In the production of urine, the process in which useful solutes in the filtrate are recaptured and transported back into the body fluids of an animal.

reactant   A substance that participates in a chemical reaction and becomes changed by that reaction.

reading frame   Refers to the way in which codons are read during translation, in groups of three bases beginning with the start codon.

receptacle   The enlarged region at the tip of a flower peduncle to which flower parts are attached.

receptor   1. A cellular protein that recognizes a signaling molecule. 2. A structure capable of detecting changes in the environment of an animal, such as a touch receptor.

receptor-mediated endocytosis   A common form of endocytosis in which a receptor is specific for a given cargo.

GLOSSARY

receptor potential The membrane potential in a sensory receptor cell of an animal.

receptor tyrosine kinase A type of enzyme-linked receptor found in animal cells that can attach phosphate groups onto tyrosines that are found in the receptor itself or in other cellular proteins.

recessive A term that describes a trait that is masked by the presence of a dominant trait in a heterozygote.

reciprocal translocation A type of mutation in which two different types of chromosomes exchange pieces, thereby producing two abnormal chromosomes carrying translocations.

recombinant An offspring that has a different combination of traits from the parental generation.

recombinant DNA technology The use of laboratory techniques to isolate and manipulate fragments of DNA.

recombinant vector A vector containing a piece of chromosomal DNA.

recombination frequency The frequency of crossing over between two genes.

red blood cell *See* erythrocyte.

redox reaction A type of reaction in which an electron that is removed during the oxidation of an atom or molecule is transferred to another atom or molecule, which becomes reduced; short for a reduction-oxidation reaction.

reduction A process that involves the addition of electrons to an atom or molecule.

reductionism An approach that involves reducing complex systems to simpler components as a way to understand how the system works. In biology, reductionists study the parts of a cell or organism as individual units.

redundancy hypothesis A biodiversity proposal that is an alternative to the rivet hypothesis. In this model, most species are said to be redundant because they could simply be eliminated or replaced by others with no effect.

reflex arc A simple circuit that allows an organism to respond rapidly to inputs from sensory neurons and consists of only a few neurons.

regeneration A form of asexual reproduction in which a complete organism forms from small fragments of its body.

regulatory element In eukaryotes, a DNA sequence that is recognized by regulatory transcription factors and regulates the expression of genes.

regulatory gene A gene whose function is to regulate the expression of other genes.

regulatory sequence In the regulation of transcription, a DNA sequence that functions as a binding site for genetic regulatory proteins. Regulatory sequences control whether a gene is turned on or off.

regulatory transcription factor A protein that binds to DNA in the vicinity of a promoter and affects the rate of transcription of one or more nearby genes.

relative abundance The frequency of occurrence of species in a community.

relative refractory period The period near the end of an action potential when voltage-gated potassium channels are still open; during this time a new action potential can be generated if a stimulus is sufficiently strong to raise the membrane potential to threshold.

relative water content (RWC) The property often used to gauge the water content of a plant organ or entire plant; RWC integrates the water potential of all cells within an organ or plant and is thus a measure of relative turgidity.

release factor A protein that recognizes a stop codon in the termination stage of translation and promotes the termination of translation.

renal corpuscle A filtering component in the nephron of the kidney.

repetitive sequence Short DNA sequences that are present in many copies in a genome.

replica plating A technique in which a replica of bacterial colonies is transferred from one petri plate to a new petri plate.

replication 1. The copying of DNA strands. 2. The performing of experiments several or many times.

replication fork The area where two DNA strands have separated and new strands are being synthesized.

repressible operon In this type of operon, a small effector molecule inhibits transcription.

repressor A transcription factor that binds to DNA and inhibits transcription.

reproduce To generate offspring by sexual or asexual means.

reproductive cloning The cloning of a multicellular organism, such as a plant or animal.

reproductive isolating mechanisms Mechanisms that prevent interbreeding between different species.

reproductive isolation Refers to the concept that a species cannot successfully interbreed with other species.

reproductive success The likelihood of contributing fertile offspring to the next generation.

resistance (R) The tendency of blood vessels to slow down the flow of blood through their lumens.

resistance gene (R gene) A plant gene that has evolved as part of a defense system in response to pathogen attack.

resolution In microscopy, the ability to observe two adjacent objects as distinct from one another; a measure of the clarity of an image.

resonance energy transfer The process by which energy (not an electron itself) can be transferred to adjacent pigment molecules during photosynthesis.

resource partitioning The differentiation of niches, both in space and time, that enables similar species to coexist in a community.

respiration Metabolic reactions that a cell uses to get energy from food molecules and release waste products.

respiratory centers Several regions of the brainstem in vertebrates that initiate expansion of the lungs.

respiratory chain *See* electron transport chain.

respiratory distress syndrome of the newborn The situation in which a human baby is born prematurely, before sufficient surfactant is produced in the lungs, causing the collapse of many alveoli.

respiratory pigment A large protein that contains one or more metal atoms that bind to oxygen.

respiratory system All components of the body that contribute to the exchange of gas between the external environment and the blood; in mammals, includes the nose, mouth, airways, and lungs and the muscles and connective tissues that encase these structures within the thoracic (chest) cavity.

resting potential The difference in charges across the plasma membrane in an unstimulated neuron.

restoration ecology The full or partial repair or replacement of biological habitats and/or their populations that have been damaged.

rest-or-digest The response of vertebrates to situations associated with nonstressful states, such as feeding; mediated by the parasympathetic branch of the autonomic nervous system.

restriction enzyme An enzyme that recognizes particular DNA sequences and cleaves the DNA backbone at two sites.

restriction point A point in the cell cycle in which a cell has become committed to divide.

restriction sites The base sequences recognized by restriction enzymes.

reticular formation An array of nuclei in the brainstem of vertebrates that plays a major role in controlling states such as sleep and arousal.

retina A sheetlike layer of photoreceptors at the back of the vertebrate eye.

retinal A derivative of vitamin A that is capable of absorbing light energy; a component of visual pigments in the vertebrate eye.

retroelement A type of transposable element that moves via an RNA intermediate.

retrovirus An RNA virus that utilizes reverse transcription to produce viral DNA that can be integrated into the host cell genome.

reverse transcriptase A viral enzyme that catalyzes the synthesis of viral DNA starting with viral RNA as a template.

rhizobia The collective term for proteobacteria involved in nitrogen-fixation symbioses with plants.

rhodopsin The visual pigment in the rods of the vertebrate eye.

ribonucleic acid (RNA) One of two classes of nucleic acids; the other is deoxyribonucleic acid (DNA). RNA consists of a single strand of nucleotides.

ribonucleoprotein A complex between an RNA molecule and a protein.

ribose A five-carbon sugar found in RNA.

ribosomal RNA (rRNA) An RNA that forms part of ribosomes, which provide the site where translation occurs.

ribosome A structure composed of proteins and rRNA that provides the site where polypeptide synthesis occurs.

ribozyme A biological catalyst that is an RNA molecule.

rickets A condition in children characterized by bone deformations due to inadequate mineral intake or malabsorption in the intestines.

right-left axis In bilateral animals, one of the three axes along which the adult body pattern is organized; the others are the dorsoventral axis and the anteroposterior axis.

ring canal A central disc in the water vascular system of echinoderms.

rivet hypothesis An alternative to the diversity-stability hypothesis of biodiversity. In this model, species are like the rivets on an airplane, with each species playing a small but critical role in keeping the plane (the ecosystem) airborne.

RNA *See* ribonucleic acid.

RNA-induced silencing complex (RISC) A complex consisting of miRNA or siRNA and proteins; mediates RNA interference.

RNA interference (RNAi) Refers to a type of mRNA silencing; miRNA or siRNA interferes with the proper expression of an mRNA.

RNA polymerase The enzyme that synthesizes strands of RNA during gene transcription.

RNA processing A step in gene expression between transcription and translation in eukaryotes; the RNA transcript, termed pre-mRNA, is modified in ways that make it a functionally active mRNA.

RNase   An enzyme that digests RNA.

RNA world   A hypothetical period on primitive Earth when both the information needed for life and the enzymatic activity of living cells were contained solely in RNA molecules.

rods   Photoreceptors found in the vertebrate eye; they are very sensitive to low-intensity light but do not readily discriminate different colors. Rods are utilized mostly at night, and they send signals to the brain that generate a black-and-white visual image.

"roid" rage   Extremely aggressive behavior brought about by androgen administration.

root   A plant organ that provides anchorage in the soil and also fosters efficient uptake of water and minerals.

root apical meristem (RAM)   The region of rapidly dividing cells at plant root tips.

root hair   A specialized, long, thin root epidermal cell that functions to absorb water and minerals, usually from soil.

root meristem   The collection of cells at the root tip that generate all of the tissues of a plant root.

root pressure   Osmotic pressure within roots that causes water to rise for some distance through a plant stem, under conditions of high soil moisture or low transpiration.

root-shoot axis   The general body pattern of plants in which the root grows downward and the shoot grows upward.

root system   The collection of roots and root branches produced by root apical meristems.

rough endoplasmic reticulum (rough ER)   The part of the ER that is studded with ribosomes; this region plays a key role in the initial synthesis and sorting of proteins that are destined for the ER, Golgi apparatus, lysosomes, vacuoles, plasma membrane, or outside of the cell.

rRNA   *See* ribosomal RNA.

***r*-selected species**   A type of life history strategy, where species have a high rate of per capita population growth but poor competitive ability.

rubisco   The enzyme that catalyzes the first step in the Calvin cycle in which CO_2 is incorporated into an organic molecule.

Ruffini corpuscle   Tactile (touch) receptors in the skin of mammals that respond to deep pressure and vibration.

ruminants   Animals such as sheep, goats, llamas, and cows that have complex stomachs consisting of several chambers.

S

saltatory conduction   The conduction of an action potential along an axon in which the action potential is regenerated at each node of Ranvier instead of along the entire length of the axon.

sarcoma   A tumor of connective tissue such as bone or cartilage.

sarcomere   One complete unit of the repeating pattern of thick and thin filaments within a myofibril.

sarcoplasmic reticulum   A cellular organelle that provides a muscle fiber's source of the calcium involved in muscle contraction; a specialized form of the endoplasmic reticulum.

satiety   A feeling of fullness.

satiety signal   A response to eating that removes the sensation of hunger and sets the time period before hunger returns again.

saturated fatty acid   A fatty acid in which all the carbons are linked by single covalent bonds.

scanning electron microscopy (SEM)   A type of microscopy that utilizes an electron beam to produce an image of the three-dimensional surface of biological samples.

scavenger   An animal that eats the remains of dead animals.

Schwann cells   The glial cells that form myelin on axons that travel outside the brain and spinal cord.

science   In biology, the observation, identification, experimental investigation, and theoretical explanation of natural phenomena.

scientific method   A series of steps to test the validity of a hypothesis. This approach often involves a comparison between control and experimental groups.

sclera   The white of the vertebrate eye; a strong outer sheath that in the front is continuous with a thin, clear layer known as the cornea.

sclereid   Star- or stone-shaped plant cells having tough, lignified cell walls.

sclerenchyma tissue   A rigid plant ground tissue composed of tough-walled fibers and sclereids.

secondary active transport   A type of membrane transport that involves the utilization of a pre-existing gradient to drive the active transport of another solute.

secondary cell wall   A thick rigid plant cell wall that is synthesized and deposited between the plasma membrane and the primary cell wall after a plant cell matures and has stopped increasing in size.

secondary consumer   An organism that eats primary consumers; also called a carnivore.

secondary endosymbiosis   A process that occurs when a eukaryotic host cell acquires a eukaryotic endosymbiont having a primary plastid.

secondary growth   Plant growth that occurs from secondary meristems and increases the girth of woody plant stems and roots.

secondary immune response   An immediate and heightened production of additional specific antibodies against the particular antigen that previously elicited a primary immune response.

secondary meristem   A meristem in woody plants forming a ring of actively dividing cells that encircle the stem.

secondary metabolism   The synthesis of chemicals that are not essential for cell structure and growth and are usually not required for cell survival but are advantageous to the organism.

secondary metabolite   Molecules that are produced by secondary metabolism.

secondary oocyte   In animals, the large haploid cell that is produced when a primary oocyte undergoes meiosis I during oogenesis.

secondary phloem   The inner bark of a woody plant.

secondary plastid   A plastid that has originated by the endosymbiotic incorporation of a eukaryotic cell containing a primary plastid into a eukaryotic host cell.

secondary production   The measure of production of heterotrophs and decomposers.

secondary spermatocytes   In animals, the haploid cells produced when a primary spermatocyte undergoes meiosis I during spermatogenesis.

secondary structure   The bending or twisting of proteins into α helices or β sheets; one of four levels of protein structure.

secondary succession   Succession on a site that has previously supported life but has undergone a disturbance.

secondary xylem   In plants, a type of secondary vascular tissue that is also known as wood.

second law of thermodynamics   States that the transfer of energy or the transformation of energy from one form to another increases the entropy, or degree of disorder, of a system.

second messengers   Small molecules or ions that relay signals inside the cell.

secretion   1. The export of a substance from a cell. 2. In the production of urine, the process in which some solutes are actively transported into the tubules of the excretory organ; this supplements the amount of a solute that would normally be removed by filtration alone.

secretory pathway   A pathway for the movement of larger substances, such as carbohydrates and proteins, out of a cell.

secretory vesicle   A membrane vesicle carrying different types of materials that fuses with the cell's plasma membrane to release the contents extracellularly.

seed   A reproductive structure having specialized tissues that enclose plant embryos; produced by gymnosperms and flowering plants, usually as the result of sexual reproduction.

seed coat   A hard and tough covering that develops from the ovule's integuments and protects a plant embryo.

seed plant   The informal name for gymnosperms and angiosperms.

segmentation   The division of an animal's body into clearly defined regions.

segmentation gene   A gene that controls the segmentation pattern of an animal embryo.

segment-polarity gene   A type of segmentation gene; a mutation in this gene causes portions of segments to be missing either an anterior or a posterior region and for adjacent regions to become mirror images of each other.

segregate   To separate, as in chromosomes during mitosis.

selectable marker   A gene whose presence can allow organisms (such as bacteria) to grow under a certain set of conditions. For example, an antibiotic-resistance gene is a selectable marker that allows bacteria to grow in the presence of the antibiotic.

selective breeding   Programs and procedures designed to modify traits in domesticated species.

selectively permeable   The property of membranes that allows the passage of certain ions or molecules but not others.

selective serotonin reuptake inhibitors   Drugs used to treat major depressive disorder that act by increasing concentrations of serotonin in the brain.

self-fertilization   Fertilization that involves the union of a female gamete and male gamete from the same individual.

self-incompatibility (SI)   Rejection of pollen that is genetically too similar to the pistil of a plant.

selfish DNA hypothesis   The hypothesis that transposable elements exist because they have the characteristics that allow them to insert themselves into the host cell DNA but do not provide any advantage.

self-pollination   The process in which pollen from the anthers of a flower is transferred to the stigma of the same flower or between flowers of the same plant.

self-splicing   The phenomenon that RNA itself can catalyze the removal of its own intron(s); occurs in rRNA and tRNA.

SEM   *See* scanning electron microscopy.

semelparity   A reproductive pattern in which organisms produce all of their offspring in a single reproductive event.

semen   A mixture containing fluid and sperm that is released during ejaculation.

semicircular canals Structures of the vertebrate ear that can detect circular motions of the head.

semiconservative mechanism The correct model for DNA replication; double-stranded DNA is half conserved following replication, resulting in new double-stranded DNA containing one parental strand and one daughter strand.

semifluid A quality of motion within biomembranes; considered two-dimensional because movement occurs only within the plane of the membrane.

semilunar valves One-way valves into the systemic and pulmonary arteries through which blood is pumped from the ventricles.

seminal vesicles Paired accessory glands in the male reproductive system that secrete fructose, the main nutrient for sperm, into the urethra.

seminiferous tubule A tightly packed tubule in the testis, where spermatogenesis takes place.

senescent Cells that have doubled many times and have reached a point where they have lost the capacity to divide any further.

sense A system in an animal that consists of sensory cells that respond to a specific type of chemical or physical stimulus and send signals to the central nervous system, where the signals are received and interpreted.

sensory neuron A neuron that detects or senses information from the outside world, such as light, sound, touch, and heat; sensory neurons also detect internal body conditions such as blood pressure and body temperature.

sensory receptor In animals, a specialized cell whose function is to receive sensory inputs.

sensory transduction The process by which incoming stimuli are converted into neural signals.

sepal A flower organ that occurs in a whorl located outside whorls of petals of eudicot plants.

septum (plural, **septa**) A cross wall; examples include the cross walls that divide the hyphae of most fungi into many small cells and the structure that separates the old and new chambers of a nautilus.

sere Each phase of succession in a community; also called a seral stage.

setae Chitinous bristles in the integument of many invertebrates.

set point The normal value for a controlled variable, such as blood pressure, in an animal.

sex chromosomes A distinctive pair of chromosomes that are different in males and females.

sex-influenced inheritance The phenomenon in which an allele is dominant in one sex but recessive in the other.

sex linked Refers to genes that are found on one sex chromosome but not on the other.

sex pili Hairlike structures made by bacterial F^+ cells that bind specifically to other F^- cells.

sexual dimorphism A pronounced difference in the morphologies of the two sexes within a species.

sexual reproduction A process that requires a fertilization event in which two gametes unite to produce a cell called a zygote.

sexual selection A type of natural selection that is directed at certain traits of sexually reproducing species that make it more likely for individuals to find or choose a mate and/or engage in successful mating.

Shannon diversity index (H_S) A means of measuring the diversity of a community; $H_S = -\Sigma p_i \ln p_i$.

shared derived character A trait that is shared by a group of organisms but not by a distant common ancestor.

shared primitive character A trait shared with a distant ancestor.

shattering The process by which ears of wild grain crops break apart and disperse seeds.

shell A tough, protective covering on an amniotic egg that is impermeable to water and prevents the embryo from drying out.

shivering thermogenesis Rapid muscle contractions in an animal, without any locomotion, in order to raise body temperature.

shoot The portion of a plant comprised of stems and leaves.

shoot apical meristem (SAM) The region of rapidly dividing plant cells at plant shoot apices.

shoot meristem The tissue that produces all aerial parts of the plant, which include the stems as well as lateral structures such as leaves and flowers.

shoot system The collection of plant organs produced by shoot apical meristems.

short-day plant A plant that flowers only when the night length is longer than a defined period.

short stature A condition characterized by stunted growth; formerly called pituitary dwarfism.

short tandem repeat sequences (STRs) Short sequences repeated many times in a row and found in multiple sites in the genome of humans and other species; often vary in length among different individuals.

shotgun DNA sequencing A strategy for sequencing an entire genome by randomly sequencing many different DNA fragments.

sickle-cell disease A disease due to a genetic mutation in a hemoglobin gene in which sickle-shaped red blood cells are less able to move smoothly through capillaries and can block blood flow, resulting in severe pain and cell death of the surrounding tissue.

sieve plate The perforated end wall of a mature sieve-tube element.

sieve plate pore One of many perforations in a plant's sieve plate.

sieve-tube elements A component of the phloem tissues of flowering plants; thin-walled cells arranged end to end to form transport pipes.

sigma factor A protein that plays a key role in bacterial promoter recognition and recruits RNA polymerase to the promoter.

signal Regarding cell communication, an incoming or outgoing agent that influences the properties of cells.

signal recognition particle (SRP) A protein/RNA complex that recognizes the ER signal sequence of a polypeptide, pauses translation, and directs the ribosome to the ER to complete translation.

signal transduction pathway A group of proteins that convert an initial signal to a different signal inside a cell.

sign stimulus In animals, a trigger that initiates a fixed-action pattern of behavior.

silencer A regulatory element in eukaryotes that prevents transcription of a given gene.

silencing RNAs (siRNAs) Small RNA molecules, typically 22 nucleotides in length, that silence the expression of specific mRNAs by promoting their degradation.

silent mutation A gene mutation that does not alter the amino acid sequence of the polypeptide, even though the nucleotide sequence has changed.

simple Mendelian inheritance The inheritance pattern of traits affected by a single gene that is found in two variants, one of which is completely dominant over the other.

simple translocation A type of mutation in which a single piece of chromosome is attached to another chromosome.

single-factor cross *See* monohybrid cross.

single nucleotide polymorphism (SNP) A type of genetic variation in a population in which a particular gene sequence varies at a single nucleotide.

single-strand binding protein A protein that binds to both of the single strands of parental DNA and prevents them from re-forming a double helix during DNA replication.

sinoatrial (SA) node A collection of modified cardiac cells in the right atrium of most vertebrates that spontaneously and rhythmically generates action potentials that spread across the entire atria; also known as the pacemaker of the heart.

siRNAS *See* silencing RNAs.

sister chromatids The two duplicated chromatids that are still joined to each other after DNA replication.

skeletal muscle A type of muscle tissue that is attached by tendons to bones in vertebrates and to the exoskeleton of invertebrates.

skeleton A structure or structures that serve one or more functions related to support, protection, and locomotion.

sliding filament mechanism The way in which a muscle fiber shortens during muscle contraction.

SLOSS debate In conservation biology, the debate over whether it is preferable to protect one single, large reserve or several smaller ones.

slow block to polyspermy Events initiated by the release of Ca^{2+} that produce barriers to more sperm penetrating an already fertilized egg.

slow fiber A skeletal muscle fiber containing myosin with a low rate of ATP hydrolysis.

slow-oxidative fiber A skeletal muscle fiber that has a low rate of myosin ATP hydrolysis but has the ability to make large amounts of ATP; used for prolonged, regular activity.

small effector molecule With regard to transcription, refers to a molecule that exerts its effects by binding to a regulatory transcription factor, causing a conformational change in the protein.

small intestine In vertebrates, a tube that leads from the stomach to the large intestine where nearly all digestion of food and absorption of food nutrients and water occur.

smooth endoplasmic reticulum (smooth ER) The part of the ER that is not studded with ribosomes. This region is continuous with the rough ER and functions in diverse metabolic processes such as detoxification, carbohydrate metabolism, accumulation of calcium ions, and synthesis and modification of lipids.

smooth muscle A type of muscle tissue that surrounds hollow tubes and cavities inside the body's organs; it is not under conscious control.

soil horizon Layers of soil, ranging from topsoil to bedrock.

solute A substance dissolved in a liquid.

solute potential (S) The component of water potential due to the presence of solute molecules.

solution A liquid that contains one or more dissolved solutes.

solvent The liquid in which a solute is dissolved.

soma *See* cell body.

somatic cell The type of cell that constitutes all cells of an animal or plant body except those that give rise to gametes.

somatic embryogenesis The production of plant embryos from body (somatic) cells.

somatic nervous system The division of the peripheral nervous system that senses the external environmental conditions and controls skeletal muscles.

somites Blocklike structures resulting from the segmentation of mesoderm during neurulation.

soredia An asexual reproductive structure produced by lichens consisting of small clumps of hyphae surrounding a few algal cells that can disperse in wind currents.

sorting signal A short amino acid sequence in a protein that directs the protein to its correct location; also known as a traffic signal.

source pool The pool of species on the mainland that is available to colonize an island.

spatial summation Occurs when two or more postsynaptic potentials are generated at one time along different regions of the dendrites and their depolarizations and hyperpolarizations sum together.

speciation The formation of new species.

species A group of related organisms that share a distinctive form in nature and (for sexually reproducing species) are capable of interbreeding.

species-area effect The relationship between the amount of available area and the number of species present.

species concepts Different approaches for distinguishing species.

species diversity A measure of biological diversity that incorporates both the number of species in an area and the relative distribution of individuals among species.

species interactions A part of the study of population ecology that focuses on interactions such as predation, competition, parasitism, mutualism, and commensalism.

species richness The numbers of species in a community.

specific heat The amount of energy required to raise the temperature of 1 gram of a substance by 1°C.

specific (acquired) immunity An immunity defense that develops only after the body is exposed to foreign substances; believed to be unique to vertebrates.

specificity Refers to the concept that enzymes recognize specific substrates.

Spemann's organizer An extremely important morphogenetic field in the early gastrula; the organizer secretes morphogens responsible for inducing the formation of a new embryonic axis.

spermatids In animals, the haploid cells produced when the secondary spermatocytes undergo meiosis II; these cells eventually differentiate into sperm cells.

spermatogenesis Gametogenesis in a male animal resulting in the production of sperm.

spermatogonia (singular, **spermatogonium**) In animals, diploid germ cells that give rise to the male gametes, the spermatozoa.

spermatophytes All of the living and fossil seed plant phyla.

sperm cell Refers to a male gamete that is generally smaller than the female gamete (egg); also called a sperm.

sperm storage A method of synchronizing the production of offspring with favorable environmental conditions in which female animals store and nourish sperm in their reproductive tract for long periods of time.

S phase The DNA synthesis phase of the cell cycle.

spicules Needle-like structures that are usually made of silica and form lattice-like skeletons in sponges, possibly helping to reduce predation.

spinal cord In chordates, the structure that connects the brain to all areas of the body and together with the brain constitutes the central nervous system.

spinal nerve A nerve that connects the peripheral nervous system and the spinal cord.

spiracle A pore on the body surface of insects that leads to the trachea.

spiral cleavage A mechanism of animal development in which the planes of cell cleavage are oblique to the axis of the embryo.

spirilli Rigid, spiral-shaped prokaryotic cells.

spirochaetes Flexible, spiral-shaped prokaryotic cells.

spliceosome A complex of several subunits known as snRNPs that removes introns from eukaryotic pre-mRNA.

splicing The process whereby introns are removed from RNA and the remaining exons are connected to each other.

spongin A tough protein that lends skeletal support to a sponge.

spongocoel A central cavity in the body of a sponge.

spongy parenchyma Photosynthetic ground tissue of the plant leaf mesophyll that contains round cells separated by abundant air spaces.

spontaneous mutation A mutation resulting from abnormalities in biological processes.

sporangia Structures that produce and disperse the spores of plants, fungi, or protists.

spore A haploid, typically single-celled reproductive structure of fungi and plants that is dispersed into the environment and is able to grow into a new fungal mycelium or plant gametophyte in a suitable habitat.

sporic life cycle *See* alternation of generations.

sporophyte The diploid generation of plants or multicellular protists that have a sporic life cycle; this generation produces haploid spores by the process of meiosis.

sporopollenin The tough material that composes much of the walls of plant spores and helps to prevent cellular damage during transport in air.

stabilizing selection A pattern of natural selection that favors the survival of individuals with intermediate phenotypes.

stamen A flower organ that produces the male gametophyte, pollen.

standard metabolic rate (SMR) The metabolic rate of ectotherms measured at a standard temperature for each species—one that approximates the average temperature that a species normally encounters.

standing crop The total biomass in an ecosystem at any one point in time.

starch A polysaccharide composed of repeating glucose units that is produced by the cells of plants and some algal protists.

start codon A three-base sequence—usually AUG—that specifies the first amino acid in a polypeptide.

statocyst An organ of equilibrium found in many invertebrate species.

statoliths 1. Tiny granules of sand or other dense objects located in a statocyst that aid equilibrium in many invertebrates. 2. In plants, a starch-heavy plastid that allows both roots and shoots to detect gravity.

stem A plant organ that produces buds, leaves, branches, and reproductive structures.

stem cell A cell that divides so that one daughter cell remains a stem cell and the other can differentiate into a specialized cell type. Stem cells construct the bodies of all animals and plants.

stereocilia Deformable projections from epithelial cells called hair cells that are bent by movements of fluid or other stimuli.

stereoisomers Isomers with identical bonding relationships, but different spatial positioning of their atoms.

sternum The breastbone of a vertebrate.

steroid A lipid containing four interconnected rings of carbon atoms; functions as a hormone in animals and plants.

steroid receptor A transcription factor that recognizes a steroid hormone and usually functions as a transcriptional activator.

sticky ends Single-stranded ends of DNA fragments that will hydrogen-bond to each other due to their complementary sequences.

stigma In a flower, the topmost portion of the pistil, which receives and recognizes pollen of the appropriate species or genotype.

stomach A saclike organ in some animals that most likely evolved as a means of storing food; it partially digests some of the macromolecules in food and regulates the rate at which the contents empty into the small intestine.

stomata Surface pores on plant surfaces that can be closed to retain water or open to allow the entry of CO_2 needed for photosynthesis and the exit of oxygen and water vapor.

stop codon One of three three-base sequences— UAA, UAG, and UGA—that signals the end of translation; also called termination codon or nonsense codon.

strain Within a given species, a lineage that has genetic differences compared to another lineage.

strand A structure of DNA (or RNA) formed by the covalent linkage of nucleotides in a linear manner.

strepsirrhini Smaller species of primates; includes bush babies, lemurs, and pottos.

stretch receptor A type of mechanoreceptor found widely in an animal's organs and muscle tissues that can be distended.

striated muscle Skeletal and cardiac muscle with a series of light and dark bands perpendicular to the muscle's long axis.

stroke The condition that occurs when blood flow to part of the brain is disrupted.

stroke volume (SV) The amount of blood ejected with each beat, or stroke, of the heart.

stroma The fluid-filled region of the chloroplast between the thylakoid membrane and the inner membrane.

stromatolite A layered calcium carbonate structure in an aquatic environment generally produced by cyanobacteria.

strong acid An acid that completely ionizes in solution.

structural gene Refers to most genes, which produce an mRNA molecule that contains the information to specify a polypeptide with a particular amino acid sequence.

structural isomers Isomers that contain the same atoms but in different bonding relationships.

style In a flower, the elongate portion of the pistil through which the pollen tube grows.

stylet A sharp, piercing organ in the mouth of nematodes and some insects.

submetacentric A chromosome in which the centromere is off center.

subsidence zones Areas of high pressure that are the sites of the world's tropical deserts because the subsiding air is relatively dry, having released all of its moisture over the equator.

subspecies A subdivision of a species; this designation is used when two or more geographically restricted groups of the same species differ, but not enough to warrant their placement into separate species.

substrate 1. The reactant molecules and/or ions that bind to an enzyme at the active site and participate in a chemical reaction. 2. The organic compounds such as soil or rotting wood that fungi use as food.

substrate-level phosphorylation   A method of synthesizing ATP that occurs when an enzyme directly transfers a phosphate from an organic molecule to ADP.

succession   The gradual and continuous change in species composition and community structure over time.

sugar sink   The plant tissues or organs in which more sugar is consumed than is produced by photosynthesis.

sugar source   The plant tissues or organs that produce more sugar than they consume in respiration.

sum rule   The probability that one of two or more mutually exclusive outcomes will occur is the sum of the probabilities of the possible outcomes.

supergroup   One of the seven subdivisions of the domain Eukarya.

surface area/volume (SA/V) ratio   The ratio between a structure's surface area and the volume in which the structure is contained.

surface tension   A measure of how difficult it is to break the interface between a liquid and air.

surfactant   A mixture of proteins and amphipathic lipids produced in certain alveolar cells that prevents the collapse of alveoli by reducing surface tension in the lungs.

survivorship curve   A graphical plot of the numbers of surviving individuals at each age in a population.

suspension feeder   An aquatic animal that sifts water, filtering out the organic matter and expelling the rest.

suspensor   A short chain of cells at the base of an early angiosperm embryo that provides anchorage and nutrients.

swim bladder   A gas-filled, balloon-like structure that helps a fish to remain buoyant in the water even when the fish is completely stationary.

symbiosis   An intimate association between two or more organisms of different species.

symbiotic   Describes a relationship in which two or more different species live in direct contact with each other.

sympathetic division   The division of the autonomic nervous system that is responsible for rapidly activating body systems to provide immediate energy in response to danger or stress.

sympatric   The term used to describe species occurring in the same geographic area.

sympatric speciation   A form of speciation that occurs when members of a species that initially occupy the same habitat within the same range diverge into two or more different species.

symplast   All of a plant's protoplasts (the cell contents without the cell walls) and plasmodesmata.

symplastic transport   The movement of a substance from the cytosol of one cell to the cytosol of an adjacent cell via membrane-lined channels called plasmodesmata.

symplesiomorphy   *See* shared primitive character.

symporter   A type of transporter that binds two or more ions or molecules and transports them in the same direction across a membrane; also called a cotransporter.

synapomorphy   *See* shared derived character.

synapse   A junction where a nerve terminal meets a target neuron, muscle cell, or gland and through which an electrical or chemical signal passes.

synapsis   The process of forming a bivalent.

synaptic cleft   The extracellular space between a neuron and its target cell.

synaptic plasticity   The formation of additional synaptic connections that occurs as a result of learning.

synaptic signaling   A specialized form of paracrine signaling that occurs in the nervous system of animals.

synergids   In the female gametophyte of a flowering plant, the two cells adjacent to the egg cell that help to import nutrients from maternal sporophyte tissues.

syntrophy   The phenomenon in which one species lives off the products of another species.

systematics   The study of biological diversity and evolutionary relationships among organisms, both extinct and modern.

systemic acquired resistance (SAR)   A whole-plant defensive response to pathogenic microorganisms.

systemic circulation   The pumping of blood from the left side of an animal's heart to the body to drop off oxygen and nutrients and pick up carbon dioxide and wastes. The blood then returns to the right side of the heart.

systemic hypertension   An arterial blood pressure above normal; in humans, normal blood pressure ranges from systolic/diastolic pressures of about 90/60 to 120/80 mmHg; often called hypertension or high blood pressure.

systems biology   A field of study in which researchers investigate living organisms in terms of their underlying networks—groups of structural and functional connections—rather than their individual molecular components.

systole   The second phase of the cardiac cycle, in which the ventricles contract and eject the blood through the open semilunar valves.

T

tagmata   The fusion of body segments into functional units.

taproot system   The root system of eudicots, consisting of one main root with many branch roots.

taste buds   Structures located in the mouth and tongue of vertebrates that contain the sensory cells, supporting cells, and associated neuronal endings that contribute to taste sensation.

TATA box   One of three features found in most eukaryotic promoters; the others are the transcriptional start site and regulatory elements.

taxis   A directed type of response to a stimulus that is either toward or away from the stimulus.

taxon   A group of species that are evolutionarily related to each other. In taxonomy, each species is placed into several taxons that form a hierarchy from large (domain) to small (genus).

taxonomy   The field of biology that is concerned with the theory, practice, and rules of classifying living and extinct organisms and viruses.

T cell   A type of lymphocyte that directly kills infected, mutated, or transplanted cells.

telocentric   A chromosome in which the centromere is at the end.

telomerase   An enzyme that catalyzes the replication of the telomere.

telomere   A region at the ends of eukaryotic chromosomes where a specialized form of DNA replication occurs.

telophase   The phase of mitosis during which the chromosomes decondense and the nuclear membrane re-forms.

TEM   *See* transmission electron microscopy.

temperate phage   A bacteriophage that may spend some of its time in the lysogenic cycle.

template strand   The DNA strand that is used as a template for RNA synthesis or DNA replication.

temporal lobe   One of four lobes of the cerebral cortex of human brain; necessary for language, hearing, and some types of memory.

temporal summation   Occurs when two or more postsynaptic potentials arrive at the same location in a dendrite in quick succession and their depolarizations and hyperpolarizations sum together.

tepal   A flower perianth part that cannot be distinguished by appearance as a petal or a sepal.

termination codon   *See* stop codon.

termination stage   The final stage of transcription or translation in which the process ends.

terminator   A sequence that specifies the end of transcription.

terpenoids   A group of secondary metabolites synthesized from five-carbon isoprene units. An example is β-carotene, which gives carrots their orange color.

territory   A fixed area in which an individual or group excludes other members of its own species, and sometimes other species, by aggressive behavior or territory marking.

tertiary consumer   An organism that feeds on secondary consumers.

tertiary endosymbiosis   The acquisition by eukaryotic protist host cells of plastids from cells that possess secondary plastids.

tertiary plastid   A plastid acquired by the incorporation into a host cell of an endosymbiont having a secondary plastid.

tertiary structure   The three-dimensional shape of a single polypeptide; one of four levels of protein structure.

testcross   A cross to determine if an individual with a dominant phenotype is a homozygote or a heterozygote. Also, a cross to determine if two different genes are linked.

testes (singular, **testis**)   In animals, the male gonads, where sperm are produced.

testosterone   The primary androgen in many vertebrates, including humans.

tetrad   *See* bivalent.

tetraploid   An organism or cell that has four sets of chromosomes.

tetrapod   A vertebrate animal having four legs or leglike appendages.

thalamus   A region of the vertebrate forebrain that plays a major role in relaying sensory information to appropriate parts of the cerebrum and, in turn, sending outputs from the cerebrum to other parts of the brain.

theory   In biology, a broad explanation of some aspect of the natural world that is substantiated by a large body of evidence. Biological theories incorporate observations, hypothesis testing, and the laws of other disciplines such as chemistry and physics. A theory makes valid predictions.

thermodynamics   The study of energy interconversions.

thermoreceptor   A sensory receptor in animals that responds to cold and heat.

theropods   A group of bipedal saurischian dinosaurs.

thick filament   A section of the repeating pattern in a myofibril composed almost entirely of the motor protein myosin.

thigmotropism   Touch responses in plants.

thin filament   A section of the repeating pattern in a myofibril that contains the cytoskeletal protein actin, as well as two other proteins—troponin and tropomyosin—that play important roles in regulating contraction.

30-nm fiber   Nucleosome units organized into a more compact structure that is 30 nm in diameter.

thoracic breathing   Breathing in which coordinated contractions of muscles expand the rib cage, creating a negative pressure to suck air in and then forcing it out later; found in amniotes.

threatened species   Those species that are likely to become endangered in the future.

threshold concentration   The concentration above which a morphogen will exert its effects but below which it is ineffective.

threshold potential   The membrane potential, typically around $-50mV$, which is sufficient to trigger an action potential in an electrically excitable cell such as a neuron.

thrifty genes   Genes that boosted our ancestors' ability to store fat from each feast in order to sustain them through the next famine.

thrombocytes   Intact cells in the blood of vertebrates other than mammals that play a crucial role in the formation of blood clots; in mammals, cell fragments called platelets serve this function.

thylakoid   A flattened, platelike membranous region found in cyanobacterial cells and the chloroplasts of photosynthetic protists and plants; the location of the light reactions of photosynthesis.

thylakoid lumen   The fluid-filled compartment within the thylakoid.

thylakoid membrane   A membrane within the chloroplast that forms many flattened, fluid-filled tubules that enclose a single, convoluted compartment. It contains chlorophyll and is the site where the light-dependent reactions of photosynthesis occurs.

thymine (T)   A pyrimidine base found in DNA.

thymine dimer   In DNA, a type of pyrimidine dimer that can cause a mutation; a site where two adjacent thymine bases become covalently cross-linked to each other.

thyroglobulin   A protein found in the colloid of the thyroid gland that is involved in the formation of thyroid hormones.

thyroxine (T_4)   A weakly active thyroid hormone that contains iodine and helps regulate metabolic rate; it is converted by cells into the more active triiodothyronine (T_3).

tidal ventilation   A type of breathing in mammals in which the lungs are inflated with air and then the chest muscles and diaphragm relax and recoil back to their original positions as an animal exhales. During exhalation, air leaves via the same route that it entered during inhalation, and no new oxygen is delivered to the airways at that time.

tidal volume   The volume of air that is normally breathed in and out at rest.

tight junction   A type of junction between animal cells that forms a tight seal between adjacent epithelial cells and thereby prevents molecules from leaking between cells; also called an occluding junction.

Ti plasmid   Tumor-inducing plasmid found in *Agrobacterium tumefaciens*; it is used as a cloning vector to transfer genes into plant cells.

tissue   The association of many cells of the same type, for example, muscle tissue.

tolerance   A mechanism for succession in which any species can start the succession, but the eventual climax community is reached in a somewhat orderly fashion; early species neither facilitate nor inhibit subsequent colonists.

tonoplast   The membrane of the central vacuole in a plant or algal cell.

torpor   The strategy in endotherms of lowering internal body temperature to just a few degrees above that of the environment in order to conserve energy.

torus   The nonporous, flexible central region of a conifer pit that functions like a valve.

total fertility rate   The average number of live births a female has during her lifetime.

total peripheral resistance (TPR)   The sum of all the resistance in all arterioles.

totipotent   The ability of a fertilized egg to produce all of the cell types in the adult organism; also the ability of unspecialized plant cells to regenerate an adult plant.

toxins   Compounds that have adverse effects in living organisms; often produced by various protist and plant species.

trace element   An element that is essential for normal function in living organisms but is required in extremely small quantities.

trachea   1. A sturdy tube arising from the spiracles of an insect's body; involved in respiration. 2. The name of the tube leading to the lungs of air-breathing vertebrates.

tracheal system   The respiratory system of insects consisting of a series of finely branched air tubes called tracheae; air enters and exits the tracheae through spiracles, which are pores on the body surface.

tracheary elements   Water-conducting cells in plants that, when mature, are always dead and empty of cytosol; include tracheids and vessel elements.

tracheid   A type of dead, lignified plant cell in xylem that conducts water, along with dissolved minerals; also provides structural support.

tracheophytes   A term used to describe vascular plants.

tract   A parallel bundle of myelinated axons in the central nervous system.

traffic signal   *See* sorting signal.

trait   An identifiable characteristic; usually refers to a variant.

transcription   The use of a gene sequence to make a copy of RNA.

transcriptional start site   The site in a eukaryotic promoter where transcription begins.

transcription factor   A protein that influences the ability of RNA polymerase to transcribe genes.

transduction   A type of genetic transfer between bacteria in which a virus infects a bacterial cell and then subsequently transfers some of that cell's DNA to another bacterium.

***trans*-effect**   In both prokaryotes and eukaryotes, a form of genetic regulation that can occur even though two DNA segments are not physically adjacent. The action of the lac repressor on the *lac* operon is a *trans*-effect.

transepithelial transport   The process of moving solutes across an epithelium, such as in the gut of animals.

transfer RNA (tRNA)   An RNA that carries amino acids and is used to translate mRNA into polypeptides.

transformation   A type of genetic transfer between bacteria in which a segment of DNA from the environment is taken up by a competent cell and incorporated into the bacterial chromosome.

transgenic   The term used to describe an organism that carries genes that were introduced using molecular techniques such as gene cloning.

transitional form   An organism that provides a link between earlier and later forms in evolution.

transition state   In a chemical reaction, a state in which the original bonds have stretched to their limit; once this state is reached, the reaction can proceed to the formation of products.

translation   The process of synthesizing a specific polypeptide on a ribosome.

translocation   1. A type of mutation in which one segment of a chromosome becomes attached to a different chromosome. 2. A process in plants in which phloem transports substances from a source to a sink.

transmembrane gradient   A situation in which the concentration of a solute is higher on one side of a membrane than on the other.

transmembrane protein   A protein that has one or more regions that are physically embedded in the hydrophobic region of a cell membrane's phospholipid bilayer.

transmembrane segment   A region of a membrane protein that is a stretch of nonpolar amino acids that spans or traverses the membrane from one leaflet to the other.

transmembrane transport   The export of material from one cell into the intercellular space and then into an adjacent cell.

transmission electron microscopy (TEM)   A type of microscopy in which a beam of electrons is transmitted through a biological sample to form an image on a photographic plate or screen.

transpiration   The evaporative loss of water from plant surfaces into sun-heated air.

transporter   A membrane protein that binds a solute and undergoes a conformational change to allow the movement of the solute across a membrane; also called a carrier.

transport protein   Proteins embedded within the phospholipid bilayer that allow plasma membranes to be selectively permeable by providing a passageway for the movement of some but not all substances across the membrane.

transposable element (TE)   A segment of DNA that can move from one site to another.

transposase   An enzyme that facilitates transposition.

transposition   The process in which a short segment of DNA moves within a cell from its original site to a new site in the genome.

transverse tubules (T-tubules)   Invaginations of the plasma membrane of skeletal muscle cells that open to the extracellular fluid and conduct action potentials from the outer surface to the myofibrils.

triacylglycerol   *See* triglyceride.

trichome   A projection, often hairlike, from the epidermal tissue of a plant that offers protection from excessive light, ultraviolet radiation, extreme air temperature, or attack by herbivores.

triglyceride   A molecule composed of three fatty acids linked by ester bonds to a molecule of glycerol; also known as a triacylglycerol.

triiodothyronine (T_3)   A thyroid hormone that contains iodine and helps regulate metabolic rate.

triplet   A group of three bases that function as a codon.

triploblastic   Having three distinct germ layers—endoderm, ectoderm, and mesoderm.

triploid   An organism or cell that has three sets of chromosomes.

trisomic   An aneuploid organism that has one too many chromosomes.

tRNA   *See* transfer RNA.

trochophore larva   A distinct larval stage of many invertebrate phyla.

trophic level   Each feeding level in a food chain.

trophic-level transfer efficiency   The amount of energy at a trophic level that is acquired by the trophic level above and incorporated into biomass.

trophic mutualism   A mutually beneficial interaction between two species in which both species receive the benefit of resources.

tropism   In plants, a growth response that is dependent on a stimulus that occurs in a particular direction.

tropomyosin   A rod-shaped protein that plays an important role in regulating muscle contraction.

troponin   A small globular-shaped protein that plays an important role in regulating muscle contraction through its ability to bind Ca^{2+}.

***trp* operon**   An operon of *E. coli* that encodes enzymes required to make the amino acid tryptophan, a building block of cellular proteins.

true-breeding line   A strain that continues to exhibit the same trait after several generations of self-fertilization or inbreeding.

trypsin   A protease involved in the breakdown of proteins in the small intestine.

t-snare   A protein in a target membrane that recognizes a v-snare in a membrane vesicle.

tubal ligation   A means of contraception that involves the cutting and sealing of the fallopian tubes in a woman, thereby preventing movement of a fertilized egg into the uterus.

tube cell   In a seed plant, one of the cells resulting from the division of a microspore; stores proteins and forms the pollen tube.

tube feet   Echinoderm structures that function in movement, gas exchange, feeding, and excretion.

tumor   An abnormal overgrowth of cells.

tumor-suppressor gene   A gene that when normal (that is, not mutant) encodes a protein that prevents cancer; however, when a mutation eliminates its function, cancer may occur.

tunic   A nonliving structure that encloses a tunicate, made of protein and a cellulose-like material called tunicin.

turgid   The term used to describe a plant cell whose cytosol is so full of water that the plasma membrane presses right up against the cell wall; as a result, turgid cells are firm or swollen.

turgor pressure   *See* osmotic pressure.

20-hydroxyecdysone   A hormone produced by the prothoracic glands of arthropods that stimulates molting.

two-factor cross   *See* dihybrid cross.

type 1 diabetes mellitus (T1DM)   A disease in which the pancreas does not produce sufficient insulin; as a result, extracellular glucose cannot cross plasma membranes, and glucose accumulates to very high concentrations in the blood.

type 2 diabetes mellitus (T2DM)   A disease in which the pancreas produces sufficient insulin, but the cells of the body lose much of their ability to respond to insulin.

U

ubiquitin   A small protein in eukaryotic cells that directs unwanted proteins to a proteasome by its covalent attachment.

ultimate cause   The reason a particular behavior evolved, in terms of its effect on reproductive success.

umbrella species   A species whose habitat requirements are so large that protecting them would protect many other species existing in the same habitat.

unconditioned response   An action that is elicited by an unconditioned stimulus.

unconditioned stimulus   A trigger that elicits an original response.

uniform   A pattern of dispersion within a population in which individuals maintain a certain minimum distance between themselves to produce an evenly spaced distribution.

uniporter   A type of transporter that binds a single ion or molecule and transports it across a membrane.

unipotent   A term used to describe a stem cell found in the adult that can produce daughter cells that differentiate into only one cell type.

unsaturated   The quality of a lipid containing one or more C═C double bonds.

unsaturated fatty acid   A fatty acid that contains one or more C═C double bonds.

upwelling   In the ocean, a process that carries mineral nutrients from the bottom waters to the surface.

uracil (U)   A pyrimidine base found in RNA.

urea   A nitrogenous waste commonly produced in many terrestrial species, including mammals.

uremia   A condition characterized by the presence of nitrogenous wastes, such as urea, in the blood; typically results from kidney disease.

ureter   A structure in the mammalian urinary system through which urine flows from the kidney into the urinary bladder.

urethra   The structure in the mammalian urinary system through which urine is eliminated from the body.

uric acid   A nitrogenous waste produced by birds, insects, and reptiles.

urinary bladder   The structure in the mammalian urinary system that collects urine before it is eliminated.

urinary system   The structures that collectively act to filter blood or hemolymph and excrete wastes, while recapturing useful compounds.

urine   The part of the filtrate formed in the kidney that remains after all reabsorption of solutes and water is complete.

uterine cycle   *See* menstrual cycle.

uterus   A small, pear-shaped organ capable of enlarging and specialized for carrying a developing fetus in female mammals.

V

vaccination   The injection into the body of small quantities of weakened or dead pathogens, resulting in the development of immunity to those pathogens without causing disease.

vacuole   Specialized compartments found in eukaryotic cells that function in storage, the regulation of cell volume, and degradation.

vagina   The birth canal of female mammals; also functions to receive sperm during copulation.

vaginal diaphragm   A barrier method of preventing fertilization in which a diaphragm is placed in the upper part of the vagina just prior to intercourse; blocks movement of sperm to the cervix.

valence electron   An electron in the outer shell of an atom that is available to combine with other atoms. Such electrons allow atoms to form chemical bonds with each other.

van der Waals forces   Attractive forces between molecules in close proximity to each other, caused by the variations in the distribution of electron density around individual atoms.

variable region   A unique domain within an immunoglobulin that serves as the antigen-binding site.

vasa recta capillaries   Capillaries in the medulla in the nephron of the kidney.

vascular bundle   Primary plant vascular tissues that occur in a cluster.

vascular cambium   A secondary meristematic tissue of plants that produces both wood and inner bark.

vascular plant   A plant that contains vascular tissue. Includes all modern plant species except liverworts, hornworts, and mosses.

vascular tissue   Plant tissue that provides both structural support and conduction of water, minerals, and organic compounds.

vas deferens   A muscular tube through which sperm leave the epididymis.

vasectomy   A surgical procedure in men that severs the vas deferens, thereby preventing the release of sperm at ejaculation.

vasoconstriction   A decrease in blood vessel radius; an important mechanism for directing blood flow away from specific regions of the body.

vasodilation   An increase in blood vessel radius; an important mechanism for directing blood flow to specific regions of the body.

vasotocin   A peptide hormone that is responsible for regulating salt and water balance in the blood of nonmammalian vertebrates.

vector   A type of DNA that acts as a carrier of a DNA segment that is to be cloned.

vegetal pole   In triploblast organisms, the pole of the egg where the yolk is most concentrated.

vegetative growth   The production of new nonreproductive tissues by the shoot apical meristem and root apical meristem during seedling development and growth of mature plants.

vein   1. In animals, a blood vessel that returns blood to the heart. 2. In plants, a bundle of vascular tissue in a leaf.

veliger   In mollusks, a free-swimming larva that has a rudimentary foot, shell, and mantle.

ventilation   The process of bringing oxygenated water or air into contact with a respiratory surface such as gills or lungs.

ventral   Refers to the lower side of an animal.

ventricle   In the heart, a chamber that pumps blood out of the heart.

venule   A small, thin-walled extension of a capillary that empties into larger vessels called veins that return blood to the heart for another trip around the circulation.

vertebrae   A bony or cartilaginous column of interlocking structures that provides support and also protects the nerve cord, which lies within its tubelike structure.

vertebrate   An organism with a backbone.

vertical evolution   A process in which species evolve from pre-existing species by the accumulation of mutations.

vesicle   A small membrane-enclosed sac within a cell.

vessel   In a plant, a pipeline-like file of dead, water-conducting vessel elements.

vessel element   A type of plant cell in xylem that conducts water, along with dissolved minerals and certain organic compounds.

vestibular system   The organ of balance in vertebrates, located in the inner ear next to the cochlea.

vestigial structure   An anatomical feature that has no apparent function but resembles a structure of a presumed ancestor.

vibrios   Comma-shaped prokaryotic cells.

villi   Finger-like projections extending from the luminal surface into the lumen of the small intestine; these are specializations that aid in digestion and absorption.

viral envelope   A structure enclosing a viral capsid that consists of a membrane derived from the plasma membrane of the host cell; is embedded with virally encoded spike glycoproteins.

viral genome   The genetic material of a virus.

viral reproductive cycle   The series of steps that result in the production of new viruses during a viral infection.

viral vector   A type of vector used in cloning experiments that is derived from a virus.

viroid   An RNA particle that infects plant cells.

virulence   The ability of a microorganism to cause disease.

virulent phage   A phage that follows only the lytic cycle.

virus   A small infectious particle that consists of nucleic acid enclosed in a protein coat.

visceral mass   In mollusks, a structure that rests atop the foot and contains the internal organs.

vitamin   An organic nutrient that serves as a coenzyme for metabolic and biosynthetic reactions.

vitamin D   A vitamin that is converted into a hormone in the body; regulates the calcium level in the blood through an effect on intestinal transport of calcium ions.

vitreous humor   A thick liquid in the large posterior cavity of the vertebrate eye, which helps maintain the shape of the eye.

viviparity   Development of an embryo within the mother, resulting in a live birth.

viviparous   The term used to describe an animal whose embryos develop within the uterus, receiving nourishment from the mother via a placenta.

V_{max}   The maximal velocity of an enzyme-catalyzed reaction.

volt   A unit of measurement of potential difference in charge (electrical force) such as the difference between the interior and exterior of a cell.

voltage-gated ion channels   Ion channels that open and close in response to changes in the amount of electric charge across a membrane.

v-snare   A protein incorporated into a vesicle membrane during vesicle formation that is recognized by a t-snare in a target membrane.

W

water potential   The potential energy of water.

water vascular system   A network of canals powered by water pressure generated by the contraction of muscles; enables extension and contraction of the tube feet, allowing echinoderms to move slowly.

wavelength   The distance from the peak of one sound wave or light wave to the next.

waxy cuticle   A protective, waterproof layer of polyester and wax present on most surfaces of vascular plant sporophytes.

weak acid   An acid that only partially ionizes in solution.

weathering   The physical and chemical breakdown of rock.

white blood cell   *See* leukocyte.

white matter   Brain tissue that consists of myelinated axons that are bundled together in large numbers to form tracts.

whorls   In a flower, concentric rings of sepals and petals (or tepals), stamens, and carpels.

wild-type allele   One or more prevalent alleles in a population.

wood   A secondary plant tissue composed of numerous pipelike arrays of dead, empty, water-conducting cells whose walls are strengthened by an exceptionally tough secondary metabolite known as lignin.

woody plant   A type of plant that produces both primary and secondary vascular tissues.

X

xenoestrogen   A synthetic compound that exerts estrogen-like actions or, in some cases, inhibits the actions of the body's own estrogen.

X inactivation   The phenomenon in which one X chromosome in the somatic cells of female mammals is inactivated, meaning that its genes are not expressed.

X inactivation center (Xic)   A short region on the X chromosome known to play a critical role in X inactivation.

X-linked gene   A gene found on the X chromosome but not on the Y.

X-linked inheritance   The pattern displayed by pairs of dominant and recessive alleles located on X chromosomes.

X-ray crystallography   A technique in which researchers purify molecules and cause them to form a crystal. When a crystal is exposed to X-rays, the resulting pattern can be analyzed mathematically to determine the three-dimensional structure of the crystal's components.

xylem   A specialized conducting tissue in plants that transports water, minerals, and some organic compounds.

xylem loading   The process by which root xylem parenchyma cells transport ions and water across their membranes into the long-distance conducting cells of the xylem, which include the vessel elements and tracheids.

Y

yeast   A fungus that can occur as a single cell and that reproduces by budding.

yolk sac   One of the four extraembryonic membranes in the amniotic egg. The yolk sac encloses a stockpile of nutrients, in the form of yolk, for the developing embryo.

Z

zero population growth   The situation in which no changes in population size occur.

Z line   A network of proteins in a myofibril that anchors thin filaments at the ends of each sarcomere.

zona pellucida   The glycoprotein covering that surrounds a mature oocyte.

zone of elongation   The area above the root apical meristem of a plant where cells extend by water uptake, thereby dramatically increasing root length.

zone of maturation   The area above the zone of elongation in a plant root where root cell differentiation and tissue specialization occur.

zooplankton   Aquatic organisms drifting in the open ocean or fresh water; includes minute animals consisting of some worms, copepods, tiny jellyfish, and the small larvae of invertebrates and fishes.

Z scheme   A model depicting the series of energy changes of an electron during the light reactions of photosynthesis. The electron absorbs light energy twice, resulting in an energy curve with a zigzag shape.

zygomycete   A phylum of fungi that produces distinctive, large zygospores as the result of sexual reproduction.

zygospore   A dark-pigmented, thick-walled spore that matures within the zygosporangium of zygomycete fungi during sexual reproduction.

zygote   A diploid cell formed by the fusion of two haploid gametes.

zygotic life cycle   The type of life cycle of most unicellular protists in which haploid cells develop into gametes. Two gametes then fuse to produce a diploid zygote.

Photo Credits

Chapter 1: Opener © Gary Kavanagh; 1.1: © Photo W. Wüster, courtesy Instituto Butantan; 1.2: © blickwinkel/Alamy; 1.3: © SciMAT/Photo Researchers; 1.4: © Robert Winslow/Animals Animals; 1.5a: © Biophoto Associates/Photo Researchers; 1.5b: © Alexis Rosenfeld/Photo Researchers; 1.5c: © Cathlyn Melloan/Stone/Getty Images; 1.5d: © Adam Jones/Visuals Unlimited; 1.5e: © Patti Murray/Animals Animals; 1.5f: © Paul Hanna/Reuters/Corbis; 1.5g: © AP Photo/Mehgan Murphy, National Zoo; 1.7: © Michael L. Smith/Photo Researchers; 1.12a: © Dr. David M. Phillips/Visuals Unlimited; 1.12b: © B. Boonyaratanakornkit & D.S. Clark, G. Vrdoljak/EM Lab, U of C Berkeley/Visuals Unlimited; 1.12c(1): © Dr. Dennis Kunkel/Visuals Unlimited; 1.12c(2): © Kent Foster/Photo Researchers; 1.12c(3): © Carl Schmidt-Luchs/Photo Researchers; 1.12c(4): © Fritz Polking/Visuals Unlimited; 1.15a: © Sierra Blakely; 1.15b: © Erkang Ai and Ahna Skop, 2009; 1.16a: © Fred Bavendam/Minden Pictures; 1.16b: © Eastcott/Momatiuk/Animals Animals; 1.16c-e: © Andrew Brookes/Corbis; 1.16e(inset): © Alfred Pasieka/Photo Researchers; 1.17a: © Age fotostock/SuperStock; 1.17b: © Laurent/Photo Researchers; 1.20: © AP Photo/Dita Alangkara.

Chapter 2: Opener © Kevin Schafer/Peter Arnold; 2.6: © The McGraw-Hill Companies, Inc./Al Tesler, photographer; 2.12b: © Charles D. Winters/Photo Researchers; 2.17: © Jeremy Burgess/Photo Researchers; 2.19a: © Norbert Wu/Peter Arnold; 2.19b: © Jerome Wexler/Visuals Unlimited; 2.20b: © Aaron Haupt/Photo Researchers; 2.20d: © Rainer Drexel/Bilderberg/Peter Arnold; 2.20e: © Ethel Davies/Imagestate; 2.20f: © Anthony Bannister/Gallo Images/Corbis; 2.20g: © OSF/Photolibrary.

Chapter 3: Opener © de Vos, A. M., Ultsch, M., Steitz, A. A., (1992). "Human growth hormone and extracellular domain of its receptor: crystal structure of the complex. *Science.* 255 (306). Image Courtesy of Daniel Gage, University of Connecticut; 3.1: © The McGraw-Hill Companies, Inc./Al Tesler, photographer; 3.11a-b: © Tom Pantages; 3.11b: © Felicia Martinez/PhotoEdit; 3.13b: © Adam Jones/Photo Researchers; 3.13c: © Adam Jones/Photo Researchers.

Chapter 4: Opener © Biophoto Associates/Photo Researchers; 4.2a-b: © Images courtesy of Molecular Expressions; 4.3a(inset): © Dr. Donald Fawcett & L. Zamboni/Visuals Unlimited; 4.3b-4b: © Dr. Dennis Kunkel Microscopy/Visuals Unlimited; 4.6a: © Ed Reschke/Peter Arnold; 4.6b: © Eye of Science/Photo Researchers; p. 74 (left): © Thomas Deerinck/Getty Images; p. 74 (middle, left): © Dr. Gopal Murt/Visuals Unlimited; 4.12a: © Charles Brokaw/California Institute of Technology; 4.12b: © Brian P. Piasecki; 4.12c: © SPL/Photo Researchers; 4.13a: © Aaron Bell; 4.13b-c: © Dr. William Dentler/University of Kansas; 4.15(inset 1): © Dr. Don W. Fawcett/Visuals Unlimited; 4.16: Reprinted by permission from Macmillan Publishers Ltd. Cremer, T. & Cremer, C. Chromosome territories, nuclear architecture and gene regulation in mammalian cells. *Nature Reviews/Genetics*, Vol. 2(4), Figure 2, 292–301, 2001; 4.17(right): © Dennis Kunkel Microscopy, Inc/Phototake; 4.19: Reproduced from *Journal of Cell Biology*, 1964, 20:473-495. Copyright 1964 Rockefeller University Press; 4.20a: © E. H. Newcomb & S. E. Frederick/Biological Photo Service; 4.20b: © Courtesy Dr. Peter Luykx, Biology, University of Miami; 4.20c: © Dr. David Patterson/Photo Researchers, Inc.; 4.21: © The McGraw-Hill Companies, Inc./Al Tesler, photographer; 4.24: © Dr. Don W. Fawcett/Visuals Unlimited; 4.25: © Dr. Jeremy Burgess/Photo Researcher; 4.26: © T. Kanaseki and Donald Fawcett/Visuals Unlimited.

Chapter 5: Opener © Tom Pantages; 5.6: © Biochemistry: The Molecular Basis Of Life. 3rd Ed. by McKee and McKee. McGraw Hill. Courtesy of Audrey M. Glauert and G. M. W. Cook; 5.7a-b: © The McGraw-Hill Companies, Inc./Al Tesler, photographer; 5.17a-b: © James Strawser/Grant Heilman Photography; 5.18a: © Carolina Biological Supply/Visuals Unlimited; 5.18b: © Carolina Biological Supply/Visuals Unlimited; 5.19(4): © Courtesy Dr. Peter Agre. From Preston GM, Carroll TP, Guggino WP, Agre P (1992). Appearance of water channels in Xenopus oocytes expressing red cell CHIP28 protein. *Science.* 256:385.

Chapter 6: Opener © Patrick Olear/Photo Edit; 6.1a: © Bob Daemmrich/The Image Works; 6.1b: © amanaimages/Corbis RF; 6.9(5): © Altman, S., (1990). Nobel Lecture: Enzymatic Cleavage of RNA by RNA. *Bioscience Reports*, 10, 317–337; 6.14: © Liu, Q., Greimann, J. C., and Lima, C. D., (2006). Reconstitution, activities, and structure of the eukaryotic exosome. *Cell*, 127, 1223-1237. Graphic generated using DeLano, W. L. (2002). The PyMOL Molecular Graphics System (San Carlos, CA, USA, DeLano Scientific).

Chapter 7: Opener © PCN Photography/Duomo/Corbis; 7.11(5): © Reprinted by permission from Macmillan Publishers Ltd. Noji, H., Yasuda, R., Yoshida, M., Kinosita K., (1997). Direct Observation of the Rotation of F1-ATPase. *Nature*, 386, (6622), 299-302; 7.12: © Custom Medical Stock Photo; 7.13: © Ernie Friedlander/Cole Group/Getty Images RF; 7.15a(left): © Bill Aron/Photo Edit; 7.15b: © Jeff Greenberg/The Image Works; 7.16a: © Chris Hellier/SPL/Photo Researchers; 7.16b: © Michael P. Gadomski/Photo Researchers; 7.17: © Naturfoto Honal/Corbis; 7.18: © James Randklev/Photographer's Choice/Getty Images; 7.19: © SciMAT/Photo Researchers.

Chapter 8: Opener © Wolfgang Kaehler/Alamy; 8.2(top): © Norman Owen Tomalin/Bruce Coleman Inc./PhotoShot; 8.2(middle): © J. Michael Eichelberger/Visuals Unlimited; 8.2(bottom): © Visuals Unlimited; 8.12b: © Reproduction of Fig 1A from Ferreira, K. N., Iverson, T. M., Maghlaoui, K., Barber, J. and Iwata, S. (2004). Architecture of the photosynthetic oxygen evolving center. *Science.* 303, 1831-1838 with permission; 8.16 (step 6): © Elin Sowle. Reprinted from Chemistry 1942-1962, M. Calvin, "The Path of Carbon in Photosynthesis." *Nobel Lectures*, Elsevier Publishing Company. Copyright (1961); 8.17a: © David Norton Photography/Alamy; 8.17b: © David Sieren/Visuals Unlimited; 8.19(left): © Walter H. Hodge/Peter Arnold; 8.19(right): © John Foxx/Alamy RF.

Chapter 9: Opener © David McCathy/SPL/Photo Researchers; 9.15(both): © Courtesy of Brian J. Bacskai, from Bacskai et al., *Science.* 260:222-226, 1993. Reprinted with permission from AAAS; 9.18(all): © Prof. Guy Whitely/Reproductive and Cardiovascular Disease Research Group at St George's, University of London; 9.19: © Wyllie, A. H., Kerr J. F. R., Currie A. R., (1973). Adrenocortical cell deletion: The role of ACTH. *Journal of Pathology.* 111, 85–94.

Chapter 10: Opener © Altrendo Panoramic/Getty Images; 10.1a: © Courtesy of Dr. Joseph Buckwalter/University of Iowa; 10.1b: © J. Gross/Biozentrum, University of Basel/Photo Researchers RF; 10.6(inset): © Dr. Dennis Kunkel Microscopy/Visuals Unlimited; 10.10: © Dr. Daniel Friend; 10.11: © Courtesy Dr. Dan Goodenough/Harvard Medical School; 10.13: © Lee W. Wilcox; 10.14: © E. H. Newcomb & W. P. Wergin/Biological Photo Service; 10.19a: © Carolina Biological Supply Company/Phototake; 10.19b: © Biodisc/Visuals Unlimited; 10.20: © Robert Brons/Biological Photo Service; 10.21: © J. N. A. Lott, McMaster Univ./Biological Photo Service.

Chapter 11: Opener © Jean Claude Revy/ISM/Phototake; 11.3b: © Eye of Science/Photo Researchers; 11.13: © Meselson M. Stahl, F. The Replication of DNA in Escherichia Coli. *PNAS.* Vol. 44, 1958. f. 4a, p. 673; 11.24: © Photo courtesy of Dr. Barbara Hamkalo; 11.26a: © Dr. Gopal Murti/Visuals Unlimited; 11.26b: © Ada L. Olins and Donald E. Olins/Biological Photo Service; 11.26c: © Courtesy Dr. Jerome B. Rattner, Cell Biology and Anatomy, University of Calgary; 11.26d: © Courtesy of Paulson, J. R. & Laemmli, U.K. This article was published in *Cell.* Vol. 12, James R. Paulson and U.K. Laemmli, "The Structure of Histone-Depleted Metaphase Chromosomes," pp. 817-28. Copyright Elsevier 1977; 11.26e-f: © Peter Engelhardt/Department of Virology, Haartman Institute.

Chapter 12: Opener © Kiseleva and Donald Fawcett/Visuals Unlimited; 12.6: © Darst, S., (2001). Bacterial RNA polymerase. *Current Opinion in Structural Biology.* 11 (2), 155-162.

Chapter 13: Opener © Daniel Gage, University of Connecticut. Appeared in Schultz, S. C., Shields, G. C. and T. A. Steitz. (1991). "Crystal structure of a CAP-DNA complex: the DNA is bent by 90 degrees," *Science.* 253:1001; 17.9b: © Courtesy of I. Solovei, University of Munich (LMU); 13.2a: © Ed Reschke/Peter Arnold; 13.2b: © Triarch/Visuals Unlimited; 13.2c: © SIU BioMed/Custom Medical Stock Photo; 13.10: © Thomas Steitz, Howard Hughes Medical Institution, Yale.

Chapter 14: Opener © Yvette Cardozo/Workbook Stock/Getty Images; 14.1a-b: © Stan Flegler/Visuals Unlimited; 14.1c: © Courtesy of Thomas Wellems and Robert Josephs. Electron microscopy and Image Processing Laboratory, University of Chicago; 14.4: © Scott Aitken, www.scottpix.com; 14.9: © Dr. Kenneth Greer/Visuals Unlimited; 14.10b: © St. Bartholomew's Hospital/Photo Researchers; 14.17(all): © Dr. Oscar Auerbach, reproduced with permission; 14.18(both): © Courtesy Dr. Ruhong Li, Molecular and Cell Biology, University of California at Berkeley.

Chapter 15: Opener © Biophoto Associates/Photo Researchers; 15.1(4): © Burger/Photo Researchers;

29.1c-e: © Lee W. Wilcox; 29.1f: © B. Runk/S. Schoenberger/Grant Heilman Photography; 29.1g: © Ed Reschke/Peter Arnold; 29.1h: © Patrick Johns/CORBIS; 29.1i: © Bob Evans/Peter Arnold; 29.1j: © Wolfgang Kaehler/Corbis; 29.1k: © Fred Bruemmer/Peter Arnold; 29.1l: © Gallo Images/Corbis; 29.2a(chara): © Lee W. Wilcox; 29.2a(Coleochaete): © The McGraw-Hill Companies, Inc./Linda Graham, photographer; 29.2b(Mesostigma): © Lee W. Wilcox; 29.2b(Micrasterias): © The McGraw-Hill Companies, Inc./Linda Graham, photographer; 29.3a: © Dr. Jeremy Burgess/SPL/Photo Researchers; 29.3b-c: © Lee W. Wilcox; 29.4(mniumSEM): © Eye of Science/Photo Researchers; 29.5: © Lee W. Wilcox; 29.7(male): © The McGraw-Hill Companies, Inc./Claudia Lipke, photographer; 29.7(mature): © L. West/Photo Researchers; 29.7(young): © The McGraw-Hill Companies, Inc./Linda Graham, photographer; 29.9-29.10a: © Lee W. Wilcox; 29.10b: © Walter H. Hodge/Peter Arnold; 29.10c: © Patrick Johns/Corbis; 29.10d: © Rich Reid/Animals Animals; 29.11a: © The McGraw-Hill Companies, Inc./Linda Graham, photographer; 29.11b: © Lee W. Wilcox; 29.12(antheridia): © Lee W. Wilcox; 29.12(blue gametophyte): © Lee W. Wilcox; 29.12(gametangium): © Lee W. Wilcox; 29.12(gametophyte): © Lee W. Wilcox; 29.12(sori): © Carolina Biological Supply Company/Phototake; 29.12(sporangium, spore): © The McGraw-Hill Companies, Inc./Linda Graham, photographer; 29.12(sporophyte): © Barrett & MacKay Photography; 29.12(youngsporophyte): © Dr. Richard Kessel & Dr. Gene Shih/Visuals Unlimited; 29.13: © Mitsuyasu Hasabe, National Institute for Basic Biology, Japan; 29.14: © Stephen P. Parker/Photo Researchers; 29.15: © Brand X Pictures/PunchStock RF; 29.16: © Photo by Steven R. Manchester, University of Florida. Courtesy Botanical Society of America, St. Louis, MO., www.botany.org; 29.18(left): © Lee W. Wilcox; 29.18(middle): © Charles McRae/Visuals Unlimited; 29.18(right): © David R. Frazier/The Image Works; 29.19: © Marjorie C. Leggitt; 29.20: © Courtesy Prof. Roberto Ligrone. Fig. 6 in Ligrone et al., *Protoplasma* (1982) 154:414-425; 29.23c: © Lee W. Wilcox.

Chapter 30: Opener © Gallo Images/Corbis; 30.3a: © Walter H. Hodge/Peter Arnold; 30.3b: © Ed Reschke/Peter Arnold; 30.4a-b: © Lee W. Wilcox; 30.5a: © Karlene V. Schwartz; 30.5b: © Wolfgang Kaehler/Corbis; 30.5c: © B. Runk/S. Schoenberger/Grant Heilman Photography; 30.6a: © Lee W. Wilcox; 30.6b: © Bryan Pickering/Eye Ubiquitous/Corbis; 30.8a: © Zach Holmes Photography; 30.8b: © Duncan McEwan/Naturepl.com; 30.8c: © Ed Reschke/Peter Arnold; 30.10a: © Unknown Photographer/Grant Heilman Photography; 30.10b: © Ken Wagner/Phototake; 30.10c: © Lee W. Wilcox; 30.11a: © Robert & Linda Mitchell; 30.11b: © Walter H. Hodge/Peter Arnold; 30.11c: © Michael & Patricia Fogden/Corbis; 30.12: © Bill Ross/Corbis RF; 30.17: © Sangtae Kim, Ph.D.; 30.18a: © Medioimages/PunchStock RF; 30.18b: © Ed Reschke/Peter Arnold; 30.20a: © James Strawser/Grant Heilman Photography; 30.20b: © Corbis RF; 30.20c: © Image released under GFDL license. Photographer Florence Devouard, France 2003; 30.21a-e: © Lee W. Wilcox; 30.21f: © Michel Viard/Peter Arnold; 30.21g: © Biophoto/Hazan Muriel/Peter Arnold; 30.21h: © Jerome Wexler/Visuals Unlimited; 30.22a: © Eddi Boehnke/zefa/Corbis; 30.22b: © Jonathan Buckley/GAP Photo/Getty Images; 30.22c: © John Colwell/Grant Heilman Photography; 30.23(Cannabis): © Phil Schermeister/Peter Arnold; 30.23(Cannabis close): © Joao Luiz

Bulcao; 30.24: © Jack Jeffrey/Photo Resource Hawaii; 30.25: © Beng & Lundberg/naturepl.com.

Chapter 31: Opener © Brian Lightfoot/naturepl.com; 31.3a: © Fig. 16, Kaminskyj, S. G. W., and Heath, I. B. (1996). "Studies on Saprolegnia ferax suggest the general importance if the cytoplasm in determining hyphal morphology." *Mycologia* 88: 20-37. The New York Botanical Garden, Bronx, NY; Allen Press, Lawrence Kansas; 31.5a: © Agriculture and Agri-Food Canada, Southern Crop Protection and Food Research Centre, London ON; 31.5b: © CDC; 31.6: © Dr. Dennis Kunkel Microscopy/Visuals Unlimited; 31.7: © David Scharf/Peter Arnold, Inc.; 31.9a: © Felix Labhardt/Taxi/Getty Images; 31.9b: © Bob Gibbons/ardea.com; 31.10: © Rob Casey/Alamy RF; 31.11: © Gary Meszaros/Visuals Unlimited/Getty Images; 31.12: © Hans Pfletschinger/Peter Arnold; 31.13: © N. Allin & G. L. Barron, University of Guelph/BPS; 31.14a: © Nigel Cattlin/Photo Researchers; 31.14b: © Herve Conge/ISM/Phototake; 31.15: © Dr. Dennis Kunkel Microscopy/Phototake; 31.16: © Courtesy Bruce Klein. Reprinted with permission. *J Exp Med.* 1999; 189: cover illustration; 31.17: © Photo credit Dr. D. P. Donelley and Dr. J. R. Leake, University of Sheffield Department of Animal & Plant Sciences; 31.18a: © Mark Brundrett; 31.19a: © Jacques Landry, Mycoquebec.org; 31.19b: © Courtesy of Larry Peterson and Hugues Massicotte; 31.21a: © Joe McDonald/Corbis; 31.21b: © Lee W. Wilcox; 31.21c: © Ed Reschke/Peter Arnold; 31.21d: © Lee W. Wilcox; 31.22: © The McGraw-Hill Companies, Inc./Linda Graham, photographer; 31.23: Thomas Kuster, USDA, FS, Forest Products Laboratory; 31.24: © Photographs by H. Cantor-Lund reproduced with permission of the copyright holder J. W. G. Lund; 31.25a: © Peres/Custom Medical Stock Photo; 31.25b: © William E. Schadel/Biological Photo Service; 31.26: Yolande Dalpé, Agriculture and Agri-Food Canada; 31.27a: Micrograph courtesy of Timothy M Bourett, DuPont Crop Genetics, Wilmington, DE USA; 31.27b: © Charles Mims; 31.28: © Peter Arnold/Alamy; 31.29: © Clemson University - USDA Cooperative Extension Slide Series, ipmimages.org; 31.30a: © Darlyne A. Murawski/Peter Arnold; 31.30b: © Mark Turner/Botanica/Getty Images; 31.31(left): © Biophoto Associates/Photo Researchers; 31.31(right): © Dr Jeremy Burgess/Photo Researchers.

Chapter 32: Opener © Visuals Unlimited/Corbis; 32.2a: © Tom Stack/Tom Stack & Associates; 32.2b: © Doug Perrine/SeaPics.com; 32.2c: © Tui De Roy/Minden Pictures; 32.12: © Dwight Kuhn.

Chapter 33: Opener © Georgie HollandAge fotostock; 33.2a: © Jand Grushow/Grant Heilman Photography; 33.5b: © Peter Parks/OSF/Animals Animals; 33.6: © Matthew J. D'Avella/SeaPics.com; 33.8: © Biophoto Associates/Photo Researchers; 33.11a: © Daniel L. Geiger/SNAP/Alamy; 33.11b: © Wim van Egmond/Visuals Unlimited; 33.11c: © Fred Bavendam/Peter Arnold; 33.13a: © Breck P. Kent/Animals Animals; 33.13b: © Kjell Sandved/Visuals Unlimited; 33.13c: © W. Gregory Brown/Animals Animals; 33.13d: © Alex Kerstitch/Visuals Unlimited; 33.14: © Sinclair Stammers/Photo Researchers; 33.15b: © Jonathan Blair/Corbis; 33.18: © B. Runk/S. Schoenberger/Grant Heilman Photography; 33.19: © Biophoto Associates/Photo Researchers; 33.20: © Johnathan Smith; Cordaiy Photo Library Ltd./Corbis; 33.22: © John Cancalosi/Peter Arnold; 33.24a-c: © NASA/SPL/Photo Researchers; 33.25a: © Duncan Usher/ardea.

com; 33.25b: © Paul Freed/Animals Animals; 33.25c: © Dr. Dennis Kunkel Microscopy/Visuals Unlimited; 33.25d: © Roger De LaHarpe; Gallo Images/Corbis; 33.26a: © David Aubrey/Corbis; 33.26b: © Larry Miller/Photo Researchers; 33.29a: © Alex Wild/myrmecos.net; 33.29b: © Christian Ziegler; 33.31: © Wim van Egmond/Visuals Unlimited; 33.32a: © Kjell Sandved/Visuals Unlimited; 33.32b: © Richard Walters/Visuals Unlimited; 33.32c: © Franklin Viola/Animals Animals; 33.34: © Leslie Newman & Andrew Flowers/Photo Researchers; 33.37a: © OSF/Photolibrary; 33.38c: © Reinhard Dirscherl/Visuals Unlimited/Getty Images.

Chapter 34: Opener © Steve Bloom/stevebloom.com; 34.2: © Pat Morris/ardea.com; 34.3a: © Breck P. Kent/Animals Animals; 34.3b: © Jacana/Photo Researchers; 34.5a: © Valerie & Ron Taylor/ardea.com; 34.5b: © Jeff Rotman/naturepl.com; 34.5c: © OSF/Photolibrary; 34.5d: © Bill Curtsinger/National Geographic/Getty Images; 34.7a: © Reinhard Dirscherl/Visuals Unlimited; 34.7b: © Andrew Dawson/Age fotostock; 34.7c: © Brandon Cole Marine Photography/Alamy; 34.8: © Peter Scoones/SPL/Photo Researchers; 34.9: © D. R. Schrichte/SeaPics.com; 34.13a: © Gary Meszaros/Visuals Unlimited; 34.13b: © Dwight Kuhn; 34.13c: © Michael Redmer/Visuals Unlimited; 34.14a: © Gregory G. Dimijian/Photo Researchers; 34.14b: © Juan Manuel Renjifo/Animals Animals Enterprises; 34.14c: © Gary Meszaros/Photo Researchers; 34.16a: © Pat Morris/ardea.com; 34.16b: © David M. Dennis/Animals Animals; 34.16c: © Jim Merli/Visuals Unlimited; 34.17: © Michael & Patricia Fogden/Minden Pictures; 34.18a: © Royalty-Free/Corbis RF; 34.18b: © J. & C. Sohns/Animals Animals; 34.21c: © Gilbert S. Grant/Photo Researchers; 34.22a: © B. G. Thomson/Photo Researchers; 34.22b: © Jean-Claude Canton/Bruce Colemen/Photoshot; 34.22c: © Sylvain Condier/Peter Arnold; 34.22d: © Brand X Pictures/Jupiter Images RF; 34.22e: © Rick & Nora Bowers/Visuals Unlimited; 34.22f: Mervyn Rees/Alamy; 34.23a: © Kelvin Aitken/Peter Arnold; 34.23b: © Charles Krebs/Corbis; 34.23c: © Anthony Bannister/Photo Researchers; 34.24a: © Royalty-Free/Corbis RF; 34.24b: © Joe McDonald/Corbis; 34.24c: © S. J Krasemann/Peter Arnold; 34.24d: © Michel Renvdeau/Age fotostock; 34.24e: © Ken Lucas/Visuals Unlimited; 34.25a: © Martin Harvey/Peter Arnold; 34.25b: © John Shaw/Photo Researchers; 34.25c: © Paul A. Souders/Corbis; 34.26a: © Dave Watts/naturepl.com; 34.26b: © Theo Allofs/Visuals Unlimited; 34.26c: © Jeffrey Oonk/Foto Naturaa/Minden Pictures; 34.28a: © David Haring/Photolibrary; 34.28b: © Lacz, Gerard/Animals Animals; 34.28c: © Martin Harvey/Corbis; 34.29a: © Joe McDonald/Corbis; 34.29b: © Creatas/PunchStock RF; 34.29c: © Royalty-Free/Tetra Images/Getty Images RF.

Chapter 35: Opener © Jeff Carroll/Age fotostock; 35.4: © Prof. Dr. Gerd Jürgens/Universität Tübingen. Image Courtesy Hanno Wolters; 35.5: © Figure adapted from (Jackson and Hake, 1999); 35.7a-b: © Lee W. Wilcox; 35.7c: © Dr. Dennis Drenner/Visuals Unlimited/Getty Images; 35.7d: © Lee W. Wilcox; 35.8a: © Lee W. Wilcox; 35.8c: © Lee W. Wilcox; 35.13a-d: © Lee W. Wilcox; 35.15: © Eye of Science/Photo Researchers; 35.16: © Figure adapted from (Jackson and Hake, 1999); 35.17: © Ed Reschke/Peter Arnold; 35.17b: © John Farmar; Cordaiy Photo Library Ltd/Corbis; 35.17c: © Steve Terrill/Corbis; 35.17d: © John Gerlach/Animals Animals; 35.18-35.19: © Lee W. Wilcox; 35.22: © Photo: Bruce Iverson; 35.23a: © Stephen Ingram/

Animals Animals; 35.23b: © Peter E. Smith, Natural Sciences Image Library; 35.26: © Lee W. Wilcox.

Chapter 36: Opener © Gerald & Buff Corsi/ Visuals Unlimited; 36.1a: © Digital Photography by Ash Kaushesh, University of Central Arkansas, Conway, Arkansas 72035 USA; Image courtesy Botanical Society of America, www.botany.org St. Louis, MO 63110; 36.1b(all): © Lee W. Wilcox; 36.11(all): © Prof. and Mrs. M. B. Wilkins/University of Glasgow; 36.12a(bottom): © Pat O'Hara/Corbis; 36.12a(middle): © Robert Maier/Animals Animals; 36.12a(top): © Pat O'Hara/Corbis; 36.12b(top and bottom): © Henry Schleichkorn/Custom Medical Stock Photo; 36.12b(middle): © Michael Gadomski/ Animals Animals; 36.13: © Lee W. Wilcox; 36.16: © Courtesy Dr. Malcolm Drew, Texas A&M University; 36.18: © G. R. 'Dick' Roberts/Natural Sciences Image Library.

Chapter 37: Opener © Dwight Kuhn; 37.2: © Walter H. Hodge/Peter Arnold; 37.3a: © Raymon Donahue; 37.3b: © Raymon Donahue; 37.4: © Royal Botanical Gardens Kew/Wellcome Trust Medical Photographic Library; 37.5: © Confocal fluorescence micrograph courtesy Simon D. X. Chuong; 37.6: © Geoff Kidd/SPL/Photo Researchers; 37.7b: © Courtesy of C. A. Stiles, University of Wisconsin; 37.7c: © Ruddy Gold/Age fotostock; 37.8: © USDA Photo; 37.13: © Photo courtesy of Jayne Belnap, U.S. Geological Survey; 37.16: © Eberhard Grames/ Bilderberg/Peter Arnold; 37.18: © J. Hyvönen; 37.18(Inset): © Photo by Birgitta Bergman, Department of Botany, Stockholm University (Sweden); 37.19: © M. Kalab/Custom Medical Stock Photo; 37.21a: © Dani/Jeske/Animals Animals; 37.21b: © Breck P. Kent/Animals Animals; 37.22: © B. Runk/S. Schoenberger/Grant Heilman Photography.

Chapter 38: Opener © Barry Mason/Alamy RF; 38.8: © James S. Busse; 38.10: © Jerry Cooke, Inc./ Animals Animals; 38.11b: © Astrid & Hanns - Frieder Michler/Photo Researchers; 38.12b: © John N. A. Lott/Biological Photo Service; 38.12c: © John N. A. Lott/Biological Photo Service; 38.13: © David Cavagnaro/Peter Arnold; 38.16: Adalberto Rios Szalav/Sexto Sol/Photodisc Blue/Getty Images RF; 38.17: © Andrew Syred/Photo Researchers; 38.19a: © B. Runk/S. Schoenberger/Grant Heilman Photography; 38.19b: © Dr. William J. Weber/Visuals Unlimited; 38.20a-38.22: © Lee W. Wilcox.

Chapter 39: Opener © E. R. Degginger/Animals Animals; 39.3b: © Lee W. Wilcox; 39.5a: © Natural Sciences Image Library; 39.5b: © Lee W. Wilcox; 39.7a: © Photo: Bruce Iverson; 39.7b: © Kate Land Photography, iamkate.com; 39.8a: © Richard Shiell/ Animals Animals; 39.8b: © Richard Jorgensen; 39.10: Burke/Triolo Productions/Getty Images RF; 39.9a-b: © Courtesy of John Innes Centre; 39.11b: © RMF/Scientifica/Visuals Unlimited; 39.12(Top): Ed Reschke/Peter Arnold; 39.14: © Courtesy J. M. Escobar-Restrepo and A. J. Johnston, University of Zurich, Institute of Plant Biology. From "Bernasconi et al. Science, Feb 13, 2004. p. 973, Fig. 2; 39.19a-b: © Lee W. Wilcox; 39.22: © Lee W. Wilcox.

Chapter 40: Opener © John Rowley/Digital Vision/ Getty Images RF; 40.2(left): Michael Abbey/Photo Researchers, Inc.; 40.2(middle): © Sinclair Stammers/ Photo Researchers, Inc.; 40.2(right): © Dr. Richard Kessel/Visuals Unlimited; 40.5(inset a): © Dennis Kunke Microscopy/Phototake; 40.5(inset b): © Ed

Reshke/Peter Arnold; 40.5(inset c): © Innerspace Imaging/Photo Researchers, Inc.; 40.5(inset d): © Dr. John D. Cunningham/Visuals Unlimited; 40.5e-f: © The McGraw-Hill Companies, Inc./Al Tesler, photographer; 40.8(left): © Dr. Stanley Flegler/ Visuals Unlimited; 40.8(middle): © Dr. Stanley Flegler/Visuals Unlimited; 40.8(right): © Dr. David M. Phillips/Visuals Unlimited; 40.10a: © Biophoto Associates/Photo Researchers; 40.10b: © Pete Oxford/Minden Pictures; 40.10c: © Thomas Deerinck/Visuals Unlimited; 40.10d: © Anthony Bannister/Photo Researchers; 40.15(inset): © Mitch Wojnarowicz/The Image Works.

Chapter 41: Opener © James Cavallini/Photo Researchers; 41.2a: © James Cavallini/BSIP/ Phototake; 41.5a: Courtesy of Dr. R. F. Rakowski, Ohio University, Athens, OH; 41.14b: © The McGraw-Hill Companies, Inc./Al Tesler, photographer.

Chapter 42: Opener © Courtesy Ann-Shyn Chiang, Tsing Hua Chair Professor/Brain Research Center & Institute of Biotechnology/National Tsing Hua University; 42.6b: © Jan Leestma, M.D./Custom Medical Stock Photo; 42.13a: © David Wrobel/ Visuals Unlimited; 42.15(both): © Dr. Scott T. Grafton/Visuals Unlimited; 42.17: © The McGraw-Hill Companies, Inc./Al Tesler, photographer.

Chapter 43: Opener © Jane Burton/Bruce Coleman/Photoshot; 43.9: © Gary Meszaros/ Photo Researchers; 43.12: © Daniel Heuclin/ Photo Researchers; 43.14a: © Eye of Science/Photo Researchers; 43.16: © Omikron/Photo Researchers; 43.17(right): © Dr. Donald Fawcett/Visuals Unlimited; 43.19b: © Royalty-Free/Corbis RF; 43.23a: © Corbis/SuperStock RF; 43.23b: © Cal Vornberger/ Peter Arnold; 43.24b: © Courtesy of Russell Jurenka, Iowa State University; 43.24c(left): © Anthony Bannister/NHPA/Photoshot; 43.24c(right): © Courtesy of Louisa Howard, Dartmouth College; 43.28a-c: © The Royal Society for the Blind of South Australia Inc.

Chapter 44: Opener © Stephen Dalton/Photo Researchers; 44.1a(inset): © Dwight Kuhn; 44.1b: © Michele Hall/SeaPics.com; 44.1c: © Georgette Douwma/Photo Researchers; 44.1c(inset): © The Natural History Museum London; 44.7: © Reprinted by permission from Macmillan Publishers Ltd: Stedman, Hansell H. et al. Myosin gene mutation correlates with anatomical changes in the human lineage, Nature, Vol. 428, Issue Number 6981, pages 415-418, 2004; 44.11a: © Don W. Fawcett/ Photo Researchers; 44.12(inset a): © Mark Richards/ PhotoEdit; 44.17a: © Dr. LR/Photo Researchers; 44.17b(both): © James C. Weaver and Paul K. Hansma.

Chapter 45: Opener © Richard Hutchings/ PhotoEdit; 45.2a: © Daniel Hornbach and Tony Deneka, Courtesy of Daniel Hornbach, Macalester College; 45.2b: © 2006 James Watt/www.norbertwu .com; 45.3a: © David A. Northcott/Corbis; 45.3b: © John Giustina/Photolibrary RF; 45.3c: © Kim Karpeles/Age fotostock; 45.3d: © Reinhard Dirscherl/ WaterFrame - Underwater Images/Photolibrary; 45.3e: © CFranke/F1Online RF/Photolibrary RF; 45.4a: © Royalty-Free/Corbis RF; 45.4b: © Pascal Goetgheluck/Photo Researchers.

Chapter 46: Opener © AP Photo/The Rockefeller University; 46.9a(inset): © Darren Bennett/OSF/ Animals Animals; 46.9b(inset): © William S. Clark;

Frank Lane Picture Agency/Corbis; 46.13: © Frank Oberle/Stone/Getty Images; 46.14: © Nutscode/T Service/Photo Researchers; 46.17(both): © Courtesy of Uffe Midtgård, University of Copenhagen.

Chapter 47: Opener © SPL/Photo Researchers; 47.5: © Dr. David Phillips/Visuals Unlimited/Getty Images; 47.7a (inset): © Dennis Kunkel Microscopy; 47.11(left): © Laurent/BSIP; 47.13(inset): © Carolina Biological Supply/Visuals Unlimited; 47.15: © Ed Reschke/Peter Arnold; 47.21: © Biophoto Associates/ SPL/Photo Researchers; 47.22(inset): © Sovereign/ TSM/Phototake

Chapter 48: Opener © Xela/Alamy RF; 48.3a: © Ken Lucas/Visuals Unlimited; 48.3b: © Courtesy Alan Cressier; 48.4a: © Hal Beral/V+W/The Image Works; 48.4b: © Jane Burton/Bruce Coleman/Photoshot; 48.5a: © B. Runk/S. Schoenberger/Grant Heilman Photography; 48.5c: © Electron Microscopy Unit, Royal Holloway University of London; 48.7(inset): © Ed Reschke/Peter Arnold; 48.9: © Ed Reschke/ Peter Arnold; 48.10b(both): Pr. M. Brauner/ Photo Researchers, Inc.; 48.17(left): © Astrid & Hanns- Frieder Michler/SPL/Photo Researchers; 48.17(right): © Dr. John D. Cunningham/Visuals Unlimited.

Chapter 49: Opener © Guido Alberto Rossi/ Photolibrary; 49.12: Steve Gschmeissner/SPL/Photo Researchers.

Chapter 50: Opener © Sovereign/ISM/Phototake; 50.6a: © S. Goodwin & Dr. Max Hincke, Division of Clinical and Functional Anatomy, University of Ottawa; 50.6b: © Bob Daemmrich/The Image Works; 50.7: © Carolina Biological Supply/Visuals Unlimited; 50.13(left, right): © 2007 Massachusetts Medical Society. All rights reserved. New England Journal of Med. Vol. 340, p. 524, 1999; 50.13(middle): © Bart's Medical Library/Phototake.

Chapter 51: Opener © David Liebman/Pink Guppy; 51.1a: © Clouds Hill Imaging Ltd./Corbis; 51.1b: © Norbert Wu/Peter Arnold; 51.3b: © Dr. Stanley Flegler/Visuals Unlimited; 51.3d: © P. M. Motta & G. Familiari/Univ. La Sapienza/Photo Researchers; 51.4: © Rannels/Grant Heilman Photography; 51.12a: © Claude Edelmann/Photo Reseachers; 51.12b-c: © Photo Lennart Nilsson/Albert Bonniers Forlag AB, A Child Is Born, Dell Publishing Company; 51.15(all) © The McGraw-Hill Companies, Inc./Jill Braaten, Photographer

Chapter 52: Opener © Matsui et al. Ethanol and Vision Development, IOVS, October 2006, Vol. 47, No. 10, p. 4591. http://www.iovs.org/cgi/ reprint/47/10/4589.pdf. Image Courtesy of Jonathan Matsui; 52.2c: © Courtesy Prof. M. Whitaker, University of Newcastle upon Tyne; 52.4(bottom): © Tom Fleming; 52.6: © Courtesy Hiroki Nishida, Biological Sciences, Osaka University; 52.10a: © Courtesy Dr. Laurence D. Etkin, University of Texas M.D. Anderson Cancer Center. With permission of Malgorzata Kloc. This article was published in Mechanisms of Development Vol. 75, No. 1-2, Malgorzata Kloca, Carolyn Larabellb, Agnes Pui-Yee Chana and Laurence D. Etkin "Contribution of METRO pathway localized molecules to the organization of the germ cell lineage," pages 81-93. Elsevier Science Ireland Ltd. July 1998; 52.10b: © F. R.Turner/Indiana University; 52.11a-d: © Courtesy Kathryn Tosney; 52.12b: © Ed Reshke/ Peter Arnold; 52.17(5): © Richard Harland, U. C. Berkeley; 52.18(all): © Courtesy Edward M. King.

Chapter 53: Opener © SPL/Photo Researchers.

Chapter 54: Opener © David Muench/Corbis; 54.1: © David M. Dennis/Animals Animals; 54.2a: © Brand X Pictures/PunchStock RF; 54.2b: © Biosphoto/Pons Alain/Peter Arnold; 54.2c: © Brand X Pictures/PunchStock RF; 54.2d: © Art Wolfe/Photo Researchers; 54.7b: © Michael McCoy/Photo Researchers, Inc.; 54.10: © Raymond Gehman/Corbis; 54.9: Jonathan Bird/Peter Arnold; 54.13a: © Heather Angel/Natural Visions; 54.13b: © Biophoto Associates/Photo Researchers; 54.15a: © Gregory Ochocki/Photo Researchers; 54.15b: © Image courtesy of FGBNMS/UNCW-NURC/NOAA; 54.16: © Virginia P. Weinland/Photo Researchers; 54.17a: © Peter Wakely/English Nature; 54.17b: © G. A. Matthews/SPL/Photo Researchers; 54.26a: © Jean-Paul Ferrero/ardea.com; 54.26b: © Theo Allofs/theoallofs.com; 54.26c: © Scott W. Smith/Animals Animals; 54.26d: © altrendo nature/Altrendo/Getty Images; 54.26e: © Tom and Pat Leeson; 54.26f: © Joe McDonald/Visuals Unlimited; 54.26g: © D. Robert & Lorri Franz/Corbis; 54.26h: © Joe McDonald/Visuals Unlimited/Getty Images; 54.26i: © Art Wolfe/Getty Images; 55.6: © Nina Leen/Time Life Pictures/Getty Images; 54.26j: © Michio Hoshino/Minden Pictures; 54.26k: © Howie Garber/Animals Animals; 54.27a: © Nature Picture Library/Alamy; 54.27b: © Stephen Frink/Corbis; 54.27c: © Jeffrey L. Rotman/Corbis; 54.27d: © Phillip Colla/OceanLight/Bruce Coleman/PhotoShot; 54.27e: © Tom and Pat Leeson; 54.27f: Larry Mulvehill/Photo Researchers.

Chapter 55: Opener © James Balog/Getty Images; 55.3a-b: © L. P. Brower; 55.4(all): © Lilo Hess/Time Life Pictures/Getty Images; 55.5: © Joe McDonald/Corbis; 55.8(inset): © Frans Lanting/Minden Pictures; 55.11a: © Tony Camacho/Photo Researchers; 55.11b: © Gregory G. Dimijian/Photo Researchers; 55.11c: © Wolfgang Kaehler/Corbis; 55.12a: © Phil Degginger/Alamy; 55.12b: © Kuribayashi Satoshi/OSF/Photolibrary; 55.12c: © J. E. Lloyd, UF Entomology; 55.13a: © Mark Moffett/Minden Pictures; 55.15: © BIOS/Peter Arnold; 55.17: © The McGraw-Hill Companies, Inc./

Peter Stiling, photographer; 55.18: Danita Delimont/Alamy; 55.19: © Raymond Mendez/Animals Animals; 55.20: © Stephen A. Marshall; 55.22b: © Frans Lanting/Minden Pictures; 55.23a: © Masahiro Iijima/ardea.com; 55.23b: © Bill Terry/Grant Heilman Photography; 55.23c: © Millard H. Sharp/Photo Researchers; 55.24: © Chris Knights/ardea.com.

Chapter 56: Opener © Mike Lockhart; 56.1a: © Paul Glendeli/Peter Arnold; 56.1b: © Nigel Cattlin/Photo Researchers; 56.1c: © AP Photo/The Baxter Bulletin, Kevin Pieper; 56.1d: © Cyril Ruoso/JH Editorial/Minden Pictures; 56.2: © W. Wayne Lockwood, M.D./Corbis; 56.3a: © Phil Banko/Corbis; 56.3b: © Fritz Polking; Frank Lane Picture Agency/Corbis; 56.3c: © Bob Krist/Corbis; 56.4a: © A. Paul Jenkin/Animals Animals; 56.4b: © John Foxx/ImageState RF/Agefotostock RF; 56.4c: © M. Watson/ardea.com; 56.15: © Jenny Hager/The Image Works.

Chapter 57: Opener © Stephen Wong & Takako Uno; 57.10a: © Dr. Thomas Eisner/Visuals Unlimited; 57.10b: © Hans D. Dossenbach/ardea.com; 57.10c: © Thomas Aichinger/V&W/The Image Works; 57.10d(left): © Suzanne L. & Joseph T. Collins/Photo Researchers; 57.10d(right): © Michael Fogden/OSF/Animals Animals; 57.10e: © Paul Springett/Alamy RF; 57.11: © Tom & Pat Leeson/Photo Researchers; 57.14a: © Jim Tuten/Animals Animals; 57.14b: Toyofumi Mori/The Image Bank/Getty Images; 57.14c: © Gilbert S. Grant/Photo Researchers; 57.14d: © Donald Specker/Animals Animals; 57.16: © Compost/Peter Arnold; 57.19: © Dan Honda/Contra Costa Times/Newscom; 57.20a: © Dynamic Graphics Group/Creatas/Alamy RF; 57.20b: © Michael & Patricia Fogden/Corbis; 57.21: © Mike Wilkes/naturepl.com; 57.22a: © E. A. Janes/Age fotostock/Maxximages.com; 57.22b: © Dwight Kuhn; 57.24a-b: © From Alan P. Dodds *The Biological Campaign against Prickly Pear*, Published under the Authority of the Commonwealth Prickly Pear Board. Brisbane, Queensland. 30th October, 1940.

Chapter 58: Opener © Wolfgang Kaehler/Corbis; 58.2: © G. R. "Dick" Roberts/Natural Sciences Image

Library; 58.6b: © Plowes Proteapix; 58.10a: © Charles D. Winters/Photo Researchers; 58.9a: © AP Photo/Gary Stewart; 58.9b: © David M. Dennis/Animals Animals; 58.11a: © Tom Bean; 58.11b: © Courtesy of Lawrence R. Walker; 58.11c: © Howie Garber/Accent Alaska.com; 58.11d: © Tom Bean; 58.12: © Wayne Sousa/University of California, Berkeley; 58.17(all): © Courtesy Dr. D. Simberloff, University of Tennessee.

Chapter 59: Opener © Juan Carlos Muñoz/Age fotostock; ; 59.1: © Stephen Dalton/Photo Researchers; 59.9: © R. T. Smith/ardea.com; 59.16: © Courtesy of Experimental Lakes Area, Fisheries and Oceans Canada. Reproduced with the permission of the Minister of Public Works and Government Services Canada, 2009; 59.19(all): © The McGraw-Hill Companies, Inc./Peter Stiling, photographer; 59.21a: © Science VU/Visuals Unlimited; 59.21b: © Provided by the Northeastern Forest Experiment Station, Forest Service, USDA; 59.25: © Frans Lanting/Minden Pictures.

Chapter 60: Opener © David Cappaert, Michigan State University, Bugwood.org; 60.1: © Willard Clay Photography; 60.2: © Heather Angel/Natural Visions; 60.4: © Pete Manning, Ecotron Facility, NERC Centre for Population Biology; 60.7a: © The Bridgeman Art Library; 60.7b: © Topham/The Image Works; 60.7c: © James T. Tanner/Photo Researchers; 60.8: © Bruce Coleman/Photoshot; 60.11: © Vicki Fisher/Alamy; 60.13: © Andrew Parker/Alamy; 60.15a: © Robert E. Barber/Alamy; 60.15b: © Rick A. Brown/rick@moosephoto.com; 60.15c: © T Kitchin & V Hurst/NHPA/Photoshot; 60.16: © Johnny Johnson/Animals Animals - Earth Scenes; 60.17a: © University of Wisconsin-Madison Arboretum; 60.17b: © Courtesy of DL Rockwood, School of Forest Resources and Conservation, University of Florida, Gainesville, FL; 60.17c: © Sally A. Morgan; Ecoscene/Corbis; 60.18a: © Corbis; 60.18b: © Tom Brownold 2006; 60.19: AFP/Getty Images.

Page numbers followed by *f* denote figures; those followed by *t* denote tables.

F

L

labia majora, 1080, 1081*f*
labia minora, 1080, 1081*f*
labor, 1085–1086, 1086*f*
lacA gene, 265, 266, 266*f*, 267*f*, 268
Laccaria bicolor, 641, 641*f*
lacI gene, 266, 266*f*, 267*f*, 268–270, 268*f*, 269*f*
Lack, David, 496, 1209
lac operator, 285
lac operon
    glucose levels, effect of, 271, 272*f*
    as inducible operon, 268
    mutations affecting, 268–269, 268*f*, 269*f*–270*f*, 285
    negative control, 266, 267*f*, 268
    organization of DNA sequences, 265–266, 266*f*
    positive control, 271, 271*f*
lac repressor, 266, 267*f*, 268, 285
lactase gene, 951–952
lactate, produced in muscle cells, 151, 152*f*
lactation, 1086
lacteal, 948, 949*f*
Lactobacillus lactis, 551*f*
Lactobacillus plantarum, 432*t*, 551*f*
lactose
    gene regulation of utilization in *E. coli*, 262, 262*f*
    lac operon, 265–271, 266*f*–272*f*
    structure of, 48
lactose intolerance, 951–952
lactose permease, 262, 262*f*, 265, 266*f*, 267*f*, 268
lacuna, 212, 212*f*
lacY gene, 265, 266, 266*f*, 267*f*, 268
lacZ gene, 265, 266, 266*f*, 267*f*, 268, 413–414, 413*f*, 414*f*
lagging strand, in DNA synthesis, 230, 230*f*, 231*f*
Lagomorpha, 721*t*
Lake, James, 660, 662
Lamarck, Jean-Baptiste, 286, 327, 472
lamellae, of fills, 1004, 1005*f*
Laminaria, life cycle of, 581*f*
laminin, in extracellular matrix, 198–199, 199*t*
lampreys, 700*t*, 702, 702*t*, 703*f*
lancelet, 694–695, 694*f*
lancet fluke (*Dicrocoelium dendriticum*), 1217
landscape ecology, 1275–1276
Langerhans, Paul, 1058
Langmuir, Irving, 99*t*
lanthanum, 205, 205*f*
large intestine, 945*f*, 950
lark bunting (*Calamospiza melanocorys*), 1181
larva, *Drosophila*, 397, 397*f*
larynx, 1008, 1009*f*
Lassar, Andrew, 404
latency, viral, 376–377
lateral gene transfer, 550. *See also* horizontal
        gene transfer
lateral line, 705, 706*f*, 896, 896*f*
lateral meristems, 745, 745*f*
Latham, Robert, 1228
Lauterbur, Paul, 886
Lavoisier, Antoine, 966, 967
law of independent assortment, 332–334, 333*f*
    nonconformance to, 354–358, 355*f*–357*f*
law of segregation, Mendel's, 331, 331*f*, 334–335, 335*f*
Lawton, John, 1266
L-dopa, 881, 1048*f*
leaching, 777, 1254
leading strand, in DNA synthesis, 230, 230*f*, 231*f*
leadwort (*Plumbago zeylanica*), 822
leaf
    anatomy, 158, 159*f*, 173*f*
    compound, 740, 740*f*
    conifer, 616, 616*f*
    description of, 731
    development, 736, 737*f*, 739–740, 743–744, 743*f*
    embryonic/seed (cotyledon), 732, 733, 733*t*

eudicot, 733*t*, 740, 740*f*
evolution of, 604–605, 604*f*
form (shape), 740, 740*f*
function, 594
modified, 744, 744*f*
monocot, 733*t*, 740, 740*f*
palmate, 740–742, 740*f*, 741*f*–742*f*
pigmentation, maternal inheritance pattern in,
        359–360, 360*f*
pinnate, 740–742, 740*f*, 741*f*–742*f*
primordium, 734*f*, 736, 739–740
shade *versus* sun, 773, 773*f*
simple, 740, 740*f*
structure, 736, 737*f*
surface features, 743, 743*f*
vegetative growth and, 732
veins, 733*t*, 736, 740–742, 741*f*–742*f*
leaf abscission, 803–806, 805*f*
leaf-cutting ants, mutualism with fungus, 1219–1220
leaf folding, 752*f*, 765, 766*f*
LEAFY protein, 816
leafy sea dragon (*Phycodurus eques*), 706*f*
Leakey, Louis, 726
learning, 1164–1166, 1165*f*, 1166*f*
    associative, 1164
    cellular basis of, 884–887
    classical conditioning, 1164
    cognitive, 1165, 1165*f*
    feedforward processes and, 845–847, 846*f*–847*f*
    habituation, 1164
    hippocampus and, 882
    observational octopuses, 678–679, 678*f*–679*f*
    operant conditioning, 1164, 1165*f*
    trial-and-error, 1164, 1165*f*
Leber's hereditary optic neuropathy (LHON), 361, 361*t*
LEC1 protein, 829
Leder, Philip, 250, 251*f*
Lederberg, Esther, 286–287, 286*f*, 386
Lederberg, Joshua, 286–287, 286*f*, 384–386
leech, 680*t*, 681, 681*f*, 942–943, 943*f*
leghemoglobin, 786, 786*f*
legumes, 624, 784–786, 785*f*
Legionella pneumophila, 560
Leishmania, 569, 570*f*
leks, 1181, 1181*f*
Leman, Luke, 452
lens, 903, 903*f*, 904, 904*f*
lentic habitats, 1159, 1159*f*
leopard frog (*Rana pipiens*), oocyte maturation in,
        308–310, 308*f*, 309*f*
Leopold, Aldo, 1279
Lepidoptera, 687, 688*t*
Lepidosauria, 702*t*, 713–714, 713*f*
leptin, 960, 969–971, 969*f*–971*f*, 1060, 1066, 1087
Leptospira jaundice, 551*f*
leucine, 55*f*
leucoplast, 87
leukemia, 295–296, 296*f*
leukocytes
    description of, 984, 985*f*
    in immune defense, 1112–1113, 1113*f*
    in inflammation, 1113–1114, 1114*f*
Levine, Arnold, 297
Lewis, Edward, 399
Leydig cells, 1078, 1079*f*, 1080
LH. *See* luteinizing hormone (LH)
Li, Changbao, 629
library, DNA, 415, 415*f*
lichens, 643–644
    as air-quality monitors, 644
    crustose, 643, 643*f*
    foliose, 643, 643*f*
    fruticose, 643, 643*f*
    photosynthetic partner of, 643, 643*f*, 644*f*

reproduction, 643–644, 644*f*
    asexual, 643–644, 644*f*
    sexual, 644
Liebig, Justus von, 1250
Liebig's law of the minimum, 1250
life
    beginning of on Earth, 5
    biology as study of, 1
    characteristics of, 2–4, 3*f*
    fossil record of, 457–459, 459*t*
    history of, 459–469, 460*f*
    organization of living organisms, 4, 5*f*
    origin of, 450–457
        deep-sea vent hypothesis, 451, 452*f*
        extraterrestrial hypothesis, 451
        reducing atmosphere hypothesis, 450–451, 451*f*
        RNA world, 453–454
        stages of process, 450–454
    unity and diversity of, 4–13
    web of, 8, 8*f*, 543, 544*f*
life cycle
    animal, 320, 320*f*
    definition of, 317
    fungi, 320, 320*f*
        ascomycete, 648*f*
        basidiomycete, 649*f*
        zygomycete, 646*f*
    plant, 320–321, 320*f*
        alternation of generations in, 811–812, 812*f*
        fern, 596*f*
        flowering, 814*f*
        moss, 592*f*
        Pinus, 614*f*
        Polygonum, 619*f*
        sporic life cycle of early plants, 591*f*
    sexual, 317, 320–321, 320*f*
life history strategies, 1197–1198, 1197*f*
life tables, 1189, 1189*t*
ligand, 112, 181, 181*f*
ligand-gated ion channels, 112, 183, 183*f*, 857*f*, 858
light
    energy, 120*t*, 158, 159*f*, 160
        absorption by electrons, 160–161, 161*f*,
            165, 166*f*
        captured by photosystems, 165–166, 166*f*
    as limiting resource for plants and algae,
            1144, 1144*f*
    photon theory of, 160
    plant requirement for, 772–774
    plant responses to, 762–764, 762*f*–764*f*
    wavelength, 160
        absorbed by water, 577
light chains, immunoglobulin, 1118–1120, 1118*f*
light gap, 772
light-harvesting complex, photosystem, 165, 166*f*
light microscope, 66–67, 66*f*, 67*f*
light reactions, 159–168, 163*f*–168*f*, 172
    overview of, 159, 159*f*
    photosystem I (PSI)
        cyclic electron flow, 163–164, 164*f*
        experimental evidence for existence of, 167–168,
            167*f*, 168*f*
        interactions with photosystem II, 162–163, 163*f*,
            168, 168*f*
    photosystem II (PSII)
        electron movement pathway through, 166, 167*f*
        experimental evidence for existence of, 167–168,
            167*f*, 168*f*
        interactions with photosystem I, 162–163, 163*f*,
            168, 168*f*
        light energy captured by, 165–166, 166*f*
        light-harvesting (antenna) complex, 165, 166*f*
        manganese cluster of, 166, 166*f*, 167*f*
        oxygen produced by, 165–166, 166*f*
        as redox machine, 166–167